A Soaring Eagle:
Alfred Marshall
1842–1924

'The already classic work of Alfred Marshall .... soaring in flight like an eagle over the others'

(Francis Ysidro Edgeworth, 'Osservazioni sulla teoria matematica dell'economia politica', *Giornale degli economisti*, second series, Volume 2, 1891, p. 232 – my translation).

'The piercing eyes and ranging wings of an eagle were often called back to earth to do the bidding of a moraliser.'

(John Maynard Keynes, 'Alfred Marshall', in *Essays in Biography*, Volume 10 of the *Collected Writings of John Maynard Keynes*, London: Macmillan for the Royal Economic Society, 1972, p. 173).

Frontispiece: Alfred Marshall, Professor of Political Economy and Administrator (from a fireplace at the University of Bristol)

Reproduced with permission from the University of Bristol Library

A SOARING EAGLE: ALFRED MARSHALL 1842–1924

Peter Groenewegen

Professor of Economics
University of Sydney,
Sydney, Australia.

Edward Elgar

Published by
Edward Elgar Publishing Limited
Gower House
Croft Road
Aldershot
Hants GU11 3HR
England

Edward Elgar Publishing Company
Old Post Road
Brookfield
Vermont 05036
USA

British Library Cataloguing in Publication Data
Groenewegen, P.D.
Soaring Eagle: Alfred Marshall, 1842–1924
I. Title
330.092

Library of Congress Cataloguing in Publication Data
Groenewegen, Peter D.
A Soaring Eagle: Alfred Marshall 1842–1924
874p.24 cm.
Includes bibliographical references and index.
1. Marshall Alfred, 1824–1924. 2. Neoclassical school of economics. 3. Economists–Great Britain–Biography. I. Title.
HB98. 2.G76 1995
330.16'7–dc20
[B]

94–37278
CIP

ISBN 185898 151 4

Printed in Great Britain at the University Press, Cambridge

Contents

List of Figures and Tables

Figures

Tables

Figures 2.1 and 2.2 reproduced with kind permission of Department of Special Collections, the Joseph Regenstein Library, University of Chicago from Coase Collection and Professor Ronald Coase. Figure 4.1 reproduced with kind permission of the Master, Fellows and Scholars of St John's College, Cambridge from *From the Foundation to Gilbert Scott, A History of the Buildings of St John's College, Cambridge*, Cambridge: for the College, 1980, end ground plan 1862. Figure 6.1 reproduced with kind permission of the Syndics of Cambridge University Library from Marshall's personal copy of J.S. Mill's *Principles of Political Economy* (CUL, Marshall.d.62). Figure 6.2 reproduced with kind permission of the editor and publishers from *Early Writings of Alfred Marshall 1867–1890* edited by J.K. Whitaker, London" Macmillan for the Royal Economic Society, 1975, Vol. 2, p. 5. Tables 10.1, 10.2 and 10.3 reproduced with minor variations with kind permission of the editors from *Scottish Journal of Political Economy*, 37 (1), February 1990, pp. 53, 54, 56, as owners of the copyright. Table 12.1 reproduced with minor variations with kind permission of the editor and the publishers from *Early Writings of Alfred Marshall 1867–1890*, edited by J.K. Whitaker, London: Macmillan for the Royal Economic Society, 1975, Vol. 1, pp. 89–90.

List of Illustrations

Frontispiece: Alfred Marshall, Professor of Political Economy and Administrator (from a fireplace at the University of Bristol commemorating its first two Principals, Alfred Marshall and Sir William Ramsay). Reproduced with permission from the University of Bristol.

Photographs 1, 2, 11, 12, 21, 26, 51 and 52 reproduced from *Memorials of Alfred Marshall*, edited by A.C. Pigou, Macmillan, 1925 with permission of the Faculty of Economics and Politics, Cambridge University and the Marshall Library. Photographs 3, 5, and 8 reproduced with kind permission of the Principal and Fellows of Newnham College. Photographs 4, 6, 7, 14, 18, 23–5, 27–8, 33, 34, 38, 39, 50 and 51 reproduced with permission of the Faculty of Economics and Politics, Cambridge University and the Marshall Library. Photographs 9–10 reproduced with kind permission of the Merchant Taylors' School from F.W.M. Draper, *Four Centuries of Merchant Taylor's School 1561–1961*, Oxford University Press, 1962, plates pp. 96–7 and the Headmaster. Photograph 13 reproduced with kind permission of Mr H.C. Edwards, Secretary of the Old Cliftonian Society, from *Clifton College 1862–1912*, Bristol, Van Dyke Printers, 1912, Plate 8 and the Headmaster. Photograph 15 reproduced with permission of the Master, Fellow and Scholars of St John's College, Cambridge from *From the Foundation to Gilbert Scott, A History of the Buildings of St John's College, Cambridge*, Cambridge, for the College, 1980, Plate X. Photograph 19 reproduced from John Maynard Keynes, *Essays in Biography*, London: Rupert Hart Davies, 1933. Photograph 20 reproduced with permission of Cambridge University Press from Mary Paley Marshall, *What I Remember*, Cambridge University Press, 1947, Plate 11. Drawings 29, 30 reproduced with kind permission of the University College, London, Library, from the Sir William Ramsay Papers. Photograph 35 reproduced with kind permission of the University of Bristol from Basil Cottle and J.W. Sherborne, *The Life of a University*, for the University, J.W. Arrowsmith Ltd., 1959, Plate 2. Photograph 41 reproduced from *Punch*. Photograph 42 reproduced from *Harwich Express*, 5 December 1908. Photograph 43 reproduced from *Yorkshire Herald*, 20 February 1909. Photograph 44 reproduced from Lord Avebury, *Free Trade*, Macmillan, 1904. Photograph 45 from John Maynard Keynes, *Essays in Biography*, Volume 10 of *The Collected Writings of John Maynard Keynes*, 1972, Plate 10. Photograph

46 reproduced with kind permission from Macmillan and Company, Limited from A.S. and E.M.S. Sidgwick, *Henry Sidgwick, A Memoir*, 1906. Photograph 47 from Robert Skidelsky, *John Maynard Keynes. Hopes Betrayed 1883–1920*, London, Macmillan, 1903. Photograph 49 reproduced with permission of the National Portrait Gallery. Photographs 55, 56 reproduced with permission of Richard Freeman from letters preserved in the Foxwell Collection. Photographs 16, 31, 32, 36 and 54 reproduced with permission of the author. In some cases of reproduced material, it has not been possible to trace present owners of copyright despite diligent efforts to this effect, and any of those in this category with a claim to such copyright are asked to contact the author.

Abbreviations

AMCA	*Alfred Marshall Critical Assessments*, edited by J.C. Wood, London: Croom Helm, 1982
BUL	Bristol University Library
CUL	Cambridge University Library
DNB	*Dictionary of National Biography*
EEI	Alfred Marshall, *Elements of Economics of Industry*, London: Macmillan, third edition, 1899
EEW	*Early Economic Writings of Alfred Marshall, 1867–1890*, edited by John K. Whitaker, London: Macmillan for the Royal Economic Society, 1975
EOI	Alfred Marshall and Mary Paley Marshall, *Economics of Industry*, London: Macmillan, second edition, 1881
EPW	Alfred Marshall, *The Early Philosophical Writings of Alfred Marshall*, edited by Tiziano Raffaelli, Marshall Studies No. 6, Florence: Università degli studi di Firenze, Dipartmento di scienze economiche, 1990. This has been published as Archival Supplement 4, 1994, *Research in the History of Economic Thought and Methodology*, Greenwich, Connecticutt: JAI Press. All references to the work are to the original edition.
HME	*Alfred Marshall on the History and Method of Economics* (circa 1870), edited with an introduction by Peter Groenewegen, Sydney: Centre for the Study of the History of Economic Thought, University of Sydney, Reprints of Economic Classics, Series 2, No. 5, 1990
IT	Alfred Marshall, *Industry and Trade*, London: Macmillan, third edition, 1920
JNKD	John Neville Keynes, *Diaries 1864–1927*, CUL, Add 7827–7867
KMF	Keynes Marshall File, J.M. Keynes Papers, King's College Library
MCC	Alfred Marshall, *Money, Credit and Commerce*, London: Macmillan, 1923
Memorials	*Memorials of Alfred Marshall*, edited by A.C. Pigou, London: Macmillan, 1925
NCA	Newnham College Archives
OP	*Official Papers*, by Alfred Marshall, edited by J.M. Keynes, London: Macmillan for the Royal Economic Society, 1926
	Alfred Marshall, *Principles of Economics*, London: Macmillan,
P I	first edition 1890
P II	second edition 1891
P III	third edition 1895
P IV	fourth edition 1898
P V	fifth edition 1907
P VI	sixth edition 1910
P VII	seventh edition 1916
P VIII	eighth edition 1920
P IX	ninth variorum edition 1961
	edited by C.W. Guillebaud, London: Macmillan for the Royal Economic Society, Volume 2
TCC	Trinity College, Cambridge, Wren Library, Special Collections
UCL	University College London, Bloomsbury Science Library, Special Collections

Preface

My interest in economist biography was first aroused when I read Gardlund's magnificent study of Wicksell in an afternoon sitting in the Australian National University Library (Canberra) in 1961. Subsequently, this interest was heightened by a fascinating conversation with William Jaffé in Birmingham in 1972, who revealed his immense enjoyment in researching biography for his life of Walras, an enterprise which, alas, he did not live to complete. His earlier debate with George Stigler over the value of economist biography found me on the side of Jaffé, and my teaching in the History of Economic Thought over the decades has invariably included biographical material about the persons who contributed to the writing of economics. My extended teaching of Marshall's *Principles* in an economics honours seminar from the early 1970s, combined with the fascinating snippets about Marshall's life which were becoming available to supplement and to correct Keynes's 1924 Memoir and frequently highlighting the contradictory aspects of his complex character, started me thinking of attempting a Marshall biography myself. In 1983, encouraged by Skidelsky's call for a full-scale biography of Marshall (and of Sidgwick), I raised the matter with John Whitaker, then visiting Sydney for a few days and whose years devoted to Marshall studies made it plausible that he was contemplating such a project. When he replied in the negative, I decided to test the feasibility of the enterprise by spending a couple of terms in the Marshall Library at Cambridge to check whether sufficient material was available for a detailed biography. This volume attests to the results from this preliminary investigation, even though its opening chapter warns of limitations in terms of much missing data, something of which I had become fully aware during my initial inventory of the Marshall Papers. A decade later, the rest, as they say, has become history.

My personal Marshall odyssey over ten years, three of them virtually full time, has impressed on me both the joys and the trials of the biographer. I started writing in summer 1990, in Jesus College, Cambridge, with the inspiration of the 'Marshall year' and *Principles* centenary and the encouragement from contact with leading Marshall scholars at conferences in three countries. Five of these scholars, Giacomo Becattini, Ronald Coase, Bob Coats, Rita McWilliams-Tullberg and John Whitaker, promised full cooperation extending to willingness to read my first draft, a task the enormity of which they may not have fathomed when they first agreed to my request. Subsequently, one of them, and she from what Marshall called the 'weaker sex', volunteered to scrutinise my second draft as well, a matter accomplished with speed, insight and humour. The collected letters of comment from my initial readers would make a modest volume in themselves. The assistance they provided went, however, well beyond these comments. Coase gave me generous access to his extensive researches on Marshall's ancestry, now housed in the Regenstein Library at the University of Chicago, and during my brief visit to Chicago provided research assistance to help me extract its riches. He provided much other assistance as well. Becattini sent me invaluable copies of the fruits of his own Marshall researches over the years and in his office overlooking the Arno, gave several days of his scarce time to discussions of my draft, followed by copious faxes in his beautiful Italian. During three glorious days spent near the magnificent Jeffersonian University of Virginia in Charlottesville, John Whitaker enabled me to draw on his collection of copies of Marshall letters gathered for the volumes of Marshall correspondence he is editing. When required, he always stood ready to offer other tit-bits of information from his rich storehouse of Marshall knowledge. Bob Coats gave vital encouragement in an endless flow of letters from the various corners of the globe and invariably provided useful and perceptive bibliographical advice on diverse tricky problems faced by a Marshall biographer. From Stockholm and occasionally Newnham College, came a relentless stream of faxes and letters from Rita McWilliams-Tullberg, often accompanied by photocopies of material she had gathered during her long period of devotion to Marshall studies. Recently rediscovered Mary Paley Marshall notes in the Newnham College Archives were a particularly gratifying and unexpected bonus she provided in this way, because of the supplementary insights they yielded on crucial points. My debts to these five scholars and friends is very inadequately acknowledged by the occasional specific references given in the footnotes, though needless to say, the responsibility for any remaining defects of the book are exclusively mine. I also record my appreciation for a pleasant day spent with Dick Freeman at Woking, reading Marshall's letters to Foxwell, of which, together with the bulk of the Foxwell Papers, he is now the custodian.

Others read and advised on my manuscript in whole or in part. Michael White and Peter Kriesler gave insightful comments and suggestions, the former especially covering chapters in draft with his constructive annotations in red, blue and occasionally green ink. John Mack read my chapter on Marshall's undergraduate years, offering both useful advice and references on the Mathematical Tripos he himself had taken so many years later; Tiziano Raffaelli examined Chapter 5 in draft to give me the benefit of his immense knowledge on Marshall's early philosophical work; Louis Haddad read and commented on Chapter 16 covering Marshall's 'tendency to socialism'; Luigi Pasinetti read and briefly commented on Chapters 15, 20 and 21, while Geoffrey Harcourt read my chapter on Marshall's legacy for which he had earlier assisted with useful information. Both Geoff Harcourt and Peter Kriesler likewise assisted in securing splendid college accommodation during my many visits to Cambridge after 1984.

Several persons read the manuscript for style and flow. Sandra Fleischmann and my daughter Sarah read many of the early chapters for this purpose, saving me from errors in expression and syntax. This task was likewise performed by two research assistants, Mark Donoghue and Sue King, both of whom read the whole of the manuscript. They also spotted wobbly expression, faulty spelling and punctuation while Mark Donoghue in particular dug out difficult-to-find information on Marshall associates for various footnotes from Sydney University's library collection.

The assistance ungrudgingly given by libraries and archivists is another pleasure experienced by the biographer, and one which I tasted to the full. I am still amazed at the tremendous cooperation I received from people in all walks of life, who answered queries from a biographer, and sometimes about a person, of whom they had never heard. In the first instance, successive librarians and their staff from the Marshall Library must be thanked for their unstinting generosity in time and effort in helping with searches for material, photocopies and photographic reproduction. College archivists, especially from St John's, Newnham, King's and Trinity were equally generous, as were those of London libraries in a variety institutions, at Bristol University and elsewhere in England. These I also pestered with queries, often by letter from Sydney. A detailed list of such acknowledgements is provided subsequently (below, pp. 795–800), together with acknowledgement of the permissions granted to quote from manuscript or other copyright material over which these archivists have custody and property rights.

Some further specific thanks need to be recorded at this stage. The University of Sydney and its Economics Department generously provided several periods of special duties abroad to enable me to visit archival sources or to participate in conferences at which I could present segments of my Marshall research. The Australian Research Council assisted my travel with financial assistance through a grant and, more importantly, facilitated the writing of this book by awarding me a Senior Research Fellowship in 1990 which allowed me to work full time on this project from 1991. Without the last assistance, this book may never have been finished. Jack Towe provided his usual efficient special assistance on a variety of matters to assist my research and the production of this book; Chris Rauchle provided essential computer advice which allowed preparation of camera ready copy in all its finer detail, and prepared the genealogical figures for Chapter 2; Valerie Jones once again turned a flow of untidy manuscripts into beautiful word-processed pages, never complaining of the endless corrections and changes which I inflicted on her over three and a half years of hard typing. Julie Leppard provided superb editorial advice and comments from Elgar. Finally I owe a debt to my wife and children for patiently enduring the quirks of Alfred Marshall from early 1984, particularly during the final stages of the birth of this biography when correction of typescript and proofs was the order of the day, almost seven days a week, while the preparation of the index taxed the patience of even the greatest of saints.

Peter Groenewegen,
Sydney – December 1994.

1. A Life of Alfred Marshall: Introduction and Overview

Alfred Marshall, the father of modern British economics and founder of its Cambridge school, was born on Tuesday, 26 July 1842, a fairly normal, London summer's day in the mid-nineteenth century. At Westminister, both the House of Commons and the House of Lords were sitting. Third reading debates on the Colonial Passengers and Assessed Taxes (No. 2) bills, Reports on Parish Commissioners and question time engaged the attention of Members of Parliament. The Duke of Wellington introduced the second reading of the Poor Law Amendment Bill in the Lords. At Windsor, Queen Victoria and Prince Albert spent the afternoon riding in the park; the royal dinner party that evening included Lady Charlotte Dundas, Lord Charles Wellesley, Her Royal Highness the Duchess of Kent and Sir George Cooper. At nearby Eton, its Provost threw a splendid entertainment for nearly 100 guests to mark the end of the 'election speeches'. Sitting in Vice-Chancellor's Court, Sir John Wigram determined in favour of the plaintiff in the long-running matrimonial property settlement dispute of Taylor v. Pugh; the Surrey Coroner, Mr Carter, conducted an inquest into the death the day before of John Mitchell, a labourer, on the South-Western Railway at Woking Common, while in a state of intoxication. Discord Melody won the Craven Stakes at the Goodwood Races; at Lords, the annual cricket game between eleven gentlemen and eleven players was in its second day; Sheridan's *The Rivals* was playing at the Theatre Royal, Haymarket, while an evening performance of Bellini's 1831 opera *La Sonnambula* was on offer at Davidges Royal Surrey Theatre followed by a performance of Shakespeare's *Macbeth* in which the whole of Locke's witches music was to be sung by the entire opera company under its conductor, Mr Stansbury. These were the ordinary events which marked the entry of Alfred Marshall into the world.

They also marked the beginning of an unusual life. Alfred Marshall, after several false starts, became a famous economist. He is the author of the *Principles of Economics*, one of the most enduring texts on the subject, and of a number of less celebrated, companion volumes. He is the founder of the Cambridge school of economics and the person who established that peculiar brand of English neo-classical economics which combined aspects of both earlier classical thinking with the then new, marginalist economics, into a novel system of economics based on supply and demand.

Alfred Marshall was more than this. He was a noted teacher and occasional educational reformer. His academic experience embraced the traditional and ancient universities of Cambridge and Oxford as well as Bristol University College, the 'red brick' institution founded in the 1870s. He was a prominent participant in government inquiries into financial and other economic matters, and in the lengthy activities of the Royal Commission on Labour of 1891–94. He participated in learned societies and was involved in establishing the British Economic Association which did much for the professionalisation of economics from the 1890s onwards. He had strong views on socialism and feminism, on town planning and on the organisation of social welfare, on nationalism, pacifism and imperialism, all issues he more or less directly associated with his main interest in life as an economist. He was acquainted with many of the eminent personalities of his day in politics, education, the Church, the labour movement and social reform. His long life of more than eighty years spanned the relative tranquillity of Victorian and Edwardian times and the turbulent years of post-war reconstruction and adjustment to that 'great' but traumatic war of 1914–18. In short, he enjoyed a full, interesting, and in many ways, peculiar life.

A full-length biography of Alfred Marshall is long overdue.[1] This is not only because of Marshall's undoubted stature in the development of modern economics where the impact of his *Principles* continues to reverberate a century after its initial publication. His place in the history of the science to which he devoted the greater part of his lifetime has been well secured as is shown by the multitude of monographs and articles which have been devoted to his many and varied economic contributions.[2] Marshall's life, however, is of wider interest than that arising from the history of economics. It involves many features relevant to general Victorian intellectual and social history, because it not surprisingly reflected so many of the characteristics of the late Victorian thinker. For example, he shared the strong belief in human progress of many of his contemporaries, to be achieved through extending the then undoubted blessings of universal education as an essential part of the rational approach to improving the living standards and, more strikingly, the mode of living, of the working classes and parts of that great social substratum Marshall liked to describe as the residuum.[3] Much of this faith in progress, and the active endeavour to assist its realisation which it entailed, were for Marshall, as in the case of many of his contemporaries, grounded on a need to replace abandoned Christian beliefs by a reasoned and rational agnosticism. This was a typical reaction of those whose formative intellectual period coincided with the turbulent 1850s and 1860s and the crises for the established Church which these decades generated.[4]

Marshall's own crisis in religious belief, relatively mild though this was compared with that experienced by his Cambridge contemporary Sidgwick, has more interesting consequences for his biographer than simply recording one more case study of enlightened agnosticism in Victorian England. The years from 1865 to the early 1870s, when this loss of religious belief took place, cover a gradual shift in intellectual direction culminating in the initial years of what he later called his economic apprenticeship. This intellectual shift changed an intention of continuing mathematical investigations to research issues in the theory of knowledge as an attempt to come to grips with what a person can rationally believe. The metaphysical questions this raised for Marshall through his study of major contemporary works in religious controversy led him in turn to ethics and to psychology, then a burgeoning and fresh arena of scientific endeavour. It ultimately led to a study of political economy, partly to satisfy an urge to engage in social reform to raise the standards of life of the working classes. The intellectual foundations for this process were provided by the solid grind in preparing for the Cambridge Mathematical Tripos in the early 1860s combined with some philosophical reading in his postgraduate years and initially, his more senior school years.[5]

Investigating Marshall's intellectual progress also enables illumination of these heady days for the development of the moral sciences at Cambridge during the 1860s. Marshall's experience is instructive for at least two reasons. First of all, his pre-1870 writings on psychological and philosophical subjects, an area of study to which at this stage he was seriously considering devoting his life, enable some discussion of the current state of British psychological thought, dominated by Bain's texts on *Senses and the Intellect* and on *Emotions and the Will* and more particularly, the debate on the problems created for the 'associationist school' by the increased factual knowledge available on the physiological aspects of sense perception. Secondly, Marshall's participation in discussions conducted at the Grote Club provide insights into contemporary Cambridge philosophical debate. The way German idealist philosophy was influencing British philosophical thinking is one such insight, since Marshall at this time fell under the spell of Hegel's *Philosophy of History*, of interest to his later intellectual development in various ways. Informing both these seemingly disparate areas of intellectual endeavour was the enormous impact of the newly discovered science of evolution in its biological forms enunciated by Darwin and Spencer. The initial, and enduring, impact of evolution on a prominent late Victorian social scientist of Marshall's calibre is an interesting case study in itself, requiring a biographical dimension if its various manifestations, such as the eugenics movement, are to be fully grasped. It also reiterates the enormous influence of Spencer's work in these years, of which frequent reminders are in order, given the relative neglect of his thought for much of the twentieth century. Marshall's life, in short, embraced wider intellectual currents than those associated with the major developments taking place in economics at this time. These extra-economic interests also provided largely invisible, but none the less important, foundations for the economic system he constructed from the early 1880s.

Marshall's experience also captures much of interest in the history of university education in the later Victorian period, with special reference of course to the University of Cambridge with which Marshall was associated as student, lecturer and professor for the greater part of his life. Apart from the social value inherent in a sketch of a poor, and not socially well connected, undergraduate's experience in the Cambridge of the 1860s and the type of demands and rewards involved in attempting the Mathematical Tripos at that time, educational history enters Marshall's biography in other ways. Most interesting are the various reform movements with which he was associated in Cambridge, sometimes on one, sometimes on the other, side of progress. His drive towards the creation of a separate Economics and Politics Tripos successfully achieved in 1903 is one vital instance of this, important not only for its explanatory impact on attitudes to economics and business education in Britain at the time but also for the role it played in advancing the status of university lecturers in the educative process at universities such as Cambridge. His changing involvement in the advancement of the status of women students and teachers at Cambridge and general university education are of considerable interest, as are his general ideas on educational practice. Marshall's life therefore also opens a window on late Victorian university reform as practised in England at one of its leading tertiary educational institutions.

It portrays wider aspects of experience in a middle-class Victorian household as well. Marshall was a perceptive and extensive traveller, in particular leaving interesting reflections on developments in the United States as he saw them in 1875. These went beyond observations on the state of American manufacturing, trade, and protectionist opinion in its various shades. They embraced character sketches of persons he met in his travels, reflections on New York theatre performances, the life in religious 'socialist' communities and the spectacle of Niagara Falls. Marshall likewise had interests in some of the arts, particularly painting and music. This is implicitly demonstrated by the type of information he gathered in his Red Book[6] and the collection of portraits of the famous he collected for never realised scientific purposes. His life likewise illuminates Victorian middle-class reactions to socialism, alternatively recoiling in horror from its more extreme prescriptions while revealing simultaneous fascination with the new intellectual and social visions it opened up. Marshall's tendency to socialism was varied and rich, ranging as it did from passive intellectual involvement through teaching its leading ideas, to more active participation on the cooperative fringes while opposing some of its major aspects from the early 1870s and after. Marshall's life presents the rich panorama of Victorian life in many aspects, enabling wide-ranging observations on the pleasures, fears, phobias and likes of an ambitious, socially mobile, eccentric Victorian academic and intellectual.

SCOPE OF THE WORK

The various aspects of Marshall's rich and long life illustrate in the first place that his economics can only be part, albeit a significant one, of the story of his life. This economic content is dealt with in a variety of ways. It covers his activities and development as an economic thinker and writer (Chapters 6, 12 and 19), as an economics educator (Chapters 9, 10 and 15) and as a disseminator of 'sound' economic views (Chapters 11, 13 and 17). Much economic material features as well in his travels (Chapter 7), his retirement (Chapter 17), his friendships (Chapter 18), while it forms a major segment of his legacy (Chapter 20). The greater part of his biography is therefore coloured by what was, after all, his life-long interest. Such predominance of economic subject matter is not surprising for a person who has gone down in history as an early professional academic economist and one who contributed much to enhancing the standing of his discipline in the wider community.

   The arrangements of the specifically economic chapters deserve some further comment. The development of Marshall's economic thinking is divided chronologically in terms of his publications, of which the first stage incorporates the period he himself described as his economic apprenticeship. This first chapter on the phases of his economic thought is designed to highlight the widely acknowledged foundations of his economic studies, in the work of Mill, Cournot and von Thünen, Smith and Ricardo, and concludes with his first, book length publications. These are the privately printed *Pure Theory of Foreign and Pure Theory of Domestic Value* and the joint (with his wife) *Economics of Industry* published in 1879. In their respective ways, both these works indicate how far Marshall had by then departed from the views of his original mentor in economics, John Stuart Mill.

   The second phase of his economic development covers the work on his *magnum opus*, the *Principles of Economics*. This includes both the arduous road to that achievement, his strange urge constantly to revise the work, preparation of its abridgement (*The Elements of Economics of Industry*) in 1892 and his failure to complete the long-promised second volume. Chapter 12 provides the chronicle of its construction and revision rather than detailed analysis of its contents.

The last part of the saga of the *Principles* overlaps with the third and final phase of Marshall's economic development: the production of two final volumes published in 1919 and 1923 respectively are discussed in Chapter 19. It also discusses plans for a volume on progress.

Chapters 12 and 19 temporally coincide with the official Alfred Marshall, many of whose contributions to Royal Commissions were posthumously published in the edition by John Maynard Keynes of Marshall's *Official Papers*. This seems to be the more comprehensive way of presenting the development of Marshall's economic thinking by classifying it in terms of the major forms in which he published it, though this involves some sacrifice of chronology.

Departures from strict chronology are in fact a prominent feature of the organisation of the material in this biography. This is partly induced by gaps in the source material on Marshall's life. After the almost obligatory beginnings devoted to family antecedents and formal education (Chapters 2–4) followed by his early postgraduate ventures (Chapters 5 and 6), the plan for presenting the material focuses on activities only loosely chronologically arranged (travel, academic life, socialism, women's issues, clubs and learned societies, and so on). Choice of which activities are covered was determined by the available source material, not necessarily indicative of the importance they played in his life. This is discussed more fully in subsequent sections of this introduction. In short, it is the rationale of presenting Marshall's life in its various facets on which information is available. The silences in this manner of treating his life, disguised in the skeleton provided by a table of contents, become more evident as the story of his involvement with particular activities unfolds. The final chapter comments more explicitly on some of these silences and provides a vehicle for material difficult to include in earlier chapters. This strategy necessitates presentation of a broad chronological overview of Marshall's life by way of introduction.

Before doing this, a word on the choice of title is appropriate. The image of the soaring eagle is particularly apt for the biography of Alfred Marshall. This image, incidentally, was also invoked by Edgeworth, and by Keynes in his Memoir.[7] In the first instance, the eagle draws attention to Marshall's long association with St John's College, Cambridge, as undergraduate from 1861 to 1865, as resident Fellow from 1865 to 1877 and after his appointment as Professor of Political Economy at Cambridge in 1884, as non-resident Fellow from 1885 until his death. More importantly, and this was why Edgeworth and Keynes used the striking simile, the eagle points to Marshall's dominance in the economics profession from the 1880s onwards. In addition, it emphasises the ambitious spirit in the young Marshall which, as this biography suggests, made him in youth seek to excel wherever possible, perhaps in part compensation for the social inferiority he appears to have felt about his humble origins. A desire to soar like an eagle explains much of Marshall's search for a career during the late 1860s more plausibly than the *ex-post* explanations he gave in old age.

A CHRONOLOGICAL OVERVIEW OF MARSHALL'S LIFE: 1842–1924

Marshall was born in 1842 in Bermondsey, a lower-class London district. He was the second of an eventual five children of his father William Marshall, a clerical employee in the Bank of England, and his mother, Rebecca, née Oliver. His school education was completed with considerable distinction during 1852–61 at Merchant Taylors', a non-residential London public school. He excelled in mathematics, and developed a taste for it. Choice of school was dictated by the opportunity it offered to gain a scholarship to St John's College, Oxford, followed by a 'living' as Church of England clergyman. Financial assistance from an uncle, combined with his strong dislike of classical studies and growing taste for mathematics, enabled Marshall to enter St John's College, Cambridge, instead, to take the Mathematical Tripos (1861–65). He became second wrangler to Lord Rayleigh, briefly taught mathematics at Clifton College (Bristol) as relief teacher, and was elected Fellow of his college at the end of 1865. From 1865 to 1868 he earned his living by mathematical coaching, partly to repay financial obligations to his uncle. From 1865, he increasingly turned from mathematics and a career in the natural sciences, to philosophy and associated studies, psychology and political economy. In 1868 he was appointed College Lecturer in the Moral Sciences at St John's. From 1870 to early 1875 he was involved in teaching women students in the moral sciences, meeting there his future wife. His reading and teaching from the early 1870s increasingly focused on economics. He published a review of Jevons's *Theory of Political Economy* in 1872, presented a discussion of some of his mathematical theories in economics to the Cambridge Philosophical Society in 1873, published a paper on Mill's theory of value in 1876, and from the early 1870s started writing a volume (never published) on international trade. In 1875, the death of his uncle, who had financially assisted his Cambridge studies in mathematics, provided a legacy used to visit America, to investigate economic and social conditions there. In 1876 he became engaged to his former student, Mary Paley, who had completed the Moral Sciences Tripos in 1874, and who from 1875 had been teaching economics at Newnham. They were married in 1877. Under college regulations then in force, this meant resigning his Fellowship and livelihood. Their economic circumstances were such that alternative employment had to be found. Before the wedding, these were secured by successfully applying for the post of Foundation Principal and Professor of Political Economy at Bristol University College, an institution established the previous year. Marriage thereby opened a new stage in Marshall's life, ending his first long association with Cambridge for the fifteen years from 1862 to 1877.

From 1877 to 1881 Marshall held both positions at Bristol, aided from 1878 by his wife who undertook the day class in Political Economy. The years in Bristol were eventful in a variety of ways. In 1878 Marshall's mother died, within a short period of his younger brother Walter. In 1879 Marshall himself fell ill, diagnosed as stones in the kidney, requiring rest. This started a period of ill health from which, on his own account, he did not really recover for nearly ten years. That year also saw the publication of *Economics of Industry*, a textbook written jointly with his wife (second edition in 1881) and the private printing of some of his diagrammatic treatment of political economy questions. Its instigator,

Sidgwick, circulated this to various economists in England and Europe. Ill health, together with the stress of administrative work for which Marshall was not well suited, led to several attempts to resign from the Bristol position; only when a successor to the Principal position was found in William Ramsay, a newly appointed Professor of Chemistry, did Marshall resign. He and his wife spent a year on the continent, wintering in Palermo and using much of the time for writing. It was then that the *Principles of Economics* was started, a work whose construction was to occupy the whole of the 1880s. In 1882, the Marshalls returned to England and resumed their teaching at Bristol for a year. In 1883, they moved to Oxford, where Marshall replaced Toynbee as Lecturer in Economics to Indian Civil Service students at Balliol College. In 1884, his new college elected him to an Honorary Fellowship. When Henry Fawcett, the Professor of Political Economy at Cambridge died unexpectedly in November 1884, Marshall applied for the vacant chair and was duly elected. His years of exile from Cambridge were over. These years away from Cambridge were marked by his growing reputation as an economist, partly facilitated by the deaths of most prominent rivals in political economy over these years, but based largely on the quality and zeal of his teaching and high expectations of the *magnum opus* in preparation. They also witnessed his entry into public controversy over Henry George's *Progress and Poverty*, and into public policy with articles such as 'How to House the London Poor' (1884).

The years from early 1885 when he took up residence in Cambridge as its Professor of Political Economy until his retirement in 1908, form the third stage in Marshall's life. They are also the high point of his career. Most of his academic articles were published over this period,[8] he published the early editions of the *Principles* (1890, 1891, 1895, 1898 and 1907) in which all the major changes were made; gave his most important evidence to Royal Commissions (1886, Royal Commission on the Depression of Trade; 1887, Gold and Silver Commission; 1893, Commission of the Aged Poor; 1897, Local Finance Commission; 1899, Indian Currency Commission), was a member of the Labour Commission (1891–94) and wrote (1903), and had published (1908), his Memorandum on the Fiscal Policy of International Trade. These years also marked involvement with learned societies. He joined the Royal Statistical Society in 1880, the Political Economy Club in 1886 and as President of Section F of the British Association for the Advancement of Science in 1890, assisted in this formal role in the formation of the British Economic Association which became the Royal Economic Society in 1902. Much time in his professorship was devoted to expanding the role of economics in Cambridge University teaching, initially by enlarging student opportunities to take economics within the existing History and Moral Sciences Triposes and increasing the incentives for them to do so; later by instituting a separate Economics and Politics Tripos. This was approved by the university in 1903 and conducted its first examinations in 1905. With one exception his role in university affairs, other than as leader of its economics teachers, was limited. Intervention on the side of those against a mixed university at Cambridge with respect to sex and opposition to granting women the rights associated with degrees of membership of the University and even teaching to mixed classes, was the important deviation in his university work.

Marshall's retirement from the Political Economy chair in 1908 marks the final stage of his life. It started with controversy and honours: controversy over Pigou as his successor to the chair instead of his long-standing colleague and friend, Foxwell; honours, in the form of honorary degrees and an official portrait sponsored by the Royal Economic Society. Other controversies followed. Assisted by the young Maynard Keynes, Marshall criticised Karl Pearson's views on the effects of alcoholic parents on their children in the letter columns of the *Times* in 1910, a sign of his strong sentiments on heredity and eugenics. *Times* letter columns also recorded Marshall's views on the desirable treatment of Germany and things German, though not German militarism, during the First World War. Work on the companion volumes to his *Principles*, when its second volume was abandoned, was slow despite the increased free time for writing retirement had given. Part of the slow progress is explained by deteriorating health, particularly after 1914, part by the ease in which Marshall was distracted and his lack of focus on the task. In 1919, *Industry and Trade* was published as the first of these companion volumes; in 1923 *Money, Credit and Commerce* appeared as a pastiche of previous work, largely, one suspects, prepared by Mary Paley Marshall. By 1921, short-term memory loss was so far advanced that constructive work by Marshall himself was no longer really possible. A final volume on economic progress he was still contemplating in the last decade of his life remains little more than a rough draft outline. By May 1924, his final illness had set in. In July 1924, just before his 82nd birthday, he died, in the house, Balliol Croft, he had helped to design and into which the Marshalls had moved in 1886. His wife, Mary Paley Marshall survived him for two decades, just as he himself had survived many of his acquaintances and contemporaries.

A PREDOMINANTLY VICTORIAN LIFETIME

Unlike Henry Sidgwick, whose life falls precisely within the reign of Queen Victoria,[9] Marshall outlasted the Victorian era by close to a quarter century. Although he is very clearly a product of his age, the emphasis on the pace of change, which features in so much of his work, was enhanced by the rapid technological, social and political changes which took place over his lifetime, particularly those which came within its final decades and during and following the First World War. His struggle to absorb such changes is clearly visible in his writings, especially in *Industry and Trade*, one reason why this remains such an important book. The extent of the failure of Marshall's intellectual powers during the 1920s is shown by the fact that accommodating recent change is only rarely attempted in the highly anachronistic *Money, Credit and Commerce* where views on monetary problems from fifty years are intermingled in a way which suggests no change had taken place in this half century.[10] Yet, despite the fact that Marshall witnessed in his lifetime and occasionally wrote about developments such as the motor car, the aeroplane, the cinema and the gramophone, as well as the Bolshevik Revolution, the League of Nations and even the strong possibility of a second war with Germany within the generation of those who had fought the First World War, 'Marshall was in many respects a highly respected late Victorian intellectual'.[11]

The 'late' in connection with 'Victorian' is significant. As G.M. Young[12] has noted in his classic portrait of Victorian England, the 1840s and 1850s, coinciding with Marshall's childhood and school life, were the 'years of division' between the early and late Victorian periods. By the 1860s, when Marshall began enjoying the formative intellectual experience which university life can bring, the late Victorian era can be said to have started. This was still the time of political consensus on the major economic issues of the nineteenth century, foreign trade policy, the treatment of the poor and the role of the state; and the time when free trade was no longer contested by major political and economic groupings. Virtual universal acceptance of free trade, however, meant no slavish adherence to *laissez faire*. None of the leading economists of this period, and in particular the major influence on Marshall's thinking in this field, John Stuart Mill, were dogmatic supporters of the 'extreme *laissez faire*' of the Manchester School of the 1830s and 1840s. In fact, disciples of *Manchesterismus* of the 1850s and 1860s largely survived only on the European continent and in North America.[13] Only from the time Marshall reached the maturity of his forties during the 1880s, did that consensus on these three major economic issues begin to break down seriously in England, a feature of the times to which his reactions are abundantly recorded.

By way of background it is useful to recapture elements of these central Victorian decades during which Marshall grew up. These were years of social transition, culminating in what Frederic Harrison later called the 'fighting sixties'.[14] Only some of these events would have intruded on the lives of Alfred Marshall and his family directly. The Great Exhibition from 1 May to 15 October 1851 in that wondrous Crystal Palace, designed and erected to house it, would be one such event. It is difficult to imagine that the nine-or ten-year-old Alfred would not have visited with his family this exciting and amazing tribute to human scientific and technical progress as part of the vast crowds which did so. The progress of the Chartist petition in April 1848 would likewise have directly affected the Marshall household, given the Bank of England's precautions against this potential civil disturbance. 1848 was, of course, the year of European revolution, bringing the socialist spectre to the forefront of political life, particularly in its French form devised by Louis Blanc, Pierre-Joseph Proudhon, Charles Fourier and Claude Henri de Saint-Simon, authors whom Marshall was to appreciate and lecture on in subsequent decades. That eventful year sparked turmoil in nearly every country of continental Europe. It also sowed seeds of nationalism, of constitutional and social democracy, whose harvest was reaped in subsequent decades. In England, by contrast, it saw the end of Chartism as a major political force, and the concomitant beginnings of the Christian Socialist Movement with active leadership and support from Alfred's subsequent Cambridge colleagues, Frederick Maurice and Charles Kingsley, and acquaintances such as Ludlow.

The 1840s and 1850s were marked by many other significant social, political, economic, literary and scientific events. 1843 was the year of the Rochdale Pioneers and the creation of the first working-man's cooperative society, a movement of great interest to the mature Marshall. With the passing of Peel's Bank Act, 1844 marked the legislative solution to the Currency–Banking School controversy of the preceding decade. It also saw the as yet unnoticed beginnings of that literary partnership between Marx and Engels, destined to shake the world early the following century. 1845 was the year Texas joined the American Union and the start of its conflict with Mexico, which three years later added California, Arizona and New Mexico to a growing United States in time for the American republic to benefit from California's gold rushes. In 1846, abolition of the Corn Laws heralded the real beginnings of that British era of free trade Alfred Marshall so stoutly defended a half century later at the beginning of its demise. The general removal of trade restrictions marked by this and by the 1849 abolition of the Navigation Acts, signs of the decade's growing economic liberalism, took place simultaneously with increased regulation of the workplace. Factory Acts prohibited female and child labour underground in 1842, regulated hours of work for women and children in 1844 and subsequently in 1848 secured for men the ten-hour day in specific industrial sectors like the textile industry. Alfred Marshall's first decade coincided with increased economic freedom tempered by regulation and reform.

The 1850s were equally exciting. 1851 was the year of Napoleon III's *coup d'état*, marked the gold rushes in Australia, and the laying of the first submarine cable connection between England and France. In 1852, the Duke of Wellington, hero of Waterloo and Conservative Prime Minister, died; Cavour, father of modern Italy, became Premier of Piedmont, the kingdom from which a united Italy was created; the first Congress of Cooperative Societies was held in London, while the *Crédit Foncier*, that pioneering cooperative banking venture, was founded in Paris. 1853 saw the first of many budgets presented by Gladstone, and the last peacetime budget in Britain for several years. In early 1854, Britain joined France in war with Russia in the Crimea, fighting the battles of Alma, Balaclava and Inkerman, and capturing Sebastopol. Apart from growth in chauvinism and additional income tax, Crimea generated the legend of Florence Nightingale and inspired Tennyson's *Charge of the Light Brigade*, a duty from his post as Poet Laureate acquired on the death of Wordsworth in 1850. The 1856 Paris Peace Congress, which ended the Crimean War, cleared the way for further European conflict to advance the cause of Italian, German and Balkan nationalism in subsequent decades. For Britain, the decade closed with the Indian Mutiny and consolidation of its Indian Empire.

The 1840s and 1850s were also decades of reform, Blue Books and social investigation. Social and economic statistics became more widely available, assisted and encouraged by the creation of a special 'Statist' section of the British Association for the Advancement of Science in 1833, and from the appointment of official statisticians to individual government departments and major statistical enterprises by talented skilful amateur fact gatherers. Quételet, the Belgian social statistician, Le Play in France, and Porter and McCulloch in Britain, are names that spring to mind as statistical writers from whose efforts Alfred Marshall's early social studies were to benefit considerably. A first major step in parliamentary reform had been taken with the passing of the (first) Reform Bill of 1832. The next major step in parliamentary reform came in 1867. The reformed parliament, assisted either by individual private effort or increasingly by public administrator–reformers of the calibre of Edwin Chadwick, tackled problems in sanitation, public health, public education and transport. Municipal reforms and the birth of a genuine civil service which occurred in these years aided this process. The staunch individualism of economic liberalism, lauded by Herbert Spencer in his *Social Statics*, intermingled with increased government intervention in the 1850s. The last was essential for removing the cesspools from Britain's rapidly growing urban conglomerates, disclosed by parliamentary committees and from individual research such as Mayhew's survey of the London poor and underworld. These were years when cholera, typhus and railways still conquered London and provincial cities.

Reform and change also touched Church, education and the universities. Cambridge, for example, after parliamentary promptings, widened its educational horizons by adding both a

Natural and a Moral Sciences Tripos to its traditional menu of mathematical and classical honours degree studies in 1848. Headmaster Thomas Arnold was reforming educational practices at Rugby, reforms subsequently diffused over other public schools. In the 1840s, following earlier turmoil from Methodists and other Dissenters, Tractarians and the Oxford movement marched together to destroy further the hegemony of the established Church of England, as symbolised by John Henry Newman's open conversion to Roman Catholicism in 1845. In 1851 detailed research revealed what had long been suspected: communicant membership and regular attendance at church were a minority practice, confined generally speaking to the middle and upper classes. Even then, middle-class religious belief was steadily undermined by developments in scholarship and research. Examples are David Straus's *Life of Jesus* (translated into English by George Eliot) as a leading genus of the species, German biblical criticism; and the evolutionary message from works like *Vestiges of Creation* by Robert Chambers anonymously published in 1844, with its critical implications for scriptural chronology as contained in the Book of Genesis, and heralding the impact of evolution on the story of creation.

The early 1860s commenced with the American Civil War. They saw the virtual triumph of Italian unification with the coronation of Victor Emmanuel as King of Italy in its provisional capital of Florence established in 1864, and the beginnings of German unification. The road to German Empire had started with the appointment of Bismarck as Chancellor in 1862, continued with the war with Denmark enabling Prussian annexation of Schleswig and Kiel, to lead the way to final Prussian victories over Austria in 1866 and France in 1870 which crowned Wilhelm I as Kaiser in 1871. The 1860s were also years of colonial conquest. In 1861 Spain seized San Domingo, in 1862 France annexed Cochin-China and purchased Obok in Africa opposite Aden, adding Cambodia as a protectorate to its South East Asian Empire in 1864; a joint effort by the French, British and Dutch fleets attacked Japan in 1864 to open it up to trade. A beginning was also made on the unsuccessful French imperialist adventure in Mexico under Archduke Maximilian of Austria; Britain extended the boundaries of its Cape Colony by annexation to begin its South African venture and, with the ending of the second Anglo-Maori war, consolidated the British Empire in New Zealand. This marked the beginning of a scramble for colonies and an era of growing imperialism on which the nineteenth century ended. Other major social reforms on an international scale occurred in the 1860s. In Russia, Czar Alexander II emancipated the serfs by decree. In September 1862 Abraham Lincoln announced the freeing of American slaves as from the start of 1863, a decision confirmed by the thirteenth amendment in the American Constitution passed in 1865, followed in 1875 by attempts of the British navy to stamp out the traffic in indentured labour from the Pacific Islands for Queensland agriculture. Transportation of convicts to the western part of Australia was abolished in 1865. Revolutions occurred in Greece and Poland, and Hungary experienced yet another constitutional crisis, further signals of incipient nationalism and political unrest, while the 1870s started with the conflagration of the Paris Commune.

The scene in England presented by the early 1860s was considerably more tranquil. The British people joined their Queen Victoria in mourning the death in December 1861 of her husband and Prince Consort, Albert 'the Good'. Apart from this traumatic royal event, the early years of the decade were rather calm. Gladstonian finance, ushered in by the single

Finance Bill reform of 1860, tightened the control of the future Prime Minister over the national purse, and kept income tax on average at 2.5 per cent.

There was more turmoil in the English ecclesiastical sphere. Two major court battles took place concerning Anglican powers over heresy, or, more generally, unsound doctrine. The publication in 1860 of *Essays and Reviews* by seven churchmen, including Alfred Marshall's future friend and patron, Benjamin Jowett, brought two of its authors into the courts. One was charged with casting doubt upon the inspiration of the Bible, the other with impugning the eternity of the future punishment of the wicked, a charge which in 1852 had successfully brought about F.D. Maurice's dismissal from his two chairs at King's College, London. The two prosecuted authors of *Essays and Reviews* fared better; both were vindicated by the Queen in Council sitting in appeal in 1864.

There was simultaneous agitation over the Colenso Affair, involving the right of the Church to dismiss one of its bishops if found guilty of unorthodoxy. Once again, this case involved zeal in the application of critical biblical scholarship. Colenso, as Bishop of Natal, had published a study of the first five books of the Bible, which found them full of contradictions and historical inaccuracies. When dismissed from his post on this ground by his South African superior he appealed to the courts; an appeal ultimately upheld in 1866 by the Privy Council. Colenso would have been a quite familiar name to the young Alfred Marshall. Prior to his elevation to the Church, Colenso had been a second wrangler and a Fellow of Marshall's college. In addition he was author of texts on algebra and arithmetic, used by Marshall both in the Tripos and for pre-university mathematical preparation at school.

A third shock for believers came in 1865 with the anonymous publication of *Ecce Homo, A Survey of the Life and Work of Jesus Christ*. Its emphasis was on the humanist and moral features of Christian teaching, through detailed examination of the various credentials of Christ. It followed on Renan's controversial *Vie de Jésus* in 1862. Reactions varied from Shaftesbury's emotional outburst describing *Ecce Homo* as 'the most pestilential book ever committed from the jaws of Hell', Pusey's intense pain at the author's condescending if not patronising tone by which he separated Christ's humanity from his divinity, to Sidgwick's acceptance of the book as a 'great work', because of its 'surprisingly powerful and absorbing, almost sublime second constructive part'. Sidgwick added that it made 'a great sensation' at Cambridge, though the author 'keeps his secret'. By 1869 that author, John Robert Seeley, was back in Cambridge as Regius Professor of History, a chair he held until his death in 1894.[15]

Literary and scientific triumphs may also be briefly recalled. This was the age of Dickens, the Bronte sisters, Thackeray, Mrs Gaskell, Charles Kingsley, Harriet Beecher Stowe and George Eliot; of Flaubert, Turgenev, Victor Hugo, Tolstoy and Dostoevsky on the continent of Europe. Tennyson was the major British poet of the era; Emerson ruled poetry on the other side of the Atlantic; new poetic waves were stirred in France with Baudelaire.

The 1840s and 1850s were the years when John Stuart Mill produced much of his major work as did Thomas Carlyle, George Grote and Auguste Comte. It was the age of Herbert Spencer's *Social Statics*, Mommsen's *Roman History* and Buckle's *History of Civilisation*. There was much activity in emerging psychology with major publications by Alexander

Bain, Ferrier, Fechner, Helmholtz and Lotz. In 1859, Charles Darwin at last published *Origins of Species by Means of Natural Selection*; in 1871 appeared his *Descent of Man*. Their impact was tremendous.

Cultural, scientific and literary advances of the early 1860s consolidated the work of previous decades. This was the final decade of philosophical labour by John Stuart Mill; Herbert Spencer's *First Principle* announced his grand plan of constructing a general system of philosophy embracing biology, psychology, sociology and ethics; Henry Maine started an important tradition of English historical jurisprudence research by publishing *Ancient Law*. The general intellectual ferment of the 1860s is captured by the fact that this decade saw the establishment of more than 100 new reviews, of which the radical *Fortnightly* in 1865, and the more temperate *Contemporary* the year after, were the more important.

Despite the crises of 1847, 1857 and 1865, the mid-Victorian period marked substantial economic progress in England. Per capita national income in real terms climbed slowly but steadily from £18 to £24, reflecting an annual average growth rate over this period approximating a respectable three per cent. Concomitant with this progress were further reforms and a growing demand for more reform. Events in the early 1860s illustrate this. 1861 was the year the Post Office opened its savings bank facilities, thereby giving an outlet to even the lowest classes for exercising the virtues of thrift, praised so eloquently in Samuel Smiles's *Self Help*. Establishment of the limited liability company as a general form of business organisation was an opportunity created for business by a new, 1862 Companies Act. This was also the year of the 1862 London Exhibition, which, relative to its 1851 predecessor in the Crystal Palace, doubled the number of exhibiting firms from fourteen to twenty-nine thousand, a magnificent sign of the growth of British enterprise. Urban development took two steps forward. The first phase of London's underground railway system was successfully completed in 1863 by the opening of the Metropolitan Line. 1864 marked the year when Octavia Hill began her movement for housing reform in slum areas, a movement Alfred Marshall later revered and supported. Another issue later to interest the future economist was the first voluntary arrangement to settle labour disputes implemented by the Wolverhampton building trade in 1865.

The manner in which these events placed their stamp on the late Victorian intellectual Alfred Marshall is discussed later.[16] The backdrop to Marshall's mid-Victorian childhood at home, school and university, shows the soil in which his later activities took root and developed.

PROBLEMS FACING THE MARSHALL BIOGRAPHER

The problems faced by the Marshall biographer are in some ways more daunting than those confronting the biographer of anyone who died a good half century before the biographical task is commenced. The paucity of information on the formative period of Marshall's life creates one set of problems. There is very little material on family and childhood, early education and undergraduate years. Marshall was very reticent about his family and personal affairs. He maintained virtually no contact with school friends and seemed to have formed only one attachment to his fellow students when an undergraduate. Friendships appear to have begun only in 1865 when he had made his name as second wrangler, and even then these were rather limited. Secondly, much of the testimony about his early years, including that about his formative years as a student of economics, comes from reminiscences when he was well over 50, the more detailed coming from an even later stage in his life. In his biography of Augustus John, Holroyd[17] provides an apt warning that the testimony by old men about their youth is not to be freely believed. In so far as that testimony is subject to verification, much of this judgement applies to Marshall's reminiscences of old age. Whitaker has shown[18] how little Marshall correspondence survives from before 1877, the year Marshall was married at the age of 35. More than half of his correspondence for these years are the letters he wrote to his mother from America, the other half are largely associated with university affairs. Over a third of the nearly 800 letters from Marshall which appear to have survived go to Foxwell (113), John Neville Keynes (95) and his publishers, Macmillan (68), more an indication of their propensity to hoard than the nature of Marshall's correspondents. Much of relevance to Marshall's life can, fortunately, be retrieved from published and archival material, including the public records of births, deaths and marriages.

There is another problem of assessing the surviving manuscript material. The terms of Marshall's will gave literary executorship in the first instance to Professor Pigou, the successor to his Cambridge chair. They specifically requested Pigou to edit from his surviving manuscripts 'such materials as he considers to be of value, aiming at brevity, suppressing controversial matter, and also deciding in the negative when he has any doubts at all whether any matter should be published'. The surviving papers held in the Marshall Library were professionally reclassified and catalogued from the late 1980s. They show clear evidence of having been carefully scrutinised and sorted by Marshall himself in the last years before his death, an undoubted opportunity for the removal of unwanted, embarrassing and controversial material. Although this personal selection process was at least partially thwarted by his wife, Mary Paley Marshall, who occasionally managed to rescue discarded items from the wastepaper bin,[19] invariably some material was destroyed during this period.

There is perhaps significance in the fact that the unpublished fragments from Marshall's papers which Pigou included in the *Memorials* commence with Marshall's remark made in 1921 that a young man's autobiography has little of interest to offer.

> I think a young man's autobiography has seldom much interest: but observations by old men on the response of their own phases to changes in the prevailing phases of political and social ideas and sentiments during half a century or more have interested me: and, if time and strength favour, I should like to leave behind me some general notes as to my mental and socio-ethical experiences. But I think time and strength will *not* serve for this. [20]

If this intention guided the selection process of what Marshall wished to preserve among his papers, the lack of youthful observations and reminiscences in that collection is largely explained.

In addition, Marshall indicated that he did not want his personal correspondence published, although 'selections of worth' could be made public. The reason for this is straightforward. He was fully aware that in many of his more hasty epistles and notes to colleagues and friends, his guard had been down. They therefore contained views which would never have reached the pages of his books or other formal publication where endless revision and rethinking was the order of the day.[21] In the light of this, it is not surprising that much of his early family associations are shrouded in mystery. No family letters survive apart from his fairly impersonal letters to his mother from the United States. Family matters rarely creep into his surviving letters, and even then these are largely confined to comments to Foxwell marked 'private', and to a lesser extent, John Neville Keynes, his confidants of the 1870s, 1880s and 1890s. What little is known about Marshall's family derives in the first instance from the notes Mary Paley prepared for her husband's official obituary writers, John Maynard Keynes and W.R. Scott, both of which are preserved. Remaining knowledge has only been acquired from time-consuming investigation of the official records and following up any other clues which offered themselves on the subject. With respect to his family connection and other details of his birth, Marshall seems to have been extremely careful to leave as little information as possible.

THE KEYNES MEMOIR

Another daunting aspect in the task for the Marshall biographer is the splendid obituary Memoir of Alfred Marshall which Keynes prepared for the *Economic Journal*. Written in less than two months from Marshall's death on 13 July 1924, it presents a brilliant portrait of his 'master', a classic in biography widely admired by Keynes's literary friends.[*] Correspondence with Lydia Lopokova indicates how much the death of Alfred Marshall moved Keynes.[22] More importantly, their and Keynes's other correspondence, as well as the Memoir itself, indicate that Keynes had elicited important biographical material from Marshall prior to his death.[23] This makes the Memoir a particularly important document for the Marshall biographer. Its contents draw upon sources no longer accessible. In addition, its publication elicited several direct responses from Marshall's former acquaintances, information which assisted Keynes in the revisions he made to the Memoir for its publication in Pigou's *Memorials*.[24] Other items from this mass of material were noted in Keynes's collected works version of the Memoir.[25]

At the same time, the Memoir and its author strike a note of caution for the Marshall biographer. Correspondence preserved in the Marshall Library shows that Keynes had doubts about some of the material with which he was presented, particularly in relation to the activities of Marshall's father. He sought additional information to what he had been given from the Bank of England, largely unsuccessfully as it turned out. Within the Memoir itself, when the writing gets most florid, the factual material it contains often becomes thinner. Examples are Keynes's discussions of Marshall's ancestors, his alleged intention of becoming a missionary, his mathematical studies at Cambridge, aspects of Marshall's

---

[*] Lytton Strachey to Maynard Keynes, 21 October 1924, 'It was very kind of you to send me your life of Marshall, which I have read with the greatest interest and admiration. It seems to me to be one of your best works. . . . I wish there were more of such things – just the right length and esprit' (in Michael Holroyd, *Lytton Strachey. A Biography*, Penguin Books, 1979, p. 900 n.23). Lydia Lopokova to J.M. Keynes, 30 October 1924, 'Virginia [Woolf] asked me to tell you how much she admired your "Marshall", and she will write besides' (*Lydia and Maynard*, eds Polly Hill and Richard Keynes, London: Andre Deutsch, 1989, p. 243).

conversion from mathematical studies and intended physics research to political economy via metaphysics, psychology and ethics.[26] Other parts of the Memoir can be corrected by material now available. In addition, the space constraint of an obituary article for an academic economic journal meant that many important aspects of Marshall's life could not be fully elaborated.[27] The fact that the piece was an obituary imposed a constraint in itself, which Keynes in its writing minimised by blending the good with at least some of the bad. However, he occasionally followed Edgeworth's editorial advice to delete some things and to re-phrase others.[28] Nevertheless, Keynes's essay in biography on Marshall is an enormous *tour de force* and its contents have been extensively used in what follows.

No matter how greatly one admires and appreciates the quality of Keynes's Memoir as a portrait and judicious appraisal of Alfred Marshall, valuable for the shrewd critical insights of the man it contains, it cannot serve as the life of Marshall in the way John Neville Keynes and Edgeworth ingeniously suggested at the time when it first came out. The fact that Keynes's piece was an obituary is the most important. As Viner has eloquently argued in the case of Marshall,

> But Marshall is now long dead, and the rule 'De mortuis non nisi bonum' is a required rule of morals or of good manners only for men very recently dead. There would be no point therefore in treating Marshall, whether the man or his work, with special tenderness or reserve. He had, beyond doubt, his weaknesses on both counts, including some with which he may have infected his followers, so that we regard them as points of strength. I am sure also that even his virtues are not to be admired by us to the point of slavish imitation. Each generation should – and will – work out its own economics, borrowing from, reacting from, improving upon, retrograding from, that of the preceding generation. Marshall's economics is now distinctly that of a generation which is past, and is increasingly not that of our own. For one thing, it is essentially the economics of a society assumed to be free and to have its economic affairs conducted by free individuals. Freedom, whether of the economic system as such, or of individuals, has over a large part of the earth's surface either never existed or been suppressed. The appropriate economics of the day, is moreover, the economics of war and preparation for or against war, *Wehrwirtschaft*, and Marshall here has only very limited guidance to offer.
>
> It was a characteristic of Victorian, including Marshallian, public utterances that they typically ended on a double note, of assurance, on the one hand, of continuance into the future of all the well-established institutions and cherished values of the Victorian Age, and of promise, on the other hand, of continued betterment of the social conditions of mankind. Both the Victorian complacency with respect to the present and the Victorian optimism with respect to the future progress are now utterly inappropriate. As a social philosopher, Marshall is not yet merely a period piece. If he should become so in the near future, it would properly be a matter for concern, but not for surprise.[29]

It is in Viner's spirit that this first full-length life of Marshall is written. It attempts to present him, in so far as that is possible, warts and all. It is fully concerned with preserving Marshall's social philosophy, linking it with his economics to prevent both being reduced to a period piece and to enable savouring them in their full flavour.

NOTES

1. Robert Skidelsky, *John Maynard Keynes. Hopes Betrayed 1883–1920*, London: Macmillan, 1983, p. 32.
2. Many of them collected in the four volumes of *Alfred Marshall. Critical Assessments*, ed. J.C. Wood, London: Croom Helm, 1982 (hereafter *AMCA*); to which must be added the substantial volume of *Principles of Economics* centenary output. These were reviewed in the first three issues of the *Marshall Studies Bulletin*.
3. Alfred Marshall, *P* I, 1890, Book I, Chapter I; *P* VIII, 1920, Book I, Chapter I.
4. A.J. Cockshut, *The Unbelievers: English Agnostic Thought 1840–1890*, London: Collins, 1964, esp. pp. 143–9, Part II, Chapter 3.
5. Discussed in detail in Chapters 5 and 6 below, esp. pp. 113–18.
6. The Red Book, in which Marshall recorded annual economic data as well as what was happening in literature, the arts, philosophy and so on, is discussed below, Chapter 5, pp. 128–9, Chapter 6, pp. 163–4. For the portrait collection, see below, p. 128.
7. These quotations are reproduced above, facing title pages, p. ii. In 1890 *Punch* also presented Marshall as an eagle, fighting against the socialist snake in the cartoon reproduced as illustration 41.
8. These included 'On the Graphic Method of Statistics', Jubilee issue of the *Statistical Journal*, 1885; 'Remedies for Fluctuations of General Prices', *Contemporary Review*, 1887; 'The Poor Law in relation to State-Aided Pensions' and 'Poor Law Reform', *Economic Journal*, 1892; 'On Rent', *Economic Journal*, 1893; 'Consumers' Surplus', *Annals of the American Academy*, 1893; 'The Old Generation of Economists and the New', *Quarterly Journal of Economics*, 1897; 'Distribution and Exchange', *Economic Journal*, 1898; 'The Social Possibilities of Economic Chivalry', *Economic Journal*, 1907. The first five years of his professorship also saw the publication of a number of lectures and presidential addresses, including 'The Present Position of Political Economy' (1885), 'Theories and Facts about Wages' (1885), 'How far do Remediable Causes influence prejudicially (A) the Continuity of Employment (B) the Rates of Wages?' (1885), 'Co-operation' (1889) and 'Some Aspects of Competition' (1890).
9. J.B. Schneewind, *Sidgwick's Ethics and Victorian Moral Philosophy*, Oxford: at the Clarendon Press, 1977, p. 13: 'He was born on 31 May 1838, just a little less than one year before she [Queen Victoria] came to the throne, and died on 28 August 1900, about half a year before she died.'
10. Below, Chapter 19, pp. 617–18, Chapter 20, p. 760.
11. Jacob Viner, 'Marshall's Economics in Relation to the Man and his Times', *AMCA*, I, p. 242.
12. G.M. Young, *Portrait of an Age. Victorian England*, annotated edition by George Kitson Clark, London: Oxford University Press, 1977, p. 110.
13. Jacob Viner, 'Marshall's Economics in Relation to the Man and his Times', pp. 242–4.
14. Frederic Harrison, *Realities and Ideals: Social, Political, Literary and Artistic*, London: Macmillan, 1908, pp. 369–70. The remainder of this section draws heavily on G.M. Young, *Portrait of an Age*, and a wide range of general historical, and more specialist Victorian, sources.
15. Shaftesbury's reaction is cited in David L. Edwards, *Leaders of the Church of England 1828–1978*, London: Hodder & Stoughton, 1978, p. 148; Pusey's view, communicated to Gladstone, is cited from John Morley, *The Life of William Ewart Gladstone*, London: Edward Lloyd, 1908, Volume 1, p. 599; Sidgwick's reaction in a letter to his mother dated 19 February 1866, from A.S. and E.M.S., *Henry Sidgwick. A Memoir*, London: Macmillan, 1906, p. 143. No record has been left of what Alfred Marshall thought of this work by a future professorial colleague with whom he became quite friendly, or for that matter, how he reacted to these other ecclesiastic turmoils, but it seems certain he would have read *Ecce Homo* not long after its first publication.
16. Esp. Chapters 4–6 dealing with his formative years in the 1860s and 1870s.
17. Michael Holroyd, *Augustus John. A Biography*, Penguin Books, 1976, p. 438: 'It can therefore be misleading .... to reconstruct the young man from what the older man wrote a long time in retrospect'.
18. Unpublished talk to the *Principles* Centenary meeting organised by the Royal Economic Society at St John's College, 9 July 1990.
19. For details of this, see below, Chapter 20, pp. 748–9.
20. *Memorials*, p. 358 (my emphasis).
21. Alfred Marshall to Benjamin Kidd, 15 May 1895, CUL, Add 8064 M552.
22. J.M. Keynes to Lydia Lopokova, 16 May 1924, in *Lydia and Maynard*, p. 195. The letter is extensively quoted below, p. 651.
23. J.M. Keynes, 'Alfred Marshall', p. 172 n.2.
24. J.M. Keynes, 'Alfred Marshall', in *Memorials*, p. 8 n.1.
25. J.M. Keynes, 'Alfred Marshall', pp. 161 n., 163 n., 170 n., p. 174 n., p. 180 n.3 (the last two notes suggest Pigou's role in editing the original Memoir for the *Memorials*).
26. Discussed in Chapters 2–6 below.

27. Examples are Marshall's creation of the Economics Tripos, his role in the women's education issue at Cambridge, his involvement in the formation of the British Economic Association and especially, his work for government inquiries, to which this biography devotes chapters instead of the one or two paragraphs in Keynes's concise essay.
28. Discussed further below, Chapter 20, p. 740.
29. Jacob Viner, 'Marshall's Economics in Relation to the Man and his Times', pp. 253–4.

2. Family and Ancestry

Readers of the brief entry on Alfred Marshall in the 1889 biographical reference work, *Men and Women of the Time*, could have taken him, like that biblical character Melchizedec,[*] as a person who had entered the world with neither mother nor father, nor even a birthplace recorded. In the entry, which was presumably prepared by Marshall himself, date of birth is followed immediately by educational achievements and highlights of his subsequent academic career.[1] Keynes's Memoir is only a marginal improvement in this respect. His opening sentence lists date of birth, wrong place of birth, parents' names and wrong description of father's occupation as at the time of Alfred Marshall's birth. It then describes the Marshalls as a 'clerical family of the West', and indicates Marshall's great-great-grandfather was the Reverend William Marshall, a legendary parson of Herculean strength. Apart from a great-grandfather, the Reverend John Marshall, who linked Marshall to the Hawtreys (and therefore economist R.G. Hawtrey), this is as far as Keynes's discussion of ancestry went. Family fares only slightly better.

The second paragraph gives a picture of sorts of Marshall's father; subsequently there are references to one of Marshall's uncles and to one of his aunts, both on his father's side, though Keynes did not mention this. There are few other references to family. For Keynes, the eugenicist, heredity was therefore mighty only in a limited way. It explained Marshall 'the preacher' by reference to a clerical ancestry; Marshall's 'masterfulness to womankind' in terms of his father's domestic tyranny and, more implicitly, Marshall's interests in monetary and banking matters by his father's position in the Bank of England, wrongly elevated to that of cashier rather than humble clerk.[2]

Given Marshall's own strong interests in issues of heredity, in particular parental influence on their offspring, as well as his involvement in the Galtonian movement, it seems appropriate to repair this rather minuscule and partly erroneous account of family and ancestry. There is more justification for such correction than pandering to dated Galtonian tastes. The fact that Marshall deliberately tried to obscure his birthplace and hide his family background speaks volumes about an aspect of his character. It also says something about his insecurity in assuming the intellectual roles in Cambridge and Oxford to which his scholarly achievements had entitled him. This feature reveals a certain snobbishness on the part of an otherwise simple and fairly modest man.

Moreover, peculiarities in early family relationships are crucial to understanding some of his actions in later life. Examples are his attitudes to women's role in society, his staunch individualism and perhaps even the ease with which he shed the religious beliefs in which he had been brought up at home. Family relationships also played a highly significant role in his career. Both his opportunity to study at Cambridge and his travel to the United States for

---

[*] Hebrews 7:3 depicts Melchizedek as 'Without father, without mother, without descent.' It was for this reason that Jowett was given the nickname of Melchizedek when, like Marshall, he hid his family background from his college milieu at Oxford. See below, Chapter 18, pp. 687–8.

the purpose of learning about protection at first hand came courtesy of Charles, one of his father's brothers, and the uncle who features strikingly in Keynes's Memoir, albeit somewhat fictitiously. Earlier, the educational prowess he showed at school can on his own account at least partly be explained by the kindness of his Aunt Louisa, his father's only sister, who gave him extensive summer holidays in Devon. These apparently fortified the otherwise weakly boy for his strenuous studies during the remainder of the year. Marshall's family and ancestry deserve a more detailed account than they have been given in the past.[3]

AN INSALUBRIOUS BIRTHPLACE

Marshall's birth certificate reports the more salient facts. The birth took place at the house of his parents, 66 Charlotte Row, in the sub-district of Leather Market of the registration district Saint Mary Magdalene, Bermondsey in the County of Surrey at the south-east end of the City of London. In later life, Alfred was to have Bermondsey, Surrey, as well as more generally, London, recorded as his place of birth,[4] while some early biographers[5] provide the wrong attribution of Clapham, sometimes embellished with adjectives like leafy. Clapham, where the Marshall family lived in several different locations,[6] was, however, an area of residence beyond their financial reach at the time of Alfred's birth, while the even more lofty locality of Clapham Common did not become his parents' residence until a few years before his father's retirement in 1877.[7]

Marshall's birth certificate provides some details about his parents as well. His father's particulars are recorded as William Marshall, a clerk in the Bank of England. As a proud father for the second time, he also registered the birth. His mother's name was Rebecca Marshall, maiden name Oliver. His parents had in fact married just over two years previously on 13 May 1840, in the Parish Church of South Camberwell, also located south of the river Thames in the London area. Alfred was the second son of this union, his brother Charles William being born precisely eleven months after the wedding on 13 April 1841. At the time of Charles's birth, William and his young wife were residing in New Peckham, likewise in south-east London.[8] Three more children followed Alfred at rather longer intervals. His two sisters, Agnes and Mabel Louisa were born in 1845 and 1850, at Sydenham and Clapham respectively, and the last child, Walter, was born in 1853, also in Clapham.[9]

Charlotte Row, Bermondsey, was lowest on the social scale of the places in which his parents lived during their married life of nearly forty years. Their marriage apparently had not received the Marshall family blessing and a bank clerk, with appearances to keep up in his place of employment, would have found it difficult to keep a young wife and baby with a second child on the way in the more elegant surroundings of New Peckham.[10] Reference to Leather Market on Alfred's birth certificate signals the major industry of tanning for which Bermondsey was known in the early decades of the nineteenth century; the others being brewing and hat making. Charlotte Row, in fact, adjoined a place called Tan Yard, and other tanning establishments were close by. The burial ground of St Thomas's and Guy's Hospitals were situated to its northern side, a further mark of the lack of social distinction attached to Marshall's place of birth, because such burial grounds were abolished as public health risks in 1850. By then the Marshall family had long departed insalubrious Bermondsey.

A nineteenth-century account of Bermondsey explains why Marshall in later life disguised his place of birth:

> Bermondsey – the 'land of leather', as it has been called in our own day . . . has grown populous, busy, commercial. Its manufacturing prosperity, however, strikingly contrasts with the general aspect of Bermondsey. Its streets generally are but dreary looking places, where, with the exception of a picturesque old tenement, projecting its storey upon storey delicately upward, and 'fast nodding to its fall', or the name of a street suggestive of some agreeable reflection, there is little to gratify the delicate eye. Noble arches here and there bestride the streets of Bermondsey, bearing up a railway, with its engines puffing like so many overworked giants, and its rapid trains of passengers; an elegant free school enriches one part, and a picturesque church another; but they all serve by contrast to show more vividly the unpleasant features of the neighbourhood. . . . There is great industry in Bermondsey . . . for several centuries, this locality has been the center of the tanning and leather trades. . . . Hat making too, is most extensively carried on. . . . The intersection of the district by innumerable ditches gave unusual facilities for the leather manufacture, but at the same time it also entailed frightful misery on the crowded inhabitants.[11]

All facets of the leather industry were located in Bermondsey: hidesellers, tanners, leather dressers, morocco leather dressers, leather sellers and cutters, couriers, parchment makers, wool staplers, horsehair manufacturers, fell mongers, leather dyers and glue makers. Those visiting tanneries needed will-power 'to brave the appeals to [organs] of smell' from pungent odours of the tanning process and its bi-products of spent tan and other refuse used for garden manure and glue making.[12] The account of the Bermondsey leather market given in the *London Encyclopaedia*[13] quotes Dickens's comment on the place 'as reeking with evil smells' while *Mayhew's London*[14] in its discussion of the unsavoury trade of the 'pure-finders' whose product of dog-dung played a crucial part in the production of quality leather goods such as kid gloves and book covers, adds further colour to this facet of Marshall's birth-place. Although Charlotte Row, despite its unattractive location near tanneries, was still well distant from that notorious Jacob's Island, the terrible slum in Mayhew's description of mid-Victorian London, in which Dickens situated the death of Bill Sikes in *Oliver Twist*,[15] the shared location in Bermondsey added to its bad reputation in mid-Victorian Society.

The destruction of this area during the Second World War prevents a visit to the street and house where Alfred Marshall was born. However, the notoriously unsavoury reputation of Bermondsey fully explains why Marshall was so coy about his place of birth. Given his later concern with the problems of poverty which he sought to inform by visiting the poorer districts of major towns in England and Scotland, it is instructive to recall that his earliest years were spent as close to real poverty as the locations he subsequently deliberately explored when he was in his early twenties.

'AN UNSELFISH AND KINDLY INTENTIONED' FATHER: WILLIAM MARSHALL (1812–1901)

At the time of Alfred Marshall's birth, his father was working as a clerk in the Bank of England's clearing office with an annual salary of £140. By then, William Marshall was almost thirty, and had already been employed for twelve years by the Bank. His guarantors for the position in the Bank of England, then an essential requirement for entering employment in such a position of trust, entailing a surety on their part of £500 each, were both uncles on William Marshall's mother's side. One was John Bentall, resident at 37 Craven Street, Strand, by whom William Marshall had been employed in the two years before joining the Bank of England in 1830. The other was Thornton Bentall, a banker residing in Totnes, with whom William, together with his brothers and sister, had stayed after the death of their father. On his mother's side, Alfred Marshall's father was therefore well-connected with persons involved in the financial sector. Before uncovering this fascinating ancestry on his father's side, the portrait of Alfred Marshall's father is further pursued.[16]

Only few details about his father have been preserved. Largely on the basis of one of two extant photographs, Keynes described Marshall's father in the following way,

> a tough old character, of great resolution and perception, cast in the mould of the strictest Evangelicals, bony neck, bristly projecting chin, author of an Evangelical epic in a sort of Anglo-Saxon language of his own invention which found some favour in its appropriate circles, surviving despotically minded into his ninety-second year. The nearest objects of his masterful instincts were his family, and their easiest victim his wife; but their empire extended in theory over the whole of womankind, the old gentleman writing a tract entitled Man's Rights and Woman's Duties. Heredity is mighty, and Alfred Marshall did not altogether escape the influence of the parental mould.[17]

Keynes subsequently portrayed[18] Alfred Marshall himself as the victim of his father's 'masterful instincts' in the context of his homework for school. This recalled the 'affection and severity of James Mill' since William Marshall made his son do school work 'often at Hebrew', under his supervision until eleven at night. This story of parental surveillance derived from Mary Paley's notes to assist Keynes in writing his Marshall Memoir. These add that William Marshall himself was apt to sit up each night from 10.00 p.m. to 3.00 a.m. to work on his literary projects, after completing the 8.00–5.30 working day at the Bank of England. Drinking black coffee kept him awake in those nocturnal vigils. William Marshall's puritanical nature and paternal affection are demonstrated by a promise extracted from Alfred Marshall as a boy to stop studying chess problems. 'When a boy, A[lfred] suffered from terrible headaches and the only cure for them was to play chess. His father therefore allowed chess to be used for this purpose; but later on he made A[lfred] promise never to play chess. This promise was kept all through his life, though he could never see a chess problem in the newspapers without getting excited. But he said his father was right to extract this promise, for otherwise he would have been tempted to spend all his life on it.'[19]

At the suggestion of Edgeworth,[20] Keynes toned down Alfred's father's proclivity to severe discipline and the fact that he was 'somewhat of a tyrant in his family'.[21] Father William's tyranny was more vocally attested to by his grandson and Alfred Marshall's nephew, Claude Guillebaud. He described his grandfather as 'a wicked old tyrant, who, amongst other misdeeds, made my poor mother's life a misery to her for years. He refused to allow her to marry the man she fell in love with – an impecunious subaltern, and when she did marry my father, the old gentleman hated him, and made things as difficult as possible for him, merely because he married my mother. He lived with us for many years until his death, and one of my early and vivid recollections is that of dancing with joy and delight, together with my brothers, on hearing that he was at last dead.'[22]

In one of the few references to his father in correspondence, Alfred Marshall recollected this aspect of parental control. The context was an inquiry to John Neville Keynes about a governess for the children of his brother, Charles William, in which Marshall noted that his brother was 'adverse to *very* strict discipline, and so are my sister and her husband, the Guillebauds'. Alfred Marshall's explanation followed: 'My father has very strong views on the subject and is a little apt to put his views forward to the distress of my sister. My father is wonderfully unselfish and kindly intentioned. But he does not know how hard his extremely severe discipline would have made life to all of us children, if it had not been for the constant gentleness of my mother.'[23] William Marshall's disciplinary skills had been cultivated from an early age. After the death of his father, he was placed in charge of his brothers and sisters. This was when they were all living with Uncle Thornton at Totnes and when, in the striking phrase from Mary Paley Marshall,[24] 'he kept them in order with a slipper'. This wonderful story is spoiled by the fact that William Marshall's 'slipper discipline' was rather short-lived. The cause of the move to Totnes, his father's death in 1828, coincides with the year in which he was employed as a clerk by his legal custodian, John Bentall, in his London stockbroker firm.

Marshall's father's disciplinary perspectives and practices were certainly not unusual for a mid-Victorian paterfamilias. However, his later published writings on the need to revive the traditional English language of King Alfred's time, show an obsessive fascination with the instruments for inflicting corporal punishment on children. Commenting on the word, 'tanner', William Marshall noted that this word ought to be spelled as 'tawer', that is, the 'person who "taws" or dresses leather by beating and macerating it. A "tan" is a twig. Boys in Scotland in my schooldays used to be chastised by leathern thongs called "tawse".' Commenting earlier in this book on 'swipe, scourge', William Marshall noted the word's onomatopoeic qualities. 'The very sound of a wielded cane is given in this word. It is a word which I have not heard, I think, since my childhood, and is now thankfully remembered by me in connection with my faithful schoolmaster.'[25] There clearly are other characteristics apart from love of the rod pertinent to Alfred Marshall's father. He was, after all, also described by his famous son as 'unselfish and kindly intentioned' or, as Mary Paley went so far to suggest, as a person 'with great literary taste and faculty . . . of great resolution, great perception . . . and very strong Protestant [views]'.[26]

Mary Paley's appraisal of her father-in-law as a man of great faculty is not supported by William Marshall's career at the Bank of England. On joining it, he was described as 'single, free from debt, fair handwriting and quick at accounts and [has] no objection to go to a Branch Bank'. After two years in the Cash Book Office, he spent a decade in the Clearer's Office, then a further ten years in both the Bills Office and Clearer's Office, a subsequent fifteen years in the Bills Office, then four years in Supernumerary Cashiers and his final six years of service in the Cashiers' section. On 18 September 1877 he retired on a pension of £340 per annum, or two-thirds of his finishing salary of £510.[27] The relatively late appointment to the Cashiers' section explains William Marshall's generous retirement pension. It compares favourably with the £700 son Alfred obtained on becoming Principal of Bristol University College and Professor of Political Economy in the same year, a stipend he continued to receive while Professor at Cambridge. William Marshall's appointment to the Cashiers'section owed more to seniority than to merit. By the time he 'moved to the Cashiers' Section he had already served forty years in the Bank'. This final promotion accorded with Bank policy to secure staff with long service as favourable a pension as possible.[28] The fact that William Marshall could spend a substantial part of the night on his private studies shows that his work at the Bank was not very strenuous and required little concentration. In short, William Marshall had a long but very average clerical career in the Bank, gaining no distinction from his employment apart from long and honest service.

Did William Marshall's literary faculty make up for this undistinguished banking career? Keynes noted his authorship of an 'Evangelical Epic in a sort of Anglo-Saxon English of his own invention' as well as a tract on *Man's Rights and Woman's Duties*. In fact, Alfred's father published a number of such epics before and during retirement. However, the anti-feminist tract so conveniently ascribed to him to support Keynes's Galtonian thesis of 'mighty heredity', cannot be located in any major libraries. Nor was the Anglo-Saxon language William Marshall used in these epics of his own invention. In one of his books, he clearly indicated the major source of his linguistic return 'to the English of King Alfred's days':

> I am not a linguist; my authority for the essay is the dictionary of the late venerable and very learned Dr. Bosworth, amidst the columns of which I wandered in such a delirium of joy during the first months after I found out its existence as a traveller would feel on first entering a huge untrodden cavern full of the most beautiful stalactites, and of the rarest and most valuable fossils.[29]

No great originality can therefore be claimed for William Marshall's defence of old English. Its competence in transcription and linguistic explanation is, however, of a reasonable standard and the book was sufficiently meritorious to be published by Longmans, Green & Company.[30] The book held sentiments of which son Alfred would later have approved. William Marshall described Latin and Greek studies as unnecessarily 'sacrificing the health of our little children to one great idol' while a similar sacrifice to that health, exacted from 'that other great idol', metaphysics, was denounced with equal vehemence. To further the book's aim 'to provide for education in the pure English of King Alfred's day', its contents were devoted to lists of old English words, their 'Anglo-Latin distortions' in modern usage and detailed etymological and linguistic explanations of selected words in alphabetical order.[31] This practical aim detracted from the more scholarly objectives of the work, and offset the gains to child health from abandoning classical and metaphysical studies. It may, however, explain why Alfred Marshall got his name. If this is true, it makes his father's interest in old English a hobby of very long standing.

The evangelical epics which William Marshall produced by their use of old Anglo-Saxon words were designed as examples of the restoration of the English language to its 'pure', ninth-century form. They were also written to encourage a Christian life and to expose the dangers of 'popery'. The first, entitled *Lochlere*, specifically mentioned the aim of restoring old English. It also stressed the importance of the act of religious conversion for Christian life. A few lines from its last stanza illustrate both William Marshall's poetic style and his attempts at English language reform:

He now cries out to earth that day is breaking:
And he around him looks out for the Hebrew,
Who, when he comes, will as Thine own outrider
Come bringing dawn. Speed, speed the coming; speed it
Christ Drighten! [Lord God] Light of men, come Thou! – come
quickly! [32]

Although unsuccessful with the public, William Marshall published three other epics during his life-time. In 1887, he published *Rinalpho's Dream*, a poem combating the attractions of Roman Catholicism. This was followed in 1898 by *Aarbert* (with a revised version in 1899), and *Herbert* in 1901. The message of *Aarbert* was Protestant and Puritan. Its protests in support of the teaching of the Bible includes a loud and unflinching protest against 'every teaching, Ritualistic, Romish, Antinomian and Infidel which is in conflict with it'. No apology for such 'illiberality' was required on the part of the author because the language he used was no match for the 'curses' and 'calls to violence of Popery'.[33] William Marshall's theological preferences are concisely summarised in a verse from this rather long and dreary poem:

No, Aarbert! we will go to neither Rome
Nor cold Geneva; but will warm our faith
With the mild glow of worship Anglican,
Amid the pomp of rightful ritual.[34]

As this stanza implies, William Marshall's evangelicalism appears to have taken the more general form of its Victorian manifestation. It fell within the Anglican tradition of the established Church, avoiding both the theological extremes of Calvinism and Romish revival. His epic poems demonstrate a simple belief in Clapham-type evangelicalism, which held that man must personally experience God through conversion and individual acceptance of God's offer of redemption by the death of Jesus Christ. Personal conversion is the theme of at least three of William Marshall's epic poems. Claphamite evangelicals had also the duty to evangelise among their fellow men. Spreading the protestant and puritan word through his own writing became probably even more important to William Marshall when his second son, Alfred, showed no inclination to enter the career of minister his father may have wished for him.

Other autobiographical features are visible in William Marshall's literary creations. The description of Aarbert's wife, Milda, who 'follows him in self-surrender to God' notes that she was 'one of his own class, but more staid and lowly-minded, who has shared most of his experiences'.[35] As shown later, this was an ideal not matched for William Marshall in his own marriage. The poem's recurring references to bankruptcy[36] suggest William Marshall's recollections of youthful shame about his father's business failures. As poetry, these epics have little merit, and if heredity was as mighty in this respect as in the case mentioned by Keynes, then it is probably fortunate that Alfred Marshall's verses of which Mary Paley sent a sample to Keynes, are now lost.[37] Two other works by William Marshall indicate his strong, but for the time, not unusual hatred of Roman Catholicism.[38] Apart from such writings and his views on discipline, little else can be said about William Marshall's role of father and head of the Marshall household.

Alfred Marshall's correspondence from America in 1875 is addressed to his mother, and apart from the almost obligatory 'kindest love' to his father and his sisters, with which the letters invariably end, they contain few mentions of William Marshall. An exception is a letter from Niagara Falls dated 18 July. This expressed regret about the poor state of his father's feet, and wished him speedy recovery. A month later (from St Louis in a letter dated 22 August) Alfred expressed delight that his mother and father 'were getting on so well' and envy about the latter's 'musical successes'. He added, that 'if I had time, I should feel sorely tempted to endeavour to follow his example. I am extremely glad that he is going in for this form of recreation: it is probably the best he could have, and good everyway'. Unfortunately, the nature of these musical successes is not explained. They were possibly no more than a subscription to a series of concerts. Apart from confirming Alfred Marshall's liking for music, the comment points to a cultural side to his father missing from other accounts.[39] An autobiographical footnote included in *Money, Credit and Commerce*[40] points to another cultural side of his father: the fact that he used to take Alfred Marshall to the British Museum, both for instruction and amusement. It may be therefore for more than filial piety that his father is thanked for assistance 'on special points' in the first edition of *Principles of Economics*.[41]

Another aspect of William Marshall's character matches Alfred's view about his father's unselfishness and good intentions. The signs of upward mobility in the Marshall family reflected in their successive moves from Bermondsey to Sydenham to Clapham to Clapham Common have already been noted. Although these may indicate little more than his father's attempts to regain for himself the trappings of the status of 'gentleman' he had claimed for himself on his marriage certificate, they may also be seen as his attempt at generous provision of the best possible material background and opportunities for his children, within the bounds of his modest salary as bank clerk.[42] Such unselfishness and well-intentioned conduct is also visible in the financial sacrifices he made to secure the best possible education for his younger sons. The Merchant Taylors' School which both Alfred and younger brother Walter attended, was costly, even for non-boarders as the Marshall children were. In addition, Walter was given the opportunity to study at Peterhouse, Cambridge, and on the diagnosis of the 'consumption' that killed him before graduating, his final months were made easier by the stay in South Africa his father probably financed, perhaps with assistance from his sons.[43]

Little can be said on William Marshall's lasting influence on his son, Alfred. The family environment he created, in which the young Alfred grew up, left its scars. His father's influence has been blamed for Alfred Marshall's hypersensitivity to criticism in later life, associated as this was with a pathological fear of making mistakes.[44] His father's strong evangelical convictions which, judging from his poetry, bordered on the fanatical, perhaps facilitated Alfred Marshall's later loss of religious faith. Such dogmatic belief was far more difficult to defend against rational criticism at Cambridge than less fundamentalist Anglicanism. Negative influences from a very pious father on his son's religious beliefs were not uncommon in Victorian England, and a letter to Foxwell suggests that this may well have been the case.[45] However, as Mary Paley[46] indicated, his father did have sufficient faith in Alfred's ability to procure him a superior school education at considerable financial sacrifice, without which he would have been unable to qualify for Cambridge. Moreover, on the Bentall side, his father's family provided an ancestry more appropriate to Marshall's later career than the succession of clerical ancestors which Keynes's Memoir foisted on him.[47]

THE MARSHALL ANCESTRY

Alfred Marshall's father, William, was himself the eldest child in a large family of five sons and one daughter. In their status as Alfred's uncles and aunt, some of them were to play a significant role in his youth. No clergymen relatives can be found in his father's generation. However, Alfred's grandfather on his father's side, also called William, had two brothers who both became clergymen. Apart from a subsequent brother-in-law, they were Alfred Marshall's nearest relatives who were clergy. Alfred Marshall's great-grandfather, John Marshall, was Headmaster at Exeter Grammar School and an ordained minister. He is therefore the first of Alfred Marshall's direct clerical ancestors. John Marshall's marriage to Mary Hawtrey in the mid-eighteenth century, meant that Alfred Marshall was indirectly related to the twentieth-century economist, R.G. Hawtrey.[48] John Marshall's father was yet another William Marshall. He was a seventeenth-century clergyman, more remembered for prodigious feats of physical, than spiritual, strength. Thus Marshall's direct clerical ancestors are confined to a great-grandfather and great-great-grandfather, so that at best he is a very distant product of 'a clerical family from the west'.[49]

The family tree of Alfred Marshall, constructed on the basis of the available evidence (see Figure 2.1) enables a more systematic account of some pertinent features in the genetic inheritance on his father's side. As already indicated, Alfred Marshall had four uncles and one aunt on his father's side, that is, Uncles Edward, Henry, Thornton and Charles Henry as well as Aunt Louisa.

Uncle Edward (1817–62) built a career in the Navy, rising from the ranks on enlistment in 1829 to captain in 1857 via promotion to midshipman in 1830, mate in 1833, lieutenant in 1843 and commander in 1853. He served in the Mediterranean, the West Coast of Africa and the Cape of Good Hope, on ships which included the *Thunderer, Thunderbolt, Snake, Devastation* and *Sappho*. His death in 1862, aged forty-five, cut short what could have been an even more successful naval career. He left a son, Lionel, but Alfred does not appear to have kept in touch with this side of his father's family.

Uncle Thornton (1822–61) likewise had a career in the services. He was a pharmacist's apprentice in the late 1830s, studied medicine at Guy's Hospital in London, and when he obtained his Diploma of Surgery in 1843, he lived in 200 Tooley Street at Bermondsey close to his older brother William. His medical studies were facilitated by a reference from his cousin, the Rev. Dr Hawtrey of Eton. A medical career with the army took him to New Zealand and Australia. He married in Sydney in 1851, and their only child was born in Adelaide in 1852. He subsequently returned to England, living in St John's Wood where he died.

Uncle Henry (1821–80) was a man of business. He was a Calcutta merchant until the end of the 1850s, at which time he returned to England. He later operated a timber firm

Figure 2.1: The Marshall Inheritance

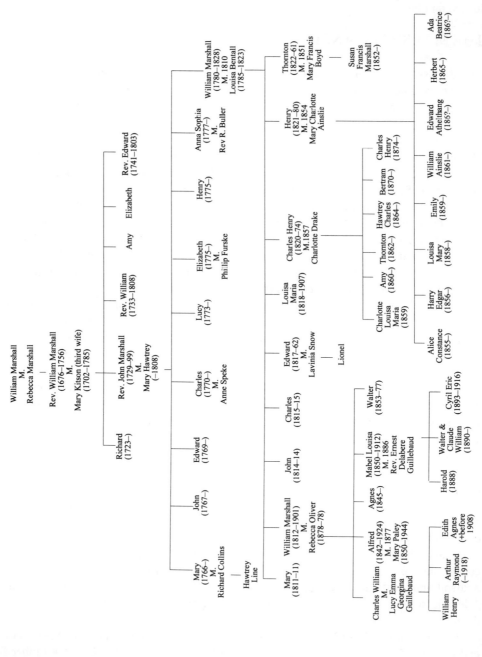

Source: Based on material in the Coase Papers, Regenstein Library (University of Chicago). Used with permission of the Department of Special Collections and Professor Coase

(Steel, Marshall & Company) from 1874, an enterprise financially assisted by his brother, Charles Henry. Uncle Henry was more important than Edward or Thornton in the life of Alfred Marshall and his family. His presence in India probably assisted the career of Alfred's older brother Charles William in the Indian sub-continent where, from age 17, he was earning his living first as an employee and ultimately as manager of the Bengal Silk Company. Alfred Marshall's letters to his mother[50] show that Uncle Henry was in contact with his brother William's family in 1875. His will, dated October 1876, named Alfred Marshall one of his executors, a further sign of the good relations between these branches of the far-flung Marshall family.

Uncle Charles Henry (1820–74), the only uncle actually mentioned in the Keynes Memoir,[51] is a most colourful character. A loan from him enabled Alfred Marshall to go to Cambridge in 1862 to study mathematics. His legacy made it possible for his economist-nephew to study American protection first hand during a summer visit to the United States in 1875.[52] As shown in Figure 2.1, Uncle Charles was the third of the five surviving sons in his grandfather's family. The story of how Uncle Charles made his money, which enabled this largesse to his talented nephew, was one which 'Alfred often told' according to Keynes. Keynes's account is quoted in full to show how facts sometimes were improved in his Marshall Memoir:

> Having sought his fortunes in Australia and being established there at the date of the gold discoveries, a little family eccentricity disposed him to seek his benefit indirectly. So he remained a pastoralist, but, to the mirth of his neighbours, refused to employ anyone about his place who did not suffer from some physical defect, staffing himself entirely with the halt, the blind, and the maimed. When the gold boom reached its height his reward came. All the able-bodied labourers migrated to the gold-fields and Charles Marshall was the only man in the place to carry on. A few years later he returned to England, with a fortune, ready to take an interest in a clever, rebellious nephew.[53]

The basis for Keynes's account was the material provided by Mary Paley. Her version which follows, indicates the degree of literary licence with which Keynes re-told the details:

> A favourite Uncle was Charles Henry, who disliked his brother William's control at Totnes, and ran away and became a cabin boy. He had great natural ability and in time made his fortune in Australia. He went to Germany without any knowledge of German, bought sheep there and took them to Australia. He also took a shepherd and paid him so much a head for every sheep that arrived safely. He engaged all the blind, halt and maimed he could get hold of at the time of the gold discoveries, and so when other sheepowners were deprived of labour by the rush to the goldfields, he managed to make a fortune out of wool.[*]

The facts about the origins of Uncle Charles's fortune are rather different. A more accurate account of his 'natural ability', foresight and 'family eccentricity' placed in the service of

---

[*] Mary Paley Marshall, 'Biographical Notes on Alfred Marshall' (KMF). German sheep imported from Saxony were quite common in the area and Charles Marshall was in Germany to buy more sheep in 1862. The cabin boy story is true to the extent that the 1841 census disclosed Charles's occupation as that of 'mariner'. Keynes'' clever transformation of Mary Paley's cabin story (significantly included in the paragraph immediately preceding Keynes's account of Uncle Charles) may be noted. It is now Alfred Marshall who 'would run away – to be a cabin boy at Cambridge, and climb the rigging of geometry and spy out the heavens' (Keynes, 'Alfred Marshall', p. 164; cf. Coase, 'Alfred Marshall's Family and Ancestry', p. 14).

rent-seeking in Australian pastures from the late 1840s is available. Nothing is known about the precise time and circumstances of Charles Marshall's arrival in Australia and how the 'cabin boy' became a pastoralist of substance. Before the gold rushes of 1851, he was already a man of considerable wealth in the Darling Downs, a pastoral district of what is now southern Queensland. This had been actively settled from the 1840s onwards, so that Uncle Charles arrived in the area at the right time. During the 1840s and 1850s, in fact until the crisis of 1866, its landowners or squatters were virtually able to 'coin money' from profitable sales of sheep for breeding or meat, as well as from the sale of wool and tallow. In August 1848, Charles Marshall was applying for leaseholds in the Darling Downs, in partnership with other settlers. By 1851, Charles Marshall was the owner of the rich property, Glengallan, which from 1855 he exploited in partnership with others, during the early 1870s with his last partner Slade. During the 1850s and 1860s he added substantially to those landholdings and invested in mining ventures. The 1851 gold discoveries in Victoria and New South Wales tightened labour supply in these colonies. They also created a 'tremendous demand for fatstock which the Downs was able to supply'. Exploitation of this rich export market was probably the reason why Charles Marshall visited the Turon goldfields in 1851 with his West Indian companion, Davson, feeding the preserver of this anecdote, Bartley, on a 'fearful and wonderful, indigestible' damper, the traditional bread made from water, salt and flour by Australian bushmen in a rough camp oven. Pastoral profits enhanced by the gold rushes of the 1850s were the means to Marshall prosperity in Australia.[54]

Labour shortages in newly settled pastoral areas were not confined to the gold rushes in the 1850s. They were endemic over the whole formative period in the Darling Downs pastoral industry. This labour problem was solved by tapping supplies from various sources. In the decades after 1840, the area sought and obtained convict labour, Chinese labour, indentured Kanaka labour from the South Pacific islands and, particularly after 1854, free immigrant labour from Germany. During the final years of convict transportation from 1848, Queensland sheep and cattle men concentrated in the southern area of that state, pressed strongly for continuing access to convict workers as a source of cheap labour, in the absence of which they claimed to have no alternative but that of importing Chinese coolies.[55]

As the good businessman–economist–entrepreneur he was said to be, Uncle Charles tapped most of these alternative sources of labour supply which were on offer. In 1849, he was in the courts seeking redress for an absconding and insolent convict servant and answered charges for a failure to pay wages and other breaches of the Master and Servants' Act. From 1850 to 1852, when gold rush-induced local labour shortages were at their height, he employed convict labour or, to use Coase's poignant phrase, the 'haltered' rather than the 'halt' and the 'lame'. When the effective ending of transportation to the eastern states in 1852 dried up the profitable supply of convict labour, he probably resorted to immigrant German, or even Chinese, pastoral labour. In 1873 and 1874, Charles Marshall's London correspondence with his partner, W.B. Slade, shows how conscious he was of the dubious morality in hiring indentured Kanaka labour by trying to disguise the fact with some ingenuity. In one of the letters, he suggested honouring a promise of supplying them with individual good behaviour medals, as apparently pledged to them when they first entered his employ. In making the suggestion, he particularly stressed the favourable newspaper publicity to be extracted from such a humane gesture. In addition, he advised his partner that such a token of esteem from their employers would demonstrate to the world that 'the boys are not treated quite as slaves'. Uncle Charles died before the importation of coloured indentured labour was prohibited in Queensland. However, in 1875 Britain responded to protests on the practice of 'blackbirding', comparable to 'the evils of the Atlantic' slave trade, by establishing a high commissioner for the Western Pacific with instructions to maintain a naval patrol to stamp out this nefarious practice.[56]

A more enterprising feature in Uncle Charles's pastoral ventures may also be mentioned. The German element in Mary Paley Marshall's account of his activities indicated correctly that German sheep imported from Saxony and elsewhere in Germany were often an important feature in the Australian sheep industry, including that of the Darling Downs. As it turned out, with crucial implications for the young Alfred Marshall's future, Uncle Charles Marshall himself was in Europe in 1862, buying prize-winning sheep in Mecklenburg. On the obligatory London leg of this visit, he undoubtedly visited his brothers residing there, regaling his nephew Alfred among others with his antipodean exploits, perhaps pulling his leg, and that of other gullible members of the family, in telling the 'yarn' of his ingenious solution to gold rush-induced labour shortage. He was also on hand to lend Alfred money for Cambridge studies. Quality sheep for breeding and wool production was a striking feature of Charles Marshall's pastoral management, and reports on the flocks at his property of Glengallan invariably stressed their excellence.

The source of Uncle Charles's fortune which so generously assisted his family, including especially nephew Alfred,[57] can therefore be described as doubly tainted. The pastoral profits from which it originated, were initially derived from his exploitation of cheap, convict labour in the years to 1852 and later from his use of the semi-slave labour of indentured Pacific Islanders in the early 1870s. This practice implied an element of shame for the Marshall family. The strong evangelical movement against the Atlantic slave trade, crowned with success in 1833, the prominence given to abolition during the American civil war in the 1860s, plus British action in 1875 to stamp out Queensland 'blackbirding', make it plausible that the Marshall family would have concealed Charles Marshall's involvement in the semi-slavery of indentured labour from which he (and subsequently they) benefited so substantially, had they known of it. For reasons like this, Uncle Charles himself had cause to keep silence and to disguise the nature of his success by telling the story 'Alfred so often told'. A colourful story for explaining how he had made his fortune in Australia was also less boring than boasting about his undoubted skills of investing in sheep, real estate and mining. A sheep-purchasing trip enabled Uncle Charles to be on hand at that crucial time in 1862 when Alfred needed his financial assistance to go to Cambridge. This part of Alfred Marshall's long suppressed family history adds extra meaning to a view expressed in the *Principles* (but removed from its third edition onwards) that 'slavery was not always entirely without advantages'.[58]

Alfred Marshall's only aunt on his father's side, Aunt Louisa, is another member of the Marshall family briefly mentioned by Keynes. In the context of his father's tendency to overwork Alfred in the evening with schoolwork, Keynes mentioned that, 'Alfred . . . used to say, his life was saved by his Aunt Louisa, with whom he spent long summer holidays near Dawlish [in Devon]. She gave him a boat, a gun and a pony, and by the end of the summer he would return home, brown and well.'[59]   In her notes for Keynes, Mary Paley added considerably to the picture of Alfred's favourite aunt, whose name, incidentally, had also been given to his favourite sister, Mabel Louisa. There she appears as an epitome of that virtuous specimen of Victorian womanhood, the spinster-sister who sacrificed her personal happiness in marriage and a chance of having her own family for the sake of serving the family as a whole. 'A[lfred] was devotedly fond of his Aunt Louisa. She made the care of her brothers and their families her first duty in life. She refused several offers of marriage because she wished to remain a centre of the large family and to keep them all together. She did this till the end of a long life.' Her brothers frequently used her as executrix in their wills and potential guardian for their offspring. From the early 1870s she moved to Clapham, hence closer to Alfred Marshall's parents. The rest of Mary Paley's notes on Aunt Louisa was reproduced verbatim by Keynes with the exception that he omitted the actual name of her cottage, that is, Kenton Cottage, near Dawlish.[60]   This explains why in his first letter from America (dated 5 June 1875), Alfred Marshall asked his mother to pass his letters and notes on his American travels to Aunt Louisa, because she 'is likely, I think, to be interested in some of them'. A list of persons to receive presentation copies of his *Elements of the Economics of Industry* in 1892 also includes her name.[61]

The parents of this extensive family, grandfather William Marshall (1780–1828) and Louisa Bentall (1785–1823), are omitted completely from Keynes's Memoir, despite the fact that grandfather William had been mentioned in Mary Paley's notes as a Paymaster in the Navy. Unlike the successful military and business careers of the sons he fathered, grandfather William appears to have enjoyed little success in enterprise. As mentioned previously, he was one of three surviving sons of John Marshall, headmaster, of whom the other two became clergymen.   Little is recorded about grandfather William until his marriage to Louisa Bentall in 1810, after which they sailed for the Cape to enable him to take up his appointment as Assistant Paymaster General to the Cape Garrison in South Africa. Grandfather William stayed in this post for a number of years, probably enjoying his life in the upper stratum of British society in this then newly acquired British colony. During the Cape period five children were born to the marriage, of whom only two survived their year of birth. They were Alfred's father, William, and Edward, the subsequent naval officer.

In March 1816, grandfather William moved to Mauritius. He first took a position with the commissionary of police. Then, in an 'ill-fated move', he purchased at public auction the farm of the battelage (or exclusive privilege of shipping and landing goods) in the harbour of St Louis. Grandfather William's expectations of monopolistic gain were not realised. The venture in fact became a financial disaster. This lack of success is explained in part because he had paid far too much for the rights of the farm. Two reasons are given for this faulty evaluation of price in grandfather William's Memorial of April 1818 to the Acting Governor in support of his request for relief in paying the first instalment on the purchase price. This explained first, he had wrongly supposed the port to be kept open until the 1 March 1820, whereas it was shut nearly two years earlier on 1 April 1818. Secondly, he alleged the market had been rigged by fictitious bidding on the part of the auctioneer, which lifted the purchase price from the $17,500 (at which grandfather William claimed real competitive bidding ceased) to the $23,000 which he eventually contracted to pay. In addition, grandfather William's financial problems were aggravated by the destruction of some of his boats and property in a hurricane during March 1818. Losses in the first year of the lease combined with the first instalment of the purchase price and the living expenses of his growing family had exhausted his original capital, amounting to the very substantial sum of £6,000. Eventually, some relief was granted. It was gradually appreciated that grandfather William was totally unable to meet his financial obligations to the Crown, and that he had completely failed to grasp the extent of the commitments into which he had so unwisely entered. In 1823, when his wife Louisa died, grandfather William left Mauritius with his young family of six children, whose ages ranged from eleven to one. He settled in Leith, Scotland and commenced a merchant venture which also appears to have failed. In any case, by 1827 grandfather William was employed as a humble clerk until his death in 1828. His gravestone's inscription, describing him as 'formerly Paymaster R.N.', explains the basis of Mary Paley's information to Keynes, and indicates a tendency in the Marshall family to enhance their social status, in this case from the reality of having been Assistant Paymaster General to the Cape garrison for half a dozen years.[62]

Apart from mentioning the name of Alfred's mother, female ancestry is ignored in Keynes's Memoir, perhaps to strengthen the misogynist overtones of its second paragraph. This is a particularly regrettable omission with respect to Alfred Marshall's paternal grandmother, Louisa Bentall. In the context of his father's career at the Bank of England, it was mentioned that the necessary guarantors were her two brothers, John Bentall, a London stockbroker and Thornton Bentall, a banker of Totnes. On the death of grandfather William in 1828, legal custody of the six Marshall orphans was given to brother-in-law John Bentall, while the children found shelter in the probably more spacious country residence of Uncle Thornton at Totnes. The fact that John Bentall provided Alfred's father William at the age of 16 with his first job as clerk in his stockbroking firm in 1828 was also mentioned. If there was any inheritance for Alfred Marshall of financial skills from his ancestry it most likely came from the Bentall side of his father's family.[63]

The potential for such inheritance is enriched by Coase's research on the antecedents of the affluent Bentalls. Louisa Bentall's father (Alfred Marshall's great-grandfather) was also a banker. Her grandfather, John Bentall (Marshall's great-great-grandfather), was a wine cooper and merchant in Colchester (Essex) who was married to an Elizabeth Thornton (see Figure 2.2). Elizabeth Thornton's family, 'was even more distinguished in business and public affairs than the Bentalls. They were merchants, bankers, members of parliament, and some of them were among the more prominent members of the Clapham Sect. Economists will immediately recognise that this means that Alfred Marshall was related to Henry Thornton, author of the *Paper Credit of Great Britain*. . . . Both Alfred Marshall and Henry Thornton were descendants of Robert Thornton, Rector of Birkin, Yorkshire, in the 17th century. Robert Thornton was Alfred Marshall's great-great-great-great-grandfather and Henry Thornton's great-great-great-grandfather.'[64] Lack of knowledge about this illustrious ancestry by Marshall's immediate family probably owed much to the business failure of grandfather William, who squandered the material inheritance from both father and father-in-law in unsuccessful commercial ventures. As a result, Keynes had to forgo rich opportunities to speculate on the genetical consequences of Alfred Marshall's family connections via the Thornton–Bentall alliance. These did not only include a major monetary economist of the early nineteenth century but, via the Forster connection (E.M. Forster was the great-great-grandson of Henry Thornton) even a tenuous association with the Bloomsbury Group.[65]

A GREATLY BELOVED MOTHER: REBECCA MARSHALL OLIVER (1817–1878)

Apart from a brief comment in its second paragraph that in exercising his misogynist proclivities, father William found 'his easiest victim' in his wife, the only reference to Marshall's mother occurs in the opening sentence of Keynes's Memoir.[66] Keynes's omissions in this regard were not from lack of interest in this side of Marshall's ancestry. The age of Freud did not permit ignoring a mother's contribution to the subject of a biography. Correspondence with Mary Paley suggests ignorance was the reason. Such ignorance extended to the son of Alfred Marshall's eldest brother, his nephew, William (see Figure 2.1). By way of nephew Claude Guillebaud, he indirectly informed Mary Paley (presumably after reading Keynes's Memoir about his famous uncle) that Keynes 'will be amused by this anecdote of Alfred's mother. William seems to know more about Alfred's mother than anyone and he says that she came from Maidstone and was the daughter of a chemist and that the Marshall family considered this a misalliance and she had to cut herself off from her own family. She was a charming woman and Alfred was devoted to her. When anything pleasant befell such as the address on the 80th birthday, he would say, "if only my mother were alive, how glad she would be"'.[67] Mary Paley's notes for Keynes in fact only mention Alfred's strong attachment to his mother. This was repeated in the notes she subsequently gave to Walter Scott to assist his biographical memoir for the British Academy.[68] Mary Paley herself had only infrequently encountered Alfred's mother. The occasion of her wedding to Alfred at which his mother was present is the single recorded occasion. Rebecca Marshall's sudden death within a year of that event, together with the young couple's move to Bristol, makes frequent meetings between the two extremely unlikely.[69]

As mentioned previously, Alfred Marshall's parents' marriage certificate indicates that Rebecca Oliver's father was a butcher, and not a chemist as nephew William had surmised. A Marshall family boycott of this wedding seems supported by the fact that the witnesses recorded for the event were both Olivers: Rebecca's brother Edward and her sister, Elizabeth.   Both her parents had died before the wedding; her father in 1833, her mother in 1838. However, when the marriage took place in May 1840, William Marshall had also been an orphan for 12 years.   Moreover, his father's brothers had been insufficiently interested in their nephews and niece to become their guardian after their brother's death, while most of his own brothers were already abroad by then. Edward was in the Navy, Henry in India, Charles Henry at sea and only Thornton, as medical student at Guy's and living in London, was a potential guest at the wedding. It is not surprising that sister Louisa's family devotion did not stretch to the long trip from Devon to London, arduous in the absence of a train connection and in any case considered most unsuitable for a twenty-three-year-old unmarried woman.

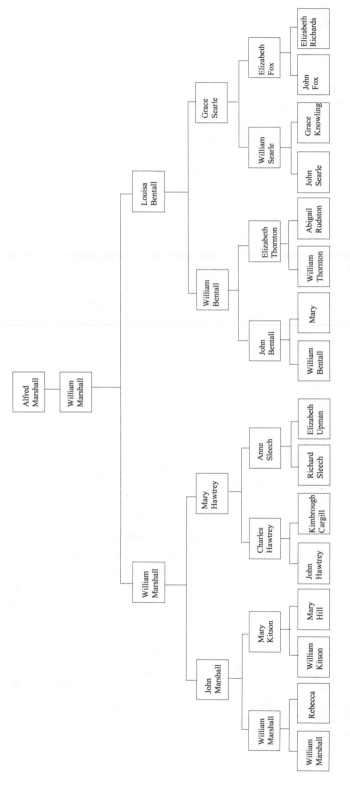

Figure 2.2: William Marshall's Ancestry

Source: Based on material in the Coase Papers, Regenstein Library (University of Chicago). Used with permission of the Department of Special Collections and Professor Coase.

The Bentall family absence is more difficult to explain on grounds other than the suggestion of misalliance, since some of the bridegroom's uncles were living in London. The family antecedents of Rebecca Oliver explain the rest. 'At the time of her marriage, Rebecca Oliver's father's family included other butchers, several couriers, at least one farmer, and a victualler (presumably an innkeeper). . . .[H]er mother, Rebecca Davenport (Alfred Marshall's grandmother), appears to have been the daughter of an agricultural labourer, . . . [who] was described as "husbandman" at the apprenticeship of his son Thomas, to a papermaker in 1786.'[70] On his maternal grandmother's side therefore, Alfred Marshall appears to have descended from agricultural labourer stock with, in the previous generation, an occasional pauper thrown in. This was an ancestry even more embarrassing than the petty tradesman stock from which his maternal grandfather's family had descended. No wonder knowledge of the Oliver side was kept well hidden in the Marshall family.

Rebecca Oliver was in fact the younger daughter in a family of seven children altogether. Oldest brother George, born in 1801, followed his father's trade of butcher, was married in 1835 and had a number of children. The second son, Edward, died in infancy. Third son James Edward was also a butcher, married with children. Fourth son Edward, born 1808, worked in the Bank of England, married but had no children. He died in 1868. A fifth son Henry, born 1810, was followed by a daughter Elizabeth in 1814, unmarried at the time of her younger sister's wedding. At the time of his birth, Alfred Marshall therefore also had four married uncles and one unmarried aunt on his mother's side. It is probable that Alfred Marshall never met any of these uncles and aunts, let alone any of his cousins on his mother's side. Possible exceptions are Uncle Edward and Aunt Elizabeth, who attended his parents' wedding.[71]

Surviving photographs of Alfred Marshall's mother, taken relatively late in her life, suggest a woman of considerable beauty. Her face in one of them also reflects much anxiety and sorrow, and perhaps prolonged illness. Her undoubted good looks provide one reason why William Marshall married her. Opportunities for meeting presented through his acquaintance with her brother Edward, a fellow employee at the Bank of England, were another.[72] She was undoubtedly a good mother to her five children. As Alfred wrote to John Neville Keynes, she frequently protected them from their father's more severe outbursts of discipline. Other epistolary references to his mother are in the eleven letters he sent her in 1875 from the United States and in letters to Foxwell.

The letters to Foxwell show Marshall's fondness for his mother and his qualities as nurse. It also shows his mother's last years were plagued by ill health. A substantial part of Alfred Marshall's January of 1875 was devoted to taking care of his mother during her recuperation from what appears to have been a long and serious illness. This was during term at Cambridge where he was lecturing for his college in the moral sciences. Marshall wrote to Foxwell on 31 January 1875 that his mother was progressing with rapid strides; a recovery bought at some personal cost to son Alfred. He 'felt more washed out' than he had ever felt before. Four days later Marshall reported how 'grateful' he was that his mother was so 'very much better'.[73] The serious nature of this illness is not only implied in the correspondence with Foxwell, it is also shown by his concern over her health the following summer when he was in America.

Only the first of these letters from America is addressed to 'my darling mother', the others commenced with 'my dear . . .', or more frequently, 'my very dear mother'. They invariably closed with 'your very loving Alfred Marshall' and passed greetings to both father and sisters. Apart from Alfred's reactions to the apparently all too few letters he was receiving from his family, the letters contain little of a personal family nature, being filled with details of his travels and in part designed to supplement the economic and other travel notes he was also making and sending home. This double function of the correspondence explains the request made in the first of the letters for his mother not to make any additional folds in the paper. Such treatment would diminish their 'standing strength' in the wooden cases in which his lecture notes were filed, 'standing up'.

Some choice of subject matter in the correspondence betrays its essentially female intended readership of mother, sisters and Aunt Louisa. Examples include the discussion of meal times and hotel prices, laundry costs, church services attended, and reference to other religious topics such as the strength of the Unitarians in Boston, their superiority to the Anglican marriage service by the express deletion of the woman's promise to obey her husband, the relative freedom of young women in Canada to manage their own affairs, the absence of a strong women's rights movement in the western part of the United States, the lack of virtue in the women living in the mining town of Nevada and accounts of excursions with various young ladies to whom he had been given letters of introduction. This is not to say that the letters were written down to his special readership. The only possible indication from which such an attitude can be inferred is in the remark that he hoped that his mother would not find the philosophical remarks inspired by his meeting with Emerson too boring. Another apology expressed regret about his difficult-to-read handwriting combined with a promise to do better in later letters (a promise which, to this reader, appears not to have been kept).

On a more personal note, there are references to things Alfred Marshall either purchased or expressly kept for his mother during his travels. These include a copy of an illustrated magazine, which he thought she might find of interest, as well as a copy of Harper's magazine specifically purchased for her; a paper containing the order of service from one of the Boston churches he attended, and some glass stereoscopic slides of Niagara Falls which he hoped would survive the return journey.

His mother used violet stationery. At one stage this made her letters easy to identify at a poste restante office to which they had been sent, unlike the elegant handwriting of the address which, Alfred advised, would have been better written in bold and large letters. Alfred frequently expressed concern over the well-being and good health of his family. More specifically, this included questions about the progress of recovery by brother Charles from an accident, concern over his father's feet and worry about his mother's apparent set-back in health 'from a walk downstairs'. These are the sum total of the letters' personal contents, apart from a characteristic warning to his sisters about the evils of excessive hymn singing to the poor. Despite their special purpose as letters of record, they nevertheless portray Alfred as a loving son and devoted brother revealing all the usual anxieties about family welfare when the writer is a long way from home. The fact they were written directly to his mother highlights the high affection in which he held her as compared to the feelings of dutiful, filial respect he had for his father. However, too much cannot be made from this fact, since it was far from unusual in Victorian times for children's correspondence with their parents to be addressed to only one of them.[74]

Rebecca Marshall died rather suddenly on the 13 June 1878 in her sixty-second year. Cause of death was officially diagnosed as chronic obstruction of the bowel accompanied by a coma of twenty hours. She died within a year of Alfred Marshall's wedding, and not long after her husband's retirement from the Bank of England to the residence selected for that purpose in Great Malvern, Worcestershire. Details on her death certificate suggest she died without the comfort of relatives, and create good reasons to believe that both husband and daughters were away at the time of her death. Alfred Marshall penned the following reaction to his mother's death to Foxwell, who had lost his mother in the same year: 'I, having just lost my own mother can feel with you. She was to me what yours was to you. And my sisters miss her as much as yours do their mother. But they are older than yours and agree with my father on most religious questions: so that they are on the whole happy.'[75] This rather unemotional letter disguises the significant impact on Alfred Marshall of his mother's death.[76]

ALFRED MARSHALL'S BROTHERS AND SISTERS

The meagre picture of Alfred Marshall's family is completed by including known facts about his relations with his brothers and sisters and their offspring. The overall picture was concisely presented by Mary Paley.

> A[lfred] had two brothers and two [sisters].
> Charles the eldest was sent to India at 17 and became manager of [a] silk factory. He married Lucy Guillebaud and had 2 sons. William now a doctor and Arthur who was killed in the [1914–18] war. Charles returned to England and died at Bathford.
> Agnes joined Charles in India and died there.
> Mabel Louisa married Reverend E. Guillebaud and had 4 sons [one] of which is C.W. Guillebaud.
> She was very musical.
> She died at Bathford.
> She and Alfred were very fond of one another.
> His sister Mabel said that he was the most wonderful nurse she had ever known. He nursed his mother through a bad illness and when I had malarial fever in Palermo [in 1882] he nursed me through it without any help though he himself was much crippled at the time.
> He loved his mother, his sister Mabel and his Aunt Louisa. I don't think that as time went on, he really cared very much for anyone else, except some of his former pupils.[77]

The oldest child, Charles William was born exactly eleven months after his parents' wedding on 13 April 1841 and about fourteen months before the birth of Alfred in July 1842. Agnes, the first daughter, was born on 25 December 1845; she was followed on 4 May 1850 by another girl, Mabel Louisa, and the youngest surviving child, once more a son, Walter, was born on 1 April 1853.[78] Alfred Marshall survived all his brothers and sisters, despite his eleven years seniority to his younger brother.

Little can be added to Mary Paley's account on Charles William Marshall. His departure for India in 1858, that is, well before Alfred went to university, may be explained by the assistance his emigration gave to his parents in meeting the education expenses of their apparently more gifted and favoured younger son. The Bengal Silk Company he eventually managed provided him with sufficient income for a comfortable retirement in England on his return, sometime after 1895. This was at Bathford, a place he made a haven for elderly Marshalls, since this was where younger sister Mabel Louisa also died after moving there with her family of four sons on the death of her husband. Charles William married Lucy Guillebaud, whose brother married his younger sister, Mabel Louisa. Three children sprang from this union, contrary to what Mary Paley recalled for Walter Scott. The one daughter, Edith Agnes, died some time between 1895 and 1907. William, the elder of the two boys, was the 'cousin William' who (wrongly) informed Mary Paley on Rebecca Oliver's antecedents. He became a doctor. Arthur Raymond, the younger son, studied mathematics and engineering at Cambridge. He died a Captain in the British Army in the military hospital at Rouen in February 1918 from wounds received the previous December.[79]

There is little more to tell about Charles William. Alfred's correspondence from America in 1875 referred to his brother's accident that summer, but whether this occurred in England or in India is not known. If India, it may explain why sister Agnes joined him there, some time after that summer, perhaps to assist in his recuperation.[80] It seems significant that he called his only daughter after her. He died in 1915. A photo taken late in his life, when he had retired to Bathford, shows a strong resemblance to father William and younger brother, Alfred, the latter perhaps heightened by their similar walrus moustache. His will also shows him to have been a person of some education. It makes separate provision for the disposal of his books, microscopes, and other scientific equipment. He may have used such tools in his business, but they more plausibly betray an interest in entymology and biology shared with many of his fellow Victorians.[81]

Alfred's younger brother, Walter, appears an equally gifted boy. He attended Merchant Taylors' School from 1866 to 1872, gaining one of its tercentenary scholarships. He matriculated for the University of Cambridge, where he entered Peterhouse as a pensioner on 15 October 1872. During his time at college, he contracted tuberculosis, was sent to South Africa for its healthy climate, and died there without graduating. As the Benjamin of the family, it seems he was the apple of his father's eye. William Marshall described son Walter as a very popular boy, being 'loved at Peterhouse, as wherever he was'.[82] A passage in the first edition of the *Principles* may have been one of those special points contributed by his father. 'Of two parents who are, so far as we can tell, equally affectionate, one will suffer much more than the other from the loss of a favourite son'.[83]

Agnes, Alfred's older sister, appears to have followed in Aunt Louisa Marshall's footsteps, if she looked after her brother in India and died there before thinking of marriage herself. Marshall's letters from America add only a little colour to this brief account. His sisters were 'to sing at the Workhouse', he recorded on 22 August, adding that he hoped 'they will not sing exclusively hymns. It is as bad for the mind to feed exclusively on hymns and suchlike as it is for the body to feed exclusively on meat'.[84] In the same letter he advised his mother to tell Agnes to address letters to him in America in 'bold, clear handwriting' as compared to her usual elegant script, to save the problems of letter identification he experienced at the St Louis Post Office.

More is known about Alfred's younger sister Mabel Louisa, his favourite sister of the two.[85] Her musical interests were one reason for this. She seems also to have been the more spirited of the two sisters. Her attempt to marry against her father's wishes has already been mentioned; as has father William's dislike of her actual marriage to the Rev. Guillebaud, the brother of brother Charles's wife. Her marriage to him in February 1886, however, provided a permanent abode for her father at the rectory of Yatesbury (Wiltshire) until his death in 1901, thereby giving him plenty of scope to tyrannise both his daughter, son-in-law and grandchildren. Four children were born of the marriage: Harold, the oldest, in September 1888, then twins Claude and Walter in July 1890 and finally Cyril, in 1893. On her husband's death in 1907, Mabel and family moved to Bathford to stay with her brother Charles, by then a widower. She died there in 1912. In his later reminiscences, Claude Guillebaud has no recollections that 'Uncle Alfred' ever stayed at their house in either Yatesbury or Bathford, though he believed that he did 'pay us a very occasional visit'.[86] Mary Paley later recalled that Alfred's relations used their Clifton house in the summers for two months while they travelled elsewhere.[87] Several letters from Alfred to his nephews Harold and Claude have survived. Moreover, as Claude Guillebaud recollected, and letters to Tanner preserved at John's College verify, Alfred Marshall was very solicitous about his nephews' education and ensured that both Walter and Claude gained places at his own college, John's, in preference to the traditional Guillebaud college of Trinity. Their entry into Cambridge was followed by occasional visits of the Guillebaud twins to Balliol Croft for meals.[88]

Family and ancestry can tell important stories about the subject of a biography. In Alfred Marshall's case their witness to his own life arises more from the curtain he chose to draw over his family history than from the all too scant facts which can be disclosed about his family and antecedents. Ignorance on Marshall's part may explain part of this. In other cases, Marshall took positive steps to keep some of his antecedents from posterity. This was done by destroying family material from his private papers, and by disguising the actual situation of his family life in such a way that no lies had to be told. Examples are his own descriptions of birthplace as Surrey or London rather than Bermondsey; and omitting his parents in autobiographical entries for reference works. This secrecy in which Marshall shrouded his family affairs and antecedents is not satisfactorily explained by a very well-developed sense of privacy, great though this may have been. It owed more to the discomfort, if not shame, felt about his origins and near relations, particularly likely as a young undergraduate at St John's and later, in the company of far more socially well-connected friends and colleagues at the Grote Club and Eranus Society. In these circles he clearly preferred just to pose as a person with no family as later friend Jowett had successfully done at Oxford.[89] In any case, this is how he would have appeared to those colleagues and friends and how he himself described the situation in the early biographical entries he produced. Only relatively late in life, when his position was secure, and the more embarrassing ancestral skeletons had faded away to the distant past, were his relatives more publicly acknowledged. Examples are support he provided for his nephews in gaining access to St John's College. However, his many uncles, cousins, aunts, and even his mother, always remained shadowy figures rarely visited or discussed, and therefore largely hidden, even from his wife.

As indicated in the next chapter, Alfred Marshall's school years and childhood cannot be described as particularly happy, perhaps further explaining why he drew a veil over this part of his life in later years. His relationship with his father was not easy, no matter how this was disguised in an occasional communication to a friend and colleague in later life. Childhood and adolescence carried the seeds for some antagonism between father and son. Examples are paternal restrictions on recreation and leisure, as well as his education, to which disputes over religious beliefs may have to be added subsequently. Alfred's strong feelings for his mother owed a great deal to her steadfast support in protecting him from his father's disciplinary excesses and her undoubtedly strong pleading on his behalf in various family matters. Her sudden death in 1878 was certainly an enormous blow to him, particularly when combined with the near simultaneous demise of younger brother Walter, whose upbringing and education so closely matched his own of the previous decade. These family circumstances made 1877 and 1878 very traumatic years for him.[90]

The important role played by women in Marshall's early life is also not easily over-emphasised. Apart from a tremendous love for his mother, Aunt Louisa and sister Mabel were the persons for whom he showed most affection, in addition to his wife. It is also significant that apart from a trip with his prospective in-laws and fiancée to Switzerland in 1876, the only relatives who appear to have accompanied him on such summer travels as an adult were his two sisters. They came with him to St Moritz in 1873, after an earlier visit there by himself in 1871.[91] On the other hand, gratitude rather than love and admiration are the likely sentiments Marshall felt towards Uncle Charles. There are no indications of visits to his Uncle Charles in London after his return from Australia in 1873. His correspondence was properly bordered in black on the occasion of his death in August 1874, a sign of respect dutifully accorded by the Marshalls on the occasion of every death amongst their close relatives. More generally, his uncles were unimportant in his life, as apparently was his older brother, explicable in terms of his departure to India at an important stage in Alfred's adolescence. The differences between Charles and Alfred in education and upbringing would in any case have prevented a close friendship between the two brothers, even though their ages differed by only fourteen months. What is known about his family relationships would not have assisted his social skills and powers of adjustment, particularly when added to those features of his background with respect to birth and ancestry which he attempted to hide. Apart from the hypersensitivity to criticism and dislike of controversy these family inheritances brought him, Alfred Marshall's lack of social confidence and grace, noticed, for instance, by William Ramsay when Marshall had risen to a situation of responsibility and leadership at Bristol,[92] can be added to this legacy. Family and ancestry are recalled in what follows, because they influence his life in some unusual and important ways.

NOTES

1. *Men and Women of the Time*, London: John Routledge, 13th edition, 1889, p. 608.
2. J.M. Keynes, 'Alfred Marshall', pp. 161–2, 163–5.

3. Exceptions are the papers on the subject by R.H. Coase: 'Did Marshall know where he was born?', *History of Economics Society Bulletin*, 7 (1), Summer 1986; 'Alfred Marshall's Mother and Father', *History of Political Economy*, 16 (4), Winter 1984; 'Alfred Marshall's Family and Ancestry', in *Alfred Marshall in Retrospect*, ed. Rita McWilliams-Tullberg, Aldershot: Edward Elgar, 1990. This chapter has benefited greatly from Professor Coase's researches. He kindly allowed me to inspect its detailed documentation in the Special Collections section of the Joseph Regenstein Library, University of Chicago, hereafter referred to as Coase papers.

4. His matriculation records show Bermondsey, Surrey as his place of birth, the place likewise recorded by Venn (*Alumni Cantabrigienses*, p. 330); biographical entries for the 12th and 13th editions of *Men and Women of the Time* (London: Routledge, 1887, p. 707, 1889, p. 608) give no place of birth while the biographical sketch he prepared in 1910 for Gustav Eckstein's project of short biographies of great economists simply gives his birthplace as London. Ronald Coase, 'Did Marshall know where he was born?', indicates that the census for 1871 lists Marshall's birthplace as 'Surrey', that for 1881 as 'Sydenham, Kent' the place where his parents lived between their residency at Bermondsey and Clapham, based on information provided by either Marshall's wife or his brother-in-law, who was staying with them in Bristol. The 1891 census gives ' Croydon, Surrey', as his birthplace, on information most likely provided by Mary Paley Marshall.

5. See John Maynard Keynes, 'Alfred Marshall', p. 161, who got it from the notes Mary Paley provided him with (Keynes's Marshall Files, King's College, Cambridge, hereafter KMF); W.C. Mitchell, 'Alfred Marshall', *Encyclopaedia of Social Sciences*, New York: Macmillan, Vol. IX, p. 155; Bernard Corry, 'Alfred Marshall', in *International Encyclopaedia of the Social Sciences*, second edition, ed. David Sills, Chicago: Macmillan and the Free Press, 1968, Vol. 10, p. 25. Surprisingly, the wrong birthplace is given in David Reisman, *Marshall's Mission* (London: Macmillan, 1990), p. 3. John Whitaker, 'Alfred Marshall, 1842–1924', gives the birthplace precisely as Bermondsey, a London suburb (*The New Palgrave*, London: Macmillan, 1987, Vol. 3, p. 350).

6. As recorded on the birth certificate of his younger sister, Mabel Louisa, and brother, Walter, and information supplied by the Bank of England for the late 1840s to the early 1860s, the Marshalls lived at 5 Russell Place, Larkhall Rise, Clapham and subsequently at Rectory Grove, Clapham, the last address being that given in the 1861 census records.

7. The death certificate of Alfred Marshall's uncle, Charles Henry, dated 11 August, 1874, records Marshall's father as the informant, with the address of 12 Victoria Road, Clapham Common.

8. The marriage certificate of William Marshall and Rebecca Oliver gives Park Road, New Peckham as the residence at the time of marriage; the birth certificate of Charles William, Alfred Marshall's older brother, gives Maismore Square, New Peckham, as his parents' address.

9. As shown on their birth certificates, Alfred Marshall's elder sister Agnes was born at Ball Green, Sydenham in Kent; his younger sister Mabel at 5 Russell Place, Larkhall Lane, Clapham, while his younger brother, Walter, was born in Clapham at the same address.

10. Clerical salaries at the Bank of England appear to have been at a low point in 1842. *Punch* (Vol. 3, p. 188), in what one historian of the Bank has described as an amusing article, then depicted Bank clerks as 'the hardest worked, the worst paid and the most polite body of men in the metropolis.' (W. Marston Acres, *The Bank of England from within 1694–1900*, London: printed for the Governor and Company of the Bank of England, 1931, Vol. 2, p. 486 n.2).

11. Edward Walford, *Old and New London. A Narrative of its History, its People and its Places*, London: Cassell Petter & Galpin, 1873–78, Vol. VI, pp. 100–101, 123.

12. *Ibid.*, p. 124.

13. Ben Weinreb and Christopher Hibbert, *The London Encyclopaedia*, London: Macmillan, 1983, p. 59.

14. *Mayhew's London*, edited by Peter Quennel, London: Bracken Books, 1984,) pp. 306–14.

15. Weinreb and Hibbert, *The London Encyclopaedia*, p. 415.

16. This draws heavily on information supplied by the Curator of Museum and Historical Research Section, Bank of England, to the author in March 1984, in addition to the Coase material cited in note 3 above.

17. Keynes, 'Alfred Marshall', pp. 162–3; this and another photo of Alfred Marshall's father are reproduced as illustrations 1 and 4. It may be noted that the later photo presents him in a much more kindly perspective.

18. Keynes, 'Alfred Marshall', p. 163.

19. Mary Paley Marshall, 'Biographical Notes on Alfred Marshall' (KMF).

20. F.Y. Edgeworth to J.M. Keynes, 30 August 1924 (KMF).

21. Mary Paley Marshall, 'Biographical Notes on Alfred Marshall' (KMF).

22. C.W. Guillebaud to J.M. Keynes, 17 November 1924 (KMF).

23. Alfred Marshall to J.N. Keynes, 4 August 1892 (Marshall Library, 1 (105)). His father was then already living with the Guillebauds at Yatesbury, the place where he also died. Marshall added that John Neville Keynes should give the intended governess (who had been employed in the Keynes family) 'the hint that she will find my sister a wiser councillor on all matters of discipline than my father: but that as he is an old man [he was then almost eighty] and not easily to be convinced, it will be generally better to pass by his suggestions rather

than actively to oppose them.' Further details on Marshall's immediate family are provided at the end of the chapter.

24. Mary Paley Marshall, 'Biographical Notes on Alfred Marshall' (KMF).
25. Augustus Hare recalled his childhood punishments administered with a riding whip, describing them as invariably 'a great deal too severe' (cited in Eugene C. Black (ed.), *Victorian Culture and Society*, London: Macmillan, 1973, pp. 201–2). Many other examples can be given. The quotations are from William Marshall's *The Past, Present and Future of England's Language*, London: Longman's Green & Company, 1877, pp. 84 and 73 respectively. On an eighteenth-century view of the Scottish schoolmaster's use of the 'tawse' see Charles Gibbon, *The Life of George Combe*, London: Macmillan, 1878, Vol. I, pp. 17–20.
26. Alfred Marshall to J.N. Keynes, 4 August 1892; Mary Paley Marshall, 'Biographical Notes on Alfred Marshall' (KMF).
27. Information provided by the Curator of Museum and Historical Research Section, Bank of England, in 1984.
28. H.O. de Fraine, *Servant of this House. Life in the Old Bank of England*, London: Constable, 1960, p. 78.
29. William Marshall, *The Past, Present and Future of England's Language*, pp. 64, 101–2. Dr Joseph Bosworth compiled the first dictionary of Anglo-Saxon English published in 1838, the abridgement of which went through several editions. See *Dictionary of National Biography* (hereafter *DNB*), Vol. II, pp. 902–3. It criticises Bosworth's work for not being in the modern philological tradition and containing many errors of detail.
30. The book received a review in *The British Quarterly Review*, January 1878, pp. 541–2. Apart from noting the inherent conservatism of the author, the review saw its objective as flawed because it ignored, 'the very first principle and necessary law which governs all language, viz., that it is a living power with an organic growth of its own, which we may call fashion or corruption, but which really is a progress wholly beyond the possibility of control'. It therefore concluded, 'the object of the essay, if well meant and earnestly advocated, is clearly impracticable. Neither in language nor in anything else does the human race permanently go backwards.'
31. William Marshall, *The Past, Present and Future of England's Language*, pp. 104–5.
32. William Marshall, *Lochlere. A Poem in Four Parts*, London: Longmans, Green & Company, 1877, p. 172. The opinions quoted in the preceding paragraph are from its preface, pp. xiv, xxi. The word in brackets is his translation of the Old English which precedes it.
33. William Marshall, *Aarbert, A Drama*, London: Swann Sonnenschein & Company, 1898, pp. 5–6.
34. *Ibid.*, p. 137.
35. *Ibid.*, p. 3.
36. *Ibid.*, pp. 112, 345 for example. Grandfather William's father's business failures are briefly mentioned in the next section of this chapter.
37. Mary Paley Marshall to John Maynard Keynes, 20 November 1924 (KMF) in which she mentions enclosing some verses which she had just found, 'the only ones which Alfred ever made'. Their loss seems likely since they can neither be found among the Keynes Papers at King's College nor in the Marshall Archive at the Marshall Library. See also Keynes to Lydia Lopokova, 21 November 1924: 'Mrs Marshall has just sent me, to look at, her husband's only poem. It isn't as good as mine! – which is something (but you mustn't ever show mine to anybody)' in *Lydia and Maynard*, p. 259.
38. See G.F.A. Best, 'Popular Protestantism in Victorian Britain', in R. Robson (ed.), *Ideas and Institutions of Victorian Britain*, London: G. Bell &Sons, 1967, Chapter 5, esp. p. 138 which indicates, 'No Popery took on a fierceness and hysteria in the early thirties . . . and was at its most intense from the middle 'thirties to the late 'seventies', starting therefore at the time when William Marshall was at a most impressionable age. See also R.H. Coase, 'Alfred Marshall's Mother and Father', pp. 525–6.
39. Marshall Archive, Correspondence File, 1:295–6. For Marshall's interest in music, see below, Chapter 21, p. 773.
40. *MCC*, p. 264 and n.2: the relevant passage is as follows: 'Egyptian bas-reliefs suggest that the *individual* man of the present time is not very much more capable, physically and intellectually, than were many of his ancestors thousands of years ago. This notion was impressed on me by my father in the British Museum seventy years ago.'
41. *P* I, p. xii, and cf. below, p. 39 and n.83, for a possible further example.
42. The low level of pay for Bank of England employees at the time of Alfred Marshall's birth was mentioned in note 10 above; the situation did not improve in subsequent decades. See H.G. de Fraine, *Servant of this House*, pp. 136–7.
43. See *Merchant Taylors' School Register*, Vol. II; *Admissions to Peterhouse or St Peter's College. A Biographical Register* (Cambridge: at the University Press, 1912). William Marshall dedicated his essay on the *Past, Present and Future of the English Language* to his son, Walter Marshall, who sought health amidst the breezes of South Africa but 'found it soon in heaven'. William Marshall as father therefore fully met the requirements of parental duty with respect to education which the young Alfred Marshall outlined in 1873 in his paper on the Future of the Working Classes (in *Memorials*, pp. 114, 117).

44. R.H. Coase, 'Alfred Marshall's Mother and Father', p. 527. Coase cites Claude Guillebaud as his authority. If true, Alfred's father may be partly held responsible for Marshall's style in writing the *Principles* with its careful qualifications designed to prevent the most remote possibility of error.

45. Cf. F.B. Smith, 'The Atheist Mission 1840–1900', in R. Robson (ed.), *Ideas and Institutions of Victorian Britain*, pp. 229–31, and see below, p. 671.

46. Mary Paley Marshall, 'Biographical Notes on Alfred Marshall' (KMF).

47. J.M. Keynes, 'Alfred Marshall', pp. 161–2.

48. J.M. Keynes, 'Alfred Marshall,' p. 162 and n.3. This draws on a letter from R.G. Hawtrey to J.M. Keynes dated 15 August 1924 (KMF) as well as on Mary Paley's notes. The last simply stated, 'A great-grandfather was John, the master of Exeter Grammar School. He married the beautiful Miss Hawtrey (of whom I have a portrait by John Downer)'. (KMF). Keynes argued Marshall gained more from the 'subtle Hawtreys' than from great-great-grandfather William.

49. Coase, 'Alfred Marshall's Family and Ancestry', p. 25 n.38.

50. Alfred Marshall to Rebecca Marshall, 5 June 1875, Marshall Archive, 1:289.

51. John Maynard Keynes, 'Alfred Marshall', pp. 164–5.

52. See below, Chapters 6, p. 173; 7, pp. 193-203, esp. 193.

53. John Maynard Keynes, 'Alfred Marshall', p. 165.

54. Coase, 'Alfred Marshall's Family and Ancestry', p. 15; D.B. Waterson, *Squatter, Selector and Store Keeper, A History of the Darling Downs, 1858–1893*, Sydney University Press, 1968, p. 13; Coase Papers (Regenstein Library).

55. Waterson, *ibid.*, p. 20; Leslie Family Letters 20 January 1850, Mitchell Library, A4094, cited in Robert Hughes, *The Fatal Shore*, London: Pan Books, 1988, p. 567; *The Australian Encyclopaedia*, fifth edition, Sydney, 1988, article 'Darling Downs'; James Jupp (ed.), *The Australian People, An Encyclopaedia of the Nation, its People and their Origins*, Sydney: Angus & Robertson, 1988, pp. 298–300, 486, 725–6.

56. Coase, 'Alfred Marshall's Family and Ancestry', pp. 17–20; Coase Papers (Regenstein Library). Colin Clark, *Australia's Hopes and Fears*, London: Hollis & Carter, 1958, p. 38.

57. Uncle Charles's help to brother Henry in setting up business in London in 1874 was noted earlier. After his death, his widow complained about the many legacies in his will she had to pay to what she appears to have considered as undeserving relatives. Coase Papers (Regenstein Library).

58. *P* I, p. 589 n.1 (eliminated from the third edition, *P* IX, p. 621).

59. J.M. Keynes, 'Alfred Marshall', p. 163.

60. Mary Paley Marshall, 'Biographical Notes on Alfred Marshall' (KMF). Her interest in the family explains the fact, noted by Coase ('Alfred Marshall's Family and Ancestry', p. 33 and n.38), that she was the only person in touch with the Hawtrey side of the family.

61. Alfred Marshall to Rebecca Marshall, 5 June 1875, Marshall Archive, 1:289. the list of presentation copies is in Marshall Archive, File 6 (2).

62. Coase, 'Alfred Marshall's Family and Ancestry', pp. 10–12. Cf. the exaggerated description of William Marshall's occupation as Chief Cashier in the Bank of England by his younger brother Charles, which was recorded by Bartley in the context of his meeting with Charles Marshall and his companion, Davson, on the diggings at Turon in 1851 (*ibid.*, p. 16).

63. Cf. Coase, 'Alfred Marshall's Family and Ancestry', pp. 20–21.

64. Coase, 'Alfred Marshall's Family and Ancestry', pp. 21–2. Coase left out the required additional 'great', since as Figure 2.2 shows, the common ancestor, Robert Thornton (1623–1697/8) was father of great-great-great-grandfather William Thornton (information from the Coase Papers, Regenstein Library).

65. *Ibid.*, pp. 22–3.

66. J.M. Keynes, 'Alfred Marshall', pp. 161–2. Even this brief statement required inquiries by Mary Paley who, at the time of Alfred's death, did not know his mother's maiden name. Her letter to Keynes of 26 July 1924 mentions 'the pedigree has been unearthed from a distant relation – I am glad to see that it gives the maiden name of Alfred's mother which I feared was lost' (KMF).

67. Mary Paley to John Maynard Keynes, 14 January 1925 (KMF). The information by William Marshall was apparently imparted by letter to his cousin Claude Guillebaud (see Coase, 'Alfred Marshall's Mother and Father', p. 520). The address on Marshall's 80th birthday is discussed below, Chapter 17, pp. 649–50.

68. Mary Paley Marshall, 'Biographical Notes on Alfred Marshall' (KMF); 'Notes for Walter Scott', Marshall Archive, Large Brown Box, Item 24. The relevant passage is quoted below, p. 38.

69. See below, Chapter 8, pp. 230–1, 234.

70. Coase, 'Alfred Marshall's Mother and Father', p. 520 and n.8.

71. Coase Papers (Regenstein Library).

72. From information supplied by the Bank of England, Edward Oliver was first employed in the Bank of England on 19 February 1829, the year before William Marshall joined. He stayed in the Bank's service until 1867, so

that he worked with his brother-in-law for the greater part of his career in the Bank, often in the same office or section. It is interesting to note that Edward Oliver, who had indeed been apprenticed to a Mr Rhodes, a druggist of Ramsgate, was recommended by a Director and subsequent Deputy-Governor and Governor of the Bank, Timothy Abraham Curtis. Edward's address of 36 Northumberland Street, The Strand, at the time of his election to the Bank in 1829, was in close proximity to the house of John Bentall (the stockbroker uncle of William), where he was living from 1828. This may explain further potential for social contact at the time for William Marshall with both Edward Oliver, and his sister Rebecca, that is, William's future wife.

73. On Marshall's proclivities as nurse, see below, p. 237; Marshall to Foxwell, 31 January and 4 February 1875 (Freeman Collection, 11, 12/229).

74. Marshall Archive, Letters 1/289–299. Two photographs of Rebecca Marshall are reproduced as illustrations 2 and 3.

75. Alfred Marshall to H.S. Foxwell, 1 September 1878 (Freeman Collection).

76. Below, Chapter 8, p. 234, Chapter 14, p. 498.

77. Mary Paley, 'Notes for Walter Scott'; virtually all of these notes were reproduced by him in the opening paragraph of his obituary for the British Academy, 'Alfred Marshall, 1842–1924' (London, Oxford University Press, for the British Academy, n.d. p. 1). However, Scott's account contains a curious addition of yet another clerical relative, a Rev. Richard Marshall of 'the same generation . . . who had a considerable reputation as a poet, but his repugnance to leave anything behind him but the best led him to burn all his MS'. No licence for this addition arises from Mary Paley's notes or from any other source with which I am familiar.

78. Information based on the birth certificates of his brothers and sisters.

79. Alfred Marshall to Raymond Marshall, 18 January 1918, in *Memorials*, pp. 495–6.

80. A letter on 20 June 1875 to his mother comments on how much he enjoyed reading Charles's letters, which enables the speculation that he had been sent his brother's letters to his parents from India. On 22 August he writes from St Louis how distressed he is about Charles's accident, adding by way of distant comfort to his mother that he trusts 'it may not be as bad as you fear'. This suggests a lack of detailed knowledge of the accident on his family's part, consistent with the fact that Charles was still in India (Marshall Archive, Letters 1:191, 1:198). The accident therefore provides a reason for Agnes's departure for India to assist Charles, as suggested in the text. The fact that author's copies of the *Elements of the Economics of Industry* were proudly sent to his father, brother Charles, sister Mabel and Aunt Louisa (Marshall Archive, File 6 (2)) indicates that sister Agnes had probably died before 1892.

81. These paragraphs draw extensively on Charles William Marshall's will, preserved with the Coase Papers (Regenstein Library). It was proved in 1915, and in codicils mentions the death of both his wife and daughter. It names Aunt Louisa as one of his executors in 1895.

82. *Merchant Taylors' School Register 1863–1934*; Thomas A. Walker (ed.), *Admissions to Peterhouse or St Peter's College. A Biographical Register* (Cambridge, at the University Press, 1912); William Marshall, *The Past Present and Future of the English Language*, frontispiece.

83. *P. I.* pp. 151–2. It disappeared in the second edition.

84. Alfred Marshall to Rebecca Marshall, 22 August 1875 (Marshall Archive, Letter 1:298). On his mother's death, Alfred wrote to Foxwell, 1 September 1878 (Freeman Collection) that his sisters agreed with his father on most religious questions.

85. C.W. Guillebaud, 'Some Personal Reminiscence of Alfred Marshall', in *AMCA*, I, p. 91. Apart from squaring with Mary Paley's opinion that 'she and Alfred were very fond of [one] another', and the remarks on the subject in her Notes for Walter Scott already quoted, a letter to Foxwell (Marshall Archive, 3/40) on 17 December 1898 supports this contention. This letter gives a detailed account of an injury Mabel Louisa suffered to her hip, and which apparently incapacitated her for a considerable length of time. The medical treatment eventually given her was first class. It included X-rays by the person who had X-rayed ('Rontgen rayed' as Marshall put it), the Prince of Wales (the later Edward VII) while his wife, Mary was staying with Mabel at the hospital before commencing holidays in Bournemouth for Christmas. This part of the letter to Foxwell is characteristically marked 'Private'. Given the lack of later family recollections of such incapacity, John Whitaker doubts the sister referred to was Mabel, though her children, it should be recalled at this stage, were then aged only from 3 to 10.

86. C.W. Guillebaud, 'Some Personal Reminiscences of Alfred Marshall', pp. 91–2; C.W. Guillebaud to J.M. Keynes, 27 November 1924 (KMF).

87. Mary Paley Marshall, MSS Notes (NCA).

88. Alfred Marshall to Harold Guillebaud, 3 October 1904 in *Memorials,* pp. 494–5, 24 December 1918 and 16 November 1920 (Marshall Archive, Large Brown Box Item 26); Alfred Marshall to Claude Guillebaud, 28 September 1904, and undated (Marshall Archive, 1/362–3), Alfred Marshall to J.R. Tanner, 3, 4 and 9 February, 1909 in St John's College Archive, S and JCC Arch. Tanner File 11/54, 59, 72, C.W. Guillebaud, 'Some Personal Reminiscences of Alfred Marshall', pp. 91–3.

89.   See below, Chapter 18, p. 687.
90.   See below, Chapter 8, p. 234, Chapter 14, p. 498.
91.   See Chapter 7 below, p. 190.
92.   Below, Chapter 8, pp. 272–3.

3. Childhood and School 1842–1861

Alfred Marshall's childhood and school life fall almost wholly within the mid-Victorian era of the 1840s and 1850s. School years started with his attendance at a Dame School 'as a small boy' in the mid-1840s, and were followed by a private establishment, perhaps of an evangelical nature, situated in Clapham. At age nine, 'he was sent to Merchant Taylors'' in early 1852.[1]

During these decades, the Marshall family's economic and social position had gradually improved. By 1845 they had left the 'slums' of Bermondsey's Charlotte Row for Bell Green, Sydenham, the place where Agnes Marshall was born on Christmas Day. Although Bell Green faced a gas works, this was undoubtedly an improvement over the tanneries adjoining Charlotte Row. Furthermore, the new address was quite distant from more working-class lower Sydenham. This gave it some genteel status, even if the new Marshall residence still lay outside the bounds of relatively affluent and middle-class upper Sydenham.[2] By 1850 the Marshalls had reached Clapham, 5 Russell Place, Larkhall Rise. The move signalled the increased affluence accompanying William Marshall's salary of almost £250 per annum from annual increments after his move to the Bank's Bills and Clearers' Office in 1842–43.[3] The 1851 Census reported that by then the Marshalls were employing a live-in servant.[4]

It was from Clapham that young Alfred made his daily trips during terms to Merchant Taylors'. That great public school[5] was then still at its original site of Suffolk Lane. This was one of the many lanes running up from Thames Street towards Cannon Street but never quite reaching it, in the part of the City lying between London and Southwark bridges. Conveniently for his early years there, it was in direct line between the river and the Bank of England, his father's place of employment. 'A[lfred] went to it by steamer or bus from Clapham.'[6] The earlier educational facilities he attended were undoubtedly situated closer to home: the Dame School probably at Sydenham; the private intermediary establishment at Clapham.

CHILDHOOD AND EARLY SCHOOLING

Given the dearth of family information, it is not surprising that Alfred Marshall's childhood and early education are a virtual blank. No careful charting of his teething and other baby problems were recorded for posterity as was lovingly done in his father's diary in the case of John Maynard Keynes. The impact of the fairly frequent parental house moving from the dislocations this involved for a youngster can therefore only be guessed at for the young Alfred Marshall, as can the effects on him of the births of his two sisters in 1845 and 1850. Little can be surmised about the Dame School which he attended when a small boy. If that establishment ran true to form, the teaching and general education he received would have been rather 'mechanical' and ineffective.[7]

Just as little is known of the 'private' educational establishment Alfred Marshall attended in the years before he entered Merchant Taylors' at age nine. At this time, about two-thirds of London's elementary schools were private. They

> flourished 'upon a deeply seated foible of the national character, the passion for the genteel or the supposed genteel. . . . A cracked piano and a couple of mouldy globes, with a brass plate on the doors inscribed with the words "Juvenile Academy" outweigh with too many parents all the merits of correct spelling and sound arithmetic.' The Church schools were at least inspected, but in the private schools there was no supervision whatever. The Newcastle Commission's London investigation reported of them that 'many are held in premises injurious to health, and quite unsuitable for school purposes', while of the teachers it was said that 'none are too old, too poor, too ignorant, too feeble, too sickly, too unqualified in any or every way, to regard themselves, and to be regarded by others, as unfit for school-keeping'. Teaching in the private schools was, in fact, 'a mere refuge for the destitute'.[8]

Irrespective of whether young Alfred's elementary schooling conformed to such a pattern, it can be safely assumed that unlike Henry Sidgwick's situation at this age,[9] there was no private governess for Alfred's elementary and preliminary education. Moreover, given his parents' own rather limited education, it seems unlikely that they were able to provide much assistance in this part of his upbringing, unless of course the schoolmaster at Leith had instilled more in father William's mind than a 'grateful remembrance' of corporal discipline. However, this education must have amounted to something. Admission to Merchant Taylors' required that at age nine, 'each boy must have at least some knowledge of the elementary parts of the Latin grammar', that is, have reached and mastered, 'the accidence' in King Edward, the 'Sixth Latin grammar' combined with an ability 'to read and write pretty well' and an expectation that 'he be acquainted with the leading facts of the early Scripture History, and with the Church Catechism'.[10] The last skills the Marshall children would have received in abundance from father William during Sunday's time of enforced devotion.

The few memories of Alfred Marshall's childhood were preserved by Mary Paley. She recalled Alfred 'said that he scarcely ever played games when a boy. His father would not let him join cricket clubs that played on Clapham Common for fear that he might make undesirable friends. At Merchant Taylors' he joined a cricket club but he had to go great distances (to Primrose Hill I think*) so he only managed to get about 10 games in three years. He tried to practice in their garden with his sister Agnes. He had a good eye and though his form was bad he could hit balls well. As he got little play, he worked with a turning lathe in a shed in the garden. He turned nine pins for his brother Walter and he loved to make useful things for his mother, e.g. a stand for her marking ink to prevent it from upsetting'.[11]

By the time he started secondary school at Merchant Taylors', little leisure time for games would have been available to him. Hours of school resemble those of today but after

---

* Mary Paley's recollection is wrong here, a possibility she herself recognised. In his statement for the *Report on Revenues and Management of Certain Schools and Colleges*, 1864, the Headmaster of Merchant Taylors', Dr Hessey, indicated that the Merchant Taylor Company rented part of Kennington Oval for school cricket for which it paid 20 guineas a year (p. 205).

school his father made him do homework up to 11.00 in the evening. For Merchant Taylors' School,

the hours of School attendance are from 9.15 in the morning till 1.0, and from 2.0 to 3.45 in the afternoon; and, altogether the boys are in School thirty-nine weeks in a year. Their holidays consist of a fortnight at Easter, about six weeks in August and September, and four weeks at Christmas. There is also a week of recess after the election day, June 11. In addition to these vacations the Head Master is privileged to grant a day's holiday four times in the year; and on the following days there is no school: – Anniversary of the death of Charles I, Ash Wednesday, Ascension Day, the Queen's birthday, the Anniversary of the Sons of the Clergy, the Anniversary of the Charity Children at St Paul's, Lord Mayor's Day, and Sir Thomas White's birthday, Saturday is the only half-holiday during the week.[12]

Given his father's strong evangelical views, Sunday would have been a day set aside for rest and devotion rather than leisure. Only the brief period after school in the afternoon and the half holiday on Saturday were therefore potentially available for play and recreation. No wonder Alfred prized the six weeks summer vacation in August and September spent with Aunt Louisa at Kenton Cottage in Dawlish. In his own words, they 'saved his life' after the overwork and long hours over the preceding thirty-nine weeks of term. The 'boat, the gun and the pony' which he could then enjoy must have been heaven after the very limited scope for pleasure and recreation allowed at home.[13] The latter were probably confined to educational excursions to places like the British Museum or family outings to major London events such as the 1851 Great Exhibition.

The high degree of deprivation on modern standards in such a childhood were general for the age. In many ways, Alfred's youth would have paralleled that of Augustus Hare. At five in the afternoon, Hare was allowed to amuse himself for a brief interlude, 'which generally meant nursing the cat'. He was forbidden 'carnal indulgences such as lollypop' by the punishment of swallowing a dose of rhubarb and soda administered by a 'forcing spoon'; and 'at a very early age' attended church initially, and for a short period only, once every Sunday and later invariably twice. 'After dinner, [he] was never permitted to amuse' himself and 'in winter had to endure a dark room after five without candles'.[14] Victorian childhood was frequently like this. However, as Annan[15] notes in the context of the childhood of Leslie Stephen, an evangelical middle-class upbringing could be joyous and happy even though pious, and need not be severe or cruel as the childhood of Hare, or, on their own account, those of Ruskin and Samuel Butler. On the available evidence, Alfred Marshall's childhood and early home life probably conformed more to the experience of Augustus Hare than that of Leslie Stephen and is perhaps well encapsulated in the following description of child and family in the Victorian age:

Father was God in that patristic universe called the home – a wrathful forbidding figure. Love for father, like love of God on the evangelical Christian model, was animated by fear. The Victorian family, revolved around the mother, the day-to-day authority who provided comfort, a haven, even an escape. Socialization defined the child's world and role. Upbringing insured acceptance, not appreciation. Children in the middle and upper classes mingled considerably with servants. They thus developed, or thought they developed, a sense of easy familiarity, understanding, and sympathy with the lower orders. From earliest childhood they proceeded to a sense of caste. The family – that congerie of father, mother, aunts, uncles, and servants – taught the creed of obedience, morality, loyalty. Discipline lay at the heart of socialization. Each child must learn order and self restraint through encouragement and suppression. Enforcement of the culture was simple and direct. Manliness, honor, duty, deference, the orderly life, God sanctioned it. The family taught it. The world approved.[16]

ENTRY TO MERCHANT TAYLORS': 1852

If Alfred Marshall entered Merchant Taylors' school aged nine as Mary Paley informed Keynes,[17] he would have joined the school in the first half of 1852 before he turned ten on his 24 July birthday. The rules of the school permitted entry at age nine at the earliest, implying that Alfred entered at the bottom, that is, the first form in the classical school. Since promotions to higher forms, the so-called classical remove, appeared to have taken place from the beginning of the quarter which started in January, or immediately after the quarter ending Christmas, it is likely that Alfred Marshall in fact started Merchant Taylors' in January 1852.[18]

As reason for this choice of school, Mary Paley gave Keynes the following explanation, much of which he reproduced in his Memoir.[19] 'His father, seeing that he [i.e. son Alfred] had ability, wanted to get him to a good school and asked a Bank Director for a nomination to Merchant Taylors'. The Director said, "do you know you are asking me for £200." But he gave it.' This account needs explanation. The choice of Merchant Taylors' for Alfred would not only have depended on its quality as a good school being, as one of the seven public schools, on a par with Eton, Harrow and Rugby. It was also the closest and, given its position as day school only, probably the cheapest. By the early 1850s, this was still an important consideration in the Marshall household.

Furthermore, the school was well-endowed with scholarships and exhibitions for St John's, Oxford. These included life fellowships at that college, quite unusual at the time and abolished in 1861, the year Alfred left school. This was a very valuable prize indeed for an able, but relatively poor son of the middle classes. It gave the school its strong appeal to 'sons of professional men, clergymen, barristers, lawyers, mercantile men, military men, clerks in public offices, and so on' as the Commission into Public Schools was informed at the start of the 1860s.[20]

Mary Paley's account of the manner in which William Marshall secured a nomination for his son is not quite accurate. The school's rules permitted nominations of students in turn to each member of its Court, comprising members and directors of the Merchant Taylor Company, a total of 40 persons. Enrolment at the school was fixed at 250 students, but this in actual fact was almost invariably exceeded by a small number. During the twenty years from 1842, enrolments ranged from a maximum 275 in 1851 to a minimum 247 in 1855, averaging 262. Since the maximum number of years school attendance was fixed at 10 years (from 9 to 19) while the normal length each boy tended to stay at school was more like 8 years, an average of approximately 30 to 35 vacancies occurred each year. On this basis, members of the Court could expect to make a maximum of three nominations every four years. Nominations had therefore considerable scarcity value. This is partly explained by the fact that the Merchant Taylor Company annually subsidised the school to the tune of two to three thousand pounds, or, on average, £10 per student per annum. For the maximum permitted term of enrolment at the school of ten years, this amounted to a potential subsidy of £100 per student. In addition, the value of a tied university college fellowship at St

John's, Oxford, to which the school gave access, potentially doubled the value of a nomination to the school by a member of the Court. This explains the sum of £200 which Mary Paley put into the mouth of the person nominating Alfred Marshall to Merchant Taylors'. Admission records for the school show that Alfred Marshall's nomination came through Bonamy Dobree, a member of the Court and Bank of England Director. How his father secured the nomination is not known; it is possible that Dobree knew members of Alfred's grandmother's family, the Bentalls.[21]

Relative to the notional value of a nomination, the fees charged by Merchant Taylors' were modest. An annual fee of £10, paid in equal quarterly instalments of £2.10s. was the major cost per student, and covered the complete educational services provided by the school. Two additional charges were payable. On first admission to the school, each boy had to pay an entrance fee of £3 to the Merchant Taylor Company. Secondly, each time he rose to a higher form, generally speaking, once a year, each boy paid a charge of 5s. to the master into whose form he was 'removed'. In addition, there was the cost for the boy's school clothing, for his lunches and fares, as well as for books and other school equipment. A contemporary of Alfred Marshall at the school described its students in 1858 as 'lay-down collared youths' as can still be observed in John Leech's picture of the Suffolk Lane school-room. It is probable that the photo of Alfred in 1855 shows him in this garb. Another account describes the boys as 'dressed, or encased, in (probably) the ugliest clothes that small boys were ever compelled to wear'. They carried a bluebook bag over their shoulders, and an ink bottle looped into the buttonhole, ink bought invariably at the school's tuckshop. When a boy moved into the sixth, he gave up his Eton-type collar and appeared in a tall hat and stick-up collar, with a black tie. Elevation to prompter or monitor entailed a swallow-tailed or evening dress coat. Alfred Marshall would have had to follow this sartorial practice. However, it is interesting to note that Marshall's schoolfriend, E.C. Dermer, later recalled that Alfred Marshall invariably 'was badly dressed' at school. Schoolbooks would have amounted to an annual charge of between two and five pounds, while lunches and fares at between two and three shillings a week would have added at least a further £5 per annum for the school year of 39 weeks.[22]

A household budget for a bank clerk with a wife, four children and a maid, and an annual income of around £250, puts these school costs in some perspective and illustrates the financial sacrifice the Marshall family incurred on behalf of its gifted, favoured son. The basis for this estimate is not known, but the family circumstances fit those of William Marshall by the start of Alfred Marshall's enrolment at Merchant Taylors' in 1852. It omits several items, some of which (pew at church, charitable and religious duties, holidays and fares), the Marshall family would have incurred. The annual budget, based on costs over 1845 to 1850, is estimated as follows:

	1845 to 1850		
	£	s.	d.
Income Tax at 7d. in the £	7	5	10
Life Assurance	8	0	0
Rent	28	0	0
Taxes including Poor Rate etc.	6	0	0
Bread, 7 quarterns per week, and flour, 1 quartern per week	10	12	4

Milk, 1 quart per day	6	0	0
Butter, ½ lb. per week, at 1s.6d. per lb.	9	0	0
Cheese, 1 lb. per week	1	6	8
Meat, ½ lb. each day, at 10½ per lb.	36	0	0
Beer, 2 quarts per day	10	0	0
Tea, ¾ lb. per week, at 3s.4d. per lb.	11	18	0
Coffee, ½ lb. per week, at 1s.6d. per lb.	1	19	0
Sugar, ½ lb. per week each, at 5d. per lb.	4	10	0
Servant's wages	8	0	0
Clothing for Six Persons, Boots, Shoes etc.	50	0	0
Education for Four Children, at £8 each	24	0	0
Washing	8	0	0
Coals, Firing, Wood, etc.	10	0	0
Soap and Candles, or Light of other kind	6	0	0
Potatoes, Vegetables, Fruit etc.	8	0	0
Insurance of Furniture	1	0	0
	£255	11	10

This budget also made no allowance for illness and medical treatment, or casualties of any kind. If the clerk was sick himself, salary was reduced by the loss of his 'Morning Money', a financial incentive for punctuality. No allowance was made for spirits or wine, probably not an important item in the Marshall household; for amusements, for wear and tear of furniture, glass, or household linen. Other items need explanation because the arithmetic is unclear. On the assumptions stated, education costs should total £32. Even then, Alfred's annual school costs at Merchant Taylors' of approximately £20 was well in excess of the average £8 allowed for education per child in this bank clerk's budget.[23]

THE SCHOOL AND ITS EDUCATIONAL PROGRAMME

What was the school like in which Alfred Marshall was to spend the greater part of the next ten years of his life? In the first place, it was an old school, founded in 1561 and still housed on the site purchased by the Merchant Taylors Company for this purpose in the year of foundation. This original site had consisted of half of what was called Sussex House, being former property of the Earl of Sussex. It included 'the west gate house, a long court or yard, the winding stairs at the south end of the said court (leading as well from the court unto the leads over the chapel, as also to two galleries over the south end of the court), the said two galleries and part of the chapel.' Towards the end of Alfred Marshall's enrolment at the school in 1859, the Company purchased the other half of the site, but the plans for using this additional space to modernise the school's facilities and to create a playground were never implemented. In fact, these plans became redundant when the school moved to more suitable premises in 1875.[24]

The virtual destruction of the original building during the great London fire of 1666 meant the school in the nineteenth century reflected nothing of its Tudor heritage. Pictures of the school's exterior in Suffolk Lane illustrate both the grime and its lack of architectural beauty noted by contemporary observers.[25] They also illustrate the particular disadvantages of the London schools which were enumerated by the 1864 Commission: 'being situated in the heart of a large city, it is impossible that they should offer to the boys the same facilities for recreation and exercise as the schools situated in the country . . . the boys of St Paul's and Merchant Taylors' have no playgrounds at all, and all four [London schools] are alike cut off from the free country rambles which constitute so important a feature of the social life of the other public schools. [They do have] liberty to walk in the streets of London, which are evidently not the most desirable place for boys to spend their leisure time in. . . . The condition of the schoolbuildings and premises seem to us good; but they are greatly in need of extension, both for purposes of study and recreation.'[*]

The hour for lunch between 1.00 and 2.00 p.m. combined with the fact that no provision was made for a place where the boys could eat on the school premises, did provide some locational advantages. One former student recalled some of these from his Suffolk Lane school-days in the decade after Alfred Marshall had left the school: 'Some went to the chophouses which still existed in the neighbourhood, others to the restaurants in Cheapside. I myself went to the Chelsea Bun House opposite Fishmongers' Hall, . . . I was allowed 6d. a day for lunch. . . . Lunch never took very long, and like many other boys I spent the rest of the time in exploring the city which we got to know very thoroughly.'[26]

It is possible that young Alfred may have lunched at the Chelsea Bun House opposite Fishmongers' Hall, or perhaps at one the 'chophouses' then still in existence in the neighbourhood, and used among others, by clerks from the Bank of England.[27] The free time provided in the middle of the day enabled excursions through Dickens's, and Mayhew's, London, perhaps especially tempting for a boy whose father's strong views on suitable recreation prevented such activities in the weekend. His school's location may therefore have provided a first taste for social inquiry and observation which he so extensively indulged in later years.

The interior of the school was reached through a 'small and well kicked wicket in the main gate which led directly into a stonepaved passage'. This gave way to both the cloisters, a reminder of the Tudor origins of the school, and a stairway, 'protected by a bold balustrade'. At its top were swinging doors, over which the arms of the Company were placed. They gave access to the main part of the school, its large schoolroom. The notion of school as schoolroom is so strange to those whose education dates from a later period, that a contemporary description is not out of place: 'The school was a long and wide room, lighted on each side by a row of windows reaching nearly from the ceiling almost to the top bench. There were four tiers of benches along each side of the school, and so far as I remember it

---

[*] *Report of the Commissioners on Public Schools*, pp. 50, 205. This may explain Alfred Marshall's great love for real country, which he so strongly expressed on his first visit to Cambridge for a scholarship examination in 1861 (on which see Chapter 4). As Mary Paley recorded for Walter Scott, 'He loved the country. He told me how, when he first came to Cambridge for a scholarship exam, he walked out by the Backs to the paths to Coton and shouted with joy to find himself at last in the real country.' Cf. the following remark in the first edition of the *Principles*: 'for even two people whose antecedents are similar and who appear to be like one another in every respect will yet be affected in different ways by the same events. When, for instance, a band of city school children are sent out for a day's holiday in the country, it is probable that no two of them derive from it enjoyment exactly the same in kind, or equal in intensity.' (*P* I, 151, eliminated from edition 2 onwards).

was only the top tier that had any accommodation for writing; on the three lower rows one wrote on one's knee as best one could.'[28]

Contemporary illustrations of the schoolroom in Suffolk Lane show this mode of furnishing for the students, and hence explain the complaints from parents in the late 1840s about 'the stooping posture in which, from the lack of desks, boys were compelled to learn their lessons'. A student attending just before Marshall complained that the room 'was as ill adapted for the purpose of an examination, as can be imagined, the boys having to use the forms as desks and to kneel in front of them'. Dermer, a contemporary of Alfred Marshall and fellow monitor, recalled that 'formerly there were no desks; they seem to have crept gradually down the school, and in 1852 the First and Petty Forms still had to do without them'. Although he and young Alfred therefore experienced the hardships of previous generations in their initial two years, accommodation steadily improved for them as they were 'removed' to higher classes until ultimately they reached the exclusivity and luxury of the monitors' table in their final year at school.[29]

Some other physical features of the school can be mentioned. On the left-hand side of the schoolroom, there was 'a large open grate, burning coal, protected by a stout iron cage at which unpopular boys and chestnuts were roasted during the dinner hour'. This form of winter heating was a luxury introduced into the school only at the start of the century, implying inadequate provision of chimneys and therefore an additional cause for smoke and soot in the school's environment. Winter months also meant illumination by candles, a necessity heightened by the grime accumulated on the high windows which, in the illustrations, tend to give the room its attractive appearance. Candles were provided by the school at the boys' expense. Gas lighting was introduced in the Upper School by 1850.[30] Heating and lighting was required during a very substantial portion of the total school year, and further worsened the generally unsatisfactory hygienic conditions of the schoolroom.

Improvements which took place in the 1850s were associated with the zeal for educational reform brought to the school by its headmaster, the Reverend James Augustus Hessey. Hessey was headmaster from 1845 to 1870, that is, for the whole period of Marshall's attendance. His appointment came after a very distinguished academic record, first at the school and then at Oxford, followed by prolonged service to the Church.[31] His reforming bent is very visible in the statement on school policy he prepared for the Commission on Public Schools and Colleges, and in the various improvements he introduced to the school's syllabus. Before taking up his appointment, Hessey had arranged for changes in the school's organisation with his predecessor. The number of forms was increased from eight to ten, English history and geography were added to the syllabus, and fees were raised to the £10 per annum Alfred Marshall's parents were charged for their son's education. In his first years as headmaster, Hessey reformed the method of examining, revised the school times to the 9.30 start and 4.00 finish with the one hour off for lunch which Alfred Marshall experienced, made the election of monitors* subject to proper

---

* Monitors, of which there were eight in the school during Marshall's time, were the intellectual elite of the school. They occasionally assisted with the education of the younger boys and also had disciplinary responsibilities (*Report*, p. 263–4). They were given special privileges to match their exalted status, as E.C. Dermer recalled in his letter to Mary Paley Marshall, 19 November 1924 (KMF). Dermer was second in the monitor list in 1861. Alfred Marshall, was third monitor. For the origin of the term, see James Bowen, *A History of Western Education*,

competition, and obstinately campaigned to secure more appropriate facilities at the school for boys to eat their lunch.

Most importantly for the future prospects of Alfred Marshall, in 1850 Hessey appointed the Rev. J.A.L. Airey, a second wrangler from Cambridge, as one of the masters in mathematics. This greatly strengthened mathematics teaching at the school. As the Public Schools Commission reported in 1864, 'the amount of mathematics taught in the school, and the time given to them (no less than the whole afternoon on five days in the week) are considerably above what we have found in any other school.'[32]

Hessey also actively campaigned for a change in the school's location and, until this was realised, for further improvements in the accommodation of students at the Suffolk Lane premises. He strongly argued against the 'miserable dark position and want of circulation of air' from the school's situation and the unsatisfactory educational conditions of the by then outdated schoolroom. His efforts meant Alfred Marshall and his fellow students enjoyed access to desks from their third year onwards, and separate classrooms in the higher grades of the school. In short, Alfred Marshall's subsequent career owes much to the reforming zeal of this persistent, courageous and very effective innovative headmaster.[33] In 1877, he recalled his headmaster and asked him to provide a testimonial when he applied for the position of University College Principal at Bristol. Some of its fulsome praise bears quoting:

I have much pleasure in bearing my testimony to the ability, vigour, and general merits of Mr. Marshall, M.A., one of my former pupils. Mr. Marshall received his education from me at Merchant Taylors' school and at his leaving in June 1861, after a very distinguished career, and obtaining our chief Mathematical Prize, and the position of Third Monitor, was offered a scholarship at St John's College Oxford . . . with characteristic independence and conscious of his mental power, he declined this opening and accepted a Parkin's Exhibition of smaller value, which is given annually to the best Mathematician leaving for Cambridge, he determined to trust his fortunes in that University. He was not mistaken. . . . The courage and judgement which have marked his own course would be invaluable when applied to the guidance of a rising institution. I may add that I have a high opinion of Mr. Marshall's integrity and sense of duty, and that I am persuaded that he would more than justify the greatest expectations that could be formed of him.[34]

Even with the changes to the syllabus introduced of the 1840s and early 1850s, the school remained within the contemporary public school tradition of providing what was essentially a classical education. Study of the languages of Greece and Rome occupied the greater part of the morning classes (from 9.30 to 1.00) not only to teach grammar, or the logic of common speech, but also composition and translation, and the rudiments of etymology. In addition, study of the classical literature was then seen as providing the best introduction 'to the intellectual and moral world we live in, and of the thoughts, lives, and characters of those men whose writings or whose memories succeeding generations have thought it worthwhile to preserve.'[35] In the fourth year, or the lower division, French classes were added to the morning school hours and, a more unusual feature of Merchant Taylors', from

---

London: Methuen, 1981, Volume 3, pp. 293–5; G.M. Young, *Portrait of an Age*, p. 71 n.* suggests the system was used at Charterhouse for some time.

the sixth form, study of Hebrew was added to the syllabus.* Arithmetic and writing formed part of the junior school, and were studied exclusively in the afternoon, between 2.00 and 4.00 p.m.. This changed to mathematics studies proper from the fourth form. Drawing lessons were given to the mathematics class for two hours a week in the two higher years. These presumably taught mechanical drawing rather than art. The teaching of history and geography was combined with the morning teaching of language, while a substantial part of the Monday morning was set aside for religious instruction such as scriptural history. In the same spirit, homework set on Saturday morning 'was strictly connected with religious subjects such as may not unfitly engage a boy's thought and time on Sunday'.[36]

The school's strong reputation for religious teaching was further enhanced by the practice of prayers from the Anglican Prayer Book four times a day (at start and finish of both morning and afternoon classes), and the headmaster's self-imposed duty to prepare boys, who had 'arrived at the proper age, for confirmation and afterwards for their first Communion, which they generally receive at his hands in the Chapel of the Hon. Society of Gray's Inn'. On average, thirty boys were annually confirmed in this way. With a total enrolment of just over 260 boys for a maximum of ten years, this implies a substantial rate of success for this part of the headmaster's work.[37]

Given its importance for Alfred Marshall's subsequent studies at Cambridge, some aspects of this syllabus need elaboration. First of all, attention can be drawn to two omissions from the syllabus about which Headmaster Hessey himself expressed regret to the Commission on Public Schools. These were natural philosophy and German.[38] The former, the Commission noted, was with only very 'slight exceptions . . . practically excluded from the education of the higher classes in England'. German was increasingly being taught in schools. The Commissioners' *Report* expressed a moderate preference for teaching French first, but recommended German for its growing practical usefulness. Teaching German was to be preferred to Italian, despite the importance of Dante for a cultured life.[39]

Alfred Marshall repaired the first of these omissions, at least in part, in the studies he took as part of the Mathematical Tripos at Cambridge. The omission of German studies was filled by subsequent private lessons in Dresden and Berlin in 1868 and 1870, and, less formally, during his many mountaineering trips in the Alps, the Tirol and Bavaria. Secondly, it should be emphasised that his school education had given him a reasonable proficiency in French. This explains the presence of a significant number of French works in his library in economics and other subjects and his ability to correspond in the language.[40]

The extensive mathematical syllabus of Merchant Taylors' School, relative to that of other public schools, needs emphasis. The headmaster's statement for the Public Schools Commission boasted of the very high standards demanded in the school's mathematical programme. This was supported by the list of examined subjects in the October 1861 examination he supplied together with a list of the books used by the head and second classes in the mathematical school. These are reproduced in an Appendix to this chapter.

---

* *Ibid.*, pp. 153–4, 156. Keynes's embellishment in adding 'often at Hebrew' ('Alfred Marshall', p. 163) to Mary Paley's statement that William Marshall 'used to make A[lfred] work with him for school up to 11 pm' (KMF) therefore has the undoubtedly unintended consequence of softening father William's harshness considerably. After all, if these late night sessions largely involved Hebrew, not begun till a boy had reached age 16 or 17, studying until 11 p.m. seems much less severe than if the practice was applied from age nine onwards.

Some of these books were written by persons who were among Marshall's Tripos examiners in 1865, that is, Walton and Todhunter; and at least one of the texts gave him an early acquaintance with the Cambridge style of mathematical examining.

The relative importance of mathematics in the school where Alfred Marshall took his first steps in this field, can also be gauged from the school's budget in 1861. In that year, the classical department accounted for £2,147 (including expenditure of £450 on items more properly allocated to the school as a whole) while the mathematical department spent £994 (or 31.6 per cent).[41]

In short, from the perspective of syllabus, Alfred Marshall later had much to be grateful for in his father's choice of school, despite his many grumbles about the excessive classical component in his education. It was another feature of the school, however, which made its choice for Alfred attractive to his father, William. This was the access to university education at Oxford or Cambridge it gave to its successful students. Particularly important were the thirty-seven out of fifty fellowships at St John's Oxford, which were attached to the school by Sir Thomas White, a member of the Court of the company at the time of the school's establishment. 'Boys elected from hence to St John's were probationary Fellows for three years, and then, if qualified and of good conduct, admitted Fellows for life'. These life fellowship opportunities provided by Merchant Taylors', similar to those offered by Eton for King's College, Cambridge, had become fully effective in 1575. They were abolished by an Order from the Privy Council under an Act of Parliament in 1861 to take effect from that year. Alfred Marshall in 1861 successfully completed his school studies which entitled him to such a probationary life fellowship.[42] His school companion, E.C. Dermer wrote to Mary Paley Marshall that 'It was a very bold act of his [Alfred Marshall] to refuse the Oxford "life fellowship" at St John's – in the very last year it was offered. I doubt if any man before him ever refused one!'.[43]

ALFRED MARSHALL AT MERCHANT TAYLORS': 1852–1861

Alfred Marshall's 'bold act' of rejecting the prize of a life fellowship at Oxford needs further comment. The opportunity of gaining this 'prize' was mentioned earlier as a major reason why his parents made such an effort to secure his nomination for the school. Keynes expanded on this by adding that entry to St John's, Oxford, 'was the first step to ordination in the Evangelical ministry for which his father designed him'. This addition needs a closer look, since a paternal wish that Marshall follow a clerical career is only emphasised by Keynes.[44] It has little support from other sources, contemporary or otherwise. It is not mentioned by Mary Paley in either her notes for Keynes or those she prepared for Walter Scott, though Scott also mentioned this possibility in his obituary.* Nor is it raised by the

---

* Cf. Keynes's entry on Alfred Marshall for the *DNB, Supplementary Volume for 1922–30*, p. 462 where it is categorically stated that Oxford 'would have meant his continuing to work at the classics, *as the first step towards the ordination, which was his father's wish*' (my emphasis). Elsewhere in his Memoir ('Alfred Marshall', p. 167), Keynes argued, once again without any evidence or support from the notes he had obtained from Mary Paley: 'In Marshall's undergraduate days at Cambridge a preference for Mathematics over Classics had not interfered with the integrity of his early religious beliefs. He still looked forward to ordination, and his zeal directed itself at times towards the field of foreign missions. A missionary he remained all his life, but after a quick struggle religious beliefs dropped away and he became, for the rest of his life, what used to be called an agnostic.' A reason for

shorter obituaries and similar notices of Alfred Marshall which appeared in Venn's *Alumni Cantabrigienses*, the *Times*, and that by his nephew, Claude Guillebaud, in the *Cambridge Review*. These simply attributed the switch to mathematical studies at Cambridge to Alfred Marshall's intense dislike of classical studies and to his love of, and ability for, mathematics discovered only towards the end of his school-days.[45] More importantly, the explanation for the career switch Alfred Marshall himself provided in several autobiographical sketches ignore this aspect of his choice. His entry in the 12th edition of *Men of the Time* of 1887 simply states that he 'was educated at Merchant Taylors' School, whence he obtained the title to a probationary fellowship at St John's College, Oxford, awarded for classical attainments, *but preferring mathematical studies* he proceeded to St John's College, Cambridge.'[46]   The carefully written and much longer autobiographical entry Alfred Marshall prepared around 1910 for a projected German reference work is even more explicit on the reasons for the career shift, but Keynes omitted this from the extensive extract of this source he quoted.   Befitting the style adopted for such reference works, Alfred Marshall wrote in the third person: 'He was educated at Merchant Taylors' school; and in 1861 under old statutes, now repealed, he obtained the title, as student of Latin and Greek to a Fellowship at St John's College, Oxford.'   At this stage, Marshall adds to the account he gave nearly a quarter of a century previously: 'When seventeen years old, however, he developed a very strong interest in Mathematics; and on leaving school resigned his title to the Fellowship at Oxford, in order to seek his fortune at Cambridge, which is the chief home of Mathematics in England.'[47]

There are good reasons for accepting Marshall's account.   It is supported by other evidence, including the independent testimony of his school companion, E.C. Dermer.

> I was a good deal surprised at the number of subjects which A[lfred] M[arshall] followed up [the ethics, metaphysics and psychology mentioned in Keynes's Memoir]. He only developed as a mathematician when he was far up in the school and it is not chiefly as a mathematician that he earned his name.   Our old 'curriculum' was very stiff – classics only and always in morning school and 10 afternoon hours a week [of mathematics] under the best master in the school (Airey, also 2nd Wrangler). I had no taste for mathematics and writhed under 'differential Calculus' as he did under Latin prose and verse.[48]

Alfred Marshall's growing fondness of mathematics while at school is well documented, as are some of the motivations for this. Mary Paley recalled,

> During A's last year or two at school, when he was able to do more what he liked, he worked at mathematics. Airy [sic!], the mathematical master said that 'he had a genius for mathematics'. His father hated the sight of a mathematical book: so when A[lfred] was walking to and from school, he had Potts Euclid in his pocket. He read a proposition and then worked it out in his head as he walked along, standing still at intervals. He thus formed the habit of turning his toes in which he did not lose for many years. He had to study mainly classics at school, including Hebrew and when he became a Monitor he was offered a classical fellowship at St John's, Oxford. But he would not accept it, for he wanted to go to Cambridge and

---

Keynes's inventiveness can be found in the opening phrase of the last sentence quoted, a motive similar to the emphasis on a clerical ancestry he also provided for Alfred Marshall without much evidence but, in this case, with a degree of support from Mary Paley's notes. Walter Scott, 'Alfred Marshall, 1842–1924', pp. 1–2) speaks of 'the straight and narrow path which his father had marked out for him through a Scholarship at St John's Oxford to the Church'.

study mathematics. He felt that he got as much out of classics as he cared for. He felt that if he went to Oxford and took mathematics there, he would not get all he wanted. So in spite of the opposition of his family, and in spite of want of funds, for his father was too poor to help further, he determined to go to Cambridge. . . . His father told him later on that he only withdrew his strong opposition to the Cambridge versus Oxford career when he found that A[lfred] was making himself ill with worry.[49]

Much of Mary Paley's account found its way into Keynes's Memoir. However, Keynes embroidered it and transformed mathematics into a symbol of general emancipation for Alfred. Keynes emphasised Marshall's pleasure 'that his father could not understand' mathematics books. Keynes then concludes on the subject with a final flourish: 'No! He would not be buried at Oxford under dead languages; he would run away 'to be a cabin boy at Cambridge and climb the rigging of geometry and spy out the heavens.'[50] Keynes's account hinting that revenge on his father was a powerful factor in Alfred Marshall's shift in careers, is also not sanctioned by Mary Paley's account. Moreover, Keynes omitted her explanation why Marshall's father eventually withdrew his opposition to Cambridge as the place of study for his son. These subtle changes appear designed to add colour to Keynes's picture of Marshall the preacher and missionary, and to the picture of his father as a domestic tyrant.

A non-clerical reason for Marshall's family's preferences for an Oxford rather than a Cambridge career is easily found. The family's relative poverty which Mary Paley mentioned, provides one clue. The Oxford Fellowship was a certainty, a guaranteed position for life, given the academic and behaviour record of young Alfred. The Cambridge alternative, as Marshall himself strikingly put it, meant 'seeking his fortune', a search moreover which needed the financial assistance through borrowing from his Uncle Charles. Though by June 1861 Marshall had gained a scholarship, the Parkin Exhibition tenable at St John's Cambridge, this was of 'less value' than the Oxford alternative. Apart from the disadvantage of needing additional finance to pursue Cambridge University studies,[51] the prospects of gaining a good enough honours result at Cambridge to obtain a fellowship at its St John's, was highly uncertain. In short, by refusing to choose Oxford and its guaranteed future, Alfred Marshall elected an uncertain prospect involving additional expense at Cambridge. For a person of relatively poor family circumstances like Alfred Marshall, such a gamble was highly risky. For someone like William Marshall, whose own career choice, unlike that of his brothers, avoided all risks by opting for the security offered by a position as clerk in the Bank of England, such a choice bordered on the insane. It threatened waste of the financial sacrifices made by him and the family in educating this seemingly wayward son. In the end, Marshall's father only consented to the switch because the effect of his opposition would have secured an even worse outcome in the form of his son's ill health. It can be added that the measure of Marshall's preference for mathematics at Cambridge over studying classics can be found (as he himself would have put it in later work on economics) by the degree of financial sacrifice involved.

Marshall's critical views of the type of classical education he had received at school need further discussion. This became a recurring theme in his life. In 1904, writing to his nephew Harold Guillebaud, then just in the sixth form at Marlborough School, Marshall criticised the relative lack of usefulness of a classical education including the mental and moral training allegedly gained from it. Marshall's letter also recalled the danger of overwork to which classical study at school, assisted by his father's bad educational practices, had unnecessarily exposed him in his youth:

> I speak with deep feeling. From six to seventeen years of age I studied practically nothing but classics. I then obtained a place in the school which entitled me to a 'close' probationary classical fellowship at Oxford. (These things are abolished now.) I spent the next five years mainly on mathematics and the next three mainly on philosophy. I have forgotten my mathematics and philosophy as well as my classics; but I am intensely grateful to them. And I am not very grateful to my classics.[52]

Marshall's hatred of compulsory classical studies at school was also recorded by others. Writing about a small dinner party he had given in April 1877, John Neville Keynes mentioned in his diary that Marshall had been 'in one of his paradoxical moods. Amongst other things he said he would give his right arm never to have learnt any classics, the time that he wasted on classics might so much more profitably have been spent on music, drawing, sculpture, a few modern languages, biology and general culture.'[53] As a young Fellow at John's in the early 1870s he publicly deplored the excessive classics requirements for a Cambridge education, proposing abolition of compulsory Greek.[54]

   During the final years of his life Marshall gave a more personal reason for his dislike of classical studies in his later school years, directed particularly at Greek:

> When at school I was told to take no account of accents in pronouncing Greek words. I concluded that to burden my memory with accents would take up time and energy that might be turned to account; so I did not look out my accents in the dictionary, and received the only very heavy punishment of my life. This suggested to me that classical studies do not induce an appreciation of the value of time; and I turned away from them as far as I could towards mathematics. In later years I have observed that fine students of science are greedy of time, but many classical men seem to value it lightly.[55]

Combined with Alfred Marshall's well-attested sensitiveness to criticism, the very heavy punishment inflicted[*] for what appears to have been an innocent, albeit foolish, mistake, may well have been the final straw in killing any remaining interest in classical studies, coming on top of the long, and unpleasant, homework sessions in the evening with his father which these studies also entailed. The autobiographical extract continues with a brief statement of the one valuable aspect that Marshall recognised in the contribution made by his headmaster to his classical education: 'my headmaster was a broad-minded man, and succeeded in making his head form write Latin Essays, thought out in Latin; not thought out in English and translated into Latin. I am more grateful for that than for anything else he did for me'.[56]

   The growing appeal of mathematical studies after Marshall turned 17 can be discussed as the other major reason for the change in direction. His 'love' for mathematical studies is

---

[*] Given the school's liberal reputation as regards punishment reflected in the *Report of the Commission on Public Schools*, pp. 205, 263 (which stated, *inter alia*, that the headmaster only very rarely, 'not once in three years' has resorted to flogging) and the reputation of his father as a martinet not known for thrift in the use of rod or slipper, it is interesting to speculate who inflicted this severe punishment and of what it had consisted. It may of course also be an example of Marshall's tendency to make exaggerated statements, a striking feature of his later conversation.

clearly visible in his manner of studying Euclid when travelling to and from school. The inclusion of the differential calculus in the Merchant Taylors' syllabus from sixth form may also have 'excited native proclivities'. The fact that Airey, the head mathematics master, taught in the senior forms supplies a further reason why Alfred Marshall grew increasingly keener on mathematical study as he advanced through the school. Apart from being 'the best master in the school',[57] Marshall would have grown fond of Airey and his subject because of the praise he received from this teacher. Mary Paley recalled Airey's comment that Marshall 'had a genius for mathematics',[58] very welcome praise for a boy sensitive to criticism. More important still to the young Marshall was the promise of gaining one of the school's eight major prizes which mathematical studies held out. A reward like this was unattainable from his classical, language or other studies given the competition from others he faced there. He did in fact win the chief Mathematical Prize in 1861. It followed mathematics prizes secured in 1857, and his very high ranking in its 1859 and 1860 examinations. The only other distinctions Marshall gained at school were a special prize in 1854 for being second in Latin grammar and a Special Essay Prize the Headmaster offered and which he shared in 1860.[59]

Praise *and* the success of being first in the class are heady stimulants for a sensitive boy. Marshall probably got little praise from his father at home. Marshall also liked winning, Mary Paley told Walter Scott in the context of the Marshalls' nightly backgammon games during marriage, he 'was much annoyed if he didn't win'.[60] In short, mathematics may also have become increasingly attractive to the young Alfred Marshall because he was good at it, so good in fact that he could beat all others, enabling himself to indulge that taste for victory which made him 'so excited over games'.[61] Irrespective of the 'love of the chase' and of the joy in puzzling out proofs and solutions to problems, coming first is a powerful motive for a boy with few friends, a domineering father sparing in praise, and a social background which, in the absence of the type of academic excellence and hard work which created monitors and prize winners, would have placed him near the bottom of the school's pecking order.

The eminence implied in being elected third monitor at Merchant Taylors' should be emphasised to avoid any impression that Marshall's successes in mathematics and his complaints about classical education suggest lack of ability and achievement in his education as a whole. It has already been indicated that monitors were the intellectual elite of the school with special privileges. At Merchant Taylors', monitors received in addition some training in public speaking. Dr Hessey mentioned this in his submission to the Public Schools Commission. Opportunities for public speaking by schoolboys 'take place twice in the year, at Christmas and in June, and are limited to the eight monitors. Dr Hessey himself superintends them, and considers them a most valuable means of bringing out boys' talents and character, and of giving them ease and self possession.' Copies of some of these speeches are preserved with other Merchant Taylors' School material from its Suffolk Lane days in the Archives of the Guild Hall Library.[62]

Alfred Marshall's school friendships also need some mention. In his old age, Mary Paley told Scott, Alfred Marshall 'often said he would have liked to have seen more of his old school and college friends'[63] but that he had lacked the strength and the time to do so effectively. Dermer's letter to Mary Paley confirms this lack of contact between the former monitors of the school so far as he was concerned. 'I scarcely ever spoke or saw him after June 11, 1861 – once or twice, when I visited Cambridge, and long after, when you came to live opposite my church.'[64] To Keynes, Mary Paley imparted that Alfred Marshall 'did not readily make friends at school' for reasons which may have something to do with his father's fears about mixing with undesirable children. She continued, 'His chief school friends were H.D. Traill and Sidney Hall, who afterwards became an artist. H.D. Trail was his chief friend, he afterwards became a monitor and Fellow of St John's College, Oxford. Traill's brother, a famous cricketer, gave him a copy of Mill's *Logic* which he and A[lfred] read at the Monitors' Table to the astonishment of Dr. Hessey the Headmaster'.[65]

The friendship with Traill is interesting. Traill was in fact Head Monitor in the school, gaining three of the eight major prizes it awarded in 1861. He became a journalist and member of the editorial staff of the *Telegraph*, the first editor of the periodical, *Literature*, and wrote several books and plays, after having been admitted to the bar on taking his B.A. and a law degree at Oxford. Either his academic success made him an attractive friend for young Alfred Marshall, or, equally likely, the reflected glory in which he basked for having as brother a famous cricketer, particularly for a boy as fond of cricket as the young Alfred Marshall was said to be. Alfred Marshall's other friend, Sidney Hall, was the eighth and last monitor in 1860–61 and, following in his father's footsteps, became an artist. He was special war artist for *The Graphic* during the Franco-Prussian War and died, aged 80, at the end of 1922. Apart from being monitors, and therefore academically gifted, Marshall's two known school friends shared other characteristics. They were both slightly younger than he was, being born in August and October 1842 respectively. Both also started at Merchant Taylors' well after the time of Marshall's initial enrolment, that is, in 1853 and 1855 respectively.[66] Mixing with slightly younger persons and with relative late-comers in their environment were features in his selection of friends Marshall later showed at college.[67]

Mary Paley's account enables the inference that Alfred Marshall's appearance and attitude to games at school did not help the cause of friendship. A photograph from 1855, probably in his school clothes, was most likely taken at the start of a new school year in September, after summer holidays in Devon with Aunt Louisa had repaired his health. This contrasts with the picture of Alfred Marshall presented by E.C. Dermer, which indicated that at school, Alfred 'always looked overworked, was small and pale, and was called "tallow candles" and was badly dressed. He did not care much for games (except cricket), was fond of propounding chess problems and did not readily make friends.'[68] Cricket, chess problems, studiousness plus the eccentricity of being badly dressed may have been a factor in his friendships with Traill and Hall. Their later artistic careers, so removed from the conventional pattern of Church and the law, may suggest similar eccentric behaviour as compared to their school peers. Marshall's reluctance to form enduring friendships stayed with him for much of his life.[69]

A few snippets about his literary tastes while at school are also available. His assiduous pursuits of the contents of Mill's *Logic* with Traill at the monitors' table, further support a growing desire during these years to abandon classical studies for a more scientific and mathematical career. Only the latter would have provided the inspiration to work through what is not an easy book for schoolboys. Those familiar with its contents will have no difficulty in sharing Hessey's astonishment that two, admittedly of the brightest, boys in his school were reading this work. Mill himself, referring to the *Logic* in his *Autobiography*, expressed the opinion that 'a treatise . . . on a matter so abstract, could not be expected to be popular; it could only be a book for students, and students on such subjects were not only (at least in England) few, but addicted chiefly to the opposite school of metaphysics'.[70] More mundane, but just as indicative of Alfred Marshall's developing tastes, was the love for Walter Scott's novels which, according to Mary Paley he developed during his schooldays and which stayed with him for the rest of his life.[71]

In June 1861, when Alfred Marshall left school, he did so with the new vocation of studying mathematics at Cambridge. Apart from the relatively strong mathematical training which his school had given him, and which had enabled him to enter for, and win, the Parkin Exhibition worth £50 per annum for four years at St John's College, Cambridge, the school had given him increased confidence and faith in his own ability. The confidence which came with the academic success he achieved at the school, together with the benefits from social contact with boys like H.D. Traill and Sidney Hall, would likewise have been of some help in the relatively lonely years which faced him as an undergraduate in Cambridge. His years at Merchant Taylors' not only made possible his matriculation to Cambridge. They eased the transition to the college life which the introverted, mother-doting, London-bred young man was to taste over the years and which brought him to adulthood. His school years in this way helped to create the man.

Enough has survived on Marshall's school years to enhance understanding of his later life and career. Contrary to Keynes's widely accepted hypothesis, explanations for his switch from classics to mathematics need have nothing to do with abandoning an ecclesiastical career, as perhaps originally intended by a domineering and evangelical father. Less emphasis on this in explaining the career switch also provides greater freedom for understanding Marshall's later abandonment of religious beliefs. Keynes's account of this experience, with as its end product the staunch, lifelong agnostic after a brief postgraduate religious crisis, is then easier to correct from the Cambridge stereotype it portrays. Lack of evidence for Keynes's speculations in this area, together with the existence of plausible alternative explanations for the abandonment of the Oxford classical career, make other speculations very possible.

It was when aged 17, that Alfred Marshall, on his own account, developed a sufficiently strong taste for mathematics to decide to concentrate on its studies as a possible future career. His eighteenth year is also important in another context. As he subsequently recalled in 1917,[72] this was the age in which he developed a method of study, useful to him for much of his later life, the inspiration for which occurred presumably during one of these lunchtime wanders through the city of London and its West End environment:

An epoch in my life occurred when I was, I think about seventeen years old. I was in Regent Street, and saw a workman standing idle before a shop-window: but his face indicated alert energy, so I stood still and watched. He was preparing to sketch on the window of a shop guiding lines for a short statement of the business concerned, which was to be shown by white letters fixed to the glass. Each stroke of arm and hand needed to be made with a single free sweep, so as to give a graceful result; it occupied perhaps two seconds of keen excitement. He stayed still for a few minutes after each stroke, so that his pulse might grow quiet. If he had saved the minutes thus lost, his employers would have been injured by more than the value of his wages for a whole day. That set up a train of thought which led me to the resolve never to use my mind when it was not fresh; and to regard the intervals between successive strains as sacred to absolute repose. When I went to Cambridge and became full master of myself, I resolved never to read a mathematical book for more than a quarter of an hour at a time, without a break. I had some light literature always by my side, and in the breaks I read through more than once nearly the whole of Shakespeare, Boswell's Life of Johnson, the Agamemnon of Aeschylus (the only Greek play which I could read without effort), a great part of Lucretius and so on. Of course I often got excited by my mathematics, and read for half an hour or more without stopping: but that meant that my mind was intense, and no harm was done.

Marshall's school life also reveals other character traits and sources of belief which strengthened in later life. Belief in the need for *useful* education is one obvious example, to which he himself drew attention in his criticism of classical studies. Concern with educational reform, including reform of the institutions in which teaching takes place, was also a lesson imparted by his school-days from the unsuitable environment of Suffolk Lane in which for so long they took place. Love of country and love of fresh air guided Alfred Marshall's future policy on housing the poor and were personally applied when choosing the location for his own residence in Cambridge. School-days also show him as a loner, a person who did not easily make friends, and who sought shelter in select family devotion and eccentricity in behaviour as part of a natural introversion.   Finally, his school experience highlights ambitions for success and a will to win, whetted by his performances in mathematics. This was, perhaps the real motive force which took him from his school to Cambridge in order to pursue mathematical honours and a scientific career.

NOTES

1. Mary Paley Marshall, 'Biographical Notes on Alfred Marshall' (KMF).
2. Data on Sydenham from Ben Weinreb and Christopher Hibbert, *The London Encyclopaedia*, pp. 852–3.
3. Information provided by the Bank of England as to salaries. Data on a bank clerk's budget for the period of 1845–50 (provided in H.G. de Fraine, *Servant of this House*, p. 137), suggests that an annual salary of £250 was fairly ample for a family with three children all aged below ten.
4. 1851 Census Report, copy preserved with Coase Papers.
5. The 'Public Schools' were named in the schedule to the Public Schools Act, 1864 (27 and 28 Vict. c. 92). 'They were Eton, Winchester, Westminster, Charterhouse, St Paul's, Merchant Taylors' (in London), Harrow, Rugby and Shrewsbury.' See G.M. Young, *Portrait of an Age*, p. 327 n.15 (by George Kitson Clark). These schools were private fee-paying schools.
6. Mary Paley Marshall, 'Notes for Walter Scott'.
7. See *Report of the Manchester Statistical Society on the State of Education in the Borough of Salford in 1835* (London: 1836), p. 14 cited in David de Giustino, *Conquest of Mind*, London: Croom Helm, 1975, p. 177.
8. Francis Shephard, *London 1808–1870: The Infernal Wen*, p. 236, citing the *Newcastle Commission*, Vol. I, p. 93, Vol. III, p. 564; Smith, *Elementary Education*, p. 303.
9. A.S. and E.M.S., *Henry Sidgwick, A Memoir*, London: Macmillan, 1906, p. 4.
10. Reports from Commissioners: 1864 (Cmnd 3288), *Revenues and Management of Certain Colleges and Schools*, Vol. 2, Appendix, pp. 249, 254.
11. Mary Paley Marshall, 'Notes for Walter Scott'.
12. Howard Staunton, *The Great Schools of England*, London: Sampson, Law & Marston, 1865, p. 239.
13. Mary Paley Marshall, 'Biographical Notes on Alfred Marshall' (KMF). They seem also to have been a sign of Bentall-type affluence, since Aunt Louisa, who had not indulged in an imprudent marriage like her older brother, would have been in a better financial position.
14. Augustus Hare, 'On Childhood and Boyhood', extracts included in Eugene C. Black (ed.), *Victorian Culture and Society*, London: Macmillan, 1973, pp. 201–10.
15. Noel Annan, *Leslie Stephen, The Godless Victorian*, London: Weidenfeld & Nicolson, 1984, pp. 16–17.

16. Eugene C. Black, 'Introduction to Socialisation: Childhood and the Family', in *Victorian Culture and Society*, p. 200.
17. Mary Paley Marshall, 'Biographical Notes on Alfred Marshall' (KMF).
18. *Report on Revenues and Management of Certain Schools and Colleges*, pp. 204, 253; the record shows he was 'admitted' 5 February 1852 (Merchant Taylors' School Probation Books, Vol. 8, Guildhall Library, London).
19. Mary Paley Marshall, 'Biographical Notes on Alfred Marshall' (KMF); Keynes, 'Alfred Marshall', pp. 162–4.
20. *Report on Revenues and Management of Certain Schools and Colleges*, pp. 50–51, 257. A check through the Register of the School on students contemporary with Alfred Marshall confirms the high incidence of the professions among parents of boys at the school.
21. Merchant Taylors' School Admissions, Vol. 2, 1825–1852; Guildhall Library, London. *Report on Revenue, and Management of Certain Schools and Colleges*, pp. 249–50, 253; Mary Paley Marshall, 'Biographical Notes on Alfred Marshall' (KMF). Details on Bonamy Dobree (1794–1863), who became Deputy Governor and Governor of the Bank, from F. Boase, *Modern English Biography*, London: 1965, Supplement to Volume II, columns 118–19.
22. *Report on Revenues and Management of Certain Schools and Colleges*, p. 251; F.W.M. Draper, *Four Centuries of Merchant Taylors' School 1561–1961*, London: Oxford University Press, 1962, esp. Chapters 13–14, pp. 134, 138.
23. Derived from H.G. de Fraine, *Servant of this House*, p. 137, who likewise finds some of the arithmetic unclear.
24. F.W.M. Draper, *Four Centuries of Merchant Taylors' School*, p. 2.
25. See Draper, pp. 153–4. One of those pictures is reproduced as illustration 9.
26. Cited in Draper, *Four Centuries of Merchant Taylors' School*, p. 139.
27. H.G. de Fraine, *Servant of this House*, p. 9.
28. Cited in Draper, *Four Centuries of Merchant Taylors' School*, pp. 134–5.
29. *Ibid.*, pp. 136–7, 148. The room is depicted in illustration 10.
30. *Ibid.*, pp. 137–8.
31. James Augustus Hessey (1814–92), *DNB, Supplement*, Vol. XXII, Oxford University Press 1949–50 reprint, pp. 840–41. In 1845 he married Emma Cazenove, daughter of R. Cazenove of Clapham, perhaps a point of contact between Merchant Taylors' School and William Marshall.
32. *Report of the Commissioners on Public Schools*, p. 204; however, evidence they collected from university people such as Price, Sedleian Professor of Natural Philosophy at Oxford, from Sir Charles Lyell and William Whewell (*ibid.*, pp. 26, 31) indicated that even this level of mathematics training was still insufficient preparation for scientific studies at university.
33. A detailed account of Hessey's reforms and an evaluation of his important headmastership is given by Draper, *Four Centuries of Merchant Taylors' School*, Chapter 14, especially pp. 151–5.
34. Rev. J.A. Hessey to Council of Bristol University College, 23 June 1877.
35. *Report of the Commissioners on Public Schools*, pp. 28, 254. It is interesting to note in this context Hessey's statement that a boy's 'knowledge of English is tested continually, though, of course, incidentally by the correctness of his oral readings, and by the spelling and construction of his translations on paper.' (*Ibid.*, p. 254).
36. *Report of the Commissioners on Public Schools*, pp. 45, 263.
37. *Ibid.*, p. 263. It is not known whether Alfred Marshall became a communicant in this way. A check with the archivist of the Society of Gray's Inn revealed that no records of these first communicants have been preserved.
38. *Report of the Commissioners on Public Schools*, p. 256.
39. *Ibid.*, pp. 31–2. On Italian, the Commissioners noted, 'to be ignorant of Italian is undoubtedly a misfortune for any man of cultivated mind. No French or German poet can be placed on a level with Dante; no poetical literature has exercised so strong or so beneficial influence on our own as that of Italy in its palmy days.' Despite their extensive travel in Italy, Marshall, unlike his wife, gained only a smattering of Italian. (Alfred Marshall's fellow economists Edgeworth and Wicksteed were of course fluent.) On this, his German lessons and the importance of French and German to his economic studies, see below, Chapters 5 and 7, and on his proficiency in Italian, Chapter 17, p. 632 and n.¶.
40. His correspondence with Levasseur and Walras provides examples of his ability to write French, and suggests his reading was better than his French composition.
41. *Report of the Commissioners on Public Schools*, pp. 203–4. If these items (rates and taxes, repairs, insurance, coals and caretakers' wages) are excluded, the share of the mathematics department in the school's budget rises to 37 per cent. The mathematical school was also responsible for the drawing classes conducted by a part-time assistant master, who taught the four more senior mathematics classes for one hour a week over two afternoons (*ibid.*, p. 255). If these were not technical drawing classes, they may have instilled the love of art into Alfred Marshall, which he cultivated in his travels at home and abroad and on which he reflected in the 1870s as well as later in life. (See below, particularly Chapter 21, pp. 773–5.)

42. *Report of the Commissioners on Public Schools*, p. 257.
43. E.C. Dermer to Mary Paley Marshall, 19 November 1924 (KMF) and cf. Rev. Dr J.A. Hessey to the University College Council at Bristol, 23 June 1877 quoted previously (above, p. 55).
44. J.M. Keynes, 'Alfred Marshall', p. 163.
45. J.A. Venn, *Alumni Cantabrigienses*, Part II, Volume IV, p. 330; *Times*, 14 July 1924; *Cambridge Review*, 31 October 1924. Other obituaries, such as that by Sanger in the *Nation and Athenaeum* (19 July 1924) do not mention the rejection of the title to an Oxford fellowship he gained under the old statutes.
46. *Men of the Time*, 12th edition, London: Routledge & Son, 1887, p. 707; the entry was reproduced unchanged in the 13th edition of 1889 and in subsequent editions of *Who's Who* in which it appeared (my emphasis in quotation).
47. 'Alfred Marshall: Professor of Political Economy, Cambridge', *AMCA*, I, p. 148 and cf. p. 151 where it is noted that the reference work for which this article was intended was projected by a Gustav Eckstein. Keynes, 'Alfred Marshall', pp. 181–2, quotes extensively from this item.
48. E.C. Dermer to Mary Paley Marshall, 19 November 1924 (KMF). Dermer's remark that Marshall's love of mathematics only developed when he was 'far up in the school' is consistent with Alfred Marshall's own recollection that he developed strong interest in the subject only at 17.
49. Mary Paley Marshall, 'Biographical Notes on Alfred Marshall' (KMF).
50. J.M. Keynes, 'Alfred Marshall', p. 164. The source of the reference to the run-away cabin boy in Mary Paley's notes on Uncle Charles was noted earlier in Chapter 2, above, p. 29 and n.*
51. These financial needs, and an estimate of the size of the loan likely to have been required from Uncle Charles, is given in Chapter 4 below, pp. 89–91.
52. Alfred Marshall to Harold E. Guillebaud, 3 October 1904, in *Memorials,* pp. 494–5. It reflects a common perspective on the lack of value in classical studies which was being put forward quite strongly from the middle of the nineteenth century onwards. See for example, *Herbert Spencer on Education*, edited by F.A. Cavenagh, Cambridge: at the University Press, 1932, pp. 4, 15, an article first published in 1859. See also George Combe, *Autobiography*, in Charles Gibbon, *The Life of George Combe*, Volume 1, pp. 17–21 and cf. David de Giustino, *Conquest of Mind*, pp. 170–72 on the general phrenologist attack on traditional classical education in Britain, which preceded, but may have influenced, that of Herbert Spencer.
53. JNKD, 16 April 1876.
54. Below, Chapter 9, p. 274.
55. A. Marshall, 'Autobiographical Fragment dated 3 October 1920,' Marshall Archive, Large Brown Box, Item 11; the whole of the relevant part is cited by Keynes, 'Alfred Marshall', p. 163 n. 4; this conforms to Dermer's recollection to Mary Paley Marshall, previously quoted.
56. A. Marshall, 'Autobiographical Fragment dated 3 October 1920', Marshall Archive, Large Brown Box, Item 11. This suggests Marshall was not aware that Hessey was largely responsible for the upgrading of mathematics in the school including the appointment of the Cambridge master, Airey.
57. J.M. Keynes, 'Alfred Marshall', p. 164; E.C. Dermer to Mary Paley, 19 November 1924 (KMF).
58. Mary Paley, 'Biographical Notes on Alfred Marshall' (KMF).
59. Merchant Taylors' School Probation Books, Vol. 8, 1845–1859, Vol. 9 (Guildhall Library, London*). Report of the Commission on Public Schools*, pp. 258–9. H.D. Traill, Marshall's closest companion at school and first monitor, gained three prizes in 1861, while two other monitors, E.C. Dermer and A. Loughborough took out one prize each and shared the French prize between them. As second wrangler from Cambridge in 1846, Airey would have provided Marshall with the information that Cambridge was a much better place for studying mathematics than Oxford.
60. Mary Paley Marshall, 'Notes for Walter Scott'.
61. *Ibid.*
62. *Report of the Commission on Public Schools*, p. 205. I am indebted to Professor Coase for bringing the Guildhall material to my attention, but unfortunately, these do not include a speech by Marshall.
63. Mary Paley Marshall, 'Notes for Walter Scott'.
64. E.C. Dermer to Mary Paley Marshall, 19 November 1924 (KMF); by 1900 Dermer had retired to Bournemouth, a place Mary Paley Marshall used to visit regularly to see her parents who had retired there, sometimes in the company of her husband. It was there that the acquaintance of the two school companions was accidentally renewed.
65. Mary Paley Marshall, 'Biographical Notes on Alfred Marshall' (KMF). H.D. Traill's famous cricket brother who gave Traill and Alfred Marshall access to Mill's *Logic* was probably W.F. Traill, who had finished his studies at Merchant Taylors' five years previously.
66. E.C. Dermer to Mary Paley Marshall, 19 November 1924 (KMF). Biographical details of H.D. Traill from *DNB, Supplement*, p. 1257 and for Hall and Traill, *Merchant Taylors' School Register 1561–1924*. Sidney P.

Hall published a volume of *Sketches from an Artist's Portfolio in 1875* (London: Sampson, Low, Marston, Law & Settrie) dedicated to the Prince of Wales and containing drawings from Italy, Russia and England as well as selected war sketches from the Franco-Prussian War.

67. See below, Chapter 5, pp. 109–10, Chapter 18, pp. 660–61.

68. E.C. Dermer to Mary Paley Marshall, 19 November 1924 (KMF); in a letter to Keynes (20 November 1924) she recalls Dermer was called 'Fanny' because he was so lady-like. The photo is reproduced as Illustration 11.

69. Below, Chapter 18, pp. 696–7.

70 John Stuart Mill, *Autobiography*, London: Longmans, Green, Reader & Dye, 1873, p. 224. Hessey may also have been astonished because of Mill's scandalous reputation including his youthful misdemeanours in the cause of neo-Malthusianism. These created scandal when Mill committed them and on Mill's death. See G.M. Young, *Portrait of an Age*, p. 227.

71. A taste he shared with many contemporaries, for example, Oliver Wendell Holmes whom Marshall met at Harvard in 1875. In 1911 Holmes wrote to the Baroness Moncheur, wife of the Belgian ambassador, 'Just now I am having one of my periodic wallows in Scott. He is also dear to most people, I suppose – but the old order in which the sword and the gentleman were beliefs, is near enough to me to make this their last voice enchanting in spite of the common sense of commerce.' (cited in Edmund Wilson, *Patriotic Gore*, London: Hogarth Press, 1987, p. 747). A similar 'periodic wallow' may have inspired Marshall's excursus into economic chivalry in 1907, an analogy of which he was very fond (reproduced in *Memorials*, pp. 323–46). It may also have come from the romantic view of the Middle Ages presented in Buckle's *History of Civilisation in England*. Marshall's literary tastes are more fully discussed in Chapter 21, below, pp. 772–3.

72. Alfred Marshall, 'Biographical fragment dated 1917', Large Brown Box, reproduced in Keynes, 'Alfred Marshall', p. 165. Keynes adds the following insightful comments: 'A power of intense concentration for brief periods, with but little power of continuous concentration, was characteristic of him all his life. He was seldom able to execute at white heat any considerable piece of work. He was also bothered by the lack of a retentive memory: even as an undergraduate his mathematical book-work troubled him as much as the problems did. As a boy he had a strong arithmetical faculty, which he afterwards lost' (*ibid.*, pp. 165–6).

APPENDIX TO CHAPTER 3:
Mathematics Texts used at Merchant Taylors' School in 1861

Head Class – 1st Section

(i)	Euclid, Books I, IV, VI, XI. 1–21
(ii)	Algebra (Hall's)
(iii)	Plane Trigonometry (Snowball's)
(iv)	Geometrical Conic Sections (Drew's)
(v)	Analytical Conic Sections (Puckle's)
(vi)	Differential Calculus; One Independent Variable
(vii)	Statics (Parkinson's)
(viii)	Dynamics (Parkinson's)
(ix)	Hydrostatics (Phear's)
(x)	Spherical Trigonometry (Snowball's)

Head Class – 2nd Section

(i)– (v), (vii),	same as for 1st Section
(vi)	Differential Calculus, to Chap. XII

Head Class – 3rd Section

(i)–(iv), (vii)–(ix) same as for 1st Section	
(v)	Analytical Conic Sections (Todhunter's)

Head Class – 4th Section

(i)–(iii), (vii),	same as for 1st Section
(iv)	Geometrical Conic Sections, Parabola and Ellipse

Second Class

(i)–(iii),	same as for Head Class

Third Class

(i)–(ii),	same as for Head Class

Fourth Class

Euclid, same as for Head Class
Algebra, to end of Progressions

Fifth Class

Euclid, Books I – IV
Algebra, to p. 105, with Problems

Sixth Class

Euclid Books I, II
Algebra, to p. 88

Seventh Class, 1st Division

Euclid, Book I, 1–20
Algebra (Scott's Bridge's elementary) to p. 43

The following books are also recommended to the Head and Second Classes: Bland's Equations. Bland's Geometrical Problems. Hind's or Lund's Larger Algebra, Gregory's Examples in the Differential and Integral Calculus, Walton's Mechanical Problems. Walton's Problems in Plane Co-ordinate Geometry. Cambridge Senate House Problems.

Source: *Report of the Commissioners on Public Schools*, pp. 255–6.

4. Undergraduate Student at St John's, Cambridge: 1861–1865

Alfred Marshall was admitted pensioner, that is, an ordinary student 'who pays for everything and enjoys no exemptions'[1] at St John's College Cambridge on 10 June 1861. He matriculated at the usual time during Michaelmas term, 1861. The certificate for admission was provided by his headmaster at the Merchant Taylors' School, the Rev. J.A. Hessey and the tutor he was assigned on admission was the Rev. A.V. Hadley, then still Mr. Hadley.[2] Sixteen students in total were admitted to St John's in June 1861. Most were of similar age, being baptised in 1842.[3] In January 1865 Alfred Marshall took the Mathematical Tripos examinations, taking out his degree shortly afterwards as second wrangler, that is, second in the first class honours list. On 6 November 1865, he was elected Fellow by his college. Alfred Marshall's period of undergraduate studies, devoted largely to mathematical studies, therefore lasted approximately three and a half years from the middle of 1861, when he had just turned nineteen, to early 1865, the year in which he turned twenty-three.

CAMBRIDGE IN THE 1860s

The University of Cambridge to which Alfred Marshall was admitted in 1861 was one of the two ancient universities in England, having been established in the twelfth century not long after its rival at Oxford. The decades prior to the 1860s had, however, seen some growth in the development of university education in England. Two colleges were founded in London in the 1820s. University College, a secular institution was created by the philosophical radicals in 1826 to widen access to university education. King's College, designed for all Christian students including Dissenters, followed in 1829; to be transformed into the University of London by statute in 1836. In 1832, legislation also created a university at Durham. A college for this purpose was duly founded in 1837, followed in 1851 by the creation of two more. 1852 likewise saw the beginnings of Owens College at Manchester, from which Manchester University subsequently evolved. Other English provincial universities did not develop until the 1870s, after legislation encouraging such development had been enacted at the end of the 1860s. These included Bristol University College, founded in 1875, which played such an important role in Marshall's future career. Scotland had its own universities: Aberdeen, St Andrews, Glasgow and Edinburgh, some from the fifteenth century. In 1851, the long-established colleges of Dublin and Belfast were united as the Queen's University in Ireland.

With the development of new universities from the 1820s and particularly the 1850s, the ancient universities commenced gradual transformation of their syllabus and operations during the nineteenth century. Some reform was internally generated but much was induced by parliamentary enquiry and legislation, which initially suggested, and subsequently imposed, change. At the start of the century both Oxford and Cambridge began to expand their syllabus and replaced oral examinations by written examinations. Little as yet was done to remove religious tests. At Oxford, these required that matriculating students had to declare their acceptance of the 39 articles of the Church of England's profession of faith, a requirement which Cambridge only applied to students on taking their degrees. Ordination remained associated with fellowships, as did celibacy, enforced through a restraint on marriage for college Fellows. The colleges, rather than a central organisation, constituted the core of the university. By 1862, for example, the University of Cambridge was only responsible for the giving of instruction by the professoriate, the holding of examinations, the conferring of degrees, prizes and scholarships and the maintenance of discipline.[4] The seventeen colleges of the university did the rest. De facto they were responsible for much of the actual teaching via the lectureships they sponsored.

In 1850, the then Prime Minister, Lord John Russell, announced his intention to establish Commissions of Inquiry into the educational system of the two universities and into the dispersion of their revenues. They reported separately in 1852. In helping to draft the Cambridge University Bill, passed in 1856, Cambridge responded less conservatively to reform than Oxford. It abolished religious tests for all degrees except those in Divinity, although 'it restricted membership of the Senate', the university's governing body 'to those Masters of Arts and Doctors who had declared themselves to be *bona fide* members of the Church of England'. Dissenters and non-believers were thereby effectively excluded from the university's government. Colleges were left free by the 1856 Act to restrict their fellowships to members of the Church of England if they so desired. St John's College did so. However, the 1856 legislation failed to repeal the Act of Uniformity passed in the reign of Charles II which required Masters and Fellows of all colleges, and Professors and Readers of the University, to sign a declaration confirming that they subscribed to the liturgy of the established Church. Not until 1871, that is, well after Henry Sidgwick's resignation from his Trinity Fellowship because of his inability to subscribe to the 39 articles and, more importantly, after many years of parliamentary wrangling and internal university controversy, was this question of religious tests for the university settled by legislation. Marriage, however, continued to remain a bar to retaining or holding a college fellowship until 1882, while ordination continued to bestow privileges such as the possibility of gaining a life fellowship in many university colleges.[5] The implications of the continuing presence of some religious tests for Marshall's career are discussed as they arise.

When Marshall entered the university, there was no entrance examination. A certificate of satisfactory completion of the school syllabus from his Headmaster secured his admission. Candidates for a first degree were, however, required to sit in the Lent term of their second year (May 1863 for Marshall) for the so-called Previous Examination, a system introduced in 1824. The subjects required for this test were few, and easy for those with a good public school education. They required knowledge of one of the gospels in Greek, a Latin and Greek classic, Paley's *Evidences of Christianity,* as well as the first three books of Euclid and some arithmetic. From 1855, candidates for an honours degree, such as Marshall, had to satisfy the examiners of the Previous Examination also in a number of additional subjects. These were exclusively mathematical and designed to increase the degree of preparedness of students entering for the Mathematical Tripos. Attempting this examination interrupted the studies of mathematical students because of the additional reading required, a matter of concern to John William Strutt (later Lord Rayleigh) who came first to Alfred Marshall's second place in the Tripos of 1865.[6]

There were of course other examinations as well.[7] The colleges, as discussed later in connection with Alfred Marshall's experiences as a student of John's, conducted regular examinations, partly for disciplinary reasons. In addition, pass students (or poll men) and honours students (those attempting the Tripos) sat for final examinations organised by the university (Senate House examinations) before they were able to take out their degree. Ten terms residence were required for both poll examinations sat in May, and for honours students who took their Tripos examinations in January rather than at the end of the academic year. The Mathematical Tripos was the most comprehensive of the examinations in Marshall's day. In 1824, a Classical Tripos had been introduced. Until 1857 no honours candidates were permitted to attempt it, unless they had first taken the mathematical examinations, noblemen only excepted. Those interested in pursuing classical studies, like Henry Sidgwick, had to take mathematical honours first, a regulation which secured him the position of 33rd wrangler as well as Senior Classic (first in the Classical Honours list) in 1858. Tripos examinations in the new honours schools of Natural Sciences and Moral Sciences, created in 1848, were first held in 1851, but a plan for a separate Theological Tripos, mooted in 1854, was not implemented until later. However, these relative newcomers to the Cambridge honours system never reached the status of the Mathematical or, for that matter, the Classical Tripos. A good honours result in these virtually guaranteed a college fellowship. In addition, their better students could reap other prizes and prestige from special competitions and examinations, which just were not available in the new Triposes. The certain university career created by a Mathematical Tripos result which was high up in the list of wranglers explains why students like Fawcett (seventh wrangler in 1856) and Leslie Stephen (10th wrangler in 1854) chose to pursue mathematical honours.[8]

The pass examinations were an expansion of the material examined in the Previous, and only a modest expansion at that. One additional part of these final degree examinations entailed compulsory attendance at lectures given by a professor (from amongst the dozen or so professors lecturing in Cambridge during the 1860s) with its question content strictly based on the subject matter of these lectures. Although it was said to be degrading for professors to have their lecture rooms filled in this way by unwilling recruits, several professors, including Fawcett,[9] liked the system and opposed its abolition in 1876. Attempts to reform this rather unsatisfactory system of education in the 1850s and 1860s failed. University members either desired not to dilute the honours schools by permitting poll men to attend honours classes or genuinely believed that the prescribed syllabus provided the general education and cultural introduction required by poll men. For pass students, a Cambridge education at this time could be seen as a finishing school, which consolidated public school learning and built character by the social relationships and elegance in the behaviour it fostered. Even with such low pass examination standards, it may be noted that until 1851 King's College permitted its scholars to proceed to a degree without taking a university examination.[10]

The career possibilities to which Cambridge, or Oxford for that matter, then gave access were at the same time as narrow as its restricted honours syllabus and as wide as the substantial educational opportunities it offered to the general reading man. A pass student could read extensively and discuss that reading just as fully in the stimulating intellectual companionship the university provided, particularly if parental financial resources and family connections had already secured favourable employment opportunities for the future. With the right connections, these could be found in politics or in the professions, that is Church, medicine, the law or public school teaching. More narrowly, a good honours degree secured a fellowship. This could lead to either an academic career or a Church living after ordination and then, with preferment, to leadership in the Church by appointment to the episcopate or to an influential and lucrative place as a major public school headmaster. There was considerable mobility between these positions. Highly placed churchmen moved freely from cathedral to academic chair or to the highest councils of the land when their ecclesiastical position secured a seat in the House of Lords. If all else failed, there were literary careers to be made, particularly following the explosion in periodicals from the 1860s. Connections helped those with less prestigious university results; high honours were essential for those without connections or a financially strong background.*

These substantial academic prizes are largely explicable in terms of the elite status a university education bestowed. In 1862, Marshall was one of 1,526 undergraduates at the University of Cambridge, of which less than one-fifth could expect a first class result. In 1865, the year he completed the Mathematical Tripos, there were a total of forty-five wranglers, a smaller number of classical firsts and only two firsts in the Moral Sciences Tripos. 1865 was not atypical in this respect. More generally, Cambridge undergraduates in 1862 accounted for only 0.2 per cent of the 20–24-year-old male population of England and Wales and a tiny 0.008 per cent of its total population. Access to this privileged community required an expensive public school education, which for a good boarding school amounted to over £100 per annum in Marshall's day, as compared with the cost of £20 his parents incurred for him to be a 'day boy' at Merchant Taylors'. On the basis of a statistical analysis for students entering Sidney Sussex College, matriculants in the 1860s came largely from clerical and professional households with the last concentrated in medicine, law and teaching.[11]   As the son of a lowly paid bank clerk, Alfred Marshall was particularly fortunate to join this select band, all the more reason why his family was so annoyed in 1861 when he abandoned the certainties for advancement inherent in the 'close' fellowship at St John's, Oxford, so hard earned by his school performance and their financial sacrifice.

---

*   As already indicated (above, note 8), this was the reason why Leslie Stephen and Henry Fawcett attempted the hard grind of mathematics honours and why Alfred Marshall, even less well connected, did the same in 1861. Stephen entered a very successful and even more industrious literary career after abandoning the Church and with it his position as university tutor; Fawcett combined politics (including the position of Postmaster General in one of the Gladstone governments) with an academic career as Professor of Political Economy at Cambridge, Henry Sidgwick's brother-in-law, Edward Benson was headmaster, academic and bishop – rising to Archbishop of Canterbury and the House of Lords; some of Alfred Marshall's later episcopal acquaintances, Westcott and Creighton, shifted happily between Church, school, university and Bishop's Palace combining erudite scholarship with theology and social politics. See also Rothblatt, *The Revolution of the Dons*, epilogue, pp. 248–50, 256–73, for a more general discussion. Marshall himself recorded that the 'advantages which those born in one of the higher grades of society have over those born in a lower, consist in a great measure of the better introductions and the better start in life which they receive from their parents.' (*P* I, p. 591; *P* VIII, p. 563).

The costs associated with a university education in the 1860s were formidable, although also rather flexible. Flexibility came from the degree of freedom allowed to individual students in the expenditure they had to incur and from the opportunities for subsidy and support from scholarships and prizes available to them before and during their period of study. The 1862 *Student's Guide to the University of Cambridge*[12] presented the full annual cost of an undergraduate student as varying from £125 to £250. This covered college bills, grocers and booksellers, travelling expenses to and from Cambridge, tradesman's bills for personal expenses and entertainments, and pocket money. It excluded the private tuition of a coach, essential for a candidate attempting high mathematical honours. These averaged £24 to £30 per annum, but could be considerably higher depending on the quality of the coach and the amount of time for which he was hired. It also excluded residence at college during vacations. This ranged from £1 to £1.5s. per week, and once again was considered an essential expense for those seeking good honours in mathematics or classics, because they had to work during the long vacation. Total annual costs for an undergraduate ranged therefore from a low £125 for a pass student to anything in the vicinity of £500 or more, a figure not unlikely if honours were attempted under a good coach by a student with affluent parents. However, the personal and social expenses, accounting for a large fraction in the 1862 Handbook's minimum expenditure of £125, could be significantly reduced by very economical students in straitened circumstances.[*]

The organisation of the academic year at the University of Cambridge needs some comment as well. This started with Michaelmas term (sometimes called October term), running from early or middle October to early or mid-December. A Christmas vacation from three to four weeks followed. Lent term (with lectures from the end of January to early March) and an Easter recess determined by the vagaries of that religious festival on the calendar, came next. The year concluded with a brief Easter term. Examinations were held either in January (the Mathematical and Classical Triposes) or May; with the Previous Examination generally conducted in that month. The Moral Sciences Tripos examination was held initially in December, later in June. Colleges such as John's ran their own examinations in December and June, as preparatory exercises subordinate to the examinations of the university, and useful both to give practice in written examination to students with little experience of such tests, and to decide college scholarships and prizes. The long summer vacation covered July, August, September and part of October. In total, term covered twenty-five weeks of the year.

The Cambridge that Alfred Marshall entered in 1861 was therefore an elite educational institution, the preserve of the educated professional classes, that is, those comfortable without necessarily being rich, and in general endowed with a good public school education.

---

[*] Rothblatt, *The Revolution of the Dons*, pp. 66–9. In this discussion Rothblatt indicates that £100 was not uncommon for a coach though £24 to £30 was more usual. Pensioners, the matriculant status of Alfred Marshall, were estimated by two college tutors in 1867 to need at least £125 to £150 per annum, with most students in their opinion spending between £180 and £210. Individual accounts of undergraduate Cambridge costs varied considerably, however. To add to the evidence on this score provided by Rothblatt (p. 67 n.3): for 1888–92, Arthur Bowley estimated his term expenses at £44 a term for 11 terms with special, non-recurring expenses of £60, of which £20 was refundable on leaving the university. For his 11-term stay at Cambridge, average annual expenses can be estimated at £145. See Agatha H. Bowley, *A Memoir of Professor Sir Arthur Bowley*, pp. 36–7.

Given the annual cost of university education this could not be otherwise. Even if kept to a minimum, the cost of an honours student residing in college, made substantial inroads into a bank clerk's salary of £250 per annum. No wonder that in Marshall's case financial assistance had to be sought from a well-to-do uncle by way of a loan, which left debts which took the second wrangler some time to repay after graduation.[13] University education also created severe acceptability problems for students from lower-middle-class families like the Marshalls. Young matriculants with no spare cash for the social amenities of undergraduate life faced considerable social problems. In a large and rich college like John's, the potential social stigma would be even greater, and in Alfred Marshall's case would not have been ameliorated by the presence of school friends from Merchant Taylors'. As explained in the previous chapter, they went to Oxford. In his early undergraduate years, if not for their whole duration, Alfred Marshall would have led the lonely existence of the outsider by school and, more importantly, by social and economic status.[14]

THE COLLEGE OF SAINT JOHN THE EVANGELIST, CAMBRIDGE

The college to which Alfred Marshall was admitted in June 1861, and which was to be his home for the next sixteen years, was then one of the newer colleges of Cambridge. In an educational institution dating back to the twelfth century, it had only been founded at the start of the sixteenth century, commencing its operations as a community of scholars in 1516, though some of its buildings were considerably older. It was the college of Wordsworth the poet, of Prime Ministers Castlereagh and Palmerston, of Claphamite evangelicals Clarkson, Wilberforce and Martyn, and reformers Samuel Whitbread and Horne Tooke. It was also the college of Frederick William Herschel, of James Joseph Sylvester and John Couch Adams, reflecting its growing reputation as the 'nursery of senior wranglers'. Those who attempted mathematical honours tended to outnumber candidates for honours in classics by about three and a half to one. In 1865, the year that Alfred Marshall was second wrangler, one third of the 45 wranglers were Johnians and twenty-four Johnians gained mathematical honours in all; only two students gained classical firsts with four in the other two classes. This was from a total number of matriculants of more than three hundred in 1861, of whom sixteen entered John's. As compared with Sidney Sussex College, for which data are available, John's College was much more aristocratic. At the end of the eighteenth century, for example, five per cent of its students were the sons of nobility and eligible, under the statutes then in operation, to take an M.A. degree without examination. During Marshall's undergraduate period this proportion had somewhat fallen and their easy access to university membership through the M.A. had already gone.[*]

---

[*]   Edward Miller, *Portrait of a College*, Cambridge University Press, 1961, Chapter 1, pp. 68–71, 72, 77–8; J.R. Tanner, *The Historical Register of the University of Cambridge*, 1917, p. 524. Miller, p. 92 adds that by 1881 the majority of undergraduates remained the sons of professional men, but sons of lawyers, doctors and men in government service outnumbered sons of clergymen. There were fewer sons of landed gentry but more businessmen's sons, and even men from families with no great wealth whose fathers engaged in 'white collar' occupations – clerks, cashiers and the like. By 1860, therefore, Alfred Marshall would still have been very much a rarity with respect to his father's background and occupation.

Figure 4.1: The Grounds of St John's College, Cambridge, Circa 1862

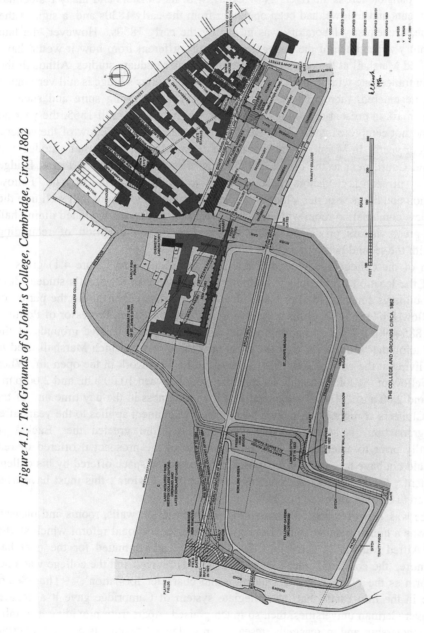

Source: Reproduced with kind permission from the Master, Fellows and Scholars of St John's College, Cambridge.

The structure of the college that Marshall entered in 1861 was as follows. The three courts, the first and original one dating from the early sixteenth century, the second and third, though separated by nearly a century, both dating from the seventeenth, had been added to by expansion across the river. New Court, with its cloisters and many residential rooms for students and fellows, had been operating from the early 1830s and, a sign of the times to come, a chemistry laboratory was in use by the early 1850s. However, the late twentieth-century appearance of the college is distinctly different from how it would have looked to Alfred Marshall at the commencement of his undergraduate studies. Although the magnificent entrance gate with its twin towers sheltering the porter's lodge is still very much like the one he entered, there was no new chapel with its imposing spire and such an important landmark in present-day Cambridge. This was not begun until 1865, the year he graduated, and not completed until 1869 when he had already been a Fellow of the college for close to four years. In Marshall's undergraduate days and after, the Master's Lodge was still in Second Court, next to the old chapel, and the new Master's Lodge, facing Bridge Street, which present-day visitors observe next to additional student and Fellow accommodation and the new porter's lodge, were architectural innovations still well into the future. The new combination room with its magnificent ceiling and the extended dining hall which now greet visitors privileged to see them, date from the period of rebuilding associated with the second half of the 1860s.[15]

The plan of the college and grounds circa 1862 (reproduced as Figure 4.1) gives an indication of the location of the college buildings as they were in Marshall's student days and that of buildings constructed after his graduation but in use either during the period of his initial fellowship (1865–77) or his second fellowship on becoming Professor of Political Economy (1885–1908). More importantly, they also show the extensive grounds of the college, including the 'wilderness' and the grass near the cloisters which Marshall used to enjoy when living at the college. 'A[lfred] always did his best work in the open air. When he became Fellow of St John's he did his chief thinking between 10.00 a.m. and 2.00 p.m., 10.00 p.m. and 2.00 a.m. He had a monopoly of the wilderness in the day time and of the New Court Cloisters at night.'[16] Although Mary Paley's comment applies to the years after 1865 and graduation, it seems unlikely that the boy who greeted the 'Backs' so enthusiastically prior to entering the university because of the prospect it offered of real country, would not have taken advantage of the enormous open space offered by his college when a student. After the bleak surroundings of Merchant Taylors', this must have been heaven indeed to be both alive and young.

A college was, however, more than mere bricks and mortar, walls, rooms and pleasant gardens. It was a human relationship. During the age of educational reform which started just before Alfred Marshall's entry into the university and continued for the next half century or more, 'the communal ideal of the College was revived and the college was once more put forth as the place of moral education and character formation'.[17] Thus Seeley could argue in the mid-1860s that the collegiate system of Cambridge gave it a decided advantage over German universities, then so much praised. Apart from providing a training ground for scholarship and increasingly, research, in colleges 'students live under a certain discipline and with a certain family life'.[18] These peculiar features of the Cambridge college are succinctly described by Rothblatt,[19]

The student was away from home, he was separated from the influences of his family and the environment which had conditioned his behaviour. He was not as completely receptive to new influences as younger boys in boarding schools, but his greater maturity meant that he could be entrusted with more responsibility. Discipline was not likely to be as onerous and unrewarding a task as it was in the schools. The student was at an age when he could appreciate advanced learning and higher ideals; and being close to the time when he would take his place in society, he was particularly anxious to benefit from the advice and assistance of his superiors. In these respects he was very responsive to collegiate influence. In the college, with its communal life and surrounded by the symbols of a long and distinguished traditions the student began to identify with what were represented as the tone and atmosphere of the place. The antiquity and beauty of the college lent it an air of historical purpose and serenity and appeared to require of the student a sense of humility and self-denial. He became desirous of living up to the ideals of the society and learned to forgo some of his own pleasures in the interests of the larger college community. At the same time, because the college was not so large that he felt lost within it, he retained a sense of his own individuality.

The character-forming proclivities of college life was something Marshall later stressed when extolling the virtues of Cambridge as a man's university.[20] Other advantages claimed for the college system by late nineteenth-century dons were 'that in Cambridge, a man's social background did not count for much . . . in the final analysis, distinction was related to intellectual merit, to personal integrity, to a sense of duty, to character to use that vague and important word.'[21] Such opportunities for rising to equality, if not superiority, to those with greater family and financial advantage acquired by birth was a spur to excellence for the poorly endowed but ambitious Cambridge student. Benjamin Jowett, the powerful Master of Balliol provided a striking, contemporary example, of its potential. These advantages also featured markedly in the advice to students on choice of college as given in the University Handbook. This stressed the importance of opportunities for gaining scholarships during study, 'decisive for students in poor circumstances', the number and conditions for fellowships offered and other positions open to its members on graduation, as well as the quality of tuition it offered.[22]

In these respects, St John's College was particularly well endowed. In the first place, it had 56 fellowships. These entailed ordination within seven years from taking the M.A. unless the incumbent also held important college or university positions. In addition, the college held the appointment of masters to seven endowed schools, including that of headmaster and second master at Shrewsbury. It also had the gift of fifty-one livings for those intending to pursue an ecclesiastical career. Moreover, it was increasing its number of lecturing positions. New Statutes in 1860 established ten college lectureships, including some in the new honours schools of Moral and Natural Sciences. The spread of inter-collegiate teaching, particularly in cooperation with Trinity College, further expanded the number of lecturing positions in the 1860s, to the particular advantage of Alfred Marshall in 1868. For those Fellows who for one reason or another wished to escape ordination, a college lectureship provided exemption from this requirement with retention of the privileges a fellowship bestowed.

For undergraduates, the college provided sixty foundation scholarships as well as a vast array of other scholarships and exhibitions, including several, such as the Wood and Hare Exhibitions, for the specific assistance of deserving students in poor circumstances. The college also offered Sizarships by annual examination,[*] and prizes of books to those who excelled in the college examinations held in December and June. In view of the prizes it offered to the successful, St John's Cambridge compared well with its Oxford counterpart, entry to which Alfred Marshall had so recklessly abandoned.[23]

The support and opportunity colleges gave to the poor but academically successful student did not mean total elimination of class distinction for undergraduates. Rothblatt[24] admits that 'quite obviously, money could buy better Cambridge accommodation and amenities, and a man's family background might guarantee his admission to the college of his choice'. More characteristically perhaps, 'sons of wealthy families', who tended to see college education as a prerogative of their 'station', 'were apt to despise their contemporaries endowed with less worldly goods'. In his undergraduate years during the 1830s, the first service given to reform by William Henry Bateson, the Master of John's during Marshall's initial period at the college, was to fight against the rules excluding sizars from the college cricket and boat clubs. Twenty years later, Samuel Butler drew attention to the concentration of the poorer undergraduates in the 'dingy, tumble-down rooms' of the labyrinth and noted 'they were rarely seen except in hall or chapel or at lecture, where their manners of feeding, praying and studying were considered alike objectionable'.[25] Even Alfred Marshall's student undergraduate status of pensioner, ranked well above sizars as it was, was starkly divided socially from the 'men of fortune' who made fellow commoners, particularly if, like Alfred Marshall, their pensioner status was underwritten by scholarships and borrowed money.

College teaching was arranged by a tutor, with college lecturers, of whom an increasing number were appointed from the 1860s onwards, responsible for the actual teaching. Tutors did not therefore have the type of responsibilities which this title now calls to mind. 'The tutor was usually responsible for admissions, for the assignment of rooms and lodgings, for advice on general expenses. He was also in charge of the college teaching programme. . . . Tutorial responsibility was least clear in the exercise of those functions which related to the moral and physical welfare of students. The tutor was supposed to be a father to the students, and some tutors performed this function remarkably well'. [26] The tutor's original teaching function had disappeared by the early Victorian period. This transformation was coincident with the increasing necessity for private tuition and coaching for students seeking high mathematical and classical honours. The loss of control over this important aspect of collegiate responsibility to private teachers, no matter how closely connected some of them were with colleges and the university, subsequently assisted the growth of college lecturing staff. Such an expansion presumed replacing private tuition through the appointment from among the Fellows of qualified persons capable of instructing both honours and pass students. The 1860s started this gradual transformation: there were increasing numbers of college lecturers being appointed, particularly at larger colleges such as Trinity and John's, but private coaching remained an important element in university education until the turn of the century. Its disappearance also needed reform of college educational methods secured by the revival of an individual and more personalised tutorial-type system as the century

---

[*]   'Sizars' were a class of students entering college and university with certain 'emoluments and exemptions in consideration of poverty'. See *Student's Guide to the University of Cambridge*, 1862, p. 44.

drew to its close. [27]

Like his years at school, Marshall's years at college were spent in an institution controlled by a reformer, William Henry Bateson, who was Master of John's College from 1857 to 1881. Bateson had gained experience with matters of university reform as secretary to the 1850 Commission of Inquiry into the 'State, Discipline, Studies, and Revenues of the University and the Colleges of Cambridge'. In 1858 he was elected Vice-Chancellor of the University. In general, he therefore took an active part in the business of the university as transacted by its Senate, of which at one stage he was also secretary. During his period of office, he was widely regarded as the head of the liberal reform party in the university, as shown by his efforts in promoting higher education for women at the university.[28]

With respect to reform in his own college, he was responsible for the change in its statutes in 1860 enabling, among other things, the expansion of its teaching staff; the abolition of various religious tests and the liberalisation of conditions for scholarships and the range of subjects in which the college examined.[29] Keynes[30] mentioned that Alfred Marshall was specifically indebted to Bateson on at least two counts. In 1868, Bateson created a special position of Lecturer in the Moral Sciences for him in addition to the two others the college already had, a 'friendly action' Marshall told Keynes, which finally determined 'the course of his life'. In 1877 Bateson wrote a strong testimonial in support of Marshall's appointment to Bristol, emphasising the great admiration he had for Marshall's character, 'which is remarkable for its great simplicity, earnestness, and self-sacrificing conscientiousness'. Bateson added that 'in his office of College Lecturer he has rendered valuable and important service, always exercising a refining influence and making his subject and his classroom attractive and popular . . . he is one who would on no account accept service where he could not work heartily and effectively'.[31] Although Bateson carried out no revolution in his college or in the university, and was sometimes missing from the more radical vanguard on specific reform issues, he broadly contributed to gradually improving the social and educational trappings of college and university.[32]

College routine for the early 1860s provides a general picture of how Alfred Marshall as an undergraduate may have spent at least part of his week during term. For a start, there were seven compulsory chapel attendances per week, at morning services held at 7.15, or as special choral services in the evening on Saturdays, Sundays and feastdays. Music was provided by a male choir 'which rushed from King's to Trinity, and from Trinity to St John's, thereby giving a brevity to the services 'which may not always have seemed undesirable to those present by conscription'. Evening services were preceded by dinner in Hall at 4.00 p.m., a regular event during the whole of term apart from the times set aside for college feasts. Dinner generally consisted 'of a joint with vegetables and college-brewed beer', which made a 'capital dinner' even if the joint was often cold by the time it reached the students, as Bishop Colenso recalled from his undergraduate days in 1832. Breakfast was the student's own responsibility, an opportunity for poorer students to practice economy, while their richer counterpart could officiate at 'lavish breakfast parties at which ham, pigeon pies and chops were served' and which could take the best part of the morning. All undergraduate students living in the colleges were daily supplied with bread and butter from the butteries.[33]

Lectures could start as early as 8.00 in the morning, were generally not given during the afternoons, and never on Sundays. Private tuition by coaches extended over longer hours. Todhunter, the famous mathematics coach from John's had classes from 8.15 a.m. to 3.00 p.m. and then again in the evening from 5.30 to 10.00 to allow time for dinner. Such hours would not have been untypical for this type of activity.[34] Afternoons were often reserved for boating or cricket, the only college sports at this time, or for riding, walking, swimming, chess or cards, according to taste and pocket. Wine parties and other social gatherings after Hall occupied the evenings for many undergraduates.[35] Those reading for honours would heavily substitute study for leisure. What is known of Alfred Marshall's undergraduate life is discussed at the end of this chapter.

THE MATHEMATICAL TRIPOS

During the 1860s, the Mathematical Tripos remained the jewel in the crown for Cambridge achievers. Its long-standing history as a rigorous test of students' intellects and their capacity for sustained hard work, together with the prizes success in its examinations offered, were the reasons for its high reputation. Over its long history, organisation and subject matter of the Tripos had undergone considerable change. Written university examinations rather than the former disputations had become the norm from 1763. By the 1840s, the Tripos became completely mathematical. The 'Little Go' or Previous Examination established in 1824 enabled the Tripos to remove the last vestiges of philosophy and theology which had for long clung to it. The form of the Tripos examination as it was to be attempted by Marshall, was regularised in 1848. In the first three days, six elementary papers were attempted. These decided whether a person was eligible to sit for the advanced, second part of the Tripos to be examined over five days in ten further papers, following a week's interval after the examinations of the first part.[36]

The second part established the order of merit in terms of men of the first class or wranglers, and that of the senior and junior optimes as men of the second or third class were respectively called. All candidates at this time were ranked in strict order of merit within these classes, which made competition for a good place particularly keen. From 1768, the Tripos examinations had been followed by examinations for the Smith's Prize, the major mathematical prize offered by the university.[37] Often described as a 'severe test of endurance',[38] the influential philosopher and Master of Trinity, William Whewell, himself a second wrangler, regarded the solid mathematical preparation the Tripos required as 'an effective discipline of the reason'. In addition, Whewell held the study of mathematics to be particularly valuable because its subject matter marked 'the sign of truth' and gave access to progressive studies in modern analytics, not only in the mathematical, but also in associated physical and even social sciences.[39] Other opinions of the merits of the mid-Victorian Tripos existed. Speaking of the Cambridge examinations in general, Rothblatt could argue,

The tripos examinations stressed method-technique, precision, logic and rigour – and method was transferable: the man who understood the principles of argument and hence how to derive generalizations from a body of factual material could subsequently teach himself any subject. If necessary, the tripos could also be defended as preparation for professional life. Mathematics and classics were of obvious value to the school-master; logic and argument were the tools of the lawyer and politician; generalization enabled the clergyman to read God's will; scientific method was essential to the physician.

The tripos was held to be scientific in ideals, content, and in its method of determining ability. Unlike Oxford, Cambridge ranked its honours men on a strict order of merit, from the senior wrangler or senior classic down. This intensified the competition for honours and made many believe that the tripos system of marking was a scrupulously objective method of selection. As Francis Galton wrote in 1869, 'the fairness and thoroughness of Cambridge examinations have never had a breath of suspicion cast upon them'. The order of merit had faults, however, that did not go unrecognized. Ranking could only be accurate within each year's grouping, making it difficult to compare men of different years who might be competing for the same college fellowship. It also reinforced the character of the tripos as an examination on set knowledge; textbooks were especially compiled to offer the student unimaginative lessons to be gotten up quickly by rote. Nowhere was there a suggestion of original synthesis, analysis or a developing frontier of knowledge. The nature of the tripos made it a useful device for controlling students. Success in the examinations required considerable advance preparation and cramming, as well as speed and stamina during the long hours of the examination week. The competition was strenuous, and bets were laid in advance as to the probable winners. 'True to their sporting instincts the English had contrived to turn even the university examinations into an athletic contest'. If a student were conscientious, if he needed the academic recognition and financial reward that the tripos could bestow, if he crammed to the point of injuring his health – particularly in his last year – he would have little time for mischief.[40]

Whether such trials of strength and endurance constituted a satisfactory mathematical education is debatable. In the context of Marshall's success as a second wrangler, and his further developments as a mathematical economist, Whitaker has argued,

Although a love for mathematics had brought Marshall [to] . . . Cambridge . . . there is little to indicate that he was a born mathematician, a Routh or a Cayley. It is true that Cambridge legend has passed on a picture of the older Marshall reading for pleasure the first and last chapters of the latest mathematical treatise and inferring the rest. But this must surely be more colourful than correct. Despite an early penchant for Euclid, there is from the first an awkwardness and hesitancy about Marshall's efforts at mathematical economics that argues against him ever having breathed wholly freely on the pinnacles of abstraction. Both Jevons and Edgeworth seem to have dwelt more comfortably in the realm of abstract logic, despite their inferiority to Marshall in mathematical training.

That a man without exceptional endowment of mathematical talent should become a high Wrangler may seem so surprising as to be improbable, but it should be observed that the Mathematical Tripos of the time involved primarily book-work and rapid manipulation, being almost as much a test of endurance undertaken for high prizes as a training for serious research in mathematics. Thus one Second Wrangler went on to become Lord Chief Justice Romer, while John Fletcher Moulton, who became Senior Wrangler in 1868 with the highest total of marks ever recorded, later became Lord of Appeal in Ordinary. Of course none of this proves that Marshall (or Romer or Moulton) was not a brilliant mathematician, diverted from his subject by other considerations or interests. But it does suggest that the common view of Marshall, as a mathematical giant who exercised great self restraint in resisting for economics sake the natural bent of is own mind, may have become exaggerated.[41]

Although later generations of mathematicians were dissatisfied with many aspects of the contents of the Tripos, it did have strong points as well. 'This mathematical training, with an emphasis upon particular functional forms, was ideally suited for someone like Marshall with his search for realism and his high hopes for the *operational* role of economic concepts such as consumer surplus.'[42] Marshall's mathematical training gave him opportunities in economics which were closed to his less mathematical colleagues.

The importance of the Tripos to Marshall's career means a more detailed discussion of the Mathematical Tripos syllabus and its examination in Cambridge of the early 1860s needs to be given. This also provides a feeling for the amount of solid study it involved. The 1862

Student's Guide to the University of Cambridge described the elementary part of the mathematical syllabus in the following terms,

> Euclid. Books I. to VI. Book XI. Props I. to XXI. Book XII, Props. I, II.
>
> Arithmetic, and the elementary parts of Algebra: namely, the Rules for the Fundamental Operations upon Algebraical Symbols, with their proofs; the solution of simple and quadratic Equations; Arithmetical and Geometrical Progression, Permutations and Combinations, the Binomial Theorem, and the principles of Logarithms.
>
> The elementary parts of Plane Trigonometry, so far as to include the solution of triangles.
>
> The elementary parts of Conic Sections, treated geometrically, together with the value of the Radius of Curvature, and of the Chords of Curvature passing through the Focus and Centre.
>
> The elementary parts of Statics, treated without Differential Calculus; namely, the Composition and Resolution of Forces acting in one plane at a point, the Mechanical Powers, and the properties of the Centre of Gravity.
>
> The elementary parts of Dynamics, treated without the Differential Calculus; namely, the Doctrine of Uniform and Uniformity Accelerated Motion, of Falling Bodies, Projectiles, Collision, and Cycloidal Oscillations.
>
> The 1st, 2nd, and 3rd Sections of Newton's Principia; the Propositions to be proved in Newton's manner.
>
> The elementary parts of Hydrostatics, treated without the Differential Calculus; namely, the pressure of non-elastic Fluids, specific Gravities, floating Bodies, the pressure of the Air, and the construction and use of the more simple Instruments and Machines.
>
> The elementary parts of Optics: namely, the laws of Reflection and Refraction of Rays, at plane and spherical surfaces, not including Aberrations; the Eye; Telescopes.
>
> The elementary parts of Astronomy; so far as they are necessary for the explanation of the more simple phenomena, without calculation.[43]

This material was generally covered in the first year, both in the college mathematics lectures and the private tuition students received. The mathematical syllabus at Merchant Taylors'[44] indicates that much of this preliminary work had already been covered by Alfred Marshall at school, some of it in greater depth than in his first year university work. The school's 1850 appointment of second wrangler Airey in this case paid handsome dividends for one of his better students, and that student was undoubtedly particularly grateful for the tremendous advantage this training was giving him relative to potential rivals in the Tripos competition within college and university.

    More difficult mathematical studies began in the second year. Potential honours students began this work during the intervening long vacation. The following topics were covered in college lectures as part of the second-year syllabus, and for honours students invariably involved work with a private tutor during long vacations.

> Differential and Integral Calculus, Differential Equations, Statics, dynamics of a Particle, the first three sections of Newton's Principia, and some portion of Geometry of Three Dimensions. They form in most colleges the Mathematical portion of the second Midsummer examination.
>
>   The long Vacation immediately following the first Midsummer Examination will enable the Student to get considerably advanced with his reading. Every Candidate for high Mathematical Honours reads during the Long Vacations with a private Tutor. By the end of the first 'Long' the Theory of Equations, the Differential and Integral Calculus, and Elementary Mechanics, should have been read. The Michaelmas Term of the second year may then be devoted to Statics and Differential Equations; the lent Term to Newton, the dynamics of a Particle, easier portions of Geometry of Three Dimensions, and the more

elementary parts of the Dynamics of a Rigid Body. The Easter Term is generally spent in revising for the College Examination the subjects read during the preceding year.[45]

Having mastered these subjects, a mastery which invariably was tested by the degree of success in the college examinations, 'the third Long Vacation is usually devoted to studying Geometry of Three Dimensions, Finite Differences, Rigid Dynamics, Formal Optics, and Hydrostatics. The Michaelmas term of the third year is usually devoted to Astronomy, Spherical and Physical; the Lent term to the theories of Sound and Light; and the Easter term to revising the subjects read in the year preceding. Most of the subjects here enumerated are lectured on in the Colleges during the third year.'[46]

Books recommended for the final part of the course, such as Parkinson's *Optics*, Hershel's *Astronomy*, Brunnow's *Spherical Astronomy*, Godfray's *Lunar Theory*, Airey's *Tracts on Planetary Theory* and on *Precessions and Nutation* as well as Todhunter's *History of the Calculus of Variations*, show that university work by this stage had gone well beyond school training. The third long vacation and third year lectures were based on their study, supplemented by reading on hydrostatics, finite differences and the theory of light, the subject of lectures by Stokes in Marshall's days as undergraduate.[47]

Third year's Easter term revision was the prelude to the work of the final half year before the examinations started on the traditional first Tuesday following 30 December. Such revision included the whole of the long vacation, Michaelmas term and that part of the Christmas vacation available for final cramming before the first paper commenced. Such revision invariably concentrated on the more difficult parts of the syllabus and, for good coaches, on taking their students through the likely sorts of problems to be set by the examiners and moderators appointed for the Tripos. Thus Strutt[48] recollected that 'he had taken care to study the idiosyncrasies of the examiners, and guessed with success some of the questions which Todhunter, who was the apostle of mathematical rigour as then understood, would be likely to set'. Such practice was common, and perfected into a fine art by the coaches whose reputations rested on their 'ability to cram an undergraduate, to drill him intensively for a high place in the examination list . . . and whose performance could be strictly measured by the number of first class honours men' he produced and which determined the fees he could charge.[49]

The sketch of the Mathematical Tripos given in the previous paragraphs draws attention to more than the subject matter to be studied. It implicitly emphasises several important features and characteristics. First of all, the work required continuous application by the student through term and vacation with little opportunity for any breaks or relaxation. Todhunter, Leslie Stephen's coach, stopped Stephen from holding office in the Cambridge Union but could not stop him from speaking in its debates, and continually exerted him to 'push on'.[50] Marshall was dissuaded from rowing in the college boat on the advice of his tutor. It would have interfered with his studies.[51] John Neville Keynes, who gave up studying for the Mathematical Tripos after a year in Cambridge, despite the pressure put on him by his parents and Henry Fawcett to continue, lamented in the pages of his diary that Cambridge mathematics cost him an average seven hours a day as compared with the five hours at London University which secured him the B.A. with first class honours and several prizes.[52]

Secondly, the *Student's Guide* stressed the need for private tuition. This was not just desirable, as was the case in preparing for all competitive examinations, it was absolutely essential for those attempting the Mathematics Tripos. 'For, although the truths which are the life-blood of the system of mathematics remain the same, yet the particular forms in which these truths are clothed depend a good deal on fashion, and consequently vary from day to day. It is therefore necessary that the student to whom the difference of a single place in the Tripos may be of the greatest importance, should be kept, as it were, floating on the summit of the wave of mathematical taste; and this can be effected for him by the pilotage of the private tutor only . . . a candidate for a high place in the Mathematical Tripos cannot dispense with the assistance of a private Tutor.'[53]

Thirdly, the appropriate study method was very important since all too often slow but steady was argued to win the race.

> The Mathematical student must be content to work slowly at first. The difficulties of his subject will vanish before patient and continued application; but it is by patient and continued application only that he can hope to attain success, as it is only by such application that he will deserve it. If he accustoms himself to pass by difficulties, without combating and conquering them, he will find them continually starting up to check his progress. He should therefore never hesitate to confess to his College or private Tutor an inability to understand any demonstration which may be put before him if he feels such an inability.[54]

After three and a half years of hard, continuous study came the final test. Table 4.1 shows a *pro forma* timetable for the 16 papers. They were taken in the space of two and a half weeks at the rate of two papers a day with an hour and a half break for lunch in between. The first, elementary part was examined in six papers over the three days ending Thursday of the first week of January in which there was a Tuesday; the other ten papers which examined the second part followed in the week containing the third Tuesday in January, starting on the Monday morning and finishing on the Friday at 4.00 p.m. for the by then, very weary candidates. This interval between the two parts was not an act of kindness to the candidates in this test of examination stamina. It enabled assessment of the first part in order to determine the candidates eligible to sit the second part, the names of whom were posted at Senate House, the main university building, before the end of that week. Tripos results were available on the Friday morning following the final day of examination and were read out to an enthusiastic and tumultuous crowd gathered at Senate House for the occasion. They were widely reported in the press, and, as already noted, enabled the settlement of wagers this competition fostered amongst members of the university community inclined to gamble.

Table 4.1 also indicates the topics to which the individual papers were devoted and the persons by whom they were examined. The first six papers contained generally only one paper devoted to problems, while the pure mathematics and other subjects of the advanced part covered

Algebra, including Theory of Equations.
Trigonometry, Plane and Spherical.
Algebraic Geometry of two and three dimensions with the modern extensions.
Differential and Integral Calculus.
Differential Equations.

The Calculus of Finite Differences.
The Calculus of Variations.
The Subjects included under the term Natural Philosophy, are limited to Statics
Dynamics of Particles and of Rigid bodies.
Hydrostatics and Hydrodynamics.
Optics.
Astronomy.
The Lunar Theory treated both analytically and by Newton's method.
The Planetary Theory.
Precession and Nutation.
The Undulatory Theory of Light.[55]

Table 4.1: Pro Forma Timetable of the Cambridge Mathematical Tripos

The first Tuesday here mentioned is the first Tuesday after Dec. 30. The Monday is the second Monday after the commencement of the Examination.

Days	Hours	Subjects	Examiners
Tues	9 to 12	Euclid and Conics	Jun.Mod. and Sen.Ex.
	1 to 4	Arith.Alg.and Plane Trig.	Sen. Mod.and Jun.Ex.
Wed.	9 to 12	Statics and Dynamics	Sen.Mod.and Jun.Ex.
	1 to 4	Hydrostatics and Optics	Jun.Mod.and Sen.Ex.
Thur.	9 to 12	Probs.in all the preced.Sub.	Sen.& Jun.Moderators
	1 to 4	Newton and Astronomy	Sen.& Jun.Examiners
Mon.	9 to 12	Natural Philosophy	Sen.& Jun.Moderators
	1 to 4	Pure Mathematics	Jun.Moderator
Tues.	9 to 12	Easy Problems	Sen.& Jun.Moderators
	1 to 4	Natural Philosophy	Sen.& Jun.Examiners
Wed.	9 to 12	Problems	Senior Moderator
	1 to 4	Pure Mathematics	Sen.& Jun.Moderators
Thurs.	9 to 12	Problems	Junior Moderator
	1 to 4	Pure Math.and Nat.Phil.	Sen.& Jun.Moderators
Fri.	9 to 12	Pure Math.and Nat.Phil.	Sen.Mod.and Sen.Ex.
	1 to 4	Pure Math.and Nat.Phil.	Jun.Mod.and Jun.Ex.

Examiners were appointed by the university on a rotating basis in order to maintain that reputation for fairness of the Cambridge Triposes. Moderators in the one year became the examiners of the following year, with new moderators consequently having to be appointed. Examiners in 1865 were William Walton and Michael Wilkinson, both from Trinity College; moderators were Johnians Isaac Todhunter and George Richardson. The first named in both categories was the senior in the respective examining teams.

How good was this syllabus for producing mathematicians and scientists? One Cambridge historian has argued that judged by the output, 'I do not think it can be said to have resulted in failure, and perhaps Cayley, Sylvester, Adams, Green, Stokes, Kelvin and Maxwell – to mention no others – were none the worse for having been compelled to go through the course.'[56] Others[57] have argued that the Tripos effectively ruined serious mathematics in England for a century, so that by the early twentieth century, Cambridge began to have second thoughts about the race to success the Tripos implied. It abolished publication of the strict order of merit and thereby its overly competitive basis. The expansion of subject matter for university studies available by that time made emphasis on such single skill testing in mathematics and associated subjects both redundant and unpopular. In 1912, Arthur Berry, one of Marshall's students and himself a high wrangler, reported substantial drops in numbers for those attempting the Tripos between 1881 and 1909 while numbers in the Natural Sciences Tripos and later the Mechanical Sciences Tripos were rising. More importantly, Berry noted that the Tripos as a system of examining was flawed:

> In the first place it is clearly very difficult to set questions suitable for a large number of candidates of very varying ability and knowledge, including some who may be the leading mathematicians of the coming generation, and others who with little aptitude for or interest in the subject, acquire the minimum of knowledge requisite for obtaining the degree. . . . Moreover, the good mathematician who would naturally at this stage of his career have a bent towards certain departments of mathematics was much discouraged from any kind of specialisation. The pure mathematician inclined to pursue the study of higher analysis would be checked by the necessity of being able to answer questions on geometrical optics . . . in the examination . . . no place is assigned to any kind of original research. The examinations tested knowledge and that limited form of originality which consisted in applying knowledge very rapidly to such application of theory as could take the form of examination questions. . . . Another serious defect . . . is the almost complete divorce between mathematics and experimental physics. [58]

Berry's more detailed account about the nature of the examinations is also worth quoting.

> The examination for the Mathematical Tripos is conducted entirely by means of printed papers of questions to be answered by the candidates in a limited time (three hours per paper), without any assistance from books or notes. The standard type of question consists of two parts; first comes a piece of 'bookwork', that is, a known theorem, the proof of which is required to be given; this is followed by a 'rider' or example, which is, at least in theory, a consequence of the 'bookwork', but is in practice not infrequently rather loosely connected with it. Before the last change in the regulations there were also set two papers of 'problems', exercises of a more difficult kind with no indication given by the 'bookwork' as to the method to be used in the solution. Such 'riders' and 'problems' are very characteristic of Cambridge Mathematics: they are to be found in abundance in any ordinary English text-book and even treatises of an advanced type.[59]

The blend of bookwork and problems enabled examiners to separate sheep from the goats in the finely tuned calculus of grading, essential for determining the merit list. Examiners tended also to look for thoroughness and quality in answers rather than the quantity of questions attempted; marks were gained for the first two of these qualities, the last was less important.[60] A salutory story about the training the work for the Tripos could provide was told by Alfred Marshall's later friend from the Bristol days and fellow-Johnian, James Wilson. He was senior wrangler in 1859, suffered a nervous breakdown afterwards, and some months later 'made the discovery that my illness had swept away all my Higher Mathematics.'[61]

A PENSIONER AT ST JOHN'S: OCTOBER 1861 TO JANUARY 1865

Alfred Marshall, admitted as pensioner to St John's in June 1861, entered the college at the start of Michaelmas term in October of that year. He was assigned Room E6 in Third Court[62] for the whole of his period as undergraduate in the college. This room overlooked the river and the 'Backs', and thereby was perhaps prone to catch the summer smells of a Cam which still acted as a general sewer for the colleges and the town. His assigned tutor was the Rev. Hadley, a senior wrangler and Smith Prize winner of 1856 and therefore potentially very useful to the fresh undergraduate from Merchant Taylors' with high mathematical ambitions. It was Hadley presumably who warned Marshall about the potential dangers for his honours ranking from joining the college boat crew, advice that was not immediately followed. Hadley possibly also advised him on problems of a social and religious nature faced by the young undergraduate in his first extended period away from mother, family and home.

Based on the record on college examination performances regularly reproduced in *The Eagle*, Alfred Marshall appears to have continued his fine academic performance of Merchant Taylors'. He did, in fact relatively even better than he had done at school, where he had finished only as third monitor, not first in the class. 'Our Chronicle' for Michaelmas Term, 1862[63] lists Alfred Marshall as first in the first class in the June first-year college examinations, ahead of all fourteen John's students who joined him as wranglers in 1865. *The Eagle* fails to record the prizes he received for this performance – first class examination results at John's generally secured the award of books for the successful candidates – but his excellent examination performance at the end of his first college year may explain Marshall's gain of the scholarship mentioned by Keynes.[64] In the second year[65] Alfred Marshall remained among the first class results. In addition, he won the Wood and Hare Prizes awarded to impecunious students for excellent performance and valued at £20. However, this is the one college examination in which Alfred Marshall did not come first. He was beaten by Alexander Wood,[66] who was third in the first class list in first year, and who, as sixth wrangler, was to become the second Johnian in the 1865 Mathematical Tripos list. Alfred Marshall's pride and ambition probably received such a shock from coming second, by now an unusual outcome, that it did not recur in his undergraduate college experience. Lent term 1864[67] saw him once more on top of the college examination list and in the Tripos list he beat his nearest college rival by no less than four places. Alfred Marshall never liked to be beaten if he could help it.

The official John's record of Alfred Marshall, undergraduate, largely stops with a reference to his Tripos results. Apart from this *Eagle* material, there is his firm, but still boyish signature in the matriculation register of the college as a tangible sign of his presence as an undergraduate,[68] and references to him as a member of the Lady Margaret Boat Club, as the college boating club was called.

For Walter Scott[69] Mary Paley recorded that 'rowing was his favourite amusement when at College. He would have rowed in his College boat, had not his tutor dissuaded him.' Marshall was elected to the Boat Club on 16 October 1861, but only appears on a crew list once during 1862.[70] Unlike the Rev. Leslie Stephen, his counterpart at Trinity Hall up the river, the Rev. Hadley as tutor at John's was clearly no believer in 'muscular Christianity' for potential first wranglers, and successfully dissuaded Marshall from persevering with his rowing. Of cricket, Marshall's great love as a schoolboy, no mention is made by Mary Paley in the context of his undergraduate student days. Perhaps the St John's College Cricket Club was too expensive both in time and money for an impecunious mathematical honours student.

Mary Paley also recorded some of Marshall's undergraduate study habits:

> A[lfred] said that he was never good at bookwork. He always worked out problems for himself. An examiner at his Tripos examn told him that his answers to bookwork were as troublesome to look over as those to the problem papers.
> He kept himself at Cambridge chiefly by scholarships and gradually paid back his debt to his uncle by coaching in mathematics. He learned the habit of concentrating by making a rule of never working more than a quarter of an hour at a time unless he got so absorbed that he forgot to stop. He always had by his side books such as Boswell's Life of Johnson or Shakespeare to read between the intervals of work.[71]

This method of study Marshall had learnt in senior school from observing a signwriter working in Regent Street. Apart from keeping his mind fresh for grasping mathematical problems, it enriched his cultural outlook by absorbing nearly all of Shakespeare's plays, the collected wisdoms of Samuel Johnson as well as Aeschylus' *Agamemnon*. In a continuation of this biographical fragment from old age, Marshall recalled that he thought the method so useful that others might benefit from it if they had a tendency to overwork, a habit into which he had been forced at school. He accordingly passed it on, 'years afterwards to Professor Jowett: and later on he told me he had advised several young Balliol men to adopt a similar practice'.[72]

Marshall left few recollections of his teachers from his undergraduate years. Did he, as would be expected under normal university arrangements, attend Professor Stokes's lectures on Optics during Michaelmas term 1864? Rayleigh recollected this as an 'epoch in his life . . . [because] . . . for the first time he was brought into contact with a leader in physical science, and one whose mode of thought and expression particularly appealed to him. Above all, he was delighted with the experimental illustrations.'[73] Absence of Marshall's reactions is regrettable because he later claimed an intention to continue work with Stokes after taking out his degree, an intention abandoned during his early postgraduate years as a young Fellow at John's.[74]

His coach for the Tripos can, however, be identified. In its Report on the 1865 Tripos results, The *Times* (30 January 1865) indicated that Mr E.J. Routh was the coach for the first ten wranglers in that year, hence including Marshall. Routh was then 'the most famous of mathematical teachers. Routh's teaching was not in the least like what is ordinarily understood by "coaching", it was in reality a series of exceedingly clear and admirably arranged lectures, given to an audience larger than that attending the lectures of many of the mathematical Professors and College Lecturers.'[75] Routh did not come cheap. His fees were £36 a year at the time Thomson attempted the Tripos (1876–80), an expense considered worthwhile for a coach who over his thirty-three years of active coaching produced 27 senior wranglers and 24 in 24 consecutive years.[76] If, as the *Times* indicated, Marshall used his services as coach, this helps to explain the time Marshall took for paying back the loan from Uncle Charles to finance his Cambridge studies.

An ambiguity about Marshall's tutor in mathematics, implied in one of the very few stories he later told about his undergraduate days, can be mentioned at this point. In his Presidential Address to the Annual Cooperative Congress of 1889, Marshall recalled,

> When I was an undergraduate, I once took to my mathematical tutor a long face and an unfinished problem. I told him I had worked at it the whole of the preceding day, and yet not done it, though the day before I had done twenty that did not look a bit harder. He was a wise man – Dr. Parkinson was his name – and he looked at me cheerily and said, 'Well, then, yesterday's work probably did you much more good than that of the day before. There is not much good in doing things you can do; but there is great good in trying to do those that you can't do, but that are worth doing.'[77]

This tutor was almost certainly Dr Stephen Parkinson (1825–89), whose memorial service at St John's in January 1889 probably sparked the recollection Marshall used in this lecture. Parkinson was senior wrangler and winner of the Smith Prize in 1845, a Fellow of John's from 1845–71 and again 1882–89, and a tutor for his college from 1864–82. His books became part of the Tripos list and during the 1850s he was teaching mathematics to Tripos candidates at his college, including the senior wrangler of 1859, James Wilson, a later friend of the Marshalls at Bristol. An anecdote told by Wilson may explain Marshall's lack of recollections about Stokes's lectures, if Parkinson as his tutor had given him the same advice as he gave Wilson six years before. 'I had wished to attend Stokes, who was lecturing magnificently on the Undulatory Theory of Light. . . . Parkinson forbade me to attend as not bearing on the Tripos sufficiently.'[78] Irrespective of whether Marshall received such advice, he eventually would have met Stokes at meetings of the Eranus Society or the Cambridge Philosophical Society which he attended in subsequent years.[79]

Marshall's financial status as undergraduate helps to assess his social standing at his college. His financial resources depended on the nature of scholarships he had won as well as his annual outlays for college expenses, out-of-term residence, private coaching, and on overheads. The last included special fees to college and university, costs of a basic outfit in terms of required academic dress, and furniture and other utensils for his college room. Using cost estimates for 1862, where necessary adjusted by special knowledge on St John's College costs, or where, as Rothblatt suggests,[80] the students' guide costs are rather on the extravagant side, Marshall's university expenses can be satisfactorily estimated.

College expenses for a year can be estimated at £70. These comprised room rental of £10 (the minimum cost at St John's at this time), tuition at £18, coals at £3.10s., meals for the 25 weeks of term aggregating £20.12s.6d., laundry £5.8s. and miscellaneous college fees totalling £5.7s.4d. For the ten terms in college until the completion of the Tripos in late January 1865, total college costs approximate to £234. If, as mathematical honours students apparently more or less had to do, long vacations, and the shorter-between-terms ones, were spent in study with a coach, out-of-term costs of at least £27 per annum (£81 for the ten-term course) can be added to this. Periods of vacation spent at home – for Christmas, for example – while lowering this out-of-term residence cost, would have enhanced annual expenses by adding costs for travel between Cambridge and London. Incidentals are modestly estimated at £20 per annum, or 60 per cent below the estimate for such expenses in the *Student's Guide*. These cover purchases of books, additional food and refreshments, replacement of clothing and similar personal expenses. Given the book prizes Marshall was winning through his college examinations, expenditure on that item was probably small. He made up for this in later years. The level of private tuition for which Alfred Marshall paid to assist his quest for honours can only be guessed at. If his coach was E.J. Routh, the annual charge may well have been the £36 per annum for three years Thomson paid in 1876 and which Bonney, who did the Tripos in 1856, also paid. This gives total recurrent expenses of £483 for the ten terms of undergraduate studies, rather higher than those incurred by Arthur Bowley nearly three decades later but when retail prices as a whole had fallen considerably.[*]

Overheads are estimated at £30.3s., of which special university and college fees accounted for more than a half. These included the St John's admission fee of £2.3s., a matriculation fee of £5, a fee for sitting the previous Examination of £2.10s. and a B.A. degree fee of £7. The *Student's Guide* estimated the minimum costs for outfitting a college room at 10 guineas of which £3 went on crockery and linen; a further £3 purchased cap, gown and surplice, then essential academic dress for undergraduates when cap and gown had to be worn all Sunday, even on a country walk, and on weekdays up to noon as well as after dark.[81] The whole of Alfred Marshall's university costs then approximate to £513.

On a *pro rata* basis, the Parkin Exhibition valued at £50 annually for a maximum four years Alfred Marshall had won at Merchant Taylors' gave him £166 for the ten terms in question. If he also obtained a Foundation Scholarship valued at £50 per annum during his first year at college, the maximum income to be added from this source is a further £150.[82] The Hare and Wood Prize, which he won in his third year, yielded a further £20. This makes a total of £336 (maximum) and £186 (minimum) from scholarship income.[¶] The potential deficit to be covered from Uncle Charles's loan may then range from a high of £327 to a low of £177. In either case it amounted to a substantial debt, while the student budget it helped to finance remained extremely modest.

A budget like this was not designed for making many college friends, because it

---

[*] T.G. Bonney, *Memories of a Long Life*, p. 16. Bowley's cost per term in recurrent expenses was £44; Marshall's on my estimate £48.6s. In real terms, given the very substantial fall in prices which took place between 1861–65 and 1888–92, Bowley's costs approximate £53 in 1861–65 pounds. Bowley's special expenses or overheads had almost doubled from the £30 estimated for Alfred Marshall to £55 of which £20 was returnable on leaving the University on completion of the degree. See Agatha H. Bowley, *A Memoir of Professor Sir Arthur Bowley*, pp. 36–7.

[¶] The gap between income and outlay also depends on whether the Hare and Wood Prize was won on more than one occasion. Given the estimated annual costs, Mary Paley's remark that Alfred Marshall had kept himself chiefly by scholarships while at university, suggests the maximum amount of scholarship income as more correct since it is close to three-quarters of total expenses; the minimum is less than 40 per cent. On the other hand, the loan took Alfred Marshall at least two years to repay, so it cannot have been too small.

provided for only the barest minimum in entertainments. No invitations to supper parties or lavish breakfasts originated from Room E6 in Third Court between October 1861 and January 1865, not even, it may be presumed, to celebrate the Tripos results in January 1865. As in the case of school, where only friendships with Traill and Hall were recorded, the only evidence of a specific undergraduate friendship Marshall made was a rowing companion from John's, Rawdon Levett.[83] This fits in with the historical record of college life at the time. The poorer students were relative outcasts in their colleges, and sons of Bank of England clerks, rare in the 1880s in the courts of St John's, would have been even more scarce amongst the John's undergraduates with whom Alfred Marshall resided in college during the early 1860s.

Social acceptance at university in such economic and family circumstances required academic success. This, together with what can be described as his general will to win, were probably enough to drive a student like Alfred Marshall to the grind involved in the Tripos competition. His undergraduate years more than likely reflected the long hours of work inherent in this sought-after achievement: study, study and more study, with little time for entertainment, sport and recreation. Lack of money in one way facilitated this lonely and Spartan existence. Apart from his temporary involvement with rowing, the entertainment and recreation Marshall enjoyed in these years was likely to have been of the solitary and inexpensive kind. Walks in the Cambridge countryside, particularly appealing to the lover of real country Marshall was as a boy, were certainly one form of recreation. Some awakening of latent musical interests by the choral music offered twice weekly in chapel may have led to another form of relaxation. That, and hard work, concisely sum up his undergraduate experience, an experience even less subject to retrospective recollection than that bestowed on his similarly lonely school-days. A contemporary ditty, recorded by John Neville Keynes[84] sums up the abstemious life for the student in search of that glittering prize of highest mathematical honours:

He who would fain a Senior Wrangler be
Must eat but little and must drink but tea
Must burn his midnight oil from month to month
And solve binomials to the $(n + 1)$th

MATHEMATICAL TRIPOS: JANUARY 1865

Climax and solution to this baneful existence came with the Mathematical Tripos. This commenced on Tuesday, 3 January 1865, with a paper on Euclidian geometry, in which as first question a geometrical construction had to be given for 'finding a point in a given straight line, the difference of the distances of which from the two given points on the same side of the line shall be the greatest possible'. The five subsequent papers, ending on Thursday, 5 January at 4.00 p.m. with a problem on Julian and Gregorian calendar correction, completed the first and elementary part of the Tripos. Unlike Lord Rayleigh, the ultimate victor in the Tripos, Alfred Marshall left no impressions in letters to his family about the degree of satisfaction and confidence these three days had given him for the trials ahead. Rayleigh had only come fifth in these preliminary papers but it is not known whether

Alfred Marshall, or someone else, was the 'formidable rival' named in Rayleigh family discussion about his chances for the senior position, prior to the start of the final test a week later.[85]

The first three days' papers sat by Marshall were basically Euclidean geometry, the conics, some elementary algebra and trigonometry, mechanics of the sort taught to undergraduates at many universities as late as the 1950s, and some physics of a similar nature. However, the overall impression they give is that candidates were expected to have a mastery of all the detail in these areas – something which gradually lost significance in mathematics education during the twentieth century.[86]

The Tripos resumed on Monday, 16 January, for its second, advanced part. This time it began with a question applying the 'principles of the parallelogram of forces' to grind on, paper by paper by paper, for the rest of the week. The later papers were full of the sorts of questions contained in English texts on applied mathematics and (theoretical) physics; some easy, some very nasty to solve even though the possible methods of solution were obvious. The work on 'higher algebra' was technical and detailed but conveyed none of the conceptual structures underlying the subject. A similar comment can be made on the other topics in 'pure' mathematics. Only in areas of the calculus do the papers imply some attempt at generality. This is not surprising. The development of structural concepts in algebra and, more generally, in mathematics generally did not begin until the mid-nineteenth century, and was then not very significant in England. The work of many of the great continental mathematicians was often neither communicated to England nor translated into English, a situation not redressed until late in the nineteenth century.[87]

It seems doubtful whether Alfred Marshall could have arranged with the college porter at John's to wake him from twenty minute naps during the lunch break between the daily two papers as Rayleigh had managed to do at neighbouring Trinity. Nor was Alfred Marshall as low down the alphabetical list of candidates. He therefore missed some of the advantage enjoyed by his rival in the earlier papers in not having the extra time during the interval when papers were being collected from candidates higher up the alphabetical list.[88] However, at 4.00 p.m. on that Friday, 20 January, Alfred Marshall's relief that it was all over bar the results was certainly as great as that of fellow examinees. What he did that evening is an interesting matter for speculation.

Whether he was in the crowds near Senate House on the morning of 27 January to hear the results is not recorded, nor for that matter whether parents, younger brother or sisters were present, after braving the expense and early rise travel to Cambridge for that purpose would have involved. Alfred Marshall's initial reaction to the result that he was second wrangler to Rayleigh is likewise unknown. Whether like Rayleigh[89] he went to see one of his fellow Johnians among the moderators to discover how he had done, is more likely, given Mary Paley's recollection that one of those examiners had told him that 'his answers to book work were as troublesome to look over as those to the problem papers'.[90] Whether that examiner also told him, as Walton from Trinity apparently told Rayleigh, that the two seniors among the examiners had forecast Rayleigh to be the senior wrangler on the basis of his performance in the first three days' papers and where Marshall was placed in these preliminary papers, is likewise a gap in the preserved record.

What Alfred Marshall thought about the *Times* leader on 30 January 1865, proclaiming as it did that there was no reason to fear that Rayleigh had obtained his honour through favouritism accorded to the heir to a peerage, can also only be guessed at. The same applies to the subsequent correspondence on the subject by a Fellow of Trinity, presumed to have been Henry Sidgwick. It would be equally interesting to have Alfred Marshall's reaction to Rayleigh's cavalier dismissal of the offer by the editor of the *Illustrated Times*, conveyed to him through his coach, Routh, to have the photographs of the two top wranglers published in that periodical,[91] always presuming of course that either Rayleigh or Routh had made Marshall aware of this offer.

Why Alfred Marshall failed to enter for the Smith Prize examinations is also not known. These started on 30 January and were won by Rayleigh, with Taylor, the third wrangler, as runner up and second Smith Prize winner. Did Alfred Marshall's nerve fail, or did he prefer not to risk being beaten twice in as many weeks in a subject in which he originally expected to come first. Because the Smith Prize examinations, as Arthur Berry mentioned,[92] required ability at original mathematical research, this may be a more important reason why Alfred Marshall did not attempt them. His gifts and talents for mathematics identified by Airey at school may not have been in that direction. The low pecuniary value of the prize, not worth the additional effort to Marshall, is another possible explanation for his failure to attempt it.

These unanswered questions about what was, after all, a highlight in a university career, emphasise how little is known about Marshall's personal reactions to what generally was regarded as a resounding success: being second wrangler in a stiff competition. This made him[93] a member of a small band of famous second wranglers, including Cambridge notables such as William Whewell, Clerk Maxwell and Lord Kelvin and two years later his own friend, W.K. Clifford, a friendship perhaps bonded by this shared experience. It bears repeating, that no comment on his feelings about the nature of the prize he had secured after all this effort and sacrifice were ever made in Marshall's later autobiographical writings. For the most detailed of these,[94] the episode is factually recorded as follows: 'He took his degree in 1865 as second in Mathematical Honours, the eminent Physicist Lord Rayleigh taking the first place. He was elected Fellow of St John's College in 1865.' *The Eagle*[95] in its Chronicle for Michaelmas 1865 expressed as its only regret that the 'young nobleman Senior Wrangler . . . was not a Johnian. It was however a very successful year for the College, as we had fifteen wranglers, and amongst them the second, Mr. A. Marshall.' However, by late January the second wrangler would undoubtedly have been told that vacancies existed among the college fellowships at St John's. Together with his result in the Tripos, his election to a fellowship in the coming November was ensured and therefore his immediate future.

For most people, their university undergraduate days are a period of grateful recollections, particularly if, as in the case of Marshall, they were crowned with considerable success at graduation. This makes the limited information on Marshall's undergraduate days all the more surprising. Explanations for this memory failure on his part are not difficult to suggest. For a poor student, dependent on scholarships, prizes and borrowed funds, prone to excessive study because obsessed with doing well, if only to prove to his family that he had been correct in rejecting the classical road to fame at Oxford, there was probably little pleasurable to remember from the experiences of those ten, long terms. Hardship, loneliness, strenuous work, undiluted by extended summer holidays at Aunt

Louisa's of the type which had made his school-days bearable; nor, it may be surmised, by frequent, if indeed any, access to the comforting role of mother and of his increasingly grown-up sisters, made this an episode in his life to be suppressed rather than cherished. Such suppression is all the more understandable when these sacrifices at first sight appeared to have been in vain. They were not crowned with the success of becoming senior wrangler, secretly hoped for, a hope all the more potent if it had sustained him during these difficult years. Although easily sufficient for securing a fellowship and university career, being *second* wrangler may have seemed to the young Alfred Marshall not much different from failure. If his liking for mathematics at school owed much to the fact he came first in it, his failure to maintain that primacy in the Tripos, particularly given his sustained record in this regard in the John's examinations, may explain why his career in mathematics or the natural sciences was almost immediately abandoned. For one without friends, if not socially outcast, as Alfred Marshall seems to have been during his undergraduate years at St John's College, the honour of coming first was a powerful inspiration, making the failure to achieve it all the more galling.

Finally, how good a mathematician did the Tripos make him? Many wranglers were undoubtedly capable mathematicians by any standard. Some performed pioneering work. The training they received pushed many into applied mathematics and physics, and others became noted pure mathematicians and geometers. One wrangler, Hardy, later argued that these achievements were often in spite of, rather than because, the training the Tripos preparation gave them.[96] Alfred Marshall was to apply his mathematics to economics with care, with caution and with a considerable degree of skill, a benefit from his Tripos experience and undergraduate period which should not be underrated though he preferred geometry more for this role than the terse language of algebra and the calculus.[97] However, his fellowship won for him by the second wrangler position, combined with the value of his mathematical training for his later career in economics, became major consolations only well after what in the first instance may have been seen as a poor reward for the long and lonely years of hard work as a relatively impoverished undergraduate.

NOTES

1.	*The Student's Guide to the University of Cambridge 1862*, Cambridge: Deighton, Bell & Co, 1862, p. 44.
2.	Rev. A. V. Hadley (1834–67), Senior Wrangler and first Smith Prize winner, 1856, Fellow of St John's 1857–65, Tutor. *The Eagle* (Vol. VI, No. 30, p. 97) records that Alfred Marshall in 1867 donated £5 to the Hadley Memorial Fund, a sign of his growing affluence at that time as well as recognition of the services rendered to him by his tutor.
3.	St John's College Admission Register, June 1861; St John's College, extract from *Biographical Register*, entry No. 2848. This shows that Alfred Marshall had been baptised on 7 September 1842, approximately six weeks after his birth. Of the 16 students admitted to St John's in June 1861, eight had been baptised in 1842, five in 1841 and of the three other entrants, one each in 1843, 1844 and 1845.
4.	*The Student's Guide to the University of Cambridge, 1862*, p. 9. Although the university also operated the library, colleges provided the main library service, the University library being open only from 2.00 to 4.00 p.m. on week-days. *Ibid.*, p. 39.
5.	D.A. Winstanley, *Late Victorian Cambridge*, Cambridge: at the University Press, 1947, pp. 36–8, 67–89.

6.   *Ibid.* p. 144. Details of the syllabus for the Additional Examination are in *A Guide to the Examinations for the Degree of B.A. at the University of Cambridge*, Cambridge University Press, 1865, pp. 7–10, and Rita McWilliams-Tullberg, *Women at Cambridge*, London: Gollancz, 1975, Appendix A. The extraordinarily high quality mathematical education Alfred Marshall had received at Merchant Taylors' would have given him a considerable advantage in the Previous and Additional Examinations. For Rayleigh, the Previous Examination proved to be 'a considerable obstacle' and on his own account, 'in the viva voce examination, the examiners who were aware of his promise as a mathematician, had some difficulty in finding a question he could answer, so that they could with decency let him pass.' Robert John Strutt, *John William Strutt, Third Baron Rayleigh*, London: Edward Arnold & Co., 1924, p. 30.

7.   See D.A. Winstanley, *Late Victorian Cambridge*, pp. 146–57; Sheldon Rothblatt, *The Revolution of the Dons*, pp. 181–7, A.S. and E.M.S., *Henry Sidgwick*, pp. 27–8, Rita McWilliams-Tullberg, *Women at Cambridge*, Appendix B.

8.   Noel Annan, *Leslie Stephen*, pp. 24–8; Lawrence Goldman, 'An Advanced Liberal: Henry Fawcett 1833–1884', in Lawrence Goldman, (ed.), *The Blind Victorian: Henry Fawcett and British Liberalism*, Cambridge: Cambridge University Press, 1989, p. 3.

9.   See Leslie Stephen, *Life of Henry Fawcett*, London: Smith, Elder & Company, 1885, pp. 123–4; Winstanley, *Late Victorian Cambridge*, pp. 180–84.

10.   Sheldon Rothblatt, *The Revolution of the Dons*, pp. 181–2.

11.   Data from *Encyclopaedia Britannica*, Edinburgh: A & C Black, ninth edition, Vol. XXIII, 1887, p. 853; B.R. Mitchell, *Abstract of British Historical Statistics*, Cambridge: at the University Press, 1962; J.R. Tanner, *The Historical Register of the University of Cambridge*, Cambridge University Press, 1917; Rothblatt, *The Revolution of the Dons*, Chapter 2, Appendix II. In connection with the matriculants at Sidney Sussex College he noted the relatively small number of aristocratic entrants to that college as compared with a college like Trinity.

12.   *The Student's Guide to the University of Cambridge, 1862*, pp. 63, 65, 72.

13.   A more precise estimate of this financial burden is presented below, pp. 89–90; partly for the purpose of establishing the debt to Uncle Charles Marshall had to repay from his financial resources over 1865–67.

14.   In retirement Marshall addressed the problem in correspondence in the context of university reform. See below, Chapter 17, pp. 639–40.

15.   Alec C. Crook, *From the Foundation to Gilbert Scott. A History of the Buildings of St John's College, Cambridge 1511–1885*, Cambridge: printed for the College 1980, esp. Chapters VII–IX; T.G. Bonney, *Memories of a Long Life*, Cambridge: Metcalf & Company, 1921, pp. 25, 53–60.

16.   Mary Paley Marshall, 'Biographical Notes on Alfred Marshall' (KMF).

17.   Sheldon Rothblatt, *The Revolution of the Dons*, p. 239.

18.   John Robert Seeley, 'Liberal Education in Universities', first published in 1867, cited in Rothblatt, *The Revolution of the Dons*, p. 175.

19.   Sheldon Rothblatt, *The Revolution of the Dons*, p. 236.

20.   Below, Chapter 14, esp. pp. 503–4.

21.   Sheldon Rothblatt, *The Revolution of the Dons*, p. 237.

22.   *The Student's Guide to the University of Cambridge, 1862*, pp. 69, 71–2, 76–9.

23.   *Ibid.*, pp. 313–17; Edward Miller, *Portrait of a College*, pp. 86–7; T.G. Bonney, *Memories of a Long Life*, p. 15.

24.   Rothblatt, *The Revolution of the Dons*, p. 237.

25.   Edward Miller, *Portrait of a College*, p. 81.

26.   Rothblatt, *The Revolution of the Dons*, pp. 196–7; T.G. Bonney, *Memories of a Long Life*, pp. 15–16.

27.   *Ibid.*, pp. 196–8.

28.   William Henry Bateson (1812–1881), *DNB*, Volume I, p. 1321.

29.   Edward Miller, *Portrait of a College*, pp. 86–94.

30.   John Maynard Keynes, 'Alfred Marshall', pp. 172 n.2, 164 n.2.

31.   The Rev. Dr Bateson to the Bristol University Council, 20 June 1877.

32.   Edward Miller, *Portrait of a College*, p. 94; Winstanley, *Late Victorian Cambridge*, pp. 70–71, 81–2 and Chapter 7, esp. pp. 289–314; T.G. Bonney, *Memories of a Long Life*, pp. 41–3.

33.   Edward Miller, *Portrait of a College*, pp. 80–82; T.G. Bonney, *Memories of a Long Life*, pp. 19–20, 23–4.

34.   Edward Miller, *Portrait of a College*, p. 87.

35.   *Ibid.*, p. 81. Cf. T.G. Bonney, *Memories of a Long Life*, pp. 17–19. Marshall's story to Fay that bowls was his sport at college, which his tutor asked him to give up, was therefore fictitious, as the reference to the raconteur's 'soft chuckle' implies. See C.R. Fay, 'Reminiscences of a Deputy Librarian', p. 88.

36.   W.W. Rouse Ball, *The Origin and History of the Mathematical Tripos*, Cambridge: E. Johnson, 1880, pp. 17–18; Robert John Strutt, *John William Strutt, Third Baron Rayleigh*, p. 33.

37.   W.W. Rouse Ball, *Cambridge Notes*, Cambridge: Heffers, second edition, 1921, p. 270.
38.   W.W. Rouse Ball, *The Origin and History of the Mathematical Tripos*, pp. 14–15.
39.   William Whewell, *On a Liberal Education in General, and with particular reference to the leading Studies in the University of Cambridge*, Part I, London: Parker, second edition, 1850, pp. 40, 56, 63–8. As mentioned in Chapter 6, Whewell analysed economic problems with the aid of mathematics in work with which Alfred Marshall became familiar during the early years of his economic studies.
40.   Sheldon Rothblatt, *The Revolution of the Dons*, pp. 182–3. The quotation from Galton is from *Hereditary Genius*, London: Macmillan, 1962, p. 59; the second quotation from Noel Annan, *Leslie Stephen*, p. 25.
41.   John Whitaker, Introduction to *EEW*, I, pp. 3–4. The Cambridge legend referred to in the quotation is quoted below, Chapter 20, p. 744 and n*. Mary Paley recalled Moulton as 'excellent at examinations. He did all the bookwork questions, writing very fast, long before anyone else and then had plenty of time for the problems' (MSS Notes, NCA). See also Peter Newman, 'F.Y. Edgeworth', in *The New Palgrave*, Vol. 2, pp. 87–8.
42.   J. Creedy and D.P. O'Brien, 'Marshall, Monopoly and Rectangular Hyperbolas', *Australian Economic Papers*, 29 (55), December 1990, p. 142.
43.   *The Student's Guide to the University of Cambridge, 1862*, pp. 83–5.
44.   Reproduced above, Appendix to Chapter 3.
45.   *The Student's Guide to the University of Cambridge, 1862*, pp. 93–4.
46.   *Ibid.*, p. 95.
47.   On Marshall's possible association with Stokes, see below, pp. 78, 126.
48.   Robert John Strutt, *John William Strutt, Third Baron Rayleigh*, p. 33.
49.   Sheldon Rothblatt, *The Revolution of the Dons*, p. 199; cf. J.J. Thomson, *Recollections and Reflections*, London: G.Bell & Sons, 1936, Ch. 2, esp. pp. 35–42.
50.   Noel Annan, *Leslie Stephen*, p. 25.
51.   Mary Paley Marshall, 'Notes for Walter Scott', but cf. a story he later told to Fay ('Reminiscences of a Deputy Librarian', p. 88); T.G. Bonney was given the same advice by his family doctor, 'You can read hard, or you can row hard, but you cannot do both.' (*Memories of a Long Life*, p. 17).
52.   JNKD, entries for 14 and 19 October 1872, 12 and 18 January 1873, July 1873.
53.   *The Student's Guide to the University of Cambridge, 1862*, pp. 97–8. T.G. Bonney, *Memories of a Long Life*, p. 16, indicates that he had a private tutor during the whole of his residence, as 'everyone who hoped to get a fairly high place in a Tripos' then did.
54.   *The Student's Guide to the University of Cambridge, 1862*, p. 98.
55.   *Ibid.*, p. 86.
56.   W.W. Rouse Ball, *Cambridge Notes*, p. 306.
57.   C.H. Hardy, *Pure Mathematics*, Cambridge University Press, seventh edition, 1938, Preface, cited by Peter Newnham, 'F.Y. Edgeworth', p. 88.
58.   Arthur Berry, 'Recent Changes in the Mathematical Tripos at Cambridge', in Board of Education, *The Teaching of Mathematics in the United Kingdom*, Part II, London: HMSO, 1912, pp. 186–8. See also Sheldon Rothblatt, *The Revolution of the Dons*, p. 252.
59.   Arthur Berry, 'Recent Changes in the Mathematics Tripos at Cambridge', pp. 185–6.
60.   *The Student's Guide to the University of Cambridge, 1862*, pp. 91–2.
61.   James M. Wilson, *An Autobiography*, eds A.T. and J.S. Wilson, London: Sidgwick & Jackson, 1932, pp. 44–52, the quotation is from p. 48.
62.   G.C. Moore Smith, *Lists of Past Occupants of Rooms in St John's College*, Cambridge, March 1895, p. 40, kindly made available to me by the St John's archivist, Dr Malcolm Underwood.
63.   *The Eagle*, Vol. III, 1863, p. 241.
64.   John Maynard Keynes, 'Alfred Marshall', p. 164 and n.1. This was probably a St John's Foundation Fellowship worth £50 per annum.
65.   *The Eagle*, Vol. IV, pp. 59, 60.
66.   Alexander Wood (1840–1917), Alfred Marshall's academic rival at John's, later became Assistant Master at Sherborne School (1867–1902). He was a Fellow of St John's 1866–74 and was ordained Deacon, Sodor and Man for Salisbury 1870, priest at Salisbury 1870. Venn, *Alumni Cantabrigienses*, Part II, Vol. VI, p. 554.
67.   *The Eagle*, Vol. IV, p. 118.
68.   Not reproduced here. It was kindly shown to me by Mr Malcolm Pratt the John's sub-librarian at the time.
69.   Mary Paley Marshall, 'Notes for Walter Scott'.
70.   Boat Club Minutes, 1857–67, St John's College Archives, Soc 26.2.1. Information supplied by Dr Malcolm Underwood, College Archivist.
71.   Mary Paley Marshall, 'Biographical Notes on Alfred Marshall' (KMF).

72. Biographical fragment, dated 18 July 1917, partly reproduced by J.M. Keynes, 'Alfred Marshall', p. 165; Marshall Archive, Large Red Box 1, Item 1. Cf. above, Chapter 3, pp. 63–4 for Marshall's own description of his method.
73. Robert John Strutt, *John William Strutt, Third Baron Rayleigh*, p. 32.
74. Below, Chapter 5, pp. 94, 126.
75. J.J. Thomson, *Recollections and Reflections*, p. 35 and see pp. 36–8 for a more detailed discussion of his teaching style.
76. J.J. Thomson, *Recollections and Reflections*, pp. 38, 42.
77. Alfred Marshall, 'Co-operation', in *Memorials*, p. 246.
78. Details from Venn, *Alumni Cantabrigienses*; James M. Wilson, *An Autobiography*, pp. 44–5.
79. See below, Chapter 5, pp. 112–3.
80. Sheldon Rothblatt, *The Revolution of the Dons*, pp. 66–9.
81. T.G. Bonney, *Memories of a Long Life*, p. 22.
82. John Maynard Keynes, 'Alfred Marshall', p. 164 n.1. Venn, *Alumni Cantabrigienses* does not record Alfred Marshall as a scholar of St John's nor do the college records I have seen substantiate a Foundation Scholarship. There was no bar of course against simultaneously holding scholarship and exhibition, as well as sundry prizes. See Rothblatt, *The Revolution of the Dons*, pp. 80–83.
83. Mary Paley Marshall, 'MSS Notes' (NCA). Marshall's friendships are more generally discussed in Chapter 18.
84. JNKD, entry for 4 October 1883.
85. Robert John Strutt, *John William Strutt, Third Baron Rayleigh*, pp. 33–5; the details of the Tripos papers are quoted from the CUL collection of examination papers. In *P* I, p. 242, *P* VIII,. p. 194, Marshall recorded 'University men even when engaged in different studies get to estimate one another's strength very closely'.
86. The last two sentences are derived from information provided by my colleague, John Mack, in the Department of Pure Mathematics at the University of Sydney. He also provided me with the 1912 Report on Mathematical Education in the United Kingdom and the contributions thereto by Arthur Berry.
87. Much of this paragraph derived from John Mack's information referred to in the previous footnote. Bonney, *Memories of a Long Life*, p. 29, recalls difficulties in remembering his 'bookwork' during the five days, and getting boggled over the riders. On the other hand, James Wilson (*Autobiography*, p. 45) recorded that after the initial shock, 'all was easy'.
88. Robert John Strutt, *John William Strutt, Third Baron Rayleigh*, p. 34. Altogether, fourteen other candidates separated the two top wranglers alphabetically, seven of them with surnames starting with M.
89. Robert John Strutt, *John William Strutt, Third Baron Rayleigh*, p. 35.
90. Mary Paley Marshall, 'Biographical Notes on Alfred Marshall' (KMF).
91. Robert John Strutt, *John William Strutt, Third Baron Rayleigh*, p. 35.
92. Arthur Berry, 'Recent Changes in the Mathematical Tripos at Cambridge', p. 187.
93. John Maynard Keynes, 'Alfred Marshall', p. 166 n.1.
94. 'Alfred Marshall, Professor of Political Economy, Cambridge', *AMCA*, I, p. 148. The text contains the obvious misprint of '1861' for 1865, as the year he took his degree.
95. *The Eagle*, Vol. IV, 1865.
96. These conclusions on mathematics derive heavily from John Mack's views, previously acknowledged. Hardy's views (in 1938) were quoted above, note 57 and p. 86.
97. On this, see Chapter 6, esp. pp. 745–7 and for the critical use the mature Marshall made of mathematics in the *Principles*, see Chapter 12 below, pp. 402–4, 412–3.

5. In Search of a Vocation 1865–1872: Postgraduate Years as a Young Fellow at John's

In November 1905, Walter Layton, one of Alfred Marshall's most prized and successful economics students at Cambridge, took down a brief autobiographical sketch which Alfred Marshall presented to his class by way of introduction to the subject of political economy. It illustrated some of the reasons why Marshall considered economic studies valuable but limited, and serves equally well as an introduction to Marshall's eventful period of postgraduate studies even if most of its economics aspects are postponed to the next chapter.

> Marshall intended to work at Maths and Physics under Stokes. Got onto Metaphy[sics] which he thought was the key to human life. Up at five in the morning to read – Kant's Critique. Got onto Ethics. As [a way of] solving practical problems got to Econ[omics]: Returned to Ethics to find what were not Metaphysics or Econ[omic]s [problems]. Found one set: How far is a man bound to express opinion when he knows that what others hold to [be] good for them to believe [is] untrue.[1]

Keynes also attended these lectures and therefore may have heard this autobiographical pronouncement. In any case, his subsequent account resembles and expands on that given by Layton. After mathematics had paid Alfred Marshall's 'arrears' by discharging the loan from Uncle Charles, Keynes recounts that Marshall now felt himself free to follow his own inclinations. An original plan of studying with Stokes was 'cut short by a sudden rise of deep interest in the philosophical foundations of knowledge, especially in relation to theology'.[2] Self-realisation of inadequate preparation may be another, more contemporary reason. In a retrospective fragment for the preface of *Money, Credit and Commerce*, Marshall further explained his tortuous road to economic studies, which filled gaps in the story Layton recorded in 1905:

> About the year 1867 (while mainly occupied with teaching Mathematics at Cambridge), Mansel's Bampton Lectures came into my hands and caused me to think that man's own possibilities were the most important subject for his study. So I gave myself for a time to the study of Metaphysics; but soon passed to what seemed to be the more progressive study of Psychology. Its fascinating inquiries into the possibilities of the higher and more rapid development of human faculties brought me into touch with the question: how far do the conditions of life of the British (and other) working classes generally suffice for fullness of life? Older and wiser men told me that the resources of production do not suffice for affording to the great body of the people the leisure and the opportunity for study; and they told me that I needed to study Political Economy. I followed their advice, and regarded myself as a wanderer in the land of dry facts; looking forward to a speedy return to the luxuriance of pure thought. But the more I studied economic science, the smaller appeared the knowledge which I had of it, in proportion to the knowledge that I needed; and now, at the end of nearly half a century of almost exclusive study of it, I am conscious of more ignorance of it than I was at the beginning of the study.[3]

Other accounts drawn from Marshall late in his life, confirms this gradual progress through the 'mental sciences' (psychology) in the late 1860s, with only minor differences. A letter to James Ward, then Cambridge Professor of Psychology and Marshall's colleague in the moral sciences, provides a more definite account:

> I would not have you think me indifferent to mental science. About as much of my time since I came to Cambridge in 1861 has been given to it as to mathematics. My zeal for economics would never have got me out of bed at five o'clock in the morning, to make my own coffee and work for three hours before breakfast and pupils in mathematics: but philosophy did that, till I became ill and my right foot swelled to double its normal size. That was in 1867. Soon after, I drifted away from metaphysics towards psychology. When Pearson asked me to lecture on Political Economy I consented; but I should have preferred philosophy, which was his subject. Shortly after the College made me a lecturer: and I added Logic and Ethics. But I always said till about 1871 that my home was in Mental Science. Gradually, however, the increasing urgency of economic studies as a means towards human well-being grew upon me. About 1871–2, I told myself the time had come at which I must decide whether to give my life to psychology or economics. I spent a year in doubt: always preferring psychology for the pleasures of the chase; but economics grew and grew in practical urgency, not so much in relation to the growth of wealth as to the quality of life; and I settled down to it.[4]

Mary Paley recollected other activities and friends gained during these early postgraduate years. She mentions Clifford and Moulton as 'his two greatest friends . . . when a young Fellow [at John's]'. They, with Alfred Marshall and another Johnian called Moss, were members of a group of seven which sometimes met to read Shakespeare;[5] an ideal society for a lover of Shakespeare as Marshall claimed to be. She later also remembered that 'the seven went a good deal to Mrs. Potts' parties. She was the reigning beauty in Cambridge. [but] Mr. Potts was so ugly that they were called "Beauty and the Beast".'[6] Marshall's membership of the Eranus Society was likewise recorded by Mary Paley Marshall, as 'a dining club in which each member paid expenses and was host and supplied the subject of discussion in turn. (Hence the name which means picnic, where each guest brings his share of the meal). Among its members were H. Sidgwick, Venn, Fawcett and Clifford'.[7] Mary Paley failed to mention the Grote Club, another Cambridge discussion society, to which Marshall, on his own account,[8] was admitted in 1867 and of whose deliberations he kept a record, part of which has been preserved.[9] However, after his degree taken in January 1865 and before his election to a fellowship in November 1865, she recorded,

> he went to Clifton College for a short time, under Percival, for whom he had an enormous veneration. There he made friends with Dakyns and also with J.R. Mozley who turned his thoughts to philosophy by suggesting that he should read Mansel's Prolegomena, which he found unsatisfactory. He then wanted to read Kant in the original and when he went to Germany he took lessons in Dresden [in 1868] and began on Kant. His teacher objected to such an unsuitable book for a beginner, but he answered, 'if it were not for Kant, I should not be learning German'. He was also much influenced by Hegel's Philosophy of History. For many years he was deep in Philosophy, and he became much interested in Psychology, and at one time he would have liked to devote himself to the subject of attention on which depends the power of concentration. He turned to Economics (as he thought for a short time) intending to return to Philosophy or perhaps to Psychology. He entered upon Economics because he was told that Economics would show him how far his aims were realizable. Bateson, the then Master of St John's was instrumental in getting him a lectureship in Moral Sciences, and he gradually settled down to Economics, though for a time he gave short courses on other branches of Moral Sciences, e.g. on Logic and on Bentham.[10]

These biographical fragments enable the construction of a rough chronology for the very important years in Alfred Marshall's intellectual development after January 1865. Illness of the mathematics master at Clifton College, a newly established public school near Bristol, created a temporary vacancy on the teaching staff which Marshall filled during the first half of 1865. Apart from Percival, Clifton's headmaster, Marshall made friends there with fellow teachers Dakyns and Mozley and, possibly, Sidgwick who examined for the school that summer. This opened doors to Cambridge society closed to him as an undergraduate. Sidgwick in turn may have introduced him to Clifford and Moulton, whom Sidgwick would have come to know as Apostles in his capacity as an 'old' Apostle from 1856 to 1865, and who, in his capacity as an 'angel', continued to attend their meetings.[11] However, Moulton, who entered John's together with Moss in 1864, may just as easily have independently become acquainted with fellow Johnian, Marshall.

No summer vacation could be afforded in 1865, money had to be earned to repay Uncle Charles with mathematical coaching. In November 1865, John's elected him Fellow of the college, and during Michaelmas term 1865 he resided in second court, Room C2 of the college. During the next two years, income from college fellowship dividends and mathematical coaching, enabled rapid repayment of his debt. He also began reading philosophy, initially inspired by Mozley and Dakyns as a result of his theological discussions and debates with them at Clifton, and later by his other new friends at the university. A sign of his growing social acceptance, he was invited to join the Grote Club in 1867. Philosophical studies became so intense that by 1867, as Marshall later claimed, his health was affected. Marshall also started economic and psychological studies that year, as well as Alpine mountaineering in Switzerland with Mozley and his brother.

In 1866, summer holidays were spent in Scotland, perhaps the year when Marshall first studied poverty in the industrial regions of the north. Subsequent holidays, especially in summer, were largely spent abroad. Marshall was in Dresden and Berlin for German studies in 1868 and the winter of 1869–70. He also enjoyed mountaineering trips in the Tirol, Bavaria and Switzerland, where nearly every summer holiday was spent until 1873. In 1868 Bateson gave him a College Lectureship in the Moral Sciences, thereby eliminating the obligation for ordination from his college fellowship. In 1872, when the Eranus Society was founded, Marshall was sufficiently well regarded in the university community to be almost immediately invited as a member.

The early 1870s likewise marked Marshall's growing involvement as a young Fellow in university and college reform. He actively participated in advancing the rights of women to education at the university, concerned himself with reform of college teaching and more general educational reform.[12] Outside the university Marshall became attracted to the cause of labour and even contributed to the socialist press. By the early 1870s, Marshall's lectures were still not exclusively devoted to economics, but increasingly, and initially reluctantly, on his own account, he began to concentrate his teaching on that subject. By 1875 he could say that his 'economic apprenticeship' has been completed, while his initial period as

Fellow at John's was brought to a close when his engagement to moral sciences student and fellow economist Mary Paley, concluded in their marriage in July 1877.[*]

What follows elaborates on Alfred Marshall's search for a vocation by tracing his intellectual development during his postgraduate years. The departure from mathematics, his religious doubts and study of theological controversy, theory of knowledge and metaphysical enquiry, ethics, human progress, psychology and economics, are part of this search. Friends, including the 'older and wiser men' with whom he became acquainted in 1865 and after, are likewise a crucial part of this story. Clifton College, the St John's fellowship and Cambridge discussion societies therefore precede the account of his intellectual odyssey, because these were the places where the friendships were made and the intellectual horizons widened. The backdrop to Alfred Marshall's adventures of the mind was the spiritual and intellectual ferment of what was called the 'fighting sixties', a decade which was a landmark in more than one sense of the word.

THE 'FIGHTING SIXTIES'

The first decade which Marshall spent at Cambridge University coincided with the fighting sixties. Frederic Harrison, who coined this phrase, concisely gave his reasons for this choice:

> Those were the days of the 'Essays and Reviews' and Dr. Colenso polemics in the Church, of the fight to open the Universities to Dissenters, the fight over National Education, about Church Rates, State Churches, and reform of the Suffrage. It embraced the period of Mr. Gladstone's ascendancy in the House of Commons and his first two ministries, the Reform Act of 1867, the Irish Church Disestablishment Act of 1869, the Education Act of 1870, the Irish Land Act of 1870 and the long struggle over the Trades-Union Laws, which was closed . . . by the Act of 1871 and 1875.[13]

In a similar vein, Arthur Balfour, the future Prime Minister, who entered Trinity College, Cambridge, in 1866 to study the moral sciences, recalled the 1860s in his autobiography as the decade of the conflict between religion and science, when the impact of German biblical criticism and Darwin's *Origin of Species* made 'every dabbler in theology and science realise these were stormy times'.[14] The court cases over *Essays and Reviews* and the Colenso affair, as well as the impact of Seeley's *Ecce Homo* were mentioned as *causes célèbres* during Marshall's undergraduate years.[15] His new friends, especially those made at Clifton College in 1865, brought such theological issues and wider social questions to his attention.

The second half of this decade was fascinating for those like Marshall who then became interested in the social and moral sciences with time to read, to study, to investigate and to discuss the many new issues the debates of the time opened up. Marshall subsequently recalled these years himself as the golden age of the Moral Sciences Tripos when some of the best young minds in the university flocked to study such issues.[16] Apart from the

---

[*]   Much of this chronology is not covered in this chapter. The economics apprenticeship from 1867 to 1875 is dealt with in Chapter 6; travels and summer vacations, including the major trip to the United States in 1875 in Chapter 7; Marshall as college lecturer at John's from 1868 to 1877 forms part of Chapter 9 while his engagement and wedding are discussed in Chapter 8.

religious controversy, educational reform issues and extension of the parliamentary franchise noted by Harrison, many other events contributed to the fighting spirit in the 1860s.

This was the heyday of the Social Science Association, a meeting place of parliamentarians, scientists, public administrators and workers seeking to secure social reform through the clarification of social issues. The Association itself had grown from 'three related movements for the wholesale reform of the legal system, the legal emancipation of women – specifically for the passage of a Married Women's Property Act to secure a woman's right to ownership and income after marriage – and for the introduction . . . of reformatory penal discipline following the end of transportation in the 1840s and early 1850s'.[17] The second half of the decade witnessed considerable revitalisation of the feminist movement. Its ending in 1869 coincided with the publication of Mill's *The Subjection of Women* and a college for women which opened at Hitchin, to eventually become Girton College, Cambridge, and an encouragement for further initiatives to extend opportunities for women's education at the universities.

The second half of the decade also saw continued strengthening of the labour movement, following on from the foundation of the International Workingmen's Organisation in 1864. In 1868 Bakunin formed the *Alliance Internationale de la démocratie sociale*; the year after the German Social Democratic Party was founded. In England, there was much agitation over trade union rights. In 1867, Karl Marx published the first volume of *Das Kapital*, the only volume to be published during his lifetime. A year later, William Morris began his literary contributions to British socialism by publishing his *Earthly Paradise*. Working-class education was not ignored in these years. Professor James Stuart from Cambridge organised the first extension courses for this purpose, a teaching initiative strongly supported by Cambridge moral scientists.

The triumphs of nationalism in Europe of this period should not be forgotten. Italy completed its unification in 1871 by the absorption of Rome as the new national capital. A unified Germany, the 'second' empire, was inaugurated by the coronation of Wilhelm I as its Kaiser in the Hall of Mirrors at Versailles. Other consequences of the German victory in the Franco-Prussian War, which Marshall experienced in Berlin, were the end of the second Napoleonic Empire in France and the short-lived Paris Commune in 1871. This, for the first time, raised the spectre of socialist revolution in Western Europe, and prepared the way for the third French Republic. In varying degrees Marshall became personally involved in several of these movements.[18]

Social, national and political revolution combined with revolution in the arts and letters and further revolution in science. In 1867, Gautier, Verlaine and Baudelaire formed Les Panassiens and the movement, *L'art pour l'art*. In 1871, the first Impressionist exhibition was held in Paris. Ibsen published his first plays, 'Brand' and 'Peer Gynt', in 1865 and 1867, and Zola's first novels began to raise a scandal in the English world. The new and the passing of the old intermingled. Dickens died in 1870, George Eliot achieved her greatest literary triumphs with *Middlemarch* and *Daniel Deronda*. Matthew Arnold published *Culture and Anarchy* in 1869 in defence of the Hellenist spirit. Some years before, Swinburne had presented a different depiction of that Greek civilisation in *Atlanta in Calydon* and *Poems and Ballads*, at the time considered scandalous works. Some of these artistic movements caught Alfred Marshall's imagination at the time, and his future wife as a student read Swinburne in secret with some of her friends.[19]

These years were equally revolutionary for a person becoming interested in economics. They included the debate over the wages fund doctrine and trade union efficacy, climaxing with Mill's recantation in the pages of the 1869 *Fortnightly Review;* geometrical illustrations in economics by the engineer Fleeming Jenkin, followed in 1871 by the publication of Jevons's *Theory of Political Economy* as a self-conscious attempt to construct a new political economy on mathematical foundations. Marshall's initial studies in economics coincided with these events.[20] This rich intellectual panorama is the backdrop to Alfred Marshall's conversion to the moral and mental sciences, which is traced in this chapter.

MATHEMATICS MASTER AT CLIFTON COLLEGE

Some time after taking out his degree in January 1865, Alfred Marshall accepted a position as temporary master in mathematics at Clifton College, then a relatively new public school.[21] This opportunity for Marshall's employment came from a turn for the worse in the respiratory illness of Charles Cay, the school's permanent mathematics master. The twenty-two-year-old graduate would undoubtedly have seized this chance with alacrity. It enabled him to earn board and living for much of the interval between graduation and election to a college fellowship in early November, hence speeding up the repayment of Uncle Charles's loan. Since temporary appointments were not recorded in the school's registers of staff and students, the precise length of Marshall's time at Clifton cannot be ascertained. It probably covered part of the first two school terms of 1865, ending in July for the summer vacation. By Michaelmas term 1865, Marshall was back in residence at John's College, housed in new rooms. The only tangible evidence of this period at Clifton is a photograph of Alfred Marshall with its 1865 masters, in which he stands capped, gowned and clean-shaven with his temporary colleagues.[22]

Brief though it was, the period at Clifton was important in Marshall's life because of the friendships it enabled him to make. Mary Paley mentioned Alfred Marshall's 'enormous veneration' for John Percival, the school's foundation headmaster and Marshall's particular friendship for two of the masters, John Mozley and Graham Dakyns. With Sidgwick examining at Clifton that summer, Marshall may also have met him at this time. These friendships need scrutiny to identify the older and wiser friends who two years later induced him to commence his economic studies.

John Percival's (1834–1918) certain influence on an impressionable Alfred Marshall in this very formative stage of this life, explains why he later held Percival in such high esteem. Percival[23] was a headmaster in the Arnold tradition, reforming, zealous in safeguarding the best interests of the boys and educationally progressive. In the early years of his appointment Percival had been very active in seeking the best possible staff for the school. When for health reasons associated with overwork, he retired from the school in 1878 while still in his early forties, he left behind him a fine institution.[24] Percival's educational interests went well beyond his position as headmaster. He was heavily involved in advancing higher educational opportunities for poor boys. He supported higher education for women assiduously: helping to establish a high school for girls at Clifton in 1876; and suggesting the creation of a Queen Victoria University for women in 1897 when women and their supporters had failed to win the right to degrees at Cambridge. He also energetically contributed to the Workers' Educational Association, the Tutorial Classes and University Extension movements.[25] Of relevance to Marshall's later academic career, Percival was actively involved in the establishment of Bristol University College during the 1870s.[26] Percival served long on its Council, and probably helped to gain his former temporary mathematics master from Clifton the position as first Principal of the College. Percival's Oxford background, with its double 'first' in Classics and Mathematics in 1858, facilitated cooperation with Benjamin Jowett in this work of establishing Bristol University College. because Jowett, an old friend and correspondent of Percival, brought in much needed financial and moral support from Oxford.[27]

Percival was a radical in his politics and extensively involved in major social issues of the day. These ranged from prevention of cruelty to animals to campaigns against the 'two great blemishes in the national life of England, the vice of drunkenness and the vice of gambling'.[28] He became a staunch defender of free trade and competition, supported schemes of imperial federation in the opening decade of the twentieth century and advocated the use of arbitration in the settlement of labour disputes and of government intervention for altering the very unequal distribution in income and wealth. In short, he was a radical social reformer Anglican clergyman of a type frequently encountered in this period.[29]

Discussion of such social issues at the social gatherings which Percival in his role as the headmaster organised for his staff in the early days at Clifton, would have left their mark on the recent mathematics graduate and unmarried temporary master. They would have introduced Marshall to factors which prevented members of the working class from leading 'a full life' and the means by which to induce 'a higher and more rapid development of human faculties', including educational reform as the means for more general social advancement. The Percivals' love of music, together with their general cultural interests, helped to fill other gaps in the education of young Alfred. After Airey at Merchant Taylors', who had opened the door to mathematics, enabling Marshall's escape from classics, Percival, as Headmaster of Clifton, may well have shown the way for Alfred Marshall to a nobler vocation, an ideal for life about which he could leisurely think after fulfilling his formal obligations to the school in teaching mathematics.[30]

Less can be said about Alfred Marshall's friendship with Henry Graham Dakyns (1838–1911). Dakyns had studied classics at Trinity College, Cambridge, from 1856 to 1860. Earlier, he had become Henry Sidgwick's 'intimate and life long friend' at Rugby where they collaborated as schoolboys in the writing of drama.[31] Subsequently, Sidgwick corresponded with him on theological issues, literature and affairs of the day, including the issues of women's education and feminism. More generally, during vacations, they travelled together in Germany and Switzerland. Hence, although no longer of the university, Dakyns remained an important part of Sidgwick's circle of friends.[32] After employment with the Tennysons as tutor for their sons, to the general satisfaction of his employers, his charges and himself,[33] Dakyns commenced teaching classics at Clifton. Subsequently he acted as housemaster until, aged in his early fifties, he resigned from the school in 1889. A description of Dakyns at Clifton in 1864, not long before Alfred Marshall befriended him, is given by the biographer of J.A. Symonds:

> Although extremely short, he was handsome and physically vigorous; sympathetic and emotional as well, he appealed to Symonds immediately. Their interests and temperaments were remarkably similar: both responded ardently to beauty, each possessed a gentleness and sensitivity which at times could sharpen into nervous irritability, and they shared a profound interest in philosophical speculation. This in Dakyns was supported by Comtism. . . . On 29 March 1864 Symonds wrote to his friend: 'You know now that to be loved is what I desire more than anything on earth. But I rarely can hope to find one so unselfish, so true, so pure as you to love me.'[34]

This description makes it easy to see how Marshall befriended Dakyns at Clifton. Dakyns's naturally friendly disposition would have drawn him to the young Cambridge graduate who joined the staff on a part-time basis in 1865, if only because of their shared Cambridge background. Marshall's youth and intelligence, combined with the recent graduate's enthusiasm and willingness to learn, would also have appealed to Dakyns. Unlike his friendship with Sidgwick and Symonds, extensively documented in reams of correspondence, no tangible evidence of Marshall's friendship with Dakyns remains, apart from the recollections of Mary Paley Marshall.[35] The potential benefits of friendship for Marshall were immense. Philosophical speculation, including an introduction to Comtist secular religion and sociology, further education in the arts about painting and music, poetry and literature, cover some of them. Encouragement to travel abroad in Germany and Switzerland, and to see for himself the beauties which this new-found friend could so eloquently describe to his other acquaintances, were others. Problems of faith and theology, especially that of dealing with religious doubts, would likewise have been part of their discussions, particularly because Sidgwick was then corresponding in detail with Dakyns on such subjects. This correspondence covered Sidgwick's re-reading of Mansel's *Bampton Lectures*, the implications of the Colenso Affair, Sidgwick's own careful biblical studies and during the period that Marshall was at Clifton, his reading of Mill's *Examination of Sir William Hamilton's Philosophy*, which had then just appeared.[36] Finally, Dakyns's friendship gave Alfred Marshall access to a Cambridge social circle which had remained closed to him while a hardworking and impecunious undergraduate. This was a circle at Trinity, Dakyns's own college and the centre of which was Henry Sidgwick, then a rising star in the Cambridge educational firmament, and a person who provided a very effective entrée into this stimulating environment for a young graduate like Marshall without connections.[37]

The third valuable friendship Marshall acquired at Clifton was that with John Mozley (1840–1932). Mozley had entered King's College, Cambridge, in 1858 from Eton, and took his degree as 12th wrangler and 5th classic in 1862. Although a fellow at King's from 1861 to 1869, Mozley had taken a job as assistant master at Clifton in 1864. He left this in the second half of 1865 to take up the appointment of Professor of Mathematics at Owens College, Manchester, thereby becoming a colleague of W.S. Jevons who, in 1866, had been appointed to its newly created Chair of Logic, Mental and Moral Philosophy.[38] When Marshall first met him at Clifton in early 1865, Mozley was a good two years older and a graduate with a double first of three years standing.

In a biographical fragment dated October 1920, Alfred Marshall recollected that he was first confronted with Mansel's orthodoxy at Clifton College and that this coincided with the time he began to question his religious faith. However, he added that he still remained orthodox in his beliefs on leaving Clifton during the summer of 1865.[39] All evidence points to Mozley as the person who introduced him to Mansel's *Bampton Lectures*. In her notes for Keynes, Mary Paley recalled him as the person who more generally steered Alfred Marshall into philosophical studies, that is, beyond those related to matters of faith, by suggesting that Marshall should read Mansel's *Prolegomena Logica, An Inquiry into the Psychological Character of Logical Processes*. In short, via Mansel's writings, Mozley generated that 'sudden rise of deep interest in the philosophical foundations of knowledge, especially in relation to theology' which helped abort earlier plans to concentrate on studies with Stokes.[40] Mozley himself in a letter to Keynes recalled the heady atmosphere of the early 1860s with respect to religious doubts. This stressed the critical impact on religious orthodoxy from various factors. In addition to Mansel's influence, these included the realisation that Genesis was not an accurate account of creation, something which Mozley ascribed to the legacy of both evolution and geological research; John Stuart Mill's remarks on the nature of modern Christianity in his *Essay on Liberty*, and the impact of biblical criticism, especially that in *Essays and Reviews*.[41] However, as discussed more fully below, Mansel's views seem to have been crucial in Marshall's change of direction in study, in the manner in which he himself described the process, and it was Mozley at Clifton who apparently put Mansel's major work into his hands.[42]

In the years immediately following Clifton, Mozley continued to exert some influence on Marshall's activities.[43] It is likely he was instrumental in getting Marshall admitted to the Grote Club, not long after he himself had been induced to join it.[44] He also appears to have introduced Alfred Marshall to the joys of Alpine mountaineering. In 1867, he and his brother were joined by Alfred Marshall for a climbing holiday in Mürren, as Mozley recollected almost fifty years later in a letter to Alfred Marshall. During this vacation they also climbed steep mountain walls in the Dolomites, a region Marshall continued to use for holidays after his marriage.[45]

Irrespective of the effects it may have had on his love of mathematics – teaching schoolboys the elements of the subject cannot have been much fun for a fresh second wrangler – the Clifton period was rich in both new experience and important friendships for Marshall. Contacts with Percival and Dakyns were renewed when the Marshalls moved to Bristol in 1877; that with Mozley had more sporadic revivals.[46] Return to St John's College in Michaelmas 1865, followed not long afterwards by his election to a fellowship, further extended Marshall's social and intellectual horizons. This nurtured the interest in social questions and the moral sciences to which he was probably first introduced at Clifton.

FELLOW AT ST JOHN'S: NOVEMBER 1865 TO JULY 1877

Marshall was back in full-time residence at St John's College from Michaelmas term 1865. On 6 November 1865 he was elected to a college fellowship, requiring reconfirmation of his membership of the Church of England, and from the beginning of 1866 moved into New Court, accommodation more in keeping with his enhanced college status. Until 1871 he occupied set 15 at the top of staircase A in New Court; in 1871 he moved to set 11 on staircase E, the rooms he kept until his marriage in 1877. Being in New Court, both sets of rooms gave him easy access to the 'wilderness' and 'the cloisters' (see Figure 4.1) where he liked to think over problems.[47] The period during which Marshall held his first college fellowship was one of reform in university and college. Its Master, Bateson, was active in the university's reform party, a former Bursar and able financial administrator, and 'one of the best and kindest of friends'.[48] Marshall's fellowship also coincided with an active rebuilding programme at St John's, involving a new Chapel, extensions to Hall, a new Master's Lodge and a new Combination Room.[49]

A Fellowship at St John's College entitled each of the 56 Fellows to important privileges. First of all, was the dividend paid to Fellows as their share of college income. Bonney, whose tenure of a fellowship at St John's extensively overlapped with that of Marshall, remembered this as a fluctuating income source. During the 1860s it rose steadily from £210 free of income tax to £300 in 1872, the maximum allowed under the College Statutes. When the effects of the agricultural depression were felt on college rents in the 1880s, these dividends started to decline. By 1894 they reached a minimum of £80.[50] For most of Marshall's initial period of fellowship they were therefore at historically high levels, giving him a level of income which speeded up his repayment of Uncle Charles's loan.

Fellows in residence in addition received a daily allowance of 4s.6d. This enabled them to defray necessary expenses of dinner, other meals, and postage charges. They were also entitled to attend the regular college feasts and to recover charges incurred with respect to visitors. Dinner for Fellows at high table was more sumptuous than undergraduate dining, but still relatively modest.

> As a rule it consisted of two courses, with cheese to follow but about twice a week it was preceded by soup or fish, a luxury introduced after 1850. On the one table, which then occupied the dais, and at which there were seats for twenty-four (with an establishment of Fellows of 56), four joints were placed. They were also served on pewter dishes, and each, as a rule, was carved by the Fellow sitting opposite, but if any one desired a second helping, which was not unusual, the dish was taken down to him by a waiter. . . . The usual vegetables were served with the joints, and on Fridays baked batter pudding with the beef. The next courses consisted of pies and puddings, varying with the season. The cheese was sent up in the old fashion – a rather large piece being put into a kind of tray, made of dark wood, running on castors.[51]

Dinner continued to start at either 4.00, 4.30 or 7.00, 7.15, the later hours when there were choral services in chapel to be attended. It was charged to Fellows on a weekly basis at 2s.1d. for the early hour, 2s.6d. or 2s.9d. for the later ones. There were two standard college feast days, on 6 May and 27 December; another feast day to mark the annual election of Fellows in November; while the college President in addition had the right to designate two feast days in Michaelmas term, one in Lent term, two in Easter term and one in the Long Vacation. Fellows could invite one guest to such feasts at the expense of the college and an additional guest at a charge of 10s.6d.

Unless a Fellow occupied a specific college position, such as Tutor, Dean (whose role included keeping order during chapel), College Lecturer, Bursar, Steward, President or

Master, his responsibilities to his college were slight. He was expected to attend chapel and to participate in the other activities of college life if he was in residence. If a Fellow of long-standing, he was likely to serve as a 'Senior' on the College Council, the college's governing body. Marshall held only two college offices in this period. In 1868 he was appointed College Lecturer in the Moral Sciences, thereby adding significantly to his annual income.[52]   He was elected College Steward on 17 March 1877, not long before his resignation as Fellow. This required him to 'superintend the purchase and supply of provisions for the public table, keep the cooks and servants to their duty, make payments as required for such purposes, and receive the sums of money due from the several members of the College, whether for Commons or other like charges'. [53]

Here was a task tailor-made for the resource-allocating economist applying his science to the management of a substantial household. Did Marshall as Steward attempt to balance the marginal utilities of cheddar versus stilton or more economically organise the provision of the college? Unlike the skilful housewife of his *Principles*, or 'the young pair' examining its annual budget, and reallocating expenditures in the light of this review, the records of St John's do not suggest that Marshall was an innovating and reforming Steward, despite the potential for reforms existing at the time in both kitchen staff management and in securing more competitive prices in purchasing supplies. Time in office, a little over six months, was perhaps too short for the application of Marshall's skills to the task of reform.[54] His successor did, however, attempt to break local monopolies in purchasing by buying from London instead of Cambridge, an experiment in management which appears to have been only partially crowned with success.[55]

For the first two years of his fellowship, that is, up to and including 1867, Alfred Marshall supplemented his fellowship income from mathematical coaching to enable more rapid repayment of the loan to Uncle Charles. During 1867 the debt was repaid and coaching, which until then occupied a sizeable slice of his day, could be abandoned.[56] Even at its maximum value of £327 as previously estimated, repayment of this loan over two and a half years would not have involved Alfred Marshall in excessive coaching. A third of his annual college dividend together with fees from half a dozen students during term would easily have wiped the slate clean over two and a half years. This even applies when additional expenses from a new life style are taken to account, such as more extensive, and later foreign, travel and the costs of building a personal library.[*]

There was plenty of time for philosophical studies, for discussion groups and for walks. It must therefore have been Marshall's inordinate appetite for acquiring philosophical understanding that made him rise at 5.00 a.m. to make his own coffee and do three hours of hard reading before teaching his private pupils. These hectic early years of philosophical study imply Marshall had forgotten the lesson imparted by that signwriter in Regent Street

---

[*]   Mary Paley recalled for Keynes that on his overseas trips from 1867 he used to take £60 to cover his expenses in what were essentially backpacking summer trips. This is discussed more fully in Chapter 7, below pp. 191–2. Books would have accounted for no more than £40 per annum at this stage of his career, since he bought books for use and not as a collector. Some of them were purchased through St John's Book Club sales, of which his copy of John Ruskin, *Time and Tide, Twenty-Two Letters to a Working Man of Sunderland on the Laws of Work*, he bought in 1870, is an example preserved in the Marshall Library.

who so impressed him as a schoolboy. He was deliberately straining his mind in this period of intellectual discovery, and in retrospect claimed this made him ill.[57]

Few new friends were made among the fellowship of St John's in these years. He did however, as Mary Paley recalled to Keynes and Keynes duly reported, enjoy the 'devotion of his gyps and College servants. He treated them like human beings and talked to them about things he was interested in'.[58] Later in life, Marshall recorded some fond memories of his association with Bateson, and of the other moral science lecturers of the college: J.B. Mayor, the first such lecturer in the university and J.B. Pearson. At this time, the last two were also members of the Grote Club.* An early manuscript notebook[59] mentions two other college Fellows: W.H.H. Hudson and T.G. Bonney.¶ His undergraduate rival Alexander Wood, who became a Fellow in 1868, does not crop up among Marshall's college intimates. Marshall therefore appears to have largely remained a loner in St John's, the Shakespeare reading group of which he was a member only excepted.[60] Generally speaking, new friends and acquaintances seem to have been made in outside activities in the various societies which Marshall joined from 1867 onwards, when mathematics teaching was no longer required for financial reasons and when moral and mental sciences were increasingly absorbing his attention. With few exceptions, his more notable friendships were made from among his students.[61]

THE GROTE CLUB, THE ERANUS SOCIETY, THE CAMBRIDGE PHILOSOPHICAL SOCIETY AND THE CAMBRIDGE 'REFORM' CLUB

From the late nineteenth century and after, the Cambridge University community bristled with discussion societies, which played a very significant part in its social and intellectual life. The Cambridge Conversazione Society, better known as 'the Apostles' or more simply, 'the Society', is perhaps the most renowned species of this genus. Its membership included many persons Marshall encountered during this period. The fact that Marshall himself had not been invited to membership as an undergraduate, the time when such invitations were made, further illustrates his lack of social connections as undergraduate at John's. Academic brilliance, school, and Jowett's opinion on Marshall's extraordinary conversational

---

* Joseph Bickerstith Mayor (1828–1916) had been admitted as sizar to St John's in 1842, was second classic in 1851 when taking his B.A., Fellow of John's from 1852 to 1864 and Professor of Classics at King's College, London, from 1870 to 1879. He was a long-standing friend of Sidgwick, perhaps because of shared school experience at Rugby. In Marshall's time he may have come up from London for occasional meetings of the Grote Club. When he was College Lecturer in the Moral Sciences, Venn does not say, but he cannot have been in that position simultaneously with Marshall. Josiah Brown Pearson (1841–95) was admitted as sizar to John's in 1860, gained a first class honours result in the Moral Sciences Tripos in 1863 and was a Fellow of St John's from 1865 to 1880. He was ordained in 1866, not long before Marshall became involved with the Grote Club, and was an unsuccessful candidate for Maurice's chair on his death in 1872.

¶ William Henry H. Hudson (1838–1916) was admitted to John's in 1857, took his degree as third wrangler in 1861, was elected Fellow in 1862 and served as mathematics lecturer in the college from 1869 to 1881; T.G. Bonney, from whose autobiography much has been quoted on life at John's during Marshall's time, became Fellow in 1859 and served as college tutor from 1868 to 1876 in succession to Hadley. Both were involved in the movement to enhance women's education at Cambridge. See below, pp. 228–9, 496.

powers,* would have made him more than eligible to join this select group of undergraduates, if social barriers including his father's occupation had not stood in the way.

The Chit Chat Club, a discussion society limiting itself to 15 members and founded in 1860, was a university society which Marshall ought to have been invited to join. Its membership drew largely on graduates associated with moral sciences and in the 1870s read like a who's who of the brightest products from its Tripos. Dilke, Carpenter and Symes were among its members in the early 1870s; Maitland was elected in 1872, the year he was Senior Moralist; Foxwell, who had gained that distinction two years previously, became an honorary member in the same year, as did William Cunningham. In May 1875, James Ward was elected. John Neville Keynes, after being a visitor at its March 1874 meeting and unwilling to accept an invitation to join the following May, later relented and joined for a year in early 1876. Later members and likewise associates of Marshall were Tanner and Leathes.[62] What is surprising from the records of this club is that during the 1870s when Marshall's credentials in the moral sciences were already substantial, he was neither invited to join nor nominated for membership by a group who at this time included several of his close friends. This shows that even among peers not expected to be hostile, Marshall was not always wanted among the company.

By 1867 some closer contacts with young intellectuals were, however, established by Alfred Marshall. Success as 'second wrangler' and subsequent election to a fellowship at St John's, built foundations for such opportunities. Clifton friendships with Mozley and Dakyns provided necessary social connections. Marshall's involvement in, and knowledge of, the moral and mental sciences further improved eligibility for several circles. In 1867, he was admitted to the Grote Club; by 1874 he was attending meetings of the Eranus Society; he gave at least one paper to the Cambridge Philosophical Society and the Cambridge Reform Club in the early 1870s; and participated with other young dons in discussing and implementing university reform.

The 'Grote Club', the first of such societies Marshall was invited to join, was named on his death after the founder of this philosophical discussion society, the Rev. John Grote, who had been Knightbridge Professor of Moral Philosophy at Cambridge from 1855 to 1866. It was 'the only thing in the nature of a speculative club or gathering in Cambridge . . . with the exception, of course, of the well known "Apostles". . . .The more regular members of this little gathering consisted of Professor Grote, J.B. Mayor, H. Sidgwick, Aldis Wright, and myself. Occasionally one or two others appeared, and after a short time J.R. Mozley of King's and J.B. Pearson of St John's joined us. . . . We used to meet once or twice a term at Grote's vicarage at Trumpington, where he hospitably entertained us at dinner, after which the evening was devoted to the reading of a paper by one of us, and its subsequent discussion.'[63]

---

*   Mary Paley Marshall, 'Biographical Notes on Alfred Marshall' (KMF). The passage in question reads: 'His extraordinary conversationalist powers, Jowett told me that he thought [Alfred] was the best talker he had ever known – though J.A. Symonds ran him hard' while earlier she had written to Keynes that she recalled a reminiscence of a fellow woman student of the early 1870s about the Sunday evenings in his rooms at John's with 'his wonderful talk and how he made the simplest subject interesting. She thinks he was the most brilliant talker she ever met and I have heard others say the same.' (undated letter, KMF).

The Rev. F.D. Maurice, as Grote's successor to the Knightbridge chair, continued with the club, which now met in the rooms of the member giving the paper. This was the practice in 1867 when Marshall was invited to participate, as he recollected in an account of the club he prepared in October 1900 for Sidgwick's biographers:

When I was admitted in 1867, the active members were Professor F.D. Maurice (Grote's successor), Sidgwick, Venn, J.R. Mozley, and J.B. Pearson. . . . After 1867 or 1868 the club languished a little: but new vigour was soon imparted to it by the advent of W.K. Clifford and J.F. Moulton. For a year or two Sidgwick, Mozley, Clifford, Moulton and myself were the active members; and we all attended regularly. Clifford and Moulton had at that time read but little philosophy; so they kept quiet for the first half hour of the discussion; and listened eagerly to what others, and especially Sidgwick said. Then they let their tongues loose, and the pace was tremendous. If I might have verbatim reports of a dozen of the best conversations I have heard, I should choose two or three from among those evenings in which Sidgwick and Clifford were the chief speakers. Another would certainly be a conversation at tea before a Grote Club meeting of which I have unfortunately no record (I think it was early in 1868), in which practically no one spoke but Maurice and Sidgwick. Sidgwick devoted himself to drawing out Maurice's recollections of English social and political life in the thirties, forties and fifties. Maurice's face shone out bright, with its singular holy radiance, as he responded to Sidgwick's inquiries and suggestions; and we others said afterwards that we owed all the delight of that evening to him. No one else among us knew enough to keep on again and again arousing the warm latent energy of the old man: for he always looked tired, and would relapse into silence after two or three minutes' talk, however eager it had been, unless stimulated by some one who knew how to strike the right chord.[64]

The account included in the Sidgwick Memoir omits an interesting autobiographical snippet. This mentioned that by 1869 or 1870, 'I had got to know some philosophy whereas in 1867 I was quite a beginner. (I had only begun to read it seriously towards the end of 1865, and had been teaching mathematics all the while.) Clifford and Moulton were still beginners.'[65]

The detailed records of meetings during 1867 which Marshall had appended to these recollections, and which were drawn from the commonplace book he kept at the time, confirm the fact that he contributed little to the debate in that year, because of his general lack of philosophical knowledge. At the 5 March 1867 meeting, for example, Marshall noted that he did not speak because he had only read 'a few pages' of Whewell's *Elements of Morality*, which was the subject for discussion. At the following meeting, held in his own rooms, Alfred Marshall read a paper on 'The Law of Parcimony', apologising at the beginning for its fragmentary nature, a sign of his limited self-confidence at this stage. However, apart from some critical comment by Sidgwick and Venn, which he handled comfortably, the paper appears to have been well received, although Sidgwick suggested later to Marshall that Maurice appeared to have been unhappy with it. By the end of 1867, at a November meeting held in Venn's rooms, Marshall was sufficiently confident to 'break in' on a conversation on Whewell with an observation on the connection between Butler and Pyrrhonism, a remark about which he later felt rather uncomfortable, believing it to have been 'offensive' to Maurice. Marshall's account of the meeting continues,

I did not play my cards well. I ought first to have said is not this the general method of Butler. Then is it not also that of Pyrrho, though the latter worked with such bad materials and made such miserable work. I did not even explain clearly that the difficulties I meant were of the practical kind, the mistakes that we made in our every day of business, &c.[66]

No accounts are unfortunately extant of the time when Moulton and Clifford attended the meetings. By then, the quality of Marshall's performances in discussion would have greatly improved, because of his more extensive philosophical study. The 1867 record only shows him as the novice in philosophy he acknowledged himself to have been thirty years later.

The records Marshall kept of these 1867 meetings also show their lighter side, reporting on the conversation over dinner and after the formal discussion of the night's paper had been concluded. For example, at the 14 March meeting, the talk was of politics, centring on reform of the suffrage then being implemented by Disraeli's new government. Remarks ranged from the likelihood of John Stuart Mill trying to press the Hare scheme of voting; the treatment by Parliament of Bright, who had so long been involved in electoral reform; Lord Cranbourne's reconciliation with Gladstone and the conservative opposition to Derby's bill. At the last meeting Marshall recorded, that of November 1867, they discussed spiritualist matters such as mesmerism (in the context of which Maurice told an anecdote about Harriet Martineau) and clairvoyance, both topics in which Maurice and Sidgwick dominated the discussion. Some gossip about plagiarism from Comte, being circulated by Frederic Harrison, drew Sidgwick's observation that comparing some passages from Isaiah and Jeremiah could lead to similar charges, the closest the record comes to any discussion of theological issues. [67]

Early meetings of the Grote Club enabled Marshall to become closer to fellow Johnians, J.B. Pearson and J.B. Mayor, both College Lecturers in the Moral Sciences.[68] Another passage omitted from the published version of Marshall's recollections of the Grote Club described Pearson as

> the chief teacher of Moral Sciences [after Sidgwick]. He was a devoted friend of J.B. Mayor, and an earnest broad Churchman. He brought many worthy, but not always able, young men, chiefly from St John's, who were preparing for Holy Orders, and thus, while maintaining the numbers of the Moral Sciences Tripos, gave it a somewhat theological tone.[69]

A theological presence more strongly marked the Eranus Society. This had been formed in 1872 by Westcott, Lightfoot and Hort, Cambridge academics and future bishops, for the purpose of interdisciplinary debate rather than theological discourse. In 1896, Sidgwick provided the following account of its functions and members for the biographer of Hort:

> its fundamental idea was that it should contain representatives of different departments of academic study, and afford them regular opportunities for meeting and for an interchange of ideas somewhat more serious and methodological than is suitable at an ordinary social gathering. Accordingly the original members included, among others, Clerk Maxwell, Seeley, [Henry] Jackson, and myself, as well as the three theologians whom I have called the nucleus. The number of the club has varied, but never exceeded twelve. It met five or six times a year in the evening at the house or rooms of one of its members. The host of the evening had the duty of reading a paper as an introduction to conversation. The range of subjects was entirely unrestricted; the general idea was that each member in turn would select a subject in which he was specially interested, and would therefore probably choose one belonging more or less to his own department of study, only not of too technical a character to be interesting to outsiders. But there was no obligation on him to choose such a subject if he preferred one of more completely general interest, such as education, politics, the mutual duties of social classes, etc.; and, as a matter of fact, we have often discussed subjects

of this latter kind. I should add that the reading of the paper was followed by conversation quite spontaneous and unregulated, not anything like formal debate.[70]

Sidgwick added that others joined the society subsequently. He mentioned Lord Acton, Professor Clifford Albutt and George Darwin, and implied that his recollection of members was by no means complete.[71] A letter by Hort to his wife in February 1874 indicates that at a meeting he addressed that month, the only absent members were Marshall, Cowell and Foster.[72] A letter in 1881 to Westcott indicates that the society by then was still active.[73] Contrary to Mary Paley's recollections for Keynes there is no record of membership of Venn, Fawcett or Clifford,[74] though Clifford as an old Apostle and friend of Maxwell would have been a likely member. Irrespective of the benefits Marshall may have received from the stimulus in the debates and conversation generated by this society, many of its members – such as Westcott, Hort, Lightfoot and George Darwin – were persons with whom he either maintained personal social contact or spasmodic correspondence on social questions.

Two other Cambridge societies with which Marshall was involved in the early 1870s can be mentioned. The first was the Cambridge 'Reform Club' at a conversazione of which he presented a paper in November 1873, dealing with 'The Future of the Working Classes'. It was published in *The Eagle*.[75] He appears also to have frequented occasional meetings of the Cambridge Philosophical Society. He presented a paper at one of these on 'The Graphic Representation by aid of a series of Hyperbolas of some Economic Problems having reference to Monopoly' while his student Henry Cunynghame demonstrated a machine for constructing such rectangular hyperbolas at the same meeting.[76] At its meetings Marshall would not only have met his more eminent colleagues in the sciences at Cambridge, but also many of the scientific luminaries of the day.

During the years Marshall became engrossed in philosophical questions, membership of the Grote Club would have been most helpful. This group included several older and wiser men, able to steer him to political economy, once his attention had been directed towards social problems and their solution. Among them were Maurice, whose Christian Socialist ideals made him fully cognisant with the importance of the subject; Pearson, who had been lecturing on it to college students; Sidgwick, who likewise was acquainted with its relevance at this stage of his career and, a person who so far has received little attention in this chapter, Henry Fawcett. In 1863, Fawcett had been elected to the chair of Political Economy at Cambridge, and this, together with his wide interests in social reform, makes him also a possible influence in directing Alfred Marshall to the subject which was to become his life's work.[77]

LOSS OF RELIGIOUS FAITH

Doubts about his religious faith some time during the second half of the 1860s appear to have been the negative factor which gradually led Marshall to the study of the moral and mental sciences which their onset generated. Personal doubts about his ability to excel in the physical sciences may be another factor, sparked by disappointment with his Tripos results.[78] Dakyns and Mozley at Clifton College were probably instrumental in starting such religious doubts by means of the philosophical discussions to which they introduced him. More specifically, Marshall's study of Mansel on Mozley's suggestion, would have opened up a whole range of epistemological, metaphysical, moral and even psychological issues. Marshall's reading concentrated on these topics for about five years after 1867, having earlier devoted much leisure time to such philosophical readings from 1865.

Mansel's writings were the most direct force in Marshall's change of intellectual direction, but their impact was undoubtedly reinforced by some of the other major factors generating unbelief and the rejection of Christian faith in nineteenth-century England. German philosophy and its impact on biblical criticism was one; the publication of Darwin's theory of evolution and the impact of other, especially geological, scientific evidence on the story of creation, was another. This dual assault on biblical truth was difficult to counter by the Anglican Church and its adherents, since its confession of faith as expressed in the thirty-nine articles was totally silent on the nature of the literal truth of scripture and its importance to faith. Absence of a definite position on this matter by those who broadly accepted these articles of faith implied that the Church could accommodate a variety of biblical positions, ranging from the most literal acceptance of every text to those humanistic interpretations which queried much of its historical accuracy and converted its gospel, in the manner of Seeley's *Ecce Homo*, to moral guidance only. The authority of scripture and Church was thereby weakened, facilitating that deliberate and conscious rejection of Christianity by Anglican intellectuals of the mid-nineteenth century. Both the doctrinal crisis inherent in the controversy over the publication of *Essays and Reviews* and the right to engage in biblical criticism which underlay the Colenso Affair highlighted a devaluation of scriptural authority to speculative knowledge. This contrasted sharply with what was increasingly seen as the certain knowledge of science. Nevertheless, irrespective of its origins, religious doubts for an intellectual in the Victorian era involved issues raised by the theory of knowledge.[79]

Despite the importance of German historical and philosophical scholarship in biblical criticism and that of evolution theory, the main inspiration to Marshall's ultimate loss of faith appears to have been his study of Mansel's *Bampton Lectures*, or to give this work its full title, *The Limits of Religious Thought examined in eight Lectures*, delivered at Oxford in 1858. The quotations from George Berkeley and Sir William Hamilton on its frontispiece reveal Mansel's strong views that the theory of knowledge lay at the heart of theological debate. Moreover, reading these lectures could easily instil in a person like Marshall a desire to further explore the philosophical and psychological issues raised by the theory of knowledge. In the 1860s religious doubt was still taken very seriously by young intellectuals. Resolving the mental conflict these doubts generated, required arduous, time-consuming study of the issues involved on their part.[*]

---

[*]   Cf. J.M. Keynes's reaction to Sidgwick's struggle with Christianity and religious doubts, during which 'He even learnt Arabic in order to read Genesis in the original' (letter to B.W. Swithinbank, 17 March 1906, in R.F. Harrod, *Life of John Maynard Keynes*, London: Macmillan, 1952, pp. 116–17.) However, Keynes's absorption in a dull memoir of Sidgwick appears to have been forgotten when he wrote his account of Marshall's loss of faith.

Mansel's *Lectures* were intended to clarify the nature and duty of Christian belief by examining the limits to knowledge from reason or thought. Right at the start, they signalled an acceptance of Berkeley's proposition that 'the objections made to faith are by no means an effect of knowledge, but proceed rather from an ignorance of what knowledge is' and an agreement with Sir William Hamilton's view, that 'no difficulty emerges in theology, which had not previously emerged in philosophy'. Even more strikingly, Mansel's intentions are shown in the preface to their first edition by approvingly quoting Berkeley's first nineteenth-century editor, A.C. Fraser: 'the theological struggle of his age, in all its more important phases, turns upon the philosophical problem of the limits of knowledge and the true theory of human ignorance.'[80] His targets moved beyond the propositions of German rationalism, that what is supernatural cannot be historical (Strauss) and that the Hegelian theory of development is the only standpoint from which the history of nations and ideas can be contemplated (Bauer and Vatke). Mansel's purpose was to 'pursue, in relation to Theology, the inquiry instituted by Kant in relation to Metaphysics; namely, *How are synthetical judgements a priori possible?*', that is, to examine the applicability of tests of experience to theological issues such as the belief in God.[81]

Mansel's discourse takes him through the limitations of the human mind to grasp the unknowable (lecture 1), the philosophical problems associated with the nature of the absolute in which he mounts a strong attack on Hegel, Feuerbach and Strauss (lecture 2, esp. pp. 43–4) and the association between the philosophy of, and the laws of the human mind (lecture 3). The analysis of reflective and intuitive religious consciousness with special reference to dependence and moral obligation as principal modes of religious intuition, because they imply conviction of the power of God and the existence of a moral law-giver, are then identified by Mansel with the goodness of God (lecture 4, which is the key lecture). Lecture 5 pursues the distinction between speculative and regulative truth, the second identifiable with religious knowledge on the basis of the argument of the previous lecture. Lecture 6 examines the nature of religious ideas on the basis of the previous argument. Lecture 7 analyses supposed moral objections to Christian doctrines in which Kant's errors in moral theory are highlighted. They also give Mansel's critical perspective on the rationalist opinions on eternal punishment.[82] Lecture 7 and the final lecture draw attention to the importance of faith as a sign not only of the operation of divine grace but also of the limits of moral reason, religious thought and the non-speculative and non-scientific nature of theology. In short, the upshot of Mansel's argument was that the human mind could neither grasp God intuitively on a priori grounds nor gain such understanding from perception and induction. Religious understanding and knowledge about God depended on revelation and belief.

Criticism of Mansel's defence of belief and revelation against reason came from several quarters. John Stuart Mill, whose theory of knowledge was based on the necessity of perception, rejected Mansel's conclusion about uncritical and unreasoned belief in searching for knowledge about God. The absence of perceived knowledge about God meant, in Mill's mind, that man possessed no evidence for believing in God.[83] A response from agnostics grounded in the physical sciences, such as Huxley, Tyndall and Herbert Spencer, agreed with Mansel's premiss that there are limits to human knowledge but disagreed with the conclusion: where knowledge is not accessible, belief cannot provide a definite answer to a rational mind and the matter at hand, knowledge of God, cannot be decided one way or the other.[84] A third response was that of Maurice, who saw Mansel's *Lectures* as an 'outrage upon philosophical method' and who was 'indignant' at Mansel's denial 'that a knowledge of the infinite is attainable by man.'[85]

The ins and outs of Mansel's theological *tour de force* need not be debated.[86] Enough has been said about the contents of his *Lectures* to reveal the invitation to hard philosophical thinking and study they offered to a person like Marshall whose acquaintance with the theory of knowledge until then had been confined to three rather limited aspects, of which the two more fundamental in his upbringing were rooted in a priori reasoning. This facet of Marshall's intellectual background needs reiteration and clarification. Marshall's first implicit introduction to epistemology came with the Anglican evangelical background of his youth, reinforced by the compulsory religious instruction at the Merchant Taylors' School. The nature and origin of religious knowledge were an essential part of this upbringing with its teaching on the authority of scripture and the importance of revealed truth. School, and more particularly undergraduate university education likewise introduced him to a second epistemological awareness: the nature and origin of mathematical knowledge, particularly in its classical form of Euclidean geometry. More specifically, the appreciation of mathematical knowledge as necessary and inevitable truth, derived axiomatically, was an aspect of Cambridge mathematical training which justified its pre-eminence in the university honours syllabus, combined as it was with the methods by which such truths could be mastered. This was a point stressed by Whewell in his defence of the value of mathematical specialisation.[87] A high wrangler in particular would have been heavily imbued by this special feature of mathematical knowledge. Apart from this practical contact with the status of knowledge from religious and mathematical training, Marshall had come to grips with more theoretical discussions of epistemology via his study of Mill's *Logic* at the monitors' table with H.D. Traill. This book dealt extensively with the proper ways of acquiring knowledge, and with methods to test its validity or truth. In particular, the young Alfred Marshall could not have missed the emphasis Mill's work gave to the different status and certainty of truths in the moral and social sciences, as against the science of nature, and to its detailed examination of the specific nature of geometrical truth.[88]

Reading Mansel's *Bampton Lectures* would have widened and deepened the epistemological perspectives of a bright graduate possessed with the type of background in the field which Marshall had by the mid-1860s. In the first place, it would have brought back to his mind some of the more difficult parts of Mill's *Logic*. More importantly, Mansel's discourse would have opened up sceptical proclivities on the nature of religious, geometrical and moral truth. In addition, Mansel's *Lectures* provided a magnificent reading list for investigating these problems further. Its references drew attention to texts in German idealistic philosophy and historical criticism, including Hegel and the young Hegelians; Kant's metaphysics and his critique of pure reason, the many writings on the philosophy of the human mind and on the theory of morals.[89] All these had to be studied if theological knowledge was to be seriously investigated. Although Marshall subsequently described Mansel's reasoning as showing him 'how much there was to defend' in religious belief, the road to that understanding to which Mansel pointed constituted the valuable part his writings played in Marshall's intellectual development. That road can be illustrated by an examination of Marshall's reading of philosophical subjects which he commenced in earnest some time during 1867.

Little can be said, unfortunately, about the precise outcome of Marshall's loss of religious faith, and the painfulness of the manner by which this process was completed. Unlike the case of Sidgwick's youthful struggles with unbelief, few clear details are available on the way Marshall's thoughts were dominated for a time by metaphysical studies before, as Keynes put it,[90] they dissolved into agnosticism and turned his mind more constructively towards ethics and the social sciences. Whether illness and the swollen right foot he recalled three decades later for Ward were the psychosomatic manifestation of a religious trauma, or simply caused by worry and overwork, cannot now be ascertained. However, once he had rejected the Christian beliefs in which he had been baptised, nurtured and almost certainly confirmed in his late teens at Merchant Taylors', he seems to have easily accommodated such absence of faith for the rest of his life. Again, unlike Sidgwick, he never seems to have suffered from continuing religious doubts, nor did he seem to have had any scruples about affirming the thirty-nine articles of faith on taking up his fellowship in November 1865 as he had done earlier on taking his degree. The last may be explained by the fact that loss of faith was not final until some time in 1874. In the context of a controversy to which Lightfoot, his fellow member of the Eranus Society, had contributed, Marshall wrote Foxwell in 1875 that by the previous year he would still have become 'excited' about such issues, 'but I became so absolutely convinced that Christ neither believed nor taught any of the leading dogmas of Christianity that I now look upon the fray with the languid interest of a mere spectator'.[91] Some days before, by way of a joke, he had sent Foxwell pages from an evangelical tract he had probably picked up at his parental home while he was nursing his mother in January 1875.[92]

Being the 'mere spectator' is the impression Marshall gave in his descriptions of church services he attended in the United States and later, during his travels in England with his wife. These present him as the detached observer of religious practices, in the manner of the student of comparative religion.[93] Details of the nature of his unbelief survive from biographical fragments written in old age, and were summarised by Mary Paley Marshall in her notes for Keynes.[94] These show a strong lack of faith in future life for a variety of reasons, an unbelief he classed with the rejection of theological dogma enshrined in articles of faith.

Marshall never rejected religion as social and moral instruction. In December 1921, Mary Paley recorded him saying that he believed more and more in religion as contrasted with theology, a view consistent with both the opinions on the utility of religion he expressed in the *Principles* and the Marshalls' membership of the Cambridge Ethical Society during the 1890s.[95] A subsequent fragment on economic ideals concerning education, opportunity and organisation of society goes so far as to conclude that such matters point 'towards the "economic religion" which claims to be a development of Christian religion appropriate to modern resources of knowledge and of organisation'.[96] Such Comte-like visions of secular religion reveal Marshall's need for a substitute religion so common in the Victorian agnostic experience once Christian belief was abandoned.[97]

One fragment in Marshall's handwriting from the late 1860s survives about the type of theological criticism Marshall himself had used in these years. It comments on Pusey's calculations[98] on the growth of population required in the 4,200 years after the flood to enable Noah's sons and their wives to produce a progeny of about 1,400 million people. Marshall demonstrated that Pusey's estimate of the required rate of multiplication was wrong. The data of the problem as stated by Pusey gave a rate of increase far in excess of the contemporary English rate. This is the only evidence available on Marshall's approach to biblical criticism as theological argument. Not surprisingly, it used his mathematical talents to make his point (much in the manner of Colenso).[99]

THE STUDENT OF 'PHILOSOPHY' FROM THE MID-1860s

Notebooks are extant which indicate the type of reading Marshall was doing from the mid-1860s and which in addition reveal other aspects of his philosophical studies. Four philosophical papers are also preserved, devoted to the theory of knowledge and psychological issues, one of which was presented at the Grote Club in early 1867. From 1868 Marshall's studies of philosophy were interwoven with his duties as College Lecturer in the Moral Sciences, hence inducing some constraints on his intellectual development from reading.

The notebooks from the second half of the 1860s contain lists of books set for study by students in the Cambridge Moral Sciences Tripos. In addition, they contain quotations, sometimes grouped under various subject headings, which likewise provide an indication of the type of material Alfred Marshall was studying at this time. At the start of the 1860s, the Moral Sciences Tripos included moral and mental philosophy (psychology), logic, history of political philosophy, political economy and general jurisprudence among the subjects on which students could be examined. The course of study to be followed was defined by means of a list of books, generally not exceeding ten in each subject area, which students were expected to master. Lists of books on moral and mental philosophy included at various times in Marshall's notebook, are given in the Appendix to this chapter.

The numerous extracts and quotations in the manuscript notebooks are identifiable with topics discussed in the four philosophical papers which he wrote at the time, while others are simply grouped by subject matter or by source. Examples of the first include quotations on the 'law of parcimony' and on the subject of man and beast (the nature of 'brutes'). Those on the 'law of parcimony' that is, 'no fact be assumed as a fact of consciousness but what is ultimate and simple', were drawn from Hamilton's *Lectures*, as is this definition. They also contained detailed cross-references to Locke's *Essay*, Bailey's *Letters on the Philosophy of the Human Mind*, Bacon's *Novum Organum*, and other books Marshall was then studying. Examples of the last are Buckle's *History of Civilisation* (specifically referred to on Reid's philosophy), Lewes's *History of Philosophy* and Mill's *Examination of Sir William Hamilton's Philosophy*.

Hobbes's *Leviathan* was used by Marshall as his major source of information on 'brutes'. It was supplemented by W. Fleming 'on laughter' from his *The Vocabulary of Philosophy*, Ferrier's *Institutes*, Aristotle (as quoted by Lewes) and Kant's *Critique of Pure Reason*. Quotations by subject matter deal with topics such as 'fundamental tendencies of the human mind', drawn largely from Hamilton and Bain; 'Self Consciousness', drawn from the same sources; and 'Genius' – national and individual – drawn from Coleridge, *The*

Friend (Section II, Essay 1) and from various eighteenth-century thinkers (Helvétius, Buffon, Cavier, Chesterfield)[100] as cited in Hamilton's *Lectures*.

At this time, Marshall also collected striking similes and metaphors in his notebooks together with other terse sayings, including some drawn from the Talmud. Their subject matter express issues of vital concern to Marshall, and some are of clear biographical interest:

> Men had learned to seek the *how* instead of the why (unattributed)
>
> Be a good hypocrite: you will never want dupes. Seem mild, cautious, religious, sincere. Be so, now and then, if you can. (Machiavelli)
>
> There are two essential causes of philosophy (i) the necessity we feel to connect causes with effects (ii) to carry up our knowledge into action. (Sir William Hamilton)
>
> Imagination disposes all things: it constitutes beauty, justice, happiness and these are the all in all the world. (Pascal, *Pensées*)*
>
> Everyman is strong enough to enforce his convictions. (Goethe)
>
> Next to exact knowledge, there is nothing so instructive as exact error. (Lewes)
>
> The profound epigram of Agassiz that the world in dealing with a new truth passes through three stages: it first says that it is not true, then that it is contrary to religion, and finally that we knew it before. (Henry Sidgwick, article on Arnold, *Macmillan Magazine* for 1867)
>
> Teach thy tongue to say, I do not know (Talmud)

A further indication of Marshall's philosophical reading in the 1860s can be gained from the references he cited in his early philosophical writings.[101] The first of these, 'The Law of Parcimony' draws heavily on the lectures of Sir William Hamilton, which provide the inspiration for the paper.[102] It also cites Mill's *Examination of Hamilton's Philosophy*, Bain's *Senses and the Intellect*, Mansel's *Prolegomena* and Ferrier's *Institutes*, works he had listed, or given extracts from, in his notebooks. In addition, its contents indicate that Marshall by March 1867 had worked through Darwin's *Origins of Species* and had studied Spencer's article, 'Mill versus Hamilton', which had appeared in the first volume of the *Fortnightly Review*.¶ The paper also refers to Condillac's *Traité des sensations*, though whether at first hand or not, is hard to say from the context.[103]

The essay on 'Ferrier's Proposition One', draws on all these references and in addition used Ferrier's article 'An Introduction to the Philosophy of Consciousness', Morell's *Elements of Psychology*, Mansel's *Metaphysics or the Philosophy of Consciousness*, Maurice's *Modern Philosophy; or a Treatise of Moral and Metaphysical Philosophy from*

---

*   This quotation from Pascal on the importance of imagination is interesting in the light of the emphasis Marshall later gave to imagination among the three required attributes for economists, that is, perception, reason and imagination, of which the last was said to be the most important. See *P* VIII, p. 43. This dated from *P* V and was derived from Marshall's *Plea for the Creation of a Curriculum in Economics and Associated Branches of Political Science*, Cambridge University Press, 1902, in *P* IX, p. 179, but in that version imagination is not ranked as strongly as Marshall subsequently did in the *Principles*.

¶   This radical and rationalist magazine had started publication in 1865, first under the editorship of George Lewes and then of John Morley. Marshall was an avid reader of this publication from its commencement and in 1876 contributed an article on Mill's theory of value. Lists of useful articles it contained during the early 1870s are preserved in the Marshall Library in his bound volumes of this journal. For a discussion of its importance to Victorian intellectual life, see E.M. Everett, *The Party of Humanity: The Fortnightly Review and its Contributors in 1865–1874*, Chapel Hill: University of North Carolina Press, 1939, especially Chapters 1 and 2.

the Fourteenth Century to the French Revolution, while it is critical of Cousin's interpretation of Locke's notion of 'reflection'.[104]

'Ye Machine', the third of Marshall's philosophical essays preserved, is largely psychological in content. Not surprisingly its main sources are Bain's two texts, and Spencer's *Principles of Psychology*. It also reveals Marshall's acquaintance with Charles Babbage's *Autobiography*.[105]

The final essay, 'The Duty of the Logician or System-maker to the Metaphysician and to the practical Man of Science', raises broad philosophical questions of methodology. It cites Kant's *Critique of Pure Reason*, Spencer's *Principles of Psychology* and Whewell's *The Philosophy of the Inductive Sciences founded upon their History*, but its background is geometrical (hence drawing on a variety of geometry texts Marshall would have used while studying for the Tripos).[106] More specifically, it focuses on the debate between Mansel and Mill on the status of geometrical axioms in the context of empirical versus extra-empirical origins of knowledge, raised in Mansel's *Prolegomena* and by Mill in his *Examination of Hamilton* and earlier in his *System of Logic*.[107]

Enumerating Marshall's reading in philosophy and associated subjects, particularly logic and psychology, is instructive in providing background to the type of work he was doing by way of self-clarification and, from 1868, in preparation of his teaching in the moral sciences. However, it cannot pretend to be a complete list of all of his reading for these formative years in the social sciences. It relies far too selectively on the little evidence which has survived from this period: a notebook or commonplace book, in part inspired by the book list for the Moral Sciences Tripos, and four essays which Marshall preserved among his papers from those he probably presented at the Grote Club.[108]

The last two of Marshall's philosophical papers, in the order they are named in this section, probably owed much to Marshall's friendship with W.K. Clifford, which started in 1868. Clifford, together with Moulton, had joined the Grote Club discussions in either late 1868 or early 1869. Both left Cambridge during the early 1870s; Clifford in 1871 to take up the Mathematics Chair at University College, London; Moulton in 1873 to pursue a very successful legal career. Alfred Marshall later recalled his 'profound admiration for Clifford' because he 'cared most for ideas . . . [while] . . . Moulton cared most for getting on in the world'.[109] By the early 1870s Clifford's ideas on non-Euclidean geometry were to have a profound impact on the end results of Marshall's studies in theory of knowledge.

THE PHILOSOPHICAL WRITINGS 1867–1869 (?)

Marshall's philosophical papers from the late 1860s were intended to illuminate some major intellectual conflicts. They were clearly inspired during his escape from religious belief through metaphysical, moral and mental philosophical studies, summarised by his search for answers to the fundamental question, 'What can I know?'.* The last of the four papers dealt specifically with this question. It examined the 'duty of the logician' in satisfying the

---

* T.H. Huxley, *Hume*, p. 48, identified this as Kant's question, that is, Kant's views on the major problem the philosopher has to solve. Kant's other two questions, 'What ought I to do?' and 'For what may I hope?', resolve into this one, ultimate question, according to Huxley.

requirements of both the 'Practical Man of Science' and the 'Psychologist', defined by Marshall as a 'sort of naturalist who, not contented with the bare existence of all the things enumerated [as logic's role], must have a theory . . . as to the mode in which they were produced'.* Marshall summarised logic's role as that of the 'surveyor' arranging the material, or agents, from which knowledge is constructed, classified under the four heads of 'requisite ideas', 'axioms and assumptions', 'powers and reasoning' and 'general methods'.[110] This paper provides the rationale for Marshall's continuing interest in the details of mental processes, his compromise conclusion on method, while in addition, it demonstrates the enormous importance he attached in these years to his study of Kant.[111]

The earlier papers deal with aspects of the functioning of the mind on a virtually purely psychological basis ('Ye Machine'), and with the subject of 'self consciousness' as consistent with the processes of mental association, when account is taken of their potential for being strengthened by the evolutionary force of natural selection. The contents of these papers implicitly reveal Marshall's cautious position on two major philosophical controversies of the period: the metaphysics of the mind–body problem and free will, as well as the virulent debate between associationists and intuitionists in explanations of mental processes, particularly in the context of the discovery of new knowledge. John Stuart Mill and William Whewell initially represented the major adversaries on these issues of a debate in which Kant's view on the subject continued to be fundamental,[112] though by the 1860s the two problems had merged into a single issue dividing authors like Bain from the more physiological psychologists such as Carpenter.

Marshall's first two philosophical papers deal with the interpretation and role of consciousness and self-consciousness as an original intuition of the mind in the ascertainment of fact. The first dealt with Hamilton's statement of the 'law of parcimony' as a law 'for the interpretation of consciousness', and already defined as stating that 'no fact be assumed as a fact of consciousness but what is ultimate and simple'. Facts of consciousness themselves are explained in terms of 'the special and derivative phenomena of mind . . . which are primary and universal'.[113] Marshall interpreted the purely phenomenal form of this law as follows. 'On the observation of any sequences of phenomena which is similar to other sequences which have been tabulated, and have thereby given rise to a phenomenal law, this newly observed sequence should be referred to the old table and not put down as the head of a new one.' Marshall argued that such a process is justified by experience, and accords with the principle that 'entia non sunt cumulanda praeter necessitatem' (Occam's razor).[114] However, he constrained the application of the 'law of parcimony' to observations and sensations which are homogeneous, thereby permitting its application to biology (Darwin's theory as the example) but not to psychology where sensations are too distinct and separate to enable use of the law. Sensations of colour and sound are dissimilar. Generally speaking, the same applies to sound and touch, though taste and smell may be fused together. This qualification of the rule is then applied by Marshall to both a criticism of its use by Bain in his analysis of the sympathetic process, and its application by Mill to

---

* Alfred Marshall. 'Duty of the Logician' in *EPW*, pp. 94–5. This follows the aphorism on the how and the why which Marshall had written in his notebooks, as quoted above (p. 119). It may also be noted that in the passage of the paper referred to, Marshall appears to identify the 'naturalist' or 'psychologist' with the metaphysician, an indication perhaps of some disillusionment with psychology at this stage.

the case of memory. In both cases, lack of homogeneity enters through the involvement of mental and physical aspects of the process. Bain attempted to eliminate this problem by completely shirking the question of self-consciousness, in the manner in which Marshall conceived it as the kind of necessary truth needed to construct chains of reasoning. This aspect of Bain's procedure was particularly deplored by Marshall. The 'law of parcimony' can also be applied to deciding the legitimate and fruitful use of analogy: Darwin's work in the *Origin of Species* was a clear case of such fruitful use. However, Darwin's method was not immediately transferable to that of the mental science of psychology. Only in cases where there is direct evidence of the evolution of a certain psychological element can this method be applied to mental process. This can be seen as an application of the 'law of parcimony' and demonstrates Marshall's initially cautious attitude to Darwinism as an aid in understanding the social sciences.[115]

Marshall's second paper dealt with 'self-consciousness' as an essential feature of man, distinguished from brutes. This was in fact a discussion of Ferrier's first proposition that, 'along with whatever any intelligence knows, it must, as the ground or condition of its knowledge, have some cognizance of itself'.[116] Ferrier's Proposition One as a synthetic, symbolic statement of the idealists' position with respect to the scientific treatment of man, can therefore be seen as a banner against the growing claims of Associationism of which Bain and Mill were the leading representatives, even though in Bain this was increasingly merged with psycho-physiological explanations. In his treatment of Bain and Ferrier, Marshall adopted a position derived from Grote. This saw the two positions as different rather than as opposites, the one grounded in the extreme physiological or physical, the other in the philosophical. Marshall indicated that he could accept many of Bain's explanations of habits and combinations of actions, of correspondences between impressions and the revivals of past impressions, all developments of the faculty of association perfectly explicable in terms of the processes of mere mechanism. However, other factors needed explanation in terms of the subjective Ego, Ferrier's 'self consciousness', such as memories and expectations. On these, Marshall thought that Bain's explanations were weaker. In short, Marshall saw truth in both Bain's and Ferrier's position in what they confirmed but not with respect to what they denied, a position which became characteristic of him in fields other than philosophy.[117]

The study of self-consciousness as ego and its relation to the external world underlying the first two philosophical papers, involving as it did problems of memory, sense fusion and sense perception in general, explains the purpose of a number of factual observations Marshall recorded in his notebooks at this time.[118] These are interesting to indicate how seriously Marshall perceived his psychological studies and are therefore quoted at some length.

In performing many actions and in taking part in many conversations, an irresistible (but generally erroneous) conviction arises that the same scene has been passed through before, under the same circumstances; and the same words having been frequently used on both occasions. Hudson[119] has not only remarked this himself, but says that everyone to whom he has talked on the subject has done the same. Question: Is this experience very common and how far is the conviction erroneous?

My hand had been supporting my chin. I put it to my forehead and had a sensation of intense warmth. My first impression was that my forehead was warm. But I speedily perceived that it was my hand which was strikingly hot. I however did not feel comfortable till I had verified this by putting my hand to my chin and again to my forehead. X? To be accounted for by the fact that I put my hand in that position to ascertain anything about warmth it is generally my forehead that is the subject of observation.

Bonney[120] looked at a man [Mor Sci] whose head was turned completely away from him. He turned around and in explanation said that he could always feel when another was looking at him. Even this is not conclusive testimony that the 'feeling' operates when the eyes of the looker are behind those of the looked. This particular case might have been accidental.

When putting away books, etc. before going to bed my eye fell on my watch lying on the table. The thought passed through my mind that I must take it into my room with me. I then closed [the] book with my left hand (my pocket kerchief was in my right) carefully putting a mark in it and thinking about using it next morning. Thus the idea of the watch was not present to my consciousness at all. When I turned from the book my attention was roused by the fact that my waistcoat watch pocket would contain no more of my kerchief I had rammed half in. N.B. I was not sleepy.*

These observations also indicate Marshall's cautious attitude to the use of experience as evidence in generalising about the nature of sense perception, thereby confirming the critical perspective he expressed in the two papers on the type of empiricism advocated by Mill.

'Ye Machine', which Marshall himself envisaged as a prelude for 'a general theory of psychology . . . capable of being developed into the true one'[121] is a direct continuation of the argument from the previous two papers. It elaborated those aspects of Bain's theory which Marshall considered to be correct. These related to the more mechanical aspects of associationist explanations which contrasted with the human attributes of the problem so usefully captured in Ferrier's Proposition One on the meaning of the self-conscious.[122] Pursuing the very substantial element of truth in Bain's position enabled Marshall to attempt construction of the mechanism of the human mind. This construction therefore relied on associationist and evolutionist neuro-psychology and neuro-physiology, that is, Grote's 'physical', so evident in the work of Bain and Carpenter as distinct from the 'philosophical' Grote saw in Ferrier. This indicates that Marshall's foot was not nearly as firmly planted in the idealist camp as his support for Ferrier's first proposition, and sympathy with Kant's position,[123] would suggest.[124] The complexities of the argument of the paper, demonstrating as it does Marshall's grasp of contemporary neurological explanation and the origins of mental automatism, need not be gone into.[125] What is important in this context are the implications it appears to have had for his subsequent intellectual development.

The paper purports to shed light on the mechanical aspects of the nature of sensations, ideas, actions, the relationship between repetitive action and memory, reasoning, deliberation and volition. Ideas are described as the province of the brain; actions, of the body. Marshall's explanatory circuit links sensations (like pressure, light, sound) to ideas of sensations. These induce ideas of action and these in turn cause action. Repeated performance of an idea or set of ideas constitutes memory. Repetition may be direct, or induced by an association of ideas, either through contiguity (thunder and lightning) or

---

* Two other observations recorded in this section of the notebooks have been omitted. One deals with the acquisition of the habit of soft breathing by watchmakers, the other comments on the seemingly inaccurate observations on the nature of waterflow Marshall overheard being made by two boys. This transformed a steady outflow from a pipe into a periodic emission of a bucketful of water from the pipe. The final observation in the text resembles a visual memory experiment recorded by Mill in his *Examination of Sir William Hamilton's Philosophy*, pp. 192–3 in the context of his discussion of the psychological theory of belief in the external world (Chapter XI).

similarity (a sensation of sound recalling sensation of a like sound). Brain (ideas) and body (action) of the machine are represented by wheels connected by bands (the nervous system) or some other motor agency like electricity or magnetism. Mediation involves complex transmission of motion; pleasurable and painful ideas and actions of the machine can be distinguished by the type of motion they cause, conflicting motions induce deliberation, volition is implied in a predominant motion.[126] Marshall then expands the analysis to consider more distinct results (actions), examines the types of habits a machine can acquire under certain conditions, and introduces the distinction between cerebrum and cerebellum to enable reasoning in the machine. Expectations of changes in the environment (the source of sensations) are then introduced, together with the notion of rapid, complex, simultaneous motions, akin to those of the chess automaton and the automaton proposed by Babbage. This possibility in mechanical action is compared with human ability (mental power) generally confined to one calculation at a time.[127]

In the final sections of the paper, Marshall extended his machine's powers by liberal education. This gave the machine access to language and communications, numbers (arithmetical operations) and ultimately geometry. It also enabled Marshall to introduce some limitations to the power of the machine, and hence to the mechanical and exclusive application of associationist psychology in the explanation of mental processes. Abstract symbols as used in algebra or in complex numbers cannot be grasped and processed by the machine.[128] A similar limitation is applied to its ability in painting. Although painting was capable of being raised by the machine to the highest degree of technical excellence, it would never be able to penetrate 'the secret springs of action' and therefore never be able to reflect these in its 'art'. Such limitations need not apply to the machine's ability in creating music, or in its study of mechanics, and practical chemistry, geology, biology and psychology. This implies a further limit to the machine's ability since for the last three sciences Marshall conceived the practical side to be rather small. The paper's final step suggests the potential for moral education of the machine via sympathy and systematised experience. This capacity is enhanced by natural selection and may be greatly developed by means of that 'sixth sense, always probably latent in man, and now coming prominently forward' by which Marshall meant the 'so-called electrical states of other persons and things'.[129]

The extensive powers accorded to the machine (instilled though they were by the simple motives of pleasure and pain, and the sympathy incited by giving pleasure) show the extent of Marshall's departure from philosophical idealism, and his proximity to the thought of Bain and Carpenter. Some room, however, remains for Ferrier's idealist notion of self-consciousness in the important mental attributes of speculative and creative thought not accessible to the machine. Relative to its associationist and evolutionist psychological content, the role for metaphysics for Marshall is thereby substantially minimised in explanations of the mind's operation. Furthermore, Marshall's retention of a strong physiological foundation in the depiction of his mechanical mind enabled him to maintain some role for volition and deliberation (free will) and to provide a solution to the controversy between a priori and empirical knowledge by the limitations he gave to his machine. Preserving some room for an idealist conception of 'self consciousness', meant that Marshall did not *completely* embrace the radical empiricism of Mill and his followers.

The limits to a priori and such empirical knowledge are the subject matter of Marshall's final philosophical paper.[130]

Although still within the theory of knowledge, and hence intimately connected with the three previous papers, Marshall's final philosophical paper has far less psychological orientation, even though it ostensibly deals in part with the duty of the logician to the psychologist *qua* metaphysician as compared with the man of science. Once again, however, the battle to be observed is that between the a priori, idealist position now firmly represented by Kant rather than by Hamilton, Ferrier or Mansel,* and the associationist, physiologically and neurologically empiricist position presented by Mill and Bain. The battlefield is now geometry, its axioms being the most obvious examples of synthetic and certain propositions. Marshall would have imbibed this with his mathematical training, influenced as it was indirectly by Whewell's views with its Kantian a priori proclivities. Mill and Bain, on the other hand, explained the wide acceptability of geometrical axioms through past experience and the association of ideas, and thereby disproved an explanation of a priori origin of such axioms by superseding it.[131]

Spencer's evolutionist philosophy once again allowed Marshall to maintain a role for the a priori and at the same time admit the importance of the associationist position based on experience. The evolutionary content in Spencer's thinking permitted an explanation of confidence in the verities of geometry by experience where such confidence was not only formed with experience but also from experience. This perspective enabled Marshall to rearrange his definitions and axioms to make them compatible with both philosophical positions. Such axioms had to be constructed according to criteria of economy, distinctiveness and intuitiveness but they needed also to be capable of leading to the construction of the defined things out of the given ideas.[132] In this manner, continued co-existence of the 'law of parcimony' with associationism was ensured.

Marshall's paper is on the verge of the debate triggered by the discovery of 'non-Euclidean geometries.'[133] As Helmholz argued, these could 'refute the claim that the axioms of geometry are in Kant's sense necessary consequences of a transcendental form, given a priori, of our intuition'.[134] Marshall's friend Clifford was in fact one of the early English mathematicians to be aware of these philosophical implications of the new discoveries, implications which Marshall appears to have quickly absorbed, perhaps because he himself had already been moving intuitively towards them. One of the new geometry's propositions was the postulate that parallel lines may meet, hence disproving the generality of Euclid's fifth postulate and suggesting the possibility that space was curved. This opened up opportunities for quite distinct geometries, none of which could be held to be a priori correct, because all were constructed on valid, logically sound bases. Living on a sphere, as the earth is, suggested more empirical criticism of Euclidean propositions. Between the North and South pole, an infinite number of lines could be constructed (the earth's longitudes) contrasting with the Euclidean proposition which admitted the possibility of

---

* This first explicit use of Kant's views in a paper by Marshall suggests that it was possibly written after the summer of 1868, which he had partly used to learn German in Dresden in order to read Kant in the original rather than in translation. Style, and confidence in the manner with which the argument is expressed, likewise suggest a reasonable interval between March 1867 and the completion of this paper. Marshall's depth of philosophical understanding is visibly greater. See Raffaelli, introduction to *EPW*, p. 31.

only one line between two points on flat space. In his paper, Marshall was not able to call attention to such startling propositions, of which he only later became cognisant.[135]

THE HARVEST FROM MARSHALL'S EXCURSUS INTO THE THEORY OF KNOWLEDGE

Marshall's journey into the theory of knowledge, initially inspired by the religious doubts sown through his reading of Mansel's *Bampton Lectures*, had a number of important consequences for his later career. The only solid evidence from which such consequences can be inferred are the four philosophical papers and the extracts from his contemporary notebooks examined in the previous sections, combined with the more limited information on the impact of new friends and the new career opportunities offered by the Moral Sciences Tripos. Why mathematics and study with Stokes was abandoned by Marshall after his Tripos result can only be guessed at. New intellectual horizons opened up by religious doubts and associated study, combined as they were with teaching career opportunities at Cambridge outside of mathematics, may have made the erstwhile plans less attractive. Stokes's strong Christian beliefs, when Marshall was losing his, may also have influenced the decision.[136] Coming second to Rayleigh in the Mathematical Tripos and advice from his examiners, may have generated fears of an inability to do original research in physics. Such factors made the alternative of 'straying' into moral and mental sciences perhaps even more appealing. New friends and religious doubts not only widened intellectual horizons within the moral sciences; this intellectual exposure combined with Percival's influence at Clifton, subsequently reinforced by contact with Maurice, Sidgwick and Fawcett, may have given an impetus to the new studies from a desire to do good through social reform.* The last would be pure speculation but for Marshall's recollections on the subject preserved from old age.

The evidence from the philosophical papers and notebooks does, however, enable some firmer conclusions about career direction by showing why Marshall may have eliminated certain subjects of further study. They also have methodological implications, aiding the understanding of his later intellectual work.

One clear inference from the content of Marshall's philosophical work is his growing impatience with metaphysical inquiry. Ultimately this turned into a strong dislike for such studies, visible in the 1880s and 1890s in Marshall's attitude to educational reform within and without the Moral Sciences Tripos. Metaphysics is of course not easy to define. The dual definition given by Marshall's later correspondent, Edward Caird,[137] provides a double reason for Marshall's later intense dislike of the subject. Caird firstly defined metaphysics as the 'science of the principles presupposed in all being and knowing'; the other meaning he gave it was that of 'theology, or the science of God'. Marshall's dislike of theology was mentioned earlier. His systematic reduction of the importance of Caird's first definition,

---

*   During the summer of 1866 Marshall had been touring Scotland, en route perhaps investigating the conditions of the poor in the industrial cities of the north. Percival, for reasons already explained in this chapter, Maurice, Sidgwick and possibly Fawcett, are all potential candidates for being those older and wiser men who, he later recalled, introduced him to the study of social problems and the relevance of political economy thereto, as discussed more fully Chapter 6, below, pp. 143–4.

vis-à-vis associationist and evolutionist psychology, has just been extensively documented from his philosophical papers. Once religious doubts were settled by abandonment of Anglican faith and the theory of knowledge by the neuro-psychological approach of 'Ye Machine', Marshall could effectively relegate metaphysics to a study fit only for idealist clergymen.

Reasons for the ultimate rejection of psychology as a suitable field for a future career can also be inferred from the contents of Marshall's philosophical papers, and are important given his later claims about love for the subject. In a letter to James Ward, Marshall indicated it was not until 1871–72 that he abandoned psychology for economics after a hard struggle.[138] Mary Paley recalled that 'at one time, he [i.e. Marshall] would have liked to devote himself to the subject of "attention", on which depends the power of "concentration"', a subject not unrelated to the type of inquiries he pursued while writing 'Ye Machine'. More striking is her recollection of the remark made by Marshall at the end of their 1923 Christmas dinner, during which 'he had been unusually silent'. This reflected the exact nature of his philosophical speculations at the Grote Club more than fifty years previously. 'I have been considering the relation of Psychology to Ontology. If I had time to live my life over again, I should have devoted it to Psychology. Economics has too little to do with ideals'.[139]

Contrary to these later recollections, effective abandonment of psychology as a career path may well have been earlier than the years 1871–72 mentioned to Ward. The shift away from pure psychology between his third and fourth philosophical paper suggests this step could have been taken as early as 1869.* Recall the high hopes of building the foundations for a new, perhaps 'the true psychology' he expressed to his audience at the Grote Club before presenting 'Ye Machine', and while it must already have been in an advanced stage of preparation. Nothing is heard of such hopes in the later paper, which returns to an area of his more proven skills, mathematics, albeit in relation to philosophy. Had he realised in the meantime that his psychological paper was simply 'following a trodden path'[140] rather than breaking substantial new ground, and that pursuit of the topic broached by 'Ye Machine' required skills in experimental psychology he simply did not possess? After all, Bain and Spencer, Marshall's major sources for 'Ye Machine', had driven the speculative aspects of the topic as far as it would go. The next step forward, as Young[141] has argued, required practical biological and physiological knowledge combined with experimental skills. In 'Ye Machine', Marshall confessed his lack of expertise in these subjects.[142] His subsequent realisation of its implications, may have effectively closed the door on further serious work in psychology as a subject to which he could personally contribute. This fits his 1920 recollection. Economics, as the subject 'most neglected by academic students' became an effective choice because psychology had to be abandoned despite 'its good practice of

---

* Although the dating of these philosophical papers cannot be precise, 1869 seems not an inappropriate date for the final paper, given the fact that Marshall's notes on the proceedings of the Grote Club, which cover nearly the whole of 1867, only mention his 'Law of Parcimony'. The other two papers are therefore likely to have been presented during 1868, Marshall in later life gave 1871–72 and 1872–73 as the years when he finally abandoned psychology, but it seems more likely that these were the years when he finally committed himself totally to economics. It is interesting to note that in the early 1870s, on Mary Paley's account (*What I Remember*, p. 18), Sidgwick was lecturing on mental philosophy, not Marshall.

progressive and suggestive studies of human nature and its possibilities'.[143] As Whitaker strikingly put it in his brief description of this part of Marshall's life, 'Economics' gain . . . exceeded . . . Psychology's loss'.[144] and his interests in psychology were gradually allowed to fade away to make room for an increasingly dominant interest.

The contents of his philosophical papers also point to a shift in method. They deprecate the value of pure speculation and intuition while raising the importance of empiricism and the gathering of facts. The major conclusions of the final philosophical paper particularly point in that direction. These rejected the universal validity of a priori and axiomatic statements, a position reinforced from the philosophical implications of the non-Euclidean geometry to which Clifford probably introduced him, while stressing the value of experience in knowledge acquisition. By the start of the 1870s he appeared to be particularly 'greedy of facts', a quality he continued to stress as crucial for the economist.[145]

One of the more peculiar manifestations of this lust for facts may be mentioned here. By the early 1870s, Mary Paley recalled, Marshall had 'made a collection of portraits, grouping them by their occupations – poets, musicians, artists, statesmen and by this means he hoped to make some generalisations which would enable him to discover the characteristics of such [persons] but he could not come to any valuable conclusions.'[146] This portrait collection can still be seen in the Marshall Archive. It comprised fifty sheets containing a maximum of ten portraits each, classified chronologically, by nationality, and by occupation. Over twenty sheets are devoted to statesmen (including royalty), four to musicians (composers), seven to painters, seven to poets, three to writers, five to divines and one each to historians, sculptors and artists. They even include the characters in the Passion Play at Oberammergau he had attended in 1871.*

Another manifestation is the 'Red Book' he constructed in 1875, 'arranged so that if a pin were run through its many pages at any given year the pin hole would show what was happening that year in Philosophy, Art, Science, Industry, Trade, etc.'[147] Walter Layton described this in his 1905 lecture notes as follows: 'Marshall has prepared a huge statistical history – if a pin is placed through a given year, it gives all the statistical information that is known about that year. Sovereigns of Europe, Political History of England, Inventions and Industry Progress, Agriculture, His. Statistics, shipping, rents, exp[or]ts, imp[or]ts of different countries, wages, trades unions, prices.'[148] This was Marshall's home-made solution (prepared with some assistance from Mary Paley Marshall) to the problem of solving the complex statistical interrelationships of many variables by inspection, as he later explained to several persons.[149] It can be seen as a practical reflection of his motto, 'The One in the Many, the Many in the One', designed to illustrate the complexity of the subject

---

*   The portraits of miscellaneous writers, which altogether make up three sheets in the collection, may serve as an example: sheet 1 contained La Fontaine (2 portraits), Charlotte Bronte, Balzac, Winckelman, Samuel Johnson, David Garrick, Richter, Mme de Stael, Chateaubriand; sheet 2, Dickens, Heine, Berthold Auerbach, George Sand, Thackeray, Carlyle (2 portraits), Trollope, Kingsley and Mrs Margaret Gatty; sheet 3, Ruskin (2 portraits), Nathaniel Hawthorne, Dr Livingstone, Miss Ethel Dahlen, G. McDonald, G.E. Casual, Mrs Stowe, Miss Sarah Cobbe and Mark Twain. Marshall's favourite novelist, Walter Scott, is included among the poets, where Heine was also appropriately included. The pictures do not seem to have a specifically phrenological purpose, as I first thought on reading about this collection, if only because they are too diverse to make reasonable observations of the shape of the skull. An amateur phrenological intent fits in well with Marshall's fascination with psychology in the 1860s. Another speculation on their purpose is offered below, Chapter 6, p. 143, Chapter 7, pp. 201, 213.

and therefore the difficulty in drawing simple statistical inferences in economics. As he told J.B. Clark in his year of retirement from the Cambridge chair, the search for facts was the difficult thing in economics if designed to make theory realistic, hence his choice of reading matter was by then largely confined to books with facts.[150]

Apart from Marshall's philosophical predilection for facts, the end of the 1860s and early 1870s more generally marked a changing attitude to history. In Cambridge, this is visible in the appointment in 1869 of Seeley to the Regius Professorship as successor to Kingsley. Although Seeley was vetted before his appointment for possible Comtist tendencies, his programme of history as a 'practical subject' allied to the 'kindred subject of political economy' gave a new importance to the subject in its role as providing training for leaders of the nation.[151] For several years in the early 1870s, Marshall himself embraced this new historical spirit, and in these years devoted much time to historical inquiry.

The contents of the philosophical papers provide no direct information on these historical studies, but sections of the contemporary moral sciences syllabus, so far not mentioned, provide some clues, as do his notebooks of the period. Among the books prescribed for moral sciences students were works such as Montesquieu's *L'Esprit des Lois*, Guizot's *History of Civilization*, Hallam's *Middle Ages* and his *History of Representative Government*. The 1862 Cambridge student handbook also drew attention to the publication of two more recent, and valuable books for students of jurisprudence: a new edition of Austin's *Lectures* and Maine's *Ancient Law*.[152] Marshall cited all these books in his writings of the period, while his reading of Buckle's *History of Civilization in England* (at least with respect to its account of Reid's philosophy) has already been noted. It was also during this time that he fell under the spell of Hegel's *Philosophy of History*.[153]

Neither do the contents of these papers highlight his strong interest in ethics and moral philosophy at the time. Marshall's notebooks contain many references to works on moral philosophy, of which the reference to Bentham's *Principles of Morals and Legislation* is the more important. Likewise, the proceedings of the half dozen or so meetings of the Grote Club he recorded in 1867 show that ethical topics featured frequently in both their formal and informal discussion. After 1868, both logic and ethics were added to political economy among the subjects Marshall taught as college lecturer, while Mary Paley recalled lectures on moral and political philosophy among his teaching in the early 1870s, the subject matter of which was largely devoted to Bentham's and John Stuart Mill's utilitarianism.[154]

One further manuscript fragment of this period can be mentioned. This is an unfinished dialogue on poetry, 'both a tribute to Kant and an implicit assertion of the relations between poetry and science'.[155] Ostensibly a defence of the modern school of poetry against the classic and, with references to the contemporary situation, of Browning against Tennyson, it enumerates the desirable qualities of good poetry in the eyes of the young protagonist. The participant in the dialogue defends the modern with 'all the uncompromisingness of youth' and it is with him that Marshall presumably wished to be identified. The subject of good poetry must be man, 'in the full power of his weakness, in the full glory of his humiliation, in the full triumph of his failures, in the full peace of the struggles, in the full life of his death', in short, 'man as he lives in the strong energy of becoming – Goethe's "werden", . . . with eyes ever fixed on the measureless blue beyond.' Style is seen as less important to good poetry.* It may be written in prose or verse, but the 'essence' of poetry, 'metaphors and illustrations', must be present to 'give clear and strong impressions'. 'The poet's voice must give no uncertain sound' and must have 'something to say which is clear and definite'.[156] Imagination and the unknown, link poetry with science and Kant, whose lesson of the intrinsic limits of the human condition Marshall was never to forget. A biographical fragment dated October 1920 records this clearly: 'Influence of Neo-Platonism on later creeds. The letter kills. The spirit gives life. Kant my guide: the only man I ever worshipped: but I would not get further; beyond seemed misty'. [157]

Apart from the influence of Kant, these autobiographical jottings just quoted recall the mottoes Marshall later placed on the frontispiece of his two major books, but which he discovered during this formative period. *Natura non facit saltum*, the motto of the *Principles*, derived from Kant according to Walter Scott,[158] and his adaptation of *The Many in the One, and the One in the Many* (that of *Industry and Trade*) from Plato's record in *Philebus* of Socrates' saying that a true understanding of the One in the Many was the gift of heaven to man. Mary Paley's recollection that he went to Dresden in 1868 to learn German in order to read Kant in the original has already been noted, as is the story that during these years Kant's *Critique* and other philosophical works were his companions on solitary mountain hikes in the summer.¶ The postgraduate period is therefore particularly important for understanding his later life. Apart from ultimately giving him his true vocation, it provided the philosophical foundations for the future work his new vocation implied. The aim was later presented in the story about his 'patron-saint': 'I saw in a shop window a small oil painting [of a man with a strikingly gaunt and wistful expression, as of "one down and out"] and I bought it for a few shillings. I set it up above the chimney-piece of my room in college and thence forward called it my patron-saint, and devoted myself to trying to fit men like that for heaven.'[159]

NOTES

1.   Layton Papers, Trinity College, Cambridge (Layton, Box 15, 15^b, p. 25).
2.   John Maynard Keynes, 'Alfred Marshall', pp. 166–7.
3.   Cited in Keynes, 'Alfred Marshall', p. 171.
4.   Alfred Marshall to James Ward, 23 September 1900, in *Memorials*, pp. 418–19. Marshall's claim about a swollen foot from mental strain and fatigue is hard to believe on the basis of present-day medical knowledge. Similar symptons were reported by Charles Darwin in a letter to Hooker circa 1859 (cited in Adrian Diamond and James Moore, *Darwin*, London: Penguin Books, 1992, p. 475).
5.   Mary Paley Marshall, 'Biographical Notes on Alfred Marshall' (KMF). W.K. Clifford (1845–79) was a student at Trinity College, a second wrangler in 1867 and was elected to the Cambridge 'Apostles' in November 1866 as member No. 165; J.F. Moulton (1844–1921) was a student at John's, senior wrangler in 1868 and was elected

---

*   It is not known whether this dialogue was written at the same time when Marshall made his own attempts at poetry, of which Mary Paley showed a then surviving sample to Keynes. See above, Chapter 2, and note 37.

¶   Mary Paley Marshall, 'Biographical Notes on Alfred Marshall' (KMF). She adds that when Marshall began his German lessons, he insisted on starting with Kant. 'His teacher objected to such an unsuitable book for a beginner, but he answered, 'If it were not for Kant, I should not be learning German'. English translations of Kant were of course available at this time, and the Moral Science Tripos recommended the Bohn edition, from which Marshall in fact quoted in his writings, as Raffaelli has pointed out to me in correspondence.

to the Apostles in June 1867 as member No. 166. Thomas Moss (1845–72) was a student at John's admitted in 1864, the same year as Moulton, fourth classic in 1868, a Fellow of John's from 1868–72 and died in New Zealand in 1872. Data from Venn, *Alumni Cantabrigienses*, *D.N.B.* and Paul Levy, *G.E. Moore and the Cambridge Apostles*, Oxford University Press, 1981, p. 307.

6. Mary Paley Marshall, 'MSS Notes' (NCA).
7. Mary Paley Marshall, 'Biographical Notes of Alfred Marshall' (KMF). It is discussed below, pp. 112–13.
8. A.S. and E.M.S., *Henry Sidgwick. A Memoir*, p. 137.
9. With the Sidgwick Papers at Trinity College, Cambridge, Add MS c. 104 65 (17).
10. Mary Paley Marshall, 'Biographical Notes on Alfred Marshall' (KMF).
11. An 'angel' was an Apostle in residence at Cambridge, absolved from attending all meetings during term. See Paul Levy, *G.E. Moore and the Cambridge Apostles*, esp. pp. 65–8
12. In the late 1860s and early 1870s Marshall published letters in the *Cambridge Gazette* (2, 9 December 1868, 14 April 1869, 10 November 1869) and in the *Cambridge University Reporter* (22 February 1871). In the first, he commented at length on proposals to reform the Previous Examination, while the last discussed the issue of celibacy among members of a college. A letter to the *Cambridge University Reporter* and a fly sheet addressed to the members of the University Senate (1 March 1871 and 22 May 1872) further debated issues in the Previous Examination, particularly the importance assigned to it of classics.
13. Frederick Harrison, *Realities and Ideals: Social, Political, Literary and Artistic*, London: Macmillan, 1908, pp. 369–70.
14. A.J. Balfour, *Chapters of Autobiography*, ed. Mrs. Edgar Dugdale, London: Cassell, 1930, p. 51.
15. Above, Chapter 1, p. 12.
16. Marshall to Foxwell, 14 February 1902 (Marshall Archive, 3:44).
17. L. Goldman, 'The Social Science Association 1857–1886', *English Historical Review*, January 1986, pp. 95–134, esp. pp. 97–9; and his 'A Peculiarity of the English? The Social Science Association and the Absence of Sociology in Nineteenth Century Britain', *Past and Present*, No. 114, February 1987, pp. 133–71, esp. p. 138.
18. Marshall's involvement with women's issues in general is discussed in Chapter 14 below; with socialism and the labour movement in Chapter 16 below, while his perspectives on the Franco-Prussian War are mentioned especially in Chapter 17, pp. 640, 642–3.
19. Marshall's literary tastes including that for George Eliot's novels, are discussed in Chapter 21 below, p. 772. Mary Paley Marshall recalled her readings of Swinborne in notes she prepared for Jane Harrison's biographer in the 1930s (NCA). Marshall defended Swinborne to Emerson in 1875 (below,p.196), and cf. below, pp. 129–30 for reference to Marshall's remarks on poetry.
20. Discussed at length in Chapter 6 below, pp. 145–54 and esp. pp. 158–60 on Jevons's *Theory of Political Economy*.
21. John Rickard Mozley, *Clifton Memories*, Bristol: J.W. Arrowsmith Ltd., 1927, p. 184, in which Mozley mentions that the teaching position at Clifton was the start of Marshall's career; O.F. Christie, *A History of Clifton College 1860–1934*, Bristol: J.W. Arrowsmith, 1935, p. 48, mentions his appointment was a temporary replacement for the sick Charles Cay.
22. Reproduced as illustration 13 from the *Jubilee Album Clifton College 1862–1912*, Bristol: Van Dyk Printers, 1912, photograph 8.
23. Much of the following draws on William Temple, *Life of Bishop Percival*, London: Macmillan, 1921, supplemented on occasion from his entry in the *DNB*.
24. Temple, *Life of Bishop Percival*, pp. 17–19, 34.
25. Temple, *Life of Bishop Percival*, pp. 41–2, 258, 259, 276–7. His services to worker education were described by his biographer (*ibid.*, p. 283) in the following terms: 'To have done something really effective towards opening to the common people the treasure house of beauty and wisdom is the true crown of Percival's never-ceasing efforts on national education.' As shown below, Chapter 18, p. 661, Mary Paley Marshall served on the Council of this girls' school in Clifton.
26. Temple, *Life of Bishop Percival*, p. 53 and see John Whitaker, 'Alfred Marshall: the Years 1877 to 1885', *History of Political Economy*, 4 (1), Spring 1972, pp. 1–5. Marshall's period at Bristol is discussed in detail in Chapters 8 and 9 below, pp. 230–7, 275–93.
27. Temple, *Life of Bishop Percival*, pp. 259–64; his friendship with Jowett was formed at Oxford, and Jowett was a loyal correspondent during Percival's headmastership at Clifton (*ibid.*, pp. 32–4). Marshall's friendship with Jowett is discussed in detail below, Chapter 18, pp. 687–95.
28. Temple, *Life of Bishop Percival*, pp. 225–34, the quotation is from p. 225.
29. Temple, *Life of Bishop Percival*, pp. 238–57. Later in life, Marshall may have possibly influenced his former mentor on some of these economic issues. And see G. Kitson Clark, *Churchman and the Condition of England 1832–1885*, London: Methuen, 1973, esp. phase III.

30. Temple, *Life of Bishop Percival*, p. 33 for the musical interests. The whole of Temple's biography shows why Marshall would have revered his first employer, who in his life exemplified many of the ideals which Marshall subsequently proclaimed. The admiration became mutual, as shown below, Chapter 17, p. 628n*.
31. A.S. and E.M.S., *Henry Sidgwick. A Memoir*, p. 13.
32. *Ibid.*, Chapter II, esp. pp. 73, 85.
33. R.B. Martin, *Tennyson. The Unquiet Heart*, Oxford: Clarendon Press, 1983, pp. 436–7, 438–9; cf. Phyllis Grosskurth, *John Addington Symonds*, London: Longmans, 1964, p. 77.
34. Phyllis Grosskurth, *John Addington Symonds*, p. 77. Dakyns is included with Marshall in the portrait of the Clifton masters of 1865 reproduced as illustration 13. The last sentence of the quotation implicitly refers to their homosexuality, the reason why Dakyns had to resign early from Clifton.
35. Apart from her notes for Keynes, already quoted, see her *What I Remember*, p. 23, where the 'Dakyns' are listed among their real Bristol friends. By then Dakyns had married, to disguise his sexual preferences so dangerous in his occupation as teacher in a leading boys' school. Whether Marshall at Clifton became aware of this side of Dakyns is not known.
36. A.S. and E.M.S., *Henry Sidgwick. A Memoir*, esp. pp. 81, 88, 91, 120, 129.
37. These included the Grote Society and perhaps the Eranus Club but more generally, the growing circle of moral sciences teachers at Cambridge outside of John's, such as Venn, Fawcett, Maurice and Aldis Wright. In this context it may be noted that Dakyns drew attention to Mozley's suitability for the Trumpington gatherings of the Grote Club; in any case Sidgwick wrote Dakyns in November 1865 that he had made sufficient 'advances to Mozley . . . to get him to join our society at Trumpington'. (A.S. and E.M.S., *Henry Sidgwick, A Memoir*, p. 131). On the last, see below, pp. 110–12.
38. See Rosamund Könekamp, *Biography of William Stanley Jevons*, in *Papers and Correspondence of William Stanley Jevons*, edited R.D. Collision Black and Rosamund Könekamp, London: Macmillan, 1972, Vol. I, pp. 46–7. Biographical details on Mozley from Venn, *Alumni Cantabrigienses*, second part.
39. Alfred Marshall, Biographical Fragment 3 October 1920, Large Brown Box, Marshall Archive. The first part is completely in note form.
40. J.R. Mozley to John Maynard Keynes, 24 November 1924 (KMF); Mary Paley Marshall, 'Biographical Notes on Alfred Marshall' (KMF).
41. J.R. Mozley to John Maynard Keynes, 24 November 1924 (KMF).
42. Given his topics of correspondence with Sidgwick as mentioned above (p. 104), Dakyns may well have added his own encouragement to the young Marshall to follow Mozley's suggestion for reading.
43. Later they drifted apart, although Marshall appears to have sent Mozley a copy of his *Elements of the Economics of Industry* in 1892 (Marshall Archive, File 6:1). Many years later, Mozley reciprocated the gesture, as discussed below (Chapter 18, p. 662).
44. Rita McWilliams-Tullberg has drawn my attention to a letter by Mozley to J.B. Mayor (21 April 1904) in which he mentioned his presence at Grote Club meetings in October term 1863, after his graduation and before joining the teaching staff at Clifton College in 1864. Sidgwick, Venn and J.B. Pearson were then apparently in regular attendance. When Mozley returned to Cambridge in September 1865, he claimed others had joined it, including Alfred Marshall and Henry Jackson. On Marshall's own account this cannot be true (below, pp. 111), while Mozley prefaced his letter to Mayor by admitting 'the dates . . . are all mixed up in my head' (Rita McWilliams-Tullberg to the author, 1 August 1991) the Mozley letter is in Trinity College Library (Add MS.c. 105.66).
45. See J.R. Mozley to Alfred Marshall, 29 September 1916, Marshall Archive, 1/89, and below, Chapter 18, pp. 661–2.
46. Mary Paley Marshall, *What I Remember*, p. 23; note 43 above.
47. G.C. Moore Smith, *Lists of past occupants of rooms in St John's College*, Cambridge, March 1895, pp. 40, 49, 58.
48. T.G. Bonney, *Memories of a Long Life*, pp. 32–3, 41–3, and see above, Chapter 4, p. 79 for a discussion of Marshall's obligations to Bateson.
49. T.G. Bonney, *Memories of a Long Life*, pp. 53–60; Alec C. Crook, *From the Foundation to Gilbert Scott: A History of the Buildings of St John's College Cambridge 1511–1885*, Chapters VIII and IX.
50. T.G. Bonney, *Memories of a Long Life*, p. 69.
51. T.G. Bonney, *Memories of a Long Life*, p. 33; the charges for particular items are from the *Steward's Notebook* for this period, St John's College Archives, S.D. 8.1.
52. A lecturer's salary added no less than £100 to the income of the incumbent; see H.F. Howard, *The Finances of St John's College, Cambridge*, Cambridge University Press, 1935, p. 194. Together with his college dividend, then close to £300 per annum, this gave Alfred Marshall an annual income of £400, with very limited immediate living expenses, a considerable advance on his father's salary even at that time. Marshall's college teaching is discussed in Chapter 9, below, pp. 268–70.
53. *Statutes of St John's College Cambridge 1860*, p. 21.

54. His successor was appointed in October 1877, but since Marshall married Mary Paley on 17 August 1877, it is unlikely that he would have exercised his duties as Steward much beyond the end of July. The resource allocation activities of housewife and the 'young pair' are discussed in *P* VIII, pp. 118–19, for example.
55. Information supplied by Dr M.G. Underwood, St John's College Archivist, to whom I am indebted for giving me access to much of the material used in this section.
56. Alfred Marshall to James Ward, 23 September 1900, in *Memorials,* pp. 418–19, quoted extensively at the start of this chapter, p. 199.
57. Alfred Marshall to James Ward, 23 September 1900, in *Memorials,* p. 418.
58. Mary Paley Marshall, 'Biographical Notes on Alfred Marshall' (KMF), John Maynard Keynes, 'Alfred Marshall', p. 213 n.1.
59. MSS Book, Large Brown Box (Marshall Library).
60. Above, p. 99.
61. As discussed below, Chapter 18, pp. 660–62.
62. Chit Chat Club, Minute Books (Cambridge University Library, Add 6151–6155.) The importance of the club for understanding Marshall's early Cambridge life was drawn to my attention by Giacomo Becattini.
63. Reproduced in A.S. and E.M.S., *Henry Sidgwick. A Memoir*, p. 135.
64. *Ibid.*, 137–8.
65. Sidgwick Papers, Trinity College, Cambridge, Add MS c.104 65 (17) the omitted quote comes from p. 2.
66. *Ibid.* p. 13, the material quoted in the preceding paragraph is from pp. 5, 6–7. Pyrrho was a sceptical philosopher who died in 275 B.C.; Butler the eighteenth-century theologian and moral philosopher.
67 *Ibid.* pp. 14–15, 17.
68. *Ibid.* p.1. John Maynard Keynes 'Alfred Marshall', p. 172 n.2, but based on a conversation with Marshall just before he died, when his memory was failing.
69. Sidgwick Papers, Add. MS c. 104(1).
70. A.S. and E.M.S., *Henry Sidgwick, A Memoir*, pp. 223–4. Lewis Campbell and William Garnett, *The Life of James Clerk Maxwell*, London: Macmillan, 1882, pp. 434, 366, allege that the foundation of the Eranus Club owed much to the desire of ex-Apostles of the 1853–57 period to meet once again on Saturday evenings for the discussion of speculative questions. This cannot be fully accepted. Although Sidgwick had been made an Apostle in 1856, Maxwell and Hort had been elected earlier in 1851 and 1852 respectively. Westcott and Lightfoot had never been 'apostles', nor of course the other members of the Eranus Society mentioned subsequently in the text. Maxwell's biographers reprint three of the papers he gave to the Society, these dealt with Determinism versus Free Will in the light of the progress of physical science (11 February 1873), on modified aspects of pain (31 October 1876) and Psychophysik (5 February 1878). *Ibid.*, pp. 434–63.
71. A.S. and E.M.S., *Henry Sidgwick. A Memoir*, pp. 223–4 and n.1. These subsequent members were Lord Acton, the historian, presumably during his period as Regius Professor of History at Cambridge; George Darwin, the subsequent Plumian Professor of Astronomy and Experimental Philosophy, and Fellow of Trinity from 1868 to 1878 after being second wrangler in 1868 to Moulton, the senior wrangler of that year; and T. Clifford Albutt, with Michael Foster a reforming force in the Cambridge medical schools of the 1870s and 1880s.
72. Sir Arthur Hort, *Life and Letters of Fenton John Anthony Hort,* London: Macmillan, 1896, Volume II, pp. 201–2. The Cowell mentioned presumably was Edward Byles Cowell (1826–1903), who had joined Trinity as a Fellow in 1867 after an Oxford education on becoming Professor of Sanskrit at Cambridge; Michael Foster (1907) was an eminent Cambridge medical teacher and scientist, whose Cambridge career at various times was strongly assisted by Sidgwick. See J.N. Langley, 'Sir Michael Foster in Memoriam', *Journal of Physiology,* 35 (3), March 1907, p. 238. Hort had earlier provided Campbell with material on the Eranus Society for the biography of Maxwell written with William Garnett. See Lewis Campbell and William Garnett, *The Life of James Clerk Maxwell*, p. 417.
73. Sir Arthur Hort, *Life and Letters of Fenton John Anthony Hort,* p. 283. Audrey Cunningham, *William Cunningham. Teacher and Friend,* London: S.P.E.K., 1950, p. 70, indicates Sidgwick invited Cunningham to join circa 1888, and mentions Professor Alexander Macalister (Anatomy), Bateson (Biology), Darwin, Sir T. Clifford Allbutt (Professor of Physics) with Maitland, Henry Jackson and Henry Sidgwick, the regular attenders. She does not mention Marshall as a member (he may by then have dropped out, given his absence from Cambridge between 1877 and 1885) but tells an amusing anecdote on Acton's rare participations in debate: an 'impassioned . . . invective against Cardinal Newman and St Charles Borromeo'.
74. Above, p. 99. Membership of the Eranus Society in any case was not recorded in their biographies, that is, Leslie Stephen, *Life of Henry Fawcett*; Frederick Pollock, 'Memoir of William Kingdon Clifford', in *William Kingdon Clifford. Lectures and Essays,* edited by Leslie Stephen and Frederick Pollock, London: Macmillan, 1879 and H.T. Francis, *John Venn. In Memoriam,* Cambridge: at the University Press, 1923.
75. Vol. 9, 1873, pp. 1–23, in *Memorials*, pp. 101–18. Previous papers sponsored by this Club in 1872 and 1873 were by Moulton, James Stuart, Sedley Taylor, Mrs Millicent Fawcett (on women's suffrage) and Sidgwick (on

justice). By 1878, a prospectus to set up a Cambridge Reform Club Building Fund indicates that the strong university association of this club had by then disappeared.

76. Proceedings of the Cambridge Philosophical Society, October 1873, pp. 318–19. See also below, Chapter 6, pp. 162–3.

77. This issue is pursued at the start of Chapter 6, below, pp. 142–5.

78. See above, Chapter 4, p. 93.

79. See A.O.J. Cockshutt, *Anglican Attitudes: A Study of Victorian Religious Controversies*, London: Collins, 1959, Chapter 1, esp. pp. 12–23. Its other chapters discuss the implications of the debate over *Essays and Reviews* and the Colenso Affair. The latter are also incisively reviewed in Geoffrey Faber, *Jowett, A Portrait with Background*, London: Faber & Faber, 1958, Capters XI and XII on *Essays and Reviews*, pp. 314–24 on the Colenso Affair.

80. H.L. Mansel, *The Limits of Religious Thought*, London: John Murray, fifth edition, 1867, frontispiece and p. xliv.

81. *Ibid.*, pp. xlvi–xlvii; Immanuel Kant, *Critique of Pure Reason*, translated by Norman Keny Smith, London: Macmillan, 1929, p. 50.

82. This was possibly one of the factors that led F.D. Maurice to attack Mansel's *Bampton Lectures* in his *Strictures on the Bampton Lectures*, to which Mansel himself replied in 1859. Maurice's criticism of Mansel was on the whole based on philosophical rather than theological argument.

83. J.S. Mill, *An Examination of Sir William Hamilton's Philosophy*, London: Longmans, Green & Company, 1865, esp. Chapters 5–7; cf. *A System of Logic*, Book III, Chapter XXI where Mill states, 'Belief is not proof, and does not dispense with the necessity of proof.' (p. 369 in the 1896 People's Edition, and cf. p. 370 where the relationship between evidence and belief is further debated.) For a detailed discussion of Mill's controversy with Mansel and the threefold nature of the type of reply Mansel's *Bampton Lectures* received, see Leslie Stephen, *The English Utilitarians*, London: Duckworth, 1900, Vol. 3, John Stuart Mill, pp. 376–7, 409–16.

84. See for example, T.H. Huxley, *Hume*, English Men of Letters, London: Macmillan, 1879, pp. 48–52; Herbert Spencer, *First Principles*, Part I, sixth edition, London: William & Norgate, 1910, esp. pp. 50, 56–7, 69. See also Bernard Lightman, *The Origins of Agnosticism*, Baltimore: Johns Hopkins Press, 1987, Chapter 1, pp. 6–9, 15–16; Chapters 2 and 3 give a detailed account of Mansel's use of Kant in his philosophy of religion and the intellectual storm caused by the publication of his *Bampton Lectures*, including therein the response of Herbert Spencer.

85. See H.L. Mansel, *An Examination of the Rev. F.D. Maurice's Strictures on the Bampton Lectures of 1858*, London: John Murray, 1859, pp. 40, 97, where Maurice's *Strictures* are quoted to this effect.

86. For a sympathetic evaluation of Mansel's theological philosophy see W.R. Mathews, *The Religious Philosophy of Dean Mansel*, Toronto: Oxford University Press, 1956. This stresses the clarity and scholarly nature of Mansel's Lectures, and the extent of his knowledge of German philosophy. The last feature is also apparent in Mansel's *Letters, Lectures and Reviews*, London: John Murray, 1873, especially the essays he wrote on the Philosophy of Kant and on Modern German Philosophy in the late 1850s. Cf. Bernard Lightman, *The Origins of Agnosticism*, p. 33.

87. Above, Chapter 4, pp. 80–81.

88. See J.S. Mill, *A System of Logic*, London: Longmans, Green & Company, 1896, Preface to the first edition, esp. p. v and Book II, Chapters V and VI, 'Of Demonstration, and Necessary Truths'.

89. Marshall's interest in Hegel's *Philosophy of History* may therefore have been sparked by reading Mansel.

90. John Maynard Keynes, 'Alfred Marshall', pp. 169–70.

91. Marshall to Foxwell, 7 February 1875 (Freeman Collection, 14/229); the whole of this letter is quoted below, Chapter 18, pp. 671 and n.*. I am indebted to Dr Underwood, the St John's College Archivist, for information about the need to affirm his faith in 1865. On the latter, see also his remarks on this issue in the 1890s, quoted below, Chapter 8, p. 246.

92. Marshall to Foxwell, 4 February 1875 (Freeman Collection, 13/229); the letter about his religious beliefs may well have been Marshall's rejoinder to Foxwell's reaction to this humour.

93. See below, Chapter 7, pp. 195–6, 209–10.

94. Discussed in some detail below, Chapter 20, pp. 737–8 which also comments in this context on features of Marshall's burial service and subsequent burial in consecrated ground (p. 743). An autobiographical sketch preserved among the Sidgwick papers at Trinity College, Cambridge (Add MS c. 96(20)) shows that the 'virgin miraculous birth' was the 'greatest hurdle' for Sidgwick's belief in the 39 articles. However, he must also have had doubts about eternal life since his lifelong research into psychical phenomena was inspired by his wish to know more directly 'proof of continuing individual existence'.

95. *Ibid.* Marshall's membership of the Ethical Society is discussed in Chapter 13 (below, pp. 447–9), and for his views on the utility of religion see *P* VIII e.g. pp. 198, 247.

96. Marshall Archive, Red Box ,1 (5): fragment written at Seavale, dated 18 August 1922.

97. See A.O.J. Cockshut, *The Unbelievers. English Agnostic Thought 1840–1890*, esp. Part II, Chapters 2–4; Susan Budd, *Varieties of Unbelief. Atheists and Agnostics in English Society 1850–1960*, London: Heinemann, 1977, Chapters 6, 9–10.

98. E.B. Pusey, preface to Daniel, p. xxii, that is, to *Daniel the Prophet, Lectures delivered at the University of Oxford with notes*, Oxford, first edition 1864, second edition 1868.

99. Marshall Library, Box 8 (1). Presumably this fragment was preserved because of its statistical demographic content. Colenso had used his knowledge of arithmetic to throw doubt on the accuracy of the Pentateuch, that is, the five books of Moses. See Geoffrey Faber, *Jowett. A Portrait with Background*, pp. 322–3.

100. Earlier Marshall had cited Samuel Johnson's views on the subject of genius: 'Large general powers operating in a particular direction', something not undescriptive of his own later work in economics.

101. These have been edited and reprinted by Tiziano Raffaelli in *EPW*. This discussion, and subsequently the brief examination of the contents of these papers, draws heavily on this excellent edition.

102. Inspiration should not be taken to mean that Marshall had first come across the 'law' in Hamilton's works; he had almost certainly first encountered it in Mansel's *Metaphysics*.

103. See Alfred Marshall, 'The Law of Parcimony', in *EPW*, p. 51 and n.155. It is very likely that Marshall may have borrowed the example of Condillac's from the account of it given in Cousin's *History of Modern Philosophy*. In any case, Marshall's comments add nothing to it as given there. See Victor Cousin, *Cours de l'histoire de la philosophie moderne*, Paris: Ladrange & Didier, 1846, new ed., Vol. I, pp. 142–5.

104. Alfred Marshall, 'Ferrier's Proposition One', in *EPW*, p. 63 and n.198.

105. Alfred Marshall, 'Ye Machine', p. 81 and n.232 for Babbage.

106. These are listed by Raffaelli in *EPW*, pp. 130–35, esp. notes 244, 245, 252, 254, 262, 267–8.

107. Cf. note 88 above.

108. There is no certainty they were all read at meetings of the Grote Club, nor can their order of writing be established with certainty. Raffaelli's introduction to Marshall's *EPW*, p. 31, is most persuasive on this point.

109. Marshall Archive, Large Brown Box, item 26 (undated). Moulton's biographer and son, J.F. Moulton (*The Life of Lord Moulton*, London: Nisbett & Company, 1922) bears Marshall's judgement out and may in fact have inspired it. Clifford's views, looked at in the next section, would have been highly congenial to Marshall. See also below, Chapter 18, pp. 661, 695, for further remarks on this friendship.

110. Alfred Marshall, 'Duty of the Logician', p. 94.

111. See *P* VIII, p. 251 n.1 (a passage also in *P* I, pp. 311–12). On method, see *P* VIII, p. 27 (a passage dating from *P* II). On his admiration of Kant, see below, pp. 129–30.

112. See Tiziano Raffaelli 'The Analysis of the Human Mind in the early Marshallian manuscripts', *Quaderni di storia dell' economia politica*, 9 (2–3), 1991, pp. 29–58, esp. pp. 29–36. The subsequent paragraphs draw extensively on Raffaelli's fascinating paper and on his excellent introduction to his edition of Marshall's philosophical manuscripts.

113. Alfred Marshall, 'The Law of Parcimony', in *EPW*, p. 48.

114. *Ibid.*, pp. 48–49.

115. Cf. Tiziano Raffaelli, introduction to *EPW*, pp. 12–13. This disappeared with the *Principles*, see below, Chapter 12, pp. 411–12, 425–6, 436.

116. Alfred Marshall, 'Ferrier's Proposition One', in *EPW*, p. 58.

117. *Ibid.*, pp. 65–7, and see Tiziano Raffaelli , introduction, pp. 15–17. It became Marshall's position in economics when combining the views of classical economics and the new marginalist views on value, on which see below, Chapter 12, p. 411 and Chapter 21, pp. 787–8.

118. Marshall Archive, Large Brown Box 5, volume of MSS notes. The notes are in Marshall's early handwriting, and the subject matter as well as the references to two contemporary Fellows of John's, suggest 1867 or 1868.

119. That is, W.W.H. Hudson, Fellow of John's from 1862 (see above p. 109 n¶).

120. That is, T.G. Bonney, Fellow of John's from 1858 (see above, p. 109 n¶).

121. Alfred Marshall, *EPW*, p. 67.

122. An interest in this problem is also visible, as Raffaelli points out, in Marshall's manuscript notes on the characteristics of 'brutes' (comparison of man and beast). As mentioned in the previous section, these largely derived from Hobbes, *Leviathan*, Chapter 3. See Raffaelli's introduction to *EPW*, pp. 13–14 and n.33, which presents Raffaelli's reconstruction of Marshall's notes on this subject.

123. But not on the neuro-physiological side where Marshall's major authority, W.B. Carpenter, remained a confirmed Kantian all his life. See Raffaelli, 'The Analysis of the Human Mind in the Early Marshallian Manuscripts', pp. 30–32.

124. Marshall's lifelong admiration for Kant is discussed below, pp. 129–30.

125. A detailed examination of its contents is given by Tiziano Raffaelli, 'The Analysis of the Human Mind in the Early Marshallian Manuscripts', esp. pp. 36–45. See his introduction to *EPW*, pp. 18–28.

126. Alfred Marshall, 'Ye Machine', in *EPW*, pp. 72–75.

136 *A Soaring Eagle: Alfred Marshall 1842–1924*

127. *Ibid.*, pp. 77–82.
128. *Ibid.*, p. 87.
129. *Ibid.*, pp. 91–3. This type of view on the 'sixth sense' may have owed something to Sidgwick's psychical researches which commenced at this time.
130. Raffaelli's commentary on this paper also notes the importance of Marshall's model of the human mind for his economic analysis in the *Principles*. Examples include the complex interpretation of market signals within the Marshallian system, the nature of his time analysis, the widening of choices as time perspectives lengthen, and, above all, in his discussion of the formation of human character. The last provides a perfect example of how in Marshall's economics, as in his psychology, man stands well above the machine. See Raffaelli, 'The Analysis of the Human Mind in the early Marshallian Manuscripts', pp. 48–52.
131. *EPW*, p. 31.
132. *Ibid.*, p. 31 and see Marshall, 'The Duty of the Logician', p. 96.
133. *EPW*, p. 31.
134. H. von Helmholz, *Epistemological Writings*, edited by R.S. Cohen and Y. Elkana, *Boston Studies in the Philosophy of Science*, Vol. XXVII, Dordrecht and Boston: Reidel, 1977, p. 18, as cited by Raffaelli, Introduction to *EPW*, pp. 31–2. Cf. Helmholtz's 'The Origin and Meaning of Geometrical Axioms' (1870), in English in *Mind*, 1876, pp. 301–21, p. 304, cited in Joan L. Richards, 'The Reception of a Mathematical Theory: Non-Euclidean Geometry in England 1863–1883', in *Natural Order, Historical Studies of Scientific Culture*, eds Barry Barnes and Steven Chaplin, London: Sage Publications, 1979, pp. 154–5.
135. R. Butler, 'The Historical Context of the Early Marshallian Work', in *Quaderni di storia dell' economia politica* 9 (2–3), 1991, pp. 279–81, Clifford used these examples in a paper he presented in February 1870 to the Cambridge Philosophical Society, where Marshall more than likely heard it. He was, as shown earlier in this chapter, in the habit of attending at least some of its meetings (Butler, p. 282). In 1875 Marshall confronted Emerson with these findings, indicating that by then he had absorbed their implications. Marshall's visit to Emerson is discussed below (Chapter 7, p. 196). On Clifford's role in spreading the new geometry in England, see Joan R. Richards, 'The Reception of Mathematical Theory: Non-Euclidean Geometry in England 1863–1883', pp. 152–6.
136. See Mrs Laurence Humphrey, *Sir George Gabriel Stokes. Memoir and Selected Correspondence*, Cambridge: Cambridge University Press, 1907, Vol. I, pp. 46–7; and for a study of Stokes's ability to blend religious belief with science, Daniel B. Wilson, 'A Physicist's Alternative to Materialism: The Religious Thought of George Gabriel Stokes', *Victorian Studies* Autumn 1984, pp. 69–97.
137. See Edward Caird, 'Metaphysic', in *Encyclopaedia Britannica*, ninth edition, Edinburgh: A & C Black, 1883, Vol. XVI, pp. 79–102, and p. 80 for the definitions quoted in the text. Caird succeeded Jowett as Master of Balliol, and in that capacity Marshall corresponded with him during 1897 on the crisis of British industry in the context of an engineering strike (in *Memorials*, pp. 398–403) and below, Chapter 16, pp. 599–600.
138. Above, p. 99, the letter was written in 1900; cf. biographical fragment dated 3 October 1920, Marshall Archive, Large Brown Box, 5.
139. Mary Paley Marshall, 'Biographical Notes on Alfred Marshall' (KMF).
140. The phrase is that of Tiziano Raffaelli, Introduction to *EPW*, p. 20. Marshall's knowledge of the psychological literature when writing the paper may have been insufficient for realising this himself. It may have been pointed out to him in the discussion of the paper at the Grote Club. My reading of histories of psychology such as J.C. Flugel, *A Hundred Years of Psychology 1833–1933*, London: Duckworth, new edition, 1959; Edwin G. Boring, *A History of Experimental Psychology*, second edition, New York: Appleton Century Crofts, 1957 and the earlier, almost contemporary to Marshall, Th. Ribon, *English Psychology*, London: Henry S. King & Co. 1873, suggests that Marshall was aware of what was being done in the type of psychology he was interested in, but that he had not, in any major way, gone beyond it. See also note 141 below.
141. See Robert M. Young, *Mind, Brain and Adaptation in the Nineteenth Century. Cerebral Localisation and its Biological Context from Gall to Ferrier*, Oxford: Clarendon Press, 1970, esp. Introduction.
142. Alfred Marshall, 'Ye Machine', in *EPW*, p. 91, where he acknowledged his ignorance of the practical side of botany, biology and physiology. Recall Marshall's diatribe in the 1870s against classics, during which he turned it into a plea for its replacement in school education by more useful subjects, including biology. Recorded in JNKD and quoted above (Chapter 3, p. 60).
143. Alfred Marshall, 'Biographical Fragment', 3 October 1920, Marshall Archive, Large Brown Box, Item 5.
144. J.K. Whitaker, Introduction to *EEW*, I p. 8.
145. *P* VIII, p. 38 (the opening sentence of Ch. IV of Book I). It dates substantially from the *P* I, p. 94 (Book I, Ch. VIII), while in a summary of a Bristol lecture, he used the phrase, 'Be always urgent for facts'. See below, Chapter 9, p. 290, and more generally, Chapter 20, p. 760.
146. Mary Paley Marshall, 'Biographical Notes on Alfred Marshall' (KMF).
147. See Mary Paley Marshall, *What I Remember*, p. 20.

148. Layton 15² p. 15 (Layton Papers, Trinity College Library, Cambridge).
149. Marshall to Bowley, 9 March 1901, in *Memorials*, pp. 422–3 and see below, Chapter 17, pp. 637–8, which reports correspondence with Moore on the subject.
150. Cf. Marshall to J.B. Clark, 14 March 1908, in *Memorials*, p. 417.
151. See Sheldon Rothblatt, *The Revolution of the Dons*, Chapter 5, esp. 169–71, 176–9; cf. Alon Kadish, *Historians, Economists and Economic Historians*, London: Routledge, 1989, esp. pp. 134–41.
152. *The Student's Guide to the University of Cambridge, 1862*, pp. 146, 149.
153. See my 'Marshall and Hegel', *Economie Appliquée*, 43 (1), 1990, pp. 66–9. As noted previously (above, note 89) Mansel's *Bampton Lectures* cited Hegel's *Philosophy of History* and mentioned its importance in German philosophy. See for example, H.L. Mansel, *The Limits of Religious Thought*, fifth edition, 1867, pp. 260–61.
154. Mary Paley Marshall, *What I Remember*, p. 18. This is discussed further in Chapter 9, pp. 268, 270–1.
155. This Dialogue is reprinted as an appendix to *EPW*, pp. 110–12. The quotation is from the introduction to the 'Dialogue', *ibid.*, p. 109. A later note explains its purpose: 'Intended to lead up to the acknowledgement of Kant as a thorough and great poet.' *Ibid.*, p. 135, n.277.
156. *Ibid.*, pp. 110–11.
157. Alfred Marshall, Biographical Fragment, 3 October 1920, Marshall Archive, Large Brown Box, 5.
158. Walter Scott, 'Alfred Marshall 1842–1924', *Proceedings of the British Academy*, Oxford: Clarendon Press, 1925, pp. 4–5, but cf. below, Chapter 12, p. 411 for other sources.
159. Cited in J.M. Keynes, 'Alfred Marshall', p.200. The picture, now preserved in the Marshall Library, is reproduced as Illustration 14.

APPENDIX TO CHAPTER 5:

Moral and Mental Philosophy Books from an early postgraduate notebook studied by Marshall during his search for a vocation.[*]

First List (circa 1867)

Among the moral philosophy works listed are: Plato's *Republic*, Aristotle's *Ethics*, Cicero's *De Officiis*, Butler's *Three Sermons*, Kant's *Grundlegung der Metaphysik der Sitten* and his *Tugendlehre*, Dugald Stewart's *On the Active and Moral Powers*, Books I and II, Whewell's *Elements of Morality* and Jeremy Bentham's *Principles of Morals and Legislation* and *Of the Civil Code*. Mental philosophy works listed include the following items: Descartes's *Discours de la méthode*, Locke's *Essay Concerning Human Understanding*, Books I, II and IV, Victor Cousin's *Philosophie du XVIIIᵉ siècle*, material on Kant and Locke, Sir William Hamilton's *Lectures on Metaphysics*, Ferrier's *Institutes of Metaphysics, Theory of Knowing and Being*, and Alexander Bain's *The Senses and the Intellect*.

This list of philosophy books differs from the Moral Sciences Tripos list for 1860s in the following ways. Marshall's list omits Cicero's *De Finibus*, Clark on the *Attributes* and on *Unchangeable Morality*, Paley's *Moral Philosophy* and Fichte's *Ethical System* as well as Plato's *Moral Dialogues* (for which Alfred Marshall substituted his *Republic*). Marshall's mental philosophy list omits Plato's *Theaetus*, Aristotle's *De Anima*, Reid's *Philosophy* as edited by Sir William Hamilton and surprisingly, Kant's *Critique of Pure Reason*. It adds the work by Ferrier and Bain, in which he was particularly interested at this stage, and provides specific chapters and parts for Locke's *Essay* and Cousin's *Philosophie*.

---

[*] These notebooks are housed in Marshall Archive, Large Brown Box, 5.

List dated May 1869

This was prepared at the end of Marshall's first academic year as College Lecturer in the Moral Sciences, covers a wider and more varied array of books of relevance to his new teaching duties. It preserves the works by Aristotle, Whewell and Stewart previously listed under moral philosophy readings; adds Mansel's *Psychology, The Test of Moral and Metaphysical Philosophy* as well as his *Prolegomena Logica*, Mill's *System of Logic*, Whateley's *Elements of Logic*, Bain's *Emotions and the Will*, and notes several works on political economy: Mill's *Principles* and Bastiat's *Harmonies économiques*. More detailed lists for logic and political economy follow: apart from Mill's *System*, Whateley's *Logic* and Mansel's *Prolegomena*, the longer logic list adds Thomson's *Laws of Thought*, Hamilton's *Lectures*, Bacon's *Novum Organum* and Whewell's *Novum Organum Renovatum*. The extended list of works on political economy adds Smith's *Wealth of Nations*, Ricardo's *Principles* and Cairnes's *Character and Logical Method of Political Economy*. Compared with the Moral Sciences Tripos list of prescribed books for this period, Marshall's list of works on logic omits Aristotle's *Categories and Analytics*, Trendelenburg's *Elementa Logices Aristolelicae* and Aldrich's logic with Mansel's notes. From the political economy list, Marshall omitted Malthus's *Essay on Population* and his *Principles*, McCulloch's *Principles of Political Economy*, Richard Jones on Rent and his *Literary Remains* as edited by Whewell, Carey's *Political Economy* and Michel Chevalier's *Cours d'économie politique*.

6. The Economic Apprenticeship (1867–1875) and After

In one of many autobiographical fragments Marshall left in old age,[1] he described the period from 1867 to 1875 when he was a young Fellow of St John's in his twenties, as his period of apprenticeship in economics. The development of Marshall's economic thinking during these years, extended to 1879, the year two major publications appeared, is the subject matter of this chapter.[2] This requires a systematic look at the reasons Marshall later gave to explain his interest in economics, more particularly his decision to specialise in it, together with an examination of his claims to originality *vis-à-vis* some of his contemporaries in economics who, like him, developed the new marginalist approach to the subject.[3]

Marshall's most important recollections about this were nearly all written in the twentieth century, after he had reached the age of sixty. The earliest was written more than thirty years after the events they describe. Most important are some letters he wrote to J.B. Clark in 1900 and 1908, a letter to Colson dating either from 1908 or 1909, and an autobiographical sketch he prepared for publication some time in 1910.[4] These retrospective accounts of his early economic studies, largely written in the years immediately following his retirement from the chair at Cambridge, focus on the details of timing and specific sources, while the autobiographical sketch also mentions Marshall's claims as to why he started these studies.

The essentials of these accounts, which differ in some matters of detail, are as follows. Sometime in 1866 or 1867, Marshall commenced the study of political economy because he felt himself 'hampered' on questions of 'practical ethics by ignorance of their economic substratum'.[5] These practical ethics questions are not explicitly identified. They probably involved issues relating to working-class improvement in its widest sense, a social problem in which Marshall was becoming increasingly interested for reasons which are also not clear, because Marshall never articulated them in writing at this time. This is a major gap in knowledge about Marshall, addressed subsequently in this chapter. Although 1867 is the year usually given for the start of Marshall's economic studies, 1866, a year he also retrospectively mentioned, seems more plausible. Two pieces of circumstantial evidence support this date. First of all, Marshall's summer vacation in Scotland that year probably included visits to northern industrial towns, implying his interests in practical ethics questions had possibly started by then, and with it, perhaps, a desire to learn more about political economy. Mill's text on political economy, which had appeared in a cheap people's edition in 1865 was the obvious choice of book for the enthusiastic beginner. Some of its contents directly addressed possibilities for improving the working classes and their future prospects. In fact, Marshall's personal copy of Mill, preserved in the Cambridge University Library[6] is the 1865 people's edition. This creates a second clue on the time

Marshall began his economic studies. Its second printing appeared in 1867, thereby suggesting that Marshall purchased his copy before its appearance in that year, that is, probably some time during 1866.

Irrespective of the year in which Marshall started reading Mill, there is no doubt whatsoever that his systematic studies of political economy started in this way. The letters to Clark and Colson then elaborate on how Marshall moved from Mill within three or four years to complete his 'main position as to the theory of value and distribution', or to put it in another way, much of the core of the theoretical system he developed in the *Principles* flowing from its original Book V. The mathematisation of Mill, 'translating his doctrines into differential equations' was the route by which Marshall retrospectively claimed to have reached his new theory. This enabled him to reject parts of Mill's *Principles*, such as the static theory of distribution in Book II in favour of its more dynamic treatment in Book IV. At the same time, he was able to identify Mill's two major analytical faults. 'He did not seem to have assimilated the notion of gradual growth by imperceptible increments; and he did not seem to have a sufficient responsibility . . . for keeping the number of his equations equal to the number of variables, neither more nor less.'

Other writers helped Marshall's critical discovery tour through Mill's *Principles*. 'I read Cournot in 1868. I know I did not read von Thünen then, probably in 1869 or 1870, for I did not know enough German'.[7] In terms of the mathematical appendix Marshall later prepared for his *Principles*, notes V, XIII–XIV, and XIV to XX leading up to XXI, were essentially completed at this time. What Marshall claimed to have been missing by the end of 1870 in terms of the mathematical skeleton as presented in the *Principles*, was the theory of utility, of elasticity, aspects of the theory of demand concerning aggregation, the theory of allocation of labour, the theory of barter geometrically illustrated and the theory of monopoly. What was in place was the theory of value in terms of supply and demand, much of the theory of production and capital, and a great deal of the theory of distribution.

The publication of *Jevons's Theory of Political Economy* in 1871 came in the middle of Marshall's apprenticeship. His first economics publication[8] reviewed Jevons's *Theory*, a simple task he claimed retrospectively because by then his studies had advanced sufficiently for him to know 'at once how far I agreed with him and how far I did not'. During the second, post-Jevons stage of his apprenticeship, Marshall 'worked a good deal at the mathematical theory of monopolies, and at the diagrammatic treatment of Mill's problem of international values'.[9] He presented the theoretical skeleton of the first at an 1873 meeting of the Cambridge Philosophical Society, and the whole was comprehensively included by 1879 in the privately printed chapters on the pure theory of domestic and international value. 'Before 1871 when Jevons's very important *Theory of Political Economy* had appeared, I had worked out the whole skeleton of my present system in mathematics though not in English.'[10] By 1879, most of the theoretical gaps had been filled in and the essentials of his system were complete.

The letters on which the argument of the previous paragraphs with special reference to Jevons is based, were explanations about Marshall's claims to theoretical priority in so far as his analytical core in political economy was concerned. This specific purpose implies several silences in their contents. The letters, for example, completely ignore Marshall's wider motivations in the study of economics. They neglect to mention his solid work on the superstructure of economics: money, fluctuations, credit, the capital market, international finance, the functions of government and public finance. They also focus rather narrowly on Marshall's main theoretical mentors in economics, Mill, von Thünen and Cournot, to which the names of Smith and Ricardo must be added as authors from whom he claimed to have learned much on scope and method. The more comprehensive autobiographical sketch of 1910 addressed these omissions at least in part. It shows that simultaneous with the theoretical research programme just outlined, Marshall critically studied 'new views of economics taken by Roscher and other German economists; and by Marx, Lassalle and other socialists.' In addition, when 'at last', implying well after 1866 or 1867, Marshall gave up 'all thought of ever returning to philosophy, he set himself to get into closer contact with practical business and with the life of the working classes. On the one side he aimed at learning the broad features of the technique of every chief industry; and on the other he sought the society of trade unionists, cooperators and other working class leaders'.[11]

The last sentence draws attention to the real revolution in economic thinking Marshall wanted to achieve. He wished to jettison the pessimistic conclusions of classical economics on the future possibilities for the working class, inherent in its perspectives on the stationary state and in the limitations implied for human progress from its laws of population and wages, which permanently tied most workers to low incomes. For this dismal prognosis Marshall wished to, and did, substitute a law of progress which included belief in the possibilities for improving human nature itself. By holding out the prospect of both material and moral amelioration for all, Marshall desired to create a vision of a more joyful political economy to eliminate the description of 'dismal' with which Carlyle had saddled it.

This quest was to be founded on two essential types of research. It required the study of technology to see what was technically feasible by way of productive improvement to break the iron laws of population and wages which had held economics in its thrall and condemned the working class to permanent misery. Marshall's enormous attachment to the prospect of long-term increasing returns is part of this economic optimism. In addition, it required study of the working class itself, particularly its more liberal elements in the cooperative and trade union movement. This would enable him to assess the extent of, and the speed in which, human character could be changed for the better. Although Mill's political economy and logic had shown the way in this venture, Marshall quickly departed from Mill in at least two ways. He substituted the conception of continuing, evolutionary progress for the notion of the stationary state. In fact, Marshall demoted the last from the endpoint in economic progress of the classics to little more than a preliminary simplifying abstraction for price theory. Secondly, he displaced the machine-like hedonism of Mill's economic man with a moral imperative. This was the duty to behave rationally in economic matters in the ordinary business of life, by instructing households to make saving and spending decisions which took account of real needs, both present and future. Work was therefore not pain for Marshall's economic beings, it was a creative activity in itself, leading to constructive developments in 'character'. Hence work and production was an economic end as important as that of consumption, and not only a means. A stress on duty to form a 'moralised capitalism' was the way in which the highest potentialities were to be achieved for mankind. This was the noble task in which he intended his new political economy to play an important, but by no means exclusive, role.[12]

These various streams directing his economic study merged in Marshall's first attempt at writing a 'special treatise on foreign trade', as one of 'a group of monographs on special economic problems'. This got no further than the first draft stage. His plan of later condensing 'these monographs into a general treatise of a similar scope to Mill's' was therefore never implemented and in fact reversed.[13] In the end, the treatise on foundations of the *Principles* preceded, and virtually swamped, the special monographs of the companion volumes he published much later. A trial run for this came with a first book, the little *Economics of Industry*, a by-product of his marriage to Mary Paley. In its preparation, he gave three years of labour to condensing in simplified form much of the first, massive fruit from his long economic apprenticeship. For this reason alone, its publication is best treated as the end of the beginning of the economist.

Discussion of Marshall's apprenticeship involves examination of the manifold influences on his economic thinking, going well beyond the theoretical 'heroes' he himself later singled out. It needs also to test the written record as retrospectively prepared by Marshall against the available evidence. In addition, the immense scope of the studies for which the apprenticeship was to prepare him had consequences in terms of ambitious publication plans, which repeatedly had to be revised. This was a lesson from his formative years in economics he never fully absorbed, as the subsequent sagas of his writing fully demonstrate.[14] This problematic scope of his economics arose largely from the wider aims he gave to his economic studies at this time, the reasons for, and circumstances surrounding which, need also to be clarified.

THE IMPETUS TO ECONOMIC STUDIES

The problems of practical ethics to which Marshall retrospectively assigned the original impetus for his economic studies were not explicitly discussed by him until relatively late in his life. Issues raised by psychology about 'the possibilities of the higher and more rapid development of human faculties', in turn introduced the question 'How far do the conditions of life of the British (and other) working classes generally suffice for fullness of life?'. In discussing this question with friends, he received the advice 'from older and wiser men . . . that the resources of production do not suffice for affording to the great body of people, the leisure and opportunity for study, and they told me to study political economy'. This advice may have been imparted through the written word as well as in conversation.

Similar advice was given by 'a friend, who had read a great deal of what are now called the Moral Sciences. He constantly said, "Ah! If you understood political economy, you would not say that." So I read Mill's *Political Economy* and got much excited about it.' The context of both pieces of advice was very similar. Marshall's 'doubts as to the propriety of inequalities of opportunity' implied difficulties for him in justifying 'the existing conditions of society', hence suggesting these needed to be redressed. After studying the 'faces of the poorest people', a sign that Marshall's concern at this stage was less with material comfort for the poor than with opportunities for giving them 'a fuller life', he resolved 'to make as thorough a study as I could of Political Economy'.[15]

It is interesting to note that Marshall himself passed on this advice to readers of his *Principles of Economics* as prospective students of political economy. Its opening pages emphasised both the problems with which he was grappling in the 1860s and the advice he was then given by others, that the 'facts and inferences . . . within the province of economics'[16] are a necessary even if insufficient part of the solution. These concerns were likewise consistent with much of the intellectual activity in which Marshall was engaged in the formative years of his economic apprenticeship. Some diverse examples suffice at this stage. They explain his early interest, and rather rapid disillusionment, with some socialists' thinking. Their solutions to redressing the existing conditions of society were simplistic, because they were 'too quick to assume that the abolition of private property would purge away the faults and deficiencies of human nature'.[17] Marshall's concern with inequality of opportunity likewise explains his strong interest at the time in the relation between standard of living and standard of life, visible in his life-long admiration for the work of Le Play, to which William Sargant's *Economy of the Labouring Classes* had probably introduced him.[18] He continued the study of this complex issue for much of his life. Studying the faces of the poor as an index of their access to a full life provided a rationale for the portrait collection of the intellectually and materially advantaged he was building up at this time. Study of the type of portraits he collected he hoped would lead to generalisations about facial characteristics by class and occupation. This could be of assistance to studying their counterpart in the faces of the poor, perhaps enabling an empirical contribution to 'practical' psychology, or to 'ethology' as the science of character. As Mary Paley later recalled, no such conclusions were in the end ever drawn, though an interest in faces of the working class is evident in the travel notes she made during the 1880s.[19]

These concerns help to explain why Alfred Marshall started his studies in economics sometime in the late 1860s; they do not necessarily explain why he decided to concentrate on economic studies at the end of the 1860s or early 1870s or, for that matter, why he never 'returned', as he later put it, to broad philosophical studies. The fact that he became 'excited' about Mill's work on the subject is ambiguous in this context. Moreover, the fact that for several years at least he studied political economy at the same time as several other social sciences, indicates concentration on economics needs more explanation than reference to concern over the future possibilities of working-class improvement, important though this reason may have been in later economic practice. It can also reasonably be asked who the older and wiser men were, and more specifically, who was the friend versed in the moral sciences, who advised him on the necessity to study political economy.

In Chapter 5, Percival, Pearson, Maurice, Fawcett and Sidgwick, were suggested as possible candidates for directing Marshall's interests towards social issues involving working-class improvement and who, in addition, could have pointed out to him the necessity of understanding political economy. All qualify as older men. Maurice was older than Marshall by a generation (37 years). Fawcett was Marshall's senior by nine years, Percival by eight, while Sidgwick and Pearson were respectively four and one year older than Marshall, who himself had turned 25 in the summer of 1867.

Percival's influence on Marshall at Clifton in 1865 was too early to galvanise Marshall into studying political economy a year or so later. J.B. Pearson, who was lecturing on political economy to moral science students before Marshall, may well have dampened Marshall's enthusiastic verbal ventures into social reform, as Marshall's later recollections imply 'older and wiser' men had done. Marshall's own critical attitude to Pearson as a moral sciences teacher may be recalled in this context.

Henry Fawcett was not the intimate of Marshall in the way he was of John Neville Keynes and, earlier, Leslie Stephen. There is no real evidence to suggest that the two were in any way close. His testimonial in support of Marshall's application for the Bristol position shows little personal warmth. The fact that he sent Marshall a presentation copy of his *Free Trade and Protection* is a sign of common courtesy rather than strong friendship. Marshall's own glowing tribute to Fawcett in his inaugural lecture is in the same vein, the remarks on the departed predecessor expected from his successor, before laying out an altogether different educational policy for his department of study. Without denying the possibility that Fawcett's opinion on subjects like cooperation and profit sharing had some importance for Marshall; Whitaker's view that Fawcett neither 'had little to offer Marshall intellectually' nor 'had a significant impact on Marshall's intellectual development' and teaching for the Tripos, seems accurate. However, some of Fawcett's published views on the poor match those which Marshall later attributed to 'older and wiser' men.[20]

Maurice's return to Cambridge life by November 1866 makes it unlikely he was a primary influence in stimulating Marshall's interest in social questions. However, Maurice probably reinforced the drift in direction of Marshall's thinking to a marked extent. His positive views on the value of political economy correspond to the advice Marshall was receiving on the importance of economic studies to the would-be social reformer. Maurice's inaugural lecture in December 1866 was probably also inspirational. It contrasted the certainty inherent in mathematical studies compared with those of human action based on a balance of probabilities, praised moral philosophy as the study of 'What manner makyth the man?' and mentioned 'chivalry, as one of the remarkable facts in the history of modern Europe'. Maurice's criticism of utilitarianism as a 'selfish self-seeking principle' or blind worship of the 'Money God' would likewise have struck a sympathetic chord with Marshall. More generally, Maurice's Christian Socialist principles, with their emphasis on co-operation and broad sympathy for the plight of the working class would have been very instructive for Marshall's self-education programme at this time.[21]

Henry Sidgwick appears the most likely candidate for 'the friend', expert in moral sciences who suggested the necessity of studying political economy if Marshall wished to pursue the issue of working-class improvement, as distinct from the 'older and wiser men' who proffered this type of advice. Sidgwick by then 'had read a great deal of what are now called the Moral Sciences' including political economy. When Sidgwick was dying of cancer in August 1900, Marshall recalled, 'the old days 1867–1877, when he was more to me than all the rest of the University', and in the official University Memorial to Sidgwick, Marshall described himself 'as wholly [Sidgwick's] pupil' in the moral sciences.[22] Sidgwick's testimonial in support of Marshall's application for the position at Bristol[23], by suggesting Marshall's dominance in Cambridge advanced political economy teaching for the moral sciences from the early 1870s, indicates that with respect to economics these roles were subsequently reversed.

Marshall's intellectual leadership in Cambridge political economy teaching by the early 1870s may explain why he decided to concentrate on political economy, irrespective of his motivation to commence reading in this subject. There is no reason to doubt his later claims that this owed much to concerns over social problems of poverty and working-class improvement and that, for at least the first few years after this interest was kindled, it remained secondary to his philosophical and psychological studies. The case for arguing that psychology as a career path was abandoned sometime in 1869 has already been made.[24] It is equally plausible that economics as a substitute career was decided on not long afterwards, particularly if by then Marshall realised how good he was at teaching the subject. None of this rules out Marshall's continuation of simultaneous reading in psychology and philosophy for some years afterwards.

Dating of Marshall's early manuscripts supports this view. The last of the surviving philosophical papers is not easily dated after 1869; his first significant and systematic economic writings date from 1870 at the earliest. In other words, only from 1870 did Marshall begin to direct his writing to this new major interest, that is, after writing had ceased on subjects connected with the human mind and psychology. Complete specialisation on economics probably did not start until the middle of the 1870s, if only because his teaching responsibilities in the early 1870s continued to include philosophical subjects. Interest in psychology remained visible until 1875. Economics' gain in capturing Alfred Marshall may therefore have owed at least as much to Marshall's will to succeed as to his desire to do good. An undated fragment preserved in the Marshall Archive, possibly from the 1920s, is illuminating: 'The instinct of the chase and the passion for victory supply the motive to much that is greatest in constructive achievement, and much that is most cruel and unscrupulous in the destruction of rivals.'[25] By the end of 1869, Marshall's economic apprenticeship seems to have started in earnest.

ALFRED MARSHALL AND THE POLITICAL ECONOMY OF JOHN STUART MILL

Any evaluation of Alfred Marshall's economic apprenticeship needs to begin by assessing the enormous influence thereon of John Stuart Mill's *Principles of Political Economy*. This follows from the earlier discussion of Marshall's letters with J.B. Clark and Colson concerning his mathematisation of Mill. A more accurate assessment of the type of excitement the reading of Mill's treatise generated in the postgraduate of 1867 can be gleaned from the annotations Marshall made to his personal copy of Mill, where those of the late 1860s can be fairly accurately distinguished from later ones through changes in handwriting. As indicated earlier, this book has been preserved. Moreover, Marshall's copy of Mill provided particularly full scope for the extensive scribbling in books Marshall occasionally liked to engage in. In the 1865 people's edition Marshall owned, each page of text is interleaved with a blank page. On some of these blank pages the mathematisation of Mill's rent theory *ex geometrico* can be seen, but hardly ever algebraically and never, strictly speaking, by way of the differential calculus.[26]

Marshall's annotations of Mill's *Principles* are most dense in the last three books. However, there are some significant early annotations in Books I and II. In Book I, the young Marshall showed strong interest in Mill's four propositions on capital (Chapter V)*, in Chapter VIII on cooperation and combination of labour (where the young Marshall at one stage inscribed three quotations from the first edition of Marx's *Capital*).[27] His most extensive comments in Book I are reserved for Chapter IX on large and small-scale production, indicating how early in his economic studies he was struck by the significance of this topic. Annotations to Book II Chapter I show his fascination with 'communism' of the Owenite variety; there are extensive comments on the economics of slavery (Book II Chapter V), but relatively little on the rest of Book II apart from Chapter XV on profits.

Book III is perhaps the most heavily annotated. Given what is now known about the young Marshall's writings on economics, this is not surprising. Many passages in the opening six chapters on value are marked, and the same applies to the preliminary chapters on money. One comment on the quantity theory of money (Book III, Chapter VIII, §2) is particularly interesting, because it contains an early algebraic formulation of the quantity theory of money:[28]

> Let α be the number of times any particular commodity of value v changes hands over the course of a year; $\underline{n}$ the average no. of times money does so, then if γ be the whole value of money,
>
> $$n\gamma = \Sigma(\alpha, v)$$

Other parts of Mill's monetary discussion, particularly that related to crises (Book III, Chapters IX–XIII) and the chapter on international value (Chapter XVIII) are marked in later hand-writing.[29] An exception includes comments on Chapter XIV, 'Of Excess of Supply', in which Sargant's *Recent Political Economy* is quoted as a critic of Mill's 'orthodoxy' on the subject. Chapter XXII on the associated subject of regulation of the currency is likewise heavily marked in the earlier handwriting.[30] This suggests that interest in social questions about the poor may have been partly inspired by the effects of the commercial crisis of May 1866, initiated by the collapse of Overend, Gurney & Co., a prominent Merchant Bank, of which some of the more visible signs may have been observed during his trip that summer to Scotland and to other parts of the industrial north.[31]

Book IV is likewise heavily annotated. This provides, for the first time, examples of geometrical transformations of Mill's theory of rent (Book IV, Chapter III) in the form of diagrams, examples of which are reproduced in Figure 6.1.[32] The most frequent annotations in Book IV occur in Chapter IV on the falling rate of profit, Chapter VI on the stationary state and Chapter VII on the 'probable future of the labouring classes', chapters particularly relevant to Marshall's burgeoning social interests at that time. Book V likewise contains a substantial number of annotations, particularly in the early chapters devoted to taxation. Many of these derive from the early 1870s or later, when Marshall was actively writing and lecturing on this topic.

---

* The young Marshall quoted Sargant's *Recent Political Economy*, p. 40, that 'English free trade measures 30 years ago caused a great demand for wheat: the Ohio farmers proceeded to grow the wheat: the demand for wheat was a demand for the labour which produced it'. This was with reference to §9 of the chapter, 'Demand for Commodities is not Demand for labour', to which the old[er] Marshall retorted in the 1890s: 'This is a good instance of the sort of proposition that Mill would rightly say, might be misunderstood.' (*Principles of Political Economy*, People's Edition, p. 49).

Figure 6.1:Marshall's Annotations of J.S. Mill, from Principles of Political Economy, *Book IV, Chapter III § 1 and 4.*

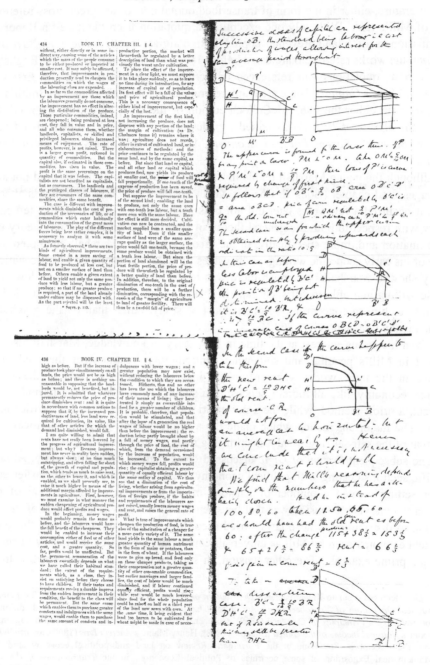

Source: Reproduced with permission from the Syndics of Cambridge University Library.

Marshall's annotations in his copy of Mill also provide useful evidence on the type of economic reading he was doing in these early years. The notes on Mill contain references to other literature, either in the form of transcribed quotations, or as direct cross-references to parts of Mill's text. With only one exception, a quotation from the Twelfth Report of the Commissioners of Inland Revenue copied from Palgrave's 1871 *The Local Taxation of England*, the works referred to are dated before 1870. All these references are English, apart from various quotations and references transcribed (in English) from the first German edition of Marx's *Capital*. There are many references in Marshall's notes to Smith's *Wealth of Nations* (in either the 1863 McCulloch edition or the 1869 edition by Thorold Rogers) and to the *Works of Ricardo* as edited by McCulloch. Marshall's notes also frequently mention Sargant's *Recent Political Economy*, 1867, a book highly critical of Fawcett's *Manual*.[*]

Although the young Marshall on his initial reading of Mill's *Principles* did not annotate the wages fund chapter (Book II, Chapter XI) in his personal copy, Thornton's attack on it when it occurred a few years later did not pass Marshall by.[33] The void this left in Mill's theory with respect to both the general theory of supply and demand as the theory of price determination and, more specifically, in the theory of wages, Marshall attempted to fill in some of his early economic writings. The wages fund debate inspired by Mill's static wages theory showed Marshall how much there was to do in economics and how few were the people willing and able to fill such gaps in theory. This fact must have provided further impetus for him to concentrate on this subject of study, rather than on the psychology he seemed ready to abandon by 1869.[34]

Given his strong interest at the time in the theory of knowledge, Marshall also showed interest in Mill's peculiar and somewhat contradictory treatment of the method of the science in the three works where Mill had discussed this. The first of these depicted political economy, like all moral sciences, as a subject whose laws were formulated by the abstract, a priori method; while the a posteriori method was reserved for verification of its truths. The major abstraction which made the a priori method proper to political economy was that of the self-seeking, wealth-maximising man, *homo oeconomicus*.[35]

The subsequent *System of Logic* discussed these matters quite differently. Although its specific sections dealing with political economy drew quite heavily on the earlier essay, its wider setting created a number of tensions in its treatment of the method of political economy. One visible tension was that between the historically relative part of the science, relating to distribution, whose laws varied according to time and place; and those parts of political economy seen by Mill as universally applicable, of which the theory of production was his prime example. The other tension, in some respects more important to the young

---

[*] Single references occur to Richard Jones's *Distribution of Wealth* of 1831, Robert Torrens's *The Principles and Practical Operations of Sir Robert Peel's Act of 1844 Explained and Defended* (in the second edition of 1857); Bonamy Price's *Principles of Currency* (1869), Goschen's *Foreign Exchanges* (in the fourth edition of 1864), Baxter's *National Income of the United Kingdom* (1868), Henry Maine's *Ancient Law* (1866), an article by Cairnes from the December 1869 issue of the *Fortnightly Review* on land and political economy, and Whewell's 'Mathematical Exposition of some doctrines of Political Economy', in the *Transactions of the Cambridge Philosophical Society* for 1829, the only known citation by Marshall of this work. By the end of 1870, Marshall's economics reading would already have included the books required for the Moral Sciences Tripos, in which he commenced teaching from the end of 1868, and on which see above, Chapter 5, pp. 118–20, 132.

Marshall, was that between the mechanical nature and the human aspects of the science. Mill drew attention to this in his plea for the establishment of ethology as a general social science of character, for whose development the empirical method was more appropriate.[36]

Mill's practical treatment of the science in his *Principles of Political Economy*, with its emphasis on 'their application to social philosophy', leaned much more to the broader aspects of method appropriate to ethology than to that abstract, a priori, mechanical method seen as most appropriate for political economy in the earlier writings.[37] Marshall, both when young *and* mature, preferred the Mill of the *Principles* to the Mill of the essay on method. He criticised the latter in his own *Principles*, while Mill's *Principles* was praised for providing the correct mixture of political economy as a social science. Mill's *Principles* emphasised the problems of humanity in discussing political economy, blended theory with the facts, and gave appropriate emphasis to the historical relativity of the subject matter.[38] Apart from the importance Mill's *Principles* exerted on Marshall's economic education because it was the first book on political economy he read, Mill's work continued to influence the development of Marshall's economic thinking over the decades to follow, despite his later criticisms of Mill.[39]

OTHER MAJOR ECONOMIC INFLUENCES AND SOURCES

After Mill, the major classical political economy books Alfred Marshall read in this period were Smith's *Wealth of Nations* and Ricardo's works. Marshall tended to use the McCulloch editions of these classics and in the case of the *Wealth of Nations* he as frequently used McCulloch's extensive notes to the text. His acquaintance with the two books was thorough. For teaching purposes he had to be familiar with both these set texts, particularly with Smith's book which tended to be the more popular with students. His notes in his copy of Mill also show how carefully he had read them. Much of the large quantity of manuscript material on Smith, and to a lesser extent on Ricardo, is substantially dedicated to the teaching task. However, the greater part of the debt Marshall owed to classical doctrine was to the version presented by John Stuart Mill, as Marshall himself indicated.[40] His strong familiarity and admiration of classical doctrine impressed itself on the organisation and content of his major economic work to an extent many later commentators found annoying.[41]

More important in this context were the work by Cournot and von Thünen. As Marshall wrote to J.B. Clark in 1900, he had studied their work as early as 1868, and 1869 or 1870, if his memory served him right. The reason why Marshall was able to study Cournot's book so early was undoubtedly due to the fact that it had been circulating in Cambridge mathematical circles from the 1840s onwards.* There is no copy of Cournot's book in the

---

* Correspondence between J.T. Graves and Whewell in 1848–49 mentioned the importance of Cournot's mathematical economics work and indicated that Graves had also brought it to the attention of Babbage. Babbage had held the Lucasian Chair of Mathematics at Cambridge from 1828 to 1839, and is said to have been a foundation member of the Cambridge Philosophical Society, at meetings of which Whewell presented his mathematical economic papers in 1829, 1830 and 1850. A Johnian mathematician, J.B. Cherriman, sixth wrangler in 1845, and a Fellow of his college for a short time, reviewed Cournot's book in a Canadian journal in

John's College Library and Marshall appears to have purchased a copy of the first edition early on. This, with his annotations, is preserved in the Marshall Library.

A pre-1870 dating of Marshall's annotations on Cournot's book is very plausible. Marshall's annotations cover aspects of monopoly theory, duopoly theory, competitive equilibrium and the effects of removal of a prohibition from trade.* Cournot's early guidance was used by Marshall to support a claim made to Walras in 1883 that 'he had anticipated all the central points of Jevons's book, and had in many respects gone beyond him'.[42] This explicitly included the matter of final utility which Marshall then claimed to have discussed in lectures prior to the appearance of Jevons's book under the title of 'terminal value in use'. An example of Marshall's use of the notion 'terminal value in use', but without using the term, is in the 1870 essay on value. 'The price P_2M_2 represents the "value in use" to those buyers who are the last induced to buy the commodity when an amount OM_2 per annum is sold, and who would not buy if the price were higher.'[43] Such usage does not imply marginal utility theory. When it is recalled that Cournot did not use utility analysis in the chapter on demand, Marshall's claims on Cournot's guidance in this respect becomes even more far-fetched. Marshall's early access to Cournot's work was a distinct advantage, but this did not extend to utility theory.[44]

Marshall never explicitly stated how he became aware of von Thünen's book. There are few references in the early writings to von Thünen's work and none which support his retrospective claim to Clark that he was reading von Thünen by 1869 or 1870. It is likely that Marshall learnt of von Thünen's importance from Kautz's discussion of his work in *Die Geschichtliche Entwickelung der Nationaloekonomik und ihrer Literatur*, which he was reading by 1870. An undated note on rent, which Whitaker suggests as a possible 1881 draft for a Chapter XII on rent of the *Principles*, bears the interesting postscript, 'Study Thünen on Rent with the aid of Roscher and Kautz on Thünen'.[45] When and how he acted on this advice is more difficult to tell, as is when he purchased the copy of *Der Isolierte Staat* preserved in the Marshall Library.[46] Another fragment gives a critical exposition of von Thünen's theory of the natural wage. Whitaker argues it 'appears to date from an early stage of Marshall's work', but no evidence is given and no time suggested.[47]

1857 as Professor of Mathematics and Natural Philosophy at Toronto University. Todhunter, who in 1875 acquainted Jevons with the importance of Cournot's book, was also a Johnian mathematician. He may well have come across the reference to the book in the Graves/Whewell correspondence, which he would have consulted with the Whewell Papers at Trinity in preparation for his biography of Whewell. See Salim Rashid, 'William Whewell and Early Mathematical Economics', *Manchester School* 45 (4), December 1977, pp. 388–9; Robert Dimand, 'An Early Canadian Contribution to Mathematical Economics': J.B. Cherriman's 1857 'Review of Cournot', *Canadian Journal of Economics*, 21 (3), August 1988, pp. 610–16, esp. pp. 613–14.

* In *EEW* II, pp. 240–48. In the context of discussing the possibility of whether these notes could have been written pre-1870, Whitaker (p. 240) notes the fact that the diagrams in the notes have price on the horizontal axis in virtually all cases. A major exception is Marshall's diagram (Figure 2 on p. 244) containing his preliminary analysis of consumer surplus. As Scott Gordon has argued, 'Why did Marshall transpose the Axes?'. *Eastern Economic Journal*, 8 (1), January 1982, pp. 34–5, Marshall's treatment of price as dependent variable (the price function form of the demand curve, p = f[Q]) fits the analysis of consumer surplus because it depicts 'the prices consumers are willing to pay for various quantities'. It may also be noted here that Graves in a paper he sent to Whewell likewise treated price as the dependent variable, criticising Mill's opposite treatment in this context. See Rashid, 'William Whewell and Early Mathematical Economics', p. 388, and see the comments on Rau below, p. 154.

The issue is of importance since Marshall later made extravagant claims on his indebtedness to von Thünen. These relate not only to marginal productivity theory and the theory of distribution in general, but to the use of the word marginal and even, in a fragment written in 1919, to marginal utility. In his letter to Clark in 1900 Marshall claimed to have got the word 'marginal' from 'von Thünen's *Grenze*', a claim which had been qualified in notes to early editions of the *Principles* by stating that although von Thünen did not actually use the word, it was 'in harmony with his method'.[48] The 1919 claim that von Thünen directed Marshall to the concept of marginal utility was justified in a similar vein. Marshall described this as one of the many 'great ideas . . . he threw out quietly . . . while chiefly concerned with agricultural problems'.[49]

The context of all of Marshall's retrospective references to von Thünen was his claim to independent discovery of the notion of the marginal method with respect to Jevons, including herein marginal utility. These always involved references to his debts initially to Cournot, and later especially to von Thünen. Such general claims on von Thünen's role in Marshall's development of marginalism were never clearly explained. Moreover, linking Cournot and von Thünen to claims of independent discovery of marginal utility seems deliberately misleading, since neither of them used the concept. Marshall was, however, specific in explicitly acknowledging von Thünen's inspiration for his distribution theory.[50] Timing of his first reading of von Thünen can be more flexible for this purpose. To demonstrate influence on his distribution theory, it is sufficient that Marshall studied von Thünen some time in the mid-1870s, which the evidence suggests he was probably doing. To make claims about the word, 'marginal' and more generally, marginalism, let alone nonsensical ones about 'marginal utility', Marshall had to be reading von Thünen by 1869 or 1870, prior to 1871 when Jevons's *Theory of Political Economy* was published. This Marshall found much more difficult to do, and the evidence is not convincing.

There is another factor in late praise Marshall later bestowed on von Thünen with great generosity. This is associated with von Thünen's method, which made him a classical author in Marshall's special sense of the word.[51] Marshall later compared von Thünen favourably with Cournot on this score, when he had become disillusioned with the lack of reality in many of Cournot's rigorous theoretical propositions.

> But my impression is that I did not derive so much of the substance of my opinions from him as from von Thünen. Cournot was a gymnastic master who directed the form of my thought. Von Thünen was a *bona fide* mathematician, but of less power: his blunder as to the natural wage is not of the same order as Cournot's little slips. But, to make up, *he was a careful experimenter and student of facts* and with a mind at least as fully developed on the inductive as on the deductive side. Above all he was an ardent philanthropist. And [since] I had come into economics out of ethics, . . . I loved von Thünen above all my other masters.[52]

It was von Thünen's love of facts, carefully blended with abstract reasoning, that especially endeared him to Marshall in later life. In 1889, he wrote to J.N. Keynes, then busily working on his *Scope and Method of Political Economy*, 'You know von Thünen's *métier* was that of agricultural reformer. His abstract economics came in by the way. He was up to his eye in facts about rye and manure and so on.'[53] Because a love of facts, when based on, and intertwined with, abstract reasoning, increasingly became Marshall's own credo in economics, this aspect of von Thünen's work is further pursued.

Von Thünen's *Isolirte Staat* begins with a simple, abstract hypothesis about a town placed at the centre of a varied, surrounding countryside, from which further hypotheses are put forward and propositions are developed into a complex analysis about location, land use, interdependence of agriculture and manufactures. Further propositions, for example, the determination of the price of grain, are then analysed under varying assumptions, and verified with data drawn from detailed calculations based on von Thünen's own estate, and on observations which took him a substantial part of his lifetime to collect.[54] Von Thünen himself explained this method as follows:

> We have now reached the point whence the present author set out on his inquiries. A deep urge compelled him to obtain a clear picture of the influence of grain prices on farming and of the laws governing these prices. This problem could be solved only by means of precise and detailed calculations on the costs of every branch of farming, based on data taken from reality; and with this end in view the author kept (and is still keeping) extremely detailed accounts on his estate at Tellow. Every single task which is undertaken at Tellow is noted in the work-book; and at the end of each year the entries are summarised to show how many people were required for mowing or harrowing, how much work one labourer or one team of horses could perform, and so on. In the same way the Tellow finance- and grain-books, when edited in association with the work-books, supply the data for working out the 'energy costs', e.g. the cost of a day labourer's family, a team of horses, or a hoeing machine. The amount and expense of the labour taken to till a field and harvest a crop gives us the production costs of this crop, and the gross product, minus the production costs, gives us the net surplus obtained from its cultivation. For the five years from 1810 to 1815, I worked out the net product of each crop, of dairying, sheep-farming, and of every branch of my estate at Tellow, and, but for 29.8 thalers annually, my findings coincided with the total net product. The findings of this calculation form the basis for all the calculations and findings in this work.[55]

Greater awareness of the importance in gathering facts and experimentation for scientific activity had only recently liberated Marshall from the basic intuitionist approach to obtaining knowledge through a priori argument. Marshall's discovery in von Thünen's work of the application of this method was therefore like a revelation to him. It conclusively showed the real possibilities for applying scientific method to his chosen subject. After all, this German philosopher–farmer had consistently applied the experimental method to the heart of economics; prices, wages, profits, rent and production and, by careful observation and gathering of facts from experience, tested his abstract hypotheses on these matters arrived at through formal deduction and introspection. The methodological appendix Marshall was to insert in the fifth edition of the *Principles* systematised his appreciation of the value of that method for economics most clearly:

> Induction, aided by analysis and deduction, brings together appropriate classes of facts, arranges them, analyses them and infers from them general statements or laws. Then for a while deduction plays the chief *rôle*: it brings some of these generalizations into association with one another, works from them tentatively to new and broader generalizations or laws and then calls on induction again to do the main share of the work in collecting, sifting and arranging these facts so as to test and 'verify' the new law.[56]

Von Thünen, however, had a further emotional connection with the young Marshall. This was his role as a great philanthropist, who, 'in the year of revolution, on 15 April 1848, felt able to carry into operation his long-conceived scheme for profit sharing' on his estate.[57] Marshall's own flirtations with socialist ideas included profit-sharing arrangements. Although Marshall's acquaintance with this notion derived largely from Mill's discussion in his *Principles*, von Thünen's embrace of such ideals was undoubtedly a further factor in retrospectively making him Marshall's 'master' in economics.[58]

OTHER INFLUENCES FROM GERMAN ECONOMICS, INCLUDING CURVES

Von Thünen was not the only German authority Marshall used during his economic apprenticeship. As he correctly claimed in 1910, early on he was attracted by the 'new views of economics taken by Roscher and other German economists' which, given Marshall's own wide perspective on nineteenth-century German economics,[59] embraced new departures in theory as well as in historical economics. Such German influence was much greater than has generally been realised, despite the fact that Marshall himself widely acknowledged its variety and its importance.[60]

In some ways, the more important of the German influences were theoretical. Following Streissler,[61] the potential impact of German economics on Marshall can be indicated as follows. Between 1825 and 1875 German economic texts blended the classical theory of growth and production with a theory of prices and distribution in which individual demand and utility generally played a significant role. This was a formulation of the 'neo-classical system in the sense it is now associated with Marshall's *Principles of Economics*, that is, half classical, half "neo"', German texts on economics, of which Marshall was reading by 1870 those by Hermann, Roscher, Rau and Mangoldt, started with goods, then wants, then the economy in terms of division of labour, organisation of industry, saving, the factors of production in terms of land, labour, capital and sometimes the entrepreneur. This structure resembles the framework of Marshall's *Principles*. Price theory was invariably handled in terms of individual prices and markets by way of supply and demand analysis. In Streissler's words,[62] these German economists 'were relatively soon satisfied that they had found sufficient causes behind supply and demand' without delving very deep into want satisfaction and cost theory. 'They always treated *one price at the time*. German economics was . . . *partial equilibrium analysis of demand and supply* par excellence.'

Some of these German authors used geometrical illustrations of supply and demand in their analyses of prices, and the remainder of this section is confined to their work. The most sophisticated attempt at this was by Hans von Mangoldt who drew demand functions and supply functions to illustrate the determination of particular market prices. Demand functions were explicitly associated with utility, with shifts in the curves explained by population growth, changes in taste and more generally, economic development and rising income and wealth. Demand curves in this analysis could be convex or concave to the origin, depending on the nature of the goods analysed, that is, whether they were luxury goods or necessities. Supply curves likewise were constructed in various shapes, reflecting differences in the behaviour of costs.[63] Unfortunately, Marshall was unable to benefit from Mangoldt's graphic analysis of supply and demand. Marshall's library shows that he only owned the posthumous edition of Mangoldt's *Volkswirtschaftslehre* which, like the second edition of *Grundriss der Volkswirtschaftslehre,* lacked any mathematical treatment or diagrams.[64] The only annotations in Marshall's copy of Mangoldt preserved in the Marshall Library are in a section dealing with the productivity of labour and the organisation of industry, in which the role of the 'undertaker' (*unternehmer*) is highlighted.[65]

Mangoldt's graphic analysis of supply and demand had been inspired by Rau's earlier but far less sophisticated treatment. This can be found in the Marshall Library, in his copy of the 1847 edition of Rau's *Grundsatze* of which he had bought a second-hand copy in Germany at what may have been quite an early stage in his economic studies. Rau thought his analysis of sufficient importance to re-state it algebraically, though this re-statement only holds for the simplified case of a linear demand, vertical supply case. More interestingly, he has price on the vertical axis and quantity on the horizontal axis, the change for which Marshall later became famous.[66] Marshall was fully aware of the significance of Rau's contribution. He lent a copy of Rau's book in early 1879 to Jevons, who was then constructing his appendix on mathematical economics; in 1910 he lent his copy of the fifth edition to Maynard Keynes, because Rau's 'curves' had come up in conversation with a Professor Liefmann, then staying with Keynes.[67] Theoretical inspiration and assistance from Germany therefore touched Marshall's analytical structure, method and 'curves', so that the importance of German economics went beyond his thinking on the role of history and humanity in good economics.

MARSHALL'S EARLY (1869–1874) INVESTIGATIONS INTO THE THEORY OF VALUE, MONEY, LABOUR, CAPITAL, RENT AND INTERNATIONAL ECONOMICS

Marshall's extant economic manuscripts of the early 1870s support the view on the nature of his early economic studies presented in the preceding sections. Their dating, difficult though it is to be precise in this matter, likewise confirm the view that when psychological writing stopped by early 1869, systematic economic writing replaced it after an appropriate lag. Some general characteristics of these early writings can first be noted. Many tend to be commentaries, re-statements or elaborations of topics raised by John Stuart Mill in his *Principles of Political Economy,* frequently assisted by the geometrical/diagrammatic technique of analysis Marshall had begun using in annotations to Mill's text. Algebra is only infrequently used and the differential calculus hardly ever.[68] Although the dating of these papers cannot be precise, the sources Marshall cited in them are invariably published before 1871 and with few exceptions are confined to the material Marshall referred to in his annotations of Mill or to the books set as required reading for the political economy segment of the Moral Sciences Tripos.[*] His Tripos lectures for the early 1870s concentrated on

---

[*]   Apart from John Stuart Mill's *Principles,* his *Essays on some Unsettled Questions* and his review of Thornton's *On Labour* in the 1869 *Fortnightly Review,* these early papers make reference to the work of Adam Smith, Ricardo's *Principles,* Malthus's work, Carey's *Principles,* McCulloch's *Principles,* Sargant's *Recent Political Economy* and William Thornton's *On Labour* (in the second edition of 1870). Apart from Sargant's book, these were all set works for the Moral Sciences Tripos. As Foxwell wrote to Jevons, 12 November 1879 (in Papers and Correspondence, V, p. 77), 'Marshall learnt and adopted a good deal from [Sargant]'. In addition, Marshall mentioned Turgot's *Réflexions* (he had bought a copy of the 1844 Daire edition of Turgot's Works at an early stage), two of Cliffe Leslie's essays (as reprinted in his *Land Systems and Industrial Economy in Ireland, England*

Mill's political economy in both the elementary and advanced segments, hence it can be presumed that much of the material in these papers was associated with his preparation for that task, a matter he took very seriously.[69] Finally, these early writings are theoretical and analytical, and rarely use factual illustration.[70]

The earliest of the economic manuscripts which appears to have survived, deals with the impact of improvements on rent. This paper is of interest because it contains Marshall's conscious decision 'to adopt curves as an engine' for analysis. The subject matter of the paper based on Mill's *Principles of Political Economy*, Book IV, Chapter III, §4, is the section in Marshall's copy where diagrams in annotations first appear.[71] These annotations form the basis of the paper, which even reproduces some of the diagrams.[72] In chronological sequence, it seems to have been followed by some short fragments on Mill's fundamental propositions on capital and fixed capital which cannot be dated beyond 1870 and which likewise were topics Marshall copiously annotated in his personal copy of Mill.[73] The essay on money which, not long before his eightieth birthday[74], Marshall himself dated 'about 1871' is very likely to have been his next production. It, like the previous two manuscripts, is a pure commentary on Mill (Book III, Chapter VIII), once again a chapter which Marshall had heavily annotated in his personal copy of Mill. These annotations provided the algebraic statement of the quantity theory of money mentioned previously.[75]

The essay on value,[76] contemporary to the essay on money, breaks new ground in the sense that it explicitly uses sources beyond Mill in determining the scope of its contents. Marshall himself was later unable to date it accurately. In December 1888 he wrote John Neville Keynes 'I can't fix the date, but I believe it was 1870. I know for certain it was before 1874.' Subsequently, in April 1892, he wrote to Edgeworth that it may have originated 'in the late [eighteen] sixties';[77] Internal evidence is not very helpful in deciding the matter more precisely, but 1870 or early 1871, the same period as the essay on money, seems to be the most likely time of writing.[78]

Because Marshall had studied Cournot by then it seems strange that there are no direct references to his work in the text. 'A nod in Cournot's direction would certainly have been appropriate when introducing the demand curve . . . [and] some trace of his influence might be suspected.'[79] The demand curve treated simply as a function of price without supporting utility argument suggests Cournot's influence, as does the definition of market provided, a definition on which Marshall later was to cite Cournot explicitly.[80] Of interest too, perhaps adding support for a late 1870–71 writing, is the fact that Marshall's diagrams are all drawn in the price-function form, contrary to Cournot's practice, and unlike Marshall's own annotations on his copy of that book, as indicated before.[81] Likewise, the brief reference to monopoly analysis which the paper makes would have owed much to Cournot's work, as Marshall's annotations on Cournot also show.[*]

---

and Continental Countries, London: Longmans Green, 1870), of which Marshall's personal copy is preserved in the Marshall Library with considerable annotations. (See *EEW*, I, p. 195 n.17.) The fact that Alfred Marshall used the second edition of Thornton's *On Labour*, which was published in the first half of 1870, assists in dating some of these early papers to late 1870 or 1871 (see *ibid*., I, pp. 185, 200 n.1).

[*] *EEW*, I, p. 152. The reference implies a separate treatment on monopolies at a later stage, which, if it was written, has not been preserved. Taken together with the neat form in which the essay on value was written, this may imply an original intention to publish on Marshall's part, aborted at a later stage. Cf. introduction to *HME*, pp. xii–xiv, and see below, pp. 164–5.

The contents of the paper on value is significant in itself because of its quite rich and already sophisticated supply and demand analysis, especially with reference to supply. A number of examples can be given. The paper criticised Ricardo's position when speaking of 'the ratio between supply and demand' because 'there cannot be a ratio between such heterogeneous quantities as supply and demand', a matter on which Mill had also criticised Ricardo.[*] Marshall linked this to a criticism of the wages fund doctrine, which relied on a similarly heterogeneous ratio in wage determination, and added the characteristic remark that Thornton's critique of the theory was to be taken as 'an addition, not a subversion of the theory of demand and supply' (p. 129). Demand and supply are then defined as functions of price, equilibrium and its stability are discussed, before a more detailed analysis of the market situations explaining the conditions underlying demand and supply is attempted. These concentrate on supply factors in terms of the time periods Marshall was to make famous in his *Principles* and raise the issue of unstable equilibria under situations of increasing returns. The paper ends by raising a number of special cases in the theory of value, including that of Thornton's fish market (p. 155) and several examples of joint supply (pp. 156–9). With reference to the discussion of the previous section, the diagrams Marshall presented with this paper bear little resemblance to those used by Rau and Mangoldt.

Subsequent topics Marshall addressed in his early economic papers were labour and wages, together with the associated problem of allotments as a form of income supplement for workers, and a paper on profits in relation to risk and other factors. These essays are noteworthy for the fact they contain no references to von Thünen although in some respects they systematically develop arguments from the essay on the theory of value whose date of writing coincides with Marshall's own recollections of when he first read von Thünen's work.[82] The piece on allotments, like so many of these early pieces, is directly inspired by Mill's treatment of the subject (*Principles*, Book II, Chapter XIII §4), though Marshall's interest in this topic may have owed something as well to Thornton's account of the reasons for labour's discontent in its rural aspects.[83] The essay on profits is also Millian in its treatment. Marshall developed Mill's ideas on risk premium and acknowledged Smith's contributions to differential profit analysis in this context. Hence early distribution analysis, among which must also be counted the 1872 essay on tithes, shows that Marshall's thinking on this subject was still essentially Millian. This also applies to the wages doctrine which continues to have a pronounced wages fund flavour though it rejects Mill's crude Book II version. None of the early writings on distribution at this stage reveal any real trace of marginal productivity ideas. As indicated previously, the state of Marshall's distribution theory by the mid-1870s suggests that his acquaintance with von Thünen's economics came later than he himself subsequently chose to remember.[84]

The last of the pre-1875 essays are devoted to several topics. One deals with the graphic solution to joint and composite demand with fixed coefficients of production. This supplements the material on joint supply in the earlier essay on value. The sophistication of its contents (it closely resembles mathematical notes XIVbis, XVII, XVIII, XX and XXI of

---

[*]   *EEW*, p. 129 (subsequent page references in brackets in this paragraph refer to the same edition). Marshall had noted Ricardo's error on this point in his own copy of Mill's *Principles* and later resolved this question of heterogeneity by treating supply and demand either in subjective (disutility, utility), or in money terms.

the *Principles*) suggests it was probably written closer to 1874 than 1870.[85]   A long manuscript essay on international trade is also extant.   This turns Mill's chapters on international values into geometry and can be dated between 1872 and 1874.   A brief note on the overall gains ('total utility') of trade, likely to have been written before 1872, and a piece on absentee landlords, with special reference to Ireland but including some anecdotal material on Australian landlords, have also been preserved.   The last may have been inspired by the experiences of Uncle Charles, who was back in London by then.   Its writing can be dated between 1872 and 1875, with 1872 or 1873 the more likely dates.   The relative maturity of the international trade essays suggests Marshall's growing interest in that direction, thereby partly explaining his choice of subject for the first project of a book.[86]

The contemporary pages from a mathematical notebook largely provide rigorous analytical support for the propositions developed in the essays on rent, tithes, wages and money, as well as more advanced solutions to problems of triangular barter in international trade.   That, and the analysis of the welfare effects of taxation and tolls in terms of consumer/producer surpluses, break important new analytical grounds not directly inspired by the scope of Mill's economics.   Dating is once again not easy as they seem to derive from the whole period of Marshall's economic apprenticeship.[87]

In combination, Marshall's essays of the early 1870s provide a systematic overview of some major topics in political economy: rent, money, value, wages, international economics.   Their development, generally speaking, relied on a systematic application of supply and demand analysis, by means of a graphical analysis which had moved well beyond its Millian origins, assisted by the guidance Marshall had obtained from Cournot's work and perhaps from German sources like Rau.   Explicit marginalist content is still limited at this stage.   It is visible in the monetary theory in which Marshall explained the demand for money in terms of an individual's desire to balance the advantages of holding assets in the form of general purchasing power (command over commodities) relative to the cost of holding less wealth in the form of interest-yielding assets. The early value theory demonstrates the usefulness of the supply and demand apparatus for explaining competitive price determination.   The time dimension of various forms of supply adjustment, including the case of falling supply curves, is already extensively recognised, as are associated problems of the stability of equilibrium, joint demand and joint and composite demand/supply.   The problems are largely Mill's, occasionally Thornton's or Ricardo's; the tools of analysis, Marshall's.   Following Cournot, there is a clear foreshadowing of the special problems of monopoly equilibrium analysis at this stage.

Marshall's early rent analysis puts the 'Ricardian' intensive margin analysis in diagrammatic form.   This illustrates simultaneous determination of the price of agricultural output and the rent of the land on which it is produced.   Marshall did this by means of a function showing declining returns to equal doses of capital and labour successively applied up to the point where the given cost of a 'dose' equals its return, that is, the point where the marginal return equals cost. This diagrammatic technique is also used to solve problems associated with the effects of improvements and of tithes on rent and agricultural prices.

Early wages theory treats demand for labour in the classical manner in terms of capital, but Marshall allows discretion to the capitalist in deciding whether capital is to be applied to wages, to fixed capital or to other purposes.   Marginal productivity is given no explicit role in explaining the demand for labour. Competition will drive wages to the discounted value of the worker's product, while the use of fixed capital is seen to depend on the rate of profit, and hence the rate of wages.

Finally, the international trade essay reveals comprehensive and systematic development of trade equilibrium by means of offer (reciprocal demand) curves, an analysis which is the most sophisticated example of Marshall's application of geometry to economic problems. Once again, much, but not all of the inspiration derived from Mill's discussion. Marshall's attempts at welfare analysis in taxation and public price theory in terms of consumer surplus by the middle 1870s are his most innovative work in the early writings with respect to substance, though all of it breaks new grounds in terms of analysis and solutions reached.[88]

Two further aspects of Marshall's early work need to be noted. First, it was highly theoretical and had none of the factual illustrations for which Marshall's work later became noted. Secondly, the material he developed in these early essays were the foundations for the major working hypotheses underlying his later work, and apart from the theory of distribution, they fundamentally remained intact in the later *Principles*. The same can be said with respect to his work on value, on rent and on international trade, though not on distribution. Although, as briefly suggested in the context of the very polished essay on value, publication may have been a motive in writing some of these essays, the fact that they were not published in this form during his lifetime owed perhaps something to contemporary developments in economics which seemed to duplicate his own efforts. Publication of Jevons's *Theory of Political Economy* and of Fleeming Jenkin's graphical analysis of labour, taxes and prices, discouraged any intentions Marshall may have had of putting his own efforts at analysis by curves into print at this stage.[*]

JEVONS, FLEEMING JENKIN AND POSTPONING PUBLICATION

In late 1871 or early 1872 Marshall was invited to review Jevons's *Theory of Political Economy* for the *Academy*, a journal founded in 1869 by Oxford scholar Dr Charles Appleton as an outlet for academic research, at a time when the notion of the academic journal was still in its infancy.[89] Marshall later[90] indicated that the editor had heard he was working in political economy on lines similar to Jevons and this was why he was asked to review Jevons's book. The *Academy*'s informant was almost certainly Sidgwick, who in 1871 was 'writing a good deal in the *Academy*, chiefly reviews of philosophical works'.[91] Sidgwick was possibly also the source of Marshall's knowledge about Jevons as an economist, though it is feasible Marshall by then was aware of Jevons's earlier contributions. These were *The Coal Question*, which had brought Jevons to public attention in 1866, and his *A Serious Fall in the Value of Gold* of 1863.

It is not difficult to see why Marshall looked forward with great excitement to Jevons's book and why, after reading it, he was disappointed. '[I]t gave me no help with my difficulties'.[92] For one who had been teaching Bentham, the material on utility would not

---

[*] Mary Paley Marshall ('MSS Notes', NCA) recalled, 'In the seventies when he first began to write his idea was to start with a series of monographs, and by 1876 he had practically completed several. The Shell Theory of Money, the Theories of Domestic and Foreign Trade and his Theory of Trade Unions. After finishing several more monographs he intended to write a Treatise. This plan was upset.'

have seemed particularly fresh or novel, though Jevons's contribution of final (marginal) utility ought to have done so.   Jevons's discussion of price determination appeared to Marshall less advanced than his own, already well-developed, supply and demand analysis. In distribution theory, where Marshall was experiencing real difficulties at the time of writing the review, little help could be gained from Jevons's book. Marshall had reached the same stage in rent theory as Jevons by 1869, through mathematising Mill *ex geometrico*, while the economics of labour and capital was seen by Marshall in his review not as a new, general theory but as 'an original treatment of a number of minor points', or as examples of the 'suggestive remarks' and 'careful analyses' which constituted the main value of Jevons's book. However, Marshall did see the mathematical and independent treatment of capital and interest as 'bold and subtle'.[93]

Jevons's reaction to Marshall's review was that it was 'more fair than that of the *Saturday Review* [but that] it contained no criticism worthy of notice'.[94] For Marshall, on the other hand, the review presented points he continued to see as important. In addition, it illustrated another aspect of that disappointment Marshall later recorded as his major reaction on first reading Jevons's book. This concerns Jevons's attack on the classics, which Marshall saw as unfounded for at least two reasons. Firstly, a point Marshall made well after the review, Jevons did less than justice to Ricardo's genius; secondly, Jevons failed to see the point Marshall himself was to make repeatedly, that the difference between the old and the new economics was one of form rather than of substance.[95] More important was Marshall's critique that Jevons in the *Theory* was insufficiently aware of the interdependence of value and distribution and that the distributional equation, price = profit + wages, needed a general equilibrium solution rather than the sequential one which Jevons proposed.[96] Marshall also criticised Jevons on aspects of his utility theory, for example, in the context of the discussion of the benefits of foreign trade.[97] However, Marshall benefited considerably from this aspect of Jevons's theory as well, particularly with respect to his thinking on the problem of measurement in political economy which his own early papers had not satisfactorily addressed. Last but not least, is the annoyance of the second wrangler at Jevons's 'occasional mathematical fumblings'. This included the confusing nature of some of Jevons's calculus and algebra.[98]

Marshall's annotations in his personal copy of the first edition of Jevons's *Theory** shed further light on some of these aspects of hs review. Marshall disagreed with Jevons's proposition that 'value depends entirely upon utility', noting 'labour is *a* cause of value' (pp. 2, 186). He also disagreed with the undue stress on consumption from focusing on utility (p. 47). The annotations reveal Marshall's strong concern with measurement at this stage. In the context of value and price, Marshall stated all such expressions required a unit of measurement (p. 83). On Jevons's rent equation (p. 207) Marshall noted 'we cannot subtract recompense from produce till we have a common measure of value'.   The annotations confirm Marshall's annoyance with Jevons's attacks on Mill, but not with those on Ricardo. Marshall only raised such objections well after he had written the review.

---

* Preserved in the Marshall Library. Page references in the text refer to this edition, where Marshall's annotation can be found. He was willing to learn from Jevons's greater knowledge of the literature, marking, for example, the references to Lardner and Tozer (p. 17) while in the bibliographies appended to the second edition, he also marked a number of books and articles as clearly of interest to him.

Referring to Jevons's comments on Mill's criticism of demand and supply as a ratio, Marshall noted, 'Mill's language is horribly slipshod but there is nothing stated in this [Jevons's argument] which Mill does not state in one form or another at some part of his accounting.' (pp. 102–3, 139). Jevons's mathematics was also patronisingly corrected in the margins of his book. For example, in the chapter on wages (p. 179), 'He does not seem to know he may divide out the Δx'. Marshall wrote a firm 'no' to Jevons's assertion, 'one pound invested for five years gives the same result as five pounds invested for one year' (p. 221). The practical reformer in Marshall likewise noted with evident distaste Jevons's attempt to measure investment by time only, 'This is a *play* result: true enough, but of no practical importance.' (p. 228). There are occasional remarks of 'good' or 'true enough', and in the section on Hearn in the final chapter (p. 263) the remark, 'True, but not Jevons'.

Although his first publication, the Jevons review clearly expressed Marshall's strong predilections 'for stating economic reasoning and results in ordinary language' while reserving the terse and clear method of graphic representation in the style of Fleeming Jenkin and Marshall himself, for their illustration.[99] Jevons's own neat diagrams, whose retention Marshall advocated, in contrast to his suggestion that calculus and algebra be removed from future editions, may disguise signs of pique at being once more beaten to the punch in this area, just as in Easter term 1870, when Foxwell showed Marshall Jenkin's 'Graphical Representation of the Laws of Supply and Demand', his face revealed 'chagrin' at being anticipated by a person whose general approach to supply and demand was so close to that used by himself.[100] Jevons's book, which strikingly demonstrated that Marshall was only one of several economists working with graphical explanations – the new tool of analysis he had so deliberately and self-consciously adopted in 1869 – may have made him realise that there was little to be gained from rushing into print with his graphical theory of value and price as contained in his 1870 manuscripts.

Personal contact between Marshall and Jevons did not eventuate until Jevons examined for the Moral Sciences Tripos in 1875. However, in 1874 Jevons did become acquainted with Marshall's 'curves', as provided by his students in their answers to the political economy papers Jevons was examining. In January 1875, Jevons wrote to Marshall how sorry he was that he had missed him the previous December and 'how interested he had been' in the answers in political economy. 'What interested me most of all however was the way in which some of them applied the graphical method no doubt according to your views. I did not understand the particulars of all the figures as some of the men in the hurry of writing seemed to think the examiners must know all about the figure if they merely sketched it out. I understand enough however to think that the way in which you had applied curves to questions of taxation and the like was very successful. I have no doubt that there is a great field open for the investigation of economy in this way and I wish you could be induced to print what you have already worked out on the subject .'[101] This was the year in which Mary Paley, Marshall's student and future wife, had an indeterminate Tripos result with two examiners voting for a result in the first class and two for the second. It was also the year when James Ward was Senior Moralist.[102] In 1875, Ward told John Neville Keynes, who followed in Ward's footsteps by becoming Senior Moralist in the 1875 Tripos examination, 'Jevons said that you floored the Logic papers and that your answers were a pleasure to read. I should fancy you pleased him better in Logic than in Economy, he evidently doesn't believe much in Marshall and was amused at your curves.'[103]   This time Marshall was present, and in fact hosted a party for the examiners,[104] at which he and Jevons may have further discussed aspects of mathematical analysis in economics, airing their differences. The possibility of this is raised both by Ward's comments to Keynes, and by subsequent correspondence between Marshall and Jevons.

A letter from Marshall in February 1875 indicates Jevons had sent Marshall his 'Mathematical Theory of Political Economy'. In thanking him, Marshall admitted that 'the substantive difference between us is less than I once supposed', an indication that the review may have been discussed.   Mill caused 'the major divergence in our views', because Marshall saw Mill's political economy as largely 'incomplete truths' instead of the fallacies perceived by Jevons. Marshall, however, conceded 'that Mill was not a constructive genius of the first order, and that, generally the most important benefits he has conferred on the science are due rather to his character than to his intellect'.[105] In 1877, Jevons wrote Marshall a glowing testimonial for the Bristol Principalship.   During 1879 the pure value theory material privately printed by Sidgwick and publication of the *Economics of Industry* fully convinced Jevons of 'Marshall's scientific powers' in economics.[106]   However, when in the context of Jevons's much-extended preface to the 1879 second edition of his *Theory of Political Economy*, Foxwell wrote that 'Marshall's work was about contemporaneous with yours . . . as to priority', explicable in terms of their 'thoroughly mathematical' presentation of their ideas, Jevons replied he could have borrowed nothing from Marshall by the time his *Theory* had first been published.[107]   Fulsome praise for Jevons from Marshall came only after Jevons's death. This included special admiration for Jevons's social essays, and, a decade or so later, the recognition in a letter to Bonar that Jevons was a genuine classical economist, on a par with the high originality of Petty, Ricardo, Hermann and von Thünen.[108]

A tribute which Marshall prepared for Jevons in the year after his death reveals his praise and admiration related to Jevons's general contributions to economics and not to his *Theory of Political Economy*. That book involved no 'startling discovery', 'was warped by his antipathy to Ricardo' and 'will lose lustre when Cournot's applications of Mathematics to Economics are better known'. The greater part of Jevons's work, Marshall argued, was 'unaffected by these blemishes', and in his applied economics, 'his full greatness is seen' because of its 'originality', 'suggestiveness' and 'wisdom'.[109]   Marshall reiterated this position some years later in correspondence with J.N. Keynes.   'I hold that Jevons's great error was that of applying to utility propositions that are only true of price . . . it is because I think he was wrong in this one point that he differed from his predecessors von Thünen and Cournot that I consider his claims to greatness do not to any considerable extent rest on his *Theory of Political Economy*'. This error related to what Marshall alleged was Jevons's 'systematic confusion between . . . Hedonics and Economics', on which Marshall had always been deliberately silent.   To avoid confusion between his notion of consumers' surplus and utility, Marshall broke this silence to convince Keynes that consumers' rent was 'a sum of money not an amount of utility' and that losses in consumers' rent from taxes can only be connected to utility losses if it is known 'the commodity taxed is one consumed by the rich by the poor or by all classes alike'.[110]   There was never an admission on Marshall's part that he learned anything from Jevons's *Theory* on the subject of utility, including aspects of its measurement on which Jevons had contributed much.[111]

Whitaker[112] draws attention to Marshall's 'less than frank position' about what he may have learned from Jevons's *Theory of Political Economy*, even if it was the 'form' of the argument, especially on utility and consumer surplus, rather than the 'substance' on which he ought to have acknowledged Jevons's contribution. On marginal utility, which facilitated the transitions of Marshall's demand theory to the mature version of the *Principles*, and on disutility of labour as treated there, such acknowledgement was only very grudgingly and spasmodically given. Marshall much preferred to discuss this question of priority in terms of obscure references to the value of his predecessors Cournot and von Thünen, who could not have been helpful on either of these topics.[113] In what was probably his last letter to Jevons,[114] Marshall recognised him as the 'chief author in abstract quantitative reasoning in economics' which may refer to either theoretical or statistical contributions.

More importantly, Jevons appears to have indirectly influenced Marshall's publishing strategy. Writing to Edgeworth the month after Jevons's death, Marshall told him: 'I sometimes wish that I had published before Jevons's book came out: as I did not, I determined to put off publishing till I could do so with satisfaction to myself; and as the cruel fates would have it, I did hardly any new work at economic curves between 1872 and 1881.'[115] The implications of these remarks seem to be as follows. Once the chance of establishing priority in the use of curves as a tool of economic analysis had completely evaporated with the publication of Jevons's elegant diagrams in the *Theory*, following as they did on the publication of Fleeming Jenkin's graphical analysis in 1870, Marshall switched publishing intentions to a treatise on international trade. This was a setting where his 'curves' could be exhibited to advantage, particularly since relatively little had been published on the subject since Mill's analysis in the *Principles* of nearly a quarter century before.*

Marshall later wrote to Maynard Keynes about the impact made by Fleeming Jenkin's graphical analysis. This came in 'some gossip' about how he became acquainted with one of Jenkin's articles,

> I had of course seen Fleeming Jenkin's first paper in *Recess Studies* 1870, but that had no bearing on the short address which I gave at the Cambridge Philosophical Society (see Proceedings for Oct. 1873) to explain the uses of H.H. Cunynghame's glorious machine for drawing rectangular hyperbolas in relation to monopoly values. In that paper, however, I explained consumer surplus (I then called it 'rent') which I thought was my own property for I knew nothing of Dupuit. I wanted it [Cunynghame's machine] of course for the curve which I afterwards called 'Compromise Benefits Curve'. Maxwell got up and said, part of the paper reminded him of Fleeming Jenkin's work, referring of course to the paper in R[oyal] S[ociety of] E[dinburgh] Proceedings for [18]71–72: and that puzzled me, for I had not seen the paper.

---

* Little on international trade was in fact published until Fawcett's *Protection and Free Trade*, London: Macmillan, 1878; Jevons, J.E. Cairnes, Bagehot and Cliffe Leslie, to mention the other great English economists who Marshall named in his inaugural lecture as having died in the twelve preceding years, published relatively little on the subject, at least in a separate treatise. Jevons did include some important material on trade in *Theory of Political Economy*, second edition, 1879, pp. 142–6, and Cairnes devoted Part III of his *Leading Principles of Political Economy* (1874) to international trade.

At last when my Principles came out, Jenkin wrote me a courteous letter, somewhat like that which Walras had written about multiple points of intersection, establishing priority of publication: and then I saw that Jenkin had gone a great deal deeper than I had gathered from *Recess Studies*.[116]

Apart from confirming Marshall's sensitivity about independent discovery and priority in connection with consumer surplus and the notion of compromise benefit, the letter has puzzling aspects. One is Marshall's claim not to have followed up Jenkins's contribution on tax incidence, particularly since he himself was working on this topic at the time. Marshall knew Clerk Maxwell from the Eranus Society. The latter, who corresponded with Jenkin, could easily have alerted Marshall to the interesting nature of this contribution which, after all, had not been published in a difficult to obtain source.[117] Jenkin's letter to Marshall appears not to have survived.

A 'FULL FRESH ENTHUSIASM FOR THE HISTORICAL STUDY OF ECONOMICS'

In a letter to L.L. Price in November 1892,[118] Marshall recalled how in 'the early seventies, when I was in my full fresh enthusiasm for the historical study of economics, I set myself to trace the genesis of Adam Smith's doctrines.' These years marked more than a thorough study of the history of economics, they also saw Marshall's search for facts relevant to economic study, contemporary and historical. The re-emergence of a genuine historical spirit in Cambridge with Seeley's appointment in 1869 to the History chair was noted earlier. Marshall may have reacted to this by a voracious reading of historical works. The summers of the early 1870s were later recorded as largely devoted to history. The philosophical position he had reached on the importance of factual analysis in the critical study of the theory of knowledge he had undertaken prior to his immersion in economic studies, would have reinforced a historical tendency. As mentioned previously, Marshall's earliest economic studies were devoid of factual material; Marshall made up for this deficiency in the final years of his economic apprenticeship in the early 1870s.[119]

One facet of Marshall's hunger for facts of this period is well illustrated in a bundle of statistical notes he collected at the time.[120] Their source varies from newspaper cuttings and extracts from periodicals like the *Economist* and the *Fortnightly Review* which Marshall by then was assiduously reading, to extracts from books and from statistical studies and reference works, official and unofficial. The data collected cover population statistics, national income and consumption data, price data, social statistics on mortality, crime and the drink question, trade and taxation statistics, data on land nationalisation, coal and water as energy sources and the power of compound interest. Sources like Sargant's *Recent Political Economy* and Marx's *Capital* are supplemented with statistical work by Seebohm, Hoyle and Hübner.[121] The difficulty of keeping these data sources manageable for reference purposes was probably one motivation for Marshall's construction of his Red Book in 1875 as a far more convenient access to contemporary economic statistics and historical data. It provided extensive economic data on an annual basis combined with information on literature, the arts, philosophy, the sovereigns of Europe and the political history of England; a cross, in short, between a statistical year book and a boy's own annual. An additional function of the Red Book was to remind Marshall of the complexity of economic causes and effects, thereby warning him off the usefulness of simple regression analysis at an early stage.[122]

The contents of Marshall's Red Book point to a fascination at this time with the more holistic aspects of history, or historicism, a fascination which probably owed much to his contemporaneous study of Hegel's *Philosophy of History*, Buckle's *History of Civilization*, Maine's early works and those of Spencer, particularly his *First Principles*. Extant notebooks for this period indicate much involvement as well with economic history. This was not confined to the study of the more modern European history from the late Middle Ages, but included material on the economic organisation of the ancient world of Asia (China, India, Persia) and the Mediterranean basin (Israel, Phoenicia and, more thoroughly, Greece and Rome). Increasingly these historical studies benefited from his growing acquaintance with the German language, begun by taking lessons in 1868, and enabling access to the works of Roscher, Rau, Knies, Kautz and other members of the German historical movement in economics. Analogous with the visible parts of the iceberg, the fruits of these historical researches were partially revealed in the historical chapters of the *Principles* which became Appendix A of the later editions of that book. In a more limited way, they were used in writing some chapters for the 1879 *Economics of Industry*.[123]

Pages in the Red Book also show considerable evidence of the study of doctrinal history, the aspect of his youthful historical enthusiasm of which Marshall had written to Price. The extent of these studies are more fully documented in a letter Marshall wrote to Foxwell. This gave advice to his former student and successor as Moral Sciences College Lecturer at John's to assist preparation of his political economy lectures. After virtually dismissing Blanqui's *History of Political Economy*, as a work by 'a good safe man, just a trifle above mediocrity', Marshall continued his advice,

> There are absolutely no English works on the suject except McCulloch, McLeod and Travers Twiss. This last is of some little use, it is out of print and extremely scarce, but it is in the Cambridge University Library. French books on Political Economy have as a rule disappointed me. Two brilliant exceptions are Lavergne's 'Les Economistes français du XVIIIe siècle – you should anyhow buy this at 7F50 and Turgot's 'Réflexions sur les richesses'. . . . There is a magnificent collection of the writings of the Physiocrats by Daire in the Univ. Library. It is out of print. It should be read *pari passu* with Lavergne. I have very often tried to read Say as a disagreeable duty; but his dullness has beaten me every time. . . . You should look at McCulloch's 'Treatise on Economic Policy', as well as his life of A. Smith, also the little article on Primitive Political Economy by Jones. If you don't read German, I can't recommend much about early medieval and ancient economic theories. But for various reasons you may be interested in working at some portions of Lecky's Rationalism and of Hallam's Middle Ages, particularly in connection with Italian economy. I believe, by the bye there is some good Pol. Econ. in Italian. I have thought of learning Italian on purpose. I forgot to mention Récherches historiques sur le système de Law par E. Levasseur 1854. . . . Levasseur is able. Of course you will look at Blanqui, commonplace as he is; the way in which he recognises the solidarity between economic phenomena and economic history is improving.[124]

That Marshall had followed his own advice is apparent from his notes on the history of economic theory and economic history preserved in the Marshall Library and from an early manuscript on the history and method of economics.[125] Designed as either a lecture or for separate publication, it perfectly illustrates Marshall's infatuation with historical economics at this time, pointing to a need for economics students to familiarise themselves with aspects of the history of economics. Although at its start, Marshall admitted that the need for such knowledge diminished with the progress of the science in question, he nevertheless argued there were three important reasons for studying the history of economic theory. It was 'likely to aid our advance as regards the abstract theory', it was essential to 'obtain a personal acquaintance with the great minds who have . . . contributed to contemporary knowledge', and thirdly, it facilitated understanding 'of the social and political phenomena of the period in which they were held'.[126] The third point emphasised more than the relativity of economic theory, because it was designed to stress the interdependence of doctrinal history with history in general.[127] The remainder of the unfinished paper illustrates this with reference to the ancient world in which Marshall demonstrates his already extensive knowledge of the historical literature achieved by the early 1870s.[128]

Although in later years Marshall substantially qualified his opinions on the relevance of history to students of economics, he never abandoned his position on the importance of factual knowledge for them. For him such knowledge invariably included historical material. Marshall's stance on this subject is indicated in his twentieth-century Cambridge economics lectures and is visible today in the prominence he gave to historical material in the pages of his *Principles*. The use he himself made of such factual material in his work, together with the various ways he sought to obtain it, are recurring subjects in his life study, starting with the preparation of the manuscript on international economics discussed later in this chapter.

PHILOSOPHICAL FOUNDATIONS: BENTHAM, HEGEL, SPENCER AND MAINE

In his *Principles*, Marshall singled out Bentham for praise as a crucial influence on the development of economics in the nineteenth century, both in his role as 'uncompromising logician' and as 'ardent reformer'. However, as Mary Paley recalled, in his lectures of the early 1870s, the important influence of Bentham – 'more influence on economics than any other non-economist' – is ascribed to his stress on measurement, of which the discussion of measurement of pleasure and pain in his *Introduction to the Principles of Morals and Legislation* is the prime example.[129] Bentham's book was an essential part of the syllabus for the Moral Sciences Tripos while study of utilitarianism was a major component of the segment the Tripos devoted to moral philosophy. When Marshall lectured on moral and political philosophy in the early 1870s, utilitarianism as originally espoused by Bentham and as revised by John Stuart Mill formed the mainstay of his lectures. Moreover, his knowledge of the subject would have benefited from discussions with Sidgwick, then writing his *Methods of Ethics*, the first edition of which was published in 1874.[130] Despite this tribute to Bentham and the close awareness of the contents and problems of utilitarian doctrine, Marshall was no 'crass utilitarian' himself. Marshall's picture of economic behaviour was sketched differently from that given in Mill's utility-maximising 'economic man'. His careful use of utility maximisation in questions of economic analysis were therefore rigidly separated from any connections with utilitarian ethics, 'let alone the psychology of hedonism or any suggestion of narrow materialism or selfish greed'.[131]

Bentham's influence on Marshall pivots on the important question of measurement in estimating the extent of human action. His own crude calculus induced Marshall's search for a measure useful to clarify aspects of human behaviour in a scientific way. The ability to use the measuring rod of money gave economics an advantage over other branches of the social sciences. 'An opening is made for the methods and the tests of science as soon as the force of a person's motives – not the motives themselves – can be approximately measured by the sum of money, which he will just give up to secure a desired satisfaction; or again by the sum of money which is just required to induce him to undergo a certain fatigue.'[132] It was Bentham's suggestion rather than his solution which was important to Marshall. Furthermore, Marshall at an early stage criticised the utilitarian creed of securing the greatest happiness for the greatest number as an empty expression. Manuscript fragments from the early 1880s query the utilitarian *summum bonum* principle for implying highly ambiguous results with respect to the precise nature of the maximand. In the *Principles*, Marshall further eroded its practical value by reference to his organicist belief that the whole may be greater than the sum of its parts.[133]

The last point introduces the influence on Marshall of Hegel's *Philosophy of History* he was carefully studying at this time. Such influence, together with that of Herbert Spencer on the 'substance of the book', was continuously acknowledged in his prefaces to successive editions of *Principles*. Very direct Hegelian flourishes are particularly visible in the unfinished paper on the history and method of economics, the 1875 lecture at Cambridge on features of American industry and the concluding sections of the 1879 Gilchrist Lecture on water as an element of the national wealth.[134] Mary Paley Marshall recollected that Marshall's lectures mixed Hegel's *Philosophy of History* in with the more general historical flavour Marshall was then giving to the theory, while not long before his death Marshall confirmed to Keynes the important impact Hegel's *Philosophy of History* had made on his thought.[135]

One reason for Marshall's undoubted fascination with Hegelian views of history was the impetus it gave to his lifelong belief in the interdependence of social science and its environment, which gives an evolutionary and biological flavour to the organic growth process which characterises its development. Less overt, but nevertheless still visible, is Marshall's continuing admiration for the bold thrust of Hegel's historical generalisation, a sign of his conscious hankering after holistic explanations for the complex interactions involved in the development of human society.[136] It cannot be definitely ascertained who first brought Hegel's work to Marshall's attention, but there is no doubt whatsoever that the German philosopher cast a spell over the young Marshall's thinking far greater than that cast over Marshall's Cambridge contemporaries at the time.[*]

---

[*]   In Chapter 5, Mansel's possible role in this was mentioned; my 'Marshall and Hegel', pp. 66–7, mentions Maurice and Sidgwick, with Jowett and T.H. Green as subsequent reinforcing influences. Sidgwick and Leslie Stephen were two students of Hegel who relatively quickly became disillusioned with his work. Henry Cunynghame, one of Marshall's prize students of the early 1870s, recalled that 'Hegel was only mentioned at this time [in Cambridge] to be sighed over and scoffed at'. If Marshall was among those doing the 'sighing' this confirms the role Hegel played in Marshall's lecturing noted by Mary Paley Marshall. See C.H. Dudley Ward and C.B. Spencer, *The Unconventional Civil Servant*, London: Michael Joseph, 1939, p. 61.

The significant influence of Spencer on Marshall's thinking cannot be repeated too often if only because it is now so difficult to comprehend. The previous chapter mentioned Spencer's influence on Marshall's early philosophical and psychological writings, while Marshall's acknowledgement of Spencer's influence on the substance of his *Principles* was mentioned in a previous paragraph. Mozley wrote Keynes that his Memoir underestimated the influence of Spencer's work on the young Marshall, particularly *First Principles*. Mary Paley Marshall also recalled he lectured her on Spencer's *Social Statics* and *First Principles*. Marshall's library contained all of Spencer's major works, including those published in the 1880s and 1890s.[137]

Direct traces of Spencer's influences in Marshall's own published work are largely confined to the *Principles*. Even these are few and relate largely to broad generalisations about life, custom and its evolution. For example, Spencer's maxim from his 'Gospel of Relaxation', that working is for life and not life for working, is approvingly quoted; the effective check on population from the growth of civilisation raised in his *Principles of Biology* is referred to as a factual finding confirmed by the data; Spencer's view of the development of physical and mental organs whose exercise gives pleasure is presented by Marshall as a beneficial outcome of natural selection. Hence Spencer's work aided Marshall's criticism and elaboration of the classical view on working-class progress.[138] However, the praise Marshall bestowed on Spencer not long after Spencer's death — 'he opened out a new world of promise, he set men on high enterprise in many diverse directions, . . . he did much more towards increasing [the] utility of English intellectual work [than Mill did]' — is tempered by other remarks in the *Principles*. Universal enterprises in the social sciences as attempted by Comte and Spencer are deprecated as unrealisable ambitions, while in some of its editions, Marshall expressed caution in the use of Spencer's *Descriptive Sociology*, useful though this work was even for economists.[139] However, such universalist perspectives in the writing of science probably appealed more to the young Marshall when he first read them, and the temptation to cover all that was relevant to an investigation was one of the snares which prevented Marshall from completing so much of his published work because of the large scale on which it was invariably planned.[140] Irrespective of the potential for such negative by-products in Spencer's influence, Marshall's endeavours to clothe his theories as much as possible with the relevant facts was a more positive response to Spencer's intellectual challenge in the 1870s.

Sir Henry Maine's importance in the development of Marshall's early economic thought also deserves attention. Marshall's notebooks of the late 1860s list Maine's *Ancient Law* and *Village Communities* as works of considerable relevance to the student of political economy. There can be no doubt that he studied these books at this time.[141] Their major impact was to reinforce Marshall's belief of the initially beneficial, subsequent detrimental, influence of custom on economic and social development, as is so clearly illustrated in the historical sketch of the growth of free industry and enterprise he provided in his *Principles*.[142] However, from the first edition, Marshall started to withdraw his generous remark on the 'conspicuous debts' Englishmen owed to Sir Henry Maine's work on the origins of law in relation to property. This was probably because the article in which he defended his historical sketch against William Cunningham, attributed his rather exaggerated views on the importance of custom in medieval rural life to the 'starting point' he had found in Maine's teaching.[143] These starting points can be more clearly seen in the references to custom, caste and village communities in the early paper on History and Method of Economics and the chapters on the organisation of industry and land tenure in the *Economics of Industry*.[144] By the eighth edition indebtedness to Maine was reduced to a general reference to 'the writings of Maine' together with those of Spencer and Bagehot's *Physics and Politics* as a guide to readers wishing to pursue the diverse importance of custom in early civilisations. However, the importance which Marshall attached to the role of custom in various parts of his economics was not affected, so that an effective impact of Maine's writings continued throughout the life of the *Principles*.[145]

Two further early influences on Marshall's economics may be mentioned at this point. The more important was the French social historian and statistician, Le Play, to whose work Marshall was probably introduced through William Sargant's *Economy of the Labouring Classes*, though later on Marshall acquired personal copies of Le Play's voluminous works.[146] Apart from the intrinsic interest of the nature of Le Play's research for a person like Marshall involved in studying the condition of the working class for the purpose of discovering means to its improvement, Le Play's unusual method of gathering facts was highlighted by Marshall in later editions of the *Principles*. Marshall described this as 'the *intensive* study of all the details of the domestic life of a few carefully chosen families. To work it well requires a rare combination of judgement in selecting cases, and of insight and sympathy in interpreting them. At its best, it is the best of all .'[147] Marshall's predilection for the method was that it potentially captured an actual representative household and not a notional one constructed from statistically average behaviour, as reflected, for example, in Quételet's 'l'homme moyen' based on normal distribution of human behaviour. Search for such real representatives of economic agents informed his attempts at aggregation in particular markets by looking for both representative consumers and representative firms. Le Play's social philosophy of individualism and self-help, his opinions on the sexual division of labour and on the importance of education, likewise appealed to Marshall and help to explain Marshall's devotion to the spirit of the Charity Organisation Society and the case study approach to social welfare it espoused.[148]

Hearn's *Plutology* is a more secondary but nevertheless interesting early influence on Marshall. Of special appeal to Marshall was the organisation of Hearn's argument in terms of wants, followed by detailed treatment of productive arrangements required to enable satisfaction of these wants. Moreover, Hearn's detailed discussion of industrial organisation and his early adaptation of Darwinian evolutionary theory in that context, together with more specific contributions on value and wages, would also have greatly interested Marshall at this stage.[149]

THE FOREIGN TRADE MANUSCRIPT AND OTHER UNPUBLISHED WORK OF THE 1870S

In early February 1877, Marshall showed John Neville Keynes part of a book on foreign trade he was writing; in July 1877 Keynes recorded the slow progress he was making in reading it, partly because he found it difficult to get a 'connected view' of the work in manuscript and partly because of Marshall's style of composition, which he found 'bad', 'or rather, no style at all'.[150] Marshall had started this book some time in 1873. By late 1876 or early 1877 the book was sufficiently advanced for a manuscript to be sent to Macmillan for their consideration. Although it was not immediately returned, Macmillan considered the book too awkward 'in both the literary form and in the actual construction' and it was sent to an independent reader. In May 1877, Macmillan returned the manuscript to Marshall, because its 'style' was perceived to lack 'vividness, and the reader is not carried along'. In addition Macmillan offered advice on how Marshall could best improve it.[151] This explains Keynes's tedium when reading it during July. Marshall's marriage in August 1877, the concomitant new responsibilities of setting up house and a new career in Bristol, together with work on the *Economics of Industry* with his new wife, meant the foreign trade volume was cast aside. Late in spring 1878 Marshall informed his publishers that it would 'never make a comfortable book in its present shape' and would be abandoned. Instead, Marshall proposed he hoped to have no less than three books ready for publication before the end of 1881. The first was a book on the method of diagrams 'applied to economic theory and including foreign trade curves', the second was a book on foreign trade for the general reader, while the third was a companion volume on trade, finance and taxation to supplement the *Economics of Industry*. A month or so previously, he had written to Foxwell that he was seriously thinking of doing his curves before the foreign trade book. Nothing came of any of these projects, though Sidgwick's private printing of the chapters on domestic and international value can be seen as a partial substitute. Alternatively, the promised book on diagrammatic method can be seen as ultimately fulfilled in the *Principles*.*

    The history of the unpublished foreign trade book was later recollected by Marshall in correspondence with Seligman and Cunynghame. The letter to Cunynghame indicates how closely connected the foreign trade project was with Marshall's desire to establish priority for at least some of his contributions. The need for Marshall to get his material into print, and thereby preserve his priority, continued to be urgent in the 1870s.[152] The contents of the proposed work included in his letter to Cunynghame is more concisely expressed in a letter to Seligman four years previously:

> In about 1873, I decided that my first book would be on International Trade, with reference to protection, etc. on the analytical and realistic sides; but not on the historical. So I began to write. . . . The work was in two parts. The first was to be addressed to the general reader; the second, in smaller type, to academic students exclusively. The second part began with an introductory chapter on my favourite theme – the One in the Many, the Many in the One; and showed how with modifications in detail the pure theory of Foreign Trade was applicable to many industrial and other problems. Then came three chapters on the pure theory of Foreign Trade; and then two on Domestic Trade. These were introduced for the purpose of leading up to

---

*   Undated draft of Marshall to Macmillan, Marshall Archive, 2/49; Marshall to Foxwell, April 1878 (Freeman Collection, Letter 44/155). From the Marshall letter to Macmillan, it appears that Fawcett's *Free Trade and Protection* may have been considered a rival (it appeared in mid-1878), a possibility Marshall denied. As Phyllis Deane points out, Mill's theory of international trade plays no part in Fawcett's book; it relied instead on general liberal economic principles and contemporary real-world illustrations, as well as its 'lively, direct and forceful style' to get its message across. See her 'Henry Fawcett: the plain man's political economist', in L. Goldman (ed.), *The Blind Victorian*, pp. 103–4. On the relationship between the projected book on diagrams and Marshall's later published work, see J.K. Whitaker, introduction to *EEW*, I, pp. 65–6.

'Consumers Rent' which I wanted to apply in an economic measure of the <u>indirect</u> effects of customs duties, whether 'Protective' or not. By June 1877, I had nearly finished a first draft of Part I and of all of Part II except for the last chapter which I found very troublesome (and which I am quite sure now I shall never write).[153]

Figure 6.2: Table of Contents of the Manuscript on Foreign Trade 1873–1877

The Theory of Foreign Trade (and other Portions of Economic Science Bearing on the Principle of Laissez-Faire)

PART I

Ch. I	[The basis for international trade and the benefits derived from it: Preliminary discussion of customs duties and the arguments for and against protection.]
Ch. II	[Monetary aspects of international transactions.]
Ch. III	[The effects on a country of changes in its productive power with and without international trade; the effects of international trade in equalising money wages; etc.]
Ch. IV	Foreign trade in its bearing on industrial and social progress.
Ch. V	Foreign trade in its bearing on industrial and social progress (continued).
Ch. VI	Taxes on foreign trade for the purposes of revenue.
Ch. VII	Protection to native industries.

PART II

Ch. I	The scope of the pure theory of foreign trade.
Ch. II	The premises of the pure theory of foreign trade. The method of diagrams. The fundamental laws of curves which represent international demand.
Ch. III	Stable and unstable equilibrium of foreign trade.
Ch. IV	Variations of international demand as affecting the rate of interchange. The incidence of customs taxes.
Ch. V	Domestic values.
Ch. VI	The total burden of a tax. Consumers' rent.
Ch. VII	[The indirect effects of customs duties, whether 'protective'or not.]
Appendices	[Cost of Production; Mill's theory of value; rent; economic measures; index of definitions.]

Source: Reproduced from *Early Economic Writings of Alfred Marshall* 1867–1890 edited by J.K. Whitaker, London: Macmillan, for the Royal Economic Society, 1975, Volume 2, p. 5, with kind permission from the editor and the publishers.

Preserved manuscript chapters of the book together with the chapters as reprinted by Sidgwick allow a reconstruction of its contents. Figure 6.2 reproduces this table of contents from the *Early Economic Writings* which also reprints the surviving portions of the book.[154] Parts and chapters no longer extant are placed in square brackets. Instead of outlining the book's rather complicated and convoluted argument, the discussion here is confined to some of its features relevant to Marshall's economic apprenticeship.[155]

As Marshall wrote to Seligman and Cunynghame, the first part of the book was designed for the general reader. It displays many of the characteristics in the development of his economics noted previously. Part of its early argument illustrates that by the middle of the 1870s when much of this material was written, Marshall had already placed his enthusiasm for historical economics behind him. Facts remained important but, as in his later warnings in the *Principles* about the use of Spencer's *Descriptive Sociology*, care had to be taken in their use. The need for correct interpretation of the complex interrelationships in the facts was a warning his readers encountered on more than one occasion (pp. 39, 52–3, 61, 95) and was something in which he had found American and other writers on protection to be not always adept.* Historical detail, often abundantly available to illustrate particular problems, needed to be properly integrated into the argument if it was to add significantly to the explanation. Despite this more cautious approach, Marshall did not completely abandon history in the writing of the foreign trade book. Flourishes of a historical nature, often reminiscent of the historical material from the *Principles*, occasionally make their appearance, indicating a continuing taste for the broad historical sweep and generalisation of which Hegel and Spencer, Maine and Buckle, had made him so fond:

> In the Middle Ages the Teutonic spirit had made men prone to guilds and other industrial brotherhoods. These were welded together under staid conditions, and Precedent (das Hergebrachte) exerted almost undisputed sway over them. But the discovery of the New World and the second birth of mechanical science instituted a new order of things. The Era of change came with irresistible force upon industry. The old organisations would not and could not bend to it, and therefore they were broken to pieces by it. Efficient organisations could not again arise until it became possible for them to accommodate themselves rapidly to each new change. It had become necessary that they should be able not only to make continual readjustments in matters of detail, but also quickly to modify their purposes: they required frequently to review their principles of action as well as to decide promptly on questions of tactics. The railway, the printing press and the telegraph have increased the rapidity with which the requirements of industry have changed but the means of communication which they have developed during the present generation are rendering possible organisations of industry adapted to the circumstances of the new era. (p. 123).

Methodological issues are also raised, of the type pertinent to the topic of diagrammatic analysis foreshadowed in the work on 'curves' which Marshall had promised to Macmillan for 1881. The following quotation ponders some of the imperfections inherent in such analysis, highlighting reservations of the type Marshall was later to express about the usefulness of mathematical economics and of which he took account in his practice. Unlike

---

* Marshall recalled this tendency of American protectionists to misuse 'pairs of statistics' to prove their case in a letter to Edgeworth of which he sent a copy to the American economist and statistician, H.L. Moore (Marshall to Moore, 5 June 1912, Moore Papers, Columbia University, see below, Chapter 17, pp. 637–8). Pages in brackets in this and the next half dozen paragraphs refer to the text of the foreign trade book as reprinted in *EEW*.

some contemporary practitioners, Marshall was painfully aware of the difficulties in applying his analytical apparatus to obtain realistic and useful results:

> The task of discovering laws by which the shapes of the curves may in any case be approximately determined does not appear to transcend the resources which the science of statistics at present affords us. It will indeed, be a long time before this task is achieved; when it is achieved, it may be worth while to hand over the curves to be manipulated by the processes of analytical mathematics: but until then, the mathematical treatment of the curve cannot lead us to any results which cannot be at once obtained from inspection of the diagrams. Even then the methods of mathematical analysis will not be able to afford any considerable assistance in the task of determining the motion of the exchange-index. For a large amount of additional work will have to be done before we can obtain approximate laws for representing the magnitude of the horizontal and vertical forces which will act upon the exchange-index in any position. Finally, even when this is done there will yet remain a further difficulty in the way of the mathematical treatment of the problem. It is necessary to inquire with considerable care into this difficulty; because it extends so far as even to impair to some extent the efficiency of the treatment of the problem by the method of diagrams. (pp. 162–3).

Many of the economic theories Marshall later made famous are included in this early work. An obvious example is the concept of consumer rent and its adaptation to the excess burden theorem in taxation (pp. 74–5, 77, 212–24). The potential impact on producer surplus of bounties and taxes is also examined (pp. 224–30), and the well-known argument about bounties on increasing returns industries financed from taxes on diminishing returns industries is presented, not only as a policy designed to enhance aggregate welfare but also to show that governments can have a legitimate interest in the manner in which people spend their incomes (pp. 230–34). In domestic value theory, the analysis covers most of the material from the early paper on value, including multiple equilibria and their stability (pp. 199–201), the irreversible nature of the falling supply curve (e.g. p. 204) and much of the other paraphernalia of Marshall's later value analysis. The pure theory of international trade presents the offer curve (reciprocal demand) analysis which graced the international trade texts until at least the late 1940s, applying these tools to problems of the gains of trade, terms of trade and the potential benefits and losses from tariffs (pp. 112–18). Contrary to what Marshall wrote to Cunynghame in 1904, there is no monopoly analysis in the book, so that the priority of the compromise benefit concept would not have been established by its publication in 1878 or 1879. The book also contains material demonstrating Marshall's perspectives on the classical economists – Smith, Ricardo and Mill – fleshing out the arguments he used in their defence against the criticism of economists like Jevons. According to Marshall, the classical writers had 'elements of truth' in most of their doctrines, but their theories were often stated 'without the conditions which are necessary to make them true'. However, at this stage he was still willing to press the case that some of Smith's doctrines at least were 'certainly fallacious' (pp. 60–61).

Concerned as it is with 'portions of economic science bearing on the principle of laissez faire', this early work also reveals many of Marshall's social concerns in economics, thereby recalling the motive which induced him to start reading in the subject. Interruptions to labourers' employment and income from trade depressions and other declines in economic activity (pp. 35–7, 43–4) are one example. Socialist remedies to such problems as proposed by Louis Blanc and, more importantly, by that 'bold and subtle genius' Lassalle (pp. 37–9) are another. The economy of high wages from the perspective of workers' efficiency and the social good (pp. 16–17, 20, 24–6, 29–31); the impact of new industries on work, life and character including the prospects of the future generation, qualified in practice by the varying impact of location on such economic, social and moral benefits of industrial development (pp. 55–8) are other topics of this nature discussed in this unfinished economic monograph. Apart from the socialist writers already mentioned,[156] the work heralds another significant new influence on his economics: Walter Bagehot. His 'masterly [1873] work', *Lombard Street* (p. 48) became a favourite with Marshall, particularly useful for enhancing his understanding of the nature of trade stagnation and financial panics beyond the confines of Mill's analysis (p. 38 n.4). He also cited Bagehot's 'Postulates of Political Economy' for its methodological content.[157]

Not surprisingly, the work also demonstrates Marshall's unshakeable belief in the virtues of free trade, not as a dogma but as a principle established by the thorough study of the benefits of trade on economic and social development. Much of the work was designed to illuminate the proposition, 'that no intelligent student of economic science denies that foreign trade freely carried on has *prima facie*, a direct tendency to increase the wealth of a country' and to controvert the view held by 'a large number of able economists, in countries other than Great Britain, that these direct and beneficial effects are liable to be outweighed by indirect effects which are injurious' (pp. 33–4). This ambitious aim explains Marshall's 1875 trip to the United States[158] and the book's failure. The book would never have reached the wider audience for which it was intended: the brilliance of the analytics of its second part was not matched by the sketchy and general nature of the first part, which made the argument not only cumbersome and hard to follow, but often unpersuasive as well.

A number of unpublished fragments from this time can also be mentioned, particularly because those devoted to taxation supplement the pioneering analysis of excess burden of the foreign trade book. One of these, 'the abstract theory of a general uniform tax', was clearly preparatory for section 4 of the second surviving chapter of what became the *Pure Theory of Domestic Value*, developing the case for the taxation of necessities on efficiency grounds which persisted as a footnote in the *Principles*.[159] It highlights Marshall's theoretical skills and his caution in applying the theorems developed to practical policy. In addition, it shows how much was lost by Marshall's many false starts in writing during the decades of the 1870s and 1880s when his analytical powers were at their greatest height.*
A note on competitive equilibrium from around the same time examines the problems raised by external effects of production on the nature of equilibrium, a problem inspired by his reading of Cournot. This was to plague him considerably and induced several attempts at resolution of what he called the 'Cournot problem', that of reconciling competitive equilibrium with increasing returns.[160]

---

* This point is strikingly illustrated by John Whitaker in his introduction to this fragment, where he notes that by the time he wrote the *Principles* Marshall had forgotten the problems in aggregating losses in consumer surplus of separate commodities raised in this little note. See *EEW*, II, p. 288.

SOME EARLY PUBLISHED WRITINGS: 1873 TO 1879

The first published fruit from Marshall's economic apprenticeship was his review of Jevons, already discussed. Marshall's two brief pages on the 'Graphic Representation by aid of a series of Hyperbolas of some Economic Problems having Reference to Monopolies' in October 1873 have also already been mentioned.[161] It was designed to introduce the machine invented by his student Henry Cunynghame[*] for constructing a series of rectangular parabolas with the same asymptotes, which its inventor himself presented as the third item on the agenda of the Philosophical Society's October meeting. The published summary of Marshall's paper goes little beyond definitions of supply and demand curves (the price – function forms) as functions of price, indirectly attributing their discovery to Cournot. It also mentions stable and unstable positions of equilibrium, and the analysis of various monopoly problems including that of profit maximisation, the last line of which foreshadowed the notion Marshall later developed as compromise benefit. Two longer essays followed. One was published in his college magazine, *The Eagle*, the other appeared in the *Fortnightly Review*. Both were inspired by Mill's *Political Economy*. These were Marshall's more important publications prior to the two books published in 1879, which signalled Marshall's successful completion of his economic apprenticeship.[162]

The Future of the Working Classes (1873). In this lecture given at a 'conversazione' of the Cambridge Reform Club, Marshall addressed the problem which originally had led him to study economics. This was 'whether the amelioration of the working classes has limits beyond which it cannot pass; whether it be true that the resources of the world will not suffice for giving to more than a small portion of its inhabitants an education in youth and an occupation in after-life, similar to those which we are now wont to consider proper to gentlemen.' This was not a question of whether all men ultimately will be equal, but whether progress ultimately will eliminate the distinction between worker and gentleman by turning all into the latter.[163] Examination of this problem led Marshall to a discussion of the meaning of working class, in which the effect of work on character was seen as the deciding characteristic. If these effects were keeping 'his character rude and coarse', he belonged to the working class. After discussing the difficulties of engaging in educational leisure activities after work for those involved in hard physical work for long hours, Marshall prescribed his solutions to the problem. These included the reduction of working hours combined with higher real incomes and the provision of state education for the young. In defence against arguments that the nation and its trade could not afford such measures, Marshall responded by pointing to the rapid growth of productivity in England over the last century, that high wages did not necessarily imply international uncompetitiveness and that

---

[*] In *P* I, p. xi n.1 (*P* IX, pp. 37–8), Marshall explained the circumstances of this invention as follows: 'Mr. Henry Cunynghame who was attending my lectures in 1873, seeing me annoyed by being unable to draw a series of rectangular hyperbolas, invented a beautiful and original machine for the purpose. It was shown at the Cambridge Philosophical Society in 1873 and to explain its use, I read a paper . . . in which I describe the theories of Multiple Positions of the Equilibrium and of Monopoly values very much as they are given below (Book V, Chapters V and VIII) . . .' (*P* VII, Book V, Chapters V and XIV). Cunynghame's biographers do not include this example of his inventiveness, but recount his assistance to Holman Hunt in making a lantern slide of a photograph of a lost picture so that the picture could be re-done. See C.H. Dudley Ward and C.B. Spencer, *The Unconventional Civil Servant*, pp. 104–5.

a state 'which has with success invested in telegraphs, should now venture to invest capital in men'.[164] Many of the propositions contained in this lecture, on the influences of work on character, the economy of high wages and shorter hours, the economic benefits of investing in human capital, the rationale for shift work as a method to raise productivity, can be found in the *Principles*.* The lecture is therefore important as a link between the ideals which brought Marshall to economics and the mature work in the *Principles* which presented the means to this ideal in a wider context while continuing to emphasise the original aim as the lofty objective of economic study. It also highlights his attempt at constructing a 'new' economic liberalism to which attention was drawn earlier.[165]

Mr. Mill's Theory of Value (1876). This essay, largely a defence of Mill against his critics (Cairnes and Jevons), enabled Marshall to explain both his 'generous perspectives' on the doctrines of the classical economists (pp. 121, 132n.)[166] and to present some of his own emendations and additions to the work of the person who, on the evidence of this chapter, more than anyone else deserves the title of being Marshall's 'master'. Marshall illustrated this by drawing a link between measurement and costs, implicit in the work of both Smith and Mill, but a 'discovery' which advanced the pure science of political economy beyond that of ethics. In contrast to economics, ethics lacked a 'system of measurement of efforts, sacrifices, desires, etc. fit for her wider purposes'. Marshall argued such measurement could be done in economics by translating incommensurable 'diverse efforts and abstinences' into measurable 'necessary expenses of production', that is, by the 'remunerative price' to the person who purchased the commodity in question. Competitive price analysis thereby provides the measuring rod of money by which the measurement problem could be solved (pp. 125–7). An advantage of this mode of stating Mill's doctrine was it entailed clarification of the terms, supply and demand. It thereby corrected the careless manner in which Mill had explained these concepts in his *Principles* until Thornton's criticism of his cavalier treatment of market values drew attention to this (pp. 128–30). In contrast to Jevons's call for a revolution to improve value theory, Marshall only corrected and clarified Mill's views, to enable them to be rescued and used as the foundation for a more correct and useful theory of value, the clue being precision in the language of measurement.¶

The Pure Theory of Foreign Trade and Domestic Value (1879). In early 1879 or perhaps late 1878, Henry Sidgwick, who had earlier borrowed Marshall's foreign trade manuscript, asked Marshall's permission to print some of the diagrammatical chapters for use at his economic discussion group at Cambridge. From Part II Sidgwick chose Chapters II, III, V and VI (see Figure 6.2), titling them *The Pure Theory of Foreign Trade and the Pure Theory*

---

* Cf. e.g. p. 113 of the paper on shift work with *P* I, p. 732 n.1; *P* VIII, pp. 695–6 n.1. R.C.O. Matthews has attributed his rather impractical suggestion for the organisation of shift work to the type of shift worked by Cambridge college servants in Marshall's time, with which by then, given his friendly attitude to the 'gyps' and college servants, he would have been very familiar. See R.C.O. Matthews, 'Marshall and the Labour Market', in *Centenary Essays on Alfred Marshall*, p. 29 n.21.

¶ Concern over measurement stayed with him in the *Principles* and was, as noted earlier in the context of Bentham (above, pp. 165–6, one of the major advantages economics was perceived to have over the science of morals. The commensurability problem in ratios had been commented on by Marshall in his copy of Mill in the context of the conception of supply and demand as a ratio. See *Principles of Political Economy*, People's Edition, 1865, Book III, Chapter II, §3, p. 270, and his annotations to Jevons's theory referred to previously above, pp. 159–60.

of Domestic Value. He provided no editing and no introduction. Sidgwick sent copies to Jevons, presumably in early 1879, for which Jevons thanked him cordially,[167] delighted to be able to see at last Marshall's 'curves' at first hand. Apart from 'adverting' to them in the preface of his second edition of *Theory of Political Economy*, Jevons also circulated spare copies from those Sidgwick had sent him. One of them reached Edgeworth, who subsequently cited Marshall's work in his *Mathematical Psychics.*[168]

As he wrote to Seligman in 1900 when sending him a copy of the Domestic Value 'to keep for curiosity's sake', Marshall was later annoyed by the wider circulation than originally intended of his unfinished work. Marshall continued,

> The substance of them . . . now entirely superseded by the corresponding chapters of my *Principles* . . . was given, in great part – in lectures very early, before the publication of Jevons's theory. The MSS do not explain themselves. . . . Then, I became seriously ill, and in 78 or 79 Sidgwick asked me to lend him the MSS. Later on he asked my leave to print some chapters for private use in the Economics Discussion Society at Cambridge. I consented. He chose Ch. II, III, V and VI. I did not know for some time afterwards which he had chosen and of course the crude draft was printed virtually without correction even of the most obvious flaws. This explains (i) their general crudity (ii) the absence of explanation of their drift (iii) the want of any reference to the real conditions of foreign trade: they were given – very badly (iv) the fact that Domestic Trade is treated *after* Foreign Trade. As [to] the MSS I withdrew entirely case II of the Foreign Trade and my whole treatment which is different from that in these Papers. Chapters I of Part II explained away a good deal of the succeeding chapters, (i.e. explained that they belonged to the economic tool shop rather than the practical workshop.)[169]

It is likely this caused some bad blood between Sidgwick and Marshall. In his letter to Seligman, Marshall seemed to convey that Sidgwick had taken advantage of his illness in seeking his permission to print the material for a private purpose and then circulated it more widely. On the first point, Marshall's recollection is wrong. Jevons received his copies of the book in February 1879; Marshall only went to London in April or May to visit a doctor for definite diagnosis of the stones in the kidney which subsequently incapacitated him for so many years.[170] Marshall himself continued to regard the papers as not having been published. A manuscript fragment of 28 September 1920, preserved among his papers, refers to a discussion of 'my unpublished papers on graphic economics' in the last chapter of Zwadski's *Les Mathématiques appliquées et économie politique* (Paris, 1914) as a 'matter . . . not worth notice unless it is taken up by some hostile important critic'.[171] The trade geometry appeared for the first time under Marshall's own name in an appendix to *Money, Credit and Commerce*, published in 1923.[172]

The Economics of Industry (1879). In October 1879, Macmillan published the *Economics of Industry* by Alfred Marshall and Mary Paley Marshall as a text for extension students in political economy. The book contained an outline of the theory of value, wages and profits, and was intended as a vindication of John Stuart Mill's political economy which, 'when properly interpreted, was true, as far as it goes'. Only in distribution theory did its authors think it necessary to depart from Mill. For this reason, the little green book for beginners has been described as containing 'a marginal productivity theory in England for probably the first time since Longfield and Butt wrote'.[173] The book sold well. It came out in a second edition in 1881, a third edition was contemplated in 1885 and a Russian translation agreed to in 1886. Prior to its replacement in 1892 by Alfred Marshall's summary of the *Principles* under the similar title, *Elements of the Economics of Industry*, it had sold 15,000 copies.[174]

Mary Paley, who became Alfred Marshall's wife in August 1877, had been invited to write the book by Professor James Stuart as a text for extension lectures. This invitation came within a year of Mary Paley's successful completion of the Moral Sciences Tripos and much later was considered to have been 'irresponsible' by Alfred Marshall.[175] When Mary Paley and Alfred Marshall were engaged in mid-1876, the book quickly became a joint product. Its first outlines were prepared in a sitting-room at Newnham, the college which employed Mary Paley for lecturing in political economy to its students. By July 1877, John Neville Keynes recorded in his diary that Alfred Marshall had become so involved in the project, he had abandoned his own work on the Foreign Trade volume and increasingly used 'we' when discussing the work.[176] After their marriage in August, the Marshalls worked on the book during their brief Cornwall honeymoon and seem to have devoted nearly all of their spare time to it during the first two years of their married life at Bristol. A sign of things to come in Marshall's career as author, substantial re-writing continually delayed publication beyond what had earlier been promised to the publishers. Moreover, intended companion volumes were never started.[177] Such re-writing came partly because the authors decided to raise the book's degree of difficulty, often by introducing complex, original material in a highly abbreviated form. Critical comments from Foxwell and Sidgwick who were reading the proofs entailed further re-writing, particularly when some of these criticisms arose from their misunderstandings of Marshall's views on aspects of monopoly and distribution theory.[178]

The book itself was divided into three parts (Books) of which the first dealt with land, labour and capital and the theory of production; the second with normal value and the third with market value. Book I commenced with two introductory chapters. The first was definitional, covering the meaning of economics or political economy, wealth, productive and unproductive. The second introduced agents of production in which the efficiency of man's work was seen as aided by machinery designed to control and harness nature, and dependent on physical vigour, knowledge and mental ability, and moral character. Chapters on capital, diminishing returns, population and poor laws, saving and accumulation, the historical development of industrial organisation, division of labour and increasing returns followed, while the book concluded with a chapter on land tenure. Book II opens with a definition of its subject matter, normal value, identified with the 'undisturbed action of free competition' in the classical manner.[*] The first two chapters of Book II then deal with the law of utility and demand (in which there is some acknowledgement of Jevons's contribution) as well as with the laws of costs and expenses of production, and supply, on lines close to Marshall's 1876 article on Mill's theory of value. Rent in itself and rent in relation to value are then discussed. This is followed by a brief re-examination of demand in

---

[*] Whitaker, Introduction to *EEW*, pp. 70–81, sees this and the treatment of distribution, as a major difference between *Economics of Industry* and the later *Principles*, one reason justifying its suppression when the *Principles* had come out. Becattini, *Invito a una rilettura di Marshall*, justified its suppression in terms of the greater maturity in subject matter of the later work, particularly in its handling of ethical matters, of evolution and cooperation (pp. ci–cxi). Cf. Keynes, 'Alfred Marshall', p. 201 who mentions Marshall's controversies over the book's treatment of value in this context.

relation to value. The second half of Book II is devoted to distribution, treated as a problem of dividing produce into wages and profits after rent and depreciation have been deducted. Successive chapters then deal with labour supply (skilled and unskilled), business power, interest, wages and earnings of management. A final chapter reiterates and summarises the theory of normal value as a necessary introduction to explaining market value, the subject of the final Book III. Major deviations from normal value are the subject matter of its first four chapters. These in turn deal with changes in the purchasing power of money and crises (the only published version of Marshall's views on this matter); sudden market fluctuations from uncertainties in supply, unanticipated changes in demand and peculiarities of production; regional deviations and those explicable in terms of custom; and deviations from normal price caused by combination and monopoly. The last subject enables a smooth transition of subject matter to three chapters on trade unions, a chapter on arbitration and conciliation, and a final chapter on the desirability of cooperative ventures in production, credit and exchange. Questions of trade, finance and taxation were postponed to the companion volume (which in the end was never started). Its status as a book for beginners dictated stylistic forms such as placing difficult passages in square brackets for easy omission on first reading, and emphasising technical terms and their definitions by bold print.

The book's footnote references to authorities cited show how familiar with the literature of political economy Marshall had become by the end of the apprenticeship period. Apart from authors on political economy whose work has been mentioned as influential on Marshall on earlier occasions in this chapter, the *Economics of Industry* introduced a number of new authors of significance in the formulation of Marshall's ideas. The more important were F.A. Walker's *The Wages Question* and T. Brassey's *Lectures on the Labour Question*. As the reviewer of the *Economist* noted, the material to which the authors referred their readers often, however, included those 'not too often read'.[179]

Although the book was favourably reviewed,[*] its authors do not appear to have been proud of their effort within a month of publication. Subsequently, Marshall spoke of the book largely as if he were its sole author. In letters to Foxwell, Marshall confessed he would like to remove the excessive quotations from Bastiat and Mill in the first book and suggested that its first three chapters in particular needed substantial re-writing and amplification, in part to raise their level of difficulty to that of later chapters. He also complained about the difficulty in writing small books, foreshadowing thereby the criticism he made of it later, summarised by Mary Paley as his view 'you cannot tell the truth for half a crown [2s.6d.]'.[180] The latter criticism was amplified on several occasions in private correspondence. In April 1900, Marshall described his experience to Seligman as 'my being drawn into writing a hollow Economics of Industry, in which truth was economised for the benefit of feeble minds'. His autobiographical sketch depicted the book as one 'forcibly

---

[*] See Cliffe Leslie's review in *The Academy*, 8 November 1879, reprinted in his *Essays in Political Economy*, second edition, London: Longmans, Green & Company, 1888, pp. 73–82; W.S. Jevons, *Theory of Political Economy*, second edition, 1879, p. xv, refers to it indirectly as having adopted the name 'economics'. Other reviews, in The *Economist*, 18 February 1880, p. 239, and in the *Westminster Review*, Vol. LVII, January 1880, p. 240, both praised it as an extension students book, capable of leading the students for whom it was intended through the works of the master, J.S. Mill, though the *Economist* at times noted 'a slight looseness of texture' and remarked that authors cited 'introduced evidence of considerable research sometimes among authors not too often read'.

simplified for working class readers' while his grudging permission for a Japanese translation in an admittedly never sent draft, referred to 'publication of matter of which I am not proud' and to the ignorance of those who suggested the book in the first place about the difficulty of 'combining simplicity with thoroughness' in economics.[181] The reasons for its 'suppression' remain a contentious issue.[182]

Publication of *The Economics of Industry* together with the extensive circulation of his privately printed 'curves', combined as these were with his professorship at Bristol following a decade of successful political economy teaching there and at Cambridge, undoubtedly showed that by 1879 Marshall had more than successfully completed his economic apprenticeship. His work was increasingly being ranked with that of the other leading English economists: Jevons, Bagehot, Fawcett and Cliffe Leslie. These were all to die in the early 1880s, the decade Marshall transformed the economics he had acquired in these formative years from the late 1860s into his *magnum opus* of the *Principles of Economics*.[183]

NOTES

1. In *Memorials*, p. 358.
2. The whole period is covered in John Whitaker, *EEW*, which prints virtually all the major early economic writings preserved in manuscript form in the Marshall Archive. This chapter relies heavily on this fine edition and its comprehensive introduction, as well as on Giacomo Becattini, *Invito a una Rilettura di Marshall*, Introduction to A & M.P. Marshall, *Economia della produzione*, Milan, ISEDI, 1975, pp. ix–cxi.
3. Two important aspects of Marshall's economic apprenticeship are left to subsequent chapters. His fact-finding trips to industrial districts during his summer holidays, or 'wanderjahre among factories' as he described this aspect of his work to Flux (letter dated 7 March 1898 in *Memorials*, p. 407) are discussed in Chapter 7; his early political economy teaching at St John's, Cambridge and in Bristol is discussed in Chapter 9.
4. That is, Alfred Marshall to J.B. Clark, 2 July 1900 and 24 March 1908, in *Memorials*, pp. 412–13, 416–17; Marshall to L.C. Colson (either 1908 or 1909) in 'Alfred Marshall the Mathematician as seen by himself', *Econometrica*, 1 (1), April 1933, pp. 221–2; and 'Alfred Marshall; Professor of Political Economy at Cambridge' (Circa 1910), *AMCA*, I, pp. 149–50.
5. 'Alfred Marshall: Professor of Political Economy at Cambridge, p. 149.
6. Preserved in its rare book library (Marshall d.61). Its annotations are discussed subsequently in this chapter.
7. Marshall to J.B. Clark, 2 July 1900, in *Memorials*, p. 413.
8. It appeared in the *Academy*, 1 April 1872 (in *Memorials*, pp. 93–100). It is discussed in some detail below, pp.158–9.
9. Marshall to L.C. Colson, p. 221.
10. Marshall to J.B. Clark, 24 March 1908, in *Memorials*, p. 416.
11. 'Alfred Marshall: Professor of Political Economy at Cambridge', p. 149.
12. This, and the preceding paragraph draw heavily on the very interesting perspective on Marshall's economics in Gareth Stedman-Jones, *Outcast London*, Oxford: Clarendon Press, 1971, esp. pp. 3–11. As a description of Marshall's new liberal research programme in economics, it explains much about the particular avenues Marshall pursued in his study and writing.
13. 'Alfred Marshall: Professor of Political Economy at Cambridge', p. 150.
14. These are respectively discussed in the other two chapters completely devoted to Marshall as an academic student and writer of economics, that is, Chapters 12 and 19 below. These form, as it were, a sequel to this chapter on economic writing.
15. Both fragments were cited by J.M. Keynes, 'Alfred Marshall', p. 171.
16. *P* I, p. 4, and see pp. 2–4 for a definition of the problem; *P* IX, p. 132 records only one minor change to these pages.

17. 'Alfred Marshall, Professor of Political Economy at Cambridge', p. 149; on Marshall's ambivalent relationship to 'socialism' and social questions in general, see below, Chapter 16, esp. pp. 570–72, 608–9.
18. Discussed more fully later in this chapter, p. 168; for Marshall's praise of Le Play, see *P* IX, p. 254.
19. Mary Paley Marshall, *What I Remember*, pp. 15–16 and above, Chapter 5, p. 128. For examples of travel records mentioning expressions on working class faces see below, Chapter 7, pp. 201, 211, 213.
20. John Whitaker, Introduction to *EEW*, pp. 14–15, 63 n.13; Alfred Marshall, 'The Present Position of Economics', in *Memorials*, pp. 152–3; Henry Fawcett, *Pauperism: Its Causes and Remedies*, London: Macmillan, 1871, p. 111.
21. Frank McClain, *Maurice, Man and Moralist*, London: S.P.K.C., 1972, pp. 71, 85; F.D. Maurice, *Casuistry, Moral Philosophy and Moral Theology: An Inaugural Lecture*, London: Macmillan, 1866, esp. pp. 22, 31, 38; F.D. Maurice, *Reasons for Co-operation*, London: J.W. Parker, 1851, pp. 19–26, 44–5.
22. See below, Chapter 18, pp. 663, 665–6.
23. H. Sidgwick to Council of Bristol University College, 20 June 1877.
24. Above, Chapter 5, pp. 127–8.
25. Marshall Archive, Red Box, 1 (5).
26. Cambridge University Library, Marshall d.61. The pagination of the People's Edition stayed uniform for all its successive printings.
27. The quotations are from Karl Marx, *Capital*, first German edition, 1867, pp. 322, 324, 353. See also below, Chapter 16, p. 578.
28. Cf. *EEW*, pp. 167–70 and n.7 for an alternative early statement of the quantity theory of money by Alfred Marshall.
29. It may be noted in the context of this chapter, that Marshall's copy of the *Principles* contains no visible reaction to Mill's use of algebra in this context, apart from marking a footnote (*Principles*, People's Edition, p. 363 n.*) where some inferences are drawn from this algebra.
30. The last cited Goschen's *Foreign Exchanges*, fourth edition, 1864, p. 73 (*Principles*, People's Edition, p. 384), the former refers approvingly to Sargent's critique of excessive savings in his *Recent Political Economy*, pp. 50–55, which was highly critical of Mill's and Fawcett's position on over supply and general gluts (*Principles*, People's Edition, p. 338). Marshall's copy of Sargant's *Recent Political Economy* in the Marshall Library is likewise annotated on this point.
31. A useful discussion of the 1866–67 depression on the London working class is given by G. Stedman-Jones, *Outcast London*, pp. 102–4, 243–4.
32. That is, Figure 6.1.
33. William Thornton, *On Labour*, London: Macmillan, 1869, Chapter 2; second edition, 1870. Marshall owned a copy of the book, preserved in the Marshall Library and heavily annotated by him. Mill's review appeared in two parts in the 1869 *Fortnightly Review*, V (New Series), May, pp. 505–18; June, pp. 680–700. They head a list of important *Fortnightly Review* articles on political economy made by Marshall and preserved in the Marshall Library.
34. On the general importance of this debate for the revision of theory, see T.W. Hutchison, *On Revolutions and Progress in Economic Knowledge*, Cambridge: Cambridge University Press, 1978, Chapter 3; and Michael White, ' "That God-forgotten Thornton" and the Laws of Supply and Demand', *HETSA Bulletin*, No. 9, Winter, 1988, pp. 16–29. Marshall's early writings on value and wages are in part a reaction to the debate, see *EEW*, I, pp. 119–60, 178–201; and G. Becattini, *Invito a una Rilettura di Marshall*, pp. xxviii–xxxvi.
35. J.S. Mill, *Essays on some Unsettled Questions*, esp. pp. 137–8, 143–4, 146, 153.
36. J.S. Mill, *A System of Logic*, Book VI Chapter IX, esp. pp. 588–94.
37. J.S. Mill, *Principles of Political Economy*, preface, and for a discussion of its effects on Marshall, Becattini, *Invito a una Rilettura di Marshall*, pp. LVII–LXI. For a detailed discussion of Mill's complex position on method, see Samuel Hollander, *The Economics of John Stuart Mill*, Oxford: Basil Blackwell, 1985, chapter 2, and for the relevance of Mill's distinction between production and distribution to Marshall's beliefs in socialism, below, p. 596.
38. *P* VIII, pp. 3–4, Book I, Chapter 2, and, for the praise of Mill, appendix B, pp. 764–6. In the first edition, all this material was located in Book I.
39. Mill's influence on Marshall's socialism is discussed in Chapter 16 below, esp. pp. 572–3, 580. See also K. Bharadwaj, 'The Subversion of Classical Analysis, Alfred Marshall's Early Writings on Value', *AMCA*, III, pp. 600–625.
40. D.P. O'Brien, 'Marshall in Relation to Classical Economics', in *Centenary Essays on Alfred Marshall*, ed. John Whitaker, esp. pp. 137–47. Selections from Marshall's extant notes on Adam Smith and Ricardo are included in *EEW*, II, pp. 253–60.
41. For example, G.J. Stigler, *Production and Distribution Theories. The Formative Period*, New York: Macmillan, 1941, pp. 63, 83 and J.A. Schumpeter, 'Alfred Marshall 1842–1924', in *Ten Great Economists*, London: Allen

& Unwin, 1952, pp. 95–7. On Marshall's peculiar treatment of Ricardo, see my 'Marshall on Ricardo', in *Essays in Honour of L.L. Pasinetti*, eds M. Baranzini and G.C. Harcourt, London: Macmillan, 1993, Chapter 1.

42. Alfred Marshall to Léon Walras, 1 November 1883, in *Correspondence of Léon Walras and Related Papers*, edited William Jaffe, Amsterdam: North Holland Publishing Company, 1965, Volume 1, p. 794.

43. *EEW*, I, p. 143.

44. Cournot, *Mathematical Principles of the Theory of Wealth*, Homewood, Richard Irwin, 1963, Chapter 4, esp. section 21, p. 38. Marshall claims of priority with respect to Jevons are discussed below, pp. 158–62.

45. *EEW*, II, pp. 319–22, the postscript is on p. 320. Whitaker suggests the Roscher book referred to is his *Geschichte der nationaloekonomik in Deutschland*, published in 1874 and Kautz's *Theorie und Geschichte der Nationalokonomik*, which was published in 1860. Roscher's *Grundlagen*, published earlier, in some editions devoted several chapters to von Thünen's work, and may have been an equally likely but earlier source of knowledge on von Thünen for Marshall.

46. Part I, the second edition of which was published in 1842, covered von Thünen's theory of agricultural intensity, location and crop zones of agricultural systems; Part II which was subdivided into two sections, contained the wage theory in the first and posthumous papers, including those on taxation, settlement policies, improvements in transport and communications in the second, respectively published first in 1860 and 1863. Marshall owned both *(Marshall Library Catalogue*, p. 87). For a discussion of the various editions available in Marshall's lifetime, see *Von Thünen's Isolated State*, edited with an introduction by Peter Hall, Oxford: Pergamon, 1969, pp. xviii–xix.

47. *EEW*, II, pp. 248–52. This criticised the natural wage theory, as Marshall likewise did in a later fragment on von Thünen quoted below. In the introduction to *EEW*, Whitaker notes Nicholson cited von Thünen, in fact on the natural wage, in his Cobden Prize essay, *The Effects of Machinery on Wages*, London: Swan Sonnenschein, 1892, p. 22, first edition in 1878, and that Marshall had introduced Nicholson on his own account to Cournot's work circa 1873, *EEW*, I. p. 18 and n.41. There is no reference to von Thünen. JNKD mentions Keynes studying Cournot in the early 1870s, but not von Thünen.

48. *P* I, p. x n.1, stated bluntly, 'The term "marginal" increment I borrowed from von Thünen.' However, in *P* II, III and IV this was reworded to 'The term "marginal" increment is in harmony with von Thünen's methods of thought and was suggested to me by him, though he does not actually use it.' (*P* IX, p. 37).

49. Alfred Marshall, 'Note on Marginal Utility, 11 December 1919', in Marshall Archive, Red Box 1 (5); Method. Cf. preface to *P* I, p. x and n.1, *P* VIII, p. x and n.1, *P* I, p. 55, n.1, did not make such an attribution. From *P* IV (p. 168n) to *P* VIII, p. 93) the attribution of marginal utility was made to von Wieser.

50. As indicated in the letters to Clark and Colson discussed at the start of this chapter. See also *EEW*, II, pp. 248–52, and H.M. Robertson, 'Alfred Marshall's Aims and Methods Illustrated from his Treatment of Distribution' in *AMCA*, III, pp. 323–4, 358–60. *P* I is particularly generous with its acknowledgements of von Thünen (for example, pp. 507, 528n., 545, 548n.1, 614 n.1, 704).

51. Alfred Marshall to James Bonar, 27 September 1898, in *Memorials*, p. 374.

52. Fragments, in *Memorials*, pp. 359–60, (my emphasis in the quotation).

53. Alfred Marshall to J.N. Keynes, August 1889, Marshall Archive 1.

54. Von Thünen, *The Isolated State*, pp. 7–22, the simple hypothesis of the isolated state and the problems it can help to solve form the first two chapters of its Part I.

55. Von Thünen, *The Isolated State*, p. 23. Von Thünen's empirical work based on his agricultural practice at his Tellow estate has now been published, edited with an introduction by E.E. Gerhard, as *Thünen's Tellower Büchführing*, Meisenheim: A.M.Glan, 1964, 2 volumes.

56. *P* VIII, p. 781.

57. See Peter Hall, introduction to von Thünen, *Isolated State*, p. xviii.

58. See below, Chapter 16, pp. 602–3.

59. *P* I, p. 70, *P* VII, p. 768.

60. References to Marshall's great admiration for the German historical school are made below, pp 164 and see Chapter 19, p. 707.

61. See Erich W. Streissler, 'The Influence of German Economics on the work of Menger and Marshall', in Bruce J. Caldwell, ed. *Carl Menger and his Legacy in Economics*, Durham: Duke University Press, 1990, pp. 31–68, esp. pp. 55–8.

62. *Ibid.*, p. 55.

63. T.M. Humphrey, 'Marshallian Cross Diagrams and their Uses before Alfred Marshall', *Federal Reserve Bank of Richmond Economic Review*, 78 (2), March/April 1992, pp. 10–11.

64. Erich W. Streissler, p. 55; Humphrey, p. 14.

65. That is, von Mangoldt, *Volkswirtschaftslehre*, Stuttgart: Engelhorn, second edition, 1868, p. 232. Generally speaking, Marshall's annotations are few and are confined to a single chapter. *P* I, p. 492, mentions Mangoldt,

together with Hermann and Senior, as author treating profit as a special class of incomes deriving from differential advantages in production but cf. *P* IX, p. 827.

66. T.W. Humphrey, pp. 5–6; Rau, *Grundsatze der Volkswirthschaftslehre*, Heidelberg: Winter, 1847, pp. 578–80 (Marshall's copy has no annotations). Its first page carries Marshall's signature as well as the name of a previous owner, dated 24 December 1852.

67. Marshall to Jevons, 30 June 1879, in *Memorials*, p. 371; that it was Marshall's copy of the eighth edition, 1868 is suggested by the entry Jevons made in the Appendix, first included with the second edition of his *Theory of Political Economy*; Marshall to J.M. Keynes, 4 December 1910 (Keynes Papers, L/M/41). The fifth and the eighth edition are listed in the Marshall Library Catalogue, p. 69.

68. Algebra is used in the 1870 fragments on fixed capital (*EEW*, I, pp. 223–4) and the early essay on wages (*ibid.*, p. 186 n.4). Use of the calculus in solving economic problems was largely confined to his analytical work in an early mathematical notebook (*ibid.*, II, pp. 270, 279–83) and in some of his annotations to his copy of Cournot (*ibid.*, II, pp. 243–4).

69. See below, Chapter 9, pp. 268–70, where Alfred Marshall's response to a St John's College survey on its lecturing is discussed. This mentions the interruption lecturing in logic would cause 'to the course of reading [in political philosophy and political economy] by which I am endeavouring to enable myself to lecture on these subjects less inefficiently' (Official responses to a request from the Master, 1872, p. 72).

70. An exception is the example on steel pens production, which uses data Marshall derived from Volume 1 of *Das Kapital*. See *EEW*, I, pp. 140–41, and for Marshall's acknowledgement of the original source of this information, Marshall Archive, Box 7 (3), 'Statistics', item 19, manufactures, where it is ascribed to *Das Kapital*, I, p. 451. Marshall's reaction to Marx is discussed more fully in Chapter 16 below, p. 578.

71. Marshall's remark on using diagrams is cited in *EEW*, I, p. 231; his annotations of Mill in this context were discussed above, pp. 145–7.

72. *EEW*, I, p. 235, Figures 4 and 5, to be compared with Figure 6.1 above.

73. That is, in Book I, Chapters IV and V of Mill's *Principles*, as was shown above, p. 146. Marshall's fragments are reproduced in *EEW*, I, pp. 212–24.

74. Marshall wrote 'Theory of Money MSS about 1871' on the envelope in which the manuscript is kept (postmarked 7 April 1922), Marshall Archive, Red Box 2(6). This is the date Keynes assigned to the paper in his 'Alfred Marshall', p. 190.

75. Above, p. 146.

76. *EEW*, I, pp. 125–59. It cites Smith on p. 125, Turgot's *Réflexions* on p. 127, Mill's *Principles* and review of Thornton on p. 129, Marx's *Kapital* on p. 140 (see note 70 above), Ricardo, Malthus and Carey's *Principles* (p. 149) and Thornton's *On Labour* (p. 155).

77. Alfred Marshall to John Neville Keynes, 8 December 1888, Alfred Marshall to F.Y. Edgeworth, 26 April 1892; both are cited in *EEW*, I, pp. 119–20.

78. *EEW*, I, pp. 120–2.

79. *EEW*, p. 121.

80. John Whitaker, introduction to *EEW*, I, p. 42; on markets, see *EEW*, p. 134 and Cournot, *Mathematical Researches*, paragraph 23. This was quoted in *P* I, p. 384, *P* VIII, p. 324.

81. See *EEW*, p. 130 and Figures 1, 2, and above, p. 150 and n*.

82. See above, pp. 150–3.

83. This chapter was also annotated in Marshall's copy of Mill's *Principles*. Thornton's discussion of the value of the labourer of allotments and rights in common land is discussed in his *On Labour*, second edition, 1870, pp. 12–14.

84. Above, p. 151.

85. *EEW*, I. p. 160.

86. *EEW*, I, pp. 260–89; on dating the three items in question see pp. 160–61, 279–80, 281–2 respectively; the example about Australian absentee landlords in England occurs on p. 282. Uncle Charles had returned from Australia to settle in London by mid-1873, and spent what turned out to be the last years of his life in England (above, Chapter 2, pp. 30–1).

87. *EEW*, II, pp. 268–83, the material on welfare effects of taxation and tolls is on pp. 279–83. In dating see esp. p. 268 and n.1 which dates some of the diagrams to 1870 on the basis of notes preserved by Foxwell, then one of Marshall's students.

88. This paragraph draws heavily on the summary of these early papers provided by John Whitaker; see introduction to *EEW*, I, pp. 42–4.

89. Jevons's *Theory of Political Economy* had been published in October 1871. For the *Academy*, see T.W. Heyck, *The Transformation of Intellectual Life in Victorian England*, London: Croom Helm, 1982, pp. 178, 215–17.

90. Alfred Marshall, undated comment on his Jevons's review, in *Memorials*, p. 100.

91. A.S. and E.M.S., *Henry Sidgwick. A Memoir*, p. 244 n.1.

92. Alfred Marshall, undated comment on his Jevons's review in *Memorials*, p. 99.
93. Alfred Marshall, Review of Jevons's *Theory of Political Economy'*, *Academy* 1 April, 1872, in *Memorials*, pp. 94, 95.
94. W.S. Jevons to J. D'Aulnis, 7 July 1874, in *Papers and Correspondence of W.S. Jevons*, Vol. IV, p. 62.
95. Alfred Marshall, 'Review of Jevons's *Theory of Political Economy'*, in *Memorials*, p. 93, cf. undated fragment in *Memorials*, pp. 99–100.
96. Alfred Marshall, 'Review of Jevons's *Theory of Political Economy'*, in *Memorials*, pp. 94–5, cf. Alfred Marshall to H.S. Foxwell, 10 January 1879 (Freeman Collection, 44/155), where Marshall referred to his problems with the theory of distribution which Jevons failed to resolve. This letter may have been in Foxwell's mind when he wrote to Jevons later that year on Marshall's originality. See below, note 107.
97. Alfred Marshall, 'Review of Jevons' *Theory of Political Economy'*, in *Memorials*, p. 95 and cf. above, p. 157, the reference to this topic in Marshall's manuscript on international trade.
98. Alfred Marshall, 'Review of Jevons' *Theory of Political Economy'*, in *Memorials*, p. 98.
99. Alfred Marshall, 'Review of Jevons' *Theory of Political Economy*, in *Memorials*, p. 99; cf. Alfred Marshall to Arthur Bowley, 27 February 1906, in *ibid.*, pp. 427–8.
100. See H.S. Foxwell to John Maynard Keynes, 24 April 1925, cited in Whitaker, introduction to *EEW*, I, p. 45 n.26.
101. W.S. Jevons to Marshall, 7 January 1875, in *Papers and Correspondence of William Stanley Jevons*, Vol. V, pp. 95–6. Marshall may have been absent from Cambridge because of his mother's illness, which kept him in London till early February as he wrote to Foxwell (17, 31 January 1875, Freeman Collection, 11,12/229).
102. See Mary Paley Marshall, *What I Remember*, p. 17; *Cambridge Historical Register*, p. 710, indicates that ten other men attempted the Tripos in that year of whom four gained second class and six, third class, results. JNKD, 15 December 1874, supposed 'that Pearson and Gardiner were the corking individuals who wanted to put her in the 2nd class'.
103. Cited in JNKD, entry for 13 December 1875.
104. *Ibid.*
105. Alfred Marshall to W.S. Jevons, 4 February 1875, in *Papers and Correspondence of William Stanley Jevons*, Vol. V, p. 100; the paper Jevons had sent Marshall was 'The Progress of the Mathematical Theory of Political Economy', read before the Manchester Statistical Society on 11 November 1874 and reprinted in its transactions for 1874–75, pp. 1–19.
106. W.S. Jevons, preface to second edition of *Theory of Political Economy*, 1897, pp. xv and xli. Jevons had sent a presentation copy to Marshall, preserved in the Marshall Library. In annotating this, Marshall particularly noted changes between the two editions (e.g. pp. 18, 62, 66, 90, 98) as well as continued criticism on the notion of trading body and aspects of the theory of distribution. Jevons's testimonial is in the form of a letter to Marshall (dated 23 June 1877). It placed Marshall 'among the most original writers in economics' on the basis of his 'forthcoming work on the theory of Foreign Trade' (*Papers and Correspondence of W.S. Jevons*, Vol. IV, pp. 204–5).
107. Foxwell to Jevons, 12 November 1879 and Jevons to Foxwell in reply, 14 November 1879 in *Papers and Correspondence of William Stanley Jevons*, Vol. V, pp. 78, 80.
108. See Marshall to Foxwell, 19 January 1883 (Marshall Archive, 3/7) and Marshall to Bonar, 27 November 1898, in *Memorials*, p. 374.
109. 'Professor Marshall on Jevons as an Economist', sent to Foxwell who was organising the memorial on 22 May 1883. The quotations are from the version included in Marshall's correspondence edited by John Whitaker, Volume 1, Letter 110. As shown in Chapter 12, Marshall was drafting his note on Ricardo at this time, below, p. 405.
110. Marshall to John Neville Keynes, 26 November and 2 December 1889 (Marshall Archive, 1:72, 1:93 (reprinted in *P* IX, pp. 260–61).
111. On this, see Michael White, 'Invention in the Face of Necessity: Marshallian Rhetoric and the Giffen Good(s)', *Economic Record*, 66 (192), March 1990, esp. pp. 3–5.
112. See Whitaker, introduction to *EEW*, p. 103, cf. pp. 46–7, 49–50, 84–5. *P* VIII, p. 101, *Memorials*, p. 128 n.3.
113. Discussed further below, Chapter 21, pp. 776–7.
114. Alfred Marshall to W.S. Jevons, 30 June 1879, in *Memorials*, p. 371.
115. Marshall to Edgeworth, 12 September 1882, Edgeworth Papers, British Library of Political and Economic Science, Coll. Misc., 470/31 M 469.
116. Alfred Marshall to John Maynard Keynes, 4 December 1910, Keynes Papers, King's College, Cambridge, File L/M/41. Foxwell later wrote to Keynes on Marshall's reaction when he showed him Jenkin's paper on supply and demand in 1870 (reproduced in *EEW*, I, p. 45 n.26).
117. Marshall's correspondence with Keynes in December 1910 recalled that at this meeting of the Philosophical Society, Clerk Maxwell told him that the matter reported by Marshall reminded him of work by Fleeming Jenkin. (Alfred Marshall to Keynes, 4 December and 12 December 1910, Keynes Papers, L/M/41, Kings

College, Cambridge. Cf. Alfred Marshall to H.H. Cunynghame, 7 April 1904, in *Memorials*, p. 449. Lewis Campbell and William Garnett, *Life of James Clerk Maxwell*, p. 336, record his friendship with Fleeming Jenkin.

118. Alfred Marshall to L.L. Price, 19 August 1892, in *Memorials*, pp. 378–9. This was a response to Price's review of the second edition of the *Principles*. He referred to some of the issues Marshall raised in this letter, see his 'Note on a Recent Economic Treatise', *Economic Journal*, 2 (1), March 1892, in *Alfred Marshall. Critical Assessments*, Vol. II, pp. 41–2.

119. Above, Chapter 5, p. 129, a record of how and where he spent some of his summers is reproduced below, p. 129, Chapter 7, p. 189.

120. Marshall Archive, Box 7 (3): Statistics.

121. That is presumably, F. Seebohm, articles on historical aspects of population in *Fortnightly Review*, 1865–1870; E.A. Hübner, *Statistische Tafel aller Lander der Erde*, Berlin, 1851, and William Hoyle, *Our Natural Resources and How they are Wasted. An omitted Chapter in Political Economy*, Manchester, 1871.

122. See Chapter 5, above pp. 128–9 and n; below, Chapter 17, p. 638.

123. See for example, *EOI*, Book I, Chapters VII, IX; *P* I, Book I, Chapters II and III, *P* VIII, Appendix A.

124. Alfred Marshall to Foxwell, 29 May 1878, 3 July 1878 (Freeman Collection, 46/155, 36/155); the material from the first letter is quoted in the text.

125. Marshall Archive, Box 5, Items 5–10, Notebooks on the History of Economic Theory and Economic History; the Lecture on the History and Method of Economics is in *ibid.*, Item 1 (f). The last has been published as *HME*. It was not included with the *EEW*.

126. *HME*, pp. 2, 5.

127. See my 'Alfred Marshall and the History of Economic Thought', *Quaderni di storia dell'economia politica* IX (2–3), 1991, Part I, esp. pp. 64–7.

128. Introduction to *HME*, pp. xv, xviii–xix.

129. *P* I, p. 58, *P* VIII, p. 760; Mary Paley Marshall, *What I Remember*, p. 19.

130. See Chapter 5 above, p. 129. In his *Methods of Ethics* (Book II, Chapter III) Sidgwick raised a number of serious problems in pleasure measurement and commensurability.

131. J.K. Whitaker, 'Some Neglected Aspects of Alfred Marshall's Economic and Social Thought' *AMCA*, I, p. 457; cf. *P* VIII, p. 17 n.1; and *P* IX, pp. 136–7 for the enormous changes this passage underwent from its first version in *P* I, p. 83 and n.1.

132. *P* VIII, p. 15, and see below for a discussion of the same subject in Marshall's 1876 article on 'Mr. Mill's Theory of Value', p. 175.

133. *EEW*, II, pp. 316–19; see also *P* VIII, p. 25, which dates from *P* II, p. 80. J.K. Whitaker, 'Some Neglected Aspects of Alfred Marshall's Economic and Social Thought', pp. 470–72, resolves some other potential conflicts in Marshall's adaptation of Benthamite views, as does Viner's classical treatment of the subject, 'Marshall's Economics in Relation to the Man and his Time', esp. pp. 245–9.

134. *P* I, p. ix; *HME*, pp. 6–7, 10–21; 'Some Features of American Industry' in *EEW*, II, pp. 355–77, esp. p. 376; 'Water as an Element in the National Wealth', in *Memorials*, esp. pp. 138–41. The last two lectures are discussed in some detail in subsequent chapters, Chapter 7, pp. 200–201, Chapter 9, pp. 292–3.

135. Mary Paley Marshall, *What I Remember*, p. 20; J.M. Keynes, 'Alfred Marshall', p. 172 n.2.

136. *P* I, p. 765, *P* VIII, p. 764; a detailed evaluation of Hegel's influence on Marshall is my 'Marshall and Hegel', esp. pp. 70–82.

137. See J.R. Mozley to J.M. Keynes, 24 November 1924 (KMF) and cf. John Maynard Keynes, 'Alfred Marshall', p. 169 where Keynes describes Spencer's *First Principles* as 'unreadable', Mary Paley Marshall, *What I Remember*, p. 19. The 1927 Catalogue of the Marshall Library lists *Principles of Biology*, 2 vols 1865, 1867; *First Principles*, second edition, 1867; *Social Statics*, 1868; *Essays: Scientific, Political and Speculative*, 3 vols 1868, 1868, 1874; *Descriptive Sociology*, 4 vols 1873–1881; *Principles of Sociology* Vol. 1, 1876, Vol. III, 1896; *The Data of Ethics*, second edition, 1879; *Study of Sociology*, 1880; *Political Institutions*, 1882; *The Man versus the State*, 1884; *Ecclesiastical Institutions*, 1885; *Factors of Organic Evolution*, 1887. However, after the Economics Tripos was established he donated many copies of Spencer's work to the Moral Sciences Library. Below, Chapter 10, p. 336 n*.

138. *P* VIII, p. 136, p. 184 n. (Marshall's remark on the factual evidence in support of Spencer's hypotheses is confined to editions 3–5, see *P* IX, p. 289 and p. 247 respectively.) For his critique of the classical view of working-class progress, see above, p. 141.

139. See *Daily Chronicle*, 23 November 1904, in *Memorials*, p. 507; and see *P* VIII, p. 770, *P* IX, p. 254 n.

140. Below, Chapter 12, pp. 422–6, Chapter 19, pp. 714–5. The complexity of Marshall's aims and a pathological fear of error are other reasons for this failure in writing. (See Chapter 21, below, pp. 784–7 and Chapter 2 above, p. 26.)

141. Marshall Archive, Large Brown Box, Item 7; the 1927 Marshall Catalogue (p. 53) lists *Ancient Law* (second edition, 1866), *Early History of Institutions* (1875), *Village Communities* (fourth edition 1881), *Early Law and Custom* (1883) and *Popular Government* (1885).

142. *P* I, pp. 12–14, *P* VIII,pp. 724–6; cf. J.K. Whitaker, Introduction to *EEW*, I, p. 72 n.18.

143. See *P* I, p. 21 n.1; another deleted reference to Maine from the first edition is on p. 54 n.2; and see Alfred Marshall, 'A Reply', in *Economic Journal* 2 (3), September 1892, p. 509. The controversy is discussed below, Chapter 13, pp. 469–71.

144. *HME*, esp. pp. 10–11; *EOI*, pp. 40–42, esp. the reference to 'Village Communities, as they are called' (p. 41), p. 60.

145. *P* VIII, p. 726 n.1. References to the importance of custom in the *Principles* are fairly frequent, see for example, 6–7, 12, 21, 61, 103, 140–41, 155–6, 182–3, 267, 392n., 531–2n., 559–60, 637–42, many of which may be associated with the researches of Sir Henry Maine.

146. That is, William Sargant, *Economy of the Labouring Classes*, London: Simpkin, Marshall and Company, 1857 which summarised many of Le Play's data and tested their accuracy against British findings on the subject. As noted previously (above, p. 154 n*), Sargant was an important early influence on Marshall's economic thinking. Marshall owned the three volumes of *La Reforme sociale en France* and the six volumes of *Les ouvriers européens*.

147. *P* VIII, p. 116.

148. See below, Chapter 11 on Marshall's association with the Charity Organisation Society, and Chapter 14, pp. 514–5 on Le Play's views on the sexual division of labour.

149. Details are given in my 'Alfred Marshall and Australian Economics', *HETSA Bulletin*, No. 9, Winter 1988, esp. pp. 1–5, 9–12, and cf. Marshall's annotation on Jevons's use of Hearn noted above, p. 160.

150. JNKD, 8 February 1877, 16 July 1877.

151. Alexander Macmillan to Alfred Marshall, 17 April 1877, 14 May 1877 (Marshall Archives, 2/36, 2/37).

152. Alfred Marshall to Henry Cunynghame, 7 April 1904, in *Memorials*, p. 449; cf. Marshall's letter to Maynard Keynes, 10 December 1910, quoted above, pp. 162–3.

153. Alfred Marshall to E.R.A. Seligman, April 1900, in J. Dorfman, 'The Seligman Correspondence', *Political Science Quarterly*, 56 (3), September 1941, pp. 408–10.

154. That is, from *EEW*, II, p. 5. The reconstructed text, interspersed by Whitaker's brief introductions to its various component chapters and parts, is given on pp. 7–236. This indicates its substantial size. The reprinted material bears out Marshall's account to Seligman just quoted that the greater part of the second Part was finished except for Chapter VII which Marshall could no longer complete by June 1877.

155. A detailed evaluation of Marshall's international trade theory is John Creedy, 'Marshall and International Trade', in *Centenary Essays on Alfred Marshall*, edited John Whitaker, Cambridge University Press, 1990, pp. 79–107. Viner's detailed account places Marshall's contributions in the wider historical context. See his *Studies in the Theory of International Trade*, New York: Harper & Brothers, 1937, esp. pp. 541–55, 570–75.

156. Marshall's views on socialism are discussed in Chapter 16 below.

157. This was first published in the *Fortnightly Review* in 1876, and Marshall later wrote an introduction to its re–issue in 1885, an episode in his life discussed in Chapter 12 below, pp. 406–7 and n*.

158. Below, Chapter 7, pp. 193–203.

159. In *EEW*, II, pp. 289–302 and probably written circa 1874. Chapter II, §4 of the *Pure Theory of Domestic Value* is in *ibid.* pp. 219–23; the footnote is in *P* I, p. 447, n.1, *P* VIII, p. 467 n.1. For a general discussion of this point, see my 'Marshall on Taxation', in *Alfred Marshall in Retrospect*, ed. Rita McWilliams-Tullberg, pp. 98–9.

160. In *EEW*, II, pp. 303–5; and see Whitaker's introduction thereto, in *ibid.*, pp. 302–3.

161. *Philosophical Transactions*, Vol. 2, October 1873, pp. 318–19; reprinted in *EEW*, II, pp. 284–5, and see above, pp. 162–3, Chapter 5, p. 113. Its significance is discussed by J. Creedy and D.P. O'Brien, 'Marshall, Monopoly, and Rectangular Hyperbolas', *Australian Economic Papers* 29 (55), December 1990, pp. 141–53.

162. This ignores his article for the *Bee-Hive* in 1874 (discussed in Chapter 16 below, pp. 574–5) and some publications in the Bristol press (discussed below, Chapter 9, pp. 289–93).

163. Marshall, 'The Future of the Working Classes', in *Memorials*, p. 102.

164. *Ibid.* passim. The quotation on state education is from p. 118.

165. Above, pp. 141–3.

166. Marshall, 'Mr. Mill's Theory of Value', *Fortnightly Review*, April 1876, in *Memorials*, pp. 119–33. Page references in brackets in this paragraph refer to this version of the article.

167. See Jevons to Sidgwick, 28 February 1879, in *Papers and Correspondence of William Stanley Jevons*, Vol. V, pp. 23–4. It is very possible that the meeting of the discussion group for which the material was privately printed was held in mid-February 1879. See Alfred Marshall to Foxwell, 14 February 1879, where he thanked Foxwell

for his 'account of Sidgwick's club. I am always glad to hear what goes on there.' (Freeman Collection, 20/9). This aspect of Marshall's relations with Sidgwick is discussed in some detail below, Chapter 18, pp. 665–7.

168. W.S. Jevons, *Theory of Political Economy*, Preface to second edition, 1879, p. xli where he refers to Alfred Marshall's 'ingenious mathematico-economic problems, expounded *more geometrico*' as 'having just been privately printed at Cambridge'. See also Edgeworth, *Mathematical Psychics*, London: Kegan Paul, 1881, e.g. pp. 25, 26 and n.1, 33.

169. Alfred Marshall to E.R.A. Seligman, 23 April 1900, in J. Dorfman, 'The Seligman Correspondence', pp. 408–10.

170. Alfred Marshall to Foxwell, April/May 1879 (Freeman Collection, 4/9).

171. Marshall Archive, Box 9 (6).

172. Below, Chapter 19, pp. 718, 719 and n*.

173. Alfred Marshall and Mary Paley Marshall, *EOI*, p. v; G.J. Stigler, *Production and Distribution Theories*, New York: Macmillan, 1941, p. 344. The last statement is quite generous to the Marshalls and ignores Jevons's contributions to the subject in *Theory of Political Economy*.

174. Rita McWilliams-Tullberg, 'Marshall's Attitude to the Economics of Industry', *Journal of the History of Economic Thought*, 14 (2), Fall 1992, pp. 257–70. Aspects of the book are also discussed below in Chapter 8 in the context of Marshall's marriage, see esp. pp. 250–55.

175. For Stuart's role in the Extension movement, see J.D.F. Harrison, *Learning and Living 1790–1960*, London: Routledge & Kegan Paul, 1961, Chapter VI esp. pp. 221–4; Mary Paley Marshall, *What I Remember*, p. 22; draft letter by Marshall, 2 May, 1910, to Japanese translator, in Marshall Archive, 3/85.

176. JNKD, 10 July 1877.

177. Alexander Macmillan to Alfred Marshall, 17 April 1877, William Jack to Alfred Marshall, 19 July 1877, Marshall Archive, 2/36, 2/41. Proposed companion volumes were alternatively called 'Trade and Government' and 'The Economics of Trade and Finance', the title mentioned in the preface.

178. Marshall to Foxwell, 26 April, 17 May, 19 May, 3 July, 27 October, 4 November 1878, 10 January, 1879 and Mary Paley Marshall, 22 September 1878 (Freeman Collection, 44/155, 49/155, 46/155, 36/155, 37/155, 33/155, 48/155).

179. Both Brassey and Walker were cited on several occasions in *The Economics of Industry*. See, for example, pp. 174, 223 for Brassey and pp. 40, 102, 118 for F.A. Walker. As shown in Chapter 7, Marshall met Walker at Yale during his trip to the United States in 1875. The *Economist*'s review appeared on 28 February 1880.

180. Marshall to Foxwell, 25 October, 2 November 1879 (Freeman Collection, 9/9, 8/9); Mary Paley Marshall, *What I Remember*, p. 22.

181. Marshall to E.R.A. Seligman, 23 April 1900, in J. Dorfman, 'The Seligman Correspondence', p. 309; Alfred Marshall, 'Alfred Marshall, Professor of Political Economy', p. 150; Marshall to Japanese translator, 2 May 1910, Marshall Archive, 3/85. The matter of this book is discussed in Chapter 8 below as an important case study of the Marshalls' intellectual collaboration during their marriage.

182. See the paper by Rita McWilliams-Tullberg cited in note 174 above.

183. Discussed in Chapter 12 below, which thereby acts as sequel to this chapter for those interested in the development of Marshall's economic theory which he published during his lifetime.

7. An Observing and Studious Traveller: Europe, Britain and the United States

The enjoyment of nature Alfred Marshall had developed as a London schoolboy generated a love of travel and vacations spent in the country as soon as he could afford it after his graduation. Initial impetus probably came from his Devon holidays as a schoolboy with Aunt Louisa but as the Marshall family grew more affluent during the late 1850s, other country holidays with his immediate family seem likely. In his first letter to his mother from America, Marshall based his expectations that Aunt Louisa would probably like to read his United States travel accounts he was sending with the letters, on the fact that 'she liked reading our journals from the lakes'.[1] From the summer of 1866 onwards, once income was assured through his fellowship, Marshall quickly adapted to the habit of Victorian academics to spend summer away from normal place of residence and employment and, when possible, to use between-term breaks in the same way.

Such excursions were not only for relaxation and rest. In his early postgraduate years, they included extended periods of seclusion during which specific subjects were mastered: for example, Dresden and Berlin were visited in 1868 and 1869–70 for the purpose of learning German; summers in Scotland and Switzerland were devoted to philosophical studies; a good deal of history was studied in the three summers from 1871 to 1873. Later, especially after marriage, some of the summers were devoted to writing. During 1869 and 1870 Marshall developed his diagrammatic treatment of economic problems; in 1874 he worked on the paper on foreign trade from which his 1876 paper on Mill's value theory and the manuscript for a book on foreign trade emerged; during his first three long vacations (1877–79) as a married man, the Marshalls worked together on *Economics of Industry*. Most of the 1880s summers were spent in developing the successive drafts of the *Principles* begun during their wintering 'holiday' of 1881–82 in Sicily.[2]

At least part of the summer travel was used by Marshall as a field trip, in which he studied industrial and social conditions in various towns and regions. By the time he was married this aspect of travel had developed into a quite specific routine, recalled by Mary Paley for Keynes and Walter Scott. These, together with some detailed notes preserved from such trips, lend colour to Marshall's reference to 'Wander-jahre among factories', designed to discover where Cournot's premises on increasing returns with respect to the preservation of competition, had gone wrong.[3]

> He spent part of his vacations in towns. . . . His plan in towns was to visit a picture gallery, and also to visit the best shop for prints and photographs of eminent men. . . . [for his] . . . collection of portraits. When in a town he would spend much time on the chief bridge, his back to the river and looking sideways, so as to see those who came along without appearing to stare. He did this chiefly in the working class quarters, and at the time when people were leaving the factories.[4]

In her notes for Walter Scott, Mary Paley Marshall added that 'In later years, when we used to visit manufacturing towns abroad and in England, we used to stand near the exit from a factory, just before closing time and watch the employees as they left work. We also frequented the market late on Saturday nights and watched the working women bargaining. We also went a great deal to Salvation Army meetings in industrial towns.'[5] Notes in Mary Paley's handwriting, made in 1885, confirm this pattern of systematic social observation. What precise generalisations and conclusions were derived from this organised but nevertheless casual empiricism, is not always clear.   An exception is Marshall's claim to Edgeworth that for some years he had systematically observed consumption of bread, and more generally, of wheat- based products, by social class in hotels, inns and through bread deliveries.   This enabled the tentative conclusion 'that the very rich eat less than half as much bread as the poorer classes;   the middle class coming midway', of relevance to demand for inferior goods.[6] Another insight into the motivation for these fact-finding tours is preserved in a fragment in the *Memorials*,

> In the years of my apprenticeship to economic studies, between 1867 and 1875, I endeavoured to learn enough of the methods of operation of the greater part of the leading industries of the country, to be able to reconstruct mentally the vital parts of the chief machines used in each, neglecting, of course, all refinements and secondary complications. This endeavour was associated with an attempt to form a rough estimate of the faculties and training needed for working each, and the strain involved therein: and, my guide – if, as generally happened he was the employer or a foreman – would generally answer my inquiries as to the wages which each was receiving. After continuing on this course for some years, I began to ask my guide to allow me to guess these wages. My error did not very often exceed two shillings a week on one side or the other: but, when it did, I stopped and asked for an explanation. Sometimes my mistake was due to the fact that the work was easier or more difficult than it appeared to me: sometimes to the fact that the demand for the work was largely seasonal, or liable to variations due to fashion and other causes; sometimes that a high grade operative was being set to rather low grade work, because his proper work was not on hand just then, and was of course being paid the wages of his proper work; sometimes that the work was a blind alley, rather low grade and not leading up to higher work; and so on. These explanations were specially conclusive when I inquired why men were doing work which seemed within the range of women. In almost every such case, it was shown that the work was more difficult, or required more strength or more prompt resource and judgement, than appeared on the surface; or that it extended on occasion into hours that were forbidden to women by law; or – and this was no uncommon occurrence in those industries in which the large majority of the operatives were women – that a man was being paid more highly than a woman would be for the same work, because he seemed to develop the qualities required for a foreman, and the business required a larger number of such men than could find employment in it without some such special arrangements.[7]

The varied purposes of the Marshalls' summer 'vacations' are explicitly mentioned in a letter written to Simon Newcomb, the American astronomer, economist and financial historian, which tried to arrange a meeting when the Newcombs themselves were visiting Switzerland. To Newcomb's suggestion that they perhaps could meet in the Engadine, Marshall responded,

> I am very sorry we cannot possibly come to the Engadine. I have come here [Sedrun, Val Tavetsch, Graubunden] in order to get more undisturbed time for writing than I could get at home, almost as much as for the change of air. We are not touring at all. We have come here straight and settled here for four weeks Hence we go in a couple of days to the next village higher up in the valley, and if all goes well, stay there

for several weeks. Then we follow a rail line direct via Göshenen to England, through Paris if the cholera is not bad there; or if it is, through Cologne. We shall stop on our way, probably at Göshenen and certainly to have some studies of industrial conditions, either in France, or if we go by the German route, in Mulhouse and elsewhere. We have a great many bookboxes and travelling by road is troublesome and expensive. So we make straight for the railway-line from Chiamutt.

Our plans are uncertain, partly because I do not know how long I shall be able to hold out without more books, partly because of some people whom we have asked to stay with us in September at Cambridge do not yet quite know their own plans.[8]

Given that the Cambridge summer vacation lasted for virtually four months from June until early October, between a quarter and a third of Marshall's adult life was spent in this type of travel. The contents of this chapter therefore cover a significant portion of his life's activities. The need for detailed discussion becomes even greater, when it is realised that some of these trips – especially his visit to the United States in the summer of 1875 and the Marshalls' recuperative trip to Europe from October 1881 to September 1882 – played significant roles in his work as an economist and social observer.

AN OVERVIEW OF TRAVEL IN MARSHALL'S LONG VACATIONS: 1866–1923

Two lists of Marshall's summer vacation activities and main travel destinations are extant. One was designed to give an approximate history of his work on 'curves', apparently prepared on his way back to Bristol in 1882 after their twelve months stay in Italy and Bavaria for reasons of Marshall's poor health. The other, in Mary Paley's handwriting, lists the various places where they spent their summers together, right up to Marshall's final illness and death in 1924. The first is quoted in the slightly edited version given in the introduction to *Early Economic Writings*,

> Long vacations: 66 Scotland, Philosophy; 67 Switzerland, ditto; 68 Dresden and Salzkammargut, curves beginning; 69 Berlin, West Tirol, Pol. Econ., A Smith, Improvements in cultivation decided me to adopt curves as an engine; 70 East Tirol, Foreign Trade curves; 71 St Moritz, miscellaneous. A good deal of history; 72 Aussee and East Tirol, chiefly history; 73 St Moritz with Agnes and May [his sisters], ditto; 74 Wales, beginning of paper on foreign trade which developed into i article on Cairnes ['Mr. Mill's Theory of Value'] ii book on Foreign trade; 75 America, Foreign Trade; 76 Switzerland, ditto; 77 Cornwall, Economics [of Industry]; 78 Ufford, ditto; 79 Torcross, ditto; 80 Clovelly, Value; 81 Salcomb, ditto; 82 Achensee, ditto.[9]

Mary Paley's list expands that prepared by Marshall himself some time in 1882. It only records final or major destinations of their summer vacation. Routes chosen to reach them and other places visited on the way are omitted. The potential extent of such omissions can be seen from the following examples. Between spending the summer of 1881 at Salcomb (South Devon) and that of 1882 at the Achensee (Bavarian Alps), the Marshalls spent nearly the whole of the intervening year in Italy. The '*rundreise*' made in summer 1892 was their only grand tour of Europe, essentially Central Europe, taking in Dresden and Prague. The list is nevertheless worth reproducing to enable an overview and some generalisations on summer destinations enjoyed by Marshall before and after marriage.

Summers: 65 nowhere; 66 Scotland; 67 Switzerland (Mürren with Mozley); 68 Dresden and Tirol; 69 Achensee [Bavarian Alps]; 70 Aussee, Bad Fush, Gross Glockner [Austria]; 71 [The] Engadine [Switzerland], Bavaria; 72 Bad Fush; 73 [Switzerland] with the girls [Marshall's sisters, Agnes and Mabel]; 74 Wales; 75 America; 76 Switzerland [with the Paleys]; 77 Land's End, Cornwall [honeymoon after the Marshalls were married in August]; 78 Ufford [with the Paleys]; 79 Torcross; 80 Clovelly; 81 Salcomb; 82 Achensee; 83 Parrog [Wales]; 84 Guernsey; 85 Lakes; 86 Cromer [Norfolk]; 87 Scotland; 88 Yorkshire; 89 Bordeaux Harbour (Guernsey); 90 Scotland; 91 Rundreise; 92 Sedrun [Switzerland]; 93 Colfosco; 94 Stuben; 95 La Grave (Dauphiné); 96 Ospitale-Ampesso Tal; 97 Hinterhein [Switzerland]; 98 Dosses – Grödner Tal [South Tirol]; 99 Radein [Bavarian Alps]; 1900 Walkerstein [South Tirol]; 01 T'Tass, Lower Grödner [Tal] Engadine; 02 Walkerstein, Grödner Tal, South Tirol; 03 Stern-Abzei Tal [South Tirol]; 04 Sheringham [Norfolk]; 05 Stern-Abzei Tal; 06 Stern-Abzei Tal; 07 Yorkshire and Cambridge; 08 Ampesso Tal; 09 Stern-Abzei Tal; 10 Weybourne [Norfolk] 11 Brixham; 12 Tustow Farm and Menstone; 13 St Martins [Thürn] South Tirol; 14 Tustow Farm; 15 Corfe Castle [Dorset]; 16 Corfe Castle [Dorset]; 17 Torquay; 18 Freshwater; 19 Weymouth [and] Southampton; 20 St Martin Thürn [South Tirol] last visit abroad; 21 20 weeks in Sea Vale, Wareham Dorset; 22 9 weeks at Sea Vale, Dorset; 23 Sea Vale July, Aug. Sept.; 24 ill from May 10 – July 13.[10]

The summer travels display some distinct patterns. Prior to marriage in 1877, Alfred Marshall largely spent his summers abroad, including a four months visit to North America in the summer of 1875. Exceptions are 1866 when, largely for financial reasons (he was still paying his debt to Uncle Charles) he visited Scotland and probably, North England industrial towns en route; and 1874 which was spent in Wales. This is probably explicable by personal concerns about health problems in his immediate family involving mother and younger brother Walter, which made foreign travel inadvisable.[11] In sharp contrast, summer holidays in the first thirteen years of married life were invariably spent in the United Kingdom. The one exception is the twelve months sojourn in Italy and Bavaria from early October 1881 for health reasons. Economy and study requirements provide the major explanation for this pattern. The first three summers after marriage were devoted to finishing *The Economics of Industry*. Holidays in the 1880s were largely devoted to composing the *Principles* but also included field trips to industrial towns, and three, slightly more exotic, vacations spent on the Channel Island of Guernsey. Between 1891 and 1909, summers were largely spent abroad. After the re-discovery of Central Europe by means of a round trip, partly revisiting places Marshall had first seen as a bachelor, the greater part of these summers were spent in secluded mountain villages, initially in Switzerland but later in the quieter and much less touristic, South Tirol. There they adopted favoured holiday destinations, to which they regularly returned. An exception in this pattern is the one holiday spent in France, but even here it is the French Alps which replaced their Bavarian, Swiss, Italian or Austrian counterparts. The two local holidays in these years are dictated by professional commitments. In 1904, the Marshalls played host to the British Association meeting in Cambridge. This meant their vacation could not be far afield. In 1907, apart from the substantial revisions for the fifth edition of the *Principles* (its preface is dated August of that year) a congress organised by the Royal Economic Society at which Marshall gave a major address, kept him in England. Health reasons, caused by growing problems with his blood pressure, dictated quieter rural holidays in England in 1910, 1912 and 1914. The First World War subsequently imposed inevitable restrictions on movements beyond the British Isles. The war years were flanked in 1913 and 1920 by the last two holidays enjoyed in the

Marshalls' much beloved South Tirol. The final three summers away, those of 1921, 1922 and 1923, all spent at Sea Vale, Dorset, were substantially allotted to the construction of *Money, Credit and Commerce* (ready for the printer by the end of the summer of 1922) and work on the final projected volume on economic progress, of which bundles of notes and a partial table of contents are the sole visible outcome.

This summary places the remaining content of this chapter in context, the comprehensiveness of which is largely dictated by the availability of material from correspondence or notes. After discussing Marshall's bachelor travel, two highlights in his travelling experience are examined. The first is the summer of 1875 spent in North America, largely in the United States; the second is the virtual twelve months from early October 1881 spent in Italy and the Bavarian Alps for health reasons. The chapter concludes with a discussion of factory trips in England in the 1880s and some reminiscences recorded by the Marshalls on activities from their European holidays during the twenty summers starting from 1891.

BACHELOR SUMMERS IN THE MOUNTAINS 1867–1876

Little is known of Marshall's first summer vacation as a graduate, which the summaries briefly indicate as including a visit to Scotland. Chapter 5 assumed it provided the first occasion for 'visiting the poorer quarters of several cities', a study of the face of poverty which initially directed his attention to economics. During the following summer Mozley and his brother introduced Alfred Marshall to the joys of Alpine mountaineering. They took him climbing in Mürren and also to the Dolomites of the Italian and Austrian Tirol. Mary Paley recollected, 'After a while, Mozley and his brother had to go home. A[lfred] described how they all drove together until their roads parted and how they drove on and left him standing and how after they were gone out of sight he gave a shout of delight of being able to be alone.'[12]   It seems that Marshall was a loner by choice from an early age.

Thereafter, Marshall's summers fell into the pattern Mary Paley Marshall later described for Keynes.

> During the years following his degree, he went abroad almost every long vacation. He took with him £60 and a knapsack, and spent most of his time walking in the High Alps. This walking, summer after summer, turned him from a weak to a strong man. He left Cambridge early in June jaded and overworked and returned in October brown and strong and upright. Carrying the knapsack pulled him upright and until he was over 80 he remained so. He even then exerted himself almost painfully to hold himself straight. When walking in the Alps, his practice was to get up at 6 and be well on his way before 8. He would walk with knapsack on his back for 2 or 3 hours and not rest till he reached some place from which he could find his way in case mist came on. He would then sit down, sometimes on a glacier, and have a long pull at some book, Goethe, or Hegel, or Kant, or Herbert Spencer, and then walk on to his next halting place for the night. This was his philosophical stage – later on he worked on his theories of domestic and foreign Trade. A large box of books was sent on from one stage to the next, but he would go for a week or more just with a knapsack. He would wash his shirt by holding it in a fast running stream and dried it by carrying it on his alpenstock over his shoulder. He did most of his hardest thinking on some of these solitary walks. These wanderjahre gave him a love for the Alps and even in 1919 [when] for the last time he went to South Tirol where he sat and worked in the open air.[13]

This was of course the time when Alpine mountaineering was 'the new sport of the upper-middle class . . . when the French railways reached Basel and Geneva, and Switzerland came to be hardly more than a day's journey from London and a fare less than ten pounds. . . . In 1855 a single climbing expedition with five porters and three guides cost a couple of friends only four pounds each.'[14] Leslie Stephen, Marshall's near contemporary at Cambridge was a noted climber. In his own college, his friend Bonney had spent many of his summers from 1859 onwards mountaineering in the Alps, a past-time he did not abandon until 1911 and which, like the Marshalls, covered the French Alps, the Bavarian Alps, the Dolomites and the Tirol as well as the Alpine beauties of Switzerland.[15]

> Marshall himself became very fond of mountain climbing and did a great deal in Switzerland without guides. He was very fond of one Alpine feat, i.e. he was the first to ascend the Gross Glockner from the Heiligenblutt side, with only one guide. He started with 2 guides and they reached the hut. The weather then got so bad that they had to stay there for the night. Early in the morning the elder guide left them to get food. When he had gone, the younger guide, after taking A[lfred] on the glacier and trying his paces said 'If you will climb the Gross Glockner I am ready.' So they went across the very narrow arrête and reached the top. It was for this dangerous arrête that two guides had been considered necessary.[16]

In the context of the difficulties of evening study for those engaged in hard manual labour, a factor Marshall mentioned in his first published paper on the future of the working classes, he illustrated the problem by reference to his own Alpine exploits, and one undoubtedly appealing to most of his Cambridge audience,

> I remember once in the Alps, after three days of exceptionally severe climbing, resolving to take a day's rest and to read a book on Philosophy. I was in good training. I was not conscious of any but physical weariness; but when the first occasion for hard thought arrived, my mind absolutely refused to move. I was immensely angry with it, but my anger was in vain.[17]

Mountaineering came to an end in 1876. After his engagement to Mary Paley was announced, Alfred Marshall's prospective father-in-law, the Rev. Thomas Paley, took him and the rest of the Paley family to Switzerland for a holiday, during which Mary, Alfred and her brother George Thomas, climbed Monte Rosa. This was a good day's climb for an experienced mountaineer, but as Mary Paley recalled, it was 'my first and last attempt at mountaineering [and although] Alfred had been an enthusiastic climber . . . he now decided to give up mountaineering'.[18] The Alps, however, were not surrendered and remained the favourite holiday spot for the Marshalls.

Large towns were of course also visited during these bachelor summer excursions. One of these was Dresden, originally, as shown in a previous chapter, to take German lessons with Sidgwick's teacher. 'When at Dresden he used to go every day to look at the Sistine Madonna, but as time went on, he got to love the Holbein Madonna more and more, and at last preferred it to Raphael's. He enjoyed the informal music at Dresden, and the immense pleasure he got from music began at this time.'* Few recollections are left from his visit to

---

* Mary Paley Marshall, 'Notes for Walter Scott'; after marriage they revisited Dresden together in 1891. The Sistine Madonna by Raphael is one of the main attractions of the Zwingler Museum, but it is not clear to which Holbein Madonna Mary Paley is referring, perhaps the Mayor Meyer Madonna, in the Darmstadt Museum. Interestingly, the two are combined for comparison in Paul Brandt, *Sehen und Erkennen*, Leipzig: Alfred Kroner,

Berlin during 1869–70 apart from brief reflections on the Franco-Prussian war made on several occasions. Whether, like Sidgwick, he also enjoyed the theatre and the magnificence of the city soon to become the German imperial capital, is not recorded, nor whether he enjoyed its magnificent art gallery which Sidgwick deprecated.[19] Likewise, no youthful recollections of Nürnberg and Munich have been preserved though the pictures in his portrait collection of the leading participants in the Oberammergau Passion Play of 1871 suggest one additional destination in the summer of that year. A letter to Lujo Brentano records that on the Marshalls' subsequent south-east route in the summers spent in the Tirol, Munich was a regular stop for changing trains, and an opportunity for Mary, sometimes accompanied by her husband, to visit its modern, secessionist, art gallery.*

AN AMERICAN TOUR: JUNE TO SEPTEMBER 1875

Marshall's extensive American visit in the summer of 1875 is undoubtedly one of the highlights of his bachelor travels. Mary Paley recalled it was made financially possible by the death in 1874 of Uncle Charles, who left him £250 in his will. Despite the amusement it brought to his relatives, 'who laughed at him', Marshall decided to spend the whole of the legacy on the American journey, which lasted close to four months. Mary Paley recalled afterwards he used to say 'he never spent money so well. It was not so much what he learnt there as that he got to know what things he wanted to learn. He was able to see the coming supremacy of the U.S., to know its causes and the direction it would take.'[20] Why four months in America exhausted a £250 legacy, Marshall explained to the Gold and Silver Commission: 'I used to spend something like 15*l*. a month when travelling in the cheaper parts of Germany. When I went to America I calculated to spend, and I did spend, exactly four times that amount. No doubt I travelled over larger distances then, but I wanted to carry three times as much money in my pocket to pay my way at American hotels as at German country inns.'[21] This part of his economic education would likewise have been impossible but for Uncle Charles's generosity.

Much is preserved of the visit, not only in the form of copious notes on American industry and the American character, but also in the form of eleven letters to his mother designed to supplement the notes on the trip he was preparing. In addition, on his return to England, he gave several lectures on America, both at Cambridge and later at Bristol.[22]

Marshall sailed from Liverpool on the steam ship, *Spain*, a vessel of 5,000 tons, with a substantial number of immigrants on board. He estimated their number at about 500, more than half German and Swedes, and including a large number of children. The trip itself was uneventful. He was seasick for a couple of days, amused at the many, rather extravagant, meals provided, from some of which he abstained, and even saw an iceberg, a rather unusual event at so low a latitude as the captain explained. He also complained about the lack of interesting ladies to converse with, but there were plenty of men of character to make up for

---

1929, pp. 300–301. Marshall's musical interests may have been awakened well before the Dresden visit both at Clifton College and at St John's. On this, see below, Chapter 21, p. 774.

* Alfred Marshall to Brentano, 13 June 1905, in H.S. McReady, 'Alfred Marshall: Some Unpublished Letters', *Culture*, Vol. XV, September 1954, p. 308. The 'secession' were a group of modern Bavarian painters who in 1892 organised their own exhibitions in Munich away from their more traditional colleagues.

this. He therefore commenced his traveller's notes with some character sketches of fellow passengers, of which those on an Irish priest and missionary returning from South Africa have been preserved.[23]

The former was described as 'amiable, erudite, with considerable dialectical power, but not otherwise powerful'. Marshall discussed philosophy with him, from which he noted that the priest confused English philosophy with the Scottish school of Reid, Stewart and Hamilton. The fact that the priest had not read Hume was seen by Marshall as a sign that his reading had 'been constrained'. In discussions of the Anglo-Irish question, Marshall found him 'a curious compound of sagacity and openness with bigotry and narrowness'.[24]

His record of conversation with the Rev. William Miller, an American Protestant missionary returning home after 20 years in Natal, showed similar characteristics. 'Though in most respects apparently fair and open . . . he spoke in uncompromising terms about the necessity of enforcing from the natives instant obedience'. Marshall also noted his bias on the Colenso Affair, and on the ignorance and thoughtlessness of 'the Kaffirs' who 'just believe whatever the missionaries tell them'. Marshall added in parentheses to this observation, that 'he would probably have been more cautious in his admissions on this subject if he had heard the conversation shortly before to the effect that the united efforts of all the missionaries who have ever been to India have not succeeded in converting one single member of the Brahmin or thinking class, and scarcely anybody at all except the most ignorant and depraved, even these being in general entirely unaffected as regards morality'.[25] Marshall in 1875 therefore neither showed signs of his father's 'anti-popish' sentiments, nor shared an evangelical fervour on the importance of missionary labour.

The ship docked in New York on 6 June. Marshall was impressed by the ship's entry into the city as 'grander in everyway than that to London' but there was 'less shipping than on the Thames'. Disembarking on Sunday may be part explanation. He likewise admired the 'glorious green' banks of the Hudson, 'set off by the colour of the houses', an impression whose vividness Marshall accounted for by 'lack of colour during the voyage'.[26] Marshall stayed only four nights in New York, intending to spend more time there on his return journey. However, he recorded first impressions in considerable detail. He was struck by the Dutch appearance of New York, as later of Albany. In other ways, he saw in American architecture the wave of the future. It was both 'original and daring', a sign that 'ere long' it may well create 'the first genuine architecture' the world has seen since 'genuine Gothic was broken up by the erudite servility of the Renaissance'. Illuminated advertising across New York streets was also admired, 'the most effective form of advertising I have ever seen'.

The first class 5th Avenue hotel he stayed at, perhaps 'the most important in the world', was likewise a new experience and the only first class hotel he patronised during the rest of his American tour. Its detailed description started with the reception desk in a gigantic foyer, the peculiar system of accounts employed, the bar ('the American drink mixer is as professional an artist as the French cook'), billiard room, newspaper room, ticker-tape connection with Wall Street, to end up with the dining and breakfast rooms upstairs, the sleeping accommodation for 1,100 persons and a lift which 'goes up and down from 7 am to midnight without stopping'. The cost: $5 a day including meals, 'not dear', Marshall justified to his parents, when for dinner every night there was a 'choice of sixty or seventy dishes, many of them very recherché'. Furthermore, he commented it was cheap relative to the $3 he paid per day for his second class hotel in Albany. This had not been 'perfectly clean', and hence offered far worse value than the superb luxury purchased in the 5th Avenue hotel for an additional $2.*

Marshall twice attended the theatre in New York. On his second night there, he went to see 'Big Bonanza' at a nearby 5th Avenue Theatre, a play 'written by an American, for Americans, about Americans'. Although it had already run for 100 days, and in Marshall's view was well acted, he noted three specific characteristics of the plot as distinctly American: '(i) it represented the businessman as a sort of deity, and the scientist as a mere nincompoop; (ii) it patronised the scientist, he was good for something, he could help to dye carpets; (iii) the main joke in the play assumed the audience to understand that you need not have "Big Bonanza" shares in order to sell them; which few of a London audience would know.'[27]

Marshall's excursion to the Union Street Theatre the next night was less rewarding. He saw 'The Orphans', an American adaptation of a French drama which, in its direct use of language, left nothing to the imagination. In addition, Marshall complained that contrary to his experience of French comedians on the French stage, 'most of the actors spoke like schoolchildren repeating a lesson'. This possibly explains why no further theatre visits are recorded in his American notes. There is, however, some comedy in a character sketch of a 'civil, intelligent, gentlemanlike, business like, elderly' shop assistant encountered in a New York hat shop. His manner of serving, which involved trying on Marshall's own headwear for fit, was described by his customer as that 'of a perfect democrat, . . . a manner absolutely free from insolence. May the habit become general'. In a rare preserved trace of that sense of humour mixed with pedantry, Marshall added, 'if it does . . . space will have to be found in their advertisement for a line "our shopmen's heads warranted perfectly clean"'.[28]

On Wednesday, 9 June, Marshall sailed down the Hudson River to Albany, a trip which reminded him of the Rhine between Bingen and Bonn, but which he preferred to the German experience because of the scenery's 'more mountainous grandeur, very much more variety, and of course, greater breadth of water'. Albany marked the beginning of the real purpose of his trip, visiting factories, a task he energetically pursued on his own account for the next two and a half days. On Saturday, 12 June, he arrived in Springfield, where the next morning he attended a church service in the Congregational Church. Although the preacher on this occasion was 'lively but of no great ability', this was to be the first of many American church services he observed as part of his general plan to study the United States way of life during the visit.[29]

Marshall arrived at Boston the following Monday, a visit which lasted for a fortnight and thereby became the longest stay in any one place during his American trip. He stayed with the President of Harvard, C.W. Eliot, and celebrated with him the centenary of the British victory at Bunker's Hill. He was also Eliot's guest at dinner at the Saturday Club, and had many conversations on politics and economics with his host. Marshall liked

---

* Alfred Marshall to Rebecca Marshall, 12 June 1875, Marshall Archive, 1/290: the letter also notes that washing at the first class hotel cost $1.50 for twelve items and that after the sea voyage, Marshall's laundry bill amounted to $4 because of the many items of dirty washing he had accumulated, including no less than 11 collars.

Boston, the most English town in America he had encountered so far, though it still had plenty of that 'American go' which he later so publicly praised in his lectures in England and which explain his preference for migrating there rather than Canada if he had to leave England. He attended a Unitarian Church service both Sundays, the second Sunday adding a Baptist service for good measure. The first made him aware of the imperfection in the Anglican liturgy. It also extracted an expression of delight because the Unitarian marriage service omitted the women's 'promise to *obey* the man'.[30]

Social highlights of the Boston visit were the Saturday Club dinner at which he met Oliver Wendell Holmes, Dean Howells and Charles Norton, and a visit to Ralph Waldo Emerson, of which he left a copious record. Through a misunderstanding, Marshall missed the lunch to which Emerson had invited him, but his host nevertheless 'was kind, no touch of hauteur about him'. He was 'also very much like his portraits [of which Marshall's collection surprisingly contains no specimen] but his eyes light up his countenance', a feature in which Marshall resembled him. They spoke about English universities, especially Oxford, with which Emerson was more familiar, during which he reminisced about a lecture by Ruskin. When Emerson asked who was currently carrying on Carlyle's literary tradition in England, Marshall replied, 'literary work of the highest order has not been done by our younger men' because the appeal of science was much greater. When pressed by Emerson for examples, Marshall mentioned Swinburne, a person 'of great literary power, whose development has been one-sided', and Clifford. Emerson interjected that there could be nothing great about 'that horrid, corporeal, loathsome Swinburne', and gave a panegyric on Tennyson and Wordsworth, adding that Shelley was 'a great genius, but . . . not a poet', a statement which infuriated Marshall.

Conversation then moved to philosophical matters, inspired by Marshall's earlier reference to Clifford as a younger man of science of great promise.

> I explained why Clifford's views about immortality, etc. might be set aside, and went on to describe him as a representative of the work of the present generation about continuity. . . . Then we talked about Clifford's interests in the problem whether two straight lines can inclose space. This was also new to E[merson]. He was amused but a trifle scornful. This piqued me. So I fired off Helmholtz's case of beings living on the surface of a sphere. He listened hard and with effort. . . . I should have dropped the matter but I had just seen him described in an American guidebook as 'the greatest living transcendentalist" so I seized the opportunity to get on the subject of Kant: and said, [Helmholtz's case] . . . seems to me to bear on fundamental questions of theology and morality. E.g. Kant says the mind may know certain moral and theological propositions certainly and a priori, for it does so know certain physical propositions. I searched his book to find what instances he gave of this; when I found that all of these were deprived of value, I changed my attitude to some extent with regard to the other propositions.

Emerson's reply stunned Marshall: 'it seems to me that Kant's argument was a trumpery one, and it is fairly matched by a trumpery answer'. Emerson only saved his dwindling reputation with Marshall when they discussed Shakespeare. Following Marshall's strong praise of the sonnets, Emerson remarked, 'There is scarcely any psychological problem more interesting than the question how a man so far ahead of others came into existence.' Marshall recalled this remark as 'the most important thing he offered to me'. Sadly, this fruitful line of talk could not be continued. Marshall had a train to catch.

Marshall's final verdict on Emerson: 'a gentle but a keen spirit, to whom Nature has not granted the power of working through her problems, but to whom she has given the rare and choice faculty of asking questions of her . . . with exquisite care and with fervent but somewhat subdued emotions'. He added no wonder that 'many women find in him their high priest'. His last comment was reserved for Emerson's house: 'comfortable, but not large, or luxurious. Plain in style, probably old. Inside: few pictures, these good'. As a visit, it undoubtedly benefited Marshall's self-confidence considerably.[31]

Cultural visits intermingled with visits to factories. Apart from Chickering's piano factory, he visited the world's largest watch factory at Waltham and its largest organ factory (Mason and Hamblin) as well as six others. He could therefore honestly write to his mother that his 'time has not ceased to be fully occupied'.[32] From the pleasures of Boston, Marshall travelled to Norwich (Connecticut) with a stop in between at Providence to enable a visit to yet another factory. At Norwich he stayed with Dr Baker, as suggested by his niece Emily Nunn, one of Marshall's Cambridge acquaintances among Newnham students in 1874–75. Her sister, who was also staying with the Bakers at Norwich, took Marshall for an evening drive. He so greatly enjoyed this experience because of her marvellous combination of 'enterprising conversation', 'earnestness' and 'sweetness', that he successfully induced her to repeat the performance the next evening.

The stay at Norwich enabled a visit to D.A. Wells, a former protectionist turned free trader, who provided him with information later used to advantage in his Foreign Trade manuscript. It also produced a meeting with Judge Samuel Bowles, 'a student of Political Economy with his eyes open, [who] took him to see several factories'. Norwich likewise permitted a weekend at Yale, where he stayed with Professor W.G. Sumner, 'a man of enormous ability . . . and with a mastery at once over principle and fact'. Marshall later claimed Sumner was 'the most instructive companion' he had met in America, a tribute all the greater since his visit to Yale included a meeting with F.A. Walker, then busily writing his *The Wages Question*. However, this meeting was, economically speaking, much less productive. As Marshall later recalled for Walker's biographer,

I have a rather vivid memory of the day on which I called on him in Boston in 1875, I think. I believe I had brought a note of introduction to him from President Eliot, so he knew what I was interested in. He sat still for a minute, saying 'I wonder what I had better talk about.' He must have known that he might talk for a week without getting to the end of what I wanted to know. But he was wont to be fond of parables, and he seemed to decide that the best thing he could do was to make me see how different fundamentally were American economic problems from British: either country might learn from the other, but the learning had to be re-distilled before it was fit for use on the other side of the herring-pond. At last he said, 'I know what I'll do,' and he fetched a book of photographs of Indians, gave it to me, talked about some of them, and his personal relations with them, and filled my mind with them. I do not recollect the details of the conversation which followed, but in some way it led up to this: 'British economics has a chief corner stone in Ricardo's theory of rent; in a sense that is universal, but the particular developments of it which are of most importance in an old country don't count for much in a land where the nominal owners of a hundred million acres or more are the people whose photographs you have just seen'.[33]

A letter to his mother also recalls a long conversation with Mrs Sumner on the relative merits of American and English girls and that the coinciding 4th of July celebrations caused annoyance because of the crackers and fireworks in the streets.[34]

The next letter to his mother, dated 10 July 1875,[35] 'Niagara Falls', records not only his disappointment at seeing this much admired natural wonder – 'a great humbug, worse than the Alps' is Marshall's manner of summing it up – but also gives accounts of a visit to the Connecticut Legislature, excursions to two communist communities – that of the Shakers at New Lebanon and the next day to the nearby settlement of Oneida – as well as further factory visits, this time in Rochester. The letter also records an ear- and toothache, which required pain-killing treatment by way of chloroform pressed to the gums, a dental affliction which returned to plague him during the final stages of his trip and for which he was given major dental treatment in New York. Given his tendency to socialism, his impressions of these religious utopias, are worth quoting:

> On Wednesday I travelled to New Lebanon the chief settlement of the Shakers. I slept at the settlement & came on the next day to Oneida, near which is the most important communistic settlement outside of the body of the Shakers. I spent five or six hours at the Community & came on to Rochester on Friday. . . . Although I had read largely about them before, the contact with communists, having thought out theories of life widely different from those in common vogue was highly instructive. I send you a paper of the Shakers. I have many of their publications. They go against the Art of 'the world'. The Spiritual Kingdom is gradually evolving music for itself; the supply of Shaker tunes is very large, a new one in almost every number of their journals, & many others besides: & gradually doubtless they will evolve a Spiritual Architecture. This was said in answer to my question why they did not spend some of the energies on adorning their buildings: these approach nearly to cubes. Yet I must confess there is a sort of picturesqueness about them when taken together with the scenery.
>
> The brother who was told off to wait upon me, & with whom I spoke more than with anyone except Elder Evans (the leader of the whole movement) was a young Swede: an angelic character. A student at a Swedish University, he had been dissatisfied with the customary views of life, & becoming interested in some account of the Shakers, he visited America in order to see them, & became convinced that here alone in the world was the spirit of early Christianity worked out in life. . . . He is cheerful though always quiet, utterly devoid of self assertion, which is more than I can say for Elder Evans. Agriculture & horticulture are the occupations that the Shakers most affect; & if you saw only the cotton frock which he wears, the brown cotton trousers clay-stained towards the feet & the rough uncouth shoes below you would think he was an ordinary agricultural labourer. But in his face you would perceive the refinement of the true gentleman. There are few men with whom I would so readily change lots as with him: but I would rathest stay where I am.[36]

Marshall treasured the Shaker publications, collected pictures of their religious dances and later regaled visitors with this aspect of his American experience.[37]

A week later, a letter from Cleveland, Ohio, briefly recounts the chief events of Marshall's week in Canada. This had been greatly assisted by 'a Mr. McKinnon, a member of the Ontario ministry'. It mentioned visits to an Agricultural College and government model farm at Guelph, and visits to factories at Hamilton and Buffalo, before the return to the States and Cleveland. Marshall obtained much useful information on the prospects for immigrants in Canada, and after his week there was ready to make some broad generalisations about the Canadian national character and Canada's economic progress. The sluggishness of the last was attributed to natural factors, especially lack of coal and the cold climate. With respect to character, Marshall thought Canadians shared 'most of the virtues of their Republican neighbours' such as 'complete absence of aristocratic exclusiveness', a high degree of self-management and independence which, Marshall said 'on good authority', even extended to young women. The last appeared 'right and wholesome' to

Marshall, even though such a view would not be shared by the average Englishman, let alone the more severe kind. The one drawback in Canadian character Marshall perceived was that they had less 'go' relative to Americans; this explains why he preferred the United States as a potential migrant destination, should the need arise, a preference previously noted in his description of the drive and bustle of America, visible even in Boston.[38]

A letter from St Louis in late August fails to mention his experiences in Chicago and omits details for the greater part of his trip to the West Coast and back. It dealt briefly with Virginia City (Nevada) where the virtual absence of 'virtuous women' was said to augur badly for the next generation of Nevadians; with San Francisco, where fortunes can be made but where 'women's rights' are not tolerated; while the Missouri, seemingly to Marshall's surprise, really is 'full of swamps, negroes, Irishmen, agues, wild luxuriant flowers and crops of [Indian] corn'. Later he recalled he had attended 'a "granger" (i.e. farmer-in-revolt) meeting in San Francisco with "the enemy" . . . the railways'. Then via Indianapolis, Cincinnati, Colombus, Pittsburgh and Philadelphia back to New York.[39] Columbus was recalled for its penitentiary and Cincinnati for the presence of 'too many', 'lower class Germans'. Pittsburgh is the 'sootiest town on this planet'.[40] Philadelphia involved discussions with protectionists. Marshall left the following account of his conversation with the American protectionist economist, H.C. Carey:

> Comfortable House. Large Drawing room. Good pictures. Hale & hearty, age 83. In dressing gown. At previous (short) interview he had burst out with, 'England always goes in for whatever suits her own interest.' I said 'I should say at once that I am an Englishman & that I find a good motive for England's conduct when you can see nothing but what is bad' voice rather derb. He was somewhat staggered: but in the second interview avoided dropping into the original line. Had been a free-trader when young. Struck by fact people moved west: attributed it to free trade which caused exportation of manure. Struck again by remnants of houses, or orchards, 'a peach tree here, an apple tree there on barren hills'. This set him to criticising Malthus. With great trouble I nailed him to the question. 'Do you reject the law of diminishing returns in an old country, the rate of agricultural progress, & the rate of emigration being given.' He could not give a direct yes: but he jumped off – why should people stay where they were born. Cairnes is diffuse & says nothing new except that things had a 'normal' value, McLeod talks nonsense. 'Oh! but English economists do not indorse McLeod.' 'Well but Chevalier does.' 'Chevalier is not trustworthy on such points." "Chevalier is a humbug: dishonest: a free-trader for gain in opposition to his convictions. McCulloch is even worse. Jevons too has written a book full of mathematical nonsense. He says value depends on utility. The jackass does not know that the utility is great only when the value is small. When Faraday first discovered how to produce electricity his methods were very expensive. There was very little of it, & therefore it did very little good: but its value was high.' 'Oh! but he does not mean total utility: he means utility per unit.' 'I don't know what he means' & he burst away to say something else. I think it was that no one knew anything who could not understand what was meant by value. 'Value depends on cost of *re*production.' I tried to nail him about this but could not succeed. I nailed him on the question why do you urge 'protection for Ireland, & yet maintain that Alabama has no right to erect custom houses round herself'. He winced: but said, 'Oh I do not *say* that Ireland ought to have protection.' He spouted at me his old views at great length. The interview lasted 2 ¾ hours: out of which he was talking 2 2/3 hours. He said his father had left Ireland because he found he would spend so much time in prison if he did not: I understood him to say that his father was a protectionist but I do not see how that is consistent with the fact that he himself was at first a free trader.[41]

These activities left Marshall no time to write. Moreover, recurrence of the toothache and advice from a Philadelphia dentist sped him to New York. His last American letter to his mother, a week before his embarkation on the *Erin* back to England, concentrated on his final confrontation with American 'industrial enterprise', that involved 'with decayed teeth'. Like so many of the others he encountered in America, it also passed with flying colours as to quality of work and efficiency of execution.[42] His American trip was over.

The fruits from Marshall's investment of Uncle Charles's legacy were substantial. The detailed letters he sent to his mother and the travel notes which accompanied them were only the first instalment. The nature and form of his traveller's notes may have been inspired by Arthur Young's travels, a firm favourite with Marshall.[43] Young's travels interspersed their economic detail, drawn more from agriculture than manufacturing, with accounts of visits to the famous in which their residential environment, pictures and all, were described in detail. Marshall's trip yielded longer-term fruits as well. Apart from influencing subsequent work on industrial development and on the threat of American competition to British industry, the more direct impact on his thinking from the American trip can be seen in a lecture he gave in Cambridge not long after his return, on 17 November 1875.[44] Appropriately titled, 'Some Features of American Industry', it demonstrates the types of conclusion Marshall was willing to draw from his industrial field work.

Befitting his audience, Marshall's lecture had as its concluding theme the ethological issue of the effect on human character from economic conditions, particularly those relating to the daily activities of mankind. Marshall noted the strong and mutual interdependence between ethical development and economic substratum, an interdependence he argued 'to be far closer than it is usually thought to be'.[45] Marshall identified two factors promoting such ethical development, both of which he explicitly associated with Hegel's notions of objective and subjective freedom from *The Philosophy of History*. The first concerns 'the peaceful moulding of character into harmony with the conditions by which it is surrounded . . . [thereby bringing it] in union with the actions, the sympathies and the interests of the society amidst which he spends his life'. Dual social outcomes are possible from this process: 'insipidity and . . . meanness' or 'sympathetic fancy, graceful enthusiasm, beautiful ideals'. The second factor, identified with Hegel's 'subjective freedom', links the individual 'education of a firm will' with 'the overcoming of difficulties', inherent in the individualistic and independent spirit of the American colonist or the spirit of that 'go' which Marshall so admired in the Americans as contrasted with their northern Canadian neighbours. Potential dual consequences of this growth include 'licentiousness and depravity' on the one hand, but 'in its higher form will develop a mighty system of law . . . the free arbitrariment of man's will be unshackled by outward restraints. Such a society will be the empire of energy, of strong but subdued enthusiasm, of grand ideals.'[46] Which factor in ethical progress predominates in any particular society, depends on 'the daily business of life', a proposition which, when recalled in the context of the opening sentence of his *Principles of Economics* – 'Political Economy, or Economics, is a study of man's actions in the ordinary business of life' – stresses the ethological objectives of Marshall's life work.[47] The 1875 trip to America elicited one of the clearest statements of the association of ethics and economics Marshall was ever to make in his lifetime, embodying a position he never consciously abandoned.

Other aspects of this lecture's conclusions stress the importance of previously mentioned philosophical foundations for Marshall's thought. One example is its recurring identification of America 'as the land of the future, where, in the ages that lie before us, the Burden of the world's history shall reveal itself'.[48] Equally prominent is the stress on the progressive elements inherent in westward movement, the key to Hegel's philosophical conception of the historical progress of civilisation ever westwards, from China to India, to Persia, to the Mediterranean countries (there also moving west from Israel and Phoenicia to Greece and then Rome), to Western Europe and ultimately across the Atlantic.[49] The lecture also dwells on the inhibiting factor of custom, in acting as a brake on the development of 'stationary societies', where Marshall identified its degenerating properties *à la* Maine with 'sanitary, economical, military and other rules having . . . continued in force after the purpose for which they were required, ceased to exist.'[50] Last, but not least, the final sentence of the lecture explicitly tied Marshall's 'ethical creed' to the 'Doctrine of Evolution' rather than to a more statical, utilitarian calculus. This was an essential emphasis for a doctrine of human progress which required the improvement in human nature as well as change in human conditions, hence also reiterating the Spencerian and Darwinian contents of Marshall's ethical beliefs.[51]

A further philosophical truth, the need for a sceptical attitude before accepting travellers' accounts as factually sound, was illustrated by Marshall's remarks on the views of relative living standards of English and American workers as presented by American defenders of protectionist trade policies.[52] Given the ethical concerns of his audience, Marshall concentrated much of his lecture on the mobility of Americans with respect to occupation and residence as a crucial feature in its moral as well as industrial development. Independence and self-assurance, the characteristic traits of the immigrant, are major explanations for this mobility; adaptability and inventiveness are some of its major outcomes, together with the democratic and non-servile spirit so visible in the American hat salesman Marshall described in his travel notes. There are, however, also less praiseworthy effects on the moral character. Mobility emphasised the value of the 'portability of money' since if a man 'makes money but loses his reputation, he can pack up his money and make it help him to earn a new reputation' (p. 364). Likewise, mobility enhanced competitiveness in economic matters rather than a more altruistic spirit of cooperation (pp. 367–9) though 'associations of citizens to meet particular emergencies' can be improved with that sense of 'local responsibility' characteristic of the practices of New England local government (pp. 364, 369). Emotional character, Marshall ventured to generalise, was signalled by the absence in outward appearance of a 'dull and insipid life' on American faces, in sharp contrast with that 'gross deadly coarseness' so visible among the European lower classes. This was the feature of American society in Marshall's view which gave it 'a strong claim to be the first country in the world' (p. 369). Marshall stoutly defended what he saw as the well-developed affectionate nature of American men and women, against frequently heard contrary opinions from observers including De Tocqueville. Independence and innovativeness in American religious movements, Marshall illustrated from the experiences with the Shaker and Oneida perfectionist communities he had visited (pp. 369–72). The high degree of economic and industrial equality then prevailing in the United States (pp. 372–3) are the last remarks before his concluding generalisations cited at the end of the previous paragraph.

Much of the factual content of the Cambridge lecture was used in the lecture on the economic condition of America which Marshall gave at Bristol in January 1878.[53] It commenced with the observation that England's future could be studied from America's present, provided that American conditions not prevalent in England were duly abstracted from. Marshall's examples were the absence in England of vast tracts of vacant territory and of 'masses of ignorant negroes and immigrants . . . entrusted with full powers of citizenship'. As reported in the press, the economic emphasis in Marshall's Bristol lecture replaced the ethical slant of its Cambridge counterpart thereby indicating Marshall's skills in adapting treatment of his topic to the needs of his audience. Within this economic content, Marshall reviewed American transport developments from rail and canal construction, potential shifts in industrial location from the North East, demographic changes, industrial training and the limited role in America for formal apprenticeships as compared to England, labour mobility, labour productivity and management practices, capital inflow, consequences of the 1873 financial crisis, illustrating the talk with 'lime light views', charts and maps.

Marshall made only spasmodic use of his American experiences in his later writings in a direct way. *Economics of Industry*, published within four years of his American visit, has only one American illustration which can be said to have been immediately inspired by the experience it provided. This is the reference to the success of American communities as a form of religious cooperation; their 'religious enthusiasm' generating the required 'spirit of brotherhood and mutual trust'. The other few references to American experience could just as easily have been derived from published sources.[54] The chapter on land in the *Principles* has a reference to his trip down 'the Missouri Valley to St Louis some years ago' and records Marshall's observation about the distance of farmers' housing away from the fertile 'river bluffs'. This only direct reference to his American trip in the pages of the *Principles* came by way of illustration that the rather poor New England soil, settled early in American development, preceded settlement of the rich river plains, as Carey had maintained against Ricardo.[55] A lecture in 1890 recalled 'Carey's splendid anger, as he exclaimed that foreign commerce had made even the railways of America run from east to west, rather than from north to south', a recollection not nearly so strikingly recalled in his notes. It also described the American visit as one 'to study American protection on the spot', the impact of which was a recurring one in Marshall's work on the subject.[56]

A reference to the lavish nature of American advertising in *Industry and Trade*[57] recalls, but appears to have owed nothing to, Marshall's New York experience nearly half a century before. Elsewhere in that study, the trip to America is directly referred to. It was argued (p. 783 and n.) that this trip alerted him to the exaggerated claims of protectionists on the effects of their policy; the importance of railroads for American economic development (p. 798 n.) and for the provision of relative luxuries like butter and canned fruit to the highly specialised cattle ranches along the Union Pacific railway (p. 805 n.).

Most benefits from the American visit were indirect. Apart from the value of comparative analysis they signalled for Marshall's subsequent work, especially in *Industry and Trade*, they left their mark on important aspects of Marshall's later thought. The stress on independence and self-assurance visible in American workers, the alertness and intelligence written on their faces as heralds of America's great industrial future, almost certainly reinforced the strong beliefs about individualism in enterprise which coloured his hostile perception of state enterprise efficiency. The trip likewise fostered his enduring belief in the benefits of free trade even when countries were in economic decline and protection seemed an easy solution. His *Memorandum on Fiscal Policy of International Trade* referred to the benefits of his American trip in that context and showed how travel in both the United States and Germany had made him aware of the growing economic difficulties England would face from declining competitiveness.[58] No wonder he later boasted how well he had spent this legacy from Uncle Charles.

A WINTER IN SICILY (1881–82)

During April or early May 1879, a London specialist diagnosed Marshall as having stones in the kidney, for the cure of which he prescribed a protracted period of rest. Poor health, together with the stress of his administrative chores as Principal of Bristol University College induced his resignation from that post in July 1881, a resignation made possible when a suitable replacement became available. The purpose of the resignation was therefore threefold. It enabled Marshall to abandon the administrative work of Principal for which he felt himself no longer capable for health reasons; it allowed the protracted rest period his doctors had prescribed for him, thereby also giving him the time to write up his economic theory in a more comprehensive form now that the primer and the curves, imperfect though they were, were out of the way and published. A two-year holiday was planned initially. This was to be spent in the country within travel distance from London; a location designed to assist his wife Mary to gain access to its university.[59] When precisely the Marshalls decided to winter in Sicily is not clear, but this project appears to have firmed in the succeeding months and came to fruition by October 1881.

Mary Paley later recalled that the choice had been made on climate, the quality of the water, and cost.[60] In some respects, it was a brave and adventurous choice, because 'up to early Edwardian times, the ordinary British or American tourist used not to venture south of Naples. Beyond this beautiful but proverbially malodorous city, the country was held to be unsafe. Between uncomfortable hotels and rapacious shopkeepers in the towns, with brigands and malaria in the country, the game was not thought to be worth the candle'.[61] However, when he was an undergraduate, Marshall's college journal, *The Eagle*, included an article on a fortnight in Sicily. This praised the comparative civilisation of Palermo, the mildness of its climate in winter, its interesting architecture and wonderful scenery, though it confirmed the discomforts to be endured in Sicilian country inns. It also suggested that the dangers from brigandage were grossly overstated and in short, highly recommended the Sicilian experience. Similar advice may have come from Henry Sidgwick, whose brother William had visited Sicily with pleasure some years before. For a Goethe lover, as Marshall purported to be, there was the additional attraction of Sicily from the praise Goethe had bestowed on the island on the basis of his Italian travels in 1786–88.[*] No matter what

---

[*] 'A Fortnight in Italy', *The Eagle*, Vol. 3, 1863, pp. 133–41, esp. pp. 140–41 on Palermo; Guercio (*Sicily, The Garden of the Mediterranean*, p. 68) indicates that in the six years ending 1899, no less than 1,092 highway robberies were reported in the province of Palermo alone, a statistic hardly designed to comfort the traveller frightened of brigands. Goethe, who visited Palermo in April 1787 and spent altogether two months in Sicily, on

determined the final decision to go to Sicily, by early October they had travelled from England to Marseilles, where they caught the steamer to Palermo, the capital city of Sicily. They arrived on 9 October, intending to stay there until March or April 1882, as Marshall informed Foxwell in one of the few letters from Sicily which appears to have survived. They would then return to England via Naples, Rome, Florence and Venice and a summer in the Bavarian Alps.[62]

Irrespective of how and when they arrived at their choice, the Marshalls did not regret having made it, and the five months they stayed in Palermo undoubtedly constituted a high point in their married life.[63] This is already obvious from Marshall's initial enthusiastic reaction in his letter to Foxwell on the delights of Palermo. Palermo, he wrote,

> is a charming place, far more lovely than we had thought. Until yesterday, it had not rained here for 8 months – this is very unusual, they generally have some rain here in late spring. So everything is very parched up: They say the country is generally at its best about December. But even then we shan't get as much as we had hoped from the gardens and the foliage of the surrounding country. For the gardens are almost all inclosed in mud walls ten feet tall; and the neighbouring country consists chiefly of rocky mountains which at present at least look as though no green things ever lived on them, unless in a few scattered patches. But the beauty of the mountains is almost beyond imagination by the eye that hath not seen. For their forms are most beautiful, and most various, full of the play of light and shade, of near distance, and middle distance, and far distance, and rich with an endless range of full deep colours: white, red and orange are the predominant colours but deep blues often come out in the shadows, and in spite of the drought there is even now sometimes a faint suspicion of green.
>
> But the town is even more wonderful than the mountains: though it is true that picturesqueness of the streets is often much in debt to a peep at a mountain through the long vistas of balconies on either side of the street. Of course we have not explored nearly all the town yet: but we have done a good deal by dint of taking an air cushion to the nearest tram, sitting there till it got to the end of its journey, and still sitting till it got back again to some other line of trams, then getting on that and sitting it out in like manner. And I think we have already seen twenty times as many picturesque bits as I have seen in any other town. It is not only that the colour is rich: but it is generally in excellent taste. At Marseilles there was a good deal of colour: but for the greater part it was simply bothersome. But here the Saracenic genius pervades everything, and the combinations are generally exquisite. In two or three shop windows in the chief city street of the town we saw a dozen blankets for beds – something like the 'Austrian' blankets; but each of them more beautiful than any blanket we had ever seen.[64]

These very favourable first impressions are Marshall's only account of their stay at Palermo. They foreshadowed a happy six months they planned to be in the town. This pleasure was made all the greater by the fact that it would be Mary's first real holiday since finishing her Tripos examination seven years previously, a time during which she intended to catch up with her reading. For that purpose, and for Marshall's own work and relaxation, they had arranged for 7 cwt (more than 350 kilograms) of books to be sent to them by sea. It was therefore not all holiday. Marshall informed Foxwell that 'meanwhile, [he] was going on with "Economic Theory" – including some curves, but making them as little prominent as possible'.[65] In fact, the birth of the *Principles* can be said to have taken place in the city of

---

the basis of his Palermo visit could pen the following praise of the island: 'To have seen Italy without having seen Sicily is not to have seen Italy at all, for Sicily is the clue to everything.' Goethe, *Italian Journey*, London: Penguin Books, 1970, p. 246.

Palermo, because 'Book III on Demand was largely thought out and written on the roof of Palermo, Nov. 1881–February 1882'.[66]

Greater detail of their enjoyable, productive and eventful five months in Sicily were recorded by Mary Paley in the section of her reminiscences devoted to what Keynes called the 'period of most unbroken happiness and perfectment of her life'.[67] The opening sentence of her account provides the basis for Keynes's inference. It also shows the mode of living the Marshalls adopted for the next five months.

> We were five months at Palermo, on a roof, and whenever I want something pleasant to think about I try to imagine myself on it. It was the roof of a small Italian hotel, the 'Olivia', flat of course and paved with coloured tiles, and upon it during the day Alfred occupied an American chair over which the cover of the travelling bath was rigged up as an awning, and there he wrote the early chapters of his *Principles*. One day he came down from the roof to tell me how he had just discovered the notion of 'elasticity demand'.
>
> From the roof we had a view of the *conca d'oro*, the golden shell of orange and lemon groves stretching a few miles inland, and of the mountains which met the sea on either side and formed a semi-circle of varied shapes. One was so remarkable that it took the fancy of the old Byzantines. They treated it as a typical mountain and in various parts of Italy it can be seen reproduced in mosaics. Perhaps the reason was that its shape fitted it to be the resting place of the ark. During many of the clear autumn days Etna, 120 miles away, was seen peeping over a saddle of the nearer mountains, its snowy peak turning pink at sunset; and out at sea were the Lipari Islands some 70 miles off pale and clear floating on the horizon, and the sea was generally so calm that it reflected cloud shapes on its green and blue and purple surface. The mountains depended for their beauty on shape and colour for they were entirely without trees. They were formerly covered with woods which used to bind the soil and prevent it being carried away by the violent torrents which rush down the mountain sides during the rainy season. This sacrifice of its future well-being to the short-sighted gain of a few individuals is one of the chief reasons that Sicily, which was once the granary of Rome, is now so poor. When we arrived in October there had been about eight months with hardly any rain, and the colour of the mountains was chiefly grey and yellow, but early in November came the first rains of winter and gradually the grey changed to green.[68]

Other things could be seen from the roof. The little courtyards of the neighbouring houses, used for cultivating vines, flowers and citrus fruit; the balconies paved with coloured tiles and over the pre-Christmas period inhabited by fattening turkeys; and busy traffic of carts in the streets below, 'gailey carved' and with 'scenes from history' and 'the lives of the saints' painted on the side, a spectacle of light and colour enhanced and glorified by the brilliant blue of the sky and the bright sunshine.

> Like the golden background of the old mosaics it [the sky] harmonises and makes beautiful bits of colour which under our grey sky would look mean and tawdry. In Sicily the yellow carts and the red handkerchief knotted on the people's heads and pink plastered houses and the bright coloured tiles and even the coloured garments and rags hanging out across the streets to dry seemed all to add to the effect; and such brilliant light brings of course deep shadows, not grey but rich purple and blue, and the buildings are generally arranged so as to cast shadows.[69]

This sample from Mary Paley's 'account of their life in Palermo reveals the sensitiveness and accuracy of [Mary Paley's] visual impressions'[70] conveyed in her water colours. This was a hobby she had begun to pursue assiduously during their Sicilian winter and its results illustrate the many summers the Marshalls spent in peaceful seclusion in the Alps, the British countryside, or elsewhere in their travels. But it was not only colour that was observed, social and economic phenomena were similarly examined; less frequently from the roof and more generally from excursions in the town and its surrounds. Some examples can be given, including those preserved in Marshall's economic writings.

Take first the observation that no 'Sicilian walks if he can help it'. This leads the observer to the conclusion that 'carriages of a sort were cheaper in Palermo than in any other town', as confirmed by the prices for town rides charged in the various Italian cities they visited during the spring of 1881. Sixty centimes was the price in Palermo, 70 in Naples, 80 in Rome and a round one lira in touristic Florence. However, an example of the caution required when using the measuring rod of money: 70 centimes in Naples is really cheaper than 60 in Palermo, 'for the distances and hills [in Naples] are great and the horses must be well fed for the work, whilst in Palermo the roads were flat and half-fed animals could manage.'[71]   On a more social slant, the foundation student of Newnham also commented on the 'strong Saracenic feeling about women' in Sicily. This meant few women ventured to walk in the streets, while 'an English lady, especially if she had pink cheeks, got more attention than was agreeable' and middle-aged, but unmarried, Sicilian maid servants thought it improper to go shopping in the markets.[72] The English lady with pink cheeks, nevertheless found the Palermo markets her favourite resort,

> for there one got all the quaintness of the place intensified, the colour and the noise. I always went there for fruit and as the price was ticketed one could not be much cheated. Grapes and pears were very good and cheap, but oranges and figs were disappointing; probably the best oranges were exported; the figs had sticks run through them and were formed into large mats, and some of the shops were entirely lined with such mats, which were very dirty, as were the raisons. In fact everything that could be dirty was so. If it were not for the absence of smoke and for the habit of using tiles instead of wood for flooring the houses would have been very dirty, and one seldom ventured to sit on chairs in the churches.[73]

More economic observations on Palermo life focused on its 'remarkable localisation of industry'. This concentrated glove shops, bootshops, watchmakers and booksellers in particular districts and specific industries like chairmaking and brass manufactures into particular streets.   A continuing legacy from the medieval guilds was how this was explained to them, perhaps by Professor Solinas, with whom they became acquainted in Palermo[74] and whose speech became so distorted during a sirocco. Forty years later, the author of *Money, Credit and Commerce* recalled such medieval influences on Palermo's industrial life on the basis of evidence he had given to the Gold and Silver Commission in 1888. Its employment aspects served his *Principles of Economics* as an illustration in all eight editions from 1890 to 1920:

> I spent a winter some years ago at Palermo; the medieval traditions of industry go on there; and everything that one reads about with regard to the clientèle of the well-to-do houses among the working-men in the Middle Ages one finds in Palermo now. If you had tried to collect statistics of want of employment you would probably have found next to none. Scarcely anybody was thrown out of regular employment because scarcely anybody ever was in it; there were none of those interruptions of employment which arise from modern forms of industry, and about which sensational articles are written in the newspapers. But I doubt whether the average employment of the handicraftsman in Palermo is more than half as great as in the East End of London in depressed times; and the average annual earnings are probably not a quarter as high. I know that there are certain cases in which hirings were made for the year and in which the employer was practically bound to give some sort of sustenance to the employé for the year, but I believe that in those

parts of the Middle Ages in which that system prevailed, the employé in return often gave up so much of his freedom that it might be questioned whether he was completely a free man. I have been struck by the objections which were brought forward at a recent meeting to discuss the existing distress, objections raised to the sufficiency of the official returns of unemployment. It was said that when people worked at their own homes, you could not prove that they were thrown out of employment because the irregularity of their employment was the rule and not the exception. If they had no work to-day they had no reason for supposing that they would tomorrow. Now those people were in the same conditions as the majority of people in the medieval times – they took a job when it came to them. They consequently never were 'out of employment'; there was nothing to get into the newspapers as it were.75

Mrs Marshall extended these economic observations to the capital scarcity of Palermo and its implications for costs and quality of work; milk prices and their consequences for the rent of land; and reflections implying the best things, such as the bread and water they enjoyed in Sicily, need not be of very high value.[76]

Given that the five months in Palermo aided Marshall's recuperation from the illness which had inspired it, later ascribed by Mary Paley to Palermo's 'absolute quiet' and 'brilliant sunshine', and completed in the following two years,[77] the Marshalls definitely received value for money from their stay in Sicily. Mary Paley also recalled later that expenses for this year abroad amounted to almost exactly £300, half of which they covered with the rent they were receiving for their Bristol house. But at that time, as she likewise noted, a few lire could buy a week's accommodation for two, breakfast included, in an old palace on the Giudecca in Venice, and meals cost one lira per head at the *trattorie* where, as in Palermo, they had most of their meals.[78]

Their stay in Palermo did generate some problems. The short sunsets with their sudden change in temperature had its dangers. They brought the chance of catching a 'chill combined with malarious vapours . . . apt to lead to fever'. Mary Paley caught such malarious fever during the latter part of their stay in Palermo, but she was capably and lovingly nursed back to health by her husband.[79] At least part of Sicily's bad reputation with the English traveller was therefore deserved. The presence of brigands imposed a further constraint on activities,

It was indeed possible to go to Monreale three miles off, for armed police were stationed all the way within shouting distance, but in every other direction there was a chance that one might be briganded and a piece of ear forwarded to friends with a message that more would follow unless a large ransom were paid. Whilst we were at Palermo Jane Harrison, who came there to study some metopes in the Museum, was staying at our hotel and she and I went for a lovely walk of about six miles round the base of Pellegrino. No harm happened to us, but on reaching home we found the whole hotel alarmed and we were soundly scolded for such foolhardy conduct.

After that I never walked out into the country but there was plenty to do in the town itself. The place I cared for most and in which I spent many hours, trying to make a picture, was the Cappella Palatina. It is small and dimly lighted by slit-like windows so that on entering from the sunlight hardly anything could be seen but a mass of dim golden shadows. Gradually, however, the wonderful beauty of outline and detail emerged. The outlines are Norman, and Saracenic workmen filled the rich colour and oriental devices. Most beautiful of all was the gold apse, out of which loomed the great Christ's head.[80]

All good things, however, come to an end. By the end of February a slow home journey was commenced. A record of this is preserved in the watercolours Mary Paley made during the spring of 1882, 'four in Capri, one in Rome, twelve in Venice and several in Bavaria and on the Rhine'.[81] More prosaically, Alfred Marshall recorded the details of the journey in terms of the progress he made on his *Principles*. This linked their stay on Capri in the second half of March to a reorganisation of Book III, and the stay in Venice around 20 April with a re-reading of Cournot. The artistic distractions of Rome and Florence (late March and early April) perhaps prevented progress on the *Principles* being recorded there, but little can be inferred from what they saw. Exceptions are a visit to the Sistine Chapel, given Keynes's recollection of the Michelangelo figures from its ceiling in the Marshalls' living-room at Balliol Croft[82] and Mary Paley's recollections of exploring Pompei at length in bath chairs and Venice by gondola because walking had to be avoided with Alfred's illness.[83]   Then on to Bavaria (Waidbruch from 19 May to 1 June, Achensee and Walchensee from 4 June until 3 August) followed by a leisurely trip up the Rhine which eventually took them to Bournemouth by 23 August for a visit to Mary's parents, and a further month's holiday.[84]

STAFFORDSHIRE POTTERY, BLACKPOOL DANCING, MIDLAND FACTORIES AND MINING IN YORKSHIRE

Recollections of the many Marshall English summer holidays are preserved in notes made by Mary Paley of 'industrial tours' of the 1880s and, less frequently, in correspondence with friends. The former cover visits to Worcester and Wolverhampton (perhaps made in conjunction with the holidays they spent in Pembrokeshire in 1883); an 1885 trip of the north of England and one in 1888 in the north-east, the last two in conjunction with holidays described in earlier summaries as in the Lake District and Yorkshire respectively. These notes[85] confirm the feature of their summers which was stressed at the beginning of this chapter: Marshall's vacations were 'sharply divided with a period of hard thought and writing among the mountains or by the sea and partly in visits to town and factories for getting to know the workers and their work'.[86]

An undated fragment, attributable to 1883 on the argument of the preceding paragraph, gave a detailed account of economic aspects of the pottery industry. This included comments on reasons for the localisation of the trade, the demand for various types of pottery, price, size of the firm, technology and labour conditions including the living conditions for employees. The main locational factor was the proximity of a crucial raw material, the presence of a special type of marl with the coal which was used in the vessels (saggars) which enclosed fine pottery in the kiln, thereby reducing risk of spoiling during the firing. The availability of suitable labour supply was a further reason. Demand for output for the works tended to be fickle, since much of it was of the luxury type, particularly geared to the American export market. The last was a specialist product, high value market, but despite a 65 per cent tariff, British porcelain was very competitive. Risk and labour costs were the major factors influencing price, the first not only from the effect of change in fashion, which tended to be sudden and final, but also from production risks during firing when expensively decorated items could break or be otherwise spoilt. Hence the importance of saggars to the industry.

Factories tended to be relatively large: Mintons employed 1,700 persons, Brown Westeads over 1,000, with economies of scale and machinery the main explanation. Another reason for this large scale was given in the *Principles*: 'the small manufacturer cannot afford even to make experiments with new patterns and designs except in a very tentative way. His chance is better with regard to an improvement in making things for which there is already a good market'.[87] A substantial proportion of women were employed, largely in unskilled, mechanical tasks and their 'apprenticed work' was confined to 'low [grade] painting and transferring'. Women also did most of the unsanitary work, such as 'scrubbing of the biscuit pottery' with its risk of respiratory illness from inhaling the ensuing dust, while dipping into glaze containing lead was an equally hazardous activity reserved for this part of the workforce. However, married women tended to return to their former place of employment, perhaps because 'on the whole, except for unhealthy dust and some heat, the occupation seemed singularly pleasant and healthy. Brown Westeads factory the pleasantest I have ever seen, surrounded by trees and rhododendrons. One maker of sanitary ware [even] had flowers hanging in windows by his workshop'. In addition, the workers' housing which the Marshalls observed was of good quality in their opinion.

The 1883 trip concluded with a visit to Wolverhampton and the Black Country, to inspect the local tool-making industry, which made a wide variety of instruments largely for export. Despite the good wages that applied to nearly all the work in this industry, the Marshalls heard considerable complaint about the incidence of drunkenness in the district but relatively little about employer problems with Trade Unions.

An account of travels in August and September 1885 indicates the scope of these trips and the hectic pace the Marshalls set themselves during such tours of inspection. The summary notes of their travels in Cumbria during August, in the vicinity of the Lake District, both indicate the territory traversed and the nature of the observations made:

August: *Coniston*: copper mines. *Kirby*: slate quarries. *Barrow*: rapid growth. Saw large steel works and beautiful factory girl. Is factory life or domestic service best (i) for the girl (ii) for the race? Wonderful floating dry dock. Saw varieties of ore. Bessemer process. Hotel and girl with charming manners. *Milton*: Iron mines. Worked in shifts 8 hours. Nice dressing room with hot and cold water heated by waste steam. Nicely built little town. Healthy industrial conditions. *Whitehaven*: Very black and disagreeable. Coal mines close to sea. Women employed at mouth of mine to screen and pick coal. Very dirty and disagreeable work. The women looked ferocious. August 15. Lancaster. Charming, rather conservative looking old town but good deal of manufacture chiefly furniture. Beautiful park with wonderful air and view. Visited Gillows. Machines for cutting square furniture. Advantages of large production make it worthwhile to have excellent design. No women employed except for sewing upholstery. The most artistic woodcarvers are Irishmen. Deaf and dumb wood carvers. August 25–27. Preston. Fine enterprising town. Most beautiful hotel we have seen. Aug. 26. Visited Horrocks spinning and weaving mills. Went in trams and walked in working people's quarter. Children dirty. Excellent houses and furniture nearly universal. Favourite ornaments: large china dogs. Quiet and respectable appearances of factory women. August 27. Visited spinning and weaving mills. Were taken over works by head manager. He preferred women to men for all work except overlooking engineers. Said they were easier to manage and cleverer with fingers. Said that present strike in cotton trade might lead to employing women to mind self acting mules. Present objection to their doing so is the amount of exercise required equal to walking 20 or 30 miles. Probably machine can be modified. He said it was common for mothers of young children to work. Said the women grew very fond of the work. Not uncommon for a family to make £4 a week. Noticed high ratio of women to men in Preston especially when over 15 years. Many Irish . . .

A five-day break in Blackpool followed, in which they observed the dancing on the pier, and on the Sunday went to a sacred concert conducted by a Salvation Army brass band. 'Much collecting of money to support the work of providing God as well as the devil with this type of entertainment took place during it, and loud hallelujahs at the news of gift of sovereign [£1].' Among the great crowd of factory workers who attended, they saw no signs of drunkenness or even drink, and they were struck by the great earnestness and sincerity of the audience and the fineness of the faces. They dined for 3d.on potato pie at the coffee palace, where the waiters, recalling their American counterparts, behaved 'on terms of equality'. Although the Marshalls lamented the fact that Blackpool was not cheaper, they praised its attractions of 'relatively open sea and tolerable sand', the very popular pier, walking and dancing, the donkey rides, steamboat excursions and the good music to be heard at the Winter Garden. However, the natural attractions of Blackpool left much to be desired and were very inferior to those of nearby Morecambe. To prepare for the continuation of factory visits in Keighley and Sheffield, during the second half of September they rested for over a fortnight at Aysgarth (1–16 September).

After this deserved fortnight's rest, factory inspections were resumed at an equally hectic pace. Keighley, 'an ideal factory town', was taken in on 16 September with a visit to a spinning-machine works. This inspired an observation on the effects of patents on machine costs – 'before patent expired a machine costing £5 to make sold for £800 and worthwhile to buy it because it enabled highly skilled and laborious work to be replaced by Irish labour at 18/–'. However, this effect was not general. The factory owner told them 'that the tendency of machinery had been to raise rather than lower the average intelligence of the workmen – that he could do much better if he could [hire] more intelligent men' and this was the view that prevailed in the *Principles*.[88] Two days later they visited Hattersley's weaving works at Keighley, with its patent machine 'driving out all others because it could drive 80 strands per minute instead of 60'. Their 'very intelligent' guide who showed them over the works disputed the advantages of technical education with them but 'gave in' on an undisclosed point 'about dyeing'. In between these visits, they went to Haworth (17 September) and Saltaire (18 September) where they could not visit the local works and instead inspected the town: 'Public washhouses coming more into use. Fine concert rooms. Good deal of dancing' but Alfred, his wife recorded, 'should prefer life at Keighley', the 'ideal factory town'.

A week in Sheffield followed. On Saturday night (19 September), after a day's walking in the town which Mary Paley succinctly described as 'black but picturesque', they 'went to all the markets. Saw a woman auctioning pots. Bought laces 12 a penny. Meat market crowded. Meat selling cheap.' On Sunday, Mary went by herself to the Salvation Army, despite 'ill-mannered people in the streets' but during the afternoon they studied together workman's houses and presumably the more elegant middle-class residences in the suburbs. The labourers' dwellings, she noted, were 'all built after the one pattern. Cheap, and with only four rooms, when there might have been five. 5/- a week rent.'* On Monday, the real purpose of the Sheffield visit commenced; inspection of the metal-working industries for which the town was famous. Once again, observations made can be linked to ideas presented in the *Principles:*

---

* These views on the need for economy of space in building can probably be linked with the personal experience the Marshalls were gaining in this field. This came by way of the design and building of Balliol Croft, from 1886 their permanent residence in Cambridge. On Balliol Croft, see Chapter 8 below, pp. 241–5.

Sept. 21st Visited Mr. Stevenson . . . at his type-founding works. He said only 6 type-founders in the U[nited] K[ingdom]. They had a monopoly and met together to fix prices of type. Price did not vary with that of raw material – lead. Just now lead very cheap. So good profits. Monopoly was due to fact that (i) workmen required long and special training (ii) enormous number of machines and variety of them required. Each of these, which made the moulds from which the type was cast had to be made by a skilled workman, and it would take an enormous time to produce a sufficient number of these matrices. . . . In type casting machines and hand labour work side by side and contrast was interesting . . . introduction of machines for casting had caused a fall in type from 5/6 to 1/10. A[lfred] suggested type should be cooled by compressed air system. Stevenson spoke about conflicts between employers and employed and said much friction could be avoided by (i) speaking to men in a body and not merely by representatives; (ii) preparing their minds for a change by giving long notice (iii) by cautious introduction of machinery and making a rule of not throwing men out of employment. He said he had no trouble beyond taking trouble in these ways and that he had affected [sic!] a reduction of 20% in own branch of trade in which wages were abnormally high. He said he did not think the introduction of machinery tended to raise the ability of workmen but rather to place skilled and unskilled on near level. This probably more true of Sheffield trade than of others, for the manual labour seemed to require higher faculties than [that working] the machines but in the cutlery and similar trades of Sheffield there seemed to be less enterprise and less high class machinery than in other trade. We were introduced to Mr. Abram Crookshank, a conservative and very strong against machinery. He declared that machine made files had not improved of late years. He said Sheffield workmen were furious because German stamped scissors were selling largely in England and showed us advertisements of Birmingham scissors at 20/- a gross. In afternoon saw Hutton's electroplate establishment. Were struck by inferiority of machinery. Women employed at scrubbery, electroplating, burnishing and packing. The scrubbing was very dirty and disagreeable work . . .

The next day the Marshalls inspected a file-making works 'and we saw all the process'. Advantages of file cutting by machine were demonstrated by the fact that hand cutting required no less than a seven-year apprenticeship while after only three hours a girl with a machine 'could cut files fairly well. Guide said that the handcutters were gradually put to machine and there earned higher wages. But that some work would always be left for handcutting in finishing.' In the afternoon the Marshalls studied the 'process for blistering steel' at Jessop's steel works, a visit during which its owner also sang the praises of the Sheffield workers. This praise was duly recorded by Marshall in his *Principles*,[89] though not in the detail with which they were provided:

On Sundays, they [the workers] would take 20 and 30 mile walks and then be fresh for work on Mondays. Fond of pidgeon flying, football and all sports. Fond of horseracing and gambling. Struck by fine physique of men as compared with those in light trades. Workmen of Sheffield as a rule fine cut and well featured.

The visit also inspired an observation on the advantages of concentrating an industry within a specific location, a major theme of the analysis of production in the *Principles*. The concentration of the metal industries in Sheffield enabled a specialist enterprise for sorting scraps and disposing of waste products, an observation generalised in the *Principles* to the statement that waste of materials 'can scarcely occur in a localised manufacture even if it is in the hands of small men.'* A visit to a further cutlery works recalled demonstrations of

---

* *P* I, pp. 339–40; *P* VIII, p. 279, once more with no change between editions. A more general indication of the influence of these holiday observations on Marshall's views on the location of industry is visible in the following quotation: 'Staffordshire makes many kinds of pottery, all the materials of which are imported from a long distance; but she has cheap coal and excellent clay for making the heavy "saggars" or boxes in which the pottery is

'hollow grinding' and a 'disappointing display of razors'. The next day they made a trip to a major steelworks where armour plating was manufactured by machines and the operation of that Bessemer steel process for which Sheffield was famous was shown to them. The tour of Sheffield concluded with a visit to Sorbey's saw-making works,

> Saw process of heating in furnace and dipping in oil after which the saw is quite brittle, whilst before it was pliable. The re-heating, or tempering, renders it elastic. This requires long practice. Then the saw is hammered to give an even surface. This also requires long practice. Polishing done by women, . . . Saw wet grinding. Dry grinding used for iron more than steel, and it only is injurious to the grinder. Mr. Sorbey told us about small masters who hire steam power for wheels – they get the steel from Sorbeys, work it up with knives with perhaps one or two assistants and make perhaps £5 a week. Sorbey, the undertaker, doing all the selling and bearing the risks. He said that [it is] very common for small men to rise to large employers, and very uncommon for business to remain in same hands for long – it got too large and turned into a company.*

A third record of an industrial tour is preserved for 1888. This covered East Yorkshire, trips to mining towns, ironworks and took in Leicester on the way back. The preserved record of this trip has the Marshalls journeying from Stockton to the nearby iron-mining villages of Brotton and Skinningrove, where the peculiarities of the miners' houses were duly noted: 'tall and very thin with broad frontage'. Then to an ironworks at Middlesbrough, where mountains of slag were said to account for a quarter of the slag in the kingdom. Trade was only slowly recovering from a severe depression, the signs of which were visible on the faces of the women and children. A visit to Stockton followed, with the customary walk among workers' houses, a tram ride to the suburbs and the observation that a Shakespeare play was showing in the theatre (but whether they went to see it, was not noted). Then to the pretty village of Norton for the train ride to Hartlepool where they saw shipbuilding and repairs involving cranes able to lift 90 tons. Sunday, 23 September, was spent in a visit to the Booths, at Gracedieu Manor. Marshall made their acquaintance two years previously when Booth was about to embark on his famous London survey of the poor.[90]   Via Leicester, they returned to Cambridge and, while in that Midlands industrial town took time off to inspect a cooperative boot factory which employed 700 men and 200 women. Social aspects recorded during this visit require extensive quotation,

> *Machinery*, very complex and interesting. One machine had a metre to record stitches and 5d. per 1000 had to be paid to owner of the *patent*, an agent coming round to inspect metre from time to time. Machines for bending the 'uppers', for button holes, for putting in eyes. The work requiring most attention was clicking, or cutting out the uppers from the hides. The manager spoke very highly of the *women*; they were employed in such work as putting eyes in, button holing and stitching, for which last work some earned £1 a week. He said the women were quick and clever and could become checkers – only the men would object – only he confessed that marriage would interfere with the training to such work, and he objected to employing married women unless in exceptional cases. The women employed were very high class looking, and looked

---

placed while being fired. . . . Sheffield cutlery trade is due chiefly to the excellent grit of which its grindstones are made.' (*P* I, p. 330; *P* VIII, p. 269, with no changes between editions.)

* Part of Sorbey's account was generalised for the Sheffield cutlery trade as a whole in *P* I, p. 358; *P* VIII, p. 296 (no change between editions); the life cycle and growth of firms in this industry which Sorbey described is different from that in the *Principles*, since a company form of organisation, more permanent by its very nature, constitutes the final stage in that growth in their informant's account. As mentioned in Chapter 19, pp. 709–10, Marshall took account of this when writing *Industry and Trade*.

very healthy and cheerful. He said that they used their money better than the young men; they earned a good deal. He said that boys often earned high wages and spent them badly. One lad of 14 earned 16/- a week; 6/- he gave to his parents for board and 10[/-] would be wasted in theatre, gambling, etc. That men often only gave their wives half their wages and wasted the rest. And that they bought unwisely – e.g. boots of delicate leather that wouldn't stand work. He said the spending of the poor on trashy things was the main cause of sweating – He said also there was a growing move for boys to bring home only a small proportion of large earnings and said it was a pity they should earn so much when so young. Then they married and expected wives to work for them. He said aged labourers' children behaved better about their earnings. Not so much subdivision in English boot factories as in American, due partly to Trades Union (the Conservatives) opposition. The manager described himself as an autocrat in matters of buying and selling, etc. said that he couldn't afford to wait for committee meeting.[*]

After noting that Leicester is the centre for working-class boot and shoe production, while Northampton is that for the 'superior kind', the manuscript breaks off on the promise to give reasons for this locational feature.[91]

The above presents only a small part of the data which the Marshalls would have gathered during their summers in England, if only because this type of social and industrial observation was a substantial part of their summer holidays both in Britain and continental Europe. The manner in which Marshall used these observations in later work has been illustrated on several occasions, largely in connection with the *Principles*. An interesting feature in this context is the longevity in the use to which these illustrations were put. Lasting the whole life of the *Principles*, they were kept long after obsolescence destroyed the value of the original observation. This indicates one danger of the casual empiricism involved in these tours of inspection.

In addition, as Whitaker[92] has noted, the process of acquiring data in this manner was far from costless. It removed valuable writing time, when much of this type of information could in any case have been more effectively gathered from books. It also demonstrated Marshall's obsession with attempting the virtually impossible, that is, 'to apprehend in all its aspects an ever-changing economic reality'. Industrial processes were of course not only studied for the sake of learning about technology and its implication for wage rates, as Marshall claimed in the autobiographical fragment quoted at the start of this chapter. The emphasis in Mary Paley Marshall's notes betrays other purposes as well, congenial to Marshall as social inquirer and reformer. Much observation was made on women's work and its consequences, and on labourers' living standards (housing, food) and standard of life (amusement, leisure, spending habits) and its effect, visible on their faces. The study of faces as social index stands out in these personal inspections, perhaps Marshall's attempt to imitate Le Play in a more casual manner. Both the methods and effects of factory production were therefore studied by the Marshalls as part of their overall social inquiry.

The facts gathered were used in the manner of von Thünen: to confirm rather than formulate new theory and new views; to illustrate all aspects of industrial practice and hence to place, wherever possible, the arguments to be presented within a context of reality. The number of times these data were directly visible in Marshall's publications are rather small

---

[*] In June 1875, Marshall had noted 'the way in which every operation is broken up into a great number of positions, the work of each individual being confined to a very small portion of the whole operation'. Marshall, 'United States Industry', Marshall Archive, Box (6) 1.

relative to the time taken to collect them. However, like the specific instance of the American tour of 1875, they informed also his views on women's issues, on socialism and social reform by providing a hidden factual basis to the views he articulated separately on these subjects.[93]

Other features of these holidays can be highlighted by quoting some brief excerpts from Marshall's correspondence. The holiday in Wales which they combined with their visit to the potteries of Staffordshire, was largely devoted to 'food, bathing, admirably sketching and river and sea boating'.[94] A holiday in the spring in Cornwall sixteen years later records cycling from Plymouth to Boxester via Fowey and Wadebridge, a mode of transport of which the Marshalls became rather fond.* A letter to Edgeworth from Bournemouth[95] concisely indicates the third type of activity Marshall engaged in during his summers: 'I am writing as I generally do in fine weather; on the cliffs. The colour here is very good: large masses of heather with pink and red; and bright yellow gorse, deep orange sandstone cliffs, and the blue sea make such a combination that it is almost too garish if it were indoors; but I think that nature out of doors can't overdo herself.' The lover of nature in this way combined with the author and serious social and industrial observer during their British, as well as European, summers.

ALPINE VILLAGES, ITALIAN LAKES AND ECONOMISTS' TEA PARTIES: THE MARSHALLS IN EUROPE

As indicated at the start of this chapter, from 1891 to 1909 with few exceptions, the Marshalls spent their summer holidays on the continent of Europe, generally in the Alps. Appropriately, their sequence of European holidays began in the summer of 1891 with what Mary Paley Marshall recollected as their *rundreise*, a journey of which only few recollections are extant. The trip, which took place from early August and mid-September at the latest,[¶] on one account took in Paris, Vienna and Germany and was designed as a delayed celebration of the publication of the *Principles* that previous year. No watercolours by Mary Paley survive for this trip presumably because they were never long enough in any one place. She herself made brief references to it in a letter to Benjamin Jowett about a month after their return to England: 'we went to Dresden on our way home and I saw the Sistine Madonna for the first time. I had no notion that the photographs of it were so inadequate – one can quite believe the story that he [Raphael] saw it in a dream. We enjoyed seeing all these towns, especially Prague.'[96] In a footnote to *Industry and Trade*, Alfred Marshall recalled some industrial features from this trip, to show that even this

---

* Marshall to Foxwell, 8 April 1897, Marshall Archive, Box 3; cf. Marshall to Cannan, 3 July 1896, where on realising that Cannan was a highly skilled cyclist, Marshall apologised for having argued with him on the subject (Cannan Papers, British Library of Economics and Political Science, 1020:100–101). Cf. Cannan, 'Alfred Marshall 1892–1924', p. 67. However, it took some time before both Marshalls were able to ride bicycles together, for reasons discussed below, p. 249.

¶ Marshall was in London as part of his duties as member of the Royal Commission on Labour until 31 July 1891; an entry in John Neville Keynes's diary for 21 September indicates that the Marshalls were by then back in Cambridge, since that evening he and his wife dined with the Marshalls at Balliol Croft. W.G. Constable, 'Art and Economics in Cambridge', p. 24, indicates Paris, Vienna and Germany as part of the tour, wrongly dating it in 1890, when, as earlier indicated, the Marshalls stayed in England for reasons of work.

excursion had not been immune from such investigations: 'In 1891, when the present writer visited some large engineering works in Bohemia, the manager said: "Look at that lad. A few months ago he was working in the country for 5s. a week. I now pay him 12s., and he is looking after three semi-automatic machines. In your country none but skilled engineers are allowed to work those machines, though no skill is needed for it: and each engineer is compelled to confine his attention to one machine."'[97] From these scant facts, it seems likely that in 1891 the Marshalls travelled from England to Paris, then to Vienna, an Austrian watering place where they met the Seligmans,[98] Prague, then, via Bohemia to Dresden and back to England via an unknown route through Germany and Holland, which probably took in Cologne. It would be nice to have detailed impressions of their tour to fill out the all too sparse knowledge about their preferences and habits of sightseeing and the other activities this enthralling route offered.

Most of the other European holidays involved far less continuous travel. Trains had made virtually all parts of Europe very accessible and when, as the Marshalls invariably did, they travelled with an enormous amount of luggage, consisting largely of the books and papers needed to assist Marshall in his writing, a longish sojourn at the one place seemed advisable. South Tirol, particularly the Dolomite region, was their favourite spot as Mary Paley later recalled.

We spent most of the Long Vacations in South Tirol which we preferred to Switzerland. For in 1890–1912 the Dolomite region was unspoilt by tourists and motor-cars, and especially in the side-valleys the people were natural and homely and we made some warm friends; of these the chief was Filomena who kept the small wayside inn at Stern in Abtei Tal where we spent three summers. She was devoted to 'der liebe Herr', and when we wished her good-bye on our last visit she said: 'We shall meet in heaven.' The hostess at another inn was very proud because one of her sons had become a priest and another the Professor of Ladinish at Vienna. He came home for the holidays and sat and drank and enjoyed life with his peasant friends, and once he brought an artist from Vienna who painted the walls of the Gastzimmer with Ladinish legends. One of them represented the mingling of the Latin and the Rhaetian elements from which the Ladinish race sprang. The Rhaetian woman agreed to marry the Latin man on condition that he should never touch her forehead, but as time went on he accidentally brushed away a fly which had settled there and she disappeared. In the side-valleys Ladinish was the usual language and many of the peasants could not speak either German or Italian.[99]

On another occasion, she recalled their 'enormous room in our Inn [at Stuben] with everything in threes: three beds, three huge tables, three life-size crucifixes.'[100]

In his letters, Marshall himself recalled other essential aspects of these trips, some of which (to Brentano and Newcomb) have already been encountered. In June 1908, he wrote to the Belgian economist Levasseur that his summer plans prevented attendance at the Paris meeting of the Institut de Statistique since he needed a prolonged period in high altitudes to improve the all too slow progress he was making in his writing. In the context of what was their first European holiday after their retirement from Cambridge economics teaching, Marshall explained,

I have already sent a hundred kilograms of books and manuscripts to South Tyrol; and I have taken berths for my wife and myself on the steamer which leaves Harwich tomorrow. I hope to write in the high mountain air (1500–1600 metres) during the summer and then to return to write here at Cambridge. You will see therefore that it is impossible for me to turn my thoughts in another direction, or to be present at the next meeting of the Institut de Statistique in Paris.[101]

Marshall's habit of open-air writing during these later Alpine holidays was also vividly recalled by Mary Paley Marshall and is captured even more eloquently in photographs of the time.

> Alfred always worked best in the open air, and especially in the high air. On rainy days he would sit on the balcony of the hay chalet and pleased Filomena by calling it her 'Sommerpalast'. On fine days he went into the woods where he had made a 'throne' with an air cushion and a camp stool which, when opened against a pile of stones, made a comfortable back to lean against; and there he would sit for hours absorbed in his writing. One day on looking up he saw a chamois standing only a few feet off. It barked and stamped and then went quietly on its way and next day it appeared again; and sometimes a cow would come from behind and breathe on his neck. He would choose the site of his 'throne' very carefully so that if possible there should be a fine view.[102]

Likewise, Mary Paley recorded the new problems they faced in arranging such mountain sojourns from the far more difficult travel situation which became the rule in post-First World War Europe. Increased passport and other documentation requirements were one part of the problem, and deprived them of a well-deserved European holiday in 1919, to celebrate the completion of *Industry and Trade*. A year later, on the last European holiday in the Tirol they were to share together, far less comfortable and reliable train travel caused them problems of personal comfort and nearly deprived the world of the volume on *Money, Credit and Commerce*.

> In July 1919 *Industry and Trade* was finished and Alfred much needed a complete change and rest. His doctor said that if possible he must go to the mountains and he went to Folkestone to be in readiness to cross whilst I was to see after passports, etc. It was very hot, and I seemed to be sitting most of the day on the steps of Consuls' houses in a crowd. Then when we succeeded in getting inside I was told that I must return to Cambridge for references from bankers or others. It was quite hopeless, so in the late afternoon I went to Folkestone and we agreed that as difficulties might be even greater on the Continent we had better stay in England that summer. Probably the mountain air would have set him up as it had done so often; he began indeed to write his third volume but he was very jaded and in June 1920 we determined to make another attempt to go abroad.
>
> When about 20 miles from Milan, at a small station, the carriage door was opened and we were told to descend as a lightning strike had begun, and that the heavy luggage was to remain in the van. With great difficulty we found a ramshackle carriage which took us and a suitcase to Milan. But when we got there no good hotel would admit us as they did not seem to like our broken-down carriage and insufficient luggage. After many vain attempts we were received by a third-class Italian hotel where we spent the next three days whilst awaiting the end of the strike. We could speak little Italian, and I don't know what would have happened but for Mr. Churchill, the English Consul. He saw how important it was to get Alfred to the mountains and said that we must not wait for the luggage (he would see to that) but leave Milan as soon as the trains began to move. He also lent us his 'messenger' who spoke English and who was to see us off. On the third morning, when the trains began to move, we went with the messenger to the station who said, 'you take hold of my coat and let him take hold of you', and he pulled our suitcase and us along through the dense mass of people in the waiting hall where the air was full of bundles and belongings flying about. He succeeded in squeezing us into a first-class carriage full of people and we were carried to Verona. We reached our destination in the Abtei Tal without much further trouble, except that the names of the stations which had been changed from German to Italian were puzzling, and we lived on the contents of the suitcase together with a few purchases. I was haunted by the idea that we might never see our heavy luggage again

for it contained all the MSS relating to what afterwards became *Money, Credit and Commerce* though, curiously enough, Alfred did not worry about this; and how I did rejoice when in the midst of a thunderstorm six weeks later the luggage reached our inn in a cart, and thanks to the Consul it had never been opened or examined. This was our last visit to the Continent for with Alfred's loss of memory and increasing ill-health I felt that we must not venture again, though he always had a hankering after the beloved South Tirol.[103]

The Austrian holidays on occasion offered opportunities for meeting with other economists. An encounter with a group of leading Austrian economists was eloquently recorded by Mary Paley's pen as well as by the camera in a rather harmonious group photo of this fortuitous gathering.

One year we discovered that in the next village were assembled a large part of the 'Austrian school' of economists. The von Wiesers, the Böhm-Bawerks, the Zuckerkandls and several others. We boldly asked the whole company to a tea party in our enormous bedroom, which was the largest and most desirable room in the inn, and we afterwards adjourned to the tent shelter in the field nearby. Filomena was proud of having such distinguished guests and got up at 4 a.m. to make fresh butter and various delicacies for the entertainment. Von Böhm-Bawerk was a wiry and agile little man, an ardent mountaineer who climbed a Dolomite almost every day. This somewhat exhausted his economic energies and he did not want to discuss the Theory of the Rate of Interest, a subject which I had rather dreaded, as he and Alfred had recently been corresponding warmly upon it. Professor Von Wieser was a noble-looking man and delightful companion with a wife and daughter to match, and I much enjoyed the return tea party which the Austrian School gave at the beautiful old peasant's house where they were spending the summer.[104]

Travel experiences in the Bavarian Alps and the Tirol were also drawn upon to illustrate aspects of the *Principles of Economics*, in the context of the localisation of industry and the custom of allowing only one son in each family to marry as a check to population. Writing in the late 1880s, Marshall recorded that 'Not very long ago travellers in Western Tyrol could find a strange and characteristic relic of this habit [one branch of production per village] in a village called Imst. The villagers had somehow acquired a special art in breeding canaries; and their young men started for a tour of distant parts of Europe each with about fifty small cages hung from a pole over his shoulder, and walked on till they had sold all.'[105] The marriage customs of European villages were illustrated by Marshall from a visit he made to the valley of Jachenau in the Bavarian Alps circa 1880, where the custom was then still in full force with rather peculiar social results,

Thus a visit to the valley Jachenau in the Bavarian Alps about 1880 found this custom still in full force. Aided by a great recent rise in the value of their woods, with regard to which they had pursued a farseeing policy, the inhabitants lived prosperously in large houses, the younger brothers and sisters acting as servants in their old homes or elsewhere. They were of a different race from the work-people in the neighbouring valleys, who lived poor and hard lives, but seemed to think that the Jachenau purchased its material prosperity at too great a cost.[106]

Craftsmen from the Grodener Tal in Tirol were also celebrated in *Industry and Trade* to illustrate both potential for drudgery and beauty in its noted woodcarving industry.[107] It could also inspire complete relaxation, as Marshall wrote to Foxwell in 1903 after his colleague's repeated request for a Tripos book list for the coming academic year:

The still peace of mountain woods has taken out my evil spirit; and I no more dream economics at night. But luckily I awakened last night and saw a picture of the list of books I had sent you. It looked too short. I thought there must be something wrong. So I looked when daylight came, and found I had omitted bodily the books on one of the slips which I had made out for the purpose some time past *

Thus pleasure mingled with work, and holidays produced book lists, illustrations for economics texts and release from the demons of everyday life.

THE FINAL ENGLISH HOLIDAYS 1921–1923: OLD HABITS DIE HARD

Marshall's last three summers were spent in Dorset, East Lulworth, not far from Corfe Castle where the Marshalls had spent two secluded holidays during the early years of the First World War. It continued their preference for the seaside, since the more western south sea coast at Brixham had been their summer resort in 1911, while Torquay was where they spent a brief 1919 summer holiday as a result of the bureaucratic frustrations of post-war continental travel. Torquay was also not far from Totnes, the place where in his youth, Marshall had recovered from the rigours of the Merchant Taylors' school year during the summer holidays of the 1850s spent with his Aunt Louisa. By this time, industrial observations were confined to leisurely inspection of the fishing boats, as he wrote to Maynard Keynes from Brixham, and by noting the vagaries of the fish market inspired by, rather than inspiring, the analysis of the price of fish he had provided well before in his *Principles*. However, instead of seeing them as pieces of fixed capital, Marshall saw fishing boats in the penultimate decade of his life as subjects for his wife's watercolours. He described his own activities as a conscious decision 'to study the evolution of sp(1911)ring [i.e. spring 1911], in Devonshire' from a long verandah belonging to the cottage they had rented, from which for variation rocks and sea in combination could likewise be studied.¶ Presumably, here too in the contemplation of nature, work was carried out on the long and arduous construction of what became *Industry and Trade* at the end of the decade, just as in the final summers of the 1920s they spent away from Cambridge, Marshall constructed *Money, Credit and Commerce* from material sometimes more than fifty years old.[108] As in the guiding ideas of his writings, Marshall maintained a high degree of continuity in holiday practice, reflecting the stability from force of habit which most people cherish. This was succinctly portrayed by Mary Paley in the final paragraph of her reminiscence, which form a most appropriate last word to this chapter, particularly when set in the context of his comments, 'only a few days before he died, "I hope you have got our lodging in Dorset for we ought to be off there in a few days".'

---

* Marshall to Foxwell, 5 August 1903 (Freeman Collection, 12/244). This was the holiday when Marshall was plagued with the Fiscal Problem in International Trade (below, Chapter 11, pp. 379–81, esp. p. 380 n.¶) and he did not want to think of book lists (Marshall to Foxwell, 31 July 1903, Freeman Collection, 5/244).

¶ Alfred Marshall to John Maynard Keynes, 18 May 1911, Keynes Papers, King's College, Cambridge, L/M/41. The analysis of the fish market in the *Principles* is in Book V, Chapter V, §4 (*P* VIII, pp. 369–71; *P* I, Book V, Chapter IV, §3, pp. 410–42). This example also illustrates the treatment of old fishing boats as fixed capital, the supply of which can only be effectively increased in the long period.

The next three summers we spent in a lovely and lonely Dorset cove called Arish Mell, where he worked away at his third volume. But after *Industry and Trade* had been finished in 1919 his memory gradually became worse and soon after his doctor told me quietly that 'he will not be able to construct any more'. And it was so, though fortunately he did not know it. For in the old days he used to come down from his study and say: 'I have had such a happy time, there is no joy to be compared to constructive work.'[109]

NOTES

1. Alfred Marshall to Rebecca Marshall, 5 June 1875, Marshall Archive 1/289. The lakes referred to could have been those visited in the summer of 1873 when Alfred Marshall took his two sisters to St Moritz, but it seems more likely that the journals referred to were written many years earlier during a family summer holiday in the Lake District.
2. Alfred Marshall, 'Historical (On the Way Home from Sicily) Approx. History of Curves', Marshall Archive: this, and a later listing in Mary Paley Marshall's handwriting providing locations for all their summer holidays until Alfred Marshall's death in 1924, are reproduced below, p. 190.
3. Alfred Marshall to A.W. Flux, 7 March 1898, in *Memorials*, p. 407, and see above, Chapter 6, pp. 141, 163.
4. Mary Paley Marshall, 'Biographical Notes on Alfred Marshall' (KMF). The picture collection was discussed in Chapter 5, above p. 128.
5. Mary Paley Marshall, 'Notes for Walter Scott', Marshall Archive, Large Brown Box, Item 26.
6. Travels in England, Marshall Archive, Red Box 1 (5); Marshall to Edgeworth, 27 April 1909, in *Memorials*, p. 438.
7. *Memorials*, pp. 358–9; the margin of error of 2s. a week he allowed effectively ranged from 12.5 per cent for junior wages to 6 or 7 per cent for skilled male earnings.
8. Alfred Marshall to Simon Newcomb, 29 July 1892, Library of Congress, Washington, MSS Division, 62 ft. shelf space, Letterbooks 4–6.
9. John Whitaker, introduction to *EEW*, I, p. 41 n.1.
10. Mary Paley Marshall, 'Summers', in Marshall Archive.
11. Chapter 2 above, pp. 36, 39, 41.
12. J.R. Mozley to Alfred Marshall, 19 September 1916, Marshall Archive, 1/89; Mary Paley Marshall, 'MSS Notes', NCA, 'Recollections of A', p. 5, for 1930s talk to the Marshall society. Hereafter referred to as 'MSS Notes', NCA.
13. Mary Paley Marshall, 'Biographical Notes on Alfred Marshall' (KMF). Her recollection of 1919 as the year of their final continental trip is wrong; it was 1920 as indicated previously. See also below, pp. 216–7 and Chapter 19, pp. 715–6.
14. Noel Annan, *Leslie Stephen. The Godless Victorian*, p. 90.
15. T.G. Bonney, *Memories of a Long Life*, pp. 60–66; earlier (*ibid.*, pp. 46–9) he described how easy the trip to Switzerland was made by the coming of the railways, though at the cost of the disappearance of much that was beautiful in the Swiss environment.
16. Mary Paley Marshall, 'Notes for Walter Scott', Marshall Archive, Large Brown Box, Item 26. *P* II, p. 79 n.1 (*P* VIII, p. 121 n.1) discusses the 'pleasure of Alpine tours' to 'young men' in the context of time preference.
17. Alfred Marshall, 'The Future of the Working Classes', in *Memorials*, p. 106.
18. Mary Paley Marshall, *What I Remember*, p. 22.
19. A.S. and E.M.S., *Henry Sidgwick. A Memoir*, pp. 54–5, 57, 60, 131.
20. Mary Paley Marshall, 'Notes for Walter Scott'.
21. *OP*, p. 44, Q. 9659.
22. Marshall Archive, Box 6 (1), and letters to Rebecca Marshall from 5 June to 25 September 1875, 1/289–299. His lectures at Cambridge and Bristol on America are discussed below, pp. 200–02.
23. Alfred Marshall to Rebecca Marshall, 5 June 1875, Marshall Archive, 1/289.
24. Marshall Archive, Box 6(1).
25. *Ibid.*
26. Alfred Marshall to Rebecca Marshall, 5 June 1875, Marshall Archive, 1/289.
27. Marshall Archive, Box 6 (1).
28. *Ibid.*

29. Alfred Marshall to Rebecca Marshall, 12 June 1875, Marshall Archive, 1/290.
30. Alfred Marshall to Rebecca Marshall, 20 June 1875, Marshall Archive, 1/291.
31. Marshall Archives 6(1). Notes on Emerson, and see Chapter 5 above, pp. 125–6 for an earlier reference to the philosophical aspects of the discussion.
32. Alfred Marshall to Rebecca Marshall, 25 June 1875, Marshall Archive, 1/292.
33. Cited in J.P. Munroe, *A Life of Francis Amasa Walker*, New York: Holt, 1923, pp. 308–9.
34. Marshall to Rebecca Marshall, 5 July 1875, Marshall Archive, 1/293.
35. Alfred Marshall to Rebecca Marshall, 10 July 1875, Marshall Archive, 1/294.
36. *Ibid.* For a detailed contemporary account of these utopian settlements, see William Alfred Hinds, *American Communities*, first published in 1878, new edition introduced by H.B. Barkes, New York: Corinth Books, 1961, pp. 81–116 on the Shaker communities and pp. 117–39 on the Oneida settlements.
37. See below, Chapter 16, p. 575 n.*.
38. Alfred Marshall to Rebecca Marshall, 18 July 1875, Marshall Archive, 1/295.
39. Alfred Marshall to Rebecca Marshall, 22 August 1875, Marshall Archive, 1/296; *IT*, p. 446 n.1.
40. Alfred Marshall to Rebecca Marshall, 5 September 1875, Marshall Archive, 1/297.
41. Marshall Archive, Box 6 (1), Sketches of Character from his American Trip: H.C. Carey.
42. Alfred Marshall to Rebecca Marshall, 23 and 25 September 1875, Marshall Archive, 1/298, 1/299.
43. Marshall by then had probably read Young's travels, on whose statistical data he drew heavily in preparing statistical notes for his students at Bristol. Most of Young's travels were in his library, see Marshall Library Catalogue 1927, p. 93.
44. JNKD, 17 November 1875; 'At the Moral Sciences Club, Marshall read a paper on American Industry'. Mary Paley, 'MSS Notes' (NCA) later recalled he gave three lectures on America, one at Cambridge, two at Bristol.
45. *EEW*, II, p. 375, cf. pp. 357–8.
46. *Ibid.*, pp. 375–6. For references to objective and subjective freedom, see Hegel, *Philosophy of History*, Sibree translation, New York: Dover Books, 1956, pp. 18–19, 40–50, 187–8.
47. *EEW*, II, p. 376, and see *P* I, p. 1, a passage only slightly altered from the fourth edition to its final form in the eighth.
48. Hegel, *Philosophy of History*, p. 86; cf. *EEW*, II, p. 355, where Marshall states in some unpublished lecture notes, 'I wanted to see the history of the future in America'. For the likely origin of these notes, see note 53 below.
49. *EEW*, II, pp. 355, 370; cf. Hegel, *Philosophy of History*, pp. 18–19.
50. *EEW*, II, pp. 374, 357.
51. *Ibid.*, p. 377.
52. Ibid., pp. 355–6. The references in brackets in the remainder of this paragraph refer to the same lecture.
53. Reported in *Western Daily Press*, 15 January 1878 and *Bristol Times and Mirror*, 15 January 1878. The text of this public lecture is not included in Appendix D of Whitaker's, 'Alfred Marshall: the Years 1877 to 1885', where many of his other Bristol public lectures are reprinted; *EEW* reproduces extracts from lecture notes which closely resemble the lecture as reported by the Bristol press, hence it may not be true that the notes were for the use of Marshall's college lectures as Whitaker assumed. See *EEW*, II, pp. 354–5.
54. *EOI*, p. 222; cf. p. 61 on farmers as landowners, p. 178 on relative profitability and prices in retail and wholesale in America as compared with England and Germany, pp. 183–4 on the Chicago and New York corn markets, and p. 221 on the use of the American term, 'engineering the business' to describe the managerial organisation function. Book III, Chapter 4, on 'Monopolies and Combinations', more generally shows the impact of Marshall's United States travel.
55. *P* I, p. 216 n.1; this footnote had disappeared in the sixth edition; see *P* IX, p. 281.
56. 'Some Aspects of Competition', in *Memorials*, pp. 258–65, esp. p. 260.
57. *IT*, pp. 295, 304n., 307n. and above, p. 194, for the reference to advertising in New York. Pages in brackets in the next but one sentence are to *IT*.
58. *OP*, p. 393. For Marshall's emphasis on the importance of individualism and initiative in enterprise in the context of socialism, see below, Chapter 16, p. 588, 593–4, 608–9.
59. Marshall to Foxwell, 24 July 1881 (Freeman Collection, 3/252); cf. Mary Paley Marshall, *What I Remember*, pp. 24–5.
60. *Ibid.*, pp. 24–5.
61. Francis M. Guercio, *Sicily. The Garden of the Mediterranean*, London: Faber & Faber, 1938, p. 11.
62. Marshall to Foxwell, 10 October 1881 (Freeman Collection, 16/150).
63. Cf. J.M. Keynes, 'Mary Paley Marshall', p. 241; 'They were months of perfect bliss'.
64. Marshall to Foxwell, 10 October 1881 (Freeman Collection, 16/150).
65. *Ibid.*
66. J.M. Keynes, 'Alfred Marshall', p. 202 n.3, and see below, Chapter 12, p. 404.

67. J.M. Keynes, 'Mary Paley Marshall', p. 240; this account is in Section IV of *What I Remember*, pp. 28–34, on which much of the remainder of this section is based.
68. Mary Paley Marshall, *What I Remember*, pp. 28–9.
69. *Ibid.*, p. 30.
70. W.G. Constable, 'Art and Economics at Cambridge', *The Eagle*, Vol. 59, 1960–63, p. 24. Use of the term 'accuracy' is appropriate when Mary Paley's descriptions are compared with similar scenes from Palermo a century later. Some of her paintings are reproduced as illustrations 23–25.
71. Mary Paley Marshall, *What I Remember*, pp. 30–31.
72. *Ibid.*, pp. 31–2.
73. *Ibid.*, p. 32.
74. *Ibid.,*. p. 29.
75. *OP*, pp. 92–3; cf. *MCC*, pp. 242–3 and *P* I, pp. 733–4 n.1, *P* VIII, p. 688 n.1.
76. Mary Paley Marshall, *What I Remember*, p. 33.
77. *Ibid.*, p. 25.
78. *Ibid.,*. pp. 25, 31.
79. *Ibid.*, p. 29 and her 'Notes for Walter Scott', where she mentioned, 'when I had malarial fever at Palermo he nursed me through it without any help, though he himself was much crippled at the time'.
80. Mary Paley Marshall, *What I Remember*, pp. 33–4. Jane Harrison was a friend from student days at Newnham.
81. W.G. Constable, 'Art and Economics at Cambridge', p. 24.
82. Alfred Marshall, 'Historical 1882: On Way Home from Sicily', Marshall Archive; J.M. Keynes, 'Alfred Marshall', p. 213.
83. Mary Paley Marshall, 'MSS Notes' (NCA), p. 14.
84. Alfred Marshall, 'Historical 1882: On Way Home from Sicily', Marshall Archive.
85. Marshall Archive, Red Box 1 (5): 'Travels in England'.
86. Mary Paley Marshall, 'MSS Notes' (NCA), p. 17.
87. *P* I, pp. 341–2; *P* VIII pp. 280–81.
88. See *P* I, pp. 574–5; *P* VIII, pp. 549–50.
89. *P* I, pp. 358–9; *P* VIII, pp. 296–7, indicating no change between editions.
90. See Belinda Norman-Butler, *Victorian Aspirations. The Life and Labour of Charles and Mary Booth*, London: Allen & Unwin, 1972, p. 88, and for a more detailed discussion of the Marshall friendship with the Booths, Chapter 18, below, pp. 695–6.
91. Some brief notes on Welsh wages and workers' living conditions are included with these notes as preserved in the Marshall Library. These possibly belong to the record of their 1883 travels, when the Marshalls had been holidaying on the coast of Pembrokeshire for part of the summer.
92. Introduction to *EEW*, I, p. 57.
93. Cf. *IT*, p. 366n., and see below, Chapter 14, p. 513, Chapter 16, pp. 575, 600.
94. Marshall to Foxwell, 22 July 1883, Marshall Archive, Box 3.
95. Marshall to Edgeworth, 12 September 1882 (British Library of Economics and Political Science, Coll. Misc. 470, M. 469).
96. Mary Paley Marshall to Benjamin Jowett, 12 October 1891, Jowett Papers, Balliol College, Oxford. Marshall's strong liking for Raphael's Sistine Madonna, which he had first seen in 1868, was mentioned above, p. 192 n*.
97. *IT*, p. 137 n.1.
98. On the basis of a letter from Sidney Webb to Beatrice Webb, 24 September 1891 which mentioned he had heard from the Seligmans how they had met the Marshalls at an 'Austrian watering place' in the summer of 1891 (*Letters of Sidney and Beatrice Webb*, edited by Norman McKenzie, Cambridge University Press, 1972, Volume 1, 1873–1892, p. 310). Parts of the letter are quoted below, p. 262.
99. Mary Paley Marshall, *What I Remember*, pp. 47–8.
100. Mary Paley Marshall, 'MSS Notes', NCA.
101. Alfred Marshall to E. Levasseur, 17 June 1908 (Arnold Heertje Collection).
102. Mary Paley Marshall, *What I Remember*, p. 48, and see illustrations 19–22.
103. *Ibid.*, pp. 49–50.
104. Mary Paley Marshall, *What I Remember*, p.48, and see illustration 18. This is discussed in more detail below, Chapter 13, pp. 476–7.
105. *P* I, p. 329 n.1; *P* VIII, p. 268 n.1 (unchanged between editions).
106. Marshall, *P* VIII, p. 182 n.1, the personal element that this was recalled from a trip in circa 1880 was not inserted until the seventh edition. Marshall's recollection in 1916 that he made the trip around 1880 is quite wrong; more likely it was made during the early 1870s when he was a frequent visitor to the Bavarian Alps.
107. *IT*, p. 808 n.1.
108. Mary Paley Marshall to J.M. Keynes, 31 July 1922 (KMF), and below, Chapter 19, pp. 715–9.

109. Mary Paley Marshall, 'MSS Notes' (NCA), [1942] Lecture to Marshall Society, p. 17; *What I Remember*, p. 50. The importance of the principle of continuity to the writing of the *Principles* is discussed below, Chapter 12, pp. 411–12.

8. The Husband (1877–1924) in an Unusual Partnership

On 17 August 1877, at the Parish Church of Ufford, County of Northampton, Alfred Marshall, who described himself on the marriage certificate as bachelor of full age, Principal of University College Bristol, residing at St John's College, Cambridge, married Mary Paley, spinster of Ufford, according to the rites and ceremonies of the established Church of England. The minister officiating was the father of the bride, the Rev. Thomas Paley; her mother, Ann Judith Paley, née Wormald, gave the bride away and acted as witness. Other witnesses included the parents of the bridegroom, William and Rebecca Marshall as well as the bride's brother, George Thomas and her married sister, Ann Elizabeth Brown. With the addition of the bridegroom's two sisters, Agnes and Mabel Louisa, these were all the nuptial guests.[1] The Marshalls contracted themselves out of the 'obedience clause' in the marriage ceremony, after the bride's father had refused to remove this from the order of service when requested to do so by his daughter and son-in-law to be. Marshall had commented favourably on the elimination of this promise from the American Unitarian marriage service in a letter to his mother from the United States. This part of the arrangements, though unusual for Victorian times, is explicable in terms of the young couple's preferences.[2] Little else is known of the marriage ceremony, except that the bride wore white, had no veil and wore only jasmine in her hair, going away 'in a cambric dress and old brown hat so as not to look like a bride'.[3] Their honeymoon was largely spent in Cornwall.[4]

Bride and groom were heavily involved in the moral sciences. Both in fact were teaching political economy at Cambridge in the year of their marriage: she at Newnham College, he at St John's. Both continued this commitment to economics teaching until retirement and jointly wrote a text on the subject. Despite these common interests, the marriage, as Keynes put it, 'was not a partnership of the Webb kind, as it might have become if the temperaments of both sides had been entirely different. . . . Yet it was an intellectual partnership just the same, based on profound dependence on the one side (he could not live a day without her) and, on the other, deep devotion and admiration, which was increased and not impaired by extreme discernment'.[*] More generally, the Marshalls partnership was praised by friends and acquaintances for its happiness and bliss. Jowett, who met them in Bristol not long after their marriage, wrote to Mary Paley Marshall eleven years later: 'I sometimes think

---

[*] John Maynard Keynes, 'Mary Paley Marshall', p. 241. Bertrand Russell, the philosopher and long-time friend of the Webbs, concisely described the nature of their partnership as follows: 'I knew Sidney [Webb] before his marriage to Beatrice Potter. But he was then much less than half of what the two of them afterwards became. Their collaboration was quite dove-tailed. . . . Their books are a tribute to their industry. . . . I do not think that Sidney's abilities would have been nearly as fruitful as they were if they had not been backed by Beatrice's self confidence' cited in Janet Beveridge, *An Epic of Clare Market*, London: G. Bell & Sons, 1960, p. 71.

that you are two of the happiest people I have ever known. In the first place you have in economics a most delightful pursuit (2) a charming society (3) a perfectly simple way of life', an observation based on close acquaintance over four terms in Oxford, and as their frequent house guest both in Bristol and Cambridge.[5] A similar impression is obtained from the reminiscences of nephew Claude Guillebaud and his wife twenty years later,[6] from student C.R. Fay[7] and several other intimates of Mary Paley Marshall after her husband's death.[8]

However, this portrait of 47 years' marital bliss can be overdrawn. The picture of Mary Paley's 'absolute devotion to her husband before and after his death', presented in so much of the written recollection and what has been called the oral tradition on the subject,[9] needs to be juxtaposed by other evidence. Mary Paley Marshall, the record shows, was a woman invariably ahead of her time, extraordinarily kind-hearted but devoid of any sentimentality. She was a working wife when this was still extremely rare in the middle classes,* and although trained in economics in the Moral Sciences Tripos in which her husband himself had taught, their intellectual cooperation was rather one-sided. This even applies to the book, *The Economics of Industry*, which had their names as joint author on its title page. The Marshalls' marriage in fact exhibited substantial tensions, going well beyond those ordinarily experienced in such unions. Some can be identified in their early married life in Bristol, and later from that shared in Cambridge. These were often, but not invariably, associated with Mary Paley's strong and progressive views on women's rights. However, such tensions were invariably sublimated through her enduring loyalty to the man she married, and who, in his own way, was devoted to her. To set the stage for this chapter, designed to portray Alfred Marshall in his role as husband, some recollections, one from not long before his death and some from well after it, indicate the difficulty in weighing up the conflicting evidence on this aspect of Alfred Marshall's life.

The first recollection, via H.M. Robertson,[10] comes from medieval economic historian, Dr Maud Sellers, a life-long acquaintance of Mary Paley Marshall going back to her Newnham College days of the early 1870s, and an occasional visitor to Balliol Croft.

> She looked on Mary Marshall as woman put upon, and she had little affection for Alfred. Indeed, from her reminiscences to me, I seem to recall one instance in which Mrs. Marshall's sense of humour may have worn a little thin. After a lunch at Balliol Croft, during a fine summer, someone remarked to Miss Sellers on the beauty of the weather and said it would be lovely to bask all afternoon in the sun. Maud Sellers replied with her customary forthrightness (and no doubt in righteous recollection of working hard throughout the heat of the day, teaching in a school in sub-tropical Queensland in another of her ventures into uncharted territory for those brought up as sheltered young Victorian women, and no doubt clad in all the layers of mid-Victorian costume which she still habitually wore in the 1920's) that in her view only very lazy people basked their time away in the sun. But just as she did so, Mary Marshall was there, waiting for them to finish their conversation in order to shoo them away, in order that Alfred could be undisturbed to bask in the garden in the sun, and she showed her annoyance. Maud Sellers, I might add, was unrepentant; she thought Marshall pampered himself and she believed that he was lazy.

---

*   '[T]he number of married women in the middle classes who combined a career with the responsibilities of family life was small. Although work *before* marriage had become respectable by the 1880s and 1890s the dichotomy between work *and* marriage persisted at least until the First World War', J.A. and Olive Banks, *Feminism and Family Planning in Victorian England*, New York: Schocken Books, 1964, p. 50.

The second recollection, of Selig Perlman, is recounted by his son.[11] When Selig Perlman was in Cardiff during 1938–39 on an exchange professorship, he was invited by Keynes to give some lectures at Cambridge, financed from funds associated with Marshall's bequest to its Faculty of Economics and Politics. Selig Perlman accepted Keynes's invitation 'with alacrity' and,

> some time in March or April 1939 he went off to Cambridge and gave the talks. Keynes then told him that he had been invited by Mary Paley Marshall for tea. My father, having deep doubts about his ability to carry on a long one-on-one conversation with Mrs. Marshall, answered Keynes by saying that he doubted that anything he had to say would interest Mrs. Marshall for as much as an hour or 90 minutes. Keynes then told him not to worry, and that he would be lucky to get so much as a word in edgewise; all he had to do was to listen to Mary Marshall (who needed audiences). So he went. He reported that the tea was on the Spartan side, and that Mrs. Marshall did all of the talking (as he had expected), but that all of the talk was about what a jealous and selfish intellectual wretch Alfred had been.

More concisely, Sir Austin Robinson in his review of Mary Paley's *What I Remember*, described the married period as the second stage of her long life. This was the time 'she was enslaved to forty years of self denying servitude to Alfred, the "fool-ometer" by which he measured the popular intelligibility of his writing, the organiser of his materials, the breakwater between himself and the irritations of life . . . why did Alfred make a slave of this great woman and not a colleague?'. The answer is not given in the pages of her recollections, since *What I Remember* is virtually silent on their married life, especially that in Cambridge from 1885.[12] Clearly, there is much to learn about Alfred Marshall in the role of husband.

THE BRIDE: MARY PALEY (1850–1944)

Like her husband, Mary Paley was a product of an evangelical household. Her clergyman father was a 'strict Evangelical, so strict that there were few if any of the neighbouring clergy with whom he could be intimate' but the last arose more from his strong opposition to gambling on horse races than theological dogmatism.[13] The household in most other respects was very liberal, quite different from that, on the available evidence, in which Alfred Marshall was brought up. Mary Paley later recalled only two signs of illiberality with respect to her own nurture. She was forbidden to read Dickens, and her father ceremonially burnt her dolls, and those of her elder sister, because 'they were making them into idols'. However, she enjoyed plenty of recreation: 'Rounders and archery and croquet' on the rectory lawns in summer, trips to London including an excursion to the 1862 Exhibition, as well as holidays at Hunstanton and Scarborough. 'We had a father who took part in work and play and who was interested in electricity and photography, and a mother who was full of initiative and always bright and amusing.'

Mary Paley's direct ancestry was also more exalted than that of her husband. Her mother, Ann Judith Wormald, was the eldest daughter of Mr Smith Wormald of Barton Hall, Barton-on-Humber, undoubtedly a line of good yeoman stock. Her father, a 27th wrangler in 1833, was elected Fellow at St John's College in 1835. After taking Holy Orders, he held the curacy at Dishford near Ripon, before being presented by his college with the Rectory of

Ufford cum Bainton in Northamptonshire in 1847. This living enabled his marriage to take place in the same year. Ufford was also the place where Mary Paley was born as the second daughter, where she spent the first twenty years of her life, where she was married to Alfred Marshall and where the Marshalls spent the summer vacation the year after they were married.

Thomas Paley came from a distinguished line of professional men and scholars. Mary Paley's grandfather had been a physician at Halifax. Her great-grandfather, William Paley, had been Fellow and tutor at Christ College, Cambridge. More importantly, he was the noted author of the *Principles of Moral and Political Philosophy* which had anticipated some of Bentham's utilitarianism and whose 'evidences', that is, *Natural Theology, or Evidence of the Existence and Attributes of the Deity collected from the Appearances of Nature,* was a compulsory part of the Previous Examination taken by all Cambridge undergraduates. Her great-grandfather had likewise taken a Cambridge degree, subsequently rising to the position of headmaster of Giggleswick Grammar School, a post he enjoyed for fifty-four years. Great-grandfather Paley provided one of the few of her ancestral credentials Alfred Marshall could match: his great-grandfather John had taken an Oxford degree and had been headmaster of Exeter Grammar School for many years.

This background explains why the Rev. Thomas Paley believed in the benefits of a good education and, unusual for the time, applied this principle to the education of his two daughters. On Mary Paley's recollections, that education was initially given at home until she was about thirteen years old. Her father taught her Latin, some Euclid and even a little Hebrew. A governess taught German and French from age nine, as well as subjects like history, geography and piano. Some of this education was rather sketchy but 'we were taught French and German pretty thoroughly and the family talked German at meals'. No wonder she became the linguist in the household at Balliol Croft. At thirteen, three years education 'of sorts' followed at a 'select school for young ladies' in a nearby town. Mary and her sister were taught 'Mangnall's Questions', 'the use of the Globes' and deportment. With this introduction to learning, her education temporarily finished.

When her sister married in 1868, Mary Paley from boredom decided to follow her example. She became engaged to an army officer in the Engineers, just before he was sent for a three-year tour of duty in India. 'During his absence, as the Cambridge Higher Local Examinations for women over eighteen came into operation in 1869, I, for want of something to do, spent my time in preparing for it.' This, as it turned out, was a momentous decision which changed her life in more ways than one. She worked with her father at divinity and mathematics, picked up her French and German with her former governess, and in 1870 and 1871 took the examination. Although she was 'floored' by a paper on conic sections, she scored distinctions in German and divinity, results good enough for the award of a scholarship for Cambridge to attend the lectures for women which had recently started there. Given these new interests, her engagement to the officer was soon broken off, a step made easier because her father had never approved of it. Her father was, however, sufficiently 'proud and pleased' with her examination result to take the radical step of letting her start at Cambridge in October 1871. Mary Paley thereby became one of the first five women students to form the nucleus student body from which Newnham College evolved.

It was this step which brought her into contact with Alfred Marshall since he was among the few college lecturers and professors then willing to give these early lectures to women.

When Mary Paley entered Cambridge in 1871, her intention was not to read for a Tripos and attempt the honours examination. Obtaining a good general education was all she wanted at this stage. With her father's advice she chose Latin, history, literature and logic, the last because her father considered it to be 'such a *safe* subject'. He placed her under the spiritual guardianship of Professor Birks, a clergyman of strong evangelical views, who had succeeded F.D. Maurice in the Knightbridge Chair of Moral Philosophy. Initially, Mary went to his church and to his 'at homes', and even taught at his Sunday School. However, Mill's *Logic*, Seeley's *Ecce Homo* and reading Herbert Spencer, combined with the general atmosphere of the place, 'gradually undermined her beliefs' and the former spiritual 'harmony' between daughter and father 'melted away'. Even more scandalously, given Morley's review in the *Fortnightly*, she and her student friends read Swinburne together.

One of her fellow students, Mary Kennedy, persuaded her to try a new subject, political economy. She reluctantly went to a lecture, but 'went to stay', for the sake of both its subject matter and its teacher, Alfred Marshall. Marshall in fact, subsequently encouraged her to take the Moral Sciences Tripos. After three years of logic, political economy, mental, moral and political philosophy, its required subjects, she did so. Her results were excellent but ambiguously recorded. In December 1874, the year that James Ward, the psychologist, was Senior Moralist, Mary Paley became the victim of a system which used four examiners but no chairman with a casting vote. She ended up with two votes for the second class and two for the first, given respectively by her four examiners, Pearson, Gardiner, Foxwell and Jevons. Her result, omitted from the official historical register of the University of Cambridge which did not start to record women's Tripos results until 1881[*] was commemorated in a humorous verse by Dr Kennedy, a classical scholar, in whose house the examinations had been taken by the women:

> Though two with glory would be cramming her
> And two with fainter praise be d—— her
> Her mental and her moral stamina
> Were certified by each examiner.
> Were they at sixes or at sevens
> Oh! Foxwell, Gardiner, Pearson, Jevons. [14]

Despite the ambiguity of her 'result', the high quality of her examination performance was sufficient for her appointment as Resident Lecturer in the Moral Sciences to the women associated with what later became Newnham College.[15]

---

[*]   *The Historical Register of the University of Cambridge, being a supplement to the Calendar*, pp. 710–12;   Mary Paley Marshall, *What I Remember*, pp. 16–17. This was Jevons's first experience with Marshall's use of curves for explaining problems in political economy (above, Chapter 6, pp. 160–1). Jevons, together with Foxwell and Pearson, set the three papers in political economy taken by Mary Paley. These are reproduced in R.C.D. Black (ed.), *Papers and Correspondence of William Stanley Jevons*, Vol. VII, pp. 132–5; see also Jevons to Foxwell, 5 June 1874 and 4 October 1874, in *Papers and Correspondence*, Volume IV, pp. 52–3, 69–70. Mary Marshall was eventually awarded 'her degree' by special dispensation in 1928. See Ethel Sidgwick, *Mrs. Sidgwick, A Memoir*, p. 244 n.1.

Despite their dissimilar backgrounds as to ancestry, Alfred Marshall and his future wife had much in common in their own experience. First was a strict evangelical upbringing which Cambridge transformed into gradual unbelief and indifference to theology, if not to religion. In addition, both had gone to Cambridge under difficult personal circumstances and each, by hard work and perseverance, had won substantial academic laurels. They shared an interest in their studies of the moral sciences, especially their specialisation in political economy. Marshall's economic studies at this stage were considerably more advanced, which is not surprising since he had been her teacher. Likewise, their seeming equality from 1875 in both being college lecturers in political economy at Cambridge was more apparent than real in important respects. Mary mainly taught women who were bent on pursuing that broad cultural education she had originally intended for herself and she may have had some Tripos students as well. Alfred Marshall excelled at instilling advanced political economy into the heads of a small and select number of honours students attempting the Tripos.   Moreover, Alfred Marshall's lectureship was underwritten by a fellowship at Cambridge's second largest college, and dedicated to teaching students who could take out their degree. This position was in sharp contrast with that of his wife. Her Cambridge academic status was officially non-existent, being a lecturer at an unrecognised college to teach students unable to take their degrees after successfully completing examinations.

COURTSHIP AND ENGAGEMENT (1872–1876)

It is tempting to say that Alfred Marshall and Mary Paley first met by accident in 1871 in the Grove Lodge Coach House classroom. The real circumstances of their first meeting were less poetic but more romantic: 'the evenings when we sat round and sewed the household linen in Miss Clough's sitting room [for reasons of economy], provided my first sight of Mr. Marshall, I then thought I had never seen such an attractive face with its delicate outline and brilliant eyes. We sat very silent and rather awed as we listened to them talking' Only afterwards did Mary see her future husband in his chosen milieu of the classroom. 'I remember that first lecture in political economy well. . . . Mr. Marshall stood by the blackboard, rather nervous, bending a quill pen which took flight between his fingers, very earnest and with shining eyes.' A year later Marshall encouraged Mary Paley and her friend Mary Kennedy to enter for the Moral Sciences Tripos. Was this the first sign of romance between the young woman student (who was then in her early twenties) and the political economy don (eight years her senior)?[16] Whether it was love at first sight as Keynes surmised[17] is difficult to say conclusively, but Mary Paley's own account of their 'courtship' showed that she took initiatives in this, as she had done in her own education. Her later reminiscences record that not only did she ask him to dance 'the Lancers', 'a round dance of complicated concentric movements'[18] with which the young don was most unfamiliar, she also attended many social evenings in his bachelor rooms at John's, which he arranged for obviously more than altruistic reasons.

Mrs. Bateson, wife of the Master of St John's, gave dances from eight to ten in the Hall of the Lodge. She would watch the dancing surrounded by her four girls in white muslin and blue sashes (one of them, Mary, became later on a distinguished historian). There were undergraduates, who we rather looked down on as 'boys' and a few dons. Once, seeing that Mr. Marshall seemed rather melancholy, I asked him to dance the Lancers. He looked surprised and said he didn't know how, but he consented and I guided him through its mazes, though being shocked at my own boldness I did not speak a word, and I don't think he did either. Sometimes our lecturers invited us to Sunday evening parties in their rooms, for five was quite a manageable number. When Mr. Marshall asked us, Miss Clough took us first to the service in St John's Chapel and then we climbed up to his rooms – the highest in the New Court. On the first of these Sunday evenings, Mary Kennedy told Mr. Marshall that he must not expect us to have our hair tidy as he had not provided a 'back glass'. He did not know what this was, but made inquiries and bought a very good one which I still use. We had tea and were offered crumpets and muffins which we consumed though with some misgivings on being told by our host that the first was 'slow poison' and the second 'sudden death'. A few suitable dons had been invited and after tea we looked at photographs which helped conversation. . . . The evening finished with a frugal supper of sandwiches and oranges.[19]

Together with fellow Johnian Hudson, Marshall had quite a few social gatherings for the women students in their college rooms on Sunday evenings. For example, when 'a Professor from Western America came with his wife to Cambridge, . . . Mr. Marshall invited us to meet them. The lady was a lawyer and told us about her practice.'[20] The moral and practical support Alfred Marshall gave her in December 1874 while she was attempting the Tripos examinations, undoubtedly further cemented a growing friendship. Courtship was interrupted by Mary Paley's departure for home in early 1875. This enabled not only a well-deserved break after the Tripos ordeal. It was also sufficiently prolonged to permit her to give a short course of elementary lectures at nearby Stamford, organised on her own initiative.[21] The last had two important results. Mary Paley herself assumed that the teaching experience she gained induced Henry Sidgwick's invitation to her to take over Alfred Marshall's lectures on political economy to women at Cambridge. Her Stamford initiative may also have encouraged Professor Stuart to ask her that same year to write a primer on political economy, the book that four years later grew into their joint publication of *The Economics of Industry*.[22] Her absence from Cambridge for early 1875 combined with Alfred Marshall's absence in the United States during the summer may have delayed things somewhat, but not for long. The start of the new academic year in autumn 1875 allowed the courtship of Mary Paley and Alfred Marshall to resume.

Alfred Marshall proposed marriage in May 1876, and they became engaged. Jane Harrison, another early Newnham student and a close friend of Mary Paley, attributed the engagement to the fact that she had stitched 'clean white ruffles' on to Mary Paley's dress that day. Harrison's biographer also explains how Marshall and Mary Paley 'achieved any real contact in that over-chaperoned academic world' by stressing it was a marriage made at Newnham, in fact 'the first Newnham romance', despite the discouragement such events received from Newnham's founders to avoid notoriety for the new college. She records Marshall as a regular attender 'at Miss Clough's large tea parties' and at the Sunday evening entertainments, 'very innocent and provincial affairs' of light refreshment and music held later in Newnham Hall. 'Clough's regimen allowed for some carefully supervised mingling with the men'.*

---

* Mary Paley Marshall, *What I Remember*, p. 22, Mary Paley's notes on Jane Harrison (NCA). Jane Harrison called Marshall 'the camel' because 'she trembled at the sight of him, as a horse does at a camel' when, against his

Their professional association as political economy teachers would also have assisted courtship. Given that John Neville Keynes did not record 'Marshall of John's is engaged to Miss Paley' until 13 July 1876, an official announcement of the engagement was probably delayed. Keynes's diary subsequently recorded social events outside Newnham at which the engaged couple were present, such as the boat races during the following May.[23]   The engagement was followed by a family trip to Switzerland in August organised by the Rev. Thomas Paley.   As recounted earlier, this led to Marshall's decision to give up mountaineering as his first sacrifice for his fiancée.[24] It was not the only one. Statutes then in force at Cambridge meant that, on marriage, Alfred Marshall had to resign his college fellowship and the lectureship at John's. Another source of income needed to be found before the couple could marry. After considering new careers in school teaching, and even the minor post of Esquire Bedell at Cambridge, Alfred Marshall applied for the position of Principal at Bristol University College, which had been advertised at £700, but only after his customary weighing up the balance of advantage had been completed. Although competition was strong, he was appointed to the post by the Council of the College on 26 July 1877.[25] Three weeks later they were married.*

EARLY MARRIED LIFE (1877–1881)

It is difficult to indicate with what expectations the young couple started their married life. Their wedding in the middle of August appears to have been preceded by house hunting in Bristol which, after some search, secured them a house in Apsley Road 'which suited them'.[26] Marshall's duties as Principal to Bristol University College virtually started from his date of appointment, 26 July 1877. He attended his first executive committee of the University's Council on 30 July 1877 just over a fortnight before the wedding. Whether he attended his second Executive Committee meeting on 18 August 1877, the day *after* their wedding, is uncertain. Its minutes mention that he pointed out necessary amendments to the University College's calendar which were accepted, and that he then learnt that looking after university appointments were an important part of his duties as Principal.   The next committee meeting did not take place until 24 September.[27]

Some unpublished notes by Mary Paley cover the honeymoon period in more detail. 'We went first to the Clifton Down Hotel as we wanted to see after the house which we had bought at my expense in Apsley Road and where certain improvements were being made, the most important being the laying down of the yard at the back in asphalt for a tennis court'. Apart from enabling them to supervise house renovations, the proximity of their

---

advice she had studied classics rather than moral science. Jane Harrison visited Sicily for her classical studies while the Marshalls were there in 1881–82, and it is interesting to speculate how she and Alfred Marshall got on at this time. No account of her stay in Palermo is preserved in June Harrison's papers at Newnham. On Marshall's courtship, see Victoria Glendenning, *A Suppressed Cry*, London: Routledge & Kegan Paul, 1969, p. 62; Sandra J. Peacock, *Jane Ellen Harrison*, New Haven: Yale University Press, 1988, p. 46. This is partly based on notes for an earlier biography by Annabel Robinson (NCA), pp. 30–32, which refer to the Marshall courtship.

* Mary Paley Marshall, *What I Remember*, p. 23, gives the wedding date as July, an error she repeated in her verbal recollections of the Bristol period recorded by M.T. Pease in 1943 (BUL, Special Collections, MSS Coll. DM 219). Foxwell wrote to J.N. Keynes, 11 August 1877, 'Marshall is to be married on Friday. He has just come up for a few days en route to Ufford where the event is to come off '(Marshall Archive, John Neville Keynes Letters, 1:16).

honeymoon hotel would have enabled Marshall's attendance at the College Council meeting as well. 'Then we went for two nights at Falmouth. After that we spent a fortnight at the Lizard and the [sic] Lands End. I preferred the Lizard because of the beautiful colouring Alfred preferred the Lands End and its fine forms. I always preferred colour and Alfred the form throughout our lives. We spent two nights in a wooden house in Kynance Cove and we then, (as always until A[lfred] had a [kidney] stone) took very long walks. When we returned to Bristol after our holiday, we spent our first Sunday in a walk to Dundry and all along its ridge. We got to Clifton in good time to settle in before Term began.'[28] However, the break was not completely devoted to leisure. A substantial part of it was spent recasting the first part of the *Economics of Industry*, on the writing of which Alfred Marshall had begun active cooperation not long after their engagement.[29]

The semi-detached house into which they moved in Bristol was part of a relatively new housing estate in fashionable Clifton, 'a prestigious residential district of Bristol' not far from the public school where Marshall had taught mathematics for some time in 1865. The house cost £1,200, capital which Mary Paley had brought to the new household, perhaps part of her share 'in the large profits as author' made by her famous great-grandfather. The house was large, because given his position as Principal, the Marshalls were expected to entertain. They therefore kept two servants – a farmer's daughter whom they paid £20 a year and a labourer's daughter whom they paid £12. During dinner parties, which invariably accompanied the regular University Council meeting held approximately five or six times per annum, they added to this relatively small staff by hiring the services of the nearby greengrocer to wait at table. Although still very small by the contemporary standards in servant numbers considered appropriate to their status, the Marshalls never kept such a large establishment again. After 1881, they made do with the one live-in-maid, the faithful Sarah Payne, who had in fact come to them in Bristol shortly after their marriage. Being one of thirteen children of a Somerset labourer, it was Sarah who initially assisted the first maid. She served them at Oxford and Cambridge until her death in 1920 and, despite the many dinner parties the Marshalls had at Balliol Croft, she managed quite well on her own.[30]

Although Mary Paley provided the finance to buy their first house, an investment they subsequently rolled over to purchase their house at Oxford and to build Balliol Croft at Cambridge, it seems to have been Alfred Marshall who bought and arranged the furnishings. Mary Paley recalled his shrewd eye for a bargain in this department, noting his college rooms at John's had been furnished from second-hand, 'beautiful things' purchased at Jolleys, at Cambridge. Such experience was clearly of use when they went to Bristol.[31] This is supported by one of Marshall's many letters to Foxwell at the time[32] in which he discussed their new piano. Marshall informed his friend that the 'case' did not matter, 'provided it is not a bright coloured wood. A dark rosewood would do as well as anything'.

Taste for such sombre colourings marked their subsequent furnishing arrangements, perhaps a source of irritation for Mary Paley who preferred the brighter colours of the Lizard and the gaily painted carts of Palermo she later described. Whether Marshall's sacrifice of colour for form caused an early marital rift is not recorded. A wedding present from friends at St John's appeared some months later, landscapes by Walton, more to the liking of the lady of the house, even though they may have had that sombre aspect which made him a popular artist in the mid-Victorian period.[33]   An acquaintance from those Bristol days later recalled the inside of the house 'with its books and pictures, and a charm and beauty of its own within . . . . which I should call aesthetic'.[34]   A different perspective on the Marshalls' taste in furnishing comes from the Ramsays, who rented the Marshalls' Clifton residence fully furnished for the twelve months they were away in Europe in 1881–82. The young Mrs Ramsay confessed to her mother she was quite pleased to leave the Marshalls' furniture when she heard in May 1882 they were returning to Bristol. When settled into their new house at the end of that year, William Ramsay wrote to his mother, 'the dining room is real modern and cosy, and has a home like feeling the Marshalls' never had'.[35]   However, it seems that the Marshalls also found it difficult to make the house perfectly suitable for their needs. The renovations arranged when they bought it in mid-1877, proved insufficient. Twelve months later, on their return in September 1878 from 'six days real holidays . . . at Lynton', Mary Paley reported to Foxwell that their 'house [was] still full of workmen. We have no sitting room but the boot room'. It did not matter much to her. Alfred would be away all day long at the college registering students and making other preparations for the coming academic year.[36]

On Mary Paley's account, their first twelve months at Bristol, which coincided with their first year of marriage, appear generally to have been happy. Marshall's health, which was to deteriorate sharply from the spring of 1879, was then still good. His work at the college was challenging and left sufficient time for socialising and even for writing on their joint book. Alfred Marshall renewed old friendships from his days at Clifton College with the Dakyns and the Percivals and they gained others from among the University Council membership and from the citizenry of Bristol. There were long walks and there was lawn tennis in the backyard. There were dinner parties and home entertainments for their students. There were musical evenings at Clifton College and the occasional houseguests. Of that year before she herself resumed her economics teaching, Mary Paley later recalled,

> We were invited out a good deal and I had much calling to do, being told that the folks at Clifton required a call at least once a term. But besides calling acquaintance we found many real friends. Among them were the Dean and Miss Elliott his daughter, the Percivals (and later the Wilsons), the Dakyns, Miss Alleyne, the Frys, the Peases, F.F. Tuckett, the mountaineer of the Dolomites, and Dr. Beddoe [their family doctor]. Some of these still remain and as true friends as ever. I was therefore pretty busy socially the first year.[37]

To Mrs Pease, Mary Paley recalled 'the delightful dinner parties which they gave when the University Council met. – Jowett, Hereford George and other Oxford Dons [such as Henry Smith, Savillian Professor of Mathematics] making witty conversation – How she used to sit and listen to their talk after dinner.'[38] This quiet and retiring behaviour in the company of what essentially were her husband's dinner guests was a feature of her after-dinner behaviour on such occasions which stayed with her all her life. It was not necessarily due to shyness. That she was initially shy in these early years at Bristol when in the company of her husband's guests is clear from William Ramsay's account of the Marshalls on their first meeting in early 1880. More generally, it gives a most unflattering account of the appearance of the Principal and his young wife. Ramsay's impressions of a student entertainment the Marshalls organised later in that year is equally unflattering. However, Mary Paley's undoubted charm grew on him on further acquaintance, and Ramsay later became 'much attached to both of them'.[39] Ramsay's successive descriptions show the changes in his reaction to the Marshalls. A letter to his mother in February 1880, after he first met the Marshalls at dinner at their house following his interview and appointment as Professor of Chemistry, described Marshall as, 'an ascetic man, all mind and no body. He hesitates in his speech, and weighs things very carefully. I think he will require management, and I think I can manage him. He can be led, if taken in the right way.' The same letter describes Mary Paley Marshall as 'a *cure* [that is, an odd or eccentric person]. Imagine a female rat, without ears and with lots of hair forming a drooping chignon behind; the rodent teeth very prominent; a habit of hugging one knee and swinging on her chair; embued with dead silence – such is the Lady-Lecturer in Political Economy. This is of course a first impression, we shall see how it remains.'[40]

Greater familiarity with the Marshalls brought a change. A week later Ramsay reported, 'I dined with Marshall again last night. Mrs. M. improved a little, and really opened out on lawn-tennis.' Ramsay obviously shared her enthusiasm for this sport since on two occasions in May he informed his parents of tennis games in the Marshalls' back-garden court. In June he drew likenesses of the couple, explaining 'I can't say it is particularly like her but it is somewhat her features. Observe her tooth in front. On the whole it is better looking than she is. Let me try Marshall. No, there is a jovial look about them which Marshall doesn't possess. I can't represent his thoughtful eye, which is really a very good one. Poor fellow. He is really very unwell. He has calcium in the kidney – quite incurable. But he says it doesn't pain him – unless he treats it unfairly – unless he walks a couple of miles.'[41]

However, Ramsay occasionally found deficiencies in the Marshalls' social graces. In November, he wrote to his father: 'At Marshall's; a lot of chemical students were there. Marshall was hopelessly embarrassed and looked at Mrs. Marshall, who was resigned. I tried to open fire, and with the help of one of our men managed to keep things going, but it was slow, slow.'[42] The cause of this social fiasco is not revealed, and it is interesting to speculate whether this was normal gaucherie on the Marshalls' part, or whether it had more immediate and less enduring causes. Keynes[43] much later recalled that on social occasions he had attended at Balliol Croft, Marshall called 'out staff directions to his wife, in unembarrassed, half embarrassed mood, with laughing high-pitched voice and habitual jokes and phrases'.

By this stage, that is calender 1880, the first year in Bristol which Mary Paley later recalled as such a pleasurable, social whirl, was well and truly over. As Ramsay mentioned in the context of his sketches of the Marshalls, joviality was a quality lacking in Marshall's countenance in 1880, a defect Ramsay implicitly attributed to the stones in the kidney which had been diagnosed during the spring of 1879. The effect this diagnosis had on their lives is clearly described by Mary Paley, though her published account diplomatically omits any reference to the inevitable bad temper and irritability which accompanied Alfred Marshall's forced abstinence from smoking, exercise, and even after dinner conversation for some time, as he confided in a letter to Foxwell.* Subject to this, and some other corrections, her account of this important Bristol storm cloud is worth quoting,

---

* Alfred Marshall to Foxwell, 10 March 1884 (Freeman Collection, 12/73). 'the next time you are coming over . . . let us know. We want much to see you: only we shall make no stranger of you; and when a meal is over, I shall

Alfred seemed fairly well until the spring of 1879. We spent that Easter vacation at Dartmouth and one morning we went to Paignton and walked by Berry Pomeroy Abbey to Tomes and then took the steamer back to Dartmouth, and as it was an intensely cold April I think he may have caught a chill. On getting home he consulted our good old friend Dr. Beddoe who discovered that there was a stone in the kidney and who said that there must be no more long walks, no more games at tennis, and that complete rest offered the only chance of cure by allowing the stone to become incysted (at the time of course an operation was not thought of). This advice came as a great shock to one who delighted so in active exercise, but he followed the doctor's orders rigidly. He was not allowed to smoke so he took to sewing and mending and he would sometimes darn with fourfold wool so that the holes became thicker than their surroundings. Later on he learned to knit stockings and they were the best I have ever had, for the heels were done with smaller needles and with double wool in order to strengthen them and the legs were perfectly shaped. Knitting was a great solace until it was forbidden by Sir Andrew Clark who feared that it might cause some nerve trouble. Alfred was very anxious that I should not suffer from want of exercise. Tennis was still to go on in the backyard, in which J.M. Wilson, then Head Master of Clifton College, often joined, and Alfred would watch the games and was full of fun at tea afterwards. But though he was always cheerful and made the best of a bad job, as soon as he knew that he must be an invalid for a length of time, he determined to give up his post as Principal. A period of complete rest seemed to be the only cure.[*]

The effects of the kidney stone on Marshall's health were long lasting. He himself argued subsequently that they removed ten years from his life through the enforced leisure they caused, a self-diagnosis confirmed to a degree by Jowett. In responding in 1891 to Mary Paley's description of their extensive European travel that summer, Jowett remarked how 'surprising' and 'wonderful' her husband's prowess was in this respect, since '10 years ago, he could scarcely walk at all'.[44] It is possible that his digestive problems of which much was heard in later years, started around this time, to earn him a reputation for hypochondria perhaps not fully deserved.[45]

Ill health was, however, not the only problem to trouble the Marshalls during their period in Bristol. It was not even the first of the various difficulties the couple had to face during their married life. Their first year in Bristol was in fact ending badly. Alfred's mother, of whom he was extraordinarily fond, died suddenly in June 1878, not long after his younger brother Walter's death in South Africa from consumption. Apart from a single letter to Foxwell, no tangible evidence of Marshall's reaction to this bereavement has been preserved, while the circumstances of his mother's death make it likely he was unable to see his mother before she died.[46] On quite a different tack, his tasks at University College were not nearly as fulfilling as he may perhaps have thought when he first, rather proudly, described himself on his marriage certificate as Principal of University College, Bristol. The manifold administrative duties which went with the post, were far more time consuming and irksome than he was probably told at the time of his interview, or, as compared to the

---

leave you to talk to my wife, and go to my knitting for an hour or so' Mary Paley ('MSS Notes', NCA, p.9) described Marshall during these final years at Bristol as a person highly 'sensitive to pinpricks'.

[*] Mary Paley Marshall, *What I Remember*, p. 24. His deprivation of exercise from walking is both a sign of the seriousness of the illness and a potential cause of that nervous irritability which from then on was increasingly associated with his behaviour. Mary Paley ('MSS Notes', NCA) noted that exercise in their 1879 summer holiday spent at a farm in Mariscombe was taken by way of a 'pony trap'. As shown in Chapter 7, above pp. 204–8, travel in Italy over 1881–82 was by cart, tram, bath chair and gondola while this necessity probably accounts for Mary Paley's extensive recollections of the price details of 'cab' costs in the various places in Italy where they stayed.

picture he could have formed of them from his previous limited experience with such work. His first year in the post was virtually completed without any assistance from other staff, and therefore left him little time for his own work. That other work included writing the little book on political economy for the Extension movement with his wife, the demands of which on his scarce free time he came to increasingly resent. Moreover, his teaching duties at Bristol seemed far less attractive than he may have expected on the basis of the admittedly, quite different Cambridge scene, even when consciously modified to take account of the distinct Bristol circumstances. Marshall appears to have enjoyed his evening classes to mature students, but his day class of 1877–78, the only year in which he himself taught it, contained only one male student in a class of twelve.[47] Again, such a possibility should have been anticipated by him, since their decision to apply for the Bristol position in 1877, necessitated though it was by their marriage, was strongly influenced by the attractions for them of the college's progressive women education policy which from the outset meant accepting men and women students on an equal footing for its courses.[48]

Pressure of administrative responsibilities together with the composition of the day class produced an important change in the Marshalls' married arrangements. On 15 May 1878, at the request of Marshall in his capacity as Professor of Political Economy at Bristol, the College Council resolved 'that he be empowered to depute Mrs. Marshall to deliver the morning lectures in Political Economy for the session 1878–79', the post to be funded, also at Marshall's suggestion, from a reduction of Marshall's own salary as Professor to £100 per annum. This decision by the Council which enabled Mary to work full-time in a salaried position as a woman married to a well-paid, professional husband needs to be seen in the context of Victorian attitudes to working, married, middle-class women. Few married middle-class women combined a career with their family responsibilities even when one of the few employment opportunities available for such persons came along. Because convention clearly opposed it, Mary Paley's appointment as a Lecturer in Political Economy, as her position was subsequently described in the Bristol University College Calender, was therefore a highly unconventional step. It confirms both the adventurous and non-conforming streaks in her make-up, other examples of which have already been noted.[49]

Marshall clearly favoured his wife's resumption of her teaching career after one year's marriage and she continued the practice at the two other universities in which he subsequently taught in the manner circumstances permitted. Mary Marshall's immense popularity among the women students at Bristol is reflected in the growth of enrolments in her day class and in reminiscences of the early days of Bristol University College. In one of these, Mrs N.F. Pease recalled,

The advent of the Marshalls made the session of 1877–78 full of interest. Mrs. Marshall's graceful charm attracted everybody and to us she represented Newnham and the cause of the higher education of women. It is difficult for this generation to realise what that cause meant to us. There were then no degree or professional examinations open to women and no college which they could enter on the same terms as men except our own. . . . . In this struggle Mrs. Marshall had taken her part and we felt indeed honoured to have her amongst us. Very early on she started a women's debating society which was so lively that on at least one occasion the debate had to be adjourned. The subject was Irish Home Rule. There was a sort of colony of cultivated and attractive Irish families then resident at Clifton and I remember the almost tearful eloquence with which their daughters combated some of us who were admirers of Parnell.[50]

The Home Rule debate episode, and perhaps the activities of the women's debating society more generally, may not have gone over well with Bristol's conservative town community, whose financial donations were essential to the survival of the new college. Irrespective of any causal relationship between the two, such donations fell, in both absolute and relative terms during 1878–79, and in relative terms in 1879–80. By 1881, the college was in a parlous financial state. The press reports on Marshall's retirement as Principal excepted financial matters from the great success the college had enjoyed under his stewardship, while Marshall's resignation from the college in the university's official history was ascribed to 'indifferent health', 'too little time for thought and writing' and his intense dislike of 'constant begging'. Marshall never found this part of his duties easy because responses from Bristol citizens were so volatile and even responded, as he once wrote to Foxwell, to the vagaries of national politics.*

Mary Paley's resumption of a teaching career as university lecturer had other implications for the Marshall marriage. Contrary to experience depicted by an 1870s family study which showed that well over half of upper- and middle-class spinsters had their first child within a year of marriage, and that nearly ninety per cent did so within the first two years,[51] the Marshalls' union remained childless. A possible explanation is that Mary Paley's unusual desire to resume working as soon as circumstances permitted induced a conscious decision on the Marshalls' part not to have a family. There is plenty of demographic evidence that from the 1870s family planning increasingly became the rule for professional and other upper- and middle-class households, while the instruments of birth control were readily available during the late Victorian period and relatively cheap for those on middle-class incomes.[52] Whether Mary's desire to continue a career was the reason for the lack of offspring in the Marshall household, or whether there was another explanation, is taken up later. It is too important an issue for their marital relationship especially in their early years at Bristol, to be ignored.[53]

One other feature of early life in Bristol needs to be mentioned in the context of their marriage. Marshall's growing dislike of his university work at Bristol may have been partly transferred to a growing resentment of his marriage. The first is well documented in a number of letters to Foxwell in which he explored job possibilities in London and Cambridge. It was exacerbated from the spring of 1879 by the constraints his illness imposed on his leisure activities as well as the drudgery involved in completing their *Economics of Industry*. Getting married was easy to depict as the direct cause of Marshall's separation from his beloved Cambridge, and from his very attractive life as Fellow at John's. He wrote to Foxwell in 1884, 'I have a grim grievance against the old Statutes that made me resign my fellowship on marrying, but the College could not help that', a remark inspired by

---

*   The *Western Daily Press*, 31 September 1881; Basil Cottle and J.W. Sherborne, *The Life of a University*, Bristol: published for the university, J.W. Arrowsmith Ltd., 1959, p. 19.   Data on donations from University College Bristol, Income Expenditure 1876–1901, BUL, Special Collections. On 20 April 1880, Marshall wrote to Foxwell how pleased he was with the Liberal election victory which had removed the Tories under Disraeli from office. He added 'we dare not canvass for money, until the heat of the Tories anger at their defeat has cooled down' (Freeman Collection, 6/151). In 1899, Marshall wrote to Hewins how much he had 'loathed' the begging part of his Bristol work which he claimed had 'nearly killed' him (in A.W. Coats, 'Alfred Marshall and the Early Development of the London School of Economics', *AMCA*, IV, p. 135).

new statutes in 1882 which enabled married men to retain their fellowships.[54] If, in addition, his wife was not fulfilling the images he may have had of the proper role for the lady in the household, some of which were subsequently reflected in his eulogies to motherhood in the *Principles*,[55] his perception of the value of the married status may have greatly diminished, thereby putting their relationship under strain. Stays by their respective in-laws in their Bristol house may not have helped.* Repercussions on his work from his wife's eccentricities, may have caused further problems. In short, Bristol, which was so intimately connected with his marriage, was later recalled as a black spot career wise, health wise and in his personal family life, given the associations it had with deaths in his family, especially that of his mother. The Bristol experience cannot have been a good foundation on which to build a particularly happy married relationship. Marshall later described his going to Bristol as the type of 'error' which 'eat[s] into a man's life . . . the most grievous deed I have ever done'.[56]

SUBSEQUENT MARRIED EXPERIENCE: PALERMO, BRISTOL AND OXFORD

The year's break from Bristol in 1881–82 provided by the winter sojourn in Palermo, the slow journey north through Italy via Naples, Florence and Venice during the spring, and a summer spent in the Bavarian Alps and Bournemouth probably did much to improve their domestic relationships. This period was later recalled by Mary Paley Marshall as one of the happiest in her life. A similar opinion is easily attributed to Alfred Marshall. Gone were the anxieties and drudgery of Bristol College administration. He had sun, clean air and a chance to indirectly commune with nature in the shape of Palermo's surrounding mountains while composing the *magnum opus* he was at last able to begin. At the same time, Mary Paley enjoyed her watercolours and sketching, her marketing and sightseeing and, for part of the time, the companionship of Jane Harrison, a close friend from her student days. Their stay may have laid the foundations for the development of an agreed life style within the Marshall household. Both parties sustained each other when necessary but, by and large, generally engaged in separate activities and amusements. The attention from his wife Marshall's health required on their arrival was fully reciprocated when later he nursed her tenderly during her recovery from malaria fever. She caught this in the latter part of their stay during the treacherous wet and cold February weather Palermo experienced that year.¶

---

* The 1881 Census Report indicates that Mary's brother George was staying with them at the time it was taken; Mary Paley's unpublished Newnham notes indicate that while they were away for two months on summer holidays from Bristol, 'our house [was left] to be occupied by Alfred's relations'. Alfred's rapport with his father-in-law was also not very good. Writing to Foxwell in April 1885 to invite him over for breakfast, Marshall added the condition, 'if my Pa in Law is not going to be with us, (I shall know tomorrow by midday) I want to ask you to breakfast on Sunday, but if he is, I dare not' (Marshall to Foxwell, 21 April 1885. Freeman Collection, 68/6). It was noted earlier that Marshall rarely accompanied his wife on her visits to her parents at Bournemouth (above, Chapter 3, note 64) a dislike which may owe something to the fact that their summer holidays in 1878 were spent with the Paleys in Ufford, her father's parish, where they were married. The seriousness of the impact for their relationship from such fairly common 'in-law' problems can only be guessed at.

¶ Mary Paley Marshall, *What I Remember*, p. 29; Notes for Walter Scott; *Cosima Wagner's Dairies*, edited by Martin Gregor-Dellin and Dietrich Mack, New York: Harcourt Brace Jovanovich, 1980, Volume 2, pp. 803–16,

The initial tensions produced by events in Bristol were partly resolved and ameliorated in that year of rest, and the more appreciated because it enabled Marshall's constructive work on his *Principles* and allowed Mary to commence her engrossing, and within the household non-competitive, activity of painting, at which she grew quite proficient.[57]

Little is known of their life together during the final year in Bristol after their year away, except that they both resumed their economics teaching. However, without the administrative hassles, and the work on their little book replaced by work on his *Principles*, life in Bristol was undoubtedly much more bearable. Return to Bristol was made possible by a donation of £250 per annum from Balliol College, perhaps more correctly described as a gift from Benjamin Jowett. £200 of this was to be devoted to paying the stipend of the Professor of Political Economy, a post to which Marshall was re-appointed.[58] Although Bristol University College probably expected Marshall's resumption of professorial duties to have been more permanent, by early 1883 the Marshalls were visiting Cambridge to discuss possibilities of gaining employment there. John Neville Keynes recorded in his diary for 21 April 1883, 'Professor and Mrs. Marshall of Bristol called upon us in the afternoon; and in the evening we met them for dinner at St John's Lodge [with Dr Charles Taylor, who had succeeded Bateson as Master on his death in 1881]. I sat next to Mrs. Marshall and enjoyed my talk with her.' Marshall wrote to Foxwell after the visit, 'you were all so good and kind at Cambridge that we almost yielded to the temptation to go there', an indication that the stay at John's included talk of a fellowship or lectureship to enable Marshall's return to his *alma mater*.[*] Not long afterwards, however, the Marshalls decided to move to a new life at Oxford. The unexpected death from meningitis in March 1883 of Arnold Toynbee, who lectured on economics to Indian Civil Service students, left a vacancy at Balliol College, and Jowett persuaded the Marshalls to take up the challenge of economics teaching at Oxford.[59] Marshall's retrospective judgement on the stay in Bristol has already been recorded. Mary Paley later noted that 'much as we liked Bristol and all our friends there, *it was a relief to go*.'[60]

The Marshalls moved to Oxford in time to commence teaching at the start of the 1883–84 academic year. Their expectation of permanency in the new position was heightened by Jowett's suggestions that the lectureship was likely to be followed by a successful attempt at Bonamy Price's Drummond Chair when it became vacant. This meant that after selling their house at Clifton, they purchased a house with a small garden at 46 Woodstock Road, Oxford. Their income now was such that their living standard rose appreciably. The Marshalls' annual income of £400 came from the £200 a year Marshall's lectureship at Balliol eventually paid, £50 a year from Mary Paley's teaching together with £150 from their (essentially her) capital. Given the prevailing consol yield of three per cent, this capital may have amounted to as much as £5000. Sarah the maid, who had returned to their service in October 1882 when they came back to Bristol, went with them to Oxford, an

---

record details of the cold weather, storms and rain which Palermo was having in February 1882, because this bad weather gave a cold to her husband and a fever to son Siegfried.

[*]   JNKD, 21 April 1883. At the end of the previous month, Marshall had announced this visit to Foxwell. The fact they were staying with Taylor at the St John's Lodge, suggests that the visit was arranged to enable discussions of a college position for Marshall. Marshall to Foxwell, 30 March 1883, Marshall Library, 3:10; Marshall to Foxwell, undated (late April 1883?), Marshall Library, 3:13.

undoubted necessity when they gave dinner parties during term. They holidayed in the Channel Islands in the one summer of their Oxford year, 'leaving the house to be occupied by relations'. Whether they were hers or his, Mary Paley did not record when she penned this reminiscence.[61]

Their stay in Oxford was pleasurable, short though it turned out to be. The record shows them to have been generally happy in their new environment. There were some complaints in Marshall's letters to Foxwell about aspects of his work. The amount of reading on India which it required particularly irked because it distracted him from his major writing task.[62] More generally, he told Foxwell when their first academic year at Oxford was nearly over,

I like Oxford very much, but I have not yet got hold of many people who are willing to go through much for the sake of econ[omic] science. I am very much hampered by not being able to go to evening meetings . . . and talk to undergraduates and others with social freedom in other ways. This makes it very hard for me to get at the right men. I do what I can but I *never* go out to a meal or have people in to see, without suffering. Otherwise, I am perfectly happy.[63]

A month later, after Balliol had elected him to an unpaid fellowship, he wrote to Foxwell to thank him for his congratulations, and for those from James Ward and McAllister, a former friend from the Eranus Society,

Balliol has raised my salary as lecturer to £200; on the ground that my teaching is not confined to Indian students. The Fellowship has no salary attached to it. But it gives all the other rights of a full Fellowship; e.g. a seat among the governing body and thus it differs from an honorary fellowship. We do very well and are absolutely happy.[64]

To the last sentence Marshall added in parenthesis: 'My wife is just now more than happy; almost mad with joy. Since I wrote this Mary has come in from Somerville Hall. She said the students are going to have a torchlight procession of triumph. She is joining in it.' Mary's happiness, and her participation in a student march, came from the announcement of a favourable vote on a students' petition presented earlier that year. This requested 'that women might be allowed to sit for some of the ordinary honours examinations. To everybody's surprise, a statute permitting [this] was carried by 464 to 321', a reason for celebration to all those concerned with achieving the rights of women to a full university education.[65]

Mary Paley therefore continued her active participation in women's issues and other social questions. Part of her account of these four, enjoyable terms in Oxford recalls this aspect, as well as some of the lighter entertainment facets of this period.

The Women's College had recently started and I had the great good fortune of getting to know Miss Wordsworth, the first Head of Lady Margaret Hall. She was wise and witty, her *bons mots* were proverbial and walks with her were a joy. Then Ruskin was at Oxford giving drawing lessons, lecturing to crowded audiences and inciting undergraduates to make roads. Toynbee Hall was being founded and the Barnetts often came to Balliol to stir up the young men to take an active part. The Charity Organisation Society had just started. Mr Phelps was Chairman and Mr Albert Dicey and Miss Eleanor Smith (accompanied by her dog) regularly attended its meetings. There was also a Society led by Mr. Sidney Ball for the Discussion of Social Questions, so the four terms of our life at Oxford were full of interest and excitement.[66]

Much of the social side of their Oxford period centred on their friendship with Benjamin Jowett, the Master of Balliol, a friendship begun during their years in Bristol when Jowett stayed with them at Clifton after College Council meetings. However, Mary Paley also recalled many of the other distinguished Balliol Fellows whom they met and befriended at this time. These included Evelyn Abbott, Lewis Nettleship, Andrew Bradley, Strachan Davidson, Albert Dicey and Alfred Milner,[*] some of whom maintained a presence in the Marshalls' life. But Oxford life was made especially pleasant for them by Jowett, 'the Master', as they continued to call him in person and in correspondence up to his death in 1893. Jowett, Mary Paley fondly recalled,

> enjoyed bringing his friends together, and almost every week-end during term he asked people to stay at the Lodge who he thought would like to meet one another or would be likely to help one another. His plan was to have a rather large and carefully arranged party on the Saturday which Arthur Sidgwick used to call a 'Noah's Ark' dinner, for so many strange animals walked in in pairs. One amusing pair was Lady Rosebery, a large lady, and the small Prince of Siam. There were the Goschens, the Huxleys, the Mathew Arnolds, Robert Browning, "Damn theology" Rogers, an Australian Prime Minister, Sir Robert Morier, Cornelia Sorabji and the Albert Greys among many others. I remember Albert Gray lying on the bank in the College garden and saying 'Aren't we swells to be staying with the V.C.?' After dinner a few select undergraduates were asked in and we had music. On the Sunday there was just the house party at dinner before the concert in Balliol Hall, and these small and intimate parties were the pleasantest. One of the most interesting conversations was with Sir Robert Morier as to 'the area within which one could lie'. And another was on the price of bread in which Mr. Mundella took an active part. There were breakfasts too at the Lodge. Mr. Asquith was at one of them and Alfred said that he had a mouth like a box, it shut so tight. The talk was chiefly on 'fads', starting with vegetarianism, going on to anti-vaccination on which Mr. Asquith had a good deal to say, especially about the people of Leicester who had been giving him trouble. Alfred suggested the Referendum as a method of dealing with "fads". The party reassembled at lunch when Mr. Asquith was very interesting in legal gossip and in his description of Parnell of whom as legal adviser he saw a great deal. He said Parnell did not seem to like Ireland, and never cared to go there. A.J. Balfour stayed there for one week-end during the Home Rule period, and as the talk was chiefly on that subject Jowett said later: 'Of course what has been said goes no further.'[67]

On their home-ground, and as an example of the carefree entertaining they were able to do at Oxford, Mary Paley's recollection of an impromptu dinner party at Woodstock Road with Jowett and Professor Vinogradoff, whose work Marshall greatly admired, is worth quoting,

> Alfred happened one day to meet Professor Vinogradoff and was so much fascinated that he asked him to dine with us and meet Jowett who had arranged to come that night. There was a little stiffness at first, as

---

[*]   *Ibid.*, p. 36. Evelyn Abbot (1843–1901) was a classical scholar, had taught for some time at Clifton College under Percival and became Jowett's biographer; Lewis Nettleship (1846–92), fellow and tutor at Balliol, author of a memoir on T.H. Green and killed in a mountaineering accident when attempting Mont Blanc; Andrew Cecil Bradley (1851–1935), Fellow and lecturer at Balliol, teaching first English and then philosophy in succession to Green; James Leigh Strachan-Davidson (1843–1916), student of Jowett and expected to succeed him as Master of Balliol, classical scholar specialising in Roman history; Albert Venn Dicey (1835–1922), Vinerian Professor of English Law from 1882 and noted constitutional lawyer; Alfred, Viscount Milner (1854–1925), founder of Toynbee Hall, private secretary to Goschen, author of memoir on Arnold Toynbee and editor of his literary remains and later greatly involved with South African affairs.

Jowett had not met Vinogradoff and as usual was shy with strangers, but as the evening went on talk became more and more free; after dinner we sat out in the little back garden under the birch tree and a full moon and then it became what Jowett called 'good', on philosophy and poetry. I never heard him talk as freely as he did that evening, and I would give much to be able to recall that conversation.[68]

The Oxford period, however, ended as abruptly as it had begun, once again as the result of a sudden death. Although by the end of four terms, the Marshalls 'had quite settled in Oxford, their small house and garden in Woodstock Road suited them well' and they both enjoyed their respective teaching, Alfred Marshall 'always felt that Cambridge was his true home'.[*] The death of Henry Fawcett on 14 November 1884 which vacated the chair of political economy at Cambridge, gave Marshall the opportunity to return. He was elected to the chair in December, and by the beginning of 1885, they were once again living in Cambridge, from 1886 in the house they built for themselves and in which they lived until their respective deaths in 1924 and 1944.

A SECLUDED CAMBRIDGE PROFESSORIAL COUPLE (1885–1924)

The position of the Marshalls as a devoted couple presented by the oral tradition on the subject rests largely on the long period of close to four decades they spent together in Cambridge. For the greater part of this, they lived in Balliol Croft, the unusual house they had built for them on the then outskirts of Cambridge at 6 Madingley Road, within easy walking distance of St John's College and only a short bicycle ride away from the gates of Newnham. Glimpses of their married life there, as it was assisted by the faithful Sarah, and based on what has been preserved in correspondence and personal recollections by Mary Paley and others, provide both support and reservations about the accuracy of that oral tradition on their married bliss. This conclusion is strengthened when the marital picture is combined with what is known about the intellectual side of their partnership.

On their return to Cambridge in January 1885, the Marshalls initially took up residence in a rented house, 'Firenze', at 17 Chesterton Road, Cambridge. Temporary though this accommodation was, the Marshalls used it extensively for entertaining friends and colleagues. John Neville Keynes, whose diaries provide much information on the subject, recorded dining at the Marshalls on 17 March 1885 with Dr and Mrs Markby of Oxford, who were responsible for his temporary lecturing post there as a replacement for Marshall; on 27 June 1885, to meet General Francis Amasa Walker and his wife and, twelve months later, for what must have been one of the last dinner parties at Chesterton Road organised by the Marshalls, to dine with L.L. Price, one of Marshall's former Oxford students, and Foxwell.[69]

Within a month of their return to Cambridge, Marshall was writing to the Bursar of St John's[70] on the possibility of leasing land from the college in Grange Road for the purpose of building his own house. The first letter in this correspondence indicates a conflict between St John's College's policy of only allowing the construction of houses with a value

---

[*] Mary Paley Marshall, *What I Remember*, p. 42. Her unpublished notes (NCA, p. 1) state, 'We had made up our minds that Oxford was to be *our* home in future. However, in 1884, Fawcett died' (my emphasis). Marshall's election to the chair and his subsequent activities as Cambridge professor are discussed in detail in Chapter 10.

in excess of £2,000 on their Grange Road property and Marshall's desire to spend only £1,000 on the house to be designed by the noted architect, J.J. Stevenson[*] and himself. Marshall defended this relatively small investment on the grounds that his 'requirements for space are small'[¶] and that his architect had advised that £1,000 is sufficient to provide a house of the size he required with a 'pleasant' architectural effect and to cover all the foreseeable extras. Given this conflict, Marshall requested the Bursar to plead with the College Council to make an exception in his case, since his inspection of the other sites available showed them to be unsuitable relative to the Grange Road site, and, if this was essential to secure its lease, he was willing to pay double the annual rent required.

By the end of April, and after an unsatisfactory outcome at the College Council, Marshall listed his site preferences as Grange Road first, then a site on the eastern end of Love Lane, and last, a Madingley Road site opposite the St John's cricket ground and then in use for lawn tennis. The same letter repeated his unwillingness to spend more than £1,000 on the house, and in support enclosed its draft plans. During May, after much further correspondence, agreement was finally reached for the construction of a £1,000 house on the Madingley Road site, with a rental of £15 a year, but with its western boundary to be straightened at college expense, an entrance to be constructed from the north, and responsibility for payment for connection to the town's main drain still to be settled. Marshall's letter of final acceptance looked to a speedy possession of the land, because he wished building to start 'in a fortnight or so'. In addition he wanted an undertaking from his nursery neighbours, guaranteed by altering their lease, that they would never 'form any manure heaps' on the eastern side of their land, that is, close to the Marshall border.

On 8 June 1885, the Bursar informed Marshall that the current tenants of the property were ready to vacate, and that the boundary would be straightened and pegged as agreed; but it was not until 16 June 1886 that the lease was signed. This was for 98 years, with a rental of £15 per annum payable half yearly, Alfred Marshall to be liable for all relevant taxes, while the house had to be painted every three years and the property needed to be insured for fire.[71] Building commenced in early July 1885, was briefly interrupted in November by an argument with the college over a ditch, but by July 1886 Marshall informed Foxwell that they should 'easily' be in the house by August, all the more important since they would then have the Walkers as their first of many house guests.[72]

The house, with its three floors, was set towards the middle of a rather irregular block of land (112' by 198' by 98' by 180'). Eventually, this setting became a spacious, tree-filled garden. No houses were built in the vicinity until the end of the century. The house in fact had no direct neighbours until the 1930s so that its overall setting was bushland and farms. A description of some of its features by Mary Paley is well worth quoting, the architect's

---

[*] J. Stevenson (1831–1908). His buildings include churches, London and country houses as well as university restoration and buildings at Oxford and Cambridge. He was also noted for his interior design of ships, a skill reflected in the fittings of the Marshall scullery. For an appreciation of his work, see *The Connoisseur,* 185 (744), February 1974, pp. 102–12; *DNB Supplement 1901–1910,* p. 414. I am indebted to Dr R.A. Green, the last private resident at 6 Madingley Road, for his reference to *The Connoisseur,* for a guided tour of the house and for drawing my attention to the Marshall correspondence with the Bursar on the purchase of the land, preserved at St John's College Archives.

[¶] Rita Mcwilliams-Tullberg suggests this could be an indication that by 1885 the Marshalls had abandoned any thought (hope) of starting a family.

mistake she mentioned relating to the initial omission of the stairwell, a fault which had to be rectified at the substantial additional cost of £200:

in 1886 Balliol Croft was built and we settled down there for good . . . the contract for the house was £900, though on account of a mistake on the part of the architect it cost £1,100. For several years it was the only house in the Madingley Road and we chose the site chiefly for its forest trees. Alfred took immense pains in planning the house and in economising space, especially in the kitchen department. He was anxious to have his study on a higher floor, as he thought that in Cambridge it was well to live as far from the ground as possible [because of the damp]. However, J.J. Stevenson, the architect, persuaded him to be content with the first floor and a balcony. . . . He loved the grass and trees but cared little for flowers, and he took a special interest in the vegetable garden. He wrote to me once: 'I have always held that a kitchen garden at its best is more picturesque than a flower garden at its best. There is more depth and serenity and unconsciousness.'*

A more systematic description of the house is as follows. From the front door, an entrance hall and small privacy foyer for removing coats, etc. were encountered first. To the right of this was a pantry and fairly sizeable kitchen; to the left a sitting- and separate dining-room (overlooking the garden) and facing it, the stairwell. Dining- and sitting-room could be combined for dinner parties of twelve guests, the maximum which could be seated. The first floor contained Marshall's study with balcony (which faced the front of the house), the front door being at the side. It also contained a bedroom (which the Marshalls used themselves) and bathroom. The final floor contained a further bedroom for guests with an adjoining dressing-room, bathroom and, under the sloping roof, a room for the maid. In addition, there was some minor attic storage space. Much of the furniture was in-built, modelled on that of a ship's cabin, and designed to save space. Maximum usable space was in fact the principle on which the house was constructed. Fire places, for example, were small, and of unusual design, as, by contemporary standards, was the kitchen. In fact, being so tiny, the house was a very unusual professorial residence. In particular, room only for *one* live-in maid provided for a servant establishment infra-dig for the household of a professional man of Marshall's status. No wonder John's College Council and its Bursar were suspicious of his building plans and unwilling to lease him a prime residential site.

The eccentricity of the house at Madingley Road was stressed in an appraisal of its features as part of a tribute to Stevenson's architecture. Although its explanation of the smallness of the house in terms of the Marshalls 'socialism' is only sustainable on a broad definition of 'socialism', its general description of the house is worth quoting. It also sheds light on Marshall's reasons for choosing Stevenson as his architect, almost certainly a legacy of his Oxford days and of his interest in the Banbury Road houses Stevenson had built in 1881 for T.H. Green and T.S. Ormond, the Bursar of St John's, Oxford.

The Banbury Road houses probably led to a commission in 1885 to design a house at No. 6 Madingley Road, Cambridge, known as 'Balliol Croft' for Arthur [sic] Marshall the great economist, who was newly arrived at Cambridge from Balliol. The three houses are all in the 'Queen Anne' manner and show J.J.

---

* Mary Paley Marshall, *What I Remember*, p. 42. Her unpublished notes (NCA) indicate more bluntly: 'Balliol Croft cost £1200 owing to (stupid) mistakes by the architect' (material in brackets crossed out in original). The *Times* obituary mentions the missing stairwell as Marshall's mistake (quoted below, Chapter 20, p. 739). Photographs of house and balcony are reproduced as photographs 31–32.

Stevenson at his best. . . . The Marshall house is a delightful eccentric, and its eccentricity reflects the tastes of the client. It is very small (the Marshalls were socialists and only had one servant), compactly planned, with the roof running in one unbroken sweep almost to the ground at the back, a midget projecting bay window from the drawing room at the side, and on the front a charmingly detailed timber verandah, on the first floor. This led off to the study and here the 'father of modern economics' with his wise owl face and little skull-cap used to sit writing his books and articles.[73]

Price's Memoirs[74] contain a further description of Balliol Croft and a less generous account of its aesthetics by the architect:

I went to stay with them more than once at Balliol Croft. They prided themselves with justice on some ingenious new contrivances in the arrangements of the house. Mrs. Marshall's love of art was evident. So was conspicuously the study in the garden for health-sustaining work in the open air; and the arrangement of the shelving of the books in the extensive representative library was noticeable. At the back, however, of their dwelling, a slanting roof stretching from the top almost, or quite, down to the ground had, so Marshall told me with grim humour, met with adverse criticism from his neighbours and from others. He had mentioned this to Stevenson the architect who told him while the house was building not to trouble as the internal accommodation was being provided just as he and his wife desired. The house completed, Stevenson then remarked 'It is perfectly hideous but I have been wanting for thirty years to make the experiment.' That it was his only house was Marshall's remonstrance, made in vain.

Guest rooms and general visitor facilities were described by Mary Paley Marshall for the benefit of the Seligmans who were visiting Europe in the summer of 1891, when she invited them to stay at Balliol Croft.

They [the guest rooms] are all small, the house not being much more than a cottage. There is our 'best room' with a double bed, adjoining is a small dressing room separated by double doors with a small bed in it. We have sometimes used this for a younger member of the same family who use the larger room. And last there is a single room not quite so small as the dressing room. If you do not mind crowding, . . . we should be glad that you should bring both of 'the children'; or perhaps you might thus be on the whole more comfortable than at a crowded hotel very insufficiently appointed . . .[75]

Alfred Marshall extended a similar invitation to stay a few years later to his friend Taussig. Unlike Seligman, Taussig seems to have taken it up in June 1895.[76] There were many houseguests at Balliol Croft over the subsequent decades. John Maynard Keynes recalled meeting Wagner and N.G. Pierson in this way,[77] his father's diaries record visits as houseguests by Giffin, Nicholson, Dunbar (from Harvard), Pantaleoni (from Rome), Moses (from California) in the context of dinner parties he attended at the Marshalls.[78] Mary Paley recalled,

During these years in Cambridge we had of course many visits from economists from the U.S.A., Germany, Italy, France and Holland. We were very fond of Professor Pierson and his wife, who stayed with us several times, and of Professor and Mrs. Taussig. Professor Edgeworth was also a frequent visitor and kept us in touch with Oxford economics, and former pupils were always welcome.[79]

Foxwell had been an occasional guest of the Marshalls at Bristol and Oxford and knew Balliol Croft sufficiently well for Marshall to intimate his familiarity with their 'three spare beds . . . one of them very small'.[80] L.L. Price was a relatively frequent former student guest, possibly because he occasionally served as examiner in the Moral Sciences Tripos. Price recalled a stay with the Marshalls at 'Firenze', the rented house where they lived in the first years at Cambridge, during which he inadvertently locked himself out from his guest room after a night at St John's:

> I dined at St John's as Marshall's guest, and after the proceedings in the large fine Combination room he, still delicate in health, went home, giving me a latch-key. Foxwell took me up into his College rooms. Late in the evening I returned to the dwelling temporarily occupied before Balliol Croft was built. I could not make the key open the door. With the idea that there was some obstructing dirt inside it I went along the road. While most houses were wrapped in darkness because their tenants had presumably gone to bed, I knocked at the door of one where a light was visible. The clergyman within, who was, I thought, preparing his sermon for the following day (a Sunday), responded in not unnatural surprise to my request for a pin to remove the dirt, but on examination we found that there was no impediment in the key [hole]. Going back again I tried to insert it with some extra force prompted by fear that I might have to spend the night between the outside door which had been left open and the inner entrance that was baffling me. But alas I broke the key and was reduced to the humiliation of ringing the bell. Whereupon Marshall came down to let me in and then I discovered to my ashamed chagrin that there were two key-holes in the hindering barrier and that failing to hit upon the right hole I had unavailingly tried the other. Such was my nocturnal adventure of which good-humouredly Marshall made fun at breakfast the next morning.[81]

Keynes's diaries also disclose names of the former pupils and friends of Mrs Marshall who stayed as houseguests, or who merely came to dinner. These included a Miss Lee, Miss Mundella, Miss Ewart, Miss Clough, Miss Sharpley, Miss Fletcher and Miss McArthur, a formidable list.[82] Mary Paley's relatives also stayed occasionally.[83] No recorded visits from the Marshall side of the family have been preserved, that is, until his nephews were old enough to attend luncheon parties at Balliol Croft when Marshall was already in retirement.[84]

However, academic economists and former students were not the only guests whom the Marshalls entertained. In the context of the Social Discussion Society, in whose meetings the Marshalls took an active interest, speakers not infrequently stayed at Balliol Croft. Mary Paley recorded this aspect of their Cambridge life for posterity,

> In connection with a Social Discussion society, which started soon after our return, we had interesting visitors, among them were Octavia Hill, Emma Cons and the beautiful Mary Clifford, one of the first women Guardians. At Bristol she used to be called 'the Guardian Angel of the Poor'. Then we had many working men to stay with us. I once took two to see King's Chapel where we sat for some time, and on my asking them what they would like to see next, one said: 'don't show us anything more so that the impression may remain.' Ben Tillett, Tom Mann, and Burnett were among our visitors and a specially delightful one was Thomas Burt.[85]

One of the trade unionists who stayed at Balliol Croft was Ben Tillett, a leader of the dockers. John Neville Keynes recorded the dinner at which Tillett was present, the other dinner guests being Dr and Mrs Humphrey, V.H. Stanton, and Harry Aves. Commenting on Maynard Keynes's Marshall Memoir, Florence Keynes later recalled this occasion in the following terms, 'your statement that "he sought the society of trade unionists, co-operators and other working class leaders" reminds of a dinner at Balliol Croft to meet Ben Tillett, then a rising young man in the labour world. I remember how he distinguished himself by paring his nails at table with a pen-knife!'.[86]

Marshall's conversation as host at such working-men's gatherings was recorded by one of these guests himself. The occasion was a visit to Cambridge in 1901 of members of the Working Man's College, a visit which included a dinner for seven of the delegates at Balliol Croft.

> We had the company of Professor and Mrs. Marshall until eleven o'clock when the Professor took us back to our quarters. At his house we talked of the power of Niagara, of the tides, the sun's rays, of electricity and the accumulator Edison had promised us; of the best forms of houses, streets, chimneys and smoke consumers; of the beauties of the Yosemite, the Mirror Lake and the cause of its stillness and of its surface being ruffled at certain varying but foreknown hours every morning, of the giant pines there and the still greater trees of California. He showed us photographs – one of the Lake, in which so faithful was the reflection that you could not tell at first that he held it upside down – and pointed out the geological wonders of the country. Then we talked of labour and capital. He advised us in the Working Men's College to get someone to continue Ludlow and the Lloyd Jones's *History of the Progress of the Working Classes, 1832–1867*. He was enthusiastic about Ludlow, and evidently valued his work highly. The names of Dent and Llewellyn Smith were mentioned; also Holyoake, but he was too old now and his knowledge of a special kind. A man was wanted whose knowledge was general of the conditions within the unions and without. He recalled having heard Maurice speak on the vexed question of signing the Thirty-nine Articles, which had to be signed at one time by all graduates at the universities. He told us that Maurice spoke against compelling men to sign them, saying that he believed them himself, and had too much respect for them to so besmirch them as to insist on their being signed by anyone who, though not really believing them, would so far swallow their scruples as to sign, in order that they might not be prevented from earning their livelihood. Then we talked of supremacy – English, German or American – of the causes of economic changes, of wars of our own, of the French and Germans and of the Americans, of our wealth produced during their troubles, of their advance since; of the relation between imports and exports, between production and importation and the sending abroad of securities and money; of the need for us to improve our methods and our education in things concerning the production of commodities, of phonographs, typewriters, hinge screws, nut and washer bolts, spokeshare irons, eyelet-hole punches, drug stores and many other things. No wonder, when we left the sweetbrier garden and passed out of the gate, that Harvey was so overcome that he disappeared in the darkness backwards into a dry ditch in such a manner that we could only see the soles of his boots. It was certainly the talk and the personal contact that we most enjoyed.[87]

During the summer, the Marshalls in absentia entertained another sort of working-class guest. After they had left Cambridge for their extensive summer vacations, the house was filled with 'poor people from Southwark, selected by the Women's Settlement' in which Mary Paley was active. They were looked after by their maid, Sarah. 'She made it possible for us to do [this act of charity for which] Alfred cared very much. . . . She welcomed and gave them a capital time and sometimes became a real friend. One of them, a delicate woman, told me how Sarah put her to sleep in the hammock and brought her tea when she woke. She said: 'It was like heaven'.[88]

In this and other ways their maid Sarah became an increasingly important part of the household. She was 'an authority' not only in all their concerns, but was as much a member of the Balliol Croft community as the Marshalls themselves. Frequent visitors, such as Benjamin Jowett, used to sit and have a chat with her in her kitchen, which some of their visitors pronounced 'the most comfortable room in the house'. Jowett's conversation with her, as Mary Paley recalled, were not only social. 'He was the only person to whom she could speak of her religious difficulties'. These were substantial because she was a member of the Plymouth Brethren, whose schisms of the early 1880s had divided an already small local congregation, so that she had only one other couple she could worship with in Cambridge. When they left, she remained as Cambridge's sole survivor of her sect, and ultimately resolved to attend the Primitive Methodist service.

Having been with the Marshalls since the early years of their marriage at Bristol from 1877, she was an institution in her own right.

> She knew more about our relations than we did; she took great interest in the friends who stayed with us and they always remembered her. She became an excellent cook and loved having great responsibilities. Though she considered it wrong to 'enjoy' herself she used to say that the happiest week in her life was when the British Association met at Cambridge and when there were about twelve at each meal; she ran the whole concern and would lie awake at nights considering the menus for the next day. At one time she was troubled by the feeling that she was not being of enough use to the world, but was consoled when she realised by good cooking she was keeping Alfred in health and was enabling him to write important books. . . . She had her faults; towards the end of her life she became a bit of a tyrant and she had fits of gloomy silence. She nearly always gave notice in November, that most trying month, but I paid no attention for I knew she would not leave. One November she said she wanted to go to Australia, and as soon as full information about the passage etc. was provided nothing more was heard on the subject. She spent little on herself. Our relations on both sides of the family left her substantial legacies, and she might have saved a good deal, but as she gave largely to her family and lent sums to so-called friends who never repaid her, she put by but little. Until the end nothing would induce her to make a will. She died in our house after a week's illness, towards the end of which she became unconscious, but as the doctor predicted, there were two short lucid intervals. One of these was used in getting her to sign a will in favour of her niece, Lizzie, who had come to nurse her, and to whom she had always intended to leave her savings; during the second Alfred came to see her (she was devoted to him), and after he left she said to me: 'He called me faithful Sarah, and what more could I want?'[89]

Life at Balliol Croft was, however, not only sweetness, dinner parties, houseguests, and general peaceful coexistence in the tranquillity of their self-designed permanent castle. There were occasional rifts in the Marshall household. The more important of these arose in the context of Alfred Marshall's increasingly conservative stance on the women's education issue, which came to a head in the fight over degrees for women at Cambridge in the 1890s. Similar differences of opinion in this household of Cambridge academics appear to have occurred over the Moral Sciences Tripos, particularly in the final drive towards a separate Economics and Politics Tripos which began after Sidgwick's death. Correspondence with Foxwell and the diaries of John Neville Keynes are the only sources of information on the frictions at Balliol Croft these matters appear to have caused.[90]

Little correspondence survives on the 1887 attempt to gain degrees for women at Cambridge, or on Marshall's reaction to Philippa Fawcett's unofficial placing as senior wrangler in the 1890 Mathematical Tripos. Mary Paley wrote in glowing terms about this triumph to Jowett.[91] However, in 1894, Marshall wrote to Foxwell about his failure to persuade the Vice-Chancellor to rescind the appointment of Girton student, Ellen McArthur, to an extension lectureship in history, because she would be teaching mixed classes. Her qualifications for the position from having obtained a first-class result in the 1885 Historical Tripos, were irrelevant to Marshall in the face of the catastrophe of women teaching mixed classes. Marshall reported his lack of success in the letter to Foxwell, an account especially interesting because it listed the various difficulties he encountered.

> I was surprised at finding, on taking stock [of possible allies] what a large proportion of my personal friends are in alliance with the extreme wing of women's emancipation. Further, my wife's association with Newnham hampers me, and on the whole I have resolved to consider for a few days before committing myself to any prominent part, beyond that which I have already taken, in this movement. I have done my share, or a good part of it. If we fight, it will be necessary to whip up non-residents, and those of a kind with whom I have not very much in common, and I am not a very good man in that part of the fight. But if others organise this fight, I will gladly play a secondary role, and will give some considerable but not very great time to it.[92]

When preparing in May 1897 for the final vote on the women's degree issue in the Senate in which non-resident M.A.'s could participate, Marshall once again appealed for Foxwell's assistance in writing an attack on those supporting degrees for women, pleading his own inability to do so. The reasons include the popularity of his wife with her Newnham students; and the encumbrances this placed in the way of Marshall's active participation.

> I would write were it not for three reasons. (a) I have done my share, (b) The fact that my wife is of Newnham, and that, bar undergraduates, three fourths of the people who come to this house are Newnham or Girton students, present or past, make it difficult for me to say anything and impossible to say something that ought to be said. (c) I have not the literary faculty. You are one of the *very few* that have it. We have a good many hard workers and hard thinkers among us: but those who are deft with their pen are mainly on the other side. . . . Soldier awake! Now is the time and you have yet to do your share. It is important work: it is just your work. Awake! Awake![93]

That the Marshall marriage survived such onslaughts on the principles they both originally had held dear together, is a tribute to Mary Paley Marshall's loyalty to her husband. A letter to Sidgwick[94] indicates agreement on a number of issues associated with the women's degree question, but disagreement on whether Cambridge should eventually become a 'mixed university'. They agreed that any move in 1887 to re-open the issue would be inadvisable, and on the principle that 'no more stringent conditions should be required of women when they are candidates for degrees than when they are candidates for degree examinations'. This single piece of evidence giving both their views indicates their differences on the main issue were fundamental. Moreover, Mary Paley's mixed teaching in Bristol, even though her classes only had a very tiny male enrolment, makes it extremely doubtful she would have sided with her husband on the Ellen McArthur mixed teaching issue. On the limited evidence, a strong suspicion of domestic friction in this matter seems highly justified.

Mary Paley appears to have been assisted in some of these difficulties by the wise council she was receiving from her many friends. One of these was Eleanor Sidgwick, the wife of Henry Sidgwick. She became Principal of Newnham as successor to Anne Clough. Her biographer records that 'Mrs. Marshall visited her friend in the evenings too, and brought her difficulties to be talked over at the Newnham fireside'.[95] The nature of these difficulties has unfortunately not been recorded, but in these years, the first decade of the twentieth century, they were probably in a large measure of domestic origin and induced by her increasingly misogynist husband. Eleanor Sidgwick, her adviser, knew Alfred Marshall well. She had worked in the laboratory with Lord Rayleigh who, in 1865, had been the senior wrangler in the Mathematical Tripos, depriving second wrangler Marshall of that distinction. As Sidgwick's wife, she was very familiar with Marshall's quarrels with her husband on reforming the Moral Sciences Tripos syllabus in the 1880s and 1890s, and on other university reform issues. She had clashed herself with Marshall in the 1897 degree for women debate, correcting his dubious statistics on the domestic role of female students and his false generalisations on the female intellect. She was therefore in a good position to ably guide her friend.

She also assisted Mary Paley Marshall on more mundane, but nevertheless not insignificant matters. For example, when bicycle riding was considered unladylike in the 1890s, because of dangers in 'disproportionate development of the leg muscles', 'ruination of the feminine organs of matrimonial necessity', and the possibility of developing 'bicycle eye' from prolonged raising of the eyes with a head lowered in the riding position,[96] Mary Paley wished to learn the use of this new mode of transport to get her more easily to work, against the wishes of her husband. However,

> Mrs. Sidgwick rode a bicycle, and rode it very well. There was an episode in early cycling days when she and a friend came to the rescue of Mrs. Marshall, – who wished to ride, against her husband's will – by riding with her, one on each side. How could Professor Marshall having seen this spectacle, continue to call bicycling harum-scarum or unwomanly? Mrs. Sidgwick was doing it.[97]

All's well that ends well, and Mrs Sidgwick's stratagem of getting Mary Paley on a bicycle proved to be a blessing in disguise by creating a new joint activity for the Marshalls. Before the resumption of lectures in 1897–98, Marshall wrote to Keynes that he and his wife 'propose to cycle every morning . . . for four or five days' during a brief country holiday; while in the spring of 1897 he told Foxwell of a long cycling holiday the two of them had enjoyed together.[98]

What repercussions the educational rifts had on their relations, is difficult to say with certainty. For the regular Moral Sciences dinner in 1898, Keynes's diary records the presence of Mary Paley by herself, then an unusual occurrence. Perhaps her husband could not face the other members of the Board in the convivial atmosphere of this regular dinner, when he and Foxwell had been the only ones amongst them who had opposed giving women their degrees. Another explanation for this absence is health, and an increasing inclination on Marshall's part to avoid dinner parties at other people's houses.[99]

In her reminiscences, Mary Paley also recorded her regular dinners without husbands as one of ten or twelve members of a Cambridge Lady Dining Society. In some ways modelled on the Eranus Society, which may be seen as its exclusively male counterpart, it met successively at the houses of individual members once or twice during term. Husbands had to eat their dinners that night either in the safety of their college dining hall or in the seclusion of their studies.[100]

Mary Paley's active support of this social retaliation by Cambridge academic wives against the male exclusiveness dominating Cambridge college and general academic life at the time, is interesting. It demonstrates once again what others would have seen as her unconventional behaviour as the wife of a late Victorian Cambridge professor. As the odd woman out in the general society to which she belonged, she sought her friends to suit her own, rather eccentric tastes. The expression of regret in her reminiscences at the decline of genuine characters in the Cambridge scene after the First World War is symptomatic of this.[101] The picture of her visit to Charles Booth's widow in 'long black robes, sandals and knitted woollen socks' tells as much of her joys in life as her association of 'the small sage green . . . *Economics of Industry*' with the pre-Raphaelite period 'when we dressed in green and had green wall paper'.[102] This recalls her student days and early years as unmarried Newnham don, a period of her life described by Austin Robinson as particularly happy,[103] when she and Jane Harrison chose William Morris wallpaper for their rooms in the then newly built Newnham. This was when, as a typical 'product of the aesthetic movement', she learnt to combine readings of Swinburne's poetry with the 'iconoclastic realism of her generation', with its spirit that delighted in destroying delusions and 'emphasising the value of critical' perspectives on all issues.[104] It made her capable of visiting the secession in Munich and undoubtedly other avant-garde art exhibitions in London.[105] To what extent her equally eccentric husband tolerated these foibles of his independent wife can only be conjectured, as can the domestic tiffs such behaviour may have occasionally induced.

Marshall's increasing dependence on his wife, combined with her loyal and generous nature, did much to preserve a relationship which, if it had been of a later era, may have collapsed under such provocations. Although for most outward observers, the partnership appeared as the happy union of kindred souls, sharing science, house and ideals, the reality may have been quite different, particularly during the 1890s and early years of the twentieth century. Marshall's stand on the women's education issue, which brought him quite publicly on the opposite side to that of his wife in the debate over degrees for women, the appointment of women to 'mixed' teaching posts, and the value of a mixed university, were certainly bones of contention at Balliol Croft. The diminished role for the Moral Sciences Tripos after the Economics Tripos was created may have been a source of other frictions. Her unconventional behaviour, which went beyond being a working wife, is part of this picture. Before concluding on these issues, the intellectual side of the partnership in the Marshall marriage needs some scrutiny.

INTELLECTUAL COOPERATION IN THE MARSHALL HOUSEHOLD

When Alfred Marshall and Mary Paley married, four years had passed since their initial teacher and student relationship. By then, they were fellow workers in the field of economics, partners in writing a book from the time of their engagement, and, for the whole of their active academic life, teachers of their subject at the three universities in which Alfred Marshall successfully found employment. The last aspect, as indicated earlier, is already a remarkable feature of their relationship. In what sense does this make their marriage an intellectual partnership? The starting-point for such discussion is the saga of their joint book, which was virtually four years in the making, enjoying a successful run in the market-place until its 'suppression' in 1892. However, many traces of the joint work can be found in the book which made the historical reputation of the dominant male partner of this economist couple.

Mary Paley's account of the association between the *Economics of Industry* and her marriage with Alfred Marshall is a useful starting-point:

When I returned to Newnham in October [1876], she [Miss Anne Clough] gave us [Mary and Alfred Marshall] a sitting-room [at Newnham] where we made the first outlines of the *Economics of Industry*, which Professor Stuart wanted as a textbook for the Extension Lectures and which with too light heart I had undertaken to write. It was published in our joint names in 1879. Alfred insisted on this, though as time went on I realised that it had to be really his book, the latter half being almost entirely his and containing the germs of much what appeared later in the *Principles*. He never liked the little book for it offended against his belief that 'every dogma that is short and simple is false', and he said about it, 'you can't afford to tell the truth for half-a-crown'.[106]

More explicit notes state that 'its Book II contains the germ of his Theory of Distribution and its Book III is almost entirely his'.[107]

Mary Paley's recollections were challenged on several occasions. Keynes wrote in his Memoir, 'In later years, Marshall grew very unfriendly to the little book. After the publication of the *Principles*, he suppressed it and replaced it in 1892 with an almost wholly different book under the same title which was mainly an abridgement of the *Principles*.' Marshall's growing dislike of the book was explicable in terms of the 'brief and imperfect manner' in which it had treated the theory of value, thereby involving Marshall in unnecessary controversies in the pages of the *Quarterly Journal of Economics*.[108] More in conformity with Mary Paley's views, Keynes added that Marshall's growing realisation of the complexity of economics meant it was not 'possible to combine simplicity with scientific accuracy', as its authors had originally hoped. Keynes concluded,

Yet these sentiments do a real injustice to the book. It won high praise from competent judges and was, during the whole of its life, much the best little text-book available. (. . .15,000 copies had been sold before it was suppressed). If we are to have an elementary text-book at all, this one was probably, in relation to its contemporaries and predecessors, the best thing of the kind ever done – much better than the primers of Mrs. Fawcett or Jevons or any of its many successors. Moreover, the latter part of Book III, on Trade Combinations, Trade Unions, Trade disputes, and co-operation was the first satisfactory treatment on modern lines of these important topics.[109]

When, twenty years later, Keynes wrote Mrs Marshall's obituary, he once again vindicated the little book, adding in its defence the views of his father, who had known the book well.[110]

A draft letter by Marshall to a Japanese student, who had translated the book in 1910 without the authors' permission, sheds further light on the fate of the little book. After exonerating this correspondent from evil intent, and explaining the difference between the 1892 *Elements of Economics of Industry* and the earlier *Economics of Industry*, Marshall continued: 'But the new volume maintains a much larger circulation than the old one. . . . Those who suggested that an educational work on economics should be written by a young student (who had obtained only a very elementary knowledge of it and did) were not economists and did not know that the task of combining simplicity with thoroughness is more difficult in this than in almost any other subject. Several scores of books have been written in the hope of doing this; but they have perished quickly. My wife and I began by trying to make the book simple.'*

The crossed-out remark about 'a young student' with only an 'elementary knowledge' of the subject invited to write an educational work was tactless and insensitive on Marshall's part. It was not really wrong for 1876 when his wife had only very recently completed her studies. Other evidence is available to illustrate the meaning of 'suppression' used by Marshall about the book. The book is not in the Cambridge University Library, nor on the open shelves of the Marshall Library (though copies are preserved in the Marshall Archive), nor is it easily found in (male) college libraries. St John's College Library, for example, does not have it. There are three copies in Newnham Library (implying that Mary Paley was an unwilling 'suppressor') and one at Girton. Moreover, a third edition had been contemplated as late as 1885 (in which, among others, J.N. Keynes was involved) while a Russian translation was permitted in 1886.[111] It can be added that the book was popular with Marshall's students until 1890, and that, on the evidence of Marshall's notes on students, it was read in 1898 by a Girton student and in 1904–5 (paradoxically) by an Economics Tripos student from Marshall's own college. His own product, however, effectively supplanted it by the end of the 1890s.[¶]

Marshall's suppression of the book in 1892 has been defended on doctrinal grounds, the ground on which he himself defended it as late as 1907–8. C.K. Hobson, who attended Marshall's lectures that year, recalled that in one of them Marshall touched 'on the suppression of the book. (I said suppression because, according to what Marshall said, he took much more positive action than merely letting the book go out of print.) Marshall was talking one day about the early trust movement in the United States. He had watched this rather closely and had come to the conclusion that the forces at work were essentially transient and that competition would re-assert itself. When later he changed his mind he suppressed the book.'[†] Becattini, using Keynes's simile from the *General Theory*, describes

---

*   Reproduced in Rita McWilliams-Tullberg, 'Economics of Industry', *History of Economic Thought Newsletter*, No. 9, Autumn 1972 (material in brackets crossed out in original), p. 15. Keynes probably saw this letter when he wrote the Marshall Memoir, since he mentions the unauthorised Japanese translation, and quotes from the introduction which Marshall prepared for the Japanese translation. See his 'Alfred Marshall', p. 201. That introduction continues, 'for the first half simplicity was given the preference but in the second no progress could be made without more accurate foundations . . . some patching was necessary: and the second half was written on lines somewhat similar to those of the *Principles of Economics*. When that was published in 1890 we saw the difficulty of keeping in circulation together opinions as divergent as some of those in this volume and that' (Marshall Archive, Large Brown Box). This incidentally totally coincides with Mary Paley's recollections quoted at the start of this section.

¶   See Peter Groenewegen, 'Alfred Marshall and the Establishment of the Cambridge Economics Tripos', *History of Political Economy*, 20 (4), Winter 1988, pp. 661, 664. John Maynard Keynes had not read the book by 1905 (*ibid.*, p. 667). It was not popular with all students, however. As Foxwell wrote to J.N. Keynes on 10 June 1881, 'I can understand . . . that Marshall's book may be difficult and unattractive to beginners. The special men don't like it: their favourite book is Adam Smith' (Marshall Archive, Keynes, 1:22). A student (*Cambridge Review*, 24 October 1889) described this 'innocent little book . . . in its modest sage-green cover' as a 'wretched little book! You who contain matter so closely packed, and on first acquaintance, so confusing: abounding with definitions so long, and travelling to all appearances in circles as complete as ever circles were.'

†   C.K. Hobson to the Librarian. Marshall Library, 21 February 1961. The letter recalls correspondence Hobson had with Keynes on this subject after Keynes had published his Memoir on Mary Paley Marshall. Hobson noted that his original letter to Keynes also mentioned that 'the word monopoly does not occur in the book, and that there is an implicit assumption that each industry consists of a number of competing firms'. The last statement is dubious

the decade after the 1879 volume, when Marshall was busily constructing his own *Principles of Economics*, as a period when very gradually, 'like a snake, he freed himself from his old skins. He surpassed the "ethical trap", he laid more stress on the evolutionary aspects, he exorcised the spectre of communism'. In short, the major work of the *Principles* replaced the earlier, and immature, *Economics of Industry*.* Whitaker likewise advances doctrinal reasons for the suppression of the earlier volume. Although the book had much of the character of a first draft of the *Principles* because it foreshadowed so many of the qualities of the later book, its treatment of the distinction between normal and market value differed substantially from the treatment in the *Principles* as did the theory of distribution. More important is Whitaker's view on the improbability 'that Mrs. Marshall contributed much, outside the opening and closing chapters, apart from literary advice and drafting' and that, in a similar sense the *Principles* can be regarded as 'a joint product' because Marshall acknowledged in its first edition, that his wife had aided and advised him at every stage of the MSS and of the proofs, and that owed a very great deal to her suggestions, her care and her judgement.[112] The role of Mary Paley in the work therefore needs further comment.

The outline of the book needs to be recalled for such an examination.[113] It was divided into three parts (books) of which the first dealt with land, labour and capital, the second with normal value, and the third with market value. Book I contains two introductory chapters and then covers the theory of production in terms of its three agents and their productivity. Book II opens with a definition identifying normal value and the effects of competition. It then deals with the law of utility and demand, expenses of production and supply, rent in itself and in relation to value, and demand in relation to value. Its second half discusses distribution as a problem of wages and profits. Book III is devoted to explanations of major deviations from normal value concluding with chapters on trade unions, arbitration and conciliation and cooperation in production, credit and exchange.

As Mary Paley recollected at the end of her life, the book was a joint production from the beginning, because its outline had been worked out together in the Newnham sitting-room after their engagement in mid-1876. This differs from John Neville Keynes's diary on the subject. He recorded on 2 December 1876 that 'Miss Paley is writing a book on Political Economy for the extension lectures'. Only six months later did he acknowledge Marshall's contribution to the project when noting 'I have rather scandalised Miss Bond by saying that [given] Marshall's matter and her own style, Miss Paley's book will probably be a great success'. By 10 July 1877 the diary indicates Marshall had abandoned his own

---

since Book III, Chapter IV of the book deals specifically with monopolies and combinations as an example of the deviation of market values from normal, competitive values. This chapter clearly treats monopoly as a rather peculiar case and sees combinations by producers as difficult to arrange. In his reply to Hobson, Keynes (31 December 1941) noted that 'Marshall may have had somewhat of a bad conscience about it [the suppression]' and that his 'ostensible reason was a pretty thin one [because] the book got out of date, like all others, as time went on.' I am indebted to Rita McWilliams-Tullberg for bringing this material to my notice. See her 'Alfred Marshall's Attitude Towards the Economics of Industry', for a more detailed discussion.

* G. Becattini, *Invito a una rilettura di Marshall*, pp. ci–cxi, the translated quotation comes from p. cix. Becattini adds that when he communicated with C.W. Guillebaud on the Italian translation of the *Economics of Industry*, for which the material quoted is an introduction, Guillebaud immediately observed 'that Marshall would not have been pleased' (*ibid.*, p. cviii n.86). Guillebaud also recalled that when his father was sent a complimentary copy of Marshall's *Principles* in 1890, he was asked to return his copy of *Economics of Industry* for 'destruction' (*P* IX, p. 12 n.c.). And see below, p. 427 n.¶.

writing for the time being and 'is now chiefly engaged on the other book. He always says "we" in talking of it and he seems to have given a very large amount of his time to it.'[114]

It will be recalled that the Marshalls' honeymoon in Cornwall had been partly devoted to the book. However, by April 1878 Marshall wrote to Foxwell that by giving it every spare minute till October they hoped to get Part I of the book in shape. By September 1878 however, proofs of that part were ready for circulation to Foxwell and Sidgwick, whose criticism involved considerable recasting of the original drafts. Correspondence from Marshall to Foxwell in late 1878 and early 1879 suggests Marshall's major problems arose from the distinction between normal and market value, and from the theory of distribution in terms of the division of national dividend (produce) into wages and profit (Jevons's problem).[115]

In early October 1879, the book was finally published and self-criticism by the authors began to appear in their letters to Foxwell. In the context of deciding where the real authorship lay, it may, however, be noted that surviving correspondence on technical points is exclusively Alfred Marshall's and that his *ex-post* criticisms of the book were largely directed at Book I. Marshall confessed his preference for removing excessive quotation from Bastiat and Mill from the first part and suggested that the first three chapters required substantial re-writing and amplification. In addition, this letter attributed the 'worse' style of Book I to the fact that writing came more easily and 'we suppose better as we went on'. More important, given his later complaints as recorded by Mary Paley, is his comment about the difficulty in writing *small* books: 'The smallness of this book has given us so much trouble that we don't want to promise to write another *small* book . . . we have, however, another plan to write an outline of economic history as a third companion volume [the projected trade and finance volume being the second one]'. In 1879, small was not beautiful for Marshall. A week later Marshall expressed regret that in view of the difficulties of Parts II and III, 'we might have pitched the key a little higher in the first chapters of Book I'.*

Criticism also came from Mary Paley Marshall: 'We are not proud of the book. We don't feel that we solved the great problem of the use of commas and we haven't been consistent in their use. But as to quotations, we think we have a theory, but perhaps it isn't the right one.' The strong ironical tone of the letter is heightened by the signature. This reads: 'yours, on behalf of the firm Alfred Marshall and Mary Paley Marshall (unlimited)', the closest either of the two ever came to describing their married life as a business partnership.[116]

Both Keynes's diaries and the Marshall–Foxwell correspondence suggest a well-intentioned take-over by Alfred Marshall, necessitated by the way he gradually raised the level of difficulty in those parts of the book for which he took prime responsibility. The book, popular though it was, consequently fell between two stools. It neither served the beginners nor the advanced market satisfactorily. Mary Paley's final comment to Foxwell

---

* Alfred Marshall to Foxwell, 25 October 1879, 2 November 1879, (Freeman Collection, 9/9, 8/9). Marshall wrote to Seligman in April 1900, 'My work [in writing] was then broken off . . . by my being drawn into writing a hollow Economics of Industry, in which truth was economized for the benefit of feeble minds.' Seligman Collection, Columbia University. However, he was happy to quote it in evidence in his response to a questionnaire from the Royal Commission on the Depression of Trade and Industry in 1886. See *OP*, p. 7 and p. 9 when he claimed the quoted material (no doubt correctly) as his own. From there it was quoted in *MCC* in 1923.

on its publication just quoted, combined with her phrase 'I realised it had to be really his book' suggests there may have been *some* resentment on her part over this outcome. As J.N. Keynes had predicted, her stylistic qualities may have ensured the book reached the audience for which it was designed, Marshall was temperamentally and stylistically incapable of achieving this.

His insistence on joint authorship is also capable of more than one interpretation. Marshall's first article 'The Future of the Working Classes' commenced with the reflection that Mill's chapter which provided its inspiration had been the joint product of Mill and his wife. This, Marshall argued, should 'awaken' us 'to the question whether the quick insight of woman may not be trained so as to give material assistance to man in ordering public as well as private affairs'. Six years later, Marshall may well have decided *Economics of Industry* paralleled Mill's Book IV, Chapter VIII; his wife's idea and his execution, with her assistance and guidance all along the way: a Millian and not a Webb-style partnership.[117]

The collaboration on the *Principles* and other economic work in the subsequent decades followed this Millian pattern, albeit to a lesser extent. Marshall's acknowledgement to Mary Paley in the first edition of the *Principles* was the most generous: 'My wife has aided and advised me at every stage of the MSS and of the proofs, and it owes a very great deal to her suggestions, her care and her judgement.' It is easy to demonstrate from the evidence[118] how arduous this proof reading task was but it suggests that Mary Paley's role in the book is more correctly described as that of the humble research assistant rather than the collaborator. For example, in the context of clarifying to Keynes his remarks on Jevons's 'systematic confusion of hedonics and economics', Marshall added in a postscript: 'My wife can't find the passage in the text quoted above. I am sure I wrote it.', while another letter indicates spelling, syntax and like mistakes were her territory.[119]

For the second edition, her contribution was reduced to the 'help and assistance from many persons' among the six of whom she was mentioned first. For the third edition, her assistance, described as 'very great' is once again separated from the others: 'first obligations' are likewise attributed to her in the fourth edition, while for the substantive changes of the fifth edition, special tribute was paid: 'My wife has aided and advised me at every stage of successive editions of this volume, and of none more than the present. Throughout each edition a very great deal has been owed to her suggestions, her care, and her judgement.' With only trivial editorial changes, this remained the form of acknowledgement for the final three editions.[120]

No thanks to Mary Paley Marshall on specific points were ever recorded in the footnotes of the *Principles*. It seems the only example of such acknowledgment in Marshall's writing which can be found is a note added to a manuscript on 'Absenteeism', written in the early 1870s. At its conclusion, Marshall notes, 'Miss Paley lays stress on the question whether their [that is, the absentee landlords'] foreign associations cause absentees to invest such savings as they make, abroad rather than at home.'[121] This seems to confirm that Mary Paley's contribution to the *Principles* was of a humble nature. In his reminiscences as Deputy Librarian, C.R. Fay records how 'the name "Mary" lives, for me, on a treasured postcard acknowledging some verbal errors in the *Principles* collected by Edwin Cannan and myself': 'thanks for the *errata*. I have handed them to Mary. The mistakes are her department. Yours A.M.'.[122]   At the Royal Economic Society meeting to commemorate the centenary of the *Principles*, Sir Austin Robinson repeated the view that Alfred Marshall treated his wife as his 'foolometer' when writing and revising his *Principles*, any passages she could not understand were to be deleted as too difficult for the general reader.[123]

Others appear to have valued her services more highly. The Marshall–J.N. Keynes correspondence indicates Mary Paley played a more substantial role in proof-reading his *Scope and Method* over 1889 and 1890. Separate comments in her hand were enclosed, and although these generally follow the thrust of her husband's remarks, they are an independent evaluation of Keynes's work. Whether this proofreading role came from Keynes's initiative or that of Alfred Marshall is not easy to say; Keynes's invitation to her seems plausible, given his earlier high opinions of her writing style relative to Alfred Marshall's.[124]

Not directly connected with her assistance to the *Principles* but conforming to the description of her work as that of an amanuensis-cum-research assistant, is Keynes's recollection that cataloguing journals by author and subject, when they had been broken up to make the special volumes Marshall prepared for his students, was 'for time out of memory, the special task of Mrs. Marshall'.[125] Her later unpublished recollections seem to negate this story. Marshall 'was a wonderful organiser of his material. Though his study might look untidy, it was perfectly arranged. His MSS were classified in portfolios and pigeon holes and he could lay his hand at once on any paper he wanted and he said that he could find any of his books in the dark. He had extraordinarily sensitive fingers, a sign of an extraordinarily sensitive nature', remarks followed by a lengthy panegyric on the neatness of his brown boxes in which he kept articles on economic subjects carefully classified and catalogued.[126] If these two tasks of cataloguing were the same, the last amounts to uncharacteristic self-praise on Mary Paley's part.

Acknowledgments to his wife similar to those in the *Principles* were recorded in the prefaces of the *Elements of the Economics of Industry* in 1892 and in the second major volume, *Industry and Trade*, first published in 1919. In 1892, 'My wife had aided and advised at every stage of the MSS and the proofs of my *Principles* and also of the present volume; which is thus indebted twice over to her suggestions, her judgement and her care.'[127]   By 1919 acknowledgement was more generous: 'Of this volume as of my *Principles* but even more than of that, I may say that my wife has aided and advised me at every stage; and that everywhere much of whatever is good is owing to her suggestions, her care and her judgement: the index is entirely her work.'[128]   Ironically, there are no acknowledgements to her or anyone else in the volume of 1923, *Money, Credit and Commerce*; ironically, since it is certain that without Mary Paley's assistance the volume would never have been completed.[129] A draft preface to a proposed final volume dated 19 March 1923 may explain this omission: 'My wife has councilled and aided at every stage of my every outpouring: and given the best part of her life to aiding me by council in all matters large and small at every stage. She refuses to allow her name to be on the title page: but that is its proper place.'[130]   Did official joint authorship bring back painful memories she preferred to forget in these final years of her marriage?

A letter to Foxwell in summer 1881, when the long leave of absence in Europe was in prospect and they were holidaying on the Devon coast, puts a different perspective on their joint work. 'I should have liked to go on with the Economics of Trade and Government because it will be such a good opportunity for Mary and me to work together. But I must do my economic theory first and she will help in that. We have a good many dreams of what we are going to do in these two years in the way of economic inductions, but very likely we shan't really manage very much of this sort.'[131] Both the expressed enjoyment at co-operation in writing the sequel of their *Economics of Industry* (induced by pleasure and pride in the launch of its second edition?) and joint fact-finding tours suggest Webb-like dimensions to the partnership at this stage. Despite the pessimistic forecasts on the latter by the then still quite ill Marshall, such inductions were undertaken in subsequent years in good measure, with important direct and indirect consequences for future work.[132]

One further, not unimportant collaboration should be noted. In her reminiscences, Mary Paley records how in her youth she learnt German from the age of nine, through a German governess who gave her and her sister regular lessons, knowledge consolidated through the practice that 'the family talked German at meals'.[133] This enabled her to prepare for her husband, whose German was probably less fluent, resumés of German books and articles for use in his writing. Generally speaking, therefore, her intellectual role, with few exceptions, evolved into one secretarial and supportive with respect to her husband's work.[*]

AN UNUSUAL PARTNERSHIP

As one of the earliest examples of a marriage between two academic economists (the earlier, only partly eligible, marriage of Henry and Millicent Fawcett springs to mind because of its interesting similarities with the Marshalls' union), the Marshalls' partnership was undoubtedly an unusual one. However, as an intellectual partnership, it was generally not an affair of intense, mental collaboration. This has just been demonstrated in the context of their, and his, writing; these were not two hearts, as was said of the Webbs, beating like one typewriter. Mary Paley's talents as an economics lecturer were undoubted, and later officially recognised when the University of Bristol conferred an honorary D.Litt. on her. Only Sidgwick appears to have cast doubt on their qualities, though Ann Carr's recollections to Maynard Keynes suggests similar features in her teaching to those of which Sidgwick complained, that is, it 'being too cut and dried'.[134] Otherwise her role in the production of Marshallian economic ideas was that of minor assistant and occasional adviser, and she invariably stayed in the background when economics was the subject at Balliol Croft. Maynard Keynes, an intimate acquaintance of the Marshall household for some prolonged periods during the final decades of its existence, emphasised this in his obituary of Mary Paley:

> She never, to the best of my recollection, discoursed on an economic topic with a visitor, or even took part in the everlasting economic talks of Balliol Croft. For a serious discussion she would leave the dining-room to the men or the visitor would go upstairs to the study, and the most ignorant Miss could not have pretended less than she to academic attainment.[135]

---

[*] Giacomo Becattini, *Invito a una rilettura di Marshall*, p. xxiii. It may be noted that Mary Paley published few pieces on economics in her own right. These are a note on a Conference of Women Workers which appeared in the *Economic Journal*, 6 (2) June 1896, pp. 107–9, and a book review of Clara Collet's essays on women's work (*Economic Journal*, 12, 1902, pp. 252–7), nearly a decade later.

A similar picture of her role at Balliol Croft is implicitly conveyed in Fay's account of their 'first, strange meeting' at the Marshall's house in 1906:

> Pigou had sent me to Marshall for an interview. He listened to me, approved the notion of what became 'Co-operation at Home and Abroad', and, spreading a row of books on his sofa, said 'Smell these, and when you've had enough, blow down the tube and Mary will bring you some tea.'
> Being quite dazed, I soon had enough, so blew down the tube.
> 'Yes, Mr. Fay?'
> 'Mary, bring us the tea, please.'
> A stately tread brought up the tray, and in walked NOT the housekeeper, but Mrs. Marshall!! I can still feel the thrill of horror that ran down my spine, when I realised who Mary was.[136]

As economists, therefore, they were hardly partners in any real sense, and unequal in training and ability, as Marshall himself in one of his letters portrayed his wife's economic capabilities in the year before they were married. To what extent this attitude to her worth as an economist was related to his steadily growing belief as he got older that women were intellectually inferior to men, is more difficult to say. His advice in 1889 to Beatrice Webb is a well-known example of the generality in which Alfred Marshall applied that belief;[137] his difficulties in accepting the examination successes by women, including those in his own Economics Tripos, are another. That this view was not accepted by Mary is implicit in another recollection by Fay,

> But of women students in general, he did not much approve. Travelling with them to Harwich one June, I said to Mrs. M. 'How well Newnham has done in the Economics Tripos." They had got a couple of firsts. Alfred in the corner, "A very unfortunate business.'
> Mrs. M. 'I'm afraid Alfred does not approve of us.'[138]

Disagreements on issues like this prevented any genuine partnership in economics, if indeed such a partnership had ever been really possible. By the 1890s if not earlier, the will and interest in such a partnership on Mary Paley's part had probably evaporated, and she may have preferred the subordinate but more peaceful role of secretarial-cum-research assistant she actually played in the construction of Marshall's manifold work. By then she had also developed her own interests in Newnham and its societies, with her own ladies dining club, her holiday hobby of water colours to match her husband's writing and was willing, without abandoning her responsibilities as a professor's wife in entertaining and like activities, to make as peaceful a coexistence as possible with her often cantankerous and hypersensitive husband.

In this context of at least partial failure of their partnership, it is useful to briefly speculate on what Marshall may have expected from his marriage. Mary Paley recalled a remark on the subject from his lectures prior to their engagement.

> As to marriage: 'The ideal of married life is often said to be that husband and wife should live for each other. If this means that they should live only for each other's gratification it seems to me intensely immoral. Man and wife should live, not for each other but with each other for some end.'[139]

Apart from economic education, there were objectives they shared over the whole of their married working life. Mary Paley Marshall frequently deputised for him in activities he wanted to engage in but for which did not have the energy. Examples are membership of the Oxford and Cambridge Charity Organisation Society, in which she was active and he was interested but where after she had attended the meetings they shared the outcome over supper or, the next morning, over breakfast. Committee meetings of the Cambridge Ethical Society of which the two were members, likewise involved her attendance, followed by his undoubtedly critical, post-mortem. 'Economic inductions' among the factories of Europe and Great Britain they shared in abundance. Of entertainments such as concert or theatre, there is virtually no evidence, apart from the context of some summer excursions. Art galleries were more generally attended together.[140]

Undoubtedly, other thoughts on marriage floated through the head of Marshall, the omnivorous reader of the early 1870s whose mind was then ranging over so many of the social sciences in the years of his courtship. For example, was his picture of married women that of Ruskin, in the lectures, *Sesame and Lilies*, which was first published in 1865. This portrayed marriage as 'only the seal which marks the vowed transition of temporary into untiring service, and of fitful into eternal love'. Ruskin added that 'the woman's power is for rule, not for battle, and her intellect is not for invention or creation, but for sweet ordering, arrangement and decision. She sees the qualities of things, their claims and their places. Her great function is Praise . . . by her office and place, she is protected from all danger and temptation . . . the man guards the woman from all this, within his house, as ruled by her.'[141]

Marshall's ideas on marriage may have also have been shaped by those of F.D. Maurice, his philosophical mentor at the Grote Club. As a consequence of 'the divine origin of society, Maurice placed the father at the centre of the family'. However, he also argued 'the wife must be distinct, and not the creature of her husband, . . . husband and wife are meant to be mutually dependent and mutually sustaining' but the tendency to 'treat women as things' was not to be counteracted 'by proclaiming their independence'.[142] It seems even more likely that Mill's essay, '*The Subjection of Women*', of which Marshall owned a first edition, influenced his opinion on the subject. On marriage, he agreed with Mill that 'marriage should be an equal condition, . . . an equal contract without the obligation of obedience'. It is, however, doubtful whether Marshall agreed with Mill's welfare argument that opening all employment opportunities to women would double 'the mass of faculties available for the higher service of humanity', while closer to home, he questioned Mill's proposition advanced in support of intellectual equality in the sexes that 'two women, since political economy has been made a science, have known enough of it to write usefully on the subject.'[143] Mill's views are therefore not the only source for Marshall's opinions on women and marriage.

Given his own taste for economic chivalry, Marshall perhaps was most at ease with Frederic Harrison's ideals on the 'future of woman': 'No decent man, much less woman, could be found to throw ridicule on the chivalrous and saintly ideal of woman as man's guardian angel and queen of the home . . . the glory of woman is to be tender, loving, pure, inspiring in her home; it is to raise the moral tone of every household, to refine every man with whom, as wife, daughter, sister or friend, she has intimate converse.'[144]   In less flamboyant language, this picture can be seen in the *Principles*.

> General ability depends largely on the surroundings of childhood and youth. In this the first and far the most powerful influence is that of the mother, when she does not abdicate it for the sake of dearly bought wages or for more selfish purposes . . . the things she can buy with her earnings are of far less importance for the health and happiness of the family than the mere material services she could have rendered them if she had stayed at home, to say nothing of her moral influence in educating the children, in keeping the household in harmony and making it possible for her husband to be cheered and soothed in his evenings at home.[145]

The little of what is known about Marshall's family life as a child suggests that a Ruskinesque (or Harrisonian) perspective, the dominant Victorian view in fact of woman's role in the home and in society, was the one conforming to the picture he himself constructed about woman's role in his own upbringing. Mary Paley's remarks for Walter Scott can here be recalled. 'He loved his mother, his sister Mabel and his Aunt Louisa. I don't think that as time went on, he really cared very much for anyone else, except some of his former pupils.'[146]   This excessive reliance on women in the formative years of his life – his mother, who saved him from possible disciplinary excesses of his father; his Aunt Louisa, whose welcome and regular summer holidays in the Devon countryside 'saved his life' as an overworked schoolboy, his sisters Agnes and Mabel, whom he took on holidays and who were his cricket companions because his older brother started work early and the younger one was perhaps too delicate – was suddenly replaced by the male society of college life at Cambridge after the equally male society at school. Did they induce in Marshall what has been called a 'Madonna complex', a reverence for women which placed them on a pedestal for remote worship?[147]   If this was the role assigned to Mary who, on the evidence, seems to have courted him rather than the other way round, a reasonable explanation for the probability of early sexual failure on his part can be found,* and some of the peculiarities in the marriage are more easily comprehended.

---

* Writing to Keynes to congratulate him on his Memoir on Marshall, Strachey speculated on whether the Marshalls used contraceptive devices ('French letters') or whether either partner was sterile, in order to explain the Marshalls' childless marriage; Keynes replied that sterility on Alfred Marshall's part soon after his marriage was the likely answer. (Cited in Michael Holroyd, *Lytton Strachey*, London: Penguin Books, 1979, p. 900n.). It has already been suggested that Mary Paley's return to permanent employment early in their marriage, makes conscious family planning a possible explanation for their childless marriage, but this would have conflicted with Marshall's coy disapproval of such method expressed in the *Principles*: 'it is best to marry moderately early provided there is sufficient self-control to keep the family within the requisite bounds without transgressing moral laws' (*P* I, p. 258; *P* VIII, p. 202). This makes impotence on Alfred Marshall's part a stronger possibility. Much of what is known of his background fits in with such a hypothesis. Aspects of his adult behaviour, for example, are easily described as a form of Jungian introversion. These are his 'extreme caution in all attitudes, activities and affective dispositions' and a 'tendency to be precise, pedantic and hypercritical', a behavioural pattern consistent with sexual impotence.   In addition, Alfred Marshall appears to have shown 'a persistent attachment to an idealised parental figure', his mother, as demonstrated by his wife's remarks to Walter Scott, again an attitude often associated with impotence.   By marrying 'an emancipated woman', one who defied convention in dress, in life style as a working middle-class married woman and in her reading, Marshall may have further risked sexual impotence.   Last but not least, their wedding night may well have ended in sexual failure.   Possible sexual ineptitude shown by both partners on this occasion, combined with the strange atmosphere of the double bedroom in the Clifton hotel (cf. J.A. Symonds, *The Memoirs*, edited by Phyllis Grosskurth, London: Hutcheson, 1984, pp. 156–8), tension and pressure of having to attend a University College Council meeting in Bristol and inspect

All this is highly speculative, given the traditional silence on such subjects in the Victorian era and the ensuing dearth of real evidence. For example, several other reasons for the absence of children in the marriage can be found. They include infertility on her part or the deliberate choice of not having children in a relationship where both partners worked in their professions. Given the secrecy about immediate ancestry that Marshall indulged in, hereditary fears may provide another reason for such a conscious choice in Marshall, the future Galtonian. Were the dog and cat at Balliol Croft, about which virtually nothing is ever heard, children substitutes in the household? Only the tombstones in the 6 Madingley Road garden for 'Fly' and 'Sheila', the names of the Marshalls' (or Mary Paley's?) dogs, as well as a solitary photograph, indicate the presence of pets in the economists' household.[148] The opportunities for guessing are endless. Much of Mary's character would have conflicted with a 'Madonna image', if Marshall had constructed this on the basis of female dominance in his nurture. Nor did she by her actions accept the domestic role for women he advocated in his writings and university scheming in conformity to the conventional views on the subject of the age.

The Marshall partnership was therefore not only unusual, it was complex. Its intricate division of labour allowed her to handle all money matters and operate the cheque book, him to design the kitchen; him to reign supreme in domestic economic debate, her to create her own intellectual world at Newnham and the Cambridge Ladies Dining Club; him to engage in constructive writing and feeding birds in his bower in the Tirol, her to sketch and watercolour with considerable distinction and make all the travelling arrangements. A sign of the eccentricity and unusual sexual division of labour in the household was that for therapeutic reasons after his illness, 'he knitted all mine and his own [socks] and black silk ones for my mother'.[149] He also felt a compulsion to advise ladies on their domestic tasks, including dusting and how to remove stains. The record also shows Marshall as a peculiar handy-man, turning wood on a lathe in his backyard workshop, inventing labour-saving gadgets which often did not work (the *Times* obituary mentioned electro-plated knives which would not cut and non-waterproof galoshes) and others which were eminently successful (the rotating mechanism of the Ark; the system of pulleys by which tea could be brought upstairs to the study through a hole in its floor and which enabled 'blackbird' to play without forcing its master to rise from his comfortable, cushioned, reclining position).[150]

There was tenderness in this marriage as well as conflict and a mutual dependence. Over the final decades of Alfred Marshall's life, the last grew into his increasing reliance on her presence and her increasing protectiveness of his need for rest, his health, his utterings and his ultimate reputation. He must often have appeared to her on calm reflection as a 'selfish and jealous intellectual wretch', but their unusual partnership also had unexpectedly

---

workmen renovating their first house the following day, are potential contributing factors for this. Such initial failure can be highly conducive to later impotence in some cases. Combined with Marshall's general poor health diagnosed from early 1879, with its symptoms of tiredness and strong requirements for rest, impotence may well have become virtually permanent. See K. Walker and E.B. Strauss, *Sexual Disorders in the Male*, London: Cassell & Company, 1954, pp. 58–9, 64–65, 85–6; 165 and, on the increasingly appreciated difficulties in making such diagnoses, Robert J. Krane, Mike B. Stroky and Irwin Goldstein, *Male Sexual Dysfunction*, Boston: Little Brown & Company, 1983, pp. 50, 81, 135–6.

tender aspects. The last are comprehensively captured in the 'pretty anecdote' Seligman confided to Sidney Webb and which he saved for posterity in a letter to his wife:

> I had dinner last night with Dr. Seligman. . . . He has been in Austria where he met Marshall (at some watering place). One pretty anecdote he had. Marshall wrote him several brief notes making arrangements etc. Opening one of these he found it addressed 'my own dear darling' and concluding 'Your affectionate Alfred'. Marshall had accidentally sent him a letter to his wife! (Dearest, I hope we may be on such terms twenty years hence, but I hope and believe that this can happen without any absorption of the life of one of us into that of the other.) But it is a revelation of a pretty, affectionate sentiment which I am glad to hear of in Marshall.[*]

NOTES

1.   Information on the marriage certificate of Alfred and Mary Paley Marshall and from Mary Paley Marshall, *What I Remember*, p. 23.
2.   Mary Paley Marshall, *What I Remember*, p. 23; above, Chapter 7, p. 196. These preferences were probably influenced by J.S. Mill's *The Subjection of Women*, London: Longmans, Green & Co., 1869, reprint of 1906, which suggested both the wrong in the obedience clause and the remedy (pp. 58,76).
3.   Mary Paley Marshall, *What I Remember*, p. 23 and n.1.
4.   Above, Chapter 7, pp. 189–90 and see below, pp. 230–31.
5.   Benjamin Jowett to Mary Paley Marshall, 19 December 1888, in Marshall Archive, 1/50.
6.   C.W. Guillebaud, 'Some Personal Reminiscences of Alfred Marshall', *AMCA*, I, p. 93.
7.   C.R. Fay, 'Reminiscence of a Deputy Librarian', *AMCA*, I, pp. 87–9.
8.   H.M. Robertson, 'Alfred Marshall', *AMCA*, I, p. 444.
9.   Giacomo Becattini, *Invito a una rilettura di Marshall*, p. xxiv. The remarks in quotation marks in this and the next sentence are from the same source.
10.   H.M. Robertson, 'Alfred Marshall', p. 444.
11.   As recounted by Mark Perlman in a letter to the author, 25 July 1991. In giving me permission to quote this account of the story, Mark Perlman repeated that this was a 'hearsay' account of what his father had told him, which he believes to be a true record of his father's experience and that, in addition, the inspiration of Mary Paley's outburst the story records may have been inspired by his father's reference during the conversation to Beatrice Webb whose *My Apprenticeship* had then only just appeared. This reference, Mark Perlman notes, may have stirred some emotions of envy coupled with anger in Mary Paley Marshall.
12.   Sir Austin Robinson, 'Review of *What I Remember*', *Economic Journal*, 58 (129), March 1948, pp. 122–4.
13.   Mary Paley Marshall, *What I Remember*, pp. 8–9. The next four paragraphs draw heavily on its first two chapters and appendix, as well as on J.M. Keynes, 'Mary Paley Marshall', pp. 232–3, a paper by Rita McWilliams-Tullberg, 'Mary Paley Marshall, 1850–1944', and notes, preserved in Newnham College. Mary Paley provided some notes for a biography of Jane Harrison, a fellow student who became an eminent classical scholar. Some of her notes for *What I Remember* have also been preserved, and some she used for a lecture on Marshall she gave to the Marshall Society in the 1930s. I owe the references to these notes to Giacomo Becattini and Rita McWilliams-Tullberg respectively.
14.   Mary Paley Marshall, *What I Remember*, p. 17.
15.   B.A. Clough, *A Memoir of Anne Jemina Clough*, London, Edward Arnold, 1897, p. 163, who wrongly gives the date of Mary Paley's appointment as 1874 instead of the more plausible 1875 Mary Paley herself recollected in *What I Remember*, p. 20. 'MSS Notes', NCA, records she lectured on her own initiative at Stamford, six lectures a week with 'papers' to a class of fifteen' and that one of her Newnham students was so good that 'I had to work hard to keep abreast of her' (p. 20).

---

[*] *The Letters of Sidney and Beatrice Webb*, edited Norman McKenzie, Volume 1, 1873–1892, Cambridge University Press, 1978, p. 310. There is other indirect evidence that they corresponded together when they were temporarily apart, for example, when he was in London with the Labour Commission. No such correspondence survives, undoubtedly destroyed with Alfred's (love?) poem Mary Paley at one stage showed Keynes (above, Chapter 2, p. 25 and n.37).

16. Mary Paley Marshall, *What I Remember*, pp. 13–14.
17. J.M. Keynes, 'Mary Paley Marshall', p. 238.
18. Belinda Norman-Butler, *Victorian Aspirations, The Life and Labour of Charles and Mary Booth*, p. 112.
19. Mary Paley Marshall, *What I Remember*, pp. 15–16.
20. B.A. Clough, *A Memoir of Anne Jemina Clough*, p. 201. In her notes (Newnham College, p. 8) Mary Paley recalled, 'Mr. Marshall asked us rather often'.
21. Mary Paley Marshall, *What I Remember*, p. 20.
22. *Ibid.*, p. 22. See Chapter 6 above, pp. 376–9 and below, pp. 250–5.
23. JNKD, 13 July 1876, 19 May 1877.
24. Mary Paley Marshall, *What I Remember*, p. 22. See Chapter 7 above, pp. 191–2 for Marshall's enthusiasm for serious mountaineering.
25. Mary Paley Marshall, *What I Remember*, pp. 22–3. Marshall's interest in the Esquire Bedell's position was noted in JNKD, 20, 25 April 1877. The Minute Book of the Council of Bristol University College (BUL, Special Collections), minutes for 26 July 1877, records Marshall's appointment on pp. 49–50. On Marshall's appointment to Bristol and his responsibilities there, see below, Chapter 9, pp. 275–7.
26. Mary Paley Marshall's account of the Marshalls' years at Bristol 1878 to 1883, Notes from Memory by M.F. Pease in 1943 (BUL, Special Collection MSS Coll. DM 219).
27. Bristol University Archive, Executive Committee Minute Book, pp. 39, 45, 49.
28. Mary Paley Marshall, 'MSS Notes' (NCA), p. 5. Material in brackets crossed out in original.
29. Mary Paley Marshall, *What I Remember*, p. 22 and see above, Chapter 7, p. 189, which records the fact that their summer of 1877 was spent in Cornwall, working on *The Economics of Industry*.
30. Mary Paley Marshall, *What I Remember*, pp. 26–7, 39–40; J.M. Keynes, 'Mary Paley Marshall', p. 245, J.K. Whitaker, 'Alfred Marshall. The Years 1877 to 1885', p. 3 n.5. (A photograph of the house, which is still standing, is reproduced as illustration 36.)
31. Mary Paley Marshall, *What I Remember*, p. 26.
32. Alfred Marshall to H.S. Foxwell, 28 January 1878, Freeman Collection, 41/155.
33. See below, Chapter 18, p. 672.
34. G.H. Leonard, Letter to *Bristol Times and Mirror*, 8 October 1924, cf. Chapter 21 below, p. 771.
35. Mrs Ramsay to her mother, Mrs Buchanan, 28 May 1882; Sir William Ramsay to his mother, 19 November 1882, in *William Ramsay, Letters and Papers arranged by Morris W. Travers*, Vol. 5 (i), UCL.
36. Mary Paley Marshall to H.S. Foxwell, 22 September 1878 (Freeman Collection, 48/155).
37. Mary Paley Marshall, *What I Remember*, p. 23.
38. M.F. Pease, 'Account of the Marshall Years in Bristol', BUL, Special Collections MSS Col DM 219.
39. M.W. Travers, *A Life of Sir William Ramsay*, London: Edward Arnold, 1956, p. 45.
40. William Ramsay to his mother, 16 March 1880, in *William Ramsay. Letters and Papers*, UCL. Disputes over administration discussed in Chapter 9 (below, pp. 281–2) demonstrates the accuracy of Ramsay's first impressions.
41. William Ramsay to his mother, 23 March 1880, 1 May 1880; to his father, 19 May 1880 and to his mother, 4 June 1880. Ramsay's drawings of the Marshalls are reproduced as illustrations 29 and 30.
42. William Ramsay to his father, 29 November 1880, in *William Ramsay. Letters and Papers*, University College London Library.
43. J.M. Keynes, 'Alfred Marshall', p. 214.
44. Benjamin Jowett to Mary Paley Marshall, 30 September 1891 (Marshall Archive, 1:58).
45. This is discussed below, Chapter 17, pp. 652–4.
46. Above, Chapter 2, pp. 38, 41, below, Chapter 14, p. 498.
47. Alfred Marshall to Foxwell, 18 June 1879 (Freeman Collection, 1/9). For details of the Bristol experience see Chapter 9 below.
48. '[B]ut both Alfred and I were anxious that I should be allowed to help in the work of the College especially as it was the first College for mixed education', Mary Paley Marshall, 'MSS Notes' (NCA).
49. Bristol University College, Council Minutes, p. 91 (BUL, Special Collections). Cf. J.A. and Olive Banks, *Feminism and Family Planning in Victorian England*, pp. 50–51, partly quoted above, p. 224, n.*.
50. N.F. Pease, 'Some Reminiscence of University College, Bristol', typescript dated 13 February 1942, BUL, Special Collections. Alfred Marshall to Foxwell, 18 June 1879 (Freeman Collection, 1/9).
51. J.A. Banks, *Victorian Values and the Size of Families*, London: Routledge & Kegan Paul, 1981, pp. 72–3.
52. *Ibid.*, pp. 97–101, 113.
53. See below, p. 260 and note *.
54. Marshall to Foxwell, 29 April 1884 (Freeman Collection, 48/123).
55. *P* I, pp. 252–3, *P* VIII, p. 198.

56.   Marshall to John Neville Keynes, 30 August 1891, Marshall Archive, 1:102.
57.   Cf. W.G. Constable, 'Art and Economics in Cambridge', *The Eagle*, 59 (1960–63), pp. 23–6; some of her Palermo sketches are reproduced as pictures 23–25.
58.   Bristol University College, Council Minutes Book, pp. 207, 210, where it was recorded in addition to Marshall's reappointment to the chair of political economy that his wife be permitted to assist him by giving day lectures. W.M. Travers, in his *Life of Sir William Ramsay*, p. 76, firmly attributes the Balliol money to Benjamin Jowett's private funds.
59.   Marshall to Foxwell, 30 March 1883, 30 April 1883 (Marshall Library, 3:10, 3:17) and Jowett to Marshall, 28 March 1883, (Marshall Library, 1:18).
60.   Mary Paley Marshall, 'MSS Notes', NCA (my emphasis).
61.   Mary Paley Marshall, *What I Remember*, pp. 26–7; Jowett to Marshall, 28 March 1883 (Marshall Library, 1:18). But cf. above, p. 237 and n.* where her unpublished reminiscences indicate it was Alfred's relations who occupied their houses during holidays at this time.
62.   Marshall to Foxwell, 22 July 1883 (Marshall Library, 3:19).
63.   Marshall to Foxwell, 10 March 1884 (Freeman Collection, 12/73).
64.   Marshall to Foxwell, 29 April 1884 (Freeman Collection, 51/123).
65.   *Ibid.*, and see Vera Brittain, *The Women at Oxford*, London: Harrap, 1960, p. 66.
66.   Mary Paley Marshall, *What I Remember*, p. 35.
67.   Mary Paley Marshall, *What I Remember*, pp. 37–8. Mary Paley must have meant an Australian State Premier, since Prime Ministers were not elected until after Federation in 1901.
68.   Mary Paley Marshall, *What I Remember*, pp. 38–9. Paul Gavrilovitch Vinogradoff (1854–1925) was a noted Russian legal and medieval historian, who was in England for his research in 1883–84. Among his English books are *Villainage in England, Growth of the Manor, Origins of Feudalism, Outlines of Historical Jurisprudence, Laws of Medieval Europe* and *Studies in Social and Legal History*.
69.   JNKD, 17 March 1885, 27 June 1885 and 6 June 1886.
70.   Alfred Marshall to the Bursar, 2 February 1885, SB21 Estate File 57, Madingley Road, St John's College Archives.
71.   Marshall to the Bursar, 28 April 1885, 16 May 1885, 26 May 1885, 9 June 1885, Bursar to Alfred Marshall, 8 June 1885, in SB21 Estate File 57, St John's Archives. This also contains a copy of the lease dated 18 June 1886. The nursery, against whose potential manure heaps Marshall wished to safeguard himself, went out of business in 1910, when the site was developed for the construction of three substantial residential dwellings.
72.   St John's College Archives, Cambridge Building Site Wallet 21, Bursar to J.A. Moyes, 27 June 1885; Marshall to Bursar, 6 November 1885; Bursar to Marshall, 10 November 1885; Marshall to Foxwell, 6 July 1886 (Freeman Collection, 42/98). The Walkers had visited them earlier together with their daughter Lucy in June 1885. See J.P. Munroe, *A Life of Francis Amasa Walker*, pp. 308–9.
73.   Mark Girouard, 'The Architecture of John James Stevenson, Part II, in *The Connoisseur*, 185 (794), February 1974, p. 109.
74.   L.L. Price, *Memoirs and Notes on British Economists*, pp. 8–9.
75.   Mary Paley Marshall to E.R.A. Seligman, 9 June, 1891, Special MSS Collection, Seligman, Columbia University, New York.
76.   Alfred Marshall to F.W. Taussig, 20 March 1895 (Harvard University Library, Taussig Papers). JNKD, 18 June 1895 records attendance at a dinner party at the Marshalls at which Taussig and Sidgwick were present.
77.   J.M. Keynes, 'Alfred Marshall', p. 214.
78.   JNKD, 13 March 1887, 9 June 1887, 5 July 1890 and 15 September 1890; Marshall to Keynes, 4 April 1896, records a visit by Brentano, the German economist, which occasioned a luncheon (Marshall Library, 1/110).
79.   Mary Paley Marshall, *What I Remember*, p. 45.
80.   Alfred Marshall to Foxwell, 22 August 1887 (Freeman Collection, 23/168).
81.   L.L. Price, *Memoirs and Notes on British Economists*, pp. 17–18.
82.   JNKD, 27 November 1887, 19 February 1888, 4 May 1895, 18 February 1900 and 4 February 1904. Misses Mundella, Sharpley and Fletcher had all gained good results in their Tripos examinations, as did Miss McArthur. See below, p. 245, and note 92.
83.   Alfred Marshall to Foxwell, 21 April 1885 (Freeman Collection, 68/6).
84.   C.W. Guillebaud, 'Some Personal Reminiscences of Alfred Marshall', pp. 91–3.
85.   Mary Paley Marshall, *What I Remember*, pp. 43–4.
86.   JNKD, 8 November 1889; Florence Keynes to John Maynard Keynes, 5 September 1924 (KMF).
87.   Reproduced in Mary Paley Marshall, *What I Remember*, pp. 44–5, and see above, pp. 70, 117, on how the matter of the thirty-nine articles had affected Marshall in his early Cambridge years.
88.   Mary Paley Marshall, *What I Remember*, p. 41.

89. Mary Paley Marshall, *What I Remember*, pp. 39–41, Mary Paley Marshall to John Maynard Keynes, 12 September 1924, (KMF). As Marshall recalled to Chapman (letter on 20 October 1904, in *Memorials*, p. 456), she had 'even worked the bulb' for a group-photograph of the Marshalls' houseguests on that occasion, and see below, Chapter 13, p. 461.

90. The issues themselves are considered elsewhere, see below, Chapter 14, esp. pp. 506–7, Chapter 15, pp. 547–8.

91. Mary Paley Marshall to Benjamin Jowett, 19 October 1891, Jowett Papers, Balliol College.

92. Marshall to Foxwell, 9 November 1894 (Freeman Collection 3/127). For background, see Rita McWilliams-Tullberg, 'Alfred Marshall and the 'woman's question at Cambridge', *Economie Appliquée* (1), 1990, pp. 220–21. JNKD, 4 February 1904 mentions he encountered Miss McArthur at dinner at the Marshalls ten years later.

93. Marshall to Foxwell, 17 April, 1897, Marshall Archive 3, (33).

94. Alfred Marshall to Henry Sidgwick, 7 June 1882 (NCA).

95. Ethel Sidgwick, *Mrs. Henry Sidgwick, A Memoir*, pp. 168–9.

96. 'Review of Frances E. Willard, *How I Learned to Ride a Bicycle*', The *Economist*, 3 August 1991, p. 78.

97. Ethel Sidgwick, *Mrs. Henry Sidgwick, A Memoir*, pp. 140–43, 168.

98. Alfred Marshall to John Neville Keynes, 30 September 1897 (Marshall Library, 1:122); Marshall to Foxwell, 8 April 1897 (Marshall Library).

99. JNKD, 10 June 1898, below, Chapter 13, p. 444.

100. Mary Paley Marshall, *What I Remember*, pp. 45–6.

101. Mary Paley Marshall, *What I Remember*, pp. 46–7.

102. Belinda Norma Butler, *Victorian Aspirations*, p. 208.

103. Sir Austin Robinson, 'Review of *What I Remember*', p. 123.

104. Mary Paley Marshall, 'MSS Notes' (NCA); Notes for Jane Harrison's biographer (NCA).

105. Above, Chapter 7, p. 193 and n*.

106. Mary Paley Marshall, *What I Remember*, p. 22.

107. Mary Paley Marshall, 'MSS Notes' (NCA).

108. J.M. Keynes, 'Alfred Marshall', p. 201. The controversies with Laughlin, Walker and Macvane appeared in the first two volumes of the *Quarterly Journal of Economics*, Volume I, 1887, pp. 359, 477; Volume II, 1888, p. 218. They dealt with the theory of value in the broader sense, since the first of these items dealt with costs in relation to value, the second with business profits and the third with the relationship of wages and profits.

109. J.M. Keynes, 'Alfred Marshall', p. 202.

110. J.M. Keynes, 'Mary Paley Marshall', p. 239. Keynes's father, John Neville Keynes, used the book as a text useful for the Tripos in his economics teaching in the period 1877–85 when the Marshalls were absent from Cambridge.

111. Rita McWilliams-Tullberg, *'Economics of Industry'*, pp. 15–17, David Collard, then editor of the *Newsletter*, added that BUL has a first edition of the book presented by the Principal of Bristol University College, who was of course one of its authors.

112. J.K. Whitaker, Introduction to *EEW*, pp. 67–83, and cf. p. 47; the quotations in the text come from p. 67 and n.3.

113. See above, Chapter 6, pp. 177–8.

114. JNKD, 2 December 1876, 15 June 1877, 10 July 1877. It may be recalled that John Neville Keynes in his entry for 17 July 1877 commented on Alfred Marshall's style, 'Marshall's style of composition is bad, or rather he has no style at all.'

115. Alfred Marshall to Foxwell, 17 and 19 May 1878 (Freeman Collection, 44/155, 38/155); Mary Paley Marshall to Foxwell, 22 September 1878 (Freeman Collection, 48/155). For Jevons's problem in distribution, see Chapter 6, above p. 159.

116. Mary Paley Marshall to Foxwell, October 1879 (Freeman Collection, 16/9).

117. Alfred Marshall, 'The Future of the Working Class' (1873), in *Memorials* pp. 101–2.

118. See below, Chapter 12, p. 410 and n*.

119. Marshall to John Neville Keynes, 2 December 1889 (Marshall Archive, 1:93); Marshall to Keynes, undated but probably January 1888 (Marshall Archive, 1:61) and below Chapter 12, pp. 410 and n*, 424–5 and n*.

120. *P* IX, pp. 37, 41, 43, 44, 54.

121. In J.K. Whitaker, *EEW,* I, p. 289 n.7.

122. C.R. Fay, 'Reminiscences of a Deputy Librarian', p. 87.

123. Oral statement made at the conference, held at St John's College, July 1990, first made in his review of '*What I Remember*', cited above, p. 225. The word, 'foolometer' was apparently invented by Sidney Smith. See L.A. Tolemache, *Benjamin Jowett*, London: Edward Arnold, second edition, 1896, p. 47. Cf., however,

Marshall to Edgeworth, 17 March 1893, in which Marshall mentions both he and his wife were incapable of understanding 'the position' presented by Edgeworth in a review, after their independent reading of it.

124.   Alfred Marshall and Mary Paley Marshall to J.N. Keynes, August 1889 (Marshall Archive) and see above, note 114.

125.   J.M. Keynes, 'Mary Paley Marshall', p. 248.

126.   Mary Paley Marshall, 'MSS Notes' (NCA), p. 18.

127.   *EEI*, p. vii.

128.   *IT*, p. xi.

129.   Mary Paley Marshall, 'Biographical Notes for Keynes' (KMF), below, Chapter 19, pp. 715–7.

130.   In *Memorials*, p. 368. Cf. H.M. Robertson, 'Alfred Marshall', *AMCA* I, pp. 442–3.

131.   Marshall to Foxwell, 24 July 1881 (Freeman Collection 3/252); this letter also mentions the appearance of the second edition of *Economics of Industry*, a pleasing sign of market success.

132.   See above, Chapter 7, pp. 208–13.

133.   Mary Paley Marshall, *What I Remember*, p. 6.

134.   JNKD, 10 June 1885. In his diary, Keynes expressed disagreement with Sidgwick's judgement on this occasion. Ann Carr to J.M. Keynes, 29 October 1944 (JMK A/44).

135.   J.M. Keynes, 'Mary Paley Marshall', p. 242.

136.   C.R. Fay, 'Reminiscences of a Deputy Librarian', p. 88.

137.   Beatrice Webb, *My Apprenticeship*, Pelican, 1938, pp. 398–400, partly cited below, Chapter 14, pp. 517–8.

138.   C.R. Fay, 'Reminiscences of a Deputy Librarian', p. 88.

139.   Mary Paley Marshall, *What I Remember*, p. 19. In 1924, having read Keynes' Memoir on Marshall, Dora Sanger, the wife of C.P. Sanger, one of Marshall's more favourite students, wrote to Keynes that when Marshall made a speech at their engagement party, 'he admonished me to serve and cherish Charlie – and of course entirely ignoring my side of the bargain'. Dora Sanger to Keynes, 22 October 1924 (KMF).

140.   Above, Chapter 7, pp. 187, 193; below, Chapter 11, pp. 357–8, Chapter 13, p. 449.

141.   John Ruskin, *Sesame and Lilies*, edited by Sybil Wragge, London: J.M. Dent & Sons Ltd., n.d., p. 111.

142.   Cited in Frank M. McClain, *Maurice, Man and Moralist*, London: S.P.C.K., 1972, pp. 94, 108–9.

143.   John Stuart Mill, *The Subjection of Women*, pp. 55, 76, 98, 110; Marshall's attack on the two women economists whose useful writings Mill praised was made in his 1897 lecture, 'The Old Generation of Economists and the New', in *Memorials*, p. 296, and see more generally on this issue, Chapter 14 below, pp. 516–8.

144.   Frederick Harrison, 'The Future of Woman', in Frederic Harrison, *Realities and Ideals*, London: Macmillan, 1906, pp. 82–3.

145.   *P* I, pp. 263, 253. Cf. F.Y. Edgeworth, 'Reminiscences', in *Memorials*, pp. 72–3.

146.   Above, Chapter 2, pp. 38–40, 41.

147.   See Anne Parsons, 'Is the Oedipus Complex Universal? The Jones–Malinowski Debate Revisited and a South Italian 'Nuclear Complex,' in *Man and his Culture*, ed. Walter Muensterberger, New York: Taplinger Publishing Company, 1969, pp. 331–89, esp. 341–350 for the 'Madonna complex'.

148.   See illustration 34; information supplied to the author by Philomena Guillebaud.

149.   Mary Paley Marshall, 'MSS Notes' (NCA).

150.   For details, see below, Chapter 17, pp. 651–2, Chapter. 20, pp. 737–8.

9. Initial Academic Experience: Cambridge, Bristol and Oxford (1868–1884)

Marshall's initial academic experience as teacher and administrator can be conveniently discussed together. This covers his period as College Lecturer in the Moral Sciences at St John's in which he increasingly concentrated on the teaching of advanced political economy (1868–77), his period as Principal and Professor of Political Economy at Bristol University College (1877–81 and, as Professor only, 1882–83), and his period as political economy teacher for four terms at Balliol College, Oxford (1883–84). The chapter therefore provides the details of Marshall's main university activities during the years of his economic apprenticeship and until his return to Cambridge as Professor of Political Economy. It therefore coincides with his marriage in 1877 and with some of the travels already discussed. Where appropriate, reference is made to public lectures he gave in this period.*

ST JOHN'S COLLEGE LECTURER IN THE MORAL SCIENCES

The first teaching experience Marshall had acquired was at Clifton College as relief teacher in mathematics in early 1865; this was followed over a period of several years by teaching mathematics as a private coach to Tripos students. In 1868, the Master of John's, Bateson, offered Marshall a College Lectureship in the Moral Sciences, a particularly generous offer given the fact that the college at that time already employed J.B. Pearson in this task. As Marshall late in his life recalled, it was 'by the kindness of my College' that academic teaching became 'my career in life'.[1]

University lecturers, or indeed other permanent university teachers apart from professors, were not appointed by the university at that time. Except for professorial lectures to pass students and private coaching for honours students, teaching was done by lecturers appointed by the colleges. At the end of the 1860s, Moral Sciences was still a relatively new Tripos. Its first candidates, who required a B.A. before they could be examined, did not attempt its examinations until 1851. Success in the Moral Sciences Tripos examinations did not admit students to the B.A. until 1861. In its early years, students for the Tripos had been few, but in the ten years or so after 1866, that is, the decade when Alfred Marshall was initially involved in its teaching, the quantity and quality of students attempting the Tripos rose significantly. This was largely because its subject matter was highly exciting for those

---

* Chronologically, it therefore coincides in part with the previous three chapters. Some of Marshall's public lectures and writings published in this period are more appropriately discussed in other chapters. These include his articles in the *Bee-Hive*, his public lectures on Henry George's *Progress and Poverty* (discussed in Chapter 16 below, pp. 574–5, 582–5) and his paper, 'Where to House the London Poor', discussed in Chapter 13 (pp. 450–1).

growing up in the 1860s. Growth in numbers was assisted as well by the entry of women into the university from the early 1870s. Initially, they entered for this Tripos in relatively large numbers because it was an area of study particulatly suitable for them if not skilled in mathematics or classical studies.[*] Even then the number of students attempting the Tripos examination rarely exceeded twenty, so that the teaching staff appointed by the colleges for teaching its syllabus remained relatively small. In 1868, when Marshall joined this small band, it included Henry Sidgwick from Trinity, J.B. Pearson from John's, John Venn from Caius and T.W. Levin from St Catharine's. Two other teachers involved in the moral sciences at Cambridge that year were Henry Fawcett, Professor of Political Economy at Cambridge since 1863, and J.F.D. Maurice, who had succeeded John Grote as Knightbridge Professor of Moral Philosophy in 1866.[2]

A questionnaire was circulated at the end of the 1871–72 academic year by W.H. Bateson as Master of the college to seek information 'on the instruction given in the College by the College Lecturers'. Its scope was quite comprehensive. It required detail on courses taught, number of lectures per course, official enrolments per course and actual attendance, the necessity for more, or fewer, lectures in particular subjects, and whether this applied to the pass, or the honours students attempting them, and suggestions for improvement in the college teaching by the lecturers.[3] On 16 October 1872, Marshall answered the questions addressed to him with 'much fullness and minuteness' because he feared the Master and Seniors of the college had 'but an imperfect acquaintance with the details of the arrangements for teaching Moral Sciences in the College'.[4]

His response to the question on courses taught indicates the following. During the two academic years of 1871–72 and 1872–73 for which he provided information, he taught Moral Philosophy (Bentham) in October term 1871, Elementary (Mill) and Advanced Political Economy in Lent and Easter terms 1872; in October term 1872 he gave three lectures a week on Bentham's Moral and Political Philosophy while in Lent and Easter term 1873, as in the previous year, he planned to give lectures on Elementary and Advanced Political Economy.[5]

Marshall succinctly reported the workload this teaching implied. His answer is so clear and precise, that it can be quoted at length.

Three lectures a week were delivered in each course. A paper of questions was given out in each week with the exception, in some cases, of the first week of the course. Students were encouraged to write their answers in my rooms. Their answers were returned to them at the commencement of the next lecture, with corrections and sometimes lengthy notes in red ink. This lecture was in every case entirely devoted to giving, with full explanations, my own answers to the questions. I made special reference to the answers sent up by the students only in those cases in which a point had been made or an error committed which might be suggestive to the rest of the class. Each student was encouraged to ask for further explanation after lecture, if the answer given in lecture, together with the written comments on his own answer, did not suffice to make the matter clear to him. By this means unnecessary repetitions were avoided; while the

---

[*] Relative to successful entrants in the Moral Sciences Tripos, not to successful women students entering for Triposes. Up to 1880, Newnham and Girton students who did so successfully numbered 36 in Classics, 27 in Mathematics, 26 in Natural Sciences, 22 in Moral Sciences, 18 in History and one each in Law and Theology (information kindly supplied by Rita McWilliams-Tullberg). Over the period in question, successful entrants to the Moral Sciences Tripos therefore constituted only 16.8 per cent of all female successful entrants to Triposes but 30.6 per cent of all successful Moral Science entrants.

written comments obviated those misinterpretations and misrecollections to which verbal corrections are liable in all subjects, but particularly in the Moral Sciences. Besides the five courses of papers given, as above described, in connexion with my five courses of lectures, it will be seen that I gave four papers specially for Questionists. These were corrected and answered in the same way as the others. From six to eight hours were occupied in writing red-ink corrections to the answers to each of these papers. . . . The examination in Moral Sciences, and the examination for College Essay Prizes, involved considerable additional work. (They are both necessary: the latter has made me acquainted with some men who promise to be successful students of Moral Sciences.) Much time – on the average probably more than three hours a week during Term – was occupied in private, but official, conversation with students on the general course of their studies, and on special difficulties. The corresponding work for a student of mathematics or Classics is performed in general by his College tutor or his private tutor. Excluding the work referred to in the last two paragraphs, I spent on my direct public work as a lecturer on the average at least seventy hours a Term. (Of course I do not include time spent directly or indirectly in preparing lectures, or in making papers of questions: or again in correcting the answers of members of other colleges.)[6]

Several features from this answer should be noted. First, Marshall's hours devoted to formal teaching during term were quite considerable, well over one hundred hours on average per term, when the minimum of thirty hours from his private, 'but official', tuition are included. In addition, he spent a considerable amount of work on college examinations and Essay Prizes. His emphasis on this time-consuming work, designed, as he explained, to discover promising students for the moral sciences, is interesting. For similar reasons, he subsequently maintained this practice during his Cambridge professorship. His personal tuition by conversation, an aspect of teaching he later much admired in the Oxford tutorial system, was seen as odd by his fellow Johnians in the early 1870s. R.F. Scott, Master of John's in 1924 and a student in the 1870s, wrote to Maynard Keynes, 'In my undergraduate days, Marshall was a bit of a mystery to us. I well remember seeing him sitting on the steps of the gate over New Court with Cunynghame by his side. It seemed so odd a method of tuition to us who were under the rule of the formal Isaac Todhunter.'[7] Much of his teaching was also given free. It earned Marshall minimal fees as compared with what he could have made as a private coach. This habit also persisted when he became Professor of Political Economy at Cambridge in 1885.

Marshall's questionnaire responses were quite specific on his student numbers. In October 1872, his Moral and Political Philosophy class drew twenty students, the Lent and Easter term courses on Political Economy attracted nine or seven respectively. Marshall conceded, however, that this estimate entailed some potential duplication from students attending both classes, while during the latter part of the Easter term, attendance became quite irregular. Most of his students, Marshall stated, were Johnians. For example, no less than seventy per cent of his Philosophy class came from his own college. This high proportion is reflected in the 1873 Moral Science Tripos list: sixty per cent came from St John's.[8] To maintain regular attendance at his classes, he saw private persuasion in conversation as the only suitable avenue; other disciplinary measures were out of the question. In order to encourage attendance by persons from other colleges at his lectures, and at lectures in the moral sciences given by other lecturers, Marshall suggested a personal approach based on better information about students' wishes and requirements. More specifically, a teacher in the moral sciences should become personally acquainted with *all* the circumstances of his students: that is, 'details of the history of his study, with the nature of the difficulties which most hamper him, with his tastes, his hopes, his aims'. Such data on individual students was essential for course planning to meet student's individual requirements. It is interesting to note that when Professor at Cambridge, he systematically collected such information on his students on cards they completed when they joined his classes, and which he had printed especially for the purpose.[9]

Marshall's other suggestion for improvement in college teaching put forward in 1873, was to allow greater specialisation for the lecturing staff. This involved greater participation by junior Fellows in the college teaching than currently was the rule, and a policy of appointment of college lecturers favouring new areas of study rather than the well-catered-for branches of mathematics and classics. A valuable by-product of this greater specialisation was better preparation for, and hence better quality lectures. This also made for greater pride in the work by the individual teacher and higher standards reached by the students. In his response, Marshall had earlier illustrated this strategy by his employment of Foxwell to give a course of lectures in Logic for him. Apart from the valuable experience this gave to Foxwell, it freed Marshall for more efficient and effective teaching on Bentham and Political Economy.[*]

This type of lecturing schedule in Political Economy was kept by Alfred Marshall for the whole of his period as Lecturer in Moral Sciences. In his correspondence with Jevons,[10] Foxwell stated explicitly that he recollected little of the content from these lectures. An exception is that in the first lectures he attended in 1869, Marshall was already arguing that wages follow similar laws of determination to rent. Foxwell's general recollections of Marshall's lectures was that Jevons had no priority over Marshall, largely from the mathematics and 'curves' both their work contained. John Neville Keynes, who attended Marshall's Political Economy lectures in both 1874 and 1875, made no comments whatsoever on their contents in his Diaries.[11] Cunynghame, who gained a first class result in the Moral Sciences Tripos of 1873, after critically commenting on the poor quality of its philosophy and logic teaching, continued: 'On the other hand, we had the best teacher on political economy. Professor Marshall was a man who made his mark.'[12] From 1874 Marshall appears to have dropped his Moral and Political Philosophy teaching responsibilities, as earlier he had done with respect to Logic. This allowed him to concentrate more fully on his teaching of advanced and elementary Political Economy. Perhaps this was a consequence of his forthright recommendations on the need for such specialisation in his replies on college teaching to the Master.[13]

Marshall's university lecturing at this time was not confined to his college teaching. He was part of the team of Cambridge academics who lectured to women when from 1870 Cambridge opened its doors to female students on an informal basis. His first lectures to women were given in Lent Term 1871[14] and, on his wife's recollections, his lectures to her on the moral sciences covered at least the same topics which he had registered as his teaching subjects with the Master of John's. Mary Paley described the contents of his lectures on Moral and Political Philosophy as chiefly 'Bentham's and Mill's utilitarianism'.

---

[*]	*Ibid.*, pp. 72, 74, and see above, Chapter 6, pp. 175 and note ¶. Foxwell, who had graduated as Senior Moralist in 1870, therefore became Marshall's protégé at an early age and in 1877 took over Marshall's teaching on his departure to Bristol. His long friendship with Marshall and the manner in which it ended is discussed in Chapter 18.

In these, he was particularly anxious to distinguish the popular (and 'trivial') meaning of utilitarianism from its important one. In addition, he emphasised the importance of Bentham's services to economics:

> There is a popular usage of the word 'utilitarian" in which utilitarian considerations are opposed to ethical or are at all events distinct from them. I have tried to show that this usage of the phrase 'a utilitarian philosophy' is so utterly trivial and foolish that it is not worth while to discuss it. I have argued that not only is ethical well-being a portion of that well-being which any reasonable utilitarian system urges us to promote, but that it is much the most important element of that well-being.' He also said that Bentham had more influence on economics than any other non-economist, his contribution being the stress laid on measurement. 'When you have found a means of measurement you have a ground for controversy, and so it is a means of progress.'[15]

In her obituary of Mary Kennedy,[16] Mary Paley recalled an incident which confirms Marshall's general practice of teaching 'curves' to his political economy classes, on which Jevons had commented in 1874.[17] This was 'the incident of the blackboard, which seemed to Mary Kennedy and me to have got too old and greasy for all the complicated economic curves. So we put our money together and bought a large handsome one. However, it refused to let the curves be rubbed out and was ignominiously set aside for the old one. Marshall's economics lectures she attended also showed many of the signs of his historical stage, which characterised his thinking in the early 1870s. Mary Paley noted that by 1873–74 political economy was already,

> the main subject on which he lectured to us. In those days books were few. There were no blue books or Economic magazines and very few text-books. Mill was the mainstay, with Adam Smith and Ricardo and Malthus in the background. Hearn's *Plutology* was thought well of for beginners. Later on we read Jevons' *Principles*, Cairnes' *Leading Principles* and Walker on *Wages*. Mixed up with the lectures on theory were some on the History of Economics, Hegel's Philosophy of History, and Economic History from 1350 onwards, on the lines of the Historical Appendices to the *Principles*. He would give half an hour to theory and half an hour to history. He was keenly interested in Economic History.[*]

Marshall lectured his women's classes on more varied subjects as well. Whether this was part of his scattered Moral and Political Philosophy course, or an aspect of the more 'popular' lectures he also gave is not certain, Mary Paley's recollections of his lectures continue,

> Herbert Spencer's *Social Statics* and *First Principles*, . . . Kant and Butler's Sermons, and Thomas à Kempis and *The Mill on the Floss*, . . . he spoke [of] with great enthusiasm. (During those years George

---

[*] Mary Paley Marshall, *What I Remember*, p. 20. Her recollections on this point contain several mistakes. She cannot have read Walker's book on *The Wages Question* for Marshall's course since it was not published until 1876 but, in fairness to her, it was then immediately adopted as a Tripos book. She confused Jevons's posthumously published (and unfinished) *Principles* with Jevons's *Theory* which was recommended reading for the advanced class. The *Economist*, the *Fortnightly Review*, the *Academy* and the *Contemporary Review*, were periodicals Marshall used systematically in his teaching. Also, if Foxwell is correct, Mill *and* Smith would have been the mainstay of Marshall's lectures, with Malthus and Ricardo in the background. In the context of Marshall's lectures at that time Jevons heard from Foxwell, Marshall 'ranks no one above Adam Smith and Mill on the whole, and his horizon was certainly formed on their writings' (*Papers and Correspondence of William Stanley Jevons*, Vol. 5, p. 78).

Eliot was at the height of her fame, and *Middlemarch* came out in thin five-shilling instalments.) In these lectures he gave us his views on many practical problems, e.g. dancing, marriage, betting and smuggling. He would say that 'Life means a deliberate choosing an aim and working to that aim, and people should regard the steady performance of their work as giving them the pleasure that they need and if excitement tends to deafen our ears to the more delicate tones then it is wrong. Relaxation has the opposite effect for it gives us greater power of appreciating delicate harmonies.' . . . He dreaded the future of betting and thought that it might be a more serious evil than drunkenness. He had a horror of smuggling. 'It is a crime of a very grave nature. It is as much worse than ordinary stealing as getting drunk in church is than getting drunk in the streets, for it is an offence against the religious feeling towards the state.'[18]

In the same paragraph from which these aphorisms are taken, Mary Paley mentioned that in May Term 1873, Marshall gave six popular lectures to women, delivered in Mr Clay's Coach House. Their official title was 'Some Economic Questions directly connected with the Welfare of the Labourer', and they attracted a large class. Mary Paley's own, very detailed set of notes of these lectures has been preserved, with his (subsequent) minor corrections. Marshall's own rough notes for the lectures are likewise extant. Their content ranged over much of political economy, from its limitations to its uses (such as disproving underconsumptionist fallacies); from trade unions to co-operation, from poverty to drink, housing to charity, from education to luxury. Mary Paley's memoirs recall 'he said much about right and wrong expenditure, especially of time', and their contents, like those of the lectures mentioned in the previous paragraph, are aptly encapsulated by her summary comment: 'He was a great preacher'.[19]

The lectures to women are particularly interesting because they reveal the nature and scope of Marshall's social concerns at a relatively early stage of their development. In addition, when their tone and content is compared with the lecture on 'The Future of the Working Classes' which Marshall gave six months later to the Cambridge Reform Club, something can be said about his already well-developed skills in adapting the message to its audience because the two exhibit very similar conclusions on their subject.[20] Both, it may be noted at the outset, reflect Mill's liberal socialist principles on the subject of workers' emancipation through education, competition and co-operation; they likewise reflect Mill's ethological perspectives, with its marriage of ethics and political economy essential for the urgent task of character building; and both exposit remedies which entail enlightened government intervention in the form of factory legislation, subsidised education and even of cultural activities such as music. In addition, both depict as an ultimate goal the transformation of the working class into gentlemen, achievable by raising the remuneration of unskilled labour through making it more scarce and by lifting the standard of life and moral character of the working man through the diffusion of higher cultural and moral values. It is a mainstream liberal platform of working-class amelioration, for which Mill and Fawcett rather than Marx laid the foundation, hence it was a vision widely shared with the contemporary reform opinion then prevalent in Cambridge.* However, Marshall's praise

---

*   The lectures do exhibit some traces of Marx's *Kapital*, both in Marshall's own notes and those taken by Mary Paley Marshall. Marshall's own notes record a remark from Homer, as cited in *Das Kapital*, p. 398, on the technology of mills as a sign of industrial progress. Mary Paley's notes contain a reference to Senior's last hour analysis in wages and profit, the tone of which may easily have come from Marx's account: 'A certain man of the name of Senior, who may well wish now that all the first part of his career were blotted out, put forward an elaborate and deliberate treatise to prove that it was the last hour the mills were kept going which alone governs

of Octavia Hill's methods introduces an emphasis on self-help as a catalyst in working-class improvement, thereby holding out possibilities for elevating human nature.[21]

Except for length, there are, however, some striking differences between the two lecturing events, despite the similarities in the thrust of their shared subject matter. Apart from the more careful and detailed exposition of points allowed in six as compared with one single lecture, together with the greater room for copious illustration open to the lecturer in that case, there is a change in tone in the lectures to women. Unlike the lecture to the male audience of the Cambridge Reform Club, reprinted for the equally male college audience reading The *Eagle*, where argument is piled upon argument in support of Marshall's case, there is a strong sense of exhortation and sermonising in the lectures to women. This difference suggests that Marshall dichotemised the nature of instruction suitable to these types of audience from an early stage in his teaching career.[22] For example, his notes distinguished what he perceived as a peculiarly 'woman's question' and dwelt specifically on what he saw as educated women's special obligations to the cause which he was outlining. This took Marshall's lectures to the more radical type of female responsibility outside the home. In Lecture V especially, Marshall exhorted ladies in the audience to take up the work which had been so well begun by Octavia Hill. Marshall fully endorsed her rules for effectively improving the lot of the poor which were based on her practical experience in city slums, in particular its fourth exhortation that 'the poor . . . need the development of every power that can open to them noble sources of joy'. These joys, as Marshall subsequently explained, encompassed 'cleanliness, independence, ability to feel shame and a capacity to pleasure from doing one's work, that is, caring for property and for children'. The spreading of such truths created special responsibilities for a modern sisterhood of dedicated persons. For their role in properly organised charity work, they needed as desirable qualities, 'a high education; a power of sympathy, ready yet restrained; leisure; and a certain restlessness which should render inactivity an evil, all these being the distinctive qualities of women in society'.[23]

Lest it be thought these lectures only contained sermons and moral uplift, some discussions of economic questions of concern to the welfare of the labourer were presented as well. The first lecture provided extensive justification of an abstract political economy as a guide to correct thinking on social questions, provided that its limitations were fully understood. Lecture III not only developed ethical arguments about the appropriate ways for spending wages, it also discussed how wages were determined, and gave explanations as to why the lowest paid were so badly paid. Likewise, the economic advantages of education, and the best ways to encourage its spread were discussed amidst homilies on the evils of alcohol and its association with long hours of hard, physical labour. Emphasis in the lectures, however, tended to be on application rather than theoretical explanation, and the right response to such knowledge from the audience was continually stressed. No wonder that Mary Paley's recollection of these lectures in her reminiscences ended so aptly by noting her husband's qualities as a preacher.

---

profits and that if the last hour were taken away, all the profits would be gone.' Marx's *Capital*, Volume I, Chapter 9, Section 3, was devoted to Senior's last hour analysis.

The wider educational objectives of this type of lecture given by Marshall during his first Cambridge period, enable comment on his alleged participation in another extra-mural lecturing activity, the University Extension movement. There has been a strong presumption of Marshall's active involvement in this movement, so much associated with Cambridge University and with Professor Stuart. Stuart had given Mary Paley the task of writing a primer on political economy for this cause, a primer which developed into their jointly published *Economics of Industry*.[24] However, there is no direct evidence of Marshall's active participation in the Extension movement. Marshall's second of two articles in the *Bee-Hive* indicates his familiarity with it, but John Holmes's reply to the first article, only suggests he had met Marshall at Halifax, a town on the Cambridge University Extension lecturing circuit at the time, and provides no evidence of direct involvement.[25] However in 1873, and possibly 1876, he examined for the Extension movement in Yorkshire and Cheltenham. Apart from some of Marshall's work at Bristol, which may be described as university extension work, there is little additional justification for claiming Marshall's direct involvement in the Extension movement.[26]

During his first period as Fellow of St John's, Marshall involved himself publicly in two issues of university educational policy and College reform. Between 1868 and 1872 he wrote half a dozen letters on desirable improvement to the Previous Examination, the compulsory examination taken by both pass and honours students in their fourth term of residence. In 1871 he addressed the rule of celibacy for holders of college fellowships. The letters on the first topic illustrate Marshall's hostility to compulsory classical studies, particularly in Greek. Their proposals reveal considerable tact in that they suggest a scheme in which Latin by itself could serve as the compulsory classical studies component. This had the advantage, Marshall claimed, of achieving for all a degree of competency in Latin 'to enable them to read Virgil and Lucretius with ease and with pleasure', thereby giving all students some real access to that classical culture which the present regulations wished to encourage. The actual outcome of the current regulations for 'non-classical men' he argued, was that they never felt comfortable to read any classical author with ease, let alone with pleasure.[27] He also commented on the benefits for people intending to take the smaller Triposes, like that of the Moral Sciences, of specialising to a greater degree at this time in mathematics and more generally, scientific method.[28]

The letter on celibacy raised an issue which later affected Marshall profoundly, the incompatibility at the time of holding a fellowship and being married. Marshall turned this discussion into a plea for a professional lecturing staff, paid by college or university, selected by peers in the discipline the person was to teach. He proposed fees from students to supplement the regular stipend, since that, together with competition from younger teachers, would ensure satisfactory performance of teaching duties. Marshall proposed retirement at 55, with opportunities for extending the period of employment in special circumstances, as well as a retirement pension funded by college and university. The whole could be financed from a diminution of fellowships under the current system. The extent to which this was an application by Marshall of Smithian perspectives on university reform to contemporary conditions is difficult to ascertain.[29]

Marshall's activities while he was college lecturer just outlined, and more especially his wider involvement in university reform causes, owed much to the guidance of Henry

Sidgwick who, as Marshall later put it, was the mentor of all the young university dons on issues of university and social reform. Just as Sidgwick had been the more important person to acquaint Marshall of the need to study political economy in 1866 or 1867, so he was his leading mentor in the moral sciences, and the person from whom Marshall and others consciously 'borrowed their opinions on University reform'. The awe in which Marshall held Sidgwick at this time is most strikingly illustrated in his account of the 1867 Grote Club meetings. A good example is Marshall's undisguised admiration of the skill, and the knowledge, with which Sidgwick drew reminiscences of his early days from an old, and tired Maurice. For this period of his life, Marshall was pupil, as well as willing supporter of Sidgwick, in all things, the teaching of political economy only excepted.[30]

ADMINISTERING A NEW INSTITUTION: MARSHALL AS PRINCIPAL OF UNIVERSITY COLLEGE, JULY 1877– SEPTEMBER 1881

Marriage in 1877 meant resignation from Alfred Marshall's college fellowship and the associated teaching position, and a move to Bristol to take up the positions of Principal and Professor of Political Economy at its new University College. In July 1881, Marshall resigned both positions to enable him to take an extended period of rest from university activities, both for the sake of his health and for his writing. This took him first to Palermo for the winter and then to other parts of Europe. At the start of the 1882–83 academic year, he returned to Bristol to serve one more year as its Professor of Political Economy on funds provided by Jowett via Balliol. Bristol activities are conveniently divided into two parts. One examines his administrative duties as Principal for the four years ending 1881; the second looks at his teaching duties as Professor of Political Economy both inside and outside the university for the five, interrupted years ending 1883.[31]

The University College at Bristol which Marshall was to serve as its first Principal originated from two factors. There was first the growing demand in England for wider university education opportunities from the late 1860s. More specifically, the Bristol venture was associated with the requirements of the Bristol Medical School (founded in 1833) for better accommodation. Initiatives from a number of Bristol's prominent citizens had set the ball rolling. These included Lewis and Albert Fry, members of that noted Quaker chocolate manufacturer's family; W.L. Carpenter, a trained engineer, partner in a soap manufacture and son of the noted physiologist/psychologist and Registrar of London University. Others involved were John Percival, Headmaster of Clifton College, under whom Marshall had briefly taught in 1865 as relief mathematics teacher. In combination with some Oxford academics, drawn largely from Balliol and New College, and including Benjamin Jowett, they organised a public meeting in 1874 which instituted an appeal for the creation and running of a Bristol University College. The appeal set a target for a capital sum of £25,000 and annual contributions of £3,000 for five years to get the enterprise going. After two and a half years, this financial target had not been reached, auguring future financial difficulties for the college. The Committee nevertheless decided to proceed with its establishment. In October 1876, it held its first classes with a staff of seven (mainly part-time) lecturers and two professors. Shaky financial foundations meant many of the early appointments were temporary. Appointment of a Principal, or chief executive of the new institution, was not actively pursued until the new college was half-way through its first year's operations.[32]

The wide-ranging duties laid down for the position of Principal reflected the small size of the institution and its poor financial circumstances. Among other things, the Principal was expected to be *ex officio* Chairman of the Educational Board (consisting of Principal and Professors), liaise between it and the University Council (and its Executive Committee), have full responsibility with the Professors for discipline and progress of the students, including sole power over their suspension and dismissal, conduct examinations where necessary and report annually on the activities of the college to its Council. If the Principal was also a Professor, the Council guaranteed a salary of £700 per annum, of which £500 was in respect of the Principal's work, £200 for that of Professor.

Alfred Marshall was appointed to the post on 26 July 1877, his thirty-fifth birthday, after stiff competition of forty initial applicants, whittled down in stages to a short-list of five who were interviewed by the Council.[33] The selection committee consisted solely of academics. One, the Professor of Mechanical Engineering from Cambridge, James Stuart, would certainly have known Marshall from his *alma mater*; the other three from Oxford would probably not have heard of the Fellow from John's. They were Jowett, Henry Smith (Oxford's Professor of Geometry) and H.B. George (a history tutor from New College). Marshall's earlier acquaintance with Percival, a member of the Council, may have helped his eventual appointment. Jowett's invitation for Marshall to stay a weekend at Balliol during the selection procedures suggests he was considered early on as one of the favourite candidates.[34]

Marshall's testimonials for the position were very impressive. They included those from three of the country's leading economists, W.S. Jevons, T.E. Cliffe Leslie and Henry Fawcett; his former headmaster J.A. Hessey (who also had excellent Oxford connections), fellow Johnians Bateson, the Master, Todhunter (who had been Moderator at Marshall's Mathematical Tripos in 1865), Bonney and Foxwell (who was also former student and fellow teacher in the moral sciences), the Principal of Newnham Hall (Anne Clough), another former student (the Rev. V.H. Stanton) and Moral Sciences Lecturer of Trinity College (Henry Sidgwick). All spoke highly of his teaching ability, his academic excellence and his character with its 'remarkable' attributes of 'simplicity, earnestness and self-sacrificing conscientiousness' and 'integrity and sense of duty'. In short, nothing was left to chance.[35]

Marshall's administrative duties started almost immediately from the date of his appointment, a matter for which the Council expressed its gratitude at the end of the year.[36] The Committee and Council Minute Books give an even wider picture of Marshall's duties as Principal than that provided in the job description. He had to suggest amendments to the University College's Calendar and correct its proofs, to decide the scholarship order of merit lists, oversee room availability in a growing institution in temporary accommodation, arrange the appointments of new academic staff and plan the college programme of popular lectures to working men and others. There were resignations at short notice from important teaching posts, requests to draw up posters for the evening lectures, work associated with a newly established building committee on whose activities he had to report in detail for the

Council, and of course the requirement to report regularly on the number of students, their average attendance at lectures, the texts being used and the portions of them worked in each session. He also had to draw up the prospectus for lectures, construct new regulations for the award of some scholarships and the contents of some classes and attend (and chair in some cases) meetings of the Education Board, the Executive Committee and the Council. In the first year all these tasks, together with teaching, were carried out by Marshall without any assistance whatsoever. The Council did not appoint a clerk to act as the Principal's secretary until the 15 May 1878, so that Marshall by himself had to handle all administrative aspects of the college, which by then had over 300 day and evening students, excluding those at the Medical School. No wonder he wrote to Foxwell that during term college business left him little time for anything else, and that the appointment of the secretary would hopefully mean 'less Principal's work next year than this one'. The day lectures, which from 1878 were taken by Mary Paley Marshall, amounted to less than 'a tenth part of the work' while he could 'hardly get five minutes in the day outside the lecture room in which to think about Pol[itical] Econ[omy]'.[37]

Marshall's annual report for 1878 emphasised two factors of crucial importance to the college's initial development. First, it mentioned the educational successes which were being achieved, in terms of the growth of student numbers, and the college's increasing reputation, activities and standards reached by its students and staff. It then switched to the concomitant need for better accommodation, since inadequate room was the major constraint on the college's further development. Lack of finance, however, made it difficult to remedy such accommodation shortages at this stage. The best the annual meeting could do in 1878 was to thank Bristol's mayor for the present, temporary accommodation he was providing for the college at low cost and to point out how easily a rich city like Bristol should be able to raise funds for more appropriate buildings.[38]

Despite assistance from the newly appointed secretary, and the fact that Mary Paley was taking over the day class teaching responsibilities during 1878–79, Marshall's work at the college continued to be onerous. Only 'six days of *real* holidays' had been taken by the Marshalls during September 1878 before the start of the new session, but the accumulated college work and the preparation of an inaugural address meant that sustained leisure for writing and other activities was little more than a distant prospect.[39] A month later, Mary Paley conveyed to Foxwell[40] that pressure of other work had meant a rush job on Marshall's inaugural, that consequently he was 'not at all proud of it' and 'stoutly resisted sending [a copy of it] to Mr. Sidgwick'.

By mid-February 1879, illness intervened to make Marshall's duties even more onerous. Marshall's doctor had 'shut him up at home' and 'forbidden him to do anything for a week'. 'When he lets me out I must give the Gilchrist Lecture that ought to have been given in November'. On a more hopeful note, the letter referred to the appointment by the College Council of an architect, who 'will, I trust, soon build, but there is some doubt about it.'[*] By

---

[*] Alfred Marshall to Foxwell, 14 February 1879 (Freeman Collection, 20/9). The Gilchrist Lecture referred to, 'Water as an Element in National Wealth' (reproduced in *Memorials*, pp. 134–41) was part of a series of seven planned public lectures on water endowed by the Gilchrist Trust, of which six were given. Its contents are discussed below, pp. 292–3. Marshall in fact delivered it five times during March: in Bridgewater on 11 March, Bristol on 12 March, Trowbridge on 13 March, Frome on 26 March and Newport on 28 March. See J.K.

April, a stone in the kidney was diagnosed as the source of the trouble, and virtually complete rest was prescribed. However, Marshall wrote to Foxwell that his London doctor 'says I will in all probability be nearly as strong as ever by the end of the summer'.[41] This was not to be. Six months later, the 'first telephone in Bristol was set up by a scientist at the College between their home and the College' to facilitate communications for the relatively immobile Principal and to enable him to do his work uninhibited at home.[*]

Marshall's optimism about a speedy recovery from his illness, based though it was on London medical opinion, was therefore premature. However, by October 1879, Mary Paley reported that although he appeared to her stronger then he had been for some time, 'he seems only just able to go through his work', presumably because 'the College is flourishing and the entries are plentiful'. Two months later, further slow progress was reported, partly ascribed to the fact that their plans had now at last been settled.[42] These plans related to the feelers Marshall had been putting out in St John's College earlier that year to explore opportunities for returning to Cambridge in some capacity. In the event, these proved unworkable and they became less necessary when Bristol was prepared to make clerical appointments to ease his administrative burdens. During October, Marshall wrote to Foxwell indicating the indecision on his part about their immediate future, an indecisiveness which two months later Mary mentioned as being removed,

> I have put off visiting the Master [Bateson, of John's], because I do not wish to trouble him as long as I do not know my own mind. And a suggestion has been made here that some of my work can be taken from me – that which I think properly belongs to the secretary – my income being reduced. I could easily give up £100 or £200 a year, and shall stay if anything of this kind can be managed. But I don't think it can: meanwhile time is going on fast. Sidgwick writes that there are practically no Moral Sciences men. So I sup[pose] it would not do for me to think of coming back as a Mo[ral] Sc[iences] lecturer. But in my last year at Cambridge I had a large class (22) more than half of which consisted of best historical men. Do you think St John's would have me as a Historical Sciences Lecturer with the understanding that I looked after the men generally, and taught Economic History, Economics and perhaps Political Philosophy including Bentham.[43]

Lack of prospects at Cambridge together with a favourable Council decision on further administrative assistance on 19 November, meant that he stayed on at Bristol for nearly a further two years after submitting his resignation on grounds of ill health.[¶] When Marshall

---

Whitaker, 'Alfred Marshall: the Years 1877 to 1885', pp. 24–5, Committee Minutes Book, 16 November 1878, p. 97. A previous series of Gilchrist Lectures covered topics associated with heat.

[*] Mary Paley Marshall to Foxwell, 14 December 1879 (Freeman Collection, 19/4): 'we are going to have a telephone wire between our house and the college so that he may administer from afar'. The quotation is from 'Account of the Marshall Years at Bristol 1877 to 1883' by Mary Paley Marshall, Notes by M.F. Pease, 1943 (BUL, Special Collections MS DM 219). The Marshalls use of new technology in Bristol is further illustrated in these notes by their 'introduction of gas fires – then a new invention', and one which much surprised Jowett during one of his visits to the Marshalls there. He in fact asked where they got their excellent coal from, since his fire had kept burning all night. In his work as Principal, Alfred Marshall also used an electric pen (purchased in 1877–78 at a cost of £8.8s., which presumably allowed both faster and neater writing and enabled the preparation of more multiple copies from carbon paper. Examples of writing using this unusual instrument are preserved in the college's Minutes Books and in copies of statistical information he prepared for his Bristol students preserved in the Marshall Archive, Red Box. One is reproduced as illustration 56.

[¶] Council Minutes Book, 19 November 1879. 'A letter from the Principal tendering his resignation on account of the state of his health having been read and discussed, it was resolved that, 'The Council are very desirous of

eventually departed from the college in September 1881 after actually resigning his Principal's position some months before, he explained his change of heart as follows: 'it was represented to him that there were many works of organisation only half way on, and that to leave them would mean the breaking up of a number of things that ought to be pulled through'.[44] As Whitaker suggests, there were probably also solid fears on the Council that the resignation of the Principal at this critical stage in the college's affairs would sap public confidence, particularly important when the deterioration of its financial affairs during the 1879–80 session is taken into consideration.[45]

A letter to Foxwell in October 1879 indicates the types of options the Marshalls were considering to leave Bristol. After rejecting Foxwell's generous offer of sharing half his salary with the Marshalls to enable their return to Cambridge, Marshall stated they would be able to live for a considerable period on their own savings, if he resigned.

We should indeed lump the first five years 1877–1881 together, and consider that as we had done more of our share of money making in the first half, we might do less in the second half. After a rest, I should look out for some work, perhaps in Cambridge, perhaps in Scotland or anywhere in fact. During this year or two we may perhaps live in an out of the way farm house but it is not unlikely we should live in lodgings in Cambridge during part of the year, so that I might have the use of the University Library and Mary might have access to Newnham. Mary is indeed urging me very strongly to resign unconditionally in order that we may do this. And if [I] consulted my own inclination, I should as things are not feel justified in going away from this College in its present state if the Council wanted me to stay and were to relieve me of the Secretarial part of my work. As to my being made a Fellow, I never thought that possible for a moment[46]

In short, with the reduction in duties agreed to in principle at the November Council meeting, Marshall was happy to stay a little longer and see the college through the difficult period it was then facing, hence not endangering its delicate growth over the previous years to which he had devoted so much of his own energies.

Financial problems were the major reason for this difficult period for the college. A deterioration of the college's financial affairs during 1879–80 can be noted, associated with a temporary, as it turned out, drying up of donations and subscriptions in that year in both absolute and relative terms. Coincident college building activities also made inroads on its finances, partly because the reduction in its capital meant a smaller interest contribution to annual income. This was a minor worry as compared with what was happening to donations and subscriptions. In Marshall's first year as Principal, donations and subscriptions of over £3,000 were received, in line with the original annual target. These covered over 70 per cent of recurrent outlays and amounted to two-thirds of college income. The following year, 1878–79, donations and subscriptions declined to just over £2,500, that is, under half of income and outlays, while in the year ending September 1880, although this source of income had recovered to £2,730, it was now only a quarter of outlays in that year (of which half, or over £5,500, was devoted to building) and less than a third of recurrent income, half the building costs being financed from capital account. Fees were the only steadily growing

retaining Mr. Marshall's services and request him to continue in office for another year. They are willing to allow him to make arrangements which would relieve him of a portion of his duties the details of the arrangements to be approved by the Chairman.' The Council in addition resolved, 'That in view of a probable rearrangement of the duties of the Principal, the Local Executive Committee be empowered to consider and if necessary to re-arrange the duties and salaries of the secretary and clerk.' Council Minutes Book, pp. 128, 131.

income source for this period: they rose from £1,150 in 1877–78 to £1,817 in 1878–79 and £1,960 in 1879–80. Finances subsequently recovered. The general progress of the college, including most noticeably its building programme, generated substantial donations in the year ending 30 September 1881. They were in excess of £20,000 so that at the end of the year in which Marshall left Bristol, funds had been more than sufficient to cover the year's building outlays of £6,200 and to enable purchase of nearly £4,000 by way of new investments of East India annuities.[47] Marshall's responsibilities with respect to the actual financial affairs of the College seem to have been small. However, as he wrote to Foxwell,[48] he was involved in the regular 'begging' for funds from the Bristol citizenry on which both running and expansion of the college depended and as he later recalled to Hewins, his 'duties as advertiser in chicf were especially onerous' while he was at Bristol University College. It was also a task for which his 'personal disinclination . . . and loathing . . . is beyond conception. What I had to do of it at Bristol nearly killed me.'[49] Public relations, socialising and fund raising, were not really his forte.[50]

For almost a further two years after his aborted resignation, Marshall plodded on with his administrative tasks, watching the gradual growth of the institution he was superintending in terms of students, staff and eventually from 1880, accommodation. For example, the staff of two professors and seven (largely part-time) lecturers he had found on his arrival, grew during his period as Principal to eight professors (including himself) and seven lecturers (including his wife). One of the new appointees, William Ramsay, who replaced the foundation Professor of Chemistry, became the means of Marshall's eventual escape from the Principal's position at Bristol. As Marshall wrote to Lady Ramsay on the occasion of her husband's death, 'the new Professor of Chemistry began his work – and by the middle of November [1880] I knew I was free. For a true strong MAN had come to the College, and young as he was, I knew that its destinies were safe in his hands.'[51]

Student numbers were also growing. Day and evening students respectively amounted to 132 and 172 in 1877–78, a total of 304; they rose to 155 and 360 in 1880–81, totalling 515. Earlier on they had peaked in 1878–79 at a total of 720 made up of 316 day students and 404 students attending classes in the evening. This peak figure was felt to be grossly inflated, given the sporadic nature of enrolments (often for one term only) of students in that year. A better index was that of fee-paying students per term: these grew steadily from 1,082 (for the three terms of 1876–77) to 1,119 (1877–78), to 1,772 (1878–79) and 1,824 (1879–80), the last year of Marshall's tenure as Principal for which these data were presented in college Annual Reports.[52] Scholastically, the quality of the college was also improving. This growth was reflected in the gradual, but consistent, rise in the number of students awarded honours in their examinations, whose names were recorded by subject in the annual College Calendar.[53]

Marshall presented a detailed account of the nature and type of student the college was attracting in the evidence he gave in December 1880 to the Commission on Higher Education in Wales and Monmouthshire.[54] Amongst other things, this indicated the presence of 'articled pupils' to engineering firms (Q. 18,168–9); the fact that the many women who attended day classes were 'chiefly the daughters of the best families in the town', but that this applied less fully to male students, because the 'sons of the richest inhabitants of Bristol still go to Oxford and Cambridge' (Q. 18,165). Marshall also told the

Commission that three-quarters of the day students were 'between the ages of 18 and 22' but that many of the evening students were of 'mature age', often engaged in business (Q. 18,186). There were also relatively few boarders at the college, but in the absence of residential colleges and more reliable data, this was difficult to ascertain precisely. In the context of this discussion of non-Bristol students, Marshall also indicated that as part of his duties, he was 'prepared to give help to any student who wanted to find lodging' provided the student took the initiative of making such a request (Q. 18,194–7). In short, by 1880, student numbers were sufficiently large for the college to seek the services of a Registrar. His appointment later that year ensured a further effective reduction in Marshall's workload as Principal. Marshall, therefore, proposed financial support for the appointment, offering a reduction in his own salary, a gesture which the Council refused.[55]

Two further episodes from Marshall's period as College Principal are worth recounting. The first concerns a detailed report Marshall prepared for presentation to the Executive Committee of the Council on 20 June 1881, relating to additional building requirements of the college and their location. A draft of the report had been placed before a meeting of the staff, so that Marshall was 'authorised to say that in the form in which it now stands, it represents their opinion as well as my own.' The Report then records some general deficiencies in the existing building programme. It first notes underestimation of the number of lecture rooms required and overestimation of their proposed height; the appropriate conclusion reached by the Report was to stress the desirability of assigning separate lecture rooms to each of the twelve departments of study in the college. The Report also argued for the necessity of providing for a university library in the building plans; in its absence, the Report proposed a temporary solution for supplying students with essential library facilities. Existing plans should cater more adequately for practical and laboratory work in natural history and chemistry was also stressed in the Report. The last request suggests possible input of Ramsay, input explicitly acknowledged in the context of proposed alterations to the laboratory's design attributed to him. Its contents likewise drew attention to future requirements of physics and engineering for such facilities. Marshall advised the Committee of the desirability to locate the Medical School's dissecting rooms outside the main buildings: the additional room this yielded ensured satisfactory space for the college for some time to come.[56] The Report is interesting for at least three reasons. The first is its reflection of Marshall's emphasis on the need for adequate library facilities for students, a matter with which he also concerned himself greatly as Professor at Cambridge. Secondly, there is its explicit appreciation of the quality of Ramsay's advice in planning college affairs; while thirdly, the fact that the Report had been accepted (and amended) by a staff meeting showed Marshall's ability to learn from earlier mistakes in the handling of staff. Such mistakes had been made in relation to a review of college examination procedures, an episode from which he also came to respect the strength of Ramsay's will-power, initiative, and character. This interesting episode of his administration concerning an essential aspect of academic freedom, can now be examined.

Earlier the wide responsibilities of the Principal with respect to examinations were briefly noted. These were apparently interpreted by Marshall as a duty to scan individual examination papers written by students to maintain consistency of standards in the marking, especially useful for making decisions on scholarships. This practice was apparently (and reluctantly) accepted by the other academic staff until the appointment in February 1880 of Ramsay as Professor of Chemistry. In October 1880, Ramsay wrote his mother that he had made 'a protest against the staff having to give in exam papers to Marshall'. He continued,

> It is done nowhere else, and is a sort of espionage, which strikes me as very unprofessional. It is supposed to be a check on marking, but it quite fails. For how can Marshall be a judge of all subjects? He isn't omniscient. He is apparently greatly riled at my giving in the protest and has addressed me as *Prof.* Ramsay. I reply: My dear Marshall. I don't intend it the least personally, and many of the Council, and nearly all the staff agree.[57]

A fortnight later, he reported, 'The question of exam[ination] papers comes off on Saturday, and will be hammered out then. I suppose Marshall and I are on quite good terms. I took good care to make the row official'.[58] Ramsay's letter to the Council was not only official, it was diplomatic: 'I beg respectfully to protest against the custom which I find is practised in the University College, Bristol, of it being required of the staff to submit their corrected examination papers to the Principal. I have of course delivered up my papers, but I cannot assent to the propriety of the course'.[59] The Council on 17 November debated the matter on the basis of a Principal's Report. This indicated Marshall had involved the Educational Board, of which he was Chairman, in the dispute. The Council resolved to ensure 'appropriate standards', and left the achievement of this difficult objective to *all* members of the academic staff, who were, as far as possible, to be supplied with copies of the requisite examination papers.[60] Hence a staff meeting settled the matter before it got to the Council, and Ramsay wrote afterwards, 'everyone agreed with me [on the new method], even Marshall himself.'[61] The episode reveals an authoritarian tendency in Marshall's academic rule when in a position of power, as well as an ability to bow to the inevitable, features of his academic administration also visible during his tenure as Professor at Cambridge. The leadership role which Ramsay clearly took in this matter, was probably the factor which made Marshall realise in November 1880 that Ramsay was the means of his escape from Bristol University.

Marshall's correspondence with Foxwell shows that during 1880 such escape was never far from his mind. In debating his attempt at resignation in November 1879, it will be recalled the Council had asked him to continue his services as Principal for one year only in the first instance. In April 1880, Marshall therefore asked Foxwell, 'N.B. If you hear any rumour as to the chance of there being a vacancy for the professorship of pol[itical] econ[omy], will you kindly let me know at once.' This may have referred to correspondence of two years before in which Marshall wrote his 'beloved Fox' that he 'thought Fawcett wouldn't go off for another year [and that] I always intended to run when he did go off'.[62] On 21 November 1880, when his full year of service as Principal was well and truly over, he expressed interest in applying for the chair at London University College (for which Foxwell, who got it, and Cunningham were also applicants), but by 29 November he realised he was too late to put in his application. By beginning of December, Marshall consoled himself with the thought that he would not have liked taking his wife to London, even though 'she vows she would like it for herself. She is doing a great work here. I don't see how she could be replaced'.[63] However, by the middle of 1881, the Marshalls revived their plans for living some years on their savings and their writings, as Marshall had mooted in earlier letters to Foxwell, particularly since Ramsay became increasingly more attractive as his potential replacement.

On 4 July 1881, Ramsay wrote to his father,

> Marshall has been commissioned to sound me as to whether I will accept the Principalship here, keeping of course my present professorship. He says that he has long been in bad health and that the worry of the post wears him out. He wants to write on his own subject, and feels himself drifting back. He and Mrs. Marshall propose to retire into private life and to write books and study. He said that his means permitted of that with great economy. . . . My answer was: – 'I am first a chemist. I won't take it if it seriously interferes with my prospect of doing scientific work' – His reply was that it wouldn't. It hadn't interfered with his, and that I should get additional help.[64]

Travers was not really fooled by Marshall's untruth about the inroads administration made on original work. His comments on Marshall's reasons for resignation, reasons Marshall confirmed in the actual letter of resignation he sent to the Council show this, and are perceptive in other ways. Travers attributed Marshall's inability to combine administrative and original work to the fact Marshall was highly disorganised and a solitary worker; whereas Ramsay who, as the record shows, did much original research work in his years at Bristol, was highly organised and able to collaborate. 'Marshall, though ably seconded by his wife, herself an economist, was essentially a solitary worker', only drew on her talents for minor research and secretarial assistance.[65]

However, Marshall saw the prospects of his resignation as relief, and once the die was cast, welcomed it as an opportunity to be 'for the first time for a very long while surprisingly happy and free from anxiety'. The two years of retirement they proposed, at this stage still in the country, would mean an improvement in health by escaping from the drudgery of the external work in public relations and entertaining, so essential a part of his task given the poor financial circumstances of the college. This work, though it 'would not toss a strong man at all, makes me not only unhappy but also to a great extent useless for the rest of the day, and very often for the next day or two.' In contrast to Travers's views, Marshall also hoped this period of retirement would provide greater opportunities for intellectual cooperation with his wife.[66]

On 18 July, the Council of University College, Bristol, accepted Marshall's resignation with regret, and in its resolution expressed 'high appreciation of the great ability, energy and devotion to the interests of the college displayed by him and Mrs Marshall during the whole period of their connection with the institution, and to express the heartiest wishes for their future welfare, and especially for the restoration of Professor Marshall's health'.[*] Although Marshall's resignation was formally accepted on 18 July, Ramsay was not appointed as his successor by the Council until 27 September and Marshall's resignation as Principal therefore did not take effect until the first of October 1881.[67] The delay was caused by

---

[*] Council Minutes Book, 18 July 1881, pp. 179, 181. Marshall's letter of resignation read in part, 'The part of my work which lies within the walls of the college presents no difficulty; but all the external work is extremely burdensome to me . . . the result is that while on the one hand I am almost entirely neglecting studies which I am most anxious to pursue I am on the other unable to push the interests of the college outside its walls with anything like the energy with which they could be pushed by a stronger man' (*ibid.*, p. 180).

William Ramsay's marriage that summer and his subsequent honeymoon which he did not want to interrupt by attending college Executive Committee meetings. When the Ramsays returned from their honeymoon on 28 September, they not only took over the Marshalls' external duties with respect to entertaining, they also rented their house in which the Marshalls had exercised those social responsibilities over the previous four years.[68]

A gathering of former political economy students at Bristol on 29 September, recorded their gratitude to the Marshalls for having given them the 'great advantage of studying this most wide-reaching, important and interesting science of Political Economy under one who is at once so completely its master and so enthusiastically devoted to it as you are. We shall never forget the very pleasant hours which we have spent with you over this most interesting study'.[69] Apart from the printed copy of the address which the students presented to their former Principal and teacher as a momento of his work in Bristol, they prudently presented to his wife the sum of £113.18s., which they had collected among themselves as a tangible expression of concern for their welfare during the coming years of unpaid retirement.[70] By early October the Marshalls were in Palermo. It was to be three years before administrative academic duties were once more laid on Marshall's shoulders after his election as Professor of Political Economy at Cambridge in December 1884.

Over the longer run, the University College at Bristol commemorated the services of its first Principal in other, tangible ways. Marshall received an Honorary Doctorate from Bristol in 1911. The *Bristol Times* reported on the occasion of the celebration of the college's golden jubilee, that a fireplace in private rooms (originally those of the Vice-Chancellor) carried oaken carved heads of Alfred Marshall and Sir William Ramsay in recognition of the services rendered by these, its first two Principals. The Wills Building erected in 1925 long after the Marshalls departed, likewise carries a tangible monument to Bristol's foundation Principal and Professor of Political Economy in the shape of a gargoyle. Few economists and academic administrators can have their services recorded for posterity in such an unusual, if not unique, manner.[71]

PROFESSOR OF POLITICAL ECONOMY AT BRISTOL: 1877 TO 1881, 1882 TO 1883

The address presented to Alfred Marshall by his students at his farewell from Bristol in September 1881 focused attention on his other major activity at the University College. As its foundation Professor of Political Economy, he was responsible for the teaching of the subject, a responsibility which, after the first year, he shared with Mary Paley. Alfred Marshall took the day students for his first year only, subsequently confining himself to evening teaching. Mary Paley later recalled about his Bristol evening classes, that they were largely

> attend[ed] by business men, trade unionists and a few women; they were less academic than those at Cambridge; and were a mixture of hard reasoning and practical problems illuminated by interesting sidelights on all sorts of subjects. Later on Lady Jebb told me that she went to his lectures because they supplied 'such good after-dinner conversation'. And there were plenty of jokes mixed in. One member of the class, Herbert Grundy, could not take in a joke at once, but a loud guffaw used to be heard like thunder a minute or so later.[72]

Although no record survives of the jokes which entertained Marshall's Bristol students, his course outlines and textbook lists are preserved in the Bristol University College Calendar and Syllabus. In addition, a set of rough notes for lectures he gave on 'The Economic Influence of Government' in 1879–80 can still be studied in the Marshall Library.[73] Both outlines and notes illustrate the depth and range of Marshall's lecture material. In contrast to the impression his later students gave of his teaching, the material he lectured on at Bristol seems to be highly organised and systematic. The notes for the nine lectures suggest that his Bristol students in 1880 were given a broadranging, and an occasionally theoretically demanding, overview of the subject. They also indicate that the material on Bentham's political and moral philosophy he had used as a moral sciences lecturer at Cambridge was not being wasted at Bristol.

After raising the general question of the functions of government, at once broad and compact, and general as well as those related to property, Marshall presented the functions of the state in a historical framework. This initially involved the three stages of ruling chiefs, absolute kings and constitutional monarchy. Chiefs, although replaced if they did not do what people liked, had no sense of trusteeship, and custom rather than system decided their function in individual cases. Absolute monarchs were trustees of God rather than of the people, but the exercise of their government's functions rested on personal predilections with respect to war and private luxury. The gradual evolution of constitutional monarchy developed principles of justice and equality, first for the ruling castes, then more generally. By the time of Bentham, the state was involved in poor laws, the expenses of public worship and the cultivation of arts and sciences. The French Revolution 'popularised' notions that 'the state exists for the people' and that 'all people are equally important'.[74]

The second lecture dealt with private property in relation to government, indicating that private property was a relatively new institution. It was reported that Smith's notion of a natural human right to the produce of labour was questioned by Bentham, and could in any case only apply to what is grown on the land. Even this was too simple. A market for corn, for example, required transport, hence taxes for roads. Bentham's views on property were then developed, in terms of his aims of subsistence, abundance, equality and security.

The third lecture discussed the implications of security and equality for taxation. Security of property was of crucial importance, votes to defend the security of property in times of war therefore needed the special difficulties of a two-thirds vote. Marshall then turned to how the primary aim of security of property was reconciled with the demand for equality in taxation. The joint stock principle of taxation suggested proportionality in terms of the citizen's share of national wealth; however, it also sometimes suggested that taxes should be levied to 'equalise wealth as far as possible without creating great alarm'. This last proposition raised further problems. First, lowering taxes on the poor expanded population and therefore not happiness; secondly, 'a division of taxes to make men nearly equal' would produce only a very low average income per head, which Marshall estimated at £35. Marshall's conclusions from this lecture were summarised as follows: 'don't take all taxes off working man but (i) spend state money on raising him, and (ii) be careful how far state money is spent [on] luxuries of the rich, the most extravagant of which is war'.[75]

The fourth lecture was devoted to detailed discussion of Smith's four canons of taxation, as a prelude to more general analysis of taxation principles in the remaining five lectures. Lecture 5 discussed the compatibility of differential duties and free trade, and reflected on tax collection. Lecture 6 explored more fully various forms of direct taxation. It expressed a preference for taxes on expenditure over taxes on income, because of their promotion of thrift; it objected to taxes on property as taxes on thrift; and supported modest progressivity in income taxes by exempting 'necessary income'. Although more elegantly demonstrated, these propositions indicate the debt Marshall owed to Mill on the subject. The final three lectures further analysed property taxes, customs duties and presented some rules for optimal taxation. Under the last topic, Marshall proposed that 'other things being equal, a tax on a commodity which obeys the law of diminishing returns is good, for the tax raises price, diminishes consumption, therefore diminishes cost of production of that produced under the [least] favourable circumstances, [and] therefore raises the price by less than [the] tax. Also [it] can be provided [to inflict] small injury to consumer's rent [surplus].'[76] The lectures succinctly present in an organised way many of the concerns in taxation which Marshall later presented in his very few published writings on the subject,[77] and show that in this case at least, he was quite capable of presenting carefully planned, systematic lectures on a specific topic without wandering off on various tangents.

That Marshall was also an inspiring teacher at Bristol, a quality his later lecturing seems to have fully preserved, was recollected by one of his first students at Bristol, Miss Marion Pease. After mentioning that her first experience with political economy had been the evening lectures by Marshall's predecessor, P. Hallett,[78] whose text had been Millicent Fawcett's *Political Economy for Beginners*, she felt that she 'knew all about the subject' and it was

> therefore in a somewhat patronising mood that I entered the large double lecture room with its great bow window, on a dark October afternoon in 1877 to hear Mr. Marshall's inaugural lecture. He spoke without notes and his face caught the light from the window while all else was in shadow. That lecture seemed to me the most wonderful I had ever heard. He told us of his faith that economic science had a great future in furthering the progress of social improvement, and his enthusiasm was infectious. I think the whole audience must have listened as breathless as I did.[79]

Others recollected his elementary course on political economy which used Mill as the textbook. 'He dealt with the method of political economy and its relation to other sciences, with the material and mental and moral elements of national wealth, with the causes and consequences of competition. He went much beyond Mill, . . . when he discussed the connection between a man's daily work and his character; and – for it was the days of the Charity Organisation Society – with the proper aims of public and private charity.'[80] The last sentence about his Bristol lectures points to another continuity with his Cambridge lecturing practice: the temptation to use the lecture platform as pulpit for presenting his views on the role political economy played in ethology and in guidance for the practical decisions of everyday life. In addition, these introductory lectures dealt with the theory of production in terms of division of labour, population growth and capital accumulation; the theory of value defined as the causes determining rent, prices, wages and profit; trades unions and cooperation; the use and abuse of luxury; and issues in money, banking, trade, government and taxation in which market fluctuations and commercial crises, the incidence of excise and custom duties, rates and taxes, were systematically explored in a preliminary way.[81]

In the evening courses he gave at Bristol, Marshall lectured on money, banking and foreign trade in the sessions of 1878–79 and with some changes, again in 1880–81; in 1879–80 he presented lectures on economic progress and the material already discussed at some length from his extant lecture notes on the influence of government. An impression of the contents of the other courses is so succinctly given in the outlines Marshall prepared for the *Calendar*, that they can be extensively quoted:

> MONEY AND BANKING – The nature and functions of money. Medieval notions about money. The causes that determine the value of money. The early history of Banks. The Bank of England. The gradual growth of the English money market. Joint Stock Banks. Bill Brokers. The Clearing-house. The Stock Exchange. The relation of the English money market to those of other countries. The influence of credit on prices: its nature and extent. Commercial fluctuations: the history of crises 1800–1880. Banking Reform. A standard of value for deferred payments: bimetallism.
>
> FOREIGN TRADE – The benefits of trade, whether domestic or foreign: the use of a special theory of foreign trade. The balance of imports and exports. Why England's imports exceed her exports. The Exchanges. The character of England's foreign trade: the resources and requirements of her competitors and customers. The causes which enable one country to undersell another. England's trade prospects. The influence of England's foreign trade on the character of her people, and in particular on the relations between her capital and labour. The difference between the effects which foreign trade produces on an old and a new country. American arguments for Protection.
>
> Text-books for the lectures: – Mill's *Political Economy*, book iii; Jevons on *Money*. Consult also Bagehot's *Lombard Street*, Goschen's *Foreign Exchanges*, Walker's *Money in relation to industry*, Gilbart's *Principles of Banking*, Wilson's *Resources of Modern Countries*, Fawcett's *Free Trade and Protection*, Text-book for the classes, Marshall's *Economics of Industry**
>
> *Economic Progress*, its nature and results. Its influence on prices, on wages, and on interest in the past, present and future. Modern forms of speculation and trade combinations. Monopolies. Rings on the Stock Exchange. The principle that 'each man is led by his own interests to that employment of his capital and labour which is most advantageous to the society among which he lives.' Limitations of this principle: in particular those due to trade combinations.[1]

Some aspects of Marshall's teaching methods need to be mentioned. The contents of his courses as shown in these outlines emphasise one aspect of his teaching method: the judicious mixture of theory and applied economics which suited the mature age audience of his evening lectures. The mathematical argument his lectures occasionally contained[82]

---

* J. K. Whitaker, 'Alfred Marshall: The Years to 1877 to 1885', pp. 45-6. The outline of the course of money and banking differs only slightly from the outline for 1878–79, largely in terms of the manner in which the contents are set out. See *ibid.*, pp. 43-4. The lectures were preceded by a more general one-hour class, in which the principles of the science were outlined with the assistance of their new text, *The Economics of Industry*, which had been published in October 1879. Note the placing of the apostrophe in Marshall's in the outline, given the discussion of the previous chapter and which, as Principal, it was Marshall's dity to check and correct when reading the proofs.

¹ J.K. Whitaker, 'Alfred Marshall: The Years 1877 to 1885', p. 44:P the summary of the segment of the course on government has been omitted. On the basis of this course outline, Whitaker (*ibid.*, p. 34) suggests that during his period at Bristol Marshall had time to develop a theory of economic growth, which rather vaguely provides the unifying framework for *The Economics of Industry*, and which became the equally implicit but mich more precise theoretical framework for the *Principles*. See also his 'The Marshallian System in 1881: Distribution and Growth', *Economic Journal*, 84 (333), March 1974, pp. 1-17. The matter is further discussed in Chapter 12 below, pp. 403-4.

similarly reflected at least part of these students' background in the engineering works and like industries in which they were employed. He himself was proud of this achievement, as he explained in his evidence to the Committee on Higher Education in Wales,[83] when he noted an interesting feature of his college's experiment with evening classes. There were no formal entry requirements, students who found they could not cope with the material presented in classes, dropped out of the course (Q. 18,245). Notwithstanding this, the evening classes largely duplicated the work required from the day students (Q. 18,246). In this context, Marshall defended also the wide range of courses offered at Bristol University College, a necessity if students were to be attracted to its courses in adequate numbers (Q. 18,347). This policy perhaps also explains why his own courses ranged so widely in terms of material covered, dealing with topics on which he afterwards never produced 'an authoritative account'.[84]

Marshall also assisted his students in gaining access to study material, essential, given the absence of satisfactory library facilities at the college which has already been mentioned. Apart from lending freely from his own bookstock, a practice he maintained at Cambridge on a rather generous scale, he provided his evening students with summary statistics. These included time series on wheat and silver prices; Young's estimate of the national income of England; Gregory King's estimates, as reproduced by Chalmers; population data from the census; statistics on English rents compiled from sources such as Davenant, Bellers, Arthur Young, Wakefield and McCulloch; Baxter's 1867 estimate of national income; taxation statistics and data on wages, prices and consumption per head.[85]

Although Marshall's resignation meant the courses in question were never given by him,[86] his lecture outline for the 1881–82 session is particularly interesting. It reflects a desire to come to grips with the wider aspect of distribution theory and its practical application to prospects for working-lass improvement, an issue of overriding concern to him. The lecture outline emphasises themes which remained an important feature of Marshall's teaching and writings over the decades to come, and is therefore reproduced in full:

SESSION 1881–2: THE THEORY OF WAGES AND ITS APPLICATION
Tuesdays 7–9. The subjects of this course will be:
I.   THE THEORY OF WAGES: – Land, labour and capital as agents of production. The growth of population and capital. Division of labour. The law of value. The distribution of the total income of the country into the shares of land, labour and capital. Unskilled labour, skilled labour and business management. The rate of interest. Normal wages and market variations of wages.
II.   APPLICATIONS OF THE THEORY and consideration of some closely allied practical problems. History of the Gilds. Trades Unions: their past, present and future. Arbitration and conciliation. Co-operation. The history of socialism. Property and Land Tenure. The right methods of public and private poor-relief. National Education. National Recreation; the Factory Acts. The incidence of taxation on the working classes. How wages are affected by variations of commercial prosperity and by changes in the purchasing power of money. Government as an employer of labour and as a manager of railways and other commercial enterprises. The limits of the *Laissez Faire or non-interference* principle.
Text books – Marshall's *Economics of Industry*; Mill's *Political Economy* (especially Book IV, ch. vii, and Book V.) consult also Walker on *Wages*, Thornton on *Labour*, Howell on *Trades Unions*, Brentano on *Gilds*, Holyoake on *Co-operation*, Crompton on *Arbitration*.[87]

Marshall's leave from Bristol lasted for only one year. Money made available to Bristol University College from Balliol, or more accurately, Jowett, enabled his return in September as Professor of Political Economy. William Ramsay wrote to his parents in May 1882 that 'Marshall is to return next October', a move the University College Council endorsed at its regular May meeting.[88] The lectures Marshall gave as Professor of Political Economy in 1882–83 covered a day course in advanced political economy (taught jointly with Mary Paley, each taking a one-our lecture per week) as well as his more usual evening classes. The programme for the latter, as outlined in the *Calendar*, provided for an illustration of the theory of value by means of the economic history of England for the last hundred years, an exercise foreshadowing the chapter on the influence of progress on the theory of value which featured in the last book of his *Principles* and reminiscent of his favourite Book IV in Mill's *Principles of Political Economy* which dealt with the same theme.[89] Once again, both outlines are of sufficient interest to be reproduced in full:

SESSION 1882–83: ADVANCED COURSE with MRS. MARSHALL.
Some of the subjects of the elementary course will be treated more fully, and in particular the history and the practical applications of the science will be discussed at greater length. The instruction on Mondays will be given by Professor Marshall, that on Wednesdays, will be given by Mrs. Marshall and will relate chiefly to Adam Smith's *Wealth of Nations*. *Text books*: Adam Smith's *Wealth of Nations*; Mill's *Political Economy*. The following also may be read: – Ricardo's *Principles of Political Economy*; Bagehot's *Lombard Street*; Goschen's *Foreign Exchanges*; Fawcett's *Protection and Free Trade*; Leone Levi's *History of English Commerce*.[90]
SESSION 1882–83: THE THEORY OF VALUE ILLUSTRATED BY THE ECONOMIC HISTORY OF ENGLAND DURING THE LAST HUNDRED YEARS.
Tuesdays 7–9. In this course an explanation will be given of the chief changes that have taken place in prices, wages and profits in England from the invention of the steam engine to the present time; and an inquiry will be made as to the influence which these changes have exerted on the sum total of human happiness. The instruction given in the regular 'classes' will be adapted to the wants of beginners. Some theoretical difficulties will be discussed with advanced students in extra classes which will be held from time to time as occasion requires. The first lecture, which will be open to all, will be on 'The Economic Condition of England a hundred years ago'. It will be given from 7 to 8 on Tuesday, October 10th. Text books. – Mill's *Political Economy*; Marshall's *Economics of Industry*. Consult also Leone Levi's *History of English Commerce*.[91]

Marshall's teaching duties at Bristol also included giving a number of public lectures. As mentioned in the last lecture outline, it was a convention that the first lecture of the session given by a professor was in the form of a public lecture and open to all. It was this type of lecture which Mrs Pease attended in October 1877 and described as Marshall's inaugural. His inaugural, however, was not given until a year later, as Mary Paley had written to Foxwell in letters already quoted.[92] Both 'inaugurals' were reported in the local press in considerable detail, which suggests Marshall had himself provided their texts.[93] The first dealt with the 'Aims and Methods of Economic Study', the second with 'Some Aspects of Modern Industrial Life'. Since the first represents a clear statement of his 'credo as an economist' and the other one of his several pleas for a new, more appropriate form of education, their contents need some examination.

The opening section of Marshall's lecture on the 'Aims and Methods of Economic Study' recalls the methodological first lecture of the six he gave to women at Cambridge in

1873. It defines the scope of economics in terms of human conduct and well-being relative to the acquisition and ownership of wealth. The strength and weakness of economic science are then illustrated. This is done first in terms of its inability to experiment as compared with the natural sciences, then in terms of the misuse of its laws to which its findings are more prone than those of most others.[*] However, as long as its limitations are properly understood, the more important of which Marshall stated was its inability to 'be the guide to life', it is one of the more useful of sciences. To quote the report of the lecture,

> Does political economy, then, give us no help in such matters? Yes, when it is used and not abused. But political economy is abused when any one claims for it that it is itself a guide in life. The more we study it the more we find cases in which man's own direct material interest does not lie in the same direction as the general well-being. In such cases we must fall back on duty. What political economy will enable us to do is to show men the grave evils they are inflicting on others; but when that is done, all we can say is – do unto others what you would that they should do unto you. Political economy will help us rightly to apply the motive force of duty, but the will to do one's duty must come from another source. Still political economy will doubtless show, in many cases, that selfish action is also foolish and suicidal. And on the whole it does show, in almost every case, that when a man adopts action which injures others, he injures himself more than he thinks he does.[94]

The lecture then briefly mentions the value of economic study to the science of ethology, or the formation of human character; 'suffice it to say that during the best hours of six days in the week . . . character is being formed in the workshop'. In summary, the lecture concluded:

> The method of political economy is that of every successful science. Pursuing it you must (1) collect facts; (2) arrange them under laws; (3) apply laws to practice; (4) correct your law, make it more accurate where you can, broader where you can. Be always urgent for facts. But no fact is any good unless it is alive; make it alive by seeing how your laws bear upon it; how it helps to prove, or elucidate, or correct your law. As to motives for the study. Study it not to be able to sprout economic dogma, but to obtain power – power which, when you know all about any practical question in which there is an economic element (and there is in most) will enable you to reason more clearly than you otherwise could. Study it to trace the vast forces that have moulded the characters of nations and have determined their history. Study it to see whether the aid you give to those in distress is so given as to leave behind it a hidden mischief. Study it to enable you to see how far anyone in seeking his own advantage is injuring others, and whether if he is injuring others he is not also bringing, in the long run, evil on himself.[95]

Marshall further elaborated on this theme in his introductory lecture to the political economy class, likewise reported in the press the day after it was given. After going through the various topics which would be covered in the course (as outlined in the *Calendar*) Marshall repeated his belief that 'reasoning from economic laws is such dangerous work', and explained why this was the case:

---

[*] See J.K. Whitaker, 'Alfred Marshall, the Years 1877 to 1885', p. 50. Marshall's examples of wrong applications are of interest. One concerned the (wrong) suggestion by people that there are insufficient resources for the extension of education, the other dealt with the wrong inference from natural economic harmony, when suggesting the impossibility of injuring others without injuring themselves. Its falsity was demonstrable from trade union behaviour, as was done in *EOI* (Bk. III, Ch. VIII, §1, pp. 206–7) and subsequently in *P* I, pp. 430–34, *P* VIII, pp. 382–6.

Firstly, there may be some imperfections about the statement of the laws; secondly, people may have made a blunder in their reasonings from them. But there is another source of error in obtaining practical conclusions which is ten times as important as these two put together, and that is, the difficulty of finding out what are the economic laws which are applicable to any particular case. There is an economic law which is popularly expressed by saying: Wages and prices will always find their own level. This means that wages in employments of equal difficulty tend to equality, so that if people can move perfectly easily from one to another without any difficulty whatever, the wages in these two must be equal, unless, indeed, one of them is more disagreeable or dangerous than the other.[96]

However, despite this easy misuse, many economic laws developed by able thinkers over a long period of time, had been severely tested. These therefore seemed 'now as certain as the propositions of Euclid'. In spite of this, they still needed conscious adaptation to contemporary and local conditions, to take account of custom and the need to do 'our own duty', and to be constantly informed by a deeper understanding of the present as history.

The greatest epoch of the world's history is that in which we are living now. Surely it is worth while to think of what is going on around us! Take trades unions for instance. Their history is a vast epic poem full of grand good and evil. Whether they attain the greatest future which is possible to them or fail of it is, . . . a matter of greater importance than the rise and fall of one half of the States with whose annals the pages of history are filled.[97]

The critical implications of conventional historical study to which Marshall referred in this closing paragraph is the theme to which he returned on a much broader canvas in his 'inaugural' of 1878, 'The Aspects of Modern Industrial Life'.[98] This lecture started with a warning of the biases of conventional approaches to classical and historical studies which tended to exaggerate the greatness of ages gone by. A more appropriate reaction to the past, Marshall suggested, was to use it as 'a means of guessing what future generations will say of our own', hence employing history as a tool to place contemporary problems in proper perspective. This is what he proposed to do in the lecture, first, by outlining 'the difficulties of modern industry'; secondly, by showing how the forces of modern science, including social science, could best be harnessed to their solution. This second part of the lecture was a plea for the important work the college was doing in providing modern education for the future leaders of Bristol. The first, by emphasising the important role of the modern businessman, entailed the presentation of a flattering picture of those who were to make the funds available for the local educational task. The inaugural arose therefore directly from what he saw as his foundation pincipal task.

The lecture's implicit aim is captured in the manuscript version preserved with the Marshall Papers, and can be quoted in full because it also gives a foretaste of the more romantic view of the morally uplifted and intellectual businessman which Marshall developed in later work:

Let us attempt to give to the businessman of Bristol that true literary education which refines the mind and broadens its interests in human life. But above all let us endeavour to educate him that his business will ever be calling forth the knowledge and the mental faculties which he has acquired at College. Let us so equip him with a knowledge of the scientific principles that bear upon the business of his after life that he may abandon rules of thumb; that he may understand for himself the reason of all that he does; that if he tries a new experiment he may be able to predict its result with tolerable accuracy, so that his experiments may not be at haphazard, but all of them near to the mark. He will not then waste his time and his substance upon new endeavours made almost in the dark, endeavours that do but discourage others. With the bright light of science guiding him on his path, he will go boldly and vigorously on, trying that which has not been done before, overcoming new difficulties, pioneering new paths. He will thus not only help to cause this country of England and this town of Bristol to hold a front place in the first van of industrial progress. But further, because he has pursued those studies which will be called into play in his business, therefore his business will every day give him scientific problems which he will glory in solving because they are problems; therefore he will be helped by his business, he will almost be forced by his business, to lead an intellectual life. Though a businessman, nay rather because a businessman, he will play an important part in making this age a great intellectual age.[99]

Apart from the forward-looking perspective on business education which Marshall presented here, and which he later also outlined in his evidence to the Committee on Welsh education,[100] the lecture demonstrated the increasing foresight and decisive action by the entrepreneur which the growing forces of competition would require. If England could not meet this challenge, 'then America will', and the education of men for business would assist England in this great task.[101] The lecture therefore broaches major issues the mature Marshall was to tackle at Cambridge. He developed them theoretically in arguments in the *Principles* on competition and the need for business organisation; he attempted to give them practical effect in the educational reforms he introduced in his new Tripos.[102]

Marshall also gave lectures at Bristol aimed at a wider public than that generally associated with its University College. Some of these were associated with, if not inspired by, the University Extension movement. The lectures on heat and water financed by the Gilchrist Trust seem to fall into this category. They were spread over a substantial regional audience from being repeated five times at different locations by each lecturer. Moreover, they were directed at a working-class audience, were examinable for those who wished to be tested, something encouraged by the incentive that good performance enabled free attendance at Bristol University College evening classes. The unity gained from their very general subject matter, first heat and then water, made them appear as miniature, self-standing courses. Marshall explained these wider aims in some detail to the Committee on Higher Education in Wales.[103] Other examples of this type of lecture are 'The Economic Conditions of America', and the three lectures on Henry George's *Progress and Poverty*. These were also officially supported by the university and in part designed to enhance working-class attendance at its evening lectures.[104] Marshall's 1879 Gilchrist Lecture on 'Water as an Element of National Wealth' is conveniently discussed at this stage to round off the account of Marshall's lecturing experience at Bristol.

The economic content of this lecture appears light, but raises many crucial issues. Whitaker's[105] concise summary uses Marshall's remark that 'in estimating a nation's wealth, mistakes are likely to be made – firstly, because many of nature's best gifts to man are not included at all in the inventory; and secondly because the inventory under-rates the importance of everything which is so plentiful as to have a low market value.' Part of the lecture was therefore a commentary on problems in national income accounting, a topic which greatly interested Marshall at the time, judging from the statistics he handed out to his Bristol students. More theoretically, it was a modern application of Ricardo's distinction between value and riches, modern in the sense that improvements to urban water supplies were an important national investment. Much of the lecture was devoted to the various economic uses of water, in which Marshall demonstrated his erudition in seeking out curious facts. Its final part looked at the broader social and historical consequences of water in determining national life and character; a rather Hegelian historical touch, clearly inspired by Marshall's reading of his *Philosophy of History*.[106] The lecture is typical of Marshall's Bristol period. It provides application of simple economic propositions, drawing on the facts and placing them within a broad, historical perspective. Marshall's historical period had finished by then in the sense of active, general research on historical topics. The value of that research to his work continued. It is visible in the gloss he put on his arguments both in lectures and in his writing.

The high moral tone Marshall took in some of his Bristol lectures in respect of the duty to society of citizen and businessman, enables a further generalisation of his lecturing style: Marshall tended to use the lecture podium also as pulpit. That feature of his Bristol work was succinctly noted by James Wilson in a letter he wrote to Mary Paley Marshall a few days before their departure for Sicily. Wilson had succeeded Percival as Headmaster of Clifton and hence became part of the Marshalls' social life in Bristol. He was earlier encountered in the context of Marshall's Mathematical Tripos as a Johnian first wrangler and student of Parkinson, though he had left his college before Marshall was elected to its fellowship in 1865.[107] Wilson's letter captures Marshall the preacher in practice:

> I preached a sermon a little time ago where the burden was that religion was the caring much and caring always for one's duty and that all that we call religious was but accessory to this end. And no one has been of late years such a religious teacher to me as the later Principal of University College. Whether he finds help for his life where I do I know not, and it is a matter of secondary importance. In what is primary he has long been my master. I most earnestly hope that he will have health and strength to continue his work. He has certainly filled his life with great interest. . . . I hope both his pupils and yours (I am in both classes) will not forget what they have learnt, and yet you will be multiplied in small reflected lights [108]

TUTORIAL FELLOW AT BALLIOL COLLEGE, OXFORD: 1883–1884

If their generous reappointment of Marshall to the Political Economy chair in May 1882 had led the Council of Bristol University College to a belief that this situation was to be more or less permanent, within twelve months this perception turned out to be mistaken. Death intervened by creating a vacancy at Oxford, to which the Marshalls all too willingly escaped. Eighteen months later, a further death enabled a return to Cambridge, the spiritual home for which Marshall had longed from the time marriage had forced his exile from its hallowed portals. William Ramsay, Bristol's new Principal, saw Marshall's successive moves in these years as signs of his naked ambition. On 29 April 1883, he wrote to his parents,

> The latest news is that Marshall is going to leave us, to retire to Oxford. He has been offered a lectureship at Balliol College, not worth much momentarily but . . . he told me that the present Prof. of Pol. Econ. Price is nearly 80 years of age. M[arshall] has a pretty knack of doing what appears unselfish with a due regard for contingencies. He got at the same time an offer to lecture at Cambridge, I forget in what

capacity, but as he explained he would have had to share the honours there with about a dozen others, whereas at Oxford he reigns second to only one, and he an octogenarian.[109]

Ramsay was not altogether sorry, even though Marshall 'is a nice fellow', he wrote to his father in May when Council had approved Marshall's resignation.[110] When Marshall's election to the Cambridge chair was reported in Bristol, Ramsay wrote to his father: 'Marshall . . . has been appointed Prof. of Political Economy at Cambridge, succeeding Fawcett. . . . I believe he was waiting for the shoes of the Oxford man, but lo! Cambridge has become vacant first. Bonamy Price, the Oxford man is over 85 years old!!'[111] Irrespective of the ultimate motives, the Marshalls departed Bristol for Oxford in the middle of 1883.

The cause for the vacancy at Oxford's Balliol College, the death of Toynbee, provides perhaps more cogent reasons for the move to Oxford than Marshall's ambitions for a chair at one of the ancient universities. A letter to Foxwell, confirming his acceptance of the appointment to Oxford offered to him a fortnight previously,[112] claimed that a sense of duty influenced the decision. Cambridge was well supplied with economics teachers, while at Oxford there were 'vast flocks of untended sheep without (economic) shepherds'. Although Marshall was sceptical about his ability to attract many students in a place which did not treat economics as a serious study, they nevertheless had the feeling 'that we ought to go'.[113] The vision of Marshall as the good shepherd takes on further meaning in the light of the picture of his Bristol teaching presented by Wilson of which, it may be presumed, the Master and Fellows of Balliol College had not been kept in ignorance. A preaching economist, with social aspirations of the type Marshall espoused, was not only a good person to fill the vacancy left by Toynbee, it matched yet another loss that Balliol had recently suffered in the death of T.H. Green, Oxford Professor of Moral Philosophy, almost exactly the year before (26 March 1882). All three, Toynbee, Green and Marshall, have been depicted as prime representatives of the new liberal perspective of the 1870s. As a branch of idealism, this repudiated hedonism and conceived of progress as a boundless and beneficent process.[114]

Marshall's adoption of this new liberal perspective to social reform was part of his economic apprenticeship and almost certainly developed quite independently of its Oxford adherents, Toynbee and Green.[115] Like them, it recognised the duty of the social reformer to moralise competitive capitalism, a matter which Marshall had broached in his Bristol classes when demonstrating the need for both moral and intellectual business men. In contrast to the old, Manchester-style liberalism, the new liberals acknowledged the problems inherent in a competitive and individualist society. These they sought to ameliorate through social action. Action by the state in this vision of improvement came in only as a last resort. Community action was to be achieved through voluntary associations; trade unions, cooperative societies, charity organisation societies, social discussion groups and an ethical movement concerned with the inculcation of social duty. For much of his life, Marshall supported such communal institutions in various ways.[116] The overriding aim was to remove inequality and distress by lifting standards to those reached by the lower middle class, to turn workers into 'gentlemen', as Marshall had put it in 1873.[117] Jowett, as Master of Balliol and friend of the Marshalls for close to six years would have been well aware that

Marshall's social and moral perspectives strongly resembled those of his recently deceased Balliol College Fellows.[118] In this sense, the period at Oxford supplemented and deepened tendencies in Marshall's economic education while for Oxford and Balliol it provided a replacement of two of its earnest lost sons.

The moral climate at Oxford would therefore have been particularly exhilarating to Marshall, given his own views on social reform and improvements and the means to achieve it. However, and this needs emphasis, he cannot have learned much from Toynbee and Green in this respect, apart from their greater examples of practice by actually working for the poor in the slums of the East End. Marshall preferred his wife to do such active community work with the University Settlement and the Charity Organisation Society and came closest to directly aiding the poor by letting a small and select number of them stay in Balliol Croft during the summers under the watchful eye of Sarah, the maid. For Toynbee he had admiration, but not as an economist; for Green he had respect but of a kind which makes it difficult to speak of wholehearted admiration. It is instructive to note in this context that the reference to Green's *Prolegomena to Ethics* was not inserted into the *Principles* until the third edition, and that in this, and the subsequent edition, Marshall implicitly described Green's position on economics and ethics as rather 'uncompromising'.[119] With respect to Toynbee, Marshall saw him as a modern Saint Francis, 'the founder of a new order, the leader of a new and more direct attack on the evils of the age', but apart from his reference to Toynbee as 'one of the noblest of the rising generation' of economists, Marshall's *Principles* only mentioned him as one of many English economists who replaced the mechanical elements of the science with an emphasis on the human.[120]

Aspects of Marshall's stay in Oxford have already been discussed.[121] The concern here is with the teaching Marshall had to do. This was initially geared to students for the Indian Civil Service, but as he explained to Foxwell after he had been elected to an unpaid fellowship at Balliol, he was attracting a wider range of students than those.[122] His lecture outline covered similar material to that given in Bristol, as is made clear in a printed prospectus for the 1884–85 academic year in which Marshall had planned to give these separate courses, presumably on lines similar to those he had given the previous year. This outline is as follows:

I   General Course:
         Michaelmas term – Production, Rent and Value.
         Lent term – Distribution, Money and Foreign Trade.
         Easter term – Economic Progress and the Function of Government.
II   Economic theory: Michaelmas term only.
III   Advanced Course: Lent term only.[123]

More information is available on the Advanced Course in a letter Marshall wrote to J.N. Keynes, who replaced him at Oxford for the year after Marshall's appointment to the Cambridge chair. It indicates the following subject matter for the Advanced Lectures to the best of Marshall's recollections:

i   difficulties in the Theory of value, and of wages and rent with special reference to Mill Bk IV

ii   further working out of the theory of crises and over-production

iii   the difficult parts of the theory of taxation, with special reference to the problems started by Adam Smith in Book V. . . . I had proposed to give half the time to this because questions of taxation open up all the earlier difficulties and are therefore specially well suited for a revision course: also I had said next to nothing about them in the 'Economic theory' course.[124]

Marshall's appointment, and subsequently his lectures, were well received at Oxford. The *Oxford Magazine* reported on 17 October 1883 that Marshall's course outline promised 'he was going to be an active teacher'. After a month of lectures, it noted at the end of November, that Oxford had 'gained a very accomplished lecturer as well as a learned economist in Alfred Marshall'. The report continued,

His lectures, delivered without the use of notes and with considerable impressiveness of voice and manner, have been well attended in spite of the collision of the hour with that of many Halls. Mr. Marshall enlivens the course of his lectures with little excursions on various points. Thus, in dealing with Socialism last week he entered on the amount of income necessary for men of different rank and occupation. A careful consideration of his own circumstances had led Mr. Marshall to fix the minimum for a bachelor fellow at £300, including £60 for four months' travelling, but not horse exercise, which might in some cases be necessary.[125]

L.L. Price, one of the three good students Marshall taught in his year at Oxford, as he later recalled to John Neville Keynes,[126] described Marshall's lectures as being

somewhat discursive, based, so far as they were based at all, on notes, and not embodied in any formal written shape, and there were frequent, apparently extempore, digressions, seemingly prompt at the moment. But the discourses (or observations) were vividly alive and wonderfully instructive. One went away each time with something stimulating to think over. It might indeed puzzle or seem hard, but it was hard grit.[127]

Price in addition recorded some other facets of Marshall's teaching practice. He apparently checked the class roll each class during which, 'perhaps from democratic sympathy, which assuredly he frequently evinced, he hurried over the name of the Duke of Newcastle, one of not a few notable listeners'. Price also enjoyed Marshall's 'at homes' for informal discussions, a 'pleasant added benefit' in which Mrs Marshall joined.[128] Although Marshall was elected to a fellowship at Balliol a year after his original appointment, gaining all privileges from that position apart from the salary, he apparently found it difficult to meet informally with students outside the teaching situation.[129] His emolument at Oxford was not ungenerous. He was paid initially £60 a term plus tuition fees based on the number of students he was teaching which amounted to £26.13s.4d.[130] With respect to teaching, Marshall was also greatly impressed with the personal tutorial system at Oxford, which he tried to introduce into Cambridge some years after his return.[131]

Fawcett's death opened up that opportunity of returning to Cambridge, an opportunity for which Marshall had been waiting since 1878. Oxford therefore enjoyed its 'accomplished' economist's 'accomplished' lectures for only four terms, congratulating him, as the *Oxford Magazine* put it in January 1885 on his appointment, but lamenting the fact that they felt he would be a hard man to replace.[132]

NOTES

1. Biographical Fragment, dated 3 October 1920, Marshall Library, Large Brown Box. It may not only have been Bateson's kindness. The appointment of 'agnostic' Marshall to teaching moral sciences may have balanced that of Pearson, who brought a strong theological emphasis to the moral sciences, as Marshall recalled (above, Chapter 5, p. 112).
2. See D.A. Winstanley, *Late Victorian Cambridge*, Chapter 4; A.S. and E.M.S., *Henry Sidgwick. A Memoir*, Chapter 3; Cambridge University, *Historical Register, being a Supplement to the Calender*, pp. 703–10; J.M. Keynes, 'Alfred Marshall', p. 172 n.2. Levin and Pearson initially taught political economy as well as Marshall.
3. Questionnaire on College Teaching issued by the Master of St John's College, Cambridge, 10 June 1872 (St John's College Library).
4. Responses to Questionnaire on College Teaching at St John's College Cambridge, Chapter 14, p. 65 (St John's College Library).
5. *Ibid.*, pp. 65–6.
6. Responses to Questionnaire on College Teaching at St John's College, Cambridge, pp. 67–8.
7. R.F. Scott to J.M. Keynes, 23 October 1924 (KMF). Marshall's thoughts on teaching are explored in more detail below, pp. 292–4 and especially Chapter 10, esp. pp. 316–17.
8 Responses to Questionnaire on College Teaching, pp. 69–70, *Historical Register*, p. 709.
9. Responses to Questionnaire on College Teaching, pp. 70, 73–4, and see below, Chapter 15, p. 555.
10. Foxwell to Jevons, 12 November 1879, in *Papers and Correspondence of William Stanley Jevons*, Vol. 5, p. 78; in a letter to the Master of St John's, Foxwell explained that part of the advanced political economy course for the moral sciences syllabus was described as 'the diagrammatic expression of [Economic] Problems in Pure Theory, together with the General Principles of the Mathematical Treatment to such Problems', a part of the syllabus only Marshall was really capable of teaching. Foxwell to Taylor, Master of St John's, 6 October 1881, St John's College Archives, D104:109.
11. JNKD, 21 April 1874, 2 February 1875. However, on 13 March 1875 he commented, 'Marshall has been speaking very highly indeed of some of the papers I have done for him, even in lectures', a practice Marshall had described as part of his teaching method (above, pp. 268–9).
12. C.H. Dudley Ward and C.B. Spencer, *The Unconventional Civil Servant*, London: Michael Joseph, 1938, p. 61. Cunynghame said philosophy teaching at Cambridge 'was a hundred year's behind its time. I do not believe there was anyone in the whole University who understood Kant, and Hegel was only mentioned to be sighed over or scoffed at. We wasted time over such rubbish as Hamilton's lectures on philosophy and [Mill's Logic].' On at least one of these subjects there was little improvement in the next few years. J.N. Keynes recorded in his diary on 13 June 1874 that he also thought 'Venn's lectures on Hamilton useless'. Cunynghame's services to Marshall's work on monopoly were recorded at the Cambridge Philosophical Society in 1873. See above, Chapter 6, pp. 162–3.
13. This at least is the impression given by Keynes's *Diaries* because Sidgwick lectured to him on these, and other, subjects during 1874 and 1875.
14. B.A. Clough, *A Memorial of Anne Jemima Clough*, London: Edward Arnold, 1897, p. 61, and see above, Chapter 8, p. 228.
15. Mary Paley Marshall, *What I Remember*, p. 19.
16. Mary Paley Marshall, 'Obituary of Mary Kennedy' (1940), cited in Rita McWilliams-Tullberg, 'Mary Paley Marshall 1850–1944', p. 26 n.47.
17. Jevons to Marshall, 7 January 1875, *Papers and Correspondence of William Stanley Jevons*, Vol. 4, pp. 95–6.
18. Mary Paley Marshall, *What I Remember*, p. 19. The material on marriage omitted here was quoted in the previous chapter.
19. *Ibid.*, pp. 19–20.
20. Marshall Archive, 'Lectures to Women', Easter Term 1873; the lecture he gave on The Future of the Working Class in November 1873 was discussed in Chapter 6 above, pp. 174–5.
21. See above, Chapter 6, pp. 141–2.
22. See Eugenio Biagini, 'Marshall's 1873 Lectures to Women', *Quaderni di storia dell'Economia politica*, IX (2–3), 1991, pp. 335–41, esp. 338–9.
23. Marshall, 'Lectures to Women', Lecture V, 23 May. For a critique of Octavia Hill's approach as a reaction to the experience of the 1860s, see G. Stedman-Jones, *Outcast London*, pp. 193–6, 256–61.
24. See, for example, John Whitaker, 'Alfred Marshall: The Years 1877 to 1885', *History of Political Economy*, 4 (1), Spring 1972, p. 4 n.9 and p. 39 n.3. It is interesting, that Stuart's *Reminiscences* make no reference to the Marshalls, although Marshall by the time of its publication had gained an enormous reputation compared to his

status as junior Fellow of St John's College when they first met. Marshall's testimonials for the position of Principal at Bristol also make no reference to such experience despite the fact that the one by Foxwell, listed its author as a former extension lecturer.

25. Royden Harrison, 'Two Early Articles by Alfred Marshall', *Economic Journal*, 73 (291), September 1963, pp. 423 n.5, 430. Their content is discussed in Chapter 16, below, pp. 574–5.
26, CUL, Minutes of the Local Examination Syndicate (Information supplied by Rita McWilliams-Tullberg). John Whitaker, 'Alfred Marshall: The Years 1877 to 1885', p. 25; the Bristol activities are discussed below, pp. 275–93.
27. *Cambridge University Gazette*, 2 December 1868, 14 April 1869.
28. *Cambridge University Gazette*, 9 December 1868.
29. *Cambridge University Reporter* (successor to the *Gazette*), 22 February 1871; Adam Smith, *The Wealth of Nations*, Book V, Chapter I, Article II, 'Of the Expense of the Institutions for the Education of Youth', Oxford: Clarendon Press, 1976, esp. pp. 760–64; and cf. *IT*, p. 98.
30. Above, Chapter 5, p. 112, and see below, Chapter 18, pp. 663–4.
31. This part, and the section on Oxford, draw heavily on John Whitaker's detailed contribution on this aspect of his life, 'Alfred Marshall: the Years 1877 to 1885'. In addition, I am also much indebted to Mr Michael Richardson from the Special Collections Department of Bristol University Library, who greatly helped my inspection of Bristol University's extensive holdings of materials relating to this aspect of Marshall's career.
32. Basil Cottle and J.W. Sherborne, *The Life of A University*, Bristol: published for the University of Bristol by J.W. Arrowsmith Limited, 1959, Chapter 1, pp. 1–10.
33. Bristol University Council, Committee Minute Book, pp. 30–31, 35–7, Council Minute Book, p. 35 (BUL, Special Collections).
34. J.K. Whitaker, 'Alfred Marshall: The Years 1877 to 1885', pp. 4–5, and notes 9, 11; Mary Paley Marshall, *What I Remember*, p. 36, and see below, Chapter 18, p. 688.
35. (BUL, Special Collections). The quotes here are from Bateson's and Hessey's testimonials respectively; extracts from them, and from those by Sidgwick and Jevons, were quoted previously, above Chapter 3, p. 55, Chapter 4, p. 79, Chapter 6, pp. 144, 161.
36. Council Minute Book, 7 December 1877, p. 67 (BUL, Special Collections).
37. Committee Minutes, and Council Minutes Books, pp. 45–90, 66, respectively; Alfred Marshall to Foxwell, 27 May 1878 (Freeman Collection, 49/155); and see Chapter 8 (above, pp. 235–6) for other aspects of Mary Paley Marshall's Bristol teaching appointment.
38. Report of Annual Local Meeting of the Governors, 21 November 1878, in Council Minutes Book, pp. 112–14 (BUL, Special Collections).
39. Mary Paley Marshall to Foxwell, 22 September 1878 (Freeman Collection, 48/155).
40. Mary Paley Marshall to Foxwell, 10 October 1878 (Freeman Collection, 47/155); Marshall's inaugural lecture is discussed below, pp. 289–92.
41. Alfred Marshall to Foxwell, undated, presumably March/April 1879 (Freeman Collection, 4/9).
42. Mary Paley Marshall to Foxwell, October 1879, 14 December 1879 (Freeman Collection, 16/9, 19/9).
43. Alfred Marshall to Foxwell, 18 October 1879 (Freeman Collection, 12/9).
44. As reported by *Western Daily Press*, 30 September 1881. It is interesting to speculate whether duty would have won over self-interest if job opportunities had been better at Cambridge.
45. J.K. Whitaker, 'Alfred Marshall: The Years 1877 to 1885', p. 9. Jowett did his hardest to get the Marshalls to stay. This is discussed below, Chapter 18, p. 689.
46. Marshall to Foxwell, 25 October 1879 (Freeman Collection, 9/9).
47. University college, Bristol, *Income and Expenditure 1876–1901* (BUL, Special Collections).
48. Alfred Marshall to Foxwell, 20 April 1880, Freeman Collection, 9/252. This was written in the worst financial year of the college during Marshall's tenure as Principal.
49. Alfred Marshall to W.A.S. Hewins, 12 October 1899, in A.W. Coats, 'Alfred Marshall and the Early Development of the London School of Economics: Some Unpublished Letters', *Economica*, N.S. 34 (3), November 1967, p. 412.
50. See below, Chapter 15, for further illustrations. An example is his letter to the *Times*, 30 October 1879, correcting some misleading reporting about the college in its pages.
51. M.W. Travers, *A Life of Sir William Ramsay*, p. 45. Ramsay's first reactions to the Marshalls were reported above, Chapter 8, pp. 232–3.
52. College Annual Reports, November 1878, November 1881, in Council Minutes Book, pp. 134, 160 (BUL, Special Collections).
53. *University College, Bristol: Calendars and Syllabus*, Bristol: J.W. Arrowsmith, various years.

54. 'Minutes of Evidence on Higher Education in Wales and Monmouthshire' in Committee on Intermediate and Higher Education in Wales, *Parliamentary Papers*, Vol. XXXIII, 1881, c–3047, 3047–1, Marshall's evidence given on 20 December 1880 appears on pp. 767–79.
55. Council Minutes Book, 9 September, 17 November 1880, pp. 152, 156; Committee Minutes Book, 23 August, 20 September 1880, pp. 152, 153. Cf. J.K. Whitaker, 'Alfred Marshall: The Years 1877 to 1885', p. 9 and n.29.
56. Executive Committee Minutes Book, pp. 171–7. The Report is dated 11 June 1881.
57. William Ramsay to his mother, 13 October, in Sir William Ramsay – Letters and Papers arranged by Morris W. Travers, Vol. 3, in *The Ramsay Papers* (UCL).
58. William Ramsay to his mother, 1 November 1880, *ibid*.
59. William Ramsay to Bristol University College Council, in Council Minutes Book, pp. 154–5.
60. Council Minutes Book, 17 November 1880, p. 157.
61. William Ramsay to his mother, 9 November 1880, in *Letters and Papers arranged by Morris W. Travers*, Vol. 3. It was written after the staff meeting which arranged for the compromise adopted by the Council.
62. Alfred Marshall to Foxwell, 20 April 1880, 28 March 1878 (Freeman Collection, 9/252, 40/155).
63. Alfred Marshall to Foxwell, 21 November, 29 November and 5 December 1880 (Freeman Collection, 6/252^{II}). In his evidence to the Committee on Higher Education in Wales (Q. 18,249) he explained why he considered his wife Mary indispensable to the work of the college.
64. M.W. Travers, *A Life of Sir William Ramsay*, pp. 55–6.
65. M.W. Travers, introduction to *Letters and Papers of Sir William Ramsay arranged by Morris W. Travers*, Vol. 5 (Parts 1 and 2), University College Library, London. This was discussed in Chapter 8 above, pp. 235–7.
66. Alfred Marshall to Foxwell, 29 July 1881 (Freeman Collection, 3/152),. quoted above, Chapter 8, pp. 256–7.
67. Council Minutes Book, 27 September 1881, pp. 182, 183.
68. See J.K. Whitaker, 'Alfred Marshall: The Years 1877 to 1885', pp. 10–11. He adds (p. 10 n.34), 'Ramsay's wife had not previously visited Bristol and, meeting the Marshalls for the first time, was "sorry they are going to be away this winter", particularly because he now liked Mary Paley "so much".'
69. 'Address to Professor Marshall, M.A., Principal of University College, Bristol', in *The Western Daily Press*, Bristol, Friday, 20 September 1881; the original with the signatures of 75 students is preserved in the Marshall Library.
70. H.S. Foxwell to the Master of John's (Taylor), 15 October 1881, St John's College Archives, D104:110, in which Foxwell also indicated that 'mental worry, partly connected with the finance, and partly with the disagreeable personalities of one or two non-university men on the staff at Bristol, was a principal cause of his illness and resignation.' The collection amounted to 30s. per student on average, a very handsome donation.
71. *Bristol Times and Mirror*, 20 March 1926, letter to the author from Mr Michael Richardson, Special Collections, University of Bristol Library, 11 June 1991, who writes, 'There is a gargoyle of Marshall at the roof line of the Wills Memorial Building', as verbally communicated by Don Carleton, a historian of Bristol University. The Bodlian is an exception to the last sentence. The fireplace portrait is reproduced above as Frontispiece.
72. Mary Paley Marshall, *What I Remember*, pp. 23–4.
73. Extracts of these lecture notes are in *EEW*, II, pp. 379–85; the lecture course outlines from the Bristol University Calendars are reprinted in J.K. Whitaker, 'Alfred Marshall: The Years 1877 to 1885', Appendix B, pp. 42–7. In what follows, use is made of these reprints as well as of the original notes preserved in the Marshall Library.
74. *EEW*, II, p. 379.
75. *EEW*, II, p. 382. Another estimate of an average income level from egalitarian policy is given below, Chapter 16, pp. 589–90 and n.*.
76. *EEW*, II, pp. 384–5.
77. Cf. Whitaker's introduction to these lecture notes, in *EEW*, II, pp. 377–8. For a detailed discussion of Marshall's views on taxation, Peter Groenewegen, 'Marshall on Taxation', in *Alfred Marshall in Retrospect*, edited Rita McWilliams-Tullberg, Chapter 6. For his later work on tax policy, see below, Chapter 11, pp. 371–6, Chapter 16, pp. 597, 608, Chapter 17, pp. 645–6.
78. P. Hallett, or more correctly, Thomas George Palmer Hallett (d. 1919) had studied medicine in London and in 1874 had published an influential paper on taxation, 'The Income Tax Question', which is appraised in F. Shebab, *Progressive Taxation*, Oxford: Clarendon Press, 1953, pp. 165–72. He was an acquaintance of Jevons, as Jevons wrote to his wife in 1875 (*Papers and Correspondence of William Stanley Jevons*, Vol. IV, p. 128).
79. M.F. Pease, 'Some Reminiscences of University College', February 1942 (BUL, Special Collections, pp. 6–7). Contrary to what she recalled, this was not Marshall's inaugural but the first lecture of the new session.
80. George H. Leonard, 'Professor Alfred Marshall', in *Bristol Times and Mirror*, 7 October 1924.
81. Course Outline for Introductory Course, Session 1877–78, in J.K. Whitaker, 'Alfred Marshall: The Years 1877 to 1885', pp. 42–3.

82. Some examples of such use of mathematical argument can be found in his Bristol lectures on government, concerning the subject of taxation. See *EEW*, II, pp. 382–3.

83. Parliamentary Papers, Vol. XXXIII (1881), pp. 767–79. Some of this is also reflected in his thoughts on education eventually published in 1919. See *IT*, esp. pp. 95–9, 351–4.

84. J.K. Whitaker, 'Alfred Marshall: The Years 1877 to 1885', p. 19.

85. Marshall Archive, Box 8 (6): Statistics for Bristol students.

86. Instruction in political economy at Bristol in that year was given by Mortimer Wheeler and William Sidgwick, Henry Sidgwick's elder brother, who was then at Merton College, Oxford. William Sidgwick had lectured on logic and political economy at Oriel College in 1867–68. The replacements promised to 'endeavour as far as possible, to carry out the syllabus already published', a rather difficult undertaking.

87. J.K. Whitaker, 'Alfred Marshall: the Years 1877 to 1885', p. 46.

88. William Ramsay to his mother, 12 May 1882, to his father 27 May 1882, in *William Ramsay. Letters and Papers arranged by Morris W. Travers,* Vol. 5 (i), pp. 27, 29; Bristol University College Council Minutes, 24 May 1881, pp. 207, 210 show Marshall's reappointment at a fixed salary of £200 plus one-quarter of his students' fees, as well as Mary Paley's reappointment as lecturer in the day classes.

89. *P* I, Book VII, Chapter XIII, *P* VIII, Book VI, Chapters XII and XIII, Marshall to J.B. Clark, 2 July 1900, in *Memorials*, p. 413 and cf. above, Chapter 6, p. 146.

90. J.K. Whitaker, 'Alfred Marshall: the Years 1877 to 1885', p. 43.

91. *Ibid.*, pp. 46–7.

92. Above, p. 277.

93. These lectures are reprinted from local press reports in J.K. Whitaker, 'Alfred Marshall: The Years 1877 to 1885', Appendix D.

94. *Ibid.*, p. 50.

95. *Ibid.*, p. 51.

96. *Ibid.*, p. 52.

97. *Ibid.*, p. 53.

98. There are two versions of this lecture. A newspaper report from the *Western Daily Press* and the *Bristol Times and Mirror* for 8 October 1878, in an edited version by John Whitaker, 'Alfred Marshall: The Years 1877 to 1885', pp. 53–61; which also used a manuscript version, described in Mary Paley's handwriting as Marshall's inaugural from the Marshall Archive (Box 6 (1) Loose Items), to correct what appeared to have been misprints.

99. From the manuscript version, as quoted by Whitaker, 'Alfred Marshall: The Years 1877 to 1885', p. 23.

100. Parliamentary Papers, Vol. XXXIII (1881), pp. 769–79, esp. Q. 18,219–20.

101. See J.K. Whitaker, 'Alfred Marshall: The Years 1877 to 1885', especially pp. 55–61.

102. Below, Chapter 15, pp. 556–7 and see *IT*, pp. 95–9, 353–4 and Appendix K.

103. Parliamentary Papers, Vol. XXXIII (1881), pp. 768–9, Q. 18,182–18,185.

104. See J.K. Whitaker, 'Alfred Marshall: The Years 1877 to 1885', pp. 24–5; William Ramsay to his mother, 16 February 1882 in *William Ramsay. Letters and Papers Arranged by Morris W. Travers,* Vol. 5 (i), p. 43 (University College Library, London). The American lecture is discussed above, Chapter 7, p. 262; the Progress and Poverty lectures below, Chapter 16, pp. 582–5.

105. J.K. Whitaker, 'Alfred Marshall, The Years 1877 to 1885', p. 25.

106. See my 'Marshall and Hegel', in *Economie Appliquée*, 43 (1), 1990, esp. pp. 74–6.

107. See above, Chapter 4, p. 87, Chapter 8, p. 232.

108. James Maurice Wilson to Mary Paley Marshall, 29 September 1881 (Marshall Archive, 1:109).

109. William Ramsay to his father, 29 April 1883, in *William Ramsay. Letters and Papers arranged by Morris W. Travers,* Vol. 5 (i), p. 47.

110. *Ibid.*, p. 48.

111. *Ibid.*, Ramsay to his father, 16 December 1884. Bonamy Price was then 78, and died three years later in 1881, when Marshall persuaded J.N. Keynes to apply for the chair. See below, Chapter 18, pp. 682–3.

112. Balliol College, Oxford, *Balliol College Register*, 1875–1903, entry for 14 April 1883; Marshall's acceptance was therefore relatively quickly decided as compared to his usual standards.

113. Marshall to Foxwell, 30 April 1883 (Marshall Archive, 1:39); Marshall to J.N. Keynes, 30 April 1884 (Marshall Archive, 1:74). Keynes noted in his diary (1 May 1883) that he found Marshall's letter 'very unexpected'.

114. G. Stedman-Jones, *Outcast London*, pp. 6–8. On Toynbee, see Alon Kadish, *Apostle Arnold*, Durham: Duke University Press, 1988, Chapters 4, 6 and 7; on T.H. Green, Melvin Richter, *The Politics of Conscience*, London, Weidenfeld & Nicolson, 1964, esp. Chapter 5.

115. See above, Chapter 6, pp. 141–2.

116. See below, Chapter 11, pp. 357–8, Chapter 13, pp. 447–9, 455–8, and especially Chapter 16, pp. 608–9 where the relationship between the new liberalism and his 'tendency to socialism' is discussed at some length.

117. Above, p. 174.

118. On Jowett's possible impact on Marshall's economics, see below, Chapter 18, pp. 693–4.
119. *P* III 78n., *P* IV 78n.; deleted from *P* V. See *P* VIII, p. 17n and *P* IX pp. 136–7.
120. 'The Present Position of Economics', in *Memorials*, p. 152; *P* VIII, p. 765 where Toynbee's name was inserted from the third edition; see also Kadish, *Apostle Arnold*, pp. 234–5.
121. Above, Chapter 8, pp. 238–41.
122. Marshall to Foxwell, 29 April 1884 (Freeman Collection, 49/123).
123. Preserved in the Marshall Scrapbook, Marshall Library.
124. Marshall to J.N. Keynes, 16 February 1885 (Marshall Library, 1:64).
125. *Oxford Magazine*, 28 November 1883 in Marshall Scrapbook, Marshall Library, and for a discussion of this, Alon Kadish, 'Marshall on Necessaries and Travel', *History of Economic Thought Newsletter*, No. 26, Spring, 1981, pp. 15–19.
126. Marshall to J.N. Keynes, 20 January 1902 (Marshall Library, 1:125). The other two students were Gonner and Harrison, but Price was Marshall's favourite. His occasional presence at Balliol Croft was reported above, Chapter 8, pp. 244–5. Marshall had apparently reported on Price's quality to Percival while he was in Oxford. L.L. Price, *Memories and Notes on British Economists*, p. 8 n.
127. L.L. Price, *Memories and Notes on British Economists*, p. 8.
128. *Ibid.*, pp. 8–9.
129. Marshall to Foxwell, 29 April 1884 (Freeman Collection, 48/123).
130. Alon Kadish, 'Marshall on Necessaries and Travel', p. 16; his total financial situation at Oxford was discussed above, Chapter 8, p. 238.
131. Marshall to J.N. Keynes, 30 September 1897 (Marshall Archive, 1:112).
132. *Oxford Magazine*, 21 January 1885 in Marshall Scrapbook, Marshall Archive.

10. The Professor at Cambridge: 1885–1908

Alfred Marshall returned to Cambridge as its Professor of Political Economy in January 1885. He was then 43 years old, and had been away from his old university for eight and a half years. For the rest of their lives he and his wife resided permanently in Cambridge from January 1885; from mid–1886 in the house they had built for themselves on its outskirts, Balliol Croft. This period of almost forty years was close to half a lifetime and for twenty-three years it coincided with his tenure of the Political Economy chair. This chapter is devoted to Marshall's more routine academic responsibilities as Cambridge professor in teaching and administration, omitting his involvement in syllabus reform leading up to the separate Economics and Politics Tripos and his participation in university issues associated with women's education.[*] Its story therefore starts with background surrounding his election to the Cambridge chair.

THE CAMBRIDGE PROFESSORSHIP IN POLITICAL ECONOMY

The title of Professor of Political Economy was conferred for the first time by the University of Cambridge on 21 May 1828. Its recipient was George Pryme, a Fellow of Trinity College, who had been lecturing on political economy at the university since 1816. Pryme's teaching secured him the title of Professor of Political Economy against some formidable opposition, including that of William Whewell, the powerful Master of Trinity College. No permanent Professorship of Political Economy was established in 1828, Pryme only gained the title. For the next 35 years he laboured assiduously to have a permanent chair established. Two events aided his persistent campaign. In 1833 he was elected as an honorary member of the London Political Economy Club, 'because of his position as Professor of Political Economy at Cambridge',[1] a recognition of the importance of the office by the first, and then still the only organisation of economists in Britain. Secondly, the introduction of a Moral Sciences Tripos by the university in 1848 gave Political Economy the status of an examination subject for honours, enhancing the potential value for it of a permanent chair. Not until October 1863 did the university's Senate finally vote to make the professorship permanent. 'The holder was to be paid £300 a year plus a share of student fees' and his duties were defined as 'to explain and teach the principles of Political Economy, and to apply himself to the advancement of that science'.[2] Pryme's judicious, simultaneous resignation brought success to his final move in the Senate to gain permanence for the chair. It enabled a vote on principle, without any hint of possible favour to a present

---

[*] These are dealt with in Chapters 15 and 14 respectively while other activities coincident with his professorship, such as involvement in royal commissions, completing and revising the *Principles*, active participation in learned societies and academic controversy are dealt with in Chapters 11–13 respectively. The present chapter continues his story as teacher and administrator begun in Chapter 9.

incumbent. Whewell now acknowledged Pryme's real service to the university. Political Economy had become sufficiently important to the university to make the absence of a chair intolerable.[3]

The now permanent chair of Political Economy was contested in November 1863 by four candidates: J.B. Mayor, a Fellow and Moral Sciences Lecturer of St John's; Leonard Courtney, also of John's and a former Professor of Political Economy at University College, London; H.D. McLeod, banker and economic writer and Henry Fawcett, Fellow of Trinity Hall, who had just published his *Manual of Political Economy* which had been well received in the reviews. Fawcett won. His victory was ascribed to the split in the John's vote, assisted by his recently published political economy text. He had also been well supported by strong testimonials from persons eminent in the field, including Robert Lowe, Thorold Rogers, R.H. Mills, G.W. Norman, W. Newmarch, W.T. Thornton, J.S. Mill and Herman Merivale. These praised Fawcett's new book and attested his debating skills at the Political Economy Club to which he had been elected in 1861. Membership of the Social Science Association and Fawcett's close friendship with Mill added further to his credentials for the position.[4]

Until his death in 1884 Fawcett gave an annual series of lectures as Professor of Political Economy during his statutory period of eighteen weeks in annual residence. Stephen, his friend and biographer described Fawcett's lectures as 'forceful and lucid' expositions of the leading principles of political economy.[5] Fawcett regarded these as relatively few in number and, by their simplicity, capable of being imparted to people of average intelligence. His lecture audience included a 'large share of the compulsory attendance of poll men' (or pass students). Until 1876, these were obliged to attend a certain quota of professorial lectures before being eligible to take their degree. Fawcett's lectures were like his text; clearly expressed, with unambiguous propositions of economic theory, applied with few qualifications to current controversies and debates. Some of Fawcett's lectures themselves became books or articles. Examples are *The Economic Position of the British Labourer* in 1865, 'State Socialism and the Nationalisation of Land' in 1883 and, perhaps the most important, *Free Trade and Protection* in 1878. He was, in short, an applied economist, who took received doctrine as more than adequate for explaining current economic problems. He was not, 'actively engaged in pushing back the frontiers of economic knowledge; [n]or indeed, did he stimulate any formal opposition from academic economists.'[6] His status as Professor and M.P. enabled him to speak with authority on the subject, not only in the lecture halls but in the wider community. Fawcett therefore carried out his minimal professorial responsibilities adequately according to the regulations then in force.

University reform in 1877 affected the requirements for pass students on compulsory attendance at some professorial lectures. More significantly, they changed the role and powers of professors within the university structure. The 1877 Statutes, which became law in 1882, therefore also touched on the chair of Political Economy. It became one of three in the Special Board of Moral Sciences, the others being the Knightbridge Professorship of Moral Philosophy, in which Sidgwick succeeded Birks in 1883, and the Chair of Mental Philosophy and Logic, then vacant, and in fact not filled until James Ward's appointment in 1897. The annual stipend for professors was raised to £700, subject to a reduction of £200 if the professor held a headship or college fellowship. Concomitantly, the professor's statutory duties were much extended. After 1882, they were to include 'research and the advancement of knowledge in his department' and 'to give lectures in every year'. Professors had to report annually to the appropriate Special Board of Studies, in this case the Moral Sciences Board, on 'the number of lectures given . . . during the preceding year, and the times of delivery, together with the number of weeks in each of the three terms during which he had resided in the University'.[7] When Marshall was elected as Fawcett's successor in December 1884, this set of regulations defined his new responsibilities, and induced an early quarrel with former friend, now professorial colleague, Henry Sidgwick.

ELECTION TO THE CHAIR OF POLITICAL ECONOMY: 13 DECEMBER 1884

Fawcett's death on 7 November 1884 set in motion a new procedure for selecting his successor, contained in the statutes which came into force in 1882. It provided for a selection committee of nine, hence abolishing the practice of election by resident M.A.s which had given Fawcett the position. The new committee consisted of the Vice Chancellor (*ex officio*), and eight members appointed by the Senate. Two were appointed on its own recommendations; three each on recommendation from the General Board of Studies and from the Special Board of Studies in which the chair was situated, in this case the Moral Sciences Board.[8]

Electors for the Political Economy chair in 1884–85 were as follows: Chairman was Vice-Chancellor, N.N. Ferrers, Master of Caius College. The two Senate nominees were Professor James Stuart MP, Trinity College Fellow, and a member of the selection committee which appointed Marshall Principal of Bristol University College and H.J. Roby, a manufacturer and former Fellow of John's. The General Board of Studies was represented by the Rev. V.H. Stanton, Trinity College, Henry Sidgwick, the Knightbridge Professor, both of whom provided testimonials for Marshall when he applied for the Bristol job and R.H. Palgrave, a banker and writer on political economy. Finally, the Special Board of Studies was represented by three Johnians: Leonard Courtney MP, the unsuccessful candidate for the Cambridge chair in 1863; Foxwell, Marshall's close friend who had also provided a testimonial on his behalf to the Bristol selection committee; and Alfred Marshall himself. Apart from the Vice-Chancellor and Palgrave, the Committee consisted exclusively of persons from Trinity and John's, the substantial representation from the latter being noted with some pride in its college journal.[9] It also contained two persons who applied for the position when it unexpectedly became vacant on Fawcett's death, that is, Marshall and Palgrave.

This last aspect of the selection committee caused a flurry of activity at 46 Woodstock Road, Oxford, then the Marshall residence. To remedy the situation of being both selector and candidate, which had already resulted in his receipt of McLeod's 'strong' testimonials for the position, Marshall decided to write to the electors that he himself was going to be a candidate, since he considered this was not a suitable task for the Vice-Chancellor. It is possible that Marshall by then had not seen the selection committee as announced by the *Cambridge University Reporter* the previous month. In any case he feigned ignorance of whether Foxwell was an elector. Nevertheless, Marshall asked Foxwell at the same time to post a letter to Palgrave telling him of Marshall's candidature, presumably because of his membership on the selection committee. Marshall also told Foxwell that, if successful, the Master of John's had promised his re-election to a fellowship, which made him 'feel like a swallow getting back to its old eaves'.[10] Shortly afterwards, Marshall urged Foxwell to stand. He had already done this with other former moral sciences students, William Cunningham and J.S. Nicholson, because Marshall could not 'bear the thought of your standing out on my account'.[11] Neither Foxwell nor Nicholson followed Marshall's suggestion, presumably because they themselves had only recently been appointed to their own respective chairs at University College, London, and Edinburgh.

The next few days Marshall seemed to have entertained some doubt about whether he should be a candidate 'for the post I have so much coveted'. This resulted in 'sleepless nights', and careful weighing up of the pros and cons. Among the latter he possibly counted the morality of deserting Balliol, which had made him a Fellow only six months before, and the candidature of Palgrave, whom he seems to have regarded as his strongest rival. However, after seeking advice from two close friends (Jowett, and someone else at Oxford?), by 20 November his mind was made up in favour of standing. By the start of December he wrote to Foxwell, 'so far as human things can be certain, it is absolutely certain I am a candidate'.[12]

Apart from Marshall, Cunningham, Palgrave and McLeod, there were two other candidates. One was T.W. Levin, since the 1860s a St Catharine's College Lecturer in the Moral Sciences, including Political Economy. The other was a Johnian, the Rev. H.E. Hoopell, a 40th wrangler in 1855, followed by honours in the Moral Sciences in 1856, and, at the time of the election, Principal of Winterbottom Nautical College. Neither presented strong competition. The same can be said for McLeod, at 64 the oldest of the candidates and the last of four candidates in 1863 when Fawcett had won the post. His many publications were outweighed by both age and heretical economic opinions.

Alfred Marshall's other two competitors were decidedly stronger. Palgrave, at 58 the oldest candidate after McLeod, had a formidable reputation as an author and banker involved in public affairs. His lack of formal university qualifications was more than offset by a prize winning essay on local taxation, two books on banking and his evidence on behalf of the country Bankers Association to a House of Commons Select Committee on Banks of Issue. Mary Paley Marshall recalled him as the only strong competitor,[13] presumably remembering her husband's worries about his application at the time. The youngest candidate, William Cunningham, was only 36 against Marshall's 43. He was also considered 'a favourite candidate'. A Doctor of Science from Edinburgh and Senior Moralist with Maitland in 1872, he had already finished two books on economics: *Growth of English Industry and Commerce* published in 1882 and *Economics and Politics* completed by November 1884, the date in the preface, but not published until 1885. However, he himself realised that when Marshall announced his candidature, 'his chance had gone' because 'Marshall had an established reputation; Cunningham had been one of Marshall's pupils and had found him a most stimulating teacher.'[14]

Marshall's undoubted credentials for the position made him front runner, even though, by the end of 1884, his publications were still few in number. His decade of experience as

Moral Sciences Lecturer for St John's, his position as Principal and Professor of Political Economy at Bristol, followed by his appointment to Oxford, outclassed the other candidates in the new age of reformed universities where professors were expected to teach. Within two years of his appointment, one of the electors, Foxwell, claimed for Marshall the honour of being the greatest living writer on the subject in England. His *Economics of Industry* had been very useful in reconstructing the science and his influence as teacher extended even wider, with 'half the economic chairs in the United Kingdom . . . occupied by his pupils'.[15] With such credentials, undoubtedly confirmed by strong testimonials, 'Marshall's election was a foregone conclusion, no other choice was possible'.[16]

On the little evidence available, it may, however, not have been a foregone conclusion. Foxwell, an elector present at the meeting at Caius College Lodge on the afternoon of 13 December to appoint the new professor, kept his friend John Neville Keynes closely informed of the proceedings by means of the excellent postal system at the time. During the afternoon, Keynes received a postcard from Foxwell, indicating 'It is by no means certain, will let you know as soon as possible'. It was not until evening that Keynes heard the result, 'Marshall is elected', with the runners up, perhaps indicating the selectors' order of merit – Palgrave, followed by McLeod, Cunningham, Levin and Hoopell. On 14 December, Keynes recorded that Foxwell had told him 'the electors have agreed to divulge nothing concerning the P[olitical] E[conomy] election'. Foxwell also confided that at the meeting each elector 'seems to have made a little speech concerning the merits of each of the candidates', and that, like John Neville Keynes, he did not estimate 'Cunningham particularly highly'.[17] Foxwell also telegraphed the result to Marshall in Oxford. In thanking him, Marshall indicated he did not wish 'to know details . . . [because] it is always best not even to be able to guess who have voted against one'.[18]   Sidgwick was much more circumspect. His published diary entry simply noted that on 13 December, 'we elected Alfred Marshall Professor of Political Economy'.[19]

A number of newspapers recorded Marshall's success. The following Monday the *Times* mentioned that at Gonville and Caius Lodge on the afternoon of Saturday, 13 December, 'the selectors had chosen Mr. Alfred Marshall, M.A. of St John's College and lecturer at Balliol College, Oxford'. The Bristol press reported likewise the next day. Other periodicals recorded the appointment later. On New Year's Day, 1885, The *Educational Times* argued Marshall's appointment to be 'one to which absolutely no exception can be taken', and noted 'that Mrs. Marshall (née Paley), late student of Newnham College, is, like Mrs. Fawcett, also an economist. Professor Marshall's well known Economics of Industry was written in conjunction with his wife.' When term started, university magazines noted the event. The *Cambridge Review* reported that the Vice-Chancellor's start-of-term address welcomed 'back one of our own old members', a welcome The *Eagle* endorsed the following month when announcing that 'our former Fellow and Lecturer, Mr. Alfred Marshall, had been elected to succeed the late Professor Fawcett in the Chair of Political Economy'. At Oxford, its magazine congratulated Marshall 'on his promotion', expressing regret at the loss this imposed on their own establishment.[20]

Before Marshall could take up his appointment, which he intended to do as soon as possible during January 1885, two things had to be done. He had to find a temporary replacement for his Oxford lectures to cover the remainder of the academic year and make arrangements for his own Cambridge teaching with Sidgwick as Head of the Moral Sciences Board. A visit to Cambridge in mid-December tackled both tasks. However, while arranging his Lent term teaching, he severely quarrelled with Sidgwick. From the account left by the two protagonists and other evidence, the quarrel related to aspects of Marshall's required teaching and to some other matters on which Sidgwick, as chairman of the Moral Sciences Board, wished to regulate Marshall's academic behaviour. Some days after the quarrel, Sidgwick recorded the following account in his diary:

> He came here on December 17, called on us, heard my view of the lectures required, then suddenly broke out. I had produced on him the impression of a petty tyrant 'dressed in a little brief authority' (Chairman of the Board of Moral Science) who wished to regulate, trammel, hamper a man who knew more about the subject than I did. I tried to explain, and we parted friends; but the explanation was imperfect, correspondence ensued, and on Tuesday (23) I received from him a long and very impressive letter, analysing my academic career, and pointing out that the one source of failure in it was my mania for over-regulation. The result of this had been that my energies had been frittered away on details of administration, and on the effort to give a wretched handful of undergraduates the particular teaching that they required for the Moral Sciences Tripos. He contrasted my lecture-room, in which a handful of men are taking down what they regard as useful for examination, with that of [T.H.] Green, in which a hundred men – half of them B.A.'s – ignoring examinations, were wont to hang on the lips of the man who was sincerely anxious to teach them the truth about the universe and human life. I have left out the partly courteous, partly affectionate – for Marshall is an old friend – padding of the letter, by which he meant to soften the pressure of these hard truths, but this is the substance.[21]

Marshall reported his side of the story to Foxwell the following day. Unfortunately, the account is rather cryptic relying as it does on 'enclosed papers' which do not seem to have been preserved. However, Marshall saw 'the whole affair as an unexpected worry; that has rather upset me'. Then, after swearing Foxwell to secrecy on the matter, and expressing the wish it would be 'all right before long', Marshall stated the hub of the argument as follows: 'It is enough to have to fight his wish to regulate my lectures on his model' but stressed he did not wish to see 'any personal element' introduced into 'the official controversy'.[22]

Much of this problem appears to have arisen from a view expressed by the Moral Sciences Board on the responsibilities of the new Professor of Political Economy, which it had been asked to give by the university's General Board of Studies. It required a minimum of 48 lectures annually, with a smaller number permissible after the Professor had submitted special reasons to the Board. At least for one term, this teaching should 'form part of the regular teaching provided for undergraduates' in which it 'should be supplemented with written examinations' and 'a due amount of personal supervision'. On the available evidence, Marshall saw this as over-regulation of his lectures by Sidgwick and an intrusion on his authority as Professor of Political Economy. This intrusion was all the more unwarranted because it related to teaching of the subject in which Marshall was the specialist, with very broad experience. Moreover, Sidgwick who had been teaching political economy at Cambridge, had failed to draw the number of students which Marshall considered the subject was capable of attracting. The reference to T.H. Green's classes probably expressed Marshall's dissatisfaction with the requirement he had to devote a prescribed proportion of his teaching to undergraduates, rather than to attracting as wide a range of students who were interested in political economy as he possibly could. Marshall may also have been annoyed that he could not confine his teaching to advanced students. Official resolution of the problem was not achieved until the Special Board Meeting of 4 March 1885, chaired by Foxwell and held in the Vice-Chancellor's room, presumably to ensure neutrality of chair and terrain to settle the conflict between the two professors.[23]

A further letter to Foxwell on 23 December confirms that the Moral Sciences Board resolutions were at the heart of the quarrel. It indicated Marshall particularly objected to be 'regulated' into setting examination papers, for which he could find no authority in the statutes but about which he would take no official action unless other professors took the lead. In any case, he informed Foxwell, Sidgwick and he 'were at peace again. He is very good, in spite of his "regulating".'[24] An entry in Keynes's diary for January 1885 suggests the quarrel may also have had something to do with Marshall's plans for extending his horizons beyond the immediate sphere of the moral sciences, by attracting students from as wide a range of background as possible.[25] This programme of enhancing the status of political economy was publicly announced by Marshall in his inaugural the following February, in a statement which Sidgwick interpreted as a 'declaration of war'.[26]

The second task Marshall had set himself for his Cambridge December visit was more easily achieved. John Neville Keynes recorded on 18 December that the Marshalls had called on his wife, Florence, who wrote of the visit, 'I must first of all tell you that I do not at all wonder at your enthusiasm for him. He is a most delightful man. You need not be jealous, husband, for the chief reason why I speak so warmly of him is because he said such nice things about you and seemed so genuinely interested in all that concerned you'.[27]

The aim of this flattery was to cajole Keynes to apply for the Oxford post Marshall was vacating on a permanent basis or, in the short run, to take his place for the last two terms of the academic year. As shown earlier,[28] Keynes consented to temporarily relieve Marshall at Oxford; however, he did not wish to take it as a permanent position. This episode reveals two character traits of Marshall which persisted in his subsequent participation in university intrigues: his deviousness and his, to many persons infuriating, habit of never taking no for an answer when pushing stubbornly forward to his goal. Deviousness is shown by Marshall's request that Keynes not reveal in Oxford that the first suggestion for his application came from Marshall; Marshall's stubborn persistence is recorded in the sequence of telegrams and letters on 20, 22, 23, 29 (two telegrams after hearing that Keynes had written he did not wish to apply) and 30 December, ending with the suggestion, which Keynes accepted, that he take the position on a temporary basis. Even then, after Mary Paley entered the fray on her husband's behalf, it took several more exchanges of correspondence before Keynes stopped the requests by telegraphing Marshall on 12 January 1885 that his mind was made up.[29] By early February, the arrangements for Keynes's temporary position were finalised, and the lectures he gave on method became the basis for the book he published on the subject five years later.[30] By this time, the Marshalls had well and truly settled back in Cambridge in their rented accommodation at 17 Chesterton Road, and Marshall's thoughts were focused on the inaugural lecture he intended to give later that month.

THE PRESENT POSITION OF ECONOMICS: MARSHALL'S INAUGURAL LECTURE

Marshall's first notice as Professor in the *Cambridge University Reporter* announced his intentions to give an inaugural lecture on 24 February. The Senate approved this at its meeting on 19 February and the lecture was delivered at Senate House on the afternoon of the scheduled day. As had been the case of his Bristol inaugural, Marshall's chosen theme for the lecture concerned the uses of economics, both in practice and in education, and the special place it deserved in the Cambridge syllabus. It thereby provided a review of the present state of the science within its own literature, within the requirements of national policy and within the university, the last providing the intended climax to the lecture which so devastated Sidgwick when he heard it. The contents of the lecture are important in explaining Marshall's subsequent activities as professor and need to be discussed in some detail.[*]

Marshall first paid the customary tribute to his predecessor.[¶] He noted Fawcett's death to be but one of many among the eminent economists who had died over the last twelve years, that is, Mill, Cairnes, Bagehot, Cliffe Leslie, Jevons, Newmarch and Toynbee. He then defined his topic for the afternoon as follows. It was an attempt 'to give a short account of the province of the economist, . . . and of what Cambridge may best do in it' (pp. 152–3). Marshall first corrected what he saw as a wrong perspective on the changes which were taking place during the present generation of economists. Such changes had few associations with quarrels over appropriate method. Induction and deduction were both necessary. Instead, these changes derived from the 'discovery that man himself is in great measure a creature of circumstances and changes with them'. (p. 153). This discovery had enabled the social sciences, aided by biology, to demonstrate that 'growth of knowledge and earnestness' could make 'deep and rapid changes in human nature'. The classical economists had ignored such possibilities of change in people and institutions, the socialists had perceived them in general, as was recognised in the work of John Stuart Mill. Recognition of a changeable human nature allowed the critique of economics if used as dogma. Developments of Smith's theory of normal (natural) value 'by Ricardo, Cournot, Hermann, Jevons and others' enabled better understanding of 'those causes which act with tolerable uniformity' (pp. 154–8). Such theoretical developments allowed economics to be described as a science facilitating reasoning 'about the motives of human action which are measurable' by money, replacing its former status as a science of wealth. However, reasoning about measurable motives could never be identified with dogma, with a ready-made 'body of concrete truth'. Political economy was an engine for the discovery of concrete truth' analogous to the theory of mechanics (pp. 158–9). Hence, discussion of economic man as a selfish maximiser of gain was to be avoided, and the many other motives

---

[*] It was published by Macmillan in May 1885 and widely reviewed. It was reprinted in *Memorials,* pp. 152–74, the text to which reference is made in this section by page references placed in brackets in the text.

[¶] *Memorials*, pp. 152–3. As Phyllis Deane has noted, 'Henry Fawcett: the Plain Man's Practical Economist', pp. 106–7, 'What Marshall [really] thought of his predecessor is difficult to say', Fawcett's views on the simplicity of economic principles and the ease of their application undoubtedly appalled him. Marshall had used Fawcett's *Manual* for teaching at Cambridge, not necessarily of his own volition.

to human action identified by scholars such as Cliffe Leslie were to be included, especially since they could nearly always, in varying degrees, be measured by money. Although the task of developing economic theory and analysis on this basis was immense, too little had as yet been done. 'Very few fields offer so important and rich a harvest to scientific enterprise' (pp. 162–3).

Marshall claimed his explanation of recent changes in economics required defence against two objections. One set came from the followers of Comte and Comtists as well as from some historians who found fault with attempts to separate economics from social science in general. The other described political economy's real task as developing its argument directly from history without any need to resort to economic theory. Both types of objection were firmly rejected by the new Professor of Political Economy. The first was disposed of by Marshall's argument that absence of any real, unified social science made separate development of economics essential. The second was rejected by his observation that 'facts by themselves are silent' and need a theory for their interpretation. Reverting back to his belief in a changing human nature, continual change in human affairs implied for Marshall that uniformities tended not to exist as permanent 'universals' in economics and the social sciences, and could therefore not be induced from the facts (pp. 163–7). Given the importance of deciding contemporary debate on issues such as protection versus free trade, and determining appropriate wage levels, examining the relevant economic phenomena to these issues required both careful study of the facts with the assistance of theoretical knowledge. Theory needed to be acquired with facts. History could not stand alone. Even medieval economic history could be enriched by this approach to economic study (pp. 167–71).

This brought Marshall to his second subject in the lecture, the relation of Cambridge to the work required of economic science. The difficulties of this work made Cambridge, the place where 'exceptional genius' could be found in such relative abundance, an ideal university for the practice of such study. Unfortunately, Marshall argued, the present position of political economy in the syllabus of the Moral Sciences made this impossible. Acknowledging the important services the Moral Sciences and its Tripos had made, and were still making in the world, Marshall saw existing Moral Science Tripos arrangements nevertheless as insufficient in supplying the economic workers in the numbers required for solving world problems. Other forces were hampering the growth of economic studies at the university as well. These included the traditional dislike of university men in studying the 'selfish' pursuit of wealth, irrespective of whether it was designed to train them for service in the world of business. Marshall repudiated this view as short-sighted. More wealth was required to end 'dirt and squalor and misery' and raise moral and mental standards of the working classes by providing better house room, more leisure and less hard physical work. Likewise, the tone of business could be raised by the entry of university-trained graduates, and factory life could be made 'more pleasant and beautiful'. These tasks should not be left to 'impetuous socialists', 'ignorant orators' or well-meaning do-gooders. It needed the professional rather than 'amateurish and earnest' application of the talents possessed by the Cambridge scientific community. Economics, in short, needed the same 'weighty seriousness' Cambridge reserved for some of its other studies (pp. 171–3). The lecture ended on a famous appeal to the Cambridge community of scholars, which underwrote Marshall's ambitions for his new position in the years to come,

> It will be my most cherished ambition, my highest endeavour, to do what with my poor ability and my limited strength I may, to increase the numbers of those, whom Cambridge, the great mother of strong men, sends out into the world with cool heads but warm hearts, willing to give some at least of their best powers to grappling with the social suffering around them; resolved not to rest content till they have done what in them lies to discover how far it is possible to open up to all the material means of a refined and noble life.*

It is easy to see Marshall's inaugural lecture as a blueprint for developing within Cambridge the status of economics, his own 'area of knowledge', a task made all the more necessary by the prejudice against its study which still existed among many members of the university. The whole thrust of the lecture seems designed to achieve this by demonstrating both political economy's recent theoretical advances and its application to urgent contemporary problems. Apart from labour conditions and the free trade–protection debate, these included the resurgence of socialism in what were seen as its various manifestations. These ranged from Henry George's land policies to Hyndman's Social Democratic Federation, with both of which Marshall had already done battle at Oxford and elsewhere.[31] Whether the plans he announced by 1885 involved establishing 'a separate School and separate Tripos in Economics and associated branches of Political Science'[32] is more difficult to say. They did undoubtedly declare his interests in modifying the current syllabus of the Moral Sciences Tripos to secure a greater place for economic studies, as well as his intentions to give economics a wider Cambridge audience than secured by its place in the Moral Sciences and Historical Triposes. Many of his later professorial ventures in university administration and controversy were directed to this end.

As already indicated, Sidgwick was one person who interpreted Marshall's inaugural in this way. His memory of their stormy encounter the previous December undoubtedly assisted this. Marshall's words proclaimed syllabus battles, a crystal-clear intention to those like Sidgwick versed in the ways of the university and its Moral Sciences Tripos, although they were expressed in a 'courteous' manner.[33] Sidgwick's diagnosis of Marshall's intentions proved to be correct. Marshall's return as Professor of Political Economy brought many years of in-fighting at the Moral Sciences Board which alienated him from erstwhile friends and colleagues as he sought to impose his views on the appropriate place of economics on his university.[34]

William Cunningham, defeated rival for the Cambridge chair, reacted unfavourably to the lecture for different reasons. As Maloney[35] put it, he saw Marshall's attack on economic history and historical economics 'as a personal and public affront'. Cunningham felt particularly frustrated since Marshall's criticism of his 'line of study' could not be answered, because Cunningham did not want to damage his current standing with Marshall by public criticism of his inaugural. Seven years later Cunningham felt less constrained by such niceties. In the pages of the *Economic Journal* and elsewhere he attacked what he saw

---

*   Alfred Marshall, 'The Present Position of Economics', p. 174. Keynes recorded in his Memoir of Marshall (p. 224 n.2), that Jowett took 'strong exception' to the phase about 'Cambridge, the great mother of strong men'. Years later Marshall ended his last lecture on the same note (below, Chapter 17, pp. 620–21).

as Marshall's misuse of economic history in the context of which he answered some of the remarks in the inaugural he had found so offensive.[36] John Neville Keynes appears to have enjoyed the lecture. 'Mother went with me to hear Marshall's inaugural lecture which I thought was a decided success. I hear however that he caused displeasure (for different reasons) to Cunningham, Sidgwick and Ward.'[37]   Although this cannot be said with certainty, as one of the initiated, Ward had also undoubtedly grasped the implications of Marshall's lecture for friction at the Moral Sciences Board of which he was a prominent member.

The lecture was printed as a separate pamphlet and extensively reviewed. The *Academy* (28 March) noted, 'it is not without significance that Professor Marshall has introduced into the title of his inaugural the term "economics" in place of "political economy"'.   The *Scotsman* (4 April) rightly described the lecture as 'an historical review, a statement, a prophecy, a defence and an appeal'. The *Leeds Mercury* (27 May) drew attention to the fact that his argument should persuade working-class leaders that the 'teaching of political economists are [not] selfishly directed against the rights and interests of labour'.   Even foreign journals took note of the lecture.   R. dalla Volta described the inaugural in *Economista* (25 August 1885) as 'an important contribution'.

The most noteworthy review, however, was published in the *Times* (30 May 1885). This said nothing about Marshall's intended educational reforms at Cambridge, but concentrated on his plea for enhancing the value of economics and his views on the older generation of economists. On the former it regretfully noted Marshall's need to defend economics in the mid-1880s, as compared with the mid-1830s, thinking here perhaps of political economy's practical victory in the new Poor Law of 1834. The *Times* however, criticised what it saw as Marshall's over-emphasis on the merits of the method of the elder economists rather than on the many results of these methods which still held true.   In particular, it carefully examined Marshall's claim that 'the elder economists' did not have 'that faith in the possibility of a vast improvement in the condition of the working classes the moderns possess'.   Marshall defended himself on the last count by explaining this claim more fully. He did so by indicating the different perspectives of present economists on the importance of rising wages for the future possibilities of workers.   High wages, if wisely spent, were a source of greater efficiency for the worker and could therefore be permanent in their effect. Hence, in contrast to the Malthusian doctrine espoused by the older generation of economists, Marshall saw the possibility of a permanently higher wage level, gradually enabling destruction of that vicious cycle of poverty which featured so strongly in the older doctrines.[38]

Marshall's inaugural is therefore an important part of his writings for more than just its declared intent in university reform with respect to economics.   It also presented his general position on economics.   This spelt out the development of the science as he saw it; its practical value for business, social reformers and political, including working-class, leaders; its appropriate methods; and its overriding objective in gradually securing the amelioration of the working class to the status of gentlemanly life which he had been advocating from the beginning of his academic career.   Many of these grander themes are pursued in subsequent chapters.   Moreover, Marshall's pride about the contents of this lecture as compared to his assessment of the quality of its Bristol equivalent, is illustrated by the use he later made of it in the pages of his *Principles*.[39]

LECTURING AT CAMBRIDGE 1885–1908

Marshall's administrative work and teaching responsibilities as Professor, greatly enhanced by the recent university reforms, can now be discussed. Much more is known about the contents and style of his lecturing as Professor in Cambridge than is the case for his earlier period at Cambridge, that at Bristol, and at Oxford. Apart from the many comments his students have left, there are sets of student lecture notes extant from courses he gave during the early 1890s and in the first decade of the twentieth century.[40] However, fewer of Marshall's own lecture notes have survived for this period than is the case for his earlier Cambridge and Bristol teaching. This is partly explained by the publication of his *Principles* in 1890, which enabled him to discourse more freely on those parts of the subject from which he believed his better students would benefit most. His own book removed any necessity for him to engage in that teaching 'as textbook', which he so explicitly deplored.[41] Another explanation for the absence of Marshall's lecture notes this time is provided by Mary Paley Marshall:

He rarely used notes except for lectures on Economic History. He sometimes made a few notes before he went to lecture, and thought over them on his way to the class. He said that the reason why he had so many pupils who thought for themselves was that he never cared to present the subject in an orderly and systematic form or to give information. What he cared to do in lectures was to make the students think with him. He gave questions once a week on a part of the subject which he had not lectured over, and then answered the question in class. He took immense pains in looking over the answers, and used red ink on them freely.[42]

Fay's reminiscences of Marshall's lectures in 1903 are more anecdotal but likewise suggest the disorganised nature of their contents.

I went to one or two of his lectures in my 2nd year – as a result of the first I bought a large Fiscal Blue Book. At the second Marshall arrived with his umbrella, the Fiscal Blue Book and a copy of The Times, the last two in a bag which he kept by the side of the desk. 'I make it a rule never to talk politics', he began, 'but this last speech of Mr. Joseph Chamberlain is . . . really . . .' and for the rest of the hour we listened to an apology for free trade. . . . I was a B.A. when I attended his last course of lectures. He pretended he was nervous of so learned a man as myself!! The lectures were on 'Trade and Industry'. I remember most distinctly one on Venetian glass, after which we had a correspondence on the demerits of modern glass by comparison with the exhibits of old work at Murano . . . [At another of these lectures] . . . he had been explaining the constructive services rendered to the Cartels by Austrian Jews.[43]

Walter Layton, who obtained first class honours in the first and second parts of the Economics Tripos in 1906 and 1907 respectively, 'soaked himself' in Marshallian economics by attending Marshall's lectures for all three of his undergraduate years. In his unpublished memoirs he wrote:

It may be thought that this was overdoing it since his lectures were supposed to be for part II of the Tripos but I do not think I shall be exaggerating if I said he never once repeated himself. It was commonly said amongst the undergraduates that he took his text out of that morning's Times and talked about anything that had struck him in the day's news. It would be nearer the mark to say he gave us the benefit of his current thinking on the book he was writing on industry and commerce.[44]

This suggests Marshall's style had changed little since the time Fay was attending his lectures.

The most detailed and systematic recollections of Marshall's lectures come from E.A. Benians (a fellow Johnian and subsequent Master of Marshall's college) who attended Marshall's classes in 1900–1, and from Sydney Chapman, one of Marshall's better students of the 1890s. Both are worth quoting at length since the flavour of the description is difficult (if not impossible) to summarise faithfully:

The fame of Marshall drew a large throng, which was evidently not what he desired. Amongst the first sentences in his opening lecture I remember: 'If you have come to me for the knowledge with which to pass the Tripos, you will certainly fail. I know more than you and I shall defeat you. You had better go elsewhere.' This won all hearts. But the first lectures were a sifting process, and we soon settled down to the term's work with about half the original number. Marshall's style was not popular and he was at his best with a small class. He did not impart information, but sought to awaken understanding. One gave up note-taking in despair. From seventy lectures or more I brought away half-a-dozen of a more ordinary type. I doubt if the originality of Marshall's ideas could ever be vindicated, as that of Adam Smith's had been, from a student's notes. The connection of Marshall's thought was hard to follow. There was something elusive and baffling, though always stimulating, in his style which stirred the mind, but except for a telling phrase or unexpected illustration, left little in the memory. His manner was easy, as of a person talking, and he seemed supremely happy in the lecture-room. Memory still recaptures the man coming into his room in the Divinity School, his head bent forward as if in thought, mounting his platform with a little fluster of manner, leaning on his desk, his hands clasped in front of him, his blue eyes lit up, now talking easily, now chuckling over some story, now questioning his class, now pausing impressively, with rapt expression, his eyes in a far corner of the room, now speaking in solemn prophetic tones of some problem of the future – the feeding of India, the prospect of England maintaining her greatness, the banishment of poverty from the world.

He had a singular power of illustration. His mind was stored with facts, though they never came out except in their subsidiary place. He dived into the remote past, or drew on recent statistics, on letters in the papers, on some play then being performed, on his own observation. He was never out of touch with life. . . . Humour played an important part in his lectures. He had good stories, and no one enjoyed their fun more than himself. He sometimes brought notes, though I doubt if he ever followed them; and even when he announced beforehand the topics of a lecture, he would often depart altogether from them, pursuing some new train of thought that had suddenly suggested itself to him. Occasionally he invited questions or remarks, but few people were ever bold enough to speak under Marshall's intent and expectant gaze. . . . .He was certainly a unique teacher. He seemed to grip the mind of his hearer and force it through unaccustomed exercises, with many a violent jolt and breathless chase. He loved to puzzle and perplex you and then suddenly to dazzle you with unexpected light. 'Ages of darkness and moments of vision', was one description of his lectures, I remember. But the vision was worth it, and was not to be appreciated without the preliminary bewilderment. . . . What we brought away from Marshall's lectures was certainly not any ordered knowledge of economics, not enough, as he had predicted, for passing an examination, but perhaps an awakened interest, a little more insight, the memory of some moment of illumination and a sense of the importance of economics.[45]

Chapman compared Marshall's performance as a lecturer (likewise described as unplanned and unsystematic) with his qualities as teacher.

> Was he also a good lecturer? Yes and No. I remember at a dinner once when, during a somewhat formless speech, one of my neighbours, who was a practised speaker, remarked to me 'there is a technique about these things.' Marshall had no technique, whether in manner, arrangement or illustration. I never heard him give a lecture which he had constructed like a work of art. So I suppose one ought to say that he was not what is commonly called a good lecturer to large or uninstructed audiences. Yet, even then, he could not help making the impression he wanted to make. In the case of small classes of serious students, however, the answer to the question would be emphatically in the affirmative. Marshall's method with them was thinking aloud and not uncommonly on what he had been thinking about in his own work. Consequently one got the best that could be got from a lecture, not only illumination on a particular theme but also a lesson in how economic theorising should be done. I attended all Marshall's lectures over a period of three years. And I had in addition, after I was definitely committed to economics, the privilege of long talks with him in his study once a week at least, sometimes in connection with one of the essays I had written for him and sometimes in connection with the extensive course of reading he was putting me though. He had most generously given me the run of his library. It was from these talks that I gained most and saw further into his mind.
>
> Whether Marshall was an accomplished lecturer or not, beyond question, he was a great teacher, which is far more important. What constitutes a great teacher, it is not easy to define. The best approach to a definition is by way of results. A teacher to be great must inspire, and further he must have the gift of so imparting his ideas that they get rooted in his pupils as if they were their own. How this is done does not matter. It may be done differently by different people, but all great teachers must have individuality. Marshall certainly had it. I recall in particular his surprising way of putting things, which cracked your shell of commonplace beliefs. How he got to inspire I cannot say – the deepest things in personal relations are the most difficult to fathom – but how he succeeded is evident from the number of economists he created. He certainly made you feel that what you thought mattered a great deal. He was tremendously in earnest.[46]

Chapman's views on Marshall's teaching correspond closely to those of near contemporaries D.H. Macgregor[47] and Fred Pethick-Lawrence. The latter's account, quoted below, confirms Marshall's power to inspire in the classroom and his habit of straying not infrequently into political territory.

> In my fifth year I decided to branch out in a new direction and attended the lectures on economics by Alfred Marshall. Of all the men with whom I came in contact at the University none made a greater impression on me than he, and his lectures were not only illuminating but inspiring. While he insisted that the 'laws' of economics were statements of fact like the 'laws of nature', and not commands to be obeyed like Acts of Parliament, he really cared passionately that a knowledge of economics should be applied to bettering the lot of humanity and in particular of the underdog. He held strong political views and every now and again expressed them. It was a fascinating sight to see the little man standing with his back to the wall facing his class and letting himself go, with a twinkle in his eye which suggested that he realised he was perhaps stepping outside the proper role of a Professor of the University. I remember in particular one of his dicta made shortly after the Jameson raid, to the effect that Mr. Joseph Chamberlain was a negative asset to the country which he assessed at several hundred million pounds![*]

---

[*] F.W. Pethick-Lawrence, *Fate has been Kind*, London: Hutchinson, 1943, p. 34. Although, as noted in Chapter 9, John Neville Keynes left no record of his impressions of Marshall's lectures in his diary, he recorded on 11 May 1885: 'Florence [his wife] is going to Marshall's lectures. They are popular and very interesting. He has a class of more than fifty'. On 25 April he recorded her impressions of the first lecture as 'very entertaining' and substantially devoted to 'the influence of climate on character'. In addition, on 5 December 1890, he noted a

It is interesting to compare these recollections of Marshall's lecturing style with what Marshall wrote to Gonner to explain his own methods of teaching and the role of the lecture as against the textbook in economics. This long quotation shows that Marshall had quite specific aims in his unsystematic presentation of lecturing material.

Methods of teaching, of course, vary, but I will explain my own private hobbies. That of course does not come to much by itself. But it seems to be what you want in this particular letter.

I recognise the existence of students whose minds are merely receptive; and who require of their teachers to render plain their path in the systematic study of a text-book; or even to speak an elementary text-book at them if they cannot or will not find the time to read a text-book for themselves. But I always warn such students away from my lecture room.

Even my more elementary teaching makes no pretence at being systematic, but aims at teaching certain dominant ideas and representative problems more fully than would be possible if every side of the subject had to be discussed equally. If I think the class are merely listening and not thinking for themselves, I try to lead on until they have got pretty well into the middle of a real difficulty and then help to find their way out. I say very little about method; but I endeavour in every advanced course of lectures to work out rather fully a difficult example of almost every important method, having generally set, a week before, a question bearing on the example, so that they will know its difficulties before I begin.

My aim is thus to help them to acquire a delicate and powerful machinery for scientific investigation, without requiring them to attend long courses of lectures. For that is what graduates generally do not care to do. Some people say that books have superseded oral teaching, at all events for able students; I don't think they have. But I think able students are injuriously treated when a chapter of a book is spoken to them. It ought to be printed, and given to them to read quietly. But the best way to learn to row is to row behind a man who is already trained; the learner's body moves by instinctive sympathy with his. And so the trained teacher should, I think, work his own mind before his pupils' and get theirs to work in swing with his. The graduate picks up the swing quickly. But he often wants a good deal of personal advice. I am 'at home' for six hours in every week to any student who chooses to come to see me; and graduates generally come more frequently than others. The initiative in the conversation rests with the student; but if he is interested in any matter, I pursue it at length, sometimes giving an hour or more to a point which is of no great general interest, but on which his mind happens to be troubled; and I give much time to detailed advice about reading.

Of course the great hope in the background is that some of them will go on to do original work.[48]

This extract from Marshall's letter to Gonner presents the basic features of his lecturing style, including the suggestion that a good textbook is required before students can be safely exposed to such unsystematic lecturing practice. This may explain why prior to publishing his *Principles* in 1890 his lecture lists seem to indicate he was providing more systematic lectures before, as compared with after, that event. Confirmation for this belief is given in Keynes's statement:

I think that the informality of his lectures may have increased as time went on. Certainly in 1906, when I attended them, it was impossible to bring away coherent notes. . . . His lectures were not . . . books in the making. . . . But the sharp distinction which he favoured between instruction by book and oral instruction by lecture was, as he developed it, extraordinarily stimulating for the better men and where the class was not too large.[49]

___

comment on Marshall's teaching by Player, one of their students: 'Marshall he considers exceedingly interesting, but not very instructive'. Player gained a third class result in the Tripos examinations of 1893.

Guillebaud,[50] in one of his anecdotes of Marshall, suggests that Keynes's remark on the difficulty of bringing coherent notes from Marshall's lectures perceptively pointed to a deliberate stratagem on the teacher's part. 'I remember Marshall telling me that if he saw a man taking detailed notes at one of his lectures, he wrote him off as a fool; but that if he had reason to believe that the individual in question was a man of ability, he would have regarded it as a personal insult'.

A typed description of his teaching plans for 1901–2 and appended to a letter written for Foxwell provides further evidence that this was the basis for Marshall's lecturing techniques. Again, it can be quoted extensively:

> I propose to work over the main principles of economics commencing at the point where my own first volume ends; and to move rather rapidly, avoiding elementary explanations. The course will therefore not be suitable generally to students in their first and second years, unless they have already some acquaintance with the whole of the ground to be covered. But candidates for the Civil Service and other students in their third or fourth year, who have already done hard work in other subjects, and who wish to obtain in a single year something more than an elementary knowledge of economics, may find the course adapted to their requirements, provided they are able to do some preliminary reading during the summer. The minimum for this purpose is some book on the general principles of value. Jevons *Money*, Bagehot *Lombard Street*, Bastable *International Trade*. (If they take my *Principles* for the analysis of value, they may if they prefer it, omit the small print and those other parts which are marked off, see pp. 9, 475, as capable of being postponed.) Next in order may come the rest of the books in the Tripos lists, and those marked with an asterisk on the following list. Generally speaking it is better to read a small number of books carefully, re-reading the difficult parts several times than to read many books.[51]

Bowley's notes on Marshall's lectures on principles of political economy during Michaelmas Term 1891 very clearly illustrate Marshall's manner of teaching when assisted by the *Principles*. The first half dozen lectures were clearly concerned with the preliminary material of its first two books. Emphasis was placed on aspects of the historical material, with the warning that this was not overly important. The notes also show more current illustrations and more detailed explanations of some of the more difficult concepts. Only one of these preliminary lectures dealt with the definitional niceties of Book II. The next two lectures discussed consumption and demand, emphasising Jevons's error in considering consumption to be the end of economic science by postulating instead the equal importance, and interdependence, of wants and activities. The final lectures were devoted to issues in production economics as raised in Book IV and to the value theory of Book V, with the material on distribution kept for later lectures. The two lectures on production stressed evolutionary and Darwinian aspects, emphasised the substantial debt economics owed to biology, but also presented more conventional material on labour and investment. Value theory commenced with the representative firm and the 'trees in the forest' example, then illustrated the principles of supply and demand in terms of the fishing example with its potential for varying time periods.

Although these lectures appear to have followed the order of contents of the early editions of the *Principles* quite closely, they tended to avoid the presentation of theory; gone are the 'curves' that Foxwell recollected from attending Marshall's 1869 lectures and which so 'amused' Jevons as examiner of the 1874 and 1875 Tripos. Instead, they stressed philosophical, moral and applied aspects of the subject matter. The concurrent advanced lectures dealt with related topics in a more sophisticated manner, generally statistically oriented. For example, following the general lecture of 11 November 1891 on ways of using wealth, which emphasised such moral rules as 'Collective use of wealth is more pleasurable and noble than private use', 'Perhaps the best possible uses of wealth would be to purchase pictures and allow them to be seen and bequeath them to the nation', or, alternatively, using it to invest in open spaces for play and adult recreation to provide a healthier environment, the advanced lecture on 13 November discussed in detail Giffin's statistics on the growth of wealth in the United Kingdom and presented a statistical table of current wealth based on capitalised income tax data.[52]

This rather detailed summary of the course of lectures followed by Bowley in 1891 not only fits in with Marshall's own account of teaching, it can be placed within the scheme of teaching which Marshall recorded himself for his first five years as Professor at Cambridge. The bare outline of the contents is reproduced first,

Year	Term	Summary
1884–5	Easter	Distribution of Wealth
1885–6	Michaelmas	Foreign Trade and Money
	Easter	Speculation, Taxation, etc. (Mill IV and V)
1886–7	Michaelmas	Production and Value
	Lent	Distribution
1887–8	Michaelmas	Foreign Trade, Money and Banking
	Easter	Taxation, Free Trade and Protection
1888–9	Michaelmas	Production and Distribution
	Lent	Trade and Finance
1889–90	Michaelmas	Value, Money, Foreign Trade
	Lent	Fluctuations, Taxation, Economic Functions of Government[53]

Synopses of these lectures were given in the *Reporter* and recorded by Marshall himself with decreasing amounts of detail in his memorandum on general work since arrival at Cambridge, perhaps as drafts for the annual reports he was required by statute to submit to his Special Board of Studies. In the *Reporter* (21 April 1885, p. 601) his first course of lectures was described as covering 'the distribution of wealth with special reference to the causes that determine the income of different classes in England now, and to the inquiry how far the existing inequalities are unavoidable'. In his personal record, he described the course as follows:

General Course: 2 lectures per week. Treated (i) outlines of history rather fully (4 lectures). Law of D[iminishing] R[eturns], elements of the theory of rent – general outline of problem of distribution with some account of H. George's economic points, his socialism being disregarded as far as possible, so that the relation to government and to land nationalisation remains either for the next Easter term or for a separate course on Land. The theoretical difficulties [for the special class] got through were few, chiefly (i) definition of income (ii) Mill's four propositions analysis (iii) the nature of interest (iv) if land rises from the seas and rent falls what is the effect on net wealth (v) do high wages promote the use of machinery (vi) does change from circulating auxiliary capital to fixed auxiliary capital injure labourers (vii) relation between capital and rent (viii) something about metayers. But very little use was made of curves except in this last question.

The 1885 Michaelmas term lectures on foreign trade and money also contained separate general and theoretical lecture classes and received an official and informal description. The *Reporter* (13 October 1885, p. 39) described the course as 'lectures on Money, Foreign Trade, Competition and Crises with special reference to the causes and consequences of recent changes in the purchasing power of gold, to bimetallism, and to the present condition of England's commerce'. A supplementary course of one lecture a week for which no fees were charged promised to deal with the more difficult points arising in these subjects. Their content is described in more detail for his private records: 'Did pretty fully theory of money, foreign trade & exchanges, relation of imports to exports, protection & fair trade. Went rapidly through main points of theory of banking, Bank Act, Bagehot's position & bimetallism but ignored almost entirely the history of Banking & Crisis and said almost nothing on the stock exchange, nor construction, nor modern history of business'.*

The term of general lectures Bowley followed in 1891 share some of the characteristics of the general course on distribution with which Marshall started his Cambridge teaching. Its contents were, however, more specifically shaped by the subsequent publication of the *Principles*. Like the 1885 lectures, they covered the history rather fully, and avoided the use of curves. Lectures on foreign trade and money, as taken by Bowley in Lent and Easter terms 1892 and by Layton in 1904 followed the pattern of the 1885–86 lectures on money and finance although the illustrative detail Marshall gave varied considerably as a result of the passing of the years. For example, the 1892 lectures on money and trade attended by Bowley dwelt on Indian currency and finance problems; when Layton attended them in 1904 the material on fluctuations was illustrated with reference to Argentina and Australia. The 1904 lectures also paid greater attention to the role of share price fluctuations in business fluctuations. The last fact by itself is supportive of Layton's subsequent hypothesis about Marshall's lectures. This was that they reflected his massive research into commerce and industry for the book he was then preparing and which in these years involved substantial study of the stock exchange, share prices and even accounting practice, as shown by his notes on these subjects preserved in the Marshall Library.¶

---

* Marshall Archive, Large Brown Box, Item 33. For 1886–87 (Michaelmas term) this course of lectures was described in the following terms: 'The causes which determine the course of foreign trade; the terms on which it is carried on: and the underselling of one country by another. The excess of England's imports over her exports. The theory of money. The influence of the depreciation of silver on the trade with the East, International currency, Bimetallism. The organisation of credit. The English banking system and stock exchange.' The Easter term 1887 lectures on taxation, free trade and protection covered 'the ethic and economic elements in the principles of taxation. The incidence, the advantages and disadvantages of different taxes, imperial and local. The pressure of taxation on different classes of the community. The different effects of the adoption of a protective policy by different countries; the peculiarities of England's commercial position; retaliatory tariffs, commercial treaties. The project for an Imperial Customs Union. The future of Financial Reform.' Among the books to be read by students, Marshall listed Mill's and Sidgwick's *Principles of Political Economy*, Bastable's *Theory of Foreign Trade*, Jevons's *Money*, Bagehot's *Lombard Street*, Walker's *Money, Trade and Industry* and Farrer's *Free Trade and Fair Trade*.

¶ Cannan Papers, Cannan 909, esp. pp. 33–4; Layton Papers, Box 15, esp. pp. 69–95. The crisis theory in the two sets of lectures remained very much the same, and followed the pattern of that published in *Economics of Industry*. Book III, Chapter I, including Overstone's summary of such crises as cited in that chapter. Marshall's unpublished notes on speculation are reproduced and discussed in detail in Marco Dardi and Mauro Gallegati, 'Alfred Marshall on Speculation', *History of Political Economy*, 24 (3), Fall 1992, pp. 571–94.

Layton's lecture notes, together with Marshall's habit of regularly testing his students with essay questions, also support Chapman's contention that Marshall's lecture courses needed to be supplemented by considerable reading. They were also invariably accompanied by a general invitation to those interested in the subject to discuss economic problems at his home at set times included with the published lecture lists. His first notice to prospective students in January 1885 advertised this service to give advice and informal instruction for which he generally set aside a generous six hours a week per term. Like his lectures, this period of private tuition was probably just as generously extended as Fay recalled in 1925. From the 1885–86 academic year, for example, his home consultation times were extended to three hours per day from Monday to Thursday between four and seven during each full term, an invitation issued to all members of the university but later confined to all students who wished to discuss economic questions. Contrary to general practice, this informal teaching was offered free of charge.[54]

A humorous account of his home teaching is preserved in the *Cambridge Review* written by one of its recipients:

> We thank you for your kindness and readiness in solving our difficulties, if we bring them to you as you sit in your study at Balliol Croft, a study all books, with scarce room for Professor and student. You meet us at the door as we are shewn in, do not know our names, never seem to recognise that we have been before, shake hands hesitatingly, and are with some difficulty started to talk; we learn much from your talk. Or else, plunging into statistics and dragging out that great MS. volume [Marshall's Red Book] wherein are preserved figures upon figures, you will shew us curves, curves telling us of cotton and iron and rupees and measles, and to all seeming yet stranger mixtures than these. What does not that book contain; can it tell us of variations of the weather and of the boat race, whereupon you are basing a theory that we win the boat race whenever a wet Lent term provides enough water in the Cam for us to row upon; or of the relative merits of Professors and undergraduates? I daresay it can. If you told me it was all there I should feel no surprise. A wonderful volume.[55]

Marshall clearly took his teaching duties very seriously, and it is undoubtedly this quality, plus his masterly command of the subject, which gained him the reputation as a teacher his students gave him. For those in tune with his economic thinking, and the contents of his *Principles*, his lectures, unorganised as they may have been, nevertheless proved to be an inspiring experience. However, it is only by comparison with the very systematic notes Layton took from Pigou's lectures on economics which he was also attending, and which, unlike Marshall's, were filled with diagrams and occasionally, equations, that Marshall's lectures appear to be highly disorganised. Layton, unlike Keynes, seems to have had little trouble in producing substantial and generally intelligible notes from them. The different observations on his lectures Marshall attracted from these two prize students in the early years of his Economics Tripos undoubtedly reflect their decidedly different personalities and what they were looking for in the economics teaching provided.

The various accounts of Marshall's teaching by his former Cambridge students also highlight some characteristics of his personal presence in the classroom. The 'little man' is at first uninspiring. Then his eyes, undoubtedly one of his strongest and most striking features, take over, expressively twinkling as the lecture takes off. There is, in addition, the peculiar sense of humour, and an impishness in expression combined with a fluency induced by spontaneity which his writings so invariably lack. Accounts of his magnetism in the classroom conform with the view Mary Paley frequently expressed about his 'extraordinary brilliant conversation'. Once again, this is difficult to reconcile with his so often, dull prose. Mary Paley sheds light on this in one of her comments to Keynes. His habit of continual, painstakingly careful, revision removed all the life and energy from his writing. She recalled only one exception, the 'article written for the cooperative annual in 1884' during their holidays and 'in white heat. It is, I think, one of the best things he ever wrote',[56] In short, the fascination which Marshall exerted on his students in the classroom is therefore no longer retrievable except in the accounts of his teaching and conversation of which many have fortunately been left behind.

Even those who disliked him as a person saw him as a 'great and inspiring teacher', who gave the 'most brilliant lectures' in a style far removed from this published prose. Lynda Grier, who was his student during his final years as Professor at Cambridge, recorded these tributes and contrasted his lecturing style with his writing in the following manner:

As a writer he was anything but epigrammatic, but as a lecturer he was often so. 'A great man is said to talk nonsense in his own generation, sense in the next, common sense in the third.' 'The motto of the speculator is "do unto others as they would wish to do to you, only do it first".' 'A difficult sentence in Economics is one which is difficult to understand, a simple sentence is one which it is impossible to understand.'[57]

THE SIZE AND COMPOSITION OF MARSHALL'S CLASSES 1885–1908

Marshall's teaching responsibilities need to be placed in the perspective of the size and composition of his classes, on which a substantial amount of information is available. Apart from highlighting the very different situation with respect to class sizes faced by the teacher of economics in the 1880s and 1890s relative to that of a century later, this information enables some testing of Marshall's complaints about the quality of the students he was attracting to economics when professor at Cambridge. Such complaints, largely made in correspondence with colleagues and former students, involved three variants: first, the generally poor quality of students attempting economics; secondly, the decline in the numbers of young, intelligent people entering the moral sciences as compared with the 1860s; and thirdly, the excessive number of women studying political economy.

Before looking at the nature of these complaints in more detail, some background has to be provided on the sources from which Marshall drew his students. As he had emphasised in the inaugural lecture, economics students tended to come from both the History and the Moral Sciences Triposes. This had already been the case when he was John's College Lecturer in the Moral Sciences between 1868 and 1877. In addition to these normal undergraduate sources of students, from 1885 Marshall also attracted to his lectures graduate students and students preparing for the Indian Civil Service but, relative to Oxford, the last at Cambridge were rather few. Much of his administrative initiatives were directed at attracting more students to economics from all these sources. His syllabus reforms in the years after 1885 were largely designed to increase the economic content of both the History and Moral Sciences Triposes, but despite the successes he achieved in this, he was never really satisfied with the degree of specialisation in economics these syllabuses could accommodate. Marshall insisted early on that effective economic studies at Cambridge could only be provided within a separate Economics and Political Sciences Tripos, the goal he eventually achieved in 1903, and had foreshadowed in his 1885 inaugural. His perception after 1885 of the students he was attracting reinforced the urgency of his drive to enhance the status of economics teaching at Cambridge.

The following correspondence provides a sample of his views on student quality. In 1902 Marshall wrote to J.N. Keynes, 'the curriculum to which I am officially attached [i.e. the Moral Sciences Tripos] has not provided me with one single high class man devoting himself to economics during the sixteen years of my professorship'.[58] In the same year, he wrote at greater length to Foxwell:

> Up to 1880 the Mo[ral] Sc[iences] List contained the names, in nearly every year, of several men of considerable and occasionally of very high natural ability, who came to Cambridge direct from school. Then came a transitional period; and since 1890, this class of man has almost disappeared from the Mo[ral] Sc[iences] Tripos. It has become in effect a postgraduate Tripos for other Universities, with a few old men thrown in, many of them of more than average age. But the fresh strong beautiful youthful minds that used to come largely to the Mo[ral] Sc[ience] Tripos are now scarcely ever seen there. MacTaggart is an eminent exception, Wedgewood is an exception: but there are not many others . . . many of the best Historical men – especially if at Trinity – do not take up economics at all. . . . But taking only those whom I know personally, and have taken their degrees from 1890 to 1901, I think that in general ability and in scientific faculty they aggregate many times as high as the Mo[ral] Sc[ience] men of the same years who came to Cambridge . . .[59]

Marshall's memory did not serve him well on this occasion. The brilliant moral science men he had taught in the 1870s, including Foxwell, were nearly all of the type of which he was complaining to Foxwell. They had not come directly from school, but had first taken a degree at another university. More generally, this was London (Foxwell, Keynes, Ward), but sometimes it was one of the Scottish universities (Cunningham, Nicholson, the last having also gone to London). Only Henry Cunynghame and F.W. Maitland went to Cambridge as their first university and even then Cunynghame only after a period in the army. During the 1880s things deteriorated further. However, the better of Marshall's students then came via the Mathematical, and not the Moral Sciences, Tripos.

Whitaker lists Marshall's good students for the 1880s as Flux, Johnson and Berry, but these were only 'half caught' for economics; Bowley, Chapman, Sanger, Pigou and MacGregor were his leading post-1890 products. This compared most unfavourably with his Oxford experience where, within one year, he had captured Gonner, Price and Harrison.[60] A list of 'crops of students' prepared by Mary Paley Marshall adds the name of Moore Ede to the students from the 1870s; Stanley Leathes and Mrs Bosanquet (Helen Dendy) to those from the 1880s and among the 1890s she included such notables as Lilian Knowles, Bertrand Russell and Clapham.[61]

Marshall's other frequent complaints about the nature of his classes was that they contained too many women students. In 1906 he wrote to Foxwell urging him to admit Newnham and Girton students to his lectures if they were to be examined in this subject matter. But Marshall added: 'I confess I think too many of them do enter for our Triposes'. Earlier, and in the context of the women's degrees issue, he had written to Foxwell (17 April 1897) that 'three fourths of the people who came to this house (6 Madingley Road) are Newnham or Girton students present or past.[62]

Some of these pessimistic reflections on his students seem to have depended on the mood of the moment. Marshall wrote to Arthur Bowley in 1901, 'there are not a score [of Cambridge men] who are setting themselves to do it [i.e. sound economic studies]. There are not six who have equal faculties for doing it with the quiet and steadfast A.L. Bowley'.[63] However, in a letter to Chapman in 1904 Marshall boasted of the quality of his 'Adam Smith Prize lot' which included Bowley, Chapman, Pethick-Lawrence and Pigou, concluding 'I am proud of my "Cambridge stable"'.[64] The time of writing helps to explain these different perceptions of essentially the same facts. In 1901, when he wrote to Bowley, the final battle for the Economics Tripos had only just started; by 1904 it had been won. Support for the view that Marshall's perception of the actual situation depended very much on the mood of the beholder, is visible in the data on Marshall's students obtainable from the statistical records he had kept himself for various reasons.

To assist preparation of the annual returns on lectures and period of residence during term required of him as Professor, Marshall kept details of the registration of students for his classes during the three academic years from 1886–87 to 1888–89 inclusive. These classified students by sex, by Tripos and by whether they were graduate students, preparing for the Special Examination, or others. The whole of this information is shown in Table 10.1 but the following can be particularly noted. For the three years from 1886 to 1889, Marshall drew only 16 per cent of his students from the Moral Sciences Tripos, nearly a quarter from the History Tripos and less than 5 per cent from pass candidates for the Special Examination. Graduate students, for the two years for which that information is available, accounted for approximately 15 per cent, that is, slightly below his intake from moral sciences. One-third of his students were women and of these nearly two-thirds came from Newnham College. The high intake from Newnham is explicable by Mary Paley's lectures on political economy from 1885 onwards, and through Sidgwick's strong association with the college. Marshall's complaints about the excessive number of women in his classes seems therefore at least statistically justified.*

Some of his women students likewise complained about Marshall's attitude to them. For example, the following was recorded by a member of his 1900 class, Miss P.M. Sturton:

> When Professor Marshall, father of today's Political Economy, called his three women students to his home to return some papers, his remarks, though kindly, were caustic. He said the amount I had written was in reverse proportion to the importance of the subject matter; and to someone else, 'your writing takes longer to read than anyone else's, and the result is not worth it'. He then proceeded to express doubts that he had been wise in opening his classes to women students, and wondered whether perhaps the type of German

---

* The overall proportion of women students at Cambridge can be gauged from the fact that in the fifteen years from 1881 to 1896 only 689 women students gained honours results, less than 10 per cent of the male honours graduates over the same period. However, even from the end of the 1880s the number of Newnham students who took political economy were a small proportion of Newnham students. In Michaelmas 1888, less than 5 per cent; in 1889, about 8 per cent; in 1891, less than 4 per cent; and in 1897 and 1898 they were 5 and 2 per cent respectively. Extracted from Newnham Archives, student registers. And see Chapter 9 above, p. 268 and n*.

hausfrau wouldn't serve our nation better. His lectures were tremendously stimulating . . . though I never became an economist.[65]

Miss Sturton obtained Class II Division 1 in Part I of the Moral Sciences Tripos in 1903 and Class II in the second part in 1904, though her results in political economy are not recorded. Her experience was duplicated by Lynda Grier, who, together with Eva Spielman, was placed in the first class results for the Economics Tripos in 1908, a year no man achieved this distinction. Her report of a meeting at Marshall's house is worth quoting,

> He did condescend to read our papers. As might be expected, we received the most devastating comments, though I know that many of the most brilliant men in the University amused themselves by comparing notes on his most acid comments on their efforts. Once he asked us [Grier, Eva Spielman and Frances Elinor Rendel] to tea. I think Mrs. Marshall might have warned us of what would be expected. We had thought she would be there, but no, we were shown into his study where the array of books and the knowledge of those which had been written there [sic] struck awe into our souls. He gave us an excellent tea, and Eva Hubback [née Spielman] ventured to make some more or less frivolous comment on some object of interest in the room. He said he would tell us about it till we got down to serious business. Having satisfied her curiosity he said 'I leave it to you to direct the conversation'. An abysmal silence ensued. In peevish tones he repeated the remark. The silence deepened. In angry tones he said it a third time, I then, desperately, knowing that I was the eldest of those present, asked a question on something which had puzzled me, and then he was most interesting and helpful. But I gather that he told his wife what a poor lot we were, and he never repeated the invitation.[66]

For the year 1888-89, separate information is available for attendance at Marshall's advanced course of lectures. These attracted six students in Michaelmas term 1888 and seven in Lent term 1888, including one woman student. The advanced students included Flux and Chapman; the woman student was Helen Dendy from Newnham. Her results in the Moral Sciences Tripos, it is interesting to note, were recorded as first in the first class list.[67]

A list of attendances at Marshall's lectures from 1884–85 to 1888–89, but with less subdivision, is also preserved among the Marshall Papers. This is reproduced in full as Table 10.2. Table 10.3 summarizes information obtained from the registration cards which Marshall kept on his students to acquaint himself with their background and reading in economics. Data are shown for three years in the 1890s prior to the introduction of the Economics Tripos and for the four complete years of the Economics Tripos during which Marshall was professor. The data for 1890–91, 1892–93 and 1898–99 supplement the data from Table 10.1, and confirm Marshall's view that fewer students were enrolling in economics in the 1890s. The sample is too small to indicate whether history men generally exceeded moral science men nor does it seem to demonstrate that too many women were doing economics. In fact, the overall proportion of women in his classes for these three years of the 1890s declined to one-sixth, that is, half of what it had been at the end of the 1880s. The material on students taking economics courses within the Economics Tripos only partly confirms Marshall's expectations about the importance of this academic reorganisation in attracting students to economics.[68]

These data on his students enable some testing of the accuracy of Marshall's complaints about the quality of students he was attracting. The evidence clearly supports

Table 10.1: Marshall's Economics Students 1886–1887 to 1888–1889

Term	Course	Tripos and other division of study					College				TOTAL STUDENTS	Of which %		
		Moral Sciences	History	Special	Misc.[a]	Total	Girton	Newnham	Other	Total		Moral Sciences	History	Women
1886–87														
Michaelmas	Production	8	25	2	8	43	5	19	7	31	74	18.6	58.1	41.9
Lent	Distribution	7	2		16	25	1	10	4	15	40	28.0	0.8	37.5
1887–88														
Michaelmas	Foreign Trade, Money, Banking	11	2	3	12	28	–	4	–	4[b]	32	34.3	18.8	12.5
Easter	Taxation, Free Trade and Protection	6	5	3	5	19	3	12	1	16	35	31.5	25.3	45.7
1888–89														
Michaelmas	Production and Distribution	4	14	1	15	34	1	5	4	10	44	11.8	41.2	22.7
Lent	Trade and Money	5	8	n.a.	8	21	1	5	2	8	29	23.8	38.0	27.6
TOTALS		41	56	9	64	170	11	55	18	84	254	16.1	24.0	33.1

Notes

a. Miscellaneous in 1887–88 include: Indian Civil Service Examinaton, 4 in Michaelmas and 1 in Easter term: graduates, 4 in Michaelmas and 2 in Easter term. In 1888-89, Miscellaneous includes 9 graduates in Michaelmas and 4 graduates in Lent term, as well as 2 Law Tripos and 1 Theology Tripos students.

b. In Michaelmas 1887 all from Newnham. In Easter 1888, Girton 3, Newnham 12, Miscellaneous 1. In Michaelmas 1889, Girton 1, Newnham 5 and Miscellaneous 4 (15 in History Tripos and 1 in Moral Sciences Tripos). In Advanced Economic Theory 1889, 2 graduates including Flux; 1 Moral Science (male); 2 History Tripos; 1 Miscellaneous (Chapman). In Lent, 1889, 5 Newnham, 1 Girton, 2 Miscellaneous. Advanced Economic Theory, 8 males, 1 female (Helen Dendy-Bosanquet).

Source: A. Marshall, General Work Since Arrival at Cambridge, Marshall Papers, Large Brown Box, Item 33. Reproduced with permission from the editors of the *Scottish Journal of Political Economy*.

Marshall's contention that only few very able people were studying political economy and that most of these came to him either from other triposes or were graduate students. Examples are mathematicians like Berry, Bowley and Flux, or historians like Clapham and Pigou. However, this period did produce a few firsts among his students in the advanced economic theory class, of which McTaggart (1888), Sanger (1894), Chapman (1898) and Macgregor (1901) can be mentioned as of particular importance.[69]

Table 10.2: Attendances at Marshall's Lectures 1884–1885 to 1888–1889

| Year | Term | Total | Men | | Women |
			Moral Sciences	Other	
1884-85	Easter*	53	13	27	13
1885-86	Michaelmas	53	12	33	8
	Easter	34	4	20	10
1886-87	Michaelmas	74	8	35	31
	Lent	40	7	18	15
1887-88	Michaelmas	33	11	18	4
	Lent	36	6	14	16
1888-89	Michaelmas	43	4	29	10
TOTALS		336	65	194	107
Average per course		45.8	8.1	24.3	13.7

Note: * These were the lectures attended by Florence Keynes (p. 315 n.*), who thereby quite correctly estimated the attendance at Marshall's class at 'more than fifty'.

Source: Reproduced with permission from the editors of the *Scottish Journal of Political Economy*.

On the other hand, Marshall's comments on the quality of moral sciences students before and after 1880 cannot be supported from the evidence in the published results, unless very considerable qualifications are made. In the first place, his generalisation seems a very selective recollection of his experience as College Lecturer in the Moral Sciences from 1868 to 1877. This period produced a substantial number of outstanding firsts in the Moral Sciences Tripos and the total number of its students was relatively large. 1880 cannot therefore be taken as the cut-off point in this context. In fact, the period when the Moral Sciences Tripos consistently attracted a substantial number of good honours students was from 1866 to 1874. As far as men students were concerned, this period was never really

Table 10.3: Student Lists from Student Registration Forms

1890–91 to 1898–99

	Men — Moral Sciences	History	Misc.	Special	Total	Women — Moral Sciences	History	Newnham	Total	TOTAL STUDENTS	Of Which % — Moral Sciences	History	Women
1890–91	3	3	2[a]	–	8	–	–	–	–	8	37.5	37.5	–
1892–93	2	6[b]	1[c]	–	9	2	–	–	2	11	36.4	54.5	18.2
1898–99	23	8	6[d]	1[e]	38	4	–	5	9	47[f]	57.6	17.7	23.7

1904–5 to 1907–8

	Men — Moral Sciences[h]	History	Econs.	Other	Total	Women — Moral Sciences	History	Econs.	Total	TOTAL STUDENTS	Of Which % — Moral Sciences	History	Econs.	Women
1904–5	–	5	7	5	17	3	2	2	7	24	12.5	25.6	37.5	29.2
1905–6	–	5	6[g]	4	15	–	–	1	1	16	–	31.3	31.3	6.5
1906–7	–	3	2	8	13	1	1	3	5	18	55.1	16.7	27.8	27.8
1907–8	–	–	11	5	16	–	–	5[i]	5	21	–	–	76.2	23.8

Notes

a. A.L. Bowley and C.P. Sanger, both mathematicians.
b. Includes J. H. Clapham, on whose performance Marshall commented 'shows force'.
c. Includes R.L. Wedgewood (Trinity) but not reading for a Tripos.
d. 5 from Mathematics and 1 from Classical Tripos.
e. Indian Civil Service.
f. 6 of the 47 students had recorded first class results in earlier examinations in either part of another Tripos.
g. Includes J.M. Keynes.
h. As shown below, Chapter 15, pp. 547–8, moral science students could no longer take economics as a prescribed course on the introduction of the Economics and Politics Tripos.
i. Includes Lynda Grier and Eva Spielman who gained first class results in the Tripos in June 1908.

Source: Marshall Papers, Large Brown Box, Item: Notes on Students. Reproduced with permission from the editors of the *Scottish Journal of Political Economy*.

repeated in the history of that Tripos. By way of comparison, the first three years of Marshall's professorship were especially poor in first class results, as were the years immediately following 1902. Marshall was over-influenced by these circumstances when he wrote so pessimistically to Foxwell and J.N. Keynes in 1902, and two years later to Gonner. Even that 'golden age' of the Moral Sciences Tripos was not nearly as strongly founded on 'fresh young men from school' as he later complained, but included many other men who had previously attended other universities. The sad regret he voiced about the quality of students was influenced by faulty memories of what in retrospect was the exciting period in the Moral Sciences Tripos when, by coincidence, he had first become involved in its teaching.

The accuracy of Marshall's claim that too many women were taking the economics courses and the Moral Sciences Tripos and that their results were generally inferior to those of the men, also needs some comment. Women made up approximately one-third of his economics classes at the end of the 1880s (Table 10.1), a proportion that dropped to a little over a quarter in the subsequent two decades of his teaching (Table 10.2). However, it greatly exceeded the proportion of women students in the university population as a whole. The Moral Sciences Tripos itself attracted a considerable number of women, especially in the 1890s, and for two particular years (1894 and 1897) women accounted for nearly 50 per cent of those attempting its examinations. These data say more about the growing unpopularity of the Moral Sciences Tripos with men students of this generation than about its attractiveness to women students. In fact, the proportion of women students attempting the Moral Sciences Tripos also sharply declined at this time as compared with the 1870s. There is a further potential aberration in the statistics as reflected in Table 10.2. The presence of Florence Keynes at Marshall's day class in Easter term 1885 may impart an upward bias to the information on women attendance contained in them. If these data included information on interested members of the public like Florence Keynes, the proportion of women is likely to be over-stated because middle-class members of the public able to attend day-time lectures would be largely confined to women.

These women students did not necessarily lower the tone of the school in so far as quality was concerned. The proportion of first class results for men recorded from 1881 to 1906 was slightly lower (18.3 per cent) than that for women over the same period (19.6 per cent) but these proportions compare quite unfavourably with the 30.6 per cent of first class results from enrolments in the 'golden age' of the Moral Sciences Tripos of 1866 and 1874 inclusive. The evidence suggests that Marshall at this stage of his life was highly prejudiced against women students with little factual justification.[*]

---

[*] Cf. D.H. Macgregor, 'Marshall and his Book', pp. 114–15. I take the opportunity in this context to draw attention to an ambiguity in the phrase, 'first class', to which Sir Austin Robinson alerted me in correspondence. Sir Austin writes: I think Marshall was not talking about people who were classed in the First Class in a tripos examination, though the difference was not as great in his day as it is now, I am quite sure what Marshall was meaning was this. In any given year in Cambridge there are in all subjects perhaps ten or twelve first class men at most, and in the sense that they have the capacity to change the whole of their subject and their whole approach to it. In Marshall's time I doubt if there were more than four or five. He was meaning "first class" in this sense. He was lamenting the fact that the sort of people who were the top three Wranglers, the first one or two in the Classical Tripos, possibly one in the years in the Moral Sciences Tripos, were not coming when he got back to Cambridge to the

Finally, the data on Marshall's economics students enables some comments on the market provided by university students for his *Principles*, though these are obviously confined to his 'home market' of Cambridge. After its publication in 1890, Marshall consistently set his *Principles* as one of a number of general texts required to be read; but the total market this requirement provided was very small relative to the sales the book enjoyed in England. The proportion of students who claimed to have studied the *Principles* at least in part before enrolling in Marshall's classes was high in the early years of the new Economics Tripos (72.7 per cent). This compares with 42.6 per cent 1898 and just over a third on very small numbers in 1892 (36.3 per cent).[70] Some support is therefore given to the view that in his post-*Principles* teaching, Marshall increasingly presumed his students were familiar with some of the details of his text.

THE PROFESSOR AS ACADEMIC ADMINISTRATOR

Marshall's administrative career at the University of Cambridge outside his immediate duties as Professor of Political Economy cannot be described as particularly impressive. Unlike Henry Sidgwick,[71] who for the whole of his teaching life was active in the cause of university reorganisation and reform, and who, in addition, was a substantial benefactor of the university and its activities, Marshall largely avoided active participation in general university administration. When he did so, his endeavours were invariably directed at expanding the status of the study of economics within the university or enhancing its general standing in the community at large. In spite of the impression he later gave, Marshall could be an ardent controversialist when the situation required it[72] and he was equally willing to engross himself fully and wholeheartedly in academic politics, if issues such as the advancement of economics were at stake.

During his first two years as Professor, Marshall introduced some minor changes designed to benefit students of political economy, sometimes specifically with the aim to enhance its acceptability to students outside the Moral Sciences and Historical Triposes. For example, the *Reporter* notified the university community in November 1885 that 'political economy in so far as it bears upon international law' was to be included in the examination for the Whewell Scholarship open to international law students in the History Tripos. Although this sounds a minor change, its significance arose from the fact that students in subjects outside mathematics, classics and to a lesser extent the natural sciences, had little real access to college scholarships. Inclusion of some study of political economy in the examination for the Whewell Scholarship therefore provided a marginal improvement in their situation, and hence gave a slightly greater incentive to economic study.[73]

Marshall's offer to establish a general political economy prize in March 1886 can be interpreted in a similar vein: as an inducement to students to take up systematic study of the subject. The Marshall Prize, as it was first known, amounted to £15 to be spent on books. Initially for five years, it was to be awarded annually from 1887 to the student who performed best in the regular papers on Political Economy or Advanced Political Economy

---

Social Sciences. I very much doubt whether in his sense they are even now coming to the social sciences. In Marshall's sense [Maynard] Keynes was obviously first class.'

required for the Moral Sciences Tripos. Although the prize was awarded on performance in examinations within the Moral Sciences Tripos, it was open to all [men] students who wished to enter, provided they took the relevant papers. In the letter to the Vice-Chancellor containing his proposal, Marshall explained his reasons for giving the prize. Its regulations were intended to emphasise a need for widening access to examinations in political economy to students beyond those entering the Moral Sciences and History Triposes and for demonstrating the subject's relevance for students of mathematics, the natural sciences, law, and even the classics. In presenting these arguments, Marshall also impressed upon his audience of senior university administrators the fact that he saw economics as holding 'a singular position' among the sciences because of this wide-ranging relevance.[74]

When the term of five years for which the prize was approved was drawing to its close, Marshall wrote again to the Vice-Chancellor. He advocated discontinuation in order to substitute a triennial essay prize to the value of £60. The essays for this new prize were to be submitted mid-way between the triennial Cobden Essay Prize. The prize was to be awarded on the basis of reports by internal and external examiners. In this way, Marshall desired 'to work by a new route towards my old aim of attracting to the study of Economics men who are able to bring to it highly trained minds, and who may have gradually acquired, by intelligent observation of what goes on around them, a sound knowledge of contemporary economic conditions; but who, for the present at all events, cannot give their whole time to economic studies.' The Adam Smith Prize, as it became known, is still in existence, the result of the permanent endowment which Marshall offered to the university in 1913. He undoubtedly considered it as a worthwhile investment for, as Marshall wrote to Chapman, the prize had attracted substantial entries from his students of the calibre of Bowley, Pethick Lawrence, Pigou, and Chapman himself in its early years.[75]

Further examples of Marshall's attempts to make political economy studies more attractive to students can be given. One involved a change in the examination timetable designed to give students in the moral sciences slightly more time between papers, including of course their political economy papers. For such students, it was proposed they should take their afternoon papers during the Tripos week from 1.30 to 4.30 p.m. instead of the customary time of 1.00 to 4.00 p.m. while the traditional morning schedule of 9.00 to 12.00 was to be maintained.[76] This enabled students to sleep between papers, if they wished to avail themselves of such an opportunity, as indeed the senior wrangler was known to have done in the year that Marshall took the Mathematical Tripos, and the value of which Marshall may well have recalled from his own experience of that hectic time.

At any possible occasion, Marshall pressed directly for the extension of opportunities to study political economy within the university. He gained some minor, but still quite useful successes. New regulations for special examinations in political economy for the B.A. were approved in 1889[77] but as shown in Table 10.3, did not gain Marshall a large number of additional students. In 1890, Marshall succeeded in making political economy an optional paper within the Indian Civil Service Studies syllabus (provided it had not been taken previously in examinations) while it was also to be included among the subjects for examination in connection with the open competition for places in the Indian Civil Service.[78] Marshall's more significant attempts in expanding possibilities for economic studies within the Triposes for which its study was already accepted are discussed later.[79]

Concern about adequate access to library facilities for students of political economy, already apparent in his Bristol building plans modifications, was translated to Cambridge as well. Initially this involved skirmishes to gain access for students in political economy to the collection of books left by George Pryme, the first political economy professor at Cambridge, for the use of his successors and, presumably, their students. These books had been stored in boxes outside the Vice-Chancellor's room, but had apparently remained unused since they were deposited there after Pryme's death in 1868. In correspondence with Oscar Browning sixteen years after the event, Marshall recalled some stratagems he claimed to have used in order to give his students access to the books, a letter written in the context of a similar situation facing the History School à propos of the Sir James Stephen Collection (which first Kingsley, and then Seeley, had apparently appropriated for their private use).

> So I went to the Mo[ral] Sc[iences] Board and said – I am having plans made for a house with a small dining room. If you approve, I will [have] the dining room enlarged so as to carry bookshelves on two walls, and will let any one have access to the books by appointment, except when my house is full of visitors. I will also spend £50 or more on binding the books.
>   The Mo[ral] Sc[iences] Board was in its most administrative 'mood' and said that was not sufficient. There must be one day in the week on which people could come in as a matter of right. That would have deprived me of a dining room. So I built a small room. Later on the Mo[ral] Sc[iences] Board said my original proposition would do. But I have no room in my house for the collection now. The joke is that after it I found that the Mo[ral] Sc[iences] Board had no locus standi in the matter.[80]

It is difficult to give full credence to Marshall's *ex-post* recollection of this event after an interval of sixteen years, even though his proposal to extend their house for library purposes was later confirmed by Mary Paley Marshall.[81] When at its meeting of 30 April 1885, Marshall first raised the issue at the Moral Sciences Board, the type of offer he recalled to Browning was not recorded. It seems yet another example of faulty memory long after the event. The Board only resolved to ask the University Library to take charge of the collection, 'subject to the condition that the Professor of Political Economy should retain the right of removing it from the University Library at any subsequent period'.* The matter was not raised again at the Moral Sciences Board until 13 March 1886 when Marshall reported the library's unwillingness to accept the Pryme Collection conditionally, and at its subsequent meeting on 11 May 1886 the alternative strategy of housing them in lock-up boxes near the lecture rooms was agreed to by the Board, despite reservations expressed about problems of security which this solution implied. Later that month, the *University Reporter* recorded the Moral Sciences Board proposal to house the books in 'lock-up boxes' to be kept in room 5 of the Literary Schools where most of its lectures were being held, until

---

* Moral Science Board Minutes, Cambridge University Archives, Min. V 10, 30 April 1885, Item 2. In 1886 Marshall had exchanged letters with Browning about the collection, suggesting temporary accommodation in the Philosophical Society's Library with the historical books in the gallery. He estimated the books to occupy about 100 feet of wall space, and indicated that many of them were unbound paper pamphlets, Marshall to Browning, 15 October 1886, 27 October 1886, 4 November 1886 and 17 November 1886. On 17 November 1886 he also wrote to Foxwell about the large number of Pryme's pamphlets, suggesting they should be bound in volumes with a separate bookplate (Freeman Collection, 50/98). Details of the construction of the Marshall's house were provided in Chapter 8 above, pp. 241–4.

they could be more permanently housed in either the University Library or a special Moral Sciences Library. After some opposition from members of the Council of Senate as to whether such 'lock-up boxes' constituted 'due custody of the books', Marshall, and the Moral Sciences Board won the day and the books were made available to his students in economics in this way for many years. Eventually, they found their place in better accommodation, first in the Marshall Library when this was founded after Marshall's death, and then, on a permanent loan basis, in the Cambridge University Library, where they can now be found.[82]

Some correspondence Marshall had on the subject with the university Librarian survives in the university archives. In January 1891, Marshall offered the Pryme Collection once again, 'as the nucleus of a roomful of economics books' provided he gained privileged borrowing access to the collection 'for the time being', by classing such borrowing as additional to the ten books he could have out on loan from the library as a member of the University. Nothing came of this suggestion, and in October 1894 Marshall repeated the offer, adding by way of inducement that he was willing to contribute £25 towards the rebinding of some of the pamphlets or other necessary refurbishments. This was followed three weeks later with a further letter in which Marshall drew the Librarian's attention to an article dealing with 'seminars and their libraries',[83] a matter of importance in Marshall's opinion, given the university moves towards introducing advanced (graduate) studies, a proposal in which Marshall himself was actively involved as a member of the syndicate investigating the issue.

Marshall also corresponded with the Librarian on other matters. A 1905 postcard from Austria survives in which Marshall advised the Librarian against the purchase of the second edition of a French title because he had never heard of it, suggesting instead a check whether the most recent edition of Leroy Beaulieu's *Traité des finances* was in the library.[84] A year later he advised the Librarian on a more suitable classificatory scheme for the university's economics collection, in the form of a modification of the scheme proposed in the Hungarian publication, *Bibliographia Economica Universitatis*.[85] Few positive results appear to have flowed from these and like endeavours by Marshall to influence library policy,[86] nor is there any evidence that Marshall attempted at any stage to increase his influence in this area by trying to get himself elected to the University Library Syndicate.

Marshall's generosity to students with his own books may be recalled at this stage. Chapman mentioned his intense personal concern with this aspect of his better students' welfare. An even more striking reminiscence came from Fay. After Marshall had assisted him with the selection of a suitable topic for his fellowship dissertation, for which he used a very roundabout method of first reading from a long list of topics for the student to reject and then asking him to suggest one of his own, Marshall 'began prowling around the shelves, handing out books in English and German . . . about thirty in all. . . . I went away . . . staggering under an armload of books, and next day came back with a bag for the balance. I had them nearly three years.'[87]

Marshall served on few university committees during his twenty-four years as Cambridge Professor, tending to avoid them unless they dealt with issues such as course reform in which he was particularly interested.[88] In November 1894 he was appointed as a member of a university Syndicate to investigate advanced studies and research at the university. More specifically, this Syndicate had been appointed to consider, '(1) the best means of giving further help and encouragement to persons who desire to pursue courses of advanced study of research within the University, (2) what classes of students should be admitted to such courses, (3) what academic recognition, whether by degree or otherwise, should be granted to such students, and under what conditions'.[89]

This followed a previous inquiry which had looked at the subject largely in terms of enabling graduates from other universities to take existing Tripos examinations. In its first report, the Advanced Studies Syndicate proposed that advanced students should be admitted to the university, if graduates of other universities, were aged 21 years or more, and qualified to undertake advanced studies; such students to undertake either studies leading up to existing Tripos examinations or to pursue supervised research within the university in a subject for which they were qualified, and to submit a dissertation, eventually to be adjudged a distinguished piece of original research or as a record of original research. Supervision of the new procedures was to be in the hands of a Degree Committee of the Special Board of Studies in which the topic of research undertaken by an advanced student was located. Further reports proposed detailed regulations for the proposed advanced courses and research degrees, including those on admissions, minimum period of residence, fees and type of degrees to be awarded.[90]

In addition, Marshall occasionally participated in general university business by contributing to the regular debates on University Reports, a privilege granted to him by virtue of his membership of the university as resident M.A. on the university's electoral roll. Unlike Sidgwick, who took an active interest in university business, Marshall entered such debates fairly infrequently. Apart from the debates on the women's degrees issue,[91] Marshall participated in those on order of merit lists in examinations and on the postgraduate studies report, more generally confirming his participation in this way to matters which could affect the study of economics at the university.[92]

As the Professor of a subject within the Moral Sciences Tripos, Marshall was *ex officio* member of the Special Board of Studies in Moral Sciences, whose meetings he therefore attended fairly regularly. Recorded attendances in the Moral Sciences Board Minutes indicate Marshall attended approximately two-thirds of the meetings it held between 1885 and 1904, in total exceeding sixty. He was also a member on the Special Board for History and Archaeology, a group of subjects which likewise included political economy while, on the creation of the Economic and Political Science Tripos, he served on its Special Board until his retirement in 1908, in the capacity of its chairman from 1906. Regular meetings of these Special Boards were held for appointing examiners, deciding on book lists to be studied as preparation for the examinations, deciding on lecturing responsibilities for the coming year and term and, less frequently, making recommendations for syllabus changes. Apart from the one occasion already noted, Marshall never served on them in an official capacity as chair or secretary though sometimes, on 22 January 1897, for example, in the absence of Sidgwick, or Ward, he took the chair as the most senior Board member. From 1897, Degree Committee meetings were held immediately after Board meetings if there was business dealing with postgraduate studies in the moral sciences.

His performance at these Board meetings, even when there were no contentious issues at stake, was often a source of irritation. At various times, Keynes described his behaviour at its meetings as 'narrow', 'egotistical', 'a dreadful bore', 'exceedingly irrelevant' while on another occasion he recorded Marshall's absence from the meeting as enabling the Board to complete as much business in an hour as normally would take two long meetings. Finally, on hearing of Sidgwick's intention to resign as Chairman of the Moral Sciences Board, Keynes recorded, 'I should dread having Marshall at the head of the School.'[93]

In the context of Marshall's responsibilities on the Moral Sciences Board, it may be noted that he never served on it as an examiner for the Tripos after his appointment as Professor. In fact, the record shows he only once served as an examiner in the moral sciences in 1876, when J.S. Nicholson was second in the first class honours list, although during the 1870s he had occasionally examined political economy papers for the Extension and Local Examination Movement.[94] Why this was the case is not easily explained.[*] Economics examining at Cambridge from 1885 in the moral sciences was carried out by J.S. Nicholson (1885, 1890, 1891), Sidgwick (1885, 1890, 1891, 1895), J.N. Keynes (1886, 1887, 1891, 1892, 1896, 1897, 1901, 1902),[¶] Edgeworth (1893, 1894), MacTaggart (1895, 1896, 1901, 1902), L.L. Price (1898), Foxwell (1899, 1900, 1901) and Sanger (1902, 1903, 1904, 1905) and probably W.E. Johnson (1887, 1888, 1891, 1892, 1896, 1897, 1901, 1902, 1905, 1906). The presence of Sidgwick on the board of examiners for four years after 1885 suggests there was no convention against professors examining their own students, while it can also be noted that with the exception of Edgeworth, all the examiners classed competent to assess the political economy papers had been Marshall's own students at one time or another.[†] This was even more so in the examiners' lists for the Economics Tripos when it began operating from 1905. For the four Tripos examinations it conducted while Marshall was Professor, John Neville Keynes examined twice (1905, 1907), as did Pigou (1905, 1906), Clapham (1905, 1906), Chapman (1906, 1907), Macgregor (1907, 1908) and Ashley (1907, 1908), while Flux and H.O. Meredith both started examining in 1908, the year Marshall retired. Unlike several of his students, Marshall never sought appointment as

---

[*] In the discussion on a report dealing with the interpretation of a specific regulation for the Historical Tripos, Marshall stated that he 'did not care very much about Examinations. He thought they counted for too much in University life; and that the Senate spent too much time in discussing them, and too little in discussing the aims and methods of instruction' (*Cambridge University Reporter*, 13 November 1900).

[¶] Some of Keynes's remarks on his examining preserved in his diaries are worth quoting particularly in the context of Marshall's complaints of poor student quality. On 31 May 1891 he wrote, 'Looking over Part I Political Economy. Poor work except Miss Blomefield's. Welton is taking Part I papers for the Marshall Prize; but his work is not so good in quality as Miss Blomefield's.' Subsequently he recorded substantial agreement with J.S. Nicholson, his fellow examiner on the political economy papers with respect to the high marks but not on the low ones, where Keynes marked lower because (a) I mark question by question. He marks paper by paper. (b) I interpret the question more strictly and give practically no marks for irrelevancies.
I think my principles of marking brings out the most practical results.' (JNKD, 3 June 1891.)

[†] W.E. Johnson (1858–1931), the logician, philosopher and occasional economic theorist was not one of Alfred Marshall's mathematical students 'half caught' for economics, since he gained his first class result in the Moral Sciences Tripos in 1883 while Marshall was at Oxford. Johnson contributed several papers to the Cambridge Economic Club and published a paper on the pure theory of utility curves in the 1913 *Economic Journal*, as well as a number of entries in Palgrave's *Dictionary of Political Economy*. His theoretical contributions are reprinted in *Precursors in Mathematical Economics: An Anthology*, edited by W.J. Baumol and S.M. Goldfield, London: London School of Economics, Reprints of Scarce Works on Political Economy, No. 19, 1968. He examined as frequently for the moral sciences as J.N. Keynes and must, on occasion, have helped out with examining the political economy papers as well as with those on logic and philosophy.

external examiner to either London or Oxford, presumably because he did not need the additional income or, possibly, because he felt the strain and responsibility of examining to be too great.

However, irrespective of why he did not take an active role in examining, Marshall was happy to comment on other people's examination papers for the Tripos and on the final outcome. Keynes's diaries preserve a number of these observations. In connection with his examining of the Moral Sciences Tripos in 1886, Keynes recorded on 19 May that Marshall had approved of his political economy papers, and on 13 June copied in his diary some of Marshall's written commentary on the results: 'I am glad Miss Mason did not get a first. I did not dare say so before for fear I might bias you and Ward as examiners. But I thought her conceited and awfully muddle-headed. Miss Earp I liked. I am sorry for her. But as I thought P[olitical] E[conomy] was her strong subject, I hardly expected her to get a first.' Both students named in fact were recorded with results in the second class. In the context of the 1891 Tripos which Keynes also examined, he recorded Marshall as writing on 11 June: 'What you say about Welton, Duncan and Robertson fits in with my ideas of them. But I think there are some good men coming on. Miss Blomefield struck me as very attentive to all she was told and read and was good at answering questions on points which she had been taught about: but not as having much original force.'* These comments are all the more interesting since they reinforce Marshall's more general views on the type of students in the moral sciences examined previously. Last, but not least, Keynes recorded some general comments from Marshall on the quality of the political economy papers he had prepared in 1891 and 1892. Marshall described these as 'splendid', adding, 'This year we both thought Part II P[olitical] E[conomy] rather easy, and Part I rather hard. But the papers in Part II were hard enough for the victim.'[95]

These comments indicate that Marshall was not loath to make judgements on his students. Marshall was also quite willing to participate in judging for both the Cobden Prize and, later, the Adam Smith Prize, although in the context of the first he could take an inordinate time in deciding the appropriate topics, as Cannan found out when he was co-adjudicator for this prize in 1906. In the lengthy correspondence between them on this topic, Marshall confessed that 'the experience of 8 Cobden Prizes weighs heavily on me',[96] indicating his personal difficulty in carrying out this type of assessment task. His judgement of students, however, as Clapham told Keynes in 1924, could also be very exact, even if based only on his observations of student reactions in lectures. He apparently told a college tutor, 'You have two very interesting men from your college at my lecture. When I come to a very stiff bit, A.B. says to himself, "This is too hard for me: I won't try to grasp it." C.D.

---

* In the 1891 Tripos results, Miss Blomefield was placed in the First Class, Second Division of Part I, Welton was placed in the First Class of Part II though as Keynes recorded (above, p. 334 n.*), he had also attempted the political economy papers of Part I for the Marshall Prize, but less successfully on Keynes's account than Miss Blomefield had done when she sat them. Robertson (not D.H.) was placed in Division 2 of the Second Class, and Duncan in Division 1 of the Third Class in Part I of the Tripos. It is difficult to identify whom Marshall referred to when he mentioned 'good men' coming on, since Sanger (who took Part II of the Tripos in 1894) and Wedgewood who gained a First Class in Part I in 1895 are the first good men students Marshall identified elsewhere as such in the Tripos records. They may have been in history, and included students like Clapham, on whose quality Marshall commented in 1894 in correspondence with Oscar Browning. (Marshall to Browning, 10 and 11 February 1894, King's College Archives, Browning Correspondence.)

tries to grasp it, but fails. – Marshall's voice running off onto a high note and his face breaking up into his smile. It was an exact estimate of the two men's intelligences and tempers.'[97] However, willingness to judge people when no grave consequences can arise from the outcome is different from judging a person's performance in matters like a Tripos examination on which a future career may depend. Marshall's unwillingness to assume responsibilities in examining for the Tripos is a further sign of his general difficulty in arriving at important decisions.[98]

Marshall's role as university benefactor during his tenure in the political economy chair can also be mentioned. Over these years, the *University Reporter* records a number of specific donations he made for university purposes not associated with the teaching of economics. In November 1895, Marshall is recorded as donating £5 to the Engineering Laboratory; during 1899 he donated £25 to the Vice-Chancellor's general university appeal, of which he earmarked £10 for the building of a Law School, £15 for the building of a Medical School; in 1903 he undertook to support the new Appointments Board Fund by means of an annual subscription of £1.1s.[99] These donations were additional to his financial contributions for the sake of enhancing economics studies. His contributions to establish the Marshall Prize, which subsequently became the Adam Smith Prize, have already been mentioned. In addition, in the last decade of his professorship, he on occasion donated the annual sum of either £50 or £100, to pay the salaries of one or two persons he wished to lecture in economics, since direct university assistance for that purpose in the form of university lectureships in economics were not forthcoming while he held the chair.[100]

Donations in kind were also made to the University. In 1901, the *University Reporter* acknowledged the donation of a clock to the literary lecture rooms which, given Marshall's suggestions on the need of such an instrument in these rooms made several years previously, may easily have come from him.[101] More importantly, in 1906 the Moral Sciences Board of which Marshall by then was no longer a member, recorded donations by Marshall of some books for its library.[*] This handsome donation, much of which remains as part of the Philosophy Library, foreshadowed subsequent donations of books to university libraries in retirement and on death.[102]

This then was Marshall as Professor in so far as his general role as teacher and administrator was concerned. By all later accounts, he was a brilliant, because inspiring, teacher. A contemporary assessment is therefore of particular interest. An anonymous letter addressed to Marshall as teacher of political economy and printed in the *Cambridge Review* sums up a student's perception of the effectiveness of his teaching.

---

[*] According to the list Marshall provided, these included the following: 'Berkeley's Works, 5 volumes, ed. Fraser; Locke's works, 10 volumes (note the first three volumes; Essay on the Understanding, are interleaved because I expected to lecture on it at least every other year for ever more!! All in calf); Stewart's Active and Moral Powers of Man 2 Vols (bound in leather but broken backs); Lewes' Life & Mind 3rd edn. 2 vols.; also his History of Philosophy 2 vols.; Vol I of *Mind* in parts unbound; Broole's Laws of Thought; Venn, Empirical Logic; Bentham's *Works*, Vol. I being lost. (There are about ten or eleven others, I think, double columned. Ed. Bowring); Leslie Stephens, Science of Ethics; A good many of Herbert Spencer's *Works*, Spinoza's Works (ed. Willis); Whewell's *Elements of Morality*; Gollen, *Prologomena to Ethics*; all are in fairly good condition except Stewart's.

So well can I picture you to myself as you lay bare the intricacies of Normal Value to beginners, or speak to the more advanced of Banking and Money and the Economic Functions of Government. Each difficulty modestly cleared away in words that come now fast now slow, gaining emphasis by the increased quietness with which they are delivered. Nor are you without a sense of humour and the power of leavening a dull lump or so with it. When at times you stray from the narrow paths of the Science of Economics and tell us of the Stock Exchange, of 'Brums' and 'Berthas', of the peddlings of Jew and Greek, of Wall Street and American operators, you shew a touch and more of the driest wit. With eyes directed abstractedly towards the ceiling (some say you are often among the clouds), and a voice so tiny and quiet that all ears are kept astretch, is the story told. And when the eyes descend again upon the class we see by the twinkle there, that we and you are laughing together. Permit me to recall to you an occasion on which you gave notice that at the next lecture you would treat on the curves of demand mathematically for those who would please to attend, 'only an elementary knowledge of mathematics will be required', and then you gave time to those who had recently floored the additionals to preen themselves and think they would certainly come, before you observed with the upward gaze and sly air 'I don't think it will be much use for anyone to come who has not a fairly complete knowledge of differential and integral calculus.' A sadder and wiser class, among whom was I, went from that room thinking perchance that after all, elementary was a relative word.[103]

Marshall's performance as administrator was far less distinguished. Only where his special objectives and interests were at stake, could he rise to the occasion. Even here it can be said it was perseverance rather than skill and diplomacy that won out.[104] He was neither a committee man nor greatly involved in the general life of his university, and his career as Professor largely revolved around his students as did indeed much of his personal life. This personal element is invariably present in his administration work, including his major triumph, the establishment of the Economics and Politics Tripos. However, even on that personal side, Marshall's involvement was often incomplete. He was rather reluctant to involve himself in the all-important examination process, leaving that to those whose temperament was more suited to this type of decision-making. Except for library matters and a committee on postgraduate studies, his wider administrative role in the university was virtually non-existent. The Marshall Library which became his permanent memorial in the university is therefore a particularly appropriate recognition of the specific administrative service to which he persistently directed his resources.[105]

NOTES

1.   James P. Henderson, 'Just Notions of Political Economy'; George Pryme, The first Professor of Political Economy at Cambridge', *Research in the History of Economic Thought and Methodology*, 2, 1984, pp. 10–20, on which this paragraph draws extensively. The quotation in the text is from p. 6.
2.   James P. Henderson, 'Just Notions of Political Economy', p. 9.
3.   *Ibid.*, pp. 9–10.
4.   Leslie Stephen, *Henry Fawcett*, London: Smith, Elder & Company, 1885, pp. 117–22.
5.   *Ibid.*, pp. 123–5.
6.   Phyllis Deane, 'Henry Fawcett: the Plain Man's Political Economist', p. 108.
7.   *Cambridge University and College Statutes* under the Act of 1877, Cambridge: Cambridge University Press, 1883, pp. 46, 49–52, 57–60, the quotes coming from Statute B, Chapter XI, Sections 5 and 6, p. 58. For background to these new statutes and the enhanced status the new regulations gave to professors, see A.S. and E.M.S., *Henry Sidgwick. A Memoir*, pp. 264, 371–9; D.A. Winstanley, *Late Victorian Cambridge*, Chapters 5 and 7.
8.   *Cambridge University and College Statutes* 1882, Chapter IX.

9.   *Cambridge University Reporter* No. 550, October 1884, p. 36; *The Eagle*, No. 13, 1885, p. 107.
10.   Alfred Marshall to Foxwell, 15 November 1884 (Freeman Collection, 14/73).
11.   Alfred Marshall to Foxwell, 20 November 1884 (Freeman Collection, 7/73).
12.   Alfred Marshall to Foxwell, 1 December 1884 (Freeman Collection, 5/73).
13.   Murray Milgate, 'Robert Henry Inglis Palgrave', in *New Palgrave. A Dictionary of Economics*, Vol. 3, pp. 789–91, Mary Paley Marshall, *What I Remember*, p. 42.
14.   Audrey Cunningham, *William Cunningham. Teacher and Friend*, pp. 63–4.
15.   H.S. Foxwell, 'The Economic Movement in England', *Quarterly Journal of Economics*, 2 (1), October 1887, p. 92.
16.   Audrey Cunningham, *William Cunningham. Teacher and Friend*, p. 64.
17.   JNKD, 13 and 14 December 1885.
18.   Marshall to Foxwell, 13 December 1884 (Freeman Collection, 11/73).
19.   A.S. and E.M.S., *Henry Sidgwick. A Memoir*, p. 394.
20.   *Times*, 15 December 1884; *Bristol Western Daily* Press, 16 December 1884; *Educational Times*, 1 January 1885; *Cambridge Review*, 21 January 1884; *The Eagle*, Vol. 13, February 1885, p. 196; *Oxford Magazine*, 21 January 1885.
21.   A.S. and E.M.S., *Henry Sidgwick. A Memoir*, p. 394.
22.   Marshall to Foxwell, 19 December 1885 (Freeman Collection, 6/73); the papers which Marshall wanted Foxwell to return may have been drafts of the letter which Sidgwick subsequently received on 23 December.
23.   Cambridge University Archives, Moral Sciences Board, Min V 10, Minutes for 3 December 1884, 4 March 1885. The last indicates Marshall's symbolic victory since it reduced his minimum lecturing requirement to 45 lectures per annum.
24.   Marshall to Foxwell, 23 December 1884 (Freeman Collection, 9/73).
25.   JNKD, 15 January 1885.
26.   A.S. and E.M.S., *Henry Sidgwick. A Memoir*, p. 402. The inaugural lecture is discussed below, pp. 309–13.
27.   JNKD, 18 December 1884.
28.   Above, Chapter 9, pp. 295–6.
29.   JNKD, 20, 22, 23, 26, 29, 30 December, then in the context of the temporary position, 31 December 1884, followed by further correspondence and telegrams 5, 8, 11 and 12 January (a postcard *and* a letter) and Keynes's terminating telegraph informing the Marshalls his 'mind was quite made up'.
30.   JNKD, 16 February 1885; Keynes lectured on Marshall's advanced political economy syllabus at Oxford, as mentioned in the previous chapter (above, pp. 295–6).
31.   See below, Chapter 16, pp. 581–6, 590, 591.
32.   J.M. Keynes, 'Alfred Marshall', pp. 221–2.
33.   A.S. and E.M.S., *Henry Sidgwick. A Memoir*, p. 402.
34.   Discussed below in Chapter 15, pp. 534–49.
35.   John Maloney, *Marshall, Orthodoxy and the Professionalisation of Economics*, Cambridge: Cambridge University Press, 1985, pp. 99–100.
36.   Below, Chapter 13, pp. 469–71.
37.   JNKD, for 24 February 1885.
38.   As preserved in Marshall's scrapbook, Marshall Library. There were also reviews published in the *Bradford Observer* (3 April 1885) and in the Berlin *Nord-Deutsche* (by H. von Scheel, 18 March 1885). Marshall's comment on the *Times* review was in a letter to the editor, published Tuesday, 2 June 1885. The anonymous *Times* reviewer was Leonard Courtney, one of the selectors for the chair. See G.P. Gooch, *Life of Leonard Courtney*, London: Macmillan, 1920, pp. 229–31.
39.   *P* VIII, pp. 782–3, *P* IX, p. 772, and cf. *P* I, pp. 74–7.
40.   This section draws heavily on, and in part reproduces, extensive extracts from my article, 'Teaching Economics at Cambridge at the turn of the Century: Alfred Marshall as Lecturer in Political Economy', *Scottish Journal of Political Economy* 37 (1), February 1990, pp. 40–60; the student lecture notes preserved are those taken by Bowley in the Michaelmas term 1891 and Lent term 1892 sessions (British Library of Economics and Political Science, Cannan Papers – Cannan 909) and notes taken by Walter Layton from Michaelmas term 1904 (Trinity College Library, Cambridge, Layton Papers, Box 15).
41.   Marshall to Sir William Ramsay, his former Bristol colleague and successor as Principal, some time in 1914, in *Memorials*, pp. 488–9, where Marshall indicated he 'would not give a halfpenny for a testimonial by the man who dictated a text-book in his classroom'.
42.   Cited in Keynes, 'Alfred Marshall', p. 215. Keynes appended the note: 'I have papers which I wrote for him in which his red ink comments and criticisms occupy almost as much space as my answers.' (*ibid.*, p. 215 n.1). Some of these have been preserved among the Keynes Papers and are discussed in Chapter 15, below, p. 554. This was an old habit of Marshall's, as indicated above, Chapter 9, pp. 268–9.

43. C.R. Fay, 'Reminiscences', in *Memorials*, pp. 74–6. The reference to Chamberlain is explored more fully below, Chapter 11, pp. 379, 380, 383, Chapter 16, pp. 605 and n¶, 606 and n.*

44. Cited in David Hubback, *No Ordinary Press Baron: A Life of Walter Layton*, London: Weidenfeld & Nicolson, 1985, p. 48.

45. E.A. Benians, 'Reminiscences', in *Memorials*, pp. 78–80. Benians later told C.W. Guillebaud ('Some Personal Reminiscences of Alfred Marshall', p. 92), 'He had never known anyone who laughed so frequently during the delivery of his own lectures, but yet was so patently deficient in a sense of humour'.

46. Unpublished autobiography of Sir Sydney John Chapman, pp. 19–20, British Library of Economics and Political Science, M1073 Coll. Misc. 644.

47. D.H. Macgregor, 'Marshall and his Book', *AMCA*, II, pp. 115–16.

48. Marshall to Gonner, 9 May 1894, in *Memorials*, pp. 380–81.

49. J.M. Keynes, 'Alfred Marshall', p. 216. Keynes also attended Marshall's lectures in Michaelmas term 1905, above, Chapter 5, p. 98.

50. C.W. Guillebaud, 'Some Personal Reminiscences of Alfred Marshall', p. 92.

51. Alfred Marshall to Foxwell, 8 May 1901, Marshall Archive, 3:41.

52. Cannan Papers: Cannan 909, British Library of Economics and Political Science, the quotations come from pp. 18–19.

53. Marshall Archive, Large Brown Box, Item 33.

54. From 1894–95 until his retirement, he employed a junior colleague, first McTaggart, and subsequently Clapham, to mark the student papers in the Elementary Political Economy class for which a fee of £1.1s. was charged.

55. 'Letters to Lecturers', *Cambridge Review*, 24 October 1889 (unsigned and part of a series). Accounts of his 'at home' by some women students are cited below, pp. 323–4.

56. Mary Paley Marshall to John Maynard Keynes, September 1924 (KMF); Notes for John Maynard Keynes (KMF). The paper, 'Theories and Facts about Wages' was published in the Cooperative Wholesale Annual, 1885, pp. 379–88, and is discussed below, Chapter 12, p. 405.

57. As cited in Rita McWilliams-Tullberg, 'Marshall's Final Lecture, 21 May 1908', *History of Political Economy*, 25 (4), p. 607. Grier's report of Marshall's final lecture, as well as her sketch of Marshall in her draft autobiographical notes are preserved among her papers at Lady Margaret Hall, Oxford, and is discussed in more detail below, Chapter 17, pp. 620–1.

58. Marshall to John Neville Keynes, 30 January 1902, Marshall Archive, 1:125.

59. Marshall to Foxwell, 14 February 1902, Marshall Archive, 3:44.

60. See John Whitaker, Introduction to *EEW*, pp. 29, 31–3.

61. Mary Paley Marshall, 'MSS Notes' (NCA).

62. Marshall to Foxwell, 8 February 1906, Marshall Archive 3:48; 17 April 1897, Marshall Archive 3:33.

63. Marshall to Arthur Bowley, 3 March 1901, in *Memorials*, p. 423.

64. Marshall to S.J. Chapman, 29 October 1904, in *Memorials*, pp. 455–6.

65. Reproduced in A. Philips, (ed.), *A Newnham Anthology*, Cambridge: Cambridge University Press, 1979, p. 47.

66. Cited in Rita McWilliams-Tullberg, 'Marshall's Final Lecture, 21 May 1908', pp. 607–8.

67. As Helen Bosanquet, her married name, Helen Dendy wrote a number of books on aspects of social economics and after graduation played an active role in the Charity Organisation Society. See A.M. McBriar, *An Edwardian Mixed Doubles*, Oxford: Clarendon Press, 1987, pp. 10–14, for a brief biographical sketch. And see below, Chapter 14, pp. 521–3.

68. This is discussed in detail below, Chapter 15, pp. 553–6.

69. Others are Holman and Lloyd. Holman attended Marshall's Advanced Political Economy class in 1889 and gained a first in 1890; Lloyd gained a first in Part I of the Tripos in 1896 and was later appointed Professor of Economics at Toronto. Marshall's more famous students are discussed in more detail below, Chapter 20, pp. 753–8.

70. Details on sales of the *Principles* are discussed below, Chapter 12, pp. 435–6; data on student reading from Peter Groenewegen, 'Alfred Marshall and the Establishment of the Economics Tripos', pp. 654, 660, 664.

71. A concise discussion of Sidgwick's contributions to the University of Cambridge, is given by J.N. Keynes, 'Obituary: Henry Sidgwick', *Economic Journal*, 10 (4), December 1900, pp. 585–91, esp. 589–91.

72. Pigou, 'In Memoriam: Alfred Marshall', presents the conventional point on this matter (see *Memorials* esp. p. 88). Marshall's involvement in controversy is discussed below, Chapter 13.

73. *Cambridge University Reporter*, No. 610, p. 158; D.A.Winstanley, *Late Victorian Cambridge*, pp. 189–90; Moral Sciences examinations were not generally included in examinations for Scholarships, Sizarships and Exhibitions until 1890. *Cambridge University Reporter*, No. 854, 5 November 1890, pp. 148–9.

340 A Soaring Eagle: Alfred Marshall 1842–1924

74.   *Ibid.,* 4 May 1886, p. 579; 25 May 1886, p. 647; 8 June 1886, p. 719. The first Marshall Prize was awarded in 1877 to S.M. Leathes, a student from the History Tripos. McTaggart won the Prize in 1888; A.W. Flux, the mathematical economist, in 1889; and James Welton in 1891. No award was made in 1890 (*Cambridge University Reporter*, 18 June 1887, p. 849 and 18 June 1889, p. 950).

75.   Marshall to Vice-Chancellor, 24 January 1891, in *University Reporter*, 17 February 1891; *University Reporter*, 18 November 1913, pp. 247–8, and see above, p. 323.

76.   *University Reporter,* No. 643, 15 June 1886, p. 779 and on its formal approval by the Senate, *University Reporter*, No. 662, 14 December 1886, p. 274; further changes to the timing of the Tripos examinations were recorded in the Moral Sciences Board Minutes (Min. V. 10, 14 May 1890).

77.   *University Reporter* No. 809, p. 219.

78.   *Ibid.,* No. 850, 14 October 1890, pp. 92, 96–7. Marshall also stressed the importance of a good economics education for Indian civil servants in his evidence to the Indian Currency in 1899. See below, Chapter 11, p. 353.

79.   Below, Chapter 15.

80.   Marshall to Oscar Browning, 7 November 1902 (King's College Library, Browning Collection).

81.   Mary Paley Marshall, 'MSS Notes' (NCA).

82.   *Cambridge University Reporter*, 25 May 1886, p. 641, cf. No. 652, p. 49. More general aspects of Marshall's contributions to the libraries of Cambridge are discussed below, Chapter 20, pp. 750–1.

83.   Marshall to University Librarian, 5 January 1891, 7 and 29 October 1894, Cambridge University Library, Add 6463/1666, 2719, 2748.

84.   Marshall to Octavius Johnson, University Librarian, 17 August 1905 (Cambridge University Library, Add 8398/61). The book Marshall did not want the library to buy in a second edition was Stourm, *Systèmes généraux d'impôts*.

85.   Marshall to the Librarian, 6 October 1906 (Cambridge University Library, Add 4251(B)941).

86.   This even included advice on a good cabinetmaker for the construction of bookshelves. See Marshall to the Librarian, 20 February 1890 (Cambridge University Library, Add 6463/1430).

87.   C.R. Fay, 'Reminiscences', in *Memorials*, pp. 74–5. See also J.M. Keynes, 'Alfred Marshall', p. 223 and Agatha H. Bowley, *A Memoir of Professor Sir Arthur Bowley*, p. 35.

88.   Exceptions include the following: an appointment as university representative on the University, County and Town Committee for the Imperial Institute (*University Reporter*, 10 May 1887, No. 685, p. 651); and occasional membership of memorial committees for considering suitable tributes to deceased colleagues. An example is his membership of the Hort Memorial Fund Committee (*University Reporter*, 29 April 1894, p. 757).

89.   *Report of the Advanced Study and Research Syndicate* (*University Reporter*, 5 March 1895, p. 594). This followed on the *Report by the University Council on Postgraduate Studies* (*University Reporter*, 5 February 1894, p. 425). Marshall was presumably elected to this Syndicate because of his constructive contribution to the debate on advanced studies induced by the earlier Report (*University Reporter*, 6 November 1894, p. 175).

90.   *Report of the Advanced Study and Research Syndicate* (*University Reporter*, 5 March 1895, pp. 594–8), *Second Report* (*University Reporter*, 7 May 1895, p. 770), *Third Report* (*University Reporter*, 14 May 1895, pp. 790–93).

91.   Below, Chapter 14, pp. 503–7.

92.   *University Reporter*, 13 November 1900, pp. 210–12.

93.   JNKD, 11 May 1886, 23 May 1888, 23 October 1894, 2 November 1895, 3 May 1897 and cf. 22 May 1897, 11 December 1897.

94.   An examination paper for this year by Marshall, of which a copy was preserved among John Neville Keynes's files on examinations held in the Marshall Library, is reproduced as an appendix to this chapter. For his 1870s examining see Chapter 9 above, p. 269. In 1880, in his evidence to the Committee on Higher Education in Wales, Marshall claimed there was a Cambridge convention that teachers should not examine their students whom they had taught 'a short time beforehand' (Committee on Intermediate and Higher Education in Wales, 1881, Q. 18,227, p. 772).

95.   Perhaps a reference to Welton, who was one of four students attempting Part II of the Tripos in 1891, in addition to his taking of the Political Economy papers in Part I for the Marshall Prize.

96.   See Marshall to Cannan, 30 March 1905, 15 February 1906, 2 April 1906, 6 April 1906, 15 April 1906, 24 April 1906, 10 May 1906. The quotation is from the letter of 2 April (British Library of Economics and Political Science, Cannan Papers 1021).

97.   J.M. Keynes, 'Alfred Marshall', p. 224.

98.   Examples from his personal life have been given on various occasions. Above, Chapter 9, pp. 278, 279; Chapter 10, p. 305.

99.   *University Reporter*, 19 November 1895, pp. 225–6; 30 May 1899, p. 928; 24 February 1903, pp. 496–7.

100. See below, Chapter 15, p. 656, and for his donations to Newnham, Chapter 14, p. 496. His posthumous benefactions are discussed in Chapter 20 below, pp. 746–7, 750–1.

101. *University Reporter*, 5 June 1901, p. 1043; the Moral Sciences Board Minutes, Cambridge University Archive, Min. V. 10, 25 November 1898, Item 9.

102. Moral Science Board Minutes, Cambridge University Archive, Min. V. 10, 25 October 1906, where this list of books, on 6 Madingley Road notepaper, is pasted into the relevant section of the minutes, and see below, Chapter 20, pp. 750–1.

103. 'Letters to Lecturers', *Cambridge Review*, 24 October 1889 (unsigned, and part of a series of such letters).

104. See, for example, below, Chapter 15, pp. 540–7.

105. Aspects of the creation of the Marshall Library, together with a discussion of other memorials to Marshall are discussed below, Chapter 20, pp. 750–3.

APPENDIX TO CHAPTER 10

MORAL SCIENCES SCHOLARSHIP EXAMINATION

GONVILLE AND CAIUS, ST JOHN'S AND TRINITY COLLEGES
TUESDAY, April 18, 1876. 1 to 4.

POLITICAL ECONOMY

1.   WHAT are the conditions which determine the rate of increase of capital in England? What are the leading causes of the diversities in these conditions which exist in different portions of the world at the present time? What modifications would you on this account introduce into an English treatise on economic theory if you were adapting it for use in such a country as India?

2.   Enunciate Ricardo's theory of rent, stating exactly the assumptions on which it proceeds. Examine how far the conditions of the bargains actually made between the agricultural tenant and the landlord in England are represented by these assumptions.

3.   Give some account of the history and meaning of the phrase 'the natural rate of wages'. What is the nature of the evidence with regard to the existence of such a rate which has been obtained by a comparison of the prices of agricultural labour and of corn respectively during the last five centuries?

4.   What causes are extending the division of labour in England? How do they affect competition for employment between workmen of different trades?

Indicate the conditions under which the introduction of piece-work into a trade will be economically beneficial to the workmen in that trade taken as a whole.

5.   Give some account of the causes on which the average price of iron in England depends; also of the causes which govern the fluctuations of that price.

How would each portion of your answer be affected if all the iron mines of England were bought up by one company?

6.   Examine the influence exerted on the economic welfare of England by the bounty that France gives on the exportation of sugar, on the several suppositions that the bounty is and is not permanent.

Inquire whether circumstances can possibly exist in which it may be economically advantageous for a government to award a bounty on exportation.

7.   How is the value of an inconvertible paper currency determined? What determines the ratio between the amount of sovereigns and bank-notes in circulation in England? Why has this ratio increased during the last twenty years?

8.   Examine the incidence of a tax on raw produce. Examine briefly what Ricardo has said about this tax. Why are taxes on the raw material of manufactures in general to be avoided?

9.   What light does the history of village Communities throw upon the questions raised by modern socialism?

11. Giving Advice to Governments: 1886–1908

During his period as Cambridge Professor, Marshall was invited on a number of occasions to contribute to government inquiries on topics within the province of his chair. Such experience had started earlier. As Principal of Bristol University College, he had given evidence to an Inquiry into Higher Education in Wales and Monmouthshire.[1] However, the decades over which he held the Cambridge chair greatly increased his involvement in this type of activity, of which three different forms can be identified. For the earlier commissions he prepared memoranda on which he was later cross-examined. His contributions to two currency inquiries and to the Royal Commission on the Aged Poor in the 1880s and 1890s fall into this category. On other occasions he provided written memoranda to answer questions set him by the commissioners themselves or directly by members of the government. His 1886 memoranda on prices and currency for the Royal Commission on the Depression of Trade and his 1897 Memorandum on Taxation are examples. His famous paper on the Fiscal Policy of International Trade was in direct response to a request from the government. A third type of experience was gained from 1891 to 1894 when Marshall himself served as Royal Commissioner on the Labour Commission. Finally, Marshall occasionally supplied material indirectly to Royal Commissions by means of advice he gave to Commissioners among his former students. His letter to Cunynghame on food supply during war is an example of this last type of advice to government.[2]

It goes without saying that Marshall's services to government inquiries are an important part of his professional life. His evidence often contains views not present elsewhere in print, a matter particularly important to understanding his position on monetary theory and taxation.[3] Secondly, the time involved in these inquiries, particularly that associated with his lengthy involvement on the Labour Commission, helps to explain the slow progress in his academic writing. His behaviour as witness and as Royal Commissioner illuminate facets of his personality and are part of his life never before systematically studied.[4] This makes it useful to deal with these contributions in one chapter.

The heterogeneous nature of Marshall's contributions to government inquiries makes for a complex chapter. The policy issues discussed by these inquiries need to be placed in their context, which in some cases requires considerable background. Strict chronology is sacrificed in the treatment of the subject matter to enable Marshall's monetary evidence to be examined seriatum. His role with respect to the Aged Poor Commission is considered in the wider context of his association with the Charity Organisation Society. This makes the chapter also a long one, unavoidable given the importance of this work in Marshall's life and activities as Professor.

DEPRESSION OF TRADE, THE VALUE OF GOLD AND SILVER AND INDIAN CURRENCY

The evidence Marshall gave on these topics needs to be set in the rather special context of British economic history in the final quarter of the nineteenth century. The steady depreciation of silver of this period should first be noted. This was generally ascribed to the demonetisation of silver by Germany from 1873 onwards, the restriction of silver coinage by the Latin Monetary Union formed in 1874, the increasing supply of silver from the American mines and a decline in the traditional absorption power of silver by India, associated with India's growing indebtedness to England. Since India was also the major silver currency country in the British Empire, this depreciation of silver seriously impaired her economy and trade with England.[5] Secondly, this period saw a steady appreciation in the value of gold, or a steadily falling price level in a gold currency country like Britain, visible both in terms of contemporary index numbers and those estimated for the relevant period at a later date.[*6] In addition, it coincides with what some economic historians have described as the 'great depression', when British growth rates slowed dramatically in terms of industrial production and output as a whole, and when Britain became the weakest of the world's three major industrial nations after Germany and the United States. Although the generality of this phenomenon is still disputed among economic historians, there is now little doubt that after the early 1870s, British productivity and output growth slowed down significantly as compared with the previous three decades and that this trend deteriorated further in the early decades of the twentieth century.[7] Superimposed on this trend of industrial decline were the regular commercial crises and periods of depressed trade which England had experienced since 1825, and of which the enduring depression which followed the crisis of 1882–83 provided the *raison d'être* for the first Royal Commission to which Marshall gave economic evidence.[8]

These broad considerations, together with the unity in Marshall's monetary theory from its overwhelming concern with issues of the value of money, provide a degree of homogeneity in Marshall's monetary evidence, spread though it was over a period of over a decade. Changes in the value of money, or instability of the price level, manifested in this

---

*   Gold currency and silver currency countries refer to the precious metal which formed the standard for the national currency of the country in question. From the early nineteenth century, Britain had been a gold standard country. This made its paper currency convertible into gold and allowed gold coins to circulate with bank notes. By acting as the reserve for the currency, gold also regulated the quantity of paper money which it was possible to issue, and hence was argued to maintain the value of the currency and the stability of the price level. International indebtedness between gold standard countries was ultimately settled by gold flows. A silver country like India used silver instead of gold as the standard. The period after 1870 saw a rapid rise in the number of gold standard countries, causing a rise in gold values and a depreciation of silver, as well as a general world monetary shortage by the restrictions on paper currency a general gold scarcity imposed. Bimetallism sought to remedy this deficiency by proposing a dual gold and silver standard in the traditional gold–silver price ratio of 15.5:1. By restoring the market for silver, the bimetallist proposal was favourably regarded by silver-mining countries like the United States. Marshall's scheme of modified bimetallism (or symmetallism) sought to combine gold and silver as the standard in a higher ratio than this traditional one. Bimetallism, by questioning the traditional backing of the currency in Britain, became a highly controversial subject, aggravated by the fact that its consequences raised contentious issues on trade depressions and price instability. Useful discussions on these topics can be found in the *New Palgrave*, Vol. 1, pp. 243–5 for bimetallism and Vol. 2, pp. 539–45 for the gold standard.

period by a prolonged deflationary trend, underlie Marshall's contributions to all three inquiries. The various detrimental effects Marshall ascribed to such price movements likewise are present in his evidence on these subjects. However, given the terms of reference of the latter two Commissions, Marshall gave more emphasis to such effects with respect to India and Indian commerce than to causally associating a fluctuating price level and the depression of trade, which characterised Marshall's input to the first Commission. Given this association, Marshall naturally set great store on the desirability of stable prices as an object of policy. He addressed some remedies for dealing with adverse effects of fluctuations of general prices in an article published in 1887.[9] Among other things, its proposals included a tabular standard of value to ensure stability of value for longer-term business contracts by means of what would now be called indexation. This was partly designed to link price and wage stability. The paper also proposed what he called, 'modified bimetallism', subsequently described as 'symmetallism' by Edgeworth, to assist stability of the currency in the face of relative supply instability of the monetary metals. The evidence Marshall gave therefore addressed most of the current issues in monetary theory and policy at a time when he was still continuing to develop his views on these subjects.

Marshall's Memorandum for the Royal Commission on the Depression of Trade and Industry answered questions the Commission had circulated to 'experts' in April 1886. These questions concentrated on price stability, its association with currency and other factors and its effects on trade and industry. In addition, it sought opinions on shifts in the relative price ratio of the precious metals and the effects of such shifts on the trade of countries with mono-metallic currencies, especially India.[10] Marshall's answers are succinct and concise and were returned to the Commission within approximately a month from the time he had received them. Conciseness was assisted by Marshall's deliberate strategy of answering the Commission's nine questions within four broad sub-groups of his own making. These in turn dealt with the fall of the price level in recent years, or, as he preferred to call it, the rise in the purchasing power of gold or fall in general gold prices; changes in the relative price of gold and silver; the effects of price instability on trade and industry; and, finally, the effects on trade, especially that of India, of changes in the relative price ratio of the precious metals. Speed in completion was undoubtedly assisted by the fact that his answers incorporated substantial extracts from previously published writings.*

After drawing attention to Tooke's analysis of price deflation in his *History of Prices*, Marshall warned that care had to be taken when using falling production costs as an explanatory variable. Its effects were often incorporated when the issue of price changes was treated in terms of the scarcity of commodities in general, relative to the quantity of gold. Available data were insufficient to separate changes in gold price induced by changes in the relative supply of commodities from those caused by changes in the supply of gold. In explaining relative price shifts between gold and silver, Marshall developed a 'law of

---

* Extracts were included from *EOI*, Book III Chapter 1, §5 and 6, pp. 155–7 (*OP*, pp. 7–9) and from his address to the Industrial Remuneration Conference, January 1885, 'How far do Remediable Causes Influence Prejudicially (A) the Continuity of Employment (B) the Rate of Wages' in which, among other things, the remedy of the tabular standard of value was proposed (*OP*, pp. 9–11). These extracts from previously published writings account for approximately forty per cent of the Memorandum.

hoarding'. This discussed tendencies to hoard the precious metals in terms of price expectations formed on past trends. Demand for hoarding is therefore opposite to the 'law of demand for a commodity for the purpose of using it.' (*OP*, p.6). Price was not the only factor, however. For the precious metals, hoarding was also stimulated by sudden shocks to the system, such as the collapse of trade caused by a financial panic in France during 1882. Increased silver supply in this way enhanced the demand for gold and, therefore, its price relative to that of silver. In India, preferences for hoarding bullion moved from silver to gold. However, in Section 4 of the Memorandum, Marshall argued that the effects of this changed preference on Indian trade and its price level were less than was often supposed because other, unspecified, causes counteracted the devaluation effect of a relative rise in the price of gold on a silver-currency country in its trade with a gold-currency country (*OP*, pp. 15–16).

The third section of the Memorandum dealt with the main term of reference of the Commission. It started with a substantial extract from The *Economics of Industry* about the effects of falling prices on the volume of industry. Marshall described such effects as nugatory if all prices fell proportionately, a situation unlikely to be realised in practice. Experience showed that finished commodity prices changed most rapidly, raw materials more moderately, and wages least. Therefore, when prices were falling, manufacturers found it difficult to cover their costs. Marshall used this asymmetric price behaviour to explain his preference for a deflationary situation. Workers could then be expected to spend their income more wisely, because they thought it was falling in real, as well as in nominal terms. Their presumption was wrong because real wages tended to rise when prices were falling. Price instability altered income distribution more generally. Mortgage and debenture holders benefited from falling prices, active business incomes were detrimentally affected. Price stability was the remedy. It eliminated the distortions to real distribution of income caused by uneven fluctuations in prices. Because uneven price changes impaired business and the level of activity, stable prices also stabilised activity levels.[11]

Alfred Marshall proposed indexation as the remedy.[12] It enabled contracts to be written in terms of a stable unit of purchasing power. In addition, and this according to Marshall was impossible to tell on the available evidence, if price falls were largely caused by checks to the supply of gold, a further remedy was at hand in his proposal of symmetallism. This proposed a specified combination of gold and silver in bars (say, in the ratio of 1:20) as backing for the currency, in the sense that the government would sell this silver/gold combination for a fixed amount of currency. Marshall's plan, adapted from a similar proposal by Ricardo,[13] was superior to ordinary bimetallism in Marshall's view. The bimetallist solution would rapidly degenerate into an inferior form of mono-metallism, when, in a situation of falling silver prices, Gresham's Law* operated to drive gold into hoards and silver into circulation. Marshall's brief Memorandum provided much of the inspiration and content of the far more voluminous evidence he supplied to the Gold and Silver Commission.

---

* Gresham's Law simply states that when there are effectively two currencies in operation, good currency is driven out by the bad, low value money. Bimetallism, operating in both gold and silver, would drive out gold from active use when silver was depreciating in terms of gold, the relevant situation for the 1870s and 1880s. And see above, p. 344 n*.

The release of the Commission's *Report* drew an interesting letter from Marshall to the *Times* (17 January 1887). Its three points all elucidated the distributional considerations which Marshall's evidence on the effects of price changes on business activity had mentioned. One concerned the Commission's comment on the desirability of shorter working hours. Consistent with his sympathy for the working class in his evidence, Marshall argued that shorter working hours often raised efficiency, and that longer working of machines combined with shorter labour shifts should be the objective for a society where 'production is for men and not men for production', the 'great hope for the improvement of the human race'. His other points corrected the Commission's use of nominal income tax data to measure economic progress in a period of falling prices and its emphasis on profit as the major source of accumulation.

A Gold and Silver Commission was appointed by the Government in September 1886 in response to a recommendation in the *Report* by the Commission on the Depression of Trade and Industry. Its terms of reference covered similar currency questions, and emphasised the effects of changes in the value of gold and silver on India and the United Kingdom. In response to an invitation from the Commission, Marshall prepared a preliminary Memorandum on general issues (*OP*, pp. 19–31). He gave evidence over three days (19 December 1887, 16 and 23 January 1888), answering close to 500 questions (*OP*, pp. 32– 169). Subsequent memoranda covering specialised topics were prepared in support of his oral evidence.*

Marshall's preliminary Memorandum reiterated many of his general principles on money. Its starting-point portrays stable prices as the national objective. Failing that, he preferred falling to rising prices, because 'the discouragement of enterprise' from 'a slow and gradual fall' is not very great, while falling prices had highly beneficial effects on the manner in which workers spend their wages and on their living standard (*OP*, pp. 19–20). The detrimental effects of sudden price fluctuations were a more serious matter. Their social consequences were invariably 'physically and morally injurious'. Finally, the claim by farming interests that the depreciation of silver had provided a substantial bounty to Indian corn imports, was rejected by Marshall and he was severely questioned on this point during his first day of oral evidence.[14]

Marshall then provided a brief discourse on broader aspects of monetary theory and policy. First of all, this reiterated his adherence to the quantity theory as a long-term proposition linking price movements proportionally to changes in quantity of the monetary metal(s), provided other things remained equal. However this was never the case in practice. Other things, such as the quantity of token coin in limited use as legal tender, the volume of business, and methods of payment determining velocity of circulation, invariably tended to change over time. Likewise, the effect of an increased quantity of the precious metals on

---

* Marshall's evidence was subsequently carefully studied by Wicksell, who saw it as a reason for eager anticipation of Marshall's second volume of the *Principles*. Wicksell, *Interest and Prices*, translated by R.F. Kahn, Macmillan: for the Royal Economic Society, 1936, pp. 76–7 and n. In his personal copy of the original German edition, *Geldzins und Guterpreise* (Jena: Gustav Fischer, 1898, p. 69) Marshall wrote in the margin, 'I don't think we really differ', Marshall, according to Wicksell, had given 'too much emphasis on the direct influence . . . exerted by the magnitude of banking reserves on the rate of interest' (*ibid.*, p. 76 in the English edition). On further contact between Marshall and Wicksell, see below Chapter 13, pp. 473–6, Chapter 19, pp. 721–2.

credit was not straightforward; factors other than those associated with bullion were capable of inducing a credit expansion.* In the context of a Commission request to comment specifically on the feasibility of bimetallism, Marshall reiterated his grounds for preferring his own symmetallist position, discussing its derivation from Ricardo in more detail (*OP*, pp. 18–19). The symmetallist plan made Bank of England lender of last resort facilities more flexible by giving greater elasticity to the currency, the expansion of which was severely restricted under the Bank Charter Act's rigid association between the note issue and the Bank's stock of gold bullion reserves. It would also avoid the inevitable shift to monometallism which conventional bimetallism tended to generate through the operation of Gresham's Law. However, it would not, of course, eliminate price fluctuations. Hence, Marshall also urged adoption of his 1887 proposal for indexation of contracts by a 'tabular standard of value' as government policy, thereby eliminating 'much anxiety of business and irregularity of employment' (*OP*, pp. 29–31).

Marshall's oral evidence to the Commission on the first day retraced much of this ground, clarifying his position on definitional matters; the quantity theory of money; and differences between his scheme of symmetallism and the conventional bimetallist scheme. He then analysed aspects of saving and investment influenced by an influx of precious metals, largely in terms of its potential effects on the discount rate; and discussed the relationship between general price rises and trade. The long session concluded with a drawn-out discussion on the alleged association between the depreciation of silver and the bounty it was said to create on Indian imports.

As a result of this exchange, Marshall prepared a further Memorandum for the Commission, dated 13 January 1888. This elucidated his views on the relation between a fall in the exchanges and in trade with non-gold countries such as India. Although it conformed to the evidence he had given in December, its more systematic and concise arrangement facilitated further cross-examination when he gave evidence on 17 January. The Memorandum reflects Marshall's beliefs on the satisfactory nature of traditional theory for discussing these matters and, not surprisingly, it reveals that he found it much easier to explain such complex matters in the quiet of his study rather than in presenting oral evidence with its potential distractions.[¶]

Marshall's two days of evidence in January 1888 retraced earlier points and introduced new topics. His symmetallist proposals was severely scrutinised (*OP*, pp. 101–15), and Marshall's view that trade was conducted in terms of comparative costs of production was also explored, a proposition requiring little qualification in so far as its permanent effects were concerned. The specific effects exerted by trade in the precious metals via the money market were likewise probed. This enabled consideration of the impact of changes in the discount rate on prices, during which Marshall explained the influence of both monetary and

---

* Marshall had already analysed some of these issues in his earliest paper on money, discussed in Chapter 6 above, and see below, pp. 349–50 for his qualified statement on the working of the quantity theory. For a detailed analysis of Marshall's contributions of monetary theory, see David Laidler, 'Alfred Marshall and the Development of Monetary Economics', in *Centenary Essays on Alfred Marshall*, pp. 44–78. Equally useful references are Eprime Eshag, *From Marshall to Keynes*, Oxford: Basil Blackwell, 1964, and Pascal Bridel, *Cambridge Monetary Thought*, London: Macmillan, 1987, Chapter 3.

[¶] Marshall referred to the dangers of such distractions in the process of giving oral evidence in a note he afterwards inserted on his personal copy of the transcript, reproduced in *OP*, p. 48 n.1.

real factors on that rate (*OP*, pp. 126–31, esp. Q. 9,981). Marshall likewise reaffirmed his view that periods of prolonged inflation were more likely to cause distress than periods of deflation (Q. 9,819). In discussing the hardship from irregular employment, Marshall noted reliable unemployment statistics were difficult to obtain. He then criticised the widely held view that modern industry increased such employment irregularities. This was an illusion, because regular employment hardly existed prior to the development of modern industry. He illustrated this from earlier observations in Palermo, whose medieval labour market made it impossible to identify unemployment.[15] During this part of the evidence, Marshall also criticised the paucity of industrial statistics (Q. 9,817) and the dangers in hastily interpreting available employment data (Q. 9,830). His own self-assured views on this topic were based on 'personal observations ranging over many years, and a study of almost everything of importance which has been written on the subject' (Q. 9,829).

The final day on which Marshall appeared before the Commission enabled follow-up questions on his previous evidence. These reviewed the nature of money and its relation to the prices as affected by hoarding, the discount rate and like short-term factors; whether silver or gold was the better reserve metal, and Ricardo's views on this subject. Effects on non-merchandise external transactions and on the commodity trade of a silver-currency country in the face of the depreciation of silver, were points on which Marshall's evidence seemed to worry the Commission most. This is illustrated by Sir Thomas Farrer's final question, inviting Marshall to address conflicting evidence by other witnesses on the effect of the depreciation of silver on Indian imports of wheat to the United Kingdom (*OP*, p. 169). Marshall's final Memorandum first addressed this question from the perspective of general theory, before examining the extent to which the evidence received by the Commission contravened this general theoretical point of view.

Keynes's edition of Marshall's *Official Papers* does not reprint Marshall's comments on material J.S. Nicholson had prepared for the Gold and Silver Commission. This objected to what Marshall saw as Nicholson's misrepresentations of his views, in particular, Nicholson's omission of essential points from the manifold causes affecting 'the value of a bill on India [apart from] the market price of silver here'; his exclusion of silver from the exports affected by variations in the gold price of silver; and his lack of 'attention to the many lines of statistical argument' which prove 'that the prices of certain wares, and especially wheat, do fluctuate from week to week in sympathy with the gold price of silver'. It then restated Marshall's complex views on the quantity theory, admitting 'that the general level of prices is affected by many causes beside the quantity of currency'. Marshall continued,

We have to take account of (i) the volume of currency; (ii) population; (iii) the amount of goods produced per head of population, and their wealth generally; (iv) the amount of business to which any given amount of wealth gives rise; (v) the proportion of these payments that are made for currency; (vi) the average rapidity of circulation of the currency (and under this head provision may be made for the locking up of money in hoards, in bank cellars, military chests, &c.); (vii) the state of commercial and political confidence, enterprise, and credit; and this last head might be again divided. (The influence of cost of production shows itself in the amount of the metals available for currency purposes; and the anticipation of a change in the cost of production is among the many causes which determine the amount of hoarding.)

Now, since the general level of prices is determined by all these seven elements acting together, it is quite possible that one or more of them may be tending to move general prices in one direction, while yet the net result of all the forces acting on prices is to move them in the other. I do not then regard the theory as leading us to expect that an increase in the amount of currency would always or even generally cause a rise in prices, but only that it will cause prices to be higher than they otherwise would have been if all other changes of the time had gone on as they have done, but the volume of currency had not increased.[16]

The Indian trade effects of silver depreciation involved Marshall a year later in further controversy over his views on bimetallism in the January 1889 letter columns of the *Times*. This enabled a succinct re-statement of Marshall's beliefs on both bimetallism and on the relationship between the quantity theory of money and the cost of production theory as theories of the value of money. On the last, Marshall argued that, like Mill, he held to both theories because, 'either of them, when properly explained, includes the other', a position already developed in Marshall's first paper on money. With respect to bimetallism, Marshall referred readers of the *Times* to his Memorandum appended to the Final Report of the Gold and Silver Commission. He repeated his preference for that modified bimetallism (symmetallism) adapted from Ricardo's ingot plan, which permitted a silver to gold ratio of 20, or even 22:1 as against the 15.5:1 of conventional bimetallism. Echoing what he had strenuously argued in his evidence, he denied adherence to any form of bimetallism implied support for 'the doctrine that the fall in the gold price of silver gives a proportionate bounty to the Indian cultivator of wheat.'[17]

Marshall's views on monetary policy in this evidence raised hackles in other quarters. His support for government involvement in preparing a tabular standard of value to facilitate indexation of long-term prices and thereby to act as a remedy for the detrimental effects on business activity from price instability, had earlier been attacked in a leading article by the *Economist*. This described Marshall's *Contemporary Review* version either as 'an impossibility' or of 'very restricted use' and 'impracticable'. It retraced Bagehot's equally savage attack as editor of the *Economist* on Jevons's similar proposal in 1875.[18] Marshall immediately defended his proposal by writing to the editor. Noting that a practical, and therefore imperfect, tabular standard of value could be relatively easily devised, he argued this would nevertheless provide 'a tenfold better standard of value than that afforded by the precious metals' and thereby more effectively protect individuals contracting for deferred payments from price instability. Marshall then criticised the *Economist* for failing to grasp his main argument, which he summarised as follows:

(1) That evils of a fluctuating standard for deferred payments are chiefly of modern origin; but that now they are of overwhelming importance; (2) that these evils would be but very slightly diminished by the adoption of gold and silver instead of gold alone as the basis of our currency; (3) that even so rough-and-ready a tabular unit as that published by yourself from year to year would give a far better standard for deferred payments than even a stable bi-metallic currency; (4) that fixed-ratio mintage is not what it claims to be, a stable bi-metallism. I propose an alternative scheme for basing our currency on gold and silver, which, though more uncouth at first, would, I believe, be stable, and have many other advantages. . . . An authoritative tabular unit might be introduced at once for use by those who liked it in arranging for deferred payments. It would at first be on a simple basis; . . . [19]

Marshall's letter failed to convince the *Economist*. It continued to question the ease of construction which Marshall claimed for his standard.[20] Marshall was not deterred by this criticism. He reiterated his support for the proposal before the Gold and Silver Commission.[21]

In his evidence before the Indian Currency Commission in 1899, Marshall referred only briefly to his own preferred scheme of bimetallism (*OP*, p. 286) and made no reference whatsoever to the tabular standard. Marshall's omission is explained by Giffen's devastating attack on such 'fancy monetary standards'. Although this refrained from mentioning Marshall by name, it reiterated Bagehot's arguments used in 1875 to crush Jevons's venture into tabular standards, and convicted contemporary proponents on the same grounds of 'impossibility' and 'impracticality' by which the *Economist* had criticised Marshall's proposal five years before.[22] Giffen's omission of Marshall's 1887 proposal among the 'fancy' standards he was attacking is explained in a letter Marshall subsequently wrote to Foxwell, mentioning discussions with Giffen in 1887 on the difficulties in obtaining reliable price data for the purpose of constructing such standards, during which Marshall accepted Giffen's views on the subject.[23] Twenty years later, Marshall recalled to Irving Fisher that 'when Giffen uttered his vehement trumpet blast against "Fancy Monetary Standards" . . . I chaffed him about his energy; and I recollect that he said that his argument was not opposed to my scheme'.[24]

Before looking at Marshall's evidence to the 1899 Indian Currency Commission, some of his skirmishes with more conventional bimetallists, including those with his friend Foxwell, can be conveniently discussed. Marshall's letter to Foxwell mentioned in the previous paragraph arose in the context of correspondence on bimetallism to the *Times*, in which Foxwell had imputed to Giffen 'a half dishonest desire to stifle discussion'.[25] Marshall regarded this 'as absurd as well as unkind', because he greatly admired Giffen 'despite his conspicuous faults'. Not long beforehand, Marshall 'had told Foxwell [that] he wished that his party would drop the 15.5 ratio to which Foxwell answered that he had never heard any serious person propose bimetallism at any other ratio'. Not surprisingly, Marshall objected to this diagnosis, indicating he had always, and publicly, drawn 'a distinction between 15.5 and 22 [ratio] Bimetallism' and that he thought Foxwell 'had proved the former would create a panic in the City; but not the latter'.[*]

When in 1894 leading bimetallists wished to organise a supportive manifesto from economists, Foxwell's attempts to get Marshall to sign proved lamentably unsuccessful. Foxwell's correspondence with Beeton,[26] a prominent member of the Bimetallic League, on the importance of getting Marshall to sign, is so informative about Marshall's quirks in these matters that it deserves extensive quotation. On 4 April 1894, Foxwell advised Beeton that Marshall wanted to discuss the matter with Keynes, 'a very level-headed man, who, however, inclines to Marshall's side'. He continued,

---

[*] JNKD, 25 January 1890. At the Bimetallic Conference held in Manchester (4–5 April, 1888), Foxwell claimed that Marshall and Goschen 'were in the main' on the fixed ratio bimetallic side. See *Report of Proceedings*, Manchester: The Bimetallic League, 1888, p. 66. It is interesting to note that Marshall quarrelled with Foxwell during June 1890 over the role Giffen should play in the about to be formed British Economic Association (later Royal Economic Society), in which Marshall favoured, and Foxwell opposed, such a role for Giffen. (Marshall to Foxwell, 28 June 1890, Freeman Collection, 14/124), and see below, Chapter 13, pp. 464–7.

Marshall is always a man whom it is extremely difficult to work with. He is opinionated, perhaps inclined to his opinions too highly. Moreover, knowing nothing of English bimetallists, he is filled with suspicion of them. In fact he regards them as unmitigated soft money men – most unfairly of course. I showed him Houldsworth's comments on the Manifesto. This produced just the effect I expected. He fell in love with Houldsworth on the spot. He thought the temper of the comment admirable. If he could only be got to meet Houldsworth at dinner, I should not despair of his joining the League. As to argument, you might as well argue with Giffen. But Marshall is extremely kind and generous with it all. He is an odd personality – but he is a high-minded, honourable man and I should be sorry to quarrel with him. . .[27]

Three weeks later Foxwell reported that an 'unfortunate phrase' in the manifesto mentioning 'matters of detail' rather than 'some important matters of principle' not only caused 'an explosion' on Marshall's part, but had induced his refusal to sign. Foxwell concluded that the matter of the manifesto should therefore not be hurried, for 'if you alienate Marshall, you give a blow to this movement the importance of which it could be difficult to exaggerate. . . . Lunching with Marshall on Monday [17 April], he observed, during the general half hour which usually succeeds a judicious meal, "There is really not much difference between our views" but he quickly added, "But that difference is *most* important".'[28]

A month later, Foxwell wrote that he now definitely expected Marshall not to sign, and advised Beeton against attempting to invite Marshall to speak on their behalf. Foxwell could explain the reasons for this 'at large' in conversation, but in a letter the following remarks had to suffice: 'What will happen if you goad him against his will into speaking is that he will so qualify his former expressions that every practical man will regard him as really hostile to Bi-metallists . . . M[arshall] is very obstinate. If you don't seem to want him, he may come in: but the more pressure you put on him, the more he bucks up.'*

Marshall's own epitaph on the bimetallic controversy appeared in a letter to Bowley in 1901, when the controversy had died down. This succinctly explained his ambivalent position on the subject. After reminding Bowley that he himself was still a bimetallist but one 'opposed to the excrescences which the League had borrowed from the U.S. silver men', Marshall continued that it was their simplistic view of causal relations which particularly offended him. 'Without proof they assert that A is the cause of B, when it seems to me that it would be less untrue to say that B is the cause of A, and they deluge the public with these correlated curves to prove it.'[29]

It is difficult to recapture the fervour caused by bimetallism. It undoubtedly produced an early rift between Marshall and Foxwell; it was also one of Jowett's favourite topics of conversation with his friend. Mary Paley later recalled for the Marshall Society,[30] 'The Bimetallic controversy was raging [in the 1880s] and it is difficult now-a-days to realise how furious that raged. Next to Home Rule it was the most dangerous subject to discuss, and it too had to be forbidden at dinner parties.'

---

*   Foxwell to Beeton, 21 May 1894, Marshall Archive, Misc. 1:15. In his obituary of Foxwell (*Economic Journal*, 46 (4), December 1936, p. 599), J.M. Keynes mentioned that Foxwell 'took a leading part in the Bimetallic controversy, as one of the outstanding academic supporters of change, and as a friend and helper of the American authorities, General F.A. Walker and Dana Horton'. Cf. Audrey Foxwell, *Herbert Somerton Foxwell: A Portrait*, pp. 13–14, which refers to his association in this context with Sir William and Lady Houldsworth and Beeton.

Eleven years after the Gold and Silver Commission, Marshall gave evidence before the (second) Commission on Indian Currency over two days in January and February 1899. By this time, Marshall's status in the economics profession had risen considerably, and he was treated far more deferentially by the commissioners. The 1899 evidence traversed much of the same territory as that to the Gold and Silver Commission, except that emphasis on the Indian aspects of the problem became even greater. Marshall once again presented his views on the quantity theory (*OP*, pp. 267–9), on the relationship between currency, bank money and real capital, in which 'credit paper' and 'bank money' were treated as 'command' over capital 'one further stage' removed (*OP*, pp. 270, 305–6, 307) and on causes governing the rate of interest and the rate of discount (*OP*, pp. 270–74, 307–11, 322–4). Marshall's evidence approvingly cited Fisher's distinction between nominal and real interest rates (*OP*, pp. 271–2), although Marshall himself had been long aware of the importance of the phenomenon.[31] Other oral evidence was devoted to explanations of Indian prices and their effects, the importance of the Indian rate of exchange and its causes and influences, including those in stimulating foreign trade, the matter to which the Gold and Silver Commission had devoted so much attention. When at the end of the day Marshall was invited by the commissioners to give any information he considered relevant to the inquiry, he volunteered his strong belief in the need for better economic education of Indian civil servants, particularly with respect to their opportunities for taking advanced studies in political economy (*OP*, pp. 325–6).[32]

The rich content of Marshall's 'monetary' evidence, which embraced aspects of saving-investment analysis and of trade cycle theory, was not exploited by him in academic publications until the final years of his life when, with the indispensable assistance of his wife, he put together the 'pastiche' of *Money, Credit and Commerce* in the early 1920s. By then, many of his more prominent students had already moved well beyond his contributions to monetary theory in its widest sense, building on the strong foundations prepared both by him and his younger contemporaries, Wicksell and Fisher.[33]

CHARITY, THE AGED POOR, OUTDOOR RELIEF AND REFORM OF THE POOR LAW

On 5 June 1893, while still involved with his responsibilities as member of the Labour Commission, Marshall submitted a preliminary memorandum to the Royal Commission on the aged poor, on which he was subsequently questioned. This Commission had been set up by the Liberal government in November 1892 'to consider whether any alterations in the system of poor law relief [were] desirable in the case of persons whose destitution is occasioned by incapacity for work, resulting from old age or whether assistance could otherwise be afforded in those cases.'[34] Much of the inspiration for setting up the Commission came from proposals for aged pension schemes, sometimes as part of wide-ranging national insurance schemes, which were surfacing in the wake of Bismarck's comprehensive social security legislation in Germany and active debate on the issue in New Zealand. The Commission included two prominent proponents of such schemes, Joseph Chamberlain and Charles Booth. Other members were C.T. Ritchie (who chaired the session at which Marshall gave oral evidence), Joseph Arch, Lord Brassey and James Stuart, with some of whom Marshall was personally acquainted.

The Commission also included leading members of the Charity Organisation Society (C.O.S.): C.S. Loch, its energetic secretary, and Mr. Albert Pell, MP, one of its council members. The C.O.S. was itself strongly opposed to age pensions. It described pensions as vehicles for undermining the cohesiveness of the family, because they eliminated the need for children to support their parents in old age. Secondly, age pensions as a form of 'outdoor relief' (the Poor Law terminology for any pecuniary assistance to the disadvantaged as contrasted with the 'indoor relief' provided by the workhouse), if too lavishly provided, were said to increase the workhouse population since 'out relief is a preparatory school for total dependence'.[35] As Marshall informed the Commission (*OP*, p. 217, Q. 10,237), he 'had a good deal of indirect experience of the working of Charity Organisation Societies . . . as a member of them for a great many years, and at Oxford and Cambridge, my wife has been an active member of the Committee'.*

Apart from his association with the C.O.S., Marshall claimed long involvement with the area of poor law reform and general issues of poverty. By way of introduction to his evidence, he indicated 'I have devoted myself for the last twenty-five years to the problem of poverty, and . . . very little of my work has been devoted to any inquiry which does not bear on that. But I do not regard the problem of pauperism, as distinguished from the problem of poverty, as of so great importance as it seems to other people to be' (*OP*, p. 205, Q. 10,188). Alleviation of poverty through the steady progress and improvement of the working classes was undoubtedly an important element in Marshall's initial decision to commence studies in political economy and later to concentrate on them. The proposition that freeing the masses 'from the pains of poverty' was the problem that gave 'to economic studies their chief and their highest interest' was prominently displayed in the opening sections of his then recently published *Principles of Economics*, already in its second edition by 1891.[36] In 1892, Marshall had contributed two pieces on poor law reform in relation to 'state-aided pensions', the second of which in response to a criticism of the first by Bernard Bosanquet, a prominent publicist for the C.O.S. view.[37] This exchange illustrates that Marshall was at odds with C.O.S. principles on important points, and his interventions on the aged poor issue are aptly described as a 'compromise solution'[38] between the proposals of Charles Booth and the C.O.S. position. These early contributions and the nature of his association with the C.O.S. need to be explained before discussing his evidence to the Aged Poor Commission.

Marshall's earlier views on the political economy of outdoor relief were presented in the *Economics of Industry*. There he correctly diagnosed 'indoor relief' in the workhouse as highly 'unpopular', and 'outdoor relief' as liable to 'great evils' because on the whole, it has been found that wherever outdoor relief had been given freely, a large part of the population

---

* Marshall followed this remark with an interesting comment on how he and his wife discussed issues raised at these committees 'at the next meal' thereafter, while he also claimed to have diligently studied the reports on individual cases as reported by the London, and other, committees of the C.O.S. in the *Charity Organisation Reporter* and its successor, the *Charity Organisation Review*. Examples of such cases are given in Helen Bosanquet, *Social Work in London 1869–1912*, pp. 61–2, 108–15. The Marshalls' involvement with the C.O.S. is examined in more detail below, pp. 357–8.

had become idle, thriftless and base, in short, 'pauperised'. Where outdoor relief was given to the able-bodied, it tended to lower wages, unless confined to very temporary emergencies. Thus outdoor relief ought to be reformed and not abolished. Applicants for outdoor relief should carry the onus of proof by demonstrating that they deserved it, while decisions to give relief should be supported by tests such as the thrift test. Marshall concluded that provided it was possible to separate the deserving from the undeserving poor, outdoor relief should be maintained.[39]

Marshall reiterated his support for outdoor relief in a letter to the *Times* in 1886, which denied that political economy provided a general case against outdoor relief as was so often claimed. To the contrary, provision of outdoor relief was essential to prevent the breaking up of homes of 'honest workers . . . by a season of misfortune' and to save them from the workhouse. Marshall added that this opinion 'seemed to be that of all working men, without exception, the best as well as the worst' as he had found from personal observations when attending socialist lectures, where mention of cutting outdoor relief invariably drew angry reactions from all.*

Marshall's letter arose in the context of temporary relief work in times of depressed trade, a policy Marshall supported so long as wages paid were sufficiently low to encourage recipients to be always on the look-out for work elsewhere at more normal rates of remuneration. Marshall's 1892 *Economic Journal* contribution applied the case for 'outdoor relief' to the more permanent condition of the aged poor. This was undoubtedly inspired by his attendance on 15 December 1891 at a meeting of the Royal Statistical Society during which Charles Booth unfolded his scheme for aged pensions by way of conclusion to his paper on the statistical enumeration and classification of paupers.

Such proposals were by then fairly common. Apart from those of Booth and Chamberlain already noted, there were proposals by Marshall's former student, the Rev. Moore Ede, Canon Barnet and others.[40] In the subsequent discussion, Marshall was generally supportive of Booth's proposals. It 'was the best that had ever been suggested' but could be criticised on the taxation side. Marshall's objections relied on his 'excess burden' theorem. 'Because every tax cost more to the people than it brought to the State, a man was injured in paying in taxes a sum of money the net proceeds of which were to be returned to himself'. Marshall therefore preferred a combination of Booth's new public pension scheme with the principles of a reformed 'old poor law'.[41] For the occasion of

---

* Alfred Marshall, letter to the *Times*, 11 February 1886. Marshall's letter was subsequently criticised by the Rev. Llewellyn-Davis in its letter columns (16 February 1886). This induced Marshall to explain himself further to Lewellyn-Davis in a private letter (in *Memorials*, p. 373). Marshall's letter to the *Times* was approvingly referred to in two *Times* editorials (15 February and 6 March 1886) because it had so ably defended an essential feature of Poor Law administration during 'exceptional and passing distress'. The justice of Marshall's diagnosis on the unpopularity of the workhouse is illustrated by George Lansbury's recollection of his first visit to a workhouse after being elected a poor law guardian in 1893. 'It was not necessary to write up the words, "abandon hope all ye who enter here". Officials, receiving ward, hard forms, whitewashed walls, keys dangling on the waist of those who spoke to you, huge books for name, history, etc., searching and then being stripped and bathed in a communal tub, and the final crowning indignity of being dressed in clothes which had been worn by lots of other people, hideous to look at, ill-fitting and coarse – everything possible was done to inflict mental and moral degradation'. Cited by Paul Thompson, *Socialists, Liberals and Labour. The Struggle for London 1885–1914*, London: Routledge & Kegan Paul, 1967, p. 122. This differed little from George Orwell's description of the workhouse forty years later. See *Down and Out in Paris and London*, 1933, London: Penguin Books, 1975, esp. pp. 127–33.

Booth's lecture, the Marshalls were staying at the Booths' London residence (a return visit to the Booths' recent stay with them at Cambridge) and Mrs Mary Booth recorded laconically in her diary that after the lecture, Marshall and her husband only 'talked about docks', undoubtedly reflecting Marshall's contemporaneous experience on the Labour Commission. However, Mary Paley subsequently told the wife of Sir Horace Darwin in Cambridge that Marshall had thought well of Booth's proposal, and that his only objection, as far as she (Lady Darwin) understood, was that its consideration might hinder a more radical reform of the Poor Law. Marshall's reaction contrasts therefore markedly with the strong opposition Booth's plan attracted from Loch, the secretary of the C.O.S., and the lukewarm reaction of Leonard Courtney, who had also spoken at the meeting at which Booth presented the scheme. The adjourned discussion of Booth's proposal on 22 December 1891 was, however, overwhelmingly hostile to his plan. Opponents of the scheme had rallied forces against it after its initial, relatively sympathetic reception.[42]

Marshall's *Economic Journal* proposal can therefore be seen as a rescue attempt of the Booth plan by suggesting a compromise with the C.O.S. It proposed some examination as to eligibility of potential recipients of outdoor relief among the 'old who had passed their 65th birthday', dealing with their 'present resources and needs' and their previous attempts to provide for the future. This removed the universality of Booth's scheme, and thereby the excess burden taxation objections which Marshall had voiced the previous December. In addition, Marshall suggested the need for a wider inquiry before committing the nation to such a major scheme. Amongst other things, this would have to address the sixteen problems of principle with which Marshall concluded his article. These mentioned consideration of greater working-class participation in poor law administration; the desirability of freeing scarce C.O.S. resources from approving individual cases of relief for the aged poor thereby enabling them to concentrate on more difficult cases; eliminating the dichotomy inherent in Booth's scheme of stigma in public (state) charity before, but not after, the age of 65; and serious consideration of further ways of improving public relief schemes by enhancing their voluntary and insurance elements.[43]

Bosanquet's reply to Marshall did not rehearse the type of arguments his wife later raised against aged pensions.[44] For reasons of space, he concentrated on a major flaw in Marshall's paper, 'excellent in spirit' though it was. Because of Marshall's limited experience, he had misunderstood the degree of similarity between the policies on giving outdoor relief to the able-bodied (including the able-bodied aged over 65) by the formulators of the 1834 poor law reform and by current poor law administration. Marshall's lack of expertise was further reflected in the type of division of labour between C.O.S. personnel and poor law guardians in poor law administration he proposed. No outdoor relief should be automatically given, as age pension proposals implied. All cases needed individual investigation if pauperisation (putting the disadvantaged on public relief) was to be avoided. In this context, Bosanquet pointed to a London C.O.S. study opposing outdoor relief, which opposed it *'first on the grounds of humanity, then with a view to thrift, and thirdly as lowering wages'*.[45]

Marshall's 'reply to Bosanquet', despite its polite opening remarks – 'it was perhaps rash to write so short a paper as my last on so large a subject' – was as vitriolic as the reply penned eighty years before to another Bosanquet by Marshall's 'hero', Ricardo. After noting that 'many persons' supported his proposed division in the treatment with respect to outdoor relief between those over 65 and those not, Marshall vigorously attacked Bosanquet's imputation of lack of experience to explain his alleged 'misunderstanding'. Marshall indicated that it was thirteen years since he had first written on the subject (in *Economics of Industry*), and that combined with his long, and his wife's even more extensive experience with C.O.S. committee work at Oxford and Cambridge, 'I may be pardoned the presumption of thinking that Mr. Bosanquet would find that I had made myself acquainted with the teachings of experience on which he relies, and that I had considered nearly every difficulty of detail that he could suggest'. Marshall then consoled Bosanquet for not being alone in his ignorance. Rev. Llewellyn-Davis, who knew of Marshall's earlier *Economic Journal* paper only at second hand, had incautiously stated in the *Manchester Guardian* (6 April 1892) that Marshall was among those 'who do not consider consequences' whereas in the article referred to, he had gone out of his way to warn of the dangers in lax poor law administration. In particular he had only advocated 'cautious, tentative and slow extensions of outdoor relief' and assumed that 'able-bodied men would not receive this under normal circumstances'. Nor did he think, as Bosanquet implied, that the plan he proposed would lower wages, although 'lavish outdoor relief, without regard for the consequences', undoubtedly did.[46]

Marshall then turned his attack on some C.O.S. preconceptions. Bosanquet had not attempted to deny that the C.O.S. systematically fostered the belief that public relief by definition involved disgrace to the recipient and he could therefore be presumed to assess the importance of that element of disgrace far more highly than Marshall did. This perspective arose from the essentially middle-class nature of the C.O.S., which systematically ignored working-class views on the '*justice*' of giving outdoor relief in deserving circumstances. Marshall continued by noting, 'The grim comedy of excluding working-class witnesses from the Parliamentary inquiries into Poor Relief is partly responsible for this failure. . . . The arguments given from the stand-point of the well-to-do may possibly be sufficient to convince those who find it rather pleasant to believe that out-relief can be abolished without injustice, and cannot be retained without injury.'[47]

The feature of cooperation between public and private charity, so essential to his plan, had been first brought to his notice through Octavia Hill's writings, Marshall explained. This division of labour in charity administration was analogous to that in transport between trains and carts: one had great resources within restricted limits, the other was highly flexible while in command over only very small resources. Although Marshall conceded his plan 'was not the best possible, . . . what little experience there is of cordial co-operation between Charity Organisation Societies and Guardians, tends to show it is workable'. He repeated the need for a Royal Commission to assess the evidence before committing the nation to 'such an expensive new patch on our old system', a Royal Commission whose members and witnesses should include both providers and clients of charity.[48] Marshall's plea, undoubtedly assisted by 'the rapidly increasing interest taken by the public at large in the question of old-age pensions'[49] was answered in November 1892, when a Royal Commission was set up to investigate the issue from all perspectives.[50]

Marshall's reply to Bosanquet had stressed his long-standing involvement with the C.O.S. and his even longer admiration for the principles of one of its leading members,

Octavia Hill. However, although in his evidence to the Commission on the Aged Poor (*OP*, p. 217, Q. 10,237) he claimed to have been 'a member . . . for a great many years', his references to Oxford and Cambridge suggest a membership of at best a decade, that is, from the time they moved to Oxford in October 1883. This conforms to the known facts. C.O.S. Annual Reports indicate that only from 1887 did Professor Alfred Marshall become an active financial supporter of the organisation with an annual donation of £3.3s., kept up until the demise of the C.O.S. in 1912. Although Bristol had an unaffiliated C.O.S. Committee from the mid-1870s, there is no evidence that the Marshalls had joined it. In her later recollections, Mary Paley only mentioned her active attendance at meetings of the Oxford Committee.[51]   She left no personal recollections of the Cambridge Committee, but Marshall's evidence leaves no room for doubt about her active membership of both that and the Oxford Committee. The Marshall Library, in addition, houses nearly 2,000 C.O.S. case studies for the relevant period.[52]   Mary Paley's recollections, however, do mention C.O.S. members as invitees to address the women's Social Discussion Society at Cambridge, including Octavia Hill, Emma Cons and 'the beautiful Mary Clifford, one of the first women [Poor Law] Guardians'.[53]

There is also evidence of Marshall's occasionally more active, albeit reluctant, involvement with the Cambridge C.O.S. In 1901 he chaired one of its general meetings as part of the C.O.S. Annual Conference held in Cambridge that year, during which he mentioned both the negative and the more constructive work of the C.O.S. In October 1902, Marshall addressed a Conference of the C.O.S. Committee on Social Education on the subject of 'Economic Teaching at the Universities in relation to Public Well-being'.[54] Marshall's passive involvement and considerable interest in C.O.S. activities is therefore confirmed, as is his occasional critical admiration.[55]

Marshall's attitude to the C.O.S. is concisely illustrated in a letter to Charles Booth seeking his participation as a speaker to the C.O.S. Annual Conference at Cambridge in 1901: 'The annual meeting of the Charity Organisation Society is to be held in Cambridge in the middle of May: drat them! They will talk their everlasting small things blown big: not an evil, but not much a good. I have nothing to do with the arrangements but Mary is on the committee which meets to select the topics next Wednesday. And so I have got half sucked into the whirlpool.'[56]

Given this background, Marshall's contibutions to the Aged Poor Commission can be examined in context. His preliminary memorandum to the Aged Poor Commission duplicated and expanded on the 1892 *Economic Journal* articles. Not surprisingly, given Bosanquet's attack, it first of all explored the validity of postulating the continuity of present policy with the 1834 Poor Law. Marshall then briefly considered the influence of modern industrial conditions on the poor and the infirm; the difficulty in drawing generalisations about the consequences of outdoor relief on the basis of early nineteenth century experience, and the extent to which the findings of the 1834 Report were still applicable. Marshall defined the universally valid principles it had established as follows: 'That "character is the parent of comfort": that money gifts are of little avail by themselves: that relief by official routine is less discriminating than personal charity: that certainty and absence of suspicion of favouritism are advantages that outweigh a good deal of hardship;

and above all that the position of the dependent, whether in health or illness, should not be better than that of the independent worker in like case.' (*OP,* p. 201).

Marshall also explained that public outdoor relief need not necessarily reduce wages, the method of tax financing and the manner of giving relief being crucial to the outcome. If appropriate precautions were taken, 'Charles Booth's scheme would not lower wages, in spite of the heavy tax it would levy on capital'. Ethical considerations in poor relief and the 'vexed question' of the difficulty in discriminating in poor relief between 'the worthy and the unworthy' concluded his memorandum. Its final part also covered his considered verdict on the work of the C.O.S.: 'It is difficult to over-rate the debt that the nation owes to the Charity Organisation Societies. But they have some weaknesses. Their funds are limited, their action and even their existence is haphazard and their basis is oligarchic. And perhaps they under-rate the moral and economic evils of anxiety.' (*OP,* p. 203).

Marshall answered more than 250 questions on the day he appeared before the Commission, well over half from its chairman. Many of these concentrated on his plea for greater working-class involvement in both poor law administration and the work of the Commission. In cross-examination, Marshall confessed that his own discussions with working-class leaders outside of the Commission had been practically confined to no more than two persons (p. 233, Q. 10,305, p. 243, Q. 10,348).* Clarification was also sought from Marshall on the nature and details of the cooperation he envisaged in poor law administration between poor law guardians and C.O.S. Committees, especially through the Chairman's extensive questioning (pp. 210–24). During this questioning, Marshall occasionally showed himself to be rather hazy on matters of detail (pp. 211–14). There were also pertinent questions on the effects of outdoor relief on wages (pp. 224–8), confirmation of Marshall's strong belief that the working class as a whole was convinced of the necessity of outdoor relief (Q. 10,193). Loch's (the C.O.S. Secretary) twenty-five questions were largely designed to reveal Marshall's lack of detailed knowledge and experience with conditions of actual poor law administration, especially of workhouses (pp. 255–6, and cf. pp. 229–30). Modern readers, particularly those familiar with Orwell's *Down and Out in Paris and London*, will shudder at Marshall's harsh recommendations on the need for severe disciplinary treatment for tramps (*OP*, Q. 10,352, p. 143) and his hints for the need of equally severe treatment for gypsies (Q. 10,355, p. 244). This evidence, as compared with that he gave to the Monetary Commissions, reveals a Marshall less sure of himself as to detail, but always able to hold his own on questions such as the effect of outdoor relief on wages, which fell within his special province as economist.

The Aged Poor Commission had no positive outcome.[57] In fact, age pensions were not introduced until 1908, after a further Royal Commission on the Poor Law, a Departmental Committee on Old Age Pensions as well as a Special Select Committee of the House of Commons. Marshall did not give evidence to these, even though he was specifically asked to do so for the Royal Commission on the Poor Law by Professor William Smart, one of its members. Marshall's presence was nevertheless felt by the Poor Law Commission in two

---

* One of these was Thomas Burt, the trade unionist, radical M.P. and one of Marshall's working-class leader acquaintances. In May 1892 Marshall had sent him a set of questions on working-class attitudes to outdoor relief to which Burt responded in the manner Marshall later indicated to the Commission on the Aged Poor (Marshall Archive, 1/9–10).

distinct ways. A Marshallian analysis on a number of poor law problems was presented by Pigou, Marshall's successor to the political economy chair in 1908. Marshall's 1907 paper, 'The Social Possibilities of Economic Chivalry', with its emphasis on the desirability of income redistribution and the increased capacity of the nation to do this, also attracted the attention of several of the poor law commissioners. Charles Booth praised Marshall's paper for its 'profoundly true' utterances, which were translated 'into precise recommendations concerning the Poor Law' by Pigou, in the Memorandum for the Commission already referred to.[58]

THE ROYAL COMMISSION ON LABOUR 1891–94: TRADE UNIONS, MINIMUM WAGES AND IRREGULARITY OF EMPLOYMENT

On 28 February 1891 the Salisbury Conservative Government, alarmed at the growth of what has been called the 'new trade unionism',[59] announced its intention to set up a Commission on Labour, to investigate a number of important issues in labour relations which had come into prominence in the late 1880s. The Majority Report of the Commission tabled in Parliament during June 1894 summarised these issues as follows:

(1) What are the leading causes of modern disputes between employers and employed; out of what conditions of industry do they arise; and what are the effects upon them of organisations on either side?
(2) By what means of institutions can they be prevented from arising, or if they do arise, can they be most pacifically settled without actual conflict in the shape of strikes or lock-outs?
(3) Can any of these causes of dispute be wholly or partially removed by practicable legislation, due regard being had to the general interests of the country?[60]

The above elaborated the original terms of reference with which the Commission was established. The latter more simply asked the Commission to inquire into 'questions affecting the relations between employers and employed, the combinations of employers and employed and the conditions of labour, which have been raised during the recent trade disputes in the United Kingdom'. This version of the Commission's purpose links its task more explicitly to the growth of industrial unrest in 1889 and 1890. Strikes, as reported in the *Times*, rose from 37 in 1888 to 111 in 1889, while the Labour Department of the Board of Trade with its more complete records for subsequent years, estimated that from 1890 to 1899 'there were never fewer than 700 stoppages through dispute each year'.[61] This dramatic rise in labour disputes was vividly brought home to the British public by the sudden, and unexpectedly successful, industrial action of 'the match girls' in their strike against Bryant and May in 1888, by the gasworkers' industrial victory in 1889, and by the momentous dockworkers strike which, for the first time since 1797, had effectively closed the London docks. These events reflected rising political unrest among the working class, particularly in London. Striking examples of this were the 1886 Hyde Park 'riot' with its looting and overturning of carriages, and 'Bloody Sunday' on Sunday 13 November 1887, in which 1,500 police and 200 mounted lifeguards clashed with thousands of workers and middle-class radicals. Fear of the social revolution became rampant among the middle class and hastened the demise of support for *laissez faire* and self-help philosophies in the area of social welfare.[62]

In spite of this background of wide social unrest, the Commission, 'did not intend . . . to undertake an examination of the fundamental causes of wealth and poverty, or to discuss the remedies by which evils and misfortunes, not directly connected with or bearing upon industrial disputes can be met'. This explains part of its shortcomings, since the minor reforms it eventually recommended failed to meet the aspirations of the working class. The Minority Report written on behalf of the more radical working-class members by Sidney Webb reflects such problems. The Commission itself saw its brief as a fact-finding one, and eventually reported at inordinate length over the period of its existence, another cause for its lack of success.[63] The political importance assigned to it by the government can be gauged from the fact that its budget was nearly £50,000. Moreover, it numbered 27 commissioners, of whom seven were trade unionists designed to give its composition the requisite balance.[64]

Why and how Marshall was appointed to the Commission is easily documented. His prominence in the economics profession was a major factor in his appointment, particularly when combined with his experience from earlier Royal Commissions and his writings on labour problems. The last signalled appropriate sympathy with working-class improvement as a major objective of national policy. Marshall's formal invitation to join the Commission came from Arthur Balfour, the nephew of Lord Salisbury who, as Conservative Prime Minister, had the major say on appointments to the Commission. As a Cambridge moral sciences graduate and Sidgwick's brother-in-law, Balfour was familiar with Marshall's reputation and work and their association was further cemented through a Jowett dinner party in Oxford in November 1890.[65]

Why Marshall accepted the task of Commissioner is likewise easily explained. Pigou suggested in 1924 that it was Marshall, 'the tireless collector of realistic detail' who 'eagerly welcomed the opportunity of serving on the Royal Commission on Labour, on which he came into close personal touch with many representative workpeople and employers of labour'.[66] Marshall himself stressed the educative value of the experience in letters to Jowett, Taussig and others, while he later depicted it as 'the most valuable education of my life'.[67] More realistically, Mary Paley described Marshall's work on the Commission as something her husband found 'very interesting. . . but it will hinder Vol. II which has now been entered upon'.[68]

The Commission started its work in May 1891 by discussing procedures, reporting on this by the end of the month.[69] These procedures included: '(1) the taking of oral evidence; (2) the collection of written evidence in the shape of answers to schedules of questions; (3) the use of existing materials; (4) the appointment of Assistant Commissioners to collect information not obtainable by other means'. The Commission divided itself into three sub-committees to inquire into specific groups of trades: Committee A to be responsible for the mining, iron, engineering, hardware, shipbuilding and cognate trades; Committee B (of which Marshall was a member) for transport and agriculture, the term 'transport' to include shipping, canals, docks, railways and tramways; Committee C for textile, clothing, chemical, building and miscellaneous trades. More general evidence was collected by the Commission as a whole, largely during December 1892. The Commission also decided to summon trade union representatives first to state their grievances, to be followed by a statement of views from representatives of the Employers' Associations.[70]

In all, the Commission examined 583 witnesses at 151 sittings, with the evidence published periodically. The volume of evidence was so immense that it was summarised, indexed and published with an analysis of its major content. The Commission obtained much information. This came from European and North American countries, namely, Holland, Belgium, Germany, France, the United States and Switzerland, and from the 'dominions', India, Canada, South Africa, New Zealand and Australia.[71] Marshall wrote to Jowett in October 1891,[72] that the last source would be particularly useful because the 'attitude of Australians to labour questions seems to me more interesting than that of any other nation, except Englishmen: much more interesting than that of Americans'. Marshall also wrote to Jowett that the Commission had been advised 'to inquire thoroughly into women's labour', advice heeded because it appointed four lady assistant commissioners who 'prepared 19 Reports over the course of 1892 and 1893'.[73]

As could be expected, the earnest Marshall diligently attended his share of the Commission's hearings. With one exception, he was the only commissioner to attend all 17 sittings of the Commission as a whole. However, he missed eight of 46 sittings of Committee B, the sub-committee of which he was a member. In addition, Marshall attended four sittings of Committee A and three of Committee C, a grand total of 62 out of a possible 151. Marshall's attendance record was almost the perfect median: 12 commissioners attended more, and 13 attended fewer sittings than he did.[74]*

Marshall showed himself an assiduous questioner in the Commission, both when it was sitting in Committee and, even more, in the seventeen sittings of the Commission as a whole at all of which he was present. His questions covered the whole of the wide range of issues with which the Commission in practice concerned itself. These varied, as Beatrice Webb[75] put it in her caustic review of its *Final Report*, 'from the merits of piecework to the drawbacks of overtime, from sanitation of factories to irregularity of employment, from Eight-Hour Bills to employers' liability, from seamen to miners, and from women-workers to agricultural labourers', a list she could have easily extended by mentioning cooperative

---

* Marshall's involvement with the work of the Commission was spread unevenly through the year. It rarely interfered with the Marshalls' trips abroad during the summer vacation, as sittings tended to be concentrated in the first six and last two months of the year. Marshall's record of attendance was as follows: three opening sittings of Committee B in June 1891; 8 Committee B sittings in two, four-day weeks in November 1891. During January 1892, Marshall was absent from four Committee B sittings in the week commencing 24 January. Proofs for *EEI* and a head cold are the explanation (JNKD, 13 January 1892). In February and March 1892, he attended four sittings of Committee B and two of Committee C; in May 1892, two sittings of Committee A and seven of B. The Commission was not allowed to interfere with summer holidays in Switzerland, from which the Marshalls did not return until September, so that Marshall was absent from the four Committee B sittings of the first week of August. (Marshall to Newcomb, 2 and 29 August 1892, cited above, Chapter 7, pp. 188–9.) Marshall attended all sittings of the Commission as a whole. These began at the end of October (25–28) 1892, continuing during November (14–18, 29–30) and early December (1–2). Final sittings for Committee B took place in early November 1892 (2–3) while the last four of the Commission as a whole were held in the last week of January 1893 (24–27) and 2 February. In summary the Commission's sub-committees transacted their business from June 1891 to early November 1892; with the greater part of their evidence presented by the early summer of 1892; the Commission as a whole took oral evidence from October 1892 to early February 1893, before deliberating on the final Report. This was not signed by the majority of the commissioners until 24 May 1894. (Data compiled from Minutes of Evidence.)

enterprise and profit sharing, municipal socialism and fare evasion, shipping regulation and sanitary housing, workers' trains and the cost of feeding horses for London's cabs, machinery and productivity, workers' wages and living standards, arbitration and conciliation, Sunday observance and American labour statistics, productive and unproductive labour, garden cities and the defence of the legitimacy of interest as a normal business cost. Marshall's extensive questioning makes summary impossible. Hence, selection of some interesting and characteristic parts is appropriate.[76]

Whether dictated by shyness, modesty or a willingness to learn from the experience of his more practised fellow commissioners, Marshall did not start questioning witnesses until the fourth sitting day of Committee B. Marshall's first witness was Henry Quelch, a member of the Southside Labour Protection League and Steam Ship Workers Society. His questions sought information on the nature of trade unions, the average wage, and the comparative advantages of casual as against labour hired on a weekly basis on the waterfront (Q. 2,438–74). He also questioned the next witness, Joseph Falvey, another dockers' organisation trade unionist, this time on the effects of machinery on employment and on wages paid in the industry (Q. 2,650–64).

Marshall's first major witness was Ben Tillett, to whom he addressed questions in Tillett's dual capacity as one of the 'best informed on the general conditions of the dock labourer . . . [and] as a social reformer of a thorough going character' (Q. 3,641).* Marshall's questions started with seasonal factors governing dock labour, before moving to an observed unwillingness of dock labourers to take relief work in times of seasonal unemployment. Here Marshall mentioned a feature of Irish dock labour observed, according to him, by specialists on the subject, in terms of their preference for long stints of work in highly paid labour as against steady work at regular hours for lower pay. Tillett denied the accuracy of such observations, saying he 'had a drop of Irish' in his own composition and that he himself had seen 'a lot of Irishmen at regular work . . . punctual and sober' (Q. 3,650). Marshall also inquired about Tillett's views on the role of arbitration in settling labour disputes, particularly on the proposals he thought were practical 'without an organic change in the conditions of industry' or the scope of action open 'to the councils of the nation after the glorious revolution of which several Socialists have told us' (Q. 3,659–60). This was the first instance of Marshall's rather hostile approach to 'socialist witnesses' before the Commission, repeated when fellow commissioner, Tom Mann, as well as Sidney Webb and Henry Hyndman took the stand. Finally, Marshall questioned Tillett, social reformer, on the division of dock labourers between those able to live life 'like good citizens' and those forced to 'enjoy life' in more 'rough and brutal ways' (Q. 3,664), a matter which had long interested him from the point of view of the social consequences of excessive hours of labour. Tillett's answer was not comforting. 'From a rough estimate I gather 25 per cent of the dock *employés* have a decent chance to live, 25 per cent have to do

---

* Marshall's questioning of Tillett at the Commission took place approximately two years after Tillett had startled Florence Keynes with his table manners at a dinner party at Balliol Croft (see above, Chapter 8, pp. 245–6). Tillett's later *Memories and Reflections* (London: John Long, 1931, p. 160) only mentions Marshall, 'the standing authority on political economy in the period' as someone who, 'with his wife' was 'most anxious to assess the economic meaning of our great struggle' within the strike movement of the new unionism.

this heavy work which means physical incapacity in the long run, and 50 per cent are not able to live a decent life.'[77]

Although often devoted to different topics, Marshall's examination of many other witnesses during sittings of Committee B was similar in style. Contemporary assessments on Marshall's performance of this aspect of his task as commissioner are of greater interest than a summary of his practice. First and foremost these include Beatrice Webb's references to Marshall as gatherer of evidence in her review of the Commission's *Final Report*. Her general remark on the approach to working class witnesses taken by some of the commissioners can be quoted first:

> One by one the working men are brought up to give, as they believe, the facts of their own trades. Presently they find themselves entangled in a discussion on abstract economics, political philosophy, or even history, with such cultivated dialecticians as Mr. Gerald Balfour, Sir Frederick Pollock and Professor Marshall. It would have been surprising if, in these academic debates, the workmen had not frequently got worsted, quite as often when they were right as when they were wrong. The greatest triumph was to lead them by skilful questions into some logical inconsistency. This game of cat and mouse may have been interesting enough to the Commissioners; it was certainly amusing to the casual visitor to watch the dialecticians 'purring' at each other with complacency when their little pounces came off. But it aroused the deepest resentment among the working-class witnesses, and had, as the Chairman might have known, the effect of destroying any chance the Commission ever had of getting to the bottom of the questions of fact within their knowledge. The workmen, feeling as several of them have since told me, that they were from the outset treated as hostile witnesses, were afraid of making admissions that could be used against them. The result was that they gave as little information as possible, and felt, as one of them expressed it to me, that they 'had enough to do to resist attacks'.[*]

Beatrice Webb's remarks are not a very objective assessment of the treatment of witnesses by the more academic commissioners, or of the role the chair played in preventing such treatment. Tom Mann's later recollections are sufficient to cast serious doubts on Beatrice Webb's aspersions on the role of the chairman: 'The Duke made an excellent chairman. He never tried to browbeat a witness, or to take advantage of any clumsiness of expression. Sometimes, of course, a commissioner or a witness would show irascibility. On such occasions the Duke would interpose with a question that invariably damped the ardour of one or other of the disputants; but his action was so tactful that no awkwardness was left behind. The other three chairmen, one for each subcommittee, were Lord Derby, Sir David Dale, and Mr. Mundella. Sir David Dale was particularly suave and deferential to witnesses. Mundella was assertive and disposed to be argumentative . . . a practice unsuitable in a chairman.'[78] Workmen were summoned to the sub-committees to give 'the facts of their

---

[*] Beatrice Webb, 'The Failure of the Labour Commission', pp. 17–18. Cf. with her diary entry for 24 December 1892, after the Commission had been in progress for 18 months, and not long after Sidney Webb's appearance before it: 'Royal Commission on Labour a Gigantic Fraud. Made up of a little lot of dialecticians, plus a carefully picked parcel of variegated labour men, and the rest landlords and capitalists, pure and simple. The dialecticians – G. Balfour, Fred Pollock, Marshall and Courtney – have had their way. They have puzzled the workmen with economic conundrums, balked inconvenient evidence by cross questions, and delivered themselves of elaborate treatises on economics, history and philosophy to bewildered reporters, equally in the form of questions' (*The Diary of Beatrice Webb*, Volume 2, 1892–1905, edited Norman and Jeanne McKenzie, pp. 25–6). Her hostility to the Commission may not be unrelated to the fact that, as she wrote to Marshall (20 January 1892, Passfield Papers, II i(ii)116, London School of Economics) 'my socialism has lost me the sub-commissionship', that is, one of the four positions of lady assistant commissioner created by the Commission to investigate issues of women's labour.

own trade'. Their membership and attendance record does not support the practice of four 'dialecticians' which Beatrice Webb mentioned. Balfour sat on Committee A, Marshall on Committee B and Pollock (with the fourth dialectician, Sir Leonard Courtney, whom delicacy in her role as sister-in-law presumably restrained Beatrice Webb from mentioning as such in public) sat on Committee C.[*]

Beatrice Webb's picture of Marshall's treatment of working-class witnesses as attempts to trap them in inconsistencies, contradicts what he himself reported as the Commission's practice in evidence to the Royal Commission on the Aged Poor.[79] Marshall's account conforms more closely to the record of evidence which shows only one instance where he sought to draw information from an unwilling working-class witness by trying to lead him into affirming an 'economic conundrum'. The chain of questions numbered 14 in this context, the witness was Thomas Sutherst, 'a tram and bus' man and the subject of questioning the requisite wage a municipality should pay after it had 'nationalised' local public transport. During his examination, Marshall tried to get Sutherst to admit that the wage he proposed was far too high, and would result in a ridiculous number of applications for new positions which, at one stage, Marshall in his questions estimated at approximately three million. His attempt was unsuccessful as Sutherst skilfully parried Marshall's probing for the answers he wanted.[80]

Beatrice Webb's reference in her review of the Commission to 'Professor Marshall's statistical inquiries'[81] is likewise misleading in the context of Marshall's questioning as a whole. It is particularly misplaced if applied to Marshall's questioning of expert witnesses at the end of 1892, when the Commission was sitting as a whole. These included Dr Ogle, the Superintendent of Statistics in the General Registrar's Office (27 October), Dr Gould, the American Labour Statistician (2 December) and Sir Robert Giffen (24 January and 2 February 1893). Marshall was obviously well placed to ask questions about the adequacy or otherwise of industrial and labour statistics, a matter of long-standing concern for him, as shown by the fact he had raised it in his evidence before the Gold and Silver Commission.[82] Her charge is more pertinent to Marshall's attempts to gain quantitative estimates from working witnesses on things he was interested in of which his questioning of Ben Tillett is an example, and a characteristic of his questioning confirmed by Tom Mann.

Mann's recollections about Marshall as commissioner appear more in character. He saw Marshall as a 'very diligent commissioner, [who] gave close attention to all the evidence. It was obvious that his questions were carefully elaborated beforehand. The Professor had an academic and somewhat pedantic style'.[¶] In making the comment, Mann undoubtedly

---

[*] See the entry for 24 December 1892 in Beatrice Webb's diary quoted above, p. 364, n*. This mentions Courtney with Balfour, Pollock and Marshall among the Commission's dialecticians, suggesting her major attendance at the sittings of the Commission was occasioned by its hearing of her husband that month. All four 'dialecticians' were present on this occasion and their treatment of Webb conforms to the practice she generalised to their treatment of all working-class witnesses. As Mann noted later (*Memoirs*, p. 101), 'When Sidney Webb was examined by Marshall, the witness showed unmistakable signs of annoyance, and frequently replied in curt and satirical terms.' Cf. Drage, 'Mrs. Webb's Attack', p. 461, and on the manner in which Courtney was prone to take evidence, 'questioning à la Socrates', see J.S. Nicholson, *Money and Monetary Problems*, p. 404.

[¶] *Tom Mann's Memoirs*, p. 101. In this context it is interesting to note that Marshall wrote on 20 October 1891, when the Commission was about to resume in a few weeks, that 'my good friend Mr. Tom Mann has been making about as much new history at the wharves during the vacation as we have been able to unravel during the session'. Marshall to Jowett, 20 October 1891, Jowett Papers, Balliol College, Mann's correspondence with Marshall is

recalled the dogged manner in which Marshall had pursued him on the concept of 'surplus' population when he himself was examined in November 1892 before the Commission as a whole. Marshall asked him to elucidate the nature and causes of unemployment, the effects of shorter working hours on output, on wages and on the state of demand, as well as on the use workers would make of their increased leisure time, the composition of the unemployed, emigration as a remedy to unemployment and other remedies for unemployment such as the 'socialist' reorganisation of industry and of marketing. Mann's evidence lasted for three whole days, during which he faced 1,500 questions, of which Marshall contributed around 180. In many cases, Marshall's questions are as revealing as the answers and, not infrequently, considerably longer.*

Mann's appearance before the Commission was followed by that of Sidney Webb. This shows Marshall at his pedantic worst. It also confirms Mann's shrewd observation that Webb's responses revealed a considerable amount of hostility to Marshall. Excerpts from this exchange further help to explain Beatrice Webb's subsequent hostility to 'dialectician' Marshall, as does the fact that Marshall's interrogation of Webb was interspersed by supplementary questions from Courtney and Pollock and followed that by Balfour. Marshall's first round of questions concentrated on correcting what he saw as Webb's mistaken beliefs on the views of the old generation of economists, with special reference to Adam Smith and Nassau Senior. The following presents some of the flavour.

4074. You describe Adam Smith as having advocated a system of natural liberty? – Yes, in brief.

4075. That is what you may call the popular opinion of Adam Smith? – Yes, only giving it in a brief expression. Of course I am quite aware Adam Smith was not by any means so individualistic as many of those who came after him.

4076. You are aware, I suppose, that he made something like fifty first-class exceptions to the general principle of individual liberty? – I am aware of that, and I am aware that those exceptions were slurred over – I mean quite honestly and unconsciously slurred over, by some of those who followed him.

4077. You are aware that most of the modern tendencies of economics were to a certain extent anticipated by Adam Smith? – I think that is so to some extent.

. . .

4100. Ought you not therefore to regard Nassau Senior's declarations as to the Factory Acts as opinions of a man who was not a representative economist? I should be very sorry to say that Mr. Nassau Senior was not an economist.

4101. Is there any other recognised economist who spoke against the Factory Acts? – I have in my possession an extremely virulent article from the writings of Harriet Martineau to the same effect.

4102. Would you regard Miss Harriet Martineau as a recognised authority? – Miss Harriet Martineau was the source from whom a large number of the people of England derived their economic teaching and still derive it.

4103. Are you aware that Miss Harriet Martineau said that when she wrote her tales, she would not read beyond the chapter which she was going to illustrate, for fear she should get her mind confused? – It is an incident in Miss Martineau's life which I should be glad to remember.

---

preserved in the Marshall Archive (1:84–86). This shows some amusement at how Marshall used the Commission for eliciting facts about workers and their organisations, as something to be expected from 'the Professor'.
Royal Commission on Labour, *Fourth Report*, Cmnd 7063, June 1893, pp. 162–5, 218–29. See, for example, Q. 3,265–3,285 on the connection between wage increases and the level of demand, in which Marshall suggests that rather than showing an increase in demand, Mann had indicated its redistribution, with the higher wages of certain workers being precisely offset by lower profits (Q. 3,276).

4104. Are you justified, therefore, when I ask you what economists of position condemned the Factory Acts, in quoting Miss Martineau as an instance? – I would rather leave that for you to decide.

4105. Putting aside Mr. Nassau Senior and Miss Harriet Martineau, can you mention any other economist who attacked the Factory Acts? – I am strongly under the impression that Mr. McCulloch opposed the Factory Acts. Had I known that the Commission were going to inquire into the state of economic feeling in the year 1840, I would have come down better prepared; but I in my ignorance rather thought that was outside the scope of this reference.

4106. I am referring to this point merely, because so much of the evidence you have given has been devoted to indicating that the economists have rather been behind the age? – Perhaps I may say that it seems to me that there has been a change of opinion among the economists, but if Professor Marshall wishes to suggest there has not been any change, I shall be glad to withdraw that statement.

4107. I am not suggesting that there has not been any change? – Then I do not understand you to contradict my statement.[83]

After considerable questioning on the nature and extent of collective property historically contemplated, Marshall raised some general questions about the effects of collectivism with Webb. These ended with a clear indication of Webb's declaration of annoyance at the procedures adopted in this questioning by Marshall (and by Balfour, Courtney and Pollock); a remark for which he apologised the next day when the hearing resumed.

4163. Do you not think that the general adoption of collectivism would be likely to retard the growth of those mechanical appliances on which industrial progress is dependent? – No, I do not.

4164. Why? – I suggest that if I had said that I thought it would retard them I might have been asked why; but if I suggest no change would take place, it is surely for any other witness to say why it would take place.

4165. Do you think it is possible that the motives for saving might be diminished?. – It is of course conceivable, but not probable.

4166. Do you not think it is probable? – No; I think, on the contrary, the motives for saving would be increased.

4167. Do you think it is not rather an indication of the importance of individualistic motives as a lever by which capital can be accumulated that municipalities have had to borrow from private concerns means of purchasing businesses? – It appears to me that your statement is an interesting example of the manner in which collectivism increases savings.

4168. I do not quite understand why it illustrates it? – If you did not mean it to illustrate that, I will withdraw the statement.

4169. I should like to know whether you can come to-morrow? – I should be delighted to come to-morrow at considerable inconvenience in order to give any information to the Commission, but I must venture to ask to be excused from debating these things. I should be very glad to debate the matter with any Commissioner at a proper time, but I cannot presume to take up the time of the Commission by debating questions and answers. I am prepared to give any information in my power, but not to debate or argue.[84]

The next day Marshall continued his questioning of Webb on collectivism and its implications for progress, on the eight-hour day as a remedy for unemployment, on problems with the State ownership of industries like docks and tramways, and the notion of surplus population as a concept of modern Malthusianism. Marshall's over 200 questions to Webb were the greatest number he asked any individual witness, exceeding his lengthy questioning of Tom Mann earlier that week and of Giffen during the final sittings of the Commission.

A long letter written in early November 1891 from his hotel at Charing Cross to Benjamin Jowett, gives Marshall's own account of his initial experience in taking evidence:

I am now attending at Westminster Hall and hearing a great deal that is interesting, and seeing even more. We are still engaged in my Committee on the London Docks, etc.; and we hear not very much that is new about things: but we see every day very interesting persons. Yesterday, for instance, there was Colonel Birt, manager of the Millwall Docks, an able but impulsive man. . . After him, we had several rather humdrum witnesses, and two of a loud and pretentious character. Of these one was an uneducated man who liked to use long words. I am told he is an effective speaker among the low grade men with whom he has to deal; but his big words were too much for him, and not one sentence in six was grammatical, and not more than one in two was intelligible. But he declaimed away with so much pleasure to himself that at last he had to be called to order, and he is to take the night to think over the question of how many of the employers he is going to 'hold up to approbium'. This is the kind of man who brings out all of Lord Derby's excellencies: his head is always cool and clear, and he manages excellently to keep people within moderate bounds, without giving them an opportunity of going to their constituents, and saying that they were gagged . . . *

After the evidence had been taken, the *Final Report* of the Commission with its recommendations, was prepared. Before considering potential recommendations, the vast amount of evidence the Commission had gathered was reviewed in stages, in terms of the topics into which the final report was divided. These were conditions of labour; associations and organisations of employers and the employed; relations between employers and employed; conciliation and arbitration; limitation of hours of work by legislation; irregularity of employment; a labour department and labour statistics; the employment of women. Such reviews were initially drafted by Lord Devonshire as Chairman, submitted from time to time to the Commission as a whole, discussed by them, and then revised 'to make them as far as possible impartial statements of the facts, opinions and arguments with which they were intended to deal'.[85] Marshall's role in the drafting of the *Final Report* probably occurred at this stage. The minimum wage, trade unions and the irregularity of employment were the topics in which Marshall was particularly involved.[86]

On the first of these topics, the *Final Report* is exceedingly brief. 'We do not think that it has been seriously maintained on either side that the remuneration of work or rate of profit, or maximum and minimum wage rates in the general field of labour, should be fixed by law.'[1] In 1892 Marshall prepared a paper on Trade Unions, to be part of the introduction to the Report of the Labour Commission, but it was not published in this form. Part of its thrust is, however, visible in sub-section 2 of the part on Employers' and Employees' organisations in the *Final Report*.[87] Marshall's strong belief that a complete view of the effects of such organisations should fully take into account 'the interests of the community

---

*   Marshall to Benjamin Jowett, 4 November 1891, Jowett Papers, Balliol College. Years later, Marshall recalled to J.M. Keynes after his first experience with a government inquiry, 'Your experience goes on similar lines to that which I had on the Labour Commission: the preponderance of heavy minds in the management of business that can be reduced to routine is a great evil. The minds of leading working men seemed often more elastic and strong.' (Marshall to John Maynard Keynes, 12 October 1914, in *Memorials*, p. 481). His admiration for working-class witnesses on his own account shared by his fellow commissioners, was also recorded in *IT*, p. 637, n.1.

¶   *Fifth and Final Report*, p. 104. In his *Principles* Marshall endorsed the Commission's views, largely on practical grounds. These included dangers of 'malingering' and the need to implement a state welfare safety net for those not on the minimum wage. He also saw problems with the treatment to be given to families and dependents when minimum wages were in force. The only experience with minimum wage legislation was in Australia (*P* VIII, pp. 714–15 and n.1) one of the reasons why Marshall considered its experience on labour questions so important as he had earlier written to Jowett (above, p. 362).

at large', something prevented by the Commission's terms of reference, is duly reflected in the *Report*. The same goes for his strong belief in the dual role of trade unions, that is, in their 'friendly benevolent purposes'; as well as their 'trade purposes' connected with 'disputes and conflicts'.[88] In addition, his work with the Commission may have accelerated his increasing scepticism on the value of trade unions, particularly because of their 'make-work powers', a subject on which he heard much evidence and argued with trade union representatives during several sittings of the Commission.[89]

Marshall's hand is most visible in section VI of the *Final Report* dealing with irregularity of employment, particularly its subsection devoted to causes.* Its paragraph 213, which summarised the effect of the state of commercial credit on fluctuations of trade, is a striking example, as are the subsequent paragraphs (214 and 215) on seasonal employment fluctuations and the influence of sudden changes in fashions on the availability of work in the clothing trade. The distinction between temporary fluctuations in employment associated with credit cycles and more permanent imbalances in the supply of and demand for labour, although only 'a question of degree' (paragraph 218) has undoubtedly a similar source. Given his membership of Committee B, and his questioning illustrated by his examination of Ben Tillett, it is also very likely that Marshall materially assisted the drafting of subsection 2 dealing with the special case of riverside labour on the docks. The same can be said for the third subsection dealing with remedies for the problem. The balanced defence of speculative activity in mitigating trade fluctuations to match the preceding criticism of its responsibility in causing them (paragraphs 230–31), the comments on the spread of education in eliminating unemployment of the unskilled (paragraph 236), the judicious criticism of 'make-work schemes' on the London docks (paragraphs 237–8) and the emphasis on the effect of a minimum wage, if enforceable, on unemployment (paragraph 239) likewise demonstrate Marshall's substantial role in the drafting of this section. More generally, the fact that Alfred Marshall was one of the relatively few commissioners who signed the Majority Report without any reservation whatsoever, can be taken to imply that his agreement with its findings was secured by his substantial assistance in revising it to its final form. Such a supposition is strengthened when it is recalled that revisions of the Chairman's drafts were secured through written comments rather than oral discussion, a method more suited to Marshall's talents.

Marshall's cooperation in drafting the *Final Report* may help to explain the sanitised presentation of its contents and its relative lack of firm conclusions and recommendations. What recommendations there were dealt with voluntary conciliation and arbitration, the establishment of a Labour Department, improved factory inspection, and some specific issues relating to seamen and agricultural labour.[90] Few reviewers went as far as Beatrice Webb in describing the Commission's *Final Report* as 'a symposium on the Labour question' and 'a popular summary of views, opinions and arguments'.[91] However, the *Edinburgh Review*[92] noted that the success of the majority signing, by bringing together the

---

* References to the *Fifth Report* in this paragraph are given by its paragraph numbers inserted in parentheses in the text. As shown previously (note 86 above) Marshall later claimed much of this for his own in conversation with Mary Paley Marshall.

middle group of experts, the employers' representatives and the three old trade unionists, was obtained at 'the sacrifice of strength, definiteness and consistency of views in the final document'. The *National Review*, albeit prior to the publication of the *Final Report*, accurately predicted that the 'ungrateful public's reaction' to the *Report* would be like 'the girl in Landor's poem at the first sight of the sea,

Is this the mighty ocean, is this all?[93]

Even Marshall's former student, L.L. Price, although quite critical of Beatrice Webb's judgement of the quality of the Majority Report, could find little more to say in its praise than that 'the apparent paucity, caution and pettiness of its recommendations' arise from its signatories not being 'prepared for organic changes in the constitution of society' and in their recognition that 'improvement may be accomplished, and has been effected, by the steady progress of experimental methods, sometimes, no doubt assisted and inspired by the State'.[94]

Given Marshall's explicit motivation for participating in the work of the Labour Commission, what was the longer-term educative value of the *Report* as a historical document? Here opinion among the reviewers was likewise firmly divided. The *Edinburgh Review*[95] justified the enormous cost of the Royal Commission by the value it would have for future historians keen to savour its 'copious material in sixty-five volumes for living pictures of industrial and social England at the end of the Victorian epoch. . . . The 'Spirit of the Age' evidently demanded an inquiry on a large scale into all these capital and labour questions'. Beatrice Webb disagreed, citing her methodological dissatisfaction with the careless and unsatisfactory nature of the Commission's gathering and use of evidence, of which their treatment of the eight-hour day movement was the most striking example. Given that few Royal Commissions had 'spent so much money on investigation, cast so wide a net, or produced so great a bulk of printed matter', there was full justification to expect the Labour Commission might have presented . . . a body of carefully sifted materials on the problems of the day as useful, and possibly as convincing, as the celebrated Poor Law Report of 1834. As it is, their product will, but for the volumes on agriculture and women's work, rank in economic history with such humiliating failures as the Select Committee on Manufactures, Commerce and Shipping of 1833 or the Royal Commission of 1886 on the Depression of Trade'.[*]

---

[*]   Beatrice Webb, 'The Failure of the Labour Commission', pp. 2, 21. The Minority Report, signed by William Abraham, Michael Austin, James Manasley and Tom Mann, and published before the majority *Final Report*, is praised for its 'twenty closely packed pages . . . its comprehensive and far-reaching practical reforms'. Recommendations covered poor law reform, regulation of sweated trades, legal regulation of hours of work by introduction of the eight-hour day, improvement in factory legislation, better conditions for seamen and rural workers, employers' liability for accidents, assistance for the unemployed, and publicly provided sanitary housing for all citizens. These resembled trade union programmes prepared without the benefit of the Commission and even more show the weaknesses of the majority of the Commission for its 'lack of any authoritative diagnosis or definite advice' (*ibid.*, p. 8). That it had been drafted by Sidney Webb, Beatrice Webb refrained from mentioning. The *Edinburgh Review* (October 1894, p. 337) correctly surmised that the Minority Report, if not written by Sidney Webb, owed much to his direct influence. See A.M. McBriar, *An Edwardian Mixed Doubles*, p. 195, n. 177, and cf. Drage, 'Mrs. Sidney Webb's Attack . . .', esp. pp. 463–7, for a distinctly different opinion on the Commission's methods.

One of the majority commissioners, M.P. and 'old trade unionist', Thomas Burt, later remarked that the Royal Commission on Labour had been 'famous for its length, for the extent of its enquiries, and for its copious and costly Reports' but that, 'in no other respect [had it been] memorable'.* Although Marshall's words never explicitly echoed this verdict of his fellow commissioner, correspondent and friend, his practice with respect to the findings of the Commission implicitly supports Burt's sentiments. For example, the chapter on trade unions in his *Elements of the Economics of Industry* only cites the information obtainable from the Labour Commission's *Reports* as a general reference in its final footnote, stressing the 'unique authority' which its *Final Report* 'derived from the cooperation of employers and trade union leaders of exceptional ability and experience'.[96] There are few signs of influence of the Commission experience in the pages of the *Principles* but a little more can be found in *Industry and Trade*, in the context of co-partnership and co-operation.[97] The high educative value of the experience which Marshall mentioned in 1919[98] therefore refers more to what he learnt in general about human nature than to the costly, and in some respects supernumerary collection of data the Labour Commission published from the evidence. Examples are the reinforcing effects of the Commission on his views on women in the labour force, trade unions, socialism, and even investment in shares.[99] A retrospective cost/benefit analysis would have to conclude that Marshall's few benefits from his Commission work were greatly outweighed by the cost it imposed in terms of writing foregone, and that, as he wrote to Taussig.[100] the only way he could have recouped his investment was by writing a book exclusively devoted to labour problems.

CLASSIFICATION AND INCIDENCE OF IMPERIAL AND LOCAL TAXATION

In the autumn of 1897 Marshall responded to a request made to a select group of financial and economic experts by the Royal Commission on Local Taxation to answer a number of questions on the incidence and classification of taxation. Unlike the Commissions discussed earlier, where written submissions were generally followed by oral questioning, the nature of the subject matter on which the Royal Commission on Local Taxation sought guidance was such that substitution of 'paper work for *viva voce* examination', to use the phrase

---

* Thomas Burt, *An Autobiography*, London: T. Fisher Unwin Limited, 1924, p. 304. Cf. Bernard Holland, *The Life of Spencer Compton, Eighth Duke of Devonshire*, London: Longmans, Green & Co. 1911, Vol. 2, pp. 220–21, and W.H.C. Armytage, *A.J. Mundella 1825–1852*, London: Ernest Benn, 1951, pp. 293–6 and esp. p. 371 n.49. In the context of the free trade issue discussed subsequently in this chapter, Balfour, who had invited Marshall to the task, wrote about the Labour Commission,

> I have always had grave doubts about the value of a Commission to examine what I may call 'fundamentals', whether in economics or anythings [sic] else. An enquiry of this kind drags on for months, and sometimes years, and it is extremely difficult to get really competent persons to give their time to it, and when the inquiry is finished, it probably produces a series of widely divergent Reports upon all the really important issues. The Labour Commission, for example, dealt with, on the whole, far simpler problems. How many people are there who have read the report – to say nothing of the Evidence? And what degree of agreement has followed from its protracted labours? B.M. Add MSS 49856 (Balfour Papers), cited by A.W. Coats, 'Political Economy and the Tariff Reform Campaign of 1903', *Journal of Law and Economics*, 11, April 1968, p. 204).

Edgeworth employed in this context,[101] was a distinct improvement in eliciting expert opinion. It also produced a distinct gain for the student of Marshall's economics because, as Marshall indicated at the start of his comprehensive response, the nature of the questions proposed by the Commission made him think 'it best to answer a few somewhat fully, and merely to indicate my opinion as to the rest'.[102] The end product was a clear indication in written form of Marshall's position on many aspects of taxation and regional finance, of which he himself thought so highly that large parts were incorporated in an Appendix of the *Principles* from the fifth edition onwards.[103]

The terms of reference given to the Commission on its appointment explain part of the thrust of Marshall's memorandum. The Commission was 'to inquire into the present system under which taxation is raised for local purposes, and report whether all kinds of real and personal property contribute equitably to such taxation; and if not, what alterations in the law are desirable in order to secure that result' (*OP*, p. 331). The specific questions addressed by the Commission to the experts went in some ways beyond these terms of reference, concentrating as they did on basic problems in local finance. For example, they sought guidance on aspects of the meaning and classification of taxation in general, such as asking whether the 'net revenue of the Post Office should be treated as a tax'. They also sought guidance on the 'tests [to] be applied' in determining whether individual taxes or the tax system as a whole could be described as equitable, and asked for views on 'the real incidence' of the major property taxes including death duties and taxes on trade profits. Only then did they address questions on specific aspects of their terms of reference, seeking information on function and revenue assignment principles for local government and on the desirability of cost sharing with the central government in the case of some, or all, local expenditures (*OP*, pp. 329–30).

Marshall's first set of answers (*OP*, pp. 334–6) discussed general principles on the nature and classification of taxes. His starting-point was that 'taxes are paid by persons, not things', things being the conduit 'through which many taxes strike persons' in their capacity as 'owners, users, sellers, purchasers, etc. of those things'. Some taxed things were representative of a class of activities. For example, the former window tax was designed to tax houseowners in an administratively simplified way;* likewise housing taxation could be seen as representative of more general household expenditure and of living conditions in terms of 'comfort and social position'. Classifying taxes by tax base could therefore be misleading because it neglected this representative element, and hence provided spurious information on exempt activities. The last consideration could have serious consequences if it induced behavioural responses from tax payers inimical to the public good. For example, specific housing taxation as a proxy for more general household expenditure could induce curtailment of house space to the minimum and encourage frivolous spending on items not vital for a desirable standard of comfort. Finally, Marshall argued that the monopoly element in net Post Office revenue implied its treatment as a tax, but one in a separate class of its own.

---

* Given Marshall's support for the 'garden city movement' and the right of access to fresh air and light as an essential component of living standards for all, a subject pursued in Chapter 13 (below, pp. 450–2), Marshall could not refrain from condemning the window tax because it caused people to diminish 'their windows to the injury of happiness and health'.

Marshall next addressed the equity issue (*OP*, pp. 336–9), commenting on the two contemporary yardsticks then in use in the literature. The first of these was the 'joint-stock principle' that shareholders should pay in proportion to their holdings, essentially a synonym for what now would be called the benefit, or user-pay, principle applied to taxation. Marshall confined the use of this principle to cases of 'remunerative taxes', where 'the owners of property to be benefited may fitly be assessed on the "joint-stock principle".' Onerous taxes levied for general government purposes needed different treatment, and the equity consequences of such taxes had to be considered in aggregate. Such a comprehensive approach was required because specific onerous taxes tended to bear heavily on a particular class of the population, while equity of taxation needed to balance out the overall effect of all onerous taxes. In this context Marshall gave support to the progressivity principle, that is, lower average tax rates for poorer classes relative to middle classes, who in turn were required to make lower proportionate contributions relative to the rich. Relative tax contributions should be measured against net income (that is, after deducting for wear and the replacement of capital) so that the income tax was the ideal, onerous tax from the equity point of view. But, as Marshall warned at the outset, there was no definite, and simple basis for equity. An income tax was flawed by its effects on saving, which a general tax on expenditure could avoid, but such taxes invariably had technical difficulties and 'often press with disproportionate weight on the poorer classes'. Given considerations like this, Marshall concluded that 'no near approach to equity in taxation is attainable'. He suggested instead that, in tax reform, greater weight should be placed on the incentive effects of taxation on 'the energies and inventiveness of the people'; on reducing the excess burdens associated with taxes from their distorting effects on consumption and production decisions; and, as much as possible, in avoiding in tax administration uncertainty to the tax payer, 'vexatious meddling' and 'opportunities for corruption' while searching for the requisite revenue instruments. This approach to tax reform, together with the inevitable political pressure for removing unambiguously inequitable taxes from the system, would provide far better equity results in taxation than the search for the spurious perfection of an ideal equitable tax system.[*]

Marshall then addressed issues of tax incidence (*OP*, pp. 340–45). These, he said, were a subject of concern to the 'greater part of economic science', addressing as they did 'the diffusion throughout the community of economic changes which primarily affect some particular branch of production or consumption'.[¶] After distinguishing forward and

---

[*] It may be noted here that Marshall from an early stage in his career had shown much interest in the empirical studies of the incidence of the tax system as a whole which were being prepared by Baxter, Leone Levi and Jevons. These showed that while most consumption taxes on items like sugar, tea, coffee, corn and the excisable commodities of tobacco, salt, beer and spirits were regressive in their incidence, the overall tax system was progressive, as reflected in comparing per capita burdens faced by upper-class members as against those for members of the working class. A summary table of such results for 1842, 1862 and 1882 is preserved among the Marshall Papers (Marshall Archive, Box 5 (4), Miscellanea on Taxation). Using Baxter's estimates for the 1860s, Jevons had also carried out such studies as part of his applied work in tax policy. See his 'The Match Tax' and 'The Pressure of Taxation', reprinted in H. Higgs (ed.), *The Principles of Economics and Other Papers by W.S. Jevons*, London: Macmillan 1905, pp. 245–64.

[¶] It made tax incidence, according to Marshall, a superb illustration of general economic principles. This is clearly illustrated in his *Principles of Economics* and the probable reason why he incorporated so much of the Memorandum on Local Taxation into the text of its fifth edition, that is, at the first opportunity after he had

backward shifting* of a tax in terms of impact on consumption and production respectively, and indicating that a lump sum (unit) and net profit tax on a genuine monopolist were examples of the small number of taxes that could not be shifted (a tax on the 'gross revenue' of the monopolist could, however, be shifted), Marshall moved closer to the topic of greater interest to the Commission, the incidence of property taxes. This was first done from general principles. Marshall warned that the landholder was not a monopolist. A printing tax example then contrasted incidence of local from national (imperial) taxes by indicating the former could be escaped through relocation of the taxed activity. As a tax base, income from land induced different incidence effects depending on whether it could be classed as 'pure rent' or some form of profit, a matter associated with the short- or long- term effects of a particular tax measure. Marshall likewise informed the Commission that rent elements intruded in earnings of skilled workers, including those of the professions and owners of specialised appliances, at least in the short run appropriate to their specific nature, and that classification of income including property income in terms of profit or rent depended therefore on this complex element of time.

After discussing the general principles, Marshall proceeded to apply this theory to case studies of existing property taxes (*OP*, pp. 345–57). His discussion covered the imperial tax on building in general, the Inhabited House duty and the onerous (general) as well as the remunerative local rate. The complexity of the topic suggested to Marshall 'that any general statement as to the incidence of rates must be incorrect' (*OP*, p. 346) a proposition whose truth he then demonstrated by a careful analysis of the potential effects of taxes under varying assumptions. Marshall also showed his awareness of the capitalisation possibilities in property tax incidence by noting that long-established taxes on agricultural land imposed no real burden on present farmers, landowners or labourers, so that old rate burdens should only be relieved on new building and other fresh investment, in order to 'stimulate agricultural activity, give new employment to farmers and labourers, help to keep the profit on the land, and diminish our dependence on foreign imports of food' (*OP,* p. 352).

One of the few general conclusions Marshall hazarded was the universal condemnation of taxes on the transfer of property, which impinged on the all-important principle of substitution as applied especially to production (*OP*, pp. 355–6). Profit taxation, on the other hand, had a wide and evenly diffused incidence despite the fact that profits were not an economic entity but an amalgam of interest on capital, earnings of ability and work and frequently, insurances against risk, parts which tended to obey different economic laws. Taxes on profits would in any case tend to check the growth of capital and increase its migration through investment abroad (*OP*, pp. 356–7). Marshall voiced a similar objection to levying taxes on inheritance, although given the growth of wealth during the century, their effects were less adverse than expected when this type of taxation was started.[104]

The last issue Marshall broached in this memorandum (*OP*, pp. 357–60) related to function assignment, including tax assignment to local government. It also argued the case for cost sharing between the two levels of governments in this context. Here the scope for,

---

completed its preparation. See also my 'Marshall on Taxation', pp. 104-7 for a more detailed examination of this point.

* Forward shifting changes prices of the taxed commodities, backward shifting changes the income (and/or employment) of those involved in producing the taxed commodities.

and experience of, change in local government suggested the need for 'extensive experiment' and 'cautious change', leaving future generations the requisite degree of freedom in dealing with these problems when they arose. Marshall explained the portent for major change in the division of government powers in terms of the political factor of municipal socialism. This could even require extensive subdivision of governmental jurisdictions beyond the customary one of central and local, and involve experimenting with intermediate levels such as those used in the Swiss Confederation. Technical change embodied in electricity supply and improvements in transport likewise held out the promise of changes in the allocation of governmental functions. This arose from their potential impact on local spending requirements for roads and the distribution mechanism for electric power. Despite such difficulties from an uncertain future, Marshall ventured some general rules. National taxes should not be assigned locally; cost sharing was a far more suitable revenue response to an expansion of local resource requirements, particularly since this provided a mechanism of central control over the efficiency by which new tasks were conducted by local authorities. Subject to this principle, and provided they were 'first-class', local authorities should be given the greatest possible freedom to experiment with alternative revenue sources ranging from beer and spirit licences to vehicle taxes. Secondly, the national benefit content in local endeavours should always be recognised. This applied to education, to water supply and even fresh air. Without ample provision of the last, for example, and of room for 'wholesome play', the 'vigour of the people' could not be maintained relative to that of other nations. Concomitant town improvement in widening streets and providing playgrounds and open space in urban area, as well as prevention of merging urban conglomerations, implied grants in aid from the central government to secure these national benefits (*OP,* pp. 360).

On the basis of such principles, which he saw largely in terms of future application, Marshall had little to offer on immediate local finance reform (*OP,* pp. 360–64). He suggested small grants-in-aid towards the poor rate, a heavier poor rate on land with special site value as compared with ordinary agricultural land, and the imposition of a fresh-air rate for those associated urban improvements which were so dear to his heart. However, he argued that for the time being, the bulk of revenue for local government should continue to come from local rates, supplemented by some minor local taxes of the kind already mentioned in this paragraph. To ease the growing rate burden, Marshall suggested reduction in similar national taxes, such as the Inhabited House duty. An alternative was to introduce deductibility of rates from rent payments by tenants, in the same manner as they were deductible from Schedule A Income Tax. Such a division between owner and tenant liability had the backing of the highest authority, according to Marshall. The growth of local responsibility also raised distributional issues in matching tax burdens with requisite expenditure. Creating appropriate levels of government – Imperial, provincial and local – was the answer to this problem, though Marshall's reasons for this were not further elaborated beyond the preliminary remarks he had made on the subject.[105]

The direct impact of Marshall's memorandum on policy is not easy to assess, though many of his principles of local finance have attracted both theoretical and practical support over the years. The importance of his contribution was, of course, recognised in the contemporary journal literature. Edgeworth's article on 'Urban Rates' spoke highly of

Marshall's memorandum on several occasions, particularly in the context of the taxation of rent. However, he begged to differ with Marshall, albeit ever so politely, on the division of rate burden between landlord and tenant in the manner proposed by Marshall on the authority of Mill.[106] Sanger, a former student of Marshall indicated in his review of the Commission's *Report*, that as a result of Marshall's Memorandum, grants-in-aid from central to local government now had the highest authority in support, that of Professor Marshall. Given the importance of such grants to contemporary local government in Britain, Sanger's comment implies one successful outcome from Marshall's advice. Relative to local government receipts such grants almost doubled from 1899 to 1939.[107] Bickerdike's penetrating analysis of the taxation of site values chided Marshall's Memorandum for omitting to present an explicit analysis of the incidence of beneficial, or 'remunerative rates' to use Marshall's terminology. Marshall's simple invitation to his readers to reverse the analysis of onerous rates he presented was no satisfactory substitute for this. On Marshall's own account, this was far from simple because of the complexities in analysing incidence from that type of rates, as he had abundantly demonstrated.[108]

THE FISCAL POLICY OF INTERNATIONAL TRADE

Marshall's public participation in the 1903 tariff reform debate which in 1908 led to the publication in revised form of his famous *Memorandum on Fiscal Policy in International Trade*, is one of the better chronicled episodes in his life.[109] An explanation for this unusually wide interest in Marshall's policy pronouncements is that this Memorandum 'is surely one of the finest policy documents ever written by an academic economist'.[110] It was therefore a fitting climax to his distinguished career as government adviser, while its eventual publication coincided with his retirement from academic life in 1908.

The background to Marshall's Memorandum is as follows.[111] In 1897, at a conference of Colonial Prime Ministers, Joseph Chamberlain, the then Colonial Secretary, floated the notion of an Imperial Zollverein as a way to cement imperial relations. This was partly in response to Pan-Teutonic and Pan-Slavic movements then erupting in Central and Eastern Europe. British traditional support for free trade together with colonial reliance on protection of their 'infant industries' and their general economic development meant that this call for 'Imperial Preference' in trade gained little immediate support in the white dominions. A minor fiscal measure, by which the Chancellor of the Exchequer in 1902 attempted to balance the budget in the face of the heavy expenses generated by the South African war, brought the issue back to the forefront of public debate. His choice of tax was a corn registration duty, cheap to collect, predictable in its short-term consequences and far less unpopular than alternative means of additional taxation through increasing stamp duties or a higher income tax rate. In addition, this tax had been used by Peel as a revenue measure on the abolition of corn duties, so that only the more ardent Cobdenites and dogmatic adherents of the Manchester Commercial School condemned it as a violation of the 'sacred' principle of free trade. However, the new tax became linked with the Imperial Trade Preference issue when the Canadian Prime Minister saw it as a means to this end, indicating in his own Parliament that he would seek remission from the British government of the corn duty with respect to Canada. Chamberlain responded positively to the Canadian initiative, and in a well-reported speech lamented the possibility of losing 'opportunities of closer union which are offered to us by our colonies, [for the sake of] adherence to economic pedantry, and old shibboleths'.[112] The fat was well and truly in the fire.

Although Imperial Preference gained greater support at the 1902 Colonial Conference than proposals for closer colonial union, the matter continued to simmer in the public arena. In November 1902, Ritchie, as Chancellor of the Exchequer, presented arguments to the Cabinet in favour of rejecting the introduction of such a preferential system if at the expense of British free trade. However, because of the divided ministry, Prime Minister Balfour reported to the King by letter that Cabinet had decided to maintain the corn duty in the 1903 budget and to remit it in favour of the British Empire. Balfour's Cabinet summary was subsequently disputed by some of his ministers. What had actually been resolved is still difficult to ascertain. In any case, Chancellor Ritchie repealed the duty in the 1903 Budget and thereby removed this easy way of implementing Imperial Preference. The split on the issue in Cabinet now became a matter of public notoriety. Chamberlain in particular was furious, and in May 1903 launched a massive national debate through a speech to his Birmingham constituents.

Chamberlain could count on at least one staunch supporter for his policies among academic economists. This was W.A.S. Hewins, from 1895 to 1903 Director of the London School of Economics. Coinciding with the Tariff Reform debate, he resigned his position at LSE to become secretary to the Tariff Reform Commission, a body set up to collect information and propaganda for the Tariff Reform League. Some years before, Hewins had been invited by Schmoller, the German historicist and leader of the Verein für Sozialpolitik, to contribute an article on fiscal change and protection in which he was critical of free trade. More importantly, he was asked by the *Times* to contribute articles on the subject to stimulate public debate. It was these articles, as well as the ruckus in cabinet, which eventually brought Marshall into the fray.[113]

Hewins's anonymous articles – they were published under the simple by-line 'by an Economist' – commenced on 15 June 1903 with a defence of Chamberlain. Hewins's first line of defence was to indicate that the issue of Imperial Union was not a new one, even when seen in the context of an imperial customs union; it had been agitating the mind of elder statesmen like Lord Rosebery for close to a quarter century. Secondly, the older economists and Mill approved of colonial policy, especially as the great imperative in British domestic politics of finding an immigration outlet for her surplus people.

The Monday on which Hewins's first article appeared was an important day for Marshall. It marked the first meeting of the Special Board of Economics and Politics, formalising his victory in establishing the Economics and Political Sciences Tripos.[114] When Marshall read Hewins's article, his day would have been partially spoiled. Marshall was aware of its author's identity because Hewins had told him in confidence before he began his writing, thereby making Marshall's annoyance with its contents all the greater.[*]

---

[*] Alfred Marshall to Brentano, 17 July 1903, in H.W. McReady, 'Alfred Marshall on Tariff Reform 1903: Some Unpublished Letters', *Journal of Political Economy*, 63 (3), June 1955, pp. 160–61, where, writing in response to Brentano's query about who the *Times* 'Economist' was, he indicated that though he would 'have found out ere now' by himself who it was, the author had told him in strict confidence before he began the series of articles, which now prevented Marshall from disclosing his name. The February meeting of the Political Economy Club

Marshall had clashed with Hewins on earlier occasions in correspondence over aspects of Hewins's views favouring economics teaching at the London School of Economics. During this exchange of letters Marshall had taken umbrage at Hewins's downgrading of the economics teaching at Cambridge, and at his opinions on what constituted economics in general, and economic theory in particular.[115] Marshall's dislike of Hewins over what constituted good economics went back further. His personal copy of Hewins's *English Trade and Finance*, an extension students text on seventeenth-century economic history, is particularly heavily and critically annotated, a sign of his hostility to Oxford historical economics at the time.[116] Such personal factors further explain why Marshall became embroiled in the free trade debate against his own inclinations.

Following the first article in mid-June, Hewins's contributions to the fiscal question continued to appear in the *Times* in a steady but irregular stream. The second (22 June) cast doubt on the wisdom of abolishing the corn laws by raising the question whether they were still in the best British interest. The third (25 June) attacked the proposition that wages followed the cost of living as a dogma of economic theory not supported by historical fact. The fourth (Monday, 29 June) contained a further critical examination of the effects of the repeal of the Corn Laws, from which Hewins concluded that free importation could not guarantee cheapness and that British increasing over-reliance on United States grain imports in the last few years was becoming dangerous. The fifth article (4 July) argued free trade was a consequence rather than a cause of British economic progress, and that, with the observable slowing down of industrial growth in Britain, the tariff issue was ripe for re-examination, particularly since it could also be shown that growth in trade owed more to bilateral trade negotiations than to untrammelled free trade.

Two days earlier, on 2 July 1903, Theodore Llewellyn Davies, the private secretary at the Treasury to Chancellor Ritchie, wrote Marshall a 'private' and unofficial invitation to present his views on the controversy. Although special reference to Imperial Preferential Tariffs and the potential for retaliatory duties were to be essential contents, Ritchie looked also for general comment on the benefits of free trade versus protection in Britain's present circumstances and, if at all possible, Marshall's summary views about the incidence of import duties, particularly on corn, meat and dairy produce with or without imperial preference.* When Marshall received the letter, he was on holiday in Austria, explaining the delay in his response (14 July) for which he apologised. He promised he would send a brief memorandum as quickly as possible. In the meantime he referred Davies to his 1890 Presidential Address on Competition, which in part dealt with the subjects of trusts and protection. In the context of his published views on the incidence of import duties, he pointed to 1901 correspondence with the *Times* on an export duty on coal, which had been reprinted in the *Economic Journal*.[117]

---

was probably the occasion when Hewins imparted this confidence to Marshall, as they occasionally met at these meetings and were both present on this occasion. See Marshall to Hewins, 19 February 1901, in Coats, 'Alfred Marshall and the Early Development of the London School of Economics', *AMCA*, IV, p. 138; Political Economy Club, *Minutes of Proceedings*, Vol. VI, London: Macmillan, 1921, p. 137.

* T. Llewellyn-Davies to Alfred Marshall, 2 July 1903 (Marshall Archive, 1/252). Davies' letter is a masterly exercise in cajoling by flattery since it starts by indicating his awareness how busy Marshall is with work already too long delayed and concludes with the wish to hear from Lowes-Dickensen, a colleague of Marshall who assisted with the establishment of the new Tripos, about its recent successful outcome.

Marshall's personal annoyance with the Hewins articles is evident from his contemporary correspondence with Brentano, the German economist. The traumatic energy devoted to the establishment of the Tripos, about which he had been keeping Brentano informed in earlier letters, combined with the 'tariff issue', were, he complained, preventing him from enjoying his customary initial relaxation in the mountains, forcing him to commence work earlier than he had intended, and consequently, he was 'dreaming economics at night!'. Marshall informed Brentano that he had privately remonstrated with the author who, as already indicated, had made himself known to Marshall before the event, and that, although he had declined a *Times* invitation to respond on behalf of free trade, Marshall was 'currently formulating [his] own opinion on some of the chief issues which are now before the country'. This would address some of the views of 'An Economist' in the *Times*.[118]

Marshall also told Brentano that Chapman, his former student, was writing a response for the *Daily Mail*,[119] and that Bastable was engaged in preparing something. This led Marshall to point to two difficulties facing persons replying to Hewins's articles. First, their author had not proposed his own scheme. He had in fact not fully declared his position in the articles Marshall had seen, leaving it open to view him as a 'divinely inspired free trader' as well as anything else. Secondly, the articles presented their author more as a statesman than as an economist, so that any reply by an economist needed 'to mix politics with the economics'. Finally, Marshall commented to Brentano on the political situation as he saw it unfolding in the light of the debate. He thought it possible that Chamberlain would alter his current position drastically, more openly on the side of protection and against trusts; that the intervention of the *Daily Mail* against Chamberlain was significant because of the paper's enormous influence, especially in Birmingham and that, given the potential for indirect consequences favourable to protection, such as retaliatory measures and dumping, the fight could be a long one, lasting for years if not generations.[120]

Meanwhile Marshall was continuing to follow the Hewins articles as they appeared in the *Times*, perhaps sent on to the Marshalls' holiday address by the 'faithful' Sarah. Article 6 (July 11) pontificated on how difficult it was to derive empirical support from data on economic progress for either free trade or protection, while number 7 (July 16) discussed the effects of protection on German wheat prices. Marshall described this seventh article to Brentano as 'monstrous' and hoped Brentano would answer the German part. He himself could easily publish something on the effect of protection on English corn prices, as in fact he had threatened to Hewins he might do through premature publication of material destined for Volume II of the *Principles*.

Marshall also used this letter to unburden himself to his German friend about his commitment to a leading member of the Cabinet to write a response in the form of a memorandum. One part of this dealt with the incidence of customs duties, the other with the required modifications to the British fiscal system from changes experienced over the last two decades. He had sent off the first part some days before, but was still working on the second. The letter ended by indicating Marshall's continuing epistolatry contact with Hewins ' "An Economist's" letters to the *Times* are increasingly hard to reconcile with his private letters to me'.[121]

No further Hewins article appeared before Marshall wrote again to Brentano to thank him for some material he had sent, and to warn him in the context of the *Fortnightly Review* article Brentano was preparing[*] against advocating special duties on goods which enjoy export bounties. A recommendation of this nature would play right into the hands of British protectionists and thereby be the '*worst*' outcome for the cause of free trade. This was because British protectionists saw German taxes on imports as the equivalent of bounties on German competing exports, so that compensatory duties could be widely applied to protect British industry. He also told Brentano that Hewins had warned him in correspondence that this was the greatest danger in Chamberlain's campaign, because it could so easily be exploited for electoral purposes by one, such as Chamberlain, who was already demagogically inclined.[1]

Three more Hewins's articles had appeared by the time Marshall next wrote to Brentano on the subject. Article 8 (July 27) argued that changed industrial conditions would enforce an 'Imperial Policy' on British free traders and stated that such a revision of trade policy, particularly in view of its importance for defence, was of crucial importance to the British ailing iron and steel industry. Conventional arguments explaining its competitive decline in terms of high British wages were rejected by Hewins, though he accepted the force of those relating to relative freight costs and to British backwardness in technical education. An effective remedy for the last required substantial public investment. Article 9 (3 August) stated that all civilised countries had pursued protection for the greater part of their history, and that, despite the merits of free trade for a considerable part of more recent British experience, changing circumstances would force it to reconsider protection within the context of the empire. Conditions in the iron trade as the previous article had described made a system of imperial tariff preference the best possible trade policy option for Britain. Article 10 (8 August) examined the effects of free trade on British agriculture. It highlighted agricultural efficiency in Britain and associated its disadvantages with the

---

[*]   This appeared under the title, 'The Proposed Reversal of English Commercial Policy', *Fortnightly Review*, August 1903, pp. 212–21. Marshall commented on this in a subsequent letter (15 August 1903), criticising it in the following terms:

> I have just been reading your article in the *Fortnightly*: I have had no time during the last month to read anything carefully. I hope it will do good, though I believe that if the sale of German slaughter goods 'leaves thousands of workmen without bread' in England, it leaves tens of thousands without bread in Germany. I mean it makes German industry much more unstable than it does English. With this exception, I cordially and heartily concur in and admire the article. . . . One little suggestion I will venture on. The English statistics of exports and imports of *silver* are fairly trustworthy, but not those of *gold*. For English tourists, especially those who frequent the semi-Anglicised hotels, take large numbers of sovereigns in their pockets; and these escape the notice of the customs officers. All of these that are not quite full weight are sent back to England; and in most cases by Bullion dealers, who of course report them to the customs officers. No doubt a few come back in the pockets of German visitors to England; but not very many. Our net import of gold, though considerable, is therefore rather less than is indicated by the statistics.

[1]   Marshall to Brentano, 24 July 1903. In this letter, Marshall also denied that Bonar was the *Times*'s 'An Economist', Bretano's second wrong guess at the person's identity, the first being Ashley (Marshall to Brentano, 17 July 1903). Marshall would allow no further guesses since the third had to be right, and could force him to break his confidence. He solved the problems of maintaining his promised confidence by reporting to Brentano on 12 August 1903 that 'rumours are current in England that Hewins is "an Economist" of the *Times*, I pass that rumour on to you for what it is worth', a clear invitation on his part for Brentano to accept it since it was the first time he himself had mentioned a name in this context. On 2 August, Marshall wrote Foxwell (Freeman Collection, 13/224) that he was still 'not yet free from my fiscal problem correspondence'.

deplorable state of rural education, the character of rural business organisation and the condition of transport, particularly rail. Imperial Preference in food imports was the implied solution to such agricultural problems, given that the natural protection from distance would preserve a satisfactory agricultural base in the country, an outcome Hewins ardently desired for social and political reasons.

By the time this last article had appeared, Brentano was informed that Marshall had finished his Memorandum for Chancellor Ritchie. Within the following week, Marshall received proofs for the first part from London, with a request for some minor corrections.* By 25 August, Davies acknowledged receipt of Part II of the Memorandum on 22 August (postage from Austria therefore took more than ten days) and explained the fate of the Memorandum to Marshall. His remarks on the latter are worth quoting:

> And, now, as to your Memorandum generally. – When I first wrote, I had no idea that you would be able to reply so fully, and no definite arrangement was in my mind as to how your answer should be treated. But I had no hesitation about printing it at once when it came in. It is now clear that the Government does not mean to consult Economists generally in a systematic way – in fact, I do not know that any others have been consulted (unless it be the 'Times' pet!), and under all the circumstances there would be no question (even if we had your permission) of issuing your Memorandum by itself officially. So, I hope it will be satisfactory to you – as I gather from your letters it would be – that the position should stand thus: that the Chancellor of the Exchequer asked you for your views: that you communicated to him a Memorandum which was and remains altogether your property: that he printed it for his own convenience, and for his private use: that he, incidentally, for your convenience I hope, supplied you with some of the prints: but that the question of publication remains entirely in your own hands, except that he would prefer that, in case of publication, any reference to his intervention in the matter should be omitted. I needn't say that I hope you may manage to publish it soon.[122]

During the height of the Tariff controversy, Marshall's labours remained therefore hidden. Hewins's statement that, in December 1907, Balfour 'knew nothing of Marshall's memorandum, except that when Ritchie left the Treasury it was found amongst the rubbish of his office, and that he had never seen or read it',[123] therefore rings true. The extent of Marshall's revisions of the original 1903 document for its publication in 1908 is shown by comparing the 1903 version and the document reproduced in *Official Papers* from House of Commons No. 321, 1908.[124] Before broaching this topic, and the contents of the Memorandum as published, events in England from the middle of August 1903 need to be mentioned. These involved the Manifesto of fourteen economists in favour of free trade which Marshall was reluctantly persuaded to sign.

As Hewins[125] also sarcastically noted, the fact that British free trade economists did more or less nothing until their Manifesto appeared in the *Times* on 15 August 1903, that is, over two months after the appearance of his first article and when the first ten of his eventually sixteen *Times* articles had already appeared, meant that such replies were not regarded as

---

* Alfred Marshall to Brentano, 12 August 1903. This also declined an invitation to stay with the Brentano's on their way back from Austria in September and conceded he had recommended in his Memorandum, despite his personal belief in its impracticability, the possibility of levying special duties on goods dumped below cost in England (see *OP*, pp. 414–15). T. Llewellyn-Davies to Marshall, 13 August 1903, raised a query on paragraph 29 of the original Memorandum in which Davies claimed Marshall saw this price effect as negligible, though Marshall described it as probably less than the full amount of the tax. *OP*, pp. 394–5, paragraph 29, fits the point raised in Davies' letter (Marshall Archive, 1/254).

very effective. During the intervening weeks, the political debate over the issue had not died down, and was in fact warming up for the autumn when the Cabinet was to make its final decision. At the start of July 1903, the former Chancellor Hicks-Beach had established a 'Free Food League', whose opening meeting in the House of Commons had attracted the support of 54 unionist M.P.s. Letters to the press, leading articles and pamphlets abounded in the public arena. Balfour had been circulating his own 'Blue' paper, *Economic Notes on Insular Free Trade*, promising the possibility of modest fiscal reforms amidst expressions of 'polite wonder whether unqualified laissez faire was always for the best'.* Balfour's pamphlet with its hints of the end of traditional free trade, following as it did on his speech of 10 June to his constituents warning 'times have vastly changed since Peel made Britain a free trade country'[126] finally stirred some of the more dogmatic of the British free trade economists from their summer vacations to prepare a manifesto in response.

The Manifesto, whose writing was organised by Edgeworth, appeared on 15 August in the letter columns of the *Times*. Its fourteen signatories included six Professors of Political Economy (Bastable, Edgeworth, Gonner, Marshall, Nicholson and Smart), one former professor turned politician (Courtney) and seven teachers of the subject, many of whom were to become professors within the next decade or so (Bowley, Cannan, Phelps, Pigou, Sanger, W.R. Scott and Armitage-Smith). Although many of Marshall's students were among the Manifesto's signatories, there were likewise some missing names. Two of those, Chapman and Clapham, later indicated they would like to be added to this roll of free trade supporters.

The text of the Manifesto held Imperial Preference 'most probably to lead to protection' and, far from uniting the empire as had been claimed, that it would 'engender irritating controversies between the different members of the empire'. It then firmly rejected any proven link between import growth and unemployment, related taxation of food imports firmly to lower real wages and reduced living standards for British consumers, concluding that such taxes could never simultaneously expand colonial wheat-growing areas, encourage British agriculture and not injure British consumers. The last was a conscious swipe at the contents of Hewins's seventh and tenth articles, the first of which Marshall had described as 'monstrous'.

The impact of the Manifesto, 'Professors of Economics and the Tariff question' was significantly reduced from the fact that it was followed by the text of a letter by Price addressed to Edgeworth as its organiser. This explained in detail why Price was not among the signatories. Most striking was Price's charge that the fourteen were condemning a proposal before its details were known. Although this was justifiable behaviour for politicians; academic economists, trained as they were to judge such questions, reduced their authority by engaging in premature criticism.[127] Price's public reasons for this opposition to the Manifesto matched the sentiments J.N. Keynes confided to his diary,

---

* J.M. Keynes, 'Arthur Balfour', in *Essays in Biography*, pp. 43–5, cf. Leonard Gomes, p. 79. Marshall's reaction to Balfour's pamphlet is preserved in his annotations of his personal copy, consisting largely of queries on its factual content, such as his remark, 'not certain' on Balfour's proposition that protection was unlikely to grow less among the nations currently practising it. Marshall indicated the dangers of Balfour's approach as he saw them in a letter to Ritchie, 21 September 1903 (Marshall Archive, 1/258) in which he talked about the 'slippery slope' to which Balfour's modest tariff reforms were leading his government.

Fourteen teachers of economics (including Marshall and Nicholson) have written a Manifesto to the *Times* and other papers in opposition to Mr. Chamberlain's tariff proposals (which are still very much in the air). The *Times* is very angry. . . . For my part I think the issue of the Manifesto unwise and likely to injure the authority of professed economists.[128]

Marshall himself commented in detail to Brentano on his role, and that of others, in drafting the Manifesto. On 18 August he informed his friend,

It was mainly drafted by Edgeworth in consultation with Bastable and Nicholson: I having declined to draft it, because when I was asked to do so there was nothing sufficiently definite to kick against. Afterwards, when Chamberlain and his League committed themselves to the most glaring economic falsities, I changed my mind, and suggested one should be drafted in England. The first draft was sent to me about three weeks ago, but miscarried in the post. When I got the first draft there were several things which I disliked and three or four which I could not sign. So I expected to have to be left out, but Edgeworth was very good, and obtained the consent of the others to those changes about which I felt strongly. Finally Cannan – who has much literary skill – helped in verbal changes. And now I think that on the whole we may be proud of it.[129]

A week later, in the context of a furious attack by the *Times*, supported by critical letters from colleagues such as Foxwell and Palgrave, and a 'superior' answer from Hewins,[130] Marshall confessed 'that one or two phrases in it [the Manifesto] were not the best possible'. Particularly some 'blemishes in the drafting' to which he had referred in previous correspondence had left the signatories open to the charge that they wrote with professorial 'authority on matters in which there is a large political element'. He continued,

On the whole my first feeling that a Manifesto is more vulnerable than a letter by an individual remains. The Manifesto must be short, and yet must cover a large ground. And as no one feels that its wording is exactly what he would have chosen himself, no one is very eager or well qualified to defend it. Edgeworth is in some sense under special obligation to do so. But there are few men as able as he is, who would be so likely to get the worse of a controversy, even when they have the right on their side. So we just lie low, and bend our backs to the smiters.[*]

This letter in August also referred to Marshall's own contribution to the defence of free trade, by reporting to Brentano on its uncertain future. If it was to be published, he would send a copy immediately; if it were only to be 'circulated privately among the Cabinet', Marshall intended to 'bring out its substance remodelled, and enlarged, as a small book'.[131] A month later Marshall continued the tale of his own manifesto. After spending the last weeks of his Austrian holiday in its revision (he was back in Cambridge by late August[132]), to get it 'into fairly good order' from its 'horribly confused' and malproportioned state, without keeping a 'rough copy', it 'was lost in the post'. He continued his lamentations, 'Practically my summers work has been almost wasted. I shall however perhaps rewrite it

---

[*]   Marshall to Brentano, 26 August 1903. Some years later, Marshall wrote to Sir Horace Plunkett, 'I have two or three times in my life signed documents with many propositions drafted by others; and every time I have deeply regretted it.' (Marshall to Sir Horace Plunkett, 17 May 1910, in *Memorials*, p. 469).

again by aid of the original draft, expand it a little and publish it about Christmas. I am not sure at all. If I do, I will of course send you a copy'.[133]

Nothing came of this plan, despite the gravity of the political situation on which Marshall had been informed by a friend, 'much on the inside of politics'. Marshall predicted a close general election result with the Irish members perhaps holding the balance of power, and that the dumping question eventually would spell 'the ruin of free trade'. This was in the aftermath of the Cabinet split, which led to the resignation not only of Chamberlain but also of five free trade ministers, including Ritchie and the Duke of Devonshire, and a general state of political turmoil on the issue. Although saddened by the situation, particularly Chamberlain's 'cleverest appeals with selfish ignorance *all round*', he confessed himself not rough enough, nor sufficiently crude or unscientific to enter the fray in a manner which could promise success.[134] Marshall's scruples on this occasion were probably more related to the specific situation than to the nature of his personal make-up since the qualities he claimed not to have, were well demonstrated at other times.[135]

Duties with teaching the new Economics Tripos and problems in providing it with adequate teaching staff meant the Memorandum stayed unpublished, and that Marshall, though highly supportive of free trade and the exemption of food from all imposts, did so from the sidelines to avoid any further public involvement in the issue. A letter he wrote to the Secretary of the Unionist Free Food League on 19 November, 1903 indicates in public the sentiments he had privately confessed to Brentano,

> I deeply regret that I am unable to co-operate in the great work which the Union Free Food League is doing, for I have ever acted on the principle that academic economists should avoid joining leagues and should belong to no political party, unless, indeed, they give themselves largely to politics, as Professor Fawcett did. I have much sympathy with those who argue that the changes of the last half-century in the economic condition of the Western world have been immense and not wholly to the advantage of this country, and that, therefore, it is right to examine the foundations of our tariff policy thoroughly and with an open mind. About 30 years ago I became convinced that a protective system, if it could be worked honestly as well as wisely, might on the whole benefit countries in a certain stage of industrial development, and that set me on the inquiry whether a free-trade policy was wholly right for England. I have pursued that inquiry ever since, and have gradually settled down to the conclusion that the changes of the last two generations have much increased the harm which would be done to England by even a moderate protective policy, and that free trade is of more vital necessity to England now than when it was first adopted.[136]

In 1904, Marshall further declared his staunch support of free trade. A published comment dwelled especially on aspects of German competition but warned that if Britain followed Germany down the road of protection and cartellisation of industry, 'the real wages of Englishmen must fall to the German level, instead of being, as they are now, a good deal more than half as much again for labour that is not very much more efficient'. Marshall admitted that things had changed from when he first observed German industry 'in the late Sixties and early Seventies', and 'England's leadership was conspicuous'. None of these changes warranted fiscal reform to undo the policy of free trade. Tariffs likewise were not the solution to imperial problems, and in a parody on the 'little Englander' concept, he made a plea 'that our true ideal is to be found not in little Anglosaxondom, but in great Anglosaxondom'.[137]

S. Armitage-Smith, the last signature of the fourteen on the Economists Manifesto, and now a civil servant in Treasury, on 20 June 1908 heralded the Memorandum's ultimate publication nearly five years after it had first been invited. Initiative for official publication came once again from a Chancellor of the Exchequer. This time it was Lloyd George. He had come across the Memorandum in Treasury files, had been particularly impressed with Marshall's arguments on the effects of protective tariffs on the German working class, and had used this in a speech to the House of Commons in early June. In this context, Lloyd George was anxious to have the whole of the Memorandum printed and presented to Parliament, wondering whether there were any objections against this course, such as whether in the interval the paper had been published in another form.[138]

Once again, this request found Marshall in the Austrian Tirol, in that same Stern where Chancellor Ritchie, as secretary, had found him in the summer of 1903. Marshall's retirement from the Cambridge chair by the end of May 1908 meant that summer had started earlier than usual for the Marshalls, hence their presence in what by then was their favourite holiday spot in June. Marshall therefore had neither access to the Memorandum nor to the debate in the House of Commons in which Lloyd George had made use of it. His reply, nevertheless, indicated he felt duty 'bound to accede to the Chancellor's request, although in so doing I am departing from the line of procedure which I had marked out for myself, and am indeed acting somewhat inconsistently'. Marshall here reverted to the line he had taken in public in his letter of support for the aims of the Unionist Free Food League. The professional economist had to abstain from controversy of all kind, unless, as in the case of his predecessor in the Cambridge chair, Henry Fawcett, professorial duties were combined with those of the M.P. and therefore unavoidably committed 'to take an active part in political conflict'. Before giving consent to republication, Marshall pointed out that Part I of the Memorandum had been written 'in great haste' and that some of its contents written at large would soon be found in the volumes on trade on which he was currently working.[139] Marshall apparently also telegraphed his assent to the proposal, since Armitage-Smith's response dated 4 July 1908 acknowledged receipt of a telegram, at the same time accepting Marshall's conditions for republication. These involved a further clarifying note on the influence of protective duties on prices, and a new preface containing the gist of the remarks in Marshall's last letter.[140] Marshall followed up his correspondence with Armitage Smith by sending his 1903 correspondence on the Memorandum to Lloyd George's private secretary, William Henry Clark, to indicate the need to protect Theodore Llewellyn-Davies from a remark he had made about Hewins as the *Times* 'pet' and, more generally, in order to protect the privacy of all the parties to the 1903 arrangement.[141] By then, the Memorandum had been well and truly printed for the House of Commons.[142]

The published version contains both its original 1903 preface, and an additional one produced in 1908, their contents conforming to the correspondence relating thereto already quoted.[143] The first part of the Memorandum then dealt with the direct effects of Import Duties, the second part discussed England's fiscal policy from the perspective of the events over the last sixty years, that is, the time from when England abolished the corn laws to usher in the era of free trade.

The first part of the Memorandum tackles three issues. First, it presents general argument on the incidence of import and export duties on which Marshall concludes in general that the incidence falls largely on the imposing country unless special circumstances exist. Effects of tariffs on the purchasing power of money, which may be considerable if import duties are extensive relative to international trade, and the elasticities of supply and demand for the commodities traded, affect the possibility of transferring part of the burden on the non-imposing countries. Marshall then examined two practical cases of this. The first was the impact of German tariffs on German prices and wage levels; the second dealt with wheat prices in Britain before and after the repeal of the corn laws, both issues which Hewins had addressed in his 1903 *Times* articles. Marshall saw the German tariff in general as adverse to German real wage growth (*OP*, p. 379); he saw corn price behaviour after repeal of the corn laws as generally favourable to the price effects of free trade, provided that corrections were made for both changes in the relative availability of gold which had changed substantially in this period and for particularly bad harvests in the greater part of Europe. Thus high grain prices during the Crimean War were caused by interruptions to trade with Russia, Russian bad harvests and decline in the price of gold, and like those of 1867 attributable to bad harvests in America and Europe and the indifferent harvests of 1866, could not be taken as signs of the failure of repealing the Corn Laws (*OP*, p. 381).[144]

The second part of the Memorandum dealt with the more general issue of the historical relativity of the case for free trade, a matter raised by many protagonists in the debate, including both Hewins and Balfour. This opened by conceding that the great truths of trade theory, as universal as the truths of geometry and mechanics, were misapplied to transitional circumstances, as was realised in the two fundamental propositions produced by the founders of modern protective policy, List and Carey. The proposition that 'State intervention was required on behalf of pioneer industries in less advanced countries' ought to have been accepted as valid by the proponents of free trade in England. This would have enabled them all the better to deny the protectionist's first proposition, 'that Free Trade was adapted to the industrial stage which England had reached' (*OP*, pp. 386–8). Marshall then addressed the bases of the fiscal policy established sixty years ago. Its corner stones were two propositions. Free importation of goods which could have been produced domestically, only reallocated labour and did not displace it with unemployment (*OP*, p. 389). Secondly, only inconvenient import duties were to be removed. Such duties were of three types: duties on raw material imports, duties on foods and other major articles of consumption by the poor, and differential duties imposing domestic burdens far in excess of what they imposed on foreigners (*OP*, pp. 388–9). Free trade in England when it commenced was fortunate in the sense that most duties it repealed were of the inconvenient type; while British economic growth demonstrated that domestic employment growth is more advanced by a net inflow of resources, assisted through the comparative cost advantage encouraged by free trade, than it is by import replacement. Marshall added that personal research in the United States in 1875 convinced him that protection in that country owed less to the existence of infant industries than it did to political patronage for manufactures already strong (*OP*, pp. 390–94).

Marshall then concluded his paper by looking at a number of factors, often mentioned in contemporary discussion, to show changes had occurred which made a more protectionist stance the appropriate British fiscal policy. Although Marshall did not deny the force of the first of such arguments, concern with the increased maturity and responsibility of government as better able to resist special pleading in fiscal policy design, the potential for political take-over by Trade Unions and the other pressing needs for government action made it unwise to devote scarce government resources to the police of what he called 'combative finance' (*OP*, pp. 385–7). Next he denied that industrial development of America and Germany warranted the reintroduction of protection in Britain. American growth owed much to its size and wealth which Britain could never hope to duplicate; German development owed much to that internal free trade which Britain could only imitate through the, practically impossible, device of 'a commercial federation of Anglo-Saxondom' (*OP*, pp. 397–9).

Marshall then argued the overwhelming detrimental effects on *all* trading nations using tariffs (*OP*, pp. 398–402) and that England's early industrial success now imposed costs in terms of 'self-complacency', the price effects of a long-term favourable balance, but that her tradition of free trade in wage goods enabled Britain to maintain a lower labour cost structure relative to her more protectionist rivals (*OP*, pp. 402–8). For this last reason alone, free trade remained essential to continuing British industrial leadership and, when matched with the injustice of taxing the poor's consumption, made free trade in foodstuffs imperative. 'The great glory of the fiscal policy of the last two-thirds of the nineteenth century is, that it found the working classes paying a very much greater percentage of their income in taxes than the rich did, and that it left them paying a less percentage' (*OP*, p. 410).[145] To shelter British trade from excessive protection abroad, Marshall suggested severe trade reprisals if most favoured nation treatment was not reciprocally accorded to her by her trading partners. However, Marshall considered the potential for dumping by trusts and cartels as grossly over-rated in popular discussion. It was also difficult to combat since potential remedies often proved worse than the disease. Last, and on the issue which had initially started the whole controversy, Marshall stressed that the preferences in trade British colonies could offer were but small and of little general advantage. Moreover, in terms of justice, if trade assistance were to be given, it ought to go to poor India rather than rich dominions, particularly since India's commercial policy had invariably been most generous to Britain (*OP*, pp. 415–20). With this emphasis on equity in colonial trade, the Memorandum closed.

Not long after publication, Marshall's Memorandum was criticised in a leader in the *Times*. Its thrust was that Marshall's loyal defence of the 'traditional economic truths of free trade' was an uncomfortable one, since it fitted uneasily with German experience of protection, while Marshall could only criticise American protective practices on moral grounds. In the context of Britain's changed circumstances, his assurances on the employment consequences of free trade were not satisfactory. Even if all the labour displaced by imports was eventually re-employed, there was much waste in the interval of adjustment. The leader concluded, Marshall's 'truths of geometry lead him one way, but the occasional intrusion of truths of another order give him pause and force him in the other direction'. The circumstances had altered since Britain embraced free trade in the middle of the last century. Tariffs did matter.[146] The *Times* opinion was backed up by cartoons in the more popular press and elsewhere.

On Thursday 19 November, the *Times* reported a speech by Bonar Law in Cardiff, which described Marshall's Memorandum as 'frankly partisan' and mentioned it was five years old. Marshall defended himself against this charge in the *Times* letter columns of Monday,

23 November.   Marshall stated his bias in the Memorandum was that of the trained economist and then charged Bonar Law with responsibility for the Memorandum's present republication, since Bonar Law had urged this in the previous June when Lloyd George had referred to it during the debate on the Budget.   Marshall concluded that rather than re-entering public controversy in this fashion, he preferred dealing with the trade issue in the book he was writing on *National Industries and International Trade.*[147]

During 1910, the Cobden Club made overtures to republish Marshall's Memorandum for a wider audience than its official government publication could have achieved.   In view of some interest Marshall's publisher Macmillan had expressed in its eventual publication[148] and because of Marshall's growing reluctance to be mixed up in further controversy and propaganda, he did not agree to the proposal as originally made.   He consented, however, to normal quotation from his work, and was willing to accept publication of its argument in summary form, as the Cobden Club and its proposed author, parliamentarian John M. Robertson, at one stage suggested.   In 1910, Robertson published the summary of Marshall's Memorandum; in 1911, the Cobden Club published a book by J.M. Robertson with the provocative title, *The Collapse of Tariff Reform: The Chamberlain Case Exposed.*[149]   The second work vigorously attacked the views of the subject espoused by Hewins from 1903 onwards, without ever mentioning Marshall's Memorandum or Marshall by name, though parts of his argument were used in defeating his former adversary.

With this episode, the long-lasting fiscal policy controversy closed in so far as Marshall was directly concerned.   Marshall maintained his staunch belief in free trade until he died, but the battle for free trade was lost in the period of economic reconstruction after the First World War.   Revenue tariffs were then introduced as Marshall himself had feared.[150] During the 1930s depression, Marshall did not have to witness the conversion to support for tariffs of one of his favourite pupils, Maynard Keynes, on the ground that they this generated employment.   Practice therefore proved Marshall wrong in the subsequent development of British fiscal policy on international trade.   However, the issue of free trade versus protection remains as controversial at the end of the twentieth century as it was in Marshall's later years at its start.

It may be useful to conclude this long discussion of Marshall's extensive and varied experience as Royal Commissioner and adviser to government by noting two of his own judgements on this type of activity written during the final decades of his long life.   In his penultimate book on *Industry and Trade*, in the context of a discussion of competition and monopoly in transport, Marshall wrote a paragraph on the knowledge to be obtained from Commissions of Inquiry. This reflected aspects of his own experience and philosophy in these matters, especially from the early 1890s, and stressed the importance of expert knowledge in such fact-finding institutions.[151]

The other is a draft preface written for the Fiscal Policy Memorandum, dated 23 September 1903 when its official publication had already been precluded and immediate private publication was still being contemplated. These sentiments, not published during his lifetime, provide further evidence about that ambivalence and indecision which characterised so much of Marshall's life. His years as Royal Commissioner on the Labour Commission, and his active participation to share his knowledge with governments and their advisers when invited to do so, show that for him the art and the science of political economy were both important; and that those who were forging an engine for the sake of arriving at truth, could be excused for taking an occasional ride on it.

I have made it my rule to avoid taking part in the discussion of a burning political question, even if it contains a lengthy economic argument. For however clearly a professional economist may distinguish in his own mind those aspects of the question on which his studies directly bear from those on which he has no special knowledge, the distinction is apt to be ignored by partisans on either side. And if he allows himself to be drawn into the heat of the fight, he may himself lose sight of the distinction. He may at least, swerve a little from that straight path, in which the student rejoices to discover and to promulgate a new truth on a new argument that tells against his own conclusion as much as one that tells on his side. He desires to influence the public. The public will not appreciate subtle distinctions, or complex reasoning. A full discussion of the economic bases of the problem will repel them; and be ineffective. He must lighten the discussion; he must ignore many difficulties. Brought into association with experienced controversialists, he is tempted to work for their ends and to some extent for their methods. If he yields to the temptation he may even begin to adjust his light and shade so as to bring into undue prominence those facts and arguments which tell for his conclusions. His advocacy may then become effective; but at some cost of that impartial sincerity which belongs to the student. But every rule has its exceptions, and the political issues which are now chiefly before the public differ from all others of equal importance that have arisen in this country at all events during the last two generations in the extent to which the leaders on either side have formally accepted certain distinctly economic statements. . . .

And there is one further point. An economist is after all a human being, and has his affections and enthusiasms like others. I have a passion for Anglo Saxon ideals. They are chiefly developed in this country and in the United States. If I had to choose either part, I would frankly prefer the former. But I believe that Englishmen have more to learn from arguments as a part – not the whole – of the basis of their positions.[152]

Marshall's humanity itself is strikingly revealed in this long account of his official participation as government adviser, particularly in the context of his work for the Labour Commission and his writing of the Memorandum on the Fiscal Policy of International Trade. His manner of giving evidence also shows much of Marshall the person: self-opinionated, pedantic, not always sure of the details, unsure of himself when action is required and most capable when, from the comfort and safety of his Balliol Croft study, he could pontificate on the theory and general principles of the case. The contributions he made to government disclose many principles which otherwise would not have been published during his lifetime. This is especially the case with his monetary evidence and his taxation economics. Whether the time spent on this type of activity in the end was worth it, is a difficult judgement to make. Although it can be easily argued that the time involved in the Labour Commission took him from his own academic writing, and was significantly to blame for the non-appearance of Volume II of the *Principles*, his prevarications in writing were such that even had he not involved himself in this type of work, and that may have been difficult given his status, the second volume may well have remained unwritten. Be that as it may, the Royal Commissions present the Professor as witness in a variety of interesting ways, as expert and even as fact gatherer with the occasional axe to grind on his own account. They likewise enable an interesting insight into Marshall's associations with men of affairs in business, labour, government and welfare organisations.

NOTES

1. Above, Chapter 9, pp. 280–81; below Chapter 14, pp. 497–8.
2. Mary Paley Marshall, 'Notes for J.M. Keynes' (KMF), the essentials of which were reproduced in Keynes's Memoir on Marshall, p. 217; Marshall to Cunynghame, 14 June 1903 (in *Memorials*, pp. 447–8) and see J.K. Whitaker, 'The Economics of Defence in British Political Economy 1908–1914', in Craufurd D. Goodwin (ed.), *Economy and National Security: A History of their Interaction*, Durham N.C.: Duke University Press, esp. pp. 51–2.
3. See below, Chapter 12, pp. 429–30; 437; Chapter 19, p. 718.
4. J.M. Keynes, 'Alfred Marshall', pp. 207–8, gives less than two pages to this aspect of his life, largely in the context of the interruptions to his writings caused by this type of work, particularly that associated with the Labour Commission. Cf. John Whitaker, 'What Happened to the second volume of the *Principles*? The thorny path to Marshall's Last Books', in *Centenary Essays on Alfred Marshall*, esp. pp. 197–8. I have given a more detailed treatment of the subject in my 'Alfred Marshall and the Labour Commission', *European Journal of the History of Economic Thought*, 1(2), 1994, pp. 272–95.
5. See Walter Bagehot, *Some Articles on the Depreciation of Silver and Topics Associated with it*, reprinted from the *Economist*, London: Henry S. King, 1877; Robert Giffen, 'Notes on the Depreciation of Silver', in Robert Giffen, *Essays in Finance*, London: George Bell, 1882, pp. 197–207, p. 197 of which contains the summary of causes listed in the text.
6. This is demonstrable from the Sauerbeck-*Statist* index of wholesale prices, and the index of retail prices prepared by G.H. Wood in 1909, as reproduced in B.R. Mitchell, *Abstract of British Historical Statistics*, Cambridge: at the University Press, 1962, pp. 343–4, 474–5.
7. François Crouzet, *The Victorian Economy*, London: Methuen, 1982, Chapter 12, esp. pp. 372–6, 387–90 and the references there cited; S.B. Saul, *The Myth of the Great Depression 1876–1896*, London: Macmillan, 1985.
8. Feinstein's estimates of net national income show absolute declines from 1882 to 1885 with recovery starting in 1886, but such data were then of course not available. B.R. Mitchell, *Abstract of British Historical Statistics*, p. 367.
9. Marshall had presented this plan at the Political Economy Club in February 1887; it was first published in the *Contemporary Review*, March 1887 and is reprinted in *Memorials*, pp. 188–211. Marshall submitted this paper to the Gold and Silver Commission as part of his written evidence, and during the course of his oral examination by the Commission he was severely questioned on its proposals, as mentioned in more detail below.
10. *OP*, p. 3; JNKD, 19 May 1886: 'The Royal Commission are after all going to print the answers they have received to their currency questions. I have sent my answers to Marshall and he thinks them good. He has also sent me his own answers which are exceedingly interesting.'
11. Marshall's evidence on the impact of the depression on wage earners has been called 'complacent', signalling 'the remoteness of Cambridge'. H.M. Lynd, *England in the Eighteen-eighties*, London: Frank Cass, 1968, p. 121. For a critical evaluation of Marshall's trade cycle theory, largely embodied in the chapter of *EOI* from which these extracts were taken, see J.N. Wolfe, 'Marshall and the Trade Cycle', *AMCA*, IV, pp. 82–94, esp. pp. 83–4.
12. See note 9 above. In the evidence presented to the 1886 Commission Marshall reproduced an earlier version of this proposal which he had put forward in his address to the Remuneration Conference in 1885 (see p. 345 above, n*.).
13. This was a matter more heatedly discussed before the Gold and Silver Commission in 1887, discussed below, perhaps because of the criticism it had received elsewhere. For a sympathetic evaluation, see J. Bonar, 'Ricardo's Ingot Plan: a Centenary Tribute', *Economic Journal*, 33 (3), September 1923, pp. 281–304.
14. *OP*, pp. 65–85. Marshall's argument that there was no bounty involved depended on the fact that neither comparative advantage nor relative prices were affected by changes in the gold price of silver. However, he accepted the proposition that where final commodity price changes were substantially greater than those in costs, a redistribution of income would necessarily occur, a redistribution favourable to the working classes when prices were falling. See especially his answers to Q. 9,754, 9,759 and 9,762.
15. Above, Chapter 7, pp. 206–7. Marshall's point was revived in a paper by Paolo Sylos Labini, 'Precarious Employment in Sicily', *International Labour Review*, March 1964, pp. 268–85, esp. p. 271 n.2.
16. 'Note by Professor Marshall on Professor Nicholson's Paper', 30 June 1888, pp. 142–3. A copy is preserved in the Marshall Library. In his Memorandum, 'General Work since Arrival at Cambridge' (Marshall Archive, Large Brown Box, Item 33), Marshall explained he wrote his comment on Nicholson for the private use of the Commissioners only. It is therefore not included with the printed Report of the Gold and Silver Commission. Marshall also wrote this to John Neville Keynes, 23 June 1888, Marshall Archive, 1:69. For a comprehensive

account of Nicholson's monetary views, see his *A Treatise on Money and Essays on Monetary Problems*, London: A & C Black, 1895.

17. Marshall, letter to the *Times*, 25 January 1889. The letter was quoted in a *Times* editorial (17 January). This led to an exchange of letters (28, 30 January) with Chaplin, one of the Gold and Silver commissioners, who had questioned Marshall assiduously on this point (*OP*, pp. 82–5 and cf. p. 75).

18. 'Remedies for Fluctuations in General Prices', pp. 204–11; *OP*, pp. 9–16, 31; the *Economist*, 5 March 1887, pp. 303–4. As editor of the *Economist*, Bagehot had attacked Jevons's proposal for such a tabular standard in 1875. Walter Bagehot, 'A New Standard of Value', *Economic Journal*, 2 (7), September 1892, pp. 472–7 (reprinting the material originally in the *Economist*) and W.S. Jevons, *Money and the Mechanism of Exchange*, London: Kegan Paul, Trench, Trubner & Company, 1875 [1902], Chapter XXV.

19. Alfred Marshall to the *Economist*, 8 March 1887, in the *Economist*, 12 March 1887.

20. The *Economist*, 12 March 1887, p. 335.

21. Above, p. 348.

22. R. Giffen, 'Fancy Monetary Standards', *Economic Journal*, 2 (7), 1892, pp. 463–74; cf. D. Laidler, 'Marshall and the Development of Monetary Economics', p. 66 n.23.

23. Alfred Marshall to Foxwell, 17 February 1890 (Freeman Collection 6/124). Two years later, Marshall wrote Giffen (19 April 1894, Freeman Collection, 8/127) in connection with an argument he was having with Foxwell on Giffen's precise views on the construction of index numbers, on the importance of price stability as a policy objective, and on the significance of a fall in the Indian exchange for explaining declines in British trade. Giffen's response to these questions, if made in writing, has not been preserved, though a letter by Marshall to Foxwell on 1 May 1894 (Freeman Collection, 7/127) reports that Giffen in general supported Marshall's interpretation of Giffin's views and not that of Foxwell. In June 1886, Marshall had corresponded with Giffen on his symmetallist scheme (Marshall Archives, 1/284, 285), in which Giffen at that stage showed a decided interest.

24. Marshall to Irving Fisher, 15 October 1912, in *Memorials of Alfred Marshall*, p. 478. In two previous letters to Fisher, Marshall had briefly explained his 1887 scheme about which Fisher had asked, saying that it departed but little from similar schemes suggested by Lowe, Scrope, Jevons and Walras, and indicated that now (1911), he was 'even more desirous that every country should have an official "unit" of general purchasing power' (Marshall to Fisher, 16 September 1911, in *Memorials*, p. 476 and cf. his letter to Fisher, 14 October 1912, in *ibid.*, p. 477.) It may be noted that Marshall's 1912 recollection to Fisher of Giffen's views on his scheme is implicitly contradicted by his earlier letter of September 1911. This connected Marshall's scheme with the Jevonian one at which Giffen's critique had been explicitly directed. It likewise conflicts with his earlier recollections on the matter written to Foxwell in 1890. See also below, Chapter 19, pp. 720, 721.

25. These letters appeared on 16 January 1889 (Giffen) and 7 January 1889 (Foxwell's response). Giffen described it as a scandal that in the country of Locke, Adam Smith, Lord Liverpool, and Ricardo, the idea of fixed ratio bimetallism should be taken seriously. It was this phrase Foxwell attacked, and where he hinted that Giffen's remark seemed an attempt to stifle discussion.

26. Henry Beeton (1851–1934), was a prominent figure in the stockbroking community and electricity supply industry throughout his life, and a regular *Times* correspondent, in addition pursuing interests which varied from pig breeding to Reading University. Beeton became a life member of the British Economic Association in the early 1890s and was a prominent member of the Hampstead economic discussion group on which see below, Chapter 13, p. 468. During the 1880s and early 1890s, Beeton was an active participant in the Bimetallist debates and wrote two books, now largely forgotten, on the subject. In an earlier letter to Foxwell about possible publication of his Henry George Lectures, Marshall referred to a 'talk with Beeton [who] was not hard headed. He seemed to me to swallow everything in George', Marshall to Foxwell, 22 July 1883 (Marshall Archive, Foxwell 1/42).

27. Foxwell to Beeton, 4 April 1894; Marshall Archive, Miscellaneous Correspondence 1:13. W.H. Houldsworth was an M.P. at the time, whom Marshall probably met at the 1885 Remuneration Conference, see H.M. Lynd, *England in the Eighteen-eighties*, p. 116. A copy of the Manifesto is preserved in the Marshall Library.

28. Foxwell to Beeton, 24 April 1894, Marshall Archive, Misc. 1:14.

29. Marshall to Bowley, 3 March 1901, in *Memorials*, p. 423.

30. Mary Paley Marshall, 'MSS Notes' (NCA).

31. *P* I, pp. 627–8. The source was Fisher's *Appreciation and Interest*, London: Macmillan, 1896, pp. 627–8. but as Laidler ('Marshall and the Development of Monetary Economics', p. 61) has pointed out, Fisher's work developed the nominal–real distinction to shed light on the 'paradoxical empirical association between high prices and high interest rates and low prices and low interest rates' in a manner which Marshall was not to do until after he had read Fisher's book. For Marshall's later correspondence with Fisher on the tabular standard; see above, n.24; cf. Laidler, *ibid.*, pp. 71–2.

32. Marshall's efforts in enhancing the economics education opportunities at Cambridge for Indian civil servants was mentioned in Chapter 10 (above, p. 330); that Marshall expressed such desires publicly in 1899 outside the university arena is interesting in the context of his by then imminent drive for a separate Economics and Political Sciences Tripos (discussed below, Chapter 15), but see his letter to Darwin in March 1899, there quoted (pp. 539–40).

33. Below, Chapter 19, esp. pp. 717–18, and see the references cited above, p. 348 and n*.

34. *OP*, pp. 197–204 reprints Marshall's preliminary submission, pp. 205–62 print his oral evidence in cross-examination.

35. A.M. McBriar, *An Edwardian Mixed Doubles*, pp. 65–73, esp. pp. 70–71; C.L. Mowat, *The Charity Organisation Society*, pp. 140–4, Helen Bosanquet, *Social work in London 1869–1912*, London, 1914, re-issued Brighton: Harvester Press, 1973, pp. 287–95 and her, *The Strength of the People*, London: Macmillan, second edition, 1903, pp. 175, 197–202.

36. *P* I, pp. 2–4; these pages remained virtually unchanged in subsequent editions. The distinction Marshall drew in these pages between paupers and the poor was a real one in the 1890s: paupers were persons in receipt of poor law relief; the poor were defined by a poverty line in terms of income, based on the statistical work of Charles Booth. W.A. Hunter, 'Outdoor Relief: Is it so very Bad', *Contemporary Review*, 45, 1894, p. 309, gives a table based on Booth's data which shows that for five areas of London covered in Booth's study, the number of poor exceed the number of paupers by more than tenfold.

37. Alfred Marshall, 'The Poor Law in relation to State-aided Pensions', *Economic Journal*, 2 (2), June 1892, pp. 186–91; Bernard Bosanquet, 'The Limitations of the Poor Law', *Economic Journal*, 2 (3), September 1892, pp. 368–71, Alfred Marshall, 'Poor Law Reform', *Economic Journal*, *Ibid.*,, pp. 371–9. Bosanquet, an Oxford philosopher and associate of T.H. Green, resigned his Balliol Fellowship in 1881 to concentrate on social work, becoming in fact the 'theorist' and a leading 'committee-man councillor' of the C.O.S. In 1895, he married Helen Dendy, Marshall's student at Cambridge in the 1880s. See A.M. McBriar, *An Edwardian Mixed Doubles*, pp. 1–10.

38. By McBriar, *Ibid.*, p. 567, who also summarises the debate in the *Economic Journal*, ibid., pp. 67–73.

39. *EOI*, pp. 32–5. In the last paragraph, Marshall praised Octavia Hill's work, and that of like-minded volunteer social workers, in contributing to decision-making rules for discovering deserving cases, quoting the rules she had devised (*ibid.*, p. 35) which he had cited with great approval in his 1873 Cambridge lectures to women (see above, Chapter 9). His copy of her book, *Homes for the London Poor*, is preserved in the Marshall Library. For further discussion of this distinction, see G. Stedman Jones, *Outcast London*, esp. pp. 298–304.

40. E.g. J. Chamberlain, 'Old-Age Pensions', *National Review*, XVIII, No. 108, February 1892, pp. 721–39; Samuel A. Barnett, 'Poor Law Reform', *Contemporary Review*, LXIII, 1893, pp. 322–34, which reiterated a proposal, his wife later recalled (*Canon Barnett, his Life, Work and Friends*, London: John Murray, 1918, Vol. II, pp. 282–3) as first put forward in 1883; Edward Cooper, 'A National Pension Fund', *Fortnightly Review*, L, 1891, pp. 516–24 and the survey by John Graham Brooks on 'Old Age Pensions in England', *Quarterly Journal of Economics*, 6 (4), July 1892, pp. 417–35. References to Booth's scheme, to which Marshall was sympathetic, are provided later. See also *OP*, pp. 244–5, with its reference to the scheme by the Rev. Moore Ede, one of Marshall's former students. When Moore Ede was Hulsean lecturer at Cambridge in 1895, he dedicated the published version of his lectures on 'The Church and Town Problems' to 'Alfred Marshall, who by his stimulating teaching first aroused the interest of the author in social questions'.

41. Charles Booth, 'Enumeration and Classification of Paupers, and State Pensions for the Aged', *Journal of the Royal Statistical Society*, LIV, December 1891, pp. 600–643, the aged pension proposal of a 5s. a week universal benefit for those aged 65, to be financed from 1.7 per cent on the income tax was presented in the final part of the paper. Marshall's comments were reported in the *Journal of the Royal Statistical Society*, LV, March 1892, pp. 60–63.

42. Belinda Norman-Butler, *Victorian Aspirations*, p. 119, where Lady Darwin's letter (11 January 1892) and Mary Booth's diary (16 December 1891) are quoted. Loch's hostile comments were published in the *Journal of the Royal Statistical Society*, LV, March 1892, pp. 57–8 while the adjourned, highly critical discussion, was reported in *ibid.*, pp. 63–79. Ten persons objected to Booth's proposal on the grounds of either its impracticality, its incipient 'socialism' or its detrimental consequences for thrift. Marshall corresponded with Booth on the subject in 1892, of which only Booth's side appears to have survived (Booth Papers, London University Library, MS797, I/1324–5).

43. Alfred Marshall, 'The Poor Law in Relation to State-Aided Pensions', *Economic Journal*, 2 (6), June 1892, pp. 186–91.

44. As mentioned above, p. 354.

45. Bernard Bosanquet, 'The Limitations of the Poor Law', pp. 369–71; his emphasis in the last quotation. Helen Bosanquet (*Social Work in London 1869–1912*, p. 291) later indicated that Marshall's proposal to amalgamate the Charity Organisation Society with the poor law administration was 'on lines suggested in its earliest days by

Dr. Hawksley'. On 17 December 1868, Thomas Hawksley (1821–92) a medical practitioner, had read a paper on 'The Charities of London and some Errors in their administration, with Suggestions for an Improved System of Private and Official Charitable Relief'. In it, Hawksley proposed a centralised charity administration in each parish or district, with the type of cooperation between this body and the Poor Law Guardians Marshall was proposing. See C.L. Mowat, *The Charity Organisation Society*, p. 16. Marshall's discussion of outdoor relief in *EOI* was aware of such problems, which, in contrast to Bosanquet, he did not see as prohibitive.

46. Alfred Marshall, 'Poor Law Reform', pp. 371–3. The cutting from Llewellyn-Davis's article in the *Manchester Guardian* is included in the Marshalls' scrapbook preserved in the Marshall Library, as is Llewellyn-Davis's earlier clash with Marshall on the subject of outdoor relief in the 1886 letter columns of the *Times*, reported above, p. 355 and n*.

47. Alfred Marshall, 'Poor Law Reform', p. 374. In the context of his plea for involving working-class opinion in poor law reform, he reiterated his political argument on the expediency of this, previously voiced in the February 1886 letter to the *Times*.

48. Alfred Marshall, 'Poor Law Reform', pp. 377–9. Marshall's claim that his idea of cooperation between the C.O.S. and official poor law administrators derived from Octavia Hill may explain its similarity with Hawksley's proposal mentioned in note 45 above.

49. The words are J. Fletcher Moulton's, Marshall's former Johnian friend and colleague, in his article, 'Old Age Pensions', *Fortnightly Review*, N.S. No. 304, 1 April 1892, p. 465; one of the many contributions to this subject at the time. Marshall's position had been critically discussed by a number of people in the succeeding months, for example, by T. Mackay, 'The Unpopularity of the Poor Law', *National Review*, XIX, 1892, esp. pp. 763–8. It may be noted that on the other side of the Atlantic, Marshall's views were bracketed with Charles Booth's as using the 'Socialist argument' (e.g. J.G. Brooks, 'Old Age Pensions in England', *Quarterly Journal of Economics*, 6 (4), July 1892, p. 430; J.G. Brooks, 'The Future Problem of Charity and the Unemployed', *Annals of the American Academy of Political and Social Science*, July 1894, p. 12). However, working-class leader and parliamentarian, Thomas Burt, and fellow member of the Labour Commission, wrote to Marshall (10 May 1892) that he thought Marshall's contribution 'one of the most thoughtful, and altogether one of the best, things I have read on the subject. I agree with it all.' (in *Memorials*, p. 378).

50. *Times*, 18 November 1892, Belinda Norman Butler, *Victorian Aspirations*, pp. 121–2 dates the actual appointment of the commissioners at January 1893, and notes the Commission's hopelessly divided composition. The Commission was therefore doomed to failure from the start, as Mary Booth predicted at the outset. Cf. Lionel Holland, 'The Report on Old-Age Pension', *The National Review*, Vol. 31, 1898, pp. 868–85.

51. Mary Paley Marshall, *What I Remember*, p. 35. Phelps, its chairman and a teacher of political economy, visited the Marshalls on occasions in Cambridge, and was later a member of the 1905 Poor Law Commission. On the status of the Bristol C.O.S. Committee, see Helen Bosanquet, *Social Work in London 1869–1912*, p. 393. But cf. *OP* (p. 237, Q. 10,327) where Marshall seems to refer to the Bristol C.O.S. as not having established a claim to public confidence.

52. These cover the Cambridge C.O.S. activities and those of its predecessor, the Cambridge Mendicity Society from the early 1880s through the 1890s. However, since Mrs Florence Keynes was very active in the Cambridge C.O.S., this material was possibly deposited in the Marshall Library either through her, or her husband J.N. Keynes, or her son, J.M. Keynes, rather than through Mary Paley Marshall.

53. Mary Paley Marshall, *What I Remember*, p. 43. Gillian Darley, *Octavia Hill*, London, Constable, 1990, p. 264, mentions her visit to address Newnham students on 5 March, 1898. The Marshalls' involvement with such Social Discussion Societies is discussed in Chapter 13, pp. 446–7. In 1901, Octavia Hill stayed with the Marshalls at Balliol Croft in connection with the C.O.S. annual meeting held in Cambridge, discussed below (Marshall to T.C. Horsfall, 12 March 1901, Manchester City Library, Horsfall Papers.)

54. Undated paper-clipping in Marshall's scrapbook of the 1901 C.O.S. Conference in Cambridge in which Marshall's speech is reported. The C.O.S. Annual Report for 1900–1 praised 'the Cambridge Conference as excellent in every way' (London, for the C.O.S., 1902, p. 15); Marjorie J. Smith, *Professional Education for Social Work in Britain*, London: Allen & Unwin, 1965, discusses this second conference and Marshall's role in it as opening speaker (pp. 36–9). She also reproduces the whole of the speech as printed in the *Charity Organisation Review* for January 1903 (*ibid.*, pp. 93–102).

55. Reba N. Soffer's (*Ethics and Society in England*, Berkeley: California University Press, 1978, p. 276, n.19) claim that Marshall worked 'with the Cambridge poor as a Poor Law Guardian' is contradicted by his evidence to the Commission. The lists of Poor Law Guardians for the Cambridge Union as recorded in the Minute Books for 1885 to 1900 (Cambridge County Council Records Office, G/C/AM 32–5) does not support Soffer's contention.

56. Alfred Marshall to Charles Booth, 25 February 1901 (Booth Papers, London University Library, MS 797, I/5769). Booth did not attend the conference.

394 *A Soaring Eagle: Alfred Marshall 1842–1924*

57. However, cf. L. Holland, 'The Report on Old Age Pensions', p. 893, which emphasised the 1893 Commission's importance in making the case for aged pensions.
58. A.M. McBriar, *An Edwardian Mixed Doubles*, p. 255. This whole paragraph relies on his account of Marshall's indirect involvement with the work of this Poor Law Commission (see *ibid.*, pp. 254–8).
59. *Economist*, editorial 28 February 1891, p. 266; on the 'new' Trade Unionism and its association with the setting up of the Commission see H.M. Lynd, *England in the Eighteen-eighties*, pp. 244, 275–92.
60. Royal Commission on Labour, *Fifth and Final Report*, Cmnd 7421, London: HMSO, 1894, p. 8.
61. Cited in Lynd, *England in the Eighteen-eighties*, p. 266 n.*
62. For a discussion of this background, see Lynd, *ibid.*, pp. 277–8, 282–3; Paul Thompson, *Socialists, Liberals and Labour*, London, Routledge and Kegan Paul, 1967, Chapter 3, esp. p. 45; and G. Stedman Jones, *Outcast London*, Chapters 16 and 17. Hyndman, the leader of the Social Democratic Federation, in a letter to the *Times*, 13 March 1891, welcomed the appointment of the Labour Commission as a further sign that the age of *laissez faire* was at an end.
63. *Economist*, 28 February 1891, p. 266; C.L. Mowat, *The Charity Organisation Society 1869–1913*, p. 122.
64. Royal Commission on Labour, *Fifth and Final Report*, p. 8; Lynd, *England in the Eighteen-eighties*, pp. 291, 240; Arthur Balfour to Alfred Marshall, 23 March 1891, Marshall Archive, 1/2; *The Spectator*, 18 April 1891, p. 5312 and *Times*, 11 April 1891, pp. 8, 11. See also W.E. Gladstone to H.H. Fowler, 21 March 1891 (in *The Life of Henry Hartley Fowler*, by his wife Edith Henrietta Fowler, London: Hutchison & Co., 1912, pp. 254–5). On its recommendations and those of the Minority Report, see below, pp. 369, 370 and n*.
65. Balfour to Marshall, 27 March 1891 (Marshall Archive, 1/2), Jowett to Marshall, November, December 1890 (Marshall Archive, 1/55–56).
66. A.C. Pigou, 'In Memoriam', in *Memorials*, p. 85.
67. Alfred Marshall to Benjamin Jowett, 20 October 1891; Alfred Marshall to Frank Taussig, 4 October 1895, Alfred Marshall to Cannan, 21 April 1906, Alfred Marshall, preface to *IT*, p. vii, and 'Alfred Marshall, Professor of Political Economy in Cambridge', *AMCA*, I, pp. 148–51.
68. Mary Paley Marshall to Benjamin Jowett, 29 October 1891.
69. *Times*, 29 May 1891, Royal Commission on Labour, *Fifth and Final Report*, p. 3.
70. Royal Commission on Labour, *Fifth and Final Report*, pp. 3–4; and see *OP*, p. 209, Q. 10,202.
71. Royal Commission on Labour, *Fifth and Final Report*, p. 4.
72. Marshall to Jowett, 20 October 1891, Jowett Papers, Balliol College, Oxford.
73. Royal Commission on Labour, *Fifth and Final Report*, p. 4; David Rubinstein, *Before the Suffragettes*, Brighton: Harvester Press, 1986, Chapters 7 and 8.
74. Royal Commission on Labour, *Fifth and Final Report*, Appendix CLXI, pp. 363–4 which also reports the average attendance by each member of the Commission as 61 sittings.
75. Beatrice Webb, 'The Failure of the Labour Commission', *Nineteenth Century*, Vol. 36, 1894, p. 3. Geoffrey Drage, the Commission's Secretary replied to her critique in the subsequent issue, 'Mrs. Sidney Webb's Attack on the Labour Commission', *Nineteenth Century*, September, 1894, pp. 952–67.
76. Useful summaries of the massive evidence heard by the Commission are provided in T.G. Spyers (a précis writer for the Commission), *The Labour Question. An epitome of the Report and the Evidence of the Royal Commission on Labour*, London: Swan Sonnenschein, 1894 and John Rae's brief summaries on the Commission's work which appeared in the Notes and Memoranda Section of the *Economic Journal* (Vol. 1, 1891, pp. 520–24; Vol. 2, 1892, pp. 179–83, 387–92, 552–8, 731–5; Vol. 3, 1893, pp. 164–9, 339–42). The author is editing selections from Marshall's contributions to the Labour Commission for a volume designed to supplement *OP*.
77. Cf. the remarks Alfred Marshall made on this subject in his first published paper, discussed in Chapter 6 above, pp. 174–5. The substance of Tillett's estimate was reproduced in *P* VIII, p. 716. In a subsequent question (Q. 3,669) Marshall clarified what he meant by this line of questioning: 'I do not think the public in general knows that there are a very large number of people on the docks who do work which necessarily makes them bad citizens and bad fathers, because they are so exhausted by their work that it is difficult for them to abstain from drink and other coarse forms of pleasure'.
78. *Tom Mann's Memoirs*, London: The Labour Publishing Co. 1923, pp. 100–101, and cf. W.E.H. Lecky, Introduction to *Speeches and Addresses of Edward Henry, XVth Earl of Derby*, London: Longmans, Green & Co., 1894, p. xxxvii. Hyndman, another witness, recollected differently; see his *Further Reminiscences*, London: Macmillan, 1912, pp. 15–22.
79. *OP*, p. 209, Q. 10,202.
80. Royal Commission on Labour Minutes of Evidence, Group B, 10 March 1892, Cmnd 6795 VIII, pp. 329–30 (Q. 15,942–15,955).
81. Beatrice Webb, 'The Failure of the Labour Commission', p. 21.
82. See above, p. 349, and cf. his letter to A.H.D. Acland, the Liberal MP, 26 February, 1886, in *Memorials*, p. 372.

83. Royal Commission on Labour, *Fourth Report*, pp. 273–4, Q. 4,074–7, 4,100–4,107. Marshall a decade later recalled this line of questioning in a letter to Benjamin Kidd, 27 May 1902 (CUL, Add 8069/M256).

84. Royal Commission on Labour, *Fourth Report*, p. 277, Q. 4,163–9. His apology is on p. 280: 'I owe an apology to the Commission for what I am afraid was a serious lack of courtesy yesterday. I have been suffering from sleeplessness, and I wish very earnestly to apologise for what I am sure was a falling off of courtesy to the Commission, and especially to some members of it.'

85. Royal Commission on Labour, *Fifth and Final Report*, p. 7. The extent of objectivity actually achieved was admitted in the Minority Report by the 'socialists', which was almost certainly drafted by Sidney Webb. See *Ibid.*, p. 127, and the discussion below, p. 370 and n*.

86. Mary Paley Marshall, 'Biographical Notes on Alfred Marshall' (KMF), and Mary Paley to Maynard Keynes, 22 March 1926, where she wrote: 'As to the Report of the Labour Commission, I believe that the whole of VI "Irregularity of Employment" was practically his and especially its §3, pars. 227–241, also §7 of II on Effects of Trade Unions. I remember Alfred saying that he should like to have reprinted VI just it stood but that he thought he had no right to do so.' (Keynes Papers, RES/2/44).

87. See Ray Petridis, 'Alfred Marshall's Attitudes to and Economic Analysis of Trade Unions: A Case of Anomalies in a Competitive System', *AMCA*, III, p. 487. See also Royal Commission on Labour, *Fifth and Final Report*, pp. 27, 34, and cf. Mary Paley Marshall to Maynard Keynes quoted in note 86 above.

88. See Petridis, 'Alfred Marshall's Attitudes to and Economic Analysis of Trade Unions', pp. 490–92. Much of this was a commonplace in the contemporary literature on the subject and before. See, for example, one of the books Marshall tended to use on the topic himself, that is, George Howell, *The Conflicts of Capital and Labour*, London: Chatto & Windus, 1878, pp. 152–5.

89. For example, Royal Commission on Labour, *Third Report*, Cmnd 6894, February 1893, pp. 111–12 (Q. 21,874–81), *Fourth Report*, Cmnd 7063, pp. 219–20. Marshall's changing views on trade unions are discussed below, Chapter 16, pp. 599–601.

90. Royal Commission on Labour, *Final Report*, pp. 97–113.

91. Beatrice Webb, 'The Failure of the Labour Commission', p. 4.

92. *Edinburgh Review*, Vol. 180, October 1894, p. 336.

93. Observer, 'The Labour Commission', *National Review*, 1894, p. 203.

94. L.L. Price, 'The Report of the Labour Commission', *Economic Journal*, 4 (2), June 1894, pp. 445–6, 455–6.

95. *Edinburgh Review*, Vol. 180, October 1894, p. 335. For a comprehensive overview of the Commission's publications, see Spyers, *The Labour question*, Appendix, pp. 234–40.

96. Alfred Marshall, *EEI*, p. 403 n.1. As shown below, Chapter 15, Appendix B, p. 563, the *Final Report* of the Labour Commission was included among the recommended readings for economics students in 1897.

97. *IT*, pp. 291n., 293n., 855n.; I have not found any direct reference to Reports of the Commission in the footnotes to the *Principles*, but there are remarks in its pages reminiscent of the Commission's findings on certain issues, particularly in the editions proximate to the publication of the *Final Report*. See e.g. *P* IV, p. 772 on wages of men 'with grey hairs', the list of 'disturbing factors to modern industry' which includes both the 'fickleness of fashion' and the 'instability of credit' (*ibid.*, p. 776), and the consequence from 'tramway men' working shorter hours (*P* IX, pp. 709–10). Some of these views were present in Marshall's writing before the Commission.

98. *IT*, p. vii and the letters to Jowett, 4 November 1891 and Maynard Keynes, 12 October 1914, quoted previously. In connection with the Cobden Prize Topics, Marshall referred to a letter to Cannan (2 April 1906) that his 'Labour Commission experience had taught him a good deal about . . . insurance' in relation to dangerous trades. In short, the time he devoted to the Commission's work occasionally paid dividends (London School of Economics, Manuscript Room, Cannan Papers, 1021/122–6).

99. Discussed below, Chapters 14, pp. 513–5; 16, pp. 591, 599; 20, p. 746 and n*.

100. Alfred Marshall to Frank Taussig, 4 October 1895 (Taussig Papers, Harvard).

101. F.Y. Edgeworth, 'Urban Rates', in F.Y. Edgeworth, *Papers Relating to Political Economy*, New York: Burt Franklin, 1967, Volume 2, p. 151.

102. *OP*, p. 334.

103. Marshall, *P* V Appendix G; *P* VIII, pp. 794–804. For a comprehensive discussion of Marshall's views on taxation, including this Memorandum, see Peter Groenewegen, 'Marshall on Taxation', in *Alfred Marshall in Retrospect*, pp. 91–112.

104. *OP*, p. 357. Over the next decade Marshall changed his mind on the subject, as shown in Chapter 16 below, pp. 597–8.

105. An undated fragment, 'Division of Functions between Central and Local Authorities', perhaps a draft for the Memorandum on Local Taxation, survives among the Marshall Papers (Box 6 (9)) in which many similar issues are raised. Alfred Marshall also raised such issues in a later article on taxation, discussed in Chapter 17 below, p. 646.

396 *A Soaring Eagle: Alfred Marshall 1842–1924*

106. Edgeworth, 'Urban Rates', pp. 192–3, 171–4; cf. Bickerdike, 'The Taxation of Site Values', *Economic Journal*, 12 (4), December 1902, p. 478.
107. C.P. Sanger, 'The Report of the Local Taxation Commission', *Economic Journal*, 11 (3), September 1901, p. 327.
108. C.F. Bickerdike, 'The Taxation of Site Values', p. 475.
109. See A.W. Coats, 'Political Economy and the Tariff Reform Campaign of 1903', pp. 181–229; Donald Winch, *Economics and Policy. A Historical Survey*, London: Collins, 1972, pp. 64–70; J.C. Wood, 'Alfred Marshall and the Tariff Reform Campaign of 1903', *AMCA*, IV, pp. 312–26; Phyllis Deane, 'Marshall on Free Trade', in *Alfred Marshall in Retrospect*, pp. 113–32; Leonard Gomes, *Neo-classical International Economics*, London, Macmillan, 1990, Chapter 4.
110. T.W. Hutchison, 'The Jevonian Revolution and Economic Policy', in *On Revolutions and Progress in Economic Knowledge*, Cambridge: Cambridge University Press, 1978, p. 114.
111. This paragraph relies heavily on the account by Phyllis Deane, 'Alfred Marshall on Free Trade', pp. 118–19; see also Halévy, *History of the English People: Epilogue (1895–1905) Imperialism*, London: Penguin Books, 1939, Vol. I, Chapter 1, Peter Cain, 'Political Economy in Edwardian England: The Tariff Reform Controversy', in Alan O'Day, editor, *The Edwardian Age Conflict and Stability 1900–1914*, London: Macmillan, 1979, Chapter 2.
112. Cited in Deane, p. 119. Marshall's reaction to Chamberlain's speeches at the time was preserved by Fay, who was then attending his lectures. On an earlier occasion connected with the Boer War, Pethick-Lawrence strikingly recalled Marshall's estimate of Chamberlain as 'a negative asset' worth several hundred million pounds. See above, Chapter 10, pp. 313, 315, and below, Chapter 17, p. 606 n.*.
113. Phyllis Deane, 'Alfred Marshall on Free Trade', p. 120; Gerard M. Koot, *English Historical Economics 1870–1926*, New York: Cambridge University Press, 1987, pp. 174–8, and see Blanche E.C. Dugdale, *Arthur James Balfour*, New York: G.P. Putnam, 1939, p. 252, for the text of Balfour's letter to the King.
114. *Times*, 15 June 1903; Cambridge University Archives, Min. V. 114, 15 June 1903.
115. A.W. Coats, 'Alfred Marshall and the Early Development of the London School of Economics', pp. 131–41, and discussed below, Chapter 15, pp. 542–3.
116. Preserved in the Marshall Library. Cf. Alon Kadish, *The Oxford Economists in the late Nineteenth Century*, Oxford: Clarendon Press, 1982, esp. Chapter 7. The dislike appears to have been mutual. Hewins was far from complimentary about the portrait he painted of Marshall in his autobiography (*The Apologia of an Imperialist*, London: Constable, 1929, Vol. 1, pp. 26–7) despite its opening statement that he and Marshall 'were very good friends, who did not always see eye to eye'. Koot (*English Historical Economics 1870–1926*, p. 175) records Hewins's catty remark to Sidney Webb that the Germans did not consider Marshall's book 'intrinsically important'.
117. Alfred Marshall to T. Llewellyn–Davies, 14 July 1903 (Marshall Archive, 1/253). See also Marshall, 'Some Aspects of Competition', in *Memorials*, esp. pp. 258–72 and Marshall to the editor of the *Times*, 22 April and 9 May 1901, reprinted in *Economic Journal*, XI (2), June 1901, pp. 165–8. The Marshalls had left Cambridge for Austria during the week starting 5 July 1903, passing through Munich on Thursday, 9 July and reaching Stern, their final destination by the weekend.
118. Marshall to Brentano, 17 July 1903. Earlier, 18 May 1903, there had been correspondence on the matter of a German translation of the *Principles* (see below, Chapter 12, pp. 433–4), and the implications for copyright this had with respect to the subsequent volumes, of which Marshall at one stage contemplated two. The nightmares soon disappeared. By early August, Marshall wrote to Foxwell, 'The still peace of mountain woods has taken out my evil spirit and I no more dream economics at night.' Marshall to Foxwell, 5 August 1903 (Freeman Collection, 12/224), partly quoted above, Chapter 7, pp. 217–8.
119. Chapman's four articles as Professor of Political Economy at Owen's College, Manchester, appeared in the *Daily Mail* between 30 June and 11 July 1903.
120. Marshall to Brentano, 17 July 1903. Marshall's comments about the difficulty of determining Hewins's actual position and his lack of firm commitment to Chamberlain's cause arose more in the context of the sixth, and then most recent *Times* article Marshall could have seen, when writing this letter, rather than to Hewins's first piece with its fairly clear support for Chamberlain and others on Imperial Preference. Cf. Leonard Gomes, p. 74 and n. 21. According to Hewins, Marshall also refused an invitation from one of the monthlies to reply to his articles (*The Apologia of an Imperialist*, p. 67).
121. Marshall to Brentano, 24 July 1903. It is a pity that Hewins's letters to Marshall on the subject of the *Times* articles, to which Marshall referred in the P.S., appear to have not survived. There is, however, some Marshall correspondence with Hewins extant for this year. See A.W. Coats, 'Political Economy and the Tariff Reform Campaign of 1903', p. 226 and n.132, which quotes from Marshall's letter to Hewins of 14 July 1903.
122. T. Llewellyn-Davies to Marshall, 25 August 1903 (Marshall Archive, 1/255).

123. See Hewins, *Apologia of an Imperialist*, Vol. 1, p. 225, but cf. Ritchie to Marshall 14 September 1903 (Marshall Archive, 1/257) in which Ritchie reports he sent a copy to Balfour (and see note 182 below).
124. See J. Cunningham Wood, 'Alfred Marshall and the Tariff Reform Campaign of 1903', pp. 315–17 and especially 323–4 n.2 where Wood indicates he has identified the original 1903 Memorandum among Treasury Papers in the Public Records Office, simply entitled 'The Fiscal Problem' (T1/9990FB/14949), arguing that its sections are numbered quite differently and the two parts are headed in quite distinct ways. Comparison of the documents in question supports Wood's contention. The author is currently editing the 1903 version as part of a supplementary volume of Marshall's official papers, for publication by Cambridge University Press and the Royal Economic Society.
125. W.A.S. Hewins, *Apologia of an Imperialist*, p. 67.
126. See H. Young, *Arthur Balfour*, London: G. Bell, 1963, Chapter 10, the quotation from Balfour's June speech occurs on p. 213; Blanche E. Dugdale, *Arthur James Balfour*, Chapter 16.
127. *Times*, 15 August 1903; see also *Economic Journal*, 13 (3), September 1903, pp. 442–5 which lists Foxwell, Hewins, Price, Inglis Palgrave, Venn and Yule among those publicly dissenting from the Manifesto.
128. JNKD, 20 August 1903.
129. Marshall to Brentano, 18 August 1903. Michael White, 'Marshallian Rhetoric and the Giffen Good', *Economic Record*, March 1990, p. 9 plausibly suggests Marshall's reluctance to sign was overcome when Hewins published his seventh 'monstrous' article on the food aspects of the tariff controversy.
130. Marshall to Brentano, 26 August 1903. Foxwell's reply on 20 August had imputed impropriety on his colleagues from London by implying a faculty view on the subject to which he did not subscribe, a similar viewpoint taken earlier by Palgrave in his letter of 18 August.
131. Marshall to Brentano, 26 August 1903.
132. On 21 September 1903 he informed Cannan by letter from Balliol Croft that he was 'working through a large accumulation of print which I found on my recent return from the Continent' (Cannan Papers, 1021:52–3).
133. Marshall to Brentano, 29 September 1903; as Ritchie wrote to Marshall, 14 September 1903 (Marshall Archive, 1/257), Marshall's corrections to the proofs of the second part had been lost in the mail. Ritchie took the opportunity in this letter to thank Marshall warmly for his valuable contribution, the words used when he had sent Marshall's paper to Balfour. Cf. p. 381 and note 123 above, where Hewins claims Balfour told him he had never seen Marshall's Memorandum, very possible, given the Cabinet crisis which occurred at this time, and which would have occupied all of Balfour's attention.
134. Marshall to Brentano, 29 September 1903. For the Cabinet turmoil this month, see the references cited in note 126 above. Marshall's informant may have been Courtney.
135. E.g. in his 1883 lectures on Henry George, below, Chapter 16, esp. pp. 584–6; and during the 1910 debate with Pearson (below, Chapter 13, pp. 479–82).
136. *Times*, 23 November 1903.
137. Alfred Marshall, discussion of Schuster's 'Foreign Trade and the Money Market', *Journal of the Institute of Bankers*, Vol. XXV, February 1904, pp. 94–8.
138. S. Armitage-Smith to Alfred Marshall, 20 June 1908 (Marshall Archive, 1/258). The passage with which Lloyd George was particularly impressed is on pp. 37–8 of the original Memorandum.
139. Alfred Marshall to Lloyd George, 27 June 1908 (Marshall Archive, 1/259) contains a copy of a technical note on import taxes, their incidence and the purchasing power of money; 1/260 the actual reply to Armitage-Smith's invitation, both copies in Mary Paley Marshall's handwriting.
140. Armitage-Smith to Alfred Marshall, 4 July 1908 (Marshall Archive, 1/261).
141. Marshall to Clark, 22 November 1908 (Marshall Archive, 1/262).
142. *OP*, p. 365, gives 11 November 1908 as the official date of publication. All references to the Memorandum made in subsequent paragraphs are to this reprinting. The almost five months interval between request for, and actual, publication gave Marshall plenty of time for revision.
143. *OP*, p. 367, its text of the 1903 preface conforms with the original of Llewellyn-Davies letter of 2 June 1903 and Marshall's annotations thereon for ordering the contents of the material; *OP*, pp. 367–8 gives the text of the 1908 preface conforming to the letter by Armitage-Smith of 4 July 1908. The text of the second preface incorporates the spirit of Marshall's original response to Lloyd George's invitation to publish, and indicates the revising notes he wanted to make to the text as being concerned with the material included under sub-headings A, K and L, the first one dealing with the subject matter of the general note Marshall enclosed with his letter of 27 June (see above, note 139).
144. Marshall's reference to bread as a Giffen good in this context brought him into conflict with Edgeworth. See Marshall to Edgeworth, 21, 22 and 27 April 1909 in *Memorials of Alfred Marshall*, pp. 438–42. For a detailed discussion see M.V. White, 'Invention in the Face of Necessity: Marshallian Rhetoric and the Giffen Good(s)', *Economic Record*, 66(192), March 1990, pp. 1–11, esp. pp. 7–10, and below, Chapter 17, p. 634.

145. Cf. with the account of Marshall's view on fiscal equity given in his Memorandum on Imperial and Local Taxation, above p. 373.
146. *Times*, 17 November 1908.
147. *Times*, 19 November 1908; Marshall to the *Times*, 21 November 1908, published 23 November 1908. The cartoons appear as illustrations 42 and 43.
148. J.A.M. McDonald to Marshall, 22 April 1910, Marshall to J.A.M. McDonald, 23 April 1910 (Marshall Archive, 1/265–6). Macmillan became the publishers in 1926 by its inclusion in Marshall's *Official Papers*.
149. That is, J.M. Robertson, *The Fiscal Policy of International Trade, being a Summary of the Memorandum by Professor Marshall*, London: Cassel, 1910; the work mentioned in the text was published in 1911 for the Cobden Club, London: Cassel.
150. Below, Chapter 17, p. 646.
151. *IT*, p. 443.
152. Draft Preface for *Fiscal Policy of International Trade*, dated 23 September 1903 (Marshall Archive, Large Brown Box; Marshall Archive, 1/252–268).

12. The Long Haul of the *Principles:* 1881–1922

During the middle of July 1890, the first volume of Marshall's *Principles of Economics* was published by Macmillan.* This book is undoubtedly a highpoint in Alfred Marshall's economic career, embodying between its two covers much of the fruit of his life's work. Without exaggeration, it is the enduring monument to his skills as an economic thinker and became a classic in the sense he himself defined the term as work continuously inspiring future generations of workers in the subject.[1] The reviews hailed it, almost unanimously, as the major work of its generation, the worthy successor to Mill's great *Principles* (which on its appearance had gained the same accolade); if not to Adam Smith's *Wealth of Nations*, as some reviewers ventured to argue.[2]

Newspaper reviews saw the book as more than the economic treatise for the coming generation. Marshall's *Principles* had recast political economy 'as the science of social perfectibility'; it presented a 'study of industrial history unusually thorough'; its contents included 'pieces of thoroughly artistic literary workmanship' comparable to Mill's famous chapter on the futurity of the working classes; its publication ensured that 'Political Economy has ceased to be a dismal science – dismal in its subject matter, dismal in its methods, dismal in its conclusions'.[3] It was seen as exceedingly even-handed – the review in *The Speaker* saw Marshall equally 'ready to be instructed by heretical as by orthodox economists', and though the *Manchester Examiner* compared it with the work of Herbert Spencer, particularly his sociology, others, more correctly, placed Marshall's views, such as those on the state, in between those of Spencer and of the socialists.[4] The reviews were not all praise, however. One hostile review criticised Marshall's style in particular, describing it as 'excessively long-winded, verbose, repetitious'. '[A] much more serious matter than diffuseness of style', the reviewer continued, was the book's 'practice of beginning discussions and leaving them uncompleted', a practice its author tried to defend as 'the postponement of difficulties'. More pertinently, as it turned out, some reviewers noted the implications of 'first volume', displayed on the spine. The book would appear in instalments; a hazardous enterprise when, as the *Bristol Western Daily Press* commented, the publication of this volume 'had been expected for years' and, as Sidney Webb told readers of the *Star*, this first volume had been ten years in the making.[5]

Webb's comment on the gestation period of the *Principles* was decidedly accurate. Marshall had commenced its writing in earnest during 1881–82. The Marshalls had spent that winter in Palermo, followed by a spring and summer in Italy and the Alps. Sicily can therefore claim to be the birthplace of the *Principles*. Its conception, however, to stretch the

---

* David Macmillan, 'Marshall's Principles of Economics: A Bibliographical Note' (*AMCA*, II), gives the date of publication simply as July; what appears to have been the first newspaper review preserved in the Marshall scrapbook, that is, the *Pall Mall Gazette*, appeared on 19 July 1890; in its review on Thursday, 24 July 1890, the *Times* mentioned it as having been published 'this week by Macmillan and Co.'. A letter from Macmillan to Maynard Keynes (15 August 1924) gives the date as 18 July 1890, which fits with the evidence.

metaphor, occurred during the previous year while, in its essentials, the *Principles* embodied arduous research and reading for close to a quarter century. During April 1880, six months after publication of the *Economics of Industry*, Marshall wrote to Foxwell that, despite the risk of being anticipated by others, it would be wrong for him to publish hastily,[6] particularly because, as he informed Macmillan in 1887, the book he was writing 'will be the central work of my life; and I shall regard it differently from anything I have written or may write'.[7] The long writing period after even longer preparation resembles therefore the construction of the *Wealth of Nations* more than that of Mill's *Principles*. In contrast to Smith's economic masterpiece, however, the plan on which by 1887 Marshall had decided to construct his *Principles* was never finished, the projected second volume never materialised. In addition, the work experienced frequent and, up to the sixth edition, quite drastic revision, revisions which in minor form continued until the final years of its author's life. This makes it appropriate to speak of the long haul of the *Principles*. Ten years of agonisingly slow writing eventually led to the first edition.   Marshall later described his slow writing practices to Hewins in the following exaggerated way: 'he thought he wrote on average seventeen words an hour and often when he had finished one chapter and gone onto the next, the development of the argument in the new chapter forced him to scrap the former one'.[8]

The ten years of writing the first edition were followed by twenty years during which Marshall prepared five new editions (the first within twelve months of publication), and a further decade or so during which minor alterations were made to the text. The forty years involved in this process account for half of Marshall's life. This is an extraordinary record of devotion to what was, after all, only a volume of foundations or, as Marshall put it on the title page from the sixth edition onwards, 'an introductory volume'.

The book broke records other than for long preparation and frequent revision. The contract with Macmillan for its publication was instrumental in establishing the net book agreement, hence inadvertently involving Marshall, the strong supporter of free competition, in the introduction of one of the cornerstones of retail price maintenance in the British book trade, a form of restrictive trade practice which lasted for decades.[9] Furthermore, from its first publication, the *Principles* has been continuously in print with its original publishers, Macmillan. This was so unusual a feat that the frequent reprints of its final edition required after 1921 wore out the original plates by 1949. In that year, the book was reset with a different pagination for subsequent printings, including the paperback, then published for the first time.[10] The writing, publication, reception and revision of the *Principles* and evaluation of the economics of the mature Marshall follow chronologically from the economic work he did during his long apprenticeship in the subject.[11]

THE ROAD TO THE *PRINCIPLES*

In June 1879, when the *Economics of Industry* was within a few months of publication, Marshall informed Jevons[12] that he would soon begin work on 'a book of curves', of which the chapters on domestic value 'sent you by Mr. Sidgwick' will form the basis. This topic, Marshall informed his correspondent, was difficult to handle without using such an analytical device, but the remainder of the book as he then saw it would have 'curves' only in subsidiary places, concentrate on developing application of the theory and 'contribute to that work of "real"-ising of the quantitative abstract reasoning in Economics of which I recognise you as the chief author'. The privately published material on domestic value, providing the core of what initially appeared in Book V of the *Principles* together with some chapters of its Book III, became therefore the starting-point of the new work from which the rest was subsequently developed. This was the story of the writing of the *Principles* Marshall later recalled to L.C. Colson. 'The pure analytical work in Book V of my *Principles*, with a part of Book III, were the kernel from which my volume expanded backwards and forwards to its present shape.'[13]   A year or so later, around 1910, Marshall gave a similar account of the construction of his *Principles* in a somewhat more pessimistic vein. This described the first decade of his married life, 1877 to 1887, as a 'barren decade' during which 'he lost ground in his studies rather than conquered fresh' so that the *Principles* 'was based chiefly on material collected before 1878'. The chapters on domestic value are once again listed as the starting-point, and when supplemented with 'some of the requisite limitations and conditions' to bring them closer to a 'concrete study of actual conditions', they became the kernel of Book V from which his volume 'was extended gradually backwards and forwards'.[14]

The projected work did not make much progress during Marshall's final year as Principal in Bristol when, given the financial state of the College, his administrative duties were particularly pressing and onerous. In January 1880 he wrote to Foxwell that the companion volume on Trade and Finance to the *Economics of Industry* was being put off, because he had decided first to write a book on 'pure economic theory', largely because Sidgwick was 'strongly in favour of my doing the curves next'.[15]   Later that month, he reported interest in an article on the mathematics of hedonism to Foxwell, seeking advice from his friend on the issue of *Mind* in which it had been published and whether it was written 'by any chance by a man of the name F.Y. Edgeworth. Jevons has lent him my papers on economic curves and he has just written a polite letter about them in which he seems to imply that I should know who he is. But I don't. Do you?'[16]

Marshall ought to have done, however, since Edgeworth not too long before had sent the Marshalls a copy of his *New and Old Methods of Ethics*, for which Marshall had cordially thanked him in early February 1880. Perhaps because his memory in the interval had been assisted by Foxwell, Marshall wrote, 'I had heard of your paper in *Mind* and had intended to read it, but I had forgotten your name. I have now nearly read all the book you sent me and am extremely delighted by many things in it. There seems to be a very close agreement between us as to the promise of mathematics in the sciences that relate to man's action. As to the interpretation of the utilitarian dogma, I think you have made a great advance. But I have still a hankering after a mode of exposition in which the dynamical character of the problem is made more obvious, which may in fact represent the central notion of happiness as a process rather than a statical condition'.[17]   Much of this was relevant to the content of what became Book III of the *Principles*, but the context of the correspondence in which Edgeworth made his debut in the circle of Marshall's acquaintance, may also explain why he later reviewed Edgeworth's second and last book, *Mathematical Psychics*. As shown in Marshall's letters to Foxwell about his publication plans, he appears to have been in close contact with Sidgwick at this time.   This suggests Marshall probably discussed his

Edgeworth correspondence with Sidgwick, especially because its contents covered utilitarianism and ethics. Sidgwick's connection with the *Academy* was mentioned previously as probably instrumental in securing Marshall's first review, that of Jevons's *Theory*. Correspondence on Edgeworth's work with Marshall during 1880 may have induced Sidgwick to suggest Marshall as a good reviewer of Edgeworth's final book, the high mathematical content of which made review by a mathematically adept philosopher appropriate. Marshall's review of Edgeworth's *Mathematical Psychics* during early 1881 in any case shows his continuing interest in utilitarian welfare economics at this stage though, given their earlier correspondence, in an increasingly critical manner. The review therefore cemented rather than initiated a lifelong friendship.[18]

Marshall's correspondence with Edgeworth in 1880 hints at other interests in theory he was developing. His friendly 'thank-you' note in February contained some discussion of 'the meaning of the word, dynamical', another topic Marshall was interested in investigating at this time as shown in his manuscript notes on economic growth.* Marshall also commented on the relative advantages of geometry as compared with more formal mathematical analysis.

> When tackling a new problem, I generally use analysis, because it is handier: and in the book I am just going to begin to write I shall retain (in footnotes) a little mathematical analysis for questions which I can't reduce under the grasp of curves. But – partly because curves require no special training, partly because they bear more obviously on the science of statistics – I intend never to use analysis when I can use geometry.[19]

Even geometry had its difficulties for Marshall at this early stage, he confessed to Edgeworth. This links further to the analytical work he was doing on distribution and growth, and which never saw the light of day during his lifetime. In the context of problems Edgeworth had raised with him about multiple equilibria when analysing the labour market with supply and demand curves, Marshall asked clarificatory questions revealing a sceptical attitude to this technique of handling labour market questions:

> Do you mean the labour of one trade or all trades? And do you mean the supply at any instant, or do you refer to the case(s) of growth of population? My experience of the exact treatment of supply and demand in this respect has been disappointing. The intricacies of the question are so numerous, the difficulties with the time element so great, that I have never got any curves relating to it which have satisfied me for many months after I first drew them.[20]

The theme of blending pure theory and analysis with applied work in the projected volume continued to worry Marshall during the first half of 1880. He wrote to Foxwell in April that he needed to emphasise the applied side, despite the advice on the importance of his pure

---

* Marshall to Edgeworth, 28 March 1880 (British Library of Economics and Political Science, Coll. Misc. 470/M469); John Whitaker, *EEW*, II, pp. 305–6. Marshall subsequently dated this manuscript, 'around 1880'. In correspondence with the author, John Whitaker suggests around 1881 on the ground that Marshall was not 'likely to have written it in 1879 or 1880 because of illness and work pressure', while his interests in dynamical utilitarianism, perhaps more appropriately, evolutionary utilitarianism, dating back as they did to the 1870s, need not necessarily suggest at this stage a special interest on Marshall's part in dynamic economics. See a letter from Sidgwick cited in Chapter 18, below, p. 664.

theory he had received from him, Cunynghame and, earlier, Sidgwick. He added it would be wrong to publish quickly by neglecting difficulties of application for the sake of lessening the risk of being anticipated in print by others. At that stage, Marshall was giving every moment he could spare to the work, 'but with my limited strength and my college occupations that is but little'.[21] The summer of 1880, spent at Clovelly, was devoted to the topic of value, a topic which can cover both work on the dynamics of distribution and the intricacies of the mathematics of utility, consumer behaviour and demand. 'Value' also describes the core of the eventual Book V from which the *Principles* evolved. However, resignation from the position of Principal and escape from Bristol for twelve months from early October 1881, following a summer in Salcomb also devoted to the subject of value, meant the book did not even commence to approach its final shape until the Marshalls' return to Bristol at the start of the 1882–83 academic year.[22]

What else can be said about the work on value which occupied Marshall's summers of 1880 and 1881? Correspondence with Foxwell at the start of the 1880–81 academic year indicates that writing was making very little progress: 'over the last 12 months, I have practically done nothing in term time and next to nothing in vacations' even the summer being largely swallowed up by college business.[23] Early in 1881 Marshall reviewed Edgeworth's *Mathematical Psychics*. This meant revisiting the mathematics of the hedonic calculus and the indeterminacy of bilateral monopoly as illustrated in wage bargaining. Marshall's review described the general aim of Edgeworth's economic calculus as investigating 'the conditions under which the terms and extent of a contract between two people can be determined beforehand, the utility to each of them of the things with regard to which the contract is made being known'. Marshall therefore focused on Edgeworth's notion of the contract curve, and on his application of that analytical apparatus to contracts between employers and employees, tenants and landlords where the data for a determinate solution were frequently unknown. Although this was an interesting approach, it had dangers of letting the mathematics run away from 'the actual facts of economics'. However, 'if Mr. Edgeworth can prevent his theories from becoming too abstract he may do great things by them'. Edgeworth's book therefore raised the broader problem for Marshall 'whether it is *profitable* to apply mathematical reasonings in the moral sciences', the subject of earlier correspondence with Edgeworth and something which was occupying his own mind during the search for the best way of producing an economic principles.[*]

In the broad manner Marshall defined the word 'value' in his later work, the dynamical theory of growth and distribution Marshall worked on in the early 1880s, also falls under that head. The inspiration for this material has several explanations, as Whitaker has pointed out,[24] while its eventual rejection by Marshall for explicit use in the *Principles* – it does not even make the mathematical appendix in any real way – fits in neatly with Marshall's ambivalent attitude as to whether to write a book on pure theory or a more

---

[*] Marshall, 'Review of Edgeworth's *Mathematical Pychics*', *Academy*, 1 April 1881, in *EEW*, II, pp. 265–8. Marshall discussed these matters in correspondence with Edgeworth in March 1881, noting that in *Economics of Industry*, he had referred to the bargaining problems in wage determination involving trade unions, but that, as was invariably the case in his writing of that book, he had hidden the mathematical reasoning behind his conclusions. This correspondence also shows their friendship had developed sufficiently for Edgeworth to request Marshall to support his application for a chair in London with a testimonial on his behalf.

applied, factual work. His 1879 and 1880 correspondence with Foxwell and Edgeworth revealed this dilemma, which was even more apparent in his review of Edgeworth. The notes on economic growth were equally open to this type of criticism, and to the type of problems of which Marshall had warned Edgeworth in the context of using curves in labour economics.

The theory itself is an interesting attempt to formulate a neo-classical aggregate theory of economic growth. This formalised the production theory of the *Economics of Industry* together with its distributional implications, conveniently encompassed in terms of a marginal productivity explanation of wages and interest. In 1879 Marshall had lectured at Bristol on economic progress, using his adaptation of Mill's Book IV in terms of the theory he had been developing for the distribution chapters in the *Economics of Industry*. By the late 1870s or 1880, Marshall therefore had reached the stage in his economic work of which he subsequently informed J.B. Clark, 'translating Mill's doctrines into differential equations as far as they would go . . . rejecting those which would not go. I rejected the wage doctrine in Book II . . . and accepted that in his Book IV'.[25] Production functions flowed naturally from a theory which viewed output in terms of the productive combination of land, labour and capital; conclusions on distribution followed when rent was eliminated from aggregate product by the traditional Ricardian method, and the remaining 'profit and wages fund' distributed according to marginal productivity considerations probably absorbed from von Thünen. Dynamic supply considerations, affecting both quantitative and qualitative aspects of factor growth (capital accumulation, Malthusian population growth, growth of labour efficiency and change in the arts of production), ensured that the analysis did not suffer from the static limitations of which Marshall had warned Edgeworth.[26]

The manuscript theory of growth and distribution presents concepts and functional relationships rather than an attempt to find the specific properties of solutions for secular growth paths. As Whitaker points out,[27] the models are much too complex and unrestricted to lend themselves readily to such an analysis. Even the discussion of the rates of change of the variables at a point of time is not pushed as far by Marshall as it could have been. The material nevertheless constitutes a major pioneering attempt at systematisation and the analytical framework underlying the discussion informed the discursive theory of production of Book IV of the *Principles* and its distributional consequences developed within the theory of value in its final books. Marshall's abandonment of attempts at formal modelling in this case shows his growing preference for mere description of processes if this ensured closer proximity to economic reality. Preparatory work for the *Principles* during 1880 and 1881 therefore reinforced the desirability of realism as a major objective for the new work. It also assisted clarification of important concepts used in its theory of consumer behaviour, exchange, production and distribution. Although this had not produced any finished chapters, it had the advantage of removing approaches which Marshall considered undesirable.

More constructive work on the book took place during the twelve months in Europe the Marshalls enjoyed during the 1881–82 academic year, starting with their five months winter sojourn in Palermo. It was then, it will be recalled, that Marshall discovered the concept of elasticity, as an element in his theory of demand, and that he completed a preliminary version of Book III. A note taking stock of his activities during 1882, preserved in the

Marshall Library, recounts the state his *Principles* had reached after a year of work interrupted only by rest and occasional sightseeing.*

During 1883, correspondence provides further evidence of slow progress. In March 1883, Marshall wrote to Foxwell, 'I am looking forward to nearly 5 months almost uninterrupted work at my book. I shall not share the time that would be wanted for publishing my lectures on Progress and Poverty', as Foxwell and Sidgwick had been urging him to do.[28] On 8 August, he informed Foxwell he was busily writing a long note on Ricardo's theory of value, suggesting that the 1883 summer was largely devoted to clarifying many of the tricky issues involved in expounding cost of production in relation to value.[29] Given these progress reports, it seems that his end of July 1883 expectations of sending Walras a copy of the published treatise in one or two years time was based on the presumption that the scale of the work at that stage was far smaller than its actual outcome.[30]

During these years Marshall may still have intended to cover virtually the whole of economics in one *Principles* volume. The inclusion of foreign trade with monopolies by the end of 1882 supports such a view. During 1884, other writing distracted him from working on the book, though ultimately contributing to its content. In February 1884, Marshall published a paper, 'Where to House the London Poor'.[31] More useful for the progress of his *Principles* was an article for the *Cooperative Annual*, 'written in white heat' at Rocquaine Bay, Guernsey[32] which surveyed theories and facts about wages, anticipating in less formal manner the theory of distribution Marshall more fully developed in the *Principles* and which he had worked out mathematically during 1880 or 1881. In turn, this became part of a lecture he gave at the Industrial Remuneration Conference in January 1885.[33] For Marshall, these were hectic writing activities, reducing opportunities for serious work on the book during 1884, particularly when combined with his heavy teaching responsibilities at Oxford

---

* The general arrangement of the book was altered at Capri in the latter half of March 1882. That is, it was decided to put definitions at the end of the book, to have a chapter on elasticity of desires including a great part of what had been in old chapter on Demand, before chapters on value, to have a separate chapter on Market bargaining and another on joint production and joint demand. The old chapters were regrouped in skeleton for this purpose.

   Arrived at Venice about April 20. Began to re-read Cournot and to recast, so as to get somewhere near the final form, the first few chapters. Made another attempt at an introduction or preface, whichever it may turn out to be. Continued on the same lines at Waidbruch 29 May–2 June, and Achensee 4 June –>. Up to 11 June had done first draft on I Measurement II Continuity (Continuity of Definition being left quite in the rough) III Elasticity of Desires (Statistical part being left rather in the rough) IV Statement of Problem V Pure theory of equilibrium of Demand and Supply.

   Stayed at Achensee and Walchensee till August during which time recast the skeleton of chapters immediately following Ch. V. Decided to take Joint Demand and supply next, did a little at it: made a rough draft out of old material of Ch. VII on Market Bargaining, ch.VIII on Normal Expenses of Production, Ch. IX, X on Normal Earnings. Suspended work till August 23 the first day at Bournemouth.

   Then began to consider chapters on monopolies combinations and foreign trade. Slightly altered their proposed arrangement and made a rough settlement of the questions to be discussed in them; this occupied about a fortnight; then spent three weeks in making a first draft from tolerably full notes of Ch. on equilibrium of Demand and Supply continued till September 25; when suspended writing and studied economic history of England till October 17' (Historical, 1882, On Way Home from Sicily, *EEW*, Vol I, pp. 85–6).

   The inclusion of foreign trade with monopolies is interesting because it shows that by the end of 1882 this subject had not yet been relegated to a second volume. The chapters mentioned in the penultimate paragraph strongly resemble those to feature later in Book V but the skeleton outline of 1882 still substantially differed from the book published eight years later.

and, in the last two months of the year, the death of Fawcett and his election to the Cambridge chair.

1885 was better for the *Principles'* progress. This was despite the need to prepare his inaugural lecture, a paper on 'The Graphical Method of Statistics' for the Jubilee of the Royal Statistical Society, 'a little touch of malaria' caught in the Lake District where the Marshalls holidayed that summer and the preparation of plans for Balliol Croft which occupied the late spring and early summer months, and which continued to provide distractions until they moved into their new house during August 1886. The first three months of the year left time for 'general considerations as to my book, the scope of which I gradually enlarged. . . . I was gradually outgrowing the older and narrow conception of my book, in which the abstract reasoning which forms the back-bone of the science was to be made prominent and had not yet mustered courage to commit myself straight off to a two volume book which would be the chief product (as gradually improved) of my life's work.'[34] The end of 1885 required preparation for a lecture at Toynbee Hall on 'The Pressure of Population on the Means of Subsistence'. Combined with heavy teaching responsibilities during Michaelmas term (he gave 29 lectures on money and foreign trade), this left little time for further work on the book. Easter term 1886 was likewise occupied with teaching, and with writing his Memorandum of answers for the Royal Commission on the Depression of Trade. The 1885–86 academic year with the 1886 summer, although recollected as 'very uneventful', nevertheless marked major developments on the scope of the book.

> My chief work was recasting the plan of the book. This came to a head during my stay at Sheringham near Cromer in the summer [of 1886]. I then put the contents of the book in something like their final form, at least in so far as the first volume is concerned and thence onward for the first time began to try to put individual chapters into the form in which I expected them to be printed.[35]

Resumption of writing had to wait more or less until the subsequent summer, once again spent at Guernsey. Marshall informed Foxwell he had resisted the temptation to write a paper on 'Overproduction' for the British Association Meeting because of the delay it would cause to the *Principles*.[36] In February 1887, he presented his tabular standard proposal at the Political Economy Club to which he had been elected the previous June, revising it for publication in the March 1887 *Contemporary Review*. He subsequently prepared replies to criticisms of the theory of distribution in *Economics of Industry* in the *Quarterly Journal of Economics* and became rather reluctantly involved in writing a preface for Price's book on Industrial Peace, not a task 'I shall willingly undertake again'.* However, in productive and

---

* 'General work since Arrival at Cambridge', Marshall Archive, Large Brown Box, Item 33; the text of the preface to Price's book is substantially reprinted in *Memorials*, pp. 212–26. The fact that Marshall was tempted to write a preface for another man's work is surprising given his bad experience in writing a brief preface to a reprint of Bagehot's *Postulates of English Political Economy* two years previously. This episode was explained in a letter to Keynes, when the latter had apparently mentioned the preface in a draft of his *Scope and Method of Political Economy*.

> The fact is I have always been rather ashamed of the part I played as to that. I met Mrs. Bagehot at dinner, and more with a view to being polite, than of set purpose, asked her whether she had thought of publishing the two chief essays separately at a low price. She shortly afterwards wrote that she was going to do so; and asked me to write a preface implying that she relied on me to do it, in consequence of what I had said to her.

inspiring Guernsey, 'I did a great deal of writing at my book, and having arranged with Macmillan for its publication, I began just at the end of this academic year [1886–87] to send proofs to the printers; all of it, except about half of Book VI being in type, written in a form not ready for publication but ready to be put in a form for publication – I mean the matter was all there and the arrangements practically settled.'*

TABLE 12.1: DRAFT OUTLINE OF PRINCIPLES OF ECONOMICS, VOL. I, BOOK VI, VOL. II (1877)

Volume I	Book VI	Value Distribution and Exchange
	Ch. I	Introduction
	Ch. II	Central Problem
	Ch. III	Central Problem Continued
	Ch. IV	Field of Employment for Capital and Labour
	Ch. V	Rent in Relation to Value
	Ch. VI	Rent continued, Agricultural Rent, Land Tenure
	Ch. VII	Rent continued, Influence of Progress on Rent
	Ch. VIII	Earnings
	Ch. IX	Earnings continued
	Ch. X	Interest
	Ch. XI	Earnings of Management, including Cooperation
	Ch. XII	Wholesale & Retail Prices
	Ch. XIII	Secular Changes, Pressure of Population
	Ch. XIV	Conclusion, containing summary reference to influence of Trade Unions and notice of Trade Combinations etc.
Volume II	will probably contain	
	Book VII	Foreign Trade
	Book VIII	Money and Banking
	Book IX	Trade Fluctuations
	Book X	Taxation
	Book XI	Collectivism
	Book XII	Aims for the Future
		Mathematical Appendix

Source: Marshall Library, 'Historical Notes', as cited in Whitaker, *EEW*, Vol. I, pp. 89–90.

So I wrote very unwillingly. But really I am not in sympathy (intellectually) with Bagehot. He is most brilliant; but very hasty and in reading him I alternately agree and admire much and differ and admire a little. I would not go into that, partly because Mrs. Bagehot would not have liked it, partly because I had not time. The result was a short and utterly empty preface; and to speak quite frankly I am a little ashamed of having special attention called to it by your kindness. (Marshall to Keynes, 17 August 1889, Marshall Archive 3/72).

* 'General work since Arrival at Cambridge'. In April 1887 Marshall offered his work to Macmillan as covering 'about the same ground as Mill's Political Economy, . . . probably . . . of about the same length, or a little shorter. I propose to publish it in two volumes octavo; of which the first will, I hope, appear this autumn and the second about two years later'.

He enclosed a proposed table of contents (Table 12.1) and a rough draft of close to half the first volume. The letter also made quite specific proposals about copyright and the treatment of mathematics in the proposed volumes, subjects more appropriately pursued later in this chapter (Marshall to Macmillan, 12 April 1887, Marshall Archive, 1/192; Macmillan accepted the offer two days later, Marshall Archive, 1/193).

From Guernsey, Marshall told Foxwell about his reluctance to go to the British Association meeting in Manchester, despite the attraction of possibly meeting there with Menger and Böhm-Bawerk. Pleasant weather made his wife as happy in her painting as he was in his writing, and it would be hazardous to disturb the flow,

> I have got about 40 pages in type and shall go on printing until I get a 100 or so. Then I shall pause a little. I have still nearly 100 pages of Vol. I which are not yet even in first draft though I know fairly well what I am to say in them. I don't want to run the risk of having to contradict on p. 500 what is said on p. 50 more flatly than absolutely necessary.[37]

The emphasis in this burst of writing on the final Book VI of Volume I in the summer of 1887 is reflected in a draft outline of its contents (Table 12.1) prepared at the end of that vacation (1 October 1887). It shows that still much was to be altered in ordering of the material and final content, as was to be the case for the plan outline of Volume II (Table 12.1) Marshall had formally projected to Macmillan's in May of that year.

In early October 1887, John Neville Keynes was asked to assist by correcting and commenting on the flow of proofs from the printer. On the afternoon of 8 October he called on Marshall, who then asked him to read the proofsheets, indicating 'he expects to get the first volume out by Easter'. On 13 October, Keynes recorded both his own impressions of what he had been reading and Marshall's reactions to his comments, the proofs in question appearing to have been from Book I,

> I am reading the proofs of Marshall's book. It will I think come up to the high expectations that have been raised with regard to it. It is evidently the work of a man whose knowledge of the subject is profound. He wrote most gratefully for suggestions I am sending him: e.g., 'many thanks for your notes on sheet 4. Some of them are extremely important: particularly that about Bastiat's date. I thought he wrote about 1835: but was wrong. As to your constructive suggestions: I regret only the time they may cost you: to me they are great and unmixed kindness and benefits'.[38]

By the middle of November, Keynes started receiving proofsheets of the second Book, dealing with definitions. Proofs arrived steadily over the early months of 1888 when, during January and February, Keynes was involved with those of Book III and, by the start of March, with the opening chapter of Book IV.[39] For Marshall, these months were also occupied with his work for the Gold and Silver Commission, and, from February 1888 onwards, with readings proofs of Keynes's *Scope and Method of Political Economy*. By the end of the summer vacation, spent in Yorkshire, a great deal more had been done. Book V had been sent to the printers, 'Book IV being almost out of my hands'.[40] At the end of August, he wrote to Keynes, 'after long delays' caused by both printer's and his own mistakes, he was able to send the first four batches of Book IV proofs, dealing with 'Industrial Organisation' while the printers had been asked to send the fifth, on business management, directly to Keynes on completion. Marshall continued, 'There remains in Book IV a final chapter summing up the conditions of supply. Then comes Book V, short and nasty, on the 'General Theory of the Equilibrium of Supply and Demand', and then Book VI which is very much like Book II of the *Economics of Industry*. Up to the beginning of 'Organisation of Industry' is 300 pages, from there to end of the volume is 300 pages more. It's a long job.'*

The notes on work done during 1887–88 ended with the announcement of a major change Marshall did not make until later. This was to 'bring a new book on Cost of Production further considered, putting into it (somewhat simplified) discussion I had intended to keep for the later part of the Book on Normal Value'. That book, subtitled 'Distribution and Exchange', 'now became Book VII. This decision was slowly reached, and not much further progress was made during this calendar year [that is, 1888]'.[41] On 20 December 1888, the decision about the extra book was communicated to John Neville Keynes, with further revisions to this scheme announced in the middle of January 1889.[42]

In the intervening month Keynes continued to be bombarded with further proofs and prognostications of when the book would be finished. By the end of August 1888, plans for publishing Volume I by January 1889 were scrapped in favour of March 1889; in November 1888, Marshall predicted Easter as the earliest publication date. The re-shuffle of contents announced in December and revised in January set the process back further. Some of these changes may have been inspired by Keynes, who in early November 1888 complained in his diary: 'I am now working on a rather heavy instalment of Marshall's proofsheets (with the curves in the notes). The arrangement seems to be bad, and I am not altogether well satisfied with this part of the book though portions of it are very good indeed. The form of the argument and the composition want Sidgwick's finish'.[43]

For work on the *Principles* during much of 1889, Marshall himself took up the story: 'During the first four months of 1889 I worked at Book VI, finishing the first draft of the first four chapters of it and working off Book V. Meanwhile I had paid a good deal of attention to the Mathematical Appendix and got a good part of that in print. . . . The Long Vacation of which eight weeks were spent at Bordeaux Harbour, was occupied chiefly with Book VI, Chapters V and VI, and Book VII, Chapters I–V, Chapter V having been sent in MSS to the press and the 34th sheet having just reached the second (first in sheet) stage'.[44]

Delays also came from other duties. The whole of the Easter term was virtually taken up with the preparation of a Presidential Address for the Cooperative Congress at Ipswich in June. Earlier that year the Moral Sciences Board was having frequent, and often rather stormy, meetings on the new regulations for the Tripos, agreement on which was not reached until late in February. Deciding on the editor for the proposed *Economic Journal*, for which Marshall had his own preferred candidate, also took up time. At the end of May 1889, Marshall wrote to Keynes, 'My book goes slowly and just now I am not working on it at all. Cooperation has filled my mind for some time and will do so till Term is over. Book VI "Cost of Production" is partly printed but there is not much use in you seeing it till there is some more prospect of you being able to have the latter half. I expect to get my Vol. I out before Xmas or anyhow immediately after'.[45]

To enable early publication during 1890, Marshall did not wish to lecture much in October 1889, just as he had saved time in the first half of the year by missing Moral Sciences Board meetings after its deliberations over the new Tripos regulations were

---

* Marshall to J.N. Keynes, 23 August 1888 (Marshall Archive, 1/7). In the first edition it is in fact 299 pages of text. Book IV, Ch. VII, 'Industrial Organisation', starting on p. 300. The 300 pages from there to the end became 436.

completed. By the end of June, Keynes resumed correcting proofsheets for Marshall[46] and a month later, was sent some more,

> I send you the remainder of Bk VI on Cost of Production. Book VII is on the way but it limps shockingly. You will see that the first of these chapters has already had some suggestions made on them: but you can write freely on all. I shall send another copy to the press. Price's pencil notes I have not looked at. Some of his verbal amendments seem to me generally scarcely required; but he has sharp eyes and often finds errors such as 'its' instead of 'theirs' when all we others have failed to note them. *

The late decision to create a Book VI on cost of production was a major explanation of the final delays the *Principles* was experiencing, since it required both rearrangement and rewriting, not so much of the old Book V, but of the new Book VII on 'Value, Distribution and Exchange'. A comparison of the Book VII which appeared in 1890 with the outline of Book VI prepared in October 1887. Table 12.1 gives an indication of the extent of these changes. Chapter V of the 1887 Book VI, rent in relation to value, was transferred to the new Book VI, thereby drastically altering the subject matter ordering of the book on distribution. In the 1887 plan, rent preceded the discussion of capital and labour, following the manuscript on growth and distribution. This had treated the elimination of rent as the first stage of distribution theory, with wages determined by marginal productivity considerations as the second stage. The new Book VII treats labour, then interest and earnings of management followed by rent after a general survey of the problem of distribution. The two-stage theory of distribution with its reliance on the wages and interest fund of the *Economics of Industry* was abandoned for the more general application of supply and demand to distribution. The scope of the 1890 Book VII was also considerably less than that on which its equivalent Book VI had been planned in 1887 by deferring material on wholesale and retail prices, on the influence of trade unions and trade combination to Volume II. Additional chapters on labour and the earnings of capital were, however, inserted in the 1890 published version relative to the 1887 plan.[47]

The new Book VII continued to be a source of difficulties. It explains the actual publication in July 1890 from the expected Christmas publication announced six months earlier. One problem it created was the growth in size of the book. The 300 pages projected in August 1888 grew to 436, an increase of nearly fifty per cent. On 2 December 1889 Marshall lamented to the faithful Keynes, 'My book do grow: Oh! it *do* grow! B.B. Bother it!!'[¶] Work was also interrupted in the winter months because of a bout of influenza, which meant 'flabby work', only suitable for destruction.[48]

---

*   Marshall to J.N. Keynes, 23 July 1889 (Marshall Archive, 1:91). Eighteen months before Marshall had asked Keynes, 'not to bother about misprints or small points', since these were looked after by his wife and Price (Marshall to J.N. Keynes, January 1888, Marshall Archive, 1:61). Price's version of his role is as follows: 'Having the honour of being asked, with J.N. Keynes, to read the proofs of the first edition of the "Principles", I suggested some particular varying in the punctuation; Marshall told me promptly to refrain because he had his own system thereon. Of course I did henceforth; but my own small work upon the book I should wish to mention that I could realise the extreme repeated pains taken to put the final reasoning in a shape beyond reach of probably major, or even minor, justified objection', L.L. Price, 'Memories and Notes on British Economists 1881–1947', p. 10.

¶   Marshall to J.N. Keynes, 2 December 1890 (Marshall Archive, 1/93). B.B. stands for big book, the pet name the Marshalls used for the *Principles*. This was explained to Keynes by Mary Paley Marshall, 10 August 1889, Keynes Papers, Marshall Library.

Marshall sent Keynes a table of contents in April 1890, 'not for you to correct, but to show you the geography'. By then, there remained 'one chapter on supply and demand in relation to land, and one or two winding up chapters' whose contents would now 'have to leave out much of what I had wanted to get in'.[49] Marshall had earlier approved a specimen binding sent to him by Macmillans, while a letter from his publishers in early July placed a value on the extra pages Marshall had mentioned to Keynes three months before. The book was now so much larger, that Macmillan suggested its price be raised from 12s.6d. to 14s., even though the more normal price for a book of this size was of the order of 18s.[50] The Herculean task, as Whitaker put it, was over by that time and the first volume of the *Principles* was published within the second half of July 1890.[51]

THE FIRST EDITION

'It is a very handsome volume', Keynes noted in his diary on 24 July 1890 when he had received his complementary copy of the *Principles*. And so it is. Bound in the well-known Macmillan blue cloth, with simple gold lettering on the spine – Principles of Economics. Marshall. Vol. I, Macmillan & Co. – its titlepage added little more than that the author was Professor of Political Economy in the University of Cambridge; Fellow of St John's College, Cambridge; sometime Fellow of Balliol College, Oxford. It also contained a motto, *natura non facit saltum*, adopted perhaps from Kant, perhaps from Darwin's *Origins of Species*. This concisely expressed the principle of continuity applied throughout the book, which gave it 'the special character of its own' tentatively claimed for it by its author.[52]

The book's brief preface proclaimed it as 'an attempt to present a version of old doctrines with the aid of new work, and with reference to the new problems, of our age'. This evolutionary aim of adapting traditional principles to new situations, using facts and reasoning together with 'Conscience and Commonsense' to develop 'Laws of Economics as statements of tendencies expressed in the indicative mood', was the first and major expression of this 'Principle of Continuity' in Marshall's *Principles of Economics*.[53] Other ways in which the principle was applied in the work were specified in the preface. Continuity was used to highlight the lack of 'sharp lines of division between normal and abnormal conduct; normal, and current or market values, and even between incomes like rent and the interest of capital' which the book demonstrated to be only a distinction based on time. In this context, the biological spirit in which the book was written was further illustrated in an analogy designed to focus on its major theme. 'In spite of the great difference in form between birds and quadrupeds, there is one Fundamental idea running through all their frames, so the general theory of the equilibrium of demand and supply is a Fundamental Idea running through the frames of all the various parts of the central problem of Distribution and Exchange.'

The principle of continuity needed also to be applied to the use of terms, avoiding the temptation, Marshall warned in his preface, of drawing sharp lines of distinction where nature drew none. Examples from real life were the lack of distinction between things which are, and are not, capital; are, and are not, necessaries; and labour which is, or is not, productive. Aspects of this, as Coats has argued,[54] became parts of the Cambridge 'didactic style', designed to transmit more information to the initiated than to the untrained reader. Continuity of development is a further application of the principle: whether in the biological sense of Herbert Spencer or the historical sense of Hegel, both acknowledged as major influences on the substance of Marshall's work. Last but not least, there were mathematical conceptions of continuity. In particular, its application was emphasised in the marginal method, which focused on increments, as illustrated by the stable exchange equilibrium where the 'marginal increment of demand' for a thing as a continuous function is 'balanced against the corresponding increment of its cost of production'.[55]

These various perspectives on the principle of continuity elucidate the thrust of the book. The core of the book is the theory of equilibrium of demand and supply, because 'most economic problems have a kernel relating to this equilibrium'. The theory of equilibrium was, however, far from simple, depending as it did on the nature of markets to which it was applied, the time period of operation, the nature of competition and the degree of stability attached to it. Book V as it appeared in the first edition highlighted these aspects, emphasising difficulties in applying equilibrium theory to issues such as maximum satisfaction or the public good, not to mention the difficulties in its use in deciding the important contemporary question whether collective action is likely to be inferior to individual action. Prior to this discussion, demand and supply are separately explored in Books III and IV respectively. Application to the theory of distribution and exchange was dealt with in the final Book VII after special difficulties of cost in relation to value had been illuminated in Book VI. The last acted both as a supplement to Book V and as a prelude to Book VII. The first two books provided an introductory survey covering scope and method, the growth of free industry and enterprise as the fundamental characteristic of modern business, a sketch of the development of the science demonstrating the relationship of these *Principles* to previous and contemporary thought, and some definitional chapters. They stressed the evolutionary aspects of economics, including the continuity in its development and the flexibility of definition where everything is a matter of degree.

The preface highlighted two further aspects about the book's construction. Its penultimate paragraphs explained the role mathematics played in its argument. This professed the preference for geometry over algebraic analysis that Marshall had affirmed to Edgeworth at the start of the 1880s, and indicated why diagrams were placed in the footnotes as 'supplementary illustrations' because 'the argument in the text is never dependent on them'.[*] It also clarified why the 'few specimens of those applications of mathematical language' which remained in the book, because they had proved so useful for his own purposes, were banished to an appendix. If used in the text, 'a great many symbols . . . would become very laborious to anyone but the writer' while their 'chief use' was confined to writing down thoughts 'quickly, shortly and exactly' to ensure adequate 'premisses for the writer's conclusions (i.e. that his equations are neither more nor less in number than his unknowns)'.[56] This conformed to the plan Marshall disclosed to Macmillan

---

[*] Marshall was not totally consistent in this view. For example, in the context of the tax/bounty argument in the chapter on changes in supply and demand with some bearings on the doctrine of maximum satisfaction, he qualified in at least one of the footnotes the proposition that the diagrams were valuable for illustrative purposes only. This was done by warning 'some parts of the problem cannot be satisfactorily treated without their aid'. *P* I, p. 445 n.1; *P* VIII, p. 466 n.1.

in 1887 offering the publishing right of the *Principles* and foreshadowed the views on the use of mathematics in economics he wrote to Bowley sixteen years later:

> But I know I had a growing feeling in the later years of my work at the subject that a good mathematical theorem dealing with economic hypotheses was very unlikely to be good economics: and I went more and more on the rules – (1) Use mathematics as a shorthand language, rather than as an engine of inquiry. (2) Keep to them till you have done. (3) Translate into English. (4) Then illustrate by examples that are important in real life. (5) Burn the mathematics. (6) If you can't succeed in 4, burn 3. This last I did often. . . . I think you should do all you can to prevent people from using Mathematics in cases in which the English Language is as short as the Mathematical.[57]

What dictated Marshall's stand on the use of mathematics in an economics text can be variously explained. Schumpeter surmised that this practice reflected Marshall's peculiar ambition to be read by businessmen. It also reflects recognition on Marshall's part of Jowett's advice that the 'human' and 'concrete' nature of political economy made it essential that the 'language of symbols be relegated to notes and appendices'. Marshall himself had subscribed to this view in his review of Jevons. Most crucial to the decision was Marshall's growing realisation of the dangers in pursuing the logical consequences of mathematical reasoning in economics to the limit. He grasped the portent of this danger when his confidence in Cournot as economist was shaken by the wrong conclusions Cournot had drawn about the consequences of increasing returns and which could only be corrected by careful empirical investigation of the validity of the premises on which they depended. An economist's 'greed' for facts was an essential countervailing force to the thrill of the chase mathematical reasoning provided, if contact with reality of that economics was to be preserved.[58]

Marshall's final paragraph in the preface reflected the customary acknowledgement of assistance. The important but limited role Mary Paley played in this process has been mentioned earlier, as has the role of the two other proofreaders whom Marshall thanked, Keynes and Price. Other Cambridge students, Arthur Berry and Alfred Flux were thanked for assisting in preparing the mathematical appendix. The acknowledgements conclude with an expression of gratitude to his father, Mr W.H.B. Hall and the printer, C.J. Clay, for assistance on 'special points', the nature of which in the case of the first are difficult to ascertain.[*]

The thrust of the *Principles* as summarised in its preface neither does justice to its rich contents nor reveals its varied objectives. Its full flavour can only be captured by looking more generally at the broad aims Marshall had in view in its construction, a procedure which also emphasises the inherent limitation of its contents since the work published was only the first of an intended two. As a *principles* of economics, the work presented the

---

[*] *P* I, Preface p. xii. Although the reference to help from his father could be filial politeness, the fact it does not occur in the subsequent three editions when his father was still alive suggests otherwise. And see above, Chapter 2, pp. 26, 39 and n.83. Clay was the printer for Cambridge University Press, which set the type for the *Principles*, a task in which he must have been sorely tried. William Henry Bullock Hall (1837–1904) was a student at Balliol College, Oxford, and a friend of Jowett. He was called to the Bar in 1872 but never practised law. He was a Justice of the Peace in Cambridgeshire, living in Six Mile Bottom, Newmarket, not far from Cambridge. He was an authority on land issues, and acted as Marshall's consultant on the more practical details of agriculture. As shown below, Chapter 16, p. 574, Marshall may have first met him in the early 1870s.

foundations of the science, in terms of its full purpose and scope and the most appropriate method of study. In practice, Marshall tended to be broad and non-dogmatic on these issues, having little patience with methodological inquiries about best methods and the precise nature of the subject matter. 'I take an extreme position as to the *method & scope* of economics. In my new book I say of *methods* simply that economics has to use every method known to science. And as to scope, I say, "Economics is a study of man's action in the ordinary business of life, it inquires how he gets his income and how he uses it".'[59] Elsewhere in his new book he saw a dual purpose in studying economics. First was the search for knowledge for its own sake, secondly, it threw light on practical issues (p. 94).[*] In this study, 'theory must go hand in hand with that of facts' because 'facts by themselves teach nothing' (p. 94). The knowledge to be sought in economic study, as Marshall told Keynes, related to 'man's action in the ordinary business of life', and more specifically sought answers to questions like the following,

> How does economic freedom tend, so far as its influence reaches, to arrange the production, distribution and exchange of wealth? What organization of industry and trade does it tend to bring about; what forms of division of labour; what arrangements of the money market, of wholesale and retail dealing and what relations between employer and employed? How does it tend to adjust values, that is, the prices of material things whether produced on the spot or brought from a distance, rents of all kinds, interest on capital and the earnings of all forms of work, including that of undertaking and managing business enterprises? How does it affect the course of foreign trade? Subject to what limitations is the price of anything a measure of its real utility? What increase of happiness is *prima facie* likely to result from a given increase in the wealth of any class of society? How far is the industrial efficiency of any class impaired by the insufficiency of its income? How far would an increase of the income of any class, if once effected, be likely to sustain itself through its effects in increasing their efficiency and earning power? How far does, as a matter of fact, the influence of economic freedom reach (or how far has it reached at any particular time) in any place, in any rank of society, or in any particular branch of industry? What other influences are most powerful there; and how is the action of all these influences combined? In particular, how far does economic freedom tend of its own action to build up combinations and monopolies, and what are their effects? How are the various classes of society likely to be affected by its action in the long run; what will be the intermediate effects while its ultimate results are being worked out; and, account being taken of the time over which they will spread, what is the relative importance of these two classes of ultimate and intermediate effects? What will be the incidence of any system of taxes? What burdens will it impose on the community, and what revenue will it afford to the State? (pp. 95–6).

The diligent reader of the *Principles* can find answers to all of these questions from the fundamentals of economics its pages contained. These, its author concluded in the book's final paragraph, 'hold the key' to all practical questions and 'encompass the most difficult parts' of its subject matter (p. 736). Credit, foreign trade, modern developments in combinations, topics reserved for the second volume, needed to be studied before the full range of more practical issues could be properly tackled by the student of economics. Those problems, which Marshall saw as of 'particular urgency' in 1890 *and* in 1920,[60] showed economics' indissoluble links with practical ethics and with the motive which led the author of the *Principles* to tackle the study of economics. Practical problems of this kind included advantages and difficulties in limiting 'economic freedom' and property rights, the scope for

---

[*]   *P* I, all subsequent page references in brackets in this section refer to this edition.

collective action and the functions of government, not only through ownership, but through regulating the use of resources including those of 'open space, works of art, means of instruction and amusement' and, reverting to the themes of economic reform which had occupied him in his years of economic apprenticeship,

> Taking it for granted that a more equal distribution of wealth is to be desired, how far would this justify changes in the institutions of property, or limitations of free enterprise even when they would be likely to diminish the aggregate of wealth? In other words, how far should an increase in the income of the poorer classes and a diminution of their work be aimed at, even if it involved some lessening of national material wealth? How far could this be done without injustice, and without slackening the energies of the leaders of progress? How ought the burdens of taxation to be distributed among the different classes of society?
>
> Ought we to rest content with the existing forms of division of labour? Is it necessary that large numbers of the people should be exclusively occupied with work that has no elevating character? Is it possible to educate gradually among the great mass of workers a new capacity for the higher kinds of work; and in particular for undertaking co-operatively the management of the businesses in which they are themselves employed? (pp. 96–7).

Thus teacher and reformer were blended in the major instalment of Marshall's life work which appeared in July 1890. The first volume of the *Principles* was therefore never intended to be a simple text in what is now called 'micro-economics', inculcating beginners with the elements of price theory, the contribution for which it is now largely remembered. To its author, it attempted to blend all aspects of the theory of value, or of supply and demand. Value theory for Marshall encompassed the major themes of growth and progress as well as the mechanics of price determination under static competitive equilibrium. Only the former, assisted by the understanding gained from equilibrium analysis, facilitated reaching the true goal of economics: lifting the standard of life for all including the lowest now trapped in the 'residuum' and building the elevated character that would ensure the genuine progress of the nation.

THE RECEPTION OF THE *PRINCIPLES*

Despite the restricted contents of the first volume of the *Principles* from absence of the second volume, its broad objectives for economics were what delighted the audience to which it was addressed. The reviewers of the *Principles* were fully aware that this book was about social implications as well as economic principles. This gained the book wide recognition. The Marshalls' scrap-book contains cuttings from well over three dozen British newspapers and periodicals, ranging from the *Times*, the *Economist*, the *Manchester Guardian* and the *Observer* to *Justice*, the *Church Times* and the *Cooperative News*. The scrap-book also includes close to a dozen reviews from the overseas press. In addition, there were lengthy reviews in the more academic journals, as well as in the traditional quarterlies. Some of these reflected old friendships, others the making of new ones.

Old friends included Edgeworth in *The Academy*. He opened one of his reviews with the statement that the *Principles* defied its own motto, *natura non facit saltum*, because Marshall's treatise advanced 'the position of science as it were by leaps and bounds'. He criticised his friend, perhaps recalling earlier criticism received, that 'more explicit use of diagrams and symbols at some passages might have assisted one class of readers' and expressed the hope that 'the painfully small print in which the author had shrouded all his mathematical disquisitions' should be remedied in the next edition, a hope never fulfilled. More importantly, Edgeworth recalled for his readers the fact that Marshall's book demonstrated the truth of a proposition he had used first in his 1872 review of Jevons: 'just as the motion of every body in the solar system is affected by the motion of every other, so it is with the elements of the problems of political economy'.[61]   Former student J.S. Nicholson praised Marshall's book as the most important since J.S. Mill's *Principles*, and remarked of its author, 'Rarely in modern times has a man achieved such a high reputation as an authority on such a slender basis of published work; for until the appearance of the present volume his record only showed the elementary book on the "Economics of Industry", and a few occasional essays'. Nicholson also had some criticism. Despite the just recognition given to Cournot's major contribution, much of the historical topics, especially the chapters in Book I on the growth of economic freedom and the concomitant growth in the science, 'were neither adequate nor original'.[62] However, Nicholson reserved his real criticism for private correspondence with his friend, John Neville Keynes, who recorded its contents in his diary:

> on re-reading the review, I think I let him off too easily on some things. His history is vague, old-fashioned, and excessively weak; his examples are mainly of the old a priori kind or at best curious rather than important; the repetition is so great that his plan must be faulty; but if he is to cover the whole ground of what I understand by P.E., he will at the same rate take six volumes. At the same time his pure theory is extremely good and deserves the highest praise, especially because he was really the first to introduce the ideas to England. The book, however, will never do as a textbook in its present shape, and I can only recommend it for honours students.[63]

Sidney Webb confided his reactions to reviewing the book to his fiancé Beatrice Potter: 'When I left you yesterday (16 July 1890), . . . I found a message from Massingham, telling me I must review Marshall's book for the *Star*. I went straight to the Club and read right through Marshall's six hundred pages – got up, staggering under it. It is a great book, nothing new – showing the way, but not following it. For all that, it is a great book – it will supersede Mill, but it will not make an epoch in economics. Economics has still to be re-made'.[64]   His wife-to-be read the book more gradually, and then echoed several of the criticisms Nicholson had made privately. 'The last five days I have spent over Marshall – and intend to spend five more. It is a great work (not a great book). He has precipitated all the current expert economic views – sifted and analysed them – and welded them into one body of consistent doctrine – but is there much that is original? . . . His history seems to me weak, and his illustrations and generalisations about business facts not very much removed from commonplace – rather those of an "outsider". It is in statement of theory that he is strong – and in his sympathy.'[65]

The anonymous notices the *Principles* received in the reviews were on the whole also favourable, though quite variable in both their targets for praise and for criticism. The *Annual Register*[66] found 'Professor Marshall's book . . . not . . . a great original work but . . . a solid contribution, full of sympathy, knowledge, insight and wisdom, to the perplexing economic problems of the day. . . .The treatment throughout is lucid, conspicuously able, and as sympathetic as it is broad'. The *Edinburgh Review*[67] begged to differ. Great though the authority of Professor Marshall was, and this new book would only add to its lustre, its two disadvantages were immediately noted. 'This imposing volume of more than seven hundred closely printed pages is only an instalment of his work . . . books on political economy which are so published, suffer perhaps more than others. The earliest portions of an economical treatise are precisely those which present the most difficulty and the least interest in the ordinary reader. . . . Even technical readers, . . . will find many passages in the 'Principles of Economics', both difficult and dry. . . . [W]e venture to think that . . . in his efforts to be precise, Professor Marshall has contrived occasionally to be obscure.' Much of the review, however, concentrated on the favourable prospects the book held out for the working class, in 'its stress laid on the necessity of good wages', the 'double advantage' of machines in relieving hard toil and raising wages, and that, with its stress on the value of education, the evils of town living and its belief in the improvement of the character of man, the book seemed more intent to enhance the 'common weal' than the 'common wealth'.[68] The *Westminister Review*[69] noted Marshall's demand for a wider scope in economics by taking into account 'ethical forces', his respect for predecessors, and the fact that 'the arrangement of the book . . . was admirable', and recommended its readers to 'procure the book and to study it at their leisure'. After summarising its contents, the *London Quarterly Review* concluded that the *Principles* was:

> a most valuable contribution to the study of political economy. It is extremely moderate and judicious, happily devoid of that pugnacity which has so often crept into economic discussion. It will go far to show that economic science is after all more at one with itself than ordinary readers have been led to suppose of late years. Its luminous style and copious illustrations from the state of trade today should make it widely popular.[70]

The reviews of the *Principles* in the new academic journals were on the whole far more thorough in appreciating the novel features of its contents. Giddings, in the *Annals of the American Academy of Political and Social Science*[71] called its publication 'a scientific event of the first magnitude', matching the performances for their epochs of both Mill and Adam Smith. Giddings noted the various meanings Marshall gave to 'continuity' in the preface to the work, his familiarity with Hegel and Spencer, his 'plastic' views of economic science to match a human society that is 'organic, flexible and growing'. Marshall's careful and unobtrusive use of mathematics, especially diagrams, was likewise recognised, as were his theoretical contributions such as the theory of 'consumer's rent', and his generosity to contemporary writers in economics, particularly those in America.

J.B. Clark wrote an appreciative but critical review article in the *Political Science Quarterly*, possibly the most perceptive review the first edition received. It started a warm friendship, visible in their correspondence. After stating that the *Principles*' 'merit and importance justify the eulogistic reviews of it that have appeared in America and especially in England', Clark noted the increasing difficulty of the book as the argument proceeded. This stimulated questions for the reader and sometimes dissent, indicating the high quality of Marshall's book as a 'stimulus to further work'. As Clark approached 'the paramount subject of distribution', his own questioning of Marshall's theory became more frequent, and the tone of the review more tetchy. Noting Marshall's contribution to human capital theory, Clark argued this made 'a capitalist of every worker who had taken time to learn how to do anything' and thereby caused the line of distribution between labour and capital to run right 'through the very personality of man'. Clark then commented on both the Ricardian flavour and Marshall's many departures from Ricardo's treatment of rent, particularly through his extension of the concept to cover earnings of personal abilities; the welfare gains through acts of consumption, labour and waiting; and the short period earnings of machines. This generalisation of rent, Clark argued, ought to have been taken further to form the basis of 'a general law of distribution' in which interest and wages were discussed as the respective rents of 'a pure fund of invested capital' and 'a corresponding fund of labour force'. Marshall appeared to have neglected this obvious fact, and thereby, Clark argued had confused the law of substitution applying to specific forms of capital and labour with a law of distribution applying to the general capital and labour energy funds which were free to be adapted to any use.*

A number of other academic reviews dealt more specifically with Marshall's presentation of a new economics within the old forms of classical political economy. In the *Revue d'économie politique*, Schüller[72] focused on the application of the new and abstract marginal method to the old theories of production, distribution and consumption and even production theory, yielding in total a 'more profound understanding of economic phenomena'. In the *Economic Review*, Montague[73] commented that the subjects discussed in the first volume of Marshall's *Principles* matched those discussed in the first volume of Mill's, but that Marshall's arrangement was totally different, with 'value the central problem of his treatise' in the wider sense of embracing both distribution and exchange. Like Mill, Marshall aimed 'to bring the science into harmony with itself and into the most useful relation with the problems of the age' by modernising old doctrines with the introduction of new work. Marshall's book therefore mediated the old and the new in political economy, just as it successfully mediated inductive and deductive methods. Laudable though this achievement was, Montague predicted Marshall's book would not be popular because its style lacked power. 'Nothing stands out in bold relief, and the general effect of the theory is weakened by lack of detail'. Wagner[74] in the *Quarterly Journal of Economics* likewise focused on Marshall's mediating role on scope and method and of the old and the new, praising in particular his defence, if not 'rehabilitation' of Ricardo.¶ After summarising the book's contents and critically commenting on the author's optimism about the progress of the working classes expressed in its final chapter, Wagner ended on the hope 'that the second volume will follow at an early date'.

---

* J.B. Clark, 'Marshall's Principles of Economics', *Political Science Quarterly*, 6 (1), March 1891, pp. 126–51. Marshall responded at length to the review in letters to Clark dated 6 May and 6 June 1891. These stated he did not like 'to publish notes in self defence' in the journals, a rule occasionally broken as shown below (pp. 425–6, 470–1). He also wrote to Clark that he tended in his writing to avoid 'all personal criticism except when it was necessary to defend a position of his own'. The correspndence, however, failed to settle the major issues of distribution which divided Marshall and Clark, as shown by their correspondence a decade later.

¶ The title used by William Ashley for his critique of Alfred Marshall's treatment of Ricardo in the *Principles*, which was published in the *Economic Journal*, Vol. 1, September 1891, pp. 474–89. Marshall started to write a reply to Ashley, the draft of which is preserved in the Marshall Archive, but on the principle he had enunciated to J.B. Clark in correspondence (see n.* above), he did not publish it, replying instead in brief notes added at suitable points to later editions of the *Principles*.

Combined with these many and varied reviews, all carefully studied and pondered and treasured by the household at Balliol Croft, came letters of praise and criticism from friends and acquaintances. On 24 July, Jowett wrote to Marshall to acknowledge receipt of the *Principles* and to congratulate him on writing it.

It will be of great value to capitalists and to the working classes. It seems to me just what was wanted to mediate between the old political economy and the new, . . . neither employers nor employed have any reason to regard you as otherwise than a friend. Ricardo himself would not have objected to have his a priori reasonings supplemented and modified by your facts. Also I think the book excellent in an Educational point of view: It is very clear and interesting and goes back to great principles. It answers implicitly the question so often asked: 'What is the relation of Political Economy to Ethics'? I think the style admirable – I am also pleased that you have not over-loaded the subject with Mathematics, and have rather diminished than increased its technicality. Every page I open, seems to me to contain something good – e.g. pp. 369–371 – I often think of the difficulty of how to rise in life and how to lessen it – the Universities and education do something to diminish it but business much more, especially if some noble sense of philanthropy could be introduced into it.*

Other thank-you notes for the book arrived from abroad. Schmoller's letter of 6 August praised Marshall for the wide knowledge of German economics his book exhibited. From New York, Seligman described the gift as a work 'remarkable for the knowledge displayed as to the latest advances in continental researches as well as for the holding fast to what is best in the old classical doctrines and as an antidote to those extreme votaries of the historical school'. F.A. Walker, another American friend, wrote, 'More and more I enjoy, more and more I admire your work. The spirit and tone of it are admirable. The elevation and dignity of sentiment are quite as impressive as the strength and severity of the thing. You have made a great, a very great, book, which will, . . . grow more and more upon the mind of the public'. Walker commented how Marshall's studies of physics would have assisted the work because only those 'who had profoundly studied the mechanics of heat' could show so much 'insight' into economic forces and so much 'capacity' and 'restraint' in 'estimating their effects upon human society'.[75]

Private reaction to Marshall's book can be concluded by reference to some correspondence with Leslie Stephen, unfortunately not all extant, and by Higgs's comments on the book in correspondence with Foxwell. A letter by Marshall thanked Stephen for his 'kind words about my book. There are very few persons from whom such words would be more pleasant to me: I only wish I deserved them better'. He then commented on some aspects of consumer's rent which Stephen found puzzling. Stephen's reply to Marshall the following day repeated the praise he had given but added a general criticism of style, which he hoped would be of use during Marshall's preparation of the second volume,

---

* Benjamin Jowett to Alfred Marshall, 29 July 1890, Marshall Archive, 1/53. *P* I, pp. 369–71, according to its marginal notes, dealt with 'The rise of the workingman is not hindered as much as at first sight appears, by his want of capital; for the loan fund is increasing in volume and in eagerness for employment. He is hindered much by the growing complexity of business; but he may overcome these difficulties. The rise may take two generations instead of one but that is not an unmixed evil.' Much of this is reproduced in *P* VIII, pp. 307–11, with some of the modifications, especially those made in the second edition, perhaps inspired by Jowett's comments.

I think that it would contribute to greater clearness, if you made a rather broader distinction between the general principles and the modifications required by the complexity of actual circumstances. I know that this is a great difficulty and that it is a question of degree or rather of leaning to one side or other of an awkward alternative. I only mean to say that the side to which you seem to me to lean too frequently, is that of introducing the necessary qualifications rather too soon.*

Higgs wrote to Foxwell in August that he was taking Marshall's *Principles* 'in small doses to prolong the pleasure of reading him', after indicating the previous month his delight in seeing the book for the first time and that he would soon be revelling in it. The smallness of the doses Higgs was taking is revealed by the fact that by late August he had not gone far out of the first book, criticising Marshall's discussion of custom in Book I, Chapter II, 'where Marshall appealed to Sir Henry Maine, whose teaching seems to me directly opposite'.[76]

Few authors could have expected a more favourable reaction to their first major book, and undoubtedly its author was in general pleased with this outcome.[77] Much of what he had aimed to do in the book had been captured in one form or another by the reviewers; many of whom also correctly recognised its importance and the originality of many of the contributions it contained. One particular aspect raised in many of the reviews seems to have annoyed him. This was the unfavourable comment his style, and even arrangement of the book, had occasionally received. Such criticism was all the more irksome because of the care and time Marshall had spent in designing what he believed the most appropriate arrangement, a matter over which he had pondered for close to a decade and had changed his mind several times. Likewise, the criticisms of style must have annoyed him because of the trouble he had taken over this, constantly revising in the light of comments from those who had been reading his proofs. Leslie Stephen's critical views on this aspect of the book appear to have been among the few examples of such criticism addressed to him personally. John Neville Keynes kept his general disdain for Marshall's style and arrangement for the privacy of his diary,[78] as did other former students and colleagues Nicholson, Price and Foxwell. That of Price and Nicholson has already been quoted, Foxwell, in a letter to Keynes a decade after the first appearance of the *Principles*, commented on some of its shortcomings which had been recognised by several of Foxwell's London acquaintances when the book was first published.

My only important difference with you is where, agreeing with Marshall, you say that Jevons's principle of marginal utility is only of coordinate importance with the principle of cost of production. Many persons were astonished at Marshall's position on this when his *Principles* appeared. . . . the one principle is universal and fundamental, the other special and accidental . . . the exceptional cases of Marshall and Ricardo are of enormous importance in practice, and his typical case of strict mutual determination much more rarely reached than he assumes.

---

* Marshall to Leslie Stephen, 1 March 1900, British Library of Political and Economic Science, Collection Misc. 476/M1829; Leslie Stephen's correspondence with William Booth (11 November 1891) and C.B. Clark, 18 March 1891 deals with a similar issue. Stephen's complaint about consumer's rent in this correspondence and Marshall's defence are discussed below, pp. 424 and n.*; Leslie Stephen to Marshall, 2 March 1891, Marshall Archive 1/104. Marshall was particularly worried by this type of criticism, as shown in a letter to Bonar (4 February 1891, in *Memorials*, pp. 363–4) seeking advice on how he should deal with this in his second edition.

The whole system of norms and types, which may be appropriate enough to Natural Science, and the study of kinds which we have not science enough to reduce to causal relations, seems to me out of place in economics where it has done endless mischief, not merely ethical but scientific also.[79]

Despite the silence of his friends on such matters, the openness with which the reviewers and some of his less close acquaintances broached the matter of faulty style and arrangement may have been enough to induce the early revision for the second edition, which began well within six months of the publication date of the first.

INNOVATING IN COMPETITIVE RESTRAINT: THE *PRINCIPLES* AND THE NET BOOK AGREEMENT

Marshall's *Principles* did not only make history in economics, it also made, admittedly on a smaller scale, a significant splash in publishing history. The book was the first published at the so-called net price system by Macmillan, a system designed to prohibit the contemporary practice of British booksellers to offer substantial discounts to their customers. When Macmillan in 1890 decided to introduce gradually the net book system for books which they thought could withstand initial unfavourable reactions from booksellers deprived of their power over granting substantial discounts, Marshall's *Principles*, then in press, immediately came to mind. As Macmillan explained to Marshall when acquainting him of this plan, the substantial discounts offered by booksellers led to two evils. It caused book prices to be artificially high in order to permit 'substantial' discounts and it lowered bookseller profitability from the excessive price competition it induced. Abolition of the system would enable publishers to nominally lower the price of books. If, as an experiment in net pricing, the *Principles* was published under a net book agreement, it could be offered at the price of 12s.6d. net instead of the 16s. gross they had discussed earlier, with a trade price of 10s.5d. and further discounts on settlement. Given the wide sales potential of the *Principles*, Macmillan assured Marshall the experiment could not possibly harm the sale of his book. The high cost of the book as a consequence of its gradual enlargement, had already led to suggestions of a retail price which Marshall was loath to accept, since it would make his book too expensive for students of small means. It therefore made the net price proposed particularly attractive. Marshall accepted, partly because of the lower cover price it secured for his book, and partly because he was under the wrong impression that the agreement would not prevent normal cash discounts by booksellers to their clients.[80]

In the event, the net price of 12s.6d. at which the *Principles* was published in July 1890 was only achieved by Marshall's offer to contribute £20 from his own pocket to the cost of additional corrections charged by the printer. These, Macmillan reminded him in accepting the offer, had been very large. In the week after publication, Marshall revealed his worries about the acceptance of the net book agreement. He wrote to Macmillan that he still did not comprehend all its features, seeking clarification of the restrictions it placed on booksellers to offer discounts for cash purchases,[81] but left the matter in abeyance. Further developments in the book trade returned the matter to Marshall's notice. The founding of a Publishers' Association in 1896 enabled the launching of a systematic attack on the sale of books at discount. As part of this campaign, member publishers appear to have sent a circular letter to their major authors seeking their views on the subject. Marshall replied to Macmillan's request by reverting to his principle of the desirability of discounts for cash payments, 'a service to economic and moral progress' originally achieved by the co-operative movement through forcing it on unwilling shopkeepers. If asked to provide rules for a net price agreement, Marshall argued a principle of cash discounts should be included in it. However, he expressed agreement with its underlying principle that net books should be sold only at the advertised price and no others, on ordinary quarterly accounts. Just before the fourth edition was due to appear, Marshall repeated his plea to Macmillan for a more favourable treatment to cash buyers under the net book agreement, adding he was also opposed to the scheme if it unfairly increased booksellers' profits.[82]

In response, Macmillan persuaded Marshall that his type of concessions would entail effective abandonment of the net book agreement. Marshall reluctantly accepted this advice as that of the expert. Nevertheless, Marshall continued to believe that cash discounts should be given by booksellers as a matter of principle, and that bookseller margins should be lowered on scientific works to provide additional income for young, unknown authors. Marshall returned to this subject in further correspondence in 1898, and again when the publishers' war with the *Times* Book Club over the net book agreement during 1907–8 brought the issue back to the public arena. Guillebaud's judicious summing up of this long episode of correspondence between publisher and economist-author on the economics of the booktrade is a neat representation of Marshall's position on this issue. Macmillan was right in opposing discounts for cash payments in the initial years of the scheme; it would have entailed opportunities for more general discounting of the type the scheme was designed to prevent. However, Marshall was more prescient in suggesting discriminatory margins to subsidise certain types of books, a practice in bookselling which in fact developed after his death. Furthermore, Marshall's opposition to the net book scheme was never on the grounds that retail price maintenance was uncompetitive; it rested largely on his acceptance of the cooperative principle that cash payment deserved discount, and that, had he known this principle could not be easily applied under the net book agreement, he would not have accepted Macmillan's offer to sell the *Principles* at a net price of 12s.6d.[83]

FROM EDITION 1 TO EDITION 4 (1898): FIDDLING AT THE MARGIN OF IMPROVEMENT

Criticism of style and arrangement in the reviews of his book drove Marshall to prepare for a second edition before 1890 had ended. In mid-January, John Neville Keynes recorded in his diary[84] that Marshall was making 'very extensive alterations in the 2nd edition of his book' and expressed his agreement with 'Mrs. Marshall that it would have been wiser not to attempt any rewriting' at this stage. Mary Paley had in fact earlier confided her worries on this score to Benjamin Jowett, who on 30 December 1890 tried to console her by arguing that her fears were exaggerated. 'Don't fear the work of revision. It is not really laborious: the labour was in the original concoction, and great improvement is possible because the author has more command of his subject and can see his own defects when he comes fresh to them after an interval. I should like to have new editions of books greatly altered every five years.'[85] Given that in this case revisions were made after five months rather than five years, Jowett's comments may have provided less solace than intended. He was, however, right in saying revision took less time than concoction. At the end of June 1891, Keynes's diary reported his receipt of the second edition.[86]

Although as Guillebaud[87] remarked, the 'representative firm made its first official bow' in the second edition, most of the revisions to the text were 'in points of detail, and arrangement'. The re-arrangements restored subdivision of the volume to six books, thereby rejecting the scheme Marshall had introduced at such cost in time during 1888–89 by adding a separate book on cost of production. For the new edition, its chapters were amalgamated into Book V with the warning that many of them could be omitted by those whose interest in economics is 'chiefly on the social and practical side'. Marshall justified this change in the preface as follows. The new arrangement illuminated more strikingly the importance of time in economics by showing 'more clearly how time modifies the reciprocal influences of the earnings of workers and the prices of the goods made by them. For as regards fluctuations in short periods the leading role is held by prices, and a subordinate one by earnings: but as regards the slow adjustments of normal value their parts are interchanged; and the influence which price exerts on earnings, is less than that which earnings exert on prices.' Marshall added that these considerations were closely connected with alterations made to the opening and closing chapters of the Book on distribution and exchange. They had been designed to emphasise the interdependence of forces governing supply and demand for agents of production, as shown, for example, by the inclusion of wants and activities in the standard of life.[88] In the early Books, the arrangement was also significantly altered. In Book I, Chapters V–VII were re-arranged and revised to become Chapters V–VI; in Book II, Chapters III and IV were combined to make a new Chapter III so that its contents were reduced from 6 to 5 chapters; in Book III, two new chapters were added to make a total of six, largely designed to meet points of criticism his treatment of demand had received. Book IV was changed little; the final Books carried the marks of the major re-arrangement already noted, and some of their chapters, such as those in the Book on Distribution already mentioned, were re-arranged and revised. These changes produced an effective increase in the size of the book from 754 to 770 pages.[89]

The last paragraph of the preface to the second edition drew attention to a further change: Edgeworth's name appeared among those from whom Marshall received help and suggestions in preparing the second edition. Much of this help was received in the context of Marshall's note on barter (appended to Book V, Chapter 2) and in the form of a major addition to the associated mathematical note, XII bis. The last made explicit use of Edgeworth's innovation of the contract curve and drew attention to articles on the subject in the *Giornale degli economisti* by Edgeworth and Berry.[90] These additions hide a rather acerbic correspondence between Marshall and Edgeworth during the preparation of the second edition in early 1891. In his letters, Marshall charged Edgeworth, among other things, with trying to gain easy credit for 'saying something new, whereas it was not new', and of attributing an error to Marshall 'of a kind which, if he had made it, would justly shake the credit of a very great part of his book'. The last was particularly painful to Marshall because it depicted him unjustly as a person with 'a lightness of heart and an absence of a sense of intellectual responsibility', thereby shaking popular acceptance 'of those many passages which in a book of this kind are necessarily rather hard to understand'.[91] Marshall's letters also drew attention to Edgeworth's second contribution to the new edition, a criticism he had made of Marshall's formula for estimating the present value of a piano to its owner. This may explain why the section of Book III Chapter II dealing with discounting the future became a full chapter (Book III, Chapter V) with, in addition, some substantial revision of the relevant mathematical note.[92] This episode illustrates Marshall's rather rueful admission to his nephew, made much later in his life, how controversy and misunderstanding inspired many of the revisions he made to his book, all designed to clarify his real meaning of the disputed or misunderstood argument.[93]

Similar controversy and misunderstanding explain the many changes in the third edition of 1895. Prepared at the time when 'Marshall's powers as a writer were perhaps at their peak', the third edition is often considered the best version of the *Principles* in so far as freshness and enthusiasm in writing are concerned, qualities it shares with the previous two but not the subsequent five editions.[94] Marshall's preface drew attention to substantial changes to the opening chapters of Book VI on distribution, as well as to revisions in the fifth and sixth chapters of Book I; the final chapter of Book III and, in Book II, the amalgamation of the chapters on capital and income into a single chapter, thereby reducing the number of definitional chapters in that book to four.[95] It also enlarged Mathematical Notes XIV from the two paragraphs in the second edition to over six pages. From the perspective of subsequent debate it generated, the changes made to Book III, Chapter VI, are of the greatest interest. Apart from introducing the notion of Giffen good to the literature of economics, these replaced coal with tea as the commodity used to illustrate consumer surplus, while significant changes were also made in the treatment of aggregating consumer surplus for the same commodity across different consumers.[96] Elaboration of this aspect of the revisions for edition three enables further comment on the manner in which Marshall reacted to criticism.

The replacement of coal by tea was designed to eliminate problems about the requirement of constancy in the marginal utility of money income when estimating consumer surplus. Marshall's correspondence with Leslie Stephen in March 1891 shows that this was a matter troubling some of his readers, and that, in the first edition at least, he had made it insufficiently clear in the text (but not in the relevant mathematical note) that his analysis required constancy of the marginal utility of money income for strict mathematical accuracy, something which could be approximated by taking as example a commodity of less significance than coal to the ordinary household budget. He also advised Stephen that the matter had been partially redressed in the second edition by inserting an appropriate footnote. By the time the third edition was in preparation, further criticism of the concept seems to have convinced Marshall that tea was a better example in this context than coal, because expenditure on tea was a much smaller fraction of a typical household budget than expenditure on coal.[*]

---

[*] Alfred Marshall to Leslie Stephen, 1 March 1891 (British Library of Economics and Political Science, Collection Misc. 476, M1129). The note in *P* I (p. 470, last paragraph), which Marshall mentioned in this letter, shows this very clearly: 'In the discussion of Consumer's Rent, we must assume that the marginal utility of money to the individual purchaser is the same throughout.' In *P* II (p. 182 n.1) Marshall repeated this in a different manner in a note to the text, 'It is not necessary for our present purpose to take account of the possibility that the marginal utility of money to him might be appreciably altered in the course of his purchases'. By the third edition, the

During the years between the publication of the second and the third editions, other criticism of the notion of consumer surplus, partly in the context of this assumption, appeared in the literature. Among the more prominent was that by Nicholson, to which Edgeworth replied in the *Economic Journal*.[97] Marshall's alterations to Book III, Chapter 6 were largely in response to Nicholson's critique, as is shown by the several references Marshall made to it. Its new Section 4, in which the Giffen good was mentioned, was specifically directed at Nicholson's criticism, by illustrating a rare exception to Marshall's general argument. This also belittled Nicholson's critique by mentioning the 'legitimacy of the familiar scientific method' of neglecting the second order of small quantities, a rhetorical device which has been 'described as an iron fist in a velvet glove'.[98] Much subsequent interest in this section has turned on the fact that Giffen's argument to which Marshall alluded in the text of the *Principles* could not be traced; there were, however, plenty of other economic writers who were familiar with the phenomenon Marshall ascribed to Giffen. In June 1893, Marshall himself had queried the degree of accuracy in observing expenditures on basics when estimating relative household during the discussion of a paper on 'workmen's Budgets' by Higgs. He later claimed to have studied the question in detail.[99] This episode once again illustrates Marshall's motivation for revising his *Principles*: reply to criticism and explanation and re-writing of passages which had proved difficult to grasp by others.

Marshall also used the journals for defending positions he had taken in his book. The first example of this practice is a note on 'Consumer Surplus' in the *Annals of the American Academy* in response to misunderstandings in a paper by Simon Patten about the nature of the assumptions required for its analysis.[100] The second, in the *Economic Journal*, addressed a substantial number of misconceptions by the Duke of Argyll on Marshall's broad position on rent.[101] It probably induced the substantial revisions on this topic Marshall prepared for both the fourth and the fifth editions. The third was a defence against American critics of his general treatment of distribution and exchange in the first volume of his *Principles*. This article also sought to defend features of his arrangement of the contents, particularly the prominence given to historical material in the first book. Before publication of the fourth edition in 1898, Marshall wrote to Macmillan that the paper 'Distribution and Exchange' was intended to explain the *Principles*' overall plan and structure which Marshall by then thought to be definitive.[102] Marshall blamed absence of the second volume for generating such misrepresentations and careless criticisms of the already long-standing first volume. The article was needed to clarify this and to explain his first 'volume's preliminary method' more fully. Marshall elaborated the point by contrasting biological methods with mechanics, organic growth with equilibrium analysis and the stationary state, dynamics and statics, construction and theory. The historical chapters in Book I with all their acknowledged imperfections were defined as essential to emphasise the organic growth characteristics a mature economics should have, and which an economics for beginners, or a first volume of foundations, could only hint at. Marshall then

principle was firmly enshrined in the last sentence of mathematical note VI with reference to the new example of tea (see, for example, *P* VIII, p. 842). At the initial proof stage, Marshall had already needed to explain problems of the meaning and measurement of utility and consumer's rent to J.N. Keynes. Marshall to Keynes, 26 November, 2 December 1889, Marshall Archive, 1:72, 1:93, which are reproduced in *P* IX, pp. 260–61.

drew on these broad methodological issues to clarify specific misunderstandings of his position on two matters. One was market analysis in terms of amounts bought and sold as against normal problems which compared rate of production and consumption; another, the dangers of using statical analysis for very long-run problems.

During the currency of the third and fourth editions Marshall also used the technique of issuing additional corrigenda after their publication. Marshall had adopted this tactic for the third edition to make redress to Cannan for careless use in the *Principles* of Cannan's argument on the population of Liverpool. Such additional corrigenda were printed at Marshall's expense, supplied by him to Macmillan for insertion into unsold copies of the edition in question while he also took the step to send them himself to known owners of the book. During the fifth year of the fourth edition, Marshall had Macmillan print 5,000 copies of an extensive addenda and corrigenda, covering two pages of small print, to be distributed in the manner described. From the end of 1902, copies of the fourth edition were sold with this insertion. Marshall's use of this device highlights his pathological fear of making mistakes, the *raison d'être* for its introduction; and his similar obsession about avoiding 'unnecessary controversy' from misunderstanding when this could be attributed to unsatisfactory expression on his part.[103]

The fourth edition, of 1898, made relatively few changes. Its preface explained that all were 'of small compass, and, in the hope they are nearly final, the present edition has been made a large one'. Many involved rearrangements by the transfer of sections from one chapter to another; the greater part of the changes occurring in Books V and VI. Most important was the concentration of material on quasi rent within one chapter (Book V, Chapter XI), perhaps the best version of that theory in the eight editions Marshall produced. The fourth edition in fact lasted for nearly ten years, the longest time between various editions he prepared.[104]

THE *ELEMENTS OF ECONOMICS OF INDUSTRY* AND WORK ON THE SECOND VOLUME

After the second edition of the *Principles* had been published in June 1891, Marshall commenced work on a condensation of the book, which adapted it 'to the needs of junior students'.[105] This new project, which Marshall called *Elements of Economics of Industry*, followed the contents of the second edition with only one major exception: the addition of a chapter on trade unions which concluded Book VI of the abridgement. Although in July 1891 Marshall informed Macmillan that he hoped to complete this new book quickly, the chapter on trade unions was not completed until the start of 1892, when proofs were sent for comment to John Neville Keynes, and to two specialists in the field, John Burnett and T.S. Cree.* As Marshall explained to Keynes,

---

* Marshall to Macmillan, 12 June 1891, Marshall Archive, 4:3; Preface to the first edition of *EEI*, February 1892; Marshall to Keynes, 31 January 1892, Marshall Archive, 1:104. John Burnett (1842–1914), held positions on the Board of Trade, was a person sympathetic to the old trade union system, a General Secretary to the Amalgamated Society of Engineers and Assistant Secretary to the Labour Commission. He completed several works on trade union questions. T.S. Cree (1838–1919) had published *A Criticism of the Theory of Trade Unions* in 1891.

I wonder whether you can spare time to look at the enclosed proofs of a chapter on Trade Unions that I am writing for the new Economics of Industry. It is to be tacked on to the abridgment of Vol. I of Principles (I send only two thirds by this post: the rest I hope follows in the next). I have not had time to read it carefully yet, but have made a few corrections on the copy I send you. I fear I shall have to send that copy to the press, so please write on it only with soft pencil. . . . I am afraid I shall always be ashamed of this chapter, but the book is out of print, and there is no good in waiting, there are so many other things to do.*

By February 1892, the book was printed. Its 424 pages made the contents more than half that of the *Principles*. Once again, there was some haggling with Macmillan over the terms, with respect to both retail price and royalties, as well as over an additional £35 charged by the printers for an extra sheet Marshall had added to the book during its final stages of production. However, by March these problems were resolved. Marshall accepted Macmillan's offer of £50 for the first 3,000 copies sold in England, one sixth of the 4/6 retail price for the subsequent 2,000 copies (or a total of £75) and a one-tenth royalty on copies sent to America.[106] Later that month, Marshall sent his publishers a list of persons whom he wished to receive free copies, including academic economists, friends, relatives, a number of libraries and academic journals for purpose of review.[†]

---

* Marshall to J.N. Keynes, 31 January 1892, Marshall Archive, 1:104. It is interesting to speculate what Keynes would have made of the reason Marshall gave for replacing the old *Economics of Industry* with the new *Elements*. (For the former's suppression, see above, Chapter 6, pp. 178–9, Chapter 8, pp. 251–3.)

† Marshall's list favoured many of his Cambridge and other British colleagues with copies of the book. These included Foxwell, Sidgwick, John Neville Keynes, William Cunningham, Sorley and Ernest Foxwell (Foxwell's younger brother) and, outside Cambridge, economists Wicksteed, Edgeworth, L.L. Price, Phelps, Cannan, Munro, McKenzie, Gonner, Bastable, Mavor, Smart, Nicholson, Graham, Mills, Symes, as well as Berry, Cunynghame and Flux. American economists sent the book included President Andrews of Brown University, Walker, Sumner, Hadley, Seligman, Adams, Clark, Eliot, Taussig, Giddings, Ely, Patten, Jenks and Ashley (then in America); while in continental Europe its recipients included Gide, Walras and Leroy-Beaulieu in France; Cossa and Pantaleoni in Italy; Böhm-Bawerk, Menger and Sax in Austria; and in Germany, Wagner, Halle, Brentano, Cohn and Schmoller. Outside academe and economics faculty, family, colleagues and friends were sent copies. Father William, brother Charles, sister Mabel and Aunt Louisa received copies, as did father-in-law and brother-in-law Robert. From Bristol days Marshall remembered Albert and Lewis Fry, Francis Budd, as well as Wilson and Percival; copies likewise went to Benjamin Jowett; Westcott, the Bishop of Durham; Charles Booth, Leonard Courtney, Goschen, Canon Scott Holland and Sir Andrew Clark, whom Marshall occasionally consulted for medical advice. As a sign of Marshall's appointment to the Labour Commission, its secretary, Geoffrey Drage, fellow commissioners, and trade union friends Thomas Burt and Tom Mann, as well as the Dockers and General Labourers Union were provided with copies of the book. Marshall also gave copies to the Cambridge University Library, the College Libraries of Johns, Girton and Newnham; Bristol University College Library and Toynbee Hall, Burnett and Cree, whom Marshall had asked to comment on the trade union chapter received complimentary copies for their services. Reviewers in 'specialist' journals were not forgotten. These included the *Economist*, *Statist*, *Statistical Journal*, *Economic Journal*, *Economic Review*, *Journal of the Institute of Bankers* in England; the *Quarterly Journal of Economics*, *Political Science Quarterly*, *Annals of the American Academy of Sciences*, *Zeitschrift fur die Gesammte Staatswissenschaft; Jahrbuch fur Gezetsbung, Verwaltung und Volkwirtstschaft*, *Jahrbucher fur Nationaloekonomie, l'Economiste français, Revue des économistes, La Economista and Giornale degli Economisti*. A few names on the preserved lists were subsequently crossed out. Examples are Beddoe (the Marshalls' physician in Bristol), Mrs Fawcett and Ingram, Burt and Phelps, the last two appearing elsewhere on the list. A long list of leaders from the Cooperative Movement were also to be sent copies of the book (Marshall to Macmillan, March 1892: 'A list of names to whom a book should be sent', Marshall Archive, File 6 (2). (Whether Marshall accompanied this gift with the request he had earlier sent to Ernest Guillebaud, his brother-in-law as husband of elder sister Mabel, when sending him the *Principles*, is not recorded for posterity. This asked that on receipt of this volume, the return for destruction of a presentation copy of the previous *Economics of Industry* was expected. (C.W. Guillebaud, introduction to *P* IX, n.c.). However, a letter to Hewins, 29 May 1900, suggests he may have been in the habit of asking friends to return copies of the *Economics of Industry* to him for 'destruction', since it thanks Hewins 'for the first edition of the Economics of Industry' (Sheffield University Library, Hewins

The new abridgement was as favourably reviewed in 1892 as its original source had been two years previously. Most reviewers praised Marshall's decision to make his 'standard work' more accessible to the wider public, and commented approvingly on the degree of discretion with which the task of condensation had been carried out. Only the *Journal of Education* demurred from this general opinion, by expressing the thought that 'beginners . . . will find it much too difficult'.[107] The addition of a chapter on trade unions was generally described as a wise and valuable inclusion, although in the *Journal des économistes* Courcelle-Seneuil queried 'the indolence' with which Marshall had treated this important subject.

Many reviewers of the *Elements* took the opportunity to lament the passing of its predecessor co-authored with Mrs Marshall, *Economics of Industry*. The *National Reformer* explained its demise by the fact that the 1879 book no longer 'properly presents [the] views' of the author of the *Principles*; Bonar expressed regrets in *The Academy* that replacing the *Economics of Industry*, 'for the last dozen years the best short text-book for that part of the subject which it has covered', was not achieved by expansion of the subject matter covered, but rather by its further contraction. The new *Elements* therefore shared even more the 'drawback' of its predecessor and of the more voluminous *Principles* in 'being [one of] three First Volumes', a detriment assessable in terms of their omissions of 'International Trade, Banking, Currency, Bimetallism and Taxation'. Hopefully, the intended second volumes would soon rectify this shortcoming. Price in the pages of the *Economic Journal* shared these regrets about the disappearance of the old *Economics of Industry*, particularly since the new, only containing 'the framework of the central theory' together with a chapter on trade unions, did not provide the comprehensive guidance to the subject beginners looked for in such a work and an omission only remediable by the speedy appearance of the promised second volume.[108]

Progress with the second volume, so eagerly desired by the more perceptive reviewers of the *Elements*, was not very advanced by 1892. Although preparation of the *Elements* did not completely prevent work on the second volume, which was in effect started in late 1891, Marshall could report little progress to his publishers in October 1891; a far cry from his optimistic forecasts in 1887 which had predicted its completion some time during 1889.[109] Marshall's appointment earlier in 1891 to the Labour Commission with its solid schedule of sittings during the final months of 1891 and much of 1892, prevented solid work on the second volume in these years. Only in May 1893, by which time the work load associated with the Labour Commission was reduced to comments on its draft final report, did Marshall indicate to Cannan that he was 'immersed' in problems of money and foreign trade for the second volume, a task to be assisted by his lecturing schedule at Cambridge arranged by him later that year. This enabled alternate lectures each year on foreign trade and the functions of government with those on money, banking and modern markets for goods and labour; hence covering the subject matter he had provisionally outlined for the proposed contents of the second volume in 1887.[110] Influenced perhaps by the scale of the many reports of the Labour Commission which was steadily winding its way to conclusion, the

---

Papers).   Tom Mann thanked Marshall for the gift of the book, which Marshall had sent him with some other papers (Tom Mann to Marshall, 12 May 1892, Marshall Archive, 1:86).

work during 1894, as Mary Paley later recollected, began with a historical treatment of foreign trade of such immense proportions that Marshall afterwards described it as his 'white elephant'.[111] Three years later he commented on this episode in a revealing letter to Lord Acton,

> My book makes no progress. The work for it which I feel I *must* do before finishing it, grows: there is more of it ahead than there was when I finished my last volume. The history of foreign trade seduced me: I thought it exceptionally instructive for modern times: and I spent an incredible time in laboriously producing several chapters about it. And yet, after all, I find that they would make the main arrangement hang so, that I am forced to fall back on the awkward expedient of putting them into an appendix, and making frequent references to them in illustration of my argument. I made the resolve sadly, but at the same time I resolved to read as little history as possible till I had finished my main work. I find that the illustrations which I want to take from recent events alone will occupy more time than I can spare, and will fill more pages than people will have patience to read.[112]

Part of this arduous labour found its way ultimately into the two volumes Marshall published more than two decades later.[113] The years from 1897 produced new interruptions. Apart from Marshall's involvement in the women's degree issue, there were the fourth edition of Volume I, more work for Royal Commissions, that is, those on Indian currency and on local taxation, and, during the early years of the new century, Marshall's arduous campaign for a separate Economics and Political Tripos.[114] Intermittent work on Volume II was occasionally reported to correspondents. Marshall wrote Bishop Westcott in October 1899 that speculation and stock exchange fluctuations were occupying his spare time, but that this, as other work for the second volume, 'grows in difficulty in my hands'. Problems of writing, similar to those expressed to Hewins, were reported to Seligman in May 1900. 'I am lost in a mass of material relating to Trade, Money, etc. which I cannot get into order. I can't recollect what I have said in one chapter, and am constantly saying the same thing twice and wasting time.' Two years later, from the Tirol, Marshall wrote to Edgeworth that the relationship between trusts and the stability of industry was to be covered in the second volume. At the end of that year, he wrote to Macmillan that though he was pursuing the task of writing the second volume with all the resolution he could muster, lack of leisure prevented speedy progress.[115]

By 1903, the summer of which was largely devoted to the fiscal question in international trade, the original scheme for the second volume was abandoned and, as he later recollected, an alternative table of contents devised. This greatly expanded the contents as compared with the sensible outline proposed in 1887 but, relative to the scale on which the 'white elephant' was constructed, must have appeared to its author as a model of restraint. 'The order then proposed for the continuation of the *Principles* . . . was fairly settled as follows,

1. Currency (first stage)
2. International Trade (first stage)
3. Credit and its Markets
4. Produce Markets
5. Business Combinations and Monopolies, Transport Problems
6. Association and Combination in relation to Employment
7. Credit Fluctuations (including second stages of Currency and International Trade)

8.　　　The Distribution of the National Income (concluded on the basis of Book VI [VII in first edition] of my first volume)
9.　　　Public Finance.'[*]

However, as Whitaker concludes on this phase in Marshall's valiant attempt at completing Volume II of the *Principles*, 'hardly anything remains of the thousand-page rough draft of this material'.[116] Much of it was cannibalised for the final volumes, and only rough, miscellaneous notes survive from the unsuccessful labour for the ten years spent on this draft until the end of 1903. Some of these notes were included in subsequent editions of the *Principles*. An example is a new Section 9, added to the chapter on monopolies (Book V, Chapter XIV) in the fifth edition of 1907. By that time, the single volume of the *Principles* was so well established as a volume of foundations, that it could stand on its own. This was facilitated by the few references in the text of the *Principles* which referred to the second volume, and even these were generally 'never conspicuous and [invariably] vague'. By 1910, the preface to the sixth edition recognised the inevitable. In a resumé of the twenty years which followed first publication of the first volume, Marshall explicitly abandoned his proposed second volume, suggesting by way of replacement, more or less independent volumes on *National Industries and Trade* and *Money, Credit and Employment*. In recognition of this change of policy, the Volume I was removed from the spine where it had featured for the previous five editions, and the scope of the work was explicitly re-defined as a self-standing volume of foundations.[117]

Heavily entangled though it is with the writing of the second volume, the tale of the other volumes is discussed later.[118] The original and highly appropriate design of that second volume, as enunciated in 1887 and widely expected by the reviewers of the first edition as a component essential to their claim that Marshall's work was a genuine successor to Mill's, never materialised through procrastination and other diversions on Marshall's part. Even in the years immediately before his retirement from the Cambridge chair in 1908, it seems unlikely that Marshall could have completed the 1887 plan for the second volume on a par with that of the first, by blending theoretical principles with factual material and by presenting the mathematical skeleton of his framework in a series of end notes. Marshall wrote to the Austrian economist, Lieben,[119] that by 1906 he rarely used diagrams in his lectures, had forgotten much of the theory from his own completed volume, and would have been incapable of formalising and systematising into a coherent and concise framework the mass of material on trade, money, markets, fluctuations and public finance on which he had been lecturing for so long. The real tragedy of the planned 'second volume' is therefore that Marshall failed to concentrate on its writings during the early years of the 1890s, when his analytical powers still enabled him to do so. In the ten years from 1898 to his retirement it was already too late to complete his *Principles* in the manner he intended in the late 1880s.

---

[*]　Undated manuscript fragment Marshall Library; reproduced from *EEW*, I, p. 93. This mentions a very rough draft of over a thousand pages for Volume II, which had been completed by 1903. In 1897, Marshall wrote to Foxwell that he had 'consumed nearly a ream of paper on myriad drafts of the table of contents of my book' (26 April 1897, Marshall Archive, 1/58).

THE FINAL MODIFICATIONS OF THE *PRINCIPLES*: TOWARDS THE DEFINITIVE VERSION OF THE EIGHTH EDITION

The 5,000 copies of the fourth edition published in 1898 lasted for nearly a decade, all but fifty being sold by July 1907.[120] Marshall therefore commenced preparation of a fifth edition around the start of 1907, a task completed in August. This largely consisted of a rearrangement of the contents. Much of the introductory material was shifted from Book I of the text to appendices, as were many of the long notes which had concluded chapters in previous editions. A new appendix based on material published after 1898 was added.[*]

New material in the text also drew on previously published work. For example, Book I, Chapter XIV, §5 partly reproduced Marshall's 1902 *Plea for the Creation of a Curriculum in Economics and Associated Branches of Political Science*, published in the context of his drive for a separate Economics Tripos at Cambridge. Material was also added to the chapter on monopolies from drafts of the 'second' volume. Last but not least, the final chapter in this edition of the *Principles* incorporated material on trade unions, matching thereby the strategy adopted for the *Elements* in 1892 of rounding off the book on distribution with this practical and applied topic.[121] The smaller print of the appendices enabled expansion of the contents without adding greatly to the total number of pages. The new material in actual fact added therefore many new pages to the text, 'often of considerable importance in the light they throw on Marshall's system of thought, but they added no really fresh ideas'.[122]

Assistants in preparing successive new editions were also changed and duly recorded in the prefaces. Ashley, Sidgwick (from the fifth edition described as 'the late') and Taussig were continuously noted in this capacity from the third edition, Cannan and Pigou from the fourth, and Fay from the sixth.[¶] Cannan and Fay indicated in some detail their contribution to the never-ending revision process in correspondence which has survived. Cannan had joined the error-spotting team when Marshall had wrongly quoted him on the growth of the population of Liverpool, an error which resulted in Marshall's apologetic confession and the special corrigenda for the third edition.[123] Fay later recalled that for the sixth edition,

---

[*] The first four appendices of the fifth edition drew on material originally included in Book I of the previous versions. Appendix A and B essentially reprinted the historical material of Chapters II–IV of that book, a matter which Marshall had resisted in 1898 acting partly on the advice of Taussig and others (Taussig to Marshall, 21 December 1897; Marshall to J.N. Keynes, 17 October 1897) but to which he eventually succumbed. Marshall justified this change in terms of criticism offered by many of his readers that presentation of this historical material at the start of the book postponed its main subject matter for too long. Appendices C and D contained methodological material transferred from the final chapters of the first Book in the previous editions. Other appendices were based on long notes of earlier editions. Appendix E evolved from a long note on definitions of capital introduced in the fourth edition; Appendix F was a note on barter inserted at the end of Book V, Chapter II for the first four editions; Appendix H drew on a long note on stable and unstable equilibria inserted from the fourth edition in Book V, Chapter XI; Appendix I contained the long note on Ricardo from the first edition; Appendix J reproduced the long note on the wages fund and on two of Mill's fundamental propositions on capital appended to one of the wages chapters in the final book on distribution for all previous editions; Appendix K originated in the third edition, Book VI, Chapter 2, §6 from which it was moved to the wages fund note to Book VI, Chapter II of the fourth; finally Appendix L incorporated a long note on Ricardo's doctrine on the incidence of taxation and the influence of improvements in agriculture in existence from the first edition. (*P* IX, pp. 722 ff, *passim*). Appendix G on the incidence of local rates largely reprinted material from the *Memorandum on Taxation* Marshall had prepared for the Royal Commission on Local Taxation ten years before.

[¶] Others, named only once per edition, included William Bateson (presumably on topics associated with heredity); McKenzie, both for the third edition, Wickett (Toronto) and Edgerton (Ithaca) for the fourth.

Cannan used to send him regular reports of mistakes which, when they had reached a total of twenty, Fay posted on to Balliol Croft. They were then acknowledged with the postcard, 'Thanks for the Errata: I have handed them to Mary: the mistakes are her department'. Fay, however, occasionally received a demur from the perpetrator of the errors,

> I am immensely grateful. I know there *must* be errors so I get only pleasure from being shown where they are. I have adopted practically all your suggestions, except as to p. 129. I think 'yet' is implied – but ought to have been expressed – before 'he does so because': there should be only a comma after 'tea' in the next line, followed I think by 'and'.*

Such were the trials of being the devoted student of the great man

The substantial new preface to this edition prepared the way for treating the *Principles* as an independent volume of foundations, hence foreshadowing the explicit abandonment of the second volume formalised in the sixth. It also incorporated some of the methodological contents from the 1898 *Economic Journal* article on 'Distribution and Exchange', as in the following paragraphs contrasting biology and mechanics, statics and dynamics,

> The Mecca of the economist lies in economic biology rather than in economic dynamics. But biological conceptions are more complex than those of dynamics; a volume on Foundations must therefore give a relatively large place to mechanical analogies; and frequent use is made of the term 'equilibrium', which suggests something of statical analogy. This fact, combined with the predominant attention paid in the present volume to the normal conditions of life in the modern age, has suggested the notion that its central idea is 'statical', rather than 'dynamical'. But that suggestion is incorrect in any case; and it is wholly unfounded, if the terms are interpreted as in physical science. . . .
>
> Some discussions as to the methods of social sciences have seemed to imply that statics and dynamics are distinct branches of physics. But of course they are not. The modern mathematician is familiar with the notion that dynamics include statics. If he can solve a problem dynamically, he seldom cares to solve it statically also. To get the statical solution from the dynamical, all that is needed is to make the relative velocities of the things under study equal to zero, and thus reduce them to relative rest. But the statical solution has claims of its own. It is simpler than the dynamical; it may afford useful preparation and training for the more difficult dynamical solution; and it may be the first step towards a provisional and partial solution in problems so complex that a complete dynamical solution is beyond our attainment. This volume then is concerned throughout with the forces that cause movement; and its key-note is that of dynamics. . . .
>
> At the end of this second stage the area of the dynamical problem has become much larger; the area covered by provisional statical assumptions has become much smaller; and at last is reached the great central problem of the Distribution of the National Dividend among a vast number of different agents of production. The dynamical principle of 'Substitution' is seen ever at work, causing the demand for, and the supply of, any one set of agents of production to be influenced, through indirect channels, by the movements of demand and supply in relation to others, even though situated in far remote fields of industry. Our main concern is with human beings who are impelled, for good and evil, to change and progress. Fragmentary statical hypotheses are useful as temporary auxiliaries to dynamical – or rather biological – conceptions; but the central idea in a volume on the Foundations of Economics, as in any other, must be that of living force and movement.[124]

---

* Cannan Papers, 969, p. 9; Marshall to Fay, 6 October 1908, Marshall Archive, 1:51. The passage in question reads: 'on the ground that though, when a person spends six pence on a quarter of a pound of tea instead of on a stone of salt, he does so because he prefers the tea; and he would not prefer the tea if he did not know that he could easily get whatever salt he need for his more urgent requirements.' See also *P* IX, pp. 262–3.

In his review of the fifth edition, Pigou[125] extensively discussed the points of revision which Marshall had announced in the preface from which extracts have just been quoted. He also stressed the constraints imposed on interpretation of the text now that the book had become a volume of foundations, arguing that students of Marshall who attended his lectures as well as read his book were more free from misinterpretations on this score. He then emphasised the originality of Marshall's contributions on the difficulty of time, and noted the significance of the changes in the new edition from the re-arrangement through appendices and the new material on trade unions, on distribution and on monopolies added to the text.

The sixth edition of 1910 removed the visible sign that the work was intended as the first volume of two, that is, the 'Vol. I' the first five had on their spine. It, however, contained few major textual alterations. The more important was a footnote (p. 424 n.1) in which Marshall attempted to explain what he meant and did not mean by the term quasi-rent; a footnote which since then has baffled many subsequent commentators. The seventh and eighth editions were virtually identical with the sixth so that, apart from minor alterations, the text of the work settled down to the definitive text of the eighth over its final decade during its author's lifetime. Such minor changes were not ended with the final edition prepared in 1920.[126] The 1922 reprinting incorporated changes of this nature, including a reference to an article by Taussig published in 1921.[127] Even that printing certainly would have been altered had Marshall lived longer. A copy of the *Principles* preserved in the Marshall Library contains suggestions for further corrections of a minor nature which show that even as an octogenarian Alfred Marshall continued his quest to reach the perfection in expression which had eluded him for so long.[128]

The *Principles* was translated into various European languages. Problems over a German translation at the start of the twentieth century can be documented from Marshall's extensive correspondence with Brentano.[129] In April 1903 Marshall informed Brentano that a young man from Leipzig, Hugo Ephraim, wrote to him the previous July that he had translated three-quarters of Marshall's book. Completion of the translation was then suspended for a year to enable Ephraim to finish his doctorate. Ephraim nevertheless hoped to complete translation by the 'stipulated time' of April 1904! Dubious of such a timetable, given his own forecasts in such matters, Marshall now sought Brentano's involvement in the project and assistance in the translation from one of Brentano's students, Kerstner. In his typical unbusiness-like manner, Marshall had not discussed payment with the translator nor, a week or so later, did he himself wish to claim royalties from the venture. 'I shall be more than satisfied by the mere fact that the book is well translated and well published'. Only by the following July did Marshall raise copyright problems associated with the translation, including the 'little difficulty' of 'volume II (in fact, there will probably be two more volumes if I live to finish the task)'. In August, the mundane pecuniary matters of the project were finalised after customary toing and froing. Marshall initially proposed royalties at £20 per thousand copies sold after the first thousand, the same arrangement to apply for all subsequent volumes. A week later, doubts were cast on this suggestion by Marshall, on the ground his claims were too high, inspired by a counter-suggestion received in the meantime from the proposed publisher. This predicated such payments only from the second edition, after the first 1,500 copies printed for the first edition had been sold. In mid-1905 the translation appeared with what Marshall described as a very 'flattering' introduction by Brentano. It was the first of many translations of Marshall's *Principles*.*

THE SIGNIFICANCE OF THE *PRINCIPLES*

As was quoted at the start of this chapter, in 1887 Marshall wrote to Macmillan that the *Principles* would be the 'central work' of his life. Part of the truth of this remark is amply demonstrated in the long haul of effort this project imposed on him during the four decades of his life he devoted to it. The *Principles* was of course central to his life as an economist in other ways. It became his great gift and legacy for the subject to the advancement of which he gave the greater part of his life. Although he himself could occasionally deprecate its lasting importance, by inscribing a gift copy to one of his students with 'the hope that in due course he will render this treatise obsolete',[130] the work has become a classic and continues to be read. Apart from this long-run value, the work also fulfilled its short-run aims as Maynard Keynes argued,

> The way in which Marshall's *Principles of Economics* is written is more unusual than the casual reader will notice. It is elaborately unsensational and under-emphatic. Its rhetoric is of the simplest, most unadorned order. It flows in a steady, lucid stream, with few passages which stop or perplex the intelligent reader, even though he knows but little economics. . . . By this stylistic achievement Marshall attained some of his objects. The book reached the general public. It increased the public esteem of Economics. The minimum of controversy was provoked. The average reviewer liked the author's attitude to his subject-matter, to his predecessors, and to his readers, and delighted Marshall by calling attention to the proper stress laid by him on the ethical element and to the much required humanising which the dismal science received at his hands; and, at the same time, could remain happily insensible to the book's intellectual stature. As time has gone on, moreover, the intellectual qualities of the book have permeated English economic thought, without noise or disturbance, in a degree which can easily be overlooked.[131]

The tremendous status of Marshall's great book in the development of economics has been reiterated time and time again since Keynes wrote these words, most frequently at times of major anniversaries of its first publication and at those of the birth and death of its author.[132] In a very perceptive semi-centenary appraisal of the *Principles*, Schumpeter wrote that although 'Marshallian economics has [already] passed away' in the sense that by 1940 'his vision of the economic process, his methods, his results are no longer ours. . . . In another sense, his teachings can never die':

> Its influence will last for an indefinite time not only because teaching of such breadth and force merges into the inheritance of subsequent generations, but also because there is about it a peculiar quality which effectively resists decay. Reared in an atmosphere that was full of the slogans of evolutionary progress, Marshall was one of the first economists to realize that economics is an evolutionary science (although his critics not only overlooked this element of his thought but in some instances actually indicted his economics on the very ground that it neglected the evolutionary aspect), and in particular that the human nature he

---

* The 1905 German translation virtually coincided with French and Italian translations published in the same year (Italian) or over the following ones (French). They were all made from *P* IV. Spanish and Portuguese translations followed in the 1930s and 1950s respectively, the second originating from Brazil. Translations into Japanese and Chinese were also published in the 1950s. Many of these translations were regularly reprinted, indicating the longevity of interest in Marshall's text.

1. *William Marshall 'a tough old character . . . bony neck, bristly projecting chin' (p.22)*

2. *Rebecca Marshall '[a] face [reflecting] anxiety and sorrow, and perhaps prolonged illness' (p.36)*

3. *Rebecca Marshall 'A greatly beloved mother' (p.34)*

4. *William Marshall 'an unselfish and kindly intentioned father' (p.21)*

5. *Agnes Marshall 'she looked after her brother in India and died there' (p.39)*

6. *Charles William Marshall 'sent to India at 17 and became manager of [a Bengal] silk factory' (p.38)*

7. *Mabel Louisa Marshall 'She and Alfred were very fond of one another' (p.38)*

8. *Walter Marshall 'an equally gifted boy' (p.39), who died in South Africa from 'consumption'*

9. *Merchant Taylors school 'exterior in Suffolk Lane', a vision of 'grime and . . . lack of architectural beauty' (pp.52–3)*

10. *The 'school as schoolroom is [a] strange [notion] to those whose education dates from a later period' (p.53)*

11. *The schoolboy aged 13 in 1855 'a lay-down collared youth' (p.51)*

12. *Alfred Marshall in 1869. A freshly 'appointed College Lecturer in the Moral Sciences' (p.108)*

13. *The masters at Clifton College, 1865 (pp.103–6). Extreme left: Alfred Marshall; second from right, Henry Graham Dakyns. '[C]apped, gowned, and clean-shaven with his temporary colleagues' (p.103)*

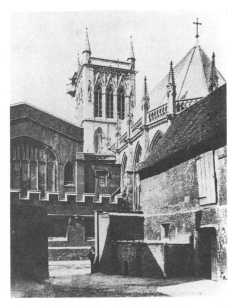

14. *Portrait of a working man –*
Marshall's patron saint who reminded
him of his true vocation in economic
studies (p.130)

15. *The College of St John the Evangelist.*
The new chapel 'not completed until 1869'
(p.76)

16. *'The Bridge of Sighs' at St John's College, joining Third and New Courts. A room*
'to catch the summer smells of [the] Cam' (p.87)

17. *Shaker Village of Mount Lebanon, New York.* 'I spent five or six hours at the Community' (p.198)

18. *With the 'Austrians' in the Tirol. Standing (from left to right): Zuckerkandl, Eugen von Böhm-Bawerk, Frau von Wieser; sitting (from left to right): Alfred Marshall, Mary Paley Marshall, Frau von Böhm-Bawerk, Friedrich von Wieser.* 'We boldly asked the whole company to a teaparty' (p.217)

19. *Alfred Marshall in the Tirol (1901)*

20. *Setting out for a day's work in the Grodner Tal*

21. *Communing with nature in the Tirol. Thinking about the next chapter (1909)*

22. *Tirol (1909) 'He . . . made a "throne" with an air cushion and a camp stool' (p.216)*

23. 'We were five months at Palermo, on a roof' (p.205)   The Cala, Palermo, from a water colour by Mary Paley Marshall (1881)

24.   'the sea was generally so calm that it reflected cloud shapes on its green and blue and purple surface' (p.205)

25.   Jane Harrison and Mary Paley 'went for a lovely walk of about six miles around the base of Pellegrino' (p.207)

26. *Mr and Mrs Marshall at the start of an unusual partnership (p.223)*

27. *'the bride wore white, had no veil' (p.223)*

28. *Principal of University College Bristol (p.230)*

29. *'an ascetic man, all mind and no body' (p.233)*

30. *'Imagine a female rat, without ears and with lots of hair . . . such is the Lady-Lecturer in Political Economy' (p.233)*

31. *A modest house with a '"pleasant" architectural effect' (p.242)*

32. *'a charmingly detailed timber verandah' to serve as study (p.244)*

33. *A study 'all books, with scarce room for Professor and students' (p.320) Mary Paley Marshall with Japanese guests at Balliol Croft, 1928*

34. *'the dog and cat at Balliol Croft' with the lady of the house (p.261)*

35. *Bristol University College, Park Row, Bristol, circa 1880.* '[I]nadequate room was the major constraint on [college] development' (p.277)

36. *6 Apsley Road, Clifton (now 31). The house where the Marshalls exercised their social responsibilities on entertaining on behalf of the College (p.284)*

37. *Balliol College, Oxford. The death of Toynbee 'intervened by creating a vacancy at Oxford, to which the Marshalls all too willingly escaped' (p.293)*

38. *Alfred Marshall circa 1885.* 'Mr Alfred Marshall . . . elected to succeed the late Professor Fawcett in the Chair of Political Economy' (p.306)

39. *Alfred Marshall circa 1890.* A relaxed pose of the Professor in his study

PRINCIPLES

OF

ECONOMICS

BY

ALFRED MARSHALL,

PROFESSOR OF POLITICAL ECONOMY IN THE UNIVERSITY OF CAMBRIDGE;
FELLOW OF ST JOHN'S COLLEGE, CAMBRIDGE;
SOMETIME FELLOW OF BALLIOL COLLEGE, OXFORD.

VOL. I.

Natura non facit saltum.

London:
MACMILLAN AND CO.
AND NEW YORK.
1890

[*All Rights reserved*]

40. *Title page of the* Principles. '*It is a very handsome volume*' (p.411)

41. *Marshall's 'virtuous fight against "the tyranny and the spiritual death of an iron-bound socialism"' as seen by Mr Punch (p.458)*

42. *Free Trade Advice as seen by the* Yorkshire Herald, *20 January 1909.* '*[An] issue . . . as controversial at the end of the twentieth century as it was in Marshall's later years*' (p. 388)

43. '*The Division of Labour*' *(*Harwich Express, *5 December 1908). '*Free importation . . . only reallocated labour and did not displace it with unemployment*' (p. 386)*

44. *A book that never was. Advertising* National Industries and International Trade *as 'in press' in 1904. 'I know I have run up a huge printers bill' (p. 703)*

In the Press.   8vo.

NATIONAL INDUSTRIES

AND

INTERNATIONAL TRADE

BY

ALFRED MARSHALL

PROFESSOR OF POLITICAL ECONOMY, CAMBRIDGE ;
HON. FELLOW OF BALLIOL COLLEGE, OXFORD

This work may be described as a study of the relations between industrial prosperity and international trade, such as the author conceives to be required as a basis of a fiscal policy adapted to the conditions of any particular country at any given time.   Towards the end of the book Professor Marshall applies the results of his investigation to the current fiscal problem in Great Britain.

MACMILLAN AND CO., LTD., LONDON.

45. Herbert Somerton Foxwell, 'a loyal, but ill-used, colleague and friend' (p.670)

46. Henry Sidgwick circa 1876, 'the "spiritual Mother and Father" betrayed' (p. 663)

47. Benjamin Jowett circa 1871, 'an economist of sorts and great influence on young men' (p.687)

48. John Neville Keynes circa 1880, a 'faithful . . . gradually disillusioned, lieutenant' (p.679)

49. *Alfred Marshall in 1917 'a sage in retirement' (p.618)*

50. *Alfred Marshall in 1908 as seen by William Rothenstein. 'He took sitting seriously, for he was vain' (pp.628–9)*

51. *Alfred Marshall in 1920, 'the sense of work well done' (p.649)*

52. *Alfred Marshall in 1920, 'wisps of white hair, and black cap on his head . . . the aspect of a sage or prophet' (p.654)*

ST JOHN'S COLLEGE, CAMBRIDGE

THE FUNERAL OF THE LATE

ALFRED MARSHALL, Sc.D.

BORN 26 JULY 1842
DIED 13 JULY 1924

EMERITUS PROFESSOR OF POLITICAL ECONOMY
HONORARY FELLOW OF THE COLLEGE

will take place on Thursday, July 17. The first part
of the Service will be held in the College Chapel at
2 p.m.

Members of the University and other friends who wish
to be present are requested to take their places in the
Chapel by 1.50.

It was his wish that no flowers should be sent.

The interment will be in St Giles's Cemetery,
Huntingdon Road.

53. *Notice of Alfred Marshall's Funeral Service 17 July 1924. 'Mourning . . . the College and University Man' (p. 742)*

54. *Marshall's gravestone, St Giles graveyard, Huntingdon Road, Cambridge. 'a far corner of its consecrated ground' (p. 743)*

1/127

1894

BALLIOL CROFT,
MADINGLEY ROAD, CAMBRIDGE. 16.X.96

Abundant thanks, Beloved Fox,
for relieving me of the fear of disgracing
the old Abline Meter. But I wanted
your letter to endorse to him: & you
have inserted irreverent remarks, that
put it hors de combat. So I have
had to extract its hints. Please
see that I have not gone wrong; & if not
front. Very sorry about your
cold. I don't think all the new
are up yet, or rather come up on

55. *Page from letter to Foxwell, 16 November 1894. 'Beloved Fox . . .'*

I find an additional reason for thinking that this
is a favourable time for retiring from any post in my
belief that you have a staff of exceptional ability;
and that you will have no difficulty in selecting from
them, should you desire it, a Principal who will
carry on the work of the College without any breach
of continuity, and with much greater chance of
success than I could have had.
Everything that could be done by yourselves or
the staff to make my post pleasant, has been done:
and I shall always feel that I owe my hearty agree-
grees to the College for having entered upon duties which
I was not strong enough to discharge. It is my one
consolation with regard to the past that in all
directions in which her influence could reach, my
wife has more than made up for my deficiencies;
and it is my chief regret with regard to the future
that her work must be lost to the College.
It is with feelings of deep gratitude for the most
generous and considerate treatment which I have
always received at your hands, that I ask your
kind permission to retire from my present post in
three months from this time.
I am, Gentlemen,
your most obliged servant,
Alfred Marshall.

T.O.

56. *A letter written with his 'electric pen' while at Bristol (p. 278n*)*

professed to deal with is malleable and changing in function of changing environments. But again, this is not what matters to us just now. What does matter is that he carried his 'evolution-mindedness' into his theoretical work. There was no air of finality about it. Unlike Mill, he would never have said that some problem or other was settled for all time to come and that there was nothing about it that called for further explanation either by himself or any other writer. On the contrary, he was fully aware that he was building an essentially temporary structure. He always pointed beyond himself and towards lands into which it was not given to himself to enter. New problems, ideas, and methods that are enemies to the work of other men, thus came to his own as allies. Within the vast fortified camp that he built, there was room – in fact, there was accommodation prepared in advance – for them all.[133]

An equally famous reassessment of Marshallian economics, written on the occasion of the centenary of Marshall's birth, elaborated the enormous impact of Marshall's book on the succeeding generations of students and teachers in the English-speaking world for the whole of the inter-war period, 1919–39, an unambiguous sign that 'its success in scientific circles was decisive and far-reaching':

> In England, it gradually acquired a position if not of such exclusive dominance as Mill's *Principles* had had in the generation after 1850, at least comparable with that. For the part of the field which it covers it became a leading text-book not only in its author's own University but wherever economics was seriously studied. A whole generation of students – more than one, indeed, as academic generations go – was brought up on it. The equilibrium of demand and supply as the all-pervasive element in the pricing process, the balancing of small increments of costs and receipts, 'marginal productivity', 'elasticity', 'substitution', the distinction between long and short periods, 'quasi-rent', 'prime' and 'supplementary' cost, the elegant and serviceable expository device of plane-curves, became the stock-in-trade of the professional economist. Ideas of this sort might very likely have permeated English political economy in any case. They were in the air. But as a matter of plain historical fact their prevalence is due to Marshall. In its country of origin Alfred Marshall's *Principles* stands with Adam Smith's *Wealth of Nations* and Ricardo's *Principles* as one of the three great watersheds in the development of economic ideas; with the usual qualifications, we may divide the history of English political economy into three distinct epochs – the Classical, the Ricardian and the Marshallian or reformed-Ricardian.
>   That the book powerfully affected theoretical economics in the United States is also evident. Thought in the 'Melting-Pot' is naturally somewhat eclectic, and in recent years one major schism at least has developed there. But both directly and through the work of such influential writers as F.W. Taussig and Prof. T.N. Carver (to name only two out of a number), the *Principles* played an important part in forming the ideas of the succeeding generation. To all appearances it must be accounted one of the foundation stones of modern American economics.[134]

The gradual way in which Marshall's *Principles* conquered the domain of economic studies in the English-speaking world to which Shove drew attention, is strikingly illustrated by the data on sales of the *Principles* provided by Macmillan.[135] Appropriately, these not only show the growing interest in Marshall's book but the growing popularity and demand for economic studies, to which its remarkable sales in the 1920s and 1930s testify. The first edition of 2,000 copies was sold out in England within the first twelve months of publication. The second edition of 3,000 copies in 1891 was half sold within its first twelve months, with over 1,000 copies sold in 1891–92 in the United States. Sales then slowed to an average of less than 500 for the next decade (1898–99, the year of the fourth edition, being an exception). The five years from 1902–3 produced sales averaging over 500 copies annually. Sales exceeded the thousand mark in the English market from 1907 to 1910, then slumped to between 700 and 800 until 1918–19, when over a thousand were sold once again. Annual sales of 2,000 were reached by 1919–20, and consistently maintained during the 1920s. Apart from 1937–38 when sales were over 2,000, sales were well below the 2,000 mark per annum for the rest of the 1930s. Nevertheless, aggregate sales of the *Principles* during that decade exceeded those made during its first two decades, while over the eighteen years *after* Marshall's death, sales matched those made over the 34 years when its author was alive. Because the book has been continuously in print, sales after Marshall's death far exceed those made during his lifetime. No wonder that more than sixty years after its first publication, Guillebaud could draw attention to the 'very remarkable fact (probably unique in the whole field of organised knowledge in all subjects) that this book should still be a standard textbook, and one that no Final Honours student in Economics could afford to neglect'.[136]

More strikingly, a statistical analysis of citations by Stigler and Friedland over the periods 1886–1923 and 1925–69 revealed that only Marshall among economists 'whose main work was done before 1900' appeared among the top 41 most frequently cited economists in the second of these periods (in fact, he ranked sixth for the first, ninth for the second) despite the substantial illusion imparted to such data through the disappearance of important ancestors from the citation index. After all, 'thoroughly successful contributions may become so widespread that authorship is first taken for granted and then forgotten'. Marshallian concepts like the 'short run, elasticity of demand, quasi-rent, and external and internal economies' are prime examples of this phenomenon in which 'proper' acknowledgement to their originator tends not to be made.[137] During the 1980s, Marshall's publications continued to attract citations at the rate of about 100 per annum, of which the *Principles* accounted for more than one half.

During the years around its centenary of publication, ideas from the *Principles* have exerted more profound influences than those generally associated with its status as major 'ancestor' of economic knowledge and enduring textbook. Three examples can be given. First is the inspiration given by Marshall's discussion of industrial organisation in Book IV of the *Principles* to the notion of industrial districts and inter-firm co-operation, particularly useful for understanding Italian industrial developments of the 1970s and after.[138] Second are attempts by a number of economists to translate Marshall's dictum that economic biology rather than economic dynamics is the 'mecca of the economist' into propositions with operational rather than didactic significance. Developments in economics and biology long after his death are assisting in bringing this dream of Marshall to reality, using means of which he had no inkling in the process of consummating a notion which he had only intuitively grasped.[139] Also methodologically orientated, is the wish to construct social economics anew on Marshallian foundations. This involves the attempt to take as point of departure for such reconstruction a work 'where the greatest number of promising options were still open'. Marshall's *Principles* has been identified as the only real candidate for this task.[140] These aspects of the book give a positive perspective to its qualities so often diagnosed as disadvantages inherent in its style. Maynard Keynes put the latter succinctly in a continuation of the remarks quoted at the start of this section. Marshall's

method has, on the other hand, serious disadvantages. The lack of emphasis and of strong light and shade, the sedulous rubbing away of rough edges and salients and projections, until what is most novel can appear as trite, allows the reader to pass too easily through. Like a duck leaving water, he can escape from this douche of ideas with scarce a wetting. The difficulties are concealed; the most ticklish problems are solved in footnotes; a pregnant and original judgement is dressed up as a platitude. The author furnished his ideas with no labels of salesmanship and few hooks for them to hang by in the wardrobe of the mind. A student can read the *Principles*, be fascinated by its pervading charm, think that he comprehends it, and yet, a week later, know but little about it. How often has it not happened even to those who have been brought up on the *Principles*, lighting upon what seems a new problem or a new solution, to go back to it and to find, after all, that the problem and a better solution have been always there, yet quite escaping notice! It needs much study and independent thought on the reader's own part before he can know the half of what is contained in the concealed crevices of that rounded globe of knowledge which is Marshall's *Principles of Economics*.[141]

As the long haul of Marshall's *Principles* so profusely demonstrates, 'the sedulous rubbing away of rough edges and salients and projections' during the continuous process of its revision, imposed costs even greater than lack of immediate clarity for its readers, important though this was as a fault conspicuous to both contemporary, and later, observers. Non-completion of the work by the failure of its second volume to eventuate was a significant part of those costs. This point is succinctly made in Stigler's critical review of the almost impossible task of preparing the *Principles*' variorum edition, over which Marshall's nephew Claude Guillebaud so loyally laboured for several decades. Although its value for Marshall scholars has been attested to once again by its frequent use in this chapter, given the manifold changes Marshall successively introduced in his *Principles*, there are many which Guillebaud's diligent efforts failed to capture. As Stigler concluded, and this is likewise a fitting conclusion to this long chapter,

In retrospect, the real culprit was Marshall. That he should have spent a large part of his professional life after 1890 in sewing small patches on, and cutting small holes in, the *Principles*, instead (for example) of writing the study of the economic functions of the state which he promised, was an utterly absurd expenditure of resources. But who has better claim than a genius to be absurd?[142]

NOTES

1. Marshall to Bonar, 27 November 1898, in *Memorials*, p. 374.
2. *Times*, 24 July 1890; *Daily Chronicle*, 24 July 1890; *The Scotsman*, 28 July 1890; *Western Morning News*, 25 September, 1890; *Dublin Evening Mail*, 27 August 1890; *Manchester Guardian*, 29 August 1890; *Weekly Review*, 1 October 1890; *The Saturday Review*, 24 January 1891, pp. 114–15; and, for a comparison with Smith, *Annals of the American Academy of Political and Social Science*, Vol. 1, July 1890–June 1891, p. 332.
3. *Pall Mall Gazette*, 19 July 1890; *Daily Chronicle*, 24 July 1890; *Glasgow Herald*, 18 August 1890; *The Dial*, October 1890, Vol. 12, p. 174.
4. *The Speaker*, 1 November 1890; *The Christian World*, 28 July 1890.
5. The one really hostile review appeared in *The Nation*, 23 October 1890, pp. 329–30; but The *Edinburgh Review*, Vol. 173, January 1891, p. 239 voiced similar criticism of poor style. The suggestion that Marshall's work was to be published in instalments appeared in the *Times*, 24 July 1890; *Edinburgh Review*, p. 238; the dangers this implied were raised in the *Bristol Western Daily News*, 1 August 1890. Webb's review in the *Star* appeared 30 July 1890.
6. Marshall to Foxwell, 20 April 1880 (Freeman Collection, 9/252).
7. Marshall to Macmillan, circa April 1887 (Marshall Archive, 1/192).

8. W.A.S. Hewins, *Apologia of an Imperialist*, Vol. 1, p. 27. In commenting on a draft chapter, John Whitaker noted Marshall's description of the slowness of his writing is exaggerated when applied to the first volume; it fits his attempts at writing the second volume much better. See below, Chapter 19, pp. 704–06.

9. David Macmillan, 'Marshall's Principles of Economics: A Bibliographical Note', p. 128; Sir Frederick Macmillan, *The Net Book Agreement 1899*, Glasgow: printed for the author, 1924; and E.T. Grether, 'Alfred Marshall's Role in Price Maintenance in Great Britain', *AMCA*, II, pp. 58–61.

10. C.W. Guillebaud, editorial introduction, *P* IX, p. 26 n.b.

11. Discussed in Chapter 6, which concludes with an account of Marshall's published writings of 1879.

12. Marshall to Jevons, 30 June 1879, in *Memorials*, p. 371.

13. Marshall to L.C. Colson, circa 1908, cited in 'Alfred Marshall the Mathematician as seen by himself', *Econometrica*, Vol. 1, April 1933, pp. 221–2.

14. 'Alfred Marshall. Professor of Political Economy at Cambridge', *AMCA*, I, p. 150.

15. Marshall to Foxwell, 14 January 1880 (Freeman Collection, 4/152).

16. Marshall to Foxwell, 24 January 1880 (Freeman Collection, 5/552). Edgeworth's article, 'The Hedonic Calculus', had appeared in *Mind*, Vol. 4, July 1879, pp. 394–408.

17. Marshall to Edgeworth, 8 February 1880 (British Library of Economics and Political Science, Coll. Misc. 470/M469).

18. F.Y. Edgeworth, Reminiscence', in *Memorials*, pp. 66–7; John Creedy, 'Marshall and Edgeworth', *Scottish Journal of Political Economy*, 37 (1), February 1990, pp. 19–20.

19. Marshall to Edgeworth, 28 March 1880.

20. *Ibid.*

21. Marshall to Foxwell, 20 April 1880 (Freeman Collection, 9/252).

22. See Chapter 7 above, pp. 189–90, 204–5.

23. Marshall to Foxwell, 10 December 1880 (Freeman Collection, 8/252).

24. *EEW*, II, p. 306.

25. Marshall to J.B. Clark, 2 July 1900, in *Memorials*, pp. 412–13.

26. *EEW*, II, pp. 309–15, reprints the text and Whitaker's valuable guide of the variables and main functional relationships, *ibid.*, pp. 306–9. A more detailed discussion of the theory in relation to Marshall's earlier thought is his 'The Marshallian System in 1881: Distribution and Growth', *Economic Journal*, 84 (333), March 1974, pp. 1–17.

27. This and the next sentence draw heavily on Whitaker's account of the theory in the manuscript (*EEW*, II, p. 309) but the broader methodological inferences drawn from this in the remainder of the paragraph do not necessarily conform to Whitaker's views.

28. Marshall to Foxwell, 30 March 1883 (Marshall Archive: Foxwell 1/35); cf. Marshall to Foxwell, 22 July 1883 (Marshall Archive, Foxwell 1/42). Marshall's Henry George lectures are discussed in Chapter 16, below, pp. 581–5.

29. Marshall to Foxwell, 8 August 1883 (Marshall Archive: Foxwell 1/43); this note, which became Appendix I of the *Principles*, was first an extensive note to Book VI, Chapter VI, 'Cost of Production', *P* I, pp. 529–36. On Marshall's original plan, it was still part of the theory of value.

30. Marshall to Walras, 23 July 1883, in *Correspondence of Leon Walras and Related Papers*, Amsterdam, North Holland, 1965, Vol. 1, letter 578, p. 781.

31. Published in the *Contemporary Review*, February 1884, pp. 224–30, and reprinted in *Memorials*, pp. 142–51. Its contents are discussed in Chapter 13, pp. 450–1.

32. Mary Paley Marshall, 'Biographical Notes on Alfred Marshall' (KMF); cf. Keynes, 'Alfred Marshall', p. 202, n.4, and see *P* VIII, p. 823 n.1, a reference which first appeared in *P* IV, p. 619 n.1, though the text of the note on the Wages Fund dates substantially from the *P* I, 1890, p. 567.

33. Alfred Marshall, 'How far do remedial causes influence prejudicially (A) the continuity of employment (B) the rate of wages', Industrial Remuneration Conference, Proceedings, January 1885. Marshall's participation in the Industrial Remuneration Conference is discussed in Chapter 16 below.

34. Alfred Marshall, 'General Work since Arrival at Cambridge', 1885–89, Marshall Archive, Large Brown Box, Item 33; extensively used by J.M. Keynes in his writing of 'Alfred Marshall', pp. 202–3.

35. 'General Work since Arrival at Cambridge', Marshall Archive, Large Brown Box, Item 33.

36. Marshall to Foxwell, 27 April 1886 (Freeman Collection, 49/98), 17 July 1886 (Freeman Collection, 51/98).

37. Marshall to Foxwell, 31 July 1887 (Freeman Collection, 22/168).

38. JNKD, 8, 13 October 1887. 'Bastiat's date' is mentioned on p. 63 n.2 (Bk. I, Ch. IV) in *P* I.

39. JNKD, 13 January, 14 April, 19 June 1888, Marshall to Keynes, January, February, March and Summer 1888 (Marshall Archive, 1/55, 1/60–1, 1/77–79 – numbering which is not in chronological order since many of these letters were not dated).

40. 'General Work since Arrival at Cambridge', Marshall Archive, Large Brown Box, Item 33.

41. 'General work since Arrival at Cambridge', Marshall Archive, Large Brown Box, Item 33.
42. Marshall to Keynes, 20 December 1888, 15 January 1889 (Marshall Archive 1/86, 1/88).
43. JNKD, 3 November 1888.
44. 'General Work since Arriving at Cambridge', Marshall Archive, Large Brown Box, Item 33.
45. Marshall to J.N. Keynes, 27 May 1889 (Marshall Archive, 1:90); JNKD, 1 December 1888, 30 January 1889, 6 and 27 February 1889; 'General Work since Arrival at Cambridge' (Marshall Archive, Large Brown Box, Item 33). The Presidential Address to the 21st Annual Congress of the Cooperative Society, simply entitled, 'Co-operation', is reprinted in *Memorials*, pp. 227–55, and discussed below, Chapter 13, pp. 455–6.
46. Marshall to J.N. Keynes, 27 May 1889 (Marshall Archive, 1/90); JNKD, 29 June 1889; Moral Science Board Minutes (Cambridge University Archives, Min. V. 140) show Marshall to have been absent at the board meetings of 27 February, 13 March, 8 May and 6 June 1889.
47. Marshall to J.N. Keynes (undated, Marshall Archive) the note on Ricardo Marshall mentioned dated back to August 1883 as previously indicated.
48. Marshall to J.N. Keynes, 2 April 1890, Marshall Archive, 1:97.
49. Marshall to J.N. Keynes, undated (late April 1890?) Marshall Archive, 1:96. A question it contained about the desirable functions of the proposed British Economic Association suggests late April, or possibly early May. See A.W. Coats, 'The Origins and Early Development of the Royal Economic Society', *Economic Journal*, 78 (310), June 1968, pp. 357–8. The quantitative estimate of this growth in the book's size was noted above, p. 409 n*.
50. Macmillan to Marshall, 27 March 1890 (Marshall Archive, 1:195), 7 July 1890 (Marshall Archive, 1:196). Marshall did not accept this suggestion of a higher price; the book was advertised in July 1890 at 12/6 net.
51. *EEW*, I, p. 92. What information there is about the precise date of publication of the *Principles* is stated above, p. 399 and n.*.
52. *Immanuel Kant's Critique of Pure Reason*, translated by N.K. Smith, London: Macmillan, 1929, pp. 248–9; Charles Darwin, *The Origin of Species*, London: John Murray, sixth edition, 1884, pp. 156, 166 and 414 where Darwin associated the confirmation of this 'old canon' with the new knowledge produced by his theory of evolution, hence the motto is partly designed to highlight the evolutionary spirit in which Marshall constructed his text. See also *P* I , preface, p. vi.
53. *P* I , preface, pp. v–vi.
54. A.W. Coats, 'Sociological Aspects of British Economic Thought', *Journal of Political Economy*, 75 (3), June 1967, pp. 710–11.
55. *P* I, pp. vi–xi.
56. *P* I, p. xi.
57. Marshall to Macmillan, April 1887 (Marshall Archive, 1/192); Marshall to Arthur Bowley, 27 February 1906, in *Memorials*, p. 427.
58. See J.A. Schumpeter, 'Alfred Marshall', in *Ten Great Economists*, ed. E.B. Schumpeter, London: Allen & Unwin, 1952, p. 97; B. Jowett to Alfred Marshall, 25 December 1884 (Marshall Archive, 1:44); Marshall to A.W. Flux, March 1898, in *Memorials*, pp. 405–6, and above, Chapter 6, pp. 158–60, for his Jevons review. For more recent discussion see R. Coase, 'Marshall on Method', Hans Brems, 'Marshall on Mathematics', both in *AMCA*, I, pp. 409–20.
59. Marshall to J.N. Keynes, Marshall Archive, 3:66.
60. Alfred Marshall, *P* VIII, 1920, pp. 41–2 reproduces the same agenda of questions.
61. F.Y. Edgeworth, 'Principles of Economics', *The Academy*, No. 956, 20 August 1890, pp. 165–6. Edgeworth had also reviewed the book in *Nature*, 14 August 1890.
62. *The Scotsman*, 28 July 1890.
63. JNKD, 24 July 1890.
64. *Diary of Beatrice Webb*, edited by Norman and Jean McKenzie, London: Virago Press and the London School of Economics, 1982, Volume 1, p. 337 entry for 27 July 1890. Webb was wrong on the size of the book, it numbers well over 700 pages.
65. Beatrice Potter to Sidney Webb, 9 August 1890, in *The Letters of Sidney and Beatrice Webb*. Vol. 1, p. 163.
66. *Annual Register*, Part II (New Series) 1891, p. 97.
67. *Edinburgh Review*, Vol. 173, January 1891, Article XI, pp. 238–9.
68. *Ibid.*, pp. 250–9.
69. *Westminister Review*, Vol. 134, July–December 1890, pp. 677–8.
70. *London Quarterly Review*, new series, XV, Oct. 1890–Jan. 1891, pp. 194–7, the quotation in the text is from pp. 196–7.
71. Vol. I, July 1890–Jan. 1891, pp. 332–7.
72. Richard Schüller, *Revue d'économie politique*, 5, 1891, pp. 404–7.
73. F.C. Montague, *Economic Review*, January 1891, pp. 115–20.
74. A. Wagner, 'Marshall's Principles of Economics', *Quarterly Journal of Economics*, 5, 1890–91, pp. 319–38.

75. Gustav Schmoller to Alfred Marshall, 6 August 1890, Marshall Archive, 1/100; E.A.R. Seligman to Marshall, 22 August 1890, Seligman Papers, Columbia University; F.A. Walker to Alfred Marshall, 16 October 1890, in J.P. Munroe, *A Life of Francis Amasa Walker*, pp. 342–3.
76. Henry Higgs to Foxwell, 22 July 1890, 23 August 1890, Clara Collet Papers, Warwick University Modern Records, MSS 29/3/13/5/3.
77. JNKD, 13 April 1891 quoted a letter from Marshall about Wagner's review article in which he described it as 'pleasant' to himself, and to Keynes for the remarks Wagner had made about Keynes's book on *Scope and Method*.
78. JNKD, 3 November 1888 when Marshall's lack of good arrangement is contrasted unfavourably with that of Sidgwick. Keynes's critical view of Marshall's lack of style was noted earlier in the context of *Economics of Industry*. See above, Chapter 6, pp. 168–9.
79. Foxwell to John Neville Keynes, 24 January 1901, J.N. Keynes papers, Marshall Library, 1:44; Marshall to Foxwell, 10 October 1878, where in the context of Foxwell's criticisms of the Marshalls' use of the word 'normal' in *Economics of Industry*, Marshall replied, ' "normal" is certainly not a satisfactory word; but after hundreds of hours thinking on the subject we cannot find a better'.
80. Macmillan to Marshall, 15 April 1890, reprinted in C.W. Guillebaud, 'The Marshall–Macmillan Correspondence over the Net Book Agreement', *AMCA*, II, pp. 256–7; this section draws heavily on this excellent article and on Frederick Macmillan, *The Net Book Agreement 1899 and the Book War 1906–08*, Glasgow University Press, printed for the author. (See pp. 14–15 in the context of the remarks made in the text.)
81. Marshall to Macmillan, 28 July 1890, in C.W. Guillebaud, 'The Marshall–Macmillan Correspondence', p. 261.
82. Marshall to Macmillan, 3 December 1897, 10 September 1898, in *ibid.*, pp. 263–5.
83. C.W. Guillebaud, 'The Marshall–Macmillan Correspondence', pp. 275–6.
84. JNKD, 15 January 1891.
85. Benjamin Jowett to Mary Paley Marshall, 30 December 1890, Marshall Archive, 1/56.
86. JNKD, 27 June 1891.
87. C.W. Guillebaud, 'The Evolution of Marshall's Principles of Economics', in *AMCA*, II, pp. 167–8.
88. *P* II, preface, pp. v–vi.
89. *Ibid.*, p. vii and n. (this is not mentioned in *P* IX).
90. *P* I, pp. 395–7, 755–6. Most of the changes referred to occur in its mathematical note, XII bis.
91. The correspondence, of which only Marshall's side is preserved, is reprinted in *P* IX, pp. 791–8. An excellent account of this debate is Peter Newman, 'The Great Barter Controversy', in *Centenary Essays on Alfred Marshall*, pp. 258–77.
92. For Marshall's original skimpy treatment of the subject, see *P* I, pp. 153–4, 737 and for the expanded version, *P* II, pp. 175–80, esp. pp. 179–80 and p. 752. Marshall's references to this dispute are in his letters to Edgeworth dated March (?) 1891 and 4 April 1891, reprinted in *P* IX, pp. 792, 795.
93. C.W. Guillebaud, 'The Evolution of Marshall's Principles of Economics', p. 167.
94. C.W. Guillebaud, 'The Evolution of Marshall's Principles of Economics', pp. 168–70, esp. p. 168.
95. *P* III, preface, reprinted in *P* IX, pp. 41–43.
96. These changes are indicated in *P* IX, pp. 258–65.
97. J.S. Nicholson, *Principles of Economics*, London: A. & C Black, 1902, pp. 63–5; F.Y. Edgeworth, 'Professor J.S. Nicholson on Consumer's Rent', *Economic Journal*, 4, March 1894, pp. 151–8; J.S. Nicholson, 'The Measure of Utility by Money', *Economic Journal*, 4, June 1894, pp. 342–7. A full discussion of this debate is given in P.C. Dooley, 'Consumer's Surplus: Marshall and his Critics', *Canadian Journal of Economics*, 16, 1983, pp. 16–38.
98. M.V. White, 'Invention in the Face of Necessity: Marshallian "Rhetoric" and the Giffen Good(s)', *Economic Record*, 66 (192), March 1990, p. 7 and more generally, pp. 5–7.
99. Discussion of Mr Henry Higgs's paper, 'Workmen's Budgets', *Statistical Journal*, LVI, 1894. pp. 286–8, esp. p. 287 where Marshall refers to the varied importance of bread in workman's budgets. His later claims came in correspondence with Edgeworth, quoted in Chapter 17 below, pp. 634–5.
100. A. Marshall, 'Consumers Surplus', *Annals of the American Academy*, III, 1893, pp. 618–21; this replied to an article by Simon Patten, 'Cost and Utility', in *Annals of the American Academy*, III, pp. 409–28.
101. A. Marshall, 'On Rent', *Economic Journal*, 3, March 1893, pp. 74–90; this replied at some length to a book by the Duke of Argyle, *Unseen Foundations of Society* which had criticised many of Marshall's views on rent in *P* I.
102. A. Marshall, 'Distribution and Exchange', *Economic Journal*, 8, March 1898, pp. 37–59. See also Marshall to Macmillan, 5 March 1898, in C.W. Guillebaud, 'The Marshall–Macmillan Correspondence', p. 264.
103. These are discussed in my, 'The Corrigenda and Addendas to Marshall's third and fourth edition of the *Principles of Economics*', *Marshall Studies Bulletin*, No. 2, 1992, pp. 3–13.

104. Preface to *P* IV, pp. v–vi; C.W. Guillebaud, 'The Evolution of Marshall's Principles of Economics', pp. 171, 183, where he argued, 'of all the editions, the fourth was the one in which the doctrine of quasi-rent was most clearly and comprehensively stated'.

105. Preface to the *EEI*, first edition, February 1892. Kadish, *Historians, Economists and Economic History*, London: Routledge, 1989, p. 160, indicates its contents were tailor-made for the new Part I of the Moral Sciences Tripos with the introduction of which its publication coincided.

106. Macmillan to Marshall, 24 February 1892, 26 February 1892 and 29 February 1892, Marshall to Macmillan, 27 February 1892, Marshall Archive, 1:202–205.

107. *Cambridge Review*, 27 October 1892; *The Guardian*, 31 August 1892; *Journal of Education*, June 1892.

108. J. Bonar, *The Academy*, No. 1043, 30 April 1892, pp. 416–17; *National Observer*, 7 May 1892; L.L. Price, *Economic Journal*, 2, June 1892, *AMCA*, IV, esp. pp. 13–14; F.Y. Edgeworth, *Nature*, 12 May 1892 and J. Courcelle-Seneuil, *Journal des économistes*, 1892.

109. Marshall to Macmillan, 3 October 1891; M.P. Marshall to Benjamin Jowett, 29 October 1891 (Balliol College Library); the 1887 outline (Table 12.1) and forecast of completion of the second volume was discussed above, p. 407 and n.*.

110. Marshall's involvement with the Labour Commission was discussed in Chapter 11, see esp. pp. 361–2 and n.*; Marshall to Cannan, 5 May, 1893, British Library of Political Economic Science, Cannan Papers Coll. 1020: 18–19; Marshall to J.N. Keynes, 30 September 1893 (Marshall Archive 1:112) and Taussig to Marshall, 21 December 1897 who advised, 'But is it not better for you to make such progress as may be with Vol. II and let Vol. I stand substantially as it is?' (Taussig Papers, Harvard).

111. Mary Paley Marshall, 'Biographical Notes for Keynes', KMF. In a letter to Macmillan, 19 March 1896, Marshall expressed an intention for the first time to issue Volume II of the *Principles* in two or more parts, thereby reporting the expansion of the work which Nicholson had predicted (above p. 416) and his wife confirmed as the reality for the mid-1890s.

112. Marshall to Lord Acton, 13 November 1897 (CUL, Add. 6443 (E) 205).

113. Alfred Marshall, *IT* , Preface, pp. vi–vii; *MCC*, for example, pp. 1–11, 98–106, 118–9 and Appendix F.

114. Discussed in other chapters, above Chapter 11, pp. 351, 353, 371–6; Chapter 14, pp. 503–07; Chapter 15, pp. 540–9.

115. Marshall to Westcott, 26 October 1899 (in *Memorials*, p. 395); Marshall to Seligman, May 1900 (Seligman Papers, Columbia University); Marshall to Edgeworth, 28 August 1902 (in *Memorials*, p. 436); Marshall to Macmillan, 13 December 1902 (Marshall Archive, 4:17).

116. John Whitaker, 'What Happened to the Second Volume of the Principles?', in *Centenary Essays on Alfred Marshall*, pp. 201–2 (the quotation is from p. 201). This section has drawn extensively on this account of the aborted second volume of the *Principles*.

117. Marshall, Preface to *P* VI, reprinted in *P* IX, pp. 55–6. The explanation starts with the splendid understatement that the first edition of the Principles 'implied' the speedy publication of a second volume. The announcement elicited a sarcastic note in the *Economic Journal* (21 September 1911, p. 496) from its editor, who compared it 'to a change in a fixed star' noticed from his 'editorial observatory'. *National Industries and International Trade*, the first of these volumes, had been advertised as 'in print' since 1904. See illustration 44.

118. In Chapter 19 below, esp. pp. 702–4.

119. Marshall to Lieben, 19 June 1906, Marshall Archive, 1:27.

120. David Macmillan, 'Marshall's Principles of Economics: A Bibliographical Note', *AMCA*, II, p. 130.

121. *P* IX, pp. 160–81, 713–21, 798–800.

122. C.W. Guillebaud, 'The Evolution of Marshall's Principles of Economics', p. 174.

123. See *P* III, p. 280 n., and above, p. 426. Cannan also recalled that Marshall solicited his and Taussig's assistance in revising for the fourth edition: Cannan, 'Alfred Marshall', in *AMCA*, I, pp. 67–9; Marshall to Cannan, 6 November 1895, 16 November 1895 (British Library of Political and Economic Science, Cannan Papers, 1020: 46–53).

124. Marshall, Preface to *P* V, reprinted in *P* IX, pp. 47–50.

125. A.C. Pigou, 'Review of the Fifth Edition', *Economic Journal*, 1907, *AMCA*, II, pp. 54–7. Its tone and content may have strengthened Marshall's resolve to have Pigou as his successor in the Cambridge chair, discussed below, Chapter 17, pp. 622–7.

126. C.W. Guillebaud, 'The Evolution of Marshall's Principles of Economics', pp. 174–5.

127. Marshall, *P* VIII, p. 99, n.2 which refers to an article by Taussig in the *Quarterly Journal of Economics* for May 1921; cf. *P* IX, p. 245 where the paragraph in question is wrongly ascribed to an insertion in the eighth edition.

128. Most of these changes are minor, apart from the one relating to the Taussig article mentioned in the previous note. For example, in *P* VIII, note 1 of page 804, it suggests deletion of 'recent' before 'Commission on Local Taxation' and its replacement by the appropriate date.

129. Marshall to Brentano, 9 and 19 April, 18 May, 5, 12 and 18 August 1903, 13 June 1906. The book appeared under the title *Handbuch der Volkswirtschaftslehre*, Stuttgart: J.G. Cotta, 1905, with an introduction by L. Brentano.

130. C.P. Sanger, 'Alfred Marshall 1842–1924', *Nation & Athenaeum*, 19 July 1924, p. 502, cf. Marshall to Fay, 15 February 1915, in *Memorials*, pp. 489–90.

131. J.M. Keynes, 'Alfred Marshall', pp. 210–12. This aspect of Marshall's legacy is discussed in greater detail in Chapter 20 below, esp. pp. 760–62.

132. That is, those of 1940 and 1990 with respect to the *Principles*, and for 1942 with respect to the centenary of Marshall's birth. Most of the contributions associated with the commemorations of the 1940s are included in *AMCA*, esp. Volumes I and II; the first two issues of the *Marshall Studies Bulletin*, 1991, 1992 contain comment on the international centenary celebrations of 1990, with full bibliographical detail.

133. J.A. Schumpeter, 'Alfred Marshall's *Principles*: A Semi-centennial Appraisal', *American Economic Review*, 1941, *AMCA*, II, pp. 100–1.

134. G.F. Shove, 'The Place of Marshall's *Principles* in the Development of Economic Theory', *Economic Journal*, December 1942, *AMCA*, II, p. 147.

135. David Macmillan, 'Marshall's *Principles of Economics*: A Bibliographical Note', pp. 130–31 presents annual sales data for the book in both the English and United States markets from 1890–91 to 1941–42, on which the material of much of this paragraph is based.

136. C.W. Guillebaud, 'Marshall's *Principles* in the light of Contemporary Economic Thought', *Economica*, May 1952, *AMCA*, II, p. 186.

137. G.J. Stigler and Claire Friedland, 'The Pattern of Citation Practices in Economics', in G.J. Stigler, *The Economist as Preacher*, Chicago: Chicago University Press, 1982, pp. 182–4. See also Patrick Deutscher, *R.G. Hawtrey and the Development of Macroeconomics*, London: Macmillan, 1990, pp. 189–92

138. For example, the contributions by G. Becattini and Fabio Sforzi to *Industrial Districts and Inter-Firm Co-operation in Italy*, edited by F. Pyke, G. Becattini and W. Sengenberger, Geneva: International Institute for Labour Studies, 1990, pp. 37–51, 74–107 and for a discussion of Marshall's role in the conceptualisation of industrial districts, Marco Bellandi, 'Il distretto industriale in Alfred Marshall', *l'Industria*, 3 (3), July/September 1982, pp. 355–75.

139. For example, Laurence Moss, 'Biological Theory and Technological Entrepreneurship in Marshall's Writings', *Eastern Economic Journal*, 8 (1), January 1982, pp. 3–13; A.L. Levine, 'Marshall's *Principles* and the biological Viewpoint: A Reconsideration', *Manchester School* (3), September 1983, pp. 276–93; J. Foster, 'Economics and the self-organisation Approach: Alfred Marshall Revisited', *Economic Journal*, 103 (419), July 1993, 975–91, and 'Biology and Economics', in *Handbook of Evolutionary and Institutional Economics*, edited G. Hodgson, M. Tool and W. Samuels, Aldershot: Edward Elgar, 1992; Brinlay Thomas, 'Alfred Marshall on Economic Biology', *Review of Political Economy*, 3 (1), 1991, pp. 1–14; G. Hodgson, 'The Mecca of Alfred Marshall', *Economic Journal*, 103 (417), March 1993, pp. 406–15. As shown in Chapter 20 below, p. 738, Marshall himself thought in 1924 it would take 1,000 years before economics was fully based on biology.

140. Neva R. Goodwin, *Social Economics: An Alternative Theory. Volume 1: Building Anew on Marshall's Principles*, Macmillan, 1991, esp. Chapter 5, p. 104.

141. J.M. Keynes, 'Alfred Marshall', p. 212.

142. G.J. Stigler, 'Marshall's *Principles* after Guillebaud', *Journal of Political Economy*, June 1962, *AMCA*, II, p. 229.

13. A Principled Controversialist and Strident Advocate

Marshall was not only the slow but painstaking composer of economic principles, the devoted teacher of economics students and the authoritative expert giving, or taking, evidence on behalf of government enquiries and commissions. If need be, Marshall was a principled, and occasionally unscrupulous controversialist, a strident advocate and earnest if not active joiner and supporter of causes of which he heartily approved. Glimpses of this side of his mature life were occasionally visible in the account so far of his academic activities in teaching, writing and giving expert advice. His involvement with the Charity Organisation Society, the Bimetallic League, the formation of the British Economic Association (later Royal Economic Society), the Cooperative Movement, the Royal Statistical Society, the British Association for the Advancement of Science, the Political Economy Club, the Society for Promoting Industrial Villages and Garden City Movement, are all cases in point.

An occasional taste for controversy on Marshall's part is also evident. A willingness to take advantage of the letter columns of the press to defend himself against misrepresentation or to make a point in favour of causes or principles to which he was strongly attached, were not infrequent during his lifetime. Even the pages of the *Economic Journal* were used by Marshall for such purposes, as when it reprinted some of his more popular material in defence of free trade or published further explanations and elucidations of tricky points in his major work. Marshall was often far removed from the position of detached observer and ivory tower recluse, the way he was presented by students turned colleagues and friends at the time of his death. Keynes's portrait of Marshall reveals little of the controversial aspect of his subject's life. It concentrated – quite wisely, given its author's constraints of time and space – on Marshall the teacher, the researcher and the expert, and how he came to be what he was. Only Keynes's emphasis on Marshall as 'preacher' with a 'mission', and the paragraphs he devoted to Marshall's involvement in 'three important movements which deserve separate mention' disturb this otherwise quite specific impression of Marshall, the academic economist and objective scientist.[1] Pigou's official reminiscences as Marshall's academic successor and literary executor go even further in this respect. Pigou paints Marshall the man as the austere scholar, devoted to truth above social reform, disdaining popularity and public acclaim. Above all, Pigou presented Marshall as a person who hated and avoided controversy and who cared only for constructive work.[2] Edgeworth associated Marshall's intense dislike of controversy with his hypersensitivity to 'adverse criticism', a characteristic to which Keynes also alluded[3] and which Jowett construed into advice beneficial for Marshall's good health, and for his reputation.[4] The record shows, however, that no matter how highly Marshall valued Jowett's advice, when the thrill of the chase came upon him, and the issue was of sufficient significance, controversy was not avoided, a point which Cannan's more detached obituary fully captures.[5]

Marshall's tastes and skill in controversy, are illustrated in this chapter in three instances all taking place during the second half of his long lifetime when the impetuosity of youth can no longer serve as an excuse for such indulgence.[*] In addition, it looks at Marshall as joiner of clubs and societies and as advancer of social causes and organisations. Most important in this context is his role in forming the British Economic Association, one of the three 'great movements' which Keynes said his Memoir had to include.[6] However, the whole range of Marshall's activities of this genre is canvassed in what follows. Much can be learned of Marshall's character from the 'clubable nature' of his life, irrespective of whether it took a passive, or more active form of involvement. There are peculiar aspects in his social life, partly related to his health, and partly to his sociability, which are reflected in the nature of his involvement in this type of activity.[7]

UNIVERSITY CLUBS AND OTHER CAMBRIDGE SOCIETIES

Earlier chapters[8] showed Marshall's involvement in university and Cambridge club and society life as confined to the Lady Margaret (St John's) Boat Club, the Cambridge Reform Club, the Grote Club and the Eranus Society. Other select societies, such as the Chit Chat Club, let alone the 'Apostles', never invited him to join. When Marshall returned to Cambridge as Professor of Political Economy in 1885, he may well have been desirous of becoming more active in this sphere of social life. However, there was a relutance on Marshall's part to go out in the evenings, which would have prevented such socialising. Whether this was caused by an unwillingness to expose himself outside of his own domestic domain for psychological or physiological reasons is difficult to say. The need to feel in full control of the social situation, only realisable in his own house and dining-room, combined with the increasing digestive problems which were plaguing him after 1879, may explain why he declined invitations to stay, or even dine, with his friends at their houses. Marshall mentioned this, by then long-standing feature of his social practice to explain to Brentano why he did not wish to stay for some days with the Brentanos at Arnberg when he and his wife were returning to England from Austria that summer. 'I have not stayed with any friends for many years. I abstain on the same ground that I decline all invitations to dinner'.[9] Nor is the record very helpful for ascertaining the extent to which this inclination interfered with social activities more generally. Re-election to a fellowship at John's enabled resumption of participating in college activities including its feasts and more regular dinners, a situation of which he took occasional advantage as shown by his correspondence with, and the diary of, John Neville Keynes.[10] In addition, a number of other Cambridge clubs and societies appear to have attracted his support, either because of their association with his field of study or for other reasons.

Several examples of the former can be found. A Cambridge Economic Club commenced its activities in 1885 with J.R. Tanner of St John's as foundation President. Marshall does

---

[*] Chapters 11 and 16 detail Marshall's controversial interventions on feminist and socialist movements, hence further demonstrating that avoidance of controversy was not a general law of behaviour for him.

not appear to have been actively involved in its membership. For example, the papers presented at its meetings preserved in the Cambridge University Library show no sign of Marshall's contributions, though in the absence of minutes of meetings or records of membership this signifies little.* Ten years later, Marshall informed Taussig of a new Economic Club, 'that is just being founded among the economics students here. Foxwell is Vice President, and I am President for this year'.[11] Marshall presented an opening address for the new club, appropriately entitled 'The Old Generation of Economists and the New'[12] in which he reviewed the salient features of nineteenth-century economics as he had found it, and prognosticated on likely developments in economics in the coming century.

Marshall's predictions for the future covered much ground. Advances in scientific techniques and understanding, including wider recognition of the complexity of economic phenomena, meant that 'never again will a Mrs. Trimmer, a Mrs. Marcet or a Miss Martineau earn a reputation by throwing [economics principles] into the form of catechism or of simple tales'. At the same time, the lessons from practice in modern physics, invariably ahead of that of the social sciences, demonstrated that knowledge about the complex phenomena of nature was often accompanied by 'a diminution in the principles required to explain them'.[¶] Despite his emphasis on the leading role of physics in science, Marshall also preserved a crucial role for history in the future of economics, provided it was seen in its Hegelian form of 'history as a whole'. Social science, Marshall argued in explanation, was synonymous with the 'reasoned history of man', and in making predictions or developing tendency statements, the social scientist was simply applying the adage that 'from what *is* we have to learn what is *becoming*, from *das Sein* we have to learn *das Werden*'. (pp. 299–300). Marshall also predicted that the predominantly qualitative analysis of nineteenth-century economics would be increasingly supplemented by quantitative analysis. For example, gains and losses of actions must be made commensurable, to make practical decisions on a sound basis. Drawing on contemporary labour market problems of securing a 'living wage' and collective bargaining as illustrations, Marshall noticed the difficulty of 'forecasting the problems which will chiefly occupy the coming generations'. He nevertheless hazarded the suggestion that growth in the size of business would be one such problem, but that in general the social problems to be faced by 'the larger and stronger strain of economists that are now following' would take on forms appropriate to their age.

---

* Papers preserved from this club, covering the years 1885 to 1887, among others include some by William Cunningham, Arthur Berry and J.E. McTaggart. They were presented to CUL by J.R.Tanner. JNKD, 8 March 1885 mentions a Political Economy Club for Students. Neither CUL, nor St John's College Library appear to have any records of the club other than those papers. I have not been able to discover whether this club continued as the Cambridge Economic Club during the 1890s. For such a club, papers by W.E. Johnson (one joint with C.P. Sanger) have been preserved. See W.J. Baumol and Stephen M. Goldfield, *Precursors in Mathematical Economics: An Anthology*, London: the London School of Economics and Political Science, 1968, esp. pp. 40–41, 313 which indicates that Arthur Berry was its President in 1891. Berry is therefore a link between the 'two' [?] clubs, though McTaggart was also continuing his interest in economics during the 1890s and could have been a member in both decades. See also Alon Kadish, *Historians, Economists and Economic History*, pp. 117–23, and his 'Marshall and the Cambridge Economics Tripos', in *The Market for Political Economy*, edited Alon Kadish and Keith Tribe, London: Routledge, 1993, pp. 137–8.

¶ Alfred Marshall, 'The Old Generation of Economists and the New', pp. 296–7 (subsequent references to the paper are inserted in brackets in the text). It may be recalled from Chapter 11 that Marshall had strongly indicated his dislike of Martineau's economics when taking evidence from Sidney Webb before the Labour Commission (above, pp. 366–7, and see below, Chapter 14, pp. 516–17.

However, as in the past, these would invariably involve 'the great task of utilising the present waste product of human effort for the production of human lives that are joys in themselves and the sources of joy'. No sudden improvement could be expected in this task, but only that steady progress 'towards the distant goal where the opportunities of a noble life may be accessible to all' (pp. 307–11).

Little is known about the fate of this new Economics Club, which was given such an auspicious start by Marshall. However, it almost certainly was a discussion group based on the more or less formal presentation of papers by pre-selected speakers, as its predecessor(s) were. The same can be said about the fate of the various Cambridge Social Discussion Societies in the activities of which both the Marshalls took considerable interest. Mary Paley Marshall recollected that one such society 'started in the 80s after his return from Oxford'.* Keynes in his Memoir mentioned visits of working-class leaders such as Burt, Tillett and Mann between 1885 and 1900, 'to fit in with meetings of the Social Discussion Society', a surmise for which he was taken to task by Roderick Clark, who claimed the society was not founded until 1903 or early 1904.[13] A Guillebaud reminiscence about Marshall indicates the society expired at the start of the First World War.[14]

The Eagle provides an early account of its meetings, confirming Marshall's involvement in an official capacity. It can be reproduced in full, particularly since some of the subjects it mentioned as being discussed were dear to Marshall's heart:

It may not be out of place in *The Eagle* to mention the Meetings for the Study of Social Questions, which, though conducted by a Committee representing the University, have been held by permission of the College Council in one of our own Lecture Rooms ever since they were started – now more than a year ago. The committee represents both the Senior and Junior element in the University. Its object has been to introduce now and again to a Cambridge audience someone able to give practical information on a subject of wide social interest. The papers have been followed by discussion, and it is believed that in this way the meetings have been of real use to those who have taken advantage of them in clearing their minds and suggesting to them new ideals in regard to important social questions. Among those who have addressed the meetings, the Rev. C.W. Stubbs, Mr. Howard Evans, and Mr. W.H.B. Hall, dealt with the position of the agricultural labourer; Mr. Ernest Hart, with Sanitary Reform; Rev. S.A. Barnett, with the Universities Settlement, and Mr. W. Ripper, of Sheffield, with Technical Education. This Term two meetings have been held; at the first a paper was read on 'Usury' by Mr. R.G. Sillar, whose views were much canvassed in the subsequent discussion. Greater harmony prevailed at the latter meeting, when Rev. H. Solly and the Rev. R. Macbeth pleaded for their project of 'Industrial Villages', as one remedy for the overcrowding of our towns and the depopulation of the country. It is to be noticed that Professor Marshall, whose return to Cambridge has been already of conspicuous advantage to these meetings, made some time ago, independently of Mr. Solly, an almost identical proposal. The members of the College who are or have been on the Committee for the Study of Social Questions are, besides Professor Marshall, Mr. H.S. Foxwell, Mr. Caldecott (now in Barbados), Mr. G.C.M. Smith, and J.R. Tanner. It would be wrong not to mention with these names Mr. Heitland who has been an unfailing friend to the cause.[15]

---

* Mary Paley Marshall, 'MSS Notes' (NCA); *What I Remember*, p. 43; Newnham College Club Letter, 1886, p. 14 confirms that sexual division was practised in social discussion as in so many other parts of Cambridge social life. Thus, Octavia Hill's visit she recalled was probably her visit to Newnham College in 1898. See Gillian Darley, *Octavia Hill*, London: Constable, 1990, p. 264. Other visitors to the women's social discussion group included Emma Cons, Mary Clifford, Henry Cunynghame, Mrs Garrett Anderson, Mr Clement Edwards and Tom Mann, who filled the hall in which he spoke. I owe this information to Rita McWilliams-Tullberg.

Marshall's role in the revived Social Discussion Society is evident from several sources. The *Daily News* reports him chairing a meeting on unemployment.[16] More interesting is correspondence between Erasmus Darwin, the secretary of the society and Marshall. In it, Marshall suggests Crooks, a recent speaker on the subject of unemployment, should be sent his expenses, because Marshall was 'a passionate admirer of Crooks' even though he disagreed with much of what he said at the meeting. For this purpose, and to cover future speakers' expenses, Marshall enclosed a cheque for £1.10s. Marshall also forwarded some material concerning a George Thody with this letter, apparently at the suggestion of Oscar Browning, the prominent tutor from King's College. Thody subsequently thanked Marshall for this service, offering to speak to the society on land tenure. This Marshall accepted, as he wrote to Darwin, provided Thody consented 'to describe the difficulties, aspirations and general experiences of the tenant farmer in his part of the world'.[17] The whole exchange of letters in 1905 reveals Marshall's participation in the Social Discussion Society as extending to suggestions for speakers and financial support, an indication of fairly active involvement in its activities on his part. There is other evidence for such support. Walter Layton's recollection, that he first met F.W. Hirst, the editor of the *Economist* during May 1908, when he 'heard him speak . . . *at Marshall's Discussion Society* on the Licencing Bill, then going through Parliament',[18] suggests Marshall's continuing prominence in the society's affairs. This may also explain the passion with which Marshall attacked his nephew, Claude Guillebaud, about his suggestion for changing the rules for a segment of the society, presumably well after his own active involvement with it had ceased as a result of his retirement from academic life:

> There existed at that time a university Social Discussion Society (it came to an end with the First World War), within which there was a smaller body consisting of some of the more active members of the society, and known as the Social Discussion Circle. A condition of membership of the Circle was an undertaking to produce a paper at some stage in the member's university career, to be read to a meeting of the Circle. I had become secretary of the Social Discussion Circle and found, like many another in a similar position, that there could be a wide gap between an undertaking and its performance. At the end of a frustrating period of unsuccessful endeavours to extract papers, I proposed at a meeting of the Circle that any member who, after being approached by the secretary and given adequate notice, failed to fulfil his obligation to produce a paper, should be required to resign from the Circle. This motion was negatived by the unanimous vote of all the other members present. I then altered the motion in the sense that the requirement should be made to apply to all those elected in future to membership in the Circle, but not to the existing members; whereupon the motion was carried unanimously. Alfred Marshall, like Queen Victoria in a different context, was not amused. He put the worst possible construction on the morals and motives of (to use his own words) 'people who were willing to impose on subsequent generations burdens which they themselves found too heavy to bear'. When he had finished his diatribe, my brother rashly remarked: 'But it is only human nature, isn't it?' I looked rather apprehensively at Marshall to see how he would react to this. He said nothing for a moment, but was clearly gathering all his forces for an explosion – and out it came: 'BRUTE NATURE!!' There was no more to be said on that subject. My brother was effectively pulverized; while for my part I decided that in future I would have to exercise still greater caution in the choice of appropriate subjects for conversation at the Marshallian dinner table.[19]

An equally prominent society with which the Marshalls were involved on their return to Cambridge, was the Cambridge Ethical Society founded in 1888. This was part of the then burgeoning Ethical Movement, established in London in 1885 by persons acquainted with the Marshalls such as James Bonar, Leslie Stephen and Bernard Bosanquet. Prospective members of this Ethical Movement were asked to agree

> in believing that the moral and religious life of Man is capable of a rational justification and explanation, apart from Authority and Tradition. They believe that there is at present great need for the teaching of a reasoned out doctrine on this subject, especially where old sanctions and principles have lost their hold.
>
> They are prepared therefore to help each other to supply this need by every suitable means. It is suggested *inter alia* that the society should endeavour to organise systematic Ethical Instruction in connection with such educational agencies as the Society for the Extension of University Teaching, Working Men's Colleges, Clubs, Co-operative Societies, and with the education of the young. It will further be the duty of the society to use every endeavour to arouse the community at large to the importance of testing every Social, Political, and Educational Question by moral and religious principles.[20]

One commentator on the Ethical Movement has noted the tension within it between those who wanted 'a philosophical discussion group combined with charitable activity, [or] a semi-political meeting [or] a religious service'. Irrespective where specific members stood in relation to these factions, the movement was imbued with replacing the loss of Christian faith by a new, rational morality. This stressed 'community and duty', 'moral redemption of the whole of man and society', religious experience in which the good and right could be worshipped, a strong belief in associating moral endeavour as essential to personal and social progress, and 'that the pursuit of the moral life was not only the supreme personal good but also the only means by which reform could be effected'.[21] In short, the Ethical Movement was tailor-made for those middle-class Victorian intellectuals who had lost their religious faith during the 1860s and 1870s but who continued to adhere to the social necessity for a religious emphasis on morals, community and duty. As one of those Victorian agnostics who still believed in the importance of religion, it therefore also quite capably filled a spiritual void for Alfred Marshall.

When the formation of an Ethical Society was proposed for Cambridge, it is therefore not surprising that Marshall was present, that he moved the vote of thanks to the organisers, and consented to membership of its organising committee.* Marshall's speech, as reported on this occasion, suggests his approach was closest to those stressing its educational and charitable role.

> Professor Marshall thought that it might be difficult to invite the general public to take part in the ordinary meetings of the society, but that it was important to bring the University and the Town more into contact with one another, and he suggested that at some future time the society for the Discussion of Social Questions and the Ethical Society might form a joint Committee to organise lectures to be delivered in some of the poorer parts of Cambridge.[22]

A detailed historical account of the activities of the Cambridge Ethical Society[23] shows that Marshall was a member of its committee for the whole of its existence, and that he and his

---

* Cambridge Ethical Society, *Report of Preliminary Meeting*, 18th May 1888, p. 22 (CUL, Add 8776). The committee elected at this meeting comprised a substantial number of persons associated with teaching the moral sciences, namely Caldecott, Cunningham, J.N. Keynes, J.S. Leathes, Marshall, McTaggart, Stanton, Stout and Ward, while Henry Sidgwick organised the foundation meeting and was President of the Society for the whole of its life. It was not of course a university society, though in a university town like Cambridge the impetus for its foundation and operation came from within the university.

wife were among the subscribing members in both 1890 and 1896, and that he never appears to have given a lecture under its auspices during these years. The Minutes of the Society[24] reveal that, after the preliminary meeting, Alfred Marshall was conspicuous by never attending a committee, or any public meeting of the society, but that he nevertheless was regularly re-elected to the former in absentia. Mary Paley, who was added to the committee on 18 October 1889, attended most subsequent committee meetings. The minutes also record a committee decision to invite either Marshall or Wicksteed to give a lecture for the society during October term 1891, an invitation not accepted by either for the stipulated time. However, the minutes do record that Wicksteed subsequently accepted the invitation and on 3 March 1892 gave a lecture on gambling. Presumably writing and revising the *Principles*, serving on the Labour Commission, as well as the pressure of normal academic duties, prevented Marshall from participating in the society's objectives in public education which he himself had so wholeheartedly endorsed at its foundation meeting.

Marshall's involvement in societies as a whole is shown in microcosm in the experience of his participation in Cambridge clubs after 1885. He was a willing joiner, a loyal subscriber, an inactive attender and rare contributor. This pattern of his association was earlier shown in the context of his membership of the Charity Organisation Society;[25] it even fits his pattern of membership of the learned societies he joined from the 1880s. It highlights a lack of willingness to take responsibility by active participation and leadership, consistent with other of his endeavours in life.

IMPROVING THE HOUSING AND THE GENERAL EDUCATION OF THE POOR

During the 1880s Marshall also became involved in societies for improving the housing of the poor and expanding the educational opportunities for the disadvantaged as an essential part of raising their living standards and standard of life. The first of these aims Marshall initially supported through his writings, which led to his association with the Society for the Promotion of Industrial Villages in the 1880s and later offered both inspiration and support for the Garden Cities movement which was initiated by Ebenezer Howard in the 1890s. The latter objective secured Marshall's somewhat reluctant involvement with the Toynbee Trust in the 1880s, support for the University Settlement movement and more enthusiastically in the British cooperative movement, to which in fact he gave intellectual and moral encouragement. Advocacy, sometimes strident and strong, mingles with these activities, occasionally rising to dominance, while advice under this general heading often permeated the footnotes in the *Principles* in the most unlikely ways.*

---

* For example, the following passage in one of the footnotes of the *Principles* dealing with a problem of domestic production in the English-speaking world:

The working-class budgets which were mentioned in Ch. IV, §8 [of the *Principles*] may render most important services in helping people to distribute their resources wisely between different uses, so that the marginal utility for each purpose shall be the same. But the vital problems of domestic economy relate as much to wise action as to wise spending. The English and the American housewife make limited means go a less way towards satisfying wants than the French housewife does, not because they do not know how to buy, but because they cannot produce as good finished commodities out of the raw material of inexpensive joints, vegetables etc., as she can. Domestic economy is often spoken of as belonging to the science of consumption: but that is only half

In 1884, Marshall was one of three contributors to a symposium on 'Where to House the London Poor' published in the *Contemporary Review*.[*] Marshall's paper succinctly discussed the historical development of industry and urbanisation, indicating energy technology in the form of water power first dispersed and then, in the form of steam power, concentrated population in urban areas. Developments in transport and communications (railways, shipping, telegraphs and reliable postal services) likewise affected the nature and necessity of urban concentration. These considerations set the background to solutions to the London housing problem according to Marshall. Housing the London poor seemed an impossible task when 'the whole area of London is insufficient to supply its population with fresh air and the free space that is wanted for wholesome recreation'. However, economically feasible and socially imaginative planning in removing inessential sections of the city's population to areas where clean air and open space could be satisfactorily provided, suggested a potential solution (p. 142). This was an appropriate vision for Marshall, the former 'slum boy', made aware of the value of access to nature through the Devon summer holidays he had enjoyed with Aunt Louisa and which had saved him from the detrimental effects on his health imposed by deprivation of fresh air and open space during the rest of the year by both location of school and, initially, parental home.

An analysis of the industrial composition of London's population suggested to Marshall that many of its industries could be economically transferred elsewhere, a process in principle facilitated by the high migratory traditions of its population. Implementation was to rely partly on economic incentives, partly on coercive rules and active encouragement[1] of emigration. It also needed initially expensive investment to provide new dwelling places from which 'a colony in some place well beyond the range of London smoke' could be best established. Objections like these required the organisational talents of a committee, whose offices were also needed to acquaint prospective employers of the advantages to them of this new village community. These benefits included lower rents, the value of garden produce, and saving workers 'from the temptation to drink that is caused by the sadness of London'. In combination, these advantages contributed to encouraging employment to flow into the new 'low wage' area of the industrial village. Employment would successively beget more employment, until the new area became self-sufficient as a provider of work opportunities. In addition, the possibility of regular commuting opened up by cheap rail travel enabled old

---

true. The greatest faults in domestic economy, among the sober portion of the Anglo-Saxon working-classes at all events, are faults of production rather than of consumption (*P* VIII, p. 119 n.1, unchanged from *P* II, p. 177 n.1.)

[*] Reprinted in *Memorials*, pp. 142-51 (references in the text are to this edition and inserted in brackets). Marshall's co-contributors to the symposium were M.G. Mulhall, the statistician, who discussed the 'ways and means' of the problem, and Elijah Hoole, a charity worker in the East End, who discussed the 'cost of tenements'. For splendid background to the London housing problem in late-Victorian England, see Gareth Stedman-Jones, *Outcast London*, Part II, esp. Chapter 11, which includes a depiction, slightly overdrawn, of his perception of Marshall's role therein.

[1] Marshall did not eschew compulsion. In a comment foreshadowing the typical 'economic rationalist' association of pain with reform, he argued: 'the suffering caused on the way would be as nothing compared with the ultimate gain; and, if the suffering could not be prevented, it should not be shirked. But there is no more urgent duty, no more truly benificent work, than to deprive progress of its partial cruelty, by helping away those who lie in the route of its chariot wheels' (p. 148). Needless to say, this was written before he had fully worked out problems associated with inter-personal comparisons of pain and pleasure, to which readers of his *Principles* were later alerted.

employment locations to be combined with new outlying residential areas where space and fresh air would be more easily and cheaply provided. 'If such plans as these be carried out, the car of progress may roll on till everyone in London is properly housed, and every house has adequate space around it; and yet its wheels may crush under them none of the industrious poor.' (p. 150).

Marshall's widely read paper brought him into contact with the Society for Promoting Industrial Villages. This had been founded in 1884 as a charitable organisation. Its moving spirit was the Reverend Henry Solly, a person active in the labour movement, social reform and, like Marshall, a great believer in the need to transform working men into gentlemen through inculcating them with the essential virtues of 'truthfulness, honour, bravery, education and courtesy'.[26] A brochure published by the society in 1885 quoted a letter by Marshall in support, endorsing the solutions it proposed as remedies for London overcrowding through the enforcement of strict sanitary regulations in cities and assisting in the migration of low-paid London workers to country areas 'where house and garden rents are cheap'. Marshall matched his moral support with a £5 contribution, supplemented a year later with a £2.2s. contribution repeated annually until 1888. In early 1885 Marshall also commented on the desirable qualities of the committees required to organise the desired new rural communities. As his 1884 paper had insisted, these committees needed to rely on the voluntary labour of private citizens because municipal endeavour would inevitably be tainted with 'jobbery' and 'imposture' (p. 150). Marshall cautiously advised that work by these committees should only be gradually expanded, a reaffirmation that haste had little room in Marshall's plans for reform. 'I think it is doubtful whether we are quite ready for the joint stock company part of the programme. . . . I would begin by not climbing too high, so as not to fear a fall'.[27]

Marshall's generosity with his advice and money for the society's activities did not stretch to joining its governing council. That privilege he gladly left to Foxwell, who by May and July 1887 himself expressed lack of enthusiasm to continue with this responsibility, given the society's clear lack of success in achieving its aims, perhaps attributable to the absence of a strong secretary such as the Charity Organisation Society had found in C.S. Loch.[28] In this context, Marshall had earlier shown willingness to help with advice from the sidelines. In June 1885 Marshall mentioned Turnbull to Foxwell as a possible secretary to the Industrial Villages Society, provided he was given a letter of introduction from Morley.[29] However, any further chance of involvement with problems of the society for Marshall and Foxwell disappeared in September 1889, when a public meeting wound up its activities.[30]

Marshall's interest in the housing question did not abate with the demise for plans of industrial villages. From its first edition, the *Principles* reminded its readers of the steady advantages gained from providing good housing to ensuring the health and strength of both present and prospective workers and of the excessive social and economic costs incurred by accommodating inessential members of the labour force in high rental urban districts such as London.[*] When Appendix G on the incidence of local rates was added to the fifth edition,

---

[*] *P* I, pp. 253–5; a slightly altered version in *P* VIII, pp. 199–200 contains the following succinct concluding paragraph on the issue: 'There is no better use for public and private money than in providing public parks and

its associated 'suggestions as to policy' did not forget his former concerns with the need for fresh air and open space as part of a healthy environment for families and their children. A 'fresh air rate' was proposed to defray 'the large public expenditure needed to secure air and light and playroom' in cities, an 'appropriate source', because it alienated at least some part of 'the extreme rights of property in land' held since time immemorial when the King as Head of State was sole landowner.[31] Last but not least, in its chapter on the consequences of economic progress, Marshall deplored the fact that despite the improvements following the period covered in evidence by Lord Shaftesbury and Miss Octavia Hill before the 1885 Commission of Housing, 'it is undeniable that the housing of the very poorest classes in our towns now [i.e. 1907] is destructive both of body and soul; and that with our present knowledge and resources we have neither cause nor excuse for allowing it to continue'.[32]

With views like this in such a prominent place in the standard economic text of the day, it is no wonder that Marshall became one of the heroes of Ebenezer Howard's Garden Cities movement. Howard sent Marshall a copy of his book, *Tomorrow: A Peaceful Path to Real Reform*, when it first appeared which, though still preserved in the Marshall Library, contains no annotations by Marshall himself. When its second edition in 1902 more clearly expressed its aims under the title, *Garden Cities of Tomorrow*, Marshall continued to be praised, as he had been in its 1898 predecessor, as an important supporter and anticipator of Howard's advanced philosophy of urban planning.[33] No correspondence between Marshall and Howard appears to have survived. However, Howard recalled meeting Marshall 'in connection with stenography work he did for Royal Commissions' and claimed to have discussed the garden city idea with Marshall.[34] Marshall's continuing interest in the movement is indicated by the fact he chaired a meeting in the Cambridge Guild Hall in February 1902 in support of its aims at which Ebenezer Howard was one of the speakers. The presence in his library of a 1909 German history of the Garden City movement's international progress, records from his lectures at the time and the note he added in 1923 to the 1884 paper in which he had first declared his interests in the housing question, are further signs of his abiding interest:

> This paper was printed and circulated widely in 1884: since then there has been a great increase in the number of children who rarely see a green field. It is true that school playgrounds have multiplied; that commons are now kept in good order; and that electric tramways and railways enable an ever-increasing number of artisans, and even of unskilled labourers, to take their families out of London occasionally during the summer. It is true also that increased care in regard to ventilation and to sanitary arrangements of all kinds have greatly diminished the evils of urban life. But natural causes tend to increase the evils, and increased care and energy are needed to combat the evils.[35]

Given its role in education of the poor, Marshall's association with the Toynbee Trust and subsequent Toynbee Hall can be conveniently discussed in this context, if only because it sheds further light on the manner in which he so often participated in worthy causes. It will be recalled that Marshall was able to leave Bristol for Oxford because Toynbee's death in

---

playgrounds in large cities, in contracting with railways to increase the number of the workmen's trains run by them, and in helping those of the working classes who are willing to leave the large towns to do so and to take their industries with them'.

March 1883 created a vacancy in teaching economics to Indian civil service students at Balliol which Marshall filled. Presumably, Marshall had first met Toynbee on his occasional visits to Jowett at Balliol after 1877. Marshall later recalled of these 'few occasions when I met him, [that] the talk always ran chiefly on social and economic questions. He was always brilliant in thought, eager in speculation; but his intellect, fresh and vigorous as it was, was not the chief part of him: the leading controlling strain of his character was emotional'.[36] For one who within two years was to praise the need for 'warm hearts and cool heads' in the service of economic and social reform, this was not a strong tribute[37] and it is interesting to note that his correspondence both shortly before and after Toynbee's death was not very complimentary to the Oxford man. On 15 February 1883 he told Foxwell in the context of his own imminent Henry George Lectures, that he had heard at fourth hand, that 'mild and gentle as Toynbee is, offence was taken at something that he said about the working classes' in the lectures on *Progress and Poverty* Toynbee had just given to a radical London audience.[38] After Toynbee's death he told Foxwell how he had declined Mrs Toynbee's request to write a notice of Toynbee *qua* economist, passing the task on to Foxwell instead.[39]

When Marshall returned to Cambridge in 1885, he chaired a meeting in St John's College on 5 February, designed to 'advocate the claims of the University Settlement in the College'. The report of this event in *The Eagle* continues,

> Professor Marshall, who was received on rising with hearty cheering, expressed the pleasure it gave him to be present on the occasion. He had had some experience of the Settlement Movement in Oxford from the commencement, and his interest in it was deepened by the fact that he had been the immediate successor of Arnold Toynbee at Balliol. He had thus had peculiar opportunities of estimating the extent of his influence, and of understanding the spirit in which he worked. It was Arnold Toynbee's interest in working men of the East End of London that primarily made him an economist. He went among those classes with the view of becoming acquainted with their wants and opinions. And so he believed that the University Settlement would most worthily fulfil its purposes, and would best do the work which he would most have desired to see done, if the residents at Toynbee Hall went there not with the expectation of teaching so much as of learning. He looked upon this as their great object. Perhaps it might sound like saying that "there was nothing like leather'; but he could not conclude without expressing his opinion that there was no subject in the present day more important for men to study than the laws of Political Economy; and it was only by such systematic study that we should see our way clear to solving the great problems that are now occupying modern society.[40]

After hearing an account of the recent establishment of Toynbee Hall from a delegation present, the meeting elected a committee on which, among others, Foxwell and J.R. Tanner were included, but not Marshall. In the autumn of 1885, Marshall did contribute to this educational institution[41] by giving a public lecture on the pressure of population. Its report in the *Malthusian*, the journal of the Malthusian League, gave a brief summary of the lecture, but more detailed contents in manuscript form have survived among the Marshall Papers.[*] In the lecture, Marshall corrected some popular misrepresentations of the principle that population could exert pressure on the means of subsistence, by qualifying this in terms of countervailing forces from both the growth of capital and the growth of knowledge

---

[*] Reproduced in *EEW*, II, pp. 386–93 (further references to this paper are given in brackets in the text).

(p. 390). A more important pressure of population growth, Marshall argued, particularly relevant for Londoners, was its pressure on fresh air, open spaces and clean water, enabling a return to the theme of the housing question (p. 391). The more important cost of this pressure of population fell on the children since it deprived them of opportunities for 'noisy, healthy play . . . where cricket may be played with hard balls, and where the joyous young creatures need not keep one eye always on the policeman' (p. 392). Migration from London and similar areas was the solution, Marshall repeated in this context: building cheap houses was not even a temporary solution since it ultimately only benefited employers' profits and landlords' ground rents.   Marshall's conclusions reiterated these points, and noted in addition that checking population growth by reducing the number of children, not only tended to lower average population quality in the world, but detrimentally affected the average quality of British population.   In addition, while it was also possible that such a policy raised average welfare, it would lower total well-being.

> If there might be in England 25 millions with an average income of £60 and 25 millions with an average income of £30, that is 50 millions with an average income of £45, and instead you have as a total 25 millions with an income of £50, or even £60, you have lowered total utility unless the existence of the second 25 million was a positive evil.[42]

Marshall's support for Toynbee Hall and the University Settlement movement, evidenced by his position as chair of the St John's meeting and his willingness to lecture on its behalf in London, is also reflected by his membership of the original Cambridge Committee for that University Settlement movement, of which Toynbee Hall was an early example.   In November 1887, a report in *The Eagle* shows him still to be part of that committee, attending a meeting at his college in aid of extending the settlement scheme.[43]   Furthermore, in the context of a meeting at Newnham College in February 1887, to talk on the settlement and Toynbee Hall, Canon Barnett recalled the 'large part' played by 'Professor and Mrs. Marshall' in organisation on behalf of the Settlement movement, among which he particularly fondly remembered a visit of a week in 1886 during which he and his wife stayed with the Marshalls.[44]   Once again, however, Marshall placed limits on his devotion to this cause. Although in early 1887 he had reluctantly accepted the task of writing a preface for Price's *Industrial Peace* on behalf of the Toynbee Trust, when Sidgwick wanted to reduce his administrative burdens through resigning from the Trust and getting Marshall to replace him, Marshall did not want to and proposed Foxwell, once again, as 'the right man for the job'.[45]   More generally, and analogous to his 'involvement' with the Charity Organisation Society, Marshall supported the settlement financially, let his wife attend committee meetings, and dissected their findings afterwards on the basis of his wife's report of the proceedings.[46]

Marshall's other social reform and working-class involvement at this time concerned the cooperative movement. His library reveals him as a keen reader of its publications and he was chosen as chairman of one of its annual congresses at the end of the 1880s. Marshall was following a Cambridge tradition here. Cooperation had been dear to the heart of F.D. Maurice, Marshall's mentor at the Grote Club. Fawcett, his predecessor in the Cambridge chair, had been an active cooperationist and had even included a chapter on the subject in his *Manual of Political Economy*. Mill had likewise sung its praises in his famous chapter on the future of the working classes, which the young Marshall so greatly admired.[47] This emphasised the features Marshall found so attractive in the cooperative movement: its implications for a union between capital and labour as opposed to conflict, and the enormous benefits the working class received from being members of a cooperative store. The last included the encouragement of thrift, their distribution of dividends policy as a form of profit sharing and, more widely, 'the most healthy social discourse between workmen' involved by their fairly frequent membership meetings. Fawcett also carefully distinguished between cooperative retail and wholesale trading ventures and cooperative production. The last occasioned far greater difficulties than organising cooperative stores. Finally, Marshall fully endorsed the manner in which Fawcett concluded the chapter: the success of the movement 'may be regarded as representing the highest ideal of economic progress'.[48]

Marshall's first published paper on the future of the working classes had briefly praised the cooperative ideal in the manner of the equal associations in trading ventures of working men so strongly supported by Mill and Harriet Taylor.[49] The 1879 *Economics of Industry* devoted its concluding chapter to the subject. This briefly covered its wide-ranging origins and history, its associations with socialism and American religious 'communities' of the type Marshall had inspected during his United States visit, the application of the co-operative principle to production and credit as well as to exchange; the advantages of co-operative stores, starting with its insistence on the principle of purchases exclusively for cash, and in the context of its final topic, the difficulties in organising cooperative workshops. The book closed with a final, one sentence paragraph, 'The plan [for co-operative workshops] will require much exercise of the Co-operative Faith; but it will be a gain to the world if many wish for it, and a great gain if they achieve it.'[50] At the end of the previous chapter,[51] the Marshalls had praised the notion of 'co-operative production' as a catalyst for 'the extension of economic knowledge and the improvement of industrial morality'.

Given such enthusiastic endorsement of the cooperative movement in a leading textbook on political economy specifically addressed to workers, the only surprise about the movement's invitation to Marshall to preside over its twenty-first annual congress at Ipswich in 1889 is that this invitation was so long in coming. Marshall's acceptance of the position entailed an opening address which he appropriately devoted to a systematic overview of the cooperative movement from the perspective of the academic economist.[52] After stating that the cooperative movement perfectly reflected 'the spirit of the age' by combining 'high aspirations' with 'strenuous activity', Marshall noted its distinguishing feature from other movements by being 'at once a strong and calm and wise business, and a strong and fervent proselytizing faith' (pp. 227–8). Its four 'cardinal doctrines of faith' were shared with other movements. Production of 'fine human beings' rather than 'rich goods' as 'the ultimate aim of worthy endeavour' was the first of these. Secondly, it held work to be not exclusively for the benefit of individual and family, but as 'work with others for some broad and high aim'. Thirdly, this high aim can be found in cooperative endeavour to remove the evils in the form of deficient incomes and opportunities from insufficient capital for the mass of the people. Finally, the strength of the working classes is in their numbers, and hence the potential for substantial, and cumulative growth, from the educational and moral development which cooperative activity entails. Speaking as an economist, this growth of cooperative trade had been understated from neglecting the fall of the price level when estimating that growth by money turnover (pp. 228, 220–21). Although Marshall saw the British as particularly adept at cooperation, there were nevertheless major problems to be faced. Avoiding the temptation to overcentralise, contrary to English traditions of freedom and local autonomy, was one of those (pp. 236–7, 240, 249–50). To be aware of difficulties in cooperative production where more serious competitive problems arose (pp. 236–8), while at the same time to approach closer to the ideal of 'labour employing capital' through profit sharing and other ways of 'warming' the interests of workers in their own business, were others. And, on a similar note to that in which he had four years earlier asked Cambridge men to take up economics, the 360 representatives of the cooperative movement present were exhorted that there was plenty of work to do for their hearts and heads (p. 255). Press reports of the speech indicated that many parts of the address were cheered by the audience, who must have realised, as the *Scotsman* stated in its report, that Professor Marshall had 'paid them the compliment of familiarising himself with the minutest details of their business interest before attempting to discuss them'.*

A number of eyewitnesses left their impressions of Marshall as public speaker at such gatherings. Holyoake, whom Marshall had acknowledged at the start of his address as a veteran co-operator, reported in the *Cooperative News*:

> Though robust in ideas and mature in wisdom, Professor Marshall is slenderly built and youthful in appearance. He has a sparkling speaking voice which seems to brighten the sentences as he speaks them. . . . On Monday afternoon, as is the custom of Presidents, Professor Marshall occupied the chair. Our Congress Proceedings are not readily mastered by a new President, but Professor Marshall made an unrivalled chairman. Alert, fertile in resource, prompt in decision, he conducted the business like a Master of Assemblies, accelerating it, getting through it without offending any susceptibility, and enabling more people to speak without disorder than have spoken before in any debate in the same time. . . . What surprised us was the tireless voice of the President, which showed no traces of fatigue from having spoken two hours in the morning.[1]

This praise is all the more telling because as a former President, Holyoake must have known the demands of the position. A less flattering picture of Marshall's presence at Ipswich was recorded by Beatrice Potter, first in the coffee room on the Sunday evening, then on his lecture itself.

---

*   *Scotsman*, 11 June 1889; the report in the *Times*, 11 June 1889, inserted cheers from the audience when Marshall enunciated the four principles underlying the cooperative faith and following his endorsement of the underlying profit-sharing philosophy of the movement. The *Economist* was less enthusiastic, commenting critically on Marshall's 'sentimental tone' in the address (15 June 1889).

[1]   *Co-operative News*, 18 June 1889, Holyoake added a sketch of an associated   tour of Cambridge under the guidance of Marshall, which can be noted here: 'Professor Marshall conducted through the University buildings and colleges the party to which I belonged. He walked backwards before us, describing what we saw. Cabs were on the streets, vehicles, bicycles, horsemen and people, but the Professor's volcanic voice went on unheeding all. . . . The groups to which I was attached were finally entertained at Professor Marshall's house, where Mrs. Marshall made us all at home.'

It it Sunday evening and we are all assembled in the long coffee room – scattered up and down in knots round a long table, some devouring cold beef and tea, others chatting together. In one of these parties, behold the hero of this year's Congress: the distinguished man whom working-men co-operators have elected to give the inaugural address, Professor Marshall of Cambridge. He looks every inch a professor. A small slight man with bushy moustache and long hair, nervous movements, sensitive and unhealthily pallid complexion, and preternaturally keen and apprehending eyes, the professor has the youthfulness of physical delicacy. In spite of the intellectuality of his face, he seems to lack the human experience of everyday life. . . . To-night, however, his desire to gain information outweighs his nervous fear of a sleepless night, and he is listening with mingled interest and impatience to the modicum of facts dealt out in the inflated and involved phrases of Mitchell, the Chairman of the Manchester Wholesale.[53]

Her critical comments on Marshall's 'carefully prepared address to the Ipswich Co-operative Congress' rested on what she saw as his refusal 'to see that the distinction between successful and unsuccessful working-class co-operation lay not in the [functional] distinction between trading and manufacturing' but depended on whether government was by consumers or producers. Furthermore, Marshall's view that successful cooperative trading did not imply success in production, was contrary to the facts as she knew them.[54] Her criticism may have been inspired by an earlier quarrel on the subject between Marshall and her fiancé, Sidney Webb; by her realisation that if Marshall was right, Fabian visions of socialism would lose much of their appeal; while her earlier associations were not designed to endear her to 'the Professor' for a variety of reasons.[*]

A year later, the *Principles* devoted several pages to cooperation. These reiterated Marshall's views on the greater difficulties of cooperative production as compared to trading expressed the year before at Ipswich, and reaffirmed his belief in the educative value of the movement, including that of preparing workers 'for the higher posts of business management'.[55] Subsequent editions curtailed these sentiments. Tribute continued to be paid to the cooperative ideal, but increasing emphasis was given to the difficulties in human nature preventing its effective realisation. Exceptions were the communities of 'small bands of religious enthusiasts' with few 'material concerns'. Marshall therefore concluded that competition with all its imperfections remained the best foundation for effectively organising economic society.[56] Whether Marshall's ardour for cooperation had cooled from his more intimate contact with the organisation which the Whitsun weekend of 1889 entailed, or whether the taunts from some of the reviewers of the *Principles* – that he was 'a socialist of the chair' believing 'collectivism and co-operation will largely replace individualism and co-operation'[57] were striking home, is not easily ascertained. However, his next Presidential Address, that to Section F of the British Association a year later, staunchly defended the virtues of competition, earning him both the praise – and a cartoon –

---

[*] Cf. Sidney Webb to Marshall, 28 February 1889, in which Webb mentions Marshall's doubts as to the practicality of socialism (letters of Sidney and Beatrice Webb, Volume 1, p. 124) largely based on the difficulties he saw in cooperative production; and see her 'The Relationship between Co-operation and Trade Unionism', first published in 1892 and reprinted in *Problems of Modern Industry*, by Sidney and Beatrice Webb, London: Longmans Green & Company 1902, pp. 192–208. A year later, a letter from Sidney Webb to Beatrice Potter, dated 15 August 1890, that is, still before their eventual engagement, and largely devoted to a discussion of Marshall's theory of rent, on its top bears the plaintive remark, 'Is Marshall altogether to replace the *Ring and the Book*? [by Robert Browning]' (*ibid.*, pp. 173–4). A more detailed discussion of the Marshall–Beatrice Webb relationship is presented below, Chapter 14, pp. 517–20.

from Mr Punch – for his virtuous fight against 'the tyranny and the spiritual death of an iron-bound socialism'.[58]

Marshall's favourable attitude to cooperation largely reflects the widespread belief of its many liberal supporters that it would make an effective antidote to more militant forms of socialism. In their *Economics of Industry*, the Marshalls had attempted to dissociate cooperation from such socialism by noting Marx's criticism that it was 'too mild a remedy for the diseases which affect society'.[59] In any case, Marshall's degree of enthusiasm for this cause was undoubtedly influenced by perceptions of the immediacy of the dangers of socialism. In this context it may be noted that while on the Labour Commission, the issue of cooperatives was rarely raised by Marshall in evidence, though a paragraph in its *Final Report*, perhaps bearing his personal stamp, refers to difficulties in establishing cooperative production and that doing so in London was particularly fraught with special problems.[60] This aspect of Marshall's involvement with the cooperative movement is best left to the evaluation of his highly ambiguous stance on socialism.[61] However, it may be noted here that when more real threats of socialism had appeared during the First World War in the shape of the Bolshevik Revolution, Marshall's attitude to the value of cooperation enterprise in post-war reconstruction grew decidedly more friendly.[62]

PARTICIPATING IN LEARNED SOCIETIES: AN INFREQUENT DISPLAY OF COLLEGIALITY

The degree of zeal with which Marshall engaged in his extra-curricular activities in social reform matched the energy with which he exercised his membership responsibilities in the more learned societies associated with his subject. In chronological order of joining, these were the British Association for the Advancement of Science, the Statistical Society and the Political Economy Club. Marshall's role in the formation of the British Economic Association, and later activity in it and in the Royal Economic Society, is given separate treatment in the next section as one of Keynes's 'three great movements' to which Marshall gave his support.

Like most of his colleagues in the scientific community, Marshall became associated as a matter of course with the British Association for the Advancement of Science, whose Section F from 1855–56 covered economic science and statistics. Apart from a number of special occasions, his involvement with the association's annual congresses was not very great, even when as Professor of Political Economy at Cambridge he would have been expected to take an active interest. For example, in July 1886 he wrote to Foxwell that he was thinking of presenting a paper on over-production to the British Association meeting but would not because it would take time from work on the *Principles*.[63] In August 1887 the pleasures of vacationing in Guernsey and the inspiration to writing this provided induced a reluctance to visit 'dusty Manchester' for the British Association meeting, despite the temptations of meeting Menger and Böhm-Bawerk, and of visits to Manchester factories. After much vacillation on Marshall's part, including room reservations in Manchester, Foxwell reported to Keynes that 'Marshall has suddenly determined not to come up to Manchester after all', thereby also forgoing the opportunity of hearing a paper by Walras.[64]

Only when he himself was elected President of Section F did he attend the meeting of the association in August 1890, giving his address on the subject of competition.[65]

Marshall introduced this topic by emphasising that on this subject as in others, dogma was being replaced by analysis. He then illustrated this proposition by various examples. The first was concerned with protection, in which limitations were conceded to the general case for free trade. His second example drew on the domestic competitive issues raised by trusts and other combinations. After recounting the qualified successes of trusts in the United States, with special reference to the Standard Oil Trust, he dwelt on their failures through immoderate pricing policies, and their detrimental effects by failing to combine central responsibility and individual energy in a balanced way. Potential conflict between competition and combination, complex though this question was, had resulted in legislative action against attempts to monopolise, of which the United States Sherman Act was a pioneering example. This followed the increasingly prevalent tendency among English-speaking economists to seek state control over non-competitive industry, including the so-called natural monopolies (or indivisible industries as Marshall preferred to call them), rather than the German road to state socialism and state management. Marshall then distinguished competition in marketing from competition in production; contrasted the economies of scale case for large combinations with the advantages of inventive energy from a multitude of independent enterprises. His concluding sections dealt with more general issues. Businessmen followed the profit motive as a sign of success rather than for the simple sake of money making for itself; economic progress required free individual responsibility with controls over the resulting inequalities of wealth through State action; socialists had under-rated the importance and difficulty of business management, and their alternative blueprints required reasoned accounts of the form of productive organisation they sought to substitute. Finally, Marshall noted the growing strength of public opinion as an element of control over business, supplementing that provided by competition, either through encouraging state action or, indirectly, in restraining business leadership by its very existence. However, to ensure public opinion exercised its control responsibly, Marshall argued it should be educated, without indicating how this was to be done. He finally apologised for his 'imperfect and fragmentary study', excusing himself with the reflection that 'every year economic problems become more complex [and] the necessity of studying them from many different points of view and in many different connections becomes more urgent'. Hence expansion of economic knowledge was imperative 'to escape, on the one hand, from the cruelty and waste of irresponsible competition and the licentious use of wealth, and on the other from tyranny and the spiritual death of ironbound socialism'.[66]

Reactions to the lecture were varied. That from *Punch* has already been mentioned.[67] This aspect of the address was also emphasised by the *Times,* which it summarised as follows: the socialist position by 'taking up the use of sweeping phrases condemning competition similar to which the older economists used in its praise . . . is therefore weak'.[68] In his diary, Keynes noted the timeliness of Marshall's address because 'its attitude to socialism was distinctly hostile';[69] others were less taken by Marshall's anti-socialist outburst. Hyndman, the leader of the Social Democratic Federation, reported in *Justice,*

Professor Marshall, who seems to be as inconsequent and verbose in his speeches as in his books, delivered an address . . . which has been rightly condemned as the merest trimming and superficial verbiage. Competition was good, co-operation was good, free trade was good, protection was good; there was trouble between capital and labour which ought not to exist, etc., etc., but not one word did Professor Marshall vouchsafe as to the solution of the problems which he did not even state correctly.[70]

Beatrice Potter's comments were equally unfavourable: 'Marshall's address was poor and disappointing after the excellence of his greater work'. This matched her picture of the whole economic section, 'deadly dull: except for the eight hours debate' and the whole permeated by 'slow-minded economists' and an absolutely 'bewildered audience steeped in the economics of forty years ago'.[71] Present-day readers of Marshall's address can sympathise with these judgements: it is overlong, general, diffuse in its judgements and never clearly focused. Its poor style, even by Marshall's standards, may be explained by the relative hurry in which it was written. He wrote to Brentano from Scotland where he spent part of the summer, that he had 'retreated [there] to hide himself from all men, to rest, and to write my address as President of Section F of the British Association. That address, alas, I have not yet begun'.[72] Both its length and the fact that Marshall did not reach the country-side of Scotland until after 10 July,[73] indicate he had given relatively little time to the customary revision and polishing. The ideas, however, survived, and at much greater length can be found in *Industry and Trade* nearly three decades later.[74]

Marshall's role of chairman for the subsequent sessions of the meeting over several days of the congress was apparently admirably fulfilled. Although the audiences were very large, the *Daily Mail* reported, 'Professor Marshall has made a capital President, ruling the section wisely and well'. On the spot, the *Leeds Mercury* reflected on the happy coincidence of Marshall in the chair in a congress that overflowed with people. The *Times* likewise noted the substantial audience. It also reported Marshall's contribution to a report of the Section by a sub-committee on measuring changes in the value of money, and proposing official preparation of index numbers on a regular basis. In joining his fellow committee members in speaking to the report, Marshall cautiously proposed establishment first of a commission to examine the proposals in detail, seeking advice from experts in business and academe, before deciding anything definite.[75] The *Times* likewise reported an occasional authoritarian flourish on the part of Chairman Marshall. A paper by a Mrs Victoria C. Woodhull-Martin, on 'The Ideal Aim of the Economist', and read by her daughter, was immediately followed by the chairman's adjournment of the session, 'without inviting discussion' from the floor as was the usual procedure.[76]

As its predecessors had done, the 1890 Section F meeting of the British Association attracted its share of foreign visitors, some of whom afterwards gathered socially in Cambridge, where they were royally entertained at Balliol Croft. Among them was Hadley, the American railway economist, whose text on the subject Marshall used in his teaching; Pantaleoni, who the year before had published Marshall's international trade diagrams in his text, *Manuale di Economia pura*; and Lujo Brentano, Professor of Political Economy at Munich and later a trusted correspondent. On 15 September 1890, Keynes recorded his presence at a dinner in Balliol Croft where Hadley, Pantaleoni, a Californian economist, Moses, as well as William Cunningham made up the dinner guests.[77]

Marshall's next involvement with the British Association was in 1904 when it met in Cambridge. This meeting was memorable for the burst of social activity it generated in the Marshall household at Balliol Croft, and for the public clash between Marshall and his former student Price over the fiscal question in international trade. Price, it will be recalled, had criticised the Economists' Manifesto in the *Times* the previous summer, and it was therefore a brave action on his part to present a paper in Marshall's home territory on 'Economic Theory and Fiscal Policy'.[78] Keynes in low key described the session on the fiscal question as 'rather a heated discussion between L.L. Price and Marshall'; Price recollected the incident more vividly forty years later, as one where 'Marshall chid me like an irate dominie flogging a naughty schoolboy, for my support of Tariff Reform'. Price saw this as a sign that Marshall had 'nursed his wrath over the ridicule in the *Times* of the damning pontifical manifesto of the Free Trade Professors against Chamberlain'.[79] The *Cambridge News* reported the high-minded tone with which the leading local economist had exacted his revenge:

> Professor Marshall, referring to Mr. Chamberlain's Policy, said he believed as a citizen, that policy would do more to break up the Empire than any proposal he had ever heard made, but he said that as an economist, he had no more authority to speak on that matter than he had to speak on the prediction of the next eclipse.[80]

Another spectator on this occasion saw things differently. Clara Collet recorded: 'Professor Marshall, . . . with his usual want of balance, made a solemn repudiation of Mr. Price's criticisms. We all felt during the morning that we were near a powder magazine which might explode any moment. But nothing beyond Marshall's speech happened although heaps of people were rather disgusted at having no opportunity of speaking.'[81]

The 'betrayal' of free trade principles by a former Oxford pupil was sweetened for Marshall by participation in the proceedings of two of his former Cambridge students. Both Flux and Bowley read papers at Section F in 1904.[82] Earlier, Marshall had expressed his delight at Flux's intention to attend the British Association Meeting, telling him that Dr and Mrs Pierson would be staying at Balliol Croft for the occasion.[83] John Maynard Keynes later recalled meeting Pierson at the Marshalls; Marshall himself recalled a dinner party during the 1904 British Association meeting to Edgeworth, saying that after dinner, 'though there were several people to whom I wanted particularly to talk, I spent the whole time – as it was my only chance – in getting from Mavor, who knew much more about it than anyone else in the world, a detailed (illustrated) account of the wheat resources of the Canadian Northwest'.[84] A photo of the house-party entertained at Balliol Croft during that hectic week (after Edgeworth had gone), was taken to commemorate the occasion, with the 'faithful Sarah', appropriately, 'holding the bulb'.[85] Marshall clearly took his duties as host seriously during this event, confining their normal summer excursion for that year to six weeks in Norfolk during July and the first half of August, a sacrifice he was not often willing to make for Section F meetings.[86] Clara Collet's diaries record Marshall's absence at both the official reception at Trinity Hall and a garden party at Girton's, though his wife and some of the distinguished economic guests were present on both occasions.[87]

In 1880, Marshall declared his intention to Foxwell of joining the Statistical Society as a life member; the records of the society showing his election to membership in January of that year, indicate that Marshall had acted on this resolve. The society unfortunately has no systematic records of members' attendance at its meetings,[88] only when Marshall participated in the discussion of the paper presented, was attendance recorded in the society's journal. A number of such occasions were mentioned in previous chapters. These included Charles Booth's paper advocating pensions in 1892 and Henry Higgs's analysis of workingmen's budgets in 1893. In 1895, Marshall participated in the discussion of Bowley's paper on the growth of average wages in England. These are the only instances of his attendance recorded in this way.[89]

Marshall participated in the activities of the society by presenting a paper on only one occasion. This was during its jubilee in 1885, an event which a new Cambridge Professor of Political Economy could not really ignore. The paper dealt with the Graphic Method of Statistics,[90] as a manner of enhancing the systematic discovery of empirical laws of cause and effect 'to be analysed by reason and tested by experience' (p. 177). This paper once again demonstrates Marshall's concern with having the necessary economic facts made available in as convenient a manner as possible, a principle embodied in the preparation of his 'Red Book' during the 1870s. It also expressed his faith in the need for quantification as an essential aid to more precise reasoning in the subject (pp. 176–80), a matter later eloquently expressed in addressing Cambridge economics students at the first meeting of their new Economics Club in 1896. However, Marshall was fully aware of the pitfalls in the graphical method when used for achieving such desirable ends. Choice of scale used in graphs and various ways of estimating average growth for variables such as population were examples provided (pp. 182–7). His last illustration implicitly referred to one of his own contributions to economics, the measurement of elasticity from empirically estimated demand curves. This induced a concluding statement of belief 'that inductions with regard to the elasticity of demand, and deductions based on them, have a great part to play in economic science' (p. 137), a forecast fully realised in the twentieth century though not always with results of which he would have approved.[91]

Marshall's association with the London Political Economy Club arose indirectly from his election to the chair of Political Economy at Cambridge which, by virtue of its rule 5, entitled him to honorary membership. This was, however, not automatic; formal application was necessary. On 27 April 1886, Marshall, who had been reading the history of the club with great interest, asked Foxwell to put him 'in the way of becoming a member, either by proposing me yourself, or by telling me how to proceed. I suppose that other things being equal it would be well that one at least of the proposers should be a member of old standing. I should like Courtney as well as anybody. I think he would be willing'.[92] At its June meeting that year, Marshall was duly elected.

This distinguished club, which had been founded in April 1821 at a meeting in Russell Square, London, with Tooke, Torrens, Mallet, Mill and Mushet among those present, within a few months boasted among its membership most leading economists including Malthus and Ricardo. It was organised as a dining–discussion club. Its first meeting had been held at the Freemason's Tavern; by the time Marshall joined, its meetings took place at the Inns of Court Hotel, Lincoln Inn's Field. Club regulations provided for seven meetings annually, in Marshall's days on the first Friday of December and February to July inclusively. The annual subscription was £5.5s. Members were drawn from business and politics and, via a special, facilitating ruling, from the growing number of professors of political economy. Discussions were on questions proposed by members.[93]

Marshall's first paper to the club has already been discussed. This was his proposal of 'remedies for fluctuations of general prices', published later in the *Contemporary Review* and used in his evidence to Royal Commissions in 1886 and 1887. It introduced the question, 'What Monetary System is best calculated to avoid the evils which are now caused by changes in the value of Gold and Silver' which Marshall had proposed for the meeting of 4 February 1887. It is also his only contribution to a meeting of the Political Economy Club of which the text has survived.[94] Over the next decade, Marshall proposed two further questions. For the December 1889 meeting he initiated discussion on 'How has the power of Trade Unions to influence rates of wages and hours of labour been affected by the social and economic changes in recent years', a contribution the discussion of which may well have influenced his subsequent appointment to the Labour Commission, as Balfour was among those present at this meeting.[95] For the 1895 meeting, Marshall proposed the more general distributional question, 'What account of the causes governing general wages are we to substitute for the so-called Wages Fund Doctrine', during which he may have ventured a preliminary reaction to the generalised distribution theory Wicksteed had published the previous year and which Marshall came closest to embracing in the pages of the third edition of the *Principles* he was then preparing.[96] For Marshall this was a most respectable contribution to the club's proceedings, and over the period in question, the frequency of his presentations was only exceeded by Giffen and matched by those from his former St John's friend, Fletcher Moulton.

The conviviality and usefulness of the proceedings – it allowed Marshall to be in contact with businessmen, men of the city and men of affairs more generally – explain his good attendance record for the club during the 23 years he stayed as member. The minutes of the club show his attendance at three meetings in 1887; one, which he chaired, in April 1888; two in 1889 and 1891, one only in 1892, then two again in 1895 and 1897; and one in 1896, 1898, 1901, 1902, 1903 and 1906, a total of 19 from a possible 161. He only resigned his membership on vacating the chair at Cambridge, before club meetings resumed in December 1908.[97]

One further association with a learned society can be briefly mentioned in this context. This concerns Marshall's unwillingness to accept Francis Galton's invitation to nominate him as one of the Vice-Presidents to the Demography Division of the International Statistical Congress under the patronage of H.R.H. The Prince of Wales, which took place in London during the week commencing 10 August 1891. Although Galton tried to make his offer as attractive as possible to Marshall, by suggesting vice-presidential duties were very flexible, Marshall's plans for the European *rundreise* he and his wife intended to make that summer, their first European trip since their sojourn in Sicily, mainland Italy and the Alps of 1881–82, made it impossible for Marshall to accept. In any case, Marshall tended to regard his summers as sacrosanct for the rest, recreation and writing opportunities they provided, and was not easily tempted away from this practice by even the greatest honours.[98]

LEADING FROM BEHIND IN CREATING AN ECONOMIC ASSOCIATION

As Coats has argued,[99] the creation of the British Economic Association in 1890 arose from gradual dissatisfaction in the 1880s with the three institutions just described which until then acted as the major public fora for economic discussion. The Political Economy Club was not suitable because of its exclusive nature; the Statistical Society was asked to broaden its economic thrust but proved not to be enthusiastic about changing its traditional role in this way; Section F of the British Association was seen as too eclectic, in that like the Social Science Association, it enabled discussions from sanitation to industrial relations, while its debates were too often encumbered, in the words of its 1885 President, Henry Sidgwick, by the overbearing 'presence of certain familiar bores'. In addition, a need was expressed for a more specialist journal in economics, akin to *Mind* and the *English Historical Review* founded in 1876 and 1886 respectively, with articles, reviews, specialist reports, notes and memoranda, and which could be suitably introduced as part of a new economic association. Although from 1885 limited finance was available for the purpose of a journal it proved difficult to find a suitable editor. As early favourite for this role, Keynes had declined the position repeatedly in 1887 and after, despite the strong invitation from Foxwell and considerable pressure exerted by Marshall. *

By April 1890 things began to move, however, partly under the spur of what was seen as the establishment of a rival venture at Oxford in the form of the *Economic Review*. A quite definite proposal for a new association and journal was then circulated among Section F committee members of the British Association. This supported an inaugural meeting, to be chaired by Goschen or Courtney, some time in the autumn of 1890 because they were unavailable during the summer months when the annual conference of the association was held. Up till then, Marshall's role in the process had been very much subordinate to the initiatives in negotiations taken by Foxwell, Palgrave and Gonner, but in 1890 both the imminent publication of the *Principles* and his presidency of Section F enabled him to take a more dominant role in the final push. Marshall also insisted on a somewhat more eclectic approach to membership and editorial policy for the new journal than Foxwell and Gonner wanted, largely to enable contributions by the type of bank directors and other leading City men of business whom he enjoyed meeting at the Political Economy Club.[100]

As President of Section F, Marshall's steps in the process of forming the society were threefold. On 10 April 1890 he circulated a questionnaire to members of the Section F

---

* JNKD, 22 January 1887, where Foxwell's approach to him to take on the editorship is recorded; 15 February 1887, which notes Marshall asking the same during a feast of John's; 13 March 1887, where he recorded that both Giffen and Marshall pressed him to become editor over breakfast at Balliol Croft. Marshall also pressed Keynes in correspondence, for example, Marshall to Keynes, 5 August 1887 and, as noted in Keynes's diary for 6 February 1889, continued to do so, despite an earlier promise not 'to worry you any more about the editorship of the *Economic Journal*'. However, Marshall wanted to give Keynes a last chance before the job was offered to Edgeworth or Price at double the salary (£100) than that first offered to Keynes in early 1887. Foxwell had apparently first suggested Keynes as editor, a proposal Marshall eagerly accepted and offered to press on Keynes. Marshall to Foxwell, 6 July, 17 July and 26 July 1887 (Freeman Collection, 42/98, 51/98, 70/168). The chance of starting an economic journal came from a donation, for the purpose of general economic education, by R. Miller, a wealthy engineer, and left over from his contribution to the 1885 Industrial Remuneration Congress. Marshall thought this money should be devoted to starting a non-popular economic journal.

Committee. This sought their advice on the functions and objectives of a new society and the necessity for its formation. It desired agreement that suggestions on suitable membership should be obtained from members of the Council of the Royal Statistical Society, the Political Economy Club and from past and present teachers of Political Economy at universities and colleges, as well as from among themselves (the Section F Committee) and from any other fit and proper persons not included in these categories.[101] As a result of further discussions in the committee, and after no less than at least four drafts, a general invitation was issued under Marshall's name to an inaugural meeting at University College, London, on 20 November. This was to discuss the proposals for society and journal. It therefore contained specific recommendations about the nature of the journal, the possibility of reprinting rare works and translating foreign books, proposals for financing the society and its activities and, even more specifically, whether membership should be wide or exclusive and what benefits it should entail, whether meetings should be frequent or few and similar details. It ended by putting forward an agenda for the meeting,

> Firstly, whether it is desirable to found an Economic Society or Association which shall undertake at once the issue of a journal; and (supposing this question to be answered in the affirmative): Secondly, whether, for the present, it shall hold any meetings other than business meetings; and if any, then at what intervals: Thirdly, what shall be the conditions of membership; and any other questions that may arise. The meeting will further be asked to appoint a committee to give effect to its decisions.[102]

Before sending this circular, Marshall had been actively campaigning for his preferred option of an open society with a wide-ranging membership. The arguments he tended to use in this cause are illustrated in a letter to Bonar, who could not be present at the November meetings and who, with Foxwell, and at that stage, Edgeworth, belonged in the exclusive membership camp:

> I am sorry you won't be present at the meeting; firstly because I think you might be converted to an open Society. No one, to whom I have spoken, except Foxwell, Edgeworth and yourself thinks a close society would be safe and the general opinion of those with whom I have conferred is that a close society would be inundated by Quacks, who could not be kept out, unless the society was so small as to be little more than a private club: but that Quacks would not care to come into a society which was open to all: and would not do much harm there, if they did come in.[103]

The inaugural meeting on 20 November 1890 was well attended. The report of it published in the first issue of the *Economic Journal* mentioned the presence of about 200 persons, among whom 63 were sufficiently distinguished to be mentioned by name. Marshall introduced the major motion for the evening, explaining both the rationale and delay in forming a society while pontificating about its more desirable aims,

> It was remarkable that England was in these matters behind other countries; but this state of things was due not to want of careful consideration of the matter, but to sad accident. For although England in 1870 had a stronger array of economists than any other country – within a few years the greater number of them were dead. Cairnes, Jevons, Bagehot, Cliffe Leslie, Toynbee, and Fawcett, whose power and originality placed them in the first rank, and who would have been the right men to take the lead in such a movement, died prematurely in the prime of life. Thus, though in 1870 England was remarkably strong, later on she was remarkably weak in economists of mark; and therefore he did not think they were to blame for not

having started this movement long ago. Happily, however, in 1890 we had a large number of very able young men at Oxford, Cambridge, and elsewhere, who were at the age at which they might be expected to write papers suitable for a journal. Thus, while others, like Mr. Palgrave and Professor Foxwell, had long taken a more cheery view of the situation, even he now felt that the time had come for the movement which they were beginning, and he no longer doubted whether it would be possible to maintain a journal at a high level of excellence. . . . He had received promises of assistance from almost every economist. Besides that, he had received a great number of suggestions from persons who were not economists, some of whom expressed the hope that the proposed Association would 'exert a wholesome influence'. That was the one thing which he hoped they would not set themselves to do. Their desire was not 'to exert a wholesome influence' in the sense of setting up a standard of orthodoxy, to which all contributors had to conform; economics was a science, and an "orthodox science" was a contradiction in terms. Science could be true or false, but could not be orthodox; and the best way to find out what was true was to welcome the criticism of all people who knew what they were talking about. In that way, indeed, he did hope they would exercise a wholesome influence on the character of economic discussion. In the past, time had been wasted in controversies which ought never to have come into existence – controversies based upon a perversion of the words of some writer, the critic interpreting them in the most foolish sense possible, and then writing long articles to prove that they were absurd when thus misinterpreted. All sciences in their early youth had been pestered by this sort of controversy, though economics had suffered more than others. The one influence which he hoped they would exercise would be that they would start from an absolutely catholic basis, and include every school of economists which was doing genuine work. He trusted that those who should control this journal would insist that all who wrote in criticism of others should take the writings of those others in the best possible sense, and in that way all schools might work amicably together, interpreting each other in the fairest and most generous manner; acting on that principle they would make sound progress.[104]

One by one the resolutions were put before the meeting and passed unanimously, only the matter of choosing a president of the new association raised a problem of principle for one of those present. George Bernard Shaw, who became a foundation member of the new association, without wishing to cast any aspersions on the manner in which Goschen had chaired the meeting, nevertheless questioned the wisdom of choosing as president anyone 'identified with any political party in the State'. In response, both Goschen and Marshall rose to speak but Goschen let Marshall speak first. Disassociating himself from Goschen's party, Marshall said he was sure 'he was expressing the general opinion when he said that it would be impossible to find any more fair and impartial man to be at their head than the present Chancellor of the Exchequer'. As chairman, Goschen expressed sympathy with Shaw's opinion, suggesting selection of president should be deferred. Marshall moved then that the matter should be fully decided by the Council after the meeting, a matter which was agreed.[*] Marshall, not surprisingly, was elected to the Council, Edgeworth became editor of the new journal as well as secretary of the new association and, as the first issue of the *Economic Journal* proudly declared, 'The British Economic Association is open to all

[*] 'The British Economic Association', *Economic Journal*, Vol. 1, No. 1, March 1891, pp. 1–14, esp. pp. 8–14. George Bernard Shaw's other claim to fame in the context of the British Economic Association is to have set up the canard that it developed from the so-called economic circle organised in Hampstead by H.R. Beeton, the close friend of Foxwell, and which some Fabians, including Shaw, as well as a number of prominent economists (Wicksteed, Foxwell, Edgeworth and occasionally Marshall) attended. The dubious foundation for this recollection by Shaw is indicated by Coats, 'Early Development of the Royal Economic Society', pp. 354–5 and n.4; Shaw's story is uncritically repeated by Shaw's official biographer Holroyd (*George Bernard Shaw*, London: Chatto & Windus, 1988, Volume 1, p. 178).

schools and parties; no person is excluded because of his opinions. The *Economic Journal* . . . will be conducted in a similar spirit of toleration.'*

Marshall, as was his wont, was not active on Council business for the new association; he in fact attended only four meetings. This adds pungency to a desire he later expressed for having less frequent meetings; he was quite willing to leave the association's business in the capable hands of Higgs, Edgeworth and a few other enthusiasts such as Foxwell and Bonar.[105] Similar reticence applied when Edgeworth too actively sought his advice in editing the *Economic Journal*. As Edgeworth himself recalled, 'New to that sort of work, I wrote to Marshall asking for advice on every small difficulty which arose, until he protested that, if the correspondence was to go on at that rate, he would have to use envelopes with my address printed on them.'[106] Little of this Edgeworth–Marshall correspondence has survived, so that neither the nature of the advice nor its frequency is easily tested.

With the early history of the association so well documented, including Alfred Marshall's relative inactivity therein, only two further matters need to be raised about his association with it. The first concerns Marshall's 'seconding' of the vote of thanks for Goschen's 1893 Presidential Address, in which he took the opportunity to distance economics from the abstract notion of 'economic man' and from 'the utilitarian theory of ethics'. His explanation was as follows. The technical use of the word 'utility' in economic theory referred to 'satisfactions' of 'man's higher as well as his lower nature', not to pleasure.

> Economics was then not utilitarian, nor intuitional; she left such questions to be decided by her mistress, Ethics. In early times Ethics did all her own work. But as she got on in the world, she delegated much of the drudgery to various servants; of whom Economics was one of the most busy. Ethics now gave herself mainly to the higher problems of the ultimate basis of duty and the correlation between its various aspects. Ethics was raising her standard; and setting ever higher and higher ideals, as tasks up to which her servants had to work.[107]

To illustrate these ever 'higher ideals', Marshall resorted to a comparison of contemporary relief of distress with that practised in 1834, the year of the new Poor Law. Free trade, encouraged by the 'good Abigail, Economics', had since then greatly improved workers' access to good, cheap bread, thereby changing the shape of poverty. Ethics was now showing how working-class cooperation could assist in removing poverty, and that, instead of 'lax out-door relief', the major cause of degradation in 1834, 'other causes of degradation, and other hindrances to the development of the higher activities of the soul' had taken their place and were in search of remedy. Unfortunately, Marshall did not elucidate these new manifestations of an old problem in his brief remarks.[108]

In 1896 Marshall was appointed Vice-President of the British Economic Association and, when Goschen in 1906 resigned as President of what by then had become the Royal Economic Society, the presidency was offered to him. Marshall declined the honour, partly because he could not spare the time to organise the society's annual congress in October

---

* 'The British Economic Association', *Economic Journal*, March 1891, pp. 1, 13. It is interesting to note that no ladies were elected to the Council, despite the fact that ten women were mentioned among the 62 persons present listed by name in the *Economic Journal* report of the meeting. These included Mary Paley Marshall, Octavia Hill and Clara Collet.

during the summer, the only time he could work satisfactorily on his writing. In any case, his wife had already reserved accommodation in the Tirol, where he liked to hide himself from interruptions in summer.[109] Marshall stayed on as Vice-President until his death in 1924; playing no real part in the administration and nurture of 'his creation', rarely attending Council meetings unless 'to achieve some specific objective of his own (as when the young Maynard Keynes was first made editor [of the *Economic Journal* in 1912])'.[110] He was content to have assisted in bringing the association and its journal into existence.

To bring this discussion of Marshall's participation in learned societies to a close, his involvement in two further economic clubs may be briefly mentioned. The first of these was the 'Economic Circle' or Hampstead Economic Discussion Society, the other its offshoot, the Junior Economic Club. The Economic Circle was itself a development from the Bedford Chapel Debating Society, whose initial membership included Henry Beeton, Philip Wicksteed, Sidney Webb, George Bernard Shaw and Graham Wallas. In October 1884 the Economic Circle transferred its meetings to Beeton's Hampstead residence, adding Edgeworth and Foxwell as new members in the process. It is therefore not surprising that Marshall, as well as William Cunningham and George Armitage-Smith, occasionally attended its regular weekly meetings. These meetings were also a good opportunity for its members to discuss the desirability of founding a British Economic Association, and may in fact have formed a ginger group to stir other, more eminent economists such as Marshall, Goschen and Giffen into action on this matter. Little is known about Marshall's attendance at the circle's meetings, though he did attend on occasions to defend his economics against hostile criticism from Wicksteed.*

The London-based Junior Economic club was formed by Clara Collet in 1890, perhaps a by-product of the more senior circle with its strong Fabian membership. It commenced activities in October with an inaugural address by Foxwell, boasted Edgeworth and Wicksteed among its membership by their special request, and used Marshall as an advisor on its formation, and as an occasional invitee at its meetings. In this context, she recorded[111] three chacteristic anecdotes about his participation in these ways:

(15 July, 1890): . . . Professor Marshall has contributed some advice. I dined with him at Toynbee Hall recently . . . (18 July, 1890); . . . I ignored Marshall's advice that we should *not* be careful about exclusions. Get all the people you can, he argues, and those who are keen and interested in economics will alone remain. It seems to me that we were better without members who would waste the time and spoil the tone of the Club. . . . (29 November, 1896) . . . Marshall writes to say: 'It was a great pleasure to meet the Club; but I hope the next time you do me the honour of inviting me, I may hear less of my own voice and more of those of others,' etc. etc. As the considerations which apply to the Census question apply in a measure to these family statistics, perhaps he would like an invitation for the 9th? . . . (16 November 1890). On June 27th I convened a meeting at the Denison Club and the Junior Economic Club was formed. Its first meeting after the vacation was held on the second Tuesday in October, and Prof. Foxwell gave an inaugural address. The next was on the second Tuesday in November. Mr. Edgeworth criticised Marshall, and Marshall answered, or rather gave his own criticisms of his work.

---

* R.S. Howey, *The Rise of the Marginal Utility School 1870–1889*, Lawrence: University of Kansas Press, 1960, Chapter XIII, esp. pp. 118–20, 121, 129–30. Marshall appears to have been invited to join the circle by Beeton (Marshall to Foxwell, 12 December 1887, Freeman Collection, 30/69), whom he had met on various previous occasions (above, Chapter 11, pp. 351–2 and n. 26). It is doubtful whether Marshall gave a firm commitment in the affirmative, and there is no evidence that he attended its meetings on any sort of regular basis.

STRIKING OUT IN CONTROVERSY: DEFENDING MARSHALL'S INTERPRETATION OF HISTORY AGAINST THE CUNNINGHAM ONSLAUGHT

The open door policy of the *Economic Journal*, which Marshall had so strenuously argued during 1890, two years later embroiled him in painful controversy in its pages. His adversary was his former student, subsequent colleague and competitor in 1884 for the Cambridge chair, William Cunninghan.[112] Immediately after Marshall's inaugural lecture, Cunningham had resisted the urge to publicly criticise Marshall for its historical extravagances, but such restraint was no longer exercised by him in the years immediately before, and after, the *Principles* was published. Marshall's willingness to interfere in the teaching of colleagues, when it fell short of his standards and desires, was applied in a demand that Cunningham as university lecturer, and therefore under Marshall's control, teach economic theory instead of economic history at least for one term a year. In 1888 Cunningham escaped Marshall's authority by resigning his university post when appointed to a college lectureship at Trinity. However, Cunningham wished for more than escape from Marshall's authority; he desired to challenge it, preferably from a position of equal stature such as the Drummond chair at Oxford to which he unsuccessfully applied that year.[*] Deprived of the chance to give an Oxford inaugural by which to blast Marshall's Cambridge effort, Cunningham used other vehicles. A paper to the British Association's Section F in 1889 criticised Marshall's stance on the historical school taken in his inaugural lecture, implied that the lecture's criticism of Comte was only an echo of Mill's earlier critique and, more devastatingly, described Marshall's 'intellectual exercise' of treating 'medieval or economic forms' of land tenure to illustrate 'Ricardo's law of rent' as on a par with the works of the Alexandrian writers in their theological stage. Cunningham added insult to injury by including Marshall's response to his criticism, prefaced by the statement that he had not realised Marshall's sensitivities on that score.[¶] Cunningham's 1891 Presidential Address to Section F of the British Association as successor to Marshall continued the fray, as had an earlier article on 'What did our forefathers mean by Rent', so that three earlier blows had been struck before the two articles were published in the 1892 *Economic Journal*.[113]

The first of Cunningham's *Economic Journal* articles implicitly criticised Marshall's qualified analogies between economics and physics, by stating that the differences in subject matter of these two sciences were sufficient to negate the force given to the analogy from their similarity of method. It then sought to destroy attempts at doctrinal history, such as that by Marshall, through showing 'old doctrines [to] have been refuted by the logic of

---

[*] JNKD, 15 March 1888; Cunningham 'is anxious to have in his inaugural lecture an opportunity of delivering a manifesto from the historical point of view in opposition to Marshall and Sidgwick'. Like Keynes, Cunningham was unsuccessful in his application, the Oxford chair went to Thorold Rogers on this occasion. Above, pp. 466–7, and see below, Chapter 18, pp. 682–3.

[¶] William Cunningham, 'The Comtist Criticism in Economic Science', in *Essays on Economic Method*, ed. R.L. Smyth, London: Duckworth, 1962, pp. 98–111, esp. pp. 99–100, 109–110. On p. 109 n.2, Cunningham stated that he had been sorry to learn Marshall had been 'aggrieved' by his criticism, so that he had offered 'to include any disclaimer Marshall might send', which in fact he did. Marshall had learned of the paper through Keynes; Marshall to Keynes, 11 October 1889 (Marshall Archive, 1:92).

events', and not simply corrected; and that no strictly economic argument can adequately explain 'the phenomena of exchange in all times and places'. These points were less suited for destroying their implicit Marshallian target.*

Cunningham's second piece attacked Marshall's economic history in the *Principles* both implicitly and explicitly. The opening paragraph presented a picture of the 'ordinary economist' assuming 'free competition and the laws of supply and demand' awakening to the actual world of industry and commerce of which he 'ought to take account' and 'professing' an extreme interest in history. In the second paragraph, Cunningham attacked the view of gradual and continuous economic progress as a characteristic of actual economic history and quipped at those without the requisite skills in weighing historical evidence who attempted to sketch 'the history of the world with easy confidence'.[114] The third paragraph explicitly condemned Marshall's *Principles* for such practice, and was immediately followed by a demonstration of the meaning Cunningham attached to his title, perverting economic history, first in terms of neglect of serious study of the facts and then their misinterpretation (p. 493). Cunningham's examples once again involved Marshall's use of Ricardo's rent theory for historical explanation (pp. 493–4) and then gradually but systematically illustrated the point of lack of serious investigation of the facts from Marshall's history in the *Principles* (pp. 495–8).

Friendship with the editor was presumably the reason why Marshall was able to respond immediately to Cunningham's criticism of the historical chapters in the *Principles*. Marshall's reply[115] rested on Cunningham's misinterpretation and misunderstanding of his purpose in these historical chapters and how they came to be written, a standard line of defence to the critics of his book. To overcome these failures in his critic, Marshall proposed to explain himself more clearly. For example, in defence of his criticised views on rent, he stated 'the fact that Ricardo's teachings on rent do not appear to him to have the same general import as they do to me. For I regard them as containing a living principle applicable, with proper modifications, to the income derived from almost every variety of Differential Advantage for production . . . while he regards them as applicable only to the rents of farms from which all the corn is taken to one market' (p. 512). Having replied to this major, and rather recursive aspect of Cunningham's criticism, Marshall then dealt with the minor points (pp. 514–17). From this discussion, Marshall concluded, 'Mr. Cunningham has discovered one sentence in which there has been a slip and which is not defensible . . . and also one wrong reference; . . . he and I differ in opinion as to Roman business, and other matters. But, speaking broadly, his criticisms proceed on assumptions that I hold opinions which in fact I do not hold, and which I believe I have not expressed; while in several cases I think I have definitely expressed contrary opinions.' (p. 517).

A note at this point indicated Marshall intended his reply to cover all of Cunningham's critical articles, not just the article preceding his reply in that issue of the *Economic Journal*. For him, it was therefore the end of the matter. The final paragraph of Marshall's reply was

---

* William Cunningham, 'The Relativity of Economic Doctrine', pp. 3–4, 5–14; the first could well have been directed at *P* I, pp. 85, 88–90, the second at phrases such as 'in all ages' which occurred in Marshall's doctrinal overview (*ibid.*, p. 51). It was more difficult to charge Marshall with lack of awareness of relativity in history, because he explicitly acknowledged how thought was liable to change with altered habits and institutions, praising Goethe, Hegel and Comte for their stress on this matter (*ibid.*, pp. 63–5).

used to mention other critics, lest they thought his reply to Cunningham suggested he did not take them seriously. Marshall stressed that changes made in the second edition, which by then had already appeared, showed this to be a wrong conclusion. However, as in the case of the critic on which Marshall's article largely focused, most of their criticism rested on misunderstandings and misinterpretations of the *Principles* which changes in wording, generally speaking, could answer (pp. 518–19).

Cunningham's criticisms are said to have hit Marshall hard. Jowett was sufficiently concerned to ask Mary Paley to ensure that Marshall did not persevere with the quarrel, writing some months later how pleased he was the debate with 'that troublesome and unsuccessful fellow' Cunningham had blown over.[116] The effect of the controversy is however, easily exaggerated, particularly long after the event. After having the Marshalls to dinner, Keynes recorded in his diary in October 1892 that 'Marshall looks and seems particularly well' adding nevertheless that he thought Marshall 'has been worried by the Cunningham controversy'.[117] Price, on recalling Cunningham's 'clamorous and doughty strokes, if on the whole they were successfully foiled, athwart some pronouncements on economic history in the *Principles*', implied in their context that Marshall did not take such 'hostile blows with calm, cool confidence, or faced assault in unruffled temper', and later associated them with Cunningham's hostility to the Economics Tripos when it came before the university.[118]

By the time Marshall's exchange with Cunningham took place, his early fascination with historical economics had greatly diminished, as had his interest in doctrinal history for its own sake. The debate with Cunningham may in fact have increased his critical position on economic history and its uses, particularly in so far as teaching it to undergraduates was concerned. However, it would not have altered his long-standing view that history was useful to economics as a supplier of facts. In the words of Kadish,[119] Marshall was more of an empiricist than a historian, and in correspondence tended to show relatively little regard for history and historical studies, except as a potential source of economics students. Thus in May 1889 he wrote to Keynes, 'I want however to keep my hold on the historical men, they are Kittle-Kattle and yet important. So I propose to adapt my general course in October and Lent terms to their needs. . . . Lectures on Advanced Economic Theory, including the higher part of Statistics, I mean all that is not suitable [for] men of the Historical type, – intelligent, more or less earnest, but not very profound.'[120]

Marshall was not always critical of history and historians. For example, he praised the quality of English economic history relative to that produced in Germany with its far greater number of students engaged in it, because 'those very few students of economics whom we get at our English universities are taught the use of inductive method in a scientific way'.[121] A few years later, he lamented to Lord Acton that 'the absence of any tolerable account of the economic development of England during the last century and a half is a disgrace to the understanding of the economic problems of our own time', a deficiency in Marshall's view which could only be repaired at London and Cambridge.[122]

Marshall's complaint to Acton reveals his special concern with more contemporary economic history. In 1902, a letter to Foxwell showed the inverse of this argument: 'No one can have a greater dislike to minute study of medieval history than I'.[123] This was no idle statement on his part. Both the first historical chapter on the growth of free industry and enterprise and, in more detail, notes on economic history preserved in the Marshall Library show that during the early 1870s he had worked on these minutiae with special reference to land tenure, the guilds and the rise of cities.[124]   By the 1890s, this itself had almost become ancient history and his preferences on useful economic history for economics students were firmly biased in favour of modern European study. Marshall's suggestions for Foxwell's lecture programme in early 1906, in connection with the Economics Tripos, made this abundantly clear. The context is duplication between Foxwell's lectures and those by Macgregor, one of the economics teaching staff, a 'waste' of the 'small strength' of teaching resources available to the new Tripos, and one which could be overcome by curtailing historical introductions in topics like money and banking. After complaining that 'the time which men spend on history is too long . . . when there are three papers on economics and only two on history' Marshall suggested that one solution to the problem he had raised, appropriate to Foxwell given 'the keen interest . . . in lectures on history' he showed at the last faculty board meeting, 'might be found in you undertaking English economic history in the nineteenth century, and giving two terms to it. That is as much time as men ought to give to lectures on the subject; really rather more, I think'.[125]

Although Foxwell refused to accept this solution,[126] Marshall's meaning about the importance of economic history expressed in his proposal was clear: recent economic history was all that economics students required. In a letter to Acton, Marshall expressed such sentiments in terms of the gratitude economists would feel towards Acton if he would turn Clapham's interest 'towards XVIII and XIX century economic history. Clapham has more analytical faculty than any thorough historian whom I have taught, and as his future work is I think still uncertain, a little force would I think turn him this way or that'.[*] 'Descriptive and simple history' provided the analytical beginnings for acquaintance with the facts, an introduction which needed to be followed by 'elementary qualitative, compound qualitative and then quantitative study of the facts' with the last qualified to those facts to which quantitative techniques could be usefully applied.[127]   The proximity of eighteenth and especially nineteenth century economic history to contemporary economic problems made it so useful for the economist as user of facts. For Marshall it was not the history as history which was important, but the factual content which some historical research could provide.

Marshall's critical perspectives on the role of economic history in the syllabus extended to his equally restrictive views on the role of doctrinal history in the economics syllabus. When preparing details of courses for the proposed Economics Tripos in 1902, Marshall wrote to Keynes that he did not at this stage wish to argue the position 'of the paper on history of economic theory'. He advised, however, that 'in Germany, even academic students have almost abandoned the study of the history of economic theory: which I think goes to the opposite extreme. But, knowing the turn of your mind, I feel sure that if you had

---

[*]   Marshall to Acton, 13 November 1897 (CUL, Add 6443(E)205). Acton must have criticised Marshall's praise of Clapham, since Marshall's letter to Acton a week later qualified his admiration for Clapham considerably. 'I had not thought of Clapham for so weighty a task yet. For he is young and immature for his age. But I am sorry he is not as good a historian as I had gathered from others that he was. Better, however, half a loaf than no bread; and as no one else in Cambridge seems to be specialising on recent economic history, I shall do what I can to secure him.' (Marshall to Acton, 19 November 1897, CUL, Add 6443:206).

been through what I have been through during the last twenty years, you would not wish to make it compulsory'.[128] Marshall's letter probably harked back to advice he had given to Foxwell in 1878 on his experience with teaching history of economic theory in Cambridge in the early 1870s. After recounting that he had spent the best part of a year in studying the subject, making voluminous notes, on which he lectured twice, he had come 'to the conclusion that anything like an elaborate treatment was not profitable for me and most unprofitable for the class, and I have seldom used my notes since'.[129] Marshall's experience did not change in the intervening years. In 1906 he told Foxwell that his long-standing practice in lending books to students revealed the unpopularity with them of history of theory. 'Not one in a hundred of those which I lend relate to it, . . . though I *always* offer such books to third year students'.[130] The fact that he preserved an overview of the growth of economic science in the *Principles*, even though less prominently in its later editions, does not conflict with Marshall's decided views. That material had quite distinct pedagogical purposes, especially for demonstrating the relativity of economics to the changing habits and institutions of the societies it was intended to inform and thereby to emphasise its association with organic growth.[131]

The last remark brings the discussion back to where it started, the controversy with Cunningham over Marshall's use of history in the *Principles* and elsewhere. That this use was quite specific to Marshall's views on studying economics is clear, and explains why the material was retained in the *Principles* and only reluctantly removed to its appendices, as discussed previously. The controversy with Cunningham left few scars, though possibly some residual bitterness on Marshall's part. It also left very few corrections to subsequent versions of the historical chapters which had been debated between them.[132]

CONFRONTING BÖHM-BAWERK ON CAPITAL THEORY: OF CLASS EXERCISES AND ALPINE ENCOUNTERS, INTELLECTUAL DEBTS AND CONTEMPORARY ECONOMISTS

Marshall's controversy over Böhm-Bawerk was of a quite different ilk to that with Cunningham. It was carried on in correspondence with others than the party directly concerned, in occasional footnotes in the *Principles* and in annotations of Böhm-Bawerk's writings made in the privacy of Marshall's study. More publicly, it formed the subject matter of an exercise Marshall set for one of his classes, and was visible when the two antagonists encountered each other face to face during a colourful Alpine meeting circa 1909.[133] Much of Marshall's hostility arose from Böhm-Bawerk's treatment of his predecessors in the critical history of interest theories although, more generally, it extended to his interest and capital theory and even his value theory. It therefore implicitly raised issues about Marshall's own intellectual debts on this score, and makes this a convenient place to explore some of Marshall's other relations with economists from Europe.

Cassel's acknowledgements of Marshall's 'very suggestive remarks' on the subject of Böhm-Bawerk's treatment of Turgot in his 1903 *Nature and Necessity of Interest*, prompted an inquiry from Wicksell as to the nature of these remarks.[134] In reply, Marshall noted he had been reading little on interest lately, whether by Cassel, Böhm-Bawerk or, for that matter Wicksell himself, but that he was probably in considerable agreement with Cassel's position on the matter, for reasons explained as follows:

> I think it is probable I am in considerable agreement with Professor Cassel. For a student, who had come to Cambridge with the opinion that the founders of Economics of all nations were inferior in common sense to most children of ten, and very much inferior to his worthy self, gave Prof. Böhm-Bawerk as his authority. I replied, 'I do not think Prof. Böhm-Bawerk has caught their real meaning. I regard personal controversies as a great waste of time; but if you will select anyone of these great writers as a test case, I will give a lecture on his doctrines of interest'. It happened that several other members of this class were present at the conversation, and the notion was approved and they selected Turgot. I therefore did – what I had not done before – compared Turgot's words with Prof. Böhm-Bawerk's account of them; I made full notes for the lecture. I read out alternately passages from Turgot and from Prof. Böhm-Bawerk's account of Turgot. I then gave Turgot and Prof. Böhm-Bawerk's book to the class and asked them to pass the books from hand to hand, adding 'a fortnight hence, I will ask the question in lecture – have I done justice to Prof. Böhm-Bawerk's treatment of Turgot'. The answer was yes! I forget details; but I think I found not only that the opinions which Prof. Böhm-Bawerk had read into some of Turgot's passages, were not really there; but also that in other sections to which discussions on these matters more properly belonged, Turgot had expressed categorically the exact opposite of the opinions attributed to him. I have lent the notes of this lecture to several persons, and I may have lent them to Prof. Cassel; though I do not recollect whether I did or not. No one who has read the notes had questioned the conclusion to which they point.[135]

Wicksell was not convinced by Marshall's reply. After checking the texts in question again, he asked if Marshall could let him have his notes on the subject.[136] Marshall declined, because he feared that if he did, he would be gradually drawn to 'waste time' on what for him was now an uninteresting matter. He would only relent and send the notes if Wicksell promised not to bring him into the controversy. Marshall added,

> I will be frank. I have decided not to answer, probably not even to read Prof. Böhm-Bawerk's criticisms on myself. I am therefore debarred from any indirect attack upon him. If I had time for personalities I should respond to his frontal attack by a frontal movement of defence. As it is I prefer to lie low, and to take without reply any chastisement he may inflict on me. But while lying low, I do not wish to shoot at him *en enfilade*. It is possible I may be *compelled* to break silence: but hope not.[137]

Wicksell must have accepted Marshall's conditions, for the following December Marshall wrote he was sending the notes exclusively for Wicksell's use. At the same time, Marshall explained he was not

> quite ignorant of what Prof. Böhm-Bawerk had said about me. My pupils occasionally bring me passages of his, and we have our little laugh at the way in which, after having misinterpreted my great masters, he misunderstands my humble self. This does not make me angry: for indeed he has always been very courteous to me, and has treated me far more generously than my masters. My only feeling of anger rises out of this: – While he was still at school, I learnt from the men whom he reviles everything which he has vaunted as a great discovery: and especially in America, he has been taken at his own valuation by people *who have never studied the great men* on whose burial places he dances his war dance. If then he accuses me of discounting backwards and reckoning interest forwards *over the same period of time* on the same economic goods (or sacrifices), why should I concern myself. A boy in a village school who made such a blunder in his arithmetic would be punished: and he knows I am a trained mathematician. If he were really earnest in his desire to know what I mean, he would turn to my mathematical notes. He would find in my Note XIII a complete solution of his mystery; which simply arises out of his neglecting the 'starting point', shown by the limits to the integral. He simply runs together and confuses a discussion in which the limits

to the integral have reference to a starting point *prior* to the events in question, with another in which the starting point is *posterior*. England is going to the bad, because we English economists have not time and strength enough to deal with the real problems of our age. How could I be right in wasting my time by controversy about such paltry personalities. One of my pupils, now a lecturer, proposed to write an answer to him. But I said 'No – you have more important things to do at present'. But perhaps he may later on.[138]

Wicksell returned the notes promptly and in early January 1905 summed up his views on Marshall's quarrel with Böhm-Bawerk. Böhm-Bawerk was wrong in his interpretation of Marshall's theory of waiting, while Marshall had interpreted him wrongly in the *Principles* on the increased productivity of lengthening the period of production. Furthermore, he disagreed with Marshall's defence of Turgot, and thought Böhm-Bawerk to be 'substantially in the right' on this subject.[139] Marshall's notes on Turgot still extant do not enable an adjudication on this part of the debate;[*] however, his annotations of Böhm-Bawerk's texts together with references to Böhm-Bawerk in the various versions of the *Principles* enable some interesting observations to be made on this correspondence, which reveal Marshall's peculiar attitude to the work of the Austrian economist.

Marshall's annotations in his copy of Smart's translation of Böhm-Bawerk's critical history of interest theory occur largely in the chapters on Turgot, Ricardo, Jevons and Say. In the Turgot chapter, two sentences are particularly noted. One of these attributes failure to Turgot for not getting 'down to the last root of interest, even if we cannot give any accurate account of why and where it fails'; the other highlights the point at which, in Böhm-Bawerk's opinion, Turgot 'made a mistake', an opinion he did not wish to force on his readers because of the complexity of the proof. Both annotations suggest Marshall's scepticism on the nature of Böhm-Bawerk's discussion. This makes it all the more surprising to read in the first two editions of the *Principles*, that Turgot's inconsistencies on interest and capital had been well demonstrated by Böhm-Bawerk. Marshall's other annotations to Böhm-Bawerk's history explain why elsewhere in these editions, Marshall drew attention to the fact that Böhm-Bawerk's 'full and able' history was marred by exaggerations on 'the difference between his own position and that of his predecessors'.[¶]

Marshall's annotations in his copy of Böhm-Bawerk's *Positive Theory of Capital* deal largely with aspects of the definition of capital which were exercising his mind at the time and which, during the early 1890s, induced changes in the note on historical definitions of capital which became Appendix E from the fifth edition. Although Marshall's annotations contain criticism of detail, for example on the treatment of Jevons's definition of capital by Böhm-Bawerk, and on his treatment of items such as houses, yachts and theatres within the

---

[*] Preserved in Marshall Archive, Box 6, Items 1 and 2. A section of them is reproduced in *EEW*, II, pp. 252–3. These notes, which Marshall probably made in the early 1870s, do not summarise in any detail Turgot's position on capital and interest, and therefore cannot be those he used for criticising Böhm-Bawerk in class and which he lent to Wicksell. For an interpretation of Turgot's theory of capital and interest which sides with that of Marshall and Cassel, see my 'A Re-interpretation of Turgot's Theory of Capital and Interest', *Economic Journal*, 81, June 1971, pp. 327–40.

[¶] Preserved in the Marshall Library. The passages in question in the Smart edition (1890) occur on pp. 65, 67. See also *P* I, pp. 550 n., 614–15 n.; *P* II, pp. 549 n. Although *P* IX notes the substantial changes made to these chapters from the third edition onwards, it does not mention the elimination of the footnote on Böhm-Bawerk's treatment of Turgot to which the text draws attention.

stock of capital, Böhm-Bawerk's summary definition of capital either as 'an aggregate of intermediate products' or as a subsistence fund, met with Marshall's approval as conforming 'very nearly' to his own definition.[140] The annotations in this book in fact show that Marshall had studied it carefully and in general was not critical of its contents.

In his correspondence with Wicksell, Marshall had stated that he had been less annoyed with Böhm-Bawerk's treatment of his own theory of capital and interest, as compared to that Böhm-Bawerk had inflicted on those who Marshall considered to be his 'masters'. This implies an acknowledgement on Marshall's part of Jevons as one of his 'masters'. It also fails to match the annotations Marshall made in his copies of Böhm-Bawerk's books, which are at their most dense and critical in connection with Böhm-Bawerk's remarks on Marshall's own theories. In addition, Marshall's comment to Wicksell in 1904, that he had not been reading much on interest by Böhm-Bawerk recently, is in potential conflict with the substantial annotations on his copy of the 1903 translation of Böhm-Bawerk's *Recent Literature on Interest 1884–1899*, particularly in the section on abstinence theories dealing with his own theory of 'waiting'.[141] In this case, Marshall's comments are peppered with hostile criticism, charging Böhm-Bawerk with misunderstanding his argument, or with writing 'sheer nonsense', or, on several occasions indicating his displeasure with the fact that Böhm-Bawerk failed to consult the more recent editions of his *Principles*, that is, those of 1895 and 1898. Of greatest interest in this context is a long critical comment which resembles the (subsequent?) correspondence with Wicksell:

> He seems not to catch the point that when a man pays a premium of £100 a year from 1860 to 1880 in order to get an annuity of say £300 from 1880 till the probable end of his life in 1895, the equation may be worked out from the basis in 1860, in which case both premia and annuity will be discounted; or from a basis of in 1880, in which case the premia will be accumulated and the annuities discounted. He ought to know that a mathematician and the experts of the first rank who read his notes in proof cannot have made a mistake for which a schoolboy of 12 would be punished.[142]

It is not unlikely that, contrary to what he wrote to Wicksell, these remarks on his work may have inspired Marshall's subsequent hostility to Böhm-Bawerk, which is also more marked in the later editions of the *Prinicples.*[*] Earlier on, Marshall had clearly shown no special grudge against Böhm-Bawerk. This is not only evident from his early comments on Böhm-Bawerk's treatment of Turgot. In 1892, Marshall had sent Böhm-Bawerk a copy of his *Elements of the Economics of Industry*; it is not unlikely that in 1890 or 1891 a copy of his *Principles* had gone to Böhm-Bawerk. In 1887 Marshall had expressed regrets to Foxwell that missing the Manchester meeting of the British Association meant forgoing the possibility of meeting with Böhm-Bawerk and Menger. Mary Paley's account of the meeting with the Austrians in the Tyrol in 1909 was quoted in an earlier chapter, including her recollection of their reluctance to talk on the subject of interest. This aspect of the

---

[*]   See for example *P* VIII, pp. 583–4 and n.1 which dates largely from *P* V; p. 790 n.1, the greater part of which dates from *P* IV and *P* VI. Later editions also reduce the number of times Böhm-Bawerk's work is mentioned. Cf. Marshall to J.B. Clark, 24 March 1908, of which the context is Böhm-Bawerk's 'rough method of thumping' in controversy, and where Marshall argued his own theory of capital was developed between 1870 and 1874 with respect to 'the details of my theoretical position . . . the time when Böhm-Bawerk and Wieser were still lads at school or college' (in *Memorials*, pp. 416–17).

encounter is more emphatically re-told by Fay in his recollection of Mary Marshall's own words in the context of his later pilgrimage to the spot where that encounter had taken place:

'You know, Mr. Fay, it was so important for Alfred not to be disturbed, and I was very upset when I heard that Professor Bohm Bawerk and his party were at an Inn on the other side. And unfortunately one day they met at the bridge.'

I gather that after a brief salutation A.M. and B.B. got down to the Rate of Interest, on which, according to A.M., B.B. held preposterous views, and things got so hot that finally Mrs. M. took her Alfred by the sleeve and Frau B.B. did ditto, and hurried them from each other's presence.

A.M. (for he was the soul of chivalry) felt that he had been rude: and so a Feast of Reconciliation was arranged. The loft was cleared of sacks and odd implements, the walls were whitewashed, and the table spread with food and flowers. The whole Bohm Bawerk colony came. Not a word was said about the Rate of Interest. Healths were drunk. Harmony reigned supreme – The landlord took me up to the loft and showed me where the feast had been, 'Er war ein tapferer Mann', and he told me how the birds used to come and sing to Marshall in his bower.[143]

A similar embarrassing encounter between Wieser and Marshall was described to von Hayek by Wieser himself. According to von Wieser, 'he and Marshall were going for several summers to a place in the Groeden Valley in the South Tyrol, knowing of each other but not formally acquainted and not wanting to meet, because neither was anxious to talk economics. Then one year Böhm-Bawerk came to visit Wieser. The former had met Marshall before, and at once introduced the two men. This led to a friendly meeting, but neither Wieser or Marshall went thereafter to the same place.'[144]

Some intriguing and unresolved aspects therefore remain of this episode in Marshall's life, during which he engaged in quiet, and occasionally amusing, controversy over Böhm-Bawerk's views in his classroom. For example, Marshall's actual annotations in his books reveal memory losses on his part when writing to Wicksell on the subject. They also reveal that Marshall made such annotations only in the English translations of Böhm-Bawerk's work he owned. This is despite the fact that the first edition of the *Principles* cited such works in German, but German versions of the work here discussed have only been preserved in the Marshall Library in later editions.[145] Had Marshall and Böhm-Bawerk met before their Tirollian encounter described by Mary Marshall as claimed by Wieser? Some of the evidence presented here smacks of a personal grudge on Marshall's side attributable to Böhm-Bawerk's later strident criticisms of his own work. However, the full story of this aspect of the controversies in Marshall's life will probably never be known.

Marshall's dealings with the other Austrians are quickly told. His limited contact with Menger is represented by two letters from Menger preserved in the Marshall Library. The first expressed doubts about Menger's ability to attend the Leeds meeting of the British Association in 1890, despite his desire to have an English seaside holiday and to meet Marshall. The second thanked Marshall for a complimentary copy of the *Principles*, and indicated that Austrian reviews of the book were likely to appear soon. A similar, but rather belated thank you, presumably for the third edition of the *Principles*, constitutes the sole epistolatry contact with von Wieser which has been preserved,[146] though Marshall allegedly redressed a grievance of Wieser in relation to the word 'marginal', which in the first edition he had wrongly ascribed to von Thünen.[147]

Marshall's association with the rival school of Lausanne were also rather peculiar. The evidence of contact with Walras in correspondence shows a rather one-sided arrangement in which Walras initiated exchanges of his writings, to which Marshall rather tardily, and sometimes rather irritably responded.[148] In July 1883, Walras sent Marshall a collection of some of his early theoretical papers, for which Marshall thanked him briefly, adding a promise to reciprocate the gesture by sending a copy of the *Economics of Industry* as soon as he and his wife had returned home from their summer holidays, a promise kept the following October.[149] This prompted Walras to send Marshall a copy of his *Elements of Pure Economics* in the first edition, the copy preserved in the Marshall Library with Marshall's annotations.[150] In his reply of thanks, Marshall raised both criticism on Walras's theory of rent and questions of priority in a rather controversial tone. He corrected Walras's implication that he had 'accepted Jevons's theory of final utility', because he 'had anticipated all the central points of Jevons's book and had in many respects gone beyond him'. In addition, an 1873 paper Marshall had read to the Cambridge Philosophical Society had anticipated 'incidentally your doctrine of unstable equilibrium', a remark Walras underlined in pencil in the original of this letter.[151]

Further correspondence is equally brief. In December 1884 a postcard from Marshall acknowledged receipt of Walras's paper on 'Monnaie d'Or'; a letter from Walras thanked Marshall for sending his inaugural lecture and referred him to Launhardt's work on mathematical economics; a postcard postmarked 8 December 1885 from Marshall provides a brief errata of Marshall's graphic method of statistics he must previously have sent to Walras; twelve months later a letter from Marshall expressed his good wishes for Walras's intentions to collect and complete his economic writings, reminding him at the same time that though he never claimed to have anticipated Jevons, neither had he learnt from him on the subject of final utility.[152] The correspondence ended as it had begun; in September 1889 Marshall thanked Walras for the new edition of the *Elements*, indicating his delight that Walras was developing 'the pure mathematical route', so contrary to his own view that mathematics should be kept in the background in a treatise of economics, because there was plenty of room for both methods for those working in the field.[153]

Marshall's annotations on Walras's work were brief, stopping at Lesson 12 of the *Elements*. They were also critical, and revealed a lack of appreciation for his colleague's work. Marshall's final annotation, dealing with the conversion of the demand curve for one commodity into the supply curve of the other geometrically, described this technique as of no use, so that Marshall believed he could ignore that page and, perhaps, the rest of the book. The *Principles*, it is well known, made few references to Walras; a practice Walras reciprocated with respect to the explicit acknowledgement of Marshall's work he made in his *Elements*.[154] It is ironical to note that one of the last, indirect references to Marshall in Walras's correspondence, a letter to Charles Rist of 1906, referred approvingly to an article by Rist in which Marshall and Pareto were represented as having continued economic work on lines initiated by Jevons, Menger and Walras thirty years before.[155]

Marshall's controversy over Böhm-Bawerk's theories illustrates the peculiar attitudes he had to issues of priority in economic thinking and to acknowledging work of other economists. The last are also strikingly demonstrated in Marshall's very peculiar relationship with Walras, which could even, from Walras's perspective on the matter, sink to censorship of his views from the pages of the *Economic Journal* via the solicited assistance of Edgeworth as editor.[156] Marshall's qualms on these matters were aired in correspondence with J.B. Clark, in which Marshall also explained when he did, and when he did not, think it worthwhile to engage in controversy with fellow economists. These comments encapsulate what he called his more 'callous' treatment of this issue in later years, thereby summarising the instances of his practice which have just been recounted:

> I have in earlier years eaten my heart out with doubt and anxiety as to what acknowledgements I should make to others. I fear I am an awful sinner; but I have grown callous. My rule has been to refer in a footnote to anyone whom I know to have said a thing before I have said it in print, even though I may have said it in lectures for many years before I knew that it had ever occurred to him: I just refer, but say nothing about obligations either way; being quite aware that people will suppose me to imply obligations. Instances are Francis Walker and Fleeming Jenkin. . . . I scarcely ever read controversies or criticisms. I have not read even a quarter of those which have been written about myself. The books, for instance, which I take to the Alps nearly every summer are almost exclusively concerned with matters of fact; though I try to read or skim any piece of analysis in which a man works to produce knowledge and not to controvert others. Thus I could not make acknowledgements to others properly: and I fall back on the plan already mentioned of referring in silence to any anticipation, of which I am aware, of a suggestion made by myself. My whole life has been and will be given to presenting in realistic form as much as I can of my Note XXI. If I live to complete my scheme fairly well, people will, I think, realise that it has unity and individuality. And a man who has lost ten of the best years of his life – from 37 to 47 – through illness, would, I think, be doubly foolish if he troubled himself to weigh and measure any claims to originality that he has. One thing alone in American criticism irritates me, though it be not unkindly meant. It is the suggestion that I try to 'compromise between' or 'reconcile' divergent schools of thought. Such work seems to me trumpery. Truth is the only thing worth having: not peace. I have never compromised on any doctrine of any kind.[157]

Marshall's casual attitude to generalisation revealed in this letter, particularly given the specific instances just documented which somewhat contradict his account, show his peculiar disposition on anticipators and predecessors, a matter noted earlier in the context of Jevons and Fleeming Jenkin.[158]

ALCOHOLISM AND HEREDITY, NATURE AND NURTURE: MARSHALL'S CONTROVERSY WITH PEARSON OVER PRACTICAL BIOMETRY

On 7 July 1910, readers of the *Times* would have seen a letter on 'Alcoholism and Efficiency' written by Marshall. This commented on a study on the influence of parental alcoholism on offspring by Miss Elderton and Karl Pearson and published by the Galton Laboratories, as summarised in the *Times* for 21 May. Against the conventional belief, this study ventured to show from the data that alcoholic parents exerted negligible detrimental influence on their offspring. This conclusion, contravening Marshall's strong beliefs on both the evils of alcohol and the importance of parental influence, undoubtedly explains why Marshall entered into controversy with its key author, Karl Pearson. Marshall justified his delay in responding to Pearson by his hope that someone 'more competent' than himself would have written on the adequacy of the statistical base by which the authors reached the 'broad conclusions' attributed to them on such a matter of 'intrinsic importance'. Marshall then promptly provided some reasons why he doubted the reported results. One of these came from 'within my own province', dealing as it did with wages and alcoholics, where Marshall argued that the conclusion reached derived from 'the choice of data' by the investigators.   As the wage statistics came only from residents in the poorest part of Edinburgh, comparable rents for individuals in the sample implied the alcoholic worker would have to earn higher wages to support his habit particularly when recorded in terms of weekly earnings, given the greater irregularity of employment associated with such persons. Marshall also questioned aspects of the studies' methodology, especially in terms of the inadequate account they took of the time element in investigating the problem.[159]

Marshall's letter drew at least two responses.   John Maynard Keynes expressed his joy at seeing Marshall's 'very damaging letter' criticising Pearson's memoir.   He also told Marshall he himself was publishing a critique in the *Statistical Journal* since his attempt to reach the letter columns of the *Times* on the subject had proved unsuccessful.   Keynes's detailed perusal of the evidence, including its original Edinburgh source, fully vindicated Marshall's conclusions reached from general principles.[160]   Pearson replied in the *Times*, criticising Marshall's letter for its statements of what 'may be' rather than 'what is' the case, and suggesting Marshall's surmise on the wage data was mistaken. Criticism, Pearson argued, should be backed by production of alternative data; this had not been done by Marshall.   Hence, despite the unanswered questions left by his study, Pearson maintained it had not been dented by Marshall's attack.[161]

Pearson's response irritated Marshall sufficiently for him to inform Keynes he would write to the *Times* again, though he was unsure of whether 'they will have patience with another demonstration'.[162]   In writing the second letter, Marshall was assisted by Keynes, who two days earlier had sent him both the proofs of his own contribution on the subject and the original report by the Charity Organisation Society from which Pearson's Edinburgh data derived.   'You will have no difficulty in showing how much evidence Pearson has had to overlook, in order to regard his sample as random.'[163]   Marshall's study of this evidence explains why his second letter to the *Times* did not appear until 2 August.   It mentioned the importance of Keynes's contribution in the *Statistical Journal*, stressing Keynes had drawn on the original Edinburgh data on which Pearson's study relied.   Marshall added that now he had himself seen these data, he was even more convinced of Pearson's errors in interpreting their wage material.   Marshall's opening paragraph reiterated that the matter was 'of far-reaching importance' and expressed the hope that Keynes's profound criticism of Pearson's work would 'be considered carefully by those interested in Eugenics'.[164]

Pearson's letter in reply came with the *Times* of 10 August.   It reiterated his criticism that Marshall had once again showed 'his inherent tendency to cite the possible instead of inquiring into the actual' as a prelude to a detailed defence of his use of the Edinburgh wage data. This defence *inter alia* accused Marshall of not retracting his 'original suggestion' as 'valueless, for it had no foundation in the *data* themselves'.   Careful analysis also destroyed Marshall's 'mere assertion' that alcoholics moved down to lower grades of work. Implicitly, Pearson charged Marshall with being amongst those of his critics who desired 'the children to be ruined in order to emphasise more markedly the wickedness of the parents', rather than sharing in the joy of one temperance newspaper which saw Pearson's analysis as proof that the 'sins of the fathers' need not always be 'visited on the children'.[165]

This was too much for Marshall, and his letter in response appeared the following week. Marshall immediately challenged Pearson's claim to have shown conclusively 'that parental degeneration has no causal relation to filial degeneration'. Given this failure on Pearson's part, economists had no need to readjust 'some of their views as to the conditions of social progress'. Pearson's irresponsibility in this matter, Marshall added, was the sole reason for breaking his 'almost absolute rule against controversial correspondence'. He then questioned once again Pearson's ability to interpret the wage data of the Edinburgh report. Despite that report's brevity, Marshall argued, these data came closer to the 'ideal Le Play had set up in social investigation' than any other comparable study Marshall had seen, praise of the data designed to highlight Pearson's ineptitude in using this splendid source. An economist, Marshall stressed, would not have made the errors of a 'mathematical outsider' like Pearson, when using them. Marshall concluded his 'wearisome letter', which he declared to be his last public word on the subject, by repeating his original argument on efficiency losses from alcoholic workers, explaining its foundation in his earlier experience on the Labour Commission, dated though some of that experience now was.[166]

Pearson's promise to deal with Keynes at a later stage came in a rather unusual form: a 26-page pamphlet 'Reply to the Cambridge economists', thereby including Marshall among his targets. Marshall's annotated copy of this pamphlet has been preserved, and his comments reveal the self-restraint he exercised by not re-entering the fray.[167] This, however, did not prevent him from sending the pamphlet to Maynard Keynes with the comment that he would not at all be adverse if Keynes finished the controversy, since his last letter to the *Times* made it impossible for him to do so. Keynes replied immediately to this invitation. Pearson's pamphlet revealed him for the 'lying, insolent fellow' he was, but its contents also left him wide open to unambiguous rebuttal by Keynes. This was best placed in the pages of the *Statistical Society Journal*, if editor Yule was willing, which Yule indeed was.[168] Marshall's encouragement of this course of action was equally quick. It was also positive in providing Keynes with some 'ammunition' on the inappropriate use of the method of least squares made by Pearson in his inquiry, for which Marshall quoted an 1866 contribution by Todhunter to the Cambridge Philosophical Society as authority. Further support of this kind was prohibited by Mary Paley Marshall, who warned Keynes a week later that Marshall's holiday in Devon should not be 'further broken into' by affairs of this nature.[169] Intermittent correspondence on the subject between Marshall and Keynes, however, continued. In November, Marshall wrote to Keynes about Galton's intervention in the *Times*, indicating that his inability to re-enter the controversy made him keen for Keynes to reply for him; subsequent letters canvassed issues related to the appropriate statistical method to be used in such social inquiry.[170]

It is not easy to conclude on the rights and wrongs of this controversy. Pearson had undoubtedly been hasty in his preliminary conclusion about the impact of alcoholic parents on their offspring, as he admitted in a subsequent study.[171] Marshall was vulnerable because his citations or paraphrasing of findings from the Edinburgh Report which featured so strongly in the controversy occasionally contained a choice of words which twisted part of the original meaning. In his annotations to Pearson's pamphlet, Marshall conceded he had sometimes gone too far on the basis of inadequate knowledge, but he categorically denied Pearson's charge that his attack on Pearson had been inspired by preconceived notions about the effects of alcohol.[172]   However, his, and Keynes's view that both Pearson's sample and methods were inadequate were, on the available evidence, correct. All the same, Marshall's initiating role in the controversy, of which Pearson reminded him in his concluding comments to his final *Statistical Journal* reply,[173] showed there was an element of truth in his charge that Marshall's preconceptions were of importance in the debate. After all, Marshall's entry into the controversy had been inspired by the importance of the issue to the views on social progress he had elaborated as economist, as he mentioned several times in his letters to the *Times*.   More specifically, it touched Marshall's tremendous concern as an economist with matters of heredity and nurture in securing the best possible demographic basis for further social progress. As Soffer has argued,[*] liberal social scientists like Marshall were annoyed when research from the eugenics laboratory run by Galton and Pearson increasingly yielded work showing 'little sensible effect of nurture, environment, and physique on intelligence'.   Such findings contradicted their specific emphasis on the importance for social progress of eliminating poverty, visible in Marshall's stress on a satisfactory standard of life for the formation and progressive development of character. This was therefore one of a number of occasions where Marshall, on being confronted with considerable factual evidence, evaded the unpalatable data either by controverting it with limited justification or by searching for authority which backed his preconceptions.[174]

Marshall's interest in these issues went back to the 1880s if not before, as is shown in various parts of the *Principles*. From its first edition onwards, and with remarkably little change except in detail in the subsequent editions, Book IV devoted one whole chapter, and parts of at least two other chapters, to issues of heredity in relation to labour supply, labour organisation and labour efficiency in which Galton's work was favourably quoted, as well as that of social Darwinists, and where, from the final three editions onwards, the 'principles of eugenics' were praised as an important input in achieving that desirable aim of slow and gradual progress.[175] Such minor changes, largely of a technical nature, were made for the third edition, probably on the advice of William Bateson, whose assistance was acknowledged in its preface. Other changes reflect new literature, since Marshall appears to have read widely on the issue; or involvement with new movements, like the Eugenics Movement just mentioned. Endorsement of its principles in the 1910 sixth edition was followed a year later by Marshall's apology to Keynes for his inability to attend a meeting of the newly formed Cambridge branch. Marshall was so delighted with its establishment that he immediately sent Keynes the composition fee for life membership.[176]

Two letters by Marshall to Bateson reveal the extent of his interest in these biological issues of genetics and heredity. The first was written the day after Marshall had attended a lecture by Bateson, 'with great interest, profound admiration and some understanding'. It raised the question for him 'why twins *when* similar are often incapable of being

---

[*]   Reba N. Soffer, *Ethics and Society in England. The Revolution in the Social Sciences 1870–1914*, p. 91, indicates Marshall was, however, not among those reforming social scientists who found it 'distasteful' that 'medical progress mistakenly prolonged the lives of those who weakened the average quality of the race stock'. See, for example, *Principles of Economics*, Book IV, Chapter V, §6, an argument present in all editions, and cf. especially the reference to J.B. Haycraft's *Darwinism and Race Progress*, London: Swann Sonneschein, 1895 (*P* VIII, p. 200 n. 1 and first inserted in *P* IV, 1898), and see below, p. 483 and n.†.

distinguished' in contrast with brothers of unequal age when compared at the same age by means of photographs.* In the context of the lecture, Marshall also asked if Bateson knew of a study called 'The Jukes', whose contents could either support or conflict with the position Bateson had advanced, and which had also frequently been quoted by those seeking 'sterilisation of the unfit'.¶ Bateson's subsequent explanation about 'the diversity of the ovum' solved much for Marshall, but a principal question remained. 'Does the similarity of (some) multiple twins indicate that the quality of the life (physical and mental, etc.) of the parents at the time of conception, and that of the mother during gestation and perhaps during suckling may possibly affect the qualities of offspring?' Nor was Marshall convinced that Bateson's facts were

> inconsistent with the belief that the *quality* of the life of the parents affects every juice and every fibre and every cell inside the genital organs as well as outside. Every rowing man knows that character is as important as physique: the Johnian freshman of my year who, judged by physique, was easily first, turned out to be *absolutely* useless. After a little while the captain of the sixth boat would not look at him; and mere 'weeds' full of pluck made it to the first boat. . . . Again, if it is true that good wheat sown year after year on barren soil degenerates, why should it not be true that the social life of many generations of parents is quite independent of any selection – affected the nerves, i.e. the quality and character of the later generations. That is all that we 'social people' want.†

Marshall's purposeful reading of evolutionary and social Darwinist literature is also brought out in his correspondence with Benjamin Kidd, the social Darwinist, whose book *Social Evolution* was greatly admired by Marshall. In acknowledging his receipt of an author's copy of its first edition, Marshall praised the work to its author as adding 'much more to the life of the thinking world during 1894 than anyone else'. With this praise, Marshall also

---

* Marshall to William Bateson, 24 October 1908 (Marshall Archive, 1:272). Bateson, a noted Cambridge biologist, occasionally gave public lectures on 'practical evolution'. In October 1908, he advertised lectures for the Natural Sciences Tripos, of which Marshall may have attended the first, and more general, introductory lecture. Marshall's limited knowledge of the subject, mentioned previously in another connection, is strikingly confirmed by the contents of this letter. The question about twins probably derived from his reading of Haycraft's *Darwinism and Race Progress*, p. 179, which Marshall annotated in his copy. 'But why do brothers differ so widely?' The birth of the Guillebaud twins in 1890 may also have inspired such curiosity. Incidentally Marshall had inadvertently signed the letter, 'Alfred Bateson', a 'Freudian' slip which his wife argued he should not correct because it showed how 'dominated' Marshall was by 'a master mind' like Bateson.

¶ That is Richard Louis Dugdale, *The Jukes. A Study in Crime, Pauperism, Disease and Heredity*, described by the editor of its first posthumous edition as 'a most important study of heredity in its relation to crime'. Marshall's liking of this book (which incidentally is not in the Cambridge University Library) came probably from its thesis that environment could modify heredity, since 'where the environment changes in youth, the characteristics of heredity may be measurably altered. Hence the importance of education'. Dugdale's findings also supported Marshall's views on the possibility of improvement in human character, the value of work and the value of family life in securing such progress (fifth edition, London: Putman, 1895, pp. 11, 55, 118, 120).

† Marshall to William Bateson, 26 October 1908 (Marshall Archive, 1:1:273). Such purposeful reading of genetics was not alien to Marshall and can be illustrated by his many annotations in his copy of Haycraft's *Darwinism and Race Progress'*, e.g. pp. 39, 41 on the first of which he noted, 'this is all I want', and on the second, 'this is not vital for my purpose'. Pearson would have been delighted to have come across the annotation on heredity and alcoholism Marshall made in his book which after expressing agreement with Haycraft's view, added 'this seems to be all I want', a confirmation of the preconceptions Marshall entertained on the subject. As an undergraduate member of the Lady Margaret Boat Club, Marshall could speak with some authority on the subject of desirable qualities in such athletes.

offered some criticism, 'without any reserve – as I would that others should do unto me'. This commenced with a biological issue associated with heredity,

> As to Weismann to begin with – I know the fault there is at best in a great measure mine. I can't make him out. I have read part of his controversy with Herbert Spencer without being convinced. One man here undertook to make the main point clear to me; but gave no satisfaction to this question. 'Given two men alike at birth, one of whom lives a vicious, self indulgent life, fills his blood with bad matter and makes the fibre of his body rotten, while the other lives a healthy, energetic but placid life; does Weismann contend that the child of the first is likely to be as good a citizen as the child of the second?' I have talked a little with Mr. Bateson on the same subject; but with no satisfactory results, though of course he knows Weismann well. On the whole, however, he seems inclined to defend Weismann on this particular point . . . we have agreed to have a thorough good talk on Weismann in relation to sociology in September. . . . As things are, I am inclined to think that the race which has prospered under the influence of natural selection through struggle, and in spite of bad provisions for the health of mind and body of young and old, might *conceivably* continue to progress under the influence of better physical and moral conditions of life, and in spite of the cessation of the struggle for survival.[177]

Apart from confirming Marshall's long-standing interest in heredity as part of his theory of social progress, this letter is interesting for a number of other points. The discussions with Bateson in September 1894 strengthen the view that Bateson was responsible for the technical changes on evolution theory in the third edition of the *Principles* mentioned previously. One of these changes is directly associated with the work of the German biologist–evolutionist, August Weismann, whose writings Marshall found difficult to understand, but of whose relative merits Bateson must have convinced him later that year. The first two editions of the *Principles* had illustrated the adaptation of Spencer's law of organ growth and pleasurable mental and physical exercise in humans or the impact of 'survival of the fittest' on organ growth in 'lower animals', by the 'long neck of the giraffe'.* The third and subsequent editions eliminated this example, presumably because Marshall had been convinced through Bateson of the validity of Weismann's Darwinian critique of the Lamarckian interpretation of this phenomenon on the basis that it assumed that such physical changes could be transmitted through heredity. However, in typical Marshallian fashion on an issue in which he believed strongly, the removal of the Lamarckian example of modification through use of the giraffe was combined with maintaining its Spencerian formulation for humans in the text, because of its importance for Marshall's theory of social progress.[178] As his subsequent correspondence with Bateson already quoted shows, Marshall was also not convinced by Bateson on Weismann's position on the impact of parental life style on offspring, the issue on which in the special case of alcoholism he went to the barricades in his controversy with Pearson. Combined with evidence already noted from his annotations in books on the subject such as Haycroft's,[179] this episode shows an occasional unwillingness on Marshall's part of abandoning theories suitable to his purpose irrespective of countervailing data or argument.

---

* *P* I, pp. 307–8 and n.1, Mathematical Note XI; *P* II, pp. 306–7 and n.1, Mathematical Note XI. The text of the mathematical note replaced the giraffe example with one about birds adopting aquatic habits which gradually increased the webbing between their toes, attributed, according to Marshall, by 'a minority of biologists . . . partly from the inherited effects of use'. *P* VI, removed this Lamarckian argument from the note (see *P* IX, p. 834).

Eight years later, Marshall further explained his moral interest in Darwinism to Kidd, at the same time indicating what Marshall 'the moralist' had found useful in Darwin from the perspective of his theory of social progress:

> For as to Darwin, he seems to me to have done what you seem to hold he has not done, emphasise the dominance of sacrifice for future generations as an, or even *the* essential element of progress. Thus the brief hints as to my ethical position given in book IV chapter VIII of my *Principles* seemed to me to be mere Darwinism (I have not developed this hint any further in print, though I talk about the matter more or less in lectures and there is another touch to the 'moralist' on p. 787 of my *Principles* [in the fourth edition].[180]

Some aspects of these remarks on the moral role of Darwinism in Marshall's theory of progress need to be stressed. One concerns the crucial importance of parental sacrifice for the progress of the race, a view which explains much of his attitude on the role of women in society, as shown in the next chapter. As Hearn had already noted in 1864,[181] the moral check to population increase through postponement of marriage was a major example of such parental sacrifice for the good of future generations, and as one only fully developed in civilised societies, a feature of human progress. Marshall added the sacrifice entailed in the parental nurturing responsibilities of providing for their offspring both a good and joyous home life and a better education than they themselves had enjoyed.[182] On a more general level, Marshall saw saving and investment as examples of this type of sacrifice so essential for the progress of future generations.[183] Moreover, 'modern', that is, evolutionary biology, had demonstrated for Marshall 'how malleable man is'.[184] This adds a different dimension to his view that economic biology was the mecca for the economist: only by adapting the features from modern biology on heredity and nurture could economists map a truly dynamic path of human and economic progress, the high ideal which underlay so much of Marshall's own economic endeavour. His limited grasp of that modern biology, also demonstrated in his discussion, explains why so little of that economic biology was ever applied to specific economic topics by him.[185]

Marshall's controversy over heredity with Pearson also neatly summarises his attitudes to advocacy and controversy. Only the highest principles, in this case parental responsibility and social progress, could induce him in later life to enter public controversy as he publicly proclaimed during its course. Defence of key features of his economic system played at least an equally dominant part, in encouraging this and other controversies in which he actively participated. The Pearson episode also illustrates the lack of scruple on Marshall's part in fighting such battles in which an occasional untruth was part and parcel of the argument. This sits uneasily with his boast to Clark, that truth was more important than peace.[186] Strident advocacy went hand in hand with the defence of high principle and, as in the case of his participation in various 'movements' (such as the eugenics movement in this instance), with the good they would do for the advance of economics both for its own sake and as a vehicle for the advance of mankind. Taking the moral high ground was a debating trick Marshall tended to use to advantage. Hence the principled controversialist and the strident advocate reveal further ambivalent features in Marshall's character in his persistent battles on behalf of causes to which he was committed on grounds of principle and which also involved him in occasional lapses from the high regard for the 'facts' the 'true scientist' should have.

NOTES

1. J.M. Keynes, 'Alfred Marshall', esp. pp. 218–23, 173, 199–200.
2. Pigou, 'In Memoriam', in *Memorials*, esp. p. 88. This is evaluated more fully below, Chapter 20, pp. 743–4.
3. F.Y. Edgeworth, 'Reminiscences', in *Memorials*, p. 69; cf. Keynes, 'Alfred Marshall', p. 199.
4. Jowett to Mary Paley Marshall, 16 October 1892 and 1 February 1893, Marshall Archive, 1:60–61.
5. E. Cannan, 'Alfred Marshall 1842–1924', *Economica*, November 1929, *AMCA*, I. p. 67.
6. J.M. Keynes, 'Alfred Marshall', pp. 218–23; The other two movements, Marshall's involvement in the women's degree issue and his role in establishing an Economics Tripos in Cambridge are discussed in Chapters 14 and 15 below.
7. Pursued further in later chapters, especially Chapter 21 below.
8. Above, Chapters 4 and 5, esp. pp. 88, 109–13.
9. Marshall to Brentano, 12 August 1903. He had earlier written to Brentano (17 September 1900) that talking 'too much officially' meant he never went to see anyone. Recall Keynes's remark (quoted in Chapter 8 above, p. 233) of Marshall giving orders at Balliol Croft dinner parties, and dominating the procedures on other social occasions at Balliol Croft.
10. For example, Marshall to Foxwell, 29 May 1886 which mentions his more than likely presence at Hall in St John's that Saturday night (Freeman Collection, 48/98); John Neville Keynes recorded in his diary for 15 February 1887, 'I dined with Marshall at a Feast at St John's' Marshall's activities as a Senior Fellow in college deliberations late in life are anecdotally illustrated by Guillebaud's 'Some Personal Reminiscences of Alfred Marshall', pp. 92–3.
11. Marshall to Taussig, 14 October 1896 (Taussig Papers, Harvard).
12. Alfred Marshall, 'The Old Generation of Economists and the New', in *Memorials*, pp. 295–311. This was delivered in Cambridge on 29 October 1896, that is, shortly after Marshall's letter to Taussig which mentions his preparation of it for the inaugural meeting of the new Economic Club; it was first published in the *Quarterly Journal of Economics*, of which Taussig was then editor.
13. J.M. Keynes, 'Alfred Marshall', p. 214, Roderick K. Clark to J.M. Keynes, 1 December 1924 (KMF).
14. C.W. Guillebaud, 'Some Personal Reminiscences of Alfred Marshall', p. 94, quoted below, p. 447.
15. *The Eagle*, Vol. 13, 1885, pp. 316–17. The reference is to Marshall's paper, 'Housing the London Poor', discussed below, pp. 450–51. The *Cambridge Review*, for example 9 March 1887, pp. 259–60 likewise carried regular reports of Social Discussion Society meetings, which reveal the extent of Marshall's involvement. I am indebted to John Whitaker for this information.
16. *Daily News*, 7 March 1909; and cf. the report of Alfred Marshall's speech at the preliminary meeting of the Cambridge Ethical Society in May 1888, which is quoted below (p. 448). See also Alon Kadish, *Historians, Economists and Economic History*, pp. 105–17.
17. Oscar Browning to Alfred Marshall, 13 March 1905; George Adams Thody to Alfred Marshall, 14 March 1905; Alfred Marshall to Erasmus Darwin, 15 March 1905; George Adams Thody to Alfred Marshall, 23 March 1905 and Alfred Marshall to Erasmus Darwin, 24 March 1905 (Layton Papers, 26–30, Trinity College Library, Cambridge).
18. See Walter Layton, *Dorothy*, London: Collins, 1961, p. 32; the quotation is from David Hubback, *No Ordinary Press Baron. A Life of Walter Layton*, London: Weidenfeld & Nicolson, 1985, p. 21 (my italics).
19. C.W. Guillebaud, 'Some Personal Reminiscences of Alfred Marshall', p. 94.
20. 'Statement of Belief' dated July 1886, sent to likely sympathisers and prospective members of the Ethical Movement, reprinted in G. Spiller, *The Ethical Movement in Great Britain. A Documentary History*, London: for the author, 1934, p. 2.
21. Susan Budd, *Varieties of Unbelief. Atheists and Agnostics in English Society 1850–1960*, London: Routledge, 1977, Chapter 9, esp. pp. 188–9.
22. Cambridge Ethical Society, Report of Preliminary Meeting, 18 May 1888, p. 21.
23. G. Spiller, *The Ethical Movement*, Chapter 3, pp. 47–56. This detailed account is based on reports in the *Cambridge Review* and on the Society's Minute Book which passed to him via Sorley.
24. Cambridge Ethical Society, *Minute Book*, CUL, Add 8776.

25. As discussed above, Chapter 11, pp. 354 and n.*, 357-8.
26. Solly Papers, British Library of Political and Economic Science, Coll. Misc. 154, Item 2g, a lecture by Solly on 'What is a Gentleman' reported in the *Lancaster Athenaeum*; Sections 4a and 4b of this collection include Solly's papers on the land and industrial village movements. For a discussion of Solly's less than altruistic motivations in starting such movements, see G. Stedman-Jones, *Outcast London*, esp. pp. 243, 260.
27. Solly Papers, Section 4B: D45, D57, D162. For further discussion of Marshall's fears of municipal socialism, see below, Chapter 16, pp. 593–5.
28. Foxwell to Solly, 15 May, 4 June 1887 (Solly Papers, D93). On Loch, see above, Chapter 11, pp. 354, 359.
29. Marshall to Foxwell, 8 June 1885 (Freeman Collection, 11/84).
30. Solly Papers D 202; Solly's contact with Kropotkin (*ibid.*, D171) may explain the presence of Kropotkin's *Fields, Factories and Workshops* in Marshall's Library in both the 1899 and 1901 editions.
31. *P* VIII, Appendix G, pp. 803–4. This came straight from Marshall's *Memorandum on Taxation* prepared for the Royal Commission on Local Taxation in 1897. See above, Chapter 11, p. 375 and cf. the remark from *P* VIII, p. 200 quoted above p. 451 and n*.
32. *P VIII*, p. 677 and n.1; a passage introduced in this form in *P* V. A similar passage was included as a note in *P* I, p. 720 n.1; and see Marshall to T.C. Horsfall, 21 February 1901, (Manchester Central Library, Horsefall Papers). For a different evaluation to Marshall's, see G. Stedman Jones, *Outcast London*, pp. 193–6, 229–30, 302–14.
33. See F.J. Osborn, introduction to re-issue of Ebenezer Howard, *Garden Cities of Tomorrow*, London, Faber & Faber, 1974, pp. 9–10. Marshall was cited on material from his 1884 paper, his *Principles* and for his proposal of a fresh air rate in the Report of the Royal Commission on Local Taxation (*ibid.*, pp. 66, 74–6, 119, 121–2, 125, 142). Charles Gide, according to Osborn the only other contemporary important economic writer who supported the movement, likewise endorsed its principles in his major economic text. See Charles Gide, *Principles of Political Economy*, second American edition, London: Heath, 1914, pp. 681–4.
34. Howard Papers, Folio 10, cited in Robert Fishman, *Urban Utopias in the Twentieth Century*, New York: Basic Books, 1977, pp. 45–6 and n.13. Howard claimed he had developed his reforms without having seen Marshall's 1884 paper.
35. That is, H. Kampffmeyer, *Die Gartenstadtbewegung*, Leipzig: Trubner, 1909; Bowley's lecture notes for 11 November 1891 (Cannan Papers, 909); Marshall's 1923 note on his 1884 paper is reproduced in *Memorials*, p. 142 n.1, and prefaced by Pigou's comment that the paper probably 'gave an impetus' to the Garden City movement. The February 1902 meeting was reported in *The Cambridge Review* (13 February 1902, p. 184) with the comment that with Marshall in the chair the scheme was more than a wild and visionary dream; and in *The Chronicle* and *The Independent Press* (14 February 1902).
36. Alfred Marshall, preface to L.L. Price, *Industrial Peace*, Oxford, 1887, pp. vii–viii, and see above, Chapter 9, pp. 294–5.
37. In his inaugural lecture at Cambridge, February 1885, in *Memorials*, p. 174; (quoted above, Chapter 10, p. 309); at its start this lecture paid tribute to Toynbee by noting that 'his death had stricken down also one of the noblest of the rising generation' (*ibid.* p. 152). In his *Principles*, Marshall only cited Toynbee's posthumously published *Industrial Revolution* once (*P* I, p. 440 n.; *P* VIII p. 392 n.) and, from *P* IV, included him in his account on the progress of economics, among those who exemplified the new 'humane' and 'high notions of social duty among economists' (*P* VII, p. 765).
38. Marshall to Foxwell, 15 February 1883 (Marshall Archive, 3:11). The traumatic experience of these lectures apparently contributed to Toynbee's premature death. A full account of Toynbee's lectures and their aftermath is presented in Alon Kadish, *Apostle Arnold: The Life and Death of Arnold Toynbee 1852–1883*, Chapter 8.
39. Alfred Marshall to Foxwell, 30 March 1883 (Marshall Archive, 3:13). Mrs Toynbee later withdrew this request in a letter to Marshall dated 5 April 1883 on the ground that the task had been admirably performed by Milner in the *Academy* for 24 March 1883.
40. *The Eagle*, Vol. 13, 1885, p. 315. The saying, 'there was nothing like leather', probably refers to the Victorian belief, so strongly espoused by Marshall's father, in the educative value of strap or cane.
41. An extensive centenary account is Asa Briggs & Anne Maccartney, *Toynbee Hall. The First Hundred Years*, London: Routledge & Kegan Paul, 1984, esp. Chapters 1 and 2; and for a more contemporary picture of its establishment, functions, and association with the University Settlement movement, W. Francis Aitkin, *Canon Barnett of Toynbee Hall*, London: S.W. Partridge & Company, 1902, esp. pp. 125–30.
42. Marshall, 'Lecture on Population', p. 393. These remarks on the impact of birth control on future generations indicate Marshall's early interest in the eugenics movement, discussed more fully below, pp. 482–5.
43. *The Eagle*, Vol. 14, 1887, p. 297; W. Francis Aitken, *Canon Barnett of Toynbee Hall*, p. 128. Marshall's fellow committee members included former Eranus associates Westcott, Seeley and Foster, as well as Cambridge University colleagues and acquaintances, Oscar Browning, William Cunningham, Foxwell, J.R. Tanner, Stanton, Sedley Taylor and Prothero.

44. *Canon Barnett. His Life, Work and his Friends* by his wife, London: John Murray, 1918, Volume 2, pp. 31–3.
45. Marshall to Foxwell, 31 January 1887 (Freeman Collection,35/69), Marshall to Foxwell, September 1887 (Freeman Collection, 26/69, 27/69).
46. Mary Paley Marshall, Newman Roll Letter, 1925. Information supplied by Rita McWilliams-Tullberg.
47. See G. Becattini, 'Henry Fawcett and the Labour Question', in L. Goodman, editor, *The Blind Victorian. Henry Fawcett and British Liberalism*, pp. 120–41, esp. p. 121; Henry Fawcett, *Manual of Political Economy*, third edition, London: Macmillan, 1869, Book II, Chapter X, pp. 241–57. J.S. Mill, *Principles of Political Economy*, Bk IV, Chapter VIII, §6; Marshall, 'The Future of the Working Classes', in *Memorials*, esp. pp. 113–14.
48. Henry Fawcett, *Manual of Political Economy*, pp. 246–8, 257, cf. Marshall's 'The Future of the Working Classes', in *Memorials*, pp. 113–14.
49. Alfred Marshall, 'The Future of the Working Classes', in *Memorials*, pp. 113–14.
50. *EOI*, Book III, Chapter X, esp. pp 225–6, 228.
51. *Ibid.*, p. 217.
52. Alfred Marshall, 'Co-operation', Presidential Address to the 21st Annual Congress of the Cooperative Movement, Whitsun weekend, June 1889, in *Memorials*, pp. 227–55 (all subsequent references to this paper in this section are inserted in brackets in the text).
53. Beatrice Webb, *My Apprenticeship*, London: Pelican edition, 1938, p. 415.
54. *Ibid.*, p. 432 n.1
55. *P* I, pp. 366–8, 641. A note to this last page refers readers to Marshall's Ipswich address.
56. *P* VIII, p. 307 (which dates from the second edition, 1891, p. 361 and eliminates any reference to the Ipswich Address) and p. 9 (dating back to the fifth edition).
57. *Observer*, 24 August 1890.
58. *Punch*, 13 September 1890, p. 123 (this cartoon is reproduced as illustration 41). Marshall's address on Competition (reproduced in *Memorials*, pp. 256–91; the words quoted by *Punch* are on p. 291 of the address, constituting its finale). Its contents are discussed below, p. 459.
59. *EOI*, p. 219 n.1.
60. One of the few exceptions of which I am aware took place on 15 March 1892 when Marshall discussed with witness F.A. Moore the opportunities for unions to take contracts in worker-organised business. *Minutes of Evidence*, Group B, Cmnd 6305, 1892, Volume 2, p. 320, Q. 18,902–3;. *Final Report*, June 1894, p. 20, paragraph 41. Cooperation and its organisation played however a significant part in the findings of the Commission, as Marshall himself later recorded (*IT*, p. 855 n.2).
61. See below, Chapter 16, esp. pp. 601–03.
62. *IT*, for example, pp. 289–95, Appendix P. In 1895, the *Economic Journal*, 5, p. 309, reported Marshall among the signatories calling attention to the work of the Labour Association, which was involved in spreading the cooperative gospel.
63. Marshall to Foxwell, 17 July 1886 (Freeman Collection, 51/89).
64. Marshall to Foxwell, 31 July, 22 August 1887 (Freeman Collection, 22/168, 23/168); Foxwell to J.N. Keynes, 26 August 1887, Marshall Archive, 1:26. Walras's paper dealt with 'A Solution to the Anglo-Indian Currency Problem'.
65. Alfred Marshall, 'Some Aspects of Competition', in *Memorials*, pp. 256–91. In December 1904, he wrote Wicksell, 'I *never* go to the British Association but in 1904 it came to Cambridge; and of course I acted as one of the hosts.' (in T. Gardlund, *Life of Knut Wicksell*, p. 343).
66. A. Marshall, 'Some Aspects of Competition', p. 291.
67. Above, pp. 457–8.
68. *Times*, 25 August 1890.
69. JNKD, 4 September 1890.
70. *Justice*, 13 September 1890.
71. *The Diaries of Beatrice Webb*, Vol. 1, p. 340.
72. Marshall to Brentano (July 1890), in H.W. McReady, 'Alfred Marshall: Some Unpublished Letters', *Culture*, September 1954, p. 304.
73. A letter to Edgeworth from Glasgow dated 10 July 1890 indicated the Marshalls' imminent departure for the Scottish countryside, the type of environment in which Marshall liked to rest, relax and write. Previous correspondence for that month was still from Balliol Croft, Cambridge.
74. Below, Chapter 19, pp. 707–12, esp. p. 712.
75. *Daily News*, 11 September 1890; *Leeds Mercury*, 11 September 1890; *Times*, 10, 11 September 1890.
76. *Times*, 10 September 1890.
77. JNKD, 15 September 1890 Bernard Moses (1846–1931) was then teaching in California, and as a product of Heidelberg and Michigan, and an admirer of Roscher's economics, would have appealed to Marshall. (Joseph Dorfman, *The Economic Mind in American Civilisation*, New York: The Viking Press, 1959, Vol. 3, pp. 96–8.)

78. Price's paper was published in the *Economic Journal*, September 1904, a sign of the 'open door' policy espoused by its editor, and, as shown below, (pp. 466–7), encouraged by Marshall. The Free Trade Manifesto was discussed above, Chapter 11, pp. 381–3.

79. JNKD, 19 August 1904; L.L. Price, *Memories and Notes on British Economists 1881–1947*, p. 14.

80. *Cambridge News*, 20 August 1904.

81. Clara Collet, *Diaries 1876–1914*, Warwick University Modern Records, MSS 29/8/1/69.

82. Flux's paper, 'Improvements and Rentability' appeared in the *Economic Journal* (15), June 1905, pp. 276–82; Bowley's 'Tests of National Progress' in the *Economic Journal* (14), September 1904, pp. 457–65.

83. Marshall to Flux, 19 March 1904, in *Memorials*, pp. 407–8.

84. J.M. Keynes, 'Alfred Marshall', p. 214; Alfred Marshall to F.Y. Edgeworth, 22 April 1909, in *Memorials*, p. 439. Marshall's discussion with Mavor on Canadian wheat was intimately connected with the fiscal question in international trade, which had so occupied him at the 1904 meeting of the British Association and on which he was then writing for his projected book on *National Industries and Trade*. See below, Chapter 17, pp. 634–5 and above, Chapter 11, p. 387.

85. Marshall to Chapman, 29 October 1904, in *Memorials*, p. 456. The photograph Marshall referred to, does not appear to have survived. An earlier chapter (above p. 247) indicated that the Marshalls' maid Sarah greatly enjoyed her duties in cooking for twelve for a whole week during the 1904 British Association meeting at Cambridge.

86. Marshall to Flux, 19 March 1904, in *Memorials*, p. 407; cf. Marshall to Wicksell, 26 August 1904, where the British Association 'Week' was described as 'most pleasant, though most fatiguing'. Cf. Marshall to Wicksell, 19 December 1904, in Gardlund, *Life of Knut Wicksell*, pp. 341, 343.

87. Clara Collet, *Diaries, 1876–1914*, Warwick University Modern Records, MSS 29/8/1/68–9. Marshall's absence from these functions is perhaps explicable in terms of his remarks to Brentano reported at the start of this chapter, p. 444.

88. Marshall to Foxwell, 14 January 1880 (Freeman Collection, 4/252); letter from assistant secretary of the Royal Statistical Society to the Author, 3 March 1992.

89. Above, pp. 355–6, 425.

90. Alfred Marshall, 'The Graphic Method of Statistics', *Journal of the Royal Statistical Society*, Jubilee issue 1885, in *Memorials*, pp. 175–87. Reference to this paper in this paragraph are inserted in brackets in the text.

91. See his correspondence with Moore, discussed below, Chapter 17, pp. 637–8; and Pigou's assessment, Chapter 20, p. 744.

92. Marshall to Foxwell, 27 April 1886 (Freeman Collection, 49/98). Foxwell had been elected in April 1882 as Professor of Political Economy at University College, London. See *Political Economy Club*, London, Macmillan, 1921, Volume 6, pp. 368, 107, 112.

93. See *Political Economy Club*, London, 1899, p. 68. At its foundation, meetings were held on the first Monday from December to June inclusively.

94. See above, Chapter 11, p. 345 and n.9.

95. As shown above, Chapter 11, p. 361, it was Balfour who issued the invitation in 1891 though, as mentioned there, Marshall and Balfour were acquainted well before this particular encounter at the Political Economy Club.

96. See *Political Economy Club Minutes, Members' Attendances and Questions*, London, 1899, pp. 19, 30, 48. Wicksteed's generalised marginal productivity theory had been published in 1894 as *An Essay on the Co-ordination of the Laws of Distribution*. As Stigler has noted ('Marshall's *Principles* after Guillebaud', in *AMCA*, II, p. 224), the third edition was the closest Marshall ever came to accepting this theory, of which he may have become more critical after taking on board some of the implications of its penetrating review in the *Economic Journal* by Flux in June 1894, pp. 308–13. An anecdote from one of Marshall's addresses to the cub was reported by Taussig in his Marshall obituary. This is cited below, Chapter 20, p. 741.

97. *Political Economy Club, Minutes, Members' Attendances and Questions*, London, 1899; *Political Economy Club*, London, 1921.

98. Francis Galton to Marshall, 3 August 1891 (Marshall Archive, 1:23); the short notice arose from the sudden resignation from the position by Dr William Ogle, because of pressure of work associated with the 1891 census.

99. See A.W. Coats, 'The Origins and Early Development of the Royal Economic Society', *Economic Journal,*78 (310),June 1968, pp. 349–71, esp. pp. 349–56; while the section title draws on Coats's earlier remark Marshall 'led British economics from the rear' ('Sociological Aspects of British Economic Thought', p. 711). This section draws heavily on its contents and on Alon Kadish and Richard Freeman, 'Foundation and Early Years', in *A Century of Economics: 100 years of the Royal Economic Society and the Economic Journal*, edited John Hey and Donald Winch, Oxford: Blackwell, 1990, pp. 23–43.

100. Kadish and Freeman, 'Foundations and Early Years', pp. 23–30.

101. Reprinted in 'The Society's Jubilee 1890–1940', *Economic Journal*, December 1940, pp. 401–2.

102. *Ibid.*, pp. 403–04, the quotation is from p. 404.
103. Marshall to Bonar, 25 July 1890, reprinted in 'The Society's Jubilee 1890–1940', *Economic Journal*, December 1940, p. 404.
104. Reproduced in *ibid.*, pp. 405–6.
105. See Kadish and Freeman, p. 32; Coats, 'Early Development', p. 365 and Austin Robinson, 'Fifty Five Years on the Royal Economic Society Council', in *A Century of Economics*, p. 163.
106. Edgeworth, 'Reminiscences', in *Memorials*, p. 69. One example is Marshall to Edgeworth, 16 February 1891 (Marshall Archive,1:307) which mentions details for the journal about its cover, bibliographical information, and a précis of past articles which Marshall advised Edgeworth was 'a big task'.
107. 'Report of Goschen's Presidential Address to the British Economic Association', *Economic Journal*, 3, September 1893, p. 389.
108. *Ibid.*, pp. 389–90. The meeting coincided with the Royal Commission on the Aged Poor to which Marshall had given evidence, above Chapter 11, pp. 353–60, esp. pp. 353–4.
109. Kadish and Freeman, p. 32; Robinson, p. 163; Marshall to T.H. Elliott, Secretary of the Royal Economic Society, 25 May 1906 (Marshall Archive, 1/25).
110. Robinson, p. 165. A few letters by Marshall to Higgs on society business have been preserved in the Royal Economic Society Archives.
111. Clara Collet, 'Obituary of Henry Higgs (1864–1940)', *Economic Journal* 50 (4), December 1940, pp. 559–61. The first two 'I's in the quotation refer to Higgs. Other members of the cub included Bonar, Aves, Robinson and Llewellyn-Smith.
112. This section relies heavily on John Maloney, *Marshall, Orthodoxy and the Professionalisation of Economics*, Chapter 5; Gerard M. Koot, *English Historical Economics 1870–1926*, esp. Chapter 7, pp. 142–55; Alon Kadish, *Historians, Economists and Economic History*, esp. Part II.
113. William Cunningham, 'What did our Forefathers mean by Rent', *Lippincott's Magazine*, February 1890; 'Nationalism and Cosmopolitanism in Economics', *Journal of the Royal Statistical Society*, December 1891, the text of his Presidential Address to Section F in 1891. His *Economic Journal* articles to which Marshall eventually replied were 'The Relativity of Economic Doctrine', his inaugural lecture as Tooke Professor of Political Economy at King's College, London (Vol. 2, March 1892, pp. 1–16) and, in direct attack on Marshall's historical chapters then in Book I of the *Principles*, 'The Perversion of Economic History', Vol. 2, September 1892, pp. 491–506. It is ironical to note that Marshall had supported Cunningham's candidature for the Tooke chair with a testimonial dated 13 April 1891.
114. Cunningham, 'The Perversion of Economic History', pp. 491–2; further references to this article are given in brackets in the text of this paragraph.
115. Alfred Marshall, 'A Reply [to Dr. Cunningham]', *Economic Journal*, 2, September 1892, pp. 567–79 – further references to this paper in the text are inserted in brackets.
116. Benjamin Jowett to Mary Paley Marshall, 16 October 1892, 1 February 1893 (Marshall Archive,1:60–61). The 'unsuccessful' in the quote undoubtedly refers to Cunningham's attempt at the Oxford chair. See p. 469 and n.* above.
117. JNKD, 16 October 1892. Earlier Marshall had written to Keynes about Cunningham's letter on rent published in the *Academy* and in the *Pall Mall Gazette* on which he did not feel inclined to comment in public because the points raised were too trivial. Marshall to Keynes, 10 October 1892 (Marshall Archive,1:106).
118. L.L. Price, *Memories and Notes on British Economists*, pp. 13–14.
119. Alon Kadish, *Historians, Economists and Economic History*, p. 131.
120. Marshall to Keynes, 27 May 1889, Marshall Archive,1:90.
121. Marshall to Keynes, 10 June 1894, Marshall Archive,1:107; cf. Marshall to Hewins, 8 February 1894, postscript (Sheffield University Library, Hewins Papers).
122. Marshall to Acton, 13 November 1897 (CUL, Add 6443(E)205).
123. Marshall to Foxwell, 14 February 1902, Marshall Archive, 3:44.
124. *P* I, Book I,Chapter II, esp. pp. 23–8; Marshall Archives, Box 5, Item 8: Middle Ages. 2 Parts. Needless to say, Marshall's studies of the period did not encompass work on primary sources.
125. Marshall to Foxwell, 8 February 1906, Marshall Archive, 1:72.
126. Marshall to Foxwell, 12 February 1906, Marshall Archive, 1:73.
127. Marshall to Foxwell, 25 January 1897, Marshall Archive, 1:49.
128. Marshall to J.N. Keynes, 6 February 1902, Marshall Archive, 1:126.
129. Marshall to Foxwell, 3 July 1878 (Freeman Collection, 36/155). These notes have been preserved in the Marshall Archive, Box 5, Items 6 (i and ii) Cf. *HME*, esp. pp. 1–7.
130. Marshall to Foxwell, 12 February 1906 (Marshall Archive, 1:73).

131. See Alfred Marshall, 'Distribution and Exchange', *Economic Journal*, 8, March 1898, p. 44 and P. Groenewegen, 'Marshall as Historian of Economic Thought', *Quaderni di Storia dell'economia politica*, IX (2–3), 1991, pp. 59–87. And see also above, Chapter 6, pp. 164–5.

132. These are documented in *P* IX, pp. 722–50, of which few changes are directly attributable to the exchange between Marshall and Cunningham. Marshall to Foxwell, 27 March 1899 (Baker Library, Harvard) presents a quite moderate view of Cunningham as teacher and economic historian.

133. In a letter to the Marshall Librarian (2 August 1971), Klaus Hennings dated this encounter at 1909 on the basis of details from a photograph taken on this occasion (this is reproduced as illustration 18).

134. G. Cassel, *The Nature and Necessity of Interest*, London, Macmillan, 1903, reissued Augustus M. Kelley, New York, 1957, pp. 22–24, esp. p. 22 and n.2. Cassel had visited the Marshalls briefly in 1901, when they may have discussed this matter together. Cassel's *Nature and Necessity of Interest* was recommended by Marshall to Macmillan. Marshall to Cassel, 18 June 1901; an undated letter by Mary Paley Marshall to Cassel around the same time (Cassel Correspondence, Royal Library, Stockholm); Marshall to F. Macmillan, 9 January 1903.

135. Marshall to Wicksell, 26 July 1904, in T. Gardlund, *The Life of Knut Wicksell*, pp. 339–40.

136. Wicksell to Marshall, 10 August 1904, in *ibid.*, pp. 340–41.

137. Marshall to Wicksell, 26 August 1904, in *ibid.*, p. 341.

138. Marshall to Wicksell, 19 December 1904, in *ibid.*, pp. 342–3.

139. Wicksell to Marshall, 6 January 1905, in *ibid.*, pp. 343–5.

140. E. von Böhm-Bawerk, *Positive Theory of Capital*, translated by William Smart, London, Macmillan, 1891, pp. 32, 38, 65–6, 70. Marshall's copy is preserved in the Marshall Library.

141. E. von Böhm-Bawerk, *Recent Literature on Interest 1884–1899*, translated by William A. Scott and Siegmund Feilbogen, New York: Macmillan, 1903, pp. 26–7, 44–5. The copy is preserved in the Marshall Library. As Michael White pointed out to me, the annotations may well have been made after some of his correspondence with Wicksell.

142. *Ibid.*, pp. 37–9 in the copy preserved in the Marshall Library. Cf. Marshall to Edgeworth, 16 February 1891, where in the context of 'discounting pleasurable events' he referred to his difference in style relative to 'Böhm-Bawerk's young lions' (Marshall Archive, 1:307).

143. C.R. Fay, 'Reminiscences of a Deputy Librarian', *AMCA*, I, p. 89; above, Chapter 7, p. 217.

144. F. A. von Hayek to C.W. Guillebaud, 5 January 1960, in Marshall Archive.

145. Marshall Library, *Catalogue*, p. 8, where the German editions of the *Critical History* and the *Positive Theory* listed are the 1914 and 1912 editions respectively.

146. Carl Menger to Marshall, 6 August 1890, 1 October 1891, Marshall Archive, 1:87–88, von Wieser to Marshall, 24 November 1895, Marshall Archive, 1:108. These letters strengthen the earlier surmise that Marshall may have sent a presentation copy of the *Principles* to Böhm-Bawerk.

147. Above, Chapter 6, p. 150 and note 43.

148. See Marshall to Walras, 20 March 1883, in *Correspondence of Léon Walras and Related Papers*, edited William Jaffé, Letter 549. Walras's, initiative in sending Marshall some of his writings may have been inspired by a letter from Foxwell, describing Marshall as our 'greatest living economist' (Foxwell to Walras, 30 December 1882, in *ibid.*, letter 544). As Whitaker surmises, Marshall may first have heard of Walras's work through Jevons. See introduction to *EEW*, pp. 103–4; J.K. Whitaker & K.O. Kynn, 'Did Walras communicate with Marshall in 1883?', *Rivista Internazionale di Scienze Economiche e Commerciale*, 23 (4), 1976, pp. 386–90.

149. Walras to Alfred Marshall, 15 July 1883, in Jaffé, ed. Letter 573; Marshall to Walras, 23 July 1883 (*ibid.*, Letter 578); Marshall to Walras, postcard postmarked 26 October 1883 (*ibid.*, Letter 592).

150. Walras to Marshall, 28 October 1883 (*ibid.* Letter 593).

151. Marshall to Walras, 6 November 1883 (*ibid.*, Letter 595 and see p. 794 n.5); this was discussed Chapter 6 above, p. 150 and see Whitaker, introduction to *EEW*, I, pp. 103–7.

152. Marshall to Walras, December 1884 (*ibid,.* Letter 618); Walras to Marshall, 2 April 1885 (Letter 644); Marshall to Walras, 8 December 1885 (*ibid,.* Letter 689); Marshall to Walras, 28 November 1886 (Letter 751). The last replies to Walras' letter to Marshall, 25 November 1886, which mentions questions of priority in connection with the notion of final utility (*ibid.*, letter 749).

153. Marshall to Walras, 19 September 1889 (in *ibid.*, Letter 922).

154. These notes have been preserved in the Marshall Library in the original, but rebound, copy of the *Elements*, the one which Walras may have sent him in 1883. For Marshall's few comments on Walras, see *P* I, pp. 149 n., 425 n., 536 the second of which notes their independent discovery of unstable equilibria; *P* VIII, pp. 101 n., 138 n., 787, 788n., 821 which removes the note on independent discovery and adds notes on the tripartite division of factors of production in Walras and on his view of capital. Walras, *Eléments*, contains three references to Marshall's work (*Eléments d'économie pure*, edited Claude Mouchot, in *Works*, Vol. VIII, Paris: Economica, 1988, pp. 21, 489, 712).

155. Walras to Charles Rist, 5 March 1906 (in *Correspondence*, ed. Jaffé, Letter 1621, Vol. 3, p. 299 and n.2).
156. See T.W. Hutchison 'Insularity and Cosmopolitanism in Economic Ideas 1870–1914', *American Economic Review*, 45 (2), May 1955, esp. pp. 10–14.
157. Alfred Marshall to J.B. Clark, 24 March 1908, in *Memorials*, pp. 416–18.
158. Above, Chapter 6, pp. 161–3; the topic is further pursued below, Chapter 21, pp. 776–9.
159. Marshall to the editor of the *Times*, 7 July 1910.
160. Maynard Keynes to Marshall, 11 July 1910 (Marshall Archive, 1:269).
161. Karl Pearson to editor of the *Times*, 12 July 1910.
162. Marshall to J.M. Keynes, 14 July 1910 (Keynes Papers, King's College, Cambridge, File C013/35).
163. Maynard Keynes to Marshall, 12 July 1910 (Marshall Archive, 1:270).
164. Marshall to editor of the *Times*, 2 August 1910.
165. Karl Pearson to editor of the *Times*, 10 August 1910.
166. Marshall to editor of the *Times*, 19 August 1910.
167. Karl Pearson, *Questions of the Day and of the Fray, Supplement to the Memoir entitled, The Influence of Parental Alcoholism on the Physique and Ability of the Offspring: A Reply to the Cambridge Economists*, London: Dulau & Company, 1910, Marshall's copy with annotations is preserved in the Marshall Library.
168. Marshall to Maynard Keynes (Keynes Papers, File CO13/35); Maynard Keynes to Marshall, 13 September 1910 (Marshall Archive,, 1:271). Keynes's reply to Pearson's pamphlet appeared in the *Statistical Journal*, LXXIV, part 1, December 1910, pp. 114–21; Pearson's reply in the subsequent issue, January 1911, pp. 221–9. For brief discussions of Keynes's part in the debate, see R.F. Harrod, *Life of Keynes*, pp. 154–5; Robert Skidelsky, *John Maynard Keynes: Hopes Betrayed 1883–1920*, pp. 223–7, who gets some of the chronology wrong and D.E. Moggridge, *Maynard Keynes. An Economist's Biography*, London: Routledge, 1992, pp. 205–7.
169. Marshall to Maynard Keynes, 14 September 1910, Mary Paley Marshall to J.M. Keynes, 21 September 1910 (Keynes Papers, File C013/35).
170. Marshall to Maynard Keynes, 2 November, 10 November and 4 December 1910, Maynard Keynes to Marshall, 31 December 1910 (Keynes Papers, File C013/35). Pigou entered the fray in 1911 in support of his Cambridge colleagues, with a carefully worded article in the *Westminister Gazette*, 2 February 1911.
171. Amy Barrington and Karl Pearson, *A Preliminary Study of Extreme Alcoholism in Adults*, London: Dulau & Company, 1910, pp. 44–5.
172. Pearson, *A Reply to the Cambridge Economists*, pp. 12, 14, 20–21, but cf. p. 483, note † below.
173. Pearson, 'Influence of Parental Alcoholism', *Journal of the Royal Statistical Society*, January 1911, p. 229.
174. Similar examples can be found in his handling of the women's issue, e.g. Chapter 14, below, pp. 515–16.
175. See *P* IV, Book IV, Chapter V §6–7; Chapter VI §3, Chapter VIII especially final paragraph. The reference to the principles of eugenics, first inserted in the *P* VI can be found in *P* VIII, pp. 248–9.
176. Marshall to J.M. Keynes, 18 May 1911 (Keynes Papers, File L/M/41).
177. Marshall to Benjamin Kidd, 6 June 1894 (Cambridge University Library, Add 8069/M251). Weismann was quoted frequently by Kidd in this book, both for his contributions to Darwinian theory and in connection with Spencer's critique of them.
178. *P* VIII, p. 247; *P* IX, p. 326; and see August Weismann, *The Evolution Theory*, London: Edward Arnold, 1904, Vol. 1, pp. 20–21 on the giraffe example, and pp. 354–5 on his criticism of Spencer's theory in this regard.
179. Above, p. 483 and note †.
180. Marshall to Benjamin Kidd, 17 May 1902 (Cambridge University Library, Add 8069/M256); the material in the fourth edition on the role of nurture and family life in economic progress to which Marshall specifically referred, first appeared in *P* II, (p. 748) and survived to *P* VIII (pp. 720–21). See *P* IX, pp. 720.
181. W.E. Hearn, *Plutology*, London: Macmillan, 1864, esp. p. 391. Marshall had studied this book at an early stage in his economic education, as shown in my 'Alfred Marshall and Australian Economics', in *HETSA Bulletin*, No. 9, Winter 1988, pp. 1–15; and on Hearn's contribution to 'evolutionary' economics, Peter Groenewegen and Bruce McFarlane, *A History of Australian Economic Thought*, London: Routledge, 1990, pp. 52–5 and the references there cited.
182. *P* VIII, pp. 720–1, a passage as shown in note 180 above, originating in *P* II.
183. Bowley's lecture notes of Marshall's lectures, 16 November 1891 (British Library of Political and Economic Science, Cannan Papers, 909, p.22).
184. *Ibid.*, p. 21, and see above Chapter 6, pp. 141, 167–8.
185. For different perspectives on Marshall's economic biology, see Brinley Thomas, 'Alfred Marshall on Economic Biology', *Review of Political Economy*, 3 (1), 1991, pp. 1–14; Geoffrey Hodgson, 'The Mecca of Alfred Marshall', *Economic Journal*, 103 (417), March 1993, pp. 406–15.
186. Above, pp. 481–2, and below, Chapter 21, pp. 786–7.

14. A Feminist *Manqué*

Marshall's ambivalent attitude to women during his lifetime was attributed by Keynes to 'mighty heredity', a direct product of inherited paternal characteristics. This perspective was based on his reading of William Marshall's portrait as that of a 'tough old character', whose 'nearest objects of his masterful instincts were his family, and their easiest victim his wife; but their empire extended in theory over the whole of womankind, the old gentleman writing a tract entitled *Man's Rights and Women's Duties*'.[1] Apart from the difficulties such Galtonian viewpoints raise, Keynes's diagnosis is based on dubious 'facts' about Marshall's father. Nevertheless, Keynes's view that 'an implanted masterfulness towards womankind warred in him with the deep affection and admiration which he bore to his own wife, and with an environment which threw him in closest touch with the education and liberation of women'[2] is close to the mark. It clearly points to the conflicting emotions on women revealed during Marshall's long life. His active support for the university education of women within the early Cambridge movement from which Newnham developed and his appointment as Principal to the first university College 'to open its doors freely to women' sit uneasily with his later opposition to women's claims for Cambridge degrees and the use of female teachers to men students, let alone strong views on the sexual division of labour based on equally staunch beliefs on the nature of women's intellect and on their duties in life. Was this the product of a 'congenital bias' gathering strength over the years until it burst out in the actions of the mature Marshall?[3] The fact that little in Marshall's life was ever so simple warns against accepting this particular hypothesis.

Unfurling the events which made Marshall a feminist *manqué* requires first revisiting some aspects of Marshall's formative years relevant to his attitudes to women and in particular addressing the question whether events in Bristol marked a turning-point in his opinions, as signalled, for example, by the evidence he gave to the Higher Education Commission in Wales and Monmouthshire.[4] Secondly, the views of the older Marshall on the women's question need to be aired. These are visible in the debates at Cambridge University in the 1880s and 1890s; in the views on sexual division of labour revealed particularly in the pages of the *Principles*, and in his relationship with and attitude to some prominent women of the time, with some of whom he was personally acquainted. Only then can it be decided whether at the end of his life Marshall is accurately described as a (relatively) courteous misogynist and a victim of contemporary (conservative) scientific beliefs.

MARSHALL AND WOMEN: THE FORMATIVE YEARS (1842–1877)

Earlier chapters have reflected occasionally on the strong feminine influences in Marshall's nurture through his mother, his Aunt Louisa and his favourite sister, Mabel Louisa. From an early age, however, such influences were counterbalanced by a rather domineering father

493

who, nevertheless, on some critical issues could be persuaded to give way; a benevolent and romantic, but also rather ruthless, Uncle Charles, whose financial largesse during life and death enabled major undertakings in Marshall's early life; and, less personal and all the more overwhelming, the exclusively masculine environment of school (tempered by home and holidays) followed by his almost monastic university and college life, where the only women Marshall would have regularly encountered were bed-makers and residents of the town. So little detail is available on these aspects of Marshall's early life that psychological hypotheses to explain his later behaviour are hazardous to say the least. What must be noted, however, is that both his formative period in this sense and his cloistered college life end with the entry of the fourth formidable woman in his life, his wife and subsequent life partner, Mary Paley. Their marriage marks a conscious transition from 'masculine' Cambridge to Bristol, where a change of attitude to women on Marshall's part appears to have taken place.

A relevant feature of Marshall's early childhood is, however, retrievable from the available evidence. This is the protective and supportive role his female relatives appear to have exercised in his youth. His mother, Marshall later recalled, often shielded both him and his brothers and sisters from their father's wrath and discipline. Through the holidays she provided in Devon, his aunt was later described as having 'saved' him from the oppressive atmosphere of school and associated homework, paternally, and nocturnally, supervised. Marshall assiduously treasured the memory of these holidays. They probably also instilled that love of country his initial home and school life gave little scope for, one which later he gained for himself in the cloisters and the 'wilderness' of St John's, the 'Backs' of his beloved Cambridge and the regular summer pilgrimages to European mountains and English countryside. Sisters also acted as the playmates of his youth, in cricket practice as a schoolboy and in holidays as a young Fellow, since the late arrival and later delicate health, of younger brother Walter, prevented him from acting in this role, just as his older brother's absence in India from an early age had done previously.[5]

A number of Marshall's other pre-marital reactions to women can be examined from his American letters to his mother. These complain of the absence of ladies with 'go' on his sea voyage, a lack of character strength not compensated for in Marshall's view by their refinement and amiability, and not at all like the female company he was used to and which had probably spoilt him on this score. He also expressed delight that the Unitarian marriage service excluded 'the woman's promise to *obey* the man' but disparagingly noted in his critical sketch of Emerson that 'many women' elevated him into 'their highpriest' because his power of working through problems was rather limited relative to the force and emotion with which he stated them. Marshall's description of the drive in Norwich with Miss Nunn is also of interest; 'an active minded, able person, with very agreeable manners age 26–32', a 'first rate tête-a-tête' and the 'delicious' 'charm' of an 'enterprising, earnest-minded woman brought up in the Country', as is the ploy by which he 'manoeuvred' to repeat the experience the next evening. Even more informative of Marshall's tastes in the opposite sex are his detailed comparison of English and American girls:

I told his [that is, Professor Sumner's] wife and sister in law that I was glad to have come to America: if only for this to discover that American girls are not entirely given up to the task of preserving their complexion: I thought this was the main business of the American girls who loaf about Europe.

They were abundantly gracious; but after some hours began to talk about the English girls whom they had met on their travels. 'The English girls are very lively [or lovely] but they are sadly unable to take care of themselves. Once on the Continent of Europe I got to know very intimately two English girls. We Americans used to make up excursion parties; large parties; but we never had any one to look after us; we were able to do that for ourselves. But all my entreaties could not induce the mother of these English girls to let them come with us when she could not go herself to watch them. American girls are much more trustworthy than English; they do not require to be watched at every turn.' This nettled me: so I said – 'English mothers do not follow their daughters about when in the presence of men in order to watch them; but in order to provide them in emergency with that protection and defense which the more self-possessed American girl has learnt to be able on all occasions to provide for herself.' They were polite and seemed to assent to this; but on thinking the matter over I could not help feeling that it is probably true that the average American girl is more trustworthy than the average English girl. Not only is she more acute and more ready, but she has herself, I think more under control.[6]

A similarly favourable comment followed 'on the thorough freedom in the management of their own concerns' for Canadian women, a situation Marshall saw as both 'right and wholesome' even if 'it would be regarded as dangerous licence by the average Englishman'. Such sentiments were not applicable to the women of Nevada, who 'have all the faults of the man; many more besides, and none of their virtues' and the absence in whom 'of the gentler virtues' boded ill for the next generation, something Marshall generalised from San Francisco experience to conclude that 'the weak point of the Far West lies in their women'. Hence Irish miners tended to import their wives from 'home'. Lack of virtue in women, Marshall also observed, 'made men more "down on", intolerant of the "Women's Rights" Movement' in Nevada than anywhere else. Other generalisations were made about factory women in the textile industry, the degree of happiness in the faces of nuns of which Marshall claimed to have made a special study, and a brief sketch of the eighteen-year-old wife of a Swiss passenger, 'gentle, pretty, simple, mild', 'open, willing to talk to others', 'a favourite on board' and occasionally the butt for the wit of her jealous, forty-five-year-old husband. Such observations, although occasionally imbued by prejudice and over-generalisation, hardly smack of the type of misogyny for which Marshall later became noted.[7]

His 1875 observations on the desirable characteristics of eligible young women shed light on his subsequent courtship in Cambridge. Mary Paley undoubtedly shared many of these characteristics, as did the circle of young women students whom he entertained in his college rooms in the early 1870s, and who shyly, and not so shyly, intruded on his social life in college and elsewhere via the dancing at the Master's Lodge occasionally organised by Mrs Bateson, the Master's wife and an active participant in the movement pioneering women's education. Such female company from university and home spoiled him for contact with the characterless and refined ladies he encountered on the ship which had taken him to America in June 1875.

Here lies perhaps one motive for his active involvement in that progressive movement for women's education in the early 1870s. Another is his intimate contact with the leaders of that movement through his membership of St John's and the Board of Studies for the

Moral Sciences. For the former, it is sufficient to recall his admiration for and friendship with the Batesons, Bonney and Hudson, more senior college fellows who were active in support of this cause, and even Johnian student Foxwell, then also involved with women's education at Cambridge.   Those in the moral sciences who initiated the organisation of lectures for women at Cambridge included Frederick Maurice, the Fawcetts, the Venns, Mayor, Sidgwick, all persons with whom Marshall was closely connected, particularly via the Grote Club. An initial enthusiasm for the feminist cause on Marshall's part provided a third and powerful motivation, particularly when those he explicitly praised on one occasion for their role in that cause, John Stuart Mill and Harriet Taylor, liberally contributed to it. Absorption of liberal principles on women's rights by the young Marshall is very visible in his comments from America defending the right to freedom over their concerns in the young women of North America and his exultation over an order of service which removed the duty to obey for the wife. No matter which of these motives predominated, or the extent to which they can be said to have been promoted by self-interest in career advancement, can gainsay the active role played by the young Alfred Marshall in the women's education movement at Cambridge during the early 1870s.[8]

Marshall's contributions of time and money in his support for women's education at Cambridge in the early 1870s can be quickly indicated. He was among the first teachers of women in the early 1870s, lecturing to them on political economy and political philosophy, and, in the words of an early historian of Newnham College, 'created and directed an enthusiastic devotion to the study of economics'.[9]   Initially, most of these courses were directed at the general population in the manner of extension lectures, but teaching to prepare women students for the Tripos soon followed, and was a task in which Marshall also took part in these formative years. He actively tried to recruit the better students for political economy: his attempt to win Jane Harrison, the subsequent classical scholar, being one of his failures, compensated for by earlier successes with Mary Paley and Mary Kennedy.[10]   His wife recalled in 1884, 'I don't think that at that time we sufficiently appreciated the immense kindness of lecturers who would give as much trouble to one or two of us as if we had been a large class of men'.[11]   Later she recalled how Marshall had been among the early 'runners' who took Tripos examination papers from Senate House where the men attempted them, to the Kennedy's house in Bateman Street where the women sat the various papers, and how effectively he had taught them economics through fortnightly papers, stiffly supervised and corrected.[12]   Marshall kept up this voluntary teaching until 1875 when Mary Paley replaced him after her appointment as resident lecturer at Newnham College in Political Economy. In addition, Marshall gave £50 to the Newnham building fund in 1874, a substantial sum and perhaps partly designed to impress the person to whom he was soon to be engaged with his devotion to the cause and to her place of employment.[13]

Marshall's task of assisting women's education at Cambridge was not all work. There were entertainments and social occasions as well.   The Sunday social evenings Alfred Marshall and fellow Johnian Hudson organised in their college rooms have already been mentioned as have the dances organised at the St John's Master's Lodge. Early Newnham students recalled the presence of Henry Fawcett and Alfred Marshall at Miss Clough's garden tea parties during the early 1870s and his attendances (with Sidgwick, Seeley,

Cayley and Jebb) at entertainments – 'very innocent and provincial affairs' – with refreshments and music. Despite the attempts by more senior organisers of the movement to prevent such things from happening, romance appeared relatively quickly among the young dons and their female students. Its first fruit was the engagement between Alfred Marshall and Mary Paley within a year of his return from the United States and her commencement at Newnham as a lecturer. A year later they were married, and left Cambridge for Bristol.[14]

THE TURNING POINT: A ROAD TO DAMASCUS AT BRISTOL?

The Marshall's sojourn in Bristol, directly associated with their marriage, turned out less well than they may have initially anticipated. At the time when Alfred Marshall applied for the Principal's position at Bristol, it seemed an optimal solution to the difficult problem of earning their living. It was a financial and academic advance as well as a glorious opportunity for doing good in a new university college in the provinces. Moreover, Bristol's progressive attitudes to education as visible in its open door to women students, were a matter of considerable appeal. It has already been indicated that for Marshall at least, such anticipated satisfactions were soon dissipated. Aspects of his work, particularly the administrative drudgery of the position of Principal, provided one cause for his early disillusionment with the situation in Bristol. Other aspects were the 'debilitating illness contracted in 1879', which cost him 'ten of the best years of his life',[15] unsatisfactory day classes consisting largely of female students which enabled his bride of one year to become a working wife in 1878; the death of his mother; the prolonged and difficult labour on a little text which he increasingly saw as a wasted and premature effort keeping him from more constructive work on the subject; and, last but not least, the growing feeling of enforced exile from Cambridge so manifest in what he described as his 'grim grievance against the old statutes that made me resign my fellowship on marrying'.[16] In sharp contrast with his wife, who late in life recollected their Bristol period with pleasure, Alfred Marshall increasingly viewed it as a cross he had to bear, imposed on him through his marriage. In a letter to J.N. Keynes in 1891, Marshall even described his acceptance of the Bristol position as the most 'grievous deed' he had ever done, because it involved an 'undertaking [to do] work for which I had not physical strength enough in combination with my own studies'.[17]

In themselves, none of these factors need to have turned him against his earlier progressive views on women's education and women's role in society. Marshall's popular lectures to women in 1873 had implicitly refuted what has been described as the 'angel of the hearth' model of womanhood, by suggesting that women had important work to do outside the home. 'Our duty is that of not demanding of our near relatives that they should do things for us which prevent their working in the world'; 'there is more to be done in the world, than just taking care of each other' in the context of the family, a reason which made it important for women to study the welfare of society, a matter on which economics had something to teach.[18] When in December 1880, Marshall gave evidence as Principal of Bristol University College to the Committee on Higher Education in Wales and Monmouthshire, this opinion changed drastically. In the context of higher education for girls, Marshall indicated that 'the number of girls who can leave home [for higher education] is really very small' because 'the best women generally speaking are women whose families require part of their time; generally they have duties to perform to their fathers and mothers and sisters and brothers that takes up some part of their time, and while a woman can give half her time for six years much more easily than a man can, she cannot give her whole time for three years as easily as a man can'.[19] Follow-up questions showed that Marshall was thinking here of college-aged girls, 17 to 23 years old, and that the best of these girls, as 'the bright lights in their families' were indispensable to these families because they not only made the 'home cheerful' but 'educate younger brothers and sisters', a matter which his experience as Principal at Bristol University College had brought home to him.[20]

The feature of Bristol University College education of women to which Marshall here referred was the opportunity for non-residential education it offered to young women, enabling them to give up six years half time with ease as against the three years full time required in the ancient universities of Cambridge and Oxford. Rita McWilliams-Tullberg has described this as the perfect Catch-22 situation: 'Girls with first class intellects could not be "spared" by their families for three years' residence at Cambridge, unless they were made of morally and socially inferior stuff. Second rate intellects should not be in Cambridge anyway. Women had either weak characters or weak brains.'[21] This explains the significance of Marshall's change of mind on the women's education question, but not the reasons why he did so. A number of hypotheses based on the Bristol experience may throw light on the latter, hence indicating why, by the end of the 1870s, Marshall was ready to be converted to the conventional model of the 'angel at the hearth'.

One of these is associated with the circumstances of his mother's death. She had died rather suddenly in June 1878 from a 'coma of about 20 hours' associated with a 'chronic obstruction of the bowels'. Her death was registered by a Sarah Thompson, a person unable to sign her name in the register as the informant. Moreover, she did not know the first name of Rebecca Marshall's husband, which is consequently left blank in the registration entry, a clear sign she was not an intimate of the family and probably a servant of sorts. These facts suggest that Marshall's mother died without her immediate family being present, her husband and daughters away perhaps on holidays with other relatives.[22] Given the literacy skills of the person present at his mother's death, it is unlikely that Alfred Marshall would have been contacted at Bristol about the sudden and fatal deterioration in his mother's health. Very little else is known about the circumstances of Marshall's mother's death. However, some of his correspondence with Foxwell and his letters from America[23] show Marshall's very strong concern over her health, as indicated by his personal involvement in nursing her during a prolonged illness in the winter of 1874–75, of which she may have still been recuperating while Marshall was in America the following summer. The experience of his mother dying without the comfort of the presence of daughters and husband, and without being contacted himself, may have easily induced some re-thinking by Marshall on female family responsibilities, leading to his acceptance of the traditional Victorian model. His inordinate fondness of his mother, combined with the fact that had his sisters been there, he would have been contacted in time to see her before she died, makes his mother's death a plausible explanation for such re-thinking. Supporting evidence for this hypothesis is at best only circumstantial.

Another possible explanation for Marshall's change of mind on women's education arises from comparisons he may have been making between his predominantly male evening class and his wife's predominantly female, day students. There are hints of this in his 1880 evidence for the Higher Education Inquiry, while comparisons with the Cambridge honours men he had been teaching advanced economics in the 1870s would have been more invidious. What little is known about these students bears this out. A previous chapter indicated that from 1878 Marshall took the evening classes in Bristol consisting of business men, trade unionists and a few women. His wife took the day class, confined with one exception to women students, and the enrolment of which she doubled in her first year of teaching by drawing women from the evening course whose female enrolment dropped sharply as a result. Apart from the controversy generated by the debating society his wife formed for those women students, which may have created doubts in Marshall's mind on the worth of such activities in the serious business of economics teaching, the Bristol experience may have taught him that a sexual division of labour in teaching was appropriate if not natural: women teachers, confined to taking the classes for women, men teaching the remainder. He subsequently recalled from this Bristol experience that despite his urging to the contrary, Bristol men had refused to attend such predominantly female classes.[24] The derogatory implications this has for the nature of his judgement of his wife's intellect conforms to his later judgements about her 'only very elementary knowledge' of the subject in 1876 when she was asked to write what became the *Economics of Industry*, an enterprise which he himself in any case largely took over and in which only the rather simple early chapters of the first part were mainly ascribed to her. Marshall's limited view of his wife's intellect is not at all contradicted by his appreciation of the 'good work' she was doing in teaching at Bristol. It likewise conforms with his views that women could not do really constructive work in economics, an attitude reflected in his wife's reported remark that the publication of Joan Robinson's *Economics of Imperfect Competition* proved Alfred to have been quite wrong on this subject.[25] Bristol teaching experience may therefore have contributed in a wider sense to Marshall's shift in opinion on women's education and women's role.

Most fundamentally, perhaps, his change in attitude on the women's issue may have been the consequence of a change in direction in his economic thinking. One of the differences between the 1879 *Economics of Industry* and the mature economic system of the *Principles* is its explicit inclusion of the importance of evolutionary forces and heredity among the variables explaining economic progress in its wider sense. Although traces of the future adherent of eugenics are visible in the earlier work, its chapters on the organisation of industry and on the division of labour lack the specific evolutionary treatment these topics were later given in the *Principles*.[26] This difference can of course be explained in terms of the requirement of a simple text for beginners as compared with those of a definitive treatise. A more plausible explanation is Marshall's desire at this time to develop a theory of economic progress in as realistic a form as possible, a task for which he may at this stage have sought inspiration in the work of Spencer and Darwin. Spencer's discussion of evolution in his *First Principles*[27] links frequently with such topics as economic progress, division of labour and industrial as well as social organisation. More interesting in this context, the task may also have induced Marshall to read, or re-read, Darwin's *Descent of*

Man, which had first appeared in 1871, when his more concentrated studies in economics took up the greater part of his time. No information is unfortunately available as to when Marshall first read this classic of evolutionary literature. If he read it as part of his preparation for a realistic account of economic progress, it may likewise have influenced his views on the natural division of labour between the sexes.

Darwin's book contains a number of remarks relevant to the point at issue, particularly in the section of the work dealing with the differences in mental powers between men and women and the possibilities for removing such inequalities through training.

> The chief distinction in the intellectual powers of the two sexes is shewn by man's attaining to a higher eminence, in whatever he takes up, than can woman – whether requiring deep thought, reason, or imagination, or merely the use of the senses and hands. If two lists were made of the most eminent men and women in poetry, painting, sculpture, music (inclusive both of composition and performance), history, science, and philosophy, with half-a-dozen names under each subject, the two lists would not bear comparison. We may also infer, from the law of the deviation from averages, so well illustrated by Mr. Galton, in his work on 'Hereditary Genius', that if men are capable of a decided pre-eminence over women in many subjects, the average of mental power in man must be above that of woman.
>
> . . .
>
> It must be borne in mind that the tendency in characters acquired by either sex late in life, to be transmitted to the same sex at the same age, and of early acquired characters to be transmitted to both sexes, are rules which, though general, do not always hold. If they always held good, we might conclude (but I here exceed my proper bounds) that the inherited effects of the early education of boys and girls would be transmitted equally to both sexes; so that the present inequality in mental power between the sexes would not be effected by a similar course of early training; nor can it have been caused by their dissimilar early training. In order that woman should reach the same standard as man, she ought, when nearly adult to be trained to energy and perseverance, and to have her reason and imagination exercised to the highest point; and then she would probably transmit these qualities chiefly to her adult daughters. All women, however, could not be thus raised, unless during many generations those who excelled in the above robust virtues were married, and produced offspring in larger numbers than other women. As before remarked of bodily strength, although men do not now fight for their wives, and this form of selection has passed away, yet during manhood, they generally undergo a severe struggle in order to maintain themselves and their families; and this will tend to keep up or even increase their mental powers, and, as a consequence, the present inequality between the sexes.[28]

Although Darwin admitted his theories wanted 'scientific precision', he was strongly convinced that sexual selection was a crucial variable in explaining differences in appearance between 'the races of man' and willing to endorse Galtonian principles of eugenics in order to ensure the improvement of the racial stock.[29] A sexual division of labour seemed therefore to be justified by evolutionary science on the basis of the highest authority. Progress of race and nation would be most advanced if actual social practice followed these findings. Before examining Marshall's specific developments of these views in the economic sphere, their application by Marshall to women's educational questions is examined. Woman's mental inferiority to man, and their specific domestic duties to the family, viewpoints Marshall implicitly articulated in 1880 to the Higher Education Commission, formed the basic underlying assumptions to his scheme of things when applying the lessons from evolution to the higher theme of economic progress or debates over degrees for women at Cambridge. When women transgressed these laws of biology, as in their demands for universal suffrage, or when seeking full rights of membership in the traditional universities, Marshall could point to the findings of science, at least as he interpreted them, in support of his principled opposition to such aberrations. However, as concluded in the previous chapter, his guidance by science in such matters was often highly selective, ignored contrary evidence and was frequently only used to confirm preconceptions to which he was deeply attached.[30]

Some factors are therefore identifiable from this Bristol experience enabling interpretation of his conversion to more traditional views on women's appropriate role in society as a veritable road to Damascus. The conjuncture of personal circumstances associated with his mother's death; the peculiar situation of women economics students and the changes in his role therein while at Bristol University College; together with the demands he made on evolution theory when constructing what he saw as the more realistic theory of economic and social theory of progress for what became Book IV of the *Principles*, could certainly well have driven him into this direction. Lack of essential detail in the extant information means such explanations can only be speculative.

WOMEN'S PLACE IN A MAN'S UNIVERSITY: THE DEBATE OVER DEGREES AND WOMEN'S PARTICIPATION IN UNIVERSITY TEACHING

As early as November 1880, in the context of a Girton College Memorial prepared for the purpose, Marshall had refused to support the granting of a B.A. to women students who had passed the requisite examinations, because the implied residence requirements would force them 'to neglect what may be their urgent duties to their families'.[31] When the degree question was raised again in 1887, Marshall, now back at Cambridge as its Professor of Political Economy, on behalf of his wife and himself objected that taking this step at this stage was premature and that, now speaking personally, if Cambridge became a mixed university, it would cease to be fully adapted to the needs of men and thereby degenerate. Fear of women's active interference in the affairs of the university was a potent argument in the fight against granting women degrees. Giving them the B.A., by leading to the M.A. would carry with it voting rights in the university and hence grant real power in university decision-making as well as access to other privileges such as the right to borrow books from the university library. Marshall was among the first to raise this spectre of petticoat government in male Cambridge.[32]

In response, a compromise was introduced, designed to give women access to degrees without immediate rights to other privileges such as university membership. This came from Sidgwick, a member of the University Syndicate (committee) appointed to draft a resolution on the subject. Fear that this more moderate approach by a faction of the women's degree movement might be successful, generated two Memorials from resident members opposed to granting women degrees. Marshall signed both Memorials, the second of which baldly expressed the hope 'that no steps will be taken by the University towards the Admission of women to Membership and Degrees in the University'.[33] Marshall's public stance against this reform, particularly damning because of his early associations with Newnham and the fact he was married to a Newnham lecturer, greatly annoyed Sidgwick. This annoyance was so great that more than three years later, Marshall could write to J.N. Keynes in the context of other quarrels with Sidgwick over changes in the Moral Sciences Tripos regulations, that his position on the Board was made all the more difficult because 'Sidgwick was already incensed with him *re* women'.[34]

Marshall's next action opposing the expansion of women's role in Cambridge arose in the context of opportunities for women to teach as university extension lecturers. In February 1893, the University Extension Lecture Syndicate had decided to invite applications for this type of position from suitably qualified women, that is, from those with a first class result in a Tripos. The first person to successfully take up this invitation was Ellen McArthur, an experienced Girton lecturer, a first in the 1885 History Tripos and later collaborator in an economic history text with Marshall's old antagonist, William Cunningham. As chairman of the Extension Lecture Syndicate, Marshall opposed the appointment on the ground that 'public lecturing to largely male audiences was unsuitable for a woman and would damage her character'.* Marshall was unsuccessful on this occasion, but during 1894, he was still very active in trying to reverse the university position on appointing women as lecturers to mixed classes. In a letter to Foxwell[35] marked '*Private*', because of his 'difficult [domestic] position' in being unable 'easily to say all I think', Marshall enlisted Foxwell's support to get the University Senate to rule on 'lecturing by women to mixed audiences'. A week later he sought his friend's advice on the wording of a Memorial on the subject he had drafted for the Vice-Chancellor.[36] When during the next fortnight he had been canvassing votes in its support, Marshall reported ruefully, 'I was surprised at finding, on taking stock, what a large proportion of my personal friends are in alliance with the extreme wing of woman's emancipation', adding that his wife's strong Newnham association made it essential for him to fight in the background. Nevertheless he was willing to 'give some considerable but not very great time' to the struggle.[37] Later that day, he reported the support of the Bishop of Durham (Westcott), the Public Orator and the University Librarian for the cause, adding that a College Head among the signatories, perhaps from Trinity or Clare, would give further strength to it.[38] Once again, this campaign was to no avail, and the battle was given up a few days later. A year later, one of Marshall's former students from Girton with a first in the Moral Sciences Tripos, preceded by her first class result in the Mathematical Tripos, and a former clerk on the Labour Commission, applied for a position as extension lecturer, asking Marshall for a reference. Marshall not only refused to do so, 'but wrote a personal letter to every member of the Board urging her non-appointment' because she was 'too young and feminine to be suitable for audiences

---

* Rita McWilliams-Tullberg, *Woman at Cambridge*, pp. 105–6; she noted this comment with the fact that Marshall as Principal of Bristol University College allowed his wife to lecture to mixed classes but, as shown previously, the cases are not exactly analogous, since the Bristol day class Mary Paley Marshall taught was predominantly female, there being only one solitary male enrolled in its first two years. The changing requirements in chaperonage at Oxford and Cambridge in 1893 and 1894 with some colleges such as Trinity requiring this at 'mixed' classes and others not, may have stirred Marshall to this frenetic campaign. (David Rubinstein, *Before the Suffragettes*, pp. 190–91). In 1895, William Cunningham and Ellen McArthur published *An Outline of English Industrial History* with Cambridge University Press.

almost wholly masculine'. He also feared her audience holding power would be determined by factors other than the contents of her lectures, an influence not altogether satisfactory.[*]

A number of less flamboyant instances of Marshall's staunch opposition to increased women's rights at the university can be recorded. In 1891, he seconded a motion moved by the Master of Selwyn College at the Moral Sciences Board that female students should not be eligible for the Arnold Gerstenberg Scholarship on the principle that women in general should not be admitted 'to a share of the emoluments of the University'. The motion was defeated 2 to 4 with Sidgwick, Johnson, Keynes and Ward voting against.[39] Marshall pursued the matter further in the debate over the regulations for the scholarship open to all members of university. The importance of higher education for women the regulations sought to emphasise, Marshall then argued, did not necessarily imply eventual near equality in numbers of men and women students at Cambridge. His preferred solution to this issue, for example, was 'the foundation of a university expressly for women'.[40] Likewise, when plans for postgraduate study were actively debated in Cambridge, Marshall hoped the word, 'men' would be used in the regulations 'if men only were meant' and that the word, 'person', ambiguously adopted by Oxford in this context, should be avoided.[41] This intervention arose from earlier comment on the subject implying postgraduate studies could be used to advance movement towards a 'mixed' university, as had already been done in the context of some scholarship regulations, such as those for the Gerstenberg Scholarship.[42]

Marshall's fiercest involvement in the battle against degrees for women at Cambridge came in the re-opening of the campaign at the end of 1895. This began with a Memorial attracting over two thousand signatories asking the University Council to appoint a new Syndicate to investigate the most appropriate way of admitting women to degrees in the university. The issue had become of greater importance, because women were disadvantaged in seeking work when their degrees had not been properly attested. Committees in support were formed, which sent Memorials in favour from 1,234 past Newnham and Girton students, 164 headmistresses and 268 other signatories gathered by Emily Davies and Marion Kennedy from interested parties outside the university. By February 1896, opposition also began to organise. Marshall took an active part in this by producing an eight page pamphlet (fly sheet) for members of the University Senate. This accepted the validity of the women's complaint in being disadvantaged by not having a degree title. By way of remedy, it therefore suggested the letters E.B.A. (*externa*) or A.B.A. (*associata*) as alternatives to the full-fledged B.A. These alternatives emphasised that women had obtained their degrees without the full benefit of residence, a matter of paramount importance, according to Marshall. Cambridge conditions of residence, although not onerous, enabled a man to concentrate on his studies without having to think about the welfare of his immediate relations.

---

[*] Rita McWilliams-Tullerg, *Woman at Cambridge*, pp. 106–7. The person in question was Miss E.E. Reid who, after her first in the Mathematical Tripos in 1891, was recorded as a first class, division 3 result in the Moral Sciences Tripos in 1892. Royal Commission on Labour, *Secretary's Report on the Work in the Office*, Appendix II p. 27 (Vol. 20, Cmnd 7421–1, 1895) mentioned her role on the Commission. The difficulties faced by women lecturers at this time are described in Jane Ellen Harrison, *Reminiscences of a Student's Life*, London: Hogarth Press, 1925, pp. 43–4. In the context of the debate over the Economics Tripos, a move he could not support, William Harcourt nevertheless hoped that such changes and fashions did not lead to 'a *female* Professor of Political Economy' (Sir William Harcourt to Marshall, 8 March 1902, Oxford, Bodleian Library).

But the same rules when applied to women have very different effects. A girl on leaving school can do many things both for parents and for younger brothers and sisters, which a lad could not do, even if he stayed at home. While the lad is almost sure to have to earn his own living by work outside the household, the girl will in nine cases out of ten be responsible later on for the household management either as a wife or sister; and concentration of nearly all her energies on merely intellectual work for three or four years is far from being the unmixed gain to her that it is to young men. But with our present arrangements, however urgent the need for her presence at home, she must keep her terms steadily under penalty of losing recognition for her work. If she decides to go her own way, and let her family shift for themselves, she gets honours; but her true life is impoverished and not enriched by them. Those whose natures are the fullest and who would turn to best account for the world whatever opportunities were afforded to them, are just those who are most likely to be deterred from coming to Cambridge for fear of this strain between their desire for knowledge with honour and their affection for those at home.[43]

In defence of his views, Marshall drew on his experience as educator in Bristol and Cambridge, including herein his participation during the 1870s in the early movement for educating women at Cambridge. This had raised doubts in his mind, especially after his return to Cambridge, as to the expediency of changes in the regulations. These arose 'not only from the point of view of women themselves', there was no doubt in his mind that the Bishop of Stepney's scheme of an Imperial University for women was the optimal solution, but more specifically from that of the interests of the university which for him were paramount.

This brings me to a difficult subject, but one on which reticence just now would be wrong. It is often said that women should pass through the same curriculum as men, in order that the attainments of the two sexes may be compared exactly in examinations: I do not think that end is desirable, I am certain it is unattainable. For examinations test receptivity and diligence in prescribed lines; and these are the strong points of women. During the last twenty-five years I have looked over nearly as many papers by women as by men, which if sent up in examination would have received very high marks; but the constructive work which has been done in after years by the women has not been comparable with that done by the men. Those very virtues which make women's influence preeminent in the family, enable them to prepare for examination with a sedulousness which belongs not to men. There is often much freshness in their treatment of illustrative instances; but in the more difficult inquiries which are reached towards the end of their studies, their work, however excellent from an examination point of view, is wanting in spontaneity as compared with that of the best men.[44]

Marshall later staunchly defended these beliefs in debate in the Senate. This partly drew on letters he had solicited from his friends Seligman at Columbia and Taussig at Harvard which suggested these leading American universities preferred granting increased privileges to their women students rather than full co-education. They also provided ammunition for correcting Mrs Sidgwick's view that at Columbia women received B.A. degrees directly from the university; such students came from Barnard College, one expressly set aside for the education of women.[*] In a speech a year later during the final debate before the vote,[45]

---

[*] *Cambridge University Reporter*, 3 March 1896, pp. 351–2; a letter from Marshall to Seligman, 30 December 1895, urged Seligman to write to the *Times*; on 13 March 1896 Marshall requested confirmation from Seligman that the Columbia University's B.A. was not open to women, on 19 March 1896 he wanted further information on the issue and a final letter on 2 April 1896 requested Seligman's authority for remarks Marshall was about to make about the status of women in various Columbia degree courses; Marshall to Taussig, 4 February 1896 sought

Marshall argued the women's education question had changed in form from the 1870s when he had actively supported the movement in Cambridge. He had found the general quality of women students from Newnham and Girton after 1885 less than what he had experienced with the 'smaller number in the 1870s', even though 'the ablest women were as able as ever'. In addition, in 1896 there were seven teaching universities with full admission to women students, in 1871 there had been none. These seven institutions open to women differed from Oxford and Cambridge in not having the residential, almost monastic form of organisation the last two had inherited from their past. This unique structure in their social life, so crucial to the educational experience these two universities provided, would be gravely disturbed by admitting large numbers of women students. This brought Marshall back to his favourite theme taught him by his Bristol experience. Many women 'cannot be spared from home duties' and most Bristol women students had therefore rejected the Cambridge plan 'compelling a woman to rush through the University course in three years'. Marshall raised two further issues in this speech in response to the Sidgwicks. He queried Mrs Sidgwick's data on the importance of a degree to a woman seeking employment; he dismissed Henry Sidgwick's aspersions on a scheme for a separate university for women. and indicated that his quarrels with Sidgwick on the issue had started on his return to Cambridge in 1885.

Marshall's pamphlet and speeches provided rallying points for what turned out to be a rapidly growing opposition to degrees for women. The opposing forces set up their own committees and organised Memorials and letter writers to the press. Battle commenced by early 1896 and was to last for over a year. Marshall himself took an active part in this, as shown in correspondence which has survived. In writing to Sir William Bate Hardy in March 1896,[46] Marshall mentioned letters he was receiving from non-residents 'inclined to go our way' which he offered to send to Hardy if they could be used in their campaign. The letter also reveals his associations with the Master of Magdalene College and Caldecott, a former Dean from St John's and moral sciences lecturer, in drumming up support for the opposition, as well as the correspondence with American economists on the subject already referred to. He was far from passive in his support for this cause, though invariably sensitive to the problems his active participation was causing on the home front at Balliol Croft.

An early battleground was found on some of Marshall's weaker propositions in his pamphlet on the subject. Mrs Sidgwick queried his statistic of ninety per cent of middle-class women spending their lives in managing a home as wife or sister, indicating that less than fifty of these women did in fact marry and that fifty per cent of former women's college students were in fact working. Marshall only tried to claw back his sweeping statistics in a private letter, reluctantly admitting a 'large element of conjecture in [his] estimates'.[47] Mrs Sidgwick also strongly defended the value of a full residential college education for women students and re-emphasised the need for them to gain proper qualifications to enable them to search for that all too often essential employment by which to earn their living.[48]

---

confirmation about what he recollected Taussig telling him the previous summer on the status of women at Harvard.

Marshall's next public exposure to the fray came during October 1896. This arose from a questionnaire the university committee, set up to investigate women's degrees, had circulated to all Cambridge lecturers about their teaching practices with respect to women. Marshall's response is not difficult to identify among the anonymous replies from teachers in the moral sciences which the committee subsequently published. His answers are distinguished by being the only ones which comment on an inherent inferiority in women's intellect, a perspective, as stated earlier, he may well have imbibed theoretically from Darwin, as well as empirically from experience in the classroom to which he had referred in the previous pamphlet. Part of his answers are worth quoting:

> As regards lectures, I consider my first duty to Members of the University and consequently endeavour to lecture as though men only were present. When lecturing to women alone, I have adopted a different manner of treating my subject which I believe to be better adapted for them. Their presence in the class prevents men from speaking freely either in answering or asking questions; it therefore makes the lectures more mechanical and similar in effect to the reading part of a book aloud than they otherwise would be.
>
> As regards the informal instruction and advice given, 'at home', I do not admit women to my ordinary 'at home', . . . but make occasional special appointments for them. I adopt this course partly because of the difficulty of getting men and women to open their minds freely in one another's presence, and partly because I find the questions asked by women generally relate to lectures or book work or else to practical problems such as poor relief. Whilst men who have attended fewer lectures and read fewer books and are perhaps likely to obtain less marks in examinations, are more apt to ask questions showing mental initiative and giving promise of original work in the future.[49]

Marshall further distinguished himself in the final debate on the Syndicate Report and the run-up to the crucial vote. The essentials of the former have already been given, the latter are revealed once again in correspondence with Foxwell. One letter in April 1897 attempted to rally Foxwell to the battle with the cry 'Soldiers Awake!', once again because constraints from Marshall's own home front, quoted in an earlier chapter, made it difficult for him at this stage to give his all to the fight. A further appeal to Foxwell the next day to assist in gathering the crucial non-resident vote ended by Marshall's exhortation that Foxwell should take 'his candle from under a bushell' and place it firmly on the top of a hill where it could be seen by all.[50] Marshall need not have worried about the final vote. When it was taken on 21 May 1897, 1713 votes were cast against any changes on the matter, compared to 662 votes for reform, almost a three to one majority. This overwhelming vote for the status quo closed the issue effectively until well after the end of the First World War.[51]

Marshall's personal cost in fighting this battle for what he saw as good principle was not small. As he had confessed to Foxwell on an earlier occasion in 1894, nearly all his personal friends were on the side of those proposing degrees for women, and nowhere was such support stronger than among teachers and students of the moral sciences. Many of these friends appear to have been very effectively alienated by Marshall's extreme stand on the issue, which went further on some fundamentals than most others on the academic side of the 'opposition' dared to go in public. There was also a domestic cost, at which an earlier chapter has already attempted an estimate, but which is also reflected in the fact that post-May 1897 dinners to celebrate the Moral Sciences Tripos results had only Mrs, and not

Professor, Marshall in attendance.* In addition, and without any other apparent explanation, it was over six months from the time the crucial vote was taken in May 1897, until Marshall showed his face again at meetings of the Moral Sciences Board.[52]

WOMEN AND ECONOMIC PROGRESS: *KINDER, KUCHE* BUT NOT *KIRCHE*[53]

When Marshall's *Principles of Economics* was published in 1890, one perceptive reviewer noted that its rich contents among other things pin-pointed the case for women staying at home.[54] It first appears in Book II dealing with 'some fundamental notions' in the chapter devoted to defining 'necessities', with special reference to 'the efficiency of an ordinary agricultural or of an unskilled town labourer'. Along with a 'well-drained dwelling with several rooms, warm clothing, with some changes of underclothing, pure water, a plentiful supply of cereal food, with a moderate allowance of meat and milk, and a little tea, &c, some education and some recreation', Marshall lastly listed 'sufficient freedom for his wife from other work to enable her to perform properly her maternal and household duties'. If deprived of any of these things, the efficiency of the labourer suffered in the same way as that of a horse 'not property tended' or a steam engine with 'an inadequate supply of coal'.[55] As an aspect of the quality of labour supply, the matter was pursued further in Book IV, Chapter V. After approvingly quoting Roscher's finding that the Jewish population of Prussia had increased faster than the Christian, though its birth rate had been lower [because] 'Jewish mothers seldom go away from their homes to work', Marshall commented on the fiscal illusion inherent in family's thinking and acting 'as though the family income was increased by all that the mother earns when she goes out to work'. Marshall's explanation was as follows:

> a little consideration would often show that the things she can buy with her earnings are of far less importance for the health and happiness of the family than the mere material services she could have rendered them if she had stayed at home, to say nothing of her moral influence in educating the children, in keeping the household in harmony and making it possible for her husband to be cheered and soothed in his evenings at home. This fact is getting to be understood by the better class of artisans and their wives; and there are not now very many mothers with young families at work in English and American factories.[56]

Here is a clear expression of Marshall's embrace of that 'Angel of the Hearth' model which guided his thinking in the women's degree debates at Cambridge.

On Marshall's death, Edgeworth succinctly argued that as in the case of Marshall's opposition to the granting of degrees to women, this perspective on women's role owed much to the leading part family life was to play in 'Marshall's ideal state',

---

* JNKD, 8 June 1896, 10 June 1897 and 10 June 1898 record Marshall being present for the first but not the other two dinners, the last of which Mrs Marshall attended by herself, at this stage a most unusual occurrence. However, such absences can be explained on various grounds. See above, Chapter 13, p. 444, where his tendency to decline invitations to dinner parties outside his own home is discussed. On 15 May 1897, Keynes expressed his forebodings about the unpleasantness caused by the fact that the degree for women issue had been raised once again prematurely, a feeling apparently shared by Mrs Sidgwick. Keynes also noted that moderate supporters of the women's cause, as he and his wife were, were alarmed about the extremist attitudes visible among the undergraduates and reported in some detail in the reference given in note 51 above.

The central figure would be the wife and mother practising pristine domestic virtues . . . [an indication] that Marshall deprecated the identical treatment of men and women. . . . In the most intimate of talks which I have had with him he expressed himself as opposed to current ideas which made for shaping the lives of men and women on the same model. In this connection he expressed strong dissent from some of Mill's treatment of sex as an 'accident'. Some loss of individual liberty, Marshall thought, should be risked for the sake of preserving the family. He regarded the family as a cathedral, something more sacred than the component parts. If I might complete the metaphor in my own words so as to convey the impression which I received: whereas the structure as it stands is not perfectly symmetrical, the attempt to make it so might result in pulling it down.[57]

Marshall's early economic writing showed relatively little interest in the condition of working women and associated issues such as women's wages, an exception being the *Economics of Industry*.[58] However, women had an important place in Marshall's mature scheme of things economic: their crucial role in the family, particularly that associated with the nurture of young children, was frequently stressed.

References to women workers are, however, infrequent in the pages of the *Principles*. The following exhaust his comments on women's work *per se*. In the context of the division of labour, women managing machine looms are said to have work far less monotonous, and calling for much greater judgements, than that associated with the former hand-loom weaver.[59] As an important industrial locational factor, textile works and other factories to give employment to women and children are said to be frequently situated in iron districts, since in their absence employment can only be found in such regions for 'strong men' and average family earnings are consequently low.[60] In the chapter devoted to general influences of economic progress, women's factory work is equated to that of children in terms of required skill, ranking below that of 'men of ordinary capacity'.[61] Last, but not least, social progress is associated by Marshall with the interest of 'the coming generation . . . in the rescue of men, and still more in that of women, from excessive work; at least as much as it is in the handing down to it of a good stock of material wealth'.[62]

Progress was only associated with the relative improvement of women's wages in the *Principles* subject to qualifications. 'The wages of women are for similar reasons [their ability to handle machines and enhanced skills from the spread of education] rising fast relative to those of men. And this is a great gain in so far as it tends to develop their faculties; but an injury in so far as it tempts them to neglect their duty of building up a true home, and of investing their efforts in the personal capital of their children's character and abilities.'[63] Apart from the reason stated, higher relative wages for women were not necessarily a good thing in Marshall's views because of their potential effect on the family wage. In a footnote added to the fifth edition,[64] Marshall discussed the connection between the family wage and the individual (male) wage in the context of minimum wage legislation for men and women workers:

The last consideration seems to have been pushed on one side largely under the influence of a faulty analysis of the nature of 'parasitic' work and of its influence on wages. The family is, in the main, a single unit as regards geographical migration: and therefore the wages of men are relatively high, and those of women and children low where heavy iron or other industries preponderate, while in some other districts less than half the money income of the family is earned by the father, and men's wages are relatively low.

This natural adjustment is socially beneficial, and rigid national rules as to minimum wages for men and for women, which ignore or oppose it, are to be deprecated.

Marshall was sceptical of the minimum wage notion for the whole of his life. The fact that only Australasia provided practical guidance on its operation at this stage was one reason. Another one was that he feared minimum wage legislation would not be made effective and hence its great benefits would not be fully secured. These benefits, it need hardly be said, were its contribution to removing much of the hardship on that class of the population which he described as 'the residuum'.[65]

The locational aspect in the family wage as included in Marshall's note just quoted was a return to a theme which he had first broached in *Economics of Industry*. The clear and succinct expression of the argument, far superior to anything on the subject in the *Principles*, make the paragraph in question worth quoting in full:

In England many women get low wages, not because the value of the work they do is low, but because both they and their employers have been in the habit of taking it for granted that the wages of women must be low. Sometimes even when men and women do the same work in the same factory, not only the Time-wages, but also the Task-wages of the women are lower than those of the men. In so far as this inequality is due to custom, it will disappear with the progress of intelligence and of the habits of competition. But more of it than at first sight appears, is due to causes that are likely to be permanent. Employers say that if a man and a woman are equally good workers, the woman is of less service in the long run. For although she is generally more anxious than a man is to merit the approval of the employer or overlooker, – she does not give up her whole mind to her work in the same way as a man does; her work is more liable to be interrupted than that of a man, and she is less likely to continue at it during her whole life; partly for these reasons, her thoughts are occupied more about her home and less about the place in which she works than his are, and she has on the whole less persistence, and less judgement and resource in cases of difficulty. Thus though the accuracy with which women follow their instructions is very serviceable in some branches of the work, the employer often prefers to have men, because he can select from them foremen and overlookers as well as workers in those branches of the business in which discretion is wanted. Again many kinds of work which are generally regarded as light, occasionally require the use of great physical strength, and perhaps the working overtime in special emergencies; and for such work women are at a disadvantage. Thus the occupations for which women are well fitted are few, and therefore overcrowded and badly paid. And this influences custom and general opinion, and causes women to be underpaid when they are doing difficult work well.[66]

As indicated previously, Marshall did not approve of high wages for women if this interfered with the crucial role women played in the family. In the first place, that role benefited the level of 'general ability' in the nation. 'General ability', a key factor in securing a productive and inventive workforce, 'depends largely on the surroundings of childhood and youth' and there 'the first, far the most important influence, is that of the mother', followed in turn by that of the father, of household servants and of the school. Marshall noted in this context that Galton's statement, 'all great men have had great mothers', is an exaggeration, since this remark can only show,

that the mother's influence does not outweigh all others; not that it is not greater than any other of them. He says that the mother's influence is most easily traceable among theologians and men of science, because an earnest mother leads her child to feel deeply about great things; and a thoughtful mother does not repress, but encourage that childish curiosity which is the raw material of scientific habits of thought.*

In addition there are longer-term influences of responsible mothers on labour supply. A beneficial effect of high wages on the death-rate may be diminished if mothers as a consequence neglect their duties to their children, while strictly necessary consumption for the reproduction of a steadily improving workforce requires that parents take good care of their children.[67] Marshall's emphasis on the importance of the essentially female role in the nurture of children as an investment in human capital is strikingly illustrated in the following remarks,

> If we compare one country of the civilized world with another, or one part of England with another, or one trade of England with another, we find that the degradation of the working-classes varies almost uniformly with the amount of rough work done by women. The most vulnerable of all capital is that invested in human beings; and of that capital the most precious part is the result of the care and influence of the mother, so long as she retains her tender and unselfish instincts, and has not been hardened by the strain and stress of unfeminine work.
>
> This draws our attention to another aspect of the principle already noticed, that in estimating the cost of production of efficient labour, we must often take as our unit the family. At all events we cannot treat the cost of production of efficient men as an isolated problem; it must be taken as part of the broader problem of the cost of production of efficient men together with the women who are fitted to make their home happy, and to bring up their children vigorous in body and mind, truthful and cleanly, gentle and brave.[68]

As shown earlier,[69] the nurturing role in families for Marshall was not confined to the mother. His was a wide notion of female family responsibility, covering both mothers and daughters. Women were therefore important in Marshall's vision of a developed society as nurturers and shapers of the future labour force rather than as workers. High wages and improved methods of production were largely useful as catalysts to free women, young and old, from the drudgery of factory and domestic labour to enable them to concentrate all the better on their family responsibilities. Such views were of course not novel in the late nineteenth century. They were echoed, for example, by Sidney Webb's evidence to the Labour Commission, which indicated that rather than prohibiting the employment of married women, 'the proper policy is to hasten the advent of such a social development in which mothers of families should be released from their present necessity of working for their living'.[70]

Marshall's strong interests in evolutionary theory, heredity and eugenics in the context of economic progress have already been mentioned.[71] These undoubtedly coloured his

---

* *P* I, p. 163 and n.1, *P* VIII, p. 207 and n.1. The reference is to Francis Galton, *Hereditary Genius*, London: Macmillan, 1892 (reprinting essentially the text of the 1869 first edition), p. 319. Marshall's paraphrase of Galton's opinion is not completely correct, since Galton's remark on the mothers of great men in fact states, 'There is a common opinion that great men have remarkable mothers. No doubt they are largely indebted to maternal influences, but the popular belief ascribes an undue and incredible share to them. I account for the belief, by the fact that great men have usually high moral natures, and are affectionate and reverential, inasmuch as mere brain without heart is insufficient to achieve eminence. Such men are naturally disposed to show extreme filial regard, and to publish the good quality of their mothers, with exaggerated praise.' But cf. Galton, *Hereditary Genius*, pp. 189, 266–72, on the parental, especially maternal influence on men of science and on divines.

views on the importance of the role of the family, so evident in parts of the *Principles*. The following quotation links parental nurture, appropriate education for the sexes and industrial, social and race progress:

> No doubt it is true that physical peculiarities acquired by the parents during their life-time are seldom if ever transmitted to their offspring. But no conclusive case seems to have been made out for the assertion that the children of those who have led healthy lives, physically and morally, will not be born with a firmer fibre than they would have been had the same parents grown up under unwholesome influences which had enfeebled the fibre of their minds and their bodies. And it is certain that in the former case the children are likely after birth to be better nourished, and better trained; to acquire more wholesome instincts; and to have more of that regard for others and that self-respect, which are the mainsprings of human progress, than in the latter case.
>
> It is needful then diligently to inquire whether the present industrial organisations might not with advantage be so modified as to increase the opportunities, which the lower grades of industry have for using latent mental faculties, for deriving pleasure from their use, and for strengthening them by use; since the argument that if such a change had been beneficial, it would have been already brought about by the struggle for survival, must be rejected as invalid. Man's prerogative extends to a limited but effective control over natural development by forecasting the future and preparing the way for the next step.
>
> Thus progress may be hastened by thought and work; by the application of the principles of Eugenics to the replenishment of the race from its higher rather than its lower strains, and by the appropriate education of the faculties of either sex: but however hastened it must be gradual and relatively slow.[72]

Only a few manuscript fragments are extant on Marshall's views on what constituted desirable education for women. One of these deals with technical, the others with higher education. The first emphasised the importance of training women for nurture, in order to raise skill levels as quickly as possible, but contains little more than a few sentences in note form,

> What women can do.
> Of course they may work as man[;] in some cases this is no doubt right.
> A washer woman ought certainly to have technical knowledge.
> That the great point is that they are trained. If they will teach their children to do whatever they do with all their might, we will soon become a skilled nation.[73]

The second is a much longer fragment headed 'The higher education of women'. It neatly supplements Marshall's views openly expressed during the debates on the issue at Cambridge.

> This does not mean the opening to them new regions of thought. Their studies are, in name at least, ambitious as they are. It means educating and applying firstly, the power of sustained close attention to one difficult point after another, and secondly, the power of consecutive thought in a large number of difficult points taken together so as to be able to realise the mutual relations of the various positions of one whole body of knowledge, thought or active feeling.
>
> These powers do not constitute originality but they are absolutely indispensable conditions of it; provided the originality is to be of any service to the world. A one sided originality such as Rousseau's, great in its effects for good but often also great in its effects for evil, can be attained by long, continued brooding over one leading thought, emotion, desire, or artistic enthusiasm [Rousseau's life was one such long continued brooding] without systematic firm-willed thinking out of difficulties.

There is every reason to believe that the reason why women have held the *first* place in so very few departments even of literature and art is that they have not, save in exceptional cases, had such a training. Whether five thousand years ago there was a distinction between the calibre of men's and women's minds, and whether there will be such a distinction five thousand years hence may be an open question. It is certain that such a distinction exists now; that women are quicker to perceive and more strengthful to feel than men; but that, on the average, they have less power of sustained concentration.[74]

In the context of women's education in general, 'The service to the world' which the fragment mentioned as such a major aim of women's higher education, needs to be narrowed to more national objectives. The steadily increasing importance Marshall attached to lifting the skills of the British workforce as part of raising its more general quality, had a narrow, technocratic meaning for him. This was associated with his growing fears about the difficulties of preserving British competitiveness in international trade against the growing industrial might of the United States and Germany. On a broader level, this fear arose from his rather pessimistic outlook on the future of the race, an outlook which he shared with many other social scientists at the time and which explains his embrace of the eugenics movement. It derived from the weakening of natural, evolutionary forces as the means of preserving the 'vigour' of the population through a variety of causes. These included medical success in eliminating some infectious diseases and the growing tendency of the better classes of society to limit the size of their families, often for selfish economic reasons. Once again, these remarks highlight responsibility and duty of the family unit for Marshall, focusing particularly on the importance of the mother in ensuring the future quality of the population. Moreover, achievement of this aim required a steady rise in the standard of life ensured through the combination of increased wealth, the wisdom of government and the growth of knowledge, a view cogently expressed in the *Principles*.

Thus, there are increasing reasons for fearing, that while the progress of medical science and sanitation is saving from death a continually increasing number of the children of those who are feeble physically and mentally; many of those who are most thoughtful and best endowed with energy, enterprise and self-control are tending to defer their marriages and in other ways to limit the number of children whom they leave behind them. The motive is sometimes selfish, and perhaps it is best that hard and frivolous people should leave but few descendants of their own type. But more often it is a desire to secure a good social position for their children. This desire contains many elements that fall short of the highest ideals of human aims, and in some cases, a few that are distinctly base; but after all it has been one of the chief factors of progress, and those who are affected by it include many of those whose children would probably be among the best and strongest of the race.

It must be remembered that the members of a large family educate one another, they are usually more genial and bright, often more vigorous in every way than the members of a small family. Partly, no doubt, this is because their parents were of unusual vigour, and for a like reason they in their turn are likely to have large and vigorous families. The progress of the race is due to a much greater extent than appears at first sight to the descendants of a few exceptionally large and vigorous families.

But on the other hand there is no doubt that the parents can often do better in many ways for a small family than a large one. Other things being equal, an increase in the number of children who are born causes an increase of infantile mortality; and that is an unmixed evil. The birth of children who die early from want of care and adequate means is a useless strain to the mother and an injury to the rest of the family. It seems *prima facie* advisable that people should not bring children into the world till they can see their way to giving them at least as good an education both physical and mental as they themselves had; and that it is best to marry moderately early provided there is sufficient self-control to keep the family within the requisite bounds without transgressing moral laws. The general adoption of these principles of action, combined with an adequate provision of fresh air and of healthy play for our town populations, could hardly fail to cause the strength and vigour of the race to improve. And we shall presently find reasons for believing that if the strength and vigour of the race improves, the increase of numbers will not for a long time to come cause a diminution of the average real income of the people.

Thus then the progress of knowledge, and in particular of medical science, the ever-growing activity and wisdom of Government in all matters relating to health, and the increase of material wealth, all tend to lessen mortality and to increase health and strength, and to lengthen life. On the other hand, vitality is lowered and the death-rate raised by the rapid increase of town life, and by the tendency of the higher strains of the population to marry later and to have fewer children than the lower. If the former set of causes were alone in action, but so regulated as to avoid the danger of over population, it is probable that man would quickly rise to a physical and mental excellence superior to any that the world has yet known; while if the latter set acted unchecked, he would speedily degenerate.

As it is, the two sets hold one another very nearly in balance, the former slightly preponderating. While the population of England is growing nearly as fast as ever, those who are out of health in body or mind are certainly not an increasing part of the whole; the rest are much better fed and clothed, and except in over-crowded industrial districts, are generally in strength. The average duration of life both for men and women has been increasing steadily for many years.[75]

The nurturing role in the family which Marshall assigned to women as their main objective in life was therefore grounded in lofty motivations associated with his views on economic progress and his fears about Britain falling behind in the industrial race. However, he said little about the effects on many family incomes if women left the workforce for this reason. As the other side of the coin, the Marshalls' factory tours of the 1880s, which so often concentrated on the nature of women's work they saw, created evidence for him on the unsavoury and unhealthy nature of that work, particularly for young mothers with children. Examples can be found in the notes Mary Paley took of their tour of inspection of the Worcestershire pottery district in 1883; Cumbria, the Lake District and Sheffield in 1885; and a visit to Leicester in 1888.[76] These findings were confirmed for him through his activities on the Labour Commission.

Marshall's membership of Committee B of the Commission devoted largely to labour conditions in transport, enabled him to enquire at some length about the consequences for children's upbringing from women working on barges. Part of his questioning concerned the 'unwomanly nature' of this work because of its nature and hours of labour, part of it consisted in ascertaining facts on the educational opportunities for the children of married couples employed in this segment of the transport industry. Its aim was to discover whether suitable methods of inspection could be found to ensure that barge children received adequate education or whether it was feasible to end women's labour on the ships. On both scores the answers Marshall received tended to be in the negative.[77] In addition, Marshall sought more general information on the attitudes of male workers to women's employment, for example, in the upholstery-making industry; and on the prohibition in certain trades against the employment of married women.[78]

At a more general level, Marshall learned much of the subject from the Commission's Reports on the Employment of Women and Women's Labour Conditions.[79] In the matter of wages, these corroborated the vast differential between male weekly wages and those paid to women and girls. This ranged from an almost threefold difference in the silk industries and the potteries to a little less than double in the retail trade, in textiles and footwear. The gradual and general rise in women's wages over time the *Principles* proclaimed, likewise found support in the statistical investigations of the Commission, particularly when interpreted in real terms. However, these data also indicated that in the three decades before 1890 the growth in male wages far outstripped the most favourable wage growth for women, contrary to the drift of the general trend in this differential Marshall had reported in the *Principles*.[80]

Marshall's hostility to married women working in factories would have been strongly reinforced by the information gathered on this subject through the Commission. Considerable evidence was collected on the deleterious effects on the health of children of married women who worked; both from 'careless nursing' on the part of working mothers and from the 'injudicious treatment' children received from their minders while the mothers were at work. Medical officers corroborated this evidence. Excessive use of sleeping draughts for quietening their charges, accidents from burns or scalds, and exposure to the influence of bad weather, were among the worst consequences of the all too frequent inexperience, youth and negligence of the child-minders. Work at home in the 'sweated' trades also had its dangers. These arose from the late and irregular hours of work for the sleep of the children, the insanitary conditions implied when home became the workplace, as well as from the ill health the long hours of work so often induced in the women engaged in it. Furthermore, the Commission found that heavy and dangerous work in the chemical and white-lead industries, as well as in nail-and chain-making, was doubly bad, by affecting both mothers and their future offspring; while the picture it painted of sanitary conditions in many work-places, and the hazards from the nature of employment in certain industries, demonstrated that many of the employment opportunities for women were highly unsuitable for those involved in the rearing of children. The summary evidence reported on this issue to the Commission elucidates the dangers to future generations Marshall diagnosed as a major cost of working women. Of course, the appropriate remedy for such evils could be found as easily in better factory legislation and its improved enforcement, as in active discouragement of the employment of married women, the path Marshall chose.

The Final Report of the Commission on the issue of employment of married women was rather cautious. Since Marshall had signed it without reservations, he must have agreed with its thrust on this subject as well. The Commission listed four objections against the employment of married women. The first of these concerned complaints that married women competed unfairly with unmarried women, since their husbands' wages enabled them to work for lower rates than their unmarried female competitors. More relevant to Marshall's views on the impact on working married women on domestic duties, the Commission reported considerable evidence that in this situation, 'homes are made comfortless, and children and husbands neglected'. This not only came from oral evidence presented by workmen, it was confirmed 'in some instances' from 'the personal inspection made by the Lady Assistant Commissioners'. Heavy labour in periods near to childbirth was likewise condemned in the case of industries such as nail- and chain-making, as were the dangers of employment of married women in white-lead works and potteries because of the effects of absorbed poison and dust to both themselves and their children. Finally, the employment of mothers in factories was condemned as generally harmful to their children. Medical evidence was cited to support a period of non-work for three months after childbirth in the interest of lowering infant mortality in specific factory districts. Legislation was not seen by the Commission as the answer to most of these complaints. Two reasons were given. The presence of young children in the family often created an economic necessity for the women to work; secondly, married women were said to prefer factory work to escape the monotony of a life exclusively devoted to domestic duties. Few other recommendations on the subject of woman's labour were presented by the Commission to ameliorate these distressing conditions apart from improvement in factory inspection.[81]

Marshall's personal experience from factory observation and practice at the university revealed to him the need for a sexual division of labour from the 'self-evident' nature of things, at least in the foreseeable future.[*] Women's 'natural' role in the family as child nurturers, mothers, comforters and guardians of a wholesome environment barred them from 'unwomanly' activities in factories and workshop. Their different mental capacities implied a distinct position for them from men with respect to the higher occupations of the professions and the arts. Ergo, their widely accepted status as home-makers in the service of the family, combined with associated, if not derivative, occupations of nursing, teaching and organised charity or social work were the best possible outcome for the type of world and society Marshall preferred to envisage. It also secured, as the scientific evidence compellingly showed to Marshall's satisfaction, the maximum benefit for the future of nation and race.

Marshall's probity in assessing these scientific findings was, however, not always what it should be on this matter about which he felt so strongly. Here a 'warm heart' ran ahead of his more usually 'cool head'. On heredity, for example, he held firmly on to his belief that good parents produced better children, despite a lack of substantiating, and much contrary, evidence on this point. His correspondence with Bateson and Kidd, and heated controversy with Pearson, show his sensitivity on this score, a sensitivity also reflected in the passage from the *Principles* quoted some paragraphs previously.[82]

Marshall likewise was not assiduous in claiming the benefits from the increased research findings on women's work available from the 1890s onwards. His ignorance of the facts was illustrated in his quarrel with Mrs Sidgwick as part of the Cambridge debates on degrees for women; a lack of detailed investigation in the relative progress of women's wages was also noted; while many of the books on the subject preserved in his library appear to have been underutilised. An early American *Cyclopaedia* of women's work, perhaps acquired during his American visit, is only slightly annotated; no annotations whatsoever grace his copy of Clara Collet's essays on *Educated Women Workers*, the essays by Gertrude Tuckwell and others on *Women in Industry* and Edith Molley's book, *Women Workers in Seven Professions*. An exception is the rather defensively marked, *Makers of our Clothes* by Carl Meyer and Clementine Black, in which Marshall either occasionally

---

[*] Edgeworth's 'Reminiscences' (*Memorials*, pp. 72–3), suggest an analogy between Marshall's views on women's degrees and on socialism in emphasising the virtues of gradual changes. The foreseeable future was very long, as implied in the five thousand years Marshall suggested in the fragment on higher education quoted earlier. Perhaps this is why another fragment (dated 23 February 1923) preserved among his papers devoted to 'Progress and Ideals' and proposing 'a constitution of Public Well-Being', includes both men *and* women drawn from medicine and business for the desired membership of a governing body for this purpose. Since these notes constitute his reflections on 'utopias', frequently from old age, they illustrate Edgeworth's analogy to perfection.

noted that he had already included the point in his *Principles*, or else that it needed to be put in.[83] Speaking generally, on the issue of women's work Marshall shows a failure to resist a temptation to which all 'responsible students of social problems' were prone, that is, taking a 'short cut to his ideal' and not accepting the world as he found it.[84] Preconceptions overwhelmed undesirable facts on social issues such as these.

SOME CASE STUDIES OF HOSTILITY TO WOMEN: ALFRED MARSHALL VERSUS HARRIET MARTINEAU, BEATRICE POTTER-WEBB AND HELEN DENDY-BOSANQUET

Marshall's lack of strict scientific objectivity on this issue just noted is also visible in the treatment he meted out to some individual women, alive or dead. Earlier instances of this were given in the context of his treatment of women economics students at Cambridge, particularly in cases when they did well, and in some aspects at least of his dealings with his wife.[85] The position Marshall took on the women's question in general can be further illuminated by discussing his treatment of three specific women, already encountered on previous occasions, in which his biases on the subject, congenital or otherwise, are further revealed.

Marshall's vehement dislike of Harriet Martineau's 'Tales' in political economy was noted in the context of both his 1897 inaugural lecture to a new economics club for Cambridge undergraduates, and in sturdy and prickly cross-examination of Sidney Webb during the Labour Commission. That questioning had dwelt largely on her views of factory legislation. It is interesting to note in this context that Marshall owned a copy of her *The Factory Controversy. A Warning against Meddling Legislation*, but that this copy contains no personal annotations.[86] However, the *Principles* show that he had also read her *Autobiography*, in which she had discussed her manner of writing the tales of political economy in some detail. His paraphrasing of her account for the first edition is accurate as far as it goes. Marshall mentioned her as an example of the 'hangers on and parasites' who, while professing to simplify economics, a cardinal sin in his hierarchy of virtues, 'really enunciated them without the conditions required to make them true'. He continued,

> Miss Martineau for instance, who wrote tales designed to enforce economic doctrines, when describing the course of reading by which she prepared herself, says: 'In order to save my nerves from being overwhelmed by the thought of what I had undertaken, I resolved not to look beyond the department on which I was engaged', (*Autobiography*, I 194). Yet she did not intend to be dishonest, as is proved by her later confession of 'a suspicion that economic doctrines might be all wrong'.[87]

Marshall's account omitted to mention that her tales had to be produced for serial publication on a regular, once-a-month basis, that these were her first professional attempt at authorship and essential for her to earn her living, factors which undoubtedly enhanced her feeling of being 'overwhelmed'. Nor did Marshall mention that in preparation, she had furnished herself 'with all the standard works on the subject of what I then took to be a science'. Such sins of omission pale into insignificance when compared to the manner in which by the eighth edition Marshall gradually transformed this relatively factual account, drawing here on his argument with Webb on factory legislation and defending his use of the word 'parasites' in terms of what he described as common German usage,

> But Miss Martineau was not an economist in the proper sense of the word: she confessed that she never read more than one chapter of an economic book at a time before writing a story to illustrate economic principles, for fear the pressure on her mind should be too great: and before her death she expressed a just doubt whether the principles of economics (as understood by her) had any validity.[88]

The removal of the reference to the source for this statement indicates Marshall was aware that he was rather careless with the truth in this description of Harriet Martineau's practice. Her autobiography gives no support whatsoever for the changes Marshall made in the final version.[89]

Beatrice Webb, née Potter, has already made her appearance on several previous occasions: in connection with Marshall's views on marriage and the Marshalls' marriage in particular, as a partial spectator at the proceedings of the Labour Commission, as an observer of Marshall during the Cooperative Congress and British Association meetings at which he gave Presidential Addresses, and as a reader of his work. When Beatrice Potter first met the Marshalls is not certain, but their acquaintance came more than likely through mutual friends such as the Creightons or the Booths.[90] Two aspects of their contact at this time are particularly relevant to the present context: their discussion about the role of women and marriage in 1889 and the correspondence between them over her book on Co-operation and her engagement to Sidney Webb some years later.

The first episode is so informative, and so entertainingly recorded by Beatrice Potter in her diary, that it can be quoted at length. The subjects raised in their conversation at this time were further pursued in 1891 *à propos* Marshall's reaction to her book on Cooperation. They also strikingly illustrate how Marshall plied his peculiar views on the sexual division of labour in conversation with acquaintances:

> Interesting talk with Professor Marshall, first at dinner at the Creightons, and afterwards at lunch at his own house. It opened with chaff about men and women; he holding that woman was a subordinate being, and that, if she ceased to be subordinate, there would be no object for a man to marry. That marriage was a sacrifice of masculine freedom, and would only be tolerated by male creatures so long as it meant the devotion, body and soul, of the female to the male. Hence the woman must not develop her faculties in a way unpleasant to the man: that strength, courage, independence were not attractive in women; that rivalry in men's pursuits was positively unpleasant. Hence masculine strength and masculine ability on women must be firmly trampled on and boycotted by men. *Contrast* was the essence of the matrimonial relation; feminine weakness contrasted with masculine strength; masculine egotism with feminine self-devotion.
>
> 'If you compete with us we shan't marry you.' he summed up with a laugh.
>
> I maintained the opposite argument; that there was an ideal of character in which strength, courage, sympathy, self-devotion, persistent purpose were united to a clear and far-seeing intellect; that the ideal was common to the man and to the woman; that these qualities might manifest themselves in different ways in the man's and woman's life; that what you needed was not different qualities and different defects, but the same virtues working in different directions, and dedicated to the service of the community in different ways.
>
> At lunch at his house our discussion was more practical. He said that he had heard that I was about to undertake a history of Co-operation.
>
> 'Do you think I am equal to it?' I asked.

'Now, Miss Potter, I am going to be perfectly frank; of course I think you are equal to a history of Co-operation; but it is not what you can do best. There is one thing that *you* and only you can do – an inquiry into the unknown field of female labour. You have, unlike most women, a fairly trained intellect, and the courage and capacity for original work; and you have a woman's insight into a woman's life. There is no man in England who could undertake with any prospect of success an enquiry into female labour. There are any number of men who could write a history of Cooperation, and would bring to this study of a purely economic question far greater strength and knowledge than you possess. For instance, your views on the relative amount of profit in the different trades, and the reason of the success of Co-operation in cotton and its failure in the woollen industry might interest me; but I should read what you said with grave doubt as to whether you had really probed the matter. On the other hand, if you describe the factors enabling combinations of women in one trade and destroying all chance of it in the other, I should take what you said as the opinion of the best authority on the subject. I should think to myself, well, if Miss Potter has not succeeded in sifting these facts no one else will do so, so I may as well take her conclusion as the final one. To sum up with perfect frankness; if you devote yourself to the study of your own sex as an industrial factor, your name will be a household word two hundred years hence; if you write a history of co-operation it will be superseded and ignored in a year or two. In the one case you will be using unique qualities which no one else possesses, and in the other you will be using faculties which are common to most men, and given to a great many among them in a much higher degree. A book by you on the Co-operative Movement I may get my wife to read to me in the evening to while away the time, but I shan't pay any attention to it,' he added with shrill emphasis.

Of course I disputed the point, and tried to make him realise that I wanted this study in industrial administration as an education for economic science. The little professor, with bright eyes, shrugged his shoulders and became satirical on the subject of a woman dealing with scientific generalisation; not unkindly satirical, but chaffingly so. He stuck to his point and heaped on flattery to compensate for depreciation.[91]

Marshall followed up this conversation in a letter to Beatrice Potter, accompanying a copy of his Presidential Address to the Cooperative Congress he had given in May. This reiterated his regrets that he had not been able to persuade her to study an aspect of women in industry, 'a path on which the broad heavy masculine foot cannot tread, and in which therefore your energetic and thorough methods of work would have a scarcity value'. He would instead have to look forward with 'joyful expectation' to her study of the co-operative movement.[92] In the meantime, Marshall's *Principles* had appeared. This included a favourable reference to her article on East End labour, in the context of division of labour in the clothing trade, of which he had apparently informed her during the earlier conversation at his house. She then noted that this 'generalisation', of which he had taken such prominent notice, was 'at any rate, . . . unconnected with the special insight of a woman's into a woman's life'.[*]

---

[*]   *P* I, p. 314 n.1; Beatrice Webb, *My Apprenticeship*, p. 400. Marshall's views on these special insights and talents of women, particularly suitable for the 'minor inquiries' into economic issues of which they were capable, have been preserved in the Marshall Library (MS note, 28 May 1894, Marshall Archive, Box 5, Item 6):

a.   abundance of leisure;
b.   interest in the concrete;
c.   interest in personal matters;
d.   sympathies;
e.   access to the Unimportant individually, but numerous and therefore important collectively;
f.   power of pursuing certain delicate inquiries relating to women and children in which a man would be out of his element.

Their next correspondence dealt with Beatrice Potter's book on the Cooperative Movement, which Marshall had been reading and on which he seemed eager to offer his comments. Marshall found the book 'far from dull' and indeed, in the second half, 'even fascinating'. His criticisms would nevertheless make her 'very angry' if she read his letter until the end. He charged her with lack of originality from uncritically reproducing views of others and with over-simplifying complex issues by ignoring too many of the possible alternatives. Marshall, however, praised what he called her own contributions in the book because they were based on her personal observations and feelings. These were 'among the most mature of all the splendid things you have done. When you are on your own ground, I learn and worship: when you are reproducing the doctrines of Mitchell and Sidney Webb and the typical Trades-Unionist, I admire the charms of your voice: but I criticise and I do not learn'[93] Beatrice Potter's response to this critique defended both her views on trade unionism, which she described as far from dogmatic, and her lack of originality on co-operation, because that quality was unnecessary in 'a practical treatise for working men, and not intended for such as you'. She also struck back with considerable skill at his opening gallantry: 'Your letter was a delightful surprise to me! I hardly expected you to read the book and certainly did not venture to hope for a letter of frank criticism. I value your criticism so much and am so sincerely anxious to learn from it that I was sorry that you had wasted 4 whole pages in saying kind things, which though they are sweet to hear, teach me nothing.'[94] However, the criticism had probably stung, just as, in August 1889, Mary Booth had had to comfort her about Marshall's criticisms of her manuscript of the 'sweating system', a part of her contribution to Booth's poverty survey of London; 'don't let dear, good Professor Marshall depress you; the best and kindest of men, but not without his fads, especially in all that concerns the capacities of our sex. He does you the compliment, in spite of this, of talking to you as if you were a man'.[95]

Perhaps with this last episode in mind, Beatrice Potter had omitted to send Marshall an author's complimentary copy of her book on the Cooperative Movement. In any case, the copy preserved in the Marshall Library with his many critical annotations contains no dedication from the author, unlike so many other books in that collection. Marshall's annotations probably express his real feelings about the book more than his letter to its author just quoted. However, many years later, Beatrice Webb noted with a degree of *schadenfreude* that Marshall had not forgotten the book more than ten years after its publication. She had heard he had told Fay, who wrote a fellowship dissertation on the subject of cooperation, that Marshall's 'only fear' about Fay's enterprise had been it 'would be over-influenced by a pernicious book written by Beatrice Potter on the subject'.[96]

Six months later, when requesting a letter of introduction from Marshall to Professor Munroe, Beatrice Potter also announced her engagement to Sidney Webb to the Marshalls. 'I feel you will not quite approve of the union of two such wicked plotters in one partnership of concentrated wisdom. But I take credit to myself that I have already moderated his views and we both aid and abet each other in our admiration of you and your work.' She hoped her forthcoming marriage would not lose her the Marshalls' friendship; it had already cost her the literary executorship of Herbert Spencer, a lifelong family and, for a long time, her own special, friend.[97] Marshall's reply was surprisingly friendly. 'I guessed it. I don't think I should always have been glad of it. But now I have a feeling it is the right thing.' After mentioning that the line dividing them was that of bureaucracy versus 'freedom of variation' rather than issues of socialism, he concluded the letter: 'I congratulate you. I don't know Mr. Webb well but have many reasons for liking and admiring him, but one is enough and that is that you like him. I am sure that you will both do good and great work, and that the world will be richer and nobler because you have lived. But what I do wish is you weren't such bureaucrats.'[98] Marshall also intimated in this letter that his wife would send her congratulations separately. Mary Paley's letter unfortunately has been lost; it apparently dealt with her views on the division of labour between married and unmarried women, a matter on which Beatrice Potter briefly commented in her reply. Beatrice Potter's letter also explained why Marshall may have guessed about the engagement. Apparently during the spring of 1891, the Marshalls had encountered both her and Sidney Webb in a Westminster teashop, a meeting which had thrown Beatrice Potter 'into confusion' in case the Marshalls had recognised Sidney Webb as the other party in what must have appeared as an intimate tête-à-tête.[99]

Subsequent correspondence is not extant. Marshall continued to cite the work of the Webbs in his *Principles* on various occasions; they almost certainly kept contact with his work.[100] The extent to which the experience of the Labour Commission soured their relations is difficult to estimate, it may easily have altered the Webbs' early, very perceptive appreciation of Marshall's worth. Despite her encounter with Marshall on marriage and research at the Creightons and Balliol Croft in March 1889, Beatrice Webb came away liking the man; Sidney Webb not long afterwards expressed feeling sorry 'for poor old Marshall, because so good a man should be so cantankerously minded in various little ways',[101] a sentiment she would have echoed when recalling another part of their conversation during the cooperative congress in Ipswich in May 1889:

'There is another question Miss Potter has to explain to us, one for which she is far more responsible' – Dent remarks in a grave tone but with a kindly light in his grey eyes – 'why she lent her influence to that appeal against the suffrage. I believe it is just this: she is satisfied with her own position because she is rich and strong; she does not see that other women need the power to help themselves which would be given by the vote.'

This I feel to be an unpleasant accusation, especially as Dent and I are old friends and he speaks seriously. But before I have time to advance any sober proposition or arguments the little Professor, in tones of nervous irritability, intervenes.

'Miss Potter sees what the women suffrage people do not see; that if women attempt to equal men and be independent of their guidance and control, the strong woman will be ignored and the weak woman simply starved. It is not likely that men will go on marrying if they are to have competitors for wives. *Contrast* is the only basis of marriage, and if that is destroyed we shall not think it worth our while to shackle ourselves in life with a companion whom we must support and must consider.'

There are two sides of that question, think I, and the celibate condition of the human race can be brought about by either party to the matrimonial contract. However, I laughingly reply: 'Mr. Marshall, I pity you deeply. You are obliged to come to the rescue of woman who is the personification of emancipation in all ways; who clings to her cigarette, if she does not clutch at her vote. Why don't you leave me to my fate? Convicted of hopeless inconsistency I might even give up smoking hoping thereby to protect myself against my rights.'[102]

This exchange sums up much about the peculiar relationship between the 'little' Professor and his female Fabian acquaintance, who was also a diligent student of his economics.

Marshall's third female antagonist to be considered was Helen Bosanquet, *née* Dendy. Her first class result in the Moral Sciences Tripos was recorded previously, as was the fact that her course of study had included the course of Advanced Political Economy Marshall provided for his better students.[103] Her subsequent writings on, and activities with, the Charity Organisation Society have also been mentioned, the likely cause of her marriage to Bernard Bosanquet, who had quarrelled with Marshall on the subject of pensions for the aged in the pages of the 1892 *Economic Journal*.[104] In 1902 she sent Marshall a copy of her *Strength of the People*, in which, on one occasion she explicitly criticised her former teacher. This queried Marshall's statement about whether there was a need for 'so-called lower classes . . . doomed . . . in order to provide for others the requisites of a refined and cultured life, while they themselves are prevented from having any share or part of that life'.[105] Helen Bosanquet raised several points in this context. First, workers who were in any true sense part of a lower class would be incapable of providing others with the 'requisites of a refined or cultured life'. Her own research had demonstrated that lowest paid workers almost invariably were engaged in producing goods and services for the consumption of their own class. Hence 'their exclusion from the life of refinement is not due to their providing it for others, but rather to their inability either to contribute to it or to partake of it'. The need for a general redistribution from the rich to the poor which Marshall's argument implied was therefore not the answer to the problem; a cultured and refined life would only come gradually to the lower sections of the working class when they started producing goods and services at a higher level for their own kind. This emphasised that 'the cultured do not benefit by the poverty of the poor, but the reverse', contrary to the impression given by Marshall's sentiments on the subject.[106]

Correspondence ensued, which Helen Bosanquet felt moved to publish in the preface of her second edition,[107] because it enabled the complex economic issues her remarks had raised to be more fully elucidated. In his letter thanking her for the book, Marshall indicated that what he had read so far made him sure he would find 'it very suggestive, when I find time to read more'. However, he wanted to 'remonstrate' over her criticism, something which he would have ignored had 'it not come from an economist'. Although he admitted other people than the rich 'consumed wastefully', and wiser spending patterns would generate better standards of life, the facts had shown him nevertheless that 'the high consumption of the rich' was excessive and necessitated a 'meagre life on the part of others'. He was also puzzled by what he called her 'invalid objection' that lower-class workers worked only for the poor, which was not at all the issue he was raising in the passage quoted. That he interpreted as saying, 'Is the share of the price of total products which goes to manual labour as large as is compatible with a wholesome and free state of society?'. He continued,

Could we by taking thought get the work of our great captains of industry and financiers done for rather less than their present huge gains? Again, I admit that costly professional services are generally paid for by the rich, and not the poor. But surely these are not the only nor even the chief highly paid services. Surely it is characteristic of those developments of manufacture which are especially American that the highest wages, salaries and profits are got by making things, and engines for making things which appeal to the demand of the working and lower middle classes.

The final paragraphs of the letter expressed general agreement with the views of his former student, praising her 'insights and sympathy' as a potentially substantial contribution to 'true progress'.

> I have always held that poverty and pain, disease and death are evils of greatly less importance than they appear, except in so far as they lead to weakness of life and character; and that true philanthropy aims at increasing strength more than at the direct and immediate relief of poverty.

Given the emphasis on freedom in his introductory chapter from which the criticised passage had been taken, Marshall also suggested that the increased importance of popular government in 'democratic economies' meant that it was becoming 'more important to dwell on the truths in Mill's *Liberty* than on those in his *Essays on Socialism*'.[108]

Helen Bosanquet's reply a few days later reveals both Marshall's authority as an economist and her courage in overcoming her 'diffidence' to criticise him on 'a point of economics'. The fact that her argument was 'less crude' than it seemed to have appeared to Marshall made it imperative for her to explain it more clearly. Her 'fundamental cure for poverty' was to raise the efficiency of the poorest workers 'as producers, consumers and in all the relations of life', the resulting increased economic prosperity for them not imposing any costs on the rest of the community. However, if the wealth of the rich *caused* the poverty of the poor, only redistribution could solve the problem, a zero-sum game she could not accept because it implied the relative fixity of the national income. None of this implied her approval of the spending patterns of the wealthy or a frivolous attitude to the evils of poverty. If she believed these evils could be remedied by 'confiscation and redistribution', she would not hesitate to advocate this; but she feared the only consequence of such a policy would be a loss of 'culture and refinement' and no decrease of 'vulgar and foolish extravagance'. The thing she objected to in Marshall's remarks was his use of 'in order to' in the passage she had quoted. This implied for her that the culture and refinement of the rich was in Marshall's view the cause of the deprivation of the poor. Her final paragraph put the matter succinctly:

> One more point: Would (I ask in real doubt) the *personal* expenditure of the rich, as distinct from that part of their wealth which is productively invested, prove to be of much importance relatively to the great numbers of the wage-earners? Would it, i.e. if divided out amongst them make any appreciable addition to their incomes? I have rather come to feel that all important economic issues rest now with the mass of the people, and that the rich – except in so far as they take part in production – are 'out of it', a negligible quantity, except (sometimes) as a bad example.[109]

In response, Marshall indicated acceptance of Helen Bosanquet's premises but not her conclusions. In illustrating the extent of the gap between them which remained, he hoped he also would show it remained 'too big'. First, Marshall always assumed it was possible to levy taxes and rates disproportionately more heavy on the rich without impairing individual effort. Secondly, he assumed significant wasteful expenditure on the part of the rich, at least over one hundred million pounds in England and probably much more.* Thirdly, municipal

---

*	Alfred Marshall to Helen Bosanquet, 2 October 1902, in *The Strength of the People*, pp. x–xi. From *P* V onwards, the first new edition after this correspondence, Marshall attributed wasteful spending of £100 million to the

and state action, limited and occasionally misdirected though it was, could nevertheless achieve some things to raise standards. Reverting to a favourite theme, he mentioned state action to provide clean air and open space, adding he would have liked expenditure to achieve such objectives equal to the cost of the South African war. He would also like a 'few thousand Miss Octavia Hills – if anybody knows where to find them' since they could cure as many social ills as a 'great deal of wise legislation'. Although he agreed neither the well-to-do nor the State could raise the poor to any significant extent, since this was a task for which self-help was largely required, both assistance by the State *and* by private individuals were required to as large an extent as possible if poverty was to be eliminated. For the last purpose, artisans, 'whose life and character are noble', held out the greatest promise.[110] A year later, Marshall repeated his view that fresh air, light and open space could be brought to poor areas without touching the necessary expenditure for their 'true well being' of the rich through excessive taxation. However, attempting this in a hurry would be dangerous, because 'it might sap the springs of freedom and energy'.[111] Informed as they were by Marshall's studies of taxation, such views appeared in the final chapter of subsequent editions of the *Principles*. These indicate a growing preference on his part for the indirect method of redistribution through the budget as against the direct legislative action and state intervention proposed by so many socialists.[112]

The exchange of letters also sheds light on some aspects of Marshall's attitudes to women in social intercourse and in the classroom. Helen Bosanquet's respectful bows to his authority, despite the fact it was over ten years since she had completed her formal economics studies at Cambridge, to some extent reflect the fear and diffidence if not terror in which his female students held him.[113] Secondly, the correspondence with Helen Bosanquet gives an example of a misunderstanding of his text on the part of a trained reader, an 'economist' as he put it in his first letter, which he never corrected in later editions of the *Principles*. Was this because his critic was a woman? The change the correspondence inspired to the text – concerning Marshall's guesstimate on wasteful expenditure by the rich on which he could secure no satisfactory data – was contained in his own defence, a defence which never conceded any error on his part, not even of style. All the errors were those of misunderstanding on the part of his female reader. There is an arrogance in this correspondence which Stigler described succinctly when commenting on it, 'A biographer must wish that Marshall had cut a better figure'.[114]

A COURTEOUS MISOGYNIST, A DEPENDENT HUSBAND AND A VICTIM OF CONTEMPORARY SCIENTIFIC BELIEF?

There seems to be much evidence that as Marshall grew older, he became more and more misogynistically inclined, even though this growing sentiment was frequently mixed with courtesy and even flattery, as shown, for example, in his relationship with Beatrice Potter. Part of this can be attributed to his deep-felt misgiving about a changing social order in

---

working class and no less than £400 million to the rest of the population, without disclosing the basis for his estimates. This suggests only a small part of the correspondence was translated into changes in the text of the *Principles*. See *P* VIII, p. 720 and *P* IX, p. 719 and see note 105 above.

which women were abandoning their traditional roles as a result of what was then seen as the cult of the modern woman, who wanted the right to a job, economic independence, smoking in public, the vote and even degrees.[115] This growing movement was particularly in conflict with his ideal vision of the family, perhaps initially instilled in him by increasingly romanticised recollections of his own youth and upbringing, the value of which was brought home to him by the likely circumstances surrounding his mother's death, the attitudes to women's higher education he gathered at Bristol and possible shortcomings in his own domestic situation after marriage from what he perhaps had expected. At home, he appears to have become increasingly a husband dependent on, what for the times, was an unusually independent and self-sufficient wife. In matters of finance, this dependence came almost with the start of married life, in travel management for the all-important summer vacations probably a little later, while in matters of obtaining domestic security, comfort and ultimately protection from wearisome guests during his final decades in Cambridge, it became the dominant aspect of their relationship. Was this a cause of repressed resentment, which he increasingly chose to take out on other representatives of the female species with whom he came in contact? These personal factors cannot be ignored in his far from attractive attitudes on the subject of women.

Such personal factors do not explain all. There was an economic rationale for his attitude to women. This based the underlying sexual division of labour he wanted to preserve on the seemingly disinterested motives about the good of the race, predicted requirements for a skilled and more efficient labour supply, and a need for lifting standards of life and character. Marshall saw all of these as crucial for securing that genuine social progress at which much of his work was directed. He was encouraged in these beliefs by his interpretation of contemporary evolutionary science as exposited by Spencer and Darwin. This was a subject the importance of which he increasingly appreciated from the 1880s onwards, as shown by the specific role he assigned it in the contents of his *Principles*. These beliefs owed even more to evolution's more fashionable offshoots from the late 1880s and beyond, especially its manifestations in Galtonian eugenics and social Darwinism. This enables him to be depicted as 'the scientist [impartially] observing [and reflecting on] his contemporaries behaviour and attitudes',[116] and modifying his findings by the latest lessons of science. Marshall's vision of woman out of the workplace and into the home for the sake of the children also drew for support on the casual, and not so casual, empiricism of his *'wanderjahre'* in factories, confirmed by evidence gained through the Labour Commission. Such a picture of the objective social scientist is also open to qualification; to the same extent as that of Marshall, the congenital misogynist which Keynes sketched after Marshall's death. Marshall's published scientific endeavours on the economic and social role for women were occasionally flawed by reluctance to accept unpalatable evidence from both the biology of inheritance and from the fact-gathering by the female assistant commissioners employed on the Labour Commission. They also suffered from his failure to take the logic of the argument to all its conclusions.

Some misogyny there therefore was, mixed in with courtesy, flattery and even chivalry for the ladies of his acquaintance, or with more open disdain and even arrogance particularly bestowed on those associated with his class-room. Misogyny combined with a faith in science, even if occasionally misapplied by the self-confessed novice in the mysteries of biology and heredity. It can also be said that Marshall found it much easier to listen to the facts as diligently gathered, for example, by that 'careful, empirical social scientist, Le Play'. Le Play's basic 'law of inequality, governing all the interesting issues concerning the two sexes' would have been music to Marshall's ears, particularly since its application to education induced the comforting conclusion that 'the truest form of education for girls was found at the domestic fireside'. Le Play's elevation of the role of family in the most desirable social structure he advocated would also have been most congenial to Marshall's way of thinking.[117] These social science 'verities' complemented Marshall's all too eager embrace of the crude applications by the eugenicists of the lessons to be learnt from what is now appropriately called the 'mismeasurement of man'.[118] Marshall the collector of pictures of the famous in the hope they would lead to conclusions which, according to his wife, they never did,[119] would have placed considerable credence on contemporary findings in craniometry when applied to higher education to women, as, for example, was done by Le Bon in 1879:

> A desire to give them the same education, and as a consequence, to propose the same goals for them, is a dangerous chimera. . . . The day when, misunderstanding the interior occupations which nature has given her, women leave the home and take part in our battles, on this day a social revolution will begin, and everything that maintains the sacred ties of the family will disappear.[120]

Marshall's attitude to women is therefore over-simplified when depicted as congenital freakishness. It also reflects the ease by which science and prejudice could be combined for the highest of motives in the work of an eminent social scientist. In the case of Marshall, there is always something of the dogmatist and the preacher in his views on the subject, disharmonious with his general stance on scientific detachment. Earlier examples given in this chapter illustrate this clearly. The rising relative wages of women and young persons, discussed briefly in the *Principles* and elsewhere in terms of technical and social progress, are in one of Marshall's more romanticist moments ascribed solely to the altruism of man.[121] More importantly, the question of the rights of women to choose whether they work or not, reflecting the assessment of some women noted in the *Final Report* of the Labour Commission that housework was a monotonous drudgery to be escaped, was never put by Marshall into later editions of his *Principles*, let alone debated. Such choices had no place in his entrenched position on the type of necessities required to obtain efficiency from the agricultural labourer or unskilled working man. Furthermore, many of his opinions on the economic and social role of woman were dictated by what he described as woman's natural mental abilities. These differed substantially from those of most men, and prevented the vast majority of women from doing constructive theoretical work, particularly in economics. When that picture started to crumble with the substantial academic successes women obtained at his own beloved Cambridge, and even in his more beloved Economics and Politics Tripos, Marshall never revised his picture of woman's mental ability in the light of the new evidence. In short, there was much unscientific prejudice, and perhaps even something 'selfish', in Marshall's support for the sexual division of labour and the arguments on which that rested. No wonder his hostility to the notion of 'modern women', threatening as it did the established monogamous institution of marriage on which that of the family rested; was able to rise to ridiculous proportions when, as reported in J.N. Keynes's diaries,[122] Marshall 'refuses to meet Miss Clough because she is in favour of woman suffrage', despite the fact that as Secretary to Newnham College, she was also his wife's effective fellow worker and friend. The respected author of the *Principles* and fighter for economics loses much dignity and scientific rectitude in his Canute-like obstruction to the advance of women in university and society. Given his early support of the movement, his is the picture of the feminist *manqué* indeed.

NOTES

1. J.M. Keynes, 'Alfred Marshall', p. 162.
2. *Ibid.* On Marshall's father, see above p. 22, while Chapter 8, pp. 223–4, suggests that Keynes's picture of marital bliss at Balliol Croft is somewhat overdrawn.
3. J.M. Keynes, 'Alfred Marshall', p. 220.
4. This is suggested by Rita McWilliams-Tullberg, 'Alfred Marshall and the "Woman's Question" at Cambridge', *Revue d'économie appliquée*, LXIII (1), 1990, pp. 209–30. This whole chapter is heavily indebted to her pioneering work on this subject, including especially her detailed study of the woman's issue at Cambridge University: *Woman at Cambridge: A Men's University though of a Mixed type*, London: Gollancz, 1975, esp. chapters 4–8. In addition, Marshall's attitudes to gender and class have been examined in Michèle A. Pujol, *Feminism and Anti-Feminism in Early Economic Thought*, Aldershot: Edward Elgar, 1992, Chapter 8, and in my 'Alfred Marshall – Women and Economic Development: Labour, Family and Race', in *Political Economy and Feminism in Victorian England*, ed. Peter Groenewegen, Aldershot: Edward Elgar, 1994, Chapter 4.
5. Above, Chapter 2, esp. pp. 39–41.
6. Marshall to Rebecca Marshall, 5 July 1875 (Marshall Archive, 1:293).
7. This, and the previous paragraph draw heavily on Marshall's letters and other papers on his American trip, to which references were given in Chapter 7 above, especially pp. 193–200.
8. See A.S. and E.M.S., *Henry Sidgwick. A Memoir*, pp. 204–7 and esp. p. 205 n.1. Marshall's admiration for Mill and his wife, Harriet Taylor, forms the eloquent introduction to his paper on 'The Future of the Working Classes', in *Memorials*, p. 101. See also Newnham College, *Record of Benefactors 1921*, printed for the College: Cambridge University Press, 1921, pp. 1–3.
9. Alice Gardner, *A Short History of Newnham College*, Cambridge: Bowes & Bowes, 1921, pp. 14, 24; B.A. Clough, *A Memoir of Anne Jemimah Clough*, London: Edward Arnold, 1897, p. 148.
10. Mirrlees typescript of Annabel Robinson's notes on Jane Harrison, NCA, p. 25; Mary Paley Marshall, *What I Remember*, pp. 20–21.
11. Mary Paley Marshall, 'The Growth of Newnham', Newnham College Club, *Cambridge Letter etc. 1884*, printed for private circulation, p. 4.
12. Mary Paley Marshall, *What I Remember*, pp. 16–17.
13. *Cambridge University Reporter*, 1874–75, p. 20; Newnham College, *Record of Benefactors 1921*, printed for the College: Cambridge University Press, 1921, p. 5. If money was the measure of motives and actions, it is interesting to note that the donation of the Marshalls in 1887 for the Clough Hall Building fund was only £25 (*ibid.*, p. 10) while the combined donation of the two for Newnham Hall amounted to £150 in 1874–75. However, in 1887 their finances may have still been recovering from the overrun in building costs for Balliol Croft.
14. Above, Chapter 8, pp. 228–30; and Mirrlees typescript, NCA, pp. 32, 34; Sandra J. Peacock, *Jane Ellen Harrison. The Mask and the Self*, London: Yale University Press, 1988, p. 46.
15. Marshall to J.B. Clark, 24 March 1908, in *Memorials*, p. 417, and above Chapter 8, pp. 233–4.
16. Marshall to Foxwell, 29 April 1884 (Freeman Collection, 48/123).
17. Marshall to J.N. Keynes, 30 August 1891 (Marshall Archive, 1:102); Mary Paley Marshall, *What I Remember*, pp. 22–7 and see above, Chapter 8, p. 237.
18. Alfred Marshall, Lectures to Women, May 1873, own notes for lecture 4; Mary Paley's notes for lecture 5; Rita McWilliams-Tullberg, 'The Male Priesthood of Economics', *Quaderni di storia dell' economia politica*, IX, (2–3), 1991, pp. 246–7.

19. Alfred Marshall, evidence to the Committee on Higher Education in Wales and Monmouthshire, Cmnd 3047–1, Parliamentary Papers Vol. XXXIII, 1881, pp. 767–79, answer to Question 18,276, p. 775, Question 18,304, p. 776.

20. *Ibid.*, answers to Questions 18,305–6, p. 776.

21. Rita McWilliams-Tullberg, 'Alfred Marshall and the "Woman's Question" at Cambridge', p. 219. She adds in brackets to these quotations, 'One wonders how Mary Paley Marshall felt to be regarded as the dull and unimportant member of her family'.

22. Older sister Agnes by then may have been in India, where she later died, as surmised in Chapter 2 above, p. 39.

23. Marshall to Foxwell, 31 January, 4 February 1875 (Freeman Collection, 12/229, 13/229); and see above, Chapter 2, pp. 36, 38 for earlier discussion associated with his mother's death. His skills as 'nurse' were attested to by his wife from the time she was ill with malaria fever in Palermo.

24. See Chapter 9 above, p. 235, cf. Chapter 10, pp. 323–4, see also *Cambridge University Reporter*, 3 March 1896, p. 551.

25. As recounted by G.C. Harcourt, 'Joan Robinson', in G.C. Harcourt, *The Social Science Imperialists. Selected Essays*, ed. Prue Kerr, London: Routledge & Kegan Paul, 1982, p. 349. Joan Robinson's presentation copy of her *Imperfect Competition* to Mary Paley Marshall is preserved in the Marshall Library, dedicated to her pioneering efforts in women's economics education. See also Rita McWilliams-Tullberg, 'Marshall's Final Lecture', p. 609 and n.7

26. *EOI*, Book I, Chapter 5, §5; Chapter 13 above, pp. 482–5.

27. Herbert Spencer, *First Principles*, Part III , §111, §114, §122, §134–5, §154, §161, §175.

28. Charles Darwin, *Descent of Man*, London: John Murray, second edition, 1906, pp. 858, 860–61; cf. pp. 923–5 and Herbert Spencer, *First Principles*, London: Williams & Norgate, sixth edition, 1919, p. 137 note* which reads as follows:

    I knew a lady, who contended that a dress folded up tightly weighed more than when loosely folded up; and who, under this belief, had her trunks made large that she might diminish the charge for freight! Another, whom I know, ascribes the feeling of lightness which accompanies vigour, to actual decrease of weight; believes that by stepping gently, she can press less upon the ground; and, when cross-questioned, asserts that, if placed in scales, she can make herself lighter by an act of will!

29. Charles Darwin, *Descent of Man*, pp. 944–6. A detailed discussion is in Eveleen Richards, 'Darwin and the Descent of Women' in *The Wider Domain of Evolutionary Thought*, edited David Oldroyd and Ian Langham, Reidel: Dordrecht, 1983, pp. 57–111.

30. Above, Chapter 13, pp. 481–2.

31. Marshall to Sarah Emily Davies, 11 November 1880 (Girton College Archives); for background to this episode see Rita McWilliams-Tullberg, *Woman at Cambridge*, pp. 70–84.

32. Rita McWilliams-Tullberg, *Woman at Cambridge, ibid.*, pp. 88–90.

33. *Ibid.*, pp. 96–7.

34. Marshall to J.N. Keynes, 30 August 1891 (Marshall Archive, 1:102).

35. Marshall to Foxwell, 21 October 1894 (Freeman Collection, 11/127).

36. Marshall to Foxwell, 29 October 1894 (Freeman Collection, 2/127).

37. Marshall to Foxwell, 9 November 1894 (Freeman Collection, 3/127).

38. Marshall to Foxwell, 13 November 1894 (Freeman Collection, 10/127).

39. Moral Sciences Board Minutes for 20 November 1891, CUL, Min. V 10.

40. *Cambridge University Reporter*, 8 March 1892, p. 600.

41. *Cambridge University Reporter*, 6 November 1894, p. 175.

42. Marshall to Foxwell, 21 October 1894 (Freeman Collection, 11/127).

43. Alfred Marshall, 'to the Members of the Senate [on degrees for women]', Cambridge, Balliol Croft, 3 February 1896, p. 5.

44. *Ibid.*, p. 6.

45. *Cambridge University Reporter*, 26 March 1897, pp. 791–6. Its opening remarks appear intended as a reply to Sidgwick's speech the year before (*Cambridge University Reporter*, 3 March 1896, p. 552) in which Sidgwick had sarcastically referred to Marshall's 'backward conversion' on the issue.

46. Marshall to Hardy, 2 March 1896 (CUL, Add 4251(B) 940); the only Hardy who was a resident M.A. in Cambridge in 1896 was Sir William Bate Hardy (1864–1934).

47. Rita McWilliams-Tullberg, *Woman at Cambridge*, pp. 115–18; 'Alfred Marshall and the Male Priesthood of Economics', pp. 252–3 which cites Marshall to Mrs Sidgwick, 16 February 1896 (NCA).

48. Rita McWilliams-Tullberg, *Woman at Cambridge*, pp. 117–18; cf. Clara Collet, 'The Economic Position of Educated Working Women' and 'Prospects of Marriage for Women', both in Clara E. Collet, *Educated Working Women*, London: P.S. King, 1902, Essays 1 and 2 (published first in 1890 and 1892 respectively).

49. As cited in Rita McWilliams-Tullberg, *Woman at Cambridge*, pp. 124–5. The original response preserved in the University Archives confirms it came from Marshall. Information supplied by John Whitaker.

50. Marshall to Foxwell, 17 April and 18 April 1897 (Marshall Archive, 1:33, 34); the first was extensively quoted in Chapter 8, p. 248.

51. Rita McWilliams-Tullberg, *Woman at Cambridge*, pp. 127–41, esp. pp. 138–9.

52. The Minutes show Marshall absent from Board meetings on 3, 10 and 28 May 1897, 16 October and 11 December 1897, recording his first attendance not until 18 January 1898 (CUL, Min. V. 10). In a letter to the *Times* (19 May 1897) Marshall valued the wear and tear of the 'weary year' of controversy at a year's salary.

53. Ascribed to the German Emperor in the 1890s. (David Rubinstein, *Before the Suffragettes*, p. 222.) This section draws strongly on my 'Alfred Marshall – Women and Economic Development: Labour, Family and Race'.

54. *Reynolds Magazine*, 30 July 1890 (cutting in Marshall's scrap-book, Marshall Archive, University of Cambridge).

55. *P* I, p. 123; *P* VIII, pp. 69–70.

56. *P* I, pp. 252–3; a much abbreviated version dates from *P* II and continued unchanged until *P* VIII, p. 199. Marshall's reference to Roscher is to his *Political Economy*, §141.

57. F.Y. Edgeworth, 'Reminiscences', in *Memorials*, pp. 72–3. In 1898, Marshall had expressed his fears about the 'drift towards New Womanhood' to Benjamin Kidd, since if this went 'too far', 'stable monogamy may be endangered', adding he didn't think it would go that far. Marshall to Kidd, 14 February 1898 CUL, Add 8069/M 254). For useful background see David Rubinstein, *Before the Suffragettes*, esp. pp. 137 ff., 220–21.

58. *EOI*, Book III, Chapter III, §7, pp. 175–7. In the following decade, Marshall's papers 'Theories and Facts about Wages' (*Cooperative Wholesale Annual*, 1885, pp. 379–88) and the 1887 'A Fair Rate of Wages' omitted the subject of women's wages altogether.

59. *P* I, p. 316; *P* VIII, p. 263.

60. *P* VIII. p. 333; this passage dates from *P* VI, p. 273.

61. *P* I p. 725; *P* VIII, p. 682.

62. *P* VIII p. 794; this passage dates from *P* VI, p. 794.

63. *P* I, pp. 727–8; *P* VIII, p. 685.

64. *P* VIII, p. 715 n.1; this passage dates from *P* V, p. 715 n.1.

65. *P* VIII, pp. 714–15; this passage dates from *P* V, pp. 714–15, and cf. above, Chapter 11, p. 368 and n.¶ for the views of the Labour Commission on this subject.

66. *EOI*, pp. 176–7.

67. *P* VIII, p. 529; this passage dates from *P* III, p. 594.

68. *P* I, pp. 592–3; *P* VIII, p. 564. Cf. *P* VIII, pp. 718–20, esp. 720 for comments on the general role of women in the improvement of human nature; amending the slightly different, and shorter, version of this passage in *P* I, pp. 730–31.

69. Above, pp. 497–8.

70. Labour Commission, Minutes of Evidence, cited in T.G. Spyers, *The Labour Question, an epitome of the evidence and report of the Royal Commission on Labour*, p. 113.

71. That is, above, Chapter 13, pp. 479–85.

72. *P* VIII, pp. 247–8. As argued in the previous chapter, this material had only been altered on detail, not on its basic thrust. Cf. with *P* I, pp. 307–9 and *P* IV, pp. 316–18.

73. Alfred Marshall, 1884 (?) fragment, 'Women and Technical Education', Marshall Library, Box 8 (1).

74. Alfred Marshall, 'The Higher Education of Women', Marshall Library, Box 8 (2). On the later recollections of Mary Paley Marshall, *What I Remember*, p. 20, an exceptional woman in literature in Marshall's scheme of things would have been George Eliot.

75. *P* VIII, pp. 201–3; as noted above, this type of passage changed greatly in detail but not in its thrust. Cf. *P* I, pp. 256–9; fourth edition, 1898, pp. 280–83, and n.72 above.

76. See Chapter 7 above, pp. 209–11, 212–13.

77. Royal Commission on Labour, *Minutes of Evidence taken before Group B*, Cmnd 6795, June 1892, Questions 15,272–305, pp. 300–1; Q. 15,362–73, p. 305; Cmnd 6894–VIII, February 1893, Q. 17,210, p. 22.

78. Royal Commission on Labour, *Minutes of Evidence taken before Group B*, Cmnd. 6894–VIII February 1893, Q. 23,888–92, p. 195; Q. 21,418–22, pp. 220–21.

79. Royal Commission on Labour, *Reports from Commissioners, Inspectors and Others*, Vol. XXXV, 1894, *Employment of Women*, esp. pp. 478–82, 507–10 on which the greater part of this and the next paragraph is based.

80. See above, pp. 508–9. There is little useful secondary evidence on this subject which would have been available to Marshall. George Hy. Wood, 'The Course of Women's Wages during the Nineteenth Century', Appendix A to B.L. Hutchins and A. Harrison, *A History of Factory Legislation*, London: P.S. King & Son, 1903, pp. 283–

4, supports Marshall's contention that generally speaking since the 1860s women's wages rose relatively faster than wages as a whole. The subsequent study by Dorothea M. Barton, 'The Course of Women's Wages', *Journal of the Royal Statistical Society*, LXXXII, Pt. 4, July 1919, pp. 508–44, provides no data on women's wage growth relative to that of men. See also David Rubinstein, *Before the Suffragettes*, Chapter 7, esp. pp. 99–100.

81. Royal Commission on Labour, *Fifth and Final Report*, Cmnd 7421, June 1894, pp. 93–4, 107–9.

82. See above, Chapter 13, pp. 482–5, and this chapter, pp. 511, 512–13.

83. Marshall Library, *Catalogue*, pp. 18, 64, which, however, does not list all the items mentioned in the text, which were personally inspected in the Library by the author. For examples of the type of annotations to Meyer and Black, *Makers of our Clothes*, London: Duckworth, 1909, see p. 195 where, in the context of low wages and innovations, Marshall noted he had made this point in the third edition of his *Principles*, while a reference on high wages and improvements on p. 192, attracted Marshall's comment, 'put in!'.

84. This draws on Marshall's remarks on the good social scientist as quoted by Pigou 'In Memoriam', in *Memorials*, pp. 83–4.

85. Above, Chapter 8, pp. 257–8, Chapter 10, pp. 323–4.

86. Listed in Marshall Library, *Catalogue*, p. 25.

87. *P* I, p. 63 n.1. The second to fourth editions withdrew direct reference to Miss Martineau in this context, perhaps in response to criticism Marshall received on the subject which has not survived.

88. *P* VIII, p. 763 n.1, first introduced in *P* V. See *P* IX, pp. 758–9.

89. Harriet Martineau, *Autobiography with Memorials by Maria Weston Chapman*, London: Smith, Elder & Company, 1877, Vol. 1, pp. 135–8, 193–200; see Vol. 2, pp. 244–5, Vol. 3, pp. 461–2 for references to her retraction of the merit of the tales and her late in life views on the science of political economy. Cf. Vera Wheatley, *The Life and Work of Harriet Martineau*, London: Seckert & Warburg, 1957, pp. 88–9 and Chapter 5.

90. See Beatrice Webb, *My Apprenticeship*, p. 397; Belinda Norman-Butler, *Victorian Aspirations*, pp. 88, 105, 112. Because their meeting at the Creightons for dinner was followed by lunch at Balliol Croft the next day, as described by Beatrice Webb in her diary for March 1889, it seems unlikely that this was the first occasion on which they met.

91. Beatrice Webb, *My Apprenticeship*, pp. 397–8.

92. Marshall to Beatrice Potter, 27 January 1889, British Library of Political and Economic Science, Passfield Papers, II(ii)204.

93. Marshall to Beatrice Potter, 11 July 1891, Marshall Archive, 1:305.

94. Beatrice Potter to Marshall, July 1891, British Library of Political and Economic Science, Passfield Papers, 1(ii)114.

95. Mary Booth to Beatrice Potter, 11 August 1889, cited in Belinda Norman-Butler, *Victorian Aspirations*, p. 105.

96. Marshall's copy of the book contains about a dozen annotations. On the comment attributed to Fay, see Beatrice Webb, *My Apprenticeship,* p. 300 n.1.

97. Beatrice Potter to Marshall, 20 January 1892, Passfield Papers, IIi(ii)116.

98. Marshall to Beatrice Potter, 22 January 1892, Passfield Papers, IIi(ii)205.

99. Beatrice Potter to Mary Paley Marshall, Marshall Archive, 1:03. The teashop encounter probably took place during one of the Marshalls' visits to London for the preliminary meetings of the Labour Commission on procedures.

100. Marshall sent them, for example, a copy of his special errata for the third edition of his *Principles* (see above, Chapter 12, p. 426 and the reference cited in its note 103).

101. Beatrice Webb, *My Apprenticeship*, p. 400; Sidney to Beatrice Webb, 17 October 1891 in *The Letters of Sidney and Beatrice Webb*, Vol. 1, p. 221.

102. Beatrice Webb, *My Apprenticeship*, pp. 210–1. This referred to her earlier opposition to women's suffrage, for which she was taken to task by Millicent Fawcett, the widow of Marshall's predecessor. See *ibid.*, pp. 400–402.

103. Above, Chapter 10, p. 324.

104. Above, Chapter 11, p. 135 and n.35.

105. That is, Helen Bosanquet, *The Strength of the People*, London: Macmillan, 1902, p. 70. Marshall's remark she criticised came from the *P* I, Book I, Chapter I, §2, p. 3, a passage preserved unchanged in the same place over all subsequent editions, and hence the 'in order' to which Helen Bosanquet objected, was not deleted.

106. Helen Bosanquet, *The Strength of the People*, second edition, 1903, pp. 70–71.

107. *Ibid.*, preface, pp. vi–xii. The two Marshall letters included in the preface but not Helen Bosanquet's response, were reproduced almost *in toto* in *Memorials*, pp. 443–5; this also adds part of a third letter by Marshall (*ibid.*, pp. 445–6) written after the second edition of *Strength of the People* had appeared.

108. Marshall to Helen Bosanquet, 28 September 1902, in *The Strength of the People*, second edition, Preface, pp. viii–ix; *Memorials*, pp. 443–4. The significance of Marshall's remark about Mill is explored more fully in Chapter 16 below, see esp. pp. 571, 593–4.

109. Helen Bosanquet to Marshall, 30 September 1902, in *The Strength of the People*, pp. ix–x.
110. Marshall to Helen Bosanquet, 2 October 1902, in *The Strength of the People*, pp. x–xii.
111. Marshall to Helen Bosanquet, 28 October 1903, in *Memorials*, pp. 445–6.
112. Marshall's attitudes to socialism and changing views on distributive tax policy are discussed below, Chapter 16, pp. 97–8, Chapter 17, pp. 645–6.
113. Above, Chapter 10, pp. 323–4; below, Chapter 15, p. 555.
114. In a letter to the author, when sending him photocopies of this material.
115. David Rubinstein, *Before the Suffragettes*, p. 137, provides a succinct definition of the 'new' woman in the 1890s.
116. John Whitaker, 'Some Neglected Aspects of Alfred Marshall's Social and Economic Thought', *AMCA*, I, p. 480.
117. M.F. Le Play, *La Reforme Sociale en France*, Tours, Alfred Mamé, seventh edition, 1887, Vol. 2, pp. 397–400, cf. p. 26 (my translation). Marshall's admiration for Le Play's work as a social scientist was mentioned above, Chapter 6, p. 168.
118. See Stephen Jay Gould, *The Mismeasurement of Man*, New York: W.W. Norton, 1981, esp. pp. 155–6, 158–9 on the dangers of biological determinism when applied to heredity and eugenicist policies. I owe this reference to Flora Gill.
119. Mary Paley Marshall, *What I Remember*, pp. 15–16.
120. G. Le Bon, 'Récherches anatomiques et mathématiques sur les lois des variation du volume du cerveau et sur leurs relations avec l'intelligence', *Revue d'Anthropologie*, Vol. 2, 1870, p. 62 (as cited by Gould, *The Mismeasurement of Man*, p. 105 in the context of a proposal by some American reformers to grant women access to higher education on the same basis as men).
121. See Alfred Marshall, 'Social Foundations of Economic Chivalry', in *Memorials*, p. 327 and cf. R.C.O. Mathews, 'Marshall and the Labour Market', in *Centenary Essays on Alfred Marshall*, p. 29.
122. JNKD, 8 April 1890. Keynes heard the story from Henry Sidgwick, who had heard it from Mrs Frances Darwin, a very close friend and confidante of Mrs Mary Marshall, thereby indicating it was a probable source of discord at Balliol Croft.

15. The Creator of a New Tripos

In 1903 Alfred Marshall achieved what he had described on his return to Cambridge in 1885 as his most 'cherished ambition', the establishment of a separate Economics and Political Sciences Tripos in which students could specialise on the subject he had so carefully fostered as its Professor. He had fleshed out this ambition in his inaugural lecture by emphasising the need to free students of economics more fully from the constraints imposed by the Moral Sciences Tripos regulations, the area of study which had initially nurtured the formal education in economics at university level in Cambridge. Over the years that followed his appointment, Marshall became increasingly aware that only the device of what would now be called a separate faculty would enable those 'who have the trained scientific minds which economics is so urgently craving [but] who have not the taste or the time for the whole of the Moral Sciences . . . to bring to bear some of their stored up force [and] add a knowledge of the economic organon to their general training. [This would aid] the great work of inquiring how far it is possible to remedy the economic evils of the present day.'[1]

Not only was the creation of the new Tripos the climax to Marshall's long and distinguished academic career at Cambridge, it was the starting-point of that Cambridge school of economics which to an extraordinary extent dominated the subject in the decades between the two world wars in virtually all its branches. That aspect of the Marshallian legacy is examined later.[2] This chapter concentrates on the campaigns Marshall had to wage in the Special Boards of Moral Sciences and History to attain his 'cherished ambition'. It thereby provides further insights into Marshall the academic politician fighting for the growth of his discipline. The years he devoted to this task, first in creating, and then in nurturing, the new Tripos in its five formative years, almost parallel the long haul of his *Principles* in terms of concentrated effort and devotion. The greatest of the three movements in which Marshall was involved as Political Economy Professor at Cambridge makes therefore an interesting chapter in his biography, and chronicles what his wife later recalled as his great, if not his main, achievement.[3]

A considerable amount of background to the story of the Tripos has already been presented. The relatively informal status of much of the early teaching in economics at Cambridge was implicit in the discussion of Marshall's apprenticeship in the subject and in that of his teaching as St John's Lecturer in the Moral Sciences from 1868 to 1877. The brief sketch of the Professorship of Political Economy at Cambridge prior to Marshall's election to the chair contains information on the growth in the syllabus of the subject for which that professor was responsible and on the Moral Sciences and History Tripos syllabus within which it was contained.[4] To set the stage for Marshall's campaigns to widen the scope for economic studies within these Triposes, the situation of economics at Cambridge as it was in 1885 is presented first. An account of Marshall's successive moves in altering the regulations of the Moral Sciences and History Tripos follows. The drive to a full-fledged economics tripos in 1901–3 is then examined, followed by a discussion of its first five years ending with Marshall's retirement in May 1908. The substantial literature available on the subject facilitates this task enormously.[5]

THE STATE OF ECONOMICS AS PROFESSOR MARSHALL FOUND IT: POLITICAL ECONOMY AT CAMBRIDGE IN 1885

When Marshall returned to Cambridge as Professor of Political Economy in early 1885, political economy was taught formally for both the Moral Sciences and the History Tripos. At that time, the subject accounted for a little less than one-third in the moral sciences syllabus for the B.A. as measured by examination requirements. Students had to take three political economy papers out of a total of ten, the other required papers being two on Logic, three on Mental Philosophy, and one each on Ethics and Moral Philosophy. The History Tripos examinations since its inception allowed one paper on the subject which from 1886 was to devote 'special attention to government action in matters of finance and industry'.[6] Although this was an expansion in the teaching of political economy when looked at over the years since Pryme had begun its informal instruction in 1816, there were a number of major encumbrances on its future growth which a skilled observer like Marshall would have been quick to notice on his return.

Although in the early 1870s, a number of prominent first class honours results were awarded in the moral sciences, coinciding with the time Marshall had been teaching its students as St John's College Lecturer in the Moral Sciences,[7] most of these bright students were not fresh undergraduates but persons who had taken university courses elsewhere, in London or Scotland, before coming to Cambridge. Examples of this genre are Foxwell, Cunningham, J.N. Keynes and J.S. Nicholson, four of the distinguished 'firsts' in Moral Sciences these years produced. However, such examples cannot be taken as but the tips of a substantially submerged iceberg of quality in the moral sciences. In 1870, Sidgwick had written that speaking of the moral sciences generally, 'the standard of a first class is low because the most able and industrious men do not devote themselves to the study', while in 1878 Sidgwick wrote to Foxwell that he 'certainly would not encourage any promising young man to try and find an opening in Cambridge in that Department'.[8] That year had recorded no result in the first class, a performance repeated in 1881, 1884 and 1885, from the six men who attempted the Tripos in each of these years. 1879 produced three firsts (including the Johnian Caldecott) from eight attempting the examination; one first in 1880 from four; one (Sorley) from three in 1882 but six (among whom Johnson and Stout) from 11 in 1883.[9] No wonder that in that stormy afternoon in December following his election to the chair, Marshall berated Sidgwick for failing to follow the example of T.H. Green at Oxford in pitching his lectures in such a way as to attract young brilliant students to this course of study.[10] Although some good women students, drawn especially from Newnham, made up marginally for these low numbers, this supplementation was not seen by Marshall as quite satisfactory.[11] Moreover, changes which had come into effect in 1883 when the moral sciences Tripos was divided into parts, allowed students for Part II to specialise in only two of the moral sciences, thereby enabling them to evade more advanced work in Political Economy.

In 1885 all history students had to take some economic theory, initially based largely on the contents of Fawcett's *Manual of Political Economy*. As noted earlier, the economics examination paper for history students was combined with economic history. To these shortcomings of the history syllabus from Marshall's perspective were added some general problems with history students. Marshall, it may be recalled, described such students as 'kittle kattle', because they were 'not very profound', though 'intelligent and earnest'. Nevertheless, history produced more economics students for him than did the moral sciences.[12] Furthermore, Cunningham excepted, Marshall's ex-officio membership of the History Board was viewed quite sympathetically, especially by its senior members. These included Seeley the Regius Professor of History and successor of Kingsley and, from 1884 when he was appointed to the Dixie Chair of Ecclesiastical History, Mandell Creighton, whom the Marshalls had befriended in Oxford. Marshall, in fact, was quite attuned to Seeley's position. In his inaugural of 1869, Seeley had called for cooperation between the Professors of History and Political Economy, because their subjects constituted a 'prominent part' for the explicit vocational target in history studies he presented to his students.[13] These features of the History and Moral Sciences Triposes, explain much of the tone of Marshall's inaugural on the subject of the role of economics in Cambridge University studies.

The teaching responsibilities in economics on Marshall's return in 1885 were divided between those of the Professor and those assigned to the various lecturers. As shown previously,[14] Marshall taught the principles of political economy ('Production, Rent, Wages, Profits and Value') during the 1880s as well as giving a survey course on money, trade and government functions over two terms. Lecturers then teaching economics included the following. Levin, a St Catharine's College Lecturer, taught the theory of money over three terms. Foxwell, a St John's College Lecturer, taught Smith, Malthus and Ricardo in the October term, the History of Socialism in Lent term together with the Elements of Political Economy, the second of which he continued during Easter term. In addition, J.N. Keynes, the only university Lecturer in the Moral Sciences, combined his substantial teaching of Logic with an Easter term devoted to papers in Political Economy, while William Cunningham taught Economic History as a university Lecturer to students of the History Tripos. Not all of these lectures were addressed to Tripos students, some were given to the pass students, or 'poll men'. Since the 1860s they had been able to take Political Economy as a special paper for their B.A. examinations, a practice encouraged by Fawcett.*

---

* *Cambridge University Reporter*, 9 June 1886, p. 762. The booklist in support of these courses was as follows: Bagehot, *Lombard Street*; Fawcett, *Protection and Free Trade*; A. and M.P. Marshall, *Economics of Industry*, Mill, *Principles of Political Economy*, and Walker's *The Wages Question* and *Money, Trade and Industry*. Students of political economy in the History Tripos were advised to read also Jevons, *The State in Relation to Labour*, to consult Roscher's *Political Economy*, and to study Part III of Sidgwick's *Principles of Political Economy*. These readings reflected the special emphasis given in this course to the economic functions of the State. Advanced students of political economy largely drawn from those attempting Part II of the Moral Sciences Tripos introduced in 1883 and from interested graduates for whom Marshall started to give special classes on his return as professor, needed to do a considerable amount of reading additional to the books prescribed for the general students. In alphabetical order, they were required to familiarise themselves with the contents of Bagehot's *Economic Studies*, Brentano's *On Guilds*, Cairnes's *Leading Principles on Political Economy*, Cournot's *Recherches sur les principes mathématiques de la théorie des richesses*, Cunningham's, *Growth of English Industry and Commerce*, Giffen's, *Stock Exchange Securities*, Goschen's *Foreign Exchanges*, Jevons's *Theory of Political Economy* and *Investigations in Currency and Finance*, Levi's, *History of British Commerce*, Leroy-

One further matter needs to be recalled by way of background. Compared with the prestigious and long-established Triposes in Mathematics and the Classics, those in which Political Economy could be taken lacked high academic standing, scholarships and prizes. This partly explains why so many of the better students avoided entry into them and why, in those initial years as Professor, Marshall attracted so few students from these fields of study. In addition, there was considerable hostility against teaching for business and commerce in the established universities of Oxford and Cambridge. This further lowered the attraction of the study of wealth, an alternative way in which the subject of political economy was described. Such handicaps had been fully acknowledged by Marshall in his inaugural lecture, and justify his concluding appeal to well-trained minds to study political economy for the good they could do in society.[15]

EXPANDING THE SCOPE OF POLITICAL ECONOMY TEACHING WITHIN EXISTING TRIPOSES: 1889 AND 1897

Marshall expanded the scope of economics teaching on two occasions within the Moral Sciences Tripos (1888–89, 1896–97) and once in the History Tripos (1897) before his final and decisive moves towards establishing an Economics and Political Sciences Tripos. Details of the syllabus outcomes are summarised in the Appendix to this chapter; arguments surrounding Marshall's case, drawn from the official record in the *University Reporter*, the minutes of the Moral Sciences Board meetings, John Neville Keynes's diaries and Marshall's correspondence, provide the basis for what follows.

According to Keynes (diary entry for 29 February 1888), initial moves to reform the structure of the Moral Sciences Tripos in 1888 came from Sidgwick, but the matter was under discussion for the whole of that month. This is clearly revealed by Marshall's correspondence with Keynes for February 1888. It put off a meeting between the two to discuss Sidgwick's proposals because of inclement weather, and explains Marshall's opposition to its contents on the ground that it enabled those attempting Part II of the Tripos to avoid political economy studies. These were the students in whom he was most interested, as he wrote Keynes on 18 February:

> I remain of the opinion I expressed to you yesterday that I should cordially concur in any slowly matured scheme for reorganising the Moral Sciences Tripos, which was approved by teachers of the other Moral Sciences, provided it made no great changes in the position which Political Economy holds: but that I should oppose uncompromisingly any proposal for diminishing its weight in the second half of the examination. I am increasingly of [the] opinion that a short study of Political Economy seldom does much good and not infrequently does much harm. It is not till a man is about to take his degree that his work at economics generally becomes of any substantial value.[16]

Beaulieu's *Essai sur la répartition des richesses*, Malthus's, *Principles of Political Economy*, Ricardo's *Principles of Political Economy*, Roscher's, *Principles of Political Economy*, Smith's *An Inquiry into the Nature and Causes of the Wealth of Nations* and Walker's *Money* (*Cambridge University Reporter*, 20 June 1885, pp. 923–4; 8 June 1886, p. 716).

Marshall added a sketch proposal of his own which, he suggested, Keynes could show to Sidgwick and other members of the Board if he liked. It provided for study of Psychology and Elements of Metaphysics, Logic, Ethics and Political Economy for Part I, of which he proposed students could either attempt three (with two examination papers in each) or, his preferred solution, that all students study the four subjects. He also proposed an examination paper on essay topics. For Part II he suggested study of five subjects: Metaphysics, Psychology, Logic, either Ethics and Politics or Sociology, and last, Political Economy and Statistics, of which each student would choose two for the examination.*

This pronounced difference of opinion induced a number of stormy meetings of the Moral Sciences Board during the following months. The different views of Marshall and Sidgwick gradually were narrowed to the question whether compulsory Metaphysics should be placed in the first preliminary part of the Tripos (Marshall's suggestion) or in the second (Sidgwick's position).¶ Deferral of the matter till October 1888 showed the friction this was causing and only when Sidgwick conceded the substantial compromise of allowing students specialising in Political Economy to avoid Metaphysics by allowing them to take Political Philosophy instead did Marshall finally accept the general position of the Board on Metaphysics in the degree structure (10 November 1888).[17] However, in early December, Marshall wanted changes in the status of the Logic examination for Political Economy specialists through the inclusion of more statistical theory. It was not until the end of January 1889 that J.N. Keynes was able to report 'fair progress with the new regulations', with agreement in sight on 6 February. Final agreement was reached on 27 February and the Moral Sciences Board Report with the new resolutions was presented to the Senate for ratification by the Vice-Chancellor shortly thereafter.

For economic studies within the Moral Sciences Tripos, the report implied the following. For the first part of the Tripos, two papers on Political Economy were to be required together with two compulsory papers for each of the two other compulsory subjects: Psychology, and Logic and Methodology. For Part II, Advanced Political Economy was changed to a special subject, taken either with Political Philosophy or the Theory of Knowledge (Metaphysics) and hence being exempted from its formerly proposed compulsion. This was the substance of Sidgwick's compromise which in the end enabled agreement. Attempting Part II was to be permitted to students from other Triposes, as Pigou and Clapham were subsequently to do after completing History. The removal of compulsory

---

* *Ibid.,* Marshall added that 'if the theory of political economy before the time of Adam Smith is to be treated at all' it should form part of Ethics and Politics (or Sociology), since there would be a strong historical element in Political Economy and Statistics if these subjects were 'treated carefully'. However, if Foxwell pushed for the early history and Sidgwick refused to take it with politics, a solution was to include it with the 'Mixed Essay papers'. This signals his difference of opinion on history of theory with Foxwell (discussed above, Chapter 13, pp. 471-3 and see below, Chapter 18, pp. 674–7). However, elsewhere he expressed different views on the importance of pre-Smithian economic theory, for example, in a letter to L.L. Price, 19 August 1892 (*Memorials*, pp. 378–9) and in a remark later recorded by Guillebaud ('Some Personal Reminiscences of Alfred Marshall', p. 96).

¶ A vote on the subject resulted in three votes for Marshall's position, three for that of Sidgwick and three abstentions (JNKD, 15 May 1888). The matter was not resolved at a more peaceful subsequent meeting of the Moral Sciences Board (15 May 1888). It was therefore deferred until October. The bitter discussion induced Sidgwick to confide an intention to resign his chair within a short term, a clear sign to J.N. Keynes of 'the low ebb which the Moral Sciences school here has now reached' (JNKD, 25 May 1888).

Metaphysics for Advanced Political Economy students was a victory for Marshall, but in the end it gained him only few additional students for Economics.[18]

During the Senate debates on these changes,[19] Cunningham opposed exemption from Metaphysics for Advanced Political Economy students because these two subjects were interdependent, particularly in a Moral Sciences Tripos where questions of social reform and the individual were so often raised. In addition, he pointed to the fact that students could already concentrate on combining Political Philosophy and Political Economy studies within the recently approved new regulations for the History Tripos, and that as such, the Moral Sciences proposals could be interpreted as a duplication of the History Tripos regulations. Marshall opposed Cunningham with the following arguments. First, the history of economics itself showed the essential independence of Political Economy from Metaphysics. Questions of method were also independent from Metaphysics. Most important, Marshall argued, was the need to create a Political Sciences school like those in the United States, enabling the combination of Political Philosophy with Political Economy studies. Because not all serious Political Economy students wanted to study History, the duplication with the History Tripos Cunningham had mentioned, could not be taken as criticism of the proposed resolutions. He concluded by saying that the Moral Sciences proposals were not completely satisfactory to him. They should basically be regarded as 'a transition stage'. In the Senate debates Sidgwick confirmed what Keynes had recorded: the part of the proposal enabling special provisions for Advanced Political Economy students had been hotly debated at meetings of the Special Board, and should be seen as a compromise which did not necessarily prevent Political Economy students from taking Metaphysics. Sidgwick also expressed agreement with 'Marshall in thinking it probable in the course of a few years . . . to construct a Political Sciences Tripos'. This prompted Marshall's affirmation that 'he had the new Tripos exclusively in view' and saw the present scheme as 'an excellent compromise'. The debate between Marshall and Cunningham has to be seen in the context of their wider conflict about the scope and method of Political Economy and Economic History, which erupted publicly at this time.[20]

The 1889 compromise lasted less than a decade. A further move to separate, and hence enable fuller development of, the 'philosophical' and 'politico-economical' branches of the Tripos was made in a report from the Special Board of Moral Sciences presented to the University Senate in May 1897. Debate over this matter had disrupted discussions at the Moral Sciences Board over the previous three years. The new regulations virtually formalised the separation of Politics and Economics from Philosophy which Sidgwick had foreshadowed in 1889 and which Marshall so strongly supported. They did this by further expanding the opportunities for Moral Sciences students to specialise in Economics. As the Report noted, 'The inclusion of Ethics in Part I of the Tripos' which was proposed, enables 'the Board to add a third paper to the two now set on Political Economy [in Part II], an extension regarded as desirable by the teachers of this subject [Marshall and Foxwell] in order to represent adequately the different parts and aspects of this important study . . . *this change will improve the whole course of preparation gone through by students of Moral Sciences whose bent lies in the direction of Economics*'.[21] The intent of this resolution was to separate Politics and Political Economy formally from Philosophy, Metaphysics, Psychology and Logic in Part II of the Tripos, thereby substantially realising Marshall's ambition to allow students from other Triposes to enter Part II of the Moral Sciences Tripos *as if* it was an Economics and Political Sciences Tripos. The new regulations formally divided Part II of the Tripos into a section dealing with Philosophy, Logic, and Psychology and a second section dealing with Political Philosophy and Political Economy. In the detailed schedule of books and courses for the subjects appended to the proposal, this part was simply divided into Politics and Advanced Political Economy.[22]

The Keynes diaries and Marshall's correspondence provide commentary on the proceedings at the Moral Sciences Board over these changes, which initially appear to have been rather inconclusive. It can be presumed that Marshall quarrelled with Sidgwick, and also with Keynes, Foxwell and other members of the Board. Marshall's letters to Keynes of the mid-1890s reveal his strong dissatisfaction with various aspects of the Moral Sciences Tripos. The number of good students he was attracting was very small, while Marshall complained in addition about the need to rely on non-specialist teachers of the subject, such as Venn and McTaggart, while he was prevented to make use of Flux's services. 'Sanger is the only student (man or women) who has taken up economics for Part II and was really worth teaching. But one Sanger, or even one Bowley, is a good recompense for 5 years work and I am content.'[23] However, a year later he talked enviously of the 400 students Brentano was attracting at Munich, more than half of them from North Germany, when telling Keynes of the manner in which Brentano had weedled 30,000 marks from the Bavarian government for books for students taking his seminar.[24]

At the same time, Foxwell was complaining to Keynes about the excessive emphasis on theory in Cambridge as against discussion of practical questions, and grumbled about low attendance at his lectures.[25] Some years later, he must have taken up this topic with Marshall in correspondence in the context of the debate over the new resolutions for the Tripos at the Moral Sciences Board. In any case, Marshall wrote to him that he did not like subdividing economic studies into theory, history and policy 'because I do not think there is any "theory" to speak of; and analysis is unprofitable when separated from the study of fact'.[26] Over the next few months the friends debated various drafts of the resolutions, resolving their quarrels over the requisite emphasis on history by Marshall's assumption 'that you intend the study of history (past and present) to be analytical'[27] and that Marshall's references to applied economics were the equivalent of Foxwell's use of 'economic policy'.[28]

Correspondence with Sidgwick on the subject has not survived; Keynes's diaries imply that debate over the resolutions in 1896–97 did not repeat the experience of the end of the 1880s, when quarrels between the two Professors had generated so much bitterness during the proceedings.[29] Marshall's absence from the final two meetings, for reasons which are not clear, speeded things up however. The final drafting of the regulations was brought quickly to a satisfactory conclusion once the difficult matters of principle had been resolved to Marshall's satisfaction. Keynes recorded about these two meetings in his diary, that because of Marshall's absence, 'in a little over an hour we got through as much as we generally manage in two long meetings' (3 May 1897) while he noted the final meeting concluded 'at a great rate, after desultory discussions over two or three years' (10 May 1897).

Final stages of the second round of Moral Sciences Board course reform debates coincided with a move for course reform within the History Tripos. This allowed Marshall to support actively a proposal to double the number of Political Economy papers to two for that Tripos thereby enhancing the potential for gaining more students in economics from that source. Although there was support for such a proposal among the historians (Tanner, for example, described the introduction of the two Political Economy papers as 'a great gain'[30]), it attracted relatively little opposition from other History Board members, including on this occasion, Marshall's erstwhile adversary Cunningham. To the contrary, Marshall enjoyed Cunningham's active support on the motions relating to Economics which, Marshall wrote Foxwell, were 'either proposed by him and seconded by me, or vice versa'.[31] Not surprisingly, therefore, Economics made substantial gains within the History Tripos. Part II offered the option of taking two Political Economy papers, both of which had to be attempted by a candidate choosing it; in addition a candidate from another Tripos taking Part II, could supplement this study of Economics with the Economic History papers from Part I. It therefore could no longer be argued, 'that Political Economy was treated cursorily and inadequately' within the History Tripos, 'and no longer suffered if the Examiner was not a specialist'.[32]

In the summary of one of his speeches during the debate given in the *Reporter,*[33] Marshall not only expressed his gratitude for the 'concessions . . . made to the subject in which he was specially interested' but also put forward what he saw as basic principles relevant to general reform of the Triposes. The Report under consideration, he argued, 'was a step towards acknowledging that the old Tripos system needed to be modified . . . so as to meet the requirement of modern study . . . to allow each student to develop his own idiosyncrasy, provided only that whatever work he did was thorough. . . . The true function of University education was to develop a man's faculties that they might continue to develop to the fullest extent in later life; and in this respect though not in all respects, the German system was superior to ours. For it gave the student a freer choice of work and would get more good by spending a year on one special subject like Political Economy than by giving three or four months to each of several subjects.' Similar arguments were to be used when within the next five years Marshall pressed for the complete independence of Economics from the Moral Sciences.

These early expansions of Economics placed heavy burdens on Marshall's personal friendships at Cambridge. The rifts with Sidgwick, begun as soon as Marshall was elected to the chair, were continued with much greater intensity during the debates over reforming the Tripos at the end of the 1880s. After a St John's feast to which Marshall had invited him, Keynes recorded that for much of its duration Marshall had attacked Sidgwick and his course proposals with 'customary exaggeration', adding the following day that Marshall had written to him immediately afterwards to explain his position more fully, presumably from fear of having gone too far in the matter the previous night. 'I have no intention of making an attack on Sidgwick's method of conducting Mo[ral] Sc[ience] Board business, unless I can not help it. Also all my indignation against him is confined to rather narrow area. It is Sidgwick as a university politician and to some extent as a writer on economics that I quarrel with. All the rest of Sidgwick I think as highly of as you do.'[34]

As usual, Keynes left no reaction to Marshall's partial equilibrium approach on the merits of Sidgwick. However, episodes like this meant that he, originally a loyal Marshall henchman, was increasingly having his patience tested by the antics of the Professor of Political Economy at the Board. Earlier during the run-up to the Tripos reforms, Keynes was already diligently recording the steadily growing friction between the senior members of the Moral Sciences Board of which he was Secretary. Keynes's sympathy was generally with Sidgwick, largely because Marshall was 'so narrow and egotistical'.[35]

Marshall's increasing stress on specialisation in Economics because 'a short study of Political Economy seldom does much good and occasionally must do harm',[36] also brought him into conflict with Sedley Taylor, a prominent university, and social, reformer, who was associated at this time with Marshall's own endeavours in the Cooperative Movement and the Society for Industrial Villages. This is visible in an exchange in the pages of the *Cambridge Review*. In it, Sedley Taylor implicitly satirised Marshall's pretensions in favour of specialisation at the university, by citing long excerpts of Mansel's *Phronisterion* written a decade previously to criticise adoption of the German professional system as a way to university reform. Marshall was not mentioned by name. However, Sedley Taylor explicitly disclaimed any intention of disparaging newly appointed staff who deprecated metaphysical and other critical studies, a clear reference to Marshall. Marshall replied to this with a satirical adaptation of his own, drawing on Mansel's *The Dynamics of a Particle*. In this contribution, Marshall sought to deflect Sedley Taylor's arguments as being either outdated or off the point, since no major reforms were intended at this stage in the change of regulations for the Moral Sciences Tripos.[37] Marshall's participation in controversies of this nature may have given him most of the changes in Tripos regulations he wanted. It was not conducive to enhancing his popularity within the university community as a whole, particularly when gaining his own way meant quarrelling with Sidgwick, a popular and widely respected university figure.

Marshall's discontent with the position of Economics at the end of the nineteenth century is concisely presented in a letter to George Darwin, designed to disclose the resource needs of Political Economy in the university to prepare for the coming century. This letter indicates Marshall's ambitions so explicitly, it can be quoted in full:

The width, complexity and thoroughness of economic methods are growing fast, as are those of other sciences. But, further, the subject matter of economics receives every year so great additions that no one person can keep pace with them in all branches of the science. Statistical science is being rapidly developed, both on its theoretical and its administrative sides; and by the comparison of international experiences a body of knowledge is rapidly growing up, which is of the first order as an intellectual training, and gives high promise of practical aid towards progress.

The urgency and all-pervading character of economic problems is shown by the fact that the legislatures and diplomatic officers of all countries of the modern world are now chiefly occupied with economic issues. Many of these are new, and must be solved by our own age for itself. The growing intelligence of the working classes and the spread of a humane spirit among all classes are causing the conditions of life and work of the people to be discussed with new eagerness; and yet what we have so far learnt is but little in comparison with what we are finding out that we ought to learn as to relations between employers and employed, fluctuations of employment, the relief of distress, and the duties of the State in regulating, and in some cases undertaking affairs of public concern. The economic element in all these questions requires patient and thorough study, that they may be handled wisely as well as boldly. To turn to another characteristic of the modern age—the progress of invention and the growth of capital are giving new power to large undertakings; and are removing some trades, especially those connected with transport, beyond the reach of individuals. Railway, electric and other enterprises at home and abroad are already almost wholly in the hands of joint stock companies, Municipalities or the Central Government itself. In old times a business might prosper, because a tradition of good management was handed down, with the business itself, from father to son. But the officials of large public and semi-public undertakings seldom inherit such a tradition; nor would it avail for the new work as fully as it did for the old. The serviceableness of academic investigations has indeed its limits; but a good grounding in economic principles is a helpful preparation for the practical work of administration of all large and especially of public enterprises, and for members of the legislature and of County Councils. It is of assistance also in the work of ministers of religion, and writers of current literature; for they are often called upon to take responsibility in matters of public concern, that are of greater economic difficulty and subtlety than appears at first sight.

In recognition of such facts, economic studies have already been placed in the first rank by the great Universities on the Continent and in America; and form a main route by which many distinguished students proceed to their degree. But in the older English Universities these studies are still relegated to an inferior place; and little encouragement is offered to students of them whether undergraduates or graduates. As a consequence there are not more than forty or fifty undergraduates belonging to each academic year, together with about twenty women students, who do any work at economics in Cambridge (I do not here reckon those who are studying economic history apart from economics); and the provision for teaching is antiquated. There is only one University chair for it; and though at present there is a lectureship in Trinity college on economic history, and one in St John's on economics, yet neither of these posts is permanently endowed. Some members of the University, whose main work lies in other directions, are giving occasional courses on economics or economic history; but there is no scope for a young man to earn a livelihood in Cambridge by preparing himself to deal with the economic problems of the coming generation. This is our most urgent need. In order to deal with the subject adequately in its present stage of development, we need to secure the permanency of our present staff, and to add one or if possible two younger men to devote themselves wholly to economic study and teaching. That is, we need one additonal Professorship or Readership in Economics, and at least one University Lectureship of, say, £200 a year. Even so, Cambridge would be less well equipped not only than Harvard and Yale, but also than some of the younger Universities of America. To take a strong instance; — the Faculty of Political Science at Columbia consists of nineteen Professors and Lecturers; and of these seven belong to the Department of Economics and Social Science; viz., two Professors and one Lecturer in 'Political Economy', one Professor in 'Political Economy and Public Finance', one Professor and one Lecturer in 'Sociology', and one Lecturer in 'Anthropology'. Five of the staff are assigned to Law, Administration and Political Philosophy taken together, and the remaining seven to general History. The courses in Economics and Social Science include, as is the custom in Germany and America, special provision for the study of Railway Problems and other branches of Applied Economics.

A further, but less urgent need, is for an economic library containing about three thousand books arranged round a room, in which advanced students can work under instruction, after the manner of the German Economic Seminar, which has already been well acclimatized in America.[38]

TOWARDS A TRIPOS OF HIS OWN: 1901–1903

Marshall's final steps to create a separate Economics Tripos were not taken until after Sidgwick's death in August 1900. Within a month, Marshall wrote to Keynes in the context of the vacant chairmanship of the Moral Sciences Board caused by Sidgwick's death, that those interested in economics and politics, 'will, I expect, soon sound the University as to the establishment of a Tripos in which those two subjects could have adequate share'.[39] It seemed unfitting to initiate such moves through the Moral Sciences Board, hence the opening gambit for a separate Economics and Politics Tripos was made through the more pliant History Board. On 8 May 1901, Marshall reported to Foxwell that he had been appointed to a committee by the History Board to report on 'how best to extend the study of modern economics and politics in the University'. Its membership consisted of A.W. Ward, the Master of Peterhouse; Lowes Dickinson, a Lecturer in Political Science; and Marshall himself. This letter to Foxwell sets out Marshall's preferred solution to the problem:

> My own hobby now is an entirely separate Tripos, as separate as are the Indian and Semitic triposes; but under the same board with the Historical Tripos as those are both under the Oriental Board. Only I would propose that this board did most of its business in two grand committees, one Historical, the other Economic and Political. The Suzerain Board would have a new title and stand in the same relation to them [the two committees] that the Nat[ural] Sc[ience] board does to its Physical and Biological Grand Committees. Possibly there might be a little economy of papers, some being set simultaneously in the Historical Tripos and the Econ[omics] and Pol[itics] Tripos. But this is a small matter. I am not sure that anything will come of it. Ward (Peterhouse) is not in Cambridge now; and nothing is in course just yet. To explain matters, I incorporated Dickinson's suggestion for the Political Papers with an amended, (perhaps I should say more humbly, 'hashed up') revision of the old scheme which you, Sidgwick, Keynes and I discussed so much some time ago. At the meeting before last, I urged that if our studies were made to give no room for what business men want, we must expect their money to go to new Universities; and we should continue money-starved. I find that some thought I was going for a 'Commercial School'.[40]

Marshall enclosed a draft plan of the proposed new Tripos or economic and political syllabus for Foxwell with the request that he show it to J.N. Keynes.[41] This also disclosed his reasons for seeking the new Tripos. A major purpose was to meet the needs of professional students in economics and politics, as well as the special needs of those intending to seek employment opportunities in parliament or local government bodies, the domestic and the Indian Civil Service, the 'higher work' in public and private business enterprises, or to exercise 'the duties of a country gentleman', and last (but certainly for Marshall not least), to engage in charitable work for 'the poor'. Marshall subsequently developed these themes on the need for creating a curriculum in economics and associated branches of political science in a number of pamphlets and speeches published during 1902 and 1903. The first of these repeated the broad thrust of the argument he had used in his inaugural lecture, about difficulties in teaching economics within the Moral Sciences Tripos, the increasing importance of securing an adequate supply of trained economists and, most importantly, provision of opportunities for persons interested in economics at Cambridge to obtain 'three years' scientific training of the same character and on the same general lines as that given to 'physicists, or physiologists, or engineers'.[42] A subsequent address concentrated on the need for economics education arising from growing complexities in business, the need in labour relations for the training of 'sympathies and the intellect' which economic studies provide, and for wider education on social questions such as housing, charity, and the causes of unemployment.[43]

However, there were other reasons as well for promoting more specialised economics training at Cambridge. Foremost was the need to develop training for the sound, analytical skills required in economists, that is, promoting the ability of 'reasoning'. Reasoning was referred to by Marshall[44] as one of three required skills for good economists, the other two being an ability for 'perception and observation' and the possession of a scientific 'imagination'. Advancement of the ability to reason clearly on complex problems, Marshall observed, was largely associated with the mature approach to study obtained from university education, the most fruitful period during which to induce good scientific and analytical habits of thought. In short, for Economics, absorption of that analytical engine for truth, with which Marshall identified the subject, was a prerequisite for its mastery.[45] As a further, and seemingly equally important reason, Marshall[46] raised the spectre that Cambridge would be left behind in the serious and important business of economics education, if it did not take steps to improve its own facilities for such education on the lines proposed. Because of development elsewhere in England, this was all the more likely if no action were taken in Cambridge at that stage. London had obtained its own School of Economics and Political Science in 1895. Birmingham had established a Faculty of Commerce; the Board of Studies of Owens College at Manchester had just approved establishment of a school of economics and politics and similar steps were under consideration at Oxford. These initiatives had been spurred by the fear that England otherwise would be left further behind American and Continental developments in economics education than was already the case,[*] while Marshall personally doubted that the London, Birmingham, and Manchester developments would address this problem in an appropriate way. His private correspondence on this subject can be usefully explored in this context.

In 1901, Marshall had deplored the relative lack of academic study in England as compared to Germany and America, noting that 'the type of students who fill German and American economic lecture rooms scarcely is to be found here'.[47] He provided no reasons in this letter, nor criticisms of the type of solution to the problem which had been adopted at Birmingham, Manchester and above all, the London School of Economics. However, Marshall was subsequently stung by comments on Cambridge in an official report on the London School of Economics prepared for the Education Department in 1898 by Hewins as the school's first Director. This made him more forthright in his comments both in private conversation with Ashley and in correspondence with Hewins. What particularly annoyed him were the emphasis on economic *theory* in the London School of Economics' scheme of things and the remarks about the state of Cambridge economics teaching Hewins had made in his report and which Marshall saw as rather 'patronising'.[¶] A letter followed, in which Marshall more than hinted at his displeasure about Hewins's remarks, but in which he also

---

[*]   A. Marshall, *A Plea* . . . , p. 11, and cf. the letter to George Darwin quoted above, pp. 539–40. An 1894 British Association Committee Report, 'The Methods of Economic Training Adopted in this and other Countries', had been prepared by William Cunningham, Gonner, Edgeworth, J.N. Keynes and Henry Higgs, and was undoubtedly a catalyst in the tertiary economics education developments just outlined. It clearly assisted, though it did not initiate, the Webbs' plans for setting up a London School of Economics. See Janet Beveridge, *An Epic of Clare Market*, pp. 14–31; and for a detailed discussion of the founding of the school, Sir Sydney Caine, *The History of the Foundation of the London School of Economics and Political Science*, London: G. Bell & Sons, 1963. In the light of Marshall's correspondence with Hewins discussed below (pp. 542–3), it is interesting to note that the 1896–97 calendar of the school lists Marshall among subscribers to funds for its library (see Janet Beveridge, p. 36–7)

[¶]   Hewins had noted that relative to Oxford, Cambridge 'economic studies have been organised up to a certain point with energy and success . . . and the teaching of Cambridge is more systematic and continuous'. Marshall's angry reaction to the Report as witnessed by Ashley was recorded by Hewins in his autobiography, *The Apologia of an Imperialist*, pp. 26–7.

acknowledged there were some faults with the system of economics education prevailing in Cambridge at the time:

> The plain fact is that I have felt rather sore since I read your account of 'the position of Economics in England' in Saddlers Educational Blue Book. Some newspaper reports of public speeches by you had fretted me a little before; but when I read that I felt that I must make a protest, in public or private, sooner or later.
>
> I think it is certain there are virtues in the London School which I do not know of, and you do; and I think it is probable that you know more about its shortcomings than I do. Nor do I blame you in the least for setting forth its merits, and leaving others to find out the deficiencies; some of which are perhaps inseparable from those merits, while others will be removed as the School grows stronger with time.
>
> But while impelled to lay stress on one side of the case as to London, it seems rather hard that you should have laid stress on the other side as regards Cambridge. I gather that you really do not know what is being done here, nor how it is being done. Taking the least important point of all, the number of lectures given, I think you would be astonished if you counted up the number that are given in the year here on subjects of the same order as those treated in the London School; I believe you would find that our number is not less than yours; though of course the proportion of them that are elementary is large; because the average age of our students is low.
>
> But the main point is that Cambridge has an idea of its own which asserts itself in spite of the partially non-Cambridge idiosyncrasies of one or two members of the staff. The incidental work which we do not advertise, but should be compelled to advertise if we were starting a new place like the London School (or to quote my own experience Bristol University College in 1879, where my duties as advertiser in chief were specially onerous) – this incidental work is very great. I regard it as the more important half of my own work; and it is governed very much by a central idea, Cambridge born.
>
> You will say – why then not write a separate and peculiar panegyric of Cambridge? I have sometimes thought that that is what I ought to have done when Saddlers Blue Book appeared. But my personal disinclination for such work, my loathing for it is beyond conception. . . . For one thing I could hardly have fully admitted that Cambridge has the faults that attach to its virtues (as well as others), without implying that in my opinion London also has those faults which attach to *its* virtues.[48]

Follow-up correspondence on the subject suggested that Marshall's motivations arose both from the fact that he was rather 'jealous . . . for Cambridge' and that he feared the London School 'would be "captured" by people acting more or less in alliance with the Fabians [even though he himself was] more in accord with some Fabian opinions and aims than are many other academic economists'.[49] This incident must have made him all the keener to press on with his scheme for separate economics and political science education from both history and the moral sciences. This is confirmed by a letter Marshall wrote to Oscar Browning in 1900. It claimed that Marshall had agreed with Sidgwick that as soon as the London School of Economics started operating, the time had arrived to make similar arrangements for the teaching of economics and politics at Cambridge.[*]

Marshall's plea for a curriculum in economics and associated political sciences had been originally addressed to the University Senate, and subsequently received considerable publicity in the press. A *Times* editorial (18 April 1902) supported Marshall's proposal for a

---

[*] Marshall to Oscar Browning, 8 July 1901, King's College Library (Browning Letters). When Balfour was asked to sign Marshall's petition in favour of setting up a university committee to investigate the new Tripos, his sister, and Henry Sidgwick's widow, Eleanor Sidgwick, asked J.N. Keynes to confirm her late husband, Henry Sidgwick, had been in favour of this proposal, as Marshall was claiming. See Eleanor Sidgwick to J.N. Keynes, 11 March 1902 (Marshall Archive, 2:87).

committee to investigate the implications of giving fuller recognition to the study of economics and politics at Cambridge. It also reported that a petition to this end had been presented to the Council of the Senate signed by many leading members of the university. The Council responded positively on 22 May 1902 by appointing a syndicate (committee) 'to inquire into the best means of enlarging the opportunities for the study in Cambridge of Economics and associated branches of political science'. Membership included the Vice-Chancellor, F.H. Chase, three members of the working party appointed to investigate the matter in 1901 (that is, A.W. Ward, Marshall, and Lowes-Dickinson), J. Westlake, the Whewell Professor of International Law, several teachers in the moral sciences (J.N. Keynes, H.S. Foxwell, Sorley, the new Knightbridge Professor of Moral Philosophy, and McTaggart, College Lecturer in History of Philosophy) and from the History School, Tanner and Leathes (both College Lecturers on Constitutional History), William Cunningham, as well as Edmund H. Parker, M.A., a lawyer and the Cambridge Borough Treasurer at the time.

The appointment of this committee was not universally applauded. In the context of the Cambridge Committee, *The Statist* (31 May 1902) editorialised against economics teaching in the universities, because of the 'utter deficiency of our present professorial system in economics' in which the teachers were 'too academic, too ignorant of real life, too far removed from the matters they treat of'. In a specific criticism of Marshall's pamphlet, it pointed to the contradiction between his view that 'economics is a science of observation' and his proposal 'that the mathematical presentation of economics should be admitted to the scheme of instruction'. The latter was part and parcel in Marshall's plan to inculcate proper methods of reasoning and analysis into economics students.[50]

Marshall's proposal for the new Tripos had therefore to be defended on a number of fronts. First, it had to be sold to his colleagues on the committee from the Moral Sciences with a strong interest in economics – Keynes and Foxwell. Disputes with Foxwell are visible in the Marshall Foxwell correspondence and dealt with the relative importance to be assigned to economic history and other historical subjects in the syllabus. They also concerned the continuing role, if any, of psychological studies in the new Tripos[*] and the relative importance to be assigned to politics. Disputes with Keynes appear to have been even greater. Keynes's diaries recorded his hostility to the new proposal when he first heard of it (31 January 1902), and gleefully noted that Marshall made a particularly bad impression at the first meeting of the committee (29 May 1902).[¶]

The proceedings of the Committee itself were arduous. For example, six months after its commencement, it circulated for the benefits of its members a number of resolutions on

---

[*] Marshall to Foxwell, January/February 1902 (Marshall Archive, 3: 43–46). The view on psychology is expressed in the letter dated 19 January 1902: 'Psychology is weaker as a science than economics, and economics is too young and weak to carry them'. This sentiment is in sharp contrast with opinions which Marshall expressed later on the relative strengths of these two social sciences, recorded previously (see Chapter 5 above, pp. 127–8; Chapter 19, p. 729 n.¶).

[¶] Correspondence (J.N. Keynes to Marshall, 29 January 1902; Marshall to J.N. Keynes, 30 January, 1902), suggests part of the disagreement arose from Marshall's too strong an emphasis on the factual, or 'inductive' side of economics, which Keynes thought misplaced for an undergraduate degree. The continuing role for economics in Part I of the Moral Sciences Tripos was also an issue, as was Marshall's general hostility to that Tripos for its treatment of Economics. The last matters are further discussed below, pp. 547–8.

which it had agreed in principle by 12 November, roughly six months after its initial appointment These numbered no less than sixteen, and in general covered issues of principle rather than detail. Such issues of principle included that Part I should have no options; that a limited specialisation in economics should be encouraged in Part II, and specific recommendations on the desirable number of papers in various subjects.[51] The Committee's final report, dated 4 March 1903, was a majority one. William Cunningham and McTaggart had refused to sign it, largely on the ground that the university catered adequately for economics teaching, apart from the provision of teaching staff which they thought should be gradually increased when circumstance permitted.[52] When the happy event occurred that there was finally sufficient agreement on the Committee to have a majority report signed, Keynes recorded his great relief that the trying business about economics was almost at an end. His diary reflects little of the nature of his later disputes with Marshall. The need to have a compulsory International Law component was one matter of dispute between them, they quarrelled over the role of Logic, while the impression Keynes gave that he saw the Economics Tripos Committee as an administrative bore rather than a major intellectual struggle, would have given further cause for friction between the two former close colleagues.[53]

Marshall's struggle for the new Tripos also gained him new supporters. Loyal assistance for his cause came from Lowes Dickinson, a strong advocate for his own 'special subject of political science'. Lowes Dickinson proved very useful in the final debate over the report, when he strongly argued the merits of the new scheme with the historians. When the new Tripos was established, he became the first secretary of the Economics Board, replacing J.N. Keynes who initially preferred to stay with his friends on the Moral Sciences Board.[54]

Reasons for the major opposition to the new Tripos from within the History School were similar to those offered by Cunningham in the context of the 1889 proposals to alter the Moral Sciences Tripos curriculum. This was revealed after the publication of the Report of the Economics and Political Science syndicate particularly during the full debate it produced in the University Council during May.[55] Before examining their critique, the contents of the committee's report can be briefly summarised.

Its preamble bears the unmistakable stamp of Marshall as shown by its resemblance to arguments he had published in the previous year. The proposed syllabus outline reveals he had been forced to accept some compromises. Part I of the proposed new Tripos consisted of three compulsory papers on Economic Principles, as well as two on General and Economic History, one on Constitutional Law and one on Essay Questions. Part II provided for no less than seven papers on General and Advanced Economics, one on Modern Political Theories, two on International Law, and two on legal principles as well as optional papers on a special subject of an applied nature to be approved by the Special Board of Studies.[56] The Economics Board was to include the Knightbridge Professor of Moral Philosophy, the Regius Professor of Modern History, the Downing Professor of the Laws of England, the Professor of Political Economy, the Whewell Professor of International Law and the Reader in Geography *ex officio*, as well as the examiners appointed for the current and last preceding year and five elected from the Senate to serve for five years.[57]

In addition to their participation in the formal debate, the historians' attack on the new Tripos was conducted in flysheets, articles, and letters in the *Cambridge Review*. Most active in this opposition was Marshall's former antagonist, William Cunningham, who produced several flysheets, a humorous interview in the *Cambridge Review* and opened the debate for the opposition in the Council's debate on the Syndicate Report. Cunningham queried the need for early and 'excessive' specialisation in economics as intended under the new Tripos, its claimed usefulness for business, the adequacy of library facilities to support serious research work in economics, and he expressed fears that the Tripos would rapidly develop into one devoted *exclusively* to economics. Last, but not least, he worried about the detrimental effects a specialist Economics Tripos would have on students taking economics subjects in the existing History and Moral Sciences Triposes.* McTaggart, Marshall's former student and teaching assistant, and like Cunningham a dissenting member of the Economics Tripos Committee, largely saw the Tripos as an unnecessary waste of resources. Opportunities for increased study of economics could have been just as satisfactorily created by allowing students to take Part I of the History Tripos followed by a modified Part II of the Moral Sciences Tripos. He also wondered where the finance for the new Tripos would come from and expressed fears about maintaining independence in economics teaching if substantial monetary gifts were provided by business interests. McTaggart's objections contained an implicit attack on Marshall's intransigence; in his view the report 'was based on the principle that *economics should give up nothing*' (McTaggart, pp. 768–9, my italics). Others opposed the new Tripos because economics lacked real complexity (Mayo, *ibid.*, p. 771); or because the subjects for the new Tripos were ill-defined, and without sound foundations (Gwatkin, pp. 771–2). Lowes Dickinson (pp. 772–3), while conceding that a new Tripos as such was redundant if changes could have been made to the existing History Tripos, argued that opposition to such changes from the History Board made the new Tripos the only practical means to secure greater analytical teachings of economic and political sciences at Cambridge.

Although other distinguished members of the Council, including the Vice-Chancellor, supported the proposal, Marshall, needless to say, provided the major reply to the opposition. This largely repeated his arguments on the wider social needs for economists and the importance of economics as a scientific area for university studies akin to physics and mathematics. Marshall recounted how his attempts of nearly two decades to teach economics within the existing Moral Sciences Tripos had been a failure for reasons he had foreshadowed in his inaugural lecture in 1885. He also referred to the overwhelming support of expert opinion his proposal had received. Apart from the view on the subject from eminent business leaders, politicians, and churchmen which Marshall had earlier circulated to the Senate[58] he indicated the signatories on a memorandum supporting his proposal as including the names of Courtney, Leslie Stephen, Roby, J.B. Mayor, Cunynghame, Nicholson, Flux, Bowley, Chapman, Aves, Wynnard Hooper, Moulton, Sanger, Clapham, Llewellyn-Davies as well as several distinguished Cambridge moralists such as Lyttleton (late Bishop of Southampton), and Caldecott, Professor of Logic and

---

* Page references and names in brackets in the remainder of this paragraph refer to participants in the debate as reported in the *Cambridge University Reporter*, pp. 763–74.

Moral Philosophy at London. The last part of Marshall's speech almost sounded like a threat. If Cambridge refused 'to do what businessmen required', then their sons would enter the new universities and Cambridge would regret this step in time when 'the rising generation of wealthy business became the loyal sons of the newer and not the older Universities'.[59]

Prior to the decisive Senate vote the debate continued with the publication of a series of flysheets from leading spokesmen for the two sides. Again opposition was concentrated in the History School which suggested a revised second part for the History Tripos as an alternative opportunity for specialisation in Economics. This argument was rebutted by Marshall in a flysheet released the day before the Senate vote was taken. Once again he appealed to the members of the university to grant students the right of three years specialisation in studying Economics and associated Political Sciences in a Tripos of their own. The previous day Pigou had joined Marshall in pressing this argument in an article opposing a History Tripos solution to the problem of economics education at Cambridge because it failed to provide the additional time the serious study of Economics required as the necessary safeguard against superficiality in such studies.[60] The Senate on 6 June 1903 approved the new Tripos's establishment with a strong vote. Most of the necessary resolutions were passed unopposed after two had passed with substantial majorities.[61] Marshall's battle for the independent status of economics studies at Cambridge for which he had been continuously fighting since his return to the university in 1885, was therefore successfully concluded.

The final push to the separate Tripos once again cost Marshall dearly in personal friendships. It has already been suggested that massive inroads were made on the goodwill Marshall still enjoyed with Foxwell and Keynes, because of the high demands his moves had been making on them. The breach with Keynes was most visible. Keynes stayed on as Secretary for the Moral Sciences Board, enabling Lowes Dickinson to become the Economics Board's Secretary. It also cost him the friendship of former student, McTaggart, once 'half won for economics', as Marshall had boasted to Keynes some years before and who, for three years, had officially assisted Marshall in his teaching duties by correcting the general papers in Political Economy. McTaggart as member of the Moral Sciences Board, moved on 19 October 1903 that Political Economy should be removed from the syllabus of Part I of the Moral Sciences Tripos. Earlier, and before the Senate vote on the new Tripos proposal had been taken, the Moral Sciences Board had removed Political Economy from Part II of the Tripos syllabus while Marshall was in the chair, part of the agreed price to be paid for the new Tripos.[62]

Although removal of Political Economy from Part II of the Moral Sciences Tripos syllabus had been agreed if a new Tripos was created, this was not the case for Part I. If Political Economy was removed from Part I of the Tripos, as McTaggart proposed in October 1903, the potential loss of students was especially serious, because this foreclosed an opportunity for Part I students to transfer to Part II of the Economics Tripos when they had successfully completed their Part I examinations. The day after McTaggart had given notice to the Moral Sciences Board that he intended to move such a motion, Marshall wrote to Keynes about tactics to combat this move. Not long after, by counting potential votes, Marshall wrote to Keynes that the situation did not look promising.[63] When McTaggart's resolution came up for discussion a fortnight later, the economics teachers represented on the Board unsuccessfully attempted its defeat by moving amendments. The first of these, moved by Keynes and Foxwell, was defeated by 4 votes to 3; a subsequent amendment by Marshall and Foxwell was defeated by 5 votes to 2; McTaggart's resolution then won 4 votes to 2, with two abstentions. Keynes was presumably among the abstentions on the final vote, with Foxwell and Marshall voting against.[64] As a consequence of this defeat, Marshall argued that the moral sciences at Cambridge should be redefined as 'Logic, Psychology, Ethics and Philosophy'.[*] This also effectively ended Marshall's long association with that Board, begun in 1868, two decades from its original foundation, and only interrupted when Marshall had been in Bristol and Oxford from 1877 to 1884.

Added to this loss in friendships, Marshall had made an enormous sacrifice in time for this cause. Apart from sitting on two special committees set up for the purposes of discussing a new Tripos, he wrote several pamphlets in its furtherance and addressed a number of meetings. Moreover, on his own account, he wrote hundreds of letters canvassing support from members of the university in order to secure the Senate vote and, more generally, to sway opinion in his favour, from outside interested parties. These included the thirty business, church and political leaders whose support he had solicited, and whose approval of the Tripos proposals he reported to the Senate. Coming on top of the many interruptions to his writing of a second volume to the *Principles* during the 1890s, this final effort for the Tripos may have given the final deathblow to that project as well. His embarkation in 1903 on an almost equally lengthy quest for a more separate and self-standing 'second' volume in any case coincided with the Tripos victory.[65] However, when seen as fulfilling the ambition of close to two decades, the costs were worth it, even though the expected fruits from the new Tripos were slow in coming and only became really visible during the final years of Marshall's life.

The last point cannot be stressed too much. In notes she prepared for a talk to economics students many years later, Mary Paley described the establishment of the Tripos as Marshall's 'great achievement', after deleting an earlier judgement that it was 'his *main* achievement'. The growing importance of Economics made its specialised, and hence separate, treatment imperative and entailed the impossibility of continuing to teach it effectively as part of either the Moral, or even the Historical Tripos. In this context, Mary Paley also recalled a lecture Marshall had given in which she claimed he had argued, 'Practically all that is economically important is less than 150 years old. $9/10^{th}$ is less than 80. ¾ is less than 25'.[66] Not surprisingly, she likewise recalled the struggle to establish the new Tripos as an arduous one but, in typical fashion, recalled that amidst all the arguments and debate of the fly sheets, Cambridge had preserved its sense of humour. Nor, even at the late stage of a few weeks before the crucial vote was taken in the Senate, had the residents of Balliol Croft lost theirs. Mary Paley records they had been greatly amused by an item published in the *Cambridge Review* summarising the case in opposition to the Tripos. This

---

[*]   Marshall to J.N. Keynes, 17 October 1903 (Marshall Archive, 1:133), in which, given the membership of the Board he implied the removal of Political Economy from the moral sciences was a foregone conclusion. When the matter came before the University Senate, Marshall mentioned the narrow vote and the fact that all economics teachers on the Board had voted against it. He particularly stressed the error in removing Political Economy from Part I of the Tripos (*Cambridge University Reporter*, 13 February 1904, p. 540).

forms a suitable finale to discussion of what, in the long run, can be seen as Marshall's main, because it was the greatest, achievement, preparing the way for a distinctive Cambridge School of Economics:

OPPOSITION ARGUMENTS [to the Economics Tripos]

1. That the proposal is a new one.
2. That it is therefore a bad one.
3. That it is asked for by people outside.
4. That it is not asked for by people outside.
5. That if it were, that would be all the more reason why they should not have it.
6. That the members of the Syndicate are amiable and well-meaning people.
7. That the members of the Syndicate are ————
8. That the British Constitution is nothing if not ancient.
9. That the middle class is being squeezed out of existence.
10. That all Political Economy is contained in Mr. Gladstone's speeches. Or if not, why not?
11. That there is really a great deal in what Dr. M —— says.
12. That the proposed Tripos is too narrow.
13. That it is too broad.
14. That it is too practical.
15. That it is not practical enough.
16. That the University is poor.
17. That it would be very dangerous to do anything that might tend to attract endowments to the University.
18. That Mr. Carnegie never studied Economics.
19. Neither did Mr. Pierpont Morgan.
20. That —— is a genius, and his opinions must therefore be worthless.
21. That —— is not a genius, and his opinions must therefore, &c.
22. That there ought to be a comma after the word —— in Regulation —— line ——.
23. That Economics ought to be spelled with a small e.
24. That people are more interested in their souls than in their stomachs.
25. That if they aren't they ought to be.
26. That you can't arrange one student in three classes.
27. That if you could, he would be none the better for it.
28. That everyone would take the new Tripos.
29. That no one would take it.
30. That anyhow we aren't going to be bullied by any Syndicate. That we intend to vote against this, and any other scheme that might be brought forward. But that no one is more anxious than we are that the study of Economics should be developed in the University. And that altogether it's a great pity.[67]

MANAGING AND ENJOYING THE NEW TRIPOS: 1903–1908

Marshall's victory in his battle for the Tripos was formally acknowledged by the University at the start of the 1903–4 academic year:

The Senate in the Easter term confirmed the recommendation of the Economics and Political Science syndicate that a Tripos (consisting of two parts) in 'Economics and Associated Branches of Political Science' should be instituted and a Special Board established to superintend these Studies. This provision for the fuller recognition of these subjects is a proof that the University is alive to the obligation which rests on it, as a place of education and as a place of research, to modify and supplement its curricula in accordance with the conditions of modern life.[68]

On 21 October 1903, a Special Board in Economics was duly appointed, consisting of the Knightbridge Professor of Moral Philosophy (Sorley), the Regius Professor of Modern History (J.R. Bury), the Downing Professor of the Laws of England (Maitland), the Professor of Political Economy (Marshall), the Whewell Professor of International Law (J. Westlake), the Reader in Geography (H.Y. Oldham), the four current and four previous year examiners, as well as five members of the Senate. The first board meeting had, however, been held on 15 June 1903, within a fortnight from the vote in the Senate establishing the Tripos. It elected A.W. Ward, the Master of Peterhouse as its first chairman and Lowes Dickinson as its first secretary, both members together with Marshall, it will be recalled, on the syndicate appointed by the History Board in 1901 to first investigate the matter.[69]

This, and subsequent meetings of the Board during 1903, also accepted an offer to finance a lectureship of £100 for three years from the Girdlers' Company, resolved that Advanced students should only be permitted to attempt the second part of the Tripos, published book and lecture lists for the courses proposed, and amended the regulations of the Adam Smith Prize to take account of its existence by substituting references to the Economics and Politics Board for that of the Moral Sciences. A Marshallian touch is visible on the new Board when it adopted the principle that the *Reporter* should announce which teachers in the new Tripos were making themselves available at home at specified periods for special tuition.[70]

The first Girdler lecturer to be appointed was Pigou, who had obtained a first in Part II of the Moral Sciences Tripos in 1900, after completing Part I of the History Tripos the year before. In 1902, when commenting on Pigou's Fellowship Dissertation at King's, Marshall had described it as a work of 'exceptional excellence'. Some months after Pigou's appointment to the Economics Lectureship, Marshall strongly defended his economic qualifications on the basis of his work in the subject for the second part of the Moral Sciences Tripos, denying any influence on Pigou from Cunningham's Economic History.[71] Earlier, Marshall had employed Pigou as a teacher of Economics for the Moral Sciences Board, much to the disgust of Foxwell, paying him a salary of £100 per annum out of his own pocket.[*] Pigou's appointment as Girdler lecturer was renewed in 1906. When the university's report for formal approval of renewal of the Girdler gift was debated, Marshall used the occasion to complain about the lack of financial support his new Tripos was receiving. Apart from his own salary as Professor, and Foxwell's salary as St John's lecturer, no university or college support was provided for its teaching, which was either done voluntarily or based on work already done for other Triposes.[72]

The business of the Board for the next two years was routine, preparing lecture lists, approving examiners, obtaining reports from the Professor on the exercise of his teaching responsibilities, amending resolutions when required and co-opting new members such as

---

[*] JNKD, 20 May 1901; on 22 May 1901 Marshall wrote to Keynes, 'Pigou couldn't duplicate him (Foxwell), and he (Foxwell) had never done what I hope Pigou will ultimately do. Pigou and I only care for the men; and I think I may truly say, for the men only, Foxwell does not seem to be able to understand this sort of aim' (Marshall Archive, 1:125). And see below, Chapter 18, p. 676 n.*.

H.D. Macgregor in February 1906. There were occasional quarrels, as over the arrangements of material in Economics and General History, in which division by countries into three classes – United Kingdom, United States and British dependencies, continental Europe – was adopted on the motion of Marshall and Lowes Dickinson, against the more chronological approach favoured by Foxwell. The breach with the Moral Sciences Board which had removed political economy from its Part I under opposition from Marshall, Foxwell and Keynes, resulted in a transfer of economics books from its library to a new economics and politics library, originally housed with the History collection. At the end of 1906, when A.W. Ward, the foundation chairman of the Economics Board declined re-election, Marshall was elected to its chairmanship, the first time he was to act in this capacity on a Special Board of Studies in his long academic career.[73]

Marshall's tenure as Chairman of the Economics Board lasted for only eighteen months. Over the 1906–7 academic year covered by his chairmanship, the Board resolved the following. It created an economics sub-committee from among its members in January 1907. More importantly, the Economics Board continually drew the attention of the General Board of Studies of the university to the paucity of resources made available to it. Unlike the position of the moral sciences, no lectureships in economics were supported from university or college funds. The Economics Board also requested a lecture room exclusively for its own use, expressing the hope that 'ultimately' it would need exclusive access to three such rooms. In addition, the Board required a 'large lecture room' to use when it arranged lectures of general interest open to the public. This last request was probably inspired by the fact that a series of such lectures on 'Rent, Profits and Wages in Agriculture, and their bearing on rural Population' given by J.S. Nicholson, had to be held in the university's Chemical Laboratories over four nights in May.[74] The Board further hinted at its poor resources by indicating its departmental library had to be combined with that of history to ensure its survival.[75] There is less to record of note for the one full academic year of 1907–8 with Marshall in the chair. Apart from Marshall's re-election to the position as chairman at the start of the academic year and his resignation as Professor in May 1908, attendance recorded for these meetings reflected some growth in the small lecturing staff for the Economics Tripos despite the lack of support given by the university. From May 1907, Benians and Fay joined its deliberations as lecturers for courses in the Tripos.[76]

Much business of the Board was of course devoted to book and lecture lists. The former are sampled in the Appendix,[77] the lecture lists are worthy of more detailed examination. That for Economics and Politics in 1904–5 listed five lecturers in Economics, four concentrating on Economic History, two on political subjects and one each on Economic Geography and General History, a total of thirteen lecturers in all. Most of these were either college lecturers or university lecturers from other Triposes. Exceptions were the Professors, of whom Marshall at that stage was the only one located within the Economics Board, and Pigou as the incumbent of the special Girdlers' lectureship. Marshall lectured that year on 'Credit and Speculation' in Michaelmas term, and on 'Problems of Modern Industry' and 'Problems in Interpreting Economic Statistics' in Lent term; Foxwell lectured in Michaelmas term on the 'Economics of Industry' and gave an 'Introduction to Nineteenth Century Economic History', while in Lent term he lectured on the 'English Classical

Economists' and 'Currency and Banking'; Johnson, the logic teacher in the moral sciences with Keynes, taught the 'Diagrammatic treatment of Pure Economic Theory' in Easter term; Green, a Caius College lecturer, taught Elementary Political Economy for the whole year; while Pigou taught a course on Economics not suitable for beginners and a general course on the Economics of Foreign Trade. Economic History was taught by Archbold, a university lecturer from History, who lectured on English Economic History over two terms; Meredith, who taught Economic and General History of Europe; Benians, whose lectures covered Economic and General History of British Colonies and Dependencies; and Macgregor who handled English and American Trade and Finance from 1800. Lectures on political subjects were given by Thornley and Lowes Dickinson; Oldham taught Economic Geography and Head lectured on General History Since 1815.[78]

The 1905–6 academic year saw few major changes in this list. Macgregor changed his lecture topic to 'The Economic Development of England from 1800'; Cunningham was listed (for that year only) as a Trinity College lecturer in both Political Economy and General History for three and two terms respectively; Sorley (from the Moral Sciences) gave one lecture a week in Michaelmas term on 'Ethics and Economics'; while Marshall lectured on Advanced Economics (3 lectures a week) for the whole year, with a special class, 'on analytical difficulties' given on Saturday mornings. This was the heaviest teaching load Marshall had ever experienced in terms of formal teaching hours, and thereby assists in explaining his bitter complaints that year about the very inadequate teaching resources for economics the university and the colleges were providing.[*]

In 1906–7, Marshall slightly reduced his lecturing load by dropping the special class on analytical difficulties (which Pigou took over), lecturing three times a week on 'National Industries and Trade' in Michaelmas term, with similar hours for lecturing on Applied Economics during the other two terms. Foxwell, who had dropped his lectures on the Classical Economists the year before, substituted a course on General Economics in Michaelmas term, continued for the subsequent two terms by Macgregor. In addition, Foxwell maintained his long-established courses on Currency and Banking and on the Introduction to Nineteenth Century English Economic History. In Michaelmas term, Macgregor taught 'Industrial Combination', while Benians added a course on American Economic History to his teaching load.[79]

The whole of Marshall's final year of teaching as Professor of Political Economy was devoted to Applied Economics. Other teaching for the Tripos during 1907–8 remained much as it had been in the previous year. Exceptions included Macgregor's Michaelmas lectures, changed for that year to deal with 'Competition and Association', and extended into the following term. There were also two new lecturers in Economic History to replace Head's more general lectures on the topic given in previous years. In Lent term, Wood (a Jesus College lecturer) lectured twice weekly on Recent English Economic History and

*   *Cambridge University Reporter*, 10 June 1905, p. 1014. In the debate occasioned by the report formally accepting the Girdlers' Company's offer to finance a lectureship mentioned previously, during which Marshall so bitterly complained about the inadequate provision of teaching resources for the new Tripos, he was also taunted by Jackson (a bitter opponent of the new Tripos), about the presence of Cunningham on the lecture list, a listing which Marshall assured Jackson was strictly for that year only and not sanctioned by the Economics Board. *Cambridge University Reporter*, 22 May 1906, pp. 960–61.

Theory; while C.R. Fay (a King's College lecturer) took twice weekly classes on English Economic History in the Nineteenth Century during Lent and the final term.[80] Hence, by the time Marshall left the care of the new Tripos to others, its teaching resources position had improved hardly at all.*

It can also be noted that student numbers for the new Tripos showed little improvement in these years relative to what the situation had been before 1903. This was in line with Cunningham's prediction that the new Tripos would make little difference to numbers of economics students enrolled at Cambridge.[81] A letter by Marshall to the Clerk (Secretary) of the Worshipful Company of Girdlers,[82] reporting on the use made of its donation for economics teaching, recorded student numbers for the first five years of the Tripos as follows:

	Part I	Part II	Total
1905	10		10
1906	4	3	7
1907	8	5	13
1908	8	9	17
1909	11	13	24

More details can be provided than numbers. The 1905 class was evenly divided between students of both sexes, recorded no first class result for Part I, one man and one woman in the first division of the second class, with two students from both sexes in the second division and the third class honours list. These unexciting results were undoubtedly discussed at the first Economics Tripos dinner attended by Keynes, Dickinson, Clapham and Pigou as examiners, in the presence of the Tanners, the Sorleys, Macgregor, Miss McArthur and Miss Ethel Glazebrook. The Marshalls were represented by Mary Paley Marshall, her husband probably absent for reasons associated with his by then long-standing practice not to accept outside dinner invitations.[83]

Prospects for the second year of the new Tripos looked even grimmer, as the raw numbers disclose. No wonder Marshall attempted so arduously that year to recruit Maynard Keynes, a fresh 12th Wrangler, to sit for Part II of the Tripos. John Neville Keynes was recording prodigious efforts on the part of his son in economics that June in connection with Marshall's *Principles*, and some months later, on Cournot's *Recherches*, while Maynard himself reported to Lytton Strachey in July he was reading 'masses of economics'. Among this, he had discovered someone he had previously not 'realised to be very good – namely Jevons . . . one of *the* minds of the century . . . with his "Investigations into Currency and Finance", a most thrilling volume'.[84] During Michaelmas term, Keynes was attending Marshall's lectures on advanced economics, and his enthusiasm for the subject became such that his father recorded in November, 'Maynard does a good deal of work for Marshall, who describes some of his answers as brilliant. I am afraid Marshall is endeavouring to persuade

---

* The Worshipful Company of Girdlers initially provided the only outside funds for teaching; the Girdlers' Lectureship it financed was in turn held by Pigou, Meredith, J.M. Keynes, and Lavington. In addition Marshall (and on his retirement, Pigou) used their own money to finance one, and sometimes two lectureships in economics. The first University Lectureship in Economics was created in 1911, the second not until 1923.

him to give up everything for Economics.'[85] To confirm such fears, Marshall wrote to J.N. Keynes in early December, 'Your son is doing excellent work in Economics. I have told him I should be greatly delighted if he should decide on the career of a professional economist. But of course I must not press him',[86] a sure sign that Marshall was doing just that.

Keynes's brief period of study in economics for Part II of the Economics Tripos is amply documented in the Keynes Papers. These include some notes from his attendance at Marshall's lectures in Michaelmas term 1905 consistent with Keynes's later remark that it was impossible to bring coherent notes back from them. This is especially evident in the single page of notes he extracted from a lecture on economics and mathematics, but less so for notes taken on 'Trade and Industry' which mention that Marshall discussed List's theory, Knies's 'corrections' of that theory, followed by Marshall's own 'corrections' of these German theorists of economic progress. The notes also indicate that Marshall discussed shifts in industrial leadership in this context, expressing regrets about British relative industrial decline, partly blamed on its poor facilities for education of business relative to Germany. A substantial number of question papers which Keynes prepared for Marshall have been preserved. As he also subsequently recalled, these were amply covered by Marshall's red ink corrections. Topics included 'Malthus and emigration', national income accounting, the cost of houseroom, estimating national prosperity by either wealth or income, variations in national employment, machinery and low wages, index numbers, modern business methods, monopoly pricing and capital theory. A number of Keynes's answers to questions on 'pure economics', drawn from the 1905 Tripos papers, have also survived. These dealt, among other things, with the stability of equilibrium, international values, long versus short periods and tax incidence. Marshall's comments reveal his increasing admiration for this gifted pupil, hence explaining his enormous regret when Keynes decided to abandon his studies for the Tripos by the end of the year.[87]

John Neville Keynes, on the other hand, recorded with some relief by the end of 1905 that Maynard was switching from economics to start preparation for the Civil Service Examinations. Marshall reluctantly accepted this situation only by May 1906, that is, not long before the Tripos examinations actually started.* By that time, Marshall may have felt himself compensated by a strong candidate in Part I of the Tripos, Walter Layton, whose first class was recorded in June 1906. Layton went on to take a first in the second part the following year, thereby marking Marshall's only male first class result while he himself was involved in teaching for the Economics Tripos.[88]

With the exception of Layton's results, there were few bright sparks among the students in Marshall's last two years of teaching for the Tripos. As Head of the Board of Examiners, John Neville Keynes recorded in June 1907 that on reading the papers in economics for Part I of the Tripos, he judged 'much of the work [to be] poor in the extreme', while after the

---

*   See D.E. Moggridge, *Maynard Keynes, An Economist's Biography*, pp. 95–7. As late as May 1906, within a fortnight before the examinations, Marshall had tried to cajole Keynes into sitting for Part II, stating 'you would probably get a first class, and that if you did not you would not injure your position, since it would be known, you had very little time for economics. But I must say no more' (Marshall to Keynes, 2 May 1906, King's College, Keynes Papers, L/M/41). He later tempted Keynes to enter for the Cobden Prize, which Keynes declined and it was not until 1909 that Keynes joined the economics teaching staff after a period in the Indian Civil Service. See below, Chapter 20, pp. 756–8 and for other aspects of Marshall's relations with Maynard Keynes, Chapter 6, pp. 162–3, Chapter 13, pp. 468, 480-2, Chapter 17, pp. 621, 643–5.

actual examiners' meeting four days later he described 'much of the work of Part I [as] quite extraordinarily bad'.* Keynes left no comment on the two students from Newnham who gained first division, second class results for Part I that year, and who annoyed Marshall so much the following year when in 1908 they gained first class results in Part II of the Tripos.¶

Marshall's own class lists for these final years based on the enrolment forms he asked students to complete show the rather mixed lot of students he was teaching. The fifteen students who commenced his economics classes at the start of the 1906–7 academic year contained one second class honours mathematics student from Cambridge; one first class Part I History Tripos student; one Moral Science Tripos Part I student; four students with satisfactory results in either the previous, or the inter-collegiate examinations; two London graduates and a number of foreign students with no recorded qualifications. The last included a Hélène Freudenberg, who honestly declared to her learned Professor, 'I am living in England for a few months and have been told it would be a great advantage to hear some of your lectures, but I have not made any special study of economics'.[89]

The number of starters in Marshall's classes had risen to 21 by 1907–8. They included a 16th wrangler, two students who had completed the Natural Sciences Tripos, two who had done likewise in Part I of the Classical Tripos and two from the History Tripos, six students who were moving to Part II of the Economics Tripos following success in Part I, as well as a number of students who had qualified through the normal entrance examinations or who, coming from abroad, qualified with degrees from universities in their own country, as did a Count Tizza with a Budapest Law degree.[90] With the exceptions noted, major successes from the new Tripos did not come until after Marshall's retirement and, more generally, when numbers started to increase after the First World War had ended.[91]

When required to do so, Marshall could put an optimistic face on relative set-backs in the progress of his Tripos of the type recorded in the previous paragraphs. He did so in his report on the Tripos to the Girdlers' Company a year after his retirement. This covered staffing issues as well as student numbers and, on the basis that if quality in both could be maintained, argued this would 'make the Cambridge School of Economics second to none in the world'.[92] Marshall was particularly pleased in this letter to report that King's College had attracted Clapham back to Cambridge, to strengthen economic history teaching as 'one of the very few living men who can treat in a masterly way the economic history of recent years'. Favourable expectations for students were founded on a record enrolment of 20 students preparing for Part I of the Tripos in 1910, while altogether 50 students were attending lectures by the economics staff, of whom ten were candidates for the Civil Service Examinations.[93]

A year later, a letter to E.S. Roberts, the Master of Caius and then Vice-Chancellor, recorded the progress of the Tripos as 'splendid' and more rapid than the experience of

---

* JNKD, 7 June and 11 June 1906. The two women students, Grier and Spielmann, as well as C.K. Hobson, were classed in the examinations as Class II, Division 1. All three continued their economics studies by taking Part II of the Tripos the following year.

¶ Fay's anecdote of Marshall's reaction to this result was recorded above (Chapter 8, p. 258); Macgregor, one of the examiners and the person who was asked to deliver the results to Marshall, recalls that because the only 'firsts were two women', he 'did not dare to linger when [Marshall] himself came to the door' on delivering the results as requested. D.H. Macgregor, 'Marshall and his Book', *AMCA*, II, p. 115. Grier's reaction to Marshall's teaching was reported in a previous chapter (Chapter 10 above, pp. 321, 324).

earlier new Triposes suggested. Marshall attributed this to 'the conspicuous ability and energy of its young staff', under-resourced and underpaid though it was, and to the demands made on its studies by businessmen and managers in private and municipal enterprises, and by the 'growing number of persons who hope to be officers of Charity Organisation Societies, Inspectors of Homes for Municipal Authorities' or to enter 'other forms of social work which bring the various classes of the nation into a mutual understanding'. Under the circumstances, Marshall could only describe it as deplorable that the Professor (Pigou) had to use a third of his income to finance lecturers from his own pocket, and that such low remuneration threatened the university's ability to retain the best of its economics staff. Despite this, the 'establishment of a connection between the studies of Cambridge and the responsibilities of after years' indicated for Marshall 'that the seed sown here may spring into full and generous life later on, instead of being dried and put by as it were, in a cabinet of memories of early life'.[94] There is no evidence that Marshall ever regretted the steps he had taken in advancing the study of economics in the manner he did, as he had foreshadowed in 1885 at the start of his career as Professor at Cambridge.

Marshall not only defended his Tripos to those who, like the Girdlers, had been among its benefactors or, like Vice-Chancellors, had it in their power to offer valuable support. In 1905, stung by some comment in the *Times* which claimed England was doing relatively little for the education of businessmen and Cambridge even less, Marshall wrote a number of letters to the editor to explain what Cambridge was, and was not, doing in this context. The first (23 November 1905) reminded the *Times* of the services it had rendered in 1902 in setting up the new Tripos, when it had supported the establishment of a committee for that purpose. The letter explained that its syllabus was geared to providing both practical, and more general, economic studies at which 'academic and business students work together'. Marshall also claimed that during its third year of operations, 'more sons of business men' than in the previous two years were preparing to enter for the Tripos, while there were other indicators of the high regard in which this course of study was held by the business community as well. These included the lectureship financed by the Girdlers' Company, the scholarship offered by Sir Henry Buckley for students from Merchants Taylors' intending to study economics at Cambridge, as well as a donation from Mr L. Cohen used to start an economics endowment fund.[95] Marshall closed by mentioning the glowing reports on Cambridge graduates from businessmen employing them, which he had received from the Secretary of its newly established Appointments Board.

Marshall's response was evidently not satisfactory to the *Times* since on 11 December it queried whether the Cambridge curriculum was able to serve its self-acknowledged objectives in business education. Deficiencies of the syllabus noted by the *Times* included absence of any explicit reference in the curriculum to 'balance sheets, sinking funds, and depreciation, goodwill, and the finance of machinery'. Marshall explained these omissions as follows.[96] In the first place, shortage of staff and resources prevented the appointment of an accountant among its teachers. Secondly, the fact that specialised economics teaching was confined to honours students and not available to 'passmen', meant that many of these areas could be adequately covered by the private reading of the students, but that, if opportunities in business education for pass students were extended, room would have to be found for detailed training 'in the forms of accounts adapted to different classes of undertakings'. Marshall concluded this second letter by repeating that for honours students such studies were inappropriate, because their current work was already sufficient for helping 'the able [British] business man to be a leader in the world'.

Marshall's remarks about the unsuitability of accounting studies for honours men drew replies in the *Times* letter columns and a final response from Marshall himself (29 December 1905). This repeated Marshall's earlier claim that accounting studies were included in the syllabus to the greatest extent possible given the very limited resources economics education was receiving. He added that raising student aptitudes for making sound judgements, so essential a part of the accountant's task, was strongly fostered in the economics training the university did provide; and that, with respect to many parts of accounting knowledge, experience gained in a firm after graduation was in any case the best teacher. Always with an eye on the main chance, Marshall concluded by inviting the correspondent to whose letter he replied, together with his business friends, to make an endowment for the Economic Board's employment of 'an expert accountant and economist', who would assist in making Cambridge more 'ideally complete' in such matters of business education. However, unlike the other business schools with which the Cambridge Tripos was alleged by Marshall to compete, such accounting staff was not hired by those involved in planning studies in economic and political science.[97]

Writing to Walter Layton in 1919 in the context of business education, Marshall boasted of the special place Cambridge had won for itself in this respect. 'Cambridge seems to be the main hope of the country. Some fatal influence seems to prevent Oxford men from uniting hard thought and perquisite study with energetic social policies. . . . No other University seems to have a curriculum comparable in scope with that of the Tripos but Manchester is strong and growing in strength, and not long ago the Head, I think he is the Vice Chancellor of the University, wrote to ask me if I could suggest a successor to Chapman. I said I could not: the cause – economists are scarce', but then added, 'for the country and the world' that Layton go to Manchester as a better use of his talents than heading a business council.[98] Interest in national education for business and the role Cambridge was increasingly playing in it delighted Marshall until the final years of his life.

In the end, the claim to fame of the new Cambridge School of Economics did not rest on the standards it set in business education. Its inter-war dominance came largely from the quality of the economics education it provided. At the birth of the Tripos in 1903, this nature of its potential contribution was clearly recognised by the *Quarterly Journal of Economics*. It reported 'this new departure in one of our oldest English-speaking universities . . . as a great advance, which will be warmly welcomed by economists generally'.[99] Two decades later, on the occasion of Marshall's eightieth birthday, a large number of the world's leading economists described the Cambridge School of Economics 'as his child', and praised this achievement as 'an inspiration to youth and council and enlightenment to age'.[100] Finally, the greatest of the many great students the Cambridge School of Economics produced in the twentieth century, one who, paradoxically, had never officially sat one of its examinations, recorded at Marshall's death the formal and informal contributions Marshall had made in creating the Economics Tripos, adding that 'to his pupils he was, and remained, a true sage and master, outside criticism, one who was their father in the spirit and who gave them such inspiration and comfort as they drew from no other source.'[101]   On this occasion, the costs of Marshall's tremendous achievement of a cherished ambition were more than matched by future benefits in an intellectual legacy that would even have astonished him had he lived to see it.

NOTES

1. Alfred Marshall, 'the Present Position in Economics', in *Memorials*, pp. 172, 174; for a detailed discussion of the contents of this lecture and the reactions of some of its audience, see above Chapter 10, pp. 310–12.
2. Discussed below, Chapter 20, pp. 753–62.
3. J.M. Keynes, 'Alfred Marshall', pp. 218–19; two of these movements, his role in the formation of the British Economic Association in 1890 and his intervention in the dispute over degrees for women were discussed in Chapters 13 and 14 above, esp. pp. 464–8, 501–7; Mary Paley Marshall, 'MSS Notes' (NCA).
4. See above, Chapter 6, pp. 160–61 especially; Chapter 9, pp. 270–73 and Chapter 10, pp. 313–21.
5. That is, John Maloney, *Marshall, Orthodoxy and the Professionalisation of Economics*, esp. Chapter 2; Stefan Collini, Donald Winch and John Burrow, *That Noble Science of Politics*, Cambridge: Cambridge University Press, 1983, Chapters 10, 11; Alon Kadish, *Historians, Economists and Economic History*, esp. Chapters 4–6; Alon Kadish, 'University Reform and the *Principles*', *Quaderni di storia dell'economia politica*, XI, 2–3, 1991, pp. 289–309; Alon Kadish and Keith Tribe, (eds), *The Market for Political Economy*, esp. Chapter 5; and my 'Alfred Marshall and the Establishment of the Cambridge Economics Tripos, *History of Political Economy*, 20 (4), 1988, pp. 627–67. Several sections of this chapter reproduce substantial parts from this last source, for which permission from its publishers, Duke University Press, is gratefully acknowledged.
6. *Cambridge University Reporter*, 17 November 1885, no. 610, p. 162. This was one of seven papers for the first part of the History Tripos. It also covered economic history, but political science was examined in a separate paper of its own.
7. Above, Chapter 9, pp. 268–70, Chapter 10, p. 322.
8. *Cambridge University Reporter*, 26 October 1870, Sidgwick to Foxwell, 2 September 1878 (Freeman Collection), cited by Collini, Winch and Burrow, p. 266.
9. *Cambridge Historical Register*, pp. 711–14.
10. A.S. and E.M.S., *Henry Sidgwick. A Memoir*, pp. 394–6. Aspects of this exchange between Sidgwick and Marshall were discussed previously in Chapter 10, above pp. 306–8.
11. For reasons explained above, Chapter 14, esp. p. 504.
12. Above, Chapter 13, p. 471.
13. J.R. Seeley, 'The Teaching of Politics', in J.R. Seeley, *Lectures and Essays*, London: Macmillan, 1895, pp. 328–9, 334–5.
14. Above, Chapter 10, pp. 303–4, 333–4.
15. Sheldon Rothblatt, *The Revolution of the Dons*, 1981, pp. 259–73, 244–7; above, Chapter 10, p. 310.
16. Marshall to J.N. Keynes, 18 February 1888 (Marshall Archive, 1:65).
17. Moral Sciences Board, Minutes, 10 November 1888 (Cambridge University Archives, Min. V. 10).
18. *Cambridge University Reporter*, 26 February 1889, pp. 481–3.
19. *Cambridge University Reporter*, 19 March 1889, pp. 593–6.
20. See Chapter 13 above, pp. 469–71.
21. *Cambridge University Reporter*, 18 May 1897, my italics in the quotation.
22. *Cambridge University Reporter*, 18 May 1897, pp. 943, 949 (and see below, Appendix to this chapter, pp. 563–4.
23. Marshall to J.N. Keynes, 2 November 1895 (Marshall Archive, 1:108) and see below, Chapter 20, pp. 754–6 for detailed discussion of the better economics students Marshall's teaching attracted at this time.
24. Marshall to J.N. Keynes, 4 April 1896 (Marshall Archive, 1:110). Marshall added in confidence that he thought Brentano 'a great success and also, between ourselves, a great jabberwock' (an allusion to the creature in the famous poem by Lewis Carroll, 'Jabberwocky').
25. H.S. Foxwell to J.N. Keynes, 14 December 1894 (Marshall Archive, 1:35). Foxwell's complaint was probably about the pass students, for whom he took major responsibility.
26. Marshall to H.S. Foxwell, 25 January 1897 (Marshall Archive, 1:49).
27. Marshall to H.S. Foxwell, 2 February 1897 (Marshall Archive, 1:50).
28. Marshall to H.S. Foxwell, 26 April 1897 (Marshall Archive, 1:58).

29. JNKD, 24 October 1894, 8 March 1897, 30 April 1897, mention board meetings but do not indicate quarrels between Sidgwick and Marshall. The May 1896 meeting in fact showed Sidgwick and Ward moving that the philosophical be completely 'separated' from the 'politico-economic' for Part II of the Tripos (Cambridge University Archives, Min V.10, 22 May 1896).

30. *Cambridge University Reporter*, 9 February 1897, p. 506.

31. Marshall to H.S. Foxwell, 18 January 1895 (presumably a mistake for 1896), Freeman Collection, 14/190.

32. *Cambridge University Reporter*, 18 May 1897.

33. *Cambridge University Reporter*, 9 February 1897, p. 510.

34. JNKD, 7 and 8 May 1888, Marshall's objections to Sidgwick's economics are discussed below, Chapter 18, pp. 665–6.

35. JNKD, 11 May 1886.

36. Marshall to J.N. Keynes, 18 February 1889 (Marshall Archive, 1:65).

37. A. Marshall, 'Mansel', in *Cambridge Review*, 7 December 1887, cited by Alon Kadish, *Historians, Economists and Economic History*, pp. 155–6, who explicitly connects the controversy to the debate at the Moral Sciences Board over metaphysics.

38. Marshall to George Howard Darwin, 24 March 1899 (printed in Cambridge University Association, *Statement of the Needs of the University*, Part I, Cambridge: Cambridge University, 1900, pp. 26–8). Correspondence with Foxwell (25 March, 27 March and 2 April 1899) suggests the letter as printed was considerably revised from the original version dated 24 March. Information supplied to me by John Whitaker.

39. Marshall to J.N. Keynes, 22 September 1900 (Marshall Archive, 1:119).

40. Marshall to Foxwell, 8 May 1901 (Marshall Archive, 3:41).

41. This is reproduced in the Appendix to this chapter, below pp. 564–5.

42. A. Marshall, *A Plea for the Creation of a Curriculum in Economics and Associated Branches of Political Science*, Cambridge, 1902, p. 11. Marshall reprinted much of its content in *P* V, Book I, Chapter IV, §5–6. Its complete text is reprinted in *P* IX, pp. 161–78.

43. A. Marshall, *Economic Teaching at the Universities in Relation to Public Well Being*, Paper presented at a Conference of Members of the Committee on Social Education, London, 1902, pp. 3–4, 6, 7–9.

44. *Ibid.*, p. 6.

45. For a detailed development of this argument, see John Maloney, *Marshall, Orthodoxy and the Professionalisation of Economics*, pp. 41–55.

46. A. Marshall, *Economic Teaching at the Universities in Relation to Public Well Being*, p. 91

47. Marshall to Richard Ely, 28 October 1901, in A.W. Coats, 'Alfred Marshall and Richard Ely: Some Unpublished Letters', *AMCA*, IV, p. 116. It was noted above (p. 537) that Marshall contemplated Brentano's 400 economics students at Munich with considerably envy.

48. Marshall to Hewins, 12 October 1899, in A.W. Coats, 'Alfred Marshall and the Early Development of the London School of Economics: Some Unpublished letters', *AMCA*, IV, pp. 134–5. The non-Cambridge idiosyncrasies of some members of the Cambridge staff presumably referred to Cunningham and to Foxwell, both of whom were strongly associated with London economics as well.

49. Marshall to Hewins, 17 October 1899 and 19 February 1901, in A.W. Coats, 'Alfred Marshall and the Early Development of the London School of Economics', pp. 136, 138–9. Marshall's degree of accord with Fabian principles can be sampled more fully below, Chapter 16, esp. pp. 571–2, 591.

50. A. Marshall, *A Plea . . .*, pp. 4–16.

51. Economics Syndicate Resolutions agreed to up to 12 November 1902 (for private circulation to Syndicate Members only (Marshall Archive).

52. Draft Report, 4 February 1903 (Marshall Archive).

53. John Maloney, *Marshall, Orthodoxy and the Professionalisation of Economics*, p. 63–5, and see above, p. 544, n.¶. Marshall's relationship with John Neville Keynes is examined in more detail in Chapter 18 below.

54. E.M. Forster, *Goldsworthy Lowes Dickinson and Related Writings*, 1973 edition, London: Edward Arnold, pp. 87–8.

55. *Cambridge University Reporter*, 10 March 1903, pp. 528–38; 14 May 1903, pp. 766–7 and see also Alon Kadish, *Historians, Economics and Economic History*, pp. 199–215.

56. The full text of the syllabus is reproduced below, pp. 565–9.

57. Membership of the first Board is given below, p. 550.

58. Alfred Marshall, 'To the Members of the Senate [on the proposed Economics and Political Sciences Tripos]', 20 May 1903; the views of some of these businessmen are summarised by John Maloney, *Marshall, Orthodoxy and the Professionalistion of Economics*, Appendix to Chapter 2, pp. 55–6.

59. *Cambridge University Reporter*, 14 May 1903; cf. Marshall to Foxwell, 8 May 1901 (Marshall Archive, 3:41), quoted above, p. 541.

60. *Cambridge Review*, 4 June 1903, pp. 346–7.

61. *Cambridge University Reporter*, 9 June 1903, pp. 933–4; Resolution 1 passed with 103 votes to 76, Resolution 5 by 75 to 10, an effective majority for Marshall of 28 as Keynes recorded in his diary (6 June 1903).

62. Moral Sciences Board, Minutes, 19 February, 9 October 1903 (Cambridge University Archives, Min. V.10).

63. Marshall to Keynes, 10 and 17 October 1903 (Marshall Archive, 1:132, 133).

64. Cambridge University Archives, Moral Sciences Minutes, Min. V. 110, Minutes for 26 October 1903; Keynes recorded in his Diary that evening: 'It is now decided to exclude Political Economy altogether from the Moral Sciences Tripos. I was in the minority in this vote'.

65. See above, Chapter 12, pp. 429–30; and below, Chapter 19, pp. 703–4.

66. Mary Paley Marshall, 'MSS Notes' (NCA), pp. 11–14.

67. *Cambridge Review*, 21 May 1903, p. 315.

68. *Cambridge University Reporter*, 1 October 1903, p. 9.

69. *Cambridge University Reporter*, 27 October 1903, p. 89. The first four examiners for the Tripos were J.N. Keynes, Lowes Dickinson, Clapham and Pigou, who thereby became *ex officio* members of the Board. Members appointed by the Senate included A.W. Ward, its first chairman (Cambridge University Archives, Min. V. 114, Minutes for 15 June 1903).

70. Cambridge University Archives, Economics Board Minutes for 14, 21 October, 18 November and 9 December 1903 (Min. V. 114), and for Marshall's early initiatives in this practice as Professor, Chapter 10 above, p. 320.

71. Marshall to Oscar Browning, 28 October 1903, King's College, Oscar Browning Papers; King's College Fellowship Elections 42: A.C. Pigou, 1902.

72. *Cambridge University Reporter*, 22 May 1906; Economics Board Minutes for 29 May 1907 (Cambridge University Archives, Min. V. 114).

73. Economics Board Minutes, Cambridge University Archives, Min. V. 114: other aspects of quarrels between Foxwell and Marshall over history were discussed in a previous chapter, above Chapter 13, pp. 471–2, and in the context of Moral Sciences Tripos reform in 1897, above, p. 537.

74. *Cambridge University Reporter*, 1 May 1906, p. 770; in November 1907 lectures were arranged on 'The Poor in Relation to the State', to be given by C.S. Hamilton, the Chairman of the Poor Law Commission which had been set up in 1906 and reported in 1909 (Cambridge University Archives, Economics Board Minutes, Min. V. 114); and on Marshall's associations with the Poor Law Commission, see above, Chapter 11, pp. 359–60.

75. Economics Board Minutes for 8 May 1907, Cambridge University Archives, Min. V. 114.

76. Economics Board Minutes for 17 May, 6 November 1907, 20 May 1908, Cambridge University Archives, Min. V. 114. The circumstances surrounding Marshall's retirement are discussed in Chapter 17 below; both Benians and Fay, who were teaching in economic history for the new Tripos from 1905 and 1907 respectively, left reminiscences about Marshall's teachings, quoted previously in Chapter 10 (above pp. 313, 314).

77. Below, pp. 562–9.

78. *Cambridge University Reporter*, 11 June 1904, p. 965.

79. *Cambridge University Reporter*, 11 June 1906, p. 1062. Foxwell's lecturing changes had been debated with Marshall in correspondence, aspects of which dealing with the importance of history for economics students were discussed previously in Chapter 13 (above pp. 471–2).

80. *Cambridge University Reporter*, 7 June 1907, p. 1014.

81. Mary Paley Marshall, 'MSS Notes' (NCA), took delight in noting that by 1930 Cunningham's prediction had been abundantly proved wrong.

82. Marshall to Clerk of the Worshipful Company of Girdlers, 2 June 1909 (Marshall Archive, 3:91).

83. JNKD, 15 June 1905; *Historical Register of the University of Cambridge*, p. 981; and see above, Chapter 13, p 444, for Marshall's remarks on this in a letter to Brentano.

84. JNKD, 28 June, 3 September 1905; J.M. Keynes to Lytton Strachey, 8 July 1905, cited in Harrod, *Life of John Maynard Keynes*, p. 106.

85. JNKD, 26 November 1905.

86. Marshall to John Neville Keynes, 3 December 1905, cited in Harrod, *Life of John Maynard Keynes*, p. 107.

87. Keynes Papers, King's College UA–4–A–2 (I am indebted to Tiziano Rafaelli for supplying me with transcripts of this material); J.M. Keynes, 'Alfred Marshall', pp. 215–16 and n.1.

88. *Historical Register of the University of Cambridge*, pp. 982–3; Layton's notes of Marshall's lectures are preserved among his papers at Trinity College, and have already been cited on several occasions. He too joined the economics teaching staff for some time and like Keynes, continued to correspond sporadically with Marshall. See below, Chapter 17, pp. 649, 651, Chapter 20, pp. 755–6.

89. Marshall, 'Notes on Own Students 1906–07', Marshall Library, Large Brown Box, Item 1.

90. Marshall, 'Notes on Own Students 1907–08', Marshall Library, Large Brown Box, Item 1.

91. In 1910, 29 students attempted the two parts of the Tripos; in 1924, the year of Marshall's death, this had more than doubled to 71; and see below, Chapter 20 (pp. 758–9), on some of the pre-First World War crop of students.

92. On the longer-term accuracy of this prediction, see below, Chapter 20, pp. 753–9.

93. Marshall to Secretary of the Girdlers' Company, 2 June 1909 (Marshall Archive, 3: 91).

94. Marshall to E.S. Roberts (Master of Caius College and Vice-Chancellor) 22 August 1910 (Marshall Archive, 3:92).

95. Sir Henry Buckley (1845–1935) was a former student of the school, and a Cambridge graduate (9th wrangler in 1868), who later made a distinguished career in the law which in 1915 gained him a peerage; Nathaniel Louis Cohen (1847–1913) was a businessman and member of the London County Council.

96. Marshall to the *Times*, 14 December 1905.

97. For a discussion of other developments in business education in British universities at this time, see Alon Kadish, *Historians, Economists and Economic History*, pp. 229–37.

98. Marshall to Walter Layton, 13 January 1919 (Layton Papers 2[37], Wren Library, TCC); Marshall's prognostication on Oxford proved to be shortsighted. By the end of the 1920s, Oxford was developing a healthy economics programme as shown by Warren Young and Frederic S. Lee, *Oxford Economics and Oxford Economists*, esp. Chapters 1–4, though with the assistance of Cambridge men (and women) such as Macgregor and Lynda Grier.

99. E.F. Gay, 'The New Economics Tripos at Cambridge University', *Quarterly Journal of Economics*, 17, 1903, p. 496.

100. 'Address on the occasion of Marshall's eightieth birthday presented by members of the Royal Economic Society', in *Memorials*, p. 497.

101. John Maynard Keynes, 'Alfred Marshall', p. 223.

APPENDIX TO CHAPTER 15

APPENDIX A: Political Economy Course Outlines for the Moral Sciences Tripos, 1889.

A. Political Economy

I. Preliminary

The fundamental assumption of economic science, the methods employed in it, and the qualifications required in applying its conclusions to practice; its relation to other branches of Social Science.

II. Production of Wealth

Causes which affect or determine
  (i)   The efficiency of capital and of labour.
  (ii)   The difficulty of obtaining natural agents and raw materials.
  (iii)   The rate of increase of capital and population.

III. Exchange and Distribution of Wealth

Causes which affect or determine
  (i)   The value of commodities produced at home.
  (ii)   The rent of land.
  (iii)   Profits and wages.
  (iv)   The value of currency.
  (v)   The value of imported commodities.
Monopolies, Gluts and crises. Banking, and the Foreign Exchanges.

IV. Governmental Interference in Its Economic Aspects

Communism and socialism: the principles of taxation: the incidence of various taxes: public loans and their results. . . .
List of books recommended on this subject:
  Marshall, *Economics of Industry.*
  Walker, *The Wages Question,* and *Land and Its Rent.*
  Mill, *Principles of Political Economy*, Books III and V.
  Jevons, *Money and the Mechanism of Exchange.*
  Sidgwick, *Principles of Political Economy*; Introduction and Book III.
  Fawcett, *Free Trade and Protection.*
The following books should also be consulted:
  Bagehot, *Lombard Street.*
  Bastable, *Foreign Trade.*
  Farrer, *Free Trade and Fair Trade.*
  Giffen, *Essays in Finance*, Second Series.
  Nicholson, *Money and Monetary Problems*, Part I.
  Rae, *Contemporary Socialism.*
  Sidgwick, *Principles of Political Economy*, Books I and II.
March 4, 1889.

Source: *Cambridge University Reporter*, 5 March 1889, pp. 506–7.

APPENDIX B: Political Economy Syllabus, 1897

A descriptive and analytical study, with special reference to the conditions of England at the present time, of

I.   Consumption. The modes of living of different classes of the community; the nature and variations of their demand for commodities and services.
II. The methods, organization, and resources of production.
III. The mutual influences of consumption and production. The population question.
IV. Markets generally. Competition, combination, and monopoly.
V.   The relative values of commodities; wages, profits and rents.
VI. The relations of imports and exports. The foreign exchanges. International trade competition. The terms of international interchange; and the distribution, immediate and ultimate, of the benefits of trade among the nations concerned.
VII. Money. Banks. Stock Exchanges. The English Money Market. The modern organizations of markets and transport. Fluctuations of credit and commerce. The policies of currency, credit, and banking in their national and international relations.
VIII. Collective bargaining in matters relating to labour; its methods, and its effects on those directly concerned and on the general public. Trade Unions. Co-operation.
IX. An elementary treatment of the following aspects of public finance, administration and control. The principles of taxation; incidence and shifting of taxes; public loans. The functions of Government, Imperial and Local, in initiating, managing and regulating enterprise; in supplying information and instruction; and in providing appliances for common use and common enjoyment. Public and private relief of the poor. The influence of Public Opinion and authority in economic matters generally. Socialism.

There will be required throughout a study of fundamental notions and their appropriate definitions; of the scope and methods of the science; and of its relations to other branches of social science.

List of the books recommended on this subject:

> Bagehot, *Lombard Street.*
> Bastable, *Theory of International Trade.*
> Dunbar, *The Theory and History of Banking.*
> Jevons, *Money and the Mechanism of Exchange.*
> Keynes, *Scope and Method of Political Economy.*
> Marshall, *Principles of Economics*, Vol. I.
> Plehn, *Introduction to Public Finance.*
> Sidgwick, *Principles of Political Economy*, Introduction and Book III.

Among the other books which may be read with advantage are the following:

> Bastable, *Commerce of Nations.*
> Booth, *Life and Labour of the People in London*. Vol. IX.
> Clare, *Money Market.*
> Giffen, *Essays in Finance*, Second Series.
> Goschen, *Foreign Exchanges.*
> Hadley, *Railway Transportation.*
> von Halle, *Trusts.*
> Labour Commission, *Final Report*, 1894.
> Levi, *History of Commerce.*
> Mill, *Principles of Political Economy.*
> Nicholson, *Money and Monetary Problems.*
> Rae, *Contemporary Socialism.*
> Sidgwick, *Principles of Political Economy*, Books I, II.

Adam Smith, *Wealth of Nations.*

Advanced Political Economy

Students will be expected to show a wider and more thorough knowledge of the subjects included in the schedule for Part I; and the papers will consist largely of questions involving considerable scientific difficulty. In particular students will be required to have a more careful and exact study of the mutual interactions of economic phenomena, especially in recent times; and to have grappled with the difficulties of disentangling the effects of different causes, and of assigning to each as nearly as may be its relative magnitude and importance. The examination will also include the following subjects: a general knowledge of economic history and the history of economic science, especially in their later stages, the science of statistics in its applications to the theoretical and practical problems of economics. Some scope will also be given for the diagrammatic expression of problems in pure theory, with the general principles of the mathematical treatment applicable to such problems.
The third paper will contain at least eight questions, of which no candidate may attempt more than four; full marks being obtainable for full answers to any two.

Source: *Cambridge University Reporter*, 18 May 1897, pp. 846–7, 949.

APPENDIX C: Marshall's Scheme for an Economic and Political Sciences Tripos, Communicated to Foxwell in 1901

Designed with a view to the needs not merely of professional students of economics; but also for those who are preparing for

(a)   Work in Parliament, or on Local Representative Bodies;
(b)   The Home of Indian Civil Services; diplomacy and the consular service;
(c)   The higher work of large businesses, public and private, including railways, shipping foreign trade and those branches of manufacture that do not require a long study of engineering and physics;
(d)   The duties of a country gentleman;
(e)   The service of the poor.

Part I
(at end of second year; all papers compulsory)

A.   *Modern History*
     (Economic & political, chiefly since 1780; to be treated broadly. Each paper to contain (say) nine questions, of which three are to be general, three distinctively economic, and three distinctively political. No one to answer more than six.)

I,2.   *United Kingdom.* (two papers)
  3.   *France and Germany.* (with some reference to the rest of Europe)
  4.   *British Possessions and the United States.*

B.   *Economics*

5,6   *A general study.*

C.   *Politics*

7.   *The existing English polity: (To include relations to colonies and dependencies.)*

D. *Essays*

Part II

(Not less than six, or more than eight papers to be taken, inclusive of the Essays. Economic students to be required to take the whole of Group A, and at least one paper from either C or D. Perhaps a corresponding rule to be made for other students.)

A. *Main Economic Course*

(A study, more detailed on the descriptive side and more advanced on the analytical side, than in Part I, of contemporary economic and social conditions; of their mutual relations and interactions and of their causes in the near past. The treatment to be international, where possible, and to require an elementary knowledge of economic geography and of statistical method.)

1. *Production: Distribution.* (Resources of different countries. Causes that govern value and the distribution of the national income. Combination and Monopoly. Trade Unions.)
2. *Money, Credit, Trade.* (Currency national and international. Banks. International Trade. Organized markets. Fluctuations of credit prices and employment.)
3. *Public business and finance. Public duties on their economic side.* (Imperial and Local Government revenues, regulations and undertakings. Economic relations and obligations of the various social classes. The organization of effort for the removal of poverty and the furthering of progress.)

B. *Secondary Economic Papers*

4. *History of economic doctrine.* (Socialism to be included.)
5. *Mathematico-economic and statistical methods.*

C. *Politics*

6. *The Structure and Functions of the Modern State*: (involving a comparative study of existing institutions)
7. *Political Philosophy.* (i.e. an examination of the nature of the State with a survey of the history of political speculation)
8. *Public International Law and existing Diplomatic Relations.*
9. *A Special Study of some existing policy*: (other than the British)

D. *Law*

10. *Mercantile Law.*
11. *Private International Law.*

E. *Essays*

Source: A typed scheme for the proposed Economics and Politics Tripos sent by Marshall to Foxwell in May 1901 after his appointment to a committee with Ward and Lowes-Dickinson to investigate possibilities for improving the possibilities for Economics and Politics studies in the university. (Marshall Papers, Cambridge, Boxes 3, 11.)

APPENDIX D: The Implemented Economics and Politics Tripos, 1905: The General Arrangement of the Tripos

The following is the schedule of the examination; the subjects marked with an asterisk are compulsory. In Part II the student must take not less than two and not more than five papers besides those which are compulsory:

Part I

1. Subject for an Essay. 1 paper*
2. The existing British Constitution. 1 paper*
3. Recent Economic and General History. 2 papers
4. General Principles of Economics. 3 papers*

Part II

1. Subjects for an essay. 1 paper*
2. General Economics. 3 papers*
3. Advanced Economics, mainly realistic. 2 papers
4. Advanced Economics, mainly analytic. 2 papers
5. Modern Political Theories. 1 paper
6. International Law with reference to existing political conditions. 1 paper
7. International Law with reference to existing economic conditions. 1 paper
8. Principles of Law as applied to economic questions. 2 papers
9. Special subject or subjects. 1 paper each.

Part I must be taken generally in the second year of residence: but a student who has already been placed in any other Tripos or Part of a Tripos may take it in his third or fourth year. Part II may be taken in the third or fourth year.
Some of the papers in each Part will include quotations from French and German writers.
The Examiners are to have regard to the style and method of the answers.

[Extracts from] Details Relating to Part I

The scheme of lectures provided by the Board for those preparing for Part I runs on well-defined lines; because every candidate has to take all the seven papers in it. As regards Economics, to which the student is expected generally to give about half his time, the courses offered are arranged, more or less, in progressive order of difficulty. He should therefore attend a full course on it in his first year and another in his second. If however, he should start with any considerable knowledge of it, he may take in his first year the course that is specially designed for the second year, and in his second year may perhaps take a more advanced course. With a view to the needs of such students, it is arranged that the course of lectures should be varied as much as possible from year to year. Every student should as a rule take two courses of history in his first year, and one in his second year.

[Extracts from] Details Relating to Part II

In Part II an attempt is made to introduce into the Tripos system some of that elasticity and freedom of choice for each individual student, which in some other Universities is obtained by a *viva voce* examination directed specially to branches of study which the candidate has selected for himself; his choice being, of course, subject to the condition that they shall be sufficiently broad, and yet have a certain unity.

The main purpose of the three compulsory papers on General Economics is to secure that those who take Part II of this Tripos after another Tripos (or a part of it), should have a sound knowledge of the main principles of Economics at large: and that those who have already taken Part I of this Tripos should not specialise even their later studies too narrowly. In addition, these papers are to lay stress on Public Finance, the Economic functions of government, and the ethical aspects of Economics generally; since all these matters are more appropriate to the later than to the earlier years of a student's career. But that work in Economics which is most distinctive of Part II must necessarily be directed into rather narrower channels; for no one can do really advanced work over the whole field. And here a double bifurcation is required.

The first bifurcation has reference to the divergent needs of active life and of professional study. Those who are preparing for public or private business, must generally be content with what study of analytical subleties they have been able to make in their past two years; in their third year they need to give their chief attention to realistic work, the facts of business life, and to the direct application of economic principles to them. Accordingly two papers, arranged specially for this class of students, are to be mainly realistic. Two similar papers are to be of a more exclusively academic character, and make provision (a) for some of the more obscure problems of value, such as those connected with the shifting and ultimate incidence of the burden of taxes; (b) for the history of Economic doctrines; and (c) for mathematical problems in Economics and Statistics. But there is nothing to prevent any student from taking all these four papers.

The second bifurcation has reference to the different groups of subjects which are included under the broad title 'Economics'. They are all ultimately connected with one another. There is scarcely any of these which can be studied at all thoroughly without some considerable knowledge of almost every other. But yet each professional student according to his bent of mind, and each man of affairs according to his work in life, will wish to give his chief attention to certain branches; and accordingly it has been arranged that, while each of the four papers on Advanced Economics shall contain some general questions, the majority of the questions in each paper shall be divided in about equal proportion among the four groups A, B, C, D, defined below:

A. Structure and problems of modern industry. Modern methods of production, transport, and marketing; and their influences on prices and on industrial and social life. Industrial combinations. The recent development of joint-stock companies. Combinations and monopolies. Railway and shipping organisation and rates.
B. Wages and conditions of employment. Causes and results of recent changes in the wages and salaries of different classes of workers, in profits, and in rents. Relations between employers and employees. Trade Unions. Employers' Associations. Conciliation and Arbitration. Profit sharing.
C. Money, credit and prices. National and international systems of currency. Banks, and banking systems. Stock Exchanges. Foreign Exchanges. National and International money and investment markets. Credit fluctuations. Causes and measurement of changes in particular prices and in the purchasing power of money.
D. International trade and its policy. The courses of trade as affected by and affecting the character and organization of national industries, trade combinations, etc. International levels of prices. International aspects of credit and currency. Foreign Exchanges. Tariffs, protective and for revenue. bounties and transport facilities in regard to foreign trade.

No one is allowed to answer more than half the questions in any one of these four papers. And consequently any one who, together with a sound knowledge of General Economics, had made a thorough study of any one of the groups A, B, C or D, would find most of his time in the examination room fully occupied with questions not very different from those which would be proposed to him in a *viva voce* examination adjusted to his requirements. Most students, however, will probably select two of the groups for about equal attention.

It is obvious that A and B will be of special interest to those who expect to be employers of labour, or landowners, or to be engaged in the service of railways, or in the administration of government, central or local. C and D, together with the latter part of A, will meet the needs of those who are to be engaged in large financial transactions, as bankers, members of the Stock Exchange, etc., while merchants and those members of manufacturing firms who are chiefly responsible for the external relations of the business rather than its internal organisation, will perhaps give their chief attention to D and part of either C or A. Those who expect to be engaged in the service of the poor will give the first place to B. The interests of any one who hopes to take part in legislation, like those of an academic student, will be specialised according to the bent of mind and character, rather than the force of external circumstances. His studies need to be broad: but he may reasonably specialise to some extent on any one, or even any two of the four.

Specimen Examination Questions

No Examination has yet been held in Part II, where the chief provision is to be made for realistic treatment of Economics. But the following questions, selected from those set for Part I in 1905 may suffice to indicate that many of the subjects, to which students are invited to give their attention, have an intimate bearing on the affairs of life; and that they appeal to such various interests as to afford a broad and liberal education.

Economics

Give a brief discussion of the advantages and disadvantages of the system of piece work; and, by reference to specific industries, show how their relative importance varies in different circumstances.

Give illustrations of the varying meaning of the term *profit* in everyday language. State how you would use the term for economic purposes, and enquire how far profit, as used by you, partakes of the nature of rent, interest, wages respectively.

Describe the function of the speculator in the organization of industry. Distinguish the speculative element in the work of the manufacturer and the wholesale merchant, and indicate the new kinds of speculation which have been made possible by modern business methods.

In constructing an ideal banking system, what elements, if any, would you take from the English, French, German, and American systems respectively?

How is the output of a monopolistic industry likely to be affected if, having hitherto been allowed to discriminate between its customers it is prevented by law from doing this? What light does your answer throw on the problem of governmental interference with the rates chargeable by railways companies?

Enumerate the principal items in the mutual indebtedness of nations, and indicate the ways in which recorded imports can increase without any corresponding increase of recorded exports.

'Le fait est que l'abondance ou la rareté de l'argent, de la monnaie, ou de tout ce qui en tient lieu, n'influe *pas du tout* le taux de l'intérêt, pas plus que l'abondance ou la rareté de la cannelle, du froment, ou des étoffes de sois.' Examine critically this statement.

Explain the process by which an alteration in the rate of discount in a country operates on the foreign exchanges. Why is a movement in the rate of exchange on Paris in London always immediately followed by a corresponding movement in the rate on London in Paris, and vice versa?

Discuss the place and functions of (a) death duties, (b) an income tax, (c) taxes on commodities, considered as parts of a general system of taxation.

Subjects for Essays

The causes and effects of the growth of large cities.
'Things are in the saddle and ride mankind'.
The influence of finance on international politics.

[Extracts from] Courses of Reading

The reading of each student is partly decided by his own choice, under the guidance of instructors who indicate the purposes and qualities of many books on each branch of his studies. But the following lists have been published by the Board as generally suitable for all candidates for Part I; while the larger lists are added of books which may with advantage be read or consulted so far as time suffices.

Economics. Students are expected to read the general treatises by Hadley, Marshall and Pierson, together with at least one of those by J.S. Mill, Nicholson and Sidgwick; Bowley, *Elements of Statistics*, Part I; Keynes, *Scope and Method of Political Economy;* Seignobos, *La méthode historique appliquée aux sciences sociales*; Bagehot, *Lombard Street*; Bastable, *International Trade*; Goschen, *Foreign Exchanges*; Clare, *The Money Market*; Dunbar, *Theory and History of Banking*; Jevons, *Money*; Jevons, *Investigations in Finance*; J.B. Clark, *The Control of Trade*; Emery, *Stock and Produce Exchanges*; Greene, *Corporation Finance*; Hadley, *Railway Transportation*; Jenks, *Trusts*; Booth, *Life and Labour in London*, Second Series (Industry), vol. 5; Gilman, *Dividend to Labour*; Jevons, *The State in Relation to Labour*; Levasseur, *La population française comparée à celle des autres nations*, vol. 3, Part 1; Bastable, *Public Finance*; Adam Smith, *Wealth of Nations*.

Source: Extracts from A. Marshall, 1906, *Introduction to the Tripos in Economics and associated branches of political science,* Cambridge, pp. 8–16.

16.   A Tendential Socialist . . . or Neo-Liberal? The Politics of Alfred Marshall

When in 1919 Marshall reviewed his 'nearly half century' of interest in industrial processes, he also explained aspects of his motivation for that type of research. Part of his interest was inspired by a desire to test the proposition that 'inequalities of pay were less arbitrary than often asserted' and were in fact more directly under the influence of 'broad, natural causes' than often understood. Such causes were, nevertheless, 'not wholly beyond human control' and amenable to modification 'to bring about a nearer approach to equality of conditions, and a better use of the products of human effort for the betterment of humanity'. Marshall continued this autobiographical segment,

> I developed a tendency to socialism; which was fortified later on by Mill's essays in the *Fortnightly Review* in 1879. Thus for more than a decade, I remained under the conviction that the suggestions, which are associated with the word 'socialism', were the most important subject of study, if not in the world, yet at all events for me. But the writings of socialists generally repelled me, almost as much as they attracted me, because they seemed far out of touch with realities: and, partly for that reason, I decided to say little on the matter, till I had thought much longer.
>
> Now, when old age indicates that my time for thought and speech is nearly ended, I see on all sides marvellous developments of working-class faculty: and, partly in consequence, a broader and firmer foundation for socialistic schemes than existed when Mill wrote. But no socialistic scheme, yet advanced, seems to make adequate provision for the maintenance of high enterprise, and individual strength of character; nor to promise a sufficiently rapid increase in the business plant and other material implements of production, to enable the real incomes of the manual labour classes to continue to increase as fast as they have done in the recent past, even if the total income of the country be shared equally by all. The average level of human nature in the western world has risen rapidly during the last fifty years. But it has seemed to me that those have made most real progress towards the distant goal of ideally perfect social organization, who have concentrated their energies on some particular difficulties in the way, and not spent strength on endeavouring to rush past them.[1]

Despite the difficulties in reconciling the penultimate sentence with the World War just concluded, these remarks accurately reflect the vagaries of Marshall's lifelong interest in socialism. For a decade or so, during the impetuosity of youth, this interest had been relatively active; it then became gradually more critical, and occasionally even hostile, partly because of Marshall's increasing theoretical problems with socialism and partly because earlier beliefs in socialism of sorts no longer fitted his social and political ideals.[2] Marshall's position on socialism, however, did not only change with age; in many respects it responded as well to the changing attitudes to socialism of his political and social environment. Evaluating Marshall as tendential socialist therefore immediately raises the problem of the meaning to be assigned to the types of 'socialism' he embraced during his long life span, and more generally, to the political views he espoused.

Segments of Victorian England could see 'socialism' in almost every radical or working-class movement just as from the 1950s there were many who could spot 'reds' under almost any conceivable type of bed. During Marshall's lifetime, those in England with a taste for radical social reform could draw 'socialist' succour in turn from the works of Carlyle and the contributions to Christian socialism by Maurice, Kingsley, Ludlow and Hughes; from the economics of Ruskin, the workshops and romances of William Morris, the semi-Marxist 'scientific socialism' of Hyndman, to the careful and often pedantic judgements based on studying the 'facts' in the essays of the Fabians with their influence on the incipient and increasingly independent political Labour Movement. What foreign element there was in British Victorian socialism came more often from the work of Henry George and its implications for land policy than from that of Marx and Engels. However, those with a penchant for studying international socialist literature were also able to draw on a long-standing French socialist tradition in the works by Saint-Simon, Fourier, Proudhon and Louis Blanc, and other German socialist perspectives from Lassalle and Rodbertus and, later in the century, the more romantic vision of socialist utopias drawn by Bellamy and Gronlund, Tolstoi and Kropotkin. It was even possible to study socialist communities in operation, often based on the religious ideals of that 'primitive communism' allegedly practised in early Christianity or to visit the temples of Owenite cooperative socialism in action in the retail, wholesale and even producer establishments of the still rapidly growing cooperative movement. Socialism meant land nationalisation and abstention, municipal tramways and public libraries, class struggle and progressive taxation.[3]

Geisner, a fictional character in a late nineteenth-century 'labour novel', while explaining socialism to a young trade unionist, simplified this complex panorama of socialism into two basic forms, the second of which, small 's' socialism, describes Marshall's socialism to perfection.

> Co-operation as against competition is the main industrial idea of Socialism. But there are two socialisms. There is socialism with a little 's' which is simply an attempt to stave off the true Socialism. This small, narrow socialism means only the state regulation of the distribution of wealth. It has as its advocates politicians who seek to modify the robbery of the workers, to ameliorate the horrors of the competitive system, only in order to prevent the upheaval which such men recognise to be inevitable if things keep on unchanged.[4]

Marshall's 'small 's' socialism' can also be described as a neo-liberalism, radical reform politics in the tradition of Millian liberalism which occasionally, as Marshall also tended to do, deigned to describe itself as socialism.[5]

Marshall in fact classified himself as largely a socialist of the Millian variety. His humanitarian and radical reformist sentiments even in youth were indisputably coloured by the Millian ideals which were then also exciting his Cambridge contemporaries in the Grote Club and on the Moral Sciences Board. Not only did Mill provide the basic inspiration for Marshall's socialism, Mill also sounded the necessary warnings against its dangers well before Marshall's old age. Marshall's advice in 1902 to his former student, Helen Bosanquet, that it was Mill *On Liberty* rather than Mill *On Socialism* which was important at the beginning of the new century when contemplating social reform, has already been quoted.[6] This is not to say that Mill was Marshall's only guide on socialism. Another autobiographical sketch, preceding that of *Industry and Trade* by a decade, recalls how Marshall 'had been attracted towards the new views on economics . . . by Marx, Lassalle and other socialists' and that, when he discovered they had 'underrated the difficulty of their problems, and were too quick to assume that the abolition of private property would purge away the faults and deficiencies of human nature', he praised the 'socialist rhapsodies' as hints at a vision splendid but rejected their socialist theories as unrealistic and practically inept.[7]

The terrain to be covered in this chapter is therefore wide. After examining Marshall's early flirtations with socialism in words and action, and the impact various socialist ideas had on him and his writings, his awareness of socialist literature is traced partly by using the contents of his lectures on socialism. Marshall's participation in controversy over, and with, Henry George, is then examined, before discussing more specific aspects of his position illustrative of his role as small 's' socialist. This covers his position on state enterprises, his decidedly anti-imperialist views, opinions on redistributive taxation and social welfare policies, profit sharing and cooperation, and the more general defence of what he later in life called 'economic chivalry', before concluding more generally on the politics of Alfred Marshall. There is a rich biographical harvest to be gleaned from Marshall's changing political perspectives, some aspects developing as he grew older while others withered and died during the final decades of his long life.

THE INCIPIENT SOCIALISM OF THE YOUNG MARSHALL: 1869–1879

Marshall's early enthusiasm for socialism largely coincided with his period of economic apprenticeship. It may even, in a sense, be said to have preceded it. This is not surprising. As he later recalled, the more he learned about economics, the more he appreciated about the difficulties of economic and social progress. Learning about economics went hand in hand with learning about the feasibility of socialist policies, no matter what impetus was given to such policies by new views on the subject or by the appearance of old and influential views such as the chapters on socialism by Mill posthumously published in the *Fortnightly Review*. As shown in the next section, the latter are better seen as inducing the more critical perspectives on socialism of Marshall's mature age. In fact, it is not difficult to argue that much of Marshall's post-1879 thinking on socialism is little more than elaborating Mill's suggestion that the exaggerations of socialism could only be rebutted by exposing their 'errors in political economy' in the form of 'ignorance of economic facts, and of the causes by which the economic phenomena of society as it is, are actually determined'.[8] This research programme conforms with the wide scope of economics presented in Marshall's *Principles*, much of which turns in a Millian manner on investigating 'all means by which the institution [of private property] may have a chance of being made to work in a manner more beneficial to that large portion of society which at present enjoys the least share of its direct benefits'.[9]

To return to the beginning. It will be recalled that Marshall's initial studies in economics were largely inspired, on his later accounts, by an interest in the question, 'how far do the conditions of life of the British (and other) working classes generally suffice for fullness of life' and by his critical attitude to justifying the existing conditions of society, particularly with respect to the impropriety of inequality of opportunity. This coincidence was recalled by Marshall forty years later when he discussed his attitude to socialism and its dependence on what this term was taken to mean:

> We are told sometimes that everyone who strenuously endeavours to promote the social amelioration of the people is a Socialist – at all events, if he believes that much of this work can be better performed by the State than by individual effort. In this sense nearly every economist of the present generation is a Socialist. In this sense I was a Socialist before I knew anything of economics; and, indeed, it was my desire to know what was practicable in social reform by State and other agencies which led me to read Adam Smith and Mill, Marx and Lassalle, forty years ago. I have since then been steadily growing a more convinced socialist in this sense of the word.[10]

These particular aspects of socialism had been addressed in Marshall's first published article on the Millian theme of the future of the working classes in which, among other things, the state was invited 'to invest capital in men' as previously it had done 'in telegraphs'.[11] Aspects of Mill's influence on these sentiments expressed in 1873, both positive and negative, are identifiable from Marshall's personal copy of Mill's *Principles*. Marshall approvingly annotated Mill's remarks about the necessity for workers' well-being of their own 'mental cultivation', such improvements in intelligence having positive effects on the growth of population, as would the associated promotion of 'the social independence of women'. Marshall also showed much interest, as indicated by his marking of passages, in issues associated with workmen's associations, the benefits of competition for progress and the effect on productivity of large-scale enterprise. The one marked disagreement with Mill on progress is an emphatic 'No!' to Mill's remark that it was highly questionable whether 'all the mechanical inventions yet made have lightened the day's toil of any human being'.[12] Earlier annotations indicate Marshall's interest in Mill's discussion of Owen's socialism in Book II, Chapter I of his *Principles*.[*]

Mill was by no means the only inspiration for Marshall's initial flirtations with socialism. It will be recalled that during the second half of the 1860s Marshall was mixing with persons close to Christian socialism such as Maurice and, to a lesser extent, Ludlow. One of his fellow members of the Eranus Society, F.J. Hort, with others, had been actively involved in establishing a working-man's college at Cambridge in 1855. Moreover, Church of England clergy, of whom so many were then produced by the ancient English universities, were also prominent in organising rural workers into an Agricultural Labour Union, a task in which Marshall was also actively involved for a short period.

From mentors like these, Marshall absorbed several radical reform ideas during his very formative postgraduate years. He learnt about the importance of cooperation in associations between working men and capitalists, the necessity of providing satisfactory opportunities for working-class education and the universities' special role therein through the university

---

[*] Mill, *Principles of Political Economy*, People's Edition, pp. 125, 127, 129, 130. Mill's comments on Owen and French socialism in this chapter distinguished small socialist communities, which he held to be practicable social experiments, from national systems of state socialism which he did not. It also raised the issue of incentives to labour under such schemes, a problem deemed to grow with the size of the experiment, as Marshall later noted more generally in his *Principles* (for example, *P* VIII, p. 9, a passage dating from *P* V).

Extension movement, and the need to assist particularly helpless sections of the working class such as agricultural labour in organising institutions for their own self-help and self-improvement.[13]   The years from 1866 to 1879, most of which Marshall himself later identified with his economic apprenticeship, also coincided with the fighting sixties as a period of reform. These years saw first political reform (the second Reform Act of 1867); subsequently trade union and industrial relations reforms, with their milestone in the 1871 Trade Union Act. This legislation was modified and improved in 1876, followed by the more liberal Conspiracy and Property Act and major changes in the Master and Servants Act in 1875, while Marshall was overseas in the United States. They also heralded a period of municipal revitalisation, urban renewal in sanitation and other public health measures, and the first legislation to establish general and free elementary public education.[14]

Details of Marshall's study of socialist literature in this period are provided subsequently; some instances of his more practical involvement with radical labour causes are required to complete the picture of the young Marshall's incipient socialism. The most striking example involves his active participation in organising East Anglian rural labour during 1872–74, largely under the inspiration of Joseph Arch's National Agricultural Labourers' Union. Local newspaper reports indicate that Marshall spoke at public meetings in support of the right of rural workers to unionise. On one of these occasions he even seconded a motion proposed by a farmer friendly to the labourer's cause, 'That the labourers who are locked-out on account of their refusal to give up their Union tickets, merit the support of all classes and that the chairman, Mr. Henry Hall, be requested to act as treasurer and to forward all subscriptions collected'. Given his newly acquired qualifications, Marshall had been asked to address the meeting on the relationship of unions to the law of supply and demand. He explained how,

> from the 'iron law' of wages, the unionists' opponents had concluded that farm workers' wages were at their natural level. Thus, if a labourer's work was undervalued, someone would come forward and offer him more. If his wages were raised artificially, they would inevitably come down again. The argument was excellent, Marshall admitted, but in the present case the reasoning was based on false assumptions. Farmers did not, as it was assumed, compete for labor, since none of the farmers with whom the labourers came into contact dared raise wages in order to attract their neighbours' men. The argument also ignored the increase in efficiency which Marshall believed would accompany wage increases. Of unionism Marshall said, somewhat cryptically, that it mingled so much harm with good that it could only be regarded as a stepping-stone to something better. However, the farmers chose not simply to attack the faults of unionism, but to proscribe the principle of combination. Some manufacturers, although they had suffered from some of the effects of unionism, had admitted that no other way was known in which men in a backward condition could take the first step forward. A union could make a man aware of the world beyond his parish boundary and show him where his labor was needed. Wages would rise and, if wisely spent would increase the efficiency of labor.[15]

Marshall also drew on his new economic expertise in the socialist cause by contributing two articles to the *Bee-Hive*, a periodical described by the Webbs as 'easily the best labour newspaper of the nineteenth century'.[16] The first of Marshall's articles, published 18 April 1874, corrected a Leeds draper and cooperator by the name of John Holmes on what Marshall saw as a mistaken perception of what 'the laws of [political economy] can teach, and what they cannot teach'. This made the point that only in some special circumstances can political economy arbitrate unambiguously on a moral question. More generally, it described political economy as a 'highly organised machinery' by which 'to discover what are the circumstances which bear upon' any particular question, the relevant facts and the most appropriate mode of their investigation, as well as the manner of reasoning by which the consequences produced by a given course of action can be accurately ascertained (p. 425). Holmes was not satisfied with Marshall's presentation of economics as essentially a 'positive science', arguing that many of its practitioners were not immune to prescribing what they saw as the correct course of action and often used the laws of political economy to support what Holmes described as 'class-sided conclusions'. Marshall's second article, 'The Province of Political Economy', published 2 May 1874, attempted to rebut these objections. Marshall admitted that many economists did what Holmes was suggesting, but that leading economists such as Mill, anxious to apply political economy to broad social questions, were also fully aware of political economy's limitations. These, Marshall argued, had been strikingly portrayed in Mill's dictum that 'a person is not likely to be a good political economist who is nothing else', and that, as his previous article had demonstrated, 'direct decisions on questions of moral principle, political economy must leave to her sister, the Science of Ethics' (pp. 427, 430). It is interesting to note that the views on scope and method Marshall dished out to radical workers in the early 1870s were little different from those he presented two decades later to all students of the subject in his *Principles of Economics*.

Marshall's study of the practice of socialism was not confined to the British Isles. His unpublished manuscript on foreign trade related how 'some years ago [i.e., some time between 1869 and 1872] I attended a meeting advertised as of "the working man's party" in Frankfurt. There were present several hundred men whose countenances were remarkably intelligent. The strictest order prevailed, and there was no excitement which could urge the speakers into unusually strong language'. But they persistently spoke of capital as 'the enemy',[17] a sentiment Marshall clearly believed to be mistaken. More importantly, Marshall studied practical socialism at the religious community level during his visit to the United States in 1875. Marshall's account of his visit to New Lebanon and the Shaker settlement at Oneida was quoted in an earlier chapter. This included his testimony of the profound impression the strong moral character and gentlemanly nature one of these 'communists' had made on him.* Marshall's experience undoubtedly influenced the view given such prominence in the opening chapter of later editions of his *Principles*: 'the history of socialist ventures, shows that ordinary men are seldom capable of pure ideal altruism for any considerable time together; and that the exceptions are to be found only when the masterful fervour of a small band of religious enthusiasts makes material concerns to count

---

* See above, Chapter 7, p. 198, where this account is extensively quoted. Cf. the recollection of Beatrice Webb's niece, described in a letter of 31 October 1899, cited by Rita McWilliams-Tullberg, 'Marshall's Tendency to Socialism', p. 101 n.77: 'I went to Mrs. Marshall on Sunday, . . . Two of the company had visited the Shaker settlement in America and Mr. Marshall, who is a queer, dry old fellow, produced the Shaker bible, a sort of revelation and law code, and several pictures of their religious dances. He stayed several weeks in the settlement while studying communism and he gave me a graphic account of some of the dances over the top of my head. I was in the bottom of a low basket chair and the performance rather alarmed me.' (Catherine Dunning-Holt, *Letters from Newnham College 1889–92* (published privately).) In fact Marshall stayed no longer than two days in these settlements.

for nothing in comparison with the higher faith'. When writing this for the fifth edition some time during 1906, Marshall's pen may have been guided by 'the angelic character' of the young Swedish student who became a Shaker, because this movement represented 'the spirit of early Christianity worked out in life'; a role Marshall would have gladly adopted had he not been happy with what he was.[18]

The last expression of Marshall's youthful views on socialism appeared in the final parts of the *Economics of Industry*. Interestingly, its second edition preface (p.vi) referred to the 'Communism . . . which prevailed among the early Christians' as the basis for economics when 'everyone always found his greatest happiness in trying to do that which was best for others', a theme to which the final chapters of the book on trade unions, industrial relations and cooperation returned in a more prosaic manner. There is little which is particularly 'socialist' in these chapters. They simply recount the benefits and disadvantages of these organisations of labour, though their tone and style reveal a broad sympathy to their existence. An example of this even-handed approach is the comparison made between guilds and unions, because the last have reproduced 'the individual self sacrifice and class selfishness' of the former. The same applies to the careful discussion of the effect of trade unions on wages. This covered the contentious issue of securing wage increases through strike action from many perspectives, emphasising that since wages depend more on the work efficiency of the labourer than on a wages fund, high wages which raise efficiency are self-perpetuating (Book III, Chapter VI). When discussing differences between the interests of individual trade union members, the long-term future of a Union and the general well-being, the Marshalls contrasted the guiding principles which settled such conflicts in practice with those inherent in communist ideals:

> The communists assumed that no one should desire to gain at the expense of an equal loss of happiness to others; but the world is not yet ready for applying in practice principles of so lofty a morality as this. The world is however ready, and working men among others are ready, to endeavour to act up to the principle, that no one should desire a gain which would involve a very much greater loss of happiness to others.[19]

In line with the sentiments Marshall had expressed in the *Bee-Hive* five years previously, solving problems concerning the conflicting interests and duties of the different classes of industry was assisted by economic reasoning as to their consequences of benefit and loss, and were most 'profitably' discussed 'from the pulpit, in Social Science Associations, in Chambers of Commerce, in Trades Councils, and in Trades Union Congresses. And there is much to be gained from all movements which tend to bring employers face to face with their employés, to talk over peacefully the economic and moral grounds of any claims that may be advanced' (p. 213).

Marshall therefore favoured the conciliation and arbitration approach to industrial relations from an early age and, as shown later, was always ready to offer advice on such matters to his bishop friends for use by them in the pulpit and in the movements which succeeded the Social Science Association as forums for social debate. Likewise, his initial endorsement of cooperation in the final chapter of the book rested on the opportunities for extending both economic knowledge and industrial morality it promised, while its links with 'the greatest of English socialists, Robert Owen', early Christianity and contemporary practice in religious communities were stressed.

The reasons underlying this approach to cooperation say much about Marshall's position on socialism in 1879. Owen was praised because of 'his unbounded belief in the latent goodness of human nature and in the possibility of forming noble characters, his earnest desire to bring out whatever power of right action men have by trusting them and appealing to their reason, his carelessness about his own interests, the unrivalled business genius and insight by which he acquired vast gains, and the generosity with which he shared them with his operatives, and otherwise devoted them to his great social aims' (pp. 218–19). Cooperation was simultaneously sharply distinguished 'from most modern socialistic schemes, by advocating no disturbance of private property, by insisting on self-help, and by abhorring state-help and all unnecessary interference with individual freedom'.[20]

Marshall's tendency to socialism, even at the end of its youthful period, could therefore peacefully co-exist with the staunch individualism of the Charity Organisation Society on many issues. It also fitted harmoniously with the romantic picture of the altruistic and dynamic businessman he was then developing on the basis of his growing acquaintance in Bristol with this type, a position not only 'romantic' but also unrealistic, because it depended so much on the selective contact with men of business his position as University College Principal made possible. The Frys, so instrumental in the foundation of that college and in its subsequent government, as Quaker businessmen were engaged in 'chivalrous' and paternalist business management from which Marshall would have learnt much. However, they were hardly typical of the species.[21]

TUNING IN ON SOCIALIST RHAPSODIES: A BRIEF FLIRTATION WITH MARX, LASSALLE AND OTHER SOCIALIST UTOPIAN VISIONS

Marshall's practical involvement with socialist causes by attending workers' meetings was combined during the 1860s and early 1870s with studies of major socialist texts. His study of Mill's *Principles* brought the early British and French schools of socialism within his ambit by alerting him to the writings of Robert Owen, Proudhon, Fourier, Saint-Simon and Louis Blanc. Travel to Germany in search of skills by which to master Kant in the original German enabled Marshall to study the scientific socialism of Marx and Lassalle at first hand. These were the bearers of nineteenth-century socialism who trotted the stage in Marshall's lectures on socialism and on the functions of government which he gave to his Cambridge students in 1886.

Marshall's acquaintance with the classics of German socialism of the mid-nineteenth century can be documented first. Forty years after the event, Marshall recalled that an interest in what was practicable in social reform had induced his studies of Marx and Lassalle. A detailed commentary on Lassalle confirms this recollection. In a discussion of industrial and social progress for his 1870s manuscript on foreign trade, Marshall raised the feasibility of Lassalle's scheme for the federation of industries as a solution to the problems of commercial depression. Marshall conceded that Lassalle's scheme made no 'Utopian demands on the generosity of man' and contained realistic arguments on the possibility of enhancing worker efficiency through improved industrial organisation. Marshall nevertheless argued it failed to treat its many difficulties satisfactorily, often by simply ignoring them. Despite these failures, Lassalle had rendered a 'conspicuous service' to economics by pointing to the 'flaw' in economic organisation 'brought about by the free play of the interests of individual producers under the sway of untrammelled competition'. Although Lassalle showed no systematic bias against foreign trade in his work, he tended to understate the difficulties it caused in smoothing industrial fluctuations while, in addition, his work illustrated the connection between those seeking to protect industry from competition and those encouraging individuals to 'look to the State . . . for guidance and protection in all matters but particularly in the ordering of daily work'.*

Marshall's first reading of Marx also took place at this time. Marshall had drawn on his reading of the first volume of *Das Kapital* while making notes on his copy of Mill's *Principles*, and in fact used Marx's book as a general historical source. Marshall subsequently recalled in correspondence that his debt to Marx was confined to this use of *Capital* for data more difficult to obtain elsewhere during the late 1860s and early 1870s than was the case afterwards. Nor was Marshall's interest in Marx sufficiently sustained to induce him to read the second and third volumes of the book, as edited by Engels, when they appeared in 1885 and 1894.¶ However, in contrast with his treatment of Lassalle, Marshall devoted considerable space in his *Principles* to rebutting Marx's system, especially with respect to what Marshall called Marx's mis-reading of Ricardo on value and wages. Marshall's broad judgement of Marx included in the first edition reflects his mature opinion on the subject equally as well: 'The strength of Karl Marx's sympathies with suffering must always claim our respect: but what he regarded as the scientific foundation of his practical proposals appears to be little more than a series of arguments to the effect that there is no economic justification for interest, while the result has been all along latent in his premisses, though shrouded in the mysterious Hegelian phrases in which he delighted.'†

Rodbertus was the third of the trio of German revolutionary socialists Marshall tended to bracket in the *Principles*. These references suggest that by the early 1890s Marshall had

---

*   *EEW*, II, pp. 37–42, esp. pp. 37–9, 41. In 1906 Marshall wrote to Foxwell that German socialism could not be satisfactorily studied from English sources and that this applied to Lassalle as well as to Marx (Marshall to Foxwell, 12 February 1906, Marshall Archive, 1:73). Marshall's library contains his personal copies of Lassalle's *System der erwobenen Rechte* (2 vols 1861), a collection of his pamphlets (covering 1863–74) and his debate with Bastiat-Schulze von Delitzsch on the Arbeiterprogramm (1863, 1864).

¶   Alfred Marshall to an unidentified person, 20 October 1889 (Marshall Archive, 1:306); Alfred Marshall to Foxwell, 12 February 1906: 'to be frank, I think no one can lecture safely on German socialism without having studied recent writings including Marx's *Capital*, Vol. II and III, and other posthumous works. I have not read them.' (Marshall Archive 1:73). The rediscovery of Marshall's copies of *Capital* in CUL supports these contentions. Barry Worrall, 'Alfred Marshall's Readings of Das Kapital, Volume I', presented at the 7th HETSA Conference, Wollongong, July 1993, has carefully documented Marshall's annotations. And see above, Chapter 6, pp. 141, 148, 163, Chapter 9, p. 272 and n.*.

†   *P* I, 620; kept in all later editions with one interesting variation. The second edition (*P* II, p. 631) uses the word 'coquetting' which Marx had used himself in this context in the Afterword to the second German edition (*P* IX, p. 713), and explicitly shows that Marshall had looked at this edition as well. Marshall's 1886 lecture notes on socialism show his capacity to criticise the core of Marx's system identified with the theory of exploitation and surplus value (Marshall Archive, Box 5, Item 1C). It is interesting to note that Marshall's description of Marx as 'the great German socialistic writer' in his first Henry George Lecture delivered at Bristol in February 1883 was to be deleted in the published version (G.J. Stigler, 'Alfred Marshall's Lectures on *Progress and Poverty*', *Journal of Law and Economics*, 12 (1), April 1969, p. 185 and n.2). Cf. *IT*, p. 7 and n.2.

only studied Rodbertus's work at second hand – through both the commentary on Rodbertus in Anton Menger's *The Right to the Whole Produce of Labour*, and Böhm-Bawerk's critical review of Rodbertus's theory of exploitation.[22] An exception to Marshall's treatment of Rodbertus drew attention to the distinction between 'individual rights in capital in a historic-juristic sense . . . and the social view of capital' and subsequently mentioned that what Marx had called 'surplus value', Rodbertus described simply as 'plus-value'. Such level of detail on Rodbertus cannot be found in all editions. Its exclusive presence in the fourth edition is explicable because Rodbertus's *Over-production and Crises*, with an introduction by J.B. Clark, was published in 1898, the year Marshall prepared the fourth edition. This translation is also the only work by Rodbertus preserved in the Marshall Library.[23] It is of some interest given Marshall's strictures to Foxwell on the importance of studying German socialism at first hand, in the context of which Marshall failed to bracket Rodbertus with Lassalle and Marx, contrary to his usual practice. Recall Becattini's hypothesis that Marshall probably relied on his wife's German expertise and was himself less fluent in German than his citation practice suggests.[24]

Marshall's first-hand acquaintance with the classics of French socialism was even more selective. Apart from Louis Blanc's *Organisation du Travail*, of which Marshall owned a copy in the fourth French edition, his acquaintance with French socialist writings was largely gained at second hand. This is also implied in the suggested reading for his 1886 lecture course on socialism. Apart from a reference to Blanc's book just mentioned, and one to Proudhon's tract, 'intérêt et principal', no reading is recommended from Saint-Simon while Fourier was to be studied via Schäffle's *Quintessence of Socialism*. This limited reading pattern conforms with the contents of his 1886 lectures. The extant notes for them only elaborate Blanc's scheme of the 'state as organiser', criticising its omission of work incentives and the essential role of competition in price determination. Marshall's reference to the French socialists in the *Principles* likewise reflects a lack of acquaintance with their writing. After mentioning the useful work done by French economics in the nineteenth century, Marshall added 'Fourier, Saint Simon, Proudhon and Louis Blanc have made many of the most valuable as well as the wildest suggestions of Socialism'.[25] This implicitly recalled his inaugural lecture in which the positive contributions of this early socialism were elaborated in terms of their views on human nature and the 'hidden springs of human action'. First Comte, and then J.S. Mill, were greatly influenced by their 'shrewd observations and pregnant suggestions . . . buried among their wild rhapsodies', an influence Marshall called 'for the greater part, wholesome'. Such positive contribution was unfortunately marred by what Marshall saw as their inadequate 'historic and scientific study', the 'extravagance' of their expression and their defective understanding of the views they were criticising. This explained why their valuable opinions on human nature were so widely ignored.[26]

Marshall's emphasis on the early socialists' crucial contribution to understanding human nature makes it strange that he appears to have made little detailed study of Robert Owen's work. His 1886 class was advised to refer to Marx on the subject, while his library only boasted Owen's *Autobiography* (presumably the basis for the panegyric on Owen in *The*

Economics of Industry already quoted) together with some tracts on Owenism.[*]   Yet the general thrust of Owen's thinking quite strikingly resembles the broad social platform of character building Marshall was constructing, with its emphasis on the improving potential of education, work and family environment on human character, especially the character of the working man. Likewise, Owen's strong association with, and contribution to, the co-operative movement ought to have stimulated Marshall to seek a greater acquaintance with Owen's actual writings. Perhaps it was the negative reaction to Owen's ideas by leading British commentators with whom Marshall was acquainted that made him think that the only part of Owen's writing worthy of study was his life.[¶]

What Marshall learnt from contemporary socialist literature can therefore be encapsulated into essentially two points. From the German socialist writings, especially Marx's *Capital*, he gathered much historical fact about conditions in factories in the manner Marx paraphrased these from blue books and similar sources. In addition, Marshall adopted their view on the interdependence of the various parts of the social organism, with its implications for the possibility of changing human nature for the better, through improving the environment in which people lived and worked. For such reasons, Marshall could tell both his student, and a wider Cambridge University audience, that socialist writers should not be seen as ridiculous and that much in fact could be learnt from their writings. However, Marshall did not accept their emphasis on the role of the state in ameliorating social conditions, and never accepted their belief in the necessity of revolution for securing major change. Apart from Marshall's own examination of these issues, his reading of Mill's chapters on socialism as published in 1879 greatly reinforced socialism's negative and positive aspects for him. These started with the identification of revolutionary socialism as essentially un-British, continued with an emphasis on the need for socialists to address the question of motivation to labour, accumulation and management under socialism, and the evils associated from its tendency to concentrate on the redistributive aspects of socialism alone. Mill's analysis of such difficulties of socialism was as important to Marshall as Mill's more positive emphasis on the virtues of socialism in these chapters. These positive aspects provided solutions for the difficulties through profit sharing, small-scale experiments in workers' and state management and the overriding need for 'a high standard of both moral and intellectual education' to prepare the population for socialism. In short, irrespective of the socialist lessons from abroad, Marshall's socialist tendencies remained predominantly British and Millian.[27]

---

[*] 1886 Lectures on Socialism (Marshall Archive, Box 5, Item 1C). In *Capital*, Volume 1, the only book by Marx which Marshall had read, Marx referred to Owen's work on about half a dozen occasions, directly quoting however, from only one of Owen's works, *Observations on the Effects of the Manufacturing System*. This makes it difficult to see what major benefits Marshall's students could have derived from this source with respect to Owen. Barry Worrall has shown that Marshall had marked these comments in his personal copy of *Capital*. For Marshall's holdings of Owen's writings, see *Catalogue*, p. 62.

[¶] For example, it is surprising that Marshall failed to look at Owen's *A New View of Society; Essays on the Formation of Character*, published in serial form from 1813 and, for the first time in a collected edition, in 1816. This may be explained by the rather casual treatment Owen had received in Mill's *Principles* relative to the treatment Mill gave to he French Socialists, a practice surpassed by Sargant's treatment which totally ignored English socialist schemes apart from some discussion of cooperation (*Social Innovators and their Schemes*, London: Smith, Elder & Company, 1858, Chapter VIII, esp. pp. 460–68).

TILTING AT GEORGIAN WINDMILLS, THE SOCIAL DEMOCRATIC FEDERATION AND THE SOCIALISM OF FABIANS AND INDEPENDENT LABOUR

The posthumous publication of Mill's chapters on socialism in 1879 may be partly explained by the warnings they contained for the coming decade about the growing socialist spectre. In particular this frightened the liberal circles who had been applauding socialist schemes in the previous decade. The 1880s were different. These were the years during which there was a dramatic change in the originators of radical social reform policy in Britain. Influence of the old radical wing of the Liberal Party started to decline, and its former role as sole agent in the reform process was eroded by initiatives from socialist organisations and an increasingly independent labour movement. Signs of conflicts to come in the 1880s were plain to see in the 1880 parliamentary sessions. These included two pieces of legislation, the Ground Game Act and Employers' Liability Act, sponsored by liberals, but, as T.H. Green put it, 'opposed in the name of freedom . . . [because they] interfered with freedom of contract'.[28] As the decade advanced, socialist organisations gradually grew in importance in setting the social reform agenda. These ranged from Hyndman's Social Democratic Federation and the Socialist League led by William Morris to the Fabian Society and forerunners of a political Labour Movement separate from Liberal parties. Opportunities for non-liberal originated reform arose from several factors. The 1884 Reform Bill further extending the franchise was one; reforms in municipal government enabling a gradual expansion of municipal control and ownership was another. By the end of the 1880s, cities like Birmingham had extended municipal ownership to cover parks and gardens, museums, art galleries, libraries, baths, wash-houses, technical schools, cattle markets, street railways and tramways, concert halls, piers, harbour dispensaries, hospitals and workers' housing. This municipal socialism, as it became known, greatly depended on public borrowing to finance these public works, as well as on increases in local property taxation.[29]

A crucial symbol of, and catalyst in, this radicalisation of social and political reform in the 1880s was Henry George. Although George himself was not a socialist, his enormously popular *Progress and Poverty* by its optimistic tone, its emphasis on the unearned increment in the return to a very visible part of private property, and the timeliness of his proposals when landownership in Ireland and Britain was an important political question, made him a convenient ally for a growing socialist movement. Although George's book had been initially ignored in Britain, by 1884 it had sold over 100,000 copies, a splendid backdrop for his extensive and popular lecture tour of Britain in that year.[30] The Henry George phenomenon brought Marshall into a more anti-socialist mode even though, as he wrote to Foxwell, he personally doubted the book's influence when he asked himself 'whether one in fifty of them [the book's purchasers] had read [*Progress and Poverty*] to the end'.[31] It also involved Marshall in public lectures in Bristol and a well-publicised clash with Henry George at Oxford a year later.

Although Marshall was later to prove rather coy about publishing the text of his Henry George Lectures, despite strong urging by Foxwell and Sidgwick,[*] he seems not to have been very reluctant to lecture on the subject in early 1883 when invited to do so, and even consented to answer questions after each lecture posed by his essentially middle-class audience. The lectures were arranged by the Evening Class Extension Committee in an unsuccessful attempt at capturing a workers' audience for the evening classes of Bristol University College. The handbills advertising the lectures as followed by discussion from the floor, aroused some anxiety among members of the College Council. A Council meeting held after Marshall's first lecture on 19 February 1883 decreed it inadvisable to practice this procedure at any further public lectures which it sponsored. Despite the controversial nature of the topic, the audience generated little heat though its size rose from 141 at the first to 194 at the third lecture and at least two working-class socialists were present among the audience.[32] The lectures themselves show Marshall willing to engage in controversy when moved to do so. George's writings had clearly antagonised him sufficiently to engage him in a public affray, not only from the lecture podium at Bristol, where it could be seen as part of his duties, but from the audience as well at the public meeting in Oxford which Henry George addressed in March 1884.[¶]

The contents of the lectures themselves are very easily summarised. They follow the strategy which Marshall had outlined to Foxwell some days before he gave the first: addressing the subject of progress and poverty and ignoring the author. The first lecture therefore disassociated progress from poverty by showing that living standards (measured by real wages) had been rising for at least the last thirty years, even for agricultural labour. Some stubborn pockets of poverty and pauperism nevertheless persisted. Marshall summarised his first lecture in two brief statements: increased wealth had not entailed increased want; secondly, what required investigation was the slow 'diminution of want' when the growth of wealth was so rapid.[33]

Marshall's second lecture was devoted to the theory of distribution, designed in particular to address the question of low wages. Following the *Economics of Industry*, the problem was discussed in two stages. Marshall agreed with George on rent determination; this left the share of capital and labour or 'the earnings-and-interest fund'. Its division

---

[*]   Marshall to Foxwell, 30 March, 22 July and 8 August 1883, in the last of which Marshall wrote: 'Sidgwick has written urging me to publish Progress and Poverty lectures. It is hard lines for one who hates controversy more than he does George to be forced into controversy: but I suppose I must do something at the beginning of next year.' His excuses for not publishing were that it would detract from his more important writing for the *Principles* and that, after the death of Toynbee in the aftermath of his Henry George Lectures, and given that Marshall was to succeed him at Oxford, he did not want to do anything with his lectures lest it cause offence in Oxford (Marshall Archive, 3:13, 3:19 and 3:20). Earlier he had written to Foxwell, 'I am in for three lectures in a workman's quarter of Bristol on Progress and Poverty. I intend to avoid talking very much about George but to discuss his subject.' (Marshall Archive, 3:10).

[¶]   Marshall to Foxwell, 10 March 1884 (Freeman Collection, 12/73); 'George disappointed me altogether. He seemed to be in earnest in a way but to have absolutely no intellectual honesty – no desire for truth, but only for victory. He never attempted – so at least every one to whom I have spoken agrees – to answer a single question. He seemed to give his whole energies to rhetorical subterfuges that would enable him to avoid answering it. These subterfuges would have gone down with an uneducated audience; but not where he was. I wish I had seen him before. I should have talked about him much less. I think him an extremely able man; quite as much as ever; but I don't see any reason for thinking that he has that kind of ability which will make a permanent impression on opinion.'

depended, Marshall argued, on the relative scarcity of labour and capital, other things being equal; while absolute size of the shares going to labour and capital depended on growth of the fund overall. This led to the crux of his views on poverty: 'if the numbers of unskilled labourers were to diminish sufficiently, then those who did unskilled work would have to be paid good wages' (p. 193), a rather different position on the subject from that presented two years earlier to Cambridge rural workers.[34] The effects of progress on income shares needed therefore further discussion. The law of productivity of land was one of diminishing returns; but this also applied to capital and labour though in a more complex way. The last proposition demonstrated George's error on fact and theory in stating wages and interest were either both high together or low together, 'for whenever population is plentiful and capital scarce, interest is high and wages low' (p. 195). Comparisons of wage and interest rate levels in Western and Eastern Europe, or in Eastern Europe and Asia, Marshall asserted, showed that George's views did not match the facts. Marshall also argued that growth in population need not necessarily lower wages if the efficiency of the population was kept up. This was achievable through increased investment, by which Marshall meant more than new machinery. A direct lesson from the early phases of the industrial revolution, where the opposite had been the rule, was that 'a well fed and well educated population is in the long run the best investment for a nation's capital' (p. 197). Apportioning blame for past mistakes, was, however, not helpful at this stage; removal of the 'shame' of continuing poverty was the thing to be achieved. The second lecture therefore resolved that though it was 'too late to get rid of poverty in our generation; . . . our children, or at all events our children's children, shall be free from it'. Managed competition, something about which 'we are learning fast', is essential to this process of achieving a 'free nation' in which 'the moral and mental strength of the great mass of the nation' can continue to rise as fast as it had done for the previous thirty years (p. 197).

Marshall's final lecture addressed the issue of whether the nationalisation of land was a remedy for poverty. Although Marshall was sympathetic to restricting the rights of private property in land for social reasons, he could not subscribe to George's plan of 'raising taxes on land so far that the State appropriated the net value of the inherent properties of the soil'. Apart from the fiscal consequences of this – Marshall, for example, doubted whether 'taking taxes off spirits would be an unmixed benefit' (p. 208) – its potential social consequences of convulsing society and risking civil war were so great, that a 'less sensational cure' for poverty should be tried. Instead, Marshall's own 'remedy for poverty' was to manage competition 'to increase the competition of capital and of the upper classes of industry for the aid of the lower classes' (p. 209). Postponement of marriage to slow population growth, emigration together with state provision 'at a nominal price' of universal quality technical education and 'first rate education to even the poorest child' with ability, were necessary steps to bend competition to this end. Cooperation, trade societies and even economists could assist the educative process of the working class, aimed at achieving 'a higher sense of duty in the community'. Marshall's concluding remarks showed what he saw as the end of this process – the 'socialist' utopia he was aiming at, in which family ties, plain living, self-help and cooperation combined to secure a better world:

Man is the perfection of nature, but woman is one step further still. Progress in general and the abolition of poverty depend above all on the strength and gentleness and purity and earnestness of the women of England. It is they that form character when it is most plastic. If the mothers of a nation are ignoble that nation must fall; if they are noble it must rise. If the men and women of England set themselves with holy purpose to make the next generation stronger in body and mind and spirit than this is, and if our children do the same by their children, the pauper will disappear, and those working men whose pay is so poor and whose work is so hard that they are cut off from the higher possibilities of life, they too will vanish away (p. 210).

The responses to questions and discussion from the floor reveal Marshall's ability in handling an audience and in playing to the gallery with considerable enjoyment and spontaneity. Commenting, for example, on the likely success of a 'socialistic movement as founded by the Apostles', Marshall replied amidst laughter and applause: 'if they had the virtues of early Christians they would have no pauperism, no misery, no property, and no trouble. Men as they were, were bound to get lazy if their laziness did not cause them much trouble. If they could get men of which this was not true, he for one would hold up his hand for socialism' (p. 191). Responding to questions about the management of competition, Marshall argued that factory legislation and regulation of dishonesty and adulteration in manufacturing were important examples of such management. He also stressed that improved organisation such as voluntary profit sharing could enhance labour efficiency considerably (p. 199). On unproductive members of society, Marshall admitted only 'those who lived on the income derived from property without putting forth efforts of their own' as falling within this category. However, he warned that without capitalists and capital, people would turn into 'savages' and existence itself would be threatened (p. 200). Only one question appears to have stumped him. A questioner drew Marshall's attention to the fact that many agricultural labourers earned less than 14 shillings a week while many more supported large families on less than £1 per week, and that Marshall's political economy solutions only seemed capable of helping the 'rich and middle classes and not the poor'. On one account, this elicited Marshall's tame agreement that such evils existed but that he could see no other remedy than those he had provided in the third lecture. The other press report stated Marshall's general agreement with the questioner about the unsatisfactory nature of the situation, but that, 'without overthrowing society and injuring the working man', only gradual improvement was possible. Dividing political economy into one for the rich and one for the poor, as the speaker had done, Marshall described as 'a rather risky thing' (p. 212).[35]

Marshall's lectures on Henry George are particularly interesting because they contain many of the key features of his 'tendency to socialism' of the small 's' variety, which he retained throughout his later life. These included his abhorrence of revolutionary measures and change, stress on the role of self-help including cooperation and other forms of working-class mutual aid, emphasis on the role of private capital and business ability in securing progress, assisted by the economic freedom from managed competition and, above all, the remedy for low wages from reducing the relative scarcity of labour, especially unskilled labour, and from improved worker efficiency through training, education, machinery and a higher standard of life. The concluding chapter(s) of the *Principles* devoted to progress highlighted this type of perspective on the removal of poverty with only one major addition in the later editions of that work: Marshall's greater acceptance of the virtues of fiscal redistributive action induced by his change of mind on the consequences of progressive taxation and the taxation of capital.[36] Marshall's choice of vehicle for expressing such sentiments has a number of peculiar features. Why choose lectures on *Progress and Poverty* to air these views? What was it about Henry George and his book that drove him to controversy on the subject? Marshall's description of George as a 'poet' and his rejection of him as 'a scientific thinker' (p. 186),[*] combined with Marshall's dislike of George's outdated economics, his unfair criticism of some of Marshall's more favourite classical economists and most importantly, his lack of grasp of the views of contemporary economics, are important clues to Marshall's choice of victim. This is reinforced by the nature of the annotations Marshall made on his personal copy of *Progress and Poverty*,[¶] and from the thrust of his critical reactions to that book in the early editions of his *Principles*.[†]

However, Marshall's annoyance with George also implied a sense of frustration in dealing with an adversary of this type. Tackling George's fallacies, he wrote to Foxwell,[‡] was 'like throwing myself against a door that is not fastened' and his hope to be enlightened by audience reaction as to 'what to attack' was dashed, since he got no inkling from his Bristol lectures as to which of George's errors had most seized the popular imagination.

This sense of frustration comes through in Marshall's dogged pursuit of his quarry when he encountered George in person at a meeting at Oxford which the American addressed in 1884. A report of the meeting showed Marshall first on the floor to open the questioning, an activity he diligently pursued for as long as the tolerant chairman of the proceedings allowed, in order to get a concise answer to his rather rambling questions. Marshall challenged George to indicate how he differed from noted philanthropists like Lord Shaftesbury, Octavia Hill, John Stuart Mill and Toynbee, to show to the audience 'one single economic doctrine in [his] book which was new and true', to confess that he, as a

---

[*] George Stigler, 'Alfred Marshall's Lectures on Progress and Poverty', p. 199, shows Marshall explained this characterisation further in response to a question from the floor. 'He did not call Mr. George a poet because he said erroneous things. He was a poet because he was poetic, and he was not a man of science because he said erroneous things.' Elsewhere in the lecture he implied George was a painter to be condemned because he 'filled his canvas with diseased subjects; . . . [a painter] is most pleasant and does most good when he paints what is beautiful and noble' (p. 186). Marshall's analogy depicts socialists as artists with warm hearts, in contrast to men of science like economists who need, and have, cool heads to get at the facts.

[¶] Preserved in the Marshall Library. For example, on Book II, Chapter II of *Progress and Poverty*, Marshall noted: 'What he says is old-fashioned and self-contradictory. He doesn't realise the difference between individual and national wealth'. Other annotations note misrepresentations of Mill and Malthus. Virtually all of Marshall's comments relate to the first three books, there are few comments or annotations on the remainder of the work which presented the non-economic part of George's argument.

[†] *P* I, p. 138 and p. 714 n. As Stigler has commented, after Henry George had criticised Marshall's *Principles* as frequently incoherently and incomprehensible, Marshall removed his own detailed criticism of George from the *Principles*, leaving only the general reference on George's eloquence and splendid description of the 'growing richness of human life as the backwoodsman finds neighbours settling around him', the sign of the poet rather than the man of science and, surprisingly shared by the 'unwonted enthusiasm' of John Stuart Mill on a similar subject. (See 'Alfred Marshall's Lectures on *Progress and Poverty*', p. 183; *P* I, p. 379, n.1, retained throughout all eight editions, though increasingly in a form designed to detract further from George's qualities).

[‡] Marshall to Foxwell, 22 July 1883 (Marshall Archive 3:19). The letter starts: 'As a general proposition, I maintain that it is more important to establish truth than to confute error, and that controversy should be left to people with sound digestions'.

completely untrained person in economics, proposed to give advice to the working class thereby unwittingly preventing them 'rising from their low position' and that this amounted to misusing his immense gifts in influencing public opinion for the better, by instilling 'poison into [working class] minds'. In response, George clearly evaded these varied challenges. He argued that Marshall was asking too many questions, and that given Marshall's claim that he had already refuted 'George's' doctrines, he was placed in the position of the British general who never acknowledged 'when he was beaten'. One question at a time was all his 'small head' and 'tired mind' could stand, a request Marshall obliged by next querying the lack of emphasis on thrift and industry in *Progress and Poverty* as means for working-class improvement. By indicating he had not intended to answer questions on the contents of *Progress and Poverty*, George likewise avoided answering this more specific question, adding by way of explanation that his memory was 'rusty' as to his book's contents because 'it was a good while since he had the pleasure of reading the book'. Marshall then challenged George's views on rent with respect to its alleged monopoly component. Amidst growing tumult among the audience, Marshall had to repeat this question again and again because George, equally repeatedly, failed to answer it, a strategy George denied when Marshall charged it directly, but which the audience accepted.[37] The surprise of Marshall's performance is the ardour with which he pursued his questioning. Marshall's disappointment with both George's Oxford performance and his lack of intellectual honesty, as reported to Foxwell, was quoted previously. His reaction resembles that recorded by J.N. Keynes after hearing a similar performance by George at the Cambridge Guild Hall before what also was essentially an undergraduate audience. This described the speech as 'inconclusive and irrelevant, but eloquent and in earnest, passionate and nervously excitable and highly wrought'.[38]

Marshall's Bristol lectures involved him in controversy with Alfred Wallace, the land nationaliser and evolutionist. This consisted of an exchange of letters in the Bristol press. The first of these charged Marshall's account of improved living conditions for labour in England with error on the basis that comparative wage data did not capture real additions to living standards from ownership of cottages, own produce, and changes in the quality of wheat. Wallace also claimed Marshall's Asian comparison was flawed since low wages there reflected low prices, while high interest matched the high risk from political and other extortion.[39] Using data from Arthur Young and from Eden, which Marshall had then only recently studied[40], it was easy for him to show that Wallace was mistaken on the first count. Marshall also rebutted Wallace's claim with respect to Asian interest rates and wages. Conceding that government was partly responsible for the first, Marshall argued that recourse by Asian governments to European capital markets for purposes such as railway construction nevertheless proved his point that capital there was scarce and interest high.[41] Wallace's reply acknowledged Marshall's likely authority on the matter of measuring living standard changes but pointed to official acceptance of his view on declining rural living standards as reported by Royal Commissions, citing also Brodrick's *English Lands and English Landlords* on the point that both Arthur Young and Malthus erred in measuring changes in the value of labour solely by the price of bread. Nor did he concede the facts about Asian wages, based as they were on his personal observations.

In the final letter of the exchange, Marshall noted Wallace's position on living standards neglected the changed purchasing power of wheat. He also stuck to his guns on low Asian wages when defined in terms of the 'food, clothing, houseroom and other necessaries, comforts and luxuries' which money wages can buy.[42] The Wallace–Marshall controversy conveys the concern in debates of this nature about the effects of capitalist progress on living standards, in which those on the side of capital invariably sought to demonstrate the potential of free enterprise to improve the living conditions for all.[43] Equally interesting, it reveals Marshall's eagerness to defend himself in print when charged, inaccurately as he usually tended to believe, with errors in publicly stated arguments. Weak digestion notwithstanding, a rapid Marshallian response could generally be expected in such cases by the antagonist in question. However, when his public stance on the issue induced an invitation from the Land Reform Union to engage in public debate with Henry George in London, Marshall declined because 'it would have upset me and prevented my doing any writing during the vacation'.[44] However, inability to count on a supportive chairman and audience as at Oxford or Bristol was probably an additional, and more important, reason.

It should be mentioned that Marshall's position on land taxation and on the unearned increment was in the final analysis not dissimilar to George's position on these subjects. This is not surprising given the support for such taxation traditionally provided by the classical economists, and the emphasis in his writings and even political leadership given by John Stuart Mill on what was known as the land question.[45] Marshall's disdain for unproductive members of the community living on an unearned increment was disclosed in his responses to the Bristol lectures; his published discussion of land taxation in the *Principles* reflects such sentiments in a more refined, policy-orientated form.

However, like George, he opposed land nationalisation. Unpublished notes 'on the State in relation to Land'[46] preserved among his papers illustrate this quite clearly. Compulsion in this, as in other matters was injurious to both individuals and State; the State could probably manage land less well than private owners could; while it would be virtually impossible to separate land from its improvements as confiscatory taxation of the unearned increments in practice implied. Marshall was willing to admit some exceptions to his anti-nationalisation stance. In India, 'where government was much wiser than the people',[47] objections to land nationalisation were less strong; state management was appropriate in the operation of public utilities often involving substantial land holdings; while the State had also a proper interest in the control of historical monuments and more generally, things of beauty. Hence land taxation was often appropriate, particularly if applied selectively and when combined with the public power to purchase. Part of Marshall's support for the land tax as a fiscal tool arose from his support for the garden city movement, where revenue raised from property taxation could be legitimately used to reduce urban overcrowding in some areas and provide resources to maintain access to clean air, open spaces and workers' garden allotments in new towns.[48]

Marshall subsequently engaged in a number of similar anti-socialist altercations, though on a smaller scale. One of these arose from his participation in the Industrial Remuneration Conference held in London over three days from 28 to 30 January 1885. This conference had been organised by the trustees of a bequest of £1,000 for the discussion of social questions left by a Scottish engineer. The trustees, who included Sir Thomas Brassey, Tom

Burt (Marshall's trade union acquaintance, perhaps made on this occasion) Robert Giffen, representing the statistical society, and Foxwell, proposed that the meeting be devoted to a discussion whether the existing distribution of income was satisfactory or not and how, if need be, it could be improved. Sir Charles Dilke acted as President of the Conference, two other M.P.s, including John Mundella, who was to join Marshall on the Labour Commission, were Vice-Presidents, and a committee drawn from the trustees, members nominated by the Statistical Society, Trades Unions, cooperative societies and chambers of commerce, selected the 150 delegates represented at the conference and the 19 speakers who addressed it over its three days. Among the participants was a good representation of the trade union leadership, and many others whom Marshall was later to encounter during his membership of the Royal Commission on Labour, either in the witness box or as fellow commissioners. The Agenda for the three days of the conference had a decidedly Georgist flavour, dealing as it did in addition to its main distributional brief with the effect on the wealth and welfare of the community from the state management of capital and land.[49]

Marshall's address on the Thursday morning dealt with employment fluctuations and wages in relation to their remedial causes, but his paper by way of appendices added his address given earlier to the Cooperative Congress on theories and facts about wages, some material on the inter-dependence of industry drawn from Bagehot's *Lombard Street*, material drawn from his discussion of London housing and, in preliminary outline, the proposal for a tabular standard of value.[50] Perhaps conscious of his very newly acquired responsibilities as Professor of Political Economy, Marshall started the proceedings by claiming he himself was a socialist 'in one sense' only, attacked what he considered to be 'social utopias', argued that ultimate good rested on a form of social organisation in which duties supplanted rights, and unambiguously condemned government activity in the economic field (pp. 173–4). Apart from what he saw as the inherent waste in government management,

A greater evil is that it deadens the self-reliant and inventive faculties and makes progress slow. But the greatest evil of all is that it tends to undermine political and through political, social morality. . . . The greatest calamity that has ever happened to the United States is the political corruption which has grown up through moneys being allowed to influence politics [and which has especially] injured the working classes. . . . Therefore, I say, let us avoid asking Government to interfere in business, whether to make employment continuous or for any other purpose, unless its action will give a very large balance of direct good (pp. 174–5).

As further effective disproof of the case made by some socialists for government intervention to remedy fluctuations in employment and low wages, Marshall then proceeded to list his own remedies for this growing problem. These included avoiding following fashion in dress; more openness in business, including the publication of tax returns; stricter penalties for bankruptcy; increasing moral indignation against gambling by the young and in business, or non-legitimate speculation; government publication of a tabular standard of value; raising the national cash reserve to remedy financial panics; official trade forecasts prepared and published by independent experts; reform of the land laws; and last but not least, more work at economic science (pp. 176–9). Many of these proposals were to feature during Marshall's involvement with Royal Commissions, others became part and parcel of his views in progress published in the *Principles*.[51] His conclusion looked forward to his last public address as Professor of Political Economy, on Economic Chivalry, and matched the lofty ideals of his final Bristol lecture on Progress and Poverty of two years before:

> The age of chivalry is not over, it is dawning now in this present generation. For now we are beginning to see how dependent the possibilities of leading a noble life are on physical and moral surroundings. However great may be our distrust of forcible socialism, we are rapidly getting to feel that no one can lay his head on his pillow at peace with himself, who is not giving of his time and his substance to diminish the number of outcasts in society and increase the number of those who can earn a reasonable income and have the opportunity of living if they will a noble life (p.183).

Marshall's paper drew indirect criticism from Mr Sedgwick (of the Boot and Shoe Riveters and Finishers Union in Leicester). Sedgwick contrasted the indirect benefits of machinery on the cost of living with its direct consequences for those employed in the affected industry: lower wages and reduced employment, a reduction in living standards far greater than the gains to which Marshall had drawn attention (pp. 209–10). A direct assault came from a Mr Rowland, representing the Cab-drivers Society. Describing Marshall as a 'bookworm' rather than a university man who had 'taken the stroke oar of the University boat'[52] and was 'thereby able to tackle the battle of life better', he mistakenly attacked Marshall's critique of gambling as disapproval of sport and similar working-class recreations. Instead, Rowland argued, Marshall should have (as he indeed had done), attacked gambling 'on the Bourse' (pp. 210–11). Not surprisingly, Marshall agreed with two-thirds of what his critic had said. However, he denied he was a 'bookworm' and in continuing his reply revealed himself as an admirer of football fans:

> As to thousands of people watching a football match, and keeping up their interest in spite of the bitter cold, it was one of the grandest things in the world. As far as a sporting paper told one how games were carried on, instead of encouraging readers to bet upon them, he had nothing to say against it. A reference to his paper would show that on this point he had been misunderstood, and that in what he said about gambling he was not speaking of the working classes chiefly; he was speaking about the gambling spirit that had invaded the most progressive countries of the world, and was a greater evil for the future than drunkenness; for though not as great an evil now, it was likely to increase while drunkenness diminished. That conviction was forced upon him fifteen years ago, when he was assisting German working men.[53] He had high ideas of what the Germans would do with their leisure; to his horror he found that a great many of them spent a great part of it in petty gambling. He also found that working men in America were being tempted away from the noble opportunities before them, and were speculating largely in mines; even servant girls were doing it. In writing the paper, however, he had not these things so much in view as he had the interruption to industry caused by illegitimate speculation in business; and that illegitimate speculation was fostered by a habit of gambling which was encouraged even among little children, who would bet on races. He maintained that reckless gambling was in all classes a great evil, and that advancing education did not stop it, although it did stop drunkenness. It was on this account a much wider and further reaching evil, and it was one that would have to be circumscribed, unless the working classes were prepared to see their industry thrown out of gear a great deal more than it had been (pp. 213–14).

The previous day, Marshall had been attacked on his intervention in the proceedings in which he claimed that statistics showed workers' living standards were steadily improving and that, with full equalisation of income, income on average per capita would amount only to £36.8s. on the available data (p. 77). This drew the response that if this effect of levelling was made widely known, that is, if full equality of income gave all families £180 a year, 'there would be a revolution at once' (p. 122).* Another worker criticised Marshall for posing the wrong question: 'the question was not whether the worker was better off than his grandfather . . . , but whether he was as well off as the resources of the country entitled him to be.' (p. 83). To that, Marshall gave no answer that has been reported.

Although Marshall on his own account continued to frequent socialist lectures during the early 1880s[54], no details of such activities have been preserved. Nor are there any accounts of a debate with Hyndman, similar to the encounter with Henry George, such as may have taken place either during Hyndman's address on socialism at Oxford University's Russell Club (30 January 1884) or when he participated in the Cambridge Union Debate on that topic the following month (5 February 1884).[55] However, Marshall's public anti-militant socialist stance continued during the whole of the 1880s. For example, after praising the early socialists for their unduly neglected insights into human nature, his 1885 inaugural lecture returned to an argument with which Marshall had tackled George in Oxford. This concerned the dangers to society of letting loose 'untrained minds' in economics to solve its visible social evils of poverty in material, industrial and moral life and environment. 'Why should it be left for impetuous socialists and ignorant orators to cry aloud that no one ought to be shut out by the wants of material means from the opportunity of leading a life that is worthy of man?'[56] Similar warnings about the danger of revolutionary action came at the conclusion of Marshall's 1887 'Plea for a fair rate of Wages'. Two years later, they took centre stage in his defence of cooperation as a scheme for working-class self-help far superior 'in practical wisdom' to others in 'developing the world's material resources'.[1]

Marshall's public stance on a more militant socialism as a means for alleviating social distress reflected the growing alarm about the spectre of working-class violence of a frightened liberal middle class sympathetic to reform. This fear had been evoked by riots in London in the mid-1880s. More important in the longer run to thoughtful social observers was the gradual transformation of unionism from the older, skilled craftsman organisations-cum-benevolent societies into a new, more aggressive union movement, embracing masses of unskilled labour on the docks, in the mines and in public utilities. When this new unionism, combined with the active formation of working-class political organisations

---

* Cf. John Saville, introduction to Industrial Remuneration Conference, *Report*, p. 41 n.83. Marshall's implication that the sum available to individuals from complete equalisation of income is a mere pittance is explicable in terms of what he described a year or so previously as the necessary minimum for a bachelor Fellow at an Oxford or Cambridge college. This he had set at £300, a sum which would enable four months travel abroad at a total cost of £60 (reported in *Oxford Magazine*, 28 November 1883 and subsequently in the *Pall Mall Gazette*, 29 November 1883, p. 4). No wonder that the *Principles* consistently argued that the necessary consumption for efficiency should be much higher for 'the highest rank of industry, including the professional classes' as compared with unskilled and even skilled manual labour (*P* I, pp. 123–4; *P* VIII, p. 70 n.2, the quantitative estimates unchanged between editions). Delicate food for weak digestions was one explanation, perhaps drawn from personal experience, for this higher cost for the thinker.

¹ In *Memorials*, pp. 212–26. Its last line reads, 'all these [suggestions for ensuring fair wages] are steps upwards. They have not the rapid pace of a revolution: but a revolution sometimes rushes backwards faster and further than it had moved forwards; and steps such as these move steadily onwards' (p. 226). 'Co-operation', in *Memorials*, pp. 227–8; its contents and implied anti-socialist sentiments were discussed above, Chapter 13, pp. 457–8.

outside the liberal fold, including explicit socialist organisations such as Hyndman's Social Democratic Federation and the more middle-class intellectual Fabian Society, these fears became particularly strong.[57] As Sidney Webb proclaimed in his 1889 historical view of the basis of socialism, 'political democracy' had been transformed into a 'complete, though unconscious socialism' while the 'old individualism' and *laissez faire* was 'gliding irresistibly into a collectivist socialism'.[58]

This socialist tide was not unresisted during the 1880s and 1890s. From the pens of two mentors from Marshall's youth came strong anti-socialist tracts: Herbert Spencer's *The Man versus the State* in 1884, followed by Sir Henry Sumner Maine's warnings on the dangers of *Popular Government* the following year. These texts became the inspiration for the staunch anti-socialist Liberty and Property Defence League with its militant *laissez faire* dogma, and provided intellectual foundations for the anti-socialist and individualist philosophies of the Charity Organisation Society, captured in the writings of Loch, the Bosanquets and in the economics sphere in particular, by Thomas Mackay.[59] They accompanied, and possibly fostered, an increasingly hostile attitude to socialism by Marshall as the 1880s gradually turned into the 1890s.[60]

How far Marshall swam with this anti-socialist movement can be seen from his performance in the taking of evidence by the Labour Commission. Marshall's hostile approach to socialist witnesses appearing before the Commission is illustrated by his questions to Ben Tillett, Tom Mann and more strikingly, Sidney Webb and Henry Hyndman, but, contrary to the claims by Beatrice Webb, Marshall rarely showed such animosity to ordinary working-class witnesses. Samples of the evidence Marshall collected from the first three have already been given;[61] some reference to Marshall's examination of Hyndman is apt in the present context. Marshall's questioning started with an attempt to get Hyndman's agreement on the improvement of workers' living standards from rising money wages combined with the favourable cost of living impact from free trade in food and productivity growth in manufacturing. This failed to budge Hyndman from his view that money wages had not risen 'very fast' and that relatively few of the century's productivity gains had accrued to labour. Next, Marshall tried to secure Hyndman's agreement on the crucial role of the capitalist, and on the necessity of interest in securing industrial growth and development. Hyndman countered this with sarcastic remarks on abstinence, particularly after Marshall referred to payment for 'deferred enjoyment', and by pointing to the greater share of the product a worker would get from a cooperative system. Marshall then changed tack to clarify a reference Hyndman had made to Marshall's own views on the detrimental effects on future generations from urban overcrowding. Marshall explained he had introduced this topic to make a number of points. First he noted that even here some improvements had taken place, largely through sanitary and other public health measures, but secondly, that urban overcrowding owed much to the selfish desires of adult workers for urban living without any concern for their offspring; but that this situation was remediable by both personal, and fiscal aid, without any need, or desire to 'revolutionise society'.

Hyndman's clever response accepted these perspectives and conceded that if the aim was to replace competition by cooperation, he and Marshall were essentially agreed.*

Marshall had also used the Commission to advance his knowledge of details about issues of social reform in which he was particularly interested. These covered the employment, and other, consequences of municipal socialism as applied to transport; aspects of conciliation and arbitration practice; the *modus operandi* of profit-sharing schemes on which the Commission had also prepared its own report; and details of cooperative enterprises in wholesale and retail trade. In addition, Marshall demonstrated considerable interest in exploring the remedies for intermittent unemployment, low wages and excessive physical labour. Some of these he addressed in his contributions to the Commission's Final Report, and were issues in which his long-standing interest was demonstrated from the contents of his lectures on *Progress and Poverty*, his address to the Industrial Remuneration Conference and to the Cooperative Congress he had chaired. His behaviour on the Royal Commission reveals his neat differentiation of ameliorating social action, which on occasions he included in 'socialism' as defined in his special way, from the more militant socialist tendencies which flourished in the 1880s and early 1890s. Thus, fitting in closely with the prevailing atmosphere, Marshall's position on socialism in the 1880s and early 1890s tended to be at its most antagonistic.

THE ECONOMIST'S SOCIALISM 'OF THE PRESENT GENERATION'

Webb's historical survey of emerging British socialism drew attention to the view of a 'competent economist . . . that all the younger men are now socialists, as well as many of the older Professors', a view endorsed, albeit equally regretfully, by Thomas Mackay in his critique of orthodox economics. Written in the 1890s, much of Mackay's remarks were directed at Alfred Marshall.[62] What were the characteristics which turned the British academic economists into the equivalent of their German *kathedersozialisten* counterpart? Marshall's attitudes to the socialist questions of the day as expressed from the late 1890s can be conveniently summarised under the rubric of small 's' socialism. This covered support for some state enterprises and municipal socialism; tax and social welfare policy for redressing social inequality and poverty; profit sharing and cooperation, as more satisfactory forms of working-class organisation than the new trade unionism. Marshall's liberalism and small 's' socialism is equally revealed in his stance on imperialism as it revived in Britain at the turn of the century. His views on some of these matters were encapsulated in a final *ex-*

---

*   *Fourth Report of the Royal Commission on Labour*, Cmnd 7963, HMSO, London, 1893, Q. 8,606–69. On the appointment of the Royal Commission, Hyndman had written to the *Times* that its investigation of 'the relations between labour and capital may be taken as yet another admission that the days of laissez-faire are at an end' (13 March 1891). He later recalled, he was 'foolish enough to offer myself as a witness', only gaining 'just a little fun out of this dull and useless and costly Royal Commission in a few of the definitions of words and phrases and statements in my evidence which I supplied at the Secretary's request'. (H.M. Hyndman, *Further Reminiscences*, London: Macmillan, 1912, pp. 14–22). This also gives a humorous sketch of the chairman's attitude to the proceedings, at odds with Mann's later recollections quoted previously (above, p. 364). Hyndman's reminiscences summed up the overall attitude of the Commission as 'eager to help the workers *in* their poverty but not *out* of it.' (*ibid.*, p. 18, my italics).

cathedra statement on 'the Social Possibilities of Economic Chivalry', encountered previously as his substitute submission to the 1905 Poor Law Commission.[63]

'Let the State be up and doing'. Marshall's position on the comparative advantages of the State in managing business enterprise was apparent in his earlier addresses on socialism and, more concisely, in the fragment dealing with the State in relation to land. These views depended on a number of propositions, often repeated in his published and unpublished writings, and to which he seems to have adhered in varying degrees over the whole of his life. The incentives to enterprise from ownership and active involvement in a business was one such principle. Private capital, as he argued time and time again, was essential for economic development. Secondly, bureaucracies established to manage state enterprise would be adverse to risk taking, and hence inimical to an essential feature of economic progress. Such bureaucracies were also prone to corruption, an argument derived from Smith, but a conclusion visible in the United States, even though modern mechanisms of publicity could do much to reduce a tendency to corruption. For Marshall these grounds provided a general presumption in favour of private capitalist enterprise and against state enterprise, though as always there were exceptions to this general rule.

When, as he realised increasingly in the last decades of his life, joint-stock companies drove a wedge between ownership and control of business, and the incentives for good management from family ownership became a thing of the past, large-scale private enterprise more and more resembled large-scale government enterprise. Such growing similarity included the managerial difficulties which were a major part of Marshall's argument against state ownership of business. Hence Marshall predicted a tendency for government business to expand, even though 'this extension brings great evils: and ought to be opposed save when it can make a strong *prima facie* case for efficiency and economy'.[64] More importantly, Marshall excepted government ownership and control over public utilities which were natural monopolies, and argued for greater leeway in government initiative at the local and municipal level, even though he drew the line well before many of the more ardent supporters of such municipal socialism. The qualified case for the former was made in one of the oldest parts of the *Principles*, the chapter on monopolies, where the dangers from public administration could be eliminated if appropriate statistical measures of public benefit were found. Even here, however, as Marshall put it emphatically in his paper on 'economic chivalry', 'When municipalities boast of their electric lighting and power works, they remind me of the man who boasted of "the genius of my *Hamlet*" when he had printed a new edition of it. The carcass of municipal electric works belongs to the officials; the genius belongs to free enterprise'.[65]

A letter to Helen Bosanquet some years earlier sheds further light on Marshall's views on the role of municipalities:

I admit that Municipal socialism has many dangers, economic and moral. I think municipalities should not speculate or employ 'direct' labour nearly as much as they already do.

I think also that public authority cannot meddle with the inside of a man's house very much without risking injury to self-reliance and wholesome independence. Municipal housing seems to me scarcely ever right and generally very wrong. Municipal free baths seem to me nearly always right.

> But the outside of a man's house is not his affair: it is the affair of the State or Municipality. The darkness and the polluted air of his surroundings narrow the life and undermine the springs of strength and independence of character for him and his wife and above all for his children, who lack play.[66]

This letter assigns one specific way in which, according to Marshall, the State should be up and doing: town planning to secure that open space of which Marshall was so fond and for the sake of which, as his letter to Helen Bosanquet continued, he would have been willing to spend the total cost of the South Africa (Boer) war then just concluded. In his subsequent pleas for 'economic chivalry', Marshall indicated that this was also one of the few government initiatives he could wholeheartedly embrace. Others were 'beauty of nature and art' which only the State could bring to the people and the provision of flexible and socially effective building regulations, the last not very costly in budgetary outlays but requiring that government 'obtain its fair share of the growing intelligence of the country'.[67]

Marshall saw government's role therefore more as that of regulator than as provider of goods and services; as a 'manager of competition', as he had put it in his lectures on *Progress and Poverty*. Securing honesty in business, quality and cheapness in its products, fairness in its dealings, and more generally, the diffusion of useful knowledge, these were the task Marshall willingly left to government, provided they did not generate what he saw as a major potential evil for the new century, an army of government bureaucrats. A fragment published in the *Memorials* concisely sums up this aspect of his views on the role of government:

> The function of Government is to govern as little as possible; but not to do as little as possible. When it governs it so far fails, as an army fails when it fights. But an army to succeed must be active; and a Government to succeed, must be ceaseless in learning and diffusing knowledge, in stimulating and co-operating.[68]

In order to limit centralised bureaucracy, Marshall wanted as large a role as possible for local initiative. His Memorandum on Taxation had made the point that such local initiatives should be fostered by central grants-in-aid from national taxation, a position likewise neatly encompassed in a fragment on government reproduced in the *Memorials*:

> The Government especially in a free country, is not an entity outside the nation, but a considerable part of the nation; and it can discharge its duties to the nation only by so arranging and developing its work as to make government itself a great education. This involves an extension of local responsibilities wherever possible. But devolution under rigid superior control is in danger of becoming mechanical and formal. The devolution that makes for organic evolution must not be limited to responsibility for carrying out details of schemes devised by the central authority; it must extend to the thinking out and the carrying out of appropriate constructive schemes in which the central ideas of the national scheme are adjusted to particular local conditions and requirements.[69]

Experimentation and potential benefits from competition by local authorities provide the rationale for Marshall's thinking on decentralisation; he strongly opposed local government as delegated administrator of central government. Education, town planning and sanitary measures provided the greatest scope for such local initiatives and experiments, but Marshall would not have disagreed with the scope for local enterprises and its rationale suggested in Leonard Darwin's Harvard lectures on the subject. These mentioned 'public baths . . . to promote health and cleanliness'; municipalisation of harbours because of the collective benefits involved were difficult to defray from tax revenue; and publicly owned abattoirs to ensure proper regard for 'sanitary and humanitarian considerations' which private meat operators were not likely to pay for. When moral and social values were placed above the strictly economic, municipal ownership was very appropriate. However, larger enterprises, such as municipal water supply, electricity and gas where only to be encouraged when private enterprise was incapable of carrying out the task effectively.[70]

The one case in which Marshall queried an established state enterprise in some detail while he was still Professor at Cambridge was the Post Office. There he saw the losses from curtailing competition as central to the issue of a state monopoly. In his address to the Industrial Remuneration Conference, Marshall had argued, 'Where, as in the Post Office, centralisation is necessary, it does better than private enterprise; but when it has had no such advantage it has seldom or never done anything that private enterprise would have done better and at less cost'.[71] When making this comment, Marshall may have been thinking of controversy over the mail service offered by his own college, St John's, which was forced to close down in 1885 by the Post Office monopoly, thus well, and not 'a little', before 1891, as he recalled in a fragment preserved by Pigou,

> A little before 1891 St John's had organized a splendid ½d. post with three times the conveniences, from the 'Varsity man's point of view, of the 1d. Royal Post. It more than paid its way, though its stamps could only be bought by Johnians. I recollect that, when it was quashed, I was set on the inquiry as to Consumers' Surplus and that I made much use of its experiences. I also went into the dependence of a cheap local parcels delivery on the right to carry local letters: taking account of the fact that it costs as much to send a book from here to Selwyn Gardens or Christ's as to California or Japan. On such bases I guessed the percentage which Consumers' Surplus was of total receipts under a free system; while postal statistics gave me a basis for aggregates. But I have forgotten details and life is short.[72]

The year 1891 may have stuck in Marshall's mind in this context because it was then that he engaged in public controversy on the issue by writing two letters to the *Times* on the Post Office and private enterprise. The first of these (24 March 1891) reiterated the large-scale and centralisation advantages which made the Post Office a state enterprise, but which did not necessitate a monopoly of all postal services. Revenue considerations were an inadequate reason for the latter because monopoly taxes were among the worst forms of taxation. In addition, some competition from private enterprise enabled scope for that inventiveness which differentiated it from public endeavour, where lethargy and reluctance to experiment were the order of the day. A follow-up letter (dated 6 April 1891), in reply to the Post Office solicitor who was his anonymous opponent in this correspondence,[73] elaborated Marshall's views on the undesirable consequences of a government postal monopoly. In this letter, Marshall conceded both the necessity of the Post Office as a state enterprise and as a state monopoly for much but not all of its business. If some local postal work was left to private initiative (such as some of the Cambridge colleges, an example he did not mention in the letter), substantial consumer gains could accrue. These Marshall assumed to exceed current post office net revenue (£2.9 million in 1895–96) on the basis of a loss he guessed to be 'at least 6s. a head' for the fifteen million persons who used the postal service (a total of £4.5 million) from their lack of access to private local postal services.* Marshall conceded his calculation was a very 'rash thing' to do, and one he probably would not have made later in his life when, as he told his nephew Guillebaud,[74] he believed 'his concept of consumers' surplus was devoid of important practical application, because it was not capable of being quantified in a meaningful way'.

Apart from highlighting the fact that Marshall's opposition to state enterprises rested on his perception of the costs imposed in terms of reduced competition and loss of initiative, the post office correspondence in the *Times* drew attention to a further Millian feature of socialism in his thinking on the subject. This was the Millian distinction Marshall drew between socialism in matters pertaining to distribution as against production. The final paragraph of his first letter mentioned his views on 'the chief dangers of socialism'. These, he argued, 'lie not in its tendency towards a more equal distribution of income, for I can see no harm in that, but in its sterilising influence on those mental activities which have gradually raised the world from barbarism', that is, the qualities he associated with business initiative and free enterprise and which the bureaucratic rule in state production would stifle and destroy. As Mill had argued in his *Principles*, economic laws governing production were not easy to set aside, in contrast to the human arrangements governing distribution which were quite amenable to alteration.[75] This Millian influence on Marshall's tendency to socialism also endured for the whole of his life.

A Volte-Face on Redistributive Taxes. Although in 1891 Marshall could rather cavalierly indicate that he saw no harm in the tendency towards a more equal distribution of income which socialists advocated, his views on the means by which this could be achieved underwent considerable change over his lifetime. Managing competition in favour of the working class through restricting population by means including emigration, combined with waiting for technical progress and education to make unskilled labour more scarce and better rewarded, was the strategy he had advocated in his Henry George lectures. Compulsory equalisation by government, as he argued before the Remuneration Conference amidst some protest, could at best achieve very limited results. However, over the longer run, when its dynamic consequences were taken into consideration, it would kill the goose that laid the golden eggs, that is, the spirit of free enterprise which produced growth in the national income available for distribution to the working class. This harked back to the reduced incentives under socialism issue which Mill had also so eloquently raised as among the chief difficulties of adopting socialism.[76]

On the expenditure side of state redistribution policies, Marshall's more generous approach to 'outdoor relief' than permitted by the outdated 1834 Poor Law, with special reference to unemployment and more importantly, old age, was discussed previously.[77] Although on this issue he was more liberal than Charity Organisation Society philosophers

---

* Albon's paper ('Alfred Marshall and the Consumer's Loss from the British Post Office') discusses in considerable detail the assumptions about demand elasticity which are implied in this 'guesstimate' on the assumption of constant unit costs in postal services, an assumption which Marshall was unlikely to have entertained for a business characterised by large-scale operations. Marshall also seems to have ignored the distributional consequences of cross-subsidisation in the single letter rate applied in the standard penny postage prevailing in the 1890s. He may have gained from the ½d postage of a letter from St John's College to J.N. Keynes or Sidgwick, but how much was he prepared to pay for a letter to Jowett at Oxford, or to Nicholson at Edinburgh?

with whom he clashed on the issue, his own scheme was considerably less generous and radical than Charles Booth's scheme for universal age pensions. Marshall saw checks on the deservedness of such 'public charity' as indispensable. This was an area to which workers from the Charity Organisation Society could effectively contribute. As he put it in his 'Social Possibilities of Economic Chivalry', relief of 'the suffering' financed from tax revenue should be confined to 'those who are weak and ailing through no fault of their own'. Compulsion, as well as assistance, were needed for those who, 'through weakness or vice, have lost their self respect, either to reform their own lives, or, at all events, to [prevent them from dragging] their children down with them'. Weakness of character remained a major cause of individual poverty and distress for Marshall, although he also admitted causes over which the poor had little control. These included sudden unemployment as well as illness and old age, for which independent workers could only prepare. Universal assistance, he argued at the start of the 1890s would cost too much and when defrayed from general taxation, would impose substantial welfare losses in the process.[78]

In the context of fiscal redistribution, it should be noted that Marshall initially did not support the notion of taxes with graduated rates, a position on which he also followed Mill's views. During the 1880s and 1890s, Marshall tended to view graduated income taxes as unjust, though like Mill he accepted that all necessary income should be exempt before taxing the remainder of income at a proportional rate. More importantly, Marshall saw income taxes as inefficient because of their disincentive effects on work, thrift and more generally enterprise, elaborating in this context Mill's notion that income taxation implied the double taxation of saving. Adverse disincentive effects applied even more to taxes on capital. These tended to check its growth and to accelerate its emigration, the traditional position of classical tax theory which abhorred all taxes on capital, and one to which Marshall steadfastly adhered until quite late in his life.[79]

His change of mind came in the aftermath of Lloyd George's 'People's Budget' of 1909. He then confessed to Lord Reay, who asked his views on the matter, that for fifteen years his teaching on death duties had been erroneous because it claimed such taxes checked the growth of capital.[80] An explanation for Marshall's change of opinion may be found in British experience with graduated death duties from 1895, the year of their introduction; none of the disastrous consequences for capital and enterprise which had been predicted from this innovation in fiscal policy did in fact eventuate. Subsequent work on taxation by Marshall during and after the First World War showed his belief in the benefits of progressive tax rates for effecting distributional justice had grown even stronger, without ever ignoring the efficiency costs such a tax policy strategy could impose.[81]

More generally, Marshall's letter to Reay linked fiscal distributional policies directly to socialism. After indicating that he did not know what a socialist budget meant, Marshall criticised the *Times*'s confusion on this point, because it substituted 'taking of property' for 'taking of money', Marshall then put forward his own views on socialist distribution:

> My own notion of socialism is that it is a movement for taking the responsibility for a man's life and work, as far as possible, off his shoulders and putting it on to the State. In my opinion Germany is beneficially 'socialistic' in its regimentation of those who are incapable of caring for themselves: and we ought to copy Germany's methods in regard to our Residuum.

But in relation to other classes, I regard the socialistic movement as not merely a danger, but by far the greatest present danger to human well-being. It seems to me to have two sides, the administrative and the financial. Its chief sting seems to lie on the administrative side.

I do not deny that semi-socialistic or Governmental methods are almost inevitable in ordinary railways etc.: though a vigorous despot in America breaks through them occasionally. But the sting of socialism seems to lie in its desire to extend these rather than to check their expansion. I believe that they weaken character by limiting initiative and dulling aspiration; and that they lower character by diverting energy from creation to wirepulling. . .

On the financial side, Socialism may be rapacious, predatory, blind to the importance of security in business and contemptuous of public good faith. But these tendencies lie on the surface: they provoke powerful opposition and reaction; and personally I fear them less than those which are more insidious. In moderation they are even beneficial in my opinion. For poverty crushes character: and though the earning of great wealth generally strengthens character, the spending of it by those who have not earned it, whether men or women, is not nearly an unmixed good. A cautious movement towards enriching the poor at the expense of the rich seems to me not to cease to be beneficial, merely because socialists say it is a step in their direction.[82]

Effects on character remained paramount for Marshall when judging fiscal measures for alleviating poverty and inequality. This induced an inevitable emphasis on self-help and mutual assistance relative to government action, no matter how justified such government action was. Marshall therefore remained in substantial, albeit incomplete, agreement with much of the philosophy of the Charity Organisation Society. Most of his early twentieth-century pronouncements on the subject suggest this, whether made in public as in the case of his address on Economic Chivalry or privately in the advice he offered to bishops and others who asked him for it.[83] This part of his essentially Victorian perspective on poverty was never abandoned even though, with persons such as Booth and the Fabians, he came to realise much more fully that factors such as casual employment, unemployment, illness and even old age were crucial variables in creating that large segment of 'deserving' poor proving to be so persistent despite all economic progress.[84]

A fragment on wealth and its distribution emphasises this human factor in Marshall's position on poverty and inequality which, despite its lack of evident success, captured him for all of his life:

Wealth exists only for the benefit of mankind. It cannot be measured adequately in yards or in tons, nor even as equivalent to so many ounces of gold; its true measure lies only in the contribution it makes to human well-being. Now, when bricks and sand and lime and wood are built up into a house, they constitute a greater aggregate of wealth than they did before; even though their aggregate volume is the same as before: and, if the house is overthrown by an earthquake, there is indeed no destruction of matter; but there is a real destruction of wealth, because the matter is distributed in a manner less conducive to human well-being. Similarly, when wealth is very unevenly distributed, some have more of it than they can turn to any very great account in promoting their own well-being; while many others lack the material conditions of a healthy, clean, vigorous and effective family life. That is to say the wealth is distributed in a manner less conducive to the well-being of mankind than it would be if the rich were somewhat less rich, and the poor were somewhat less poor; and the real wealth would be greatly increased, even though there were no change in the aggregate of bricks and houses and clothes and other material things, if only it were possible to effect that change without danger to freedom and to social order; and without impairing the springs of initiative, enterprise and energy. There is unfortunately no good ground for thinking that human nature is yet far enough improved away from its primitive barbarity, selfishness, and sloth, to be ready for any movement in this direction so rapid and far reaching as to effect with safety any great increase in real wealth by a mere redistribution of material wealth.[85]

Self-Help in the Labour Movement: Trade Unions, Cooperation and Profit Sharing.
Marshall's emphasis on self-help in alleviating poverty colours his views on the various
agencies open to the labour movement, thereby further illuminating his Millian perspectives
on socialism. Like Samuel Smiles, some of whose works he kept in his library, Marshall
identified self-help with character building and conduct, and the mark of the 'true
gentleman', the type of person into which he aimed to turn the working class from an early
stage in his career. The art of living for such true gentlemen included industry and
punctuality, thrift and politeness, healthy and frugal life, arts which the working class could
acquire both through its own institutions and through self-cultivation.[86] The early Trade
Union movement, or the 'old Trade Unionism' as it had become known by the late 1880s,
stressed associations of working men as 'the fountain of much that is noblest in human
character'. This was implied for authorities such as Howell[87] in the dual role traditionally
assigned to trade unions, combining that of voluntary organisations with combinations for
'affecting the conditions of labour'. More formally, he described the principal objects of
Trade Unions as

> (1) to procure for their members the best return for their labour in the shape of higher wages, shorter hours
> of labour, and the enforcement of certain restrictions as to the conditions of employment, which could not
> be accomplished except by means of combination; (2) to provide mutual assurance for the members by
> means of pecuniary assistance in case of sickness, accidents, death, out of work, superannuation when
> disabled by old age, loss of tools by fire, and emigration.

As Marshall discovered during his work on the Royal Commission on Labour those qualities
of the Trade Unions which he had praised in the *Economics of Industry* when he compared
unions to the old guilds, were disappearing, in the sense that the 'new' unionists focused
exclusively on the first of these objectives, often in what Marshall perceived as anti-social
ways. By the late 1890s, Marshall became in fact increasingly worried that Trade Unions
would lose their initial 'liberating and elevating influence'. He ascribed this to the growing
prominence of 'the meanest characters' in their organisations. These would destroy the
selfless endeavours of the Trade Union movement and transform it into selfish class-
action.[88] Marshall's clearest exposition of his position on the 'new' trade unionism was
written 'in confidence' to the Master of Balliol in connection with the Engineers' strike, an
exceedingly bitter and drawn-out labour dispute at the end of the 1890s. Marshall explained
that he had followed the strike with an 'interest amounting to excitement':

> I am very much of an 8 hours man: I am wholly a trade-unionist of the old stamp. For the sake of trade
> unionism, and for that of labour as a whole, I hope that the employers will so far get the better of the
> leaders of the modern unionism, that the rank and file of the workers will get to see the futility as well as
> the selfishness of the policy which their new leaders are pressing. Everywhere the tried men, who had made
> modern unionism the greatest of England's glories, have been pushed aside – sometimes very cruelly. For a
> time the Engineers adhered to moderate and unselfish courses. But lately they have used their grand
> prestige, I hold, for England's ill.
>   In Belgium, Germany, Bohemia, Hungary and Japan, crowds of men are learning to manage machines
> which a few years ago required high skill, but which have been now so improved that they will do excellent

work in the hands of a mere 'ploughman'. This tends of course to open out new kinds of mechanical work that require high skill: but England cannot keep much of that work. . . .

There is no fear whatever, not the very least, that the A.S.E. [i.e. Amalgamated Society of Engineers] will be broken up. No one wishes it: and it could not be done. But unless the A.S.E. *bona fide* concedes to the employers the right to put a single man to work an easy machine, or even two or more of them, the progress upwards of the English working classes, from the position of hewers of wood and drawers of water, to masters of nature's forces will, I believe, receive a lasting check. If the men should win, and I were an engineering employer, I would sell my works for anything I could get and emigrate to America. If I were a working man, I would wish for no better or more hopeful conditions of life than those which I *understand* to prevail at the Carnegie works now (there may be evils there, of which I do not know, but I have watched for some account of them and have found none).

The 8 hours question is of course not the real issue *at all*. The real issue lies entirely in the question whether England is to be free to avail herself of the new resources of production.[89]

Marshall's subsequent letter explained that his harsh judgement of the Trade Unions in this case owed much to his fears about England's relative economic position which he believed had been slipping over the last twenty years relative to the Americans, the nations of Central Europe such as Germany, Bohemia and Hungary, and even to Asian nations like Japan. Some of the reasons for such decline he saw as natural and inevitable, others, such as the 'dominance in some unions of the desire to "make work" and an increase in their power to do so' he regarded as an 'unmixed evil . . . and threat to national well-being'. He elaborated that these longer term considerations determined his growing hostility to unionism in England,

I have often said that T.U.'s are a greater glory to England than her wealth. But I thought then of T.U.'s in which the minority, who wanted to compel others to put as little work as possible into the hour, were overruled. Latterly they have, I fear, completely dominated the Engineers' Union. I want these people to be beaten at all costs: the complete destruction of Unionism would be as heavy a price as it is possible to conceive: but I think not too high a price.

If bricklayers' unions could have been completely destroyed twenty years ago, I believe bricklayers would be now as well off and more self-respecting than they are: and cottages would be 10 or 20% larger all round. . . .

Mr. Sinclair's letter in the *Times* of yesterday (Dec. 4) seems to me to go to the root of the matter. He illustrates one side – the American as distinguished from the Continental – of the causes that are at present making England move relatively backwards. The balance against us, allowing for the superior weight of American locomotives, comes out at about 3:1, i.e. 3 Glasgow men needed to do the work of 1 American. I should put (say) a quarter to this to account of our employers, a half to account of new-unionism, and the remaining quarter to no account at all. I mean that, when a man works in a leisurely way and for relatively short hours, he does get some gain which may be set off against the loss in his efficiency.

Leisure is good, if it is well used. But the laborious laziness, which has come into many English Government workshops, and some private ones, engenders a character to which leisure is useless.[90]

The loss of that character-building selflessness which had inspired Marshall's early admiration of the trade union movement, combined with the increase in its class-selfishness which he so deprecated, induced his growing disenchantment with this type of working-class organisation as an agency in social progress. This is the gist of the brief discussion of the role of Trade Unions in the later editions of the *Principles* which emphasises its moral and social as well as their more economic side.[91] That economic side cannot be ignored in Marshall's mature disenchantment with the unions. Marshall's fears about Britain's ability to compete effectively in the new, twentieth century against the growing competition from the United States, from Germany and from Asian nations like Japan, about which he had written to Caird, and on which he was to write not long afterwards in his analysis of the appropriate fiscal policy for international trade[92], also strongly influenced his more critical position on trade union activities.

Be that as it may. Marshall's rising disillusionment with Trade Unions as agencies in what he called social progress, based on their actual evolution and transformation which was taking place during his lifetime, may have strengthened that more romantic and idealistic streak in his make-up which hoped for the realisation of some future utopia based on cooperation.[93] Marshall's early support of, and participation in, the cooperative movement has been mentioned previously in a variety of contexts, and reinforces the picture of peculiar Millian strands in his socialism. Such beliefs were fed by the data on the miraculous growth of the cooperative movement, particularly in its trading side, as were continuously reported during the 1880s and 1890s.[94] This aspect of Marshall's character and beliefs was perceptively grasped by Beatrice Webb, an expert witness on this subject. She, after all, had seen Marshall in action at the Cooperative Congress he had chaired in 1889, had felt his reactions to her own study of the subject on several occasions, and had subsequently seen at least some of his questioning of co-operators during the sittings of the Labour Commission.[95] On 23 February 1897 she recorded in her diary,

> A flying visit to Cambridge to address the Newnham and Girton students – stayed with the Marshalls. Professor Marshall is more footling than ever. . . . For really when one talks with him and he advances his little subtle qualifications to his own slipshod generalisations, one gets irritated, almost as irritated as when, in order to controvert some 'popular' notion, he makes an astonishing assertion which bears no relation to fact. . . . He used to call himself a socialist. But the socialism he believed in was a revolt against the great industry and consisted in a far away hope in the setting up of little Co-operative productive societies or even of individual producers, anything to get relief from the bureaucracy of the great industrial machine. . . . Marshall has been forced as an economist, to accept much of our destructive criticism of the old Co-operative ideal. As an idealist anarchist, he enlists himself against the democratizing of the great machine, not because he is anti-democratic (be it said to his credit) but because he dreads and hates the great machine and fully realises that it would be enormously strengthened by having a democratic basis. So he finds himself timidly and regretfully ranging himself on the side of pure reaction in its fight with democracy.[96]

Marshall's position of 'idealist anarchism' on cooperation is visible in the remarks he later made in *Industry and Trade* when discussing guild socialism in relation to cooperation, but even here they are coloured by a pragmatic realism.[97] What is missing in this description of Marshall's economic romanticism on cooperation is the room this provided for continued competition both amongst cooperative agencies themselves and with enterprises outside the movement. Beatrice Webb recalled this Millian strand in Marshall's thinking on cooperation to Edward Pease nearly twenty years later, thereby largely redressing her earlier omission in characterising Marshall's cooperative idealism. Commenting on Pease's judgement that cooperation had succeeded, she qualified this remark by stating: 'the particular type of Co-operative advocated by Mill was a complete failure. . . . I remember Marshall telling me that the whole of his economic thought had been influenced by Mill's faith in Co-operative Production and that he still held to that faith as the ideal towards which we should work'[98]

In his famous chapter on the Futurity of the Labouring Classes, Mill had predicted co-operative production as the form of association he expected 'in the end to predominate . . . if mankind continued to improve', a form higher than the working partnership implied in profit sharing in which the capitalist continued as 'chief; and work people without a voice in the management'. The voluntary aspects of these associations together with their ability to compete 'successfully with individual capitalists' was the thing that attracted Mill to this type of human organisation, since it preserved individual liberty and the competition which Mill saw as 'useful and indispensable' and 'not pernicious'. Under such conditions, 'and assuming of course that both sexes participate equally in the rights and in the government of the association, [cooperative enterprise] would be the nearest approach to social justice, and the most beneficial ordering of industrial affairs for the universal good, which it is possible at present to foresee.'[99]

Mill's vision of cooperation enters the pages of Marshall's *Principles* in more prosaic form. Practical problems intermingle with idealist dreams, and, not surprisingly, equality of the sexes is ignored in the Marshallian vision. The 'ideal form of co-operative society, *for which many still fondly hope*, but which as yet has been scantily realised in practice' had foundered on the frailties of human nature, because the employees themselves are often not the best masters and managers of an enterprise.[100] Although by the mid-1890s Marshall could still optimistically see signs 'of the success of *bona fide* productive associations or co-partnership', realism triumphed in his economic text. In its discussion, Marshall concentrated on the more immediate virtues of such success in assisting workers to start their own business and thereby climb the social ladder, or to suggest the partial cooperative form of profit sharing as a more realistic alternative until human nature had sufficiently improved to solve the problems of ideal cooperation. Of the last he continued to dream and to write down his suggestions in old age. [101]

Profit sharing as a step towards full-blown cooperation had been recognised as such by Mill, had been advocated as a cure for harmful strikes by Fawcett and by Brassey, by Marshall's Cambridge colleague and occasional adversary, Sedley Taylor, and from the 1870s had been adopted in Britain by a small but growing number of firms.[102] As a topic, profit sharing had featured quite strongly among the papers given to the Industrial Remuneration Conference[103] and it is therefore not surprising that Marshall did not ignore this form of cooperation between owner and worker. At the Cooperative Congress in 1889 Marshall had described 'the movement towards the direct participation by the employee in the profits of the business as one of the most important and hopeful events in modern times, and as one of the best and most valuable fruits of the co-operative spirit'. The dividends paid to their members and shareholders in wholesale trading societies were similar to profit sharing, in 'providing education, opportunity and scope' for workers to become more than 'mere hands' in the enterprise.[104] It is therefore also not surprising that Marshall discussed the subject at some length in the *Principles*. In his text he described it as a mutually beneficial contract in which workers gained more than their wages, while 'the firm will find a material as well as a moral reward in the diminution of friction, in the increased willingness of its employees to go out of their way to do little things that may be of great benefit to the firm, and lastly in attracting to itself workers of more than average ability and industry'. A later chapter noted that 'there is *de facto* some sort of profit-and-loss sharing between almost every business and its employees, and perhaps this is in its very highest form when, without being embodied in a definite contract, the solidarity of interests between those who work together in the same business is recognised with cordial generosity as the result of true brotherly feeling'. Marshall added that this was 'not a very common case', perhaps because of the difficulties in organising effective profit-sharing agreements.[105] These, he had argued in another place[106] were 'a gain to all concerned when well managed . . . but it is difficult to make them, and more difficult to keep them up'. When he regarded profit sharing 'as but a step towards the still higher but much more difficult level of true co-operation'[107] the utopian elements in Marshall's visions of these forms of association as harbingers of human perfectibility and therefore a distant ideal are clearly, albeit implicitly, indicated.

An Anti-Imperialist of the Free Trade Kind. Although far removed from the problems of working-man's associations, Marshall's views on Empire in the 1890s and early 1900s are conveniently discussed in the context of assessing his political views. Against the stream of political, and increasingly economic opinion, Marshall showed himself at this time to be an anti-imperialist, an anti-jingoist and a cosmopolitan and internationalist in the Cobdenite free trade sense. Marshall's perspectives on the First World War associated with such views are discussed later[108]; his views on the Venezuelan crisis of 1895, the Boer War of 1899–1902 and the issue of Imperial Federation are discussed as part of his politics. The last topic, it will be recalled, generated frequent departures from his rule not to discuss politics in lectures[109] and brought him into an explicit political role when he prepared his paper on fiscal policy in 1903 for the benefit of the Balfour government.[110]

Marshall's first public 'anti-jingoist' act occurred in the context of the 1895 Venezuelan crisis. A frontier dispute between British Guyana and Venezuela induced intervention by United States President Cleveland who, basing himself on the 1823 Monroe doctrine, offered arbitration on the issue. Salisbury, the newly elected Conservative Prime Minister, refused. In reply, Cleveland appointed a Congressional Commission on 17 December to inquire into the matter, whose findings the United States would enforce on the two parties by armed intervention, if necessary. The British Cabinet retreated at this point and accepted the arbitration it had rejected the previous month. The matter generated much anti-American feeling in England. Sales of American bonds by British investors caused financial difficulties and were a visible sign of the hostility the dispute generated despite the community of sentiment and language between the two nations. As a person 'whose good fortune it had been to be brought in contact with the brighter side of American thought and life', Marshall thought it his duty not to stay silent on the issue. He therefore invited the readership of the *Times* to place itself in the American position, and to see the problem from an American point of view. Although he conceded that arbitration as proposed by President Cleveland 'does not give always quite the right result' and that his message to Salisbury was lacking in courtesy, he maintained that Britain was acting in an unfriendly way 'in maintaining a course which we know not to be vital to our policy, and which they [the Americans] believe to be destructive of theirs. . . . [Hence] they have a moral right to resist us by arms'. Given the anti-American feeling of the time, Marshall's action was both a courageous and a principled one, and showed his disbelief in the then increasingly common maxim, 'my country, right or wrong'.[111]

A letter to Caird two years later, already quoted in this chapter in connection with the Engineers' strike, shows that Marshall may have had an economic rationale for his 'anti-jingoism', which he did not disclose in his letter to the *Times*. A growing 'pushfulness in foreign affairs', for which Marshall gave the Egyptian crisis with France over the Upper Nile as an example, in imitation of other nations but 'with least benefit to ourselves', would entail 'expenditure on [our] Army and Navy at an ever-increasing rate'. This was bearable in a situation when British economic growth was leading the world, it was courting disaster when Britain was relatively going backwards in production.[112]

As the Boer War was to demonstrate a few years later, Britain's military unpreparedness (despite the victories won so cheaply with technology at the end of the century in the Sudan) meant that 'if we provoke a war, we must be prepared to fit ourselves for war – in plain terms to spend £100,000,000 on our army and navy, before long, and when at peace'. Bishop Westcott to whom this message was addressed, did not demur about the cost estimates; he only protested that, as a man of peace, he thought the Boer War had been inevitable and not, as Marshall implied, provoked by Britain.[113] Marshall's projected £100 million as spending required to secure genuine military preparedness for Britain can be put in context with the fact that in 1900, British defence spending amounted to £69.6 million. By then, the Boer war had already been in progress for one year while the more normal peacetime spending on defence of the 1890s averaged £35 million annually. Although the *Principles* is silent on war spending, and Marshall does not appear to have addressed the issue publicly, his letter to Helen Bosanquet quoted previously, suggests he preferred using the sum spent on the South African war (which can be estimated to have cost well in excess of £150 million) for urban renewal and the garden cities programmes to which he was so devoted.[114] For Marshall at this stage, war implied waste and resources which could be put to better use.

Marshall's opposition to the Boer War went, however, deeper than this. An entry in John Neville Keynes's diary recalls a dinner party in December 1899 'at the Marshalls' which recorded Marshall's dinner conversation as that of 'the most exasperating talker I know. He will agree with nothing you say and argues and dogmatises so as to drive one wild. He is pro-Boer and kept making innuendoes trying, but without success, to draw us into argument on the subject'.[115] Some months later, correspondence from N.G. Pierson, the Dutch economist and then Prime Minister of the Netherlands, broached the topic in a manner which secured a lengthy response from Marshall. After Pierson had informed Marshall about Dutch preoccupation with 'the horrid war in South Africa', he asked about Marshall's 'feelings . . . in this matter, though I am not inclined to believe you strongly sympathise with Mr. Chamberlain's policies'. After questioning the war's purpose and asking why the two small Boer Republics, Transvaal and Orange Free State, could not have been left alone, Pierson concluded his letter with a prediction that the war would not be quickly over because 'the Boers will never yield until they are almost exterminated'.*

---

* N.G. Pierson to Alfred Marshall, 3 April 1900, in *Memorials*, p. 410; Pierson was Prime Minister of Holland from 1897–1901, a role he combined with that of Minister of Finance, a position he had earlier occupied from 1891–94.

Marshall's response was both forthright and voluminous. After recounting the electoral successes of two pro-Boer students at the recent poll for the committee of the Cambridge Students' Union, one of them 'head of the poll . . . the highest honour which it is in the power of students to confer', Marshall developed a picture of what he believed to be the more general public opinion in England.

> English people, with all their faults, have never shown rancour to honourable opponents. They were extravagant in their wrath to the anti-Dreyfusites but they had the warmest admiration and liking for Major Marchand. As to Krüger and Cronje, their feelings are mixed: admiration for energy, ability, resource and courage is tempered by a certain doubt as to whether one can always trust in their good faith. But Joubert's honour was never called in question: and there are few English generals as popular as he was at the time of his death.[*]

With these preliminaries out of the way, Marshall broached his own views on 'this miserable war'. After confessing he did not really understand the Boer case, and thinking with certainty, that 'the continental newspapers do not understand the English case', Marshall stated that England was now ready to fight this war until the bitter end, sparing neither men nor resources. This determined war effort was 'not the work of the Jingoes; they made the war inevitable, but the determination to see the war through is as strong among most anti-Jingoes as amongst Jingoes'. Marshall was now ready to reveal his own position,

> I am myself an uncompromising anti-Jingoe, a peace-at-almost-any-price man. Chamberlain is the only Unionist public man whom I have ever thoroughly distrusted. Excepting Napoleon, I believe that England's true greatness has had no such dangerous enemy since Lord North. When a radical, he delighted to dish his colleagues even more than to flout his opponents. He is now engaged in dishing his new colleagues and flouting his old friends. He seems to thirst for power but to delight in making his enemies for the time wild with rage, and in explaining that when he said or suggested one thing, he always meant another. A more un-English character could not have been found to conduct the negotiations which led up to the war. I never trusted anything that he said about the Uitlanders' grievances and I never thought them sufficient to justify the line taken by him and by Milner.[1]

As Prime Minister, Pierson practised a cautious and distant relationship with the Boer Republics during the Boer War, at great cost to his political popularity.

[*] Marshall to N.G. Pierson, 6 April 1900 (Marshall Archive, 1:332), reproduced in part in *Memorials*, pp. 411–12. General Jean Marchand (1863–1934) played a role in the 1898 Fashoda incident associated with the diplomatic friction over the Upper Nile between France and Britain; the anti-Dreyfusites opposed the supporters of Captain Alfred Dreyfus, the only Jew then serving on the French General Staff, to secure his reinstatement from wrongful dismissal in 1895 after his conviction for allegedly being a German spy. The affair convulsed France for a decade and revealed the enormous anti-semitism in France at this time. Paul Kruger (1825–1904) was the Boers' political leader and President of the Transvaal, General Piet Cronje (1835–1911) surrendered to Lord Roberts, one of the British generals, at Paardeberg, in February 1900; General Petrus Jacobus Joubert (1834–1900) was Commander-in-Chief of the Boer forces until his death in early 1900.

[1] Marshall to Pierson, 6 April 1900, Joseph Chamberlain (1836–1914) was Colonial Secretary at the time in the Salisbury (Conservative) government; he was a *Bête-noire* of Marshall having broken with the Liberal Party over Home Rule in 1886 and, by resigning from the Cabinet in 1903 over tariff reform, he also caused severe splits in the Tory Party. (Cf. D.H. Macgregor, 'Marshall and his Book', p. 115, quoting one of Marshall's lectures, and the reference to Chapter 10 given in note 109). Lord North was the Minister chiefly responsible for the alienation of the American colonies in the eighteenth century, which led to the American war of independence and the separation of the American colonies from Britain. The comparison of Chamberlain with North, let alone Napoleon, are a typical case of Marshallian exaggeration.

Those last remarks, Marshall then explained, did not imply agreement with Pierson over the Uitlander issue. Once indignities had been perpetrated by the Boers on the Uitlanders (British settlers in the two Boer Republics), which even the South African 'blacks' were beginning to interpret as signs of British cowardice, these incidents had to be redressed. In addition, the growing military preparedness and rich mineral resources of the Boers meant that to preserve the territories of Natal and the Cape, the British would have had to maintain a standing army of 100,000 men in those colonies, an expensive policy preventable by an immediate war. Marshall concluded,

> I do not deny that these Boer armaments had their main origin in the wicked and stupid Raid, and in its equally wicked and stupid condonation by English Jingoes and by Chamberlain especially. But self-preservation is the first law of nations. . . . So though an Anti-Jingo, I say the war must go on till Natal and the Cape have security from Boer armaments. Subject to that condition, and the redress of the Uitlanders grievances, many, perhaps most, Englishmen and certainly I, would make peace tomorrow on almost any terms that the Boers might wish.*

Marshall's remarks on self-preservation as the first law of nations explain much of his stance on imperial federation and associated tariff reform. This was largely discussed in the context of his *Memorandum on Fiscal Policy in International Trade* and the main cause for his disagreement with Hewins (and indirectly Chamberlain) over the issue.[116] The original Memorandum on the subject Marshall had prepared for the government in 1903 started with a long section on preferential tariff treatment on which implementation of Imperial Federation was partly predicated. Other advantages of such a move were also widely discussed at this time. Sharing what many expected to be growing costs of defending the Empire was a reason with which Marshall would have been fairly sympathetic. The growing perception that one of the implications of Britain's declining relative economic strength was a reduction in her status as a world power unless she formed a more structured union with the white settlements of the new world (Canada, Australia, New Zealand and South Africa) was a further reason for Imperial Federation particularly when, as was the case in the years at the turn of the century, Britain was without major formal allies in Europe. Although widely considered politically impracticable, the idea of Imperial Federation resurfaced at regular intervals, often as a panacea in periods of crisis such as that of Britain's isolation in Europe, felt particularly strongly in the late 1890s; and attempts to share growing defence costs in a period of economic decline during the early years of the twentieth century.[117]

---

* Marshall to Pierson, 6 April 1900. The raid Marshall mentioned was the Jamieson Raid of December 1895, named after the leader of a small private army (police force) organised by one of Cecil Rhodes's mining companies. This invaded the Transvaal on that date in order to place it under British protection. As a staunch imperialist, Chamberlain actively supported this raid. The raid came to nothing because of Boer military strength and strong German diplomatic support in the Councils of Europe. A useful account is Elie Halévy's *History of the English People: Epilogue (1) Imperialism*, pp. 55–9 and Chapter II which present a concise account of the Boer War and its impact on British society. F.W. Pethick-Lawrence, *Fate has been Kind*, p. 34, records a lecture not long after the Jamieson raid in which Marshall claimed 'Chamberlain was a negative asset to the country which he [i.e. Marshall] assessed at several hundred million pounds!'.

The published version of Marshall's paper made the same points on Imperial Preference and Imperial Union as its 1903 predecessor.[118] Free trade, by keeping down the prices of British wage goods and hence industrial costs, would do more for preserving Britain's leadership position in the world than Imperial Union (pp. 408–12). Furthermore, the economic interests of the colonies were already such that Britain would gain far less than they from such a formal union. Colonial desires to industrialise (epitomised by their proposals to give Imperial Preference through raising the tariff for foreign countries 'without lowering it for British goods') were placed well ahead of 'the high ideal of Imperial unity' (p. 418). Britain's gain would therefore be confined to the gains she was already reaping from cheap food imports from the colonies, though the potential for cheap food imports would be reduced by constraining her access to non-imperial supplies. The Memorandum concluded with a special plea for India in this context because 'India is poor, . . . and India's commercial policy to Britain had been generous' (p. 420).

The last point enables a brief comment on Marshall's position on British rule in India. Although he had made a detailed study of Indian problems to prepare for his teaching in Oxford, and had a substantial number of Indian students* he produced very little on Indian problems, apart from the evidence he gave to currency inquiries in the 1880s and 1890s. Correspondence between him and some of his Indian students has been preserved, in some of which he was asked to give technical advice.[119] More generally, it related India's economic development problems to problems of custom and caste of the type he had addressed as early as 1870.[120] He argued that Indians should concentrate more on technical and industrial pursuits, acquiring entrepreneurial skills, than on excelling in 'mere speech making in politics and law courts' and similar general philosophising by Indians. This is concisely expressed in a letter to Manohar Làl, on 29 January 1909.

> But I do not believe that any device will make India a prosperous nation, until educated Indians are willing to take part in handling *things* as educated people in the West do. The notion that it is more dignified to hold a *pen* and keep accounts than to work in a high grade engineering shop seems to me the root of India's difficulties.[121]

It seems fair to conclude on the evidence that Marshall was not a staunch imperialist. He tended to oppose war, except as an absolute last resort. Although Marshall had his fair share of patriotism, believing in national preservation as a key principle of political life, he would have agreed with Pantaleoni's remarks on jingoism in a letter to Seligman. This criticised jingoism as offensive to free institutions, and argued that imperialism, including Italy's belated and unsuccessful attempts in Abyssinia, simply did not pay.[122] Despite his general opposition to war, Marshall was no pacifist. His correspondence on South Africa reveals this clearly. He greatly regretted the high expense of war, arguing the resources it took

---

* Marshall did not always welcome coloured students with open arms. 'My class so far', he wrote to Foxwell on 16 October 1894, 'has an unprecedented large percentage of black faces – no Japs of course – but several Africans and Indians. I don't seem to ever get inside them: if I went for the "pure empirical" method I should doubt whether they had any *an sich*. But my faint heart is sustained by faith and *a priori* deduction' (Freeman Collection, 1/127). It may be noted here that Marshall shared in fairly mild form the contemporary racist attitudes to 'weaker races' including Jews, some of which can be seen reflected in the *Principles* (for example, P VIII, pp. 761, 769); and more generally, pp. 243–6, 248–9; in *IT*, pp. 104 n., 357, 582.

would be better spent in securing domestic improvements. However, he conceded that large resources would have to be found for defence when war became inevitable. Marshall's strong belief in free trade as the best economic policy for Britain, even in this period of her inevitable, relative economic decline, implied that colonies and empire meant very little to him. The colonies offered opportunities which Britain could exploit, in migration, investment and trade, but sooner or later would go their own way, as the United States had done during the eighteenth century. Only India was excepted. He believed England had achieved much good in uniting that country, largely through improving transport and communications, as well as by the order and good government British rule had generated.* In short, Marshall's position on these issues was essentially that of the Cobdenite free trader, modified to take account of changed conditions, but nevertheless a position he shared with contemporary internationalist liberalism and which owed little to a socialist internationalist perspective.

SOCIALISM OR ECONOMIC CHIVALRY?

Marshall's final paper published as Professor of Political Economy in Cambridge addressed this question implicitly. In many ways it substituted economic chivalry for socialism while attempting to keep a foot in the socialist camp. After all, he could honestly include himself with 'nearly every economist of the present generation' who, on their belief that much of the work 'to promote the social amelioration of the people . . . is better performed by the State than by individual effort' could be classified as socialists in this sense. Marshall's role for the State was, however, a rather limited one. His lecture on Economic Chivalry, and contemporaneous writings, suggested a substantial redistributive role for the State through the Budget, which Marshall not only fully endorsed but strengthened over his lifetime by arguing that the system could tolerate considerably increased rates of graduation in income and capital taxation. On the other hand, Marshall conceded little to the State in the way of production. Exceptions covered cases where moral considerations outweighed the economic (so that private enterprise would not accomplish the task satisfactorily) or areas of natural monopoly associated with economies of scale. This was described as a Millian dichotomy in his socialist vision, one to which Marshall adhered all his life.[123]

The general case for private initiative and enterprise in production was particularly developed in that final *ex cathedra* statement. As Pigou pointed out when he debated socialism versus capitalism thirty years later, Marshall's opposition to socialism arose from his perception that in all cases where 'ceaseless invention and fertility of resource' were essential to social progress, private enterprise was best for the job, because bureaucrats abhorred the necessary risk taking. Marshall admitted in later life that joint-stock companies would stunt this inventiveness of capitalist enterprise; and Pigou added, that had Marshall lived to see the growth of government-controlled research as in the aircraft industry, he may

---

* Cf. the remark on India quoted above, p. 607; and see *IT*, pp. 23–5, 162; cf. J.C. Wood, *British Economists and the Empire*, pp. 120–21. However, in a letter to Seligman, 18 May 1905, in response to a request for information on India, Marshall confessed he knew little about the current state of affairs in that country and referred him to some ex-students, who had made their careers in the Indian civil service (Seligman Papers, Columbia University).

have changed his mind on the sterile nature of state production.[124] In addition, and again conforming with Mill, Marshall never accepted that human nature had improved sufficiently for the problem of incentives under socialism to have been solved. His questioning of witnesses at the Labour Commission (such as Webb and Hyndman) showed that Marshall believed this to have been the case with respect to incentives for accumulation and general risk-taking investments, while much of his support for profit sharing and cooperation rested on the lessons and education this would provide for engendering selfless actions in work. Once again, his writing during the last years of his life, including herein the final version of the *Principles*, demonstrates that the necessary improvement in human nature had not taken place, except in the isolated cases of small, religious communities like the Shakers. In line with his views on the desirability of a lesser degree of inequality in wealth and income, Marshall proposed that businessmen should be encouraged and stimulated by non-pecuniary incentives, that is, become embued with economic chivalry, with honours and prestige acting as substitutes for that more usual and powerful measuring rod of motives to action, money.

This romantic expectation about businessmen's behaviour, combined with the high faith he had in eventual human perfectibility, paradoxically lent a Utopian air to his schemes, making them resemble the 'wild rhapsodies' of socialists such as Fourier and Saint-Simon, which he had admired in his youth for the hope they had given him as to human improvement. A fragment from the early 1920s highlights this conflict between realism and fantasy in Marshall's ideas of progress: 'Malthus's mistake: too much on the niggardliness of nature and too little on the perfectibility of man. We must avoid his errors, but not fall into their opposites.'[125]

It is in this sense that Marshall's tendency to socialism, reinforced by his adaptation of Mill's chapters on the subject, survived until the end of his life. He was willing to accept socialist organisation conditionally as a more ideal form of society, provided it could be shown this was not *economically* harmful. All his economic studies, however, demonstrated that society for its progress depended heavily on the forces of competition, private initiative and private capital; too much in fact to permit large-scale socialist experiments in production. After experience had shown that the detrimental consequences of graduated taxes on income and capital had been exaggerated, just as had been done with respect to the disincentive effects from 'outdoor relief', Marshall adopted an increasingly progressive fiscal stance in the measures he advocated as a type of 'redistributive socialism'. This was not very different from the position of the old philosophical radicals, modified for changed circumstances or, for that matter, from Tory philanthropists whom he had praised in his Oxford challenge to Henry George, or that of small 's' socialists of the 1890s. It was not, generally speaking, the position adopted by political Labour, let alone by the more militant socialists whom Marshall occasionally encountered in person or with whose works he had come in contact as part of his general economic studies.

MARSHALL'S POLITICS

Can Marshall's political position be articulated more precisely? As an adult male he would have voted in the many general elections over the more than half century he was entitled to do so. From the late 1860s his M.A. status and membership of the university entitled him to vote for the University of Cambridge seats and later, as an adult male property owner in his constituency of residence, mostly at Cambridge but at least once in Bristol during the 1880 General Election.[126] It seems certain that his principles forbade formal affiliation with a political party. However, as indicated in a previous chapter, during the early 1870s he had actively participated in the Liberal Reform Club, in which Fawcett, the academic economist-politician, was a leading light. Given his contemporaneous political activities in organising unions in the Cambridge countryside, it seems a safe guess that Marshall, as bachelor College Fellow, would have supported the radical, Liberal reform cause when given the opportunity to do so at the Cambridge University ballot box.[127]

The vagaries in liberal politics, described by some commentators as its veritable British climax,[128] largely coincided with Marshall's lifetime as voter. The Liberals had been in office on five occasions during these years: between 1868 and 1874; between 1880 and 1885; for a few months in 1886 when the party split over Home Rule (and a dissident faction of the party formed itself into the Liberal Unionists); between 1892 and 1895; and for the whole of the period from 1906 until 1915 when Asquith organised a National Government from all major parties to strengthen the British war effort. The wide variety of liberal viewpoints over these years appears to have induced some shifts in Marshall's political opinion, especially during the 1880s and 1890s. There is, however, little direct evidence for charting his shifts in position, not even of his general political position, in the correspondence which has survived. His correspondence with the Dutch economist and liberal politician, Pierson, at the time of the Boer War, indicated Marshall's general approval, if not admiration, for the Unionist politicians, as the Conservatives were then called, in the Salisbury and Balfour governments. The exception, as he so emphatically noted, was Chamberlain, a politician he detested for his populism, his lack of principle and his disloyalty, and ultimately his attempt to betray the principle of free trade.[129] It can be noted in this context that Marshall's participation in Royal Commissions was generally associated with periods of Conservative–Unionist party rule. This applies particularly to his major involvements: the invitation to join the Labour Commission and the Cabinet request in 1903 to prepare a confidential Memorandum on the fiscal policy of international trade. This may of course be coincidence in the sense that Balfour, with his Cambridge and more general moral sciences connections was involved in both these invitations. An earlier letter to Foxwell, written during the events which led to the split in the Liberal party over Home-rule in Ireland, gives perhaps the clearest position on Marshall's party political views: 'I suppose Nature has cursed me with a cross-bended mind. For I am a Bimetallist and a Home Ruler, and yet on many points I should vote against my own side with the Mono [metallist]s or the Liberal Unionists.'[130]

Taking this remark in combination with the political predilections of Marshall spelt out in this chapter, Marshall's position can be summarised in terms of a virtual persistent adherence to the tenets of classical liberalism as they existed during his formative years. From these he never departed. The first of them was liberty, or freedom as he preferred to call it, which, as he explained to Bishop Westcott, for him was synonymous with life.[131] Three early influences on his thinking at least implanted this love of freedom: de Tocqueville, whose work he had studied in the 1870s and quoted in his lectures on America;

Hegel, whose thoughts on freedom and the duties this entailed for the citizen remained a steadfast feature of his economic writings, and above all Mill, the economist who, as he confessed to Foxwell, was particularly dear to him, because 'even when I differ from him, he seems to keep my mind in a higher plane than other writers in economics'.[132] The second was nationalism, the right to love your own country. Marshall's support for the Home Rule cause, his sympathy with the Boers and later with Germany during the First World War, with Italy in her Abyssinian tribulations trying to secure colonialist status as a new nation, and above all his overwhelming Britishness show how deeply he was imbued with this aspect of classical liberalism, tinged though it was with racist beliefs in white supremacy. Last but not least was free trade, a principle that overrode the dreams about Imperial Federation and which, for Marshall, was something from which Britain even in economic decline should never easily depart. This aspect of his liberalism was linked to his emphasis on the importance of competition, and thereby also with freedom, qualified though it was to managed competition.*

With such beliefs it is easy to see why he could never have been a capital 's' socialist, or a socialist in the more conventional sense of the word. These liberal tenets only enabled acceptance of a socialist ideal as a sign of the potential for human perfectibility and of the possibilities for the improvement of human character. Apart from this, socialist principles tended to be in conflict with Marshall's economic and political principles, more so with respect to its implications for production than for its redistributional side. Marshall's life-long economic studies, premised in part on Mill's suggestion for experiments to test how far socialism's difficulties could be overcome, revealed to him that the time for socialism had not yet come. There were as yet no real substitutes for capitalist initiative as a creator of material progress while, more generally, human motivation, given its inclinations to selfishness rather than chivalry, still largely depended on the prod of pecuniary incentives. Only the higher, because successful, businessman could be tempted to continue his effort through the moral suasion of a system of honours and other accolades of personal prestige. In the sense that socialism destroyed the vigour of the race¶ by replacing character-building self-help with assistance through the State, Marshall founded his ultimate critique of socialism on human weakness, but as these human factors and motivation drove his economic argument, the economics could never be separated from the human factor in his explanation of social progress of which his tendency to socialism formed such an important part.

Marshall's politics, therefore remained that of the liberal, following the vagaries of liberalism's shifting proximity to socialism, as liberal fears of it waxed and waned. As later in the case of Maynard Keynes[133], class and inclinations would not have allowed Marshall

---

* Alfred Marshall to Bishop Westcott, 20 January 1901 (*Memorials*, p. 394) where Marshall criticised Christian Socialists such as Maurice and Kingsley for attacking 'competition generally, without seeing in this way they were working against freedom and therefore against life'.
¶ Marshall to Benjamin Kidd, 6 June 1894 (CUL, Add 8069/M251): 'I cordially agree with you that the true danger of socialism lies in its tendency to destroy the constructive force of variation and selection, and that in the permanent interests of the race we cannot afford to diminish suffering by means that especially choke up the springs of vigour'.

to cross the divide separating liberal politics, no matter how reformist or radical, from the socialist Labour side.

NOTES

1. *IT*, Preface, pp. vii–viii.
2. Cf. Rita McWilliams-Tullberg, 'Marshall's Tendency to Socialism', *History of Political Economy*, 7 (1), Spring 1975, p. 78 for a different opinion. I have benefited greatly from reading her fascinating study of the subject. It is, however, far more easy to agree with the broad thrust of John E. Elliott, 'Alfred Marshall on Socialism', *Review of Social Economy*, 48 (4), Winter 1990, pp. 450–76.
3. Cf. G.M. Young, *Portrait of an Age*, London: Oxford University Press, 1977, pp. 167–9 and such standard contemporary references on the subject as William Graham, *Socialism New and Old*, London: Kegan, Paul, Trench, Trübner & Co., 1904.
4. John Miller [William Lane], *The Workingman's Paradise*, Sydney: Edwards, Dunlop & Company, 1892, p. 114.
5. See above, Chapter 6, pp. 141–2.
6. Marshall to Helen Bosanquet, 28 September 1902, in *Memorials*, p. 444, above Chapter 14, pp. 521–3.
7. Alfred Marshall on himself, circa 1910, p. 16. Cf. *P* VIII, pp. 8–9, 763–4, 766, 769; the first of which dates from *P* III, the others from *P* I.
8. J.S. Mill, *Chapters on Socialism*, with an introduction by Lewis S. Feuer, New York: Prometheus Books, 1987, pp. 97–8.
9. *Ibid.*, p. 146, in fact, Mill's concluding sentence of this posthumously published material on socialism. Cf. John W. Mason, 'Political Economy and the Response to Socialism in Britain 1870–1914', *The Historical Journal*, 23 (3), 1980, pp. 568–9 which draws attention to the critical nature of Mill's views on socialism.
10. See above, Chapter 6, p. 142. The quotation is from Marshall, 'Social Possibilities of Economic Chivalry', in *Memorials*, p. 334.
11. As cited above, Chapter 6, pp. 174–5. This view was not new, and can be found in Jevons, for example, *Methods of Social Reform*, London: Macmillan, 1883, p. 31.
12. John Stuart Mill, *Principles of Political Economy*, People's Edition 1865 (Marshall copy preserved in CUL, Marshall d.61), esp. pp. 458, 459, 460–61, 465, 475 and for his note of disagreement, p. 453.
13. For a detailed discussion, see G. Kitson Clark, *Churchmen and the Condition of England 1832–1885*, London: Methuen, 1973, esp. Part III; Donald O. Wagner, *The Church of England and Social Reform since 1854*, New York: Columbia University Press, 1930, esp. Chapters 3 and 4; E. Norman, *The Victorian Christian Socialists*, Cambridge University Press, 1987, esp. Chapters 1–4. For Marshall's association with Maurice and Hort see above, Chapters 5 and 6, pp. 111–13, 144.
14. See G. Kitson Clark, pp. 227–9; Alfred Marshall to Rebecca Marshall, 11 July 1875, expressed his anxiety 'to know more than the American papers tell me on the Masters and Servants Act.' (Marshall Archive, 1: 194).
15. Rita McWilliams-Tullberg, 'Marshall's Tendency to Socialism', p. 81; the whole of this paragraph draws on her account of this episode in Marshall's life, on which see also p. 80 and the references cited in its notes 15 and 16. The Hall acting as chairman was probably the Hall who advised Marshall on agricultural matters for the *Principles*. See above, Chapter 12, p. 413 and n*.
16. R. Harrison, 'Two Early Articles by Alfred Marshall', *Economic Journal*, 73 (291), September 1963, p. 422; all references to these articles in the *Bee-Hive* reprinted there are inserted in brackets in the text of this paragraph.
17. Alfred Marshall, 'The Theory of Foreign Trade', in *EEW*, II, p. 126; cf. *IT*, p. 446 n. 1, where the Frankfurt meeting 'which depicted capital as the enemy', was compared with a meeting in 'San Francisco a year or two later'.
18. *P* VIII, p. 9; the material on the young Swedish Shaker comes from the passage mentioned in note 17 above. Cf. Benjamin Jowett to Mary Paley Marshall, 11 April 1887, in which he wrote that he thought 'you and Alfred make as near an approach [in their style of living embodied in Balliol Croft] to the early Christians as is possible in the 19th century' (Marshall Archive, 1:48).
19. *EOI*, p. 211. Marshall qualified this statement with the provision that money evaluations of such gains and losses should be discounted for the wealthy to take account of the smaller relative loss in happiness involved in diminishing their income by a specific amount (*ibid.*, pp. 211–12).

20. Marshall's views on and association with the cooperative movement were discussed above, Chapter 13, pp. 455–8, and see also below, pp. 601–2.

21. On this 'romantic view of the businessman' see Rita McWilliams-Tullberg 'Marshall's Tendency to Socialism', pp. 83–4 and the reference there given to John Whitaker's analysis of Marshall's period in Bristol. The Frys became lifelong friends of the Marshalls. And see above, pp. 291–2.

22. *P* VIII, pp. 586–8, 816, 817 n.; Anton Menger's 1886 study was published in English translation in 1899 with an introduction by Foxwell. Böhm-Bawerk's *Critical History of Interest Theories* devoted a chapter to Rodbertus's theory of exploitation, followed by one on Marx, in which Böhm-Bawerk drew attention to the similarities of the views of these two revolutionary socialists.

23. *P* IV, pp. 144 n.3, 671 n.1; the 1898 translation of Rodbertus, published in Swann Sonnenschein's very popular social science series, contained (in the translator's notes) the German concepts which Marshall mentioned in these notes. This is the only Rodbertus book listed in the Marshall Library Catalogue (p. 71).

24. Above, Chapter 8, p. 257 and n.*; Chapter 13, p. 477, in the context of Böhm-Bawerk.

25. *P* I, p. 67; *P* VIII, p. 766; Marshall's 1886 Lectures on Socialism (Marshall Archive, Box 5, Item 1C) and *Catalogue*, p. 8.

26. 'The Present Position of Economics', in *Memorials*, pp. 155–6.

27. J.S. Mill, *On Socialism*, Chapter 4, esp. pp. 115–16, 131–2 and cf. the concluding paragraphs of the previous chapter, pp. 112–13, in which Mill suggested a series of experiments by which to test the practical feasibility of socialism.

28. Cited in Helen Lynd, *England in the Eighteen-eighties*, pp. 159–60; cf. G. Stedman-Jones, *Outcast London*, esp. Chapter 16.

29. Helen Lynd, *England in the Eighteen-eighties*, esp. Chapters 5, 6 and 10. Cf. Thomas Mackay, 'Municipal Socialism', in *The Dangers of Democracy*, London: John Murray, 1913, pp. 267–93, esp. 281–3, cf. his 'Democratic Finance', in *ibid.*, pp. 184–5, 217–18. These essays had originally appeared in the *Quarterly Review* during the 1890s.

30. Elwood P. Lawrence, *Henry George in the British Isles*, East Lansing: Michigan State University Press, 1957, p. 3, Chapters 2 and 3, and especially John Saville, 'The Background to the Industrial Remuneration Conference of 1885', New York: Augustus M. Kelley, 1968, pp. 14–21.

31. Marshall to Foxwell, 22 July 1883 (Marshall Archive, 3:19). Marshall's letter also noted a number of people who had fallen under George's spell but who, according to him, should have known better.

32. J.K. Whitaker, 'Marshall: The Years 1877 to 1885', pp. 25–6.

33. George Stigler, 'Alfred Marshall's Lectures on Progress and Poverty', p. 190. All subsequent references to these lectures are indicated in brackets in the subsequent paragraphs devoted to their content. The growth of wages at this time is carefully scrutinised by John Saville, 'The Background to the Industrial Remuneration Conference of 1885', pp. 25–38.

34. Above, p. 574.

35. This draws attention to the fact that the account of Marshall's lectures used here was based on two newspaper reports. These conflicted more in their reports of the discussion than on the text of the lectures, with which Marshall had probably provided them. Other examples of this practice in Bristol were noted in Chapter 9 above, p. 289.

36. *P* I, Book VII, Chapter 13; *P* VIII, Book VI, Chapters 12 and 13. The taxation issue is discussed subsequently in this chapter, and below, Chapter 17, pp. 645–6.

37. George Stigler, 'Alfred Marshall's Lectures on Progress and Poverty', Appendix, pp. 221–4; almost two-thirds of the space taken up by the report of the discussion following George's Oxford address. Cf. Elwood P. Lawrence, *Henry George in the British Isles*, pp. 69–71.

38. Marshall to Foxwell, 10 March 1884, quoted above, p. 582 n.¶; JNKD, 10 March 1884.

39. Reported in *Western Daily Press*, 17 March 1883, reprinted in George Stigler, 'Alfred Marshall's Lectures on Progress and Poverty', p. 212.

40. Much of Arthur Young's data had been used for the material on historical statistics Marshall had prepared for his Bristol students (see above, Chapter 9, p. 288); he wrote to Foxwell about his study of Eden on 22 January 1883 (Marshall Archive, 3:8). In April 1883 he sent Foxwell a copy of the statistics he had prepared with his electric pen for his Bristol students (Marshall Archive, 3:16).

41. Marshall in *Western Daily Press*, 19 March 1883, in George Stigler, 'Alfred Marshall's Lectures on Progress and Poverty', pp. 213–15. On Marshall's assertions about this in his lectures, see above p. 583.

42. A.R. Wallace in *Western Daily Press*, 23 March 1883; Marshall in *Western Daily Press*, 24 March 1883, in *ibid.*, pp. 116–17.

43. As shown above, p. 583 and n. 41, Marshall had used this argument in the Henry George Lectures. For another contemporary assessment of the importance of this issue in the fight against socialism, see Thomas Mackay, 'The Wages and Savings of Working Men', in *The Dangers of Democracy*, studies in the economic question of

the day published originally in the *Quarterly Review* 1894–1909, London: John Murray, 1913, pp. 116–55, esp. 121–4; for a more contemporary perspective see T.S. Ashton, 'The Standard of Life of the Workers in England 1790–1830', in F.A. Hayek et al., *Capitalism and the Historians*, Chicago: University of Chicago Press, 1954, pp. 123–55. It had also been used by Sargant, *Social Innovators and their Schemes*, e.g. p. 465, where he used Malthus's wheat measure, which Wallace criticised in his correspondence with Marshall.

44. Marshall to Foxwell, 30 March 1884, Freeman Collection, 49/123.

45. J.S. Mill, *On Socialism*, pp. 141–6; for a detailed discussion of Mill's active involvement with the land question, see Samuel Hollander, *The Economics of John Stuart Mill*, Oxford: Basil Blackwell, 1985, pp. 833–46; and Pedro Schwartz, *The New Political Economy of J.S. Mill*, London: Weidenfeld & Nicolson, 1968, pp. 200–6, 254.

46. Marshall Library, Box 5, Item 1D; *P* VIII, Appendix G, esp. pp. 801–04; this dates back to *P* V and drew on Marshall's Memorandum on Local Taxation discussed in Chapter 11 above (p. 375).

47. A telling phrase, in the context of Marshall's 'anti-imperialist' views discussed below, pp. 606–8.

48. See my 'Marshall on Taxation', esp. pp. 102–3.

49. Industrial Remuneration Conference, *The Report of the Proceedings and Papers at the Prince's Hall, Piccadilly*, London: Cassell & Company, 1885, re-issued New York: Augustus Kelley, 1968 with an introduction by John Saville, introduction to original Report, pp. v–xix; introduction by John Saville, esp. pp. 14–16, 38; Ellwood P. Lawrence, *Henry George in the British Isles*, pp. 37–8.

50. Alfred Marshall, 'How far do remediable Causes influence prejudicially (a) the Continuity of Employment, (b) the Rate of Wages', in Industrial Remuneration Conference, *Report*, pp. 173–86; the four appended items fill a further thirteen pages, that is pp. 186–99. All references to this paper in the next few paragraphs are inserted as page references in brackets in the text.

51. Marshall's involvement with Royal Commissions was discussed in Chapter 11 above, see esp. p. 369 which discusses his contribution to the *Final Report* of the Labour Commission on fluctuations in employment.

52. A wrong reading of Marshall who, as shown in Chapter 4, p. 88, had rowed for his College for some time.

53. Presumably while in Berlin during the winter of 1869–70; the nature of the 'assistance' Marshall claimed to have been giving is not known.

54. Marshall to the editor of the *Times*, 11 February 1886, which mentions how 'at socialist lectures' he was always struck 'with the amused smile with which the *bona fide* working men generally receive the extravagances of the orator'.

55. H.M. Hyndman, *The Record of an Adventurous Life*, New York: Macmillan & Company, 1911, pp. 324–7; Chushichi Tuzuki, *H.M. Hyndman and British Socialism*, edited Henry Pelling, Oxford: Oxford University Press, 1961, pp. 52–4; Mary Paley Marshall, *What I Remember*, p. 35: 'At Oxford he [Alfred Marshall] encountered Henry George in person . . . shortly after, another duel took place with Hyndman'

56. Alfred Marshall, 'The Present Position of Economics', in *Memorials*, p. 173.

57. G. Stedman-Jones, *Outcast London*, Chapter 16.

58. Sidney Webb, 'The Basis of Socialism: Historic', in *Fabian Essays in Socialism*, ed. G.B. Shaw, London, Walter Scott, 1889, pp. 56, 60; see also Paul Thompson, *Socialists, Liberals and Labour*, esp. Chapters 3, 6, 7.

59. Marshall had both these works in his library (Marshall Library Catalogue, pp. 53, 80); see also Kenneth D. Brown, *Essays in Anti-Labour History*, London: Macmillan, 1974, esp. Chapters 9 and 12, and John W. Mason, 'Political Economy and the Response to Socialism in Britain 1870–1914'.

60. Recall Punch's applause of Marshall the slayer of the socialist snake, above Chapter 13, pp. 457–8.

61. See above, Chapter 11, pp. 363–4, 366–7.

62. Sidney Webb, 'The Basis of Socialism: Historic', p. 59; the 'competent economist' he cited was the Rev. F.W. Aveling, though Sidgwick was also cited in this context; Thomas Mackay, 'Orthodox Economics', in *The Dangers of Democracy*, Chapter VII, esp. pp. 233–4, 239–40, among other criticisms of Marshall, asserts that: 'in the hands of its present professors, economics is not a science, it is a controversy'.

63. In *Memorials*, pp. 323–53; and see above, Chapter 11, pp. 359–60. Its title recalls Marshall's finale to his address to the Industrial Remuneration Conference quoted earlier in this chapter (above p. 589).

64. See fragment headed, 'The Future of Industry', preserved in Marshall Library, Red Box 1 (5): 'Progress and Ideals'; cf. 'Some Economic Possibilities for Economic Chivalry', pp. 333–42. Much of this was echoed in contemporary literature on the subject, for example, in Leonard Darwin, *Municipal Ownership*, London: John Murray, 1908, esp. Ch. 3, pp. 120–24.

65. *P* VIII, Book V Chapter XIV, pp. 489–93; the quotation comes from 'Economic Possibilities of Economic Chivalry', p. 339.

66. Marshall to Helen Bosanquet, 2 October 1902, in *Memorials*, p. 445.

67. *Ibid.*, p. 445; see also 'Social Possibilities of Economic Chivalry', p. 336, and Chapter 21 below, pp. 774–5.

68. *Memorials*, p. 363; cf. 'Social Possibilities of Economic Chivalry', pp. 337–9.

69. *Memorials*, p. 363; *OP*, pp. 357–60; cf. Marshall to Theodore Llewellyn-Davies, 30 October 1901, in *Memorials*, pp. 430–31.
70. Leonard Darwin, *Municipal Ownership*, pp. 95–8; cf. 'Social Possibilities of Economic Chivalry', pp. 489–95 and the treatment of government ownership in transport and research presented much later in *IT*, pp. 492–7, 502–3, 505–6, 608–9, 671–2.
71. Alfred Marshall, 'How Far do Remediable Causes . . .', in Industrial Remuneration Conference, *Report* . . . , p. 172.
72. In *Memorials*, p. 359; Robert Albon, 'Alfred Marshall and the Consumer's loss from the British Post Office monopoly', *History of Political Economy*, 21 (4), Winter 1989, pp. 679–88 dates the closure of the St John's postal service at late 1885 (*ibid.*, p. 679).
73. See Robert Albon, p. 680.
74. C.W. Guillebaud, 'Some Personal Reminiscences of Alfred Marshall', p. 96.
75. See J.S. Mill, *Principles of Political Economy*, preliminary remarks, penultimate paragraph (People's Edition, 1865, pp. 13–14).
76. J.S. Mill, *On Socialism*, pp. 117–31; Marshall favourably compared Mill's pronouncements on these subjects in both the chapters on socialism and his *Principles* with Carlyle, despite the last's humanist reputation (see 'Social Possibilities for Economic Chivalry', p. 335 n.1, cf. pp. 317–19).
77. Above, Chapter 11, esp. pp. 354–5, 356–7.
78. 'Social Possibilities of Economic Chivalry', pp. 345–6.
79. For a more detailed discussion, see my 'Marshall on Taxation', esp. pp. 101–3 and the references there cited.
80. Marshall to Lord Reay, 12 September 1909, in *Memorials*, p. 363.
81. This is more fully discussed in the next chapter, below pp. 644–6.
82. Marshall to Lord Reay, 12 September 1909, in *Memorials*, pp. 462–3.
83. 'Social Possibilities of Economic Chivalry', pp. 333–7; Marshall to Bishop Westcott, 24 January 1900, in *Memorials*, pp. 386–8; Marshall to S.D. Fuller, 21 November 1897, in *Memorials*, pp. 403–4.
84. Cf. John Saville, introduction to Industrial Remuneration Conference, *Report*, pp. 39–40; and for the battle between the Webbs and the Bosanquets (representing the Fabians and the Charity Organisation Society), see A. McBriar, *An Edwardian Mixed Doubles*.
85. In *Memorials*, p. 366.
86. Samuel Smiles, *Self Help with Illustrations of Character and Conduct*, London: John Murray, 1859; *Thrift*, London: John Murray, 1875 of which the final chapters were respectively called, 'Character – the true Gentleman' and 'The Art of Living'. For Marshall's holdings of Smiles's books, see *Catalogue*, p. 78.
87. George Howell, *The Conflicts of Capital and Labour*, London, Chatto & Windus, 1878, pp. 152–3, 180. Marshall had used this book extensively in writing the trade union chapters of the *Economics of Industry*.
88. Marshall to Bishop Westcott, 23 July 1898, 23 January 1901, in *Memorials*, pp. 384–5, 396–7, where he wrote 'the proper work of the academic student with regard to Trade Unions is that he should treat them as a special case of association in which the good of individual unselfishness is ever surrounded and apt to be vitiated by the evil of class selfishness'.
89. Marshall to Edward Caird, Master of Balliol, 22 October 1897, *Memorials*, pp. 398–9. Marshall wrote in a similar vein to Taussig, in a letter of which the front page and date have not been preserved.
90. Marshall to Edward Caird, Master of Balliol, 5 December 1897, in *Memorials*, pp. 400–1.
91. *P* VIII, pp. 702–10, much of which dates from *P* V, though occasional fragments can be found in earlier editions. For a perceptive treatment of Marshall's views on trade unions, which extensively covers the subject, see R. Petridis, 'Alfred Marshall's Attitude to and Economic Analysis of Trade Unions: a case of Anomalies in a Competitive System', in *Alfred Marshall. Critical Assessments*, Vol. 3, pp. 480–507 and his 'The Trade Unions in the Principles: the Ethical versus the Practical in Marshall's Economics', *Economie appliquée*, 43 (1), 1990, pp. 161–86.
92. *OP*, esp. pp. 397–9. Aspects of this are discussed subsequently in this chapter in the context of Marshall's views on imperialism and war. See also *IT*, esp. pp. 103, 137 and n.1, 620–21, 639–42.
93. A streak particularly visible in Marshall's notes on progress and ideals largely written during the final years of his life. For a discussion, see G. Becattini, 'Market and Communism in the thought of Alfred Marshall', *Quaderni di storia dell'Economia Politica*, 9 (2–3), 1991, pp. 161–88, and below, Chapter 19, pp. 726–9.
94. See, for example, Thomas Mackay, 'The Wages and Savings of Working Men', pp. 139–42 where he noted turnover of co-operative societies had increased twenty-four fold between 1862 and 1895, while its profits on aggregate over these decades amounted to more than £72 million. As shown in A.M. Carr-Saunders, P. Sargent Florence and R. Peers, *Consumers' Co-operation in Great Britain*, London: Allen & Unwin, 1938, the movement continued to thrive in the early decades of the 20th century.
95. See above, Chapters 11 and 13, pp. 364–5, 456–7 and Chapter 14, pp. 517–19. Examples of Marshall's taking evidence on aspects of cooperation, are his questions to F.A. Moore on 15 March 1892 (Royal Commission on

Labour, *Minutes of Evidence*, Cmnd 6795, 1892, p. 320) and his questioning of Mr Brabrook on 27 October 1892 (*Fourth Report of the Commission on Labour*, Cmnd 7063, 1893, pp. 98–9).

96. *The Diary of Beatrice Webb 1892–1905*, edited Norman and Jeanne Mackenzie, London: Virago Press, 1983, p. 109.
97. *IT*, pp. 518–20, 604–9, 854–6.
98. *The Letters of Sidney and Beatrice Webb*, edited Norman Mackenzie, Volume 3, p. 62.
99. J.S. Mill, *Principles of Political Economy*, Book IV, Chapter VIII, paragraphs 5–7, esp. pp. 775, 783–4, 794 in *Collected Works*, Vol. III; cf. his chapters on *Socialism*, pp. 105–6, 126.
100. *P* VIII, p. 305, largely derived from the text of the first edition (my italics in the quotation).
101. *P* VIII, pp. 306–6. Marshall's reference to 'more hopeful signs . . . in the last few years' was first inserted in *P* III. Marshall's reflections from old age on progress, ideals and utopias are discussed in Chapter 19, below pp. 725–30, and see the page references to *IT* in note 97 above, esp. *IT*, pp. 854–6.
102. See the references to Mill cited in note 99 above; Henry Fawcett, *Manual of Political Economy*, pp. 237–40; Thomas Brassey, *On Work and Wages*, pp. 253–60; Sedley Taylor, *Profit Sharing*, London: Kegan Paul, Trench & Co. 1884 and the authoritative treatise on profit sharing by Nicholas Gilman (London: Macmillan, 1890), which Marshall had in his library (*Marshall Library Catalogue*, p. 32). A table of British profit-sharing firms from the 1870s up to 1891 shows five such firms which commenced profit sharing during the 1870s, 24 during the 1880s and no less than 21 firms during 1890 and 1891 (see Henry G. Rawson, *Profit-Sharing Precedents*, London: Stevens & Sons, 1891, pp. vii–ix).
103. Sedley Taylor, 'How far do remediable causes influence prejudicially the well-being of the Working Classes?' and Edward D. Greening, 'Profit-Sharing and Co-operative Production', in Industrial Remuneration Conference, *Report*, pp. 251–304, 304–11.
104. Alfred Marshall, 'Co-operation', in *Memorials*, pp. 252–3.
105. *P* VIII, pp. 306–7, 626–7 (most of which date with minor revisions from *P* I–IV).
106. Alfred Marshall, 'A Fair Rate of Wages', in *Memorials*, p. 219. The nature of these difficulties probably inspired Marshall's substantial interest in *métayage* as a form of product sharing in agriculture (for a discussion see Claudio Cecchi, 'Land Tenure and Economic Progress in the Principles', *Quaderni di storia dell'economia politica*, 10 (1), 1992 pp. 585–99).
107. *P* VIII, p. 627, a remark first inserted in *P* II, and cf. *IT*, p. 856.
108. Below, Chapter 17, pp. 640–41, 647–8.
109. Above, Chapter 10, for example, pp. 313, 315.
110. Above, Chapter 11, pp. 378, 381–2, 389.
111. Marshall to the editor of the *Times*, 23 December 1895; for background to the controversy see Eli Halévy, *History of the English People*, *Epilogue (1) Imperialism*, London: Pelican Books, 1939, pp. 76–7.
112. Marshall to Caird, 5 December 1897, in *Memorials*, p. 401. On the Egyptian dispute with France and the diplomatic altercations at the time over the Upper Nile, see Elie Halévy, *History of the English People: Epilogue (1) Imperialism*, pp. 66–9.
113. Marshall to Bishop Westcott, 20 January 1901, in *Memorials*, p. 394; Bishop Westcott to Marshall, 22 January 1901, in *Memorials*, p. 396.
114. Marshall to Helen Bosanquet, 2 October 1902 (cited above, p. 594); estimates about the South African war costs are derived from B.R. Mitchell, *Abstract of British Historical Statistics*, p. 398. On Marshall's support for the Garden City movement, see Chapter 13 above, pp. 452–3.
115. JNKD, 11 December 1899; the other dinner guests included Pigou, John Carter, the Oxford economist, and the Ryles.
116. Above, Chapter 11, esp. pp. 386–7. Marshall also criticised Pethick-Lawrence on the subject, in a letter dated 12 January 1904 (in *Memorials*, pp. 453–4).
117. Memorandum on the Fiscal Problem, Treasury Document 14949, 29 August 1903 (Public Record Office T1`/9990/FB/14949), Part I, esp. pp. 5–8, 20–21. The final pages directly address the issue of closer ties between the parts of the Empire, in which it is concluded that those supporting a more real Imperial Union place political considerations above the economic ones. For a detailed discussion of the general reaction to Imperial Federation by leading British economists, see J.C. Wood, *British Economists and the Empire*, London: Croom Helm, 1983.
118. *OP*, pp. 365–420, all page references inserted in brackets in the remainder of this paragraph are to this edition. On Marshall's subsequent views on Imperial Federation, see *IT*, pp. 104–5, 159–61.
119. Marshall to Finlay Shirras, 6 July 1910, in *Memorials*, pp. 470–71.
120. Alfred Marshall, *HME*, e.g. pp. 11–14.
121. Marshall to Manohar Lal, 28 January 1909, in *Memorials*, p. 457; cf. his letter to B. Mukherjee, 22 October 1910, in *ibid.*, pp. 471–3.

122. See Pantaleoni to Seligman, 1 August 1900, in 'The Seligman Correspondence, IV, *Political Science Quarterly*, 56 (4), December 1941, p. 595. Marshall had written to Seligman on 13 March 1896 in a P.S., expressing sympathy for 'poor Italy' which had been defeated in her colonial quest for Abyssinia.

123. Marshall, 'Social Possibilities of Economic Chivalry', p. 334, and see above, p. 596. Harcourt's famous phrase, 'We are all socialists now', made in 1895 while introducing graduated death duties, suggests he was likewise implying socialism in this redistributive sense (or the socialism with a little 's' defined above, pp. 571–2).

124. A.C. Pigou, *Socialism versus Capitalism*, London: Macmillan, 1937, pp. 79–86, which in this context quoted Marshall's 'Social Possibilities of Economic Chivalry', pp. 338–9.

125. 'Outline for Book on Economic Progress: last chapter of the volume – the possible future of industry and trade', (Marshall Archive, Red Box 1(5)).

126. Marshall to Foxwell, 20 April 1880 (Freeman Collection, 9/232) in which he commented on Tory bitterness in Bristol over their election defeat and its implication for his fund-raising activities on behalf of Bristol University College.

127. Above, Chapter 6, p. 113.

128. Michael Bentley, *The Climax of Liberal Politics. British Liberalism in Theory and Practice 1868–1918*, London: Edward Arnold, esp. Chapter 1.

129. See the letter to Pierson quoted above, pp. 605–6; Marshall to Lujo Brentano, 29 September 1903.

130. Alfred Marshall to Foxwell, 27 January 1885 (Freeman Collection, 23/104).

131. Marshall to Bishop Westcott, 20 January 1901, in *Memorials*, p. 394.

132. Marshall to Foxwell, 14 April 1897 (Marshall Archive, 1:56).

133. J.M. Keynes, 'Am I Liberal?', in J.M. Keynes, *Essays in Persuasion*, London: Rupert Hart Davis, 1951, pp. 213–38.

17. A Sage in Retirement

On 20 May 1908, the Economics Board recorded Marshall's resignation as Professor of Political Economy, not long therefore, before his 66th birthday. The fact that Marshall retired during his 66th year, at the end of an academic year, has nothing to do with any statutory requirements dealing with the then retirement age of university professors. Marshall's choice was purely voluntary. It was inspired by a desire to spend more time on his writings, without the distractions provided by his responsibilities of the professorship to which, from 1906, had been added his duties as Chairman of the Economics Board. The lack of progress with his second volume, the publication date of which he had initially forecast for nearly two decades before, was something he wanted to redress, if at all possible, before old age and ill health intervened. Health reasons were also not an issue in the decision to retire: though as another factor preventing the rapid completion of work, they may have been a consideration. Thirteen years before Marshall had written to President Eliot of Harvard that his bad digestion slowed up his work on the second volume, by the constraint on concentrated effort the rest it required imposed on him,

> My health does not hamper me except indirectly. I don't see much of doctors, and I am perfectly well if I rest – without even talking or reading a newspaper – for a good hour after every meal. But this diminishes much of my time for work, and often causes relatively light special work to take up all my strength. If I had a good digestion, my Vol. II would be well on its way . . . [1]

Retirement, whether for speeding up his writing or not, was an issue which in any case had been on his mind for some time. On 8 January 1901 he wrote to Keynes in a letter marked, 'confidential', that 'I would retire if I could afford it. But I cannot. If I did I would have an income of only about £150 a year, exclusive of the rental equivalent of my house, and sundry checks from Macmillans.'[*] This implied little improvement in the Marshalls' financial situation from the time they were in Oxford in 1883, and obtained £150 annually from investment income. This is not unlikely, because consol yields had deteriorated during the intervening years in real terms. Both that, and the cost of the house which generated the (imputed) rental income, had been advanced by Mary Paley in the partnership.[2] The sundry cheques from Macmillans, given sluggish sales of the *Principles* at this time, would not have been very large.[3] Marshall's annual income in retirement would therefore be well below the

---

[*] Marshall to John Neville Keynes, 8 January 1901 (Marshall Archive, 1:22). The reason Marshall advanced in this case for his desire to resign the chair was not associated with finding more time for writing; it related to Foxwell's financial problems at the time, necessitating the sale of his library and his search for more lucrative employment than his Cambridge lectureship, perhaps as Professor at Birmingham. Marshall, who did not want to lose Foxwell at this stage, knew that the only post which could hold him in Cambridge in the immediate future was his own Professorship, were he to resign it. Marshall's concerns over Foxwell's financial position are further considered in Chapter 18 below, pp. 675–6; his degree of support for Foxwell when the chair did eventually become vacant in 1908 is discussed below, pp. 624–6.

necessary level for a bachelor Fellow he had estimated at £300 in 1883.[4] Practical thrift was clearly not a Marshallian virtue. However, a hip ailment of his sister Mabel may have cost Marshall considerably in medical expenses in previous years, while he was also paying the salary of one of the political economy teachers.[5] By 1908, such financial reasons were apparently no longer pressing for the Marshalls. More importantly, the rationale of finding time to speed up writing had become more urgent, since in early 1908 the second volume was probably as little advanced towards actual publication as it had been in 1895.

On 21 April the *Cambridge University Reporter* announced the Professorship of Political Economy was vacant by the resignation of Professor Marshall; the date of election for the chair was announced on 1 May as taking place on Saturday 30 May. Despite the late public announcement, the Vice-Chancellor had been informed of Marshall's intention to retire as early as 4 October 1907, presumably to abide with the convention of giving a full academic year's notice of such action. The reason he gave reinforces belief that it was desire to press on with his long-delayed writings which motivated the step. Significantly, he added that he had 'already passed the age of which it is generally expedient to make room for younger men', a statement which has been taken as confirmation of his desire to place Pigou in his chair.[*]

Although John Neville Keynes recorded[6] that the election of Marshall's successor was occupying Marshall's mind just before the date of election was officially announced, formal considerations of more immediate concern to Marshall's imminent retirement need to be recorded. The Economics Board at its first meeting after the Vice-Chancellor's announcement of Marshall's retirement plans passed the following resolution recording the gratitude of its members to its effective founder and undisputed *de facto* as well as *de jure* leader:

> We desire to express to Professor Marshall on behalf of this Board our deep regret on learning that he has resigned the chair which he has filled with so much lustre and with so much advantage to the University and to offer him our thanks for his services as Chairman of this Board and for the generosity with which he has for so many years supported the School of Economics destined to be long identified with his great name.[7]

Marshall's personal response to this treasured resolution was dated 30 May, the day his successor was safely elected, while his more material generosity to which the resolution also drew attention, was given further tangible expression a few days later. Marshall's thanks are preserved in the Minute Book of the Economics Board, and are worth quoting in full for the picture they give of his emotions about this important occasion:

---

[*] *Cambridge University Reporter*, 22 April 1908, p. 787; 5 May 1908, p. 835; Marshall to the Vice-Chancellor, 4 October 1907 (Cambridge University Archives), cited by T.W. Jones, 'The Appointment of Pigou as Marshall's successor, the other side of the Coin', *AMCA*, IV, p. 305 and n. 125. A notice in the *Cambridge University Reporter* (25 February 1908, pp. 615–16) on recommendations to provide better for the award of the title Professor Emeritus may have delayed the announcement. Marshall did not receive this title until 1918 (*Cambridge University Reporter*, 25 October 1918). In 1908, elections for vacant professorships tended to be called quickly. He had earlier in 1907 (January 31) communicated his intention to retire to Macmillan.

I have to express my deepest and most heartfelt thanks for the most kind and generous resolution of the Special Board of Economics and Politics which you [A.W. Ward] have just sent me. What little I have been able to do for the progress of Economics in Cambridge would have been impossible had not others co-operated genially and unselfishly. I have always been abundantly paid. Others have worked for the love of truth and for the well being of the University, with little or no material reward: and this has always seemed to me to have been one of the highest forms of chivalry.

And may I add a word of thanks to you. Your influential pleading of our cause before the Senate; and the invaluable council and guidance which you have given to the Board and to me in particular, have played a chief part in enabling the Tripos to see the light of day and to grow – as I hope and believe – to a great future.

As long as I live I shall cherish a happy and grateful remembrance of the kindness I have received from the whole Board and from no one more than you yourself.[8]

The other formal consequence of Marshall's decision to retire was his last lecture as Professor of Political Economy. It was given the day after the Economics Board recorded its gratitude for Marshall's long services to his subject. On the account of D.H. Macgregor, it was rather sparsely attended: 'there were perhaps twenty of us, including what he called "all the colts in his stable", some of the more senior of his former pupils, and a few undergraduates'.[9] One of those undergraduates, Lynda Grier, soon to head the economics honours list for the year, preserved her notes of this lecture, in which Marshall attempted 'to pull together what I have been talking about'. Although this was presumably meant to pertain only to the year's work on applied economics he had been teaching that year, the contents of the lecture as she has preserved it, suggest that Marshall, fully conscious of the historical significance of the moment, used the opportunity also to survey the essence of his life's work. In order of presentation, Marshall discussed problems of measurement; aggregation; issues of methodology including the notion of progress in economics; problems in applying consumer surplus illustrated by the case of a demand curve with rapidly varying elasticity and ending with the prediction that this technique would outlive him and his audience. Discussion of socialism and the Webbs' prescriptions for government action followed, leading into remarks on the factory acts; the economic incompetence of Miss Martineau; the essential importance of competition; problems of monopoly with special reference to railway amalgamations in Britain and attitudes to railways in Germany; lack of German democracy; the limited usefulness of international comparisons, before returning to collectivists, socialists and anarchists, movements confused in the past. It ended with *obiter dicta* describing collectivists 'as the only true Anarchists the world has ever seen' and a claim that the one way to disprove Marshall's 'main proposition, "only means by which order is maintained in the world is that standards should be set by competition", was by a unanimous agreement to fix wages "without reference to competitive forces"'. Marshall's sense of the occasion is particularly visible from his concluding remarks as recorded by Lynda Grier:

Put before us Work, Self-Sacrifice and Joy when it comes. If we do not seek it, it will come. Every man and woman must go through some self-denial. Man and woman have separate parts to play. Danger of movements. Be a little suspicious of them because people get together and become enthused.

Oxford has made movements, Cambridge has made men. 24 years ago I gave my inaugural address (Quoted it). I leave my office with a feeling of satisfaction. There is growing up a method of loving one's country more than one's party and sometimes one's party more than one's self, and[?] truth even more than one's country.[10]

Lynda Grier recorded that John Neville Keynes, perhaps in his role as Secretary of the Economics Board, perhaps as Marshall's oldest surviving pupil present at the lecture, then made a brief speech, followed by thanks from Alfred Marshall. Keynes himself noted in his diary, 'Marshall's last professorial lecture. I said a few words at the end, probably very badly.'[11] Pigou, who was almost certainly present as one of the more prominent 'colts' in the Marshallian stable, may have been thinking of Marshall's last lecture and its conclusion when he himself penned the last paragraphs of his memorial lecture following Marshall's death, with its quotation from Marshall's inaugural and its emphasis on his love of truth over party and all else.[12] No other 'colts' from that stable left records of being present at their trainer's last lecture, nor were such recollections provided by teachers of the Economics Tripos such as Lowes Dickinson, W.E. Johnson, Clapham, Fay, Meredith, Alston, Benians, Wood and Green, who could easily have been present. Maynard Keynes, soon to rejoin the Cambridge teaching staff after his short stint at the India office, was likewise not present.[13]

In the week after the election of his successor, Marshall informed the Secretary of the Economics Board of another act of material generosity on his part. The books set aside by him for the use of students were to be retained by the Board. The bookcase which housed them and for which he had paid was part of this gift. Supervision of the punctual return of these books proved to be a difficulty only resolved when the Board eventually granted formal powers to their custodian. On 27 January 1909, the Board appointed Maynard Keynes to this position[14] as a consequence of which some correspondence with Marshall ensued. A month after Keynes's appointment to oversee what was to become the Marshall Library, he received the following letter from its benefactor: 'I don't think it is worthwhile to have a separate label for those books which I have put into L.L.R.5. I never thought of such a thing being done and I cannot countenance it. But that is the only objection which I have to the enclosed label; which seems to be excellent of its kind.'[15]

A year later, on the precise anniversary of the election of his successor to the chair, Marshall congratulated Maynard Keynes on the catalogue he had prepared of the books he had donated, describing it as 'excellent' and as certain to be 'of great service'. His letter continued, 'I have a good many books, chiefly historical, which are good of their kind, and which I yet seldom use. If you had some space, I should suggest that some of them should come to you without waiting for my demise. Don't trouble to answer.'[16]

By July, he had already departed for his customary summer vacation in Europe, and was safely ensconced in the Ampezzo Tal of his beloved South Tirol. This holiday would have been enjoyed all the more now that the worries entailed by his retirement had been finally finished with. Undoubtedly, the most difficult of these had related to the election of his successor. In order to gain the success of his preferred candidate to carry on the Marshallian tradition, Marshall had sacrificed his oldest surviving friendship, with his former student and long-standing colleague of faculty and college, Foxwell. This was a price he may well not have fully anticipated as a necessary consequence of his actions to influence the choice of his successor.

REJECTING 'THE CLAIMS OF FRIENDSHIP': MARSHALL'S ROLE IN THE ELECTION OF PIGOU TO THE PROFESSORSHIP OF ECONOMICS[17]

The election of a successor to the chair of Political Economy took place not long after Marshall's official retirement. The electors at the time when the announcement of the vacancy was made, were as follows. The Vice-Chancellor, E.S. Roberts, and Master of St John's College, was in charge of proceedings *ex officio*; the eight nominated electors were A.J. Balfour, a prominent member of the university as a former prime minister; J.N. Keynes, V.H. Stanton, J.E. Sorley, R.H. Inglis Palgrave, J.S. Nicholson, Leonard Courtney and Edgeworth. Apart from the last, all of the electors had been selected for that purpose a long time ago. Three – Stanton, Palgrave and Courtney – had held this office at the time of Fawcett's death in 1884. Edgeworth, the only new elector, was in fact not appointed until 22 January 1908 by a decision of the Economics Board with Marshall in the chair. Given the reportedly close vote at the professorial election, this was a crucial appointment. It was also an early sign of Marshall's manoeuvring to gain his choice of successor, since the appointment was made after he had formally announced his resignation to the Vice-Chancellor but before that decision had been made public.[18]

By the time the election was held on 30 May, there were four candidates: Ashley, Cannan, Foxwell and Pigou. This relatively small number of candidates for a prestigious appointment is surprising. It seems that Marshall had a share in dissuading some persons from throwing their hat into the ring. A decade after the event, he wrote to his former student and one-time Cambridge lecturer, Walter Layton,

> Chapman had wanted to be a candidate for the Professorship here. I did not give him to understand that I should support him against Pigou but I urged him to stand and he decided to do so. But shortly afterwards he wrote to say that the Manchester authorities when raising his salary to £700 had understood that he undertook in return to stand by the Manchester School, so he was not free to run for the Cambridge post.[19]

The crucial aspect in this *ex post* recollection of events is Marshall's unwillingness to give Chapman a commitment of support against the person who by then would already have been known to some as his favoured candidate. Hence Marshall's suasion was, on reflection, probably taken by Chapman as purely formal, and his Manchester excuse for not standing came as a natural reaction, if not as a bargaining ploy to gain better remuneration from his employers.

Marshall also tried his hand at persuading the electors. Keynes's diary records two visits by Marshall at which he tried to do just that. The first occurred on 30 April, the day before the Vice-Chancellor's formal announcement of the vacancy in the chair following Marshall's retirement. 'Interview with Marshall on the subject of the election to the Political Economy Professorship. He speaks in the highest terms of Pigou and is clearly most anxious that he should be elected. He very distinctly does not want Foxwell to be elected. I very much wish I were not an elector'. Marshall called again on 27 May, three days before the election. On 29 May, he sent Edgeworth as his emissary to the Keynes's residence to persuade the three electors there present, Palgrave, Nicholson and Keynes, 'to discuss tomorrow's election'. Keynes recorded, 'We gathered he [Edgeworth] had been sent by Marshall. Nicholson is intensely annoyed at what he thinks Marshall's unfairness to Foxwell.'[20]

Whether Marshall tried to persuade any of the other electors in this fashion is not known. Edgeworth, who was staying at Balliol Croft at the time of the election, would certainly have followed Marshall's wishes in this, as he had done in other things, and in any case would have needed little persuasion to give his support to Pigou in this field.* Courtney was of course an old friend of Marshall, as well as a fellow Johnian and fellow member of the Labour Commission. From a letter after Courtney's death in 1918, it can be surmised that Marshall may in fact have actively canvassed him to give his support to Pigou.[†] Sorley and Stanton, the non-economist university members on the selection committee, may not have needed much persuasion to vote for Pigou, if Foxwell was right in thinking that is what they did. Sorley had been Marshall's student, had been supported by Marshall for the Knightbridge Chair of Moral Philosophy as successor to Sidgwick, and would have seen both Pigou and Foxwell in action on the Economics Board of which he had been a member from its inception. Stanton, a 20th wrangler contemporary to Marshall and a long standing Fellow of Trinity, was an early acquaintance and one with whom Marshall had been on sufficiently good terms to ask him to provide a testimonial in support of his application for the position of Principal at Bristol in 1877. This leaves the Vice-Chancellor, E.S. Roberts, and Balfour.

Foxwell had no doubt as to where the Vice-Chancellor stood *vis-à-vis* the election, particularly since as Master of St John's he had taken a strong dislike to Marshall. Foxwell wrote to Clara Collet after the election had taken place,

> It was regarded here as a moral certainty that I should be elected. 15 to 1 was Macgregor's estimate. I did not know that Marshall, as an elector afterwards told me, was moving heaven and earth to prevent my election, and raking up every conceivable thing that he thought might prejudice me. . . . The V.C. was doing all he could for me.
>
> Well, Courtney, Edgeworth, Sorley and Stanton voted against me: Nicholson, Palgrave and Keynes for me. Balfour refused to come, on the ground that it seemed to turn on politics: a curious ground for a party leader to take. If he had come and had voted for me I should have got in, in spite of Marshall, for the V.C. would have given me 6 casting votes if he had them.[21]

Balfour's role in the proceedings as elector who did not turn up, is also of interest. As an old Cambridge man and long friend of the moral sciences, Balfour was clearly in a quandary. This was worsened by the fact that the international fiscal policy matters on which Marshall had advised his government in 1903 were coming back to haunt him.

---

* Recall Edgeworth's refusal to publish a piece by Walras as editor of the *Economic Journal* at Marshall's instigation and, more generally, his slavish seeking of advice from Marshall in this position to such an extent that even Marshall grew tired of answering his correspondence (above, Chapter 13, pp. 478–9, 467).

† Marshall wrote to his widow how Courtney, among other things, 'was particularly kind and helpful to me at a time when I was lost and in need of guidance from that sound and penetrating judgement of which he was an eminent master' (Marshall to Lady Courtney, 13 May 1918, British Library of Political and Economic Science, Courtney Collection (R(S)R 1003 VIII 15(5)). This letter may refer to several instances of Courtney's support, for example, during Marshall's campaign for the Economics Tripos.

References by Asquith as Prime Minister and Lloyd-George as Chancellor of the Exchequer to Marshall's Memorandum which Balfour's Chancellor had solicited in 1903, during the parliamentary debate in the House of Commons on the Finance Bill and associated matters which had started 26 May and continued through 1 and 2 June, 1908, virtually coincided with the election for the Cambridge chair. This may have swayed Balfour to abstain from doing his duty in this case, particularly when leading players in the Cambridge election had also been prominent in public debate on the fiscal question in 1903. In any case, Balfour wrote to Hewins that he had asked the Vice-Chancellor to excuse him from taking part in the election. In reply, the Vice-Chancellor had asked for Balfour's private advice on three of the candidates, a request to which he wished to accede and on the draft of which he wanted Hewins's advice. Hewins's response failed to comment on Cannan as one of the candidates, perhaps because Hewins was a close associate of Cannan from Oxford and the London School of Economics. However, it indicated Hewins had a high opinion of the other three candidates: 'Pigou may become a great economist. . . . Ashley is by far the ablest and best equipped of the three. . . . Foxwell would be a very safe appointment and in the circumstances would probably meet with widespread approval.'[22] Given Balfour's reputation as a cautious politician, Hewins's advice would have been filtered by him to the Vice-Chancellor as support for Foxwell, as Foxwell later surmised and in fact may have even been told by the Vice-Chancellor.[23]

On the Saturday, Pigou was elected. There is no doubt that Marshall was pleased that he got what he had wanted. He hosted a celebratory dinner that evening at Balliol Croft to which the electors who did not return immediately to their home towns appear to have been invited. Keynes's diary, the source for this event, indicates both his and Nicholson's presence, and records Palgrave's departure from Cambridge not until the next day, which suggests that Palgrave was also a guest at the dinner. Edgeworth, who was staying at Balliol Croft for the election, would have been present as well. Keynes reports nothing on the evening's conversation topics, apart from Nicholson's statement 'that Marshall did not speak to him the whole evening'. The next day, Keynes recorded that Nicholson 'is very severe on Marshall's manoeuvring, and I certainly did not think that Marshall has come out of the thing well'.[24] In his letter to Clara Collet, Foxwell was less coy about Nicholson's behaviour, saying that during his Sunday visit he 'paced up and down my garden for two hours abusing Marshall'. There can be no doubt that Nicholson voted for Foxwell and against Pigou.* Keynes's comments suggest that he most likely did the same. Palgrave, as a friend of Foxwell, had no reasons to love Marshall, given Marshall's indifferent, if not hostile, response to his *Dictionary of Political Economy* project.¶

---

*   Foxwell to Clara Collet, 6 June 1908, in A.W. Coats, 'The Appointment of Pigou', p. 240. Foxwell continued his report of university reaction to Pigou's election: 'a member of the University Council has told Olive [his wife] yesterday that wherever he went in the University there was "universal execration". Cunningham's verger told my servant that he had never known C. so upset and so indignant. C referred to the business in his sermon yesterday. . . . A member of Council writes me that "this election will condemn the Cambridge School of Economics to the same level of impotence to which Edgeworth has reduced the Oxford school".' Foxwell's impression of general Cambridge hostility to the Pigou appointment was confirmed by Price, below, p. 630.

¶   I am therfore not at all convinced by Jones's hints ('The Appointment of Pigou as Marshall's Successor', esp. p. 308) that J.N. Keynes may have voted for Pigou, on the assumption that Pigou's appointment was more favourable to his son's career prospects both at King's and at the university. Confirmation of the way in which

Marshall's gloating over Pigou's success and his early notification of the mid-day events at the Vice-Chancellor's lodge that Saturday were also recollected not long after Marshall's death by an unintentional witness to these dramatic events. Roderick Clark, a Cambridge graduate, informed Maynard Keynes in the context of his Marshall Memoir, 'that the last time I saw Marshall was on the afternoon of Pigou's election as his successor. I was in Cambridge for the weekend and called on the Saturday afternoon to see him: he came to speak to me in the hall, apologising for not being able to see me because he had the Board of Electors at tea with him after the election – and I have never forgotten how his face beamed with delight as he told me that Pigou had been elected!'[25]

The only uncertainty about Pigou's election which remains is the time when Marshall switched allegiance from Foxwell to his younger protégé. Although Foxwell's role in the 1903 fiscal controversy has been depicted as the decisive factor in Marshall's switch of support to Pigou, this appears less convincing on the evidence, including from what on Marshall's part had been a very long and intimate friendship with Foxwell.[26] As indicated earlier in this chapter, by 1901 when Pigou had already been appointed as an economics lecturer against Foxwell's wishes, Marshall could still entertain Foxwell as a possible successor, for whom he claimed he would have resigned at the time in order to keep him in Cambridge. Only by 1906, and then on the basis of Webb's ambiguous evidence as to date, did Marshall appear firmly committed to the notion that Pigou should be his successor. There is no reason to doubt Webb's assertion made in writing to Ashley (shortly after his unsuccessful candidature against Pigou), that Webb 'happened to have accidently learned, a couple of years ago, that Marshall intended and expected Pigou to succeed him' and that therefore it had not surprised him that 'Marshall seems to have moved heaven and earth to exclude you [i.e. Ashley and Foxwell]'.[27]

To interpret Webb's 'couple of years' broadly, 1905 or 1906 can be seen as crucial years in this context, both very formative years in the new Tripos. By that stage Marshall would have been able to judge the relative merits of both Foxwell and Pigou for advancing his Tripos, a comparison in which the younger man would gradually have appeared as the stronger and more able for that purpose. It will be recalled that at the start of 1906 Marshall had quarrelled with Foxwell over the suitability of his lecturing for the students of the Tripos, the first time Marshall had done this so vehemently. Given the context was preparation of the 1906–7 teaching programme, it should also be recalled that at that time Marshall was sufficiently sure of Pigou's teaching to entrust him to take the class for special difficulties in economics in 1906–7, thereby relieving him of part of his extraordinarily heavy teaching load the previous year.[28] Concern for the future of his Tripos seems a more pertinent explanation for Marshall's switch to Pigou as the preferred successor, since doctrinal differences with Foxwell on many issues, including that of free trade, had been a long-standing feature of their relationship.

This explanation is strengthened by several other circumstances. Marshall's letter of resignation to the Vice-Chancellor had mentioned the desirability of a young person for the

---

Palgrave voted is much more speculative, though Foxwell's precise knowledge of how individual electors voted rings true from the circumstantial evidence already presented and from the fact that one of the electors, almost certainly Nicholson, told him in person. Votes in appointment committees at this time were never by secret ballot but were presumed to remain confidential.

chair as one reason for his retirement. This ground would have disqualified Foxwell for the position. Secondly, in his guarded letter to Maynard Keynes in April 1908, Marshall hinted that his offer of a lectureship in economics was conditional on a successor willing to pay £100 from his own pocket for the salary, something which Foxwell would not have been easily able to do, given his young family and extravagances in book buying, which were continuing unabated.[29] As a bachelor, such payments would not have been difficult for Pigou and were in fact made by him on becoming Professor.[30] Since teaching in the new Tripos depended so much on voluntary action of this nature, as Marshall reminded the Economics Board in his letter of thanks for their retirement resolution, Foxwell's election would have seriously hampered teaching resources for the new Tripos.[*] The third circumstance occurs in Marshall's remark about the electors acting as 'trustees' in the letter he wrote to Foxwell on 31 May, that is, after the election. This can only mean trustees on behalf of the university's teaching of economics, on which grounds their selection of Pigou was defensible as being in the best interests for advancing the new arrangements for economics teaching which had only so recently been made. Pigou's potential to 'be recognised ere long as a man of quite extraordinary genius' was the reason Marshall gave to Foxwell by way of explanation of 'his hope' that Pigou would be elected.[¶]

The remainder of Marshall's letter was a plea for their friendship to continue. It reminded Foxwell of its length despite their many differences of opinion. It thanked him for his support, so frequently unbegrudgingly given even when Foxwell had personal reservations on the issues in question. It is, however, difficult to ignore the element of humbug in Marshall's letter, particularly when Marshall disingenuously wrote:

> I have not heard very much about it: the proceedings of the election between 12 and 2 yesterday have been kept absolutely secret, but I have heard no one, not even among the most enthusiastic supporters of Pigou's claims, who is not deeply pained by the thought that it has not been possible to crown your long and trusty work by a high reward.
> Please do not answer this just now: for you must be feeling sore.[†]

Foxwell delayed his reply for a day, and its dignity contrasts favourably with Marshall's rather hypocritical effort to which it responded. It shows his bitterness at having 'his experience and long service' as well as feeling of loyalty to Cambridge ignored for a younger man, able though that man may be. Foxwell claimed to have no resentment for

---

[*] Marshall to Maynard Keynes, 3 April 1908 in *Collected Writings of John Maynard Keynes*, Vol. XV, p. 13. From Marshall's point of view, Pigou's appointment would also have been more staff effective, since it freed the Girdlers' lectureship he was holding for another teacher; Foxwell's St John's College lectureship, on the other hand, was not likely to be filled by St John's College with a teacher for the Economics Tripos.

[¶] Marshall to Foxwell, 31 May 1908 (Marshall Archive, 3:546). Marshall's 'hope that he would be elected' replaced his 'acted for his election' which was crossed out, a sign of bad conscience over his actions. Marshall was proved wrong over Pigou's stewardship of the Tripos in at least one respect: Pigou hated administration (see below, Chapter 20, p. 755). See also p. 441 n. 125

[†] Marshall to Foxwell, 31 May 1908 (Marshall Archive, 3:56); the humbug enters not only from Marshall's disclaimer about knowing much of the election (of which Edgeworth would almost certainly have given him a fairly detailed account), but from the 'pain' about his inability to crown Foxwell's long service with a 'high reward', given Marshall's strong opposition to Higgs's suggestion that money should be raised for a personal chair for Foxwell at Cambridge. Marshall to J.N. Keynes, 12 December 1908 (Marshall Archive 1:137) and undated (Marshall Archive, 140), and see below, p. 678.

Pigou,* though he would have preferred to have been beaten by candidates with the greater experience of Ashley or Cannan. He explained this by saying the 'slight of his failure' was likely to hinder his London teaching while it made continued Cambridge teaching impossible, with 'the stamp of incompetence so publicly branded upon me by a body of experts'. The most bitter remarks are reserved for his Cambridge friends – 'people are so polite now-a-days that it is only on illuminating occasions like this that one is able to realise what a poor figure one cuts in their real judgement'. This applied in particular to Marshall, to whom he devoted the final paragraph, 'I gather from your letter and from many other circumstances that have come to my knowledge that you are more than rejoiced at the result which I know you have worked hard for, and on which I ask to be allowed to congratulate you.'[31]

Foxwell informed the Economics Board not long afterwards that he was unwilling to continue with lectures in Cambridge, a decision he did not reverse until four years later.¶ Once again, Marshall had made a choice which he undoubtedly would have justified on the highest of principles, in this case preservation of the Tripos, at the cost of losing what certainly up to then had been his closest friend. The episode also shows him at his intriguing worst, leaving no stone unturned in order to get what he wanted. This apparently included spreading lies and slanders about his old friend and colleague.†

'A VAIN SITTER': THE ROTHENSTEIN PORTRAIT AND OTHER HONOURS

The prospects of Marshall's retirement after his long service to economics in the Cambridge chair and elsewhere also elicited a number of honours for the now elderly leader of the British economics profession. At the start of 1907, Edgeworth, presumably in his capacity as editor of the *Economic Journal,* approached Marshall on behalf of the secretary of the Royal Economic Society to gain Marshall's reactions to the idea of having his portrait painted. Edgeworth stated this idea had originated with Price and himself, had the approval of the Council of the Royal Economic Society and the support of a large number of British Professors of Economics, nearly all of whom had been Marshall's own students. Edgeworth enclosed a list of committed donors with his letter, adding that names not on it were from persons who at that stage of the proceedings 'have not been asked'.[32] Marshall's response to Edgeworth's flattering request was a mixture of false modesty and pride:

---

* A copy of Foxwell's letter to Pigou, dated 1 June 1908, is preserved among his correspondence (Freeman Collection, 11/252). It wishes Pigou well and explains one elector had told Foxwell the reason for his failure was that he was considered 'too old by the electors' for the responsible post of building up the reputation of a new Tripos in a relatively hostile university environment.

¶ Cambridge University Archive (Min. V. 114), minute for 3 June 1908; Foxwell to J.N. Keynes, 6 February 1912 (Marshall Archive, 1:44). This mentioned Marshall's note to Keynes expressing pleasure that Foxwell had resumed his activities for the Economics Board, as he had read in the *Reporter*, but since Marshall did not think it expedient to let Foxwell know himself, he asked John Neville Keynes to do it (Marshall to John Neville Keynes, 30 January 1912, Marshall Archive, 1:139). Part of Foxwell's letter is quoted below, chapter 18, pp. 677-8.

† For Foxwell's continued breach with Marshall, see below pp. 631, 650, Chapter 19, pp. 716, 724 and Chapter 20, p. 743, where the fact that he attended Marshall's funeral can be interpreted as a sign of respect for Marshall's widow.

> Your kind letter telling me that you and Price and some others wish to have my portrait painted covers me with confusion. For why should you? I am filled with gratitude. My face is not worthy to be painted, but as you will it, I may not say nay. So I fall in with your most kind and flattering suggestions and tender hearty thanks for it.[33]

A brochure seeking subscriptions not exceeding ten guineas invited potential subscribers to send their donations either to Sir T.H. Elliott, Board of Agriculture and Fisheries, the Secretary of the Royal Economic Society, or to Professor H.S. Foxwell, the secretary of the imposing committee of well over a hundred supporters of the portrait,* or to Mr L.L. Price, or to the 'Marshall Portrait Fund' which had been opened at branches of Barclay and Company at Cambridge and Oxford. By early 1908, enough had been collected to obtain the services of William Rothenstein, the eminent Edwardian portrait painter. Sittings were in progress at Balliol Croft during May, the month of Marshall's retirement with all its traumatic events. Reactions about the sittings have been preserved from artist, subject and subsequently on the end result from Marshall's closest companions, his wife and faithful maid servant, Sarah, as well as others. The sitter, whose reflections were in part designed to influence the final product, can be cited first:

> I have been so awestruck by this ponderous left hand in my photographs that I have looked over a number of loose portraits (chiefly torn out of the world's work) and I cannot find a suitable one in which left hands are shown, either loose or one enfolding the other, which I like at all. So I want to urge you to be good enough either to cut out my hand, or to let them be occupied. My own notion is to have my hat in my left hand on my knee, and my stick on my left rather like Götz at the tag in this *Secession* Catalogue. Will you kindly think over this tomorrow?[¶]

Since the final portrait in St John's College shows no hands, hats, sticks or knees, it is a safe bet that compromise on the part of the artist eliminated this problem for his sitter, although this was not the only difficulty he encountered during his sessions with Marshall. Rothenstein recollected these difficulties several decades after the event in the following terms,

> About this time I was asked to paint a portrait of Professor Alfred Marshall, who was now retiring from the chair of Political Economy at Cambridge. Marshall I was told had a broad outlook on economic subjects, but on other subjects his views were angular, his opinions all corners. In talking with Marshall one had need to be circumspect. For everything one said he took literally and met with the full weight of his pedantry the most casual remarks. I tried to speak cautiously, to be conciliatory, to be thoroughly non-committal, but in vain; no gleam of humour lightened his talk. Fortunately, he also took sitting seriously,

---

* *Proposed Portrait for Alfred Marshall.* The committee included the Duke of Devonshire as Chancellor of the University at this time, a number of other Lords including Brassey, Milner, Courtney and Reay, Bishop Hereford (the headmaster of Clifton College when Marshall acted as its mathematics master), politicians active in the Royal Economic Society such as Balfour and Haldane, various heads of colleges, office bearers from learned societies, over two dozen professors and many clerics, academics and working economists (including the Webbs).

¶ Alfred Marshall to William Rothenstein, 2 May 1908 (Houghton Library, Harvard University, BMS ENG. 1198 (981)). Götz may have been the Bavarian statesman, Ferdinand Hermann Wilhelm Goetz (1826–1915), a Bavarian elected to the Reichstag in 1887; the Secession Catalogue was probably from one of the Secession School of Painting Exhibitions at Munich which, Marshall told Brentano, he and his wife sometimes visited when they had a chance while travelling on their way south to the Tirol for summer (see above, Chapter 7, p. 793 and n.*).

for he was vain, and vain men make the best sitters. Hence I regard vanity as both the most useful and harmless of human weaknesses.[34]

Marshall had earlier tried to win Rothenstein over by presenting him with a copy of the fifth edition of his *Principles*. Rothenstein thanked Marshall for the gift, praising the nobility of its tone and reflecting implicitly on what it told about the character of the person he was about to portray. What particularly impressed him was,

> the extraordinary perception of human motives shown in it on many [a] page. What pleased me above all is that your own standard of conduct and nobility is applied to other people and that you refuse to believe that others have a much lower standard. I am always distressed when made aware of a man of high gifts and distinction looking on the rest of mankind with suspicion and contempt and the generous spirit underlying your own views of men and women does not take away from their form. It always seems to me that the pursuit of science and art is useless to anyone unless it be expressed in the form of hope; men want support for their best motives and if we can't encourage everything which is fine and good we have a very small place in the hierarchy of mankind. All I know is that I am reading your work with much inward striving and it is a very real delight to me to be made acquainted with your thoughts and views on so many matters of interest.[35]

Reading the *Principles* was not the only background research Rothenstein did on his sitter. He took the opportunity of seeing the Professor in action in his professorial milieu of the lecture room by attending Marshall's last lecture on 21 May. A year after that event he recalled in a letter to Mary Paley, 'I have a very vivid recollection of seeing him standing up there, when he gave that beautiful last lecture of his, and I am proud to think it has been allowed me to suggest something of the man who has for so many years given life to that room'.[36]

This recollection, accompanied with a reminiscence about 'the affection and kindness' shown to him during his period of work at Balliol Croft, was inspired by the advice Mary Paley had sought from him about the best firm to produce photographic prints of the portrait. Such prints were required both for presentation to subscribers to the portrait fund and for use in various parts of the university, including the lecture room where, as Rothenstein put it, 'so much of your husband's inspiration was given to the world'. This letter conflicts with the impression Rothenstein gave in his much later memoirs already quoted. It hints at affection for his 'vain sitter', not only visible in the flattering remark on the lecture and on Marshall's important work it contained, but in the reminder to Mary of 'a promise of a visit from the Doctor', as Marshall then described himself, before passing on his 'warmest regards' to them with a special request to be remembered to Sarah.[37]

Aspects of the fate of the portrait and the manner of its financing are also of interest, particularly for the light they shed on the repercussions from Pigou's appointment to the chair. The cost of Rothenstein's labour, 300 guineas (£315), of which Price as one of the fund-raisers was able to inform John Neville Keynes, had been more than adequately defrayed by the donors to the portrait fund, enabling its photographical reproductions to be easily financed. The portrait committee listed on the brochure with its 120 names had grown to nearly 200 names of actual donors even though, as was rather maliciously insinuated by Foxwell, many persons who had lent their name to the first list did not intend this costless gesture of homage to be taken as a sign of their more pecuniary support for the project at a later stage.[38]

One of these was Foxwell himself. Price's letter to Keynes indicated that Foxwell wanted nothing to do with Marshall's portrait money, leaving the responsibility of its disposal to him. Price's later reminiscences continue the story in detail, commencing with Foxwell's resignation from his position as Secretary of the Portrait Fund. Price continued,

> in answer to independent inquiry I was confirmed from an authoritative quarter in the suspicion that, while feeling in Cambridge about the Pigou appointment apparently remained sore, a public presentation of Rothenstein's picture would not get appropriate unanimity. In consequence I finished my concern with the portrait, when it was ready for transmission to Cambridge, by sending to Mrs. Marshall a list of the subscribers. She was kind enough to reply that neither he nor she 'desired public handing over', and thus the matter ended.[39]

Although this was the end of the matter for Price, it was not the end of the matter over the portrait itself. A letter from Mary Paley Marshall to Rothenstein in late 1908 acknowledged receipt of the painting at Balliol Croft. It also reported it was now hanging in their smallish dining-room and recorded the reactions to it from their household of three. These varied from Sarah's grudging admission, 'it is all right', the highest praise for a material object which apparently ever escaped her lips, Mary Paley hastened to add, to Mary Paley's quandary 'whether it is more admirable as a likeness, or as a work of art'. She added, 'the longer I look at it, the more it seems to express'. She also told Rothenstein that so far only one friend and nephew Harold Guillebaud, then a Cambridge student, had seen it. However, she intended to have many 'at homes' to enable the generous subscribers who had made the painting possible, to see it in its appropriate setting. She concluded, 'The frame seems to me very beautiful in itself and appropriate to the subject. It is indeed a noble achievement and will be my most treasured possession. It will also be associated with those pleasant days during which it was being called into being'.*

The sitter eternalised by the masterpiece also gave his reactions by way of postscript, returning to the theme with which he had originally accepted the proposal of its execution by instigator Edgeworth. 'All I have to say is that, considering the abominable material on which you had to work, I think you have made a most surprisingly good job of it in every way. I am most thankful that I have never had so difficult a task to tackle and that you had it'.[40]

The Balliol Croft dining-room turned out to be a rather temporary resting place for the portrait. Rothenstein's letter accompanying the finished portrait requested its loan for an exhibition of paintings early the following year, a request to which Mary Paley consented, though she was confused as to the precise exhibition Rothenstein had in mind.[41]   The

---

* Mary Paley Marshall to William Rothenstein, 10 November 1908 (Houghton Library, Harvard University, 6MS ENG, 1198 (981)). One of the subsequent visitors to see the portrait was John Neville Keynes who, on 14 December 1908, recorded in his diary: 'Called to see Marshall's portrait. It makes him look worn and old, but is otherwise very good.' Claude Guillebaud ('Some Personal Reminiscences of Alfred Marshall', p. 94), shared Keynes's judgement, adding additional criticism that 'the eyes in particular are quite lifeless; but it was the sparkle in his eyes which was the outstanding characteristic of Marshall's face'. He added that Marshall himself did not like it.

Economic Journal announced this event to its readers, simultaneously accounting for the disposal of the portrait fund to which so many of its membership had contributed.

> The picture of Professor Marshall, painted, as announced in our June number, by Mr. William Rothenstein, will be exhibited in the International Exhibition of Sculptors, Painters, and Gravers, which opens next January at the New Gallery in Regent Street. The total number of subscribers to the fund was one hundred and ninety-three. The balance of the fund, after paying the artist's fee, and defraying some incidental expenses, has been applied to the reproduction in photogravure of the picture on terms which will allow of the sale at a low cost ... to the subscribers to the original portrait. This work of reproduction was, on the suggestion of Mr. Rothenstein, placed in the hands of Mr. Emery Walker, who has secured an excellent likeness.[42]

The exhibition appears to have been a great success, and Marshall's portrait received at least one very favourable notice in the reviews. The *Morning Post* for 9 January 1909 reported that 'Mr. William Rothenstein's powerful portrait of Professor Alfred Marshall, [t]echnically, . . . is one of the most interesting – certainly one of the most powerful works in the new gallery'. This view was subsequently endorsed by the artist when his brief reference to the Marshall portrait in his later memoirs appeared in a chapter subheaded, 'new aims in painting', of which it and the contemporarily executed Charles Booth portrait, were taken as important examples.[43]

Marshall's dislike of the portrait meant an alternative resting place had to be found for the original. By the time this had been returned to the Marshalls during 1909, furore over the Political Economy chair had died down, and the painting was eventually accepted by Marshall's college, St John's. A letter from its then Master, R.F. Scott, conveyed the thanks of the college for this 'self denying generosity' and asked when the college could collect this new addition to its already substantial portrait collection.[44] It seems certain that at least one member of the college council among its long-standing Fellows, Foxwell, did not welcome this gift with open arms. A private communication to Maynard Keynes, explaining why he did not sign Marshall's 80th birthday letter in 1922, provides colour to the polite thank-you note of the Master preserved in the Marshall Archive:

> I did not sign the letter partly on the merits, as I thought it exaggerated and fulsome: but mainly because he played me such a dirty trick just before the election to the Professorship here that as soon as I learnt of it from Ashley, I broke off all communications with him. Long before [Marshall's eightieth birthday], and for somewhat similar reasons [Marshall's role in Pigou's election to the chair] the Master of St John's [the Vice-Chancellor on the Selection Committee] not only refused three times to subscribe to Marshall's portrait, but refused to accept it, after we had got it done, on behalf of the College. Somehow or other it got into the college and is now in the Combination Room: but there was no ceremony of acceptance.[45]

A copy was made for Mary Paley Marshall many years later for presentation to the Marshall Library where it hangs, figuratively speaking, in the shade of her own portrait executed brilliantly by Roger Fry.[46]

The reverberations over the Pigou appointment, which clouded the reception of Marshall's portrait by university and college authorities, did not prevent the appropriate award of honours in recognition of his merits awarded on this occasion by his own university and by others. On 17 June 1908, the University of Cambridge, with 13 others (including Asquith, Rudyard Kipling,* Admiral Sir John Fisher, the Duke of Northumberland, the Earl of Halsbury and two other Professors), installed him into an honorary doctorate in his own university. In the Latin oration customary on these occasions, the university's public orator mentioned the honours he had gained in mathematics, his posts at Bristol and Balliol College, his Professorship in Political Economy and his literary and other contributions to his subject. In conclusion, the orator recited two lines from Lowell's Commemoration Ode,

> The kindly-earnest, brave, foreseeing man,
> Sagacious, patient, dreading praise, not blame.

betraying both a sense of humour and irony on his part.[47]

This recognition from his own university followed, and preceded, honorary degrees and awards from other universities and overseas scientific bodies. On 13 April 1893, the University of Edinburgh had awarded him an Honorary Doctor of Laws with special reference to 'the chief monument of his great ability and learning . . . his new 'Principles of Economics', which will, it is expected, be shortly completed, and will form one of the most admirable and complete treatises on the subject in the English language'.[48] In 1904, Oxford had awarded Marshall an Honorary Doctor of Science. In 1911, Bristol included him among its first recipients of honorary degrees in the company of his successor as Principal to the University College, Sir William Ramsay, at a ceremony in October which Marshall was unable to attend. Two European universities, those of Cracow and Christiania (now Oslo) awarded him Honorary Doctorates of Jurisprudence. Only some of these honorary degrees were mentioned in the brief autobiographical sketch Marshall prepared early during his retirement for a reference book on men of science.[49]

Apart from the universities, learned societies and academies also honoured the sage from Cambridge both before and, more generally, after his retirement. The Manchester Literary and Philosophical Society conferred honorary membership on Marshall in April 1892; on 26 August 1896 the Italian Ministry of Education admitted him to the position of foreign associate in the Academia delle Scienze/Accademia dei Lincei di Roma in the category of moral, historical and philological sciences, an honour which elicited the one extant attempt of Marshall to write in the Italian language.¶ In 1902, the British Academy had elected him as one of its Fellows; on 13 June 1908 the French Academy of Moral and Political Sciences made him one of its foreign correspondents. In 1920, the Belgian Academy of Sciences paid him tribute by awarding him the prestigious Emile de Laveleye Prize, for services to

---

* Guillebaud recalled for Ronald Coase that when Marshall discovered that Kipling was to be offered an honorary degree on the same occasion as he was, he nearly decided to decline the honour on the ground that Kipling was an imperialist (letter to the author, 2 May 1991). Marshall's consistent anti-imperialist stand was discussed above in Chapter 16, pp. 603–8.

¶ Marshall's Italian letter, 1 August 1896, a copy of which is preserved in the Marshall Archive (1:365) was written in Ospitale, Cortine, in the Dolomites, the reason perhaps why Marshall took courage into his hands and wrote in a language in which, he confided to Foxwell a decade or so before, he was far from proficient. Marshall to Foxwell, 3 July 1878, Freeman Collection, 36/155: 'I believe, by the bye, there is some good Pol. Econ. in Italian. I have thought of learning Italian on purpose.' As the previously mentioned letter, and the chapter on travel above, pp. 216–17, demonstrate, this was not to be, and Mary Paley remained the proficient modern linguist at Balliol Croft.

social sciences in his writings, his teachings and his contributions to Royal Commissions, the awarding jury counting among its members former Prime Minister A.J. Balfour, the economist Charles Gide and B. Seebohm-Rowntree, the social investigator. These, and other memorabilia of his merit were initially preserved for posterity by his wife in that (literally) large brown box in the Marshall Library, from which they have only recently been removed.[50] Such are the honours and memories a long life faithfully devoted to a particular science can achieve, and which, both before, on, and after his retirement, his intellectual peers and colleagues awarded to Alfred Marshall.

PLEASURES OF VOLUNTARY RETIREMENT: LEARNING, WRITING AND CONTINUING TEACHING

Keynes describes much of Marshall's retirement activity as an opportunity to 'spend what time and strength were left to him in a final effort to gather in the harvest of his prime'. Even then, he was much distracted by long-standing habits. 'He still continued', Keynes also notes of his period 'up to the time of the [first world] war, to see students in the afternoons – though perhaps former pupils (by that time young dons) more than new comers'.[51] Keynes is among the more prominent examples. After his stint in the India Office and before the Treasury, Keynes was on quite intimate terms with Marshall during these early retirement years, a closeness not really repeated until just before Marshall's death. Fay is another example who, on these occasions both built up and gathered sagas about Marshall of which he later became the 'chief repository'. A third is Walter Layton, who joined the economics teaching staff at Cambridge in the same year as Maynard Keynes.

For Marshall, his early years of retirement were also a time for continued learning, largely through reading the ever increasing flow of books, blue books and journals which the growing economics profession was producing in this period and which often were sent to him as tributes by students. Some of Marshall's learning activities during retirement have already been mentioned. Examples are his discussions on heredity with Bateson, his membership of the Cambridge Eugenics Society and the controversy generated with Galtonians such as Pearson, if they confronted the more sacred Marshallian presuppositions on family life and nurture.[52]

The major part of his retirement writing, evolving into the two final volumes published during the last years of his life, is discussed subsequently.[53] Retirement writing began with revision and publication of the Memorandum of Fiscal Policy, his last public act of government advice.[54]

In the context of the 1909 Budget, Marshall found time to write to the *Times* in defence of his views on higher land taxation, so long as its revenue was used for urban improvement:

> it is true I did propose a small new net burden on the owners of urban land. I hold that the most important capital of the nation is that which is invested in the physical, mental, and moral nurture of its people. That is being recklessly wasted by the exclusion of, say, some ten millions of the population from reasonable access to green spaces where the young may play and the old may rest. To remedy this evil is in my opinion even more urgent than the provision of old age pensions.[55]

The subject matter of this letter to the *Times* was discussed simultaneously in correspondence with Lord Reay.[56] By way of introduction, Marshall indicated that two questions posed by a Chancellor of the Exchequer in 1903 had engaged much of his time since then, 'in writing out my answers to these questions, *with their kith and kin*'. This was why he 'paid very little attention to Budget controversies, and . . . remained silent even when my published opinions were misquoted or misinterpreted'. This prepared the way for a Marshallian caveat covering his brief comments on such a complex matter, succinctly summarised by his 'only confident dogma in economics . . . that every short statement on a broad issue is inherently false'. In addition to the questions already mentioned, Marshall's letter broached the relationship between tariff reform and employment and the importance of public investment in education, sanitation and 'providing open air play for children, etc.'[57] Despite Marshall's own description of his long letter as a 'slovenly and meagre' answer to Reay's query (it had in fact constituted a morning's work given his 'waning' powers), Reay had surprisingly few supplementary questions in response, and 'had interpreted my [Marshall's] short answers as I meant them'. Marshall answered the first of these questions on impact of foreign tariffs in part by indicating that this 'complex' and 'important' matter was receiving 'considerable space . . . in the book on *National Industries and International Trade* at which I am slowly toiling'. He evaded the question on the unproductive nature of spending on armaments by indicating he was unable to make a good judgement on armament reduction or abstention from its increase, an indication of how the importance of international tensions had grown in his mind since the Boer War period.[58]

The issue of fiscal policy in international trade, partly in relation to the Memorandum whose revision had occupied much of Marshall's first retirement summer and partly in the context of a 'distant', almost completed draft for the second volume, had earlier that year engaged Marshall in private controversy with Edgeworth. In dealing with the effect of import duties on demand, Marshall's Memorandum had touched upon the effect on demand for bread from a price rise following an import duty on wheat. In this, Marshall recalled a suggestion he had earlier attributed to Giffen, that with bread as the cheapest food, a price rise induced increased, not fewer, bread purchases, poor households effecting the necessary economies by reducing expenditure on dearer food substitutes.[59] Edgeworth had slighted this 'Giffen effect' in a book review, about which Marshall did not really want to argue. However, he wished to clarify his own position, which he felt was being slighted as well. Far from being a 'random' observation, Marshall claimed to have tested the foundations for a 'Giffen case' from careful empirical study of bread consumption by social classes:

> Ever since I saw Giffen's hint on the subject, I have set myself to compare the amounts of bread (and cake, wheaten biscuits and puddings) eaten at first class dinners in private houses and expensive hotels, with the consumption in middle class houses and second-rate hotels, and again with the consumption in cheap inns, including a low grade London hotel; and I have watched the baker's supplies to cottagers. And I am convinced that the very rich eat less than half as much bread as the poorer classes; the middle classes coming midway. This proves nothing conclusively: but it is a fair basis, I think, for a surmise as to a probability.[60]

Supply considerations could not be ignored because of their relevance to effects on price and tariffs. A longer-term rise in wheat prices from a succession of bad harvests would be initially delayed from the reduction in waste in the use of wheat in wheat-producing countries such as the United States and Australia and, over a longer time span, through adulteration of bread by the use of maize or, formerly, 'potatoes . . . when I was a boy', a point, he conceded, favouring Edgeworth's line of argument.[61] The matter had obviously irked Marshall.

The next day Edgeworth was sent a follow-up letter at much greater length. It indicated how ten years before Marshall had investigated the subject in detail in connection with Book X on markets for his second volume. This provides one reason why that volume was never finished. The book in question 'had an introductory general chapter, followed by others in detail. After working some time, I found the task too long to be made complete. So I decided to select two or three typical instances, and work them out carefully. Wheat was – for many reasons – my chief instance. My draft copy on it is about 40pp. long.'[62] Careful elaboration of the wheat case involved Marshall in reading thousands of technical pages and questioning 'every high class American' he met on the subject. During the Cambridge meeting of the British Association in 1904, he even devoted the whole of an after dinner conversation at his house to grilling the world expert on the subject of wheat resources in the Canadian North West, even 'though there were several people to whom I wanted particularly to talk'. This high opportunity cost of searching for factual truth was supplementary to the task of analysis which Marshall likewise did not neglect. Contrary to common opinion, which Marshall understood Edgeworth to endorse, price elasticity of supply was not uniform in wheat production, it depended on the nature of organising wheat production in a new country. Curiously, Marshall illustrated this argument not from his prodigious researches in North American wheat production, but from analogous instances in the production of bicycles and cement from which inferences were drawn for wheat production. He then turned to chastise Edgeworth for his treatment of demand elasticity, which perplexed him even more before, by way of conclusion, justifying his 'prodigious scrawl' from the fact that he could 'not bear to think that you suppose me to have spoken of elasticity as high for a fall yet low for a rise, without careful thought'.[63]

Edgeworth's epistolary self-defence is not extant, but its contents can be imagined from the very apologetic reply Marshall wrote in return. Seeking refuge in his state of dotage, he declined to continue the controversy before it grew too fierce. Even that excuse needed qualification for Marshall. The stupidity and slow-wittedness arising from old age were offset by the increased experience advanced years brought with them. Marshall's reference to the quality of his notes made well before he 'became a dotard', indicates his unwillingness to continue the fight and implied no concession of principle on his part. The letter also explains how conscious at this stage Marshall was of the difficulties he was experiencing in writing, and the importance and value of persevering in the task at this time.

I am trying to write out my thoughts, including of course those relating to wheat supply, without raising dust. I can't see my way through the huge difficulties of the great issue, even when there is no dust: I work ever slowly. But yet I have a notion that I really have something to say; partly on subtle points, for which my mind is now of little use, only I have a good many notes made before I became a dotard; but more on the One in the Many and the Many in the One, i.e. the relation of details to fundamentals, a matter on which the experience of age is some atonement for its stupidity . . .[64]

This concentrated exchange of correspondence over a week between the two economists, of whom Edgeworth incidentally was the younger by only three years, is particularly interesting for the insights it gives into Marshall's notoriously slow writing style. The manner in which, even during the 1890s, rapid compositional progress eluded him by the ease in which he was distracted through 'subtle points of detail' from his planned approach to develop a major topic such as 'markets', is one striking instance of this. His almost pathetic self-consciousness of 'failing strength' when still well before the age of seventy, combined with an offsetting dogged persistence not to give up, explains much of why *Industry and Trade* was not published until ten years later. The exchange of letters also shows how easily in these early years of retirement Marshall was diverted from the main task by side skirmishes which he justified to himself through puffing them up into matters essential to the preservation of socially valuable truth.[*] Marshall's reference to both Edgeworth's 'gentle criticism' and 'rude blows' in the letter ending the controversy, possibly provided the inspiration for his epigram on Edgeworth, 'Francis is a charming fellow, but you must be careful with Ysidro'.[65]

Other extant letters from this time, probably only a small remnant of the number actually written, indicate that this type of distraction was not infrequent. A long letter written from the Tirol to Louis Dumur on population decline in modern Western Europe probably cost a morning spent on the book. This was not likely to have been offset by the benefits to his French correspondent, to whom Marshall devalued the advice he was giving by suggesting 'It is very likely that I am mistaken'. For posterity, the letter provides interesting reminders of the deep-seated nature of Marshall's hobby horses on both his desired division of labour between the sexes and on the value of fresh air.[66]

A lengthy response to Sir Horace Plunkett a year later, declining his signature to support an 'impressive plea for a Country Life Institute' shows even saying 'no' was costly to Marshall from time lost in reading (he read the plea twice), and in responding at length. Here again, posterity benefited from the further insight into Marshall as social empiricist which the reply gives:

> I know a good deal of the habits of life of the rural population within an old man's cycle ride of Cambridge, say an area about 600 square miles. I doubt if there is any rural population on the continent of Europe, unless it be Scandinavia, which is so prosperous, so happy, so much given to thoughts and emotions larger and higher than those of merely local life. I attribute this chiefly to the influence of non-conformist chapels which . . . give an individuality and a holy sanction to the inner life of even the 14s. a week labourer that is very rare elsewhere. No doubt the farmer's education is generally very bad . . . but we take in, for the benefit of our servant, a weekly paper – the *Cambridge Independent Press* . . . which I often look at, as a zoologist might look at a kangaroo: and I am astonished at the width of range, the clearness and, so far as I can judge, the scientific thoroughness of its long weekly articles on things which the agriculturist ought to know.[67]

---

[*] The last paragraph of Marshall's letter to Edgeworth just quoted called for the 'steady persistent hammering' of 'fallacies' in economics, a task only possible for 'a trained thinker', and all the more necessary when even the best periodicals were not immune from stating nonsense 'fit to make Ricardo's bones rattle in their grave' (*Memorials*, p. 442).

Indian students seeking guidance by letter likewise took up valuable time. Advice given to Manohar Làl on Indian development in relation to trade policy and the need to change the attitude of India's educated classes to business was quoted previously.[68] A later letter mentioned Marshall's strong 'resolve not to publish anything about India, till I can incorporate my opinion about protection to her industries in a more general discussion'.[69] To Mukherjee, before responding to several questions at considerable length, Marshall advised by way of introduction, 'If I were to answer all the questions which are sent me, my book would never appear. As it is I shall not live to serve up to table one half of the dishes which I have partly cooked'.[*] Despite his self-awareness about the dangers for the progress of his writing of indulging such habits, Findlay Shirras was 'briefly' supplied with 'one or two things which may possibly be of interest to you' on the causes of rising prices in India, a matter Marshall had studied at considerable length during previous decades.[¶]

As befits an internationally famous sage, distracting correspondence also involved the new world. A congratulatory correspondence with Irving Fisher on his proposal for an international tabular standard of value is one example.[70] Marshall's library, and the annotations he made in Fisher's books including the complimentary copy of *Purchasing Power of Money* received from its author, show that Marshall was well equipped to make such congratulatory noises.[†] By this stage, long-established correspondence with American friends begun during the 1890s petered out to occasional exchanges of books and Christmas cards with J.B. Clark after 1908; and, with some exceptions, this likewise applies to correspondence with Taussig and Seligman.

New contacts across the Atlantic were most reluctantly undertaken. An exchange of letters with the much younger H.L. Moore (1869–1958), is a striking example that has been preserved. It arose from Marshall's delayed response to Moore's *Laws of Wages*, which its author had probably sent him on publication sometime during the previous year. Marshall explained his omission by general lack of time and, more specifically, dental troubles which had required nursing treatment at home. Having hastily skimmed the book to enable him to give some reaction, Marshall's response indicated growing impatience with its simplified mono-causal explanations. Even 'the "caeteris paribus" clause, though formally adequate, seems to me impractable'. It likewise revealed Marshall's growing doubts about the ability of statistics to measure all crucial explanatory factors. Hence Marshall strongly doubted Moore's work would produce an imminent break-through, though he applauded its attempts. With respect to his own work, Marshall repeated a familiar theme,

---

[*] Marshall to B. Mukherjee, 22 October 1910, *Memorials*, pp. 471–3; a subsequent letter (12 April 1911, in *Memorials*, pp. 473–4) refused to address the issue of protection in India in terms of a simple 'yes' or 'no', because this was as misleading an answer as when given to the celebrated question 'have you stopped beating your wife'.

[¶] Marshall to Findlay Shirras, 6 July 1910, in *Memorials*, pp. 470–71. Findlay Shirras in 1944 informed Keynes that Mary Paley had given him 'two treasures': 'one a Ricardo with Marshall's notes in her [sic] own handwriting: two, a copy of the picture in St John's of him, which she liked so much'. (G. Findlay Shirras to Keynes, 23 November 1944, KMF).

[†] Marshall's annotations on Fisher's *Purchasing Power of Money* (1911) show the strong but critical interest in monetary theory he maintained. Marshall was particularly critical of Fisher's tendency at over-simplification and over-generalisation; e.g. his comment on p. 64; 'true, but too much stress laid on one cause' and similar comments on pp. 113, 339, 343. A letter to Bonar at the time (18 June 1912, *Memorials*, p. 375) commented on his old scheme of symmetallism, first proposed during the second half of the 1880s (above, Chapter 11, pp. 346, 348–9).

My power of work is *very* small. I have half done many things which I cannot hope to publish. Talking fatigues me in a very unusual manner. And finally, it would be wrong for me to encourage you to come to Cambridge for serious conversation.

But if you are coming to Cambridge to see others, and would like to take lunch (1.30) or afternoon tea (4.15) with my wife and myself; and discuss general topics, we shall be honoured by the opportunity of making your acquaintance.

Next Friday would not suit us: but we have at present no engagement on any other day. If you write nominating a time, I will write (or if necessary wire) should that particular time be already mortgaged.[71]

As an afterthought, Marshall enclosed a critical letter on Moore's work he had previously sent to Edgeworth. It described Moore as a personal 'nightmare' and his book as 'one prolonged dancing on what has been the most tender of my beloved corns ever since 1875'. The subsequent growth of this 'corn' had been stimulated by an annoying reliance on 'statistical tables in pairs' in the arguments of American free traders and protectionists. Marshall's note to Edgeworth also asserted that simplistic analyses of this nature induced errors 'whose magnitude was not of .5 or .7 per cent but of 50 or 70 per cent'.[72] Moore declined the invitation to visit, so as not to tax its giver too much. However, he treasured the letter for its frank criticism, even though he did not accept its validity. Moore subsequently recorded that nearly ten years later Marshall thanked him for his *Generating Economic Cycles* essays in a letter which showed far greater agreement with Moore's methodology. This also claimed to have anticipated Moore in this respect some fifty years earlier when Marshall was compiling his 'Red Book'.[73]

Marshall's letter to Moore suggests that by his seventieth birthday, time was beginning to be severely rationed at Balliol Croft with respect to visitors. Fay recalled such a rationing regime from a much later visit in 1918 by Mary Paley's familiar warning, 'You won't stay too long, will you' which, when recording his last visit to Marshall in 1923, he quantified as 'the allotted ten' minutes. Prior to the First World War, Fay went to tea at the Marshall's generally once or twice a year, presumably in response to the sort of invitation Marshall sent him in 1910: 'Saturday will suit us admirably. We should sit down to our homely supper at 7.45; and a platter will be set for you, unless you write to the contrary'.[74]

Maynard Keynes was also a regular caller at Balliol Croft during Marshall's early years of retirement. Marshall was lending him books for his own use, as well as for use by the students. Their Pearson controversy over parental alcoholism and heredity generated much personal contact in 1910 and 1911, but also warnings from Mary Paley that the excitement was not good for Marshall.[75] Marshall also warmly congratulated his informal and promising student on gaining the Girdlers' lectureship in 1910 in succession to Meredith, by punning, 'I am very glad you, who have girded your own loins so well, are now well girdled'.[76] Keynes also received reports about the slow progress of Marshall's own work: 'Alas, my book proceeds as fast as Penelope's web, and I must do nothing that I can help', a lack of activity illustrated in the same letter by his successful resistance of temptation to write to the *Times* about Arlington, the Master of Shrewsbury, on 'the cruelty of being compelled to learn Euclid by heart'.*

Marshall likewise had no difficulty to find time for congratulating Walter Layton on his engagement to Dorothy, 'Mary knows her well'; to praise his work on the *Economist* while pleading with him to continue lecturing; and to give technical advice on Schedule D income tax statistics and the dangers of their use and interpretation.[77] Among such words of advice, Marshall permitted himself occasional reflections pertaining to his age. On this occasion, these were inspired by kindly compliments Layton had conveyed in one of his letters: 'When a man gets old, the most precious thing to him, almost the only thing that is precious to him outside his kith and kin, is the affection of younger men; especially when it is accompanied as it is in this case by the trust that they will achieve what he had hoped he might do, but has not done'.[78]

These years of retirement before the First World War also produced occasional excursions into university reform, particularly during 1912 when such matters were once again on the agenda in Cambridge. An undated copy of a draft letter to Henry Jackson, an active university reformer and close associate of Sidgwick, suggests a scholarship scheme with tapered financial assistance for college men, taking account of both financial need via parental income and academic merit, with provisions for anonymity to preserve individual privacy. The letter implicitly recalls Marshall's own relative undergraduate poverty and the social hardships this entailed.[79]

Some letters on university matters were also addressed that year to former student Clapham, then serving on a University Reform Committee. The first related to the role of professors and, more generally, of teaching staff and academic appointments procedures. It gave Marshall's definition of 'professorial' as fitting those involved in 'advanced study combined with high grade teaching'.[80] Six months later, Marshall addressed the issue of working-class students at Oxford and Cambridge. After expressing a desire to attend the meeting on reform called for university members, something he intended not to indulge, Marshall gave views somewhat different to his letter to Jackson on this subject. Given substantial difficulties experienced by working-class students in the traditionally residential system of Oxford and Cambridge, because they could never be 'on equal terms with other students without inordinate expense', such students should be encouraged to attend non-residential universities where they could compete more equally. Oxford and Cambridge should compensate for this defect in meeting national obligations by concentrating their public funds on studies geared to influence future national well-being. Studies directed largely at the past should be financed by 'private purses of the well-to-do'. Inadequate scientific secondary education due to opposition by traditionalist headmasters made even this solution difficult, because useful university studies required good scientific background. Marshall did not place economics among subjects suitable for inclusion in the secondary school curriculum; a view probably based on his growing belief in the complexity of the

---

* Marshall to Maynard Keynes, 2 July 1911 (Keynes Papers, L/M/41); Penelope's web was an unfortunate but apt analogy. While awaiting the return of her husband Ulysses, that mythical lady undid at night what she had woven during the day to prevent having to choose a new husband from her many suitors, as she had promised to do as soon as her handwork was finished. The headmaster mentioned in the text was later referred to in an Appendix to *IT*, p. 820, n.1.

subject he so frequently expressed to others at this time. In conclusion, Marshall stressed the individual nature of his communication; it was not addressed to Clapham in his official capacity, even though it was also not 'private'.[81] As 1912 drew to a close, the former professor had therefore well and truly retired from active participation in university affairs.

A PRINCIPLED WAR EFFORT: 1914–1919

On 4 August 1914 Britain and Belgium declared war on Germany in response to the German invasion of Belgium which had begun the previous day. A week later, on 12 August, Britain and France declared war on Austria. The First World War began in earnest not long thereafter, shattering beliefs in modern rationalism as a force for peace and civilisation. As Marshall had feared, heavy rearmament in the two countries had led the way to the catastrophe, assisted by an increasing jingoism feeding a popular belief that only British naval and military might could prevent a German thrust for European supremacy and leadership in world trade. 'Sea power is the last fact which stands between Germany and the supreme position in international commerce' was how Benjamin Kidd put the position in the *Fortnightly Review* in April 1910; 'It is not free trade, but the prowess of our Navy . . . our dominant position at sea . . . which has built up the British Empire and its commerce' was the more blunt approach of the *Times* on this subject.[82] Preparatory pre-war sentiments from such revered authorities would have already caused strong reverberations in the Marshall household before the conflict; the eruption of war itself at the beginning of August 1914 created even greater turmoil at Balliol Croft. Not only did the outbreak of war terminate their almost annual summer excursions to the beloved South Tirol, an area to become one of the major war zones after Italy's declaration of war on the allied side in August 1915; but it brought conflicts from soul searching over divided loyalties into their almost Germanomanic lives.

Such soul-searching conflicts came to the fore in two letters Marshall sent to the *Times* during the first month of war. The first, dated 22 August, after pointing out that the war was one of self-defence as well as assistance to Belgium and France, appealed for avoidance of 'acrimony', 'lurid tales' and other forms of sensationalism to make 'denunciation of the Germans' more attractive and popular.

> Those who know and love Germany, even while revolted at the hectoring militarism which is more common there than here, should insist that we have no cause to scorn them, though we have good cause to fight them. For instance, tales of their shooting civilians in cold blood should never be repeated without inquiring whether the laws of war had been broken by hostile action on the part of non-combatants. I was in Berlin in the winter of the Franco German war, and my friends complained bitterly of the willingness of Englishmen to believe that civilians who had not so offended, had been ill-treated by them. As a people I believe them to be exceptionally conscientious and upright, sensitive to the calls of duty, tender in their family affections, true and trusty in friendship. Therefore they are strong and to be feared, but not to be vilified. . . . It is therefore our interest as well as our duty to respect them and make clear we desire their friendship, but yet to fight them with all our might.[83]

A second letter later that week showed that Marshall's strong love for things German had not made him a pacifist. Just before the start of the conflict, he had refused to sign a petition against British entry into the war on the ground that 'the question of peace or war must turn on national duty as much as on our interest. I hold that we ought to mobilise instantly, and announce that we shall declare war if the Germans invade Belgium; and everybody knows they will'. Marshall continued his letter by stating his 'professorial duties' had made him aware of the German danger as early as 1900, when he 'came across the *Alldeutscher Atlas*, a clear manifesto of the Pan-Germanic League' in which several countries were painted Germanic to the surprise of their residents. He had also discussed this question with 'German and Austrian military men'. However, 'inflaming passions' about German atrocities would do nothing 'towards securing victory, . . . may very greatly increase the slaughter on both sides' and alienate German workers 'averse to wars of exploitation, [but] exasperated by insults to the fatherland'. In answer to the correspondents who had inspired his second letter, Marshall concluded by saying the real cowards were those who vented their courage 'on the reckless use of offensive adjectives'.*

Marshall's strong fear of the growing danger of chauvinism as a consequence of hostilities, was not his only humane response to the war. A letter to J.T. Sheppard at King's College in October demonstrated the Marshalls' desire to do something for Belgian refugees within their limited powers,

> I cannot talk for more than a short time without suffering from 'blood pressure' and therefore my wife and I are cut off from the power of offering hospitality to Belgians. But my wife has just gone to the Claphams to inquire as to your work for them, and [to] find out whether we might be allowed to help them through you. She has just returned with the recommendation: 'offer to pay the expenses of half-a-Belgian'. We would like to do that if we may. Will you tell me what and [where] I should remit.[84]

The plight of civilians in war-time affected Marshall in other ways. A letter to the *Times* in October 1914 addressed the issue of the rights and responsibilities of the civilian population towards an invading army. In it, Marshall indicated support for the *Times*'s plea for disseminating accurate information on this point, to prevent the difficulties in this regard being faced in Belgium where the government had not had the time to arrange for this. Once again, the letter reveals Marshall's even-handed approach in apportioning blame in this aspect of the conflict:

> There are scoundrels in every nation and in every army. The criminal population has been known to promote disorder and conflagration in order to cloak plunder; and soldiers of the same class may incline to goad peasants into fury in order that the 'punishment' of a village may remove obstacles to looting. But it seems that many troubles were caused by soldiers who were not scoundrels, but had lost full control of themselves through drink. Sometimes firing at random, sometimes provoking an outburst of anger, . . . they have inaugurated carnage for which they had no desire, but for which they were determined not to be held responsible. Confused in their memories, they made up easily stories which were accepted by their officers in preference to the perhaps not wholly consistent explanations of terrified peasants speaking in a strange tongue.[85]

---

* Alfred Marshall to the editor of the *Times*, 26 August 1914; an example of the hostility Marshall's partial defence of Germany aroused is given in a letter to Bertrand Russell by a 'John Bull' in 1915 which classed Russell with Pigou, Marshall and others of 'that pro-German ilk in Cambridge', Bertrand Russell, *Autobiography*, London: Unwin Paperbacks, 1978, p. 272.

Other correspondence during the war touched on more technical matters which fell within the scope of Marshall the economist. A letter to Lewis Fry[86] commented on the risks of war-associated unemployment from redirected domestic spending, either as the result of government policy or from war-induced shortages. Examples included the following. A redirection of luxury spending, which Marshall supported as a matter of continuing national, as well as war policy, should be carried out gradually to enable 'employments that are subservient to luxury [to] be depleted gradually, without shock and with no considerable hurt to anyone'. Marshall defined luxury spending as all personal outlays unnecessary 'to keep you (and your family's) physical and mental energies at their highest', a view shared with Marshall's 'patron saint', Abbé, the manager of the German Zeiss works.[87] There were also more immediate substitution possibilities. Inessential domestic staff, unless too old to change 'vocation', could be employed at the western front; private chauffeurs could be used to drive convalescing soldiers around the country. The principle of substitution could likewise be applied to alleviate shortages in essential consumption goods (sugar, food grains, milk) where both need and education were desirable criteria in determining rationing policy. Milk shortages, for example, should fall least on children and invalids; grain shortages should be met by changing eating habits for the educated, less easily achieved by those without 'elastic minds', as well as by eliminating their unnecessary use in manufacturing beer and spirits.

More generally, Marshall did not fear war-time unemployment, provided sea routes were kept open. Post-war adjustment in the labour market would be more difficult, because substitution would be constrained, but not eliminated, by the job-specific skills of labour engaged in war work. Building and construction unemployment could be expected to grow during the war, as pre-war contracts were completed. This problem needed imaginative post-war planning, since Marshall expected post-war dwelling construction to shrink in size as an essential part of the adjustment to lower post-war living standards entailed by the massive costs of the war effort. A post-script introduced a topic of growing importance in discussions of post-war settlement:

> In forecasting conditions after the war, I have made no allowance for an indemnity from Germany. Though I think she should be forced to pay for the havoc she has wrought in Belgium and France, I think also that the world does partially endorse Germany's charge that we alone among her enemies are influenced by sordid commercial considerations; and partly for this reason I hope that all *our* demands will be concentrated on lasting security against her military pretensions.[88]

Marshall's post-script also apologised for the 'slovenliness' of his letter, which he ought to have re-written. However, his ability 'to work only for a very short time without a break' was his implied excuse for not doing so. This more generally made him avoid letters and conversation to prevent his 'long promised book' from going even more slowly than implied by his good 'but feeble' health.[89]

By 1919 Marshall modified his general opposition to a German war indemnity for Britain to qualified support for modest war reparations. Writing to Bonar, he explained such modest retribution was best exacted by transfers of territory and German overseas investment rather than by goods. His reasoning was more 'moral' than economic. Referring to Giffen's analysis of the French indemnity to Germany following the Franco-Prussian War, he recalled that at the time he had formed the impression Giffen had exaggerated its detrimental economic consequences for Germany. Marshall had seen its costs largely in terms of the growth in German jingoism this tangible sign of victory had produced. This had inspired over-confidence in German businessmen, which was only eliminated through the trade depression which excessive reparations had helped to generate.[90] Marshall added he was strongly tempted to publish his opinions on current financial and social problems and also 'on the strange compound of good and evil in the character of the German population'. Given the spirit of revenge concomitant with the drawn-out Versailles peace negotiations only just completed, Marshall justified the second endeavour by the fact that 'most people who write on the subject seem never to have associated, as comrades, with Germans and to recognise only the evil'. Neither plan unfortunately was feasible: 'my strength fails fast; and I have much half ready material, belonging to my special province, which will need to be cremated on my funeral pyre. So I dare not write controversy on matters as to which I have no direct responsibility'[91]

Similar issues had been raised during the war in private and public correspondence. He wrote to Taussig in 1915 that although he loved 'the Germans through it all', it was necessary to seize and hold German colonies because of their military rather than economic significance for Germany and he defended Britain's naval blockade against neutral shipping to Germany. Marshall expressed grave fears about the future because 'the outlook is evil. I think more about the next war, in some moods, than even about the present'.[92] Earlier correspondence that year with Maynard Keynes elaborated these fears. A naval blockade designed to starve Germany entailed substantial costs for the coming British generation: 'I shall not live to see our next war with Germany; but you will, I expect'. In addition the current naval blockade ensured that in that next war Germany would heavily engage in submarine warfare to destroy Britain's power of successfully imposing a naval blockade.[93]

Marshall wrote to Keynes in early 1915 that a lack of detailed knowledge about defence matters prevented him from going public on war-related issues, 'lest I do mischief'.[94] By the end of that year, however, Marshall had been provoked sufficiently to address readers of the *Times* on the adequacy of German milk supplies for her children and other helpless sections of its population. The letter was inspired by an article the *Times* had published that day, reproduced from the *Cologne Gazette*. This attempted to generate hatred of Britain by pointing to the hardship the blockade was causing to the welfare of innocent and defenceless sections of the German population. Marshall queried this assertion, using long-standing boasts by German economists on the adequacy of domestic milk supply from superior agricultural methods and from the source and nature of German dairy imports, most of which required no sea transport. Diversion of dairy fats to military use by 'manufacturers of glycerine for explosives', Marshall suggested, was the more plausible cause of milk shortages, particularly since America had been Germany's largest source of supply 'of lard and oleo-margarines'. Marshall's recollections of unreasonable German food blockade policies at the conclusion of the siege of Paris during the Franco-Prussian War made him less sympathetic to German suffering on this occasion.[95] The authority of the letter may, however, have been somewhat diminished by Marshall's confession the next day that his data on quantities of fat imports into Germany had inadvertently substituted millions for thousands, though the effect of this change tended to assist his argument by increasing the high degree of self-sufficiency in fats the German data revealed.[96]

Aspects of war finance and associated conscription issues also occupied Marshall during the early years of the war. A stream of letters to Maynard Keynes during 1915 and 1916 dwelt on the need for increasing taxation, a requirement he would, if useful, be willing to support by writing to the *Times*.[97] Marshall also warned Keynes of the dangers of over reliance on the American capital market for raising war loans, and the inflationary potential for the United States from excessive British gold exports.[98] It also suggested alternative remedies to compulsory acquisition of British-owned United States' investments for use as war loans and proposed a national forced savings scheme. Twelve-hour shifts 'and the huge sums of money' these placed at the disposal of young workers, seemed to Marshall a 'national calamity of the first order' unless this excessive growth of income was channelled to boosting national savings and facilitate financing the war effort. Marshall added that this course of thinking had been started by a 'message from Lavington sent through Pigou'.[99]

A month later Marshall proposed strong fiscal disincentives for those seeking to evade the responsibility of military service. Knowing the delicate nature of this subject among 'his' Cambridge economists, Marshall introduced the matter gently to Keynes, who himself had in a sense evaded such duties by employment in 'war work' in the Treasury.[100]

> There are a few people who – from temperament and other causes – are as averse to serving in the army that they would almost rather die at once than serve; they are often brave, but they would be depressing influences in the ranks. But many, perhaps most of them, are patriotic and unselfish. They serve as a screen to shirkers and ne'er-do-wells of all sorts.
>
> The well-to-do used to protect themselves by allowing a man to escape conscription by paying the expenses of a substitute. But this plan favours the rich and is an insult to the poor.
>
> Like objections do not seem to lie against the proposal that any unmarried man of military age, who is not needed by the country at home, and is unwilling to go to the front, may be exempted from conscription if he contributes (say) *one third* of his total income (in addition to general taxation) to the services of the war.
>
> Some mitigation might be needed for special cases: e.g. that of a man earning less than £1 a week, and supporting invalid near relatives.
>
> It seems to me that such an arrangement would fulfil Asquith's pledge and bring into the army nearly all those who ought to be in it.
>
> If you think it advisable, I will write to the *Times*.[*]

Since Marshall did not write to the *Times* on this matter,[¶] it seems likely that Keynes advised against it, perhaps conscious of the problems that this would create for his Bloomsbury friends. Marshall's next letter agreed with this advice but repeated his support

---

[*] Marshall to Maynard Keynes, 24 December 1915, Keynes Papers, L/M.41. Asquith's pledge to which Marshall referred had been given during the debates in December 1915 over the reintroduction of conscription. As reported in the *Times*, 23 December 1915, Asquith promised that 'four million is the limit to the number of men who may at any one time be found in the strength of the army'.

[¶] In fact, Marshall did not write again to the *Times* until November 1917 when he controverted Conan Doyle's strategy for a national campaign to generate hatred against the Germans. However, a letter on 19 August 1916, simply signed 'Alfred Marshall', can probably be attributed to him. This passed on a message from an officer serving in Mesopotamia seeking assistance in supplying the 'rank and file' of the army there with 'minor comforts and luxuries which do so much to lighten the tedium and cheer the spirits of their comrades on other fronts'.

for substantial increases in taxation, seeking this as 'a way out, in case the pledge which Derby led Asquith into giving, be thought absolutely binding'.[101] However, Marshall did write strongly in support of increased war taxation to the *Economist* and, in response to the invitation of a Mr Dawson that year, contributed an article on 'National Taxation after the War' to a volume on *After-War Problems*, in which a similar plea for increasing taxes was made as an essential aspect of post-war reconstruction.

In his letter to the *Economist*, Marshall suggested increased taxation of alcohol and selective taxes on articles of ordinary consumption such as meat, for example, administered at the slaughter-house. Major reliance would have to be placed, however, on raising taxes on income and capital. Capital taxes imposed for the duration of the war would have very limited adverse consequences, because war made capital migration difficult, and a temporary tax in any case would not encourage such a response to any large extent. Income tax increases, given the current system, would raise major problems of equity:

> A further increase in the intensity of the income-tax will, of course, aggravate the inequalities of its burdens on people with like incomes, but unlike responsibilities and no thorough remedy for these evils can be worked out during the stress of war. But while maintaining the unity of joint incomes for husband and wife for the purpose of assessment, allowances of varying degrees might be made at once for all the members, adult and young, who depend on the family income.[102]

Marshall's more substantial contribution addressed equity in taxation on a broader level. This contribution had been elicited from Marshall with considerable difficulty. Dawson's first request for it as editor of a volume on post-war policy had been declined, though with considerable regret because Marshall acknowledged it had 'special attractions' for him. Reasons given were the familiar inability to work fast and the further delays acceptance would cause to the volume, *National Industries and Trade*, which had been advertised as in the press 'about seven years ago' but which was still far from completion. Dawson must have repeated the offer, perhaps encouraged by Marshall's remark on the appeal it had for him. A plea by the Cambridge University Senate asking members of the university to offer as much national service as possible, encouraged Marshall's eventual decision to accept. By June 1916 Marshall reported considerable progress to Dawson, mentioning the costs of his contribution in terms of time, and the length to which the chapter was growing. In his response, Dawson advised Marshall 'to write freely' without worrying about a space constraint. Such attitude signalled to Marshall that Dawson recognised the exceptional scope and complexity of the topic assigned to him.[103]

The chapter published in 1917 is in two parts. The first dealt with the appropriate level of taxation after the war and its distribution; the second with taxes on imports in the new international situation Britain would face at the conclusion of the war. Marshall tackled the problem of the least detrimental distribution of the increased tax burden essential for post-war adjustment by listing the available and potential instruments in order of preference. Marshall's preference was for an income tax with increased graduation of rates. He warned, however, of two difficulties in this measure. The first related to the problem of equity to which his letter to the *Economist* had drawn attention; the second to the detrimental consequences for much needed post-war accumulation from the double taxation of saving inherent in an income tax. If savings could be exempted from income tax, and liability adjusted for the number of persons dependent for their support on the income to be taxed, 'ideal perfection' could be achieved. Marshall also advocated some new taxes. A graduated house duty was a potential, though imperfect, proxy for the direct expenditure tax he was supporting through suggesting the exemption of saving from the income tax. In addition, the chapter proposed supplementary and mildly graduated taxes on hotels and restaurants, on domestic servants, on motor cars and on advertising,* and warned of the dangers of taxes on some commodities because they tended to be liable to 'inverse graduation', or regressivity with respect to income.

The second part of the chapter addressed the dangers of taxing imports as a device to raise revenue. Marshall first of all mentioned adverse effects of such taxes on domestic cost structure, especially that of exporters. The imposition of import duties would also adversely affect the foreign demand for British exports, while there were difficulties in using such taxes to achieve a favourable alteration in the terms of trade for Britain. Marshall then argued against taxes on imports as a measure of protection for British industry, using the familiar argument that these would not enable British industries to recover competitive ground already lost and were not defensible in the case of agriculture as a potential defence requirement. As he had done before in 1903, Marshall rejected the plea for a scheme of Imperial Preference requiring higher duties on other countries. Ethico-political considerations together with economic considerations combined to reinforce the conclusion that 'a broad system of Protective duties would deprive Britain of that economic strength' which enabled her to meet the costs of war. Any benefits of the policy were confined to a few sections of industry only. Such benefits would be bought 'at the cost of much greater injury to the people at large' from curtailing economic growth required to finance war pensions and for reducing that 'mountain of war debt' so potentially disastrous for future generations.[104] Marshall therefore held firmly to his free trade position, despite the earlier plea made in the chapter for measures designed to increase 'the cohesion of the British Empire, and of the great alliance which has been recently strengthened, and purified in blood'.[105]

Marshall addressed a final issue of post-war finance in what was his last letter to the *Times*. This criticised the lottery element proposed in Premium Bonds as a betrayal of the national birthright for a very small financial gain. It reiterated his intense dislike of gambling as at best 'a barren amusement' and not infrequently 'marring lives' by the 'morbid craving for excitement' it induced. Marshall's evidence rested on testimony from 'thoughtful Germans and Austrians' who attributed to the absence of gambling in British life the chief source of its national strength, and his subsequent inspection of 'continental gaming resorts' where he was 'much impressed by the unwholesome nervous expression of the faces to be seen there'.[106]

---

* Alfred Marshall, 'National Taxation after the War', in *After-War Problems*, edited W.H. Dawson, London: Allen & Unwin, 1917, esp. pp. 320–28 (a segment of this chapter has been reprinted in *Memorials*, pp. 347–52). Marshall's increasingly critical perspectives on advertising, which may have influenced his proposal for its taxation, are also evident in *Industry and Trade*, see, for example, pp. 306–7. In 1916 Marshall wrote to Heckscher how much he admired direct taxation, and how he would like to see it extended to greater sections of the working class. Marshall to E.F. Heckscher, 28 January 1916 (Kungl. Biblioteket, Stockholm).

Marshall's last and unofficial contribution to the war effort was recorded by C.R. Fay,

> In 1918, when the Germans had broken our Fifth Army, I was sent home to lecture to the Staff School at Caius. I was then at the G.H.Q. Machine Gun School and we were trying to get more machine guns out of the War Office. At the instigation of my Colonel I drafted an unofficial and unlawful memorandum to present to General Smuts, an honorary Fellow of my College. I sent a draft of it to Marshall. About 10 minutes after I arrived home the telephone bell rang and I heard Marshall's voice saying 'Have you got a pencil? It will probably take about ten minutes.' 'But can't I come round?' I said, 'I can't hear you very well.' 'All right – all right, come at 10.30, but you must not stay long.' When I arrived he greeted me with, "I am not prepared to argue, just write; and he dictated a new draft of my memorandum, which was obviously an immense improvement. 'You might have ruined your whole career by putting it that way,' he said, "what you are really trying to say is in your appendix." Incidentally he displayed a perfect mechanical knowledge of the differences between a Vickers and Lewis gun, on which my tactical argument was based.[107]

In an important sense, Marshall's interest in, and active personal involvement with, the economic, moral and even military aspects of the war cost him dearly in terms of lost time for writing. Moreover, this was a cost only very imperfectly recovered from the published contents of his final two volumes. Unfortunately, the war also imposed more personal losses on the Marshalls. A letter to his nephew Arthur, the younger son of older brother Charles, wounded at the front during December 1917 and to die of his wounds within weeks after this letter was written, shows the impact this family bereavement had on the old and childless uncle,

> How good and strong you are under your grievous pains! The latest news of you is always the news of the day, rivalled only by the inch high headings – if there are any – over the war news in the 'Times'. Poor dear lad! It is sad that you are thus struck, and in parts of the body that are specially sensitive and self-willed. But all brave soldiers, when hit, have the consolation of being able to say, "it was for my country": and in this war there is even more to be said. The whole world – other than Germany – is in a sense "the country" of those who are fighting for a future of peace: you suffer on behalf of the world; and the world will be grateful to you in coming times. Even should the worst befall and the world seem to darken before you, you can say "*Dulce et decorum est pro patria mori*".[108]

At a much lower level, the vastly increased difficulties in post-war travel prevented renewal of their regular excursions to the South-Tirol except for one more, rather traumatic, trip,[109] though age and rapidly failing health were as much to blame for this summer deprivation as were the change in the international order which post-war adjustment brought in its wake. It was fortunate Marshall did not live to see the full effects of these post-war events which by the end of the 1920s were rapidly gaining momentum to fulfil the gloomy expectations of a second world war with Germany which he had predicted in letters to Taussig and Keynes as early as 1915. This pessimism is underlined by his rather belated thank you to Maynard Keynes for sending him his *Economic Consequences of the Peace*, the anti-revenge contents of which provided him 'with exceptional pleasure and profit'.[110] Such sentiments from the leading colt of his growing Cambridge stable fitted in well with his own principled war effort designed to calm anti-Germanic community feeling, an endeavour largely conducted in the correspondence pages of the *Times*. Well into his 75th year, this induced him to tackle as noted an adversary as Sir Arthur Conan Doyle in the interest of preserving humane values in times of war:

> Sir Conan Doyle in your issue of today suggests that the position of Britain and her Allies would have been stronger now if they had made the development of hatred against Germany a chief aim of their policy. By doing always what seemed to us to be right we have enlisted the sympathy of the world on our side, and therefore we are strong; but we should lose much of that sympathy if we cultivated hatred as a weapon of war. Clear, well-authenticated statements of German cruelty ought no doubt to be published without reserve. But to foster hatred as an end would strengthen the position of pacifists whose noble sentiments seem to me to make for a premature peace which would inflict a disaster almost unparalleled in history in the coming generation.*

Three years later to the day, Mary Paley Marshall recorded a sentiment on the subject of German war guilt expressed by her husband in the privacy of Balliol Croft, when engagement in public controversy on his part had finally ceased,

> Talking at breakfast as to how the notion of bringing the Kaiser to justice had died out, A[lfred] said he doubted whether anything the Kaiser had done was as bad as what England had done in the conquest of India. In the end that had probably been good for India as it had prevented her from tearing herself to pieces by internal war. But A. could imagine the Kaiser believing that it might be for the good of the world that Europe should all be brought under the German yoke and turned into a brotherhood of nations. Of course for a time an army would have to be kept up on the Eastern frontier as Russia was not yet civilised and the European brotherhood would have to assemble a strong navy to conquer England's fleet and then Europe would be a happy family with no more war, so that in a century or so the Kaiser might imagine that he would be looked upon as the world's greatest benefactor.[111]

TRYING TO KEEP IN TOUCH WITH FORMER STUDENTS: THE NEVER-ENDING STRUGGLE FOR TIME OF THE RETIRED PROFESSOR

Not long after Marshall's death, Mary Paley Marshall recalled for Walter Scott[112] that apart from immediate family, Marshall only 'really cared very much for . . . some of his former pupils. He often said that he would have liked to have seen more of his old school and college friends, but that he had not strength for keeping up old friendships and also for his work'. Immediate family of whom he had been particularly fond were disappearing fast: his favourite Aunt Louisa had died in 1907 aged 89, while favourite sister Mabel followed in 1912. Two of his younger nephews died during the war: Arthur from war wounds as mentioned before; Cyril, the youngest son of his sister Mabel at age of 22 in 1915. Hence a small number of former students and fellow teachers of economics supplied the solace of friendship in Marshall's old age.

---

* Marshall to editor of the *Times*, 28 December 1917. This responded to the letter by Sir Arthur Conan Doyle published 26 December 1917 (the day on which Marshall's letter was dated), which after recounting the details about some German atrocities with respect to British prisoners of war, stated such incidents should be publicised because 'Hate has its own uses in war'. The letter then suggested as an official strategy adoption of systematically publishing German war crimes, particularly in the 'Sinn Fein districts of Ireland, and in the hotbeds of Socialism and Pacificism in England and Scotland'.

Such friendships were maintained through correspondence and occasional visits, of which the first especially showed how affectionately Marshall followed the careers of his favourite economics students and appreciated the honours they received in public life. Thus warm congratulatory letters left Balliol Croft during 1917 when first Maynard Keynes and then Walter Layton had their war service recognised by the award of a C.B. and C.B.E. respectively.[113] Their writings on economics and related subjects were similarly acknowledged by words of praise from their former teacher. In 1915, Captain Fay was praised for his 'fascinating study' of *Life and Labour 1800–1850* with the aside that 'a thousand years hence, 1920–70 will, I expect, be *the* time for historians'.[114] A year later, Pigou was congratulated for 'the brilliancy and "go" of your book', praise tempered by Marshall's expression of fear that the complexities of interdependence and the difficulties these raised were not always stressed by Pigou with the requisite clarity.[115] Before the war, praise had gone to Maynard Keynes for journal articles and his contributions on Indian currency while after the war such praise was continued when Marshall had been able to savour his *Economic Consequences of the Peace* and *Tract on Monetary Reform*. Receipt of the last brought the additional comment that given his fairly imminent departure from this world, he 'would ask newcomers to the celestial region, whether you have succeeded in finding a remedy for currency maladies'.[116]

Praise also went the other way. Marshall's eightieth birthday on 16 July 1922 was marked by the Royal Economic Society through an address signed by its leading members. This indicated the massive debt the new generation of economists owed to its founder, particularly those associated with the Cambridge School of Economics he had created, and more generally the British economists whom he had inspired by his stature and practice in education and other service to the State. Its brief message of congratulation, apart from assuring Marshall of the 'affectionate esteem' of so many of his former students and other admirers of his work, and wishing him 'continuing power and happy days and the sense of work well done', sang his praises in the following terms:

> You have held up through a long life, with single aim and steady purpose, a high scientific ideal; to look through the sign to the thing signified, to shun the superficial and the plausible, and never to be content with the good when the better may still be attained. You have given inspiration to youth and counsel and enlightenment to age. The School of Economics at Cambridge is your child; on the Labour Commission and in your evidence before the Gold annd Silver and other Commissions you have rendered important direct service to the State and have advanced Economic Science. But it is as a master of method and a path-breaker in difficult regions that we, the signatories of this letter, desire especially to greet you. Through you, British economists may boast among their foreign colleagues that they have a leader in the great tradition of Adam Smith and Ricardo and Mill, and of like stature.[117]

The signatories, starting with the names of Lord Haldane as President and Arthur Balfour as Vice-President of the Society, included 34 professors and former professors, many of them either persons with whom Marshall had corresponded or former students, together with 53 other teachers and practitioners of economics in public service or business. These also were drawn from close associates at various important junctures of his life, or from former students, both direct and indirect. The last were represented by Lavington, D.H. Robertson and Shove, members of his school of economics who knew him through his books rather than through his personal instruction; former direct students in this list included John Neville and Maynard Keynes as well as women students Marian Pease (from his Bristol days) and Lynda Grier. German economics was represented by Brentano and Schumpeter, Swedish economics by Cassel, American economics by Carver, Fisher, Hadley, Seligman and Taussig, French economics by Gide and the moral sciences by Sorley.

This imposing list of signatories has some surprising as well as less startling omissions. Among former eminent foreign correspondents, J.B. Clark and Wicksell are notable for their absence, explicable in terms of their non-membership of the Royal Economic Society. Equally striking, and perhaps a sign of a growing insularity of British economics by the 1920s, are the absence of names from the Italian, Dutch, Lausanne and, apart from the two exceptions mentioned, German and Austrian, schools. There are also interesting missing names among former students. The omission of Foxwell has already been amply explained; absence of Layton, surely then a member of the Royal Economic Society, is more difficult to fathom. The recipient of this warm congratulatory message accepted it with pleasure and gratitude. However, he could not resist the temptation of a brief final sermon on the scope of the subject he had both rejuvenated and re-defined:

> The address, which you have sent to me on my eightieth birthday, fills me with gratitude and joy. It is all too kind; but I am so avaricious that I would not give up a jot of it.
>
> It is true of almost every science that, the longer one studies it, the larger its scope seems to be; though in fact its scope may have remained almost unchanged. But the subject-matter of economics grows apace; so that the coming generation will have a much larger field to study, as well as more exacting notions as to the way in which it needs to be studied, than fell to the lot of their predecessors. The Chinese worship their ancestors: an old student of economics may look with reverential awe on the work which he sees young students preparing themselves to do.
>
> If I have helped in putting some young students on the way to grapple with the economic problems of the coming age, that is far more important than anything which I have been able to do myself: and, resting on the hope that I have done a little in this direction, I can depart in peace.[118]

In a sense, this was a formal good-bye from the profession Marshall had helped to create, and accepted as such by the now octogenarian resident of Balliol Croft. Final contact with two of his former students, to whom in many ways he appears to have been closest in these final years, and who recorded the occasion in writing, conveys a similar sentiment. These recollected that farewells to their former 'master' were spread out over twelve months, a consequence of the geographical diffusion of these two so very different scribes. They capture what appear to be the essentials of the lifestyle to which the economic thinker had been reduced in this final year of his long life. Fay, who gathered Marshalliana to promote a picture of Marshall's 'intense humanity and the affection he gave and inspired' for those who could only know 'him from his books', recalled that final visit some time in 1923 in his official reminiscences for the Marshall *Memorials*:

> Last year, before I came out again to Canada, my wife and I had tea with him for the last time. He told us of the small legacy which he devoted to his tour of America fifty years go. I made one short remark about the monotony of modern industrialism, whereupon he jumped up and began to picture the romance of modern steel. But I had broken my promise to Mrs. Marshall, for I had been with him two minutes over the allotted ten. So I rose to go, but he anticipated us and slipped out into the garden.[119]

Keynes's moving letter of May 1924 to his future wife, Lydia Lopokova, two months before Marshall's actual death, graphically recorded the impressions his last visit left with him, and the substance of which enriched a small part at least of that memoir by which Keynes commemorated the man who had made him, as so many others, into economists:

> I have been touched this afternoon. I had news that my old master [Alfred Marshall] who made me into an economist (the one who had an 80th birthday two years ago – you will remember his photograph) could not live much longer; so I went to pay him a last visit. Lying in bed in his night cap he looked like an old sage, which is what he is, – very Chinese. His voice was weak but he told me how he first came to study economics, and how such study was a sort of religious work for the sake of the human race. He was still able to laugh, but he has no memory for what happens now and has probably forgotten my visit already. I held his hand hard, and then went to speak to his old wife who has given all her life to helping him to do his work. She is calm and wise. He is now rather like a child and is often troublesome. He will do what the doctor tells him but not what she or the nurse says, and he calls out that, though he may be weak, he 'won't be bossed by women'.[120]

Other details of these last years and months were described by Mary Paley Marshall. These highlight some features of both the mode of Marshall's working and of his relaxation during the final decade of his retirement, which ended with his last illness. After mentioning that Scott's novels were the 'only story books he cared to have read aloud . . . during his last illness', and his enjoyment at winning their nightly backgammon games and annoyance if he lost, she continued,

> A great joy to him during the last 10 years of his life was an autopiano driven by electricity. With great difficulty I persuaded him to buy it, for he would never indulge in luxuries for himself. It gradually became his great solace. He invented a plan, by means of strings and pulleys for starting and stopping a tune whilst lying on the sofa and he would often play a sonata over and over again and it was nearly always a Beethoven. Towards the end of his life, he sat and worked a great deal in the Ark, a large revolving shelter fitted up as a study. It was so large and heavy that it could not be turned in the usual way from outside so he arranged for it to be turned from the inside by a handle and cogwheels so that a child could move the whole thing. He took a great delight in mechanical contrivances and declared that if he were landed on a desert island, with tools and men, he could construct most kinds of machinery.*

Two years later, she recalled these joys of Marshall's last years in a long letter to Walter Layton, in response to his message that the Ark was capable of repair. This not only recollected the necessity of this instrument to accommodate Marshall's passion for working outdoors, acting therefore as the successor to the 'balcony adjoining the study [followed by] . . . a small revolving shelter which was passed on to me when we got the Ark'. Its summer counterpart was the more portable shelter constructed for the Tirol and left there for its recurring use when year after year they returned for the summer. The letter also provides details of its origins and *modus operandi*,

---

* Mary Paley Marshall, 'Notes for Walter Scott', Marshall Archive, Large Brown Box, Item 26; cf. C.R. Fay's recollections that after dictating his memorandum on machine guns in 1918, Marshall said before Fay left, 'You may spread the cushions, and turn on Blackbird' (his automatic piano), and having complied with that commandment, 'as I shut the door, [I] glanced back to see him as if a Crusader at rest, with arms folded and eyes shut' ('Reminiscences of a Deputy Librarian', p. 90).

I find that we got it [the Ark] from Boulton and Paul in Norwich in 1910 and from that time till a few days before his death, in fact as long as he was able to walk at all, he sat in it. It was fitted up with book shelves, a revolving book case, a rocking chair and nests of boxes where he kept his MSS. In winter he wore a furlined coat and warm mittens and the tin and fur shoe kept his feet warm. The plan of turning it round from the inside was his own invention.

His Ark and his Blackbird (he always liked to give names to his things), i.e. an excellent electric piano, were his two great joys in life. He used to lie on a sofa and with an arrangement of pulleys and strings he could make the piano play to him without getting up. During the last few years he was not allowed to do constructive work for more than an hour at the time, then he laid down and Blackbird played to him and after half an hour he got up quite refreshed and ready for work. He nearly always played Beethoven and had about 200 rolls of his works.*

ILLNESS AND GROWING RECLUSE

Marshall's steady withdrawal from society during his retirement has been amply documented in this chapter, and in correspondence was ascribed by him to the deleterious effects of excitement and other stimulus from visits and conversation on his feeble strength and weak constitution. Keynes suggested that after 1882, when Marshall's health had been substantially restored after the illness originating with the stones in his kidney first diagnosed in early 1879, 'he remained for the rest of his life somewhat hypochrondiacal and inclined to consider himself on the verge of invalidism. In fact, his constitution was extremely tough and he remained in harness as a writer to a very advanced age. But his nervous equilibrium was easily upset by unusual exertion or excitement . . . his power of continuous concentration on difficult mental work was inferior to his wishes and he became dependent on a routine of life adapted ever to his whims and fancies'.[121] Keynes's remark about Marshall's 'strong constitution', seems somewhat exaggrated.¶ It tallies poorly with what little is known about Marshall's youthful constitution, with its persistent headaches to be cured by chess problems, absence of games, and pale features and light frame which earned him the nickname at school of 'tallow candles'.[122] Marshall's own recollections of his early post-graduate years in the 1860s, admittedly well after the event, suggested detrimental consequences for his health from a tendency to overwork, but such symptoms failed to prevent his arduous alpine excursions during the summers which tended to restore his health and strength for the start of each new academic year in October.[123]

'Weakness of digestion which', Keynes stated, 'had troubled him all his life, [and] increased in later years', may have been associated with the effects of illness from kidney stones which had been diagnosed in 1879. During his initial period of recuperation, correspondence with Foxwell about Marshall's after-dinner habits, which entailed seclusion and rest for at least an hour after meals with enforced relaxation through knitting, appear symptomatic of this affliction, one also frequently associated with a nervous disposition.[124]

---

*   Mary Paley Marshall to Walter Layton, 4 November 1926 (Marshall Archive, 1:328). Walter Layton in fact inherited this contraption; 'Blackbird' ended up at Newnham College (*Newnham College Letter*, 1945). Information supplied by Rita McWilliams-Tullberg.

¶   C.R. Fay, in commenting on Keynes's Memoir, remarked, 'Your article on A.M. was *brilliant* and all true except the line about the "tough constitution", but I take it your imp moved you there! and memories of his scandalous treatment of Sidgwick', C.R. Fay to Maynard Keynes, 13 November 1924 (KMF).

However, by the 1890s, Marshall was claiming that his digestive problems forced him to rest for about an hour after each meal, and it was probably this necessity which curtailed social activity by making it difficult for him to accept private dinner invitations and invitations to stay with friends.[125] Medical opinion has insufficient evidence about Marshall's symptoms to make a precise retrospective diagnosis. However, there is general agreement that at the time of diagnosis of the kidney stones, operations for their removal were hardly ever recommended and that in the absence of this more modern treatment the problem would have been severely debilitating. Moreover, psychosomatic factors are likely to have been present as well, suggested by the chess games as cures for headaches, while Marshall's nervous disposition may account for much of his digestive problems. Sir Andrew Clark, whom Marshall occasionally consulted, was famous for the treatment of dyspepsia and a 'beloved physician of brainworkers' who, Marshall suggested in his *Principles*, were prone to suffer from digestive problems. Digestive ailments provided also a useful shield to protect domestic privacy, avoiding unwanted visits and loss of independence from lodging with others. On the other hand, the type of digestive problem of which Marshall complained is consistent with the gall bladder complaint which was listed in 1924 as the chief cause of his death.[126]

Indigestion aside, from the late 1880s Marshall's health was sufficiently robust to stand considerable cycling and walking excursions, not only in the vicinity of Cambridge as Marshall recalled in 1910 to Sir Horace Plunkett, but in Devon and Cornwall in the 1890s during the Marshalls' English holidays.[127] These two-wheeled, and walking expeditions, were remarked upon by their old friend, Benjamin Jowett, as signs of how much Alfred Marshall's health had changed for the better from those years when he first knew them in Bristol. They also give some credence to an underlying more robust constitution in this middle stage of Marshall's long life.[128] Cannan later commented on how different the Marshall of the early 1890s was in physical stature to the seemingly older man with 'one foot in the grave' whom he recalled 'creeping along the Apsley Road' when he was a boy in Bristol.[129] However, by 1901, Ludlow expressed surprise at hearing that health prevented Marshall from 'going about'.[130]

Inability to sustain prolonged concentration, especially on difficult mental problems, as well as possession of a non-retentive memory, had troubled Marshall from an early age.[131] The first failing was increasingly mentioned in Marshall's correspondence from the mid-1890s, as indicated in his letter to Eliot quoted at the start of this chapter. This failing became a more prominent source of complaint during his retirement when feebleness and lack of strength were increasingly blamed for the effective brake they put on his progress in writing. Other examples of failing memory were provided earlier. Marshall himself wrote to Wicksell. 'I am ashamed of having forgotten what you said long ago about the currency. But as I forget what I have written even a week ago, I may be pardoned for forgetting others' words.'[132]

Mary Paley Marshall recalled for Keynes that after 1919 Marshall's health began to give way more seriously. 'He suffered from acidity and nausea which I believe was the beginning of his final illness, and his memory began to fail though he did not know it. On this account, I did all I could to hasten the appearance of *Money Credit and Commerce*, especially as Dr Bowen told me in 1921 that his working life was over and that he was incapable of constructive work. During the last year he was beginning to realise that his memory was failing him and he often said "how glad I am that *Money, Credit and Commerce* is out". Since *Money, Credit and Commerce* appeared, he has been trying to prepare a little old MSS and his early pamphlets, etc. for publication.'[133]

That final illness itself was described on the death certificate. This listed causes of death as cholecystitis (inflammation of the gall bladder, probably caused by obstruction of the cystic duct by a stone) combined with senility and cardiac failure.[134] The impact of these diseases inevitably had been gradual. High blood pressure had been diagnosed by 1914, the associated arteriosclerosis (hardening of arteries) explains the worsening memory loss much better than an appeal to Alzheimer's disease.[135] Senility and loss of memory became particularly bad during the 1920s. Grasp of this progress is important when clarifying Marshall's role in the publication of that third and last volume, of which he was so proud.[136] A self-diagnosis not long after his 79th birthday indicated,

> Acidity and sick feeling somewhat abated.
> Tendency of work to bring on feeling of pressure in the head, accompanied by weariness is increasing; and it troubles me.
> I must work on so far as strength permits for about two full years (or say four years of half time) if that is allowed to me; after that, I can say, *nunc dimitis*.
> I care little for length of life, for its own sake. I want only so to arrange my work as to increase my chance of saying those things which I think of chief importance.[137]

Marshall's struggles to implement this desire for the years after 1921 are discussed in the context of his final volumes.[138] By looking at the constraints on his intellectual activity his years of retirement gradually imposed, the increasing difficulties of this writing task are more easily grasped. His years of retirement also raised questions about his ability to sustain enduring friendships. These final years appear as almost friendless, apart from the crucial and sustaining companionship of his wife, a few remaining near relatives from amongst his nephews, and a handful of the more recent and loyal of his students who visited him, when either the opportunity or the inclination presented itself. In these final years of recluse and ill health, 'with the deep-set and shining eyes, wisps of white hair, and black cap on his head, he bore, more than ever, the aspect of a sage or prophet'.[139]

NOTES

1. Marshall to President Eliot of Harvard, 3 September 1895 (Marshall Archive, 3:315); it declined Eliot's offer of a visiting professorship at Harvard.
2. Above, Chapter 8, pp. 231, 238–9, 241–3.
3. Above, Chapter 12, p. 435.
4. Above, Chapter 16, p. 590 and n*. However on retirement, St John's may have resumed fellowship dividends, not paid while he was Professor.
5. Above, Chapter 2, p. 40 and n. 85, Chapter 15, pp. 550–51.
6. JNKD, 30 April 1908. This entry confirms Marshall's concern over his succession and his preference for Pigou for the post, as discussed below, pp. 625–6.

7. Letter by A.W. Ward to Marshall, 20 May 1908, in his capacity as acting chairman of the Economics Board (Cambridge University Archives, Min. V. 114, minutes for 20 May 1908), the original is preserved in the Marshall Archive (1:107). Ward had been the Board's first chairman, also had been chairman of the History Board's committee which first publicly floated the idea of a separate Economics and Politics Tripos, and had assisted the scheme through the university, as discussed in Chapter 15 above.

8. Marshall to A.W. Ward, 30 May 1908 (Cambridge University Archives, Min. V. 114, pasted in with minutes for 20 May 1908).

9. D.H. Macgregor, 'Alfred Marshall and his Book', *AMCA*, II, p. 115; Macgregor was finishing his teaching at Cambridge in that session, departing not long after for the Professorship at Leeds. An unlikely attender at the Lecture was William Rothenstein, then painting Marshall's portrait (see below, p. 629).

10. Quoted from its reproduction in Rita McWilliams-Tullberg, 'Marshall's Final Lecture, 21 May 1908', pp. 614–15; this also gives details of the student life and subsequent career of its reporter, Lynda Grier. The quotation from Marshall's inaugural is likely to have been its final paragraph, for reasons suggested in note 12 below.

11 JNKD, 21 May 1908. The suggestion in the text that Keynes was the oldest of Marshall's students present implies the absence of Foxwell, Cunningham and James Ward from the lecture.

12. Pigou, 'In Memoriam', delivered on 21 October 1908 at Cambridge in commemoration of Marshall's death in July that year, in *Memorials*, pp. 89–90; this quoted the final paragraph of Marshall's inaugural (in *ibid.*, p. 174) more than likely the passage Marshall himself had quoted in his final lecture. For Marshall's inclusion of Pigou in his 'Cambridge Stables', see Marshall to Chapman, 29 October 1904, in *Memorials*, p. 456, the others being Bowley, Pethick-Lawrence and Chapman himself.

13. Neither the reminiscences of Pethick-Lawrence and Chapman, nor the biographers of Lowes Dickinson and Layton indicate such presence, nor do subsequent reminiscences by Benians, Clapham, Fay and others on the teaching staff. Maynard Keynes's absence can be surmised from his *Collected Writings*, Vol. XV, pp. 13–15, which indicates that Marshall had been in touch with him as early as 3 April 1908 about a possible lectureship in economics to be financed by either himself or his possible successor; Keynes's presence at the lecture would undoubtedly have been recorded in his father's diary.

14. Cambridge University Archive (Min. V. 114) entries for 2 June 1908, 27 January 1909.

15. Marshall to Maynard Keynes, 26 February 1909 (Keynes Papers, L/M/41). The label read: 'Presented by Alfred Marshall. Professor of Political Economy 1885–1908'.

16. Marshall to Maynard Keynes, 30 May 1909 (Keynes Papers, L/M/41). The foundation of the Marshall Library is discussed in Chapter 20 below, pp. 750–51.

17. This issue has been much debated in the literature, by A.W. Coats, 'Political Economy and Tariff Reform', pp. 225–8; Ronald Coase, 'The Appointment of Pigou as Marshall's Successor: Comment'; A.W. Coats, 'The Appointment of Pigou as Marshall's Successor: Comment'; both in *AMCA*, IV, pp. 222–44; and T.W. Jones, 'The Appointment of Pigou as Marshall's Successor: The Other side of the Coin', in *ibid.*, pp. 302–11.

18. *Cambridge University Reporter*, 24 April 1908, p. 800; Cambridge University Archive (Min. V. 114), 22 January 1908.

19. JNKD, 30 May 1908 lists the four candidates; Marshall to Walter Layton 13 January 1919, Layton Papers, Trinity College, Layton 2[37]. In his *Memorials and Notes on British Economists 1881–1947*, p. 15 Price recalled Ashley had told him 'he had been in some sense stimulated by Marshall to become a candidate, or understood that he was not dissuaded from this step'.

20. JNKD, 30 April 1908, 27 May 1908, 19 May 1908.

21. Foxwell to Clara Collet, 6 June 1908 reproduced in A.W. Coats, 'The Appointment of Pigou', pp. 239–40. The letter is partly reproduced in her diary (Warwick University Library, Modern Records Centre, MSS 29/8/1, pp. 122–3); Foxwell to Fay, 28 March and 12 May 1908 (Marshall Archive, 1:14–15) supports Foxwell's certainty of being elected at this time.

22. A.W. Coats, 'Political Economy and Tariff Reform', pp. 227–8 which reproduces the relevant Balfour–Hewins correspondence dated 28 May; *Hansard*, House of Commons Debates, 26 May, 1–2 June 1908 and see above, Chapter 11, p. 385, where these parliamentary debates are linked to the official publication in 1908 of Marshall's 1903 Memorandum.

23. If Foxwell was as friendly with the Vice-Chancellor as his letter to Clara Collet already quoted suggests, this may well have been the case, particularly if Balfour had adopted the typical politician's reaction to Hewins's advice by opting for the safe candidate in his advice to the Vice-Chancellor.

24. JNKD, 30 and 31 May 1908.

25. Roderick K. Clark to J.M. Keynes, 1 December 1924 (KMF).

26. A.W. Coats, 'Political Economy and Tariff Reform', p. 228; cf. Audrey Foxwell, *Herbert Somerton Foxwell: A Portrait*, Cambridge: Harvard University Press, 1939, p. 9; Marshall's long friendship with Foxwell is explored in more detail in Chapter 18, below.

27. Sidney Webb to Ashley (undated), in A.W. Coats, 'Political Economy and Tariff Reform', p. 228 n.37.
28. For details, see above, Chapter 13, pp. 472–3, Chapter 15, p. 552.
29. Below, Chapter 18, pp. 675–6.
30. Above, Chapter 15, p. 556.
31. Foxwell to Marshall, 1 June 1908, a copy preserved among Foxwell's other correspondence (Freeman Collection, 11/252). Marshall's copy of the original, not surprisingly, failed to be preserved among his own correspondence.
32. F.Y. Edgeworth to Marshall, 9 February 1907 (Marshall Archive, 1:22).
33. Marshall to F.Y. Edgeworth, 11 February 1907 (Marshall Archive, 1:23).
34. *Men and Memories. Recollections of William Rothenstein 1900–1922*, London: Faber & Faber, 1934, p. 130.
35. William Rothenstein to Marshall, 21 April 1908 (Marshall Archive, 1:98).
36. William Rothenstein to Mary Paley Marshall, 14 May 1909 (Marshall Archive, 1:94).
37. *Ibid.*, One of the photographs now greets those entering the current premises of the Marshall Library within the Faculty of Economics and Politics at the University of Cambridge, a display arranged by its 1992 librarian, Donald Ross. That Mary Paley followed Rothenstein's detailed advice on the subject given in this letter is shown in the extract from the *Economic Journal* quoted below, p. 631.
38. L.L. Price to John Neville Keynes, 23 June 1908 (Marshall Archive, 2:72).
39. L.L. Price, *Memories and Notes on British Economists 1881–1947*, pp. 15–16.
40. Marshall to William Rothenstein (postscript to the previous letter); C.W. Guillebaud, 'Some Personal Reminiscences of Alfred Marshall', recalled Mary Paley telling him 'that Alfred himself did not like it [the portrait] . . . because he considered it did not do proper justice to his brow'. (pp. 93–4).
41. Mary Paley to William Rothenstein, 10 November 1908.
42. *Economic Journal*, News and Notes, December 1908, p. 669.
43. *Morning Post*, 9 January 1909 (preserved in Marshall Scrapbook, Marshall Archive); William Rothenstein, *Men and Memories*, pp. 130–33, *Cambridge Review*, 25 February 1909: The Rothenstein Marshall portrait 'will stand out as one of the best modern works that our Colleges possess'.
44. R.F. Scott (Master of St John's College) to Mary Paley Marshall, 11 December 1909 (Marshall Archive, 1: 102); considerations such as those mentioned in the previous note may have persuaded the College Council of the desirability of accepting the gift.
45. Foxwell to Maynard Keynes, not dated (Keynes Papers); my attention was drawn to this item by R.M. O'Donnell. The message sent by Keynes on behalf of the Royal Economic Society on Marshall's eightieth birthday is included in *Memorials*, pp. 497–9, with Foxwell one of the more prominent absences from the signatories which otherwise read as a virtual Who's Who of contemporary British economists. See below, pp. 649–50.
46. Donald Ross, 'An Unusual Commitment, Alfred and Mary Marshall and the establishment of the Marshall Library 1903–44', *Quaderni di storia dell'economia politica*, 9 (2–3), 1991, pp. 327, 329.
47. Public Orator's speeches in presenting the Chancellor with recipients of honorary degrees, Cambridge, 17 June 1908 (Marshall's copy preserved in the Marshall Library).
48. University of Edinburgh, Honorary Doctors of Law, 13 April 1893 (preserved in the Marshall Library). With reference to the quoted segment from the oration, it is interesting to record that the *Westminster Gazette*, 19 March 1908, printed a letter expressing the hope that 'retirement will bring the . . . Alfred J. Thorogood second volume' (preserved in Marshall scrapbook), an interesting indication also of how Marshall's social philanthropy was by then ironically contemplated in some London circles.
49. Alfred Marshall on himself, *AMCA*, I, p. 148. A more complete list is in Marshall's entry in the *Balliol College Register*, Oxford: University Press, 1914, p. 324.
50. The greater part of this and the preceding paragraph draws largely on this source of information in the Marshall Library.
51. J.M. Keynes, 'Alfred Marshall', pp. 225–6 and n. 4.
52. Above, Chapter 13, pp. 479–82.
53. Below, Chapter 19, completely devoted to these two volumes.
54. Above, Chapter 11, pp. 385–8.
55. Marshall to the editor of the *Times*, 16 November 1909.
56. Above, Chapter 16, pp. 597–8.
57. Marshall to Lord Reay, 12 November 1909, in *Memorials*, pp. 461, 464–5; it is interesting to note that Marshall's 'only confident dogma in economics' was repeated in a letter to Lewis Fry, 7 November 1914, in *Memorials*, p. 484, and see below, Chapter 20, p. 741.
58. Lord Reay to Marshall, 14 November 1909, Marshall to Reay, 15 November 1909, in *Memorials*, pp. 465–7; and see above, Chapter 16, pp. 597–8.

59. *OP*, p. 382, Section 25. The notion of Giffen goods was first introduced in the third edition of the *Principles*, 1895, p. 132; as mentioned in Chapter 12 above, p. 424.

60. Marshall to Edgeworth, 21 April 1909, in *Memorials*, pp. 438–9; Edgeworth's review of R. Rea, *Free Trade in Being*, appeared in the *Economic Journal*, 19 March 1909, pp. 102–6.

61. Marshall to Edgeworth, 21 April 1909, in *Memorials*, p. 439.

62. Marshall to Edgeworth, 22 April 1909, in *Memorials*, p. 439; this subject for Book X of Volume II was not in the original plan, but conforms to the outline Marshall recalled in 1903. See above, Chapter 12, Table 12.1 and pp. 429–30.

63. Marshall to Edgeworth, 22 April 1909, in *Memorials*, pp. 439–42. Mavor, the expert referred to in the text, was cited on the subject in *IT*, p. 749 n.1.

64. Marshall to Edgeworth, 27 April 1909, in *Memorials*, p. 442.

65. Recorded by John Maynard Keynes, 'Francis Ysidro Edgeworth', in *Essays in Biography*, p. 265.

66. Marshall to Louis Dumur, 2 July 1909, in *Memorials*, pp. 459–61.

67. Marshall to Sir Horace Plunkett, 17 May 1910, in *Memorials*, pp. 459–61; the quotation is from p. 460.

68. Above, Chapter 16, p. 607.

69. Marshall to Manohar Làl, 28 January 1909, 22 February 1911 in *Memorials*, pp. 456–8.

70. Marshall to Irving Fisher, 16 November 1911, 14 and 15 October 1912 (in *Memorials*, pp. 474–8). The fact that the last letter followed the preceding one by a day, a phenomenon evident earlier in the letters to Edgeworth during 1909 reinforces the impression that Marshall's memory by then was already slipping badly. The Fisher correspondence was previously mentioned in Chapter 11, above p. 351.

71. Marshall to H.L. Moore, 5 June 1912 (Moore Collection, Butler Library, Columbia University). Marshall's library contained this and three other works by Moore (*Marshall Library Catalogue*, p. 59).

72. Marshall to Edgeworth (undated, but some time in 1911/12) included with Marshall's letter to Moore, 5 June 1912 (Moore Collection, Butler Library, Columbia University).

73. Moore to Marshall, 6 June 1912 (copy in Moore's handwriting with notes after the event in Moore Collection, Butler Library, Columbia University); Marshall to Moore, 15 February 1921 (Moore Collection, Butler Library, Columbia University). On Marshall's 'Red Book', see above, Chapter 5, pp. 128–9.

74. C.R. Fay, 'Reminiscences of a Deputy Librarian', p. 89; cf. p. 88: 'I used to have tea with them at the summer house. Marshall took nothing. 'Mother M.' (as I always thought of her) poured out and served me with two rounds of buttered bun, sipping a cup herself'; C.R. Fay, 'Reminiscences', in *Memorials*, pp. 76–7; Marshall to C.R. Fay, 27 January 1910 (Marshall Archive, 1:32).

75. Above p. 633, Chapter 6, pp. 162–3 and Chapter 13, pp. 480–81.

76. Marshall to Maynard Keynes, 14 June 1910 (Keynes Papers, L/M/41).

77. Marshall to Walter Layton, 28 September 1909, 2 December 1910, 4 September 1911 (Layton Papers, Trinity College, Layton 2^{32-34}).

78. Marshall to Walter Layton, 28 September 1909 (Layton 2^{32}).

79. Marshall to Henry Jackson (undated, Marshall Archive, 1:32) and see above, Chapter 4, pp. 89–91 for relevant aspects of Marshall's undergraduate experience.

80. Marshall to J.H. Clapham, 17 May 1912 (Marshall Archive, 1:13).

81. Marshall to J.H. Clapham, 4 November 1912 (Marshall Archive, 1:14).

82. Cited in Norman Angell, *The Great Illusion*, London: William Heinemann, 1911, pp. 14–15.

83. Marshall to the editor of the *Times*, 22 August 1914.

84. Marshall to J.T. Sheppard, a Fellow of King's from 1906 and later its Provost, 12 October 1914 (King's College Library, Sh. 4.5 letter 2).

85. Marshall to the editor of the *Times*, 28 October 1914.

86. Marshall to Lewis Fry, 7 November 1914, in *Memorials*, pp. 484–6.

87. For Marshall's more detailed appreciation of Abbé and the Zeiss works, see *IT*, pp. 353–4, where the practice quoted was discussed from the perspective of its application as a means to enhance efficiency through appropriate working conditions. Cf. Marshall to Pigou, 12 August 1916, in *Memorials*, p. 434: 'I regard unnecessary motor car hiring as exceptionally unpatriotic'

88. Marshall to Lewis Fry, 7 November 1914, in *Memorials*, p. 487.

89. *Ibid.*, pp. 484, 487.

90. Marshall to James Bonar, 8 August 1919, in *Memorials*, pp. 375–7; cf. *IT*, pp. 93, 770; Giffen's 'The Cost of the Franco-Prussian War of 1870–71', was reprinted in his *Essays on Finance*, London: George Bell and Sons, 1879, pp. 1–81, of which pp. 41–55 were explicitly devoted to the war indemnity Germany had extracted from France.

91. Marshall to James Bonar, 8 August 1919, in *Memorials*, p. 377.

92. Marshall to F.W. Taussig, 31 March 1915, in *Memorials*, pp. 490–91.

93. Marshall to Maynard Keynes, 21 and 22 February 1915, in *Memorials*, pp. 482–3.
94. Marshall to Maynard Keynes, 21 February 1915, in *Memorials*, p. 482.
95. Marshall to the editor of the *Times*, 29 and 31 December 1915.
96. Marshall to the editor of the *Times*, 31 December 1915.
97. Marshall to Maynard Keynes, 14 October 1915, Keynes Papers, King's College, L/M/41.
98. Marshall to Maynard Keynes, 25 October 1915, Keynes Papers, L/M/41.
99. Marshall to Maynard Keynes, 15 November 1915, Keynes Papers, L/M/41.
100. Leon Edel, *Bloomsbury. A House of Lions*, Harmondsworth: Penguin Books, 1981, pp. 201–5; R.F. Harrod, *The Life of John Maynard Keynes*, Chapter VI, Robert Skidelsky, *John Maynard Keynes, Hopes Betrayed 1883–1920*, pp. 289–97, esp. pp. 296–7.
101. Marshall to Maynard Keynes, 4 January 1916, Keynes Papers, L/M/41.
102. Marshall to editor of the *Economist*, 30 December 1916, p. 1228.
103. Marshall to W.H. Dawson, 20 February, 5 June and 18 November 1916 (Marshall Archive, 1:274–6).
104. Alfred Marshall, 'National Taxation after the War', pp. 329–45; the brief quotations are drawn from its concluding pages, pp. 344–5.
105. *Ibid.*, p. 328.
106. Marshall to the editor of the *Times*, 17 November 1919.
107. C.R. Fay, 'Reminiscences', in *Memorials*, pp. 76–7; an alternative account of this anecdote is in C.R. Fay 'Reminiscences of a Deputy Librarian', *AMCA*, I, pp. 89–90.
108. Marshall to Captain Arthur Raymond Marshall, 18 January 1918, in *Memorials*, p. 495. Arthur Marshall died at Rouen Hospital on 2 February 1918.
109. See above, Chapter 7, pp. 216–17.
110. Marshall to Maynard Keynes, 29 January 1920 (Keynes Papers, L/M/41).
111. Fragment dated 26 December 1920, in Mary Paley Marshall's handwriting (Marshall Archive, Large Brown Box, Item 26).
112. Mary Paley Marshall, 'Notes for Walter Scott', Large Brown Box, Item 26.
113. Marshall to Maynard Keynes, 9 June 1917 (Keynes Papers, L/M/41); Marshall to Walter Layton, 23 September 1917 (Layton Papers, Layton 2^{35}). *IT*, p. 644, n.1, proudly recorded a similar honour to S.J. Chapman, C.B.E.
114. Marshall to C.R. Fay, 23 February 1915, in *Memorials*, pp. 489–90.
115. Marshall to A.C. Pigou, 12 April 1916, in *Memorials*, pp. 433–4; the book in question was Pigou's, *The Economy and Finance of the War*. For detailed documentation of Marshall's critical annotations on another of Pigou's books, see K. Bharadwaj, 'Marshall on Pigou's *Wealth and Welfare*', *Economica*, February 1972, pp. 32–46.
116. Marshall to Maynard Keynes, 9 March and 8 October 1914, in *Memorials*, pp. 479–80; 29 January 1920 and 19 December 1923, Keynes Papers, L/M/41.
117. Reproduced in *Memorials*, p. 497, which also prints the complete list of signatories on which comments in the following paragraphs are based.
118. Marshall to Maynard Keynes, 27 July 1922, in *Memorials*, p. 499.
119. C.R. Fay, 'Reminiscences', in *Memorials*, p. 77.
120. Maynard Keynes to Lydia Lopokova, 16 May 1924, in *Lydia and Maynard*, edited Polly Hill and Richard Keynes, London: Andre Deutsch, 1989, p. 195.
121. John Maynard Keynes, 'Alfred Marshall', p. 178.
122. John Maynard Keynes, 'Alfred Marshall', p. 163 and see above, Chapters 2 and 3, pp. 22, 62.
123. Marshall to James Ward, 23 November 1900, in *Memorials*, p. 418, Mary Paley Marshall, 'MSS Notes' (NCA).
124. Marshall to Herbert Foxwell, 10 March 1884 (Freeman Collection, 12/73).
125. Marshall to Eliot, 3 September 1895 (quoted above, p. 618); Marshall to Brentano, 12 August 1903, quoted above, Chapter 13, p. 444, and the letter to Moore, above, pp. 637–8. Acworth, writing to Marshall on 20 April 1902, referred to the value of the 'mastication-to-destruction school of hygienists' (Marshall Archive, 1:113).
126. I have benefited from medical opinion from a number of Australian retrospective diagnosticians (Drs Cobcroft, Grandivia and Leavesley) whose assistance I here gratefully acknowledge. Contemporary views on kidney diseases were derived from *Clinical Lectures on subjects connected with Medicine, Surgery and Obstetrics*, selected by Richard Volkmann, London: Sydenham Society, 1876, esp. pp. 195–211; *British Medical Journal*, 30 October 1880, pp. 708–9; 12 February 1881, pp. 223–4; 10 October 1880, pp. 549–50. I am indebted to Rita McWilliams-Tullberg for reminding me of Marshall's dealings with Sir Andrew Clark.
127. Marshall to Sir Horace Plunkett, 17 May 1910, in *Memorials*, p. 468; Marshall to Foxwell, 8 April 1897 (Marshall Archive, 1:55). Marshall wrote to Phelps (11 April 1897, Oriel College, Phelps Papers) that 'almost the only after-result of my great illness, which now remains, is a susceptibility to chills in those parts of the body which were inflamed for many years'

128. Jowett to Mary Paley Marshall, 30 September 1891, 7 August 1893 (Marshall Archive, 1:58, 62).

129. E. Cannan, 'Alfred Marshall 1842–1924', in *AMCA*, I, p. 66.

130. J. Ludlow to Marshall, 6 June 1901 (Marshall Archive, 1:82).

131. John Maynard Keynes, 'Alfred Marshall', pp. 165–6; see also Chapters 3 and 4, pp. 63–4, 88.

132. Marshall to Wicksell, 8 April 1916 (Lund University Library, Wicksell Collection). The letter had been wrongly addressed , was returned. and then sent back again.

133. Mary Paley Marshall, 'Notes for Maynard Keynes' (KMF).

134. Alfred Marshall, death certificate, the cause of death was certified by Dr. Charles H. Budd, and not by the Dr Bowen who had been treating him in 1921.

135. Marshall to J.S. Sheppard, 12 October 1914 (King's College, Sh. 4.5 Letter 2); Marshall to Macmillan, 25 August 1917 (cited below, Chapter 19, pp. 705–6. Hypertension, arteriosclerosis and memory loss are closely associated.

136. Mary Paley Marshall, 'Notes for Maynard Keynes' (KMF), quoted in the previous paragraph.

137. Fragment dated 13 September 1921 (Marshall Library, Large Brown Box).

138. Chapter 19 below, esp. pp. 704–6, 716.

139. J.M. Keynes, 'Alfred Marshall', p. 231.

18. The Friend

Close personal friendships do not feature largely in Marshall's long life. Keynes recounted that Marshall did not easily make friends at school, perhaps because of his father's fear of unwholesome influence from such sources. His subsequent undergraduate years appear equally barren of enduring friendship, probably attributable to the difficulties relative poverty placed in the way of such friendships, as he hinted when discussing the position of working class boys at Oxford and Cambridge in later years.[1] An exception is Rawdon Levett, a fellow member of the St John's Boat Club.[2] It is not even easy to find many college friendships formed in those more carefree years as a bachelor Fellow of John's, when income was sufficiently plentiful to permit foreign travel and social gatherings for Cambridge friends, and there were no grave family encumbrances to impinge on his freedom. Limited though it was, these years did produce some evidence of incipient but firm social relationships with Fellows at his own college, Bonney and Hudson, cemented perhaps by their active involvement in the women's education movement. Earlier, Marshall's brief employment at Clifton College acquainted him with Percival, Mozley, Dakyns and perhaps Sidgwick, relationships which became closer at later stages of his life. His college period also produced friendships with Clifford, Moulton and Moss, and, of much longer duration, with his own former students, Herbert Foxwell and John Neville Keynes. A list of friends prepared by Mary Paley Marshall mentions these names and adds Wilson, Albert and Lewis Fry for Bristol, Jowett and Henry Smith for Oxford.[3] Subsequent professional ties to match initial personal and social connections made some of these the more enduring friendships of his life.

Four of the friendships mentioned so far, those with Sidgwick, Foxwell, Keynes and Jowett, are more fully examined in this chapter as case studies of the course which friendships with Marshall tended to take. The first three show the difficulty Marshall had in sustaining lifelong friendships. The Marshalls' friendship with Jowett, the Master of Balliol, is an exception because of its lifetime duration. It commenced with the Marshalls' move to Bristol, survived close proximity for four terms at Balliol, ending with Jowett's death in 1893, and was commemorated in the only obituary Marshall ever wrote.

Features of some of the other friendships mentioned in the opening paragraph can be briefly recalled from earlier chapters. For Marshall's few school friendships, the authority is fellow monitor, Dermer, with whom Mary Paley gained accidental contact during her parental visits to Bournemouth. Dermer recalled Marshall's friendships with the eccentrics of the Merchant Taylors' monitors' table; the later historian and journalist, Traill and the artist Hall, famous for his Franco-Prussian war paintings. Neither friendship was kept up after school, nor was Marshall apparently anxious to resume the earlier relationship with Dermer when his casual encounter at Bournemouth with Mary Paley Marshall made this possible.[4]

The authority for the college friendships formed by Marshall as a young Fellow of John's, is largely that of his wife's later recollections. She, it will be recalled, informed Keynes that Clifford and Moulton were Marshall's 'two greatest friends' at this time, Clifford, 'first and foremost'. It is certain that Marshall for some time was closely associated with these bright young Cambridge men, slightly his junior. Moulton and Clifford were regular associates at the Grote Club, and were also part of a 'Johnian clique' of seven, which met, among other things, to read Shakespeare. She, and Foxwell, later recalled that Marshall, Moulton and Clifford formed the 'inner circle' of this Johnian group.[5] These friendships do not appear to have made a lasting impact, in so far as encouraging their duration is concerned when this 'clique' broke up on the departure of Moulton and Clifford from Cambridge. In addition, neither Clifford's nor Moulton's biographers recall Marshall in this status, a telling point since their biographies were written at a time when Marshall had already attained sufficient fame to be worthy of mention in such accounts. Clifford, it will be recalled, had died rather young, but there is evidence that Marshall kept up with his mathematical prowess, as indicated by Marshall's account of his conversation with Emerson while in the United States in 1875 in which he defended Clifford as one of England's able young minds.[6] In later life Moulton was in renewed contact with Marshall as a member of the Political Economy Club, but apart from one casual reference to his existence in Marshall's correspondence, there is no further suggestion that intimacy of the kind expected from former close college friends continued during the later stages of their lives.[7]

To the examples of friendship with Dakyns, Percival and Mozley begun at Clifton College, may be added that with James Wilson. The last was gained through Clifton College during the Marshalls' stay in Bristol, a period which consolidated friendship with Percival and Dakyns. Once again, evidence on the degree of contact maintained with these friends is slender. The Dakynses, the Wilsons and Percival were part of a group with whom the Marshalls were involved socially as well as professionally at Bristol, and which also included Albert and Lewis Fry. In 1881, Wilson wrote to Mary Paley when the Marshalls were about to leave Bristol for a prolonged stay in Europe that their departure created a gap in Bristol society; and then, to the subsequent astonishment of Mary Paley Marshall, appears not to have written again until after her husband had died in 1924.[8] The Dakynses do not appear to have kept up any contact after the Marshalls left Bristol. Even the degree of friendship Marshall had developed with Dakyns in 1865 while at Clifton College is not clear, though the acquaintance may have been very important for him.[9] With Percival, contacts were maintained for longer. Marshall's initial encounter with him as Headmaster of Clifton was renewed at Bristol, where Percival was a member of the University College Council; and then at Oxford, when the Marshalls moved there until the end of 1884. Bristol contacts would have been greater than just through the university; the Percivals were both active in the Clifton Girls' School, of whose Council Mary Paley was also a member. There were other, casual contacts in later life from mutual interests, possibly in the same way that Marshall discussed matters of economic policy and industrial relations with others among his episcopal acquaintances.[10]

Of these early friendships, the case of Mozley is by far the more interesting. Begun at Clifton College in 1865, Mozley seems to have exerted considerable philosophical influence on the young Alfred Marshall over the following two years at Cambridge. Mozley appeared as the most likely person to have introduced Marshall into the Grote Club; he definitely introduced him to the joys of Alpine mountaineering in the summer of 1867, giving Marshall his first taste of the Dolomites.[11] Marshall wrote to him during 1916, as indicated by Mozley's letter in reply which has been preserved. Marshall's letter was probably to thank Mozley for the gift of his book, *The Divine Aspects of History*, which Cambridge University Press had published that year in two volumes. Its subject matter is consistent with the tone of Mozley's reply, which invited Marshall to read its short chapter dealing with China and Japan. The reply also suggests Marshall discussed youthful reminiscences appropriate to their age, reflecting among other things on the death of their common friend Sidgwick and pontificating on 'the Unknown', a subject which was beginning to intrigue Marshall at that time. Mozley's quotation from Marshall's letters of two sentences on this subject enable some of its flavour to be captured,

> I have come to the conclusion that the Unknown probably has concerns in which this world plays a part almost as insignificant as that played by a single small insect in the history of this minute world. . . . Every year my reverence to the unknown becomes deeper, my consciousness of the narrow limitations of all the knowledge in this world becomes more oppressive, and my desire to add to that quantity something that will count, though it is a microscopic fraction of that microscopic whole, becomes stronger.[12]

These remarks prompted Mozley to introduce the subject of God as the 'Unknown' into his letter, combined with remarks on the power of prayer, perhaps an explanation why Marshall failed to continue correspondence with this voice from his past. Mozley's letter also mentioned the fact that Marshall's political economy had preserved both strands of the Millian endeavour, 'the scientific side, . . . and the emotional and expansive side, in which it aims at improving human affairs', a polite reciprocation of interest in Marshall's work. Only towards the end of the letter did Mozley introduce matters of a more personal note. These concern an almost rhetorical inquiry whether Mrs Marshall knew his sister-in-law, Mrs Nutt, of Millington Road, Cambridge (a street not far from Newnham College), and promised to inquire about the Marshalls' nephew, through his son Kenneth, who appears to have been a clergyman.[13] Although their correspondence was not continued, Mozley was sufficiently interested when Keynes's Memoir was published, to send suggestions for minor corrections, which Keynes in fact incorporated in later versions.[14] Perhaps correspondence like this produced that flicker of regret which Mary Paley recorded when her husband lamented his inability of keeping up with the friends from his youth.[15]

Some further observations on these friendships are in order. Many appear to have received more encouragement from Mary Paley Marshall than from her husband, to whom such friendships initially belonged. Her recollections frequently preserved the very existence of these friendships and it was to her that in later years these former acquaintances, especially those from Bristol, tended to write.[16] Unlike her outgoing personality, so evident from her life after 1924, Alfred Marshall's isolated life as thinker and scholar tended to shun intimate friendships. He preferred to observe mankind from the distance, and mixed with it only directly in the immediate context of his work and professional interests. Even the more intimate relationships over the prolonged periods of his long lifetime with Sidgwick, Foxwell, Keynes and Jowett, appear to fall into this category to a surprising extent.

HENRY SIDGWICK: THE 'SPIRITUAL MOTHER AND FATHER' BETRAYED

When on 26 November 1900, some months after the death of Sidgwick, Marshall spoke at the official meeting organised by the university to consider a suitable memorial for its great son, he justified his claim to speak on this occasion by indicating he was

> in substance his pupil in Moral Sciences, and . . . the oldest of them in residence. I was fashioned by him. He was, so to speak, my spiritual father and mother: for I went to him for aid when perplexed, and for comfort when troubled; and I never returned empty away. The minutes that I spent with him were not ordinary minutes; they helped me to live. I had to pass through troubles and doubts somewhat similar to those which he, with broader knowledge and greater strength, had fought his way; and perhaps of all the people who have cause to be grateful to him none has more than I.[17]

Marshall's speech went on to mention his admiration for Sidgwick's strong moral principles on duties and responsibilities, stressed Sidgwick's attitude of trusteeship to his financial and other resources shared philanthropically for the good of others, and his remarkable work on political economy, the third Book on the Functions of Government of which was 'by common consent, far the best thing of its kind in any language'. As conclusion, Marshall recalled how, as part of a group of young students from a different college, he had nevertheless idolised Sidgwick for his reforming spirit, as the 'Captain of the whole school' and the leader of the young Reform Party in the university. ' [M]y first desire on every new question was to know how Sidgwick would vote and why. One voted confidently and cheerily when led by him; but doubtfully and anxiously when on the other side. For even when one could not follow him, one knew that his opinions were the embodiment of a great idea'.[18]

Stripped of some of the rhetoric expected of such occasions, Marshall's tribute nevertheless incorporates some essentials of the vagaries of his relationship with his slightly senior colleague and mentor in the moral sciences. These vagaries related to Marshall's perception of Sidgwick as a rival in writing a political economy text at the time Marshall had begun constructing his own, and as the university reformer with whom after 1885 he increasingly tended to disagree. Marshall's early encounters with Sidgwick were discussed previously.[19] It was surmised that Marshall more than likely first met Sidgwick through his membership of the Grote Club, to which Marshall himself had probably been introduced through Mozley, though he may have met him at Clifton as early as 1865. It was argued also that Sidgwick was instrumental in nurturing his interest in the moral sciences and for steering him towards the study of political economy to foster Marshall's understanding of material constraints in the drive towards human improvement which had initially inspired Marshall's interest in these sciences. Sidgwick likewise initially generated Marshall's involvement in various issues of university reform including that of syllabus, religious tests and the education of women. These early associations and influences from the decade

1867–77 frequently crossed Marshall's mind during the months intervening between the time he realised the serious nature of Sidgwick's final illness and Sidgwick's death.[20]

From its beginnings, however, there was the occasional critical tone in the relationship between the two men. As early as 1868, in his correspondence to the *Cambridge Gazette* on syllabus reform for the Previous Examination as proposed by Sidgwick, Marshall had departed from his friend's proposal in detail by arguing for greater opportunities to specialise in Latin at the expense of dropping compulsory Greek. He wholeheartedly endorsed Sidgwick's pleas for improved mathematical and scientific studies at this level.[21] Such minor disagreements, perhaps best interpreted as declarations of independence by the younger man, are also evident in the only letter between the two friends preserved from this period.[22] The more substantial part of this related to some disagreement over evolution and the ability of its consequences to impose limitations on Benthamism. For Marshall these arose from the need of utilitarianism to be supplemented by historical sociology and the requirement of dynamical conceptions for a philosophy of jurisprudence. The context of the letter reveals that Marshall had by then already begun his questioning of economic man as a vehicle of abstraction useful for social and moral analysis, from both the evolutionary and historical standpoint, partly under the influence of Marx and Hegel, from whose work he was learning during his period of historical work during the early 1870s. By 1871, Sidgwick had become less enamoured with such influences, and defended more traditional views of utilitarianism in his teaching and, more generally, for determining practical rules of politics.[*]

Given the lack of preserved correspondence, the relationship between Marshall and Sidgwick for much of this period needs to be reconstructed from other sources. Earlier chapters have recounted how in the first place the two would have met regularly in connection with their mutual membership of the Special Board of the Moral Sciences, sharing both its formal and more social aspects. Their involvement with organising women's education in Cambridge during the early 1870s likewise implied regular meetings between the two, including 'running' Tripos papers to women candidates at examination time and, more congenially, at social occasions such as the garden and other parties they frequented at Newnham and, more often, its predecessors in Regent Street and Merton Hall. Further social occasions for meeting came from mutual membership of discussion societies. These included the Grote Club in the late 1860s, and meetings of the Eranus Society during the 1870s. After Sidgwick's marriage, there were also occasional dinner parties at their house. These Marshall attended on at least one occasion, an event recorded by John Neville Keynes in his diary for 23 March 1877. As Marshall recalled in 1900, Sidgwick by then was still his mentor, adviser and aid, guiding his younger colleague and even, it was previously suggested, assisting him in 1872 by procuring for Marshall the opportunity to write his first book review for the *Academy*.[23]

---

[*] Marshall, it will be recalled, was at this stage lecturing on the utilitarianism of Bentham and Mill as part of his moral sciences teaching, possibly subjecting them to Comtist, Hegelian, and perhaps even Marx's, criticism. This teaching took place during what was described earlier as his historical period of the early 1870s (see above, Chapter 6, pp. 166–7; Chapter 9, pp. 268–9). For Marx on Bentham, which fits the context of Sidgwick's letter, see *Capital*, Vol. 1, Moscow Foreign Languages Publishing House, 1959, pp. 176 and esp. 609 n.1, where Marx stated, 'Had I the courage of my friend, Heinrich Heine, I should call Mr. Jeremy [Bentham] a genius in the way of bourgeois stupidity'. Barry Worrall, 'Alfred Marshall's Reading of Das Kapital', shows the footnote was marked by Marshall in his copy of the first edition.

In 1877, Marshall's acceptance of the position of Principal and Professor of Political Economy at Bristol University College, an appointment which Sidgwick had aided by his glowing testimonial praising Marshall's skills as a political economist, altered their relationship by the sheer force of geographical distance. However, from the evidence in contemporary correspondence with Foxwell, contact between Sidgwick and the Marshalls continued unabated during this period of exile from Cambridge. None of this correspondence has been preserved, and few letters between the two are extant. From the middle of 1878 Sidgwick was involved in reading the proofs of the *Economics of Industry*, making valuable suggestions for rearranging some of the material, in the context of which some disagreements between the two over aspects of economics started to surface.[*] Such minor disagreements turned into annoyance when some months later Marshall felt slighted by Sidgwick's reference to Jevons's unique solution to the indeterminacy problem in distribution once the wages fund theory was removed. This ignored, Marshall testily pointed out to Foxwell, his independent discovery of this solution at least half a decade previously. Before writing his review of Jevons, Marshall explained, he 'had been already in the habit of thinking of wages as the discounted value of produce'.[¶]

Quarrels over Sidgwick's views on economics worsened during the following months. By that time, Marshall had probably learned either from Foxwell or from another source[†] of Sidgwick's intentions to write a *Principles of Political Economy*. This created the potential threat of Sidgwick becoming a serious rival in Cambridge should Fawcett's chair fall vacant. In early 1878 Marshall had been speculating on the latter with Foxwell, seeing it as a potential escape route for him from Bristol. Marshall would have also fully realised that Birk's appointment to the Knightbridge chair removed effective promotion opportunities for Sidgwick apart from the other Moral Sciences chair for which he was eligible.[‡] Marshall subsequently blamed his debilitating illness, diagnosed in February 1879, for the ease with which he had he consented to Sidgwick's request to publish his material on domestic and international value, thereby giving Sidgwick access to his extensive unpublished manuscript

---

[*] Mary Paley Marshall to Foxwell, 10 October 1878 (Freeman Collection, 47/155), Marshall to Foxwell, 4 November 1878 (Freeman Collection, 35/155): 'I send you part of the proof of that chapter on rent which we have cut out of Book I on Sidgwick's advice . . . for what Sidgwick and you call monopoly value we treat along with market values. . . . I think Sidgwick's paper is admirably written, of course I agree with *almost* every word of it' (my emphasis in the quotation). Sidgwick had written a paper on Mr Mill's theory of value, distinguishing therein between scarcity and monopoly value, which is no longer extant. It was written for private circulation in a Cambridge discussion club he had formed, in which Foxwell among others was participating, and may have been preparation for the text on political economy he was then contemplating.

[¶] Marshall to Foxwell, 10 January 1879 (Freeman Collection, 44/155). The remark offensive to Marshall occurred in a paper on the wages fund Sidgwick had written, and of which an expanded version appeared in the *Fortnightly Review*, 26, September 1879, pp. 401–13, the offending passage occurring on p. 411.

[†] A.S. and E.M.S., *Henry Sidgwick. A Memoir*, p. 341. Foxwell was the likely source of this information, as suggested by Marshall to Foxwell, 10 January 1879 (Freeman Collection, 44/155): 'Thank you for your account of Sidgwick's club. I am always glad to hear what goes on there.' The club is the one mentioned in note * above. Its members may have been discussing the three papers on aspects of economics which Sidgwick published in the *Fortnightly Review* during 1879.

[‡] Marshall to Foxwell, 28 March 1878 (Freeman Collection, 40/155), and see above, Chapter 9, pp. 282-3. Sidgwick did not succeed Birks to the chair until 1883 having contested it unsuccessfully against Birks in 1872 when it had become vacant on Maurice's death. Marshall would have recalled Sidgwick's sense of disappointment on this occasion, which Sidgwick would have shared with him as he had done with others, describing Birks' election on one occasion as a 'catastrophe' (see E.S. and A.M.S., *Henry Sidgwick. A Memoir*, pp. 260–5).

on international trade. This became a source of considerable annoyance, particularly when Marshall realised from subsequent correspondence with Jevons and Edgeworth that his material had been more widely circulated than its ostensible 'private printing' for internal consumption in Cambridge.[24] Sidgwick's three essays on political economy which appeared in the *Fortnightly Review* in 1879 were therefore not kindly received by the exile in Bristol who, in writing to Foxwell, vented his irritation on the matter at least once: 'Of course I have spent part of the last ten years in considering the question raised in Sidgwick's article on method and have views more or less satisfactory on most of them. (I agree with him more than I do with most writers on the subject: but it does not seem to me that he has gone quite to the bottom of the subject.)'[25]

Another source of irritation with Sidgwick at this time, was his role as the bearer of bad news for which, in Marshall's view, he must share at least part of the blame. Marshall wrote to Foxwell in October 1879,

> Sidgwick writes that there are practically no Moral Sciences men. So I suppose it would not do for me to think of coming back as a Mo. Sci. lecturer. But in my last year at Cambridge I had a large class (22) more than half of which consisted of the best historical men. Do you think St John's would have me as a Historical Sciences lecturer with the understanding that I looked after the men generally and taught economic history, economics, and perhaps political philosophy including Bentham etc.[26]

It will be recalled that nothing came of this suggestion and that the Marshalls obtained refuge from Bristol by going to Europe for a year from October 1881. Earlier that year, Marshall had heard stories about the writing of Sidgwick's *Principles of Political Economy*, which caused some awkwardness with Foxwell and John Neville Keynes. Keynes recorded the following missive from Marshall in his diary entry for 9 February 1881:

> Foxwell says that you are helping Sidgwick with his economics book. Sidgwick and I differ on some questions of literary morality; for one thing we would not agree in a discussion as to the use he (not you) would be at liberty to make of your notes of my lectures: and on hearing that he had asked you to help him on his book I asked Foxwell to give you my views on the subject. I don't know whether he has had an opportunity of doing so.[*]

Sidgwick's *Principles* did in fact not appear until April 1883. Little is known of Marshall's initial reaction to the work, but he should have been pleased with the quite generous acknowledgement given of his work in its preface. This referred not only to the material on value Sidgwick had privately printed in 1879, but also to its source, the unpublished manuscript on foreign trade, and to the book published with Mary Paley Marshall, *Economics of Industry*.[¶] By the time it was published, more friendly correspondence

---

[*]   JNKD, 9 February 1881, the original is reserved in the Marshall Library (Marshall Archive, 1:75). Keynes added after the transcription of the letter: 'am immensely sorry for all that this implies. Personally, however, so far as I can remember, I have never shown Sidgwick any of what I regard as Marshall's most original work.' A month or so later, after Sidgwick had secured for Keynes the Secretaryship of the University Council, he wrote in his diary (30 March 1881): 'If I ever worship any human other than Florence [his wife], it will be Sidgwick'.

[¶]   Henry Sidgwick, *Principles of Political Economy*, London: Macmillan, 1883, preface, p. v and n.1; cf. Marshall, *Principles of Economics*, first edition,1890, preface p. xii and n. It may be mentioned here that Marshall wrote detailed comments in his copy of the second edition (1887) of Sidgwick's book, often noting therein differences

between the two had in any case resumed. As Keynes recorded in his diary in May, Sidgwick had been informed at an early stage of the Marshalls' move to Oxford, while it will be recalled that Sidgwick had also been pressing Marshall in 1883 to publish the lectures on *Progress and Poverty* he had given at Bristol. The Marshalls' residence in Oxford enabled further personal contact with Sidgwick. Sidgwick was in the habit of attending the Ad Eundem dinners there, held on a regular basis to foster better relations between the two English universities. Marshall also frequented these while in Oxford. Finally, Sidgwick's election in November 1883 to the Knightbridge chair of Moral Philosophy removed a serious rival for the Cambridge Political Economy chair were that to fall vacant, though Marshall's anxiety to return to his alma mater was considerably reduced now that Oxford had enabled him to leave hateful Bristol.[*]

Marshall's return to Cambridge in 1884 as elected successor to Fawcett marked the beginnings of a fifteen-year period of stormy relations between the two moral sciences professors, interspersed though it was with more peaceful interludes. Although Sidgwick had probably voted for Marshall in the chair selection committee,[27] a quarrel ensued between them on a number of matters when Marshall visited Cambridge a few days after his election to discuss his teaching responsibilities for the coming terms with Sidgwick as Chairman of the Moral Sciences Board. As shown previously,[28] this quarrel concerned appropriate teaching styles and professorial responsibilities, during which Marshall laid claims to authority as *the* Cambridge economist, against any pretensions Sidgwick may have entertained on the matter. However, after some heated correspondence and an equally warm personal encounter, Marshall could report to Foxwell before the week was out: 'So Sidgwick and I are at peace again. He is very good, in spite of his "regulating".'[29] Before two months had passed, they were at loggerheads again, this time over matters of course reform on which Marshall had outlined his intentions *ex cathedra* in his inaugural lecture.[30]

The substance of these quarrels on course reform, and those on the women's degree issue and women's rights in the university more generally, have been discussed already.[31] The friction this generated between Marshall and Sidgwick is fully captured in Keynes's Diary, which provides a running commentary on the degree of antagonism between his two friends in these early years of Marshall's return to Cambridge. 4 March 1885: 'Moral Science Board. I trust the present friction between Sidgwick and Marshall will wear off'. 19 April 1885: 'Called on Marshall and stayed with him for three hours.. . . The state of things between him and Sidgwick is really becoming very painful'. 11 May 1886: 'Moral

---

between that and the first edition. The first edition of his own *Principles*, while not ignoring Sidgwick's book, only referred to it on four occasions. There is a critical note to Sidgwick's treatment of the gains of trade as analysed by Mill and Ricardo (*MCC*, p. 328 n.). Marshall would have been pleased to have known that in their respective first year of publication, his *Principles* outsold Sidgwick's by a ratio of more than 2:1. JNKD, 29 April 1884 gives the first year sales figures for Sidgwick's book as 1,000; Macmillan, 'Marshall's Principles of Economics: A Bibliographical Note', p. 130, gives the 1890–91 sales figures for Marshall's *Principles* as 2,017.
[*] Marshall to Foxwell, 8 August 1883 (Marshall Archive, 3:20); JNKD, 1 May 1883, Marshall to Foxwell, 7 November 1883 (Marshall Archive, 3:23). Keynes noted in his diary on 3 November 1883, 'At last Sidgwick is in his proper place, having been elected to the Knightbridge Professorship'.

Sciences Board. The friction between Sidgwick and Marshall seems to be getting worse. I sympathise with the former. The latter is so narrow and egotistical.'*

Keynes's diary records no further quarrels between Marshall and Sidgwick until two years later when moral sciences syllabus reform to improve the position of political economy studies was once more on the agenda. On 8 May 1888, Marshall confessed to Keynes that his antagonism to Sidgwick was confined to a relatively narrow area: Sidgwick as the 'reforming "University politician" and to some extent as a writer on economics. . . . All the rest of Sidgwick I expect I think as highly of as you do.'¶ Given his evaluation in 1900 of what Sidgwick meant to him, this confession entailed a typical piece of Marshallian humbug. When the university reformer and the writings of economics were removed, what was left for Marshall to revere in Sidgwick was his memory of past services. Nevertheless, May 1888 was heated at the Moral Sciences Board. A week later after a meeting on 15 May, Keynes recorded in his diary, how 'painful to other members of the board . . . the form of the conflict of opinion between Sidgwick and Marshall is'. Ten days later, his diary recorded with relief that contested matters had been postponed until the start of the 1888–89 academic year.[32] The quarrelling then resumed in full force until, to Keynes's surprise, a Sidgwick compromise offer to force a solution was accepted by Marshall, so that the resolutions incorporating the changes were passed the following year.[33]

During the two years of peace on the Moral Sciences Board, reflected in the silences on Marshall–Sidgwick quarrels in Keynes's diary for much of the 1886–87 and 1887–88 academic years, a battle between the two friends erupted on another front. A letter from Marshall in 1887 informed Sidgwick that Marshall himself did not want a mixed university at Cambridge. It also informed Sidgwick that both Marshall and his wife believed re-opening the women's degree question in Cambridge at this stage was premature, Marshall adding it also raised issues quite separate from that of women as candidates for degree examinations for him, because the former raised the question of women's membership rights in the university.[34] Marshall's 1887 views were consistent with the change of heart he had on the matter while at Bristol, and differed from what Sidgwick expected from his earlier experience with Marshall on women's education at Cambridge during the early 1870s. Before their more substantial disagreements over the women's issue, that is, over the appointment of women extension lecturers to mixed classes which lasted from 1892 to 1894 and the reconsideration of the women's degree question in 1896–97, there were other rifts between the two. For example, in April 1890, Keynes noted with some incredulity a report

---

*   JNKD, entries for dates indicated in text. Marshall wrote to Foxwell on 29 May 1886 (Freeman Collection): 'Sidgwick came to me after last Board meeting and spoke thusly: "If you and Foxwell think that the Advanced P.E. papers would be improved by having the history of early economic theory and the history of early economic facts taken out of it and put into early Pol:Phil: I will consent: though I am not anxious for the change".'

¶   JNKD, 8 May 1888. Keynes made few references to Marshall's disagreements over Sidgwick's economics in this period. An entry in the Keynes diary for 6 February 1885 mentions that Keynes debated Sidgwick's theory of international trade with Marshall, 'He says he cannot see anything in the theory, and I have been trying to make clear my version of it.' On 18 March 1891 Marshall queried the suitability of Sidgwick's Book III of his *Principles of Political Economy* for the pass students (Marshall to John Neville Keynes, 18 March 1891, Marshall Archive, 1:101). However, by 1902 Marshall described part of Sidgwick's economics 'as quite off the rails' (Marshall to Edgeworth, 28 August 1902, in *Memorials*, p. 435).

by Ward that Marshall and Sidgwick had openly quarrelled. The occasion was probably the university debate over new regulations for the Previous Examinations.[35]

It should be noted that criticism of each other was by then mutual and did not only originate with Marshall. As evidence of Sidgwick's tendency to 'regulate' in the early years after Marshall's return to Cambridge as Professor, a letter to Foxwell shows that on the basis of his perusal of the political economy papers, Sidgwick queried whether the 'men are actually taught' the 'statistical verification' and suggestions of economic 'uniformities' contained therein, and what sort of reading was prescribed on these subjects.[36] A couple of years later Marshall complained to Foxwell that Sidgwick was pressuring him to take his place on the Toynbee Trust, an honour he could well do without, given his other commitments at the time, and which he passed to Foxwell instead.[37] Despite Keynes's admiration for Sidgwick, he recorded another painful quarrel on the Moral Sciences Board between Sidgwick and Marshall in 1894 for which, in this case, he blamed Sidgwick rather than Marshall.[38]

There were also happier occasions in the relationship between the two professorial colleagues during this period. Keynes's Diary records a number of dinner parties at Balliol Croft during the first half of the 1890s in the presence of Sidgwick, often to meet visiting American economists such as Dunbar or Taussig, or for more general purposes.[39] Personal relations between the two were likewise sufficiently good for discussions to take place between the four economics members of the Board (Marshall, Sidgwick, Keynes and Foxwell) to sort out potential problems prior to formal Board meetings.[40] Marshall could also show himself sensitive to Sidgwick's feelings on occasions when their relationship showed brittleness from previous altercations. On one such occasion, when Sidgwick was already incensed with him over women, Marshall had tried his hardest not to 'intensify and perpetuate the conflict' at what he described as the considerable personal cost of not advancing the resolution of his preference.[41] He was also happy enough to give Sidgwick precedence in choice of lecture hours, perhaps more a sign of his respect for the seniority of the Knightbridge chair than for its then incumbent.[42]

By the second half of the 1890s, that is, for the final half dozen years of Sidgwick's life, the situation between them deteriorated sharply. As shown previously, the major issue which made the final break inevitable was over the women's degree question.[43] These problems were compounded by some further debate associated with Tripos syllabus reform in 1897, as a result of which the two seem to have effectively disappeared from each other's lives in so far as that was possible. By the time of Sidgwick's final illness, Marshall's rejection of his erstwhile 'spiritual mother and father' was complete. Marshall's last letter to Sidgwick effectively summarises the early friendship and its more recent ending, hinting at his desire for a death-bed reconciliation:

I thought you were weary and in need of rest when you came here a few days ago: but I had no notion you were ill. Mary told me yesterday that you needed surgical aid; and Maitland has just sent me a sad note. The cross currents of University Policy have recently made some distance between us. But I should like to tell you now that the feeling of admiration and affection with which I regarded you, the nearest realisation of my dreams of goodness and true heroism during my earlier life at Cambridge, have never died out. You have never ceased to be to me a unique and great life, a very large part of the University ...[44]

Sidgwick's reply was 'most kind and generous' when it came a few days later, as the Marshalls were about to start for the Tirol for their usual summer vacation.[45] By the time they returned, Sidgwick had died (18 August). On 7 October 1900, Marshall sent a small photograph of Sidgwick to his wife, with the words, 'I send a royal face to where it should be'.[46] However Sidgwick's ghost was not easily exorcised from Marshall's life, nor did the university and wider social sciences community readily forgive him for his treatment of Sidgwick over the last decade of his life.[*] Showing considerable tact, Edgeworth offered the task of writing Sidgwick's obituary for the *Economic Journal* to John Neville Keynes, who fulfilled it with elegance and style.[¶] Marshall's desires for a Cambridge economics in his own image, together with a dogged adherence to other 'principles', was a major force destructive of their old friendship. Moreover, Marshall's return to Cambridge in 1885 on an equal footing as his former mentor, may have brought latent jealousies and rivalries to the fore, which Marshall could indulge much more easily in his newly won position of authority as Professor of Political Economy. By then, Sidgwick was no longer needed in the manner Marshall relied on him in his first decade as graduate at Cambridge, permitting Marshall to trample on Sidgwick's feelings in pursuit of his own ambitions with respect to economics.

HERBERT SOMERTON FOXWELL: A LOYAL, BUT ILL-USED, COLLEAGUE AND FRIEND

Seven years Marshall's junior, Foxwell commenced studies for the Moral Sciences Tripos at Cambridge as a St John's student in 1868, after graduating that year as a London B.A. This was the year Marshall had started his duties as St John's College Lecturer in the Moral Sciences, thereby making Foxwell one of Marshall's first students in his chosen field of endeavour. The few recollections of Marshall's lectures in these early years are therefore largely from Foxwell's pen.[47] In December 1870, Foxwell was ranked Senior Moralist in the Tripos; in 1874 St John's elected him one of its Fellows, following this a year later with appointing him to a Lectureship in the Moral Sciences. For the greater part of his life as Fellow, including the early years of Marshall's fellowship until 1877, Foxwell and Marshall had rooms opposite each other in New Court. Their first correspondence dates from the period circa 1873. It started with some 'fatherly advice' from Bonney via Marshall. This queried the advisability of Foxwell absenting himself for a term from the college to go north for the purpose of extension lecturing when his fellowship had not been decided.[48] A

---

* Examples are Marshall to Foxwell, 28 May 1901 (Freeman Collection, 9/217) in which Marshall apologetically defended his practice of ranking candidates for selection to academic positions against that of Sidgwick; Marshall to John Neville Keynes, 22 September 1900 in connection with choosing Sidgwick's successor as chairman of the Moral Sciences Board: 'I am anxious that nothing disagreeable should happen just now' and 3 November 1900: 'I hope you will keep the Knightbridge Professor's lectures at the head of the list' (Marshall Archive, 1:119–120); cf. the reaction in JNKD, 26 September 1900: 'Marshall has given way and Ward will now be elected'. Marshall's use of Sidgwick's name in his final campaign for the separate Economics Tripos was discussed previously, Chapter 15 above, p. 543 and n*.

¶ JNKD, 17 September 1900; he declined the task initially and had to be re-invited the following month when he accepted (*ibid.*, 1 October 1900). The obituary appeared in *Economic Journal*, 10 (40), December 1900, pp. 585–91. It was most deservedly admired by W.E. Johnson, by James Ward and by others (JNKD, 30 October, 21 and 24 November 1900). Edgeworth compared Keynes's effort favourably with Marshall's obituary of Jowett and asked him to write more on Sidgwick (Edgeworth to Keynes, October 1900, Marshall Library, Keynes 1:12–13).

stream of correspondence between the two followed, resulting eventually in the greatest number of Marshall letters to any one person which have been preserved. This correspondence abruptly ended in May 1908 when Marshall supported Pigou rather than Foxwell as his successor to the Political Economy chair.[49]

The early letters of this budding friendship reveal an easy and close relationship between the two young academics. Those from 1874 and 1875 touch on both academic and more personal matters. With very few exceptions, letters to Foxwell contain the only references to his own family which Marshall permitted in correspondence. A letter on August 1874 commented on holidays in Switzerland, mentioned Marshall's wish to visit Geneva, 'the mother of the two strongest enthusiasms the world has seen since Catholicism degenerated from a faith into a creed', and remarked on Foxwell's experiences as extension lecturer that year.[50] In January 1875 Marshall advised his colleague on Tripos books, with special reference to works on cooperation, communism and Owen ('Shäffle the best') and they reported on his mother's recovery from illness, in which Marshall had assisted by exercising his nursing skills, foregoing sleep and making him exceedingly tired. The second of these letters also indicated the friends were in the habit of exchanging jokes. On this occasion, Marshall's inability at thinking up his own jokes given the circumstances of his mother's illness, made him include some from a person he described as 'England's greatest humorist'. The enclosures in question were extracts from an evangelical tract, a source of jokes in abundant supply in his parental household, given his father's religious preferences.[51] Two further letters of 1875 commented on aspects of the Tripos book list. The topics in question were stock broking and joint-stock banking, on which Marshall advised his knowledge was confined to what he had learnt from Bagehot's *Lombard Street*. The second of these letters also contains one of the few personal comments on his religious beliefs to be found in Marshall correspondence, a sign of the intimacy of his relationship with Foxwell,

> It seems to me that Lightfoot gains many victories on small points, but the matter does not excite me. A little while ago, shortly before S.R. was published, I got excited about it: and I became so *absolutely* convinced that Christ neither believed nor taught any of the leading dogmas of Christianity that I now look upon the fray with the languid interest of a mere spectator.[*]

The next two years were virtually devoid of correspondence. Proximity of their college rooms removed a need for this type of communication. Correspondence, however, resumed after the Marshalls' marriage on 17 August 1877, necessitated by Marshall's consequent move to Bristol. As Foxwell informed John Neville Keynes a few days before the marriage took place, this meant he would take over from Marshall responsibility for the political economy lectures in the Tripos.[¶]

---

[*] Marshall to Foxwell, 7 February 1875 (Freeman Collection, 14/229); 9 April 1875 (Freeman Collection, 15/129). The Lightfoot mentioned was Bishop J.B. Lightfoot, Hulsean Professor of Divinity at Cambridge from 1861 to 1879. The reference is to his *Essays on Supernatural Religion*, which had appeared in the *Contemporary Review* over late 1874, early 1875, and which replied to W.R. Cassels, a Bombay merchant, on *Supernatural Religion: An Inquiry into the Reality of Divine Revelation*, which had been published anonymously in May 1874.

[¶] Foxwell to John Neville Keynes, 11 August 1877 (Marshall Archive, Keynes Papers, 1:16). The letter suggests that Foxwell was one of the few Cambridge persons whom Marshall had trusted with the precise date and place of

Marshall's departure for Bristol provided the opportunity for a special gift to friend Foxwell: 'I send you my rosewood reading desk. I love it too much to sell it and I cannot use it at Bristol. You once praised it, so you may learn to love it.' (This sentiment was endorsed by the new bride, with the words 'read and approved'.)[52]

The flow of Foxwell correspondence over the next few years discussed progress on the *Economics of Industry*, advised on books and reading to assist Foxwell's preparation for his enhanced teaching responsibilities, and later weighed up a series of alternative strategies for leaving Bristol.[53] They also provided the Marshalls with Cambridge gossip. In addition, they contain much material of a more personal nature, signifying the closeness of the friendship. For example, a P.S. to one letter, mentioned a piano the Marshalls wished to purchase. This expressed a colour preference for its case, confirming Marshall's taste for darker colours, especially things rosewood.[54] Three months later, a P.S. from Mary Paley Marshall expressed thanks to Foxwell for his contribution to the St John's farewell gift to the couple, a pair of pictures by Walton, and a pleasure to look at as well as a charming reminder of their friends.[55] Sorrows were likewise shared by the correspondents. Marshall informed Foxwell of his mother's death in 1878 and reciprocated condolences on Foxwell's family bereavements during that year and early in the next.[56] Foxwell subsequently shared in the details of Marshall's illness from 1879 in a way few others did and, seemingly alone among their Cambridge friends, visited them occasionally in Bristol.[57]

The Marshalls' actual departure from Bristol showed further signs of the intimacy of their friendship with Foxwell and the generosity with which the sentiment was returned by their friend. Correspondence between Foxwell and the then Master of St John's College, Taylor, demonstrated Foxwell's willingness to make sacrifices on his friend's behalf to facilitate departure from Bristol. The first of these letters suggested a scheme by which the college would pay Marshall half of Foxwell's own lecturer's salary for which in return Marshall would share with him the very limited moral sciences teaching. The second letter revealed Foxwell's concern over the Marshalls' finances in 1881, given the collection which raised well over £100 from Marshall's former Bristol students. This had been prudently, and confidentially, handed to Mary Paley Marshall to assist financing what was at that stage still planned as an indefinite period of retirement on the continent.[58] It is also characteristic that the one detailed Marshall letter from Palermo on their life there which has been preserved, is written to Foxwell.[59]

When the Marshalls returned to England in the autumn of 1882, first to resume their teaching positions for a year at Bristol, then for their four-term stint at Oxford, correspondence with Foxwell resumed at full strength. Once again, they were exchanging academic advice as well as gossip and news from their respective environments. Early segments of the 1883 correspondence reveal the beginnings of Foxwell's penchant for book collecting, which by then had started in earnest. An amusing incident, demonstrating Marshall's naivety in the matter of rare books, relates to his request on behalf of his wife for Foxwell's spare copy of Cantillon's *Essai*, then only recently 'rediscovered' by Jevons. The

---

his wedding, something of which John Neville Keynes, at this stage a much lesser intimate of Marshall, had not been informed.

following explains the background and Marshall's response to what must have been Foxwell's panic-stricken reaction to the initial request:

> Don't vex yourself about Cantillon. I should not read it myself just now, if I had it. It is altogether outside my present line of work. Only Mary is going in for the History of Economic Theory and was fascinated by what Jevons said of him. If we come to Cambridge at Easter, no doubt she will borrow it and read some of it. On no account send it by railway. When I wrote I did not know the book was so precious, though now I think of it, I ought to have known.*

Earlier letters on this subject mention rare books which Marshall was interested in: these include Eden's *State of the Poor*, which he had ordered from Meggs, the rare book sellers, an order he had subsequently cancelled; Malthus's *Definitions of Political Economy*, and Hamilton on the Public Debt.[60]

Much of the contents of this phase in their correspondence was mentioned in the context of Marshall's lectures on *Progress and Poverty*, Toynbee's death and the prospects of succeeding him at Oxford, and his teaching and associated activities there.[61] Of special interest here are its more human touches. A visit by Foxwell in January is implied in the message, 'We forgot to give you your Sicilian plate when you were here', an indication that Foxwell was among those remembered when the Marshalls purchased momentos for their friends in Palermo the previous winter.[62] More interesting is Marshall's advice to Foxwell in his role as editor of Jevons's 'Investigations into Currency and Finance', a task which occupied him much longer than had originally been anticipated by Jevons's widow. Marshall's advice specifically addressed the issue of updating Jevons's statistics and the dangers of reproducing some of his results when these departed from more accessible price data (albeit for other commodities) from the *Economist*.[63] Marshall returned to this subject in his last letter to Foxwell, when he was preparing the chapters on index numbers for his *Money, Credit and Commerce* in March 1920, during which,

> I have referred to the first edition of Jevons *Investigations* – a most wonderful book which is not known as it should be. On its p. 130 (p. 122 of Ed. II), I find a pencil comment: – 'The foot-note seems out of place: it seems to belong to an earlier page'. Also on p. 129 the reference to an extraordinary rise in prices between 1833 and 1843 is difficult. I think perhaps 1843 is a misprint for 1840. I trouble you with this, because I think I may claim to be, after you, the most ardent worshipper of Jevons still living . . . and yet once, Cairnes was more in repute than Jevons.¶

Despite the flattering, implicitly conciliatory and almost grovelling tone of Marshall's letter, Foxwell followed Marshall's advice written across the top of this first letter from his former

---

* Marshall to Foxwell, a postcard post-marked 9 February 1883 (Marshall Library, Foxwell 1:32). Jevons's article, 'Richard Cantillon and the Nationality of Political Economy', had appeared in the *Contemporary Review*, 39, January 1881, pp. 20–27; Marshall purchased his own copy of the book in 1889 for the princely sum of £7, or 20 per cent of his 1885 estimate of the per capita income which would result from complete income equalisation in Britain (above, Chapter 16, p. 598 n.*). Marshall's copy of Cantillon is preserved in CUL (Marshall d.37).

¶ Marshall to Foxwell, 13 March 1920 (Freeman Collection 19/42). In this context, *MCC*, p 27 n. and 29 n. refer to Jevons's pioneering work on index numbers, the second reference specifically mentioning Investigations in *Currency and Finance*, Marshall's remark in the letter just quoted about the peculiarity of situating the note on p. 130 seems justified.

friend since 1908, by not troubling himself to give an answer. As shown previously, even two years later Foxwell was still bitter enough about Marshall's shabby treatment of his candidature for the chair in 1908 to refuse his signature to the message of good wishes presented by the Royal Economic Society on the occasion of Marshall's eightieth birthday.[64]

In line with the adage that absence makes the heart grow fonder, the first signs of such rifts in the long-standing friendship did not really begin until Marshall's return to Cambridge as the professor responsible for its political economy courses. It may be recalled that principle was strong enough on Marshall's part after Fawcett's death for Marshall to urge Foxwell and Nicholson to contest the vacancy, perhaps safe in the knowledge that both had been recently 'chaired' respectively in London and Edinburgh. Foxwell, on this occasion a member of the selection committee, was certainly a vote in favour of Marshall,[65] a decision he never publicly affirmed or disowned, but the import of which he telegraphed to Marshall in Oxford the moment he was able to do so. Even then, it still took some time before disagreements publicly surfaced on the side of either party and, it should be said, in neither case did controversy between them result in breaking off friendly, or social, relations. There was also an openness between them which permitted good-natured criticism.[*]

Some of these altercations occurred in the matter of selecting Tripos books in economics. In 1881, Foxwell had criticised *Economics of Industry* to Keynes as being too difficult and therefore unpopular with the pass students; in 1890 he expressed a preference for Marshall's *Principles*, then not yet published, over elementary primers such as that by Jevons, indicating he had expressed a compromise preference to 'Professor Marshall' for Walker's *First Lessons in Political Economy*, which had appeared in 1889.[66] There were many other altercations between them over choosing appropriate Tripos books, a task both of them took very seriously. Real difficulties over this issue, however, did not arise until much later. The first major doctrinal rift between the two concerned bimetallism, if Marshall's earlier criticism of Foxwell's tendency to dismiss the importance of Ricardo and Mill is ignored.[¶] Foxwell's unsuccessful attempts to get Marshall to sign a petition in support of bimetallism were reported earlier, as were other exchanges between them on this subject involving Giffen[†] while Marshall in later years occasionally brought this older bone of contention back into his correspondence with Foxwell as well as with others.[67]   On

---

* 'If the Goddess of Truth had touched me with her want and said – enumerate the chief virtues and defects of H.S.F.'s teaching, I should have put on the short list on the bad side: Too great a delight in questions that have lost reality: something of a neglect of real problems, especially on their statistical side.' (Marshall to Foxwell, 27 November 1895, Freeman Collection, 13/228). Cf. above, Chapter 13, p. 472, Chapter 15, p. 537 for more serious manifestations of this type of difference of opinion.

¶ Marshall to Foxwell, undated (possibly March 1893, 1894) Freeman Collection, 3/224; Marshall to Foxwell, 22 July 1883 (Marshall Library, Foxwell 1:42), and earlier, Mary Paley Marshall, 25 September 1878: 'Alfred is very glad you are beginning to like the worthy Ricardo. He always seems to me to be the backbone of the science.' (Freeman Collection, 39/155) and Foxwell to John Neville Keynes, 25 January 1892 'I disagree profoundly with Marshall on many points, especially in regard to Ricardo, Mill, economic method, and consumption' (Marshall Library, Keynes, 2:101).

† Above, Chapter 11, pp. 351–2; also Marshall to Foxwell, 27 January 1895 (Freeman Collection, 23/104) and JNKD, 24 April 1894; 'called on Marshall . . . who is having a wrangle with Foxwell over bimetallism and appealed to me to arbitrate'.

Foxwell's account, they also tended to disagree on political questions but the nature of these differences of opinion is not clear.[68]

In general, however, Foxwell continued to act as Marshall's dutiful ally. Examples are their cooperation on the formation of the Royal Economic Society, and in connection with issues associated with the women's university question during the 1890s.[69] Much of this assistance arose from Foxwell's sense of loyalty and respect for his Professor, the last in part directed at the authority of the chair and the responsibilities for the subject this entailed. After a rather critical dissection of the book list for the Tripos in 1890, Foxwell explained to Keynes, 'I give my opinions as requested, but I should certainly not wish to press them against those of Professor Marshall, who is responsible for the subject in the University'.[70]

With the passing of the 1890s this loyalty and sense of duty started to wear a little thin. For example, in the context of a meeting date Marshall wanted to fix in connection with Moral Sciences Board business, Foxwell wrote to Keynes, 'I should have thought my engagements were to Marshall's in the proportion of 5:1. But if he cannot change his hour, perhaps I had better: as I cannot possibly change the day.'[71] In 1897, when course reform was discussed at the Moral Sciences Board, Keynes noted in his diary, 'Marshall generally represents Foxwell as agreeing with him, but when we have them both together, they seldom agree.'[72] The substantial number of letters on these matters which flowed between Foxwell and Marshall at this time indicate the nature and extent of such disagreements. They dealt with the arrangements for the examination of Part I of the Tripos as well as with the description of the syllabus. Some of the letters revealed misunderstandings of the regulations on Marshall's part for which he was big enough to apologise, others gave copious explanations of the minutiae of Marshall's position.[73] The issue antagonised both Keynes, who bitterly complained about Marshall's time-wasting at the Board meetings, rejoicing at the speed of the proceedings in his absence[74] and Foxwell, who clearly expressed his ambiguous feelings about his 'chief' in a letter to Keynes at the time:

> I believe I generally agree with the core of Marshall's thought and opinion, except on politics, but I almost invariably disagree with his emphasis. I do not think his sense of proportion good; and I believe he is led astray by an irresistible inclination to paradox, very characteristic of the smart–intellectual set, Clifford, Moulton, etc – among whom he mixed in his younger days: . . . Still, he is an excellent fellow, most able, honourable and kindly, whom I for one am proud to have as my chief here. Even his weaknesses are amiable.[75]

That amiability on Marshall's part and the loyalty it generated in Foxwell came to the fore again on several occasions at the turn of the century. The former is visible in the advice and strong support Marshall was willing to give his friend in the recurring crises over Foxwell's library, resolved for the first time in the middle of 1901 by intervention of the Royal Economic Society. The latter is visible in Foxwell's staunch assistance, despite opposition to its detail, in securing Marshall's long-desired Economics Tripos.

Foxwell's proclivities in book collecting were mentioned earlier. By the late 1880s, they were rising to gigantic proportions. Keynes' diary recorded with awe in December 1887 that Foxwell had spent £2,000 on his library. Foxwell therefore lived up to the full to his motto imparted to Maynard Keynes decades later: 'I have often regretted *not* buying a book, but have *never* regretted buying one'. Such sentiments were not matched by his income, which Maynard Keynes on the same occasion estimated as never to have reached £1,000 annually.[76] Overdrafts from his bank financed the deficit and when in 1897 these had grown so large and the library was under threat of having to be disposed of, Marshall offered frank, and what he considered, very impertinent advice, in order to save both the library for Foxwell and Foxwell from himself. This entailed settling the library on Foxwell's wife, lowering his rate of acquisition, and repaying the bank by writing for newspapers, a step which went against all of Marshall's inclinations,[77] because it pandered to journalists, a set of persons Marshall intensely disliked.[78]

Marshall's advice seems not to have been followed, because during 1901 Foxwell's financial crisis was back in full force, as Marshall wrote to Keynes at the start of that year. Marshall's remark on sacrificing his chair for Foxwell in this context, had it been financially possible for him, was mentioned previously.[79] His more credible request to Keynes was to investigate the possibilities of the university finding Foxwell a personal Readership. Marshall's fears of losing Foxwell to Birmingham on this occasion did, however, not prevent him from writing a glowing testimonial in support of his friend, thereby reinforcing a feeling that Marshall was less than serious about making this sacrifice for Foxwell.[80] In the end, the matter came to nothing: by May 1901 the Worshipful Goldsmiths' Company offered to purchase Foxwell's library on behalf of London University, keeping it intact as an important collection and providing funds for additions as, and when, the oportunity arose.[81]

Foxwell's support for Marshall's moves in establishing the new Economics Tripos during 1902–3 has already been discussed, as have some of Marshall's disagreements with Foxwell during the early years of the twentieth century prior to his retirement. The last included Foxwell's disagreement with Marshall over the appointment of Pigou as economics lecturer,[*] Foxwell's 'paranoia' about attacks on him by Marshall over lecture clashes at

---

[*] This brought on general complaints from Marshall about Foxwell in a frank exchange of views (Marshall to Foxwell, 14 May 1901, Freeman Collection):

> I am distressed at your returning to the position of hostility to my attempt to get time for advanced lectures and for study. I thought you had been in a great measure convinced by the long and weary explanations, which I gave you some time ago, partly in writing and partly in conversation. But I will go over the ground again.
>   When I returned to Cambridge in 1885, I proposed to lecture exclusively to students who had either attended your lectures (or someone else's) or had learnt in the study of mathematics, or elsewhere, how to go to the root of the matter. But I was soon met by two difficulties: your lectures did not cover the ground of a 'general course'; and as no papers were set in them, students did not get to learn their own weakness, and I had often to begin from the beginning. So I went to you and asked you if you would make your elementary course cover the whole subject, and set papers in connection with it. You raised two objections: you were busy in London and with your books, and had no time to look over papers; and being yourself, no longer a very young man, you did not care to take the position of preparing men for my (as well as your own) advanced lectures. I admitted the force of the latter objection: and proposed that in alternate years you should give a systematic advanced course; and that I should do the same, taking of course the elementary course when you took the advanced, and vice versa. You said the college would object – I forget the exact reason you gave; I recollect only that I thought the college would have cordially approved.
>   So I, with very small power of work, had for many years to do *the whole* of the drudgery side of economic teaching. I believe there has never been anyone, as old as I, who has had to do the whole of the drudgery for so large a subject. The women's papers were the worst, because the longest though almost all of them had been to Mary's lectures before coming to me. Sometimes after looking over papers for two days consecutively, morning and afternoon, I felt so sick in body and mind that I could hardly hold myself up.

times when the Moral Sciences lecture timetable was settled for new academic years; Foxwell's letter to the *Times* in 1903 criticising the free trade manifesto signed by Marshall and eleven other economics teachers, and matters associated with Foxwell's lecturing style and type of lectures offered during the early years of the new Tripos.[82] The last of these issues, demonstrating Marshall's growing worries of the appropriateness of Foxwell's old-fashioned economics for the students of his new Tripos, together with the financial implications for its teaching resources were Foxwell to be elected to the chair on his retirement, were probably decisive when by 1906 Marshall decided to throw his support behind the young Pigou rather than the almost sixty-year old Foxwell as the more suitable leader for his new Cambridge School of Economics.[83]

The blow to Foxwell of this rejection was all the greater because as the years wore on he had become increasingly conscious of the sacrifices required from him in his support for Marshall. Two letters by Foxwell to Keynes, one before, and one well after the election of Marshall's successor, clearly express this growing awareness:

Many thanks for the trouble you have taken. I did not expect much success with Marshall: his arrangements are always the best possible and the results of infinite calculation! . . . However, I always say the professor ought to be the head of the school, and control the arrangements. I do not believe in Committee government. Therefore I raise no objection.[84]

I return Marshall's note. It has an unpleasantly false ring about it . . . I have no doubt that he is glad now, as he always has been, that others should help in work that he despises and neglects, I mean in providing for the poll men, for examinations, and in correspondence with the outside world. But for the people who thus oblige I believe he has in his inner feeling a very honest contempt: and in any rate he has

---

Twice more I went to you and implored you to lift some of this work from my shoulders; twice you refused, and the second time in words that hurt me so that I decided never to ask anything of the kind again. As to your advanced lectures: – you told me that the subjects on which you had elected to lecture suited you. You had chosen them before I returned: and would adhere to them. You did not ask whether I would have liked any other division. But I did not complain. I simply avoided going into detail on those subjects on which I knew you were lecturing at length. This did not seriously inconvenience me: but I had to tell my women students, who were not admitted to your lectures, that they must read some things, especially the History of Banking for themselves. I thus did everything I possibly could to make the machine work smoothly . . . [After using McTaggart and Clapham for assessing his students' essays, Marshall decided to use Pigou since Clapham had too much of a historical mind.]

At that time I understood that your books were going to London, that you wd follow, and that I should be left without any assistance. So I sounded Pigou tentatively; and, finding him not averse, I brought the matter before the Mo. Sc. Board. All agreed that the plan was excellent, and definitely approved it. (I do not know whether an entry was made on the minutes of not.) After that had been done, I made a contract with Pigou to pay him £100 for the delivery of lectures in 1900–1, on condition that he should not undertake anything in the intervening year which would interfere with his preparing himself for his work. He has acted on this.

Later in the next October Term I heard to my surprise that you had at last begun to set papers yourself. Had I known that you would do that, and had I been sure that you would stay in Cambridge, I should perhaps have applied to the Board for leave to cease my General Lectures, without providing a substitute. Perhaps I might have asked Pigou to prepare himself to give a course on International Trade and Government, two subjects which you entirely omit.

I am therefore much pained by your saying 'Pigou's appointment is of course a direct attack on my lectures, but it is a bread and butter question with me, and I am bound to fight it out: so that it is as well that the issue should be joined from the first'. For as I told you a year ago I put on Pigou solely to do that which I had three times implored you to do.

Marshall also raised the matter in letters to J.N. Keynes, 22 May 1901, and tried to patch up the quarrel with Foxwell on 25 May 1901.

left me in no sort of doubt as to the value he sets on any service it is in my power to render. However, his opinion doesn't affect me in one way or the other. I do not think judgement his strong point.[85]

The difference in tone between these two letters reflects the bitterness generated between the two men over Pigou's election to the chair. In the months immediately after the election, that dislike appears to have become mutual, as evident in Marshall's correspondence with Keynes and Higgs in December 1908 over the possibility of creating a personal chair for Foxwell at Cambridge by a subscription organised through the Royal Economic Society. Surviving correspondence reveals not only Marshall's initial involvement in this scheme, but also that six months later, the election of Pigou rather than Foxwell was still a sore point in the relevant economic circles. On 5 December Marshall wrote to Keynes,

> Just after I left you, I recollected that the saying 'if x is not elected, it must be a party job' was not spoken to my wife; but to a very responsible lady not especially interested in the issue, who met my wife shortly afterwards, and told it to her with scorn. My wife confirms this.[86]

A week later Marshall wrote again to Keynes criticising Foxwell for his bad judgement on financial matters and his retirement from Cambridge teaching. Given Foxwell's views on Marshall's judgement, this was a perfect case of the pot calling the kettle black. However, more serious accusations followed, the first distorting reality in order to enable Marshall's withdrawal from supporting Higgs's proposal to raise funds for Foxwell's chair.

> Foxwell wrote me in June[87] declaiming against electors who set aside the cause of friendship. I shuddered. I did not answer; but that was the forerunner of trouble. Even if Foxwell were still in his prime, I should hesitate to put him on the same intellectual level with Clapham [if a second professorship in economics became available]. I now leave the matter in your hands. For the sake of Auld Lang Syne, I will stretch my academic conscience as far as it will go. But it has a stiff neck. It may be well that you should have learnt at an early stage how far my benevolent neutrality towards Higgs' proposal is likely to reach. I am clear that I cannot actively support it in its present form.[88]

Earlier Marshall must have spoken more warmly to Higgs of the proposal since Higgs wrote to Keynes on 14 December, 'Marshall has spoken to you on the subject of a proposal to raise a fund for the endowment for a chair for Foxwell at Cambridge. Would you mind telling me whether a guarantee would be sufficient or whether the University would require cash down? My idea would be to obtain, if possible, guarantees of £700 a year for 7 years.'[89] An undated letter from Marshall to Keynes indicates how stiff Marshall's 'academic conscience' turned out to be. It informed Keynes in no uncertain terms that in his view a second chair for Foxwell would set an 'undesirable precedent'.[90]

No wonder the formerly warm friendship was never re-kindled. Marshall's unsuccessful atempts at this, including his futile attempt in 1920 in his letter about Foxwell's edition of Jevons's *Investigations on Currency and Finance*, have already been mentioned.[91] A complimentary copy of *Money, Credit and Commerce* in 1923, did, however, elicit Foxwell's formal acknowledgement. Close as this was to Marshall's ultimate deathbed, this was not the type of reconciliation which Marshall had secured from Sidgwick just before his death. By 1908 Foxwell clearly had had enough of his former friend's principles and the cost they imposed on him. The last word can be left with Foxwell's daughter, who succinctly summarised the post-1884 evolution of the Marshall-Foxwell friendship in the reminiscences she wrote about her father:

> In 1884 Alfred Marshall returned to Cambridge as Professor of Political Economy in succession to Henry Fawcett, his election receiving the eager support of H.S. Foxwell. Marshall's work he greatly admired: it had a mathematical foundation without being submerged therein, for its author had been second to Lord Rayleigh in the Mathematical tripos. But two such keen men as Marshall and Foxwell could hardly have been expected, working in the same institution, to see eye to eye in all departments of a rather controversial domain. Even their fields of interest clashed; and Money, Socialism, and Economic History – H.S. Foxwell's three main hobbies – had to give way to the more abstract Theory, in which Marshall was the leading spirit. Again, the controversy between Free Trade and Protection led to acute differences, including public discussion in which H.S. Foxwell was prominent in opposition to Marshall. The former felt, too, that Professor Marshall, who had signed the Manifesto of Economists perhaps against his better judgement, never forgave him for replying to it in a letter to the *Times*. H.S. Foxwell, partly as a result, was not chosen as successor to Marshall, when the latter retired from the chair in 1908, and this remained a great disappointment to him, though he was no longer young.[92]

JOHN NEVILLE KEYNES: FROM FAITHFUL, TO GRADUALLY DISILLUSIONED, LIEUTENANT

John Neville Keynes was ten years younger than Marshall, being born in 1852. Like Foxwell, he commenced his university education by first studying at London, and then, on the advice of Fawcett, a family friend, to read for the Mathematical Tripos at Cambridge. This choice of subject appeared wise to gain necessary financial support from a scholarship for his studies. Despite his first class results in the two parts of the B.A. at London, Keynes found the hard grind of Cambridge mathematics less than congenial, requiring, as it did, far more work than his London studies had done. By January 1873 he therefore desired to switch to the Moral Sciences. Although Fawcett strongly advised against this, he started attending Moral Sciences lectures from October 1873. An early and lasting friendship with James Ward, who in January 1873 had won a Trinity Scholarship for the Moral Sciences, was probably influential in finalising the switch. Another factor was his reading of Mill's *Principles of Political Economy* over August, which Keynes found very interesting. During his first term he attended lectures by Sidgwick on Ethics and by Venn on Inductive Logic. It was not until April 1874 that he decided to pursue political economy studies, of which Marshall, as shown previously, was by then the leading teacher of advanced students. Their first meeting was graphically recorded in Keynes's diary: 'Called on Marshall of John's – lecturer on Pol. Econ.; found him lying in his tub'. How many other students Marshall first encountered in this way, history does not record. However, the meeting produced Keynes's attendance at Marshall's lectures for that term and again in 1875. By that time, Marshall's new student had become very proficient and Keynes recorded with some pride: 'Marshall has been speaking very highly indeed of some of the papers I have done for him, even in lectures.' By way of trial for the Tripos, Keynes had sat the political economy papers in London set by Fawcett in June 1875. In the following December, after completing the week of ten gruelling papers in Logic, Philosophy and Economics, he was awarded the result of First Moralist.[93] When the honours list had been announced, Keynes recorded a visit by

Ward first to Foxwell's rooms and then to Marshall's, Jevons, Sidgwick and Venn also being present:

> Marshall put it: 'You have a very clear mind'. [Ward told him]: 'Jevons said that you floored the Logic papers and that your answers were a pleasure to read: he evidently doesn't believe much in Marshall, and was amused by your curves. Foxwell praises your precision, but says you shirk difficulties and lack originality in philosophy. Foxwell was decidedly moderator.' I sat between Venn and Marshall and they were both enthusiastic. All agreed that Pembroke ought to give you a Fellowship and Marshall thinks you ought to lay yourself out for Economic History, a subject that wants doing thoroughly both for the Moral and the History men, and there is nobody to do it. Marshall thinks that if the Moral Sciences men together with Seeley, Hammond and Fawcett were to back you up in this, some work could be found worth your doing, worth it possibly in a pecuniary sense, and certainly in every other. . . .[94]

This entry is particularly interesting for two things. It contains Foxwell's prophetic judgement that Keynes had a tendency to avoid difficulties. This character trait was displayed through his whole life, in which level of ambition reached invariably well below that permitted by his talents. It also shows Marshall's eagerness to dispose of Keynes's future in a manner based on Marshall's opinion where he was most needed in both the service of economics and of Marshall, something which was also repeated on several occasions over Keynes's lifetime.

Despite his better results in Logic, Keynes appears to have been initially won over by Marshall for Economics. In early 1876, Keynes recorded he was busily coaching students in Political Economy, but his election in August to a Fellowship at his College, Pembroke, meant that by the end of that year, such work was no longer financially necessary. The party to celebrate the Moral Sciences results in December 1876 had Keynes in attendance in Marshall's rooms, where he learned that Mary Paley was writing a political economy primer for the Extension movement. Earlier he had recorded her engagement to Marshall 'of Johns', and that he himself had been given the opportunity to write such a primer. As almost immediate fulfilment of Foxwell's judgement, two months later the task had started to pall, and he was able to get out of the commitment by early 1877.

During 1876 Keynes's relationship with Marshall was still in its infancy, judged by the infrequency of Keynes's diary references to him for that year. It strengthened during 1877. In February, Marshall asked Keynes to read the manuscript on international trade he had been writing over the previous years; he also urged Keynes, as thirty years later he was to do his son, Maynard, to enter for the Cobden Prize Essay with the topic 'The Effects of Machinery on Wages'.[*] In April, Marshall was seeking Keynes's support in canvassing for the Yeoman–Bedellship as potential Cambridge employment when he got married. This was abandoned as undesirable by Marshall not long after and replaced in July by his much more practical application for the position of Principal and Political Economy Professor at Bristol.

---

[*]   JNKD, 8 February, 8 March and 25 April 1877; Marshall to Maynard Keynes, 14 October 1906, Keynes Papers, L/M/41; Nicholson, who had gained a first in the Moral Sciences Tripos the year after Keynes, did in fact win the Cobden Essay Prize competition for this topic, the first to be held at Cambridge rather than Oxford where the prize originated. Skidelsky's perceptive comment says much on Marshall's relations with Keynes father and son by presenting Maynard Keynes as Marshall's 'annointed successor' motivated by a feeling 'he had to make up for his father's failure to satisfy Marshall's hopes' (*John Maynard Keynes, The Economist as Saviour 1920–1937*, London: Macmillan, 1992, p. 422).

The 1877 entries also display Keynes's first critical observations on their evolving friendship:

25 April 1877: Marshall . . . advises me strongly not to send in what I have written about Cliffe Leslie in my Cobden Essay. But I am not at all sure that I shall take his advice . . . 26 April 1877. : . . I have a small dinner party – Alfred West, Myers, Marshall, Foxwell, Prothero, Nicholson and Seymour Thompson. After dinner we adjourned to Orpens. Marshall was in one of his most paradoxical moods. Amongst other things he said he would give his right arm never to have learnt any classics, the time that he wasted on classics might so much more profitably have been spent on music, drawing, sculpture, a few modern languages, biology and general culture.[95]

A degree of spitefulness is visible in some entries of Keynes's 1877 diaries. For example, Foxwell's critical judgement of Keynes's philosophical skills as shown in his Tripos papers and confided to him by James Ward is repaid by a description of Foxwell's lectures as 'an utter failure'. Marshall's praise, recorded in July, that Keynes was 'the best political economist he had recently had to teach', with its qualification that Keynes's style was 'inferior', was countered a few weeks later by Keynes's entry that after reading Marshall's trade manuscript for some weeks, he believed Marshall had 'no style at all'.* The Marshalls' departure for Bristol in August eliminated their presence from Keynes's diary for more than three years, an absence seemingly matched by lack of correspondence. This contrasts sharply with the steady flow of letters between Foxwell and Marshall over this period, and what appears to have been quite considerable correspondence with Sidgwick.[96]

Contact with Marshall was briefly resumed in February 1881 when Keynes asked Marshall to support his application for the Political Economy chair at London's University College, an application not proceeded with. In accepting this request, Marshall inquired whether Keynes had been helping Sidgwick's writing on political economy by giving access to his notes from Marshall's lectures, an episode discussed earlier.[97] Marshall wrote a glowing testimonial for Keynes. It praised Keynes as having 'a great natural genius for economic science', 'wide knowledge of its subject matter' the quality of 'a clear and powerful thinker', a thorough 'intellectual character', 'strong originality' aimed at lasting work, in short, 'an economist of the very highest promise'. In addition, Marshall reported Keynes's 'lucid and invigorating' teaching and 'personal qualities . . . to make him a source of great strength' to any organisation which employed him.¶ When three years later Keynes sent him a copy of his first book, *Studies and Exercises in Formal Logic*, Marshall praised it as 'a beautiful specimen of thorough Cambridge work and likely to be of very great service'.[98] In the meantime, Keynes had been kept informed by Foxwell, and subsequently by Marshall himself, of their desire to return to Cambridge. On 13 February 1882, he

---

* JNKD, 13 December 1875, 16 June, 10 and 27 July 1877. Marshall's compliment on Keynes as student could have been rather left-handed. Nicholson was the only noted economist whom Marshall by then had taught after Keynes, while James Ward, Henry Cunynghame, William Cunningham and Frederick Maitland were the only real quality candidates in economics over the previous three years.

¶ Marshall to John Neville Keynes, 8 February 1881; Marshall to University College, London, 9 February 1881 (Marshall Library, Keynes Papers); and see above, p. 666. On 1 May 1883, Keynes recorded 'an unexpected letter from Marshall' in which Marshall congratulated him on becoming examiner in London, informed him of his imminent move to Oxford, and expressed gratitude for 'one of the pleasantest facts in their lives . . . that you really and heartily did wish us to come back to Cambridge'.

recorded in his diary, 'if Mrs. Marshall comes into residence [at Newnham], I shall not lecture at Newnham any more'; while in April 1883, as mentioned previously, he recorded the Marshalls' abortive visit to Cambridge from Bristol to canvas a college lectureship for Marshall from the Master of St John's.[99]

Closer friendship therefore only developed when the Marshalls returned to Cambridge, much to Keynes's delight. Part of this was associated with Marshall's solid praise for Keynes as economist. This, it will be recalled, came to the fore again at that time because Marshall wanted Keynes to replace him at Oxford.[100] The enthusiastic reception of Marshall given by Florence, Keynes's wife, on her first meeting with him, followed by her enjoyment of his first course of lectures, would have aided this growth of good relations. Keynes's diary bears positive witness to such growth in the busy round of dinner parties they attended at the Marshalls, though its pleasures were marred by Keynes's nagging worries about the quarrels between Marshall and his even closer friend Sidgwick.[*]

The friendship took on a more intimate turn when Marshall invited Keynes to read the proofs of the *Principles*, just as ten years earlier he had been asked to read Marshall's trade manuscript. This task commenced in early October 1887 and involved Keynes in an enormous amount of work over the next two and a half years, much of its essentials preserved in correspondence. It was shown earlier[101] that Keynes's task was that of critical proofreader, advising on points of theory and clarity of expression and explanation. This contrasted with the more mundane proofreading roles assigned to Price and Mary Paley, designed to catch printer's and other spelling errors, as well as more formal mistakes in grammar, syntax and punctuation. Thus Keynes was consulted on the plan to create seven Books for the first edition instead of the original six, and was questioned in detail on problems associated with the measurement of utility and consumer surplus. By 1888 proofs and their reading became a reciprocated activity between Balliol Croft and 5 Harvey Road, the Keynes residence, with corrected galleys of the *Principles* flowing one way and proofs from Keynes's *Scope and Method*, critically perused by both Alfred and Mary Marshall, going to the other.

The second flow of proofs had partly originated with another attempt by Marshall to have Keynes appointed in Oxford. The occasion this time was the death of Bonamy Price, the incumbent of its Drummond Chair. On hearing this news, Marshall immediately wrote to Keynes how pleased he was to hear Keynes intended to be a candidate, tempered though the pleasure was from the sadness 'on personal and patriotic grounds'; given its implication of losing Keynes from Cambridge. That day Keynes noted sardonically in his diary that this was the first occasion he had heard he had made his mind up on the matter, particularly

---

[*]   Above, Chapter 10, pp. 307–8, Chapter 15, pp. 534–7, and this chapter, pp. 667–8. JNKD, 17 March 1885, 27 June 1885, 6 June 1886, 13 August 1886, 15 February 1887, 9 June 1887 and 27 November 1887, record dinner parties Keynes attended in the presence of Marshall, either at his residence or in his company at St John's; this compares favourably with the dinners Keynes attended in Sidgwick's company except for the fact that unlike the Marshalls, the Sidgwicks occasionally came to Keynes's house. Marshall's digestive problems, as indicated previously, may explain this lack of reciprocated hospitality. For an alternative view, see John Maloney, *Marshall, Orthodoxy and the Professionalisation of Economics*, p. 64.

since any consideration of it on his part was overshadowed by his limited eligibility from having as yet published nothing on economics.*

Marshall's first letter, with its encouraging untruth on the matter, was followed by the usual barrage of letters and conversations in persuasion even though, as he warned in a letter the next day, 'Rogers is the first favourite'.[102] Sidgwick gave similar advice and warning, while Foxwell, seemingly more concerned for his second alma mater, urged him not to apply, for the sake of the moral sciences as well as his son. If Keynes was successful, Foxwell wrote, Maynard 'may grow up flippantly epigrammatical and end by becoming a proprietor of a gutter gazette or the hero of a popular party; instead of emulating his father's example, becoming an accurate, clear-headed Cambridge man'[103] Keynes's diary and correspondence with Marshall disclose the gradually unfolding story: continually changing favourites for the position (from Rogers to Phelps to Rogers again) as part of weighing up Keynes's chances; initiatives and gossip from Marshall after visits to Oxford and London; the candidature of two contestants of the 1884 Cambridge election, Palgrave and Cunningham, as well as possibly Laveleye from across the Channel; and the checking of testimonials when Keynes at last applied in February 1888.[104]

To assist Keynes's application, Marshall took proofs from his book on *Scope and Method* with him to Oxford on a visit to the Master of Balliol, Benjamin Jowett, while urging Keynes to also send copies to the electors. Marshall thought the proofs 'excellent' in general. However, he suggested a need to relegate to footnotes 'references of a controversial nature to the opinions of individuals' especially those it seems, pertaining to Bonamy Price.¶ Marshall's Oxford trip was less successful than he had hoped; electors whom he had wanted to canvass being absent. Keynes sent off his application on 21 February, noting when getting his testimonials together, he found Marshall's 'far too flattering'. A note some days later from Marshall described the testimonials as 'few, but vigorous'. There is a note of relief when Keynes recorded that he heard a month later in Stuttgart, that the favourite Rogers had been elected, so that this Marshall-induced trial was over.[105]

Other trials involving Marshall were continuing. Little more need be said about Keynes's many reactions to the disagreements between Marshall and Sidgwick on the Moral Sciences Board over course changes. Such tribulations were combined with increasingly vigorous criticism from Balliol Croft over his proofs. In February 1888, as a result of a more careful reading, Marshall promised to give additional suggestions, especially on Keynes's treatment of the Germans. Two months later, Marshall's comments on Keynes's first two chapters 'depressed me very much. He practically wants me to give a year studying the Germans and then rewrite entirely. On one or two points I think he is right that if I say anything at all, it ought to be made more thorough. He also thinks that some of the

---

* JNKD, 13 January 1888. In commenting on a draft, Rita McWilliams-Tullberg queried why Marshall did not urge Foxwell to apply. The latter's chair in London was one reason, while as hinted in the next paragraph, Foxwell's love of Cambridge work was probably too strong to enable him to leave his *alma mater*. Marshall himself ranked Keynes and Foxwell equally in order of probability, not merit. (JNKD, 2 February 1888).

¶ JNKD, 2 February 1888. Keynes provided the Oxford selectors also with testimonials from Browne, his superior at the Local Examinations and Lectures Syndicate, J.S. Nicholson and an old one from Fawcett (entry for 18 February 1888). Sidgwick had declined to be named as a reference, because his brother William who, it may be recalled had succeeded the Marshalls as Lecturer in Political Economy at Bristol for one year, was a candidate for the position.

points I raise for discussion are obsolete.' Marshall's letter which had caused the depression was subsequently supplemented by two lengthy enclosures of detailed criticism from the inhabitants of Balliol Croft. These drew attention to so many places where either elucidation, a shift to footnotes, omission or simplification was in order, that the Marshalls provided a table of symbols to simplify their identification.[106]

There was also less aggravating contact in these months. In March 1888, after Rogers's election to the Oxford chair had been announced, Marshall and Foxwell started their pressure, renewed periodically until 1890, to get Keynes to accept the position of editor of the new economic journal they were contemplating, at an honorarium of £100 per annum. Their efforts proved unsuccessful as Keynes was not to be moved by their pleas, despite their listing of the position's advantages with which they tried to tempt him.[107] There were also requests to Keynes as Secretary of the Moral Sciences Board to alter Marshall's lecturing schedules to facilitate his writing programme; and they attended Johnian feasts and other dinners together. However, given the trials of the Moral Sciences Board masticating its new resolutions, there was an increasing weariness about long conversations in the relationship on Keynes's part, because Marshall 'is so faddy, and because he attaches such importance to trifles'.[108] Keynes's respect for Marshall's intellect and strengths as an economist, his ingrained subservience to his superiors combined with the mutual benefits from reading each other's proofs, undoubtedly consolidated the friendship during the late 1880s.

During 1889, Marshall identified more problems in Keynes's book, especially over method. Very long letters in August and September criticised Keynes's position on his appreciation of economists such as Cliffe Leslie and Ricardo, defended the quality of English statistical research from Arthur Young and Eden to Porter, Tooke, McCulloch and McPherson, and indicated substantial methodological differences which made it difficult for Marshall to comment on the 'more orderly' presentation of Keynes's argument. Much of the September letter covered Marshall's new-found belief in continuity with its implications for non-rigid views on scope and method, which had been embodied in the opening Books of his *Principles*. 'I never discuss any line of division or demarcation except to show that nature has shown no hard and fast lines, and that any lines man draws are merely for the convenience of the occasion: and should never be treated though they were rigid.'[109] A letter in November 1889 drew attention to differences over the position on method attributable to Mill, criticising the usefulness of 'economic man' as an abstraction, and was followed by Marshall's clarification of his notion of consumer surplus and the measurement of utility.[110] Keynes's role in the production of the *Principles* by then had effectively ended, a role which in its subsequent many revisions became relatively small and in the end, non-existent.* The Marshalls' role in criticising Keynes's proofs ended about a year later.¶

---

*   For example, his involvement in the second edition was minimal, requiring proofreading over only one or two months, while after the fourth edition he, together with a number of others, was consulted on whether to shift the historical chapters from Book I to appendices as Marshall in fact did in the fifth edition. See above, Chapter 12, pp. 422–3, 431 n*.

¶   JNKD, 18 July, 22 September 1890 ('I think this chapter is excellent. Its illustrations are numerous and suggestive; and its whole style is forcible, clear and effective') and 2 October 1890 ('I think this chapter is *very* interesting to advanced students; but it is more critical than constructive, and is perhaps not so well suited to

The more happy notes on which Marshall and Keynes ended their mutual criticism of each other's *magnum opus* were matched by the increased number of dinner parties they attended together in the early 1890s, again largely in the small dining-room of Balliol Croft. Such occasions were undoubtedly multiplied in number from the duties associated with Marshall's Presidency of Section F of the British Association and his concomitant responsibilities in assisting in getting the proposed British Economic Association off the ground. At this stage Tripos problems were not on the agenda, hence there were no long drawn out meetings at which Marshall pontificated with boring and rambling speeches on the principled changes he wished to advance. The only clouds on their horizon which Keynes recorded in these years were major disagreements between all those involved on the nature of the political economy examination as part of the open competition for the Indian Civil Service, and his apologetic and retrospective notification to Marshall that he had sought admission to the new degree of D.Sc. by virtue of his recently published book.[*]

Another cooperative venture tying the two colleagues together can be noted. Their correspondence reveals that for many years Keynes and Marshall shared their respective subscriptions to the *Statist* and the *Economist*. The first of these arrangements was to have ended in 1900 when Keynes informed Marshall he no longer required to take the former on his own account. However, Marshall indicated his continuing willingness 'in any case to send you the *Economist*', while Keynes appears to have kept up his subscription to the *Statist*.[111] There was also much swapping of collegial and other advice between the two friends. In Marshall's case this tended to concentrate on matters economic, in the case of Keynes it was largely confined to things administrative. There were of course exceptions. For example, in 1888 Keynes and his wife called on the Marshalls to discuss Venice in preparation for their Italian trip that summer. In 1892, Keynes assisted the search for a governess for Marshall's sister Mabel and her growing young family, by recommending their own former governess Miss Laxton, a recommendation which Marshall accepted with the words, 'I did not know any house from which I would rather have a governess than yours'.[112]

However, these years also saw negative references to Marshall multiply in the diaries, particularly from the mid-1890s. Fanned by new problems on the Moral Sciences Board between Sidgwick and Marshall, and Marshall's increasingly frequent, ill-advised and conservative interventions on the women's issue at Cambridge, Keynes more and more depicted him as 'a dreadful bore', 'exceedingly irrelevant' or similar epithets. This situation gradually worsened, stimulated by Keynes's growing fulfilment as university administrator rather than scholar and researcher. This enhanced his pain from inefficient and unproductive

---

beginners as the notes. They are extremely interesting not perhaps a few of them might be developed a little more.'

[*] JNKD, 14 April and 5 May 1891, John Neville Keynes to Marshall, 3 May 1891 (Marshall Archive, 1:69). On the degree matter, Marshall replied: 'I will at present only say, I think you have done right'. A subsequent letter in 1891 (Marshall Archive, 1:99) is signed:

> Yours with
> Congratulations re D.Sc.
> Condolences re grip,
> apologies re proofs

the reference to proofs for the second edition making a late May or early June date likely for this letter.

Board meetings, while lowering the compensating value of important subject matter and tolerance from his undoubted respect for Marshall's scientific achievements.[113] Mutual dinner parties over these years were likewise diminishing in number. Moreover, Keynes's references to such occasions in his diary increasingly give the impression that he and his wife largely served as token colleagues at the Balliol Croft dinner table, particularly when there were foreign visitors whom the Marshalls needed to entertain.

As Maloney has noted, Keynes's reactions to the long committee grind involved in establishing the new Economics Tripos, are satisfactorily summarised as a 'time-consuming bore' and 'the only part of his administrative duties he ever really disliked'.* In this way, Keynes's declining intellectual involvement with the university can be seen as one major factor explaining his increasing irritation with Marshall. Other potent influences steering him in this direction came from Marshall's attitudes and stance on the women's issue at Cambridge, totally contrary to the views on this subject of the Keynes household. In addition, there was what Fay later described to Maynard Keynes as 'Marshall's scandalous treatment of Sidgwick',[114] the person on the Moral Sciences Board to whom Keynes was undoubtedly closest, and Marshall's final hostility to, and criticism of, the notion of a moral sciences Syllabus *per se*. The last two factors especially cannot be under-rated.

Later, Keynes greatly feared the effect of Marshall's growing influence on his son in trying to steer him to economics.[115] As Keynes became increasingly embroiled in his 'congenial' administrative work for the university, whose social life he enjoyed so much, unfulfilled intellectual hopes and ambitions induced him more and more to nostalgia about the good old days of the moral sciences, of which he had enjoyed the tail-end as a student and reaped the temporary fame of being its 1875 First Moralist. This sentiment is very evident in a speech Keynes made in 1927 on the occasion of the unveiling of his portrait at Pembroke, his old college:

> My University career was largely influenced by men, senior to myself, from whom I received stimulus and encouragement in my undergraduate days. Of those whose unfailing kindness I remember with gratitude I may mention Dr. Searle, my Tutor, afterwards Master of this College. I would also mention Henry Fawcett, who was one of the first to turn my thoughts in the direction of Cambridge, Alfred Marshall, one of my earliest lecturers, and Henry Sidgwick, to whom beyond all others I owe my interest in Moral Science, and my settlement in Cambridge. Dr. Sidgwick's friendship, helpful criticism, and encouragement continued to the end of his life, and are among my most valued memories.[116]

The memories of Fawcett and Marshall the lecturer, together with the glowing tribute to Sidgwick, say it all. Relations with Marshall from the beginning were based on his role as teacher and later, senior colleague: respectful, admiring, dutiful, befitting the earnest and rather dull young man John Neville Keynes seemed to have been. Such feelings gradually diminished as the young man grew up. They ultimately disappeared when he became increasingly faced by his former mentor's less attractive sides and Keynes lost interest in

---

* John Maloney, *Marshall, Orthodoxy and the Professionalisation of Economics*, pp. 63–4. The chapter from which these perceptive remarks are quoted is, however, often overdrawn, particularly its concluding paragraphs (pp. 64–5) where his observations on the contents of Keynes's diaries are inaccurate to say the least. The whole discussion tends to omit the mutual intellectual cooperation over the *Principles* and *Scope and Method* over the years from 1887 to 1891.

Marshall's intellectual endeavours. In the end, formal duty was all that remained of the relationship. Even that was severed by Marshall's retirement from the university by eliminating his rights of call on Keynes's duty and responsibility as administrator. After 1908, Alfred Marshall rapidly faded from John Neville Keynes's diaries and from his life.

BENJAMIN JOWETT: AN ECONOMIST OF SORTS AND GREAT INFLUENCE ON YOUNG MEN

Benjamin Jowett, the Master of Balliol, was undoubtedly a great influence on Alfred Marshall, though when they first met in Oxford in the summer of 1877, Marshall at 35 was no longer a young man. Jowett, however, was 25 years older. Jowett's influence permeated aspects of Marshall's mature economics as well as many of his values in later life. From its favourable beginnings in Oxford and Bristol, Marshall's relationship with the venerable Master of Balliol grew into a close friendship, the warmest and most enduring which Marshall appears to have experienced. Perhaps it was a replacement father figure that Marshall, like so many others, found in the venerable 'Master of Balliol'. Their association was no doubt assisted by the generous help Jowett provided to the Marshalls during the many difficulties they faced at Bristol and the escape route from there he eventually opened up for them at Oxford for four terms before, in 1885, they were able to return for good to their beloved Cambridge. That this friendship survived until Jowett's death in 1893 is attributable to his strong liking for the couple, explicable in terms of the very gradual and the particularly close rapport he built with Mary Paley Marshall, and the genuine admiration and feeling of affection he had for Alfred Marshall. Many of the more formal aspects of their relationship need not be recovered in detail,[117] the friendly benevolence and influence of the older man on the young and socially inexperienced couple placed momentarily under his wing, is suitably pursued in this context.

   The roots of this unusual friendship lay undoubtedly in the striking similarities between the two men. Faber's splendid portrait of Jowett with background[118] facilitates such comparison. The following descriptions of Jowett can easily be applied to Marshall:

He never learned to play, to make love, to break down the barriers of reserve in himself and others. He never sowed any wild oats or kicked over the traces. Fearlessly as he used his mind upon religious dogma, metaphysical systems, educational questions and national affairs, he was apt to be less courageous in face of orthodox moral assumptions . . . (p.36). 'without father, without mother, without descent', Jowett's young contemporaries said of him at Balliol. The nickname of Melchizedec stuck to him for many years. . . . When the Master of Balliol died half a century later, full of years and honour, his biographers were confronted with the difficult task of constructing his family history . . . (p. 44). [H]is attitude towards his family was pathological. He did his duty, he hated the existence of the duty. He rarely spoke or wrote about his family or childhood. (p.45). Jowett seldom – if ever – mentioned his school days, except to disparage the education he had received. This was unfair, for he owed his whole career to the . . . scholarship which the teaching [at his school] helped to win. (p.73). All the accounts of him as a school boy tell the same story. A pretty looking, gentle, delicate boy, with a round smooth face and very bright eyes, who kept to himself and to his books. (p.74). His notion of perpetual self improvement may be illusory. . . . It is at least a noble illusion (p. 402).

To what extent Jowett, or for that matter Marshall himself, grasped such similarities in their make-up, is impossible to know. Jowett's approach to strangers on first meeting, described in the case of Marshall by Jowett's original biographers, suggests that Jowett's general probing attitude to new acquaintances may well have achieved this. The occasion was the invitation Marshall received from Jowett to visit Balliol following his application to the position of Principal and Professor of Political Economy at Bristol University College:

> though they walked and talked together nearly the whole of the Sunday, the subject of University College was never alluded to. They talked about architecture, about Herbert Spencer, about theology at Cambridge, and many other things, and it was only when Marshall was leaving that Jowett said, 'I don't know how this election may turn out, but at any rate I am glad to have made your acquaintance'. This was the beginning of an intimate friendship with the Marshalls, which added much to the happiness of the last years of his life.[119]

Conversation created another strong bond between the two men. Mary Paley Marshall[120] recalled of the relationship between Jowett and her husband, 'Jowett spoke of him as "the most disinterested man I have ever known". Jowett loved talking to A[lfred] and used to bring out his note book and take notes of the conversation when he stayed at Balliol Croft. He said that A's conversation was so interesting – more so even than Symonds who J[owett] said had a wonderful flow of conversation'.

The warmth of that friendship has been well documented in their subsequent correspondence and Mary Paley's recollections. The latter recalled her first meeting with the 'master', as they soon learned to call him, and also graphically described his subsequent stays in their house at Bristol, and other aspects of their relationship:

> My first sight of the Master was at a dinner party given by the Percivals at the Clifton College School House. He sat with Mrs. Percival at one end of a long table, I as bride sat with Dr. Percival at the other. I did not know who the little man with a pink face and white hair was, but after dinner Mrs. Wollaston, noted for her sharp sayings, told me that it was the Master of Balliol, adding that he represented to her 'light without warmth'. He and Henry Smith were on the Council of the College, they came regularly three times a year to its meetings and generally stayed at our house, and these visits were a delight. They were such a well-fitting pair and seemed so happy together, for though Jowett was rather shy and silent unless with a congenial companion, he was quite at his ease with Henry Smith who was the most brilliant and humorous talker I have ever met. I used to sit up with them and Alfred till well after midnight. They might begin by discussing College affairs, but soon would reach wider subjects, and whatever they talked about was lit up by some humorous remark from Henry Smith. They insisted on leaving by an early train next morning to be in time for their College lectures, and as Alfred was not strong enough to get up early I had to pour out tea at a seven o'clock breakfast and was very shy and silent; but they were so kind and gay even at that hour, that I was made happy too. It took me about five years to feel quite at ease with Jowett, for his shyness was a difficulty but after a while we got on quite well and only talked when we wanted to. I sometimes took walks with him and he would make a remark now and then and fill up the gaps by humming little tunes. He always liked to talk about architecture. In later years he and I spent an afternoon at Ely Cathedral and he seemed to be absolutely happy there. 'I call this sublime', he exclaimed at the entrance to the southern transept. He had often stayed there and knew every detail. He made us describe any cathedrals we had visited, Chartres being a special favourite.[121]

A few years after Jowett's death, Mary Paley recalled his love of cathedrals for his biographers, the visit to Ely Cathedral being remembered there and in a letter to him subsequent to that visit that mentioned 'how seeing Cathedrals seems to do one more good than seeing anything else, to leave more behind than either scenery or painting'.[122] Her architectural reminiscences says much about the Marshalls' relationship with Jowett, and of their tastes in things other than economics:

> During the latter years of his life he paid an annual visit to Cambridge, and he always spent a good deal of his time there in wandering among the buildings. He never came to Cambridge without paying a visit to King's Chapel. His feeling for the outside was almost as enthusiastic as for the inside. The deep light and shade of the round Church came second in his affections. He used to say that the most important things in architecture were 'first proportion, then shadow'. He was constantly urging us to go and see fine architecture; and he was shocked when we once told him that we had spent a summer within thirty miles of St David's without paying it a visit. He put Cologne, on the whole, first among cathedrals. Its perfection and unity of plan had something of the same charm for him that King's Chapel had. But he was also fond of buildings of quite another kind. Chartres, for instance, with its rich glass and fascinating inconsistencies, was one of his chief favourites. In July 1891, he and I made a long-planned expedition to Ely. . . . He made the remark that if it had not been for the Reformation we should probably have had little Norman or or Early English left in our cathedrals; for it came just at a time when the earlier styles were being pulled down fast to make way for the later. On our way home we amused ourselves with arranging the English cathedrals in order of merit. He put Westminster Abbey first. A pet scheme of his was to line one of his rooms with the finest pictures of cathedrals he could get.[123]

Jowett's initial correspondence with the Marshalls was formal. It dealt with Marshall's intended resignation from Bristol University College for reasons of health, and warned the Marshalls against making hasty decisions. The letter also widened the Marshalls' options, by asking them to consider the possibility of continuing to teach at Bristol without undertaking the more irksome Principal's responsibilities. It ended on a perceptive personal note, indicative of their developing friendship: 'I am sorry to hear of your illness independently of the consequences of it for the college. This kind of illness though not dangerous is depressing and one cannot help fancying oneself at times worse than one really is. I hope that you and Mrs. Marshall will come and pay me a visit as soon as you can'.[124]

A follow-up letter a month later expanded on the advice Jowett had given earlier, after thanking Marshall for an offer to send him *Economics of Industry* on publication. It mentioned a further solution to their problem by appointing a Vice-Principal of Marshall's own choosing and paid from his salary, thereby eliminating his administrative load. In addition, Jowett poured some realistic cold water on the Marshalls' rather romantic vision at this time of living in rural seclusion to enable full-time writing, particularly as it was difficult to devote a whole lifetime to writing for financial as well as inspirational reasons. Although Jowett did not claim to know their financial circumstances, he stressed both the 'anxiety' and 'monotony' from living 'off a small income', and suggested expectations of relief from a suitable vacancy at Cambridge were not realistic.[125] When the Marshalls eventually did resign in July 1881, to depart for Sicily in October, Jowett expressed his regret. More importantly, he provided a safety valve by offering to attempt arrangements through which they could come back as teachers of political economy, a proposal which had met with the approval of the two persons on the College Council with whom he had discussed it.[126] When Marshall replied favourably to this suggestion, quibbling only over the too generous salary mentioned, Jowett hinted at yet a further future possibility: drawing 'their thoughts to Oxford' by holding out the prospect of the Drummond chair there as a reasonable one, given Bonamy Price's age.[127] How the Marshalls came to Oxford, Jowett's role therein and in their subsequent pleasant period of Oxford residence, has been told already in detail; correspondence came back as a sign of their friendship with the Marshalls' return to Cambridge.[128]

The day of Marshall's election to the Cambridge chair, Jowett expressed both sadness and joy at their imminent departure, thanking the addressee Mary Paley for her 'affection and kindness' to him. He also asked her to warn Marshall of the dangers in overloading his *Principles* with mathematical symbols. A week or so later, the thanks and the warning were repeated to Marshall himself in a letter which also sought advice on his successor at Oxford: 'Which is the most sensible man and which is the best teacher – Keynes or Cunningham?'. Although Marshall's response was not preserved, it is not difficult to guess, given the considerations presented earlier in this chapter.[129]

From then on the correspondence settled down to that relaxed exchange of gossip between old friends. Mary Paley was the more favoured addressee of Jowitt's letters, presumably because she wrote more often and more interestingly. In 1885 Jowett thanked Alfred for sending him the Remuneration Conference Paper, for news of their settling in, and mentioned his current reading of biography. Its general invitation for a visit to Oxford was made very specific early the following year, inviting them for a weekend from 23 January to meet Mr and Mrs Humphrey Ward and Welldon, the new Master of Harrow. A letter right at the end of 1886 commented further on the use of symbols in political economy, education of women at Oxford, the new Master of Trinity, a new year's gift for them of Tolstoi novels and how he looked forward to a spring visit during which he could hear Marshall's views on bimetallism.[130] Subsequent letters mentioned visits to Cambridge, a stay with Tennyson and vacations, requested a favour for a friend's daughter and prospective student of Newnham, complimented its author at length on the appearance of his *Principles* and repeatedly pressed for return visits to Oxford by the Marshalls.[131]

Preserved correspondence from the Marshalls during October and November 1891 is rich for illustrative purposes of their friendship. This took place when Jowett was recovering from his first heart attack, the seriousness of which he himself had played down as 'a slight attack of the heart – not dangerous, I think, but it requires rest and care. It is a good warning to me. Did you ever hear the story of a man who asked his physician whether he was not dangerously ill? "No sir, but you are dangerously old".'[132] Earlier that summer, he had given Mary Paley Marshall advice not to involve herself in parapsychological experiments of table-turning, in which the Sidgwicks and others of their acquaintance were heavily involved. Such unscientific practices had 'split families . . . and interfered with the power and higher interest of Cambridge'.[133] A month or so after his heart attack, a letter in his secretary's handwriting because he 'had been unwell', arrived at Balliol Croft, not long after the Marshalls' return from their extensive Central European trip that summer to celebrate the success of the *Principles*. 'I rejoice to hear how vigorous you and the Professor have been. About you, who 16 or 18 years ago climbed Monte Rosa, I am not surprised, but for the Professor who 10 years ago could scarcely walk at all, this progress is wonderful.' After warning them not to overdo things, he advised on books he had read:

Erewhon, and biographies of Sir Robert Peel and Lord Althorp, the first of which he warmly recommended to Mary Paley.[134]

During October, half a dozen long letters went from Balliol Croft to Balliol College. These followed a visit to the convalescent Jowett on Friday 10 October, after which Marshall had returned home to Cambridge, while Mary Paley had gone on to London to visit her mother. A letter from Alfred Marshall on 11 October opens the round. It is deliberately 'gossiping' by retailing how he had passed Jowett's message and all the news to Mrs Horace Darwin, how McTaggart had won his fellowship and perhaps also a wife, how delighted they were that Jolliffe had gained a fellowship at Corpus and Jebb had become their M.P. from Cambridge. It concluded by explaining a Jowett influence on their furniture re-arrangements:

> Whenever we make any changes in our furniture we always think how you will like it: that gives us a standard to live up to. And just before we got to know that you were ill, it had been settled to have a row of photographs of Greek and Roman busts, all along the central bookcase of my study. Cato and Portia holding hands are to be in the middle, four Greek heads on the right and four Roman on the left. And my chief thought at the time was that perhaps you might like them; and whenever I look at them, I think how glad I shall be to show them to you. For I know I am going to.[135]

Two letters from Mary Paley followed. The first, the day of her return from London, recounted aspects of their summer travels not mentioned in her previous letter, including her impressions of the Sistine Madonna in Dresden. It ended with the thought that after admiring all these beautiful towns such as Dresden and Prague, she liked Oxford best of all, when she saw it again the week before. Her appreciation of the seriousness of his illness on that visit made her want to tell him, 'how it has been one of the best things in our lives that you have allowed us to be your friends . . . and you are constantly in our thoughts'.[136] A week later she mentioned how anxiously they both awaited news about him from Oxford, before communicating her gossip. This mentioned their mutual acquaintance, Ethel Bowen, with whom she 'talked a great deal about you'; Phillippa Fawcett's postgraduate work with Darwin after topping the Mathematical Tripos that year; and Jebb, their new parliamentarian, whose civic duty at Ely sparked recollections mentioned earlier of their joint visit that summer to its cathedral.[137] The next day Alfred Marshall's letter recalled their visit to him now over a week ago, how brave and cheerful Jowett had seemed even though in pain, and how, 'I could not help feeling a wicked little impertinent wish at the bottom of my heart that I had a Kodak, to take a photograph of you, just as you were. I've got your photograph on my mantelpiece now, just as Mary has the framed picture of you in her room. Both are good to look on, but neither is so good as you were on the Friday. Now I will gossip a little.'[138]

Three letters by Mary Paley rounded off the correspondence with Jowett that month. These mention her dining club meeting at Mrs George Darwin's, during which she heard a story told by Mrs Jebb similar to those of Mrs Lyttleton, the novelist, whose brother Jowett had assisted years before; the Senate vote on compulsory Greek for the 'little go' won by a 'flood' of country clergymen who streamed into Cambridge for the occasion, much to the disgust of husband, Alfred; improvements in the health of Professor Seeley; the fact that 'there are fifteen brides in Cambridge this term, several from Newnham and Girton', and a wish that their own doctor, Donald McAlister could take Jowett in hand, since whoever he touched was sure to get well. The Labour Commission and her belief it would gravely hamper Alfred's second volume, end her trio of late October letters; the last subject taken up from London by Alfred while on Commission business in a letter dated early November.[139] Two further letters from Mary Paley, expressing her delight at the news from Oxford that Jowett was 'decidedly better' and even taking rides through the town, end this fascinating, though non-random, sample of letters preserved from the Marshalls' correspondence with their much loved 'Master' and 'Patron Saint'.*

On 23 September 1893, Jowett died of a heart attack similar to that which had spared him two years before. His final letters to the Marshalls of the intervening years complained about the infrequency of their visits; expressed disbelief at a rumour he had heard that Mary Paley had visited Oxford in the spring of 1892 without visiting him; and gave succour and advice during Marshall's controversy with William Cunningham in the *Economic Journal* and elsewhere. In his very last letter, he discussed the relevance of Marshall's work on bi-metallism, comparing it favourably with the outdated monetary thinking of his beloved Ricardo and Lord Overstone; acknowledged Mary Paley's account of their 1893 summer vacation in the Dolomites while regretting the end of his own 'walking days' which had been reduced from over twenty to less than one mile a day. However, he claimed he nevertheless could still do a 'good deal of work' and concluded that, on all accounts, the college was still 'very prosperous' under his leadership. This final letter, written a month or so before his death, also mentioned the joy they had given him. 'It refreshes me always to hear from you, and you kindly seem never to forget me'.[140]

Edgeworth invited Marshall to write Jowett's obituary for the *Economic Journal*. Its final paragraph says much about what Jowett meant to Marshall, sentiments only very imperfectly reflected in the few preserved letters they exchanged.

> But after all, this influence on the economic life of England was quite as much through his faculty of making people want to know the right thing, and to do it, as by his own direct work. His sincerity was infectious. He knew how to get hold of what was best in men, and to make them good citizens. He cared not whether they were of high birth or low estate provided only he could see in them a possible power of good in the world after he should have left it. A very great number of those who are forming public opinon today, or discharging high duties for the State, have learnt from personal contact with him, that money, though a good servant, is a bad master; and that private advantage is but poor exchange for the sense of having worked faithfully for one's country. His own college responded bravely to the calls he made on it. There are few foundations, either at Oxford or Cambridge, which have less material resources than Balliol: but he, continuing the good work of others, endowed it with that wealth of unselfish devotion and energy by which it has attained its unique position.[141]

Although the opening sentence of Marshall's obituary said Jowett made no claim to be an economist in any special sense of the word, the following paragraphs and the passage just

---

* Mary Paley Marshall to Benjamin Jowett, 6 and 15 November 1891 (Jowett Papers, Balliol College, Oxford). They discuss Australian labour relations, socialism and a visit and lecture by Charles Booth to Newnham. The letters from the Marshalls to Jowett are invariably addressed 'dear Master', 'my very dear master', while Alfred Marshall's letter of 11 October 1891 refers to Benjamin Jowett as his 'patron saint', an accolade of respect he rarely awarded. For other occasions see above, Chapter 5, p. 130, Chapter 17, p. 642.

quoted indicate considerable points of contact between the two men, including economics. 'The late Master of Balliol', Marshall wrote, subconsciously stressing the gap in age between them, had learnt his economics 'from Ricardo direct, before the days of Mill's *Political Economy*, . . . the last teacher of economics who has done so'. Jowett's economics teaching was special in other ways:

> He had various ways of teaching. Sometimes coming upon some young man of force and promise who had not quite the right training for his mind, or had not found in his other studies the right incentive to hard work, the Master would give him a book on political economy to read, and get him to come in from time to time to talk over his reading. Sometimes he would take one student alone, sometimes two or three together; and he did this up to the end, even in the last year of his life. While Tutor of Balliol he used to give short courses of set lectures on political economy, though he did not continue these after he became master; and he more than once preached on the right use of wealth. His teaching on the subject was admirably adapted to guide and stimulate; it was full of shrewd common-sense, and pithy hints as to details; and, at the same time, brought home to his hearers the responsibility under which money is spent, and led them towards high ideals in its use.[142]

These are some of the influences of the Master of Balliol on his erstwhile colleague, the 'Master' of Balliol Croft, demonstrating why he was so deserving of Marshall's honorific title of 'patron saint'. Marshall was greatly taken by aspects of Oxford teaching he had encountered during his terms at Balliol, taking them back with him for later introduction to Cambridge at an opportune moment.* Did Marshall learn his 'preaching on the right use of wealth' also from this, as well as from his other, patron saints? Recall the picture of the working man, bought in his youth for a pittance and displayed on his college room mantle-piece, as he later did with Jowett's portrait, to remind him of his never-ending duties in the making of economics.[143] The two shared 'masters' in Plato and Ricardo, for their 'wisdom and foresight', and for seeing reality in ideas and being 'fearless of paradox'. They likewise shared 'hobbies' in controversy over the currency, modern views on socialism and social reform, and 'in working men who were gentlemen in thought and feeling'. There is much autobiography in Marshall's description of Jowett's work in relieving the 'economic difficulties in the way in getting a first rate education':

> his public efforts, both at Oxford and in connection with Bristol University College, to diminish them [difficulties in getting a first rate education] are well known; and a great part of his own income flowed by secret channels towards the same end. But he looked less to academic teaching than to the introduction of a noble spirit in business, as a means of bringing out the best faculties of those whose start in life had not been favoured by fortune. Plato's socialistic ideas possessed his mind; he made a careful study of contemporary socialistic thought when preparing to write the last edition of his introduction to Plato's *Republic*; and there is much that is instructive to the economist in his introduction to others of the *Dialogues*.[144]

---

* Marshall to John Neville Keynes, 3 September 1897 (Marshall Archive, 1:112): 'I have some notion of beginning tentatively the Oxford system of essays where the writers come and read aloud. I think that is the only way I see for combining my obligations to the relatively many who want to prepare for papers on political economy and to the absolutely very few [among those taking my advanced classes].'

A number of Jowett's more specific influences on Marshall's political economy of the *Principles* were mentioned in the context of Marshall's preparation of that book. These included Jowett's worries about the over-use of mathematical reasoning on the subject, advice he was pleased to see Marshall had taken to heart in writing his *'opus magnum'*. Jowett's other praise of the *Principles* communicated to its author, included his admiration for Marshall's even-handedness on capital and labour, essential since political economy was the friend of both; Marshall's blending of theory and fact to which 'Ricardo himself would not have objected'; the great philosophical principles underlying the work including its adherence to Hegelianism; its clear demonstration of the complex but essential relationship between economics and ethics, and the stress on the proper role of education and business in elevating life.[145]

Jowett's 1841 notebook preserved at Oxford illustrates the potential for other broad methodological influences on the Marshall of the *Principles*. Its contents emphasise the limitations and uncertainty of political economy as a science, in part a result of its relativity in time and space. It shows an overall view of political economy stressing its differences with, and subordination to, religion and morals, its potential value to the poor by the possibilities of intervention it holds out for the betterment 'of the temporal condition of the lower classes', and its needs for this reason to stress 'the benevolent feelings of mankind which it . . . appears to slight'. Its strength in the ability of analysing statistical data for creating criteria for judgement needs to be combined with taking 'a large and extended view of [its scope]', covering commercial crises and war, as well as the more usual topics. Last but not least, Jowett saw political economy as particularly valuable in its role 'as a check to the radical disturbers of the present state of things and [to demonstrate] what is really possible with reference to improvement'.[146] Were these among the topics broached in the lengthy discussions 'until well after midnight' which Mary Paley remembered from their Bristol days, or were they raised later in the many opportunities for quiet conversation Marshall's brief appointment at Oxford allowed? Some of these sentiments undoubtedly reinforced Marshall's earlier beliefs, when he was contemplating and slowly constructing his own great work during the 1880s.[147]

Association with Jowett therefore provided true friendship at last. Its more solid foundations were based on a similarity of original circumstances: embarrassing family background and lonely school-days, a basic drive to do good with young men of their own choosing, a desire to influence in the background and to lead from behind rather than active involvement in the corridors of a power, a life of earnest duty and practical philanthropy catering to advance their own tastes and preferences. The serious side of the friendship with its concerns over political economy, education and human improvement was leavened by mutual aesthetic delights in the architecture of cathedrals at Ely and Chartres, the sculpture of the classics, the paintings of the Renaissance, and poetry and literature. More importantly, Marshall's friendship with Jowett was not cluttered with the almost daily and routine professional contact which gradually soured and eventually destroyed his Cambridge friendships with Sidgwick, Foxwell and Keynes. It was also a shared friendship, sustained by and involving both the husband and wife. It thereby provided a complementary relationship which enabled both to draw inspiration from Jowett's manifold talents. Their 'master' of Balliol, who had come into their life at the start of their marriage and life together, provided them with crucial guidance and companionship over the next fifteen years, which Mary Paley towards its end so aptly described as 'one of the best things' in their lives. For Marshall, Jowett probably was the father he wished he had had, as well as a friend, adviser, guide and 'patron saint' to look up to.

A FAILURE IN FRIENDSHIP AS LONELY, EGOCENTRIC INTROVERT?

The vagaries of Marshall's friendships just uncovered make it tempting to conclude on this note. His failures in friendship with Sidgwick, Foxwell and Keynes seem substantiated by the successful exception of that with Jowett. Such a judgement, however, would be hasty, even for the egocentric introvert which Marshall undoubtedly was. He was capable of building up strong, but inevitably not lasting relationships. Examples are his friendships with Clifford, Moulton and Mozley, not to mention those with Dakyns, Levitt and Moss about which there is so little information. Insufficient is known about some of his other relationships. Marshall's ambiguous, almost love–hate acquaintance with the Webbs, especially wife Beatrice, is one of those, already frequently encountered.[148] More interesting is the Marshalls' more enduring friendship with Charles and Mary Booth, snippets of which also flitted across previous pages from various activities more distant from Cambridge life. The last fact gives perhaps a clue to its ability to survive, as in the case of the much better documented friendship with Jowett, and contrary to the fate of his Cambridge friendships, large and small.

Friendship with the Booths was initiated by advice Marshall gave Charles Booth on his proposed poverty survey. Letters on this were exchanged in October 1886, though who took the initiative in this exchange is not clear from the letters preserved. This was followed by an exchange of books and articles, as well as of views on subjects of mutual interest, such as industrial villages and aspects of what Booth described as the 'constructive' part of Marshall's analysis on how to house the London poor.[149] Personal meetings arising from business mentioned in these letters, were followed by contact of a more social type. There was a visit to the Booths' Gracedieu Manor in September 1887 to break the routine of Yorkshire factory visits; a stay at their London house when the Marshalls attended a meeting of the Statistical Society to hear Charles Booth unveil his aged pension plan; some return visits to Balliol Croft were likewise recorded.[150] More relaxed occasions for exchanging ideas intermingled with correspondence and advice on the Labour Commission. During its sessions Marshall questioned his friend on aspects relevant to its work, an examination conducted in a distinctly friendly way,[151] a role reversed before the Royal Commission on the Aged Poor to which Marshall gave evidence in June 1893. This, it will be recalled, questioned Marshall's proposals for poor relief published in the *Economic Journal*, on which he and Charles Booth had corresponded earlier.[152]

During the new century, contact between the Marshalls and the Booths continued more sporadically. Marshall's invitation to Booth to address the Charity Organisation Society's annual conference in Cambridge was previously quoted; an earlier address by him to the students of Newnham was mentioned by Mary Paley Marshall in a letter to Jowett.[153] More complimentary exchanges of their publications took place as they grew older. Marshall greeted the seventeenth volume of the London Poverty Survey, *Notes on Social Influence and Conclusion*, with thanks for sending him 'your angelic book, holy and beautiful outside and in'. Marshall's letter praised its continuing 'constructiveness' and urged Booth to publish a volume more directly pointing 'to action . . . for the sake of all, for knowledge, for progress, for ideals – and I will throw in, though somewhat irreverently, for Booth'.[154]

The fact that, for Marshall, Booth joined the wrong side in the tariff debate which erupted in May 1903, siding with Chamberlain rather than with unadulterated free trade, explains the prolonged silence which ensued between them over the next four years. This was only broken when, in an attempt to restore communication between them in 1908, Booth wrote with how much delight he had read Alfred Marshall on economic chivalry in the *Economic Journal*, so much better than the 'incomplete' newspaper report he had read of the speech. His letter broached recent lack of personal contact – 'it is so wretchedly long since we have met and talked, that I hardly know [how long]' – combined with a strong wish for its renewal: 'we must meet'.[155] This was apparently not to be, though communication by letter was resumed. For example, a letter from Booth in 1913 looked forward to Marshall's volume, and thanked him for a 'too kind, too good, and too generous' response to his 'crude' pamphlet on *Industrial Unrest and Trade Union Policy*, lacking as it did in practical value.[156] Three years later Booth had died, and condolences flowed to his widow in separate appreciations from the Marshalls:

> I write a line to express my sympathy with you, and yours, and my grief at the loss which the world has suffered. Mr. Booth's name is imperishable, it will live not only in history, but in popular language, as we speak of an Achilles, a Socrates or a Parsival. He was strong and gentle, wise and simple, earnest and placid, resolute and tolerant: he was broad in his conceptions; and minutely careful in his unparalleled mastery of details. To know him was an education; it was also one of the chief honours and pleasures of my life.[157]

Characteristically, Mary Paley dwelled on the times 'when you and he and we have been together, and the talks and the pleasant things that happened here [Balliol Croft] and at Gracedieu and at Cumberland Place'.[158] Such reminiscences she revived during a single visit to Charles Booth's widow, when she too had lost her husband.

> Mrs. Marshall, the wife of the professor, and dear friend of long ago, arrived to stay wearing long, black robes, sandals and knitted woollen socks. It is hard to say whether Baba was bored by the economics and statistics of the past or whether she wanted to emphasise another side of life; whichever it was, she inundated Mrs. Marshall with county gossip. When at last conversation came round to more familiar ground the two widows, very pink in the face, rebutted each other's statements with phrases beginning 'Charlie always said', and 'Alfred much disliked'. The visit was not a success. I felt sorry for Mrs. Marshall and her lost expression. No doubt she was relieved to get back to her tricycle in Cambridge.[159]

However, Mary Paley wrote on the death of Mary Booth to one of her daughters, how unfortunate it was that old age had 'prevented us from meeting during the last few years . . .'.[160] In widowhood, as well as before, Mary Paley showed greater ability to sustain friendships than her husband.

Alfred Marshall's need for such friendships was in any case limited, treasured though such friendships sometimes were. The end of that with Jowett was unpreventable. His other great friendship, with Foxwell, after its break-up, was beyond repair, despite Marshall's feeble attempts at reconciliation. In the end, relatives, work and some recent students, counted for more with him than former friends of school and college, regrettable though that absence seemed occasionally in old age. When, apart from his nephews, relatives had passed away, and ability to work was steadily weakening, only recent students stayed loyal. Like Jowett was advised to do in his last years, Marshall tried to fill his old age as much as possible with young men and, occasionally, their wives. The extent of his continuing ties with Fay, Layton and Maynard Keynes was shown in the previous chapter. But when even this grew too much, and time for visits became more strictly rationed, the elderly recluse sought company in Beethoven piano rolls and in the romantic stories enjoyed in his youth, re-read to him by his faithful companion and wife.

Marshall's failure at friendship tells much about his personality, combining a need to be loved with a fear of rejection, dependence on human contact with firm adherence to dogmatically held principles, and in the end a capacity for only sustaining a friendship with a father figure of similar background, an ageing bachelor with no family ties of his own, but whose values and principles Marshall could share unreservedly and devotedly. The fact that Jowett was also not a rival in the widest sense of that word, and distant from Marshall's sphere of authority for the final years of its duration, explains further why this was the only real friendsip Marshall managed to preserve.

NOTES

1. J.M. Keynes, 'Alfred Marshall', pp. 165–6, cf. above, Chapters 3, 4, pp. 61–2, 88, 91 and Chapter 17, p. 639.
2. Mary Paley Marshall, 'MSS Notes' (NCA).
3. *Ibid.*
4. See above, Chapter 3, pp. 61–2.
5. Mary Paley Marshall, 'MSS Notes' (NCA); Foxwell to John Neville Keynes, JNKD, 20 April 1897.
6. Above, Chapter 7, p. 196. That Marshall kept up with Clifford's mathematical investigations was also noted in the earlier discussion of Marshall's philosophical studies during the late 1860s, above Chapter 5, pp. 125–6.
7. Above, Chapter 5, pp. 99–100, and see Alfred Marshall to Sir William Ramsay, 9 December 1914, in *Memorials*, p. 488, where Moulton is described as not being a member of 'the old gang of the government'. Moulton contributed in 1908 to Marshall's portrait fund, as indicated on the brochure its Committee issued, and had earlier supported Marshall's quest for his new Tripos (above, Chapter 15, p. 546).
8. James Wilson to Mary Paley Marshall, 19 September 1881 and 30 December 1929 (Marshall Archive, 1: 109–10); in 1924 she sent Keynes some letters from Wilson, 'only meant for my eyes', indicating him to be a correspondent aged 88 years, letters which undoubtedly commented on the subject of Keynes's Memoir. Mary Paley Marshall to Maynard Keynes, 20 November 1924 (KMF).
9. See above, Chapter 5, pp. 104–5.
10. See above, Chapter 5, pp. 103–4, Chapter 9, pp. 275, 277; Percival also contributed to the Marshall Portrait Fund in 1908 according to the brochure issued by its committee. Marshall's correspondence with Bishop Westcott on such matters, was quoted above, Chapter 16, pp. 599, 611 and note *. Westcott was a former Cambridge colleague and fellow member of the Eranus Society (above, Chapter 5, pp. 112–13).
11. See above, Chapter 5, pp. 105–6.
12. J.R. Mozley to Marshall, 29 September 1916 (Marshall Archive, 1:89). Cf. J.M. Keynes, 'Alfred Marshall', pp. 229–30; and some of the remarkable passages on such subjects in his final volumes: for example, *IT*, p. 665; *MCC*, p. 101 n.1.

13. J.R. Mozley to Marshall, 29 September 1916; Marshall's nephew in question may have been on active military service. Possibilities include Raymond Arthur, or one of the sons of his sister Mabel (but not Claude Guillebaud, who had been found medically unfit for active military service).

14. John Maynard Keynes, 'Alfred Marshall', p. 170, n.1.

15. Mary Paley Marshall, 'Notes for Walter Scott', quoted above in Chapter 17, p. 648.

16. This may be because her recollections from their time in Bristol were fonder than those of Marshall, for reasons already discussed on several occasions; above, Chapter 8, pp. 234–7; Chapter 14, pp. 497–9.

17. *Cambridge University Reporter*, 7 December 1900, p. 320.

18. *Ibid.*, p. 321. Marshall finished his speech with a brief quote from Mark Antony's tribute to Brutus at the conclusion of Shakespeare's *Julius Caesar* (Act V, Scene V) ending with the remark, 'This was a man'.

19. See above, Chapter 5, pp. 110–13; Chapter 6, p. 144.

20. Marshall to John Neville Keynes, 4 September 1900 (Marshall Archive, 1:118).

21. Marshall to *Cambridge Gazette*, 2 and 9 December 1868, 4 April 1869; *Cambridge University Reporter*, 1 March 1871, pp. 222–3.

22. Henry Sidgwick to Marshall, summer [i.e. July or August] 1871; Sidgwick Papers, Trinity College, Add MS c.100^{96}.

23. See above, Chapter 6, p. 158 and cf. Chapter 12, p. 403 in connection with his review of Edgeworth's *Mathematical Psychics*.

24. See above, Chapter 6, pp. 175–6.

25. Marshall to Foxwell, 2 November 1879 (Freeman Collection, 6/79). The article 'Economic Method' had appeared in the *Fortnightly Review*, February 1879, XXV, pp. 301–18; an article, 'What is Money', appeared in the April issue (XXV, pp. 563–75).

26. Marshall to Foxwell, 18 November 1879 (Freeman Collection, 7/9).

27. Marshall to Foxwell, 13 December 1884, A.S. and E.M.S., *Henry Sidgwick. A Memoir*, p. 394.

28. Above, Chapter 10, pp. 306–8.

29. Marshall to Foxwell, 29 December 1884, A.S. and E.M.S., *Henry Sidgwick. A Memoir*, pp. 394–5.

30. See above, Chapter 10, pp. 310–11.

31. See above, Chapters 14, 15.

32. JNKD, 15 and 25 May 1888, the second of which notes his fears about the possibility of Marshall becoming Chairman of the Moral Sciences Board if Sidgwick resigns his chair.

33. See above, Chapter 15, pp. 534–6.

34. Marshall to Henry Sidgwick, 7 June 1887 (NCA) and see above, Chapter 14, pp. 501–2. In the 1897 Senate debate on the women's degree question, Marshall indicated his disagreement with Sidgwick on women's university education started with his return to Cambridge in 1885. Above, Chapter 14, pp. 504–5.

35. JNKD, 8 April 1890.

36. Henry Sidgwick to Foxwell, 8 May 1885 (Freeman Collection, 69/6).

37. Marshall to Foxwell, 23 and 25 September 1887 (Freeman Collection, 26/69, 27/69). Marshall was busy with writing his *Principles*, the Gold and Silver Commission, and was preparing several other things for publication at this time. See above, Chapter 12, pp. 406–7.

38. JNKD, 6 February 1894.

39. JNKD, 5 July 1890; 26 November 1892; 18 June 1895.

40. Marshall to John Neville Keynes, 18 March 1891 (Marshall Archive, 1:101).

41. Marshall to John Neville Keynes, 30 August 1891 (Marshall Archive, 1:102).

42. Marshall to Keynes, 10 October 1892, 30 September 1897 (Marshall Archive, 1:106; 1:112).

43. See above, Chapter 14, esp. pp. 501–5.

44. Marshall to Henry Sidgwick, 30 May 1900 (Sidgwick Papers, Trinity College, Add MS c. 94.114).

45. Marshall to Henry Sidgwick, 6 June 1900 (Sidgwick Papers, Trinity College, Add Ms c.94.115).

46. Marshall to Mrs. Sidgwick, 7 October 1900 (Sidgwick Papers, Trinity College, c. 103^{81}).

47. See above, Chapter 6, pp. 154 n.*, 160; Chapter 9, p. 170.

48. Marshall to Foxwell, circa 1873 (Freeman Collection, 27/136).

49. See above, Chapter 17, pp. 622–7.

50. Marshall to Foxwell, 10 August 1874 (Freeman Collection, 9/89).

51. Marshall to Foxwell, 27 and 31 January, 4 February 1875 (Freeman Collection, 11–13/229).

52. Marshall to Foxwell, 11 September 1877 (Freeman Collection, 19/71); the letter is headed, St John's College, Cambridge.

53. See above, Chapters 8, 9, pp. 236–7, 254, 282–4.

54. Marshall to Foxwell, 28 January 1878 (Freeman Collection, 41/155).

55. Mary Paley Marshall to Foxwell, 26 April 1878 (Freeman Collection, 43/155). The list of subscribers to the present had come via Bonney, a Fellow of John's, and a friend of Marshall.

56. Marshall to Foxwell, 11 September 1878, 14 February 1879 (Freeman Collection).

57. Marshall to Foxwell, April/May 1879, 19 October 1879, 20 November 1879, 6 and 14 December 1879, give an indication of the regularity of the reports on first the diagnosis of the illness, then of the slow and gradual recovery of the patient over the first year of its course.

58. Foxwell to Taylor, Master of St John's College, September and 15 October 1881 (St John's College Archives, D104:109–110) and above, Chapter 9, p. 284 and n. 70.

59. Marshall to Foxwell, 10 October 1881 (Freeman Collection, 16/150); substantial extracts from the letter were quoted in Chapter 7, p. 204. The only other Marshall letter from Palermo which seems to have survived is a brief note to Bastable, sending him a copy of the privately printed Domestic Value Paper with explanations as to its limitations and origins (Belfast, Trinity College, Bastable Papers: Marshall to Bastable, 15 December 1881).

60. Marshall to Foxwell, 22 January and 1 February 1883 (Marshall Library, Foxwell 1:30–31).

61. Above, esp. Chapters 9 and 16, pp. 236–9, 581–6.

62. Marshall to Foxwell, 1 February 1883 (Marshall Library, Foxwell 1:31).

63. Marshall to Foxwell, 1 February 1883 (Marshall Library, Foxwell 1:29); Jevons's *Investigations into Currency and Finance* was published in 1884 with a lengthy introduction by Foxwell and a preface by Jevons's widow, which suggests that when she offered Foxwell the task, she had no idea of the labour she was inflicting on him (Preface, p. xviii).

64. Above, Chapter 17, p. 631.

65. Above, Chapter 10, p. 306.

66. Foxwell to John Neville Keynes, 20 June 1881, 3 May 1890 (Marshall Library, Keynes, 1:22, 32).

67. Marshall to Foxwell, 17 December 1898 (Marshall Library, 1:63); 10 May 1901 (Marshall Library, Foxwell, 1:65).

68. JNKD, 20 April 1897, cited below, p. 675.

69. Above, Chapter 13, pp. 464–7, Chapter 14, pp. 506–7, Chapter 8, pp. 247–8.

70. Foxwell to John Neville Keynes, 3 May 1890 (Marshall Library, Keynes, 1:32).

71. Foxwell to John Neville Keynes, 14 December 1894 (Marshall Library, Keynes, 1:35). Marshall to Foxwell, 2 November 1895, showed how much Marshall relied on Foxwell on such occasions.

72. JNKD, 8 March 1897.

73. Marshall to Foxwell, 23 and 24 February, 21 March 8, 14, 18 and 26 April 1897 (Marshall Library, Foxwell, 1:52–58).

74. See above, Chapter 15, pp. 534–9.

75. Reproduced in JNKD, 17 April 1897. Cf. Foxwell to Beeton on bimetallism, cited above, Chapter 11, for a similar evaluation of Marshall.

76. JNKD, for 21 December 1887; John Maynard Keynes, 'Herbert Somerton Foxwell (1848–1936), *Economic Journal*, 46, December 1936, pp. 604–5. J.N. Keynes had advised Marshall of his worries over Foxwell's library as early as August 1891 (Marshall to John Neville Keynes, 30 August 1891, Marshall Archive, 1:102).

77. Marshall to Foxwell, 7 September 1897 (Marshall Library, Foxwell 1:61).

78. Mary Paley Marshall, 'MSS Notes' (NCA).

79. Above, Chapter 17, pp. 618–19 and n.*.

80. Marshall to John Neville Keynes, 8 January 1901, Marshall Archive, 1:122; for an extract of Marshall's testimonial, see J.M. Keynes, 'Herbert Somerton Foxwell', p. 591.

81. J.M. Keynes, 'Herbert Somerton Foxwell', p. 605.

82. Above, Chapter 15, pp. 550, 551–2, Chapter 11, pp. 382–4.

83. Above, Chapter 17, pp. 615–17.

84. Foxwell to John Neville Keynes, 6 October 1900 (Marshall Library, Keynes, 1:40).

85. Foxwell to John Neville Keynes, 6 February 1912 (Marshall Library, Keynes, 1:44). As explained in Chapter 17 (above p. 627 n.¶), Foxwell's letter commented on a note Marshall had written to John Neville Keynes indicating how pleased he was Foxwell was returning to teach in Cambridge. He told Keynes he could show it to Foxwell, perhaps hoping it would lead to a reconciliation.

86. Marshall to J.N. Keynes, 5 December 1908 (Marshall Archive, 1:136).

87. Foxwell's letter was quoted previously, above, Chapter 17, pp. 626–7, and illustrates Marshall's penchant for exaggeration.

88. Marshall to J.N. Keynes, 12 December 1908 (Marshall Archive, 1:137).

89. Henry Higgs to J.N. Keynes (presumably in his official capacity as University Registrar), 14 December 1908 (Marshall Archive, 2:100).

90. Marshall to J.N. Keynes, undated (Marshall Archive, 1:140).

91. Above, p. 673, Chapter 17, pp. 626–7.

92. Audrey Foxwell, *Herbert Somerton Foxwell: A Portrait*, p. 9. As shown in Chapter 20 below p. 743, Foxwell was present at Marshall's Funeral Service.

93. Robert Skidelsky, *John Maynard Keynes. Hopes Betrayed 1883–1920*, pp. 7–13; the quotations from Keynes's diary come from the entries for 18 April 1874 and 13 March 1875.

94. JNKD, 13 December 1875.

95. JNKD, 25 and 26 April 1877. On Marshall's long-standing hatred of a classical school education, see above, Chapter 3, pp. 59–60.

96. Above, pp. 665, 692.

97. Above, p. 666.

98. Marshall to John Neville Keynes, 15 February 1884.

99. JNKD, 13 February 1882, 21 April 1883. Cf. that for 31 August 1884, where Keynes records he heard from one of Toynbee's students that Marshall had been elected to a Fellowship at Balliol.

100. Above, Chapter 10, p. 308.

101. See above, Chapter 12, p. 408–11.

101. JNKD, 14 January 1888.

103. JNKD, 16 January 1888.

104. JNKD, 17, 18, 21, 24, 28 and 31 January 1888.

105. JNKD, 15 March 1888.

106. JNKD, 18 February and 21 April 1888. Marshall's subsequent long letter, April 26, 1888, was accompanied by extensive critical notes on Keynes's proofs from both him and Mary Paley (Marshall Archive, 1:67).

107. JNKD, 17–20 March, 1888, Marshall to John Neville Keynes, 17 March 1888, above, Chapter 13, p. 464 and n.*.

108. JNKD, 11 November 1888.

109. Marshall to John Neville Keynes, two letters dated simply August 1888, one September 1888. Marshall's principle of 'continuity' as developed in the *Principles* was discussed above, Chapter 12, pp. 411–12.

110. Marshall to John Neville Keynes, 17 and 26 November, 2 December 1889.

111. Marshall to John Neville Keynes, 4 April 1896 (Marshall Archive, 1:110), 22 September 1900 (Marshall Archive, 1:119). On 27 September 1908, Marshall confessed he now found the *Statist* also less useful, and deplored the deline in quality of the *Times* (Marshall Archive, 1:135).

112. JNKD, 21 April 1888; Marshall to Keynes, 4 August 1892 (Marshall Archive, 1:105).

113. JNKD, for example, 24 October and 2 November 1894.

114. C.R. Fay to J.M. Keynes, 13 November 1924, cited above, Chapter 17, p. 652 and n.¶.

115. Above Chapter 15, pp. 553–4.

116. Florence Ada Keynes, *Gathering Up the Threads. A Study in Family Biography*, Cambridge: Heffers, 1950, pp. 109–10.

117. See above, Chapters 8 and 9, pp. 240–41, 276–7; Chapters 11 and 12, pp. 361–2, 367–8, 419, the last of which records Jowett's reaction to the publication of Marshall's *Principles*.

118. Geoffrey Faber, *Jowett. A Portrait with Background,* London: Faber & Faber, second revised edition, 1958, page references to this edition are inserted in brackets in the portmanteau quotation below.

119. E. Abbott and L. Campbell, *The Life and Letters of Benjamin Jowett*, London: John Murray, second edition, 1897, p. 61.

120. Mary Paley Marshall, 'MSS Notes' (NCA).

121. Mary Paley Marshall, *What I Remember*, pp. 36–7. Her account from the same source of their association at Oxford was quoted above, Chapter 8, pp. 240–1.

122. Mary Paley Marshall to Benjamin Jowett, 12 October 1891 (Jowett Papers, Balliol College, Oxford).

123. E. Abbott and L. Campbell, *The Life and Letters of Benjamin Jowett*, pp. 72–3.

124. Benjamin Jowett to Alfred Marshall, September(?) 1879 (Marshall Archive, 1:37).

125. Benjamin Jowett to Marshall, 6 October 1879, (Marshall Archive, 1:38) and cf. above, Chapter 9, pp. 282–4, 288–9.

126. Benjamin Jowett to Marshall, 16 July and 9 August 1881 (Marshall Archive, 1:39–40).

127. Benjamin Jowett to Marshall, 21 August 1881 (Marshall Archive, 1:41); Jowett repeated these sentiments in 1883 when Bonamy Price was up for re-election (Benjamin Jowett to Marshall, 28 March 1883, Marshall Archive, 1:42).

128. Above, Chapter 9, pp. 293–4; the long levity of Bonamy Price was noted above pp. 682–3.

129. Benjamin Jowett to Mary Paley Marshall, 14 December 1884, Jowett to Marshall, 25 December 1884 (Marshall Archive, 1:43–44) and above, Chapter 12, p. 419, and cf. pp. 412–13.

130. Benjamin Jowett to Mary Paley Marshall, 22 February 1885, 5 January and 30 December 1886 (Marshall Archive, 1:45–7).

131. Benjamin Jowett to Mary Paley Marshall, 11 April, 3 July and 19 December 1888, 6 January 1889 and 22 May 1890; Jowett to Marshall, 24 July 1890 (Marshall Archive, 1:48–53); the last letters were quoted above, Chapter 12, pp. 419, 422–3.

132. Cited in Geoffrey Faber, *Jowett*, p. 421. Jowett had in fact had a near fatal coronary thrombosis, and was very ill for some time.
133. Benjamin Jowett to Mary Paley Marshall, 23 July 1891 (Marshall Archive, 1:57).
134. Benjamin Jowett to Mary Paley Marshall, 30 September 1891 (Marshall Archive, 1:58); the summer trip of 1891, their central European '*rundreise*' was discussed above, Chapter 7, pp. 214–15, largely on the basis of Mary Paley's reply.
135. Marshall to Benjamin Jowett, 11 October 1891 (Jowett Papers, Balliol College, Oxford).
136. Mary Paley Marshall to Benjamin Jowett, 12 October 1891 (Jowett Papers, Balliol College, Oxford). For more on its contents see Chapter 7, pp. 214–5.
137. Mary Paley Marshall to Benjamin Jowett, 19 October 1891 (Jowett Papers, Balliol College, Oxford).
138. Marshall to Benjamin Jowett, 20 October 1891 (Jowett Papers, Balliol College, Oxford). The gossip mentioned concerned the Labour Commission, to which Marshall had been appointed the previous spring; its contents were quoted previously in that context, Chapter 11, pp. 367–8.
139. Mary Paley Marshall to Benjamin Jowett, 22, 26, 29 October 1891, Alfred Marshall, 4 November 1891 (Jowett Papers, Balliol College, Oxford). The Labour Commission news Marshall discussed with Jowett was extensively quoted above, Chapter 11, pp. 367–8.
140. Benjamin Jowett to Mary Paley Marshall, 10 June and 16 October 1892; 2 January and 7 August 1893 (Marshall Archive, 1:59–62); the controversy with Cunningham was discussed previously, Chapter 13 above, pp. 469–71 in the context of which some of Jowett's remarks from these letters were quoted.
141. Alfred Marshall, 'Benjamin Jowett', in *Memorials*, pp. 293–4.
142. *Ibid.*, p. 292.
143. J.M. Keynes, 'Alfred Marshall', p. 200. In 1914, Marshall referred to Abbé, the manager of Zeiss as his 'patron saint' (Marshall to Lewis Fry, 7 November 1914, in *Memorials*, pp. 484–6).
144. Alfred Marshall, 'Benjamin Jowett', p. 293.
145. Above, Chapter 12, pp. 414–15, 419.
146. Much of this discussion of Jowett's 1841 notebook draws on Warren Samuel's unpublished paper, 'Benjamin Jowett's Connections with Political Economy', with its copious quotations from this notebook, assistance here gratefully acknowledged.
147. Mary Paley Marshall, *What I Remember*, pp. 36–7.
148. Especially Chapter 14, above, pp. 517–20.
149. Charles Booth to Alfred Marshall, 18 and 20 October 1886 (London University Library, Booth Papers, MS797, I/1310–12). For Marshall's involvement with the housing question and industrial villages see above, Chapter 13, pp. 449–52.
150. Above, Chapter 7, p. 212, Chapter 11, pp. 355–6.
151. Royal Commission on Labour, *Fourth Report*, Cmnd 7063, London: HMSO, 1893, 30 November 1892, Q. 5,592–626; Charles Booth to Marshall, 25 May 1894 (Booth Papers, MS797, I/1352).
152. Above, Chapter 11, p. 359, Charles Booth to Alfred Marshall, 27 April and 3 May 1892 (Booth Papers, MS797 I 1324/1325).
153. Above, Chapter 11, p. 358, this chapter, p. 692 n.*.
154. Marshall to Charles Booth, 31 March 1903 (Booth Papers, MS797 I/5770).
155. Charles Booth to Marshall, 21 April 1907 (Booth Papers, MS797 I/1715) and for further context to this letter, above Chapter 11, pp. 359–60.
156. Charles Booth to Marshall, 10 November 1913 (Booth Papers, MS797 I/2037).
157. Marshall to Mary Booth, 24 November 1916 (Booth Papers, MS797 I/5771).
158. Mary Paley Marshall to Mary Booth, 24 November 1916 (Booth Papers, MS797 I/5772).
159. Belinda Norman Butler, *Victorian Aspirations*, p. 208.
160. Mary Paley Marshall to 'Meg', 2 October 1939 (Booth Papers, MS979, I/5773).

19. Some Final Volumes: 1919–1924

Marshall's retirement had been inspired by a desire to press on with his writing. His slow progress with this has already been frequently mentioned. Work on the second volume of the *Principles* was very unhurried, unfocused and subject to much change and delay. By 1911 it had been perceptively likened by Marshall to Penelope's web, never-ending by choice. After retirement, its official abandonment was announced in 1910 by the removal of 'Volume I' from the spine of the *Principles* in its sixth edition. This also announced the alternative strategy of producing several companion volumes to the book of 'foundations' the *Principles* then became.[1]

Even by publication of the seventh edition in 1916, this aim had not been achieved. In that war year, the obligation to write a chapter on post-war taxation policy, reluctantly accepted as part of his personal war effort, distracted Marshall even further from completing the task in hand. It compounded the interruptions to his writing from correspondence and added to its growing difficulties from weakness of will, constitution and eventually, increased ill health. He therefore wrote by way of its preface:

> It is now twenty-six years since the first edition of this volume implied a promise that a second volume, completing the treatise, would appear within a reasonable time. But I had laid my plan on too large a scale; and its scope widened, especially on the realistic side, with every pulse of that Industrial Revolution of the present generation, which has far outdone the changes of a century ago, in both rapidity and breadth of movement. So ere long I was compelled to abandon my hope of completing the work in two volumes. My subsequent plans were changed more than once, partly by the course of events, partly by my other engagements, and the decline of my strength: and I am now engaged in writing an independent work, which is to extend to more than one volume, on *Industry and Trade*. It is designed to cover a considerable part of the ground over which I had originally hoped to travel: but it will be directed mainly to a study of the causes which have brought about the present methods and organisation of business; to the influences, which they exert on the quality of life; and to the ever widening problems to which they give rise.[2]

Even this plan was not fulfilled. When in 1919 *Industry and Trade* appeared, it was as a single volume, 'designed to be followed by a companion volume, which is to be occupied with influences on those conditions exerted by the resources available for employment; by money and credit; by international trade; and by social endeavour'.[3] This promised volume was eventually published in 1923. However, what was now called 'the third of a group' of books, only imperfectly achieved the aim of 1919. It brought together material on money and credit, international trade, and fluctuations in trade, industry and credit, a miscellaneous but inter-connected collection assembled largely from earlier work. Hope springs eternal in the human breast, and in August 1922 when the preface of *Money, Credit and Commerce* was dated, its author, with old age pressing upon him, and only a little progress to report on the task, could still express the wish 'that some of the notions, which I have formed as to the possibilities of social advance, may yet be published'.[4] A fourth companion volume never did appear. Its embryo was for long preserved in little strips of notes, sown together with string, among so many of the other manuscripts in the Marshall Library.[5]

The preparation and content of these three companions are examined in this chapter. Their status is in many ways nominal when compared with the great first volume which so proudly preceded it. They are true companions in their neat bindings of Macmillan blue cloth, their gold lettering on the spine, and even their size. Appropriate size for number three was only achieved by the device of the extra thick paper used in printing *Money, Credit and Commerce*, given its half normal quota of less than four hundred pages. In their content, the group is highly differentiated. Keynes made this point delicately, but precisely, in his very honest appraisal of this 'great effort of will and determination on the part of one who had long passed the age when most men rest from their labour'. *Industry and Trade*, he continued:

> is altogether a different sort of book from the *Principles*. The most part of it is descriptive. A full third is historical and summarises the results of his long labours in that field. The co-ordination of the parts into a single volume is rather artificial. The difficulties of such co-ordination, which had beset him for so many years, are not really overcome. The book is not so much a structural unity as an opportunity for bringing together a number of partly related matters about which Marshall had something of value to say to the world. This is particularly the case with its sixteen Appendices, which are his device for bringing to birth a number of individual monographs and articles. Several of these had been written a great number of years before the book was issued. They were quite well suited to separate publication, and it must be judged a fault in him that they were hoarded as they were. . . . *Money Credit and Commerce* was . . . published in 1923. . . . The book is mainly pieced together from earlier fragments, some of them written fifty years before. . . . It shows the marks of old age in a way which *Industry and Trade* did not. But it contains a quantity of materials and ideas, and collects together passages which are otherwise inaccessible . . . . or difficult of access. . . . Up to his last illness, in spite of great feebleness of body, he struggled to piece together one more volume. It was to have been called *Progress: its Economic Conditions*. But the task was too great . . .[6]

The tale of the final volumes starts, however, in 1903 when, instead of a formal second volume, Marshall planned continuation of the *Principles* on a more lavish scale. A volume on *National Industries and International Trade* was now the intention, to be largely taken, as he wrote to Macmillan, from the existing manuscript for his second volume.[7] In 1904, Marshall wrote to Flux who had offered to read proofs, that the first half of the new work was concerned with 'the causes and nature of industrial leadership treated historically as well as analytically', the second with international trade, with a number of appendices and application to more 'current issues: coming towards the end'.[8] Two months later in May 1904, he advised Flux of growing difficulties with his writing. The Tariff controversy, in which Marshall had been embroiled the year before, had implications for the size of the book, by lessening 'demand for short books' on the subject. His own plan must therefore become larger. He also reported that having completed his writing on German industrial problems, he could start on those in the United States, making Part I of the book approximately two hundred pages long. Only after that was finished, would he be able to commence the second part on international trade.[9]

Marshall wrote to Cunynghame at this time[10] that he had promised Macmillan 'to keep the text of the book . . . (not the *appendices*) in a form as attractive as I can to the practical man', while he wrote to Macmillan that his plan was to fully emphasise 'the industrial conditions which underlie the fiscal issues of the day'. Hence he would also have to deal with 'large industrial aggregations' such as trusts and cartels.[11] The origins of the second companion volume to the *Principles* were therefore from the start closely inter-twined with the fiscal controversy over international trade, which was not to be finally resolved for Marshall until events forced him to revise the 1903 *Memorandum* for publication in 1908. The years following 1904 until his retirement tell the familiar tale of a book growing in scope and slowness of work, partly from the growth and complexity of the 'realistic' side of the material, partly from pressures of other work. In January 1907 Marshall wrote the first formal notification to his publisher that the original scheme of a two-volume *Principles* was no longer operational and would be abandoned. This step is revealed in the nature of the new material introduced for the appendices initiated in the fifth edition of the *Principles* later that year but, as indicated earlier, was not formally acknowledged until the sixth edition of 1910 removed Volume I from its spine and title page. Marshall's retirement year of 1908 therefore entailed a cleaner slate for future work in two important ways. During it, the *Memorandum on Fiscal Policy of International Trade* was published, 'which makes me more free', Marshall wrote to Macmillan,[12] 'to keep the controversial element in *National Industry and Trade* very low'. Secondly, with Marshall's personal abandonment of the plan for a second volume of the *Principles*, all the formal constraints it implied for the current book disappeared, leaving him free to develop the material for the *Industry and Trade* volume without any encumbrances.

FROM VOLUMES ON NATIONAL INDUSTRIES AND TRADE TO INDUSTRY AND TRADE: 1909 TO 1919

Despite the effective removal of much controversial material from the work, by 1910 Marshall reported to his patient publisher that difficulties with the analytical side of the book from reduced mental agility, together with the need for the 'realistic part' of the work to be rewritten once every decade, implied little ground for optimism for imminent completion of the task. Part of the explanation was also the growing scale of the work,

> I think the book may run to about 1000 pages. Later on I will give you a closer estimate and ask you whether it should appear as one volume or two. I do not like to prophesy, But I hope – in spite of the sluggishness of my weary old brain – to begin to print again before the end of this year and to publish before the end of the next. I have tried your patience sorely.[13]

Although Marshall's dislike of prophecy proved to be warranted, one aspect of the projected work remained constant. Appendices would deal with 'complex analysis or hard reasoning' in order to get 'the book read by practical men without spoiling it from the rigidly scientific point of view'.

A visitor that summer from America confirmed these optimistic expectations about progress, adding that the book would not really be the second volume of the *Principles*, but would 'deal with International values, protection, and I know not what other subjects'.[14] Even Macmillan was infected with an incautious note of optimism, writing in May 1913 that they looked forward to going 'to press' in autumn with two volumes of *National Industry and Trade*, with Volume III, perhaps the volume foreshadowed earlier as *Money, Credit and Employment*, to follow as soon as possible thereafter.[15] The book's progress, however, became a victim of war. In April 1916, a very busy year for Marshall due to other projects,[16] he once again had to report slow progress to Macmillan, for the first time outlining the events as they were to actually unfold over the remaining years of his life. Change of title to *Industry and Trade* was, however, not announced until November of that year:

> I make very slow progress with my new book. I have now got nearly the whole of the first volume into slips: but if the thing is ever finished, it will run to three volumes, each about three fourths as long as my *Principles*.
> I am dropping 'national' and calling it 'Industry & Trade'. Vol. I consists of:
> Book I   Origins of the present problems of Industry and trade (a historical introduction)
> Book II   The organization & administration of business (very realistic)
> Book III   Tendencies to monopolistic aggregation.
> Vol. II is to be on International & some monetary problems. Most of it is typewritten. Vol III exists only in fragments & old material. It is designed to cover social & governmental applications of the other two etc.
> About three years ago I found myself unable to do much work. I found that diseased gums had brought on blood pressure. I fell into able hands, & am in relatively good health, though I cannot work much. But I find that what I wrote before I knew I was ill is not satisfactory: & I cannot expect to bring out Vol. II, without much re-writing.
> I had therefore proposed to suggest that Vol. I should come out as soon as ready. But in view of the war my own inclination is now distinctly to wait & bring out Vols I and II together.
> If I do not finish Vol III (I am now in my 74th year), I propose to arrange that it should be converted in large measure into a collection of essays &c. already published, & selected with a view to the main purpose, which I propose for the volume, if I should be able to complete it.[17]

Macmillan readily agreed to Marshall's plan of publishing the two proposed volumes together, adding that this strategy made it best to postpone publication until after the war. However, this plan had also to be abandoned as over-optimistic.[18] Marshall soon reported the final chapters of Volume I were giving him trouble, and by the end of 1916 forecast the following scenario, necessitated by both the weakening of his intellectual powers and the complexity of the material. Volume I, concerned with 'Origins and Problems with the present industrial structure, with special reference to its monopolistic tendencies' was to be ready for publication by Easter 1917; Volume II, because it needed considerable re-writing, would unfortunately have to be postponed indefinitely. Because of this postponement, some drastic alterations had to be made to the material of Volume I dealing with the history of international trade policy, all of which was now to be shifted to appendices. In reporting this, Marshall continued,

> I must wrap myself in the white sheet, & hold the candle of the penitent when I pass to speak of my new work. For I know I have run up a huge printers bill on it. . . . I will not narrate the history of my vacillations as to scope and arrangement of the work. They have been caused partly by external events; partly by my tardy recognition of the magnitude of the task proposed: but chiefly by the mental inertia caused by 'blood pressure' before I knew that such a malady existed, & by the extreme slowness of work

which I am told is the only condition under which I can hope to work at all. So long as I obey orders, I am in excellent health.[19]

This announcement coincided with the firm adoption of *Industry and Trade* as the apposite title for the work. By June 1918, Marshall informed Macmillan the volume was advanced sufficiently to expect it to be ready by early autumn, and once again explained delay by the desire to make it as topical as possible. This meant including all the shifts in policy which were coming out of Whitehall 'at an unprecedented pace'. A crucial aspect in this context was the Whitley Report, one of the many *'embarassement des richesses'* in the form of official papers and blue books which was plaguing him, and which, among other things, entailed that the last chapter had to be re-written four times.[20]

An amusing sidelight in this long saga of changed plans and continuous drastic revision to proofs was that Marshall was annoyed when Macmillan refused to place 'Volume I on the title page'. However, after some consideration, he accepted this decision, on which Macmillan, not surprisingly, stood firm. However, he had one more try at getting some acknowledgement from them that this was only the first of two volumes:

I think you are right about dropping the words 'Volume I'. There is enough matter in semi-final form for my second volume to be printed, even if I should be unable to do anything more at it. I propose to speak of it in my Preface to this volume as a companion volume: and perhaps to indicate, more or less precisely, that its title will probably be *'Industry and Trade*, a study of the organization of employment, of international trade, and of other influences on the conditions of various classes and nations'. I cannot think of any other fitting titles on the backs than 'Industry and Trade' in both cases. The companion volume might have ** on its back: & perhaps this might have a single asterisk.[21]

Although Macmillan agreed to the asterisk, the device they were then using on Taussig's *Principles of Economics*, no such asterisk appeared on the published first edition; Macmillan was no longer prepared to take risks of this nature in the less certain publishing environment after the First World War.[*] In June 1919, the last corrections were sent off from the Marshall household at Balliol Croft, where they had been attended to by Mary Paley, after nephew Claude Guillebaud could no longer work on proofs because of his transfer to war duties at Whitehall. Apart from Flux who, as indicated previously, had assisted in the earlier versions of this long gestating work, the preface acknowledged assistance from Dr Clapham in safe-guarding the quality of Marshall's historical ventures for the first part of the book and for its early Appendices. In August 1919, the first printing of 2,000 copies were in the bookshops and sold sufficiently well for a second 'edition' to be required by December of that year.[¶]

---

[*] Macmillan to Marshall, 24 October 1918 (Marshall Archive, 2:22). In this context, John Whitaker has noted, 'A corrected copy of the first edition of *Industry and Trade* in the Marshall Library has an asterisk inked on the spine, Marshall did not give up easily!' ('What happened to the Second Volume of the *Principles*?', p. 213 n.74).

[¶] *IT*, p. ix. Proofs had been produced steadily since 1904, and were not confined to the final proofs issued in 1919. Macmillan to J.M. Keynes, 8 September 1924 (KMF) indicates that the December 1919, second edition, printing was 3,000 copies; a further 2,000 were printed for the 'third edition' of 1920, and again in 1921, followed by a further 3,000 in 1923, a total of 12,000 copies printed before Marshall's death. This is almost double the number printed for the first three editions of Volume I of the *Principles*, an indication of the growth of both the discipline and the stature of the author.

A STUDY OF INDUSTRY AND TRADE IN A CONTEMPORARY SETTING: CONTENTS AND RECEPTION

Marshall's *Industry and Trade* is a substantial book. It is a volume slightly longer than the final editions of the *Principles*, having close to 900 pages, of which over 850 pages are text including appendices. Its three books deal respectively with 'origins of present problems of industry and trade', 'dominant tendencies of business organisation', and 'monopolistic tendencies, their relation to public well being'. About a quarter of the text is devoted to its sixteen appendices. Half of these are historical in nature, for reasons already explained; others are methodological (Appendix A). More generally, they offer clarification of the text to which they refer, in some cases reprinting material published elsewhere, such as the 1905 letter to the *Times* on business education which forms the basis for Appendix K. The book's sub-title, 'A study of industrial technique and business organisation; and of their influences on the conditions of various classes and nations' indicates the unity of subject matter for the work, a unity which its author clearly emphasised in the introductory chapter to the book:

> The present Volume as a whole may be regarded as concerned first with the origins of modern industrial technique and business organization; secondly with the parts played by particular nations in developing them; and thirdly with the problems rising out of that development. These problems are considered in Book II, with little or no reference to monopolistic tendencies; which are dealt with in Book III. In Books II and III there is an ever-increasing drift towards consideration of the harmonies and discords of interest among the several sections of a nation, and between each of those sections and the nation as a whole.[22]

The first book is therefore essentially historical, drawing on Marshall's growing appreciation of the work of Ashley and of 'the late Professor Schmoller', specifically mentioned in this context in the preface.[23] Contrary to the view that Marshall was hostile to work of members of the historical school, whether from England or Germany, especially that of the younger German historical school led for so long by Gustav Schmoller, *Industry and Trade* clearly demonstrates his affinity to such work when appropriate to the task at hand. The different paths to industrial leadership taken by the countries used as case studies in that first book, illustrate the importance of this influence not only for understanding German economic development, but also for France, the United States and even England. For example, Marshall's position on mercantilism which Appendix D examined in detail, largely in relation to what he perceived as the exaggerated and hence erroneous views of Adam Smith, show a clear preference for the more balanced account from what was then the recent scholarship of Ashley and Schmoller. This was supplemented by his own rather detailed reading of mercantilist tracts, drawing particularly on those readily accessible to him because they had been reprinted by McCulloch for the Political Economy Club.[24]

The book also illustrates the value of the motto, 'The many in the one, the one in the many' as an organising principle for this diverse material which indicates the varied ramifications of specific aspects of historical development on present problems of industry and trade. As may be recalled from earlier correspondence with Edgeworth, this principle of interdependence and interaction was intended by Marshall to be the major strength of the work, a matter to which attention was drawn in both the preface and introductory chapter.[25]

Combined with the problem of 'so interpreting the past that it may be a guide to the future', this type of complexity made this work so difficult to construct for Marshall, particularly when, both during the war, and even more in its immediate aftermath, the facts of the present to be interpreted, continually kept changing. His heroic attempts to keep up with the 'realistic part' of things were at least one of the reasons for the inordinate delay in completing the book.

Book I more specifically indicated how particular aspects of national development in various countries had influenced its contemporary pattern of industry and trade. This discussion draws on geographical factors influencing industrial concentration; technical innovation and progress, as assisted by scientific research and education and the institutions designed to foster these; access to, and development of, means of transport and communication; as well as broad national characteristics, and the nature of government policy, including the very topical one of war.[*] Relevant national characteristics range from proclivities in fashion and engineering discovered among the French, to German leadership in industries where laboratory work and academic training were of great importance, and the American quality of enterprise and risk taking induced by its migrant population and wide open spaces. The role of government policy in industrial development enabled the introduction not only of the vexed question of protection and industrial growth, but also of policies encouraging regional free trade, such as the classic example of the German *Zollverein* and the potential for this in a possible British federation of nations incorporating the members of her far flung Empire. Marshall's evaluation of government policy in this context also covered more specific policies on labour relations, capital accumulation and credit supply, education and scientific co-ordination as well as more regulatory activities in sectors of industry.

The internationally comparative slant of the book meant considerable attention could be given to the possibility of halting the decline of British industry, so evident to Marshall and of such concern to him from the end of the previous century. It also allowed him to speculate a little on future outcomes in industrial leadership. The last emphasised the difficulties in making such a forecast; accentuated by the increasing speed of change. After reconfirming his earlier faith in the future of the United States, Marshall found 'in Japan a bold claimant for leadership in the East on lines that are mainly western', stressing similar advantages of geography on which Britain had drawn in the past. More remotely, Marshall predicted the possibility of 'great futures' for China and Russia, and saw even signs of future economic and industrial greatness for India. His general conclusion is not easily controverted: 'there is no sure ground for thinking that industrial leadership will remain always with the same races, or in the same climates, as in recent times; nor even that its general character will remain unaltered'.[26]

---

[*] In this context, Marshall did not only draw on the impact of past wars on industrial development, but more specifically on the experience provided by the recent world war. Its importance in this context was shown by the greater awareness of the need for formulating a national science policy; as a force in standardisation and specialisation; an influence on railway organisation and more generally, on transport and communication developments; as a factor bearing upon wages and working conditions; while war experience also provided Marshall with analogies and other illustrations for his argument. See, for example, *IT*, pp. 2, 79–85, 87–8, 99, 129, 224–8, 491–2, 593, 741–2, 700.

Book II dealt with contemporary problems of business organisation, in particular with 'the growth of massive production, and the ever increasing size of the representative unit in almost every branch of industry and trade'. As Marshall had written to Flux twenty years before, this was one of his 'chief hobbies', which had driven him to frequent inspections of factories in many summer vacations, and had generated his concept of the 'representative firm' as a possible resolution to the conflict between competition and increasing returns from growth in scale. It had also forced him to delve into the analysis of supplementary costs and long-term supply price, including their relationship to fluctuations in credit and prices, topics whose development he saw as crucial for his Volume II, then still firmly on the agenda.[27] It is therefore not surprising that the subject of increasing returns covered virtually the whole of Book II and, with special reference to monopoly policy, parts of Book III of *Industry and Trade*. Much of this material can also therefore be seen as supplementing the theoretical discussion of production in Book IV of the *Principles*, and its implications for competition, supply price and price determination discussed in its Book V and some of its appendices.[28]

Industry and Trade pays specific attention to developing the realistic side of this problem, which had engaged Marshall for much of his life, and which, unlike some later practice,[29] he did not seek to avoid but wished to face head on. Its first chapter relates the problem of industrial structure and size to the extent of the market, reviewing the theory and emphasising some of its inherent conceptual difficulties. Subsequent chapters are then free to deal with more specialised subjects. Standardisation and the associated development of machinery and mechanisation introduce more detailed discussion on technical influences on the size of the firm. The subject of marketing is then introduced. This highlights Marshall's realistic awareness that the firm was a selling as well as a producing unit, while manufacturing industry also entered markets as buyers of materials and other resources to use as its inputs. A variety of aspects of the marketing problem is covered. These include the 'constructive speculation' which is the major feature of 'organised produce markets', a topic which enabled Marshall to display his knowledge of the wheat industry, of which he had earlier informed Edgeworth in a different context.[30] Broad problems of general marketing are then discussed, from both the cost side and the consumption side, showing its growing necessity in industrial development and emphasising the importance of locational decisions in limiting such essential marketing costs. Developments in retail trade are discussed next, showing Marshall's concern over the implications of this part of production on industrial structure and industrial costs, and emphasising competitive practices of branding goods, trade marks and advertising.[31] Marketing is of special significance to this analysis because it is subject to enormous possibilities for increasing returns.

The final chapters of Book II discuss aspects of business organisation less directly related to the production and marketing processes for particular commodities. The first of these dealt with the advantages and disadvantages of joint-stock companies, where disadvantages included dangers of bureaucratisation when control is divorced from ownership. The next chapter deals with financial aspects of investment, both in terms of longer-term capital requirements financed by share issues, and the provision of short-term capital needs through bank credit. Discussion of the organisational talent requirements of modern management are considered next, in the context of which the role of business education is examined; issues of scientific management in the special way that term was then being used in the United States are then evaluated, together with other contributions scientific organisation can make to the improvement of business practice. The issues discussed are practical and informed by current literature. References are largely confined to material from the decade before the war, an explicitly admitted shortcoming of the German material. The book and its predecessor are clearly intended to provide a useful analytical matrix for understanding all aspects of business organisation in an open, competitive economy, in the way they were revealing themselves in the period before the war. The permanent value of such an analytical framework can be grasped in terms of the definition of industrial organisation economics offered in the early 1970s by a leading exponent, because it is a definition which in the broad captures the essentials of Marshall's book:

> Industrial organisation describes the way in which the activities undertaken within the economic system are divided up between firms. As we know, some firms embrace many different activities; while for others, the range is narrowly circumscribed. Some firms are large; others small. Some firms are vertically integrated, others are not. This is the organisation of industry or – as it used to be called – the structure of industry. What one would expect to learn from a study of industrial organisation would be how industry is organised now, and how this differs from what it was in earlier periods; what forces were operative in bringing about this organisation of industry, and how these forces have been changing over time; what the effects would be of proposals to change, through legal actions of various kinds, the forms of industrial organisation.[32]

The last lines of this quotation mention the type of normative issues Marshall raised, largely in the final chapter of Book II and in the discussion of monopoly in Book III. The rest summarises the previous two Books in the way in which their message was absorbed by followers of Marshall both in Cambridge and elsewhere who developed his theme of the need to understand both the structure and organisation of industry in its ever-changing patterns. In this sense, Marshall's *Industry and Trade* is not simply the descriptive opus Keynes described. It is a research programme of continuing value to economists interested in the 'realistic' side of things. Accepting the need for such a research programme is essential for making reasonable policy decisions, the reason why Marshall from the outset of his labours, so very deliberately placed 'application to current issues' at the end. The facts and the analysis of industrial structure, which required an essential historical dimension, preceded of necessity the matters concerning restructured markets under conditions of monopoly which formed the subject of Book III.[33]

The third Book begins with a general discussion of the various influences of monopoly on prices in which Marshall took care to stress the dangers of artificially distinguishing competition from monopoly. 'The fiercest and cruellest forms of competition', he argued, can be found in non-free markets, in which a giant firm was striving for a monopoly position. Cartels and similar regulative institutions were other instances of the large grey area between competitive and monopolistic policy and institutions. Last but not least, Marshall saw public advantages as well as disadvantages in monopoly, particularly in industries in which there were longer-term opportunities for exploiting increasing returns to scale.[34]

This led him logically to the next chapter, discussing issues of monopoly taxation as a way of reaping such benefits for the public, and to a lengthy, four chapter analysis of competition and monopoly in transport. These bristle with more technical analysis designed to illustrate the extent of, and need for, government regulation or ownership of such industries, a vexed question at the time, and one leading directly into the more general issue of principle involved in controlling the market power of trusts and cartels. For reasons of the superiority of their data, Marshall initially concentrated on United States experience in discussing policies of maintaining competition against trusts, thereby stressing the importance of adequate information before embarking on a legislative programme to combat undesirable monopolistic practices. His United States example of such efforts in trust building and attempts at their legislative control and regulation drew on steel, oil, tobacco and railways. These experiences were then contrasted with German pre-war practice in organising and controlling cartels, giving illustrations from appropriate German industries and emphasising the importance of German banking institutions in this process.

The three penultimate chapters of Book III seek to do the same for British industrial experience with combinations and trade associations. These are compared with more developed American and German practice, and stress the importance of both regulatory needs and developments for British industry, the public benefit and the national interest, provided that appropriate safeguards are in place. Marshall's policy recommendations for Britain favoured regulatory devices over state ownership, particularly when they involved cooperative arrangements enabling representation from various sections of society. The last chapter more specifically developed such class aspects of these problems to which the sub-title of the book and the most recent actual developments and initiatives in Britain were drawing his attention.

It is not difficult to see why Marshall found this such a difficult chapter to write. It attempted to bring together various strands of industrial policy, some of which he only slightly touched upon in the preceding chapters of the Book. The discussion shows the importance of the ideal of social progress in Marshall's forward-looking thinking at this time, a tendency on his part so strikingly evident in the optimistic and idealistic last *ex cathedra* address on 'Social Possibilities of Economic Chivalry', so much of which was simultaneously incorporated in the strengthened 'new' final chapter of the *Principles* from its fifth edition onwards.[35]

The final chapter of *Industry and Trade* discusses in turn many of Marshall's social 'hobby horses' and prejudices. It commences with the impact of education and technical progress on manual work and the standard of life, one of Marshall's earliest social concerns. It then condemns trade unions for encouraging anti-social work practices inimical to productivity growth which Britain so greatly required, if it was to retain its competitive advantage. Cooperation between capital and labour is then examined, during which older schemes of profit sharing and co-partnership were praised and the case was put that control of business organisation should stay with the risk bearers. Marshall next focused on the economic role of the State, that 'most precious of human possessions', noting that it 'being a brave borrower' rather than accumulator of capital meant curtailment of its economic activities in industry, since capital shortages were certain to be predominant during post-war reconstruction. Marshall's earlier conclusion on this topic therefore continued to reassert itself: 'Collective control of industry would be unfavourable to the best selection of men for its most responsible work.' This principle has implications for competition policy as the best way of controlling the 'juggernaut' of combination and monopoly; provided it was leavened by that equality of opportunity which allowed competition by merit and encouraged associations aimed at enriching life in the higher public interest. The National Guilds of the Whitley Report, particularly as elaborated by G.D.H. Cole, were therefore opposed by Marshall as potential controllers, co-ordinators and organisers of industry. Instead, he preferred regulating the 'present economic system' through the 'unseen hand' of the market, even if its 'discipline' may sometimes be too 'harsh'. Its removal, however, by government created controls and regulation, would allow society to 'drift into chaos, from which relief can be found only in a military despotism'.[36]

So much for the immediate future of post-war reconstruction. For the more distant future, Marshall conceded there was 'room for large hopes'. These arose from education, technical progress, encouragement of free enterprise and redistributional fiscal policy, the factors underpinning his 'tendency to socialism' announced in the preface. Seen in historical perspective, much social progress had already taken place. More importantly, it was continuing. Marshall's concluding paragraph to the book transformed the more mundane, factual account of industry and trade, supplementary costs and marketing, increasing returns and competition, trusts and cartels, into a higher, future perspective. This was the type of vision his more cynical but equally visionary pupil, Maynard Keynes, was to drench with cold water in the phrase, 'in the long run we are all dead'. Given his own proximity to that state, Marshall had no qualms about a final clarion call on the brightness of future possibilities:

> Organic life on this little planet, which has been inhabitable for only a few thousand years, may indeed perhaps claim to have made fair progress, morally as well as physically, in a minute fraction of the period during which the stellar universe is known to have been nearly in its present form. Other planets, which have been suitable for the maintenance of organic life during much longer periods, may have gone a long way towards solving socio-economic problems, of which we are only able to touch timidly the outskirts. In particular they may have probed many of those responsibilities of the individual to the State and of the State to the individual, as to which we have learnt so much in the last few generations, that we appear to have made some considerable way towards fathoming the depths of our ignorance. But it seems that, the longer we ponder, the greater must be our diffidence in prediction, and the more profound the awe with which we regard the divine government of the Universe.[37]

Given the sentiments of the final chapter, combined with the more general attack on government ownership and control in the chapters dealing with monopoly, particularly in transport, it is not surprising that the book was badly received by the socialist side of politics. In the *Daily News*, R.H. Tawney took Marshall to task for condemning state ownership and nationalisation without any real demonstration, empirically or otherwise, that industry, as currently organised, 'performs its functions with reasonable efficiency'.[38] The *New Statesman*, perhaps a trifle unjustly, condemned the book for ignoring the wage-earner, adding that it offered little on the subject of cooperation. The Church was more supportive, even in episcopal pronouncements on its relation to socialism. It praised Marshall's defence of economics against wrong social criticism. This was an essential contribution, because removal of 'popular prejudice against economic science' was imperative when 'the measure of success which any programme of social reform can secure will finally be determined by its fidelity to economic principles'.[39] Fifty years before, this tune had lured Marshall into joining the band of economists.

The rest of the vast press reviews that the book received were more laudatory. The *Liverpool Post* (16 November 1919) stated 'Dr. Marshall's treatment has a breadth and humanity which confounds those who cling to the belief that economics is the dismal science'; The *Daily Mail* (3 September 1919) pronounced Marshall from this book to be 'a truth seeker, not a peddler of panaceas'; this was endorsed by the *Anglo-Spanish Trade Journal* (30 January 1920) in its comment that Marshall 'never writes for display, but always with the singleminded desire to present the truth accurately; . . . [this induces] an extreme cautiousness in expressing decided opinions [and reveals his] scrupulous intellectual honesty'. On a more elevated plane, the *Highway* (December 1919) ventured the opinion that Marshall's new book compared favourably with the much earlier *Principles of Economics*. This judgement was shared by the *Westminister Gazette* (1 November 1919) which found 'the long years of waiting amply justified' and the *Durham University News* (July 1920), 'The debt which economics owes to the work of Dr. Marshall was great already; the present volume makes it well nigh incalculable'. Less earnest Oxford greeted the book as 'worthy of his high established fame', blessing it for an absence of the customary 'curves' (*Oxford Magazine*, 20 February 1920); more seriously, the *Economist* (13 December 1919) contrasted 'the complete touch with realities' of the author, thanks to Blue Books, and other official and trade publications, with the lack of reality in contemporary socialism, which Marshall had raised in the autobiographical segment of his preface. Perhaps the reviewer was thinking here of the ample use the author had made of the *Economist* itself, as one of its long, and distinguished, subscribers. Only the *Times Literary Supplement* (8 January 1920) reacted unfavourably, largely because of the pro-German sentiments the book contained, particularly with respect to German university education. This half delighted, rather than annoyed the author: 'I was afraid of being condemned as overrating German deficiencies, so there is some comfort'.[*]

Academic reviews would have been more carefully scrutinised at Balliol Croft, especially when they came from 'young colts' in Marshall's slowly expanding Cambridge stable. Pigou reviewed the book for the *Economic Journal*. The range of topics it covered, 'no less than the author's rivalled mastery of the subject' made it impossible for a single review to grapple with 'this mine of learning and engine of power'. All that Pigou therefore could do in the eight pages the *Journal* had set aside for him, was to make a 'rough inventory' of its 'comparative history of many countries, [discussion of] the detailed technique of many industries, elaborate realistic analysis, . . . all welded together into an ordered whole'.[40] In the *Indian Economic Journal*, H.S. Jevons praised the publication of

---

[*] This paragraph draws extensively on the newspaper scrapbook of the Marshalls preserved in the Marshall Library, which also contains Marshall's hand-written comment on the *Times* review just quoted. On the use Marshall made of the *Economist* in writing *Industry and Trade*, see, for example, pp. 347 n.2, 440 n.1 and esp. p. 577 n.1 where Marshall stressed how helpful long files of the *Economist* were for examining certain problems. The one criticism of Marshall's knowledge of industrial facts came from the *Yorkshire Observer* (6 September 1919), a criticism Marshall corrected in the later editions.

Industry and Trade, as 'an outstanding event', even though it was not 'the intended second volume'. Jevons complimented the author particularly on its style, 'the care and accuracy of thought which has gone into every sentence', as well as into the setting out and general arrangement of its contents, picking illustrating samples of special appeal to his Indian readers.[41] From the many European reviews the book received, Charles Gide's notice for the *Revue d'économie politique* provides an interesting example. He described the publication of a new book by Marshall as 'The most rare of events', not experienced since 1890, and all the more novel because parts of it had been in print since 1904. Reflecting contemporary French economic tastes, akin to those in some Oxford circles, he noted the book had no algebra or diagrams to frighten readers. Instead, their appetites were whetted by a display of its rich contents: 'industrial characteristics of various countries, concentration of industry, trusts, machinery, the Taylor system of scientific management, influence of monopoly on price, railways, co-operation and nationalisation'. In addition, Gide expressed admiration, supported by select quotation, that the author had maintained a remarkable even-handedness on all these subjects.[42] The Royal Statistical Society saw the book as 'an enzyme or ferment of men's minds, precipitating new conclusions out of stagnation' and as a 'trebly distilled essence of all the author's vast knowledge and experience gleaned in half a century of varied and intimate intercourse with men and things'.[43] Finally, Gerald Shove, a Cambridge economist of the new generation, drew attention to the 'immense erudition' of the book's author, and to 'his knowledge and understanding of industry as probably wider and more penetrating than any other living economist can command'. Nevertheless, the book was 'never overloaded with detail', avoided 'the temptation to give undue prominence to a piece of information because it is curious' and presented 'a well-balanced picture of the main forces and tendencies which were at work in the organisation of business on the eve of the war'. As a sign of the change in post-war tastes in economic writing, Shove, however, deplored the book's 'moral tone' as its least satisfactory feature, no matter how elevated. This, in his view, had to be avoided in the reporting of 'non-moral science'.[44]

The penultimate feature of the book stressed by Shove marked its strengths and weaknesses as contemplated more recently. Despite the sneering tone adopted by at least one commentator on Marshall's acquaintance both with businessmen and the ways of business, the author's erudition in writing this book as a study of pre-world war organisation of industry has rarely been matched for its wealth of contents and relevant factual information.[45] As an 'engine of power', to use Pigou's apt phrase, its qualities have lasted remarkably, as an earlier quotation from Coase's work in the 1970s demonstrated. Another commentator in 1990 has argued: 'Marshall's coverage was extremely broad. Comparison of *Industry and Trade* with a 1970 classic like Sherer's *Industrial Market Structure and Economic Performance* shows that virtually all the topics covered in the later book are at least touched on by Marshall.'[46] The methodological fashion of a later generation made it easy to dismiss Marshall's efforts 'with a mixture of impatience and amused patronage'.[47] Examples are Shove's plea for 'non-moral science', and Robbins's later condemnation of cluttering the theory of production with realistic facts as a waste of time, better spent in his view on a priori theorising, given the rapid obsolescence of 'factual' books like Marshall's to which Shove had referred. The poverty of theory in industrial economics was its sad consequence; practitioners were content to manipulate cost and revenue curves, the use of which Marshall had so hestitantly pioneered, without the need ever to set foot in a factory or to read a trade journal. Rediscovery after the 1970s of Marshall's conceptual treasure house contained in this classic of applied economics has yielded rich methodological, as well as practical dividends.[48] In addition, *Industry and Trade* demonstrated the seriousness of its author to use the two legs of 'deduction and induction' suggested by Schmoller and recommended by institutionalists old and new, as the indispensable, and only really fruitful, way of scientific advance, in spite of its manifold difficulties.[*]

Wife Mary, who had seen *Industry and Trade* through the press, is permitted the last word on the second volume, which encapsulates its birth and its conception:

> [A]t Stuben . . . he devised a Treatise which reminds . . . of the [giant] scheme which Adam Smith projected. For he also left fragments of a great work. . . . As time went on he [that is, Marshall] became convinced that he was working on too large a scale. One gets glimpses in *Industry and Trade* of the amount of material he amassed. He wrote a quantity on the History of Money, of Banking, of Railways, on the details of Scientific Management and of Cartels and Trusts: but gradually he boiled down this mass of material, or filled the Waste Paper Basket, and in its more manageable form it at last appeared as *Industry and Trade*. Still, the time had only been partly wasted, for his intimate knowledge of men and things drew the attention of Business Men. Mr. Pearce at the University Press told me he had never known such demand for a big and serious book. He said it might have been a 'Shilling Shocker'.
>
> It appeared in 1919 and it was his last constructive work.[49]

CONSTRUCTING THE THIRD COMPANION: 1919–1922

A third companion to the *Principles* was actively contemplated while the second was still in preparation. In fact, it was more or less conceived as its direct offspring, designed 'to cover a considerable part of the ground over which I had originally hoped to travel'. In the last full decade of Marshall's life, it had been alternatively mentioned as *Money, Credit and Employment* in 1913, as dealing with international trade and some monetary problems in 1916 when *Industry and Trade* could no longer accommodate the first of these topics satisfactorily, and as 'a study of the organisation of employment, of international trade, and of other influences on the conditions of various classes and nations' in 1918.[50] These alternative, and successive, strategies indicate the precise nature of the final product. It is largely a pastiche, pieced together, as Maynard Keynes put it, from earlier fragments of various vintages, much of it from the 1870s and 1880s, some of it drawing on lecture notes of the final decades of teaching, some of it using contemporary publications which fell into Marshall's hands. The element of pastiche is particularly evident in the last two of its four books, and in the more technical appendices. These demonstrate a loss of strength of which

---

[*] Alfred Marshall, 'Social Possibilities of Economic Chivalry', in *Memorials*, p. 323. Attention was drawn at the start of this section to Marshall's acknowledgement of Schmoller and Ashley in the preface of *Industry and Trade* while his use of such historical research indicated a skill noted with respect to the appendices by at least one reviewer: 'Incidentally, they show that the "theorist" is not necessarily unfitted for the work of the "historian" (*Journal of the Royal Statistical Society*, 83, March 1920, p. 296). This view was shared by economic historian Clapham, whose assistance Marshall had also acknowledged in the preface. In 1924, he wrote that though 'Marshall was not a historian, . . . he saw exactly the range and possibilities of his instruments that he was forging' (J.H. Clapham to Maynard Keynes, 1 August 1924, KMF), and see his 'Marshall and Dutch Shipbuilding', *AMCA*, IV, pp. 28–30.

he himself was increasingly aware, initially from reduced mental agility, and later, memory span. They also indicate his wife's enormous hand in its preparation. A draft preface for a 'final volume' strikingly attests to this: 'She refuses to allow her name to appear on the title page; but that is its proper place'. The irony in the fact that this was his one book in which her assistance was not acknowledged in the preface, was noted when discussing the nature of the Marshalls' intellectual partnership which, in these years especially, was especially crucial to completing the task at hand.[51]

In October 1919, perhaps stimulated by the publication and reception of *Industry and Trade*, Marshall reported to Macmillan 'I have already made a little progress with the semi-final draft of the companion Volume'.[52] Mary Paley later recorded about this time that it was then that Marshall's memory was beginning to fail rapidly, coinciding with the early symptoms of his final illness, and that in 1921, she had been advised by their doctor that Marshall's effective 'working life was over and that he was incapable of constructive work'. This recollection of what was, after all, only recent experience, fits comfortably with the few known facts about the writing of *Money, Credit and Commerce*. It also implies her major role in that writing, which she modestly described to Maynard Keynes as 'doing all I could, to hasten its appearance'.[53]

In September 1919 Mary Paley wrote to Layton that they had had no real holiday for many months. They had only just finished with the proofs for *Industry and Trade*, when after a brief period of rest to recover his strength, Marshall had begun writing again. 'He is now engaged on money and foreign trade for which he has a great deal of material in quite an advanced stage'.[54] In March 1920, Marshall's final letter to Foxwell showed him involved with index numbers, a topic covered in Book I, Chapters II and III, in the published version of the book.[55] Mary Paley's correspondence with Keynes suggests the summer vacations spent in Dorset in that year and the next two, were times when the greater part of the book was put together. As usual, a time of relaxation and good weather for working in the open air, was the best for writing: 'He is now working on *Money, Credit and Commerce*, much of which is about 50 years old.'[56] By the time that was written the task was nearly over, to their mutual relief. 'How glad I am that *Money, Credit and Commerce* is out', Marshall said frequently in his last twelve months.[57]

The book had the usual premature announcement when its author communicated with his publishers. The preface of the official final edition of the *Principles* stated in October 1920 that a third volume, '(on Trade, Finance and Industrial Future) is far advanced, the three volumes [together being] designed to deal with all the chief problems of economics so far as the writer's powers extend'.[58] This announcement demonstrates that even at this late stage the contents of the volume had not yet been finally settled, an indecision confirmed by the preservation in the Marshall Library of alternative draft title pages dating from around this time:

1.   Industry and Trade Volume II. A study of the organization of modern commerce and finance. And of their influences on the conditions of various classes and nations; with special reference to the economic possibilities of the future.
2.   Commerce and Finance; The Economic Future. A companion volume to Industry and Trade.
3.   Money, Commerce and Finance: The Economic Future. A study of organization, national and international.[59]

By then, circa 1920, Marshall's health no longer realistically permitted presentation of the material implied in these titles in any co-ordinated way. From the contents of the published book, it appears that his powers of construction were sufficiently robust to complete in a fashion the first 190 pages of the book and their associated appendices. Thereafter, scissors and paste wielded by Mary Paley Marshall increasingly took over, guided no doubt by the mass of draft material which Marshall had been selecting from his unpublished papers, and about which he wrote to Macmillan at the end of 1921:

I am now in my eightieth year: & I have a huge mass of M.S.S. in various stages of preparation for printing. They fall in the main under two heads:–
A.   Currency, the Money Market and International Trade.
B.   Functions of Government and Possibilities of Social advance.
A is practically ready to go to press & will consist mainly of matter that has not yet appeared in print.
B will consist mainly of reprints: & while A is passing through the press, I propose to make arrangements for B's being printed – after my departure if necessary.[60]

Undoubtedly as a result of his wife's assistance, 'the material under A was now prepared for publication with a speed that seems remarkable after the long history of delay'.[61]   Only Mary Paley's major input at this stage can explain this. Within twelve months, that is, by December 1922, Marshall reported that the whole of *'Money, Credit and Commerce*, is now out of my hands'. The book was published in February 1923 in a printing of 5,000 copies.[62]   Its historical vagaries are strikingly captured in the preface to the almost simultaneous reprint of *Industry and Trade*, dated March 1923: 'meanwhile a study of Money; Business Credit; International Trade: and Fluctuations of Industry, Trade and Credit, has been published under the title *Money, Trade and Commerce*'.[63]

CONTENTS AND RECEPTION OF A VOLUME UNDULY DELAYED

Irrespective of the uncertainty as to the proper title, the preface to the 1923 edition of *Industry and Trade* correctly indicated the four parts into which the new book, *Money, Credit and Commerce*, was divided. As was the case with Marshall's other volumes, a number of appendices, in total nine, completed the book. Its relatively short length, 369 pages including index, was noted previously, as was the feature of its construction in frequently reprinting previously published material, the relative importance of which rose sharply for the last eight chapters commencing with Book III, Chapter IX. By contrast, some of the earlier part of the book was less directly and obviously based on old material. References to comparatively recent, that is, post-1914 work, are few. They are confined to an official report, Maynard Keynes's two books on the Versailles peace treaty, A.W. Kirkaldy's *British Finance During and After the War* which reproduced much official material and, by way of notes to further reading on structural unemployment and fluctuations, Pigou's *Economics of Welfare* and H.S. Jevons's *Future of Exchange and the Indian Currency* were recommended.[64]

The first note to the introduction indicated the 'present volume and that on *Industry and Trade* were designed to supplement one another'. Not surprisingly, a half dozen or so references throughout its contents made the nature of this supplementation more explicit, either by warning the reader of duplication between the two volumes, or by giving the necessary cross-reference.[65] As Laidler put it concisely, *Money, Credit and Commerce* is in many ways less than a companion to the former volume, it is best seen as 'an old man's record of past contributions, not an account of new ones'.[66] Moreover, much of what had been novel and original in that past work, often written during the early decades of Marshall's life as economist, had 'found expression in the work of others', in particular, that of his Cambridge students, direct and indirect.[67] Laidler's comments are confined to the monetary contents of the work. They can be applied equally to the material on international trade, the exception being that the diagrams of Appendix J to Book III, Chapter VIII, had been first published, with some exceptions, in Pantaleoni's *Principles of Pure Economics* and in the privately printed *Pure Theory of International Value* which Sidgwick had organised in 1879.[68]

Marshall's more regularly published work which was substantially drawn upon in the new book came from both his official contributions and from the material he had published in journals, conference proceedings and his earliest books. The former drew essentially on the evidence to Royal Commissions and on his 1908 Memorandum on the Fiscal Policy of International Trade. Some details need to be given, since these borrowings have never been systematically explored. Evidence Marshall had given in late 1888 and early 1889 to the Gold and Silver Commission, and in early 1899 to the Indian Currency Commission, was frequently referred to, and sometimes extensively quoted.[69] This was not surprising. Marshall had been long in the habit of using this material as references for his students, 'the oral tradition' cast in print, as it were.[70] Given the close connection between the development of the later volumes and the tariff controversy, it is not surprising that the international trade part of *Money, Credit and Commerce* drew heavily on the published Memorandum. Substantial parts of two chapters from Book III reproduced sizeable segments from its contents.[71] The fact that Marshall did not use material from the Labour Commission also needs some comments. Aspects of Book IV dealing with business and associated employment fluctuations could easily have drawn substantially on its Part VI, which Mary Paley later claimed had been largely written by her husband. However, his qualms about reproducing this material because it was part of the agreed Report and therefore embodied joint effort, prevented such direct reference.[72]

In order of its date of initial publication, non-official published work by Marshall reproduced in *Money, Credit and Commerce* was as follows. First were extracts from *Economics of Industry*, reproducing parts of its chapter on changes in the value of money in Book IV, Chapter I, dealing with credit fluctuations. Other material from this chapter had earlier been reproduced by Marshall in his evidence to the Royal Commission on the Depression of Trade.[73] The final pages of text in *Money, Credit and Commerce* reproduce a substantial part from Marshall's speech to the Industrial Remuneration Conference; hence the third volume's concluding sections replicate material written for a conference held in January 1885.[74] A paragraph from a statistical appendix was drawn from Marshall's article for the 1885 Jubilee issue of the *Statistical Journal*. This dealt with a method of analysing complex statistical interrelationships he had earlier mentioned in *Industry and Trade*, and discussed in correspondence with H.L. Moore.[75] Marshall also drew extensively on his

Tabular Standard of Value proposal, published in the 1887 *Contemporary Review*, possibly because it resembled the scheme Fisher had put forward in his *Purchasing Power of Money*. Its resuscitation followed some decades of silence on the subject, in the wake of criticism by first the *Economist* and, later, by Giffen.[76] Even passages from the *Principles*, so very readily accessible, were reproduced. Appendix A §4 reprinted its celebrated Appendix F on barter; Appendix D on interest and profits drew heavily on its Book VI, Chapters VII and VIII. More appropriately, there were also frequent cross references to what *Money, Credit and Commerce* described as 'the first volume of the series'.[77] The last published work from which Marshall reproduced material was the chapter on post-war fiscal policy he had published in 1917. The material in question came in Book III, Chapter XI, §2, dealing with general considerations of the incidence of taxes on imports, thereby perhaps explaining why Pigou did not reproduce that part of the original chapter in the extracts he published in *Memorials*.[78]

More usefully, *Money, Credit and Commerce* also drew on Marshall's early unpublished work. Its Book IV, Chapter I, and associated Appendix C, reproduced the essentials of his first paper on money, which was roughly dated at 1871. As Keynes argued, the 1923 version had considerably less 'strength of exposition and illustration', though he also recalled that the exposition of the cash balance theory he had heard Marshall deliver in lectures in 1906 was accompanied by 'very elegant diagrams', perhaps including that of Appendix C.[79] The very substantial and analytical Appendix J drew extensively on the pure theory of international trade diagrams, which had 'percolated out to the world, particularly through the writings of Pantaleoni, Edgeworth, Cunynghame and Flux' and which, two decades before, he had described as 'set to a definite tune, that called by Mill'. In 1904, given his promise to Macmillan that he would keep his companion volumes in as 'attractive a form to the practical man' as possible, he thought it improbable he would ever publish them.[80] However, by the time Book III, Chapter VIII had been reached some time in 1921 or 1922, whose dozen pages covered the abstract theory of international trade as developed by Mill and Ricardo, with their lack of 'bearing on pressing practical problems', the temptation could probably not be resisted to accompany this omittable chapter with an even longer technical appendix. It would help to fill out an otherwise far too slender book to act as third of the series.*

The contents of *Money, Credit and Commerce* can now be briefly discussed. The self-standing introduction focused more on the 'commerce' aspects of its contents than on the matters of money and credit to which three of its books, but less than half of its contents, are devoted. Most of the introduction discussed issues of nationality and factor mobility as the rationale for a separate theory of international values, but its concluding paragraph linked foreign trade to money supply and to the value of the monetary metals.

Book I dealt with the elements of the theory of money, beginning with a discussion of its nature and functions (Chapter I), continuing with the definition and measurement of its

---

* As indicated previously, the following chapter marked the beginning of more substantial reproduction of previously published material, suggesting that at this stage Mary Paley's role in constructing became more important. Given the strong likelihood that this trade material and some of the earlier trade chapters were available in good drafts from earlier versions, it was probably Mary Paley who was unable to resist the temptation of adding thirty pages of analytical appendix at this stage to increase the size of the book by almost eight per cent.

general purchasing power, including problems associated with index numbers (Chapters II and III) and a chapter on the national currency requirements for a country (Chapter IV). Chapter IV sets out the Cambridge cash balance equation in words, the relationship between the quantity of money and the price level enshrined in the quantity theory of money, pointing to its limitations and lack of generality. By relating price and business instability, it not only linked its contents to Book IV on business and employment fluctuations, but pointed to the importance of a tabular standard of value by which to safeguard longer-term contracts from destabilising changes in the price level. Although the discussion of Chapter IV briefly mentioned both convertible and inconvertible paper currencies in its sixth sub-section, emphasis throughout was on metallic currencies. These were discussed in detail in the final chapters of Book I, which surveyed the historical development of silver and gold standards in currency and the issue of conventional bimetallism and the twist given it in Marshall's symmetallist proposal. Appendices A–C expanded on both the historical and analytical content of these chapters. On the evidence of Marshall's last letter to Foxwell and internal evidence, it seems likely that this material was ready for the press some time during 1920.[81]

Book II examined business credit, supplementing the material on this subject in *Industry and Trade* (Book II, Chapters VIII and IX) on Joint Stock Companies and their financing, the last of which was summarised in Appendix D. Its first chapter dealt largely historically with the development of modern capital markets, the relationship between interest (the discount rate) and the rate of profit (largely drawn from the discussion of this in the *Principles*, also abstracted in Appendix D), and the relationship between interest and the price level. The four pages of Chapter II briefly described aspects of the finance of joint-stock companies, either by loans or by shares. Chapter III covered the development of the British banking system, a discussion supplemented by Appendix E, which dwelt particularly on the development of the Bank of England during the nineteenth century. A brief chapter on the Stock Exchange, emphasising its rapidly growing role in both the domestic and international capital market, brings the Book to a close. Notes on these subjects preserved in the Marshall Library, dating largely from the late 1890s and first decade of the twentieth century, show how much of Marshall's significant insights and research on these topics were lost when their formal exposition was prepared for publication some time during 1920 or 1921.[82]

Book III in its early chapters reproduced much overflow material from the original drafts for *Industry and Trade*. The opening chapters (I and II) discussed the influence of transport developments on trade in a manner closely allied to the introductory material of the previous volume, as well as the major characteristics of international trade, including its benefits. Chapter III, to which Appendix F is largely attached, dealt with the development of British external trade. Its final revision was not completed until some time in early 1922, as shown by its last footnote which mentions January 1922 as the last date on which index numbers from the *Economist*'s series were available.[83] Chapter IV discussed the balance of exports and imports, largely drawing on very old material but marginally updated at a later stage.[84] Chapter V dealt with the foreign exchanges, supplemented by Appendix G, material seemingly drafted initially in the early years of the twentieth century but given the semblance of greater modernity by brief references to Keynes's 1922 *Revision of the Treaty* and Kirkaldy's up-to-date collection of official data.[85] The next three chapters, together with the associated appendices H and J, discussed aspects of the pure theory of international trade, developed from the views of Mill and Ricardo during the early 1870s, and revised at various stages during the 1890s and after by means of editorial notes.[86] As indicated earlier, the final chapters of Book III on import duties, protection and international financial issues were largely reconstructed from the material published in 1908 and 1917 on the fiscal policy of international trade and from the evidence to the currency commissions at the end of the 1880s and 1890s. They reveal only very limited attempts at updating.

This leaves Book IV on fluctuations of industry, trade and credit, whose brief contents of less than thirty pages link back to the discussion of the first two books. Its first two chapters examined irregularity of employment in early times (Chapter I) and more recently, as the result of technological change (Chapter II), the greater part of them drawing on material dating back to the 1880s. Chapters III and IV related credit fluctuations to business fluctuations, emphasising the growing international aspects of this phenomenon, the impact of which could only be reduced by growing international monetary 'solidarity'.[87] Discount rate manipulation by the Bank of England, provided it was sufficiently prompt, was discussed as the only real remedy to fluctuations; partly because of its strong associations with price levels, including the prices of securities. The final sections reverted to the association between price instability and business fluctuations, an opportunity to draw attention once again to the device of stabilising long-term contracts in terms of official units of general purchasing power. The concluding section provided the usual lofty ending with which Marshall liked to conclude his books, drawing in this case on the concluding paragraphs of the material he had prepared for the Industrial Remuneration Conference.[88]

An interesting footnote to the composition of *Money, Credit and Commerce* is provided by an item preserved in the Marshall Papers. This, Mary Paley recalled, was only rejected as unsuitable for inclusion in the book after much hesitation. Its contents are associated with the stabilisation policy issues raised in the final chapters of the book, particularly its international aspects. After reference to the 'obsolete foolishness of wars among great nations' and the difficulty of getting agreement on the merits of particular definitions of purchasing power, the following proposal for an appropriate uniform standard of purchasing power was proposed:

> The standard of uniform purchasing power should have regard to quantity of effort required rather than the quantity of enjoyment obtained: and that the supply of currency should therefore be so regulated that the average remuneration of a given amount of labour of standard quality should be taken as the unit of general purchasing power.[89]

This remark can undoubtedly be associated with criticism of Fisher's scheme which a previous note, dated 30 March 1916, described as unworkable because 'it cannot be made international', a note made *after* a visit by Wicksell to discuss the possibility of securing international agreement on maintaining price stability after the war. Wicksell recalled this visit as a 'long conversation with Marshall: *nota bene* that it was he who was talking all the time'. After the visit, reiterating his scepticism about the practicability of Wicksell's plan for international price stability, Marshall wrote to Wicksell: 'When I get to Utopia, I think, I shall lay some project of the sort before the public: but not in this world', a remark he may have recalled when he rejected the item for *Money, Credit and Commerce,* marking it 'Utopia'.*

Even after eliminating utopian flourishes, the book cannot be said to have been well received. The Marshall scrapbook records nearly three dozen reviews in newspapers and weekly periodicals, most of them embarrassingly brief or non-committal. A few examples suffice. The *Edinburgh Review* included *Money, Credit and Commerce* among a total of seven books in a fifteen-page article titled, 'The Gold Standard', but only quoted Marshall's remark that 'An ideally perfect unit of purchasing power is not merely unattainable, it is unthinkable'.[90] Equally polite and uninformative, the *Annual Register* greeted this 'new book from the pen of Dr. Marshall as [an] event . . . and the third of a series of Economic Treatises which have long won for themselves the position of standard works on all aspects of economics'. After noting the topicality of its contents, money, credit and international trade, it assured 'the ordinary reader who desires to follow the economic trend of affairs . . . will find delight in the freshness of his treatment of one aspect of economic life which is of special interest to every citizen'.[91] More honestly, the *Athenaeum* remarked this was yet another 'story to his great edifice of economic science', but expressed disappointment at the rather dated nature of the contents. The trade theory was little more than the impractical theorems of Ricardo and Mill in modern dress, while the remainder rested very much on the assumption of a gold standard which no longer existed. Only aspects of Marshall's evaluation of protection and free trade gave the book some relevance for problems of post-war reconstruction but the final chapters were far 'less helpful on the grave malady of cyclical depression'. The book also had too much faith in the automatic 'play of economic forces through market competition' particularly when 'ignorance, sluggishness, and poverty, on the one hand, monopoly and combinations, on the other' prevented such free play of competitive forces, thereby making the book's prescriptions even more redundant.[92]

As editor of the *Economic Journal,* Edgeworth only trusted himself to review this most recent book by the Society's venerable Vice-President and co-founder. As could have been expected, the review is careful, humorous, critical and politely reverent:

---

* Marshall Library Red Box, 2 (3): item headed Fisher's Purchasing Power Proposal (30 March 1916). This criticism of the Fisher proposal may have been inspired by Wicksell, who had criticised it on these grounds in a paper in 1913 (reproduced in *Lectures on Political Economy,* London: Routledge & Kegan Paul, 1934, Vol. 2, pp. 225–8). Wicksell visited Marshall some time in March 1916 to discuss international cooperation to secure world price stability (see T. Gardlund, *Life of Knut Wicksell,* p. 294). Marshall's reaction to the scheme is contained in a letter to Wicksell (8 April 1916, Wicksell Papers, Lund University Library):

I am to this extent in agreement with your suggestion, that I think international understandings as to rates of discount may play an important part in the business of the world in the distant future. But I doubt the possibility of exercising any *permanent* influence or interest, whether nationally or internationally, by the action of the banks.

I don't object to Government notes being printed on silver; but I don't like them being printed on gold, as I have indicated in print; I think that if even [ever?] international agreements for the regulation of prices are made, they should perhaps take the form of a central committee to arrange for the taxation of gold at the mines, when prices are too rising; the proceeds of the tax being so distributed that it does not press hardly on any gold-producing district. Then we could keep the kilo of gold in its present (peace) position, as the unit of international currency. If gold runs short, on the other hand I would call in some kilos of silver to help it, *if necessary.*

In this volume Dr. Marshall has brought together the substance of his earliest writings and the results of his latest reflections. Not all economists could with equal credit have confronted their present and past views. The confidence of youthful theorising might contrast too sharply with the caution that comes of experience. But with Dr. Marshall facts and theory have been ever kept in close co-ordination; united as a body and soul. Contrasted with the majority of abstract theorists he resembles that venerable sage to whom it was granted, in a world of shadows, [to be wise amidst flitting shadows].[93]

Its next half dozen pages illustrate this opening tribute. The reviewer points to the abstract elegance and realistic problems for economic analysis of the quantity theory, given in its Cambridge variant developed by the author before the Gold and Silver Commission in 1888, and expounded to his students at Cambridge in lectures for two decades thereafter. Marshall's treatment of index numbers and problems of measuring the value of money are then discussed in detail, Edgeworth noting some omissions in connection with their methods of calculation and representation as compared to Marshall's earlier writings. To practising statisticians, Edgeworth recommended Marshall's sampling as leading to more adequate reflections on the nature and extent of price changes over time. Aspects of trade analysis follow, together with praise for the geometric apparatus adopted to handle it, equally suitable for the explanation of labour market problems. This, regretfully, had focused the review 'on the more difficult parts of the book'.

There is, however, no want of plain-sailing, excellent concrete descriptions of various matters covered by the title. The author has been well advised in rehearsing elementary considerations for the sake of completeness. He thus provides a royal road to precious mines which have been hitherto almost inaccessible. To complete the metaphor, sign-posts on this route require to be corrected at two or three points. We refer to certain lapses of pen or typewriter which, however, obviously unintentional, might perhaps embarrass a new-comer. With this slight emendation the high-road will be like that which the prophet praises, such that the wayfarers, though fools, shall not err therein.

Leading by easy routes to the most difficult parts of economic science, this work is destined to be a powerful aid to scientific education. It would not have been improved by discussing in greater detail – or otherwise than by exposition of the relevant general principles – the burning questions of the present hour. If much of it might have been written in the 'eighties of last century, much of it will be read in the 'eighties of this century.[*]

Another Oxonian and old acquaintance, James Bonar, reviewed the book for the Royal Statistical Society. 'If the famous *Principles* of 1890 was a book of discovery, the present is a book of revival and reminiscence.' Bonar then commented on the variety of sources of Marshall's thinking utilised in the book, and reminded his readers that the work under review was the second of a trilogy, of which the last, 'on the influence of social endeavour' was yet to come. Despite the old-fashioned nature of the monetary discussion, the 'unprejudiced' reader 'will rather be surprised that so much stands firm'. The trade section is both the major and the most important part of the book, particularly the famous diagrams, now presented complete after having, 'like sugred sonnets, passed from hand to hand among his private friends'. Thinking of his readership, Bonar indicated that the book contained much of interest for statisticians on index numbers and on trade statistics, before a

---

[*] *Ibid.*, p. 204. This was an audacious and unrealised forecast given the overwhelming tendency in the economics profession in the 1990s not to read books more than a decade old, if they read books at all.

concluding paragraph dwelt on the 'old clearness and force' of the book's style, the lack of imagery except for a 'dainty footnote' (now describable as early 'science fiction'), and a lack of 'buoyant optimism' if not gloom in the concluding chapter, which Bonar failed to identify with its 1885 source.[94] Cambridge reviewers were noticeably absent, presumably because this book so clearly showed 'the marks of old age' in their master, as *Industry and Trade* had not done.[95]

The reception of the book by the vast array of colleagues and friends who had been sent complimentary copies of the book by its author, as revealed in their letters of thanks, appears to share the semi-embarrassment by which the volume was greeted by its reviewers. The thank-you's, with few exceptions, are perfunctory. Among the twenty-two letters of this nature preserved in the Marshall Library, most are little more than obligatory acknowledgements of the gift. Some former friends and long-standing colleagues added personal comments. Edgeworth saw book and contents as a sign of their long-standing friendship. H.S. Jevons noted with delight that the famous trade graphs at last saw the light of day under Marshall's own name. Gide expressed regret that they had never met. Taussig saw the book as further evidence of Marshall's extraordinary ingenuity in solving problems. A Japanese student, H. Oshima, having read the book not long after its publication, expressed gratitude to Marshall for the role his books had played in his personal education. Former students like Chapman and Pigou mentioned keen anticipation of the next book, which they hoped he would have the strength to complete. Most pleasing perhaps for the male resident of Balliol Croft was the brief communication from Foxwell thanking him for the gift of the book, perhaps a belated recognition of the praise its author had bestowed on him during its preparation for the labours he had exerted in editing Jevons's *Investigations in Currency and Finance* for the press.[96]

Unlike *Industry and Trade*, the third companion did not have a long life in print. Outdated before publication, it was only once reprinted by its original publisher and few universities would have used it as a text. An exception was Macgregor, who in 1935 used it in his Advanced Economics Seminar at Oxford.[97] As the reviewers hinted politely, the book was a curiosity shop of old material suggesting what might have been, had it been published earlier. For contemporary students of the Cambridge oral tradition in monetary theory, it is not even a good guide to Marshall's teaching on these subjects in his prime. Keynes's authoritative statement that it lacked vigour and strength relative to the 1906 lectures on money he had attended, and which must have further encouraged his growing interest in monetary topics, indicates this clearly. So do the original sources from which so much of the book was constructed. Not only the evidence and the analytically rigorous material on international trade of the 1870s and the tariff controversy, the early paper on money, and the frequently reprinted analysis of depressions in *Economics of Industry* testify to this loss. It can also be seen in the many fragments on banking and credit, on stock exchange, shares and speculation, dating from the twenty years when work on the 'second volume' could still have been completed. The lack of focus of which Marshall complained to Foxwell in 1897 when he was still a sprightly 54 year old captures this loss and its virtual inevitability:

I know I do not focus my work enough. Dicey gave me the same advice as you do. . . . I think I might focus more if I could give time to it. But I want to get my difficulties solved before I die. I know I can't do that, but every day I give to form keeps me back from that, and that is the only thing I really care for . . . [98]

A FINAL VOLUME ON PROGRESS

The final companion to the volume of foundations the *Principles* provided, was to be a book on economic progress. This was alternatively described as a volume dealing with the 'economic future' in terms of national and international organisation, or 'functions of government and possibilities of social advance'. An early outline from the 1920s includes all these subjects:

Book I	The Nature of E[conomic] P[rogress]
I	Introductory conditions of E.P.
II	Various tendencies of E.P.
III	Interactions among the tendencies of E.P. Note on
	diagrams in lower type
IV	Sectional interests in E.P.
Book II	Functions & Resources of Government in regard to E.P.
	Intrody.
	Currency
	Stability of Credit
	Taxes
	I[nternational] T[rade] competition
	Commercial policy
Book III	The Economic Future
	Influences of E.P. on the quality of life
	Retrospect & prospect
	Ideal & Attainable. Poverty.[99]

The logic of this outline is immediately apparent from the programme for the contents of the second volume Marshall had outlined in 1887 and again in 1903.[100] The two companion volumes published in 1919 and 1923 covered the subject matter designated for the first three Books of Volume II in the older scheme, that is, those on foreign trade, money and banking, and trade fluctuations; and, perhaps more realistically, virtually the first seven topics of the 1903 scheme. Those covered the three topics of 1887 but inserted between them material on 'produce markets, business combinations, monopolies, transport problems, labour associations and combinations' which featured so strongly in *Industry and Trade*. Under the 1903 scheme, this only left for the fourth and final volume distributional issues supplementary to the treatment of the last Book of the *Principles*, and public finance. Under the 1887 plan, the final volume needed to embrace the remaining half of the projected six books, that is, those on taxation, collectivism and on aims of the future. However, deductions of this nature based on plans at least two decades old when the last volume was finally started, counted for little with a person unable to focus clearly on his writings and one, moreover, who confessed while temporally in between these outlines, that he had 'consumed nearly a ream of paper on myriad drafts of the table of contents of my book'. At the same time, Marshall then envisaged economics as comprising four broad divisions,

I	Consumption
II	Production
III	Value (in relation between the two)
IV	What you [Foxwell] call Policy and I call Applied Economics. [101]

A simple outline like this clarifies the meaning of 'a volume of foundation', the sub-title Marshall bestowed on his *Principles* from the fifth edition onwards. The *Principles* covered three-quarters of the subject in elementary fashion from the point of view of the basic foundation of supply and demand. However, if the word 'value' was to be taken broadly as Marshall intended, when writing this letter *à propos* changes in the moral sciences syllabus, 'so as to include international trade, I should like to include also Money and Commercial Fluctuations. I don't like markets to be separated from these last. I hold that markets in general belong to the broad outlines of value; but that markets in particular with realistic details should come just before Commercial Fluctuations and just after a general description of the Money Market'.[102] On these principles, the organisation of the later volumes was also flawed, since the general description of the money market in *Money, Credit and Commerce*, though preceding the general discussion of capital market and commercial fluctuations, came after the detailed and realistic discussion of specific markets in *Industry and Trade*. Even in outline, 'the one in the many, and the many in the one' was difficult to get right for its ardent practitioner, because the scope on which he was working was so inordinately large.

The design for the final volume, no matter what specific form it took, appeared to fit in with the fourth and last branch of the subject, as Marshall had outlined it to Foxwell. It also came last from the manner in which Marshall had organised the contents of previous books, including the first, *Economics of Industry*. That, it may be recalled from previous discussions of cooperation, had ended by stressing the 'gain to the world', if many desired strongly to exercise 'the Co-operative Faith', and the '*great* gain if they achieve it'.[103] The subsequent volumes likewise ended on a noble tone even if, for the 1923 effort, that had to be recycled from an 1885 speech. The final book dealing with the 'higher theme of progress' as Marshall had called it in the *Principles*, was to bring the whole construction of his economic edifice to a suitably elevated conclusion. Hence the remnants of this final story, not to be completed by its architect, are appropriately classified among the bundle of his papers, collectively entitled as 'Progress and Ideals'.[104] In this way, it marks full circle for the young mathematician at Cambridge, who had turned to economics in 1867 as a key to unlock the secret of progress, in the sense of fitting ordinary human beings for a higher form of life.[105]

These papers and fragments, most of them written during the 1920s, but some as early as 1903, dealt with attainable ideals, utopias, the relationship between economics and ethics, the requirements for economic progress and the true meaning of human progress as Marshall saw it. Some of this material is fairly structured, some of it is epigrammatic or little more than a loose collection of points. Some are notes commenting on recent literature, other parts are written without the benefit of any source material, during that disastrous final summer holiday in the Tirol when the Marshalls' luggage of books and papers had been misplaced.[106] What coherence remains in the material comes from the framework its author provided in the draft outlines of his final book. At the same time, these disjointed reflections on the purpose of his life's work provide a kaleidoscopic overview of his past aims and ambitions, coloured with the impressions of contemporary events. For example, there are fragments containing his lifelong ambiguity on the virtues of socialism, and his constant devotion to lifting the standards of life. They show continuing 'hard thinking' on the cultural, educational, ethical, psychological and economic forces making for an evolutionary process of that character improvement which for Marshall was the essence of human progress. They are marked by recent events like the Bolshevik revolution, the horrors of war and schemes for guild socialism and workers' control as well as the advent of cinema and gramophone. They recount old policies and dreams of good housing and fresh air.

The width of the proposed final inquiry is captured by a fragment headed, 'Ye route to ordered progress towards Utopia', written in 1922. It emphasised provision of 'a cultured life for all who care for it', education for all – youth, men and women – and saving by the state.* An introductory fragment for the book on progress listed development of mental and moral faculties as the wider part of the topic; increasing man's command over material requisites for moral and mental well-being as the narrow part. 'True human progress is in the main an advance in capacity for feeling and for thought, yet it cannot be sustained without vigorous enterprise and energy. A certain minimum of means is necessary for man's well being, something more than that minimum is necessary for a high class life' This difference between minimum necessary and the standard of comfort required for a high standard of life implied economic progress. Marshall defined the essential conditions for such progress as follows:

> Economic Progress depends in great measure on the courage as well as the sound judgement with which business risks are taken. Recent developments of business, especially the form of joint stock undertaking, are mitigating some of these risks. . . . the ability to handle difficult practical problems, with foresight and imagination, with courage, resolution and ability, has never been the exclusive property of any stratum of the people. Many of the most capable rulers of Asia as well as of Europe have come from the lower rank of the people, and in our own time the American working classes have perhaps contributed [more] largely to the supply of best business genius of the world from the whole population of any other country.[107]

The importance of this factor in economic progress had been too often overlooked by 'ardent social reformers: they recognise the necessity of capital . . . and they assume, with some measure of justice, that the workers themselves will be able to supply a good deal of faculty for routine management. But they do not seem to recognise that industrial progress is dependent on the right selection of ventures' This affirmed the message of the theory of production in the *Principles*. Capital accumulation and organisation of business were essential to make the most of the natural agents of production of land and labour, a combination of factors whose mutual interdependence generated prospects for improvement in each and everyone. A fragment from 1920 developed this interdependence from the distribution of progressive industries among the nations, the benefits from improvements in transport and communication for advanced and backward nations, the internationalisation of technology, and the proposition that while advanced mechanical appliances had failed to

---

* Marshall Archive, Red Box, 1 (5), fragment dated 27 April 1922. The last aspect is clearly utopian since as recently as 1919 Marshall had stressed the reality of the state as borrower rather than accumulator (above, p. 711).

stimulate mental faculties in the artisan, the predominance of routine in staple manufactures had not detrimentally affected the impact of individuality and creative faculty on which industrial leadership depended.[108]

Other fragments on the possible future of industry and trade, devoted to subjects for the final part of the volume, returned to themes which Marshall had canvassed in his Economic Chivalry address. These stressed the need for idealism with its components of unselfishness and self-sacrifice for others, not just for relatives but for groups ranging from trade unions to nation, local region and posterity in general; the need for comforts and necessaries, but not for large wealth. The last, Marshall argued, was generally only valued for the power it gives, a quality in the successful pursuit of material well-being which could be harnessed to reduce detrimental incentive effects from steep income and wealth taxation. Economic motivation, though measurable by the yardstick of money, need not be based on money and material wealth alone.[109]

The interdependence of higher ideals and economic progress was also addressed in a fragment written in early 1922. Its ultimate aims were to be generally available to all, apart from the last:

(a)   health, physical, mental and moral. This implies adequate food and warmth, interest in the well being of relations and friends and the exercise of affectionate [faculties];

(b)   opportunity for (i) healthy exercise of faculties (he should be able to say with quiet pride – I have done a good day's work);

(c)   scope for initiative;

(d)   recreation of a kind adapted to his faculties – beginning with skittles (under cover) rising to cricket and football, and the simplest yet almost fullest pleasures: walks by daylight or artificial light;

(e)   creative work that exercises rare higher faculties.[*]

Another fragment explored the aims listed under (d) and (e) a little further, indicating the time Marshall spent thinking about these wider issues in progress going well beyond the strictly economic, as that was later defined:

> Art for the sake of art is a most worthy purpose of human endeavour and literature is perhaps the highest form of art. Art of all kind needs to be enlarged without stint. But, in quite a different plane, knowledge of nature is becoming a dominant power in the world. Knowledge of human nature is a most important pursuit for its own sake . . .
>
> Thus our ideals are: work for all intelligent [people] but not carried to the length to exhaust the strength and energies (unless of course under the pressure of exceptional emergency). This is not a rule for the student or the artist, where a divine frenzy is on him, he must let it have its head. . . . Comic and even coarse picture palace entertainment (or even advance on them by which the automatic reproduction of highly skilled speech and song are made accessible at low charge) are likely to have greater value than purely intellectual delight. But still real progress will be made if the coarser (and most socially expensive) pleasures of eating and drinking fall into the background to those which exercise faculties of intelligence and thought. . .[110]

The man who in his last year of life went back to the wisdom of Plato's *Republic* – 'He said he was going to look at Plato's *Republic*, for he should like to try and write about the kind

---

*   Marshall Library, Red Box, 1 (5), 'Ultimate Aims', dated 16 February 1922. It is headed '(e) must be only for the few, and available for all'; there is no (ii) included under (b) in the manuscript as preserved.

of republic Plato would wish for had he lived now' – also left fragments on desirable form of government for his last book.[111] On the possible democratic control of industry in the future, he reiterated the view that progress depended on risk taking so that 'the rapid democratisation of industry was uncertain [of benefit] as to the population at large'. Nor was it as urgent as current proposals such as the Whitley Report presumed, because the 'present control of industry is largely in the hands of men, who have risen from the ranks'.[112] In 1923 he also drafted a constitution for public well-being. This comprised a committee of medical men and women as well as people drawn from business, to be appointed for six years with one-sixth retiring annually, salaried for those who required it, but others 'to be encouraged to direct his or her salary to be paid to any institution which he or she selects'.[113] Here was a legacy on rule by meritocracy on true Platonic lines, with no room for the economist to advise on the importance of material feasibility.*

A number of other fragments from this period demonstrate Marshall's reappraisal of the importance of economics relative to other social and moral sciences. In February 1924 he had pencilled 'the psychological basis of Economics must include the action of many classes of motives, including ethical motives', a relationship he had previously explored more fully in a listing of points where ethics intervened in economic problems. This very explicit account of ethics in relation to economics can be reproduced in full:

1. Underselling
    Consumer League: should the consumer insist on standard wages being paid. If so, how is the standard to be set. By the Trade Unions?
2. How much of his income may a person spend on
    (i)   his own gratification (other than necessaries for efficiency)
    (ii) those of his family.
3. Is the above affected by the question whether his income is inherited or earned by himself.
4. Ought the community to interfere to secure
    (i)   steadiness of work
    (ii) comfort in old age
    (iii) comfort and necessaries for poor children (training, e.g. free meals)
    (iv) fresh air
    (v)   good homes for all or good and cheap homes
5. What rules with respect to the consumption of alcohol and stimulants should be enforced by public opinion and law (cf. economic aspects of liquor problem).
6. Is it right to diminish the death rate among the children of improvident and worthless parents, while leaving those children to be educated in vice, account being taken of the extent to which it may be necessary to levy for the purpose taxes which retard the age of marriage and otherwise diminish the birth rate among those classes whose children are likely to become good citizens.
7. Given that specialisation of tasks increases the resources available for living a full life by the community at large and that in some cases unspecialised work is more educative for the individual, what is in practice the comparative strength of these two tendencies and how ought opinion and law to be governed thereby.

---

* On Christmas Day 1923 Mary Paley recorded that after long reflective silence for the whole of their dinner, Marshall had said, 'If I had time to live my life over again, I should have devoted it to Psychology. Economics has too little to do with ideals; if I said much about them, I should not be read by businessmen.' ('Notes for Keynes', KMF).

8.   To what extent is gambling wrong? Would it be right to boycott newspapers that give much place to betting news? What forms of risk taking in business are necessary for society; which are doubtful, which are to be condemned as gambling?

9.   The morality of competition generally.

10.   The morality of the axiom caveat emptor, considered with reference to judicial and private standards; also with [respect] to dealings in which (a) both sides are experts (b) one side is not expert. The duties of shopkeepers in setting forth the disadvantages of their wares; of joint stock company directors, auditors, etc.

11.   Adulteration. Should we use none but linen paper? Where is the line to be drawn between that and paper made of rags?[114]

Conceived in this manner, a book on progress would have required another lifetime, if it was to be explored in the mass of detail and at the leisurely pace in which Marshall was in the habit of constructing his major writings. Alas, as the last published volume already fully demonstrates, no real constructive work was possible over these last years of Marshall's life. The notes on progress and ideals remained fragments of considerable intrinsic interest as to possible research agendas, and are tangible reminders of what might have been.

By December 1922 the realisation of this situation had dawned sufficiently on Marshall for him to write to Macmillan: 'I have no intention of writing anything new: but I am lazily collecting various selected essays, etc. for publication after my death if not before.'[115]

This letter is interesting for more than just the message that the final companion volume had been abandoned before the third was actually published. It indicates that during 1922 and 1923 Marshall went systematically through his papers, checking what was valuable, dating items wherever possible, and perhaps destroying items which were either embarrassing or which he did not wish posterity to see for other reasons. Those who have observed the nature of the Marshall Papers in their original state, have been left with the strong impression that a sanitising operation was carried out on them, initially by Alfred Marshall himself, later by Pigou as his literary executor, and by Mary Paley Marshall. What was preserved, generally speaking, has the distinct appearance that it was meant to be preserved. The references to fragments at this time rescued by Mary Paley from the waste-paper basket[116] supports the view that selective destruction of unwanted material was part of Marshall's activities over these last years. More constructively, he left prospective titles for the collection and draft prefaces, of which the following have been preserved, 'Economic Progress: Its methods and its possible future. Essays by Alfred Marshall[;] Essays on Economic Progress: and other matters, by Alfred Marshall', accompanied as usual with draft prefaces for the new volume':

Nearly all the substance of the present essays has been before the public for a good many years. But most of them are to be found only in the Official Reports of Royal Commissions of Inquiry; or else in back numbers of the *Economic Journal* or some other periodical. They are collected here in a form that is less difficult of access than their original sources: care being taken to indicate the few substantial differences that exist between the present reissues and their originals.[117]

In addition, Marshall inserted minor textual amendments in his own hand on off-prints of various articles, and added little explanatory notes to assist those who would complete the editorial task.[118] Marshall himself did not live to complete it. However, his literary executor, Pigou, prepared a volume of his published writings, combined with extracts from letters and other unpublished material, and prefaced by a series of reminiscences by his former students and friends. These *Memorials of Alfred Marshall* published in 1925 therefore fulfilled Marshall's wishes in more than the legal testatory sense. In 1926, his most famous pupil, Maynard Keynes, on behalf of the Royal Economic Society which Marshall had helped to create, published a substantial part of his *Official Papers* for Royal Commissions and other government purposes.[119] The final volumes that did appear were therefore very much posthumous.[*]

'THWARTED ASPIRATIONS AND FAILED INTENTIONS' [120]

The saga of the final volumes is both instructive and sad. It is instructive that a person with Marshall's developed sense of duty and responsibility could not discipline himself sufficiently to focus on a work which had been given a clear outline as early as 1887 even though the form in which it was to be presented kept changing continuously. A number of factors were at work to explain this incipient failure. The ease by which Marshall wittingly let himself be distracted both in the 1890s and after retirement, needs little reminder. Premature revisions of Volume I, valuable work for the Labour and other Commissions, the temptation of correspondence and conversation, the war, all took their toll in thwarting aspirations. Secondly, the scope of the 'second volumes' was pitched far too wide at the outset, as shown when comparing their content with the neat symmetry of Volume II mark 1887 (Table 12.1) with its six Books, equal in number to the plan for the first volume at that stage. Defining and ordering of content was difficult, particularly if, befitting the realistic nature of applied economics, the topics had to be handled in considerable depth. The story of a second volume which became a white elephant, a history which almost repeated itself in the period of retirement with respect to *National Industries and Trade* tells the difficulty Marshall had in coping with such problems. The war in itself caused difficulties other than the many distractions to which it gave rise. It changed the reality of the world about which Marshall had been writing. Although valiant attempts were made in the time before publishing *Industry and Trade* to take account of factors of war and post-war reconstruction, the task was only imperfectly achieved, as its reviewers noted. When *Money, Credit and Commerce* appeared, its factual obsolescence was even more unkindly referred to in some reviews, only old friends recalling with gratitude and surprise how much of value and interest remained in its contents.

The last factor introduces the sense of sadness by which this aspect of Marshall's life has to be contemplated. How the mighty have fallen, can be read in the silences which accompanied the perfunctory acknowledgements by so many recipients of the third volume in 1923, as shown by the substantial sample of such missives preserved in the Marshall Library. Equally disheartening is comparing the young, vigorous Marshall of the early

---

[*] Not until 1975, after John Whitaker collected and edited the greater part of Marshall's early economic writings for publication in a two volume edition with a valuable introduction, did they become accessible to the general public. He is currently (1994) completing a three volume edition of the Marshall correspondence. Both these enterprises can be seen as much needed supplementation of Pigou's efforts in 1924–25. A supplementary edition of official papers, to include what Keynes inadvertently, or intentionally, omitted from them, is in preparation by the author.

paper on money, presenting his views in the witness box or writing them down with a clarity which only the spur of haste in the occasion could give them* with the tired simplifications in summary and pastiche of their brief counterparts in *Money, Credit and Commerce*. Examining the bundle of papers on 'Progress and Ideals' reproduces such sentiments in a higher degree. What a misfortune, that fear of not being read by businessmen not only kept rigorous mathematics when it could still be done in the small print of footnote or appendix, but likewise kept the ideals, sometimes at a fairly carefully enunciated level, at an even less visible level for a general public by hiding them in the first of two substantial red boxes long kept in the Marshall Library. How different would the Marshallian legacy be presented, if this material had been inserted with care in the published work of the founder of the Cambridge School. Such reference to what might have been, permits the use of failure in this context of Marshall's last volumes.[121]

Yet even then, the actual legacy is great. The contemporary relevance of aspects of *Industry and Trade* has been pleaded persuasively and with authority by experts in the field of industrial organisation. The same cannot be said for *Money, Credit and Commerce*, which remains a curiosum in the writing of economic treatises, as well as marking a belated return in a marital partnership in the reconstruction of some of its former intellectual content. Although the hoard of material on progress and ideals is rightly dismissed as a 'fiction', if interpreted as a significant draft for a projected last work,[122] the importance of this miscellanea of casual observation and occasionally systematic notes as a 'mine' of economic 'treasure'[123] is as great in some respect as in its more finished companions. As his former student, C.R. Fay, recalled with some glee after his 'master's' death[124] there is nothing more comforting than to hear from a great technician how limited and imperfect the forged tools actually are, and how dangerous they become when they fall into the hands of those unaware of such shortcomings. The legacy of Marshall is only enriched by recollecting that the solid foundations of the *Principles* ought to have been the invisible support for a realistic economic superstructure which explained and clarified the problem of economic progress in the grand manner in which Marshall envisaged it.

NOTES

1. See above, Chapter 12, pp. 432–3; the reference comparing his second volume to Penelope's web was made in a letter to Maynard Keynes in 1911; see above, Chapter 17, pp. 638–9.
2. *P* VII, 1916, p. v; Marshall's war effort was discussed in Chapter 17 above, esp. pp. 640–46.
3. *IT*, preface, p. v.
4. *MCC*, pp. v–vi.
5. As part of his papers 'On Progress and Ideals', Marshall Library, Red Box, 1 (5), 'Outline for Book on Economic Progress'. Modern archival methods have removed the string and altered the arrangements of the notes.
6. J.M. Keynes, 'Alfred Marshall', pp. 227–8, 230–31.

---

* Mary Paley Marshall recalled for Keynes how splendidly the address for the Industrial Remuneration Conference had been written, 'in white heat'. This made it, in her view, 'one of the best things he ever wrote'. ('Notes for Keynes', KMF). Was this the reason why some of its eloquence was reproduced to conclude Marshall's final volume?

7.　Above, Chapter 12, pp. 429–30; the concluding paragraphs of this section and much of the next draws heavily on John Whitaker, 'What Happened to the Second Volume of the *Principles*? The Thorny path to Marshall's last Books', esp. pp. 203–21. As early as 1904 an advertisement for a book of this title announced it was in press (see illustration 44).

8.　Marshall to Flux, 19 March 1904, in *Memorials*, pp. 407–8; Flux is thanked in the preface of *Industry and Trade* for greatly assisting in the early work on the book, Preface, p. ix.

9.　Marshall to Flux, 26 May 1904, in *Memorials*, pp. 408–9. As it was published, Book I of *IT* was slightly less than the two hundred pages projected, totalling 177 pages to be precise.

10.　Marshall to Henry Cunynghame, 28 June 1904, in *Memorials*, p. 454.

11.　Marshall to Macmillan, 16 November 1904, Marshall Archive, 4:25.

12.　Marshall to Macmillan, 17 November 1908, Marshall Archive, 4:38.

13.　Marshall to Macmillan, 5 March 1910, Marshall Archive, 4:45.

14.　J.B. Clark to E.R.A. Seligman, 26 October 1910, in J. Dorfman, 'The Seligman Correspondence', *Political Science Quarterly*, 56 (3), 1941, p. 411 n.47.

15.　Macmillan to Marshall, 14 May 1913 (Marshall Archive, 2:14); preface to *P* VI, 1910, p. vi.

16.　Above, Chapter 17, pp. 645–6.

17.　Marshall to Macmillan, 5 April 1916, 3 November 1916 (Marshall Archive, 4:53–54), the quotation is from the first letter. Marshall had complained in 1914 to Sheppard about his blood pressure problems (above, Chapter 17, p. 641).

18.　Macmillan to Marshall, 16 April, 1916, Marshall Archive, 2:16.

19.　Marshall to Macmillan, 25 August 1917 (Marshall Archive, 4:57); cf. *IT*, p. 12. The early appendices giving historical background are B to G, pp. 681–784.

20.　Marshall to Macmillan, 8 and 11 June 1918 (Marshall Archive, 4:59, 60). On Marshall references to the Whitley Report, see *IT*, pp. 643–5 and in connection with scientific management, pp. 393–4.

21.　Marshall to Macmillan, undated (Marshall Archive, 4:72).

22.　*IT*, p. 8.

23.　*IT*, p. vi.

24.　*IT*, Appendix D, esp. pp. 719–21.

25.　Marshall to Edgeworth, 27 April 1909 (in *Memorials*, p. 442); discussed in Chapter 17 above, pp. 634–61.

26.　*IT*, Book I, Chapter VIII, §6, pp. 159–62, the quotation in the text is from p. 162. On Marshall's early appreciation of the industrial strength and future of the United States, see Chapter 7, above, esp. pp. 200–2.

27.　Marshall to Flux, 7 March 1898, in *Memorials*, pp. 406–7.

28.　See esp. *P VIII*, Book IV, Chapters VIII–XIII, Book V, Chapter IV, §5, 6, Chapters V, XII and Appendix H, and Chapter XIV.

29.　See my 'Adam Smith and the Division of Labour', *Australian Economic Papers*, 16 (29), December 1977, esp. pp. 173–4, where some of such later practice is unfavourably contrasted with Marshall's.

30.　Discussed above, Chapter 17, pp. 634–5; see also *IT*, pp. 258–64, Appendix E, Sections 1 and 2, Appendix I.

31.　Marshall's discussion of the social costs of advertising in this chapter may have inspired his proposal for a tax on advertising published in 1917 (see Chapter 17, above, p. 646). On Marshall's earlier admiration for United States advertising, see Chapter 7, p. 194.

32.　R.H. Coase, 'Industrial Organisation: A Proposal for Research', in Victor R. Fuchs (ed.), *Policy Issues and Research Opportunities in Industrial Organisation*, New York: National Bureau of Economic Research, 1972, p. 60.

33.　*IT*, p. viii, where Marshall stated, 'The hopes and the fears of humanity in these matters [regulation of output or more general actions for sectional rather than national advantage] underlie a great part of Book III, to which Books I and II are introductory'.

34.　*IT*, pp. 395–6, 399, 405–6.

35.　Discussed in some detail in Chapter 16 above, pp. 608–9, and see *P* IX, p. 703: 'this chapter [Book VI, Chapter VII] in its present form, substantially dates from the fifth edition . . . there was no corresponding chapter in the first four editions' though it incorporates material from Book VII, Chapter XIII of the first edition and Book VI, Chapter XII of the second edition.

36.　*IT*, pp. 636–60, the quotations come from pp. 647, 648, 652, 659–60.

37.　*IT*, p. 665.

38.　*Daily News* (13 October 1919).

39.　*New Statesman* (13 September 1919), Bishop of Hereford, 'The Church and Socialism', *Edinburgh Review*, 231, January 1920, p. 8.

40.　A.C. Pigou, 'Marshall's *Industry and Trade*', *Economic Journal*, 29, December 1919, pp. 443–50.

41.　H.S. Jevons, 'Industry and Trade', *Indian Economic Journal*, 3 July 1920, pp. 125–30.

42. Charles Gide, 'Industry and Trade', *Revue d'économie politique*, 33, 1919, pp. 780–85 (my translation of the quotations).

43. H.W. McCrosty, 'Industry and Trade', *Journal of the Royal Statistical Society*, 83, March 1920, pp. 292–6.

44. G. Shove, 'Modern Economics', *The Athenaeum* (31 October 1919), pp. 1119–20; his plea for keeping morals out of economics was criticised in subsequent correspondence (*The Athaneum*, 14 November 1919, p. 1198) replied to by Shove (*The Athaneum*, 28 November 1919, p. 1269).

45. John Maloney, 'Marshall and Business', in *Alfred Marshall in Retrospect*, ed. Rita McWilliams-Tullberg, pp. 179–97, esp. with respect to *Industry and Trade*, pp. 183–4, 189, 192, 194–5. As shown earlier, Chapter 7, esp. pp. 187–9, 197–200, 208–13, Marshall's factory inspections were far more thorough than Maloney's account implies; a point likewise made by Denis O'Brien, 'Marshall's Industrial Analysis', *Scottish Journal of Political Economy*, 37 (1), February 1990, esp. pp. 63–7.

46. Above, p. 710 and Denis O'Brien, 'Marshall's Industrial Analysis', p. 62.

47. *Ibid.*, p. 62.

48. See for example, A. Abouchar, 'From Marshall's Cost Analysis to Modern Orthodoxy: Throwing out the Baby and keeping the Bath', *Economie appliquée*, 43 (1), 1990, pp. 119–43; Giacomo Becattini, 'The Marshallian Industrial Districts as a Socio-economic Notion', in *Industrial Districts and Inter-firm Co-operation in Italy*, pp. 37–51; Brian Loasby, *The Mind and Method of the Economist*, Aldershot: Edward Elgar, 1989, Chapters 4–6.

49. Mary Paley Marshall, 'MSS Notes' (NCA).

50. Above, pp. 702–3.

51. J.M. Keynes, 'Alfred Marshall', pp. 230–31, quoted above, p. 703. Cf. the fragment draft of a preface, in *Memorials*, p. 368 and Chapter 8, above, p. 256.

52. Marshall to Macmillan, 20 October 1919 (Marshall Archive, 4:73).

53. Mary Paley Marshall, 'Notes for Keynes' (KMF).

54. Mary Paley Marshall to Walter Layton, 10 September 1919, Trinity College, Layton Papers, Layton 2[38].

55. Marshall to Herbert Foxwell, 13 March 1920 (Freeman Collection, 19/42), it was quoted in part in Chapter 18, above p. 673.

56. Mary Paley Marshall to Maynard Keynes, 31 July 1922 (KMF), written from Sea Vale, East Lulworth, Dorset, the place where they spent the last three summers together on holiday (above, Chapter 7, pp. 218–19).

57. Mary Paley Marshall, 'Notes for Keynes' (KMF).

58. *P* VIII, preface, p. xii.

59. Cited in Whitaker, 'What Happened to the Second Volume of the *Principles*?', p. 215.

60. Marshall to Macmillan, 28 December 1921 (Marshall Archive, 4:85).

61. John Whitaker, 'What happened to the Second Volume of the *Principles*?', p. 216.

62. Marshall to Macmillan, 1 December 1922 (Marshall Archive, 4:86).

63. *IT*, Preface to March 1923 reprint, p. ix. The contents are summarised as they appear, but the title had clearly not yet been fully settled.

64. See *MCC*, p. 31 n.2 for a reference to the 1920 *Labour Gazette*; pp. 84 and 315 for a reference to Kirkaldy's book; pp. 121 and 140 for reference to Keynes's *Economic Consequences of the Peace* and *Revision of the Treaty*; p. 245 to the works of Pigou and H.S. Jevons mentioned in the text while a note on p. 129 makes use of the price index series regularly published in the *Economist*.

65. *MCC*, p. 1 n.1; cross-references to *Industry and Trade* occur on pp. 72, 73, 89, 99, 107, 132, 208, 245, 246, 311 n.

66. David Laidler, 'Alfred Marshall and the Development of Monetary Economics', in *Centenary Essays on Alfred Marshall*, p. 44.

67. John Maynard Keynes, 'Alfred Marshall', p. 190; see also, pp. 179–80, 189–95. The Cambridge beneficiaries of Marshall's oral tradition in monetary theory included Pigou, Lavington and Keynes especially. This is demonstrated in detail in Eprime Eshag, *From Marshall to Keynes*, Oxford: Basil Blackwell, 1963; Pascal Bridel, *Cambridge Monetary Theory* and, for a more concise statement, see Laidler, 'Alfred Marshall and the Development of Monetary Economics', p. 44.

68. *MCC*, p. 330 n.1 and cf. above, Chapter 6, pp. 175–6.

69. See *MCC*, notes on pp. 45, 67 and 229 which refers to use at these points to particular parts of the two sets of evidence; Book II, Chapter I, §3; Book III, Chapter XII Book IV,Chapter II,§3, a paragraph on p. 255 and Appendix G (pp. 315–20) reproduce verbatim substantial parts of this evidence.

70. *Marshall Library Catalogue*, pp. 103, 166 indicate that it held three copies of the Gold and Silver Commission evidence and two copies of that given to the Indian Currency Commission.

71. See *MCC*, pp. 195–7 (pp. 372–5); 198–200 (371–2); 213–17 (388–93); 219–20 (393–4); 220–21 (395–6); 221–3 (397–9) and 223–4 (396–7). Pages in brackets refer to the reproduced text of the memorandum as printed in Marshall's *OP*.

72. Labour Commission, *Final Report*, 1894, Prt VI, pp. 73–87; Mary Paley Marshall to Maynard Keynes, 22 March 1926; 'I remember Alfred saying that he should have liked to reprint VI just as it stood, but that he thought he had no right to do so.' (Keynes Papers, RES/2/44).

73. *EOI*, Book III, Chapter I,§3; *MCC*, pp. 249–51 and see *OP*, pp. 7–9.

74. *MCC*, pp. 260–61 (pp. 173–4, 176, 177–8), 262–3 (pp. 180–8, 182–3); the pages in brackets being to Marshall's speech to the Industrial Remuneration Conference, Report of the Proceedings. The footnote drawing attention to this source is wrong on two counts: the conference was not held in 1899 as the note implies; the material did not come from the appendices to Marshall's address, as it asserts (*MCC*, p. 160 n.1).

75. *MCC*, pp. 310–11; 'The Graphic Method of Statistics', in *Memorials*, pp. 178–9; and see *IT*, Appendix G, p. 784 n.1. The method, and its origins, were raised in correspondence with Moore quoted above, Chapter 17, pp. 637–8.

76. *MCC*, pp. 19–20, 65 n.1 and cf. pp. 36–7. Fisher's scheme had appeared in his *Purchasing Power of Money*, and gave rise to some correspondence with Marshall on the similarity between the two schemes (above, Chapter 11, pp. 351, 353); the criticism of Marshall's tabular standard by the *Economist* and, indirectly by Giffen, was mentioned above, Chapter 11, pp. 350–51.

77. *MCC*, pp. 269–72, 285–94, 234 and for another example of such a cross-reference, p. 245. *P* VIII had been reprinted as recently in 1922 with very minor revisions.

78. *MCC*, pp. 211–13; Alfred Marshall, 'National Taxation after the War', pp. 330–32; the second part of the chapter from which this material came, was omitted in the extracts Pigou reprinted in *Memorials*, which only contain a segment of its first part.

79. J.M. Keynes, 'Alfred Marshall', pp. 190–91; Chapter 6, above, pp. 146, 151; the material is reproduced in *EEW*, I, pp. 165–77.

80. John Whitaker, introduction to 'Pure Theory of International Trade', in *EEW*, II, pp. 114–1; Marshall to Henry Cunynghame, 28 June 1904, in *Memorials*, p. 451.

81. This letter was quoted previously, above p. 716; and Chapter 18, p. 673. The most recent source cited in Book I is the March 1920 *Labour Gazette*.

82. Marshall Library, Red Box 2 (1) and (2); in July 1922 Marshall wrote on a bundle of these stock exchange notes how interesting they were to read and how much he had forgotten about the topic since the time they were made. For analysis of their contents, see Marco Dardi and Mauro Gallegati, 'Alfred Marshall on Speculation',in *History of Political Economy*, 24 3), 1992, pp. 571–94, which reprints some of Marshall's material in an appendix.

83. *MCC*, p. 129 n.1, Appendix F, particularly its Sction 2 (pp. 310–11). As shown earlier, it had drawn on Marshall's 1885 paper on the graphical method of statistics. Its inclusion can be more precisely dated because it was probably one of the last parts of the book to be revised. A fragment on this subject preserved in the Marshall Library (Red Box (5): (Method))is dated at Sea Vale, 26 August 1922, that is shortly before the finished manuscript was sent to Macmillan.

84. *MCC*, p. 138 n.1; this supplements 1907 data on the trade balance with data for 1918.

85. *MCC*, pp. 140 n.1, 315 n.1.

86. *MCC*, pp. 328–9 n. This gives the most recent reference in that appendix as Edgeworth's 1894 article on the pure theory of international trade. Appendix J is explicitly designated (p. 330 n.1) as coming from the early trade manuscript. Some minor editing took place in 1921 (p. 337 n.1) and probably before (p. 352 n.1).

87. Marshall's remark on international 'solidarity' is interesting in the context of his previous recognition of the difficulties in securing international cooperation on such matters (see below, pp. 721–2).

88. This was quoted previously in Chapter 16, above pp. 588–9; and on the lofty endings of the previous volumes, see above, pp 414–15, 712.

89. Marshall Library, Red Box, 2 (3), Item headed 'Utopia' and rejected for *Money, Credit and Commerce* some time in 1920–22. In commenting on a draft of this chapter, John Whitaker noted that in his view, this was Marshall's decided opinion from the 1890s at least.

90. *Edinburgh Review*, 237, April 1923, p. 406.

91. *Annual Register*, 1923, p. 36.

92. *Nation and Athenaeum*, 28 April 1923.

93. F.Y. Edgeworth, 'Money, Credit and Commerce', *Economic Journal*, 33, June 1923, p. 198, the material in parenthesis is an allusion to Plato and a free translation of Edgeworth's original Greek.

94. James Bonar, 'Money, Credit and Commerce', *Journal of the Royal Statistical Society*, 86, May 1923, pp. 430–33, the 'dainty footnote' referred to is in *Money, Credit and Commerce*, pp. 101–2, and subsequently attracted the attention of Keynes ('Alfred Marshall', p. 230 n.1).

95. John Maynard Keynes, 'Alfred Marshall', p. 230.

96. Marshall Archive, Items 1:150–172, above Chapter 18, p. 673.

97. Warren Young and Frederic S. Lee, *Oxford Economics and Oxford Economists*, p. 72.

98. Marshall to Foxwell, 14 April 1897 (Marshall Archive, Foxwell: 1:56).
99. As cited in John Whitaker, 'What Happened to the Second Volume of the Principles?', p. 217.
100. These outlines were reproduced in Chapter 12 above, pp. 407, 429–30.
101. Marshall to Foxwell, 26 April 1897 (Marshall Archive, 1:58).
102. *Ibid.*
103. *EOI*, p. 228, and see above, Chapter 13, pp. 455–6.
104. Marshall Archive, Red Box, 1 (5).
105. See the introduction to Chapter 6 above, pp. 139–43.
106. See above, Chapter 7, pp. 216–17.
107 Marshall Library, Red Box 1 (5), 'Outline of a book on Economic Progress'.
108. Marshall Library, Red Box 1 (5), 'Outline of a Book on Economic Progress', 'Fragment on the Influence of Economics on the Quality of Life', dated 23 July 1920.
109. Marshall Library, Red Box 1 (5), 'The Possible Future of Industry and Trade'; the contents of Marshall's 'Social Possibilities of Economic Chivalry' were discussed above, Chapter 16, pp. 608–9.
110. Marshall Library, Red Box 1(5), 'The Possible Future of Industry and Trade'.
111. Mary Paley Marshall, 'Notes for Keynes' (KMF); this was a comment Marshall had made on 2 October 1923 and which she had noted down.
112. Marshall Library, Red Box (5), fragment dated 27 November 1921. This was the view taken in *IT*, as mentioned above, pp. 711–12.
113. Marshall Library, Red Box 1 (5), 'Committee for Public Well-being', dated 23 February 1923.
114. Marshall Library, Red Box 1 (5). This substantial paper probably dated from the turn of the century, as suggested by aspects of its subject matter which resemble comments in Marshall to Bishop Westcott, 23 July 1898, in *Memorials*, p. 383.
115. Marshall to Macmillan, 1 December 1922, Marshall Archive, 4:86.
116. John Maynard Keynes, 'Alfred Marshall', e.g. p. 171 n.1.
117. As cited in John Whitaker, 'What Happened to the Second Volume of the *Principles*?', pp. 217–18.
118. See *Memorials*, e.g. pp. 101 n., 142 n.
119. Marshall's will and Pigou's literary executorship are more fully discussed below, Chapter 20, pp. 745–8.
120. This phrase is taken from the concluding section of John Whitaker's 'What Happened to the Second Volume of the *Principles*?', p. 218, a paper from which the writing of this chapter has benefited greatly.
121. John Whitaker, 'What Happened to the Second Volume of the *Principles*?', p. 221.
122. *Ibid.*, p. 220.
123. The phrase used by John Maynard Keynes to describe these last volumes ('Alfred Marshall', p. 228) perhaps recalling the phrase Pigou had used in his review of *Industry and Trade* (above, p. 713).
124. C.R. Fay, 'Reminiscences', in *Memorials*, p. 77.

20. The Last Years and Legacy

Alfred Marshall died at home on 13 July 1924, a fortnight before his eighty-second birthday. The death certificate listed three causes of death: cholecystitis, senility and cardiac failure. The informant was nephew Claude Guillebaud who provided this as the first of a number of services he was to perform for the Marshalls after the death of his famous uncle. The funeral took place four days later. It consisted of a brief College Chapel service at St John's, followed by interment in St Giles Cemetery, Huntingdon Road. On 18 October 1924, probate was granted on Alfred Marshall's will made in 1908, apart from subsequent amendments by codicil. It was granted to his wife as sole executrix. She was therefore to look after her husband's material affairs in death as she had done for much of his life.

The causes of death provide some clues about the nature of Marshall's life following his eightieth birthday. Senility had gradually set in from the early 1920s. This was associated with rapidly worsening short-term memory loss from 1921, though poor memory had been a growing problem during the years following retirement. Hypertension, diagnosed in 1914, likewise worsened steadily, inducing dizzy spells and fatigue after excessive stimulus and excitement. The gall-bladder ailment with its nausea, acidity and heightened problems with digestion was perhaps the final instalment of an affliction which had plagued Marshall consistently from the late 1870s. This final illness, about which otherwise very little else is known, lasted for several months. Mary Paley recorded it had started on 10 May 1924. During it, Marshall was largely bedridden, and, as he told Maynard Keynes at its beginning, this placed him at the mercy of his wife and his nurse. Keynes's description of that last visit, on 16 May 1924, mentioned him in bed with his night cap on, 'weak in voice, still able to laugh', no short-term memory left to speak of and 'now rather like a child, . . . often troublesome'.[1]

Glimpses of Marshall's last years were preserved by Mary Paley Marshall's record of her husband's sayings. These dwelt on the past and the future, on what had been and what might have been, frequently taking on a perhaps not surprisingly, spiritual tone. The last is evident in Marshall's reflections on musical preferences and revealed taste in pictures, as well as in his utterances on a future life. A chronological sample presents the overall picture:

26 July 1920 – Alfred's birthday when he was 78. He said he did not much want a future life. He spoke of the idea many have of heaven as a place where one spends one's time praising God. Singing praises would be an infinite yawn. . . . If you believe in a future life, you can't be disappointed, for if there isn't one, you won't know there isn't. I don't care for living except to work.

He said that he was glad to have done all he could to help the world on. I asked him whether he would not like to return to this world at intervals of (say) 100 years to see what was happening. He said he should like it from pure curiosity. He said, 'If in another 100 year's time I meet some newcomer, the first question I should ask would be: how has the exhaustion of coal been met?'

'My God is not the God of the whole world. He is the God of this Universe. So I can never get into touch again with those who regard the world and the universe as nearly the same.'

737

'My own thoughts turn more and more on the millions of worlds which may have reached a high state of morality before ours became habitable, and the other millions of worlds that may have a similar development after our own has become cool and our world uninhabitable.'

His greatest difficulty about believing in a future life was that he did not know at what stage of existence it could begin. One could hardly believe that apes had a future life or even the early stages of tree dwelling human beings. Then at what stage could such an immense change as a future life begin?

24 September 1920 – Looking around the dining room he remarked on the large proportion of pictures of theological subjects. The reasons for this were (a) that at the time when theological feeling was strong, art was the chief career open to the ability of this country and many who in these days would have gone into science and other careers, became artists. (b) At that time the chief way of appealing to the multitude was by works of art, which could be seen by the many. As soon as printing became general, the multitude could be got at by books . . .

26 December 1921 – At breakfast we were considering what new rolls we would get for the autopiano (which was the greatest solace to him during the last 10 years of his life). He said he was getting to like sacred music more and more. He had given up theology, but believed more and more in religion, of which Christianity was the latest development. He said lately, 'religion seems to me an attitude'.

3 December 1922 – His favourite poets are Goethe, Shelley and Shakespeare.

23 February 1923 – 'As men become old, they become extinct volcanoes' [analogous to Gladstone's last government] but inside the fire with 'a closed vent [is] a purer white heat.'

7 January 1924 – Alfred said that 1000 years hence economics would be entirely different from the science it is today and would probably be based on biology.[2]

The gradual diminution in number of these dated fragments among Marshall's papers in his last years resemble the intermittent flickerings of a shrinking candle, the final extinction of the pure white heat in that dead volcano of the old man. Visits and general social intercourse were by then also fast drying up. Solitary walks, brief country holidays, sessions with 'Blackbird' for Beethoven and sacred music, reminiscences of former days, old acquaintances from college days, former likes of psychology, and study in the 'ark' for rediscovering Plato's *Republic* as a guide to the future, likewise drew slowly to a halt. When the end at last came on Sunday, 13 July 1924, relief mingled with sorrow as the arduous trial of the final care of a difficult patient and husband was over for doctor, nurse and wife. The economist, college man, preacher and master was no more.

THE MOURNING OF A RENOWNED ECONOMIST

The press recorded the passing of the 'doyen of English economists' and one of that 'small band whose privilege it is to add to the renown of their country and their generation', with suitably lengthy obituaries befitting the standing of the deceased. The *Times*, perhaps recalling its letter columns during the First World War, noted Marshall had immensely 'broadened the study of economics beyond the narrow field to which Fawcett and his predecessors confined it . . . [partly by] bringing the science into contact with the stream of Teutonic thought of which we were in insular ignorance'. It stressed Marshall's devotion to economics teaching, his gathering 'around him of a band of able and enthusiastic students', his 'delicate health' preventing him from taking part in more general university business and going into society, but compensated for by 'the delightful and constant hospitality toward the students' he and Mrs Marshall exercised at their house. After praising the *Principles* as the major of his many economic writings, his contacts with leaders of labour and business, and services to the State, it pictured Marshall as a

mathematician, a statistician, a linguist, a student of history past and present, . . . well enough informed to understand the views of all his contemporary economists. Like his fellow-Johnian, Lord Courtney, he took a somewhat perverse delight in differing from almost everybody upon some subtle consideration which had occurred to him alone – not always, it must be confessed, of great relative or practical importance. This quality betrayed itself in amusing ways in private life. He had his table knives electro-plated to spare the labour of polishing, but they ceased to cut. He devised a form of boot with elastic webbing over the instep to save the labour of fastening, but found the rain penetrated to his feet. He devised the plans for his house in Madingley Road so as to provide each room with sunshine, but omitted to include stairs in the plan![3]

The *Guardian*, in a judgement with which Marshall would have disagreed,[4] saw his great 'contribution as reconciling the conflicting claims of cost and utility' and enriching its equilibrium analysis from the mathematics of Cournot and von Thünen. It argued that Marshall's work was greater on general price determination than on the theory of distribution, that his evidence had enriched the work of the Gold and Silver Commission in 1888 as had likewise been done in 1903 for public debate over Tariff reform by the 'Memorandum on Foreign Trade' . However, 'his personal contribution as educationist was of supreme value. Cambridge was the principal training school of economics teachers in this country, and for several decades Marshall was the controlling influence in Cambridge economics'.

The *Economist's* obituary appraised both the longer-term and short-run effects of Marshall's work. After noting his secluded retirement for the last sixteen years, in such sharp contrast with 'the living personality' of thirty or forty years ago, it remarked that 'everyone whose study of work leads them into the field of economics, realises that by the death of Marshall we have lost one of the intellectual giants'. His theory of supply and demand, of economic surpluses, of money and prices, made him comparable to 'the three or four great names which have made English economics a power all over the world'. That power was enhanced by his attributes as 'teacher, and as a man'. His influence over his students was mainly due to 'personal qualities' and the infinite pain he took with them to extract the best possible work from them. He was 'A great theorist' who 'humanised economics',

But Marshall was not without his weaknesses, which were far more apparent to his colleagues in university administration than to his students. His love of paradox, his pleasure in discovering unexpected grounds for differing with the general view, and a certain love of combat made him a difficult colleague to work with, and caused a certain bitterness in his relations with those who gave their adherence to a different school of economic thought. With greater tact his influence might have been even greater at Cambridge than it was. Marshall also suffered throughout most of his life from lack of a robust constitution, and he could never have achieved great results but for the unremitting care of his wife, who was also one of his first students, the joint author of one of his earliest works, and a collaborator and assistant in the larger volumes which embodied his teaching.[5]

Two other former students wrote briefer obituaries.[6] C.P. Sanger, representing the generation of the 1890s, recalled his visit to Marshall's study as student, 'a room with a balcony, looking south, tea placed on a stool between him and his Professor' to suggest 'those who had never the good fortune to be his pupils cannot realise those remarkable qualities' Marshall had. 'Unscrupulous fairness rather than his learning and critical powers' created this strong affection, and combined with the economics were sufficient to compensate for the less pleasant foibles with which he was afflicted. Apart from his opposition to women's degrees at Cambridge, he had other, more 'charming weaknesses . . . a delightful smile when he was going to make a joke. He was interested in all the details of life. He was rather fussy. He would explain to ladies how they ought to dust their rooms and what was the best thing for taking out a stain. But he was always sympathetic, encouraging, and eager'.[7] Nephew Guillebaud, student and member of the Cambridge School his uncle had created, recalled the contributions and the weaknesses. 'He was fond of his saying that his chief concern was to discover the causes of the causes of things'. The unfortunate postponement of the works following the *Principles*, which invariably failed to do justice to his 'pioneer work', were less than the loss to Cambridge of his qualities as a teacher. There he 'was at his best, [because his] powerful personality came out to the full in his conversation'. More than his books, the influence of his teaching spread the views of his distinctive Cambridge School across the oceans, into public affairs, and to the leaders of working-class opinion. Above all, 'the great corpus of fundamental principles which he built up have left an enduring mark on economic thought which will never be effaced'.[8]

Obituaries in the academic journals followed. The genius with which Keynes sketched his 'master' for the *Economic Journal* has already been frequently drawn upon. Keynes's father, an expert on its subject, commented enviously on both the speed with which his son had written it, and the accuracy of the final outcome. Edgeworth, as Keynes's co-editor, praised the Memoir 'as a great success. It is not a mere eulogium but a portraiture', one moreover which brought out, 'the half ingenious, half absurd personal element in the man', as the newspaper obituaries had also attempted to do.[9] Other obituaries of this genre came from former friends and colleagues of academe, on both sides of the Atlantic.

The quality of Keynes's Memoir was undoubtedly much assisted by the enormous help Marshall's widow had given him, both by way of notes and conversations, and by giving him access to Marshall's papers. Only W.R. Scott among other obituary writers was favoured by her in this way, perhaps because he was writing the official notice for the British Academy, and therefore creating an important part of the historical record. Later biographers must be grateful for these notes, preserving aspects of Marshall's life which otherwise would have been irretrievably lost.[10]

Scott's obituary in many ways supplements Keynes's more famous Memoir. It dwelt to a greater extent on family and formative influences, including school, university and philosophical background of his early training and later work, all of which marked his subsequent career as writer and teacher of economics. It is filled with interesting insights:

> He was slow to criticise, and in fact for this and other reasons a tract on 'The silences of Alfred Marshall' might have more than biographical interest. His character was complex, for, in addition to his devotion to truth, he was intensely sensitive. He felt deeply if he was misconceived, and this reflected back on himself in anxious wondering if he could so amend his wording as to preclude the possibilities of mistakes by his readers. . . . Up to the end of his life, he was keenly interested in the Economic Section [of the British Academy]. He wrote not long ago, 'I worship the suns that will shine more brightly when I am in my last

bed', in connexion with his hope that means might be devised by which the Academy would encourage promise as well as crown performance. . . . In 1919, he wrote, 'my health is good but my power of work decreases because my memory is vanishing. I can't recollect, when I get half-way through a page, what I had meant to drive at'.[11]

Cannan, equally conscious of Keynes's 'charming sketch' of Marshall, chose to fill his obituary with his personal recollections of Marshall. 'When a schoolboy in the Fifth or Sixth, I knew him by sight as the Principal of University College, Bristol. He was then about thirty-seven, but looked to me very old and ill. . . . I can see him now, creeping along Apsley Road . . . in a great coat and soft-black hat . . . the next time I saw him, [in 1890], he appeared thirty or forty years younger than I remembered him a dozen years before.' In July 1896, they quarrelled about aspects of cycling in Edgeworth's presence at All Souls. Later they quarrelled about mistakes in the *Principles*, which Cannan assiduously hunted out. Marshall's self-assessment as 'querulous and dyspeptic' was used by Cannan to make the pertinent judgement on Marshall's 'determination to write a complete exposition of general economics' by describing it as an impossible aim. 'The tragic air which is so marked in the best portrait of him, that I have never been able to suffer it on my own wall, always suggests that he is thinking, "If they would *only* let me alone, I could get on with my book". . . . He would have done better for himself and for economics if he had given his life to advancing and defending and developing what was new doctrine'.[12]

Taussig, Marshall's old friend from Harvard, and one of America's major Marshallians, described Marshall's death in the *Quarterly Journal of Economics* as creating 'a vacancy that will long wait to be filled'. After enumerating Marshall's published work, of which the last two volumes were described as 'an anti-climax', he appraised it as the writings of a person with strong feelings 'against half-baked work, pot-boilers, anything rapidly thrown off' and where a perception of limited physical and mental strength implied 'he must give all he had to perfected work of a kind that had promise of lasting significance'. Marshall's keen awareness of the complexities of the actual world, a significant explanatory factor in the delays in his writing, were illustrated by an anecdote from the Political Economy Club:

> Professor Marshall was addressing us, when our reverent silence was broken by some rash opponent who interjected half a dozen words of objection. 'All short statements are wrong', said the professor. 'Is that one?' asked Courtney, and the incident closed with laughter.

Taussig then reminded his readers of the benefits in committing oneself occasionally to short statements, showing that long and complex constructions, even in the *Principles*, were not always models of clarity and truth. In spite of this stylistic shortcoming, the achievements were great. He 'opened new paths, established a tradition, founded a school'. Taussig particularly stressed Marshall 'the man of science'. Marshall combined 'the two things needed for the advancement of economic science, strict and severe reasoning from premises, [together with] an understanding of the limitations of deductive reasoning, a recognition of the complexities of the actual world, a hunger for facts'.[13]

Bonar's obituary reminded readers of the *Journal of the Royal Statistical Society*[14] of Keynes's recent 'noble biography' before highlighting certain qualities of the man and his work. 'He passed into economics through religion and philosophy, and we are not surprised to find him warmly appreciative of Jowett', wrote the Oxonian, who earlier had recalled Marshall's role in stirring up 'economic study at Balliol' as successor to Toynbee. The obituary stressed the unity of Marshall's writing, its 'wonderful well-balanced judgement' and 'patient analysis, acute reasoning and learning'.

> If it be asked how much of his work will stand, the provisional answer may be that we are too near to it to judge. On the other hand, Marshall lived long enough to put his teaching to the proof over a generation of men. . . . We hardly think of Marshall as founder of a School; he has influenced all Schools of English speaking economists. . . . His place will be fixed by posterity. If some fringes drop, his robe of honour will still be ample enough to preserve his fame. No economist since Mill has had higher homage, or kept it so nearly unabated over a long life.[15]

Thus spoke both press and economists in 1924 at the loss of their long-standing leader.

MOURNING MARSHALL THE COLLEGE AND UNIVERSITY MAN

St John's College organised the funeral service of its distinguished Fellow in the College Chapel on Thursday, 17 July, at 2.00 in the afternoon. It invited members of the university and friends to share in the service and pay homage to Alfred Marshall by their attendance there, and later at the graveside in the cemetery of St Giles, Church of England. By the express wish of the deceased, no flowers were to be sent.[16]

The service itself was conducted by the Dean of St John's, the Reverend J.M. Creed, assisted by the Reverend J. Guillebaud, a relation by marriage. The opening sentences of the service, rendered by the College Choir, were by William Croft and Henry Purcell, presumably their setting to music of the funeral service rediscovered in 1921. This was followed by the chanting of Psalm 39, beginning:

> I said I will take heed of my ways, that I sin not with my tongue: I will keep my mouth with a bridle, while the wicked is before me. I was dumb with silence, I held my peace, *even* from good; and my sorrow was stirred. My heart was hot within me, while I was musing the fire burned; *then* spake I with my tongue, Lord, make me to know mine end, and the measure of my days, what it *is*, *that* I may know how frail *I am*. Behold thou hast made my days *as* an handbreadth; and mine age is as nothing before thee; verily, every man at his best state is altogether vanity . . .[17]

The lesson was then read by the Master of St John's, Sir Robert Scott, followed by singing of the hymn,

> O God, our help in ages past,
> Our hope for years to come,
> Our shelter from the stormy blast,
> And our eternal home!

words not particularly appropriate to the self-confessed agnostic about the possibilities for a future life of some years before. An address followed and at the conclusion of the service, the organist, Dr Cyril Rotham, by special request, played Beethoven's Funeral March, a fitting farewell for the ardent lover of Beethoven piano sonatas.

The *Cambridge Daily News* reported the chief mourners as the widow, Mrs Marshall, together with a few close friends and relatives. The Vice-Chancellor of Cambridge University was represented by the Master of St John's, The Vice-Chancellor of Bristol University, by Dr Broad. Oxford and Balliol were not represented to remember a former honorary Fellow and teacher. The report of the other mourners present makes interesting reading for absences as well as those present, showing for a number of them a spirit of forgiveness appropriate to such occasions. Most were university dignitaries, former students and colleagues, from Cambridge and its colleges, and elsewhere. The record shows that among those present were former colleagues and students: D.H. Macgregor, W.R. Sorley, James Ward, J.H. Clapham, J.E. McTaggart, Dr Ellen McArthur, Arthur Berry, H.S. Foxwell, J.M. Keynes, W.T. Layton, and A.H. Lloyd, of whom Foxwell and Ellen McArthur were particularly forgiving. John Neville Keynes's absence is rather surprising.

The burial took place in the graveyard of St Giles, Huntingdon Road, a final resting place not too distant from the house at 6 Madingley Road where Marshall had lived close to half of his life. The grave is in a far corner of its consecrated ground, marked by a simple granite surround, inscribed equally simply, 'Alfred Marshall 1842–1924'. It can only be surmised whether this form of burial and order of service reflected a less sceptical approach to future life in the deceased than that recorded for posterity. Perhaps it signalled a recovery of that religion, in which his belief had been strengthening from late 1921, fostered by a growing liking of sacred music and, possibly, other things spiritual.[*]

The start of a new term brought a formal memorial address by Pigou, an 'In Memoriam' falling to him as the occupant of the chair Marshall had 'made famous'. The sermon-like tone of the speech is brought out in the close of its opening paragraph, 'The voice is silent, the work done. In reverence and gratitude we take our leave of him'.[¶] The greater part of the address concentrated on Marshall's view of economics as theory and practice. It explored its links with philosophy in Marshall's early study, its enduring goal of social improvement, its intimate contact with 'realistic detail', its tight analysis underlying seemingly 'platitudinous arguments' and its attributes as 'tools' in the making and 'an organon of enquiry'. Then, after praising Marshall's dislike of controversy and preference for intellectual cooperation in constructive work, his love of truth and mistrust of popular approval, Pigou ended on an earnest high note, appropriate to the Victorian spirit of the eulogium:

> I come then to my concluding word. The Master whom we all revere is dead: full of honour, full of years, his life-work done: and you to whom I speak, many of you, have less than a quarter of his age. If it were possible I should wish to stand as an interpreter of his spirit to you in your youth and to hand on some message, not unworthy of his thought and of his life. We are set together in the world for a little time. Of

---

[*] Illustration 54. Marshall's burial is in sharp contrast to the funeral of Mary Paley Marshall almost twenty years later. She was cremated, and her ashes were scattered in the garden of their house, Balliol Croft (John Maynard Keynes, 'Mary Paley Marshall', p. 250).

[¶] A.C. Pigou, 'In Memoriam: Alfred Marshall', *Memorials*, p. 81. Keynes described the occasion in a letter to Lydia Lopokova, 24 October 1924: 'I now come from Pigou's Memorial Lecture on Marshall. . . . The lecture went down very well with the audience (which included Mrs. Marshall and "two elderly ladies who were the very first to attend his lectures about 54 years ago"); but I didn't like it very much. Being too much like a sermon itself, it brought out all the feeblest side of old M. and then said that was what we ought to admire' (*Lydia and Maynard*, p. 241).

what lies behind and beyond we may frame guesses, we may, if we can, cherish hopes, but we *know* nothing. One thing, however, is certain for us: the lives here – the brief lives – of multitudes of our fellow-men are shadowed with sorrow and strained with want. It is open to us, if we will, to stand aside, or to hinder or to help. If we would help, there are many ways. One way is the way of thought and study and the building up of knowledge. That was the way he took. It is the way for some, but not for all, of you, and the message of his life is not only for those who follow that way. Whatever way you choose, choose it with your whole heart. Follow the star that leads you: follow without turning, whatever the toil, whatever the pain. Do not hoard your life: spend it; spend it on an aim outside yourselves, the worth of which you feel. It may be that that way you will save your life, it may be you will lose it. But, save it or lose it, you will have saved or lost it well:

> O young mariner, you that are watching
> The grey magician with eyes of wonder,
> This is Merlin, and he is dying,
> This is Merlin who followed the gleam.
> * * * * *
> After it: follow it: follow the gleam.[18]

Pigou's 1924 memorial lecture indicated at the outset that the time was not yet ripe 'for any attempt to estimate with accuracy, or fullness, what Marshall accomplished for the advancement of economic science'.[19] Almost thirty years later, the 1899 Chancellor's gold medallist for an 'Ode to Alfred the Great', now himself Emeritus Professor of Political Economy at Cambridge, was the Marshall lecturer for that year.[20] Pigou decided to fulfil his role by acting as 'liaison officer' between the generations, as 'one of the few survivors whom Marshall actually taught'. The lectures recorded new praise of the other great Alfred, whom Pigou described as a revelation to him when first experienced. This praise was presented in six sections, commemorating the mathematical methods, statistics, elasticities, the rate of interest, utilities and attitudes towards socialism. This second instalment of Pigou's 'In Memoriam' provides a link to Marshall's legacy, the major concern of this chapter, and one with which Pigou was personally connected as literary executor.

Pigou's first segment sought to assess Marshall's possible reactions to the vast increase in mathematical reasoning in the literature, fully apparent by the early 1950s. It suggested two reasons why Marshall would have regretted this trend. Difficulty of communication to the intelligent layman was one, danger of faulty emphasis and simplification of reality was another. The last, Pigou argued, was a criticism to be taken seriously from a second wrangler. However, 'if any practical line of mathematical attack would indirectly help realism, he would have been its enthusiastic friend'.* On statistics, Pigou reminded his audience of Marshall's warning that to be useful, 'they must be well organised and intelligently used', while users needed also to be constantly aware of the limitations of a statistical method with respect to the unquantifiable, so often crucial to good argument.[21] Pigou then switched attention to some of Marshall's contributions to theory. There were problems in applying Marshall's contribution of the idea of elasticity to economic analysis:

---

*   A.C. Pigou, *Alfred Marshall and Current Thought*, pp. 5–12; cf. 'In Memoriam', p. 81: 'There was a tradition when I was an undergraduate – I do not know what foundation of truth it had – that, when a difficult mathematical treatise came his way, Marshall's method was to read the first chapter and the last chapter, and then to stand in front of the fire and evolve for himself the middle'. The problem with this type of awe accorded by a 'first' in the Historical Tripos (Pigou) for a high wrangler (Marshall) was discussed in Chapter 4, above, pp. 81, 91.

these arose from an asymmetry in its application to demand and supply, and from its time dependency in both cases.[22] On the rate of interest, Pigou used Marshall's work to criticise both the *tone* of Keynes's attack on his predecessors and its lack of justice with respect to Marshall's work. This came from the fact that Keynes had ignored Marshall's monetary analysis, which he had so admired in his 1924 Memoir.[23] Particularly interesting are Pigou's observations on Marshall's welfare economics, coming as they do from a master in the field. They are largely confined to the meaning of, and problems in, measuring utility. This had not been given the serious consideration it deserved by Marshall, but he nevertheless had interesting things to say on the necessary conditions for making statements about the utility of groups.[24] Finally, Pigou reviewed Marshall's thought in relation to socialism, a matter Pigou had earlier touched upon in the late 1930s. Marshall would have welcomed the fiscal push for greater equality in income distribution in post-Second World War Britain. Marshall was not very frightened of fiscal disincentives, except for those of a high income tax on saving; this sharply contrasted with his fears of the detrimental impact on productivity and enterprise 'from the deadening influence of bureaucratic methods'. Hence Marshall opposed nationalisation on principle, except in the case of natural monopolies, and only applauded government activity where it could carry out the task more efficiently: 'planning in advance for the development of cities, the simplification of law, the education of British farmers in the best and most hygienic methods practised abroad; above all, the prevention, or at least the limitations, of anti-social practices in all industries in which competition is not an effective regulator'.[25] Pigou could not help himself by concluding once again on the earnest Victorian note so dear to his, and to Marshall's, spirit. To destroy the possibility of any vision of Marshall as a 'dry intellectual machine', he retold the story of Marshall's patron saint in the shape of a working-man's portrait, 'now in the Marshall Library', and designed to show the 'mixture of philanthropist and scientist'. This was a modern, 'Ecce Homo': 'There you have the man.'[26]

A GENEROUS TESTATORY DISPOSITION

Marshall's last will and testament was prepared in the context of his retirement in 1908.* It left all of his property unconditionally to his wife, in the full confidence 'that she will dispose of it in accordance with the general plan hereafter'. This disposal was subject, however, to any modifications she cared to make in accordance with subsequent arrangements they had agreed upon, even if these were not put in writing. The will gave Mary Paley Marshall absolute discretion in these matters and any separate distributions she wished for after his death were not to be challenged. In short, Marshall's will was designed

---

* A copy of both Marshall's will and that of his wife was kindly placed at my disposal by Donald Ross as Librarian of the Marshall Library. It is dated 13 June 1908, has one minor codicil added in July 1919, while probate was granted on 18 October 1924. As indicated, Mary Paley was made sole Executrix under Marshall's will, but in case of dispute, or if he survived his wife, Mr George Knowles Paley, Marshall's brother-in-law and a barrister, as well as Mr Arthur Peters, the Marshalls' solicitor from the firm, Rosenlain, of Clifton and York, were to act as executors. The will was witnessed by William Rothenstein, who was painting Marshall's portrait in 1908 and by their maid, Sarah Payne, who also witnessed the 1919 codicil.

to create a single estate in the event of them both dying together or if, as was the case, she died after him.

The greater part of Marshall's estate at that stage consisted of four classes of assets. These included the remainder of their 99-year lease of Balliol Croft, a lease with nearly eighty years' life when the will was made; investments in various stock exchange securities,* Marshall's very substantial library of books, magazines and official reports which he kept at home,¶ and last, his copyright in books published or yet to be published. Other personal effects of furniture and pictures were not of great importance in the context of his other assets and were to be disposed of by extra-testatory written instructions. In 1924 the estate was valued for probate at £13,001; this placed a rather conservative estimate on the value of Marshall's copyright which, from the relatively substantial sales of the *Principles* over the next two decades, greatly increased in value, thereby ultimately enhancing the value of his major bequests.[27]

The disposition of the property was as follows. The estate was to be charged in the first instance with a number of specific legacies, free of duty. £100 was to go to the Library of Newnham College outright; a Post Office Annuity of £26 for life was to be paid to their maid, the faithful Sarah Payne† and a similar annuity of £5 to their gardener Mr Ellis, while the executors named in the will were to be paid £100 each. From the residual of the estate, but excluding both the books and magazines and Marshall's copyright, one-quarter was set aside for a dozen close relatives, and three-quarters, together with the copyright, was to go to the university, 'to be applied to the promotion of advanced economic studies in such manner as the University may resolve'.

Although the will therefore gave the university considerable discretion over the manner by which it was to advance economic studies, as testator Marshall could not refrain from offering a number of characteristic suggestions. Reflecting the most pressing need at the time the will was made, Marshall recommended enlargement of the economics teaching staff as the first priority for any such disposal but if, by the time the will came into operation, the need for staff had already been adequately met, scholarships to promote research by senior students in economics were proposed as a suitable alternative in disposing of the money. With the, for him, disastrous results of the 1908 Tripos still very freshly in mind, three-quarters of such studentships were to be reserved for male students, one in four was to be reserved exclusively for students from Newnham. Under no circumstances were such

---

* Marshall's talents as investor are not well documented. A letter to Sir William Ramsay in 1914 specified one investment in shares by Marshall, of what he described then as 'some of my small means'. These were shares in the Dundesland Iron Ore Co., bought because Marshall was 'impressed by the personality of Sir David Dale', a fellow member of the Labour Commission and involved with the firm. The letter disclosed Marshall's 'disgust' when he found the company was consulting 'Edison for a method of dealing with ore' and 'terrified', when the Directors had to ask Krupp' chemists to carry out essential experiments to assist their operations (Marshall to Ramsay, 1914, in *Memorials*, pp. 488–9). In 1898, Marshall wrote to Foxwell that he invested his 'little all in shares, not in debentures' (Marshall to Foxwell, 17 December 1898, Marshall Archive, 3:40).

¶ Donald Ross, 'An Unusual Commitment: Alfred Marshall and Mary Marshall and the Establishment of the Marshall Library 1903–44', *Quaderni di storia dell'economia politica*, IX (32–3), 1991, p. 321 and n.24 estimates the holdings of the Library in 1927 at approximately 4,000 items. On this basis, Marshall's personal library in 1908 probably held well in excess of 2,000 volumes.

† Sarah Payne did not survive Alfred Marshall. She died aged 58 and in their service in 1920, after a brief illness (see above, Chapter 8, pp. 246–7).

studentships to be 'open to competition by men and women simultaneously'.* Marshall's personal library 'in so far as it was considered to be serviceable by the Board of Economics' was to be given to the university for use by the Board, with the right to sell or otherwise dispose of any book judged no longer effectively useful. Together with the gift Marshall made of the books he had already placed at the disposal of his students from the time he returned to Cambridge as Professor, these were to form the nucleus of what in 1925 officially became known as the Marshall Library.[28]

Provided Mary Paley did not survive her husband, the portion of the Marshalls' residual estate reserved for family was to be disposed of as follows. After dividing it into sixteen equal parts, one-eighth of the residual was to be given to each of the Marshalls' surviving brothers and sisters. In 1908, these still included Marshall's brother Charles William and sister Mabel Louisa, and Mary's sister Ann Eliza and brother George. One-sixteenth was reserved for the benefit of their eight nephews and nieces. In 1908, these included the two sons of his brother Charles, that is, William Henry and Arthur Marshall; the four sons of Mabel Louisa – Harold, Walter, Claude and Eric Guillebaud – and the two daughters of George Paley, Edith Hope and Aelfrida Violet. Four of the named family beneficiaries died before Alfred Marshall, namely his brother and sister, and one each of their children, in both cases their youngest, Arthur Marshall and Eric Guillebaud. Their shares were to go equally to the eight surviving family members under this provision of the will.

The final, and from the perspective of posterity, the key feature of the will, was the manner in which Marshall proposed to dispose of his literary remains. The will appointed Pigou as his literary executor, 'with the request that he will kindly edit such material as he considers to be of value, aiming at brevity, suppressing controversial matter and also deciding in the negative when he has any doubt at all, whether any matter should be published'. The manuscripts bequeathed to Pigou on these conditions not only comprised Marshall's unpublished papers, 'including any new book that may be in the press' at the time of his death, but also 'a good many letters' Marshall had preserved in 'envelopes bearing the names of their authors'. Although Marshall at the time he made his will thought 'that very few indeed have any public interest now', he gave permission to Pigou 'to publish a small selection of them'. If Pigou was unable to carry out these tasks, the papers together with the responsibility for selection and publication, were to be transferred to Alfred William Flux. The 1919 codicil directed that Marshall's nephew Claude Guillebaud be associated on equal terms with Pigou and that similar arrangements were to apply 'to any other work which I may have advanced some way towards being ready for publication', an addition perhaps recognising Guillebaud's services in proofreading for *Industry and Trade* and fears about Pigou's own vigour which had greatly deteriorated in the aftermath of the First World War.[29]

As Pigou explained in the preface to the *Memorials of Alfred Marshall*, this volume was his attempt 'to carry out the trust with which Dr. Marshall honoured' him, only departing from the letter of these instructions in two ways. The first was his inclusion in Part I of the

---

* It will be recalled that to Marshall's annoyance, two women had topped the 1908 Economics Tripos list, above pp. 258, 555 n¶; Marshall's dedication to separate education of the sexes from the late 1870s was discussed previously, Chapter 14 above, pp. 503–4.

book of a series of reminiscences by Edgeworth, Fay and Benians, prefaced by Keynes's obituary from the *Economic Journal* with some minor revisions, and concluded by his own Memorial Lecture of October 1924. Secondly, he had interpreted his brief in publishing worthwhile extracts from letters broadly, though obviously not nearly as broadly as the number of these letters indicates. Even then, what has been called his 'ruthless' execution of Marshall's wishes, was at the considerable cost of suppressing material not immediately publishable after Marshall's death, irrespective of its potential value for future historian and biographer.* Some of this material Pigou returned to either Mary Paley Marshall or to Guillebaud, as is evident from items reproduced in the *Memorials* preserved in the Marshall Library. Others disappeared when Pigou in the 1950s systematically destroyed his own papers before his death.¶

Pigou was, however, not the only source for leakage of Marshall's personal papers during the 1920s. 'There is evidence that Marshall examined his notes several times in his old age, commenting on their worth and possible uses – comments which are usually dated'; but 'this [dating was] not done systematically or, it appears, always correctly'.[30] Given the fact that Marshall himself relentlessly suppressed material about his family and early life and destroyed all family correspondence with virtually no exception,† it seems improbable that these final sortings were carried out without the destruction of what he considered unwanted or unimportant material. How representative the surviving Marshall Papers are, is therefore difficult to know, though it can be concluded without hesitation that the collection preserved is highly selective overall, if only from the complete elimination of personal material relating to family.‡ A letter from Sir Frederick Pollock to Mary Paley Marshall in 1925 suggests a further possible leakage from the material. It implies that Mary Paley Marshall may have returned the originals of letters to Marshall to those of his correspondents who were still alive at the time. In this letter, Pollock thanked Mary Paley Marshall for his letters to Marshall that she had returned to him, but he sent back a letter he had written to Marshall in 1891 in which he commented on the *Principles of Economics*, presumably because of the value it may have had for her. If Mary Paley Marshall had practised such returns of correspondence to their senders more generally, it explains why so much of Marshall's correspondence was dispersed.[31]

---

* John Whitaker, 'The Early Manuscripts of Alfred Marshall', *History of Economic Thought Newsletter*, No. 1, 1968, pp. 7–9, *AMCA*, IV, p. 144; both Edgeworth and Mary Paley Marshall had urged Keynes to suppress material about Marshall's father in his Memoir, particularly all references to 'slipper discipline' (see above, Chapter 2, pp. 22–3). That Keynes gave in is shown in Edgeworth to Maynard Keynes, 30 August 1924, which urged the removal of this material at the proof stage, and Claude Guillebaud to Maynard Keynes, 27 November 1924, which expressed disappointment that on this subject Keynes had succumbed to his aunt's pressure (KMF).

¶ John Whitaker, 'The Early Manuscripts of Alfred Marshall', p. 144; in 1984 Sir Austin Robinson put this more bluntly to the author by saying, 'Pigou burnt the lot!'.

† His letters to his mother from America in 1875 are the valuable exception. Another illustration of an urge to censor material was the removal of the first twenty pages, largely covering the Bristol period, from the scrapbook which Mary Paley had prepared, presumably from their marriage onwards.

‡ As shown in Chapter 2, much family background and even his place of birth was kept hidden from Mary Paley or was romanticised. This can be seen in Mary Paley Marshall to Cousin Ainsley, 17 November 1924 (in the collection of the late George Stigler), and her letter to Maynard Keynes, 14 January 1925, reporting some partly erroneous material on Marshall's mother which she had obtained from her nephew, William Marshall. Mary Paley also destroyed Marshall's poetry which she showed Keynes in 1924.

There are also possibilities of leakages from the material both before, and after, it found its permanent place in the Marshall Library. When some of it was deposited in the library, and by whom, is not clear from the historical record. Nor was it ever catalogued in any fashion until the late 1960s, when Rita McWilliams undertook the task, within the constraints of the form in which it was housed in the library. There is evidence that some material was on loan to select individuals on a long-term basis: an example is Marshall's note-book from early postgraduate days, which was lent to Claude Guillebaud in 1938, 'to be returned when he has done with it'.[32] How much was lent this way, and then not returned?

To indicate how and why other material went missing from the collection, the case of Part I, Chapter VII of the abandoned international trade manuscript provides an interesting illustration:

> A portion of this was included with the rest of the surviving manuscript of the volume. But several pages had been removed, cut in half, renumbered, and incorporated with notes on a different subject. Fortunately, there was no difficulty in recognising the lost pages, but the manuscript, as it survives, still remains incomplete. In other cases too, manuscripts had to be pieced together from scattered fragments. In some cases not all fragments could be found: in others, the surviving portion appeared to end prematurely. The truth seems to be that Marshall retained these early manuscripts partly out of sentiment, but partly because he felt that he might still be able to use them. In such an eventuality he seems to have had little compunction about cannibalisation.[33]

Not until early 1989 were the Marshall papers placed in the care of a trained archivist, Dr Francis Willmoth. She imposed an order on the material based on what she saw as a rational basis, since, 'to the archivist's dismay, there was little evidence of the originator's order as to how he had kept his papers, except for those items in two red boxes, to which Marshall had himself referred'. The following general principle guided the re-ordering of the Marshall papers from 1989: 'the distinction between what are properly Marshall's papers and what are not; by any apparent order imposed on the papers by their originator and by any rational, imposed order that makes the papers more meaningful'.[34]

The current subdivision of the Marshall Papers housed in the Marshall Library, which gives a reasonable indication of its coverage, has been summarised as follows:

1. Correspondence (the biggest single part of the collection having some 350 items in it).
2. Records relating to teaching.
3. Lectures.
4. Notes in hard covers (mostly pre 1890).
5. Notes in bundles and loose (mostly post-1890).
6. Writings: drafts and annotated proofs; annotated pamphlets.
7. Graphs, charts, and tables.
8. Papers relating to the creating of the Tripos.
9. Personal history (including items relevant to Mary P. Marshall).
10. Photographs.
11. Supplementary materials relating to Marshall's biography.[35]

This list excludes two items of great importance. The first are the substantial number of books from Marshall's private collection housed in the library, many of them with his annotations or with authors' inscriptions in complimentary copies. By 1992 considerable progress had been made to combine together in one place a collection of Marshall's own books, whether annotated or not, with the intention of replicating his library. Secondly, there is the collection of Mary Paley's watercolours, made during their European and English holidays, and a graphic record of the places in which Marshall tried to do so much of his writing. It is gratifying that a number of steps have now been taken to keep this most personal part of the legacy for posterity.[36]

LEGACY I: THE MARSHALL LIBRARY

Marshall's strong involvement in making adequate economics readings available to his students, and his constant checks on what they in fact read, makes it understandable why his will did so much for improving library facilities. Donald Ross[37] recalled in this context how student visits to Marshall's house invariably involved tea and books, with the latter, as Fay reminisced, a more enduring feature of the visit to Balliol Croft. Library concerns were first visible in Marshall's inclusion of more satisfactory library facilities in the building plans for Bristol University College. They continued on his return to Cambridge as Professor, as shown by the arrangements he secured through the Special Board of Moral Sciences to make the Pryme collection more accessible to his students, and by creating lending facilities outside the lecture rooms from his own books for students as the effective beginnings of a Moral Sciences Library. For Marshall books were important, even though he himself increasingly concentrated for the purpose of study on those filled with facts.

The library which had grown from these humble beginnings was in 1925 called the Marshall Library of Economics to give more appropriate recognition to its major benefactor. It therefore lost the last trace of that old association between Marshall and Sidgwick of making informal library arrangements for the benefit of their moral sciences students. When the new Economics Tripos was created, a separate economics 'library' had already been formed. Early in its life, Marshall had donated his more philosophical books to the Moral Sciences Library, while books on economics he had made available to students in the new Tripos became the nucleus of a new Economics and Politics Library. In 1908 Marshall donated these books to the university for the use of the Board, an example soon followed with similar gifts from former students, Arthur Berry and Charles Sanger. In 1909, from growing worries over the security of the books under the rather informal borrowing arrangements, the special Board appointed a guardian for their safe-keeping, in the first instance, Maynard Keynes. It will be recalled that on his appointment, Keynes also suggested that Marshall's books in the collection should be appropriately marked by a book plate, a suggestion unfortunately not carried out. From 1909 to 1911 the library was maintained from the 'private generosity' of Professor Pigou, and from 1911 with a support grant voted by the University Senate, initially at an annual rate of £20. At the same time, given the very unsatisfactory nature of the university library holdings of economics and associated books, the University's Library Syndicate on 25 May 1910 indicated it would welcome a regular system of recommending books by a member of the Economics Board, a task likewise assigned to Maynard Keynes.[38] By the time of Marshall's death, the economics library had therefore enjoyed official status for some time, by being one, albeit one of the smallest, of the 34 university libraries. Its annual expenditure of £21 per year compared to an average of over £80 per library for the university in 1923/24, reflected the still quite small size of Economics Faculty and students. This library allocation was also small relative to the monetary resources devoted to teaching economics (£4,034.14s.10d.), an indication of shifting priorities. By 1924, the library's collection nevertheless had grown sufficiently large to warrant better accommodation than that able to be provided by the Literary Lecture Room 5 where it had been housed well before Marshall's retirement.

Apart from a £100 legacy to the Newnham Library, Marshall's will provided for donation to the university of those of his books required by the Special Board of Economics for the use of economics students. When the grant of probate was imminent, Mary Paley Marshall informed the Vice-Chancellor of the bequest, which she had embellished with what turned out to be an essential monetary variant of her own making:

> I am proposing that such of my husband's books as I do not want, and as the Economic Board may select from his Library, should be offered to the University for the use of Economic students, together with £1,000 (with the liberty to spend either capital or income), to be used by the University in expenses connected with such books, and with any arrangements which may be made for facilitating economic research ...[39]

The gift both necessitated and facilitated the move to new premises. On 28 April 1925 the library was established under its new name in space rented from Newnham College; it appointed a librarian from faculty staff, in the first instance D.H. Robertson, together with an assistant librarian. Mary Paley Marshall's role in the 'new' library was not to be that of mere conduit of her husband's and her own financial bequests. In February 1925, Keynes reported he had 'been to tea with Mrs. Marshall this afternoon. She is now beginning to get afraid of being bored and (age 75) wants me to get her appointed as one of the Librarians of the new Marshall Library.'[40] Such an official appointment did not come immediately, but a printed catalogue of the library's holdings published in early 1927 acknowledged her 'heavy labour' in its compilation, as well as the pecuniary services she and her late husband had rendered the library over the years. Her continued involvement in library work until not long before her death, as well as the subsequent growth of the library,[41] are at least in part indirect consequences of Marshall's legacy, a 'benefaction . . . in accordance with wishes [and actions] of Dr. Marshall during his life time. The Marshall Library is a fitting memorial to his work and influence, and to his never failing interest in the progress of economic studies in Cambridge.'[42] Apart from the name, the collection of his papers, and his books, that legacy continues to enrich the Marshall Library and the members of the Faculty of Economics and Politics at Cambridge by the now relatively very diminished financial contributions the royalties from his books make to its financial upkeep.

SOME OTHER MEMORIALS: LITERARY REMAINS, THE MARSHALL SOCIETY AND THE MARSHALL LECTURES

The *Memorials of Alfred Marshall*, in the form of reminiscences and obituary, published papers, unpublished fragments and selected correspondence, were published by Pigou as

Marshall's successor and literary executor in 1925. The book constitutes a further important instalment of his intellectual legacy, curtailed and abbreviated though it is in some respects. In 1926, Marshall's *Official Papers*, as edited by Maynard Keynes, were published by Macmillan for the Royal Economic Society, a memorial to the work Marshall had done for various Royal Commissions and other government inquiries while Professor of Economics but without real recognition of his costly and lengthy involvement with the work of the Labour Commission. Fifty years later, the Royal Economic Society supported the publication edited by John Whitaker of many of Marshall's early economic writings which, generally speaking, had remained unpublished. In 1961, it had done likewise with the intermittent labour over more than three decades on the variorum edition of the *Principles* by Marshall's nephew, Claude Guillebaud. Marshall's correspondence in three volumes, edited by John Whitaker, is the most recent contribution by the Royal Economic Society to the preservation of the literary heritage of one of its founders. Other of Marshall's early fragments and lectures have been published, reflecting contributions beyond those immediately concerned with economic analysis. These include the philosophical papers, an unfinished early paper on the method and history of economics, as well as the notes of his 1873 lectures to women taken by Mary Paley Marshall, with emendations in Marshall's hand.[43] There is as yet no collected edition of his works, but fuller appreciation of the variety and extent of Marshall's literary remains may make such a task more imperative, particularly since what has been done is still some way distant from being complete.

Two other memorials bestowed by Faculty and students on their effective founder can be mentioned as an ongoing part of the legacy. The first of these, which would have been particularly pleasing to Marshall, was the formation of the Marshall Society as a vehicle for discussing economic and social issues by undergraduates. It continues to hold regular meetings to this day. Its foundation President, P. Sargent Florence, informed Mary Paley Marshall of this event in the following way:

> I am delighted to be able to tell you that the new society that is being spontaneously formed by undergraduates, for the study of social questions, in which Dr. Marshall took such a lively interest, has decided to call itself, 'The Marshall Society'. As its first President, this gives me particular pleasure, and the Executive Committee has generously allowed me to write to you personally of the title we have chosen before it is made public.
>
>   The aims of the society are to bring together all members of the University and of Newnham and Girton Colleges who are interested in social questions and further such interests and to study these questions unbiased by political and religious prejudice, and I trust we shall not be unworthy of Dr. Marshall's name.[44]

In addition, and to facilitate the discussion of similar questions, the Faculty of Economics and Politics in 1932 established the Marshall Lectures as a regular event in its calendar of activities. These institutionalised an earlier practice of inviting a distinguished economist, generally from outside Cambridge, to give a number of lectures (at least three) during full term. The Faculty's invitees were asked to address a topic of their own choosing but within an area of economic, economic history, or wider social, interest. A feel for the nature of these lectures, which likewise are ongoing, can be gathered from the introductory remarks by one noted Marshall lecturer during the 1967–68 academic year:

It would be a great privilege, under any circumstances, to be invited by the Faculty Board of Economics and Politics to give the Marshall Lectures. It is a very special privilege under the circumstances that surround me, since I have wandered for a decade and a half in the wilderness of academic administration. I like to believe that Professor Marshall would have understood my predicament. He served for four years as Principal of University College of Bristol. At the end of this time (and with the added inspiration of a kidney stone) he sat in the sun in Italy for a year recovering from the experience.

Approaching these lectures I wrote to a friend who had given them on an earlier occasion, asking for the published text. He replied that he had no published text, not because the lectures were out of print, he regretted to say, but because they were never written. He said this was just as well. He came here with detailed notes of a technical nature on a very narrow subject. He said he found himself before what he called a 'heterogeneous' audience. He advised me to make my remarks for the audience. These lectures are thus intended 'for the general reader'. They deal with the changing institutional context of economic activity rather than with economics proper.[45]

LEGACY II: THE CAMBRIDGE SCHOOL

'Professor Marshall's personal and indirect influence has been even more widespread than his book [*The Economics of Industry*]. Half the economic chairs in the United Kingdom are occupied by his pupils, and the share taken by them in general economic instruction in England is even larger than this.'[46] Foxwell wrote this assessment of the 'economic movement in England' in September 1887 at the start of Marshall's professorial career at Cambridge, and before the publication of the *Principles*. Less than forty years later, when Marshall's career as economics teacher had ended by his death, Maynard Keynes as a student from literally the next generation, in the sense that his father had also been taught by Marshall, reiterated Foxwell's message: 'It is through his pupils, even more than his writings, that Alfred Marshall is the father of economic science as it exists in England today . . . through pupils, and the pupils of pupils, his dominion is almost complete . . . [Moreover in both a formal and] informal sense Marshall was founder of the Cambridge School of Economics.'[47] Although in the longer run less enduring, this part of his legacy, of which Marshall himself was highly conscious, is, in its overall impact, perhaps the most important of his many gifts to economics.[48]

An undated fragment preserved among the Marshall Papers reveals that Marshall himself was prone to reflect on the Cambridge School, and the contribution his students were making to economics teaching in Britain and parts of its Empire:

Even before a distinct curriculum in Economics and associated branches of Political Science was instituted at Cambridge, the influence of the Moral Sciences, and indirectly the mathematical curricula made itself felt in promoting thoroughness: and a great part of the leading teachers are Cambridge men. Thus in Edinburgh University and University College London economic teaching is directed by Nicholson and Foxwell, who are of middle age. And Chapman at Manchester, Clapham at Leeds, Lloyd at Sheffield, Hamilton at Cardiff, Jenkyn Jones at Aberystwyth are young Cambridge men responsible for what may become important economic schools. Other Cambridge men are Flux at Montreal and Bowley at the London School of Economics, who are certainly among the ablest living Economists, also Sanger at University College, London and Macgregor, and after Christmas – Meredith – at Manchester. . .[49]

This document is not only interesting for the light it sheds on Marshall's preoccupation with such matters: it illuminates the extent and duration of the Marshall school, by pointing in the first instance to the 'middle-aged' professors among his earliest students, that is, Foxwell and Nicholson. However, their intellectual independence, together with their critical agnosticism on crucial aspects of Marshall's work disqualifies them as Marshallian disciples and apostles. Although Foxwell as a loyal Cambridge man showed considerable *esprit de corps* with his Professor, both from the duty of friendship and from his status in Cambridge as non-professorial colleague, an attitude shared to a lesser extent by J.S. Nicholson,[50] they are difficult to include in a Cambridge school as fully fashioned by Marshall. The case of John Neville Keynes, also of their generation, is different in at least some respects. Marshall was unsuccessful in getting Keynes to Oxford on a permanent basis, so unlike Foxwell and Nicholson, Keynes never worked outside Cambridge, for reasons explored earlier. However, some differences in method aside, Marshall did for some time turn him into an important proselytiser of his political economy, at least during the period Keynes was engaged in the teaching of that subject in Cambridge while Marshall was in Bristol and Oxford, but again, one without permanent influence.[51] Mary Paley was another academic economist taught by Marshall at this time. Her role in spreading the Marshallian message need not be recapitulated.[52]

The next generation of Cambridge men caught for economics by Marshall in varying degrees, and mentioned by him in his *compte rendu* as teacher of teachers, were drawn from mathematics during the 1880s and 1890s. They were Arthur Berry, Alfred Flux, Arthur Bowley and Charles Sanger.[53] Three took part for brief periods in some Cambridge teaching before moving on to other universities or other fields. Two produced textbooks: Flux, an introductory *Economic Principles*, with an interesting mathematical appendix; Bowley, a standard text on statistics as well as a comprehensive overview of mathematical economics from Cournot to Pigou. Flux and Bowley were largely teachers of statistics; Berry and Sanger both taught mathematical economics, the former at Cambridge from 1891 to 1900, when his place was taken for many years by the logician W.E. Johnson; the latter part-time at University College, London and the London School of Economics. Both also wrote articles on mathematical economics associated with important aspects of Marshallian theory, some jointly with W.E. Johnson. Flux's introductory text reveals him as the most ardent Marshallian loyalist of this generation and first wave of the Cambridge School: 'No Cambridge student of economics in recent years can fail to have gained inspiration from contact with Professor Marshall, and the writer is conscious of a very special obligation to the teacher to whom he owes his chief guidance in economic study.' The sincerity of this tribute is affirmed by the fact that Marshall's *Principles*, or his other writings, invariably feature among the reading suggested at the start of each and every chapter.[54] Equally instructive for the light it sheds on the working of the Marshallian school at the start of the twentieth century, is one of the few articles in the *Economic Journal* by Sanger: 'The Fair Number of Apprentices in a Trade'. Almost simultaneously, this Marshallian theme is treated in both a rigorous and inter-disciplinary manner, and presents a notable example of the combinations, abstract and concrete, deductive–inductive and economic analysis–statistical–institutional which are the hallmark of the school in action.[55]

A student generation removed, largely from within the Moral Sciences Tripos, produced a subsequent wave of teachers of economics. The first of these was Sidney Chapman, who, in the footsteps of his master, showed a strong affinity for balancing theoretical sensitivity with an interest in facts, and who produced elementary texts as well as studies of industry which Marshall both admired and used in his own work. Although he never taught at Cambridge, Chapman held chairs at Cardiff and Manchester before entering the civil service.[56] The second of this group was Pigou. His writings likewise married theory and facts but generally not between the same set of covers, the exception being his *Principles and Methods of Industrial Peace* and, much later, his *Industrial Fluctuations*. His role in the Cambridge School needs no further emphasis, except to recall two potential disappointments Marshall may have had about this student whom he had so elevated. These were Pigou's total lack of administrative capacity and, probably much more importantly for Marshall and for posterity, his dangerous tendencies towards theoretical dogmatism and over-simplification.[57] D.H. Macgregor is the third in this generation, a graduate from the moral sciences, the author of a monograph on *Industrial Combinations*, and a teacher of both economic principles and applied economics in the early years of the Tripos. He moved to Leeds as successor to Clapham, then to Manchester and, from 1922 to Oxford. Like the other members of this generation of the Marshall school, Macgregor blended theory and fact in true Marshallian fashion, contributing to industrial economics in an evolutionary and realistic manner which greatly appealed to Marshall.[58] There were other, more minor lights, as well as students who became economic historians. They include Clapham, who returned to Cambridge from Leeds in the year of Marshall's retirement; Lloyd at Toronto; Hamilton, at Cardiff; Meredith, who went to Belfast in 1911; and Jenkyn-Jones, who taught political science and subsequently political philosophy at Aberystwyth.[*]

Excluding Marshall's informal teaching of Maynard Keynes at this time, the Economics Tripos under Marshall's professorship produced two students who became university teachers for some time: Walter Layton and Lynda Grier. Lynda Grier, who had been placed first in the 1908 Economics Tripos, continued her academic career at Leeds, and later at Oxford. During 1915 she briefly taught at Cambridge, filling in for Maynard Keynes, unable to give his lectures that year due to pressures of Treasury work.[59] Walter Layton, the best of the male graduates in the Economics Tripos when Marshall was teaching, taught at Cambridge from 1908 to the start of the First World War. He was a practical economist of the Marshall stamp, interested in blending facts and theory. As an undergraduate, he wrote an article on Argentina as a source of British food supply for the *Economic Journal* in 1905.

---

[*] Clapham has already been frequently encountered in these pages; he became Professor of Economic History at Cambridge in 1928, an appointment Marshall would have applauded. In 1922 he wrote his famous paper, 'Of empty Economic Boxes' for the *Economic Journal*, criticising the lack of concern for reality in some Cambridge theoretical pronouncements, from a perspective with which Marshall would also have been in sympathy. The others were lesser lights. H.O. Meredith became Professor of Economics at Belfast from 1911–46, writing a text on economic history; Lloyd was Professor of Economics at Toronto from 1909–15, also publishing an economic history monograph, then returned to Britain to make a career for himself in the civil service; C.J. Hamilton, Lecturer in Economics at Cardiff 1902–8, and then, after an interval of public service and appointment as Dunkin Lecturer at Oxford in 1912, pursued an academic career in economics at Calcutta (1913–18) and Patna. William Jenkyn-Jones taught political science at Aberystwyth from 1904–12, the last four years as Professor, before switching to philosophy, which he taught as its Professor from 1912–32.

In his years as Cambridge lecturer, he published two monographs, *Introduction to the Study of Prices* in 1912 and *Relations of Labour and Capital* in 1913. He then moved on to civil service, headed the Iron and Steel Federation for a brief period, worked for some time with the League of Nations, before making his career in the press, initially as editor of the *Economist* and later as chairman of the *News Chronicle*. Layton's claim to academic distinction rests on his *Study of Prices*, the preface of which expressed his 'indebtedness to the teaching and inspiration of Dr. Alfred Marshall, [as] evident to all who are acquainted with recent economic thought in England'.[60]

Fay is another important Marshall student of this generation, studying economics through the History Tripos. Combined with his lack of theoretical talent, this made it not surprising that he returned to post-1700 economic history in his subsequent teaching and writing in Canada, although he taught general economics during his brief period as teacher for the Cambridge Tripos. As shown earlier, while still under Marshall's direct influence, he contributed historically, and internationally, comparative studies on important Marshallian themes such as cooperation and *Life and Labour in the Nineteenth Century*.[61] Benians, like Fay, falls also within this category: a student of Marshall, whose reminiscences of his teaching were preserved in Pigou's *Memorials*, a brief period of teaching for the Economics Tripos, and then, continued Cambridge residence crowned by becoming Master of Marshall's college, St John's.[62]

The monographs written by some of these students were part of their output which Marshall valued most, particularly if, as in the case of Chapman's work, they had the quality of being 'both a realistic-impressionist study of human life, and an economic treatise'. It was such work in fact that Marshall's students were producing in the incipient beginnings of the Cambridge School. Apart from the works by Chapman, Pigou and Fay already mentioned, they included Pethick-Lawrence's *Local Variations in Wages* (1899) and Bowley's *Wages in the United Kingdom in the Nineteenth Century*, 'examples of true and proper economics, as Marshall would say, rivalling the factual studies being produced in America and Germany', and not infrequently inspired by either the Cobden Essay Competition, or by Marshall's own Adam Smith Essay Prize.[63]

The most important economist Marshall taught in his final decade as Professor in Cambridge was Maynard Keynes. By his teaching for the Economics Tripos from 1908 to 1914, Keynes also became the major link, together with Pigou, in creating a younger Cambridge School of pupils inducted into the Marshallian way not by Marshall himself but by his leading students. It is well known that Keynes had no formal qualifications in economics. His formal economics training consisted of attending Marshall's and Pigou's lectures and supervisions for a term or so, combined with considerable reading, including therein Marshall's major writings.[64] Keynes's continuing contact with Marshall when he started teaching economics at Cambridge in 1908, undoubted guidance on the subject from his father, and above all, the appeal for him of Marshallian economics as a vehicle for understanding the way an economy actually works, made the young Maynard Keynes a Marshallian *pur sang*. This went beyond a general embrace of Marshallian doctrine. For example, it fostered in Keynes a Marshallian attitude to his students: one of strong loyalty to them and a willingness to inculcate by discussion and debate, in which the young especially were nurtured and encouraged. Some of this is reflected in Keynes's introduction for that very Marshallian enterprise, the Cambridge Economics Handbook:

> The Theory of Economics does not furnish a body of settled conclusions immediately applicable to policy. It is a method rather than a doctrine, an apparatus to draw correct conclusions . . . its modes of expression are much less precise than those provided by mathematical and scientific techniques. . . . The main task of the professional economist now consists, either in obtaining a wide knowledge of *relevant* facts and exercising skill in the application of economic principles to them, or in expounding the elements of his method in a lucid, accurate and illuminating way. . . . Even on matters of principle there is not yet a complete unanimity of opinion amongst professors. Generally speaking the writers of these volumes believe themselves to be orthodox members of the Cambridge School of Economics. At any rate, most of their ideas about the subject and even their prejudices, are traceable to the contact they have enjoyed with the writing and lectures of two economists who have chiefly influenced Cambridge thought for the past fifty years, Dr. Marshall and Professor Pigou.[65]

Although Pigou was undoubtedly important in Keynes's formative years as an economist, it was Marshall's influence which stayed dominant. Keynes's emphasis in his introduction for the Cambridge Handbooks on the virtue of economics' relative imprecision, contrasts sharply with the formal mathematisation in which Pigou liked to indulge when writing theory. As Vaizey has perceptively put it, Pigou tried to present those parts of his system which 'Marshall left untidy and allusive' in a way which made them unambiguous, precise, 'clear and, often enough, banal'.[66] This difference in style between the founding fathers of the Cambridge School was already apparent in their lectures in 1905 when Layton attended them; while Pigou's attempts at tidying Marshall's theory by simplification annoyed Marshall personally on several recorded occasions.[67] This highlights the important distinction between Marshall and the Marshallians, particularly those Marshallians who developed Pigou's neat theorems, the actual foundations of which were only partly visible in the volumes of principles and applied economics as qualified in the way Marshall had left them to his students. Vaizey's account of Keynes and the Cambridge School continued by driving a wedge between Marshall and Pigou in this context.

> Keynes swallowed all of Marshall, though he rejected two sets of doctrines developed by Pigou. One was an excessive reverence for the price system; he regarded it as a purely pragmatic matter whether or not prices were the best allocative mechanism. The other, infinitely more important, was that he followed Marshall's hints and unsystematised notions about the rate of interest and money into a rejection of the idea that capitalism tended to sustain an equilibrium rate of employment provided that wage levels were sufficiently flexible.[68]

Although overdrawn to some extent, Vaizey's account captures important differences between Marshall and Pigou as influences on Keynes. These suggest a picture of Marshall as the proverbial prophet whose message falls on barren soil within his own country, in this case, the Cambridge economics as developed by Pigou. Pigou lost part of Marshall's message on method, conceptualisation, the nature of abstraction, style and vision, issues from Marshall's economic legacy which are briefly pursued at the end of this chapter. Keynes's *General Theory* contains more Marshall than Pigou, and hence Marshall is actually being criticised far less than Pigou. Keynes himself implicitly made this distinction between the two in the preface to the Japanese edition of the *General Theory*:

> Alfred Marshall, on whose *Principles of Economics* all contemporary English economists have been brought up, was at particular pains to emphasise the continuity of his thought with Ricardo's. His work largely consisted in grafting the marginal principle and the principle of substitution onto the Ricardian tradition; and his theory of output and consumption as a whole, as distinct from his theory of the production and distribution of a *given* output, was never separately expounded. *Whether he himself felt the need for such a theory, I am not sure. But his immediate successors and followers have certainly dispensed with it and have not, apparently, felt the lack of it* . . . [69]

Keynes's remarks focus on an uncertainty in the conclusions to be drawn from Marshall's economics, which is missing in the work of some of his more immediate successors. This is not to say, of course, that Marshall, consciously and totally, abandoned Say's Law, rejected a role for the rate of interest in balancing the operations of the capital market, or saw saving as a consequence rather than as an engine of accumulation and growth. As Negishi has argued in the context of differentiating a non-Walrasian tradition in economics of impeccable pedigree, there are important Marshallian foundations of Keynesian macro-economics. Two aspects stand out. One is Marshall's lesser emphasis on the virtues of market clearing, relative to his contemporaries from this school of Lausanne. The second is his much greater awareness of the monetary nature of economic life and activity, than most of his contemporaries appear to have had.[70]

Despite this need to differentiate Marshall from the Marshallians as represented by Pigou, the impact of his work on the first groups of Economics Tripos students after his retirement was immense. In the production of Cambridge economists by means of Cambridge economists which took place before the First World War, when Keynes and Layton incidentally dominated the economics teaching to a greater extent than Pigou,[71] the year 1911 produced Lavington and Shove; 1912, Hubert Henderson and Dennis Robertson; 1913, Claude Guillebaud; and 1914, P. Sargent Florence, as the top of a rich crop. Marshall's intellectual grandchildren, produced by his students at one remove, became more Marshallian than Marshall, in both a pejorative and more generally descriptive sense. Pejorative is apt, because at least some of them, some of the time, adopted a Marshallian faith as something close to religious dogma; descriptive, because they took over and developed the vast Marshallian research programme of unfinished work the 'master' had bequeathed.

The 'pejorative' sense in which 'Marshallian' can be applied to these early members of the Cambridge School, is illustrated *in extremis* in the obituary of Lavington:

> Lavington was the most orthodox of Cambridge economists. The whole Cambridge School is supposed, by some people, to be dominated by the teaching of Marshall, and it is true that Marshall's analysis is broadly accepted as the background of economic thought. But Lavington went much further than this. He seemed almost to believe in the literal inspiration of Marshall's *Principles*. His own work on the Capital Market was designed to fill in the details of one corner of Marshall's broad picture, but he held that the work of economic analysis had been practically completed, once and for all, by Marshall and that only the application of that analysis to practical problems remained to be done. 'It's all in Marshall' was one of his favourite dicta. [72]

Others were equally prone to exaggerated devotion to the 'master'. A striking example is contained in D.H. Robertson's *Lectures on Economic Principles*, published towards the end of his life. These proudly and unashamedly proclaimed their Marshallian pedigree:

> Marshall's work is over sixty years old, and parts of it naturally bear evidence of that fact. But nobody has ever succeeded in replacing it, and every time I look at it I am astonished again at its freshness and wisdom. But it is a deceptive book. Here is what Pigou said about it in an address delivered soon after Marshall's death. The first time one reads the *Principles* one is very apt to think that it is all perfectly obvious. The second time one has glimpses of the fact that one does not understand it at all. If then one reads some other book on the same subject and comes back to it, one discovers at the third or fourth reading that in those platitudinous sentences difficulties are faced and solved that elsewhere are not perceived at all or are slurred over. One discovers behind the smooth sentences, which hide it like a facade, an engine of polished steel. . . . When one discovers that one did not know beforehand everything that Marshall has to say, one has taken the first step towards becoming an economist! But Marshall's book, even over the range with which it deals – and in reading it it is important to remember that it was intended as the first volume of three of four – needs supplementng in certain topics. [73]

Guillebaud was in the same mould. In 1952, he argued that Marshall's *Principles* could not be neglected by final honours students, because of its qualities in forging tools for understanding actual problems, its strong association with dynamics and forces of change and its unwillingness to drive theory to its logical conclusions when this meant losing touch with reality. More interestingly, Guillebaud could report a general student perspective that with respect to Marshall's economics, 'there was nothing to unlearn'.[74] The element of truth in Guillebaud's partly uncritical devotion flows from the qualities of Marshall's book with respect to economic method and scope.

Together with Keynes and Pigou, this band of pre-First World War Cambridge economic students were also Marshallians in the sense that they actively worked on the Marshallian research agenda. That had been set over the years by Marshall's syllabus for teaching economic principles with their emphasis on a number of specific problems. Included were applied and theoretical problems in monetary economics, in international trade theory and policy, in business fluctuations, labour economics, public finance and economic progress, in the economics of socialism and the role of the state in economic life, in industrial structure and organisation, in wealth and welfare. Only few of these issues were dealt with in Marshall's published writings; his teaching pointed to the many problems which remained to be solved. More importantly, it indicated the 'Penelope's web' qualities of the enterprise of economic research. Rapid change of the modern world, which had trapped the quest for realism in his own enterprise of *Industry and Trade*, made the economist's research task an ongoing one if it was to stay in touch with the facts which gave theory and analysis the necessary air of reality. Such continuous contact with the world was essential not only for the explanatory powers of the economics, it was crucial for any application of its contents to social and other problems.[75] Marshall himself wrote to Fay, that this aspect of economics, the continuous change of its subject matter, made it so fascinating: 'It drives me wild to think of it. I believe it will make my poor *Principles*, with a lot of poor comrades, into waste paper. The more I think of it, the less I can guess what the world will be like fifty years hence.'[76]

Marshall's economic writings did not only have an impact on Cambridge economists. They also influenced economic history, sociology and even geography. The crop of academic economic historians Marshall inspired through his Cambridge teaching has already been mentioned. It may be noted that even Pigou on occasion ventured contributions to what he called contemporary British economic history; while many historians continue to hold part of Marshall's insights in high regard.[77] The rich sociological element in Marshall's writings was elaborated by Talcott Parsons in the early 1930s and both well before this, and afterwards, has been appreciated by social investigators of the calibre of the Webbs.[78] Last but not least, the association of Cambridge geography with the Economics Tripos syllabus in the early years of its existence undoubtedly left marks in terms of its later development. Examples include its 'real concern for and emphasis on human geography, . . . pioneering concern for the study of processes . . . and the high emphasis given to field work'. Its associations with Cambridge economics are equally visible from the inclusion of economic and commercial geography in the initial syllabus of the 1880s, and were reciprocated in Marshall's awareness of the importance of climate and geography in economic explanation.[79]

The last considerations have focused increasingly on the more enduring aspects of Marshall's work. These were inherent in his style of doing economics, and live on in his writings on economics, 'waste paper' though some of these now are with respect to contemporary economic reality. Such enduring features in Marshall's work give it its classical quality, that of continually influencing in various ways the manner of thinking about today's economic problems. This methodological legacy from Marshall's work has various dimensions which remain vibrant. Some of these may be briefly discussed as more tangible features of the enduring legacy he left in his work.

First is the requirement that economics needs to be in constant touch with the facts, if only because its contents itself change with the facts. This is the feature of economics as a moral and social science differentiating it in general from the 'natural sciences' and which, for Marshall made economic biology the mecca of good economists. It gives the form of Marshall's economics a dynamic quality, even if the substance hardly ever actually achieves it. At an elementary level it is visible in the emphasis Marshall himself invariably placed on the problem of time, and in the difficulties this created for economic argument. Economics can only benefit from being constantly reminded of this important characteristic.

Second, there is Marshall's emphasis on *useful* abstraction, so visible in his emphasis on the utility of partial equilibrium. This also gave his economics much of its imprecision and widened its scope in an indefinite way, because it enabled inclusion of the relevant features to the problem at hand and permitted an elasticity of terminology which many have found confusing. To put this in another way, precision in economics on Marshall's terms is only achieved by over-simplification, which either negates any importance a proposition may have for application, or turns it into banal trivia. The abstractions inherent in mathematical economics are particularly prone to such consequences and its practitioners need to be perpetually on guard against limitations of this type. The same applies to the empty formalism in timeless general equilibrium analysis: its neat theorems are nothing but elegant reminders of 'the one in the many and the many in the one', of little practical value for grasping solutions to genuine economic problems.

Third, Marshall's views on the objectives of economics were never constrained by a positivist agenda of normative/positive economics. Too much has been made in some circles[80] of the fact that Marshall (with Jevons and Macleod) changed the name of his subject from political economy to economics; his research agenda in the opening Book of his *Principles of Economics* very explicitly covered both explanation and prescription. For Marshall, economists do not only have to explain their world, they have an unambiguous duty to assist in changing it for the better. The high hopes Marshall had placed on consumer surplus in this context, dashed though they were by his growing realisation of its practical problems and difficulties, illustrate the dialectical relationship in Marshall between explanation and engineering for change.

The last point needs some elaboration because it has been too often misunderstood. Marshall's abandonment of the term, 'political economy' in favour of economics for the titles of his books, was largely based on his fear that emphasis on political had the potential to associate the subject undesirably with party-political considerations rather than with national objectives.[81] It was never intended as a means to narrow the scope of the subject or to divide it artificially into an 'art' and a 'science'. Marshall's social aims for the subject were far too broad for this, and he fully endorsed Mill's rebuke of Comte that 'a person is not likely to be a good economist, who is nothing else'.[82] This is not to deny that on this subject as on many others Marshall was ambivalent in his aims and, occasionally, particularly when it suited his argument, could support the position of economist *qua* economist. Examples are the controversy he conducted on the subject in the *Bee-Hive* in 1874 and much later, the *ex cathedra* pronouncement he made to justify his participation in the 1903 Tariff controversy.[83] Not for nothing did Marshall describe economics as the hand maid of ethics and filled the preliminary chapters of his *Principles* with a research agenda which embraced both social and what now would be called pure economic concerns, hence explaining why he toyed at one stage with calling his subject, social economics.[84]

Finally, economics is conceived by Marshall as a 'box of tools', a method of thinking. It is not a system of ready-made propositions by which economists can turn the world into the image of their textbooks. The toolbox enables systematic classification of relevant factors, as well as selecting appropriate methods of analysis. The foundations provided by the *Principles* generalised these factors into forces of supply and demand, production and consumption, activities and wants. These classificatory categories exhibit problems of interdependence: consumption influences production just as production determines consumption; supply determines demand, and demand, supply; activities generate wants, just as wants generate activities. Needless to say, the Marshallian system only reduced supply and demand to simple functional relationships of price under the most heroic assumptions, difficult to use and difficult to apply in a meaningful way. The theory of value is not a simple shorthand for relative price determination; for Marshall it was a shorthand by which to describe the complex contents and dynamic interdependence of his two groups of economic causes and effects.

The Cambridge economist who died in July 1924 still lives through his work and the method he instilled into his abler students. The Marshallian legacy to the Cambridge School remains one of its most valuable attributes, provided it does not degenerate into a sterile dogmatism, as it occasionally did. Such dogmatism about scope and method was in any case alien to the long-term inhabitant of Balliol Croft, sensitive to criticism and wary of controversy on these subjects as he was, and set in his ways and moral principles as he could so infuriatingly appear to his contemporaries and to later generations who can only know him from his works. In spite of these failures, part of his legacy remains invaluable, and will, 'like an existing yeast, ceaselessly' ferment the economic cosmos.[85]

NOTES

1. J.M. Keynes to Lydia Lopokova, 16 May 1924, in *Lydia and Maynard*, p. 195. The greater part of this letter was quoted above, Chapter 17, p. 651, in the context of a discussion of Marshall's deteriorating health during retirement and before.
2. Mary Paley Marshall, 'Notes for Keynes' (KMF); Marshall Archive, Large Brown Box, Item 26; Red Box, 1 (5), 'Progress and Ideals'.
3. The *Times*, 14 July 1924.
4. *The Manchester Guardian*, 14 July 1924; cf. G.F. Shove, 'The Place of Marshall's Principles in the Development of Economic Theory', pp. 133–4.
5. The *Economist*, 19 July 1924, pp. 90–91.
6. Although anonymous, the hand of J.S. Nicholson is possible in the *Guardian* Obituary, that of J.N. Keynes in those for the *Times* and *Economist*.
7. C.P. S[anger], 'Alfred Marshall', *The Nation and Athenaeum*, 19 July 1924, p. 502.
8. C.W. G[uillebaud], 'Alfred Marshall', *The Cambridge Review*, 31 October 1924, p. 58.
9. John Maynard Keynes, 'Alfred Marshall 1842–1924', *Economic Journal*, 34 (135), September 1924, pp. 311–72; John Neville Keynes to John Maynard Keynes, 5 September 1924; F.Y. Edgeworth to John Maynard Keynes, 6 September 1924 (both argued no 'life' was now needed since all of importance in Marshall's life had been mentioned in the Memoir, a perhaps correct assessment at the time of Marshall's death); A.O. Stenson, Master of Magdalene College, to John Maynard Keynes, 17 November 1924 (KMF). And cf. above, Chapter 1, pp. 15–16.
10. These are the notes she prepared for Keynes and Walter Scott, which have been so frequently used in this biography. For their generous acknowledgement of this assistance, see J.M. Keynes, 'Alfred Marshall', p. 161 n.1; Walter Scott, 'Alfred Marshall 1842–1924', from the Proceedings of the British Academy, London, Oxford University Press, 1924, p. 1 n.1. And cf. above, Chapter 1, pp. 14–15.
11. Walter Scott, 'Alfred Marshall 1842–1924', pp. 9, 10–11, 12.
12. E. Cannan, 'Alfred Marshall', in *AMCA*, I. pp. 66–70. The portrait is presumably the photographic reproduction of the Rothenstein portrait discussed in Chapter 17 above, pp. 629, 631.
13. F.W. Taussig, 'Alfred Marshall', *Quarterly Journal of Economics*, 39 (1), November 1924, pp. 1–14.
14. James Bonar, 'Alfred Marshall', *Journal of the Royal Statistical Society*, 88, January 1925, pp. 152–6.
15. *Ibid.*, pp. 155–6.
16. St John's College, Cambridge, *The Funeral Service of the Late Alfred Marshall*, Sc.D (KMF), (see illustration 53).
17. From the report in the *Cambridge Daily News*, 18 July 1924, on which this and the following paragraphs rely. The quotation from Psalm 39 is that of the Authorised Version, Psalm 39:1–5.
18. Pigou, 'In Memoriam', p. 90.
19. *Ibid.*, p. 81.
20. H.G. Johnson, 'Arthur Cecil Pigou 1877–1959', in Elizabeth S. Johnson and Harry G. Johnson, *The Shadow of Keynes*, Oxford: Blackwell, 1978, p. 175; A.C. Pigou, *Alfred Marshall and Current Thought*, London: Macmillan, 1953, pp. 3–4. The establishment of the position of Marshall lecturer is discussed later in this chapter, below, pp. 752–3.
21. Pigou, *Alfred Marshall and Current Thought*, p. 15. Pigou, when making these points, probably recalled the extracts from Marshall's letters to Bowley on problems of the statistical method he had reprinted in his *Memorials*, esp. pp. 419–27, 429.
22. *Ibid.*, pp. 18–23.
23. *Ibid.*, pp. 26–36, and see below, p.757 for Vaizey's comments on this.
24. *Ibid.*, pp. 37–48.

25. *Ibid.*, pp. 49–63; and see Chapter 16, esp. pp. 608–9, in which reference to Pigou's earlier views on the subject is made.

26. Pigou, *Alfred Marshall and Current Thought*, pp. 64–5; the story of this 'patron saint' was discussed above, Chapter 5, p. 130.

27. *The Times*, 24 October 1924, Gross value of the estate was £13,001, net personalty £12,811.

28. The Marshall Library is discussed more fully below, pp. 750–51.

29. Above, Chapter 19, p. 706; for a discussion of the effects on Pigou of the war, see Harry Johnson, 'Arthur Cecil Pigou', p. 178 and cf. Sir Austin Robinson, 'Keynes and his Cambridge Colleagues', in *Keynes, Cambridge and the General Theory*, eds. Don Patinkin and J. Clark Leith, London: Macmillan, 1977, p. 30.

30. Rita McWilliams, 'The Papers of Alfred Marshall', *AMCA,* IV, p. 194; John Whitaker, 'The Early Manuscripts of Alfred Marshall', p. 144, n.4.

31. Sir Frederick Pollock to Mary Paley Marshall, 2 December 1925; Sir Frederick Pollock to Alfred Marshall, 17 January 1891 (Marshall Archive, 1:91–92). A letter dated 1 December 1925 to F.W. Taussig (Taussig Papers, Harvard), shows the Pollock case was not an isolated one.

32. Marshall Library, Large Brown Box, Item 5.

33. John Whitaker, Appendix to *EEW*, II, pp. 395–6.

34. Donald Ross, 'An Unusual Commitment', p. 331.

35. *Ibid.*

36. *Ibid.*, pp. 332–3. (Three of Mary Paley Marshall's watercolours are reproduced as illustrations 23–25).

37. *Ibid.*, p. 311.

38. *Ibid.*, and see 'Marshall Library of Economics', *Cambridge University Reporter*, 99, 28 March 1969, the two sources on which the remainder of this section relies heavily.

39. Mary Paley Marshall to Vice-Chancellor, 14 October 1924, in *Cambridge University Reporter*, 14 October 1924, p. 122.

40. John Maynard Keynes to Lydia Lopokova, 24 February 1925, in *Lydia and Maynard*, p. 295.

41. For a discussion of her further services to the library see John Maynard Keynes, 'Mary Paley Marshall', pp. 247–50; Donald Ross, 'An Unusual Commitment', pp. 325–7, 329; C.W. Guillebaud, 'Mary Paley Marshall', *The Eagle*, LIX, No. 255, April 1960, pp. 27–8.

42. Marshall Library of Economics, *Catalogue*, 1927, introduction.

43. For details, see above, p. xi.

44. P. Sargent Florence to Mary Paley Marshall, 13 February 1927, Marshall Archive, 1:27.

45. Clark Kerr, *Marshall, Marx and Modern Times – The Marshall Lectures 1967–68*, Cambridge University Press, 1968, p. 1. *Cambridge University Reporter*, 29 November 1932, pp. 427–8; the lectures have been given annually since 1933–34 apart from the Second World War years (1940–45). More prominent early Marshall lecturers have included: Sir Arthur Salter (1933–34), R.H. Tawney (1934–35), R.G. Hawtrey (1937–38), Jacob Viner (1946–47), Lionel Robbins (1947–48), Gunar Myrdal (1950–51), Jan Tinbergen (1951–52), Pigou (1952–53), Talcott Parsons (1953–54), J.R. Hicks (1954–55), W. Fellner (1957–58), E. Lundberg (1958–59), H.J. Habakkuk (1959–60), D.H. Robertson (1960–61), E.H. Phelps–Brown (1961–62), T.W. Swan (1962–63), R.M. Solow (1963–64), R. Prebish (1964–65), E.A.G. Robinson (1965–66), S. Kuznets (1968–69), K. Arrow (1969–70), P. Sweezy (1970–71), Roy Harrod (1971–72), and M.H. Dobb (1972–73).

46. H.S. Foxwell, 'The Economic Movement in England', *Quarterly Journal of Economics*, 1 (1), 1887, p. 92.

47. John Maynard Keynes, 'Alfred Marshall', pp. 224, 223–4.

48. The volume of literature on the Cambridge School is immense. Material most helpful for writing this section was G. Becattini, 'Alfred Marshall e la vecchia scuola economica di Cambridge', in *Il Pensiero economico: temi, problemi e scuole*, edited by G. Becattini, Turin: UTET, 1990, pp. 275–310; David Collard, 'Cambridge after Marshall', in *Centenary Essays on Alfred Marshall*, pp. 164–92; Austin Robinson, 'Cambridge Economics in the Post-Marshallian Period', in *Alfred Marshall in Retrospect*, pp. 1–7.

49. Marshall Library, Large Brown Box. There are conflicting messages about the dating of this fragment. The reference to 'after Christmas' with respect to Meredith suggests 1910 as the time of writing, since he left Cambridge for Belfast (not Manchester) in early 1911; on the other hand, Macgregor replaced Clapham at Leeds in mid-1908, in time for the 1908–9 academic year, while Flux left Montréal in 1908, making a pre-1908 dating possible.

50. See above, Chapter 18, pp. 674–5, and John Maloney, *Marshall, Orthodoxy and the Professionalisation of Economics*, pp. 80–81.

51. Above, Chapter 18, pp. 682–3, Chapter 12, pp. 408–11.

52. Above, Chapter 8, esp. pp. 230, 235–6, 250–57.

53. These have all been frequently encountered on previous occasions as students, colleagues, advisers, associates and friends. Brief biographical sketches can be obtained from the articles on Berry, Bowley, Flux and Sanger in

the *New Palgrave*, while some of the mathematical contributions by Berry, Flux and Sanger are reprinted in *Precursors in Mathematical Economics*, eds William Baumol and Stephen M. Goldfield.

54. A.W. Flux, *Economic Principles*, London: Methuen, 1904, p. v; second edition, 1923.

55. G. Becattini, 'Alfred Marshall e la vecchia scuola economica', p. 297 (free translation by the author).

56. *Ibid.*

57. Above, Chapter 17, p. 649; David Collard, pp. 182–3, and my 'Alfred Marshall and the Establishment of the Cambridge Economics Tripos', p. 650.

58. Above, Chapter 15, pp. 552–3; F.S. Lee, 'D.H. Macgregor and the Firm', mimeographed, and kindly supplied by him to the author in September 1985.

59. See Rita McWilliams-Tullberg, 'Marshall's last Lecture'; David Collard, 'Cambridge after Marshall', p. 170.

60. David Collard, 'Cambridge after Marshall', pp. 175–6; W.A. Layton, *An Introduction to the Theory of Prices*, London: Macmillan, 1912, p. vi.

61. David Collard, 'Cambridge after Marshall', pp. 176–7, gives a brief appreciation of Fay in this context. His conclusion that Fay was largely outside the Marshallian organon because he was more a story-telling historian than a scientific investigator is less true of Fay's first two studies, those on cooperation and on life and labour.

62. Benians's appreciation of Marshall's teaching was quoted above, Chapter 10, p. 314 and on his teaching in the Tripos, see Chapter 15, p. 552. He subsequently moved back to history as College Lecturer and later as University Lecturer (1926–34). He was elected Master of St John's in 1933 and was Vice-Chancellor of Cambridge University, 1939–42.

63. G. Becattini, 'Alfred Marshall e la vecchia scuola economica di Cambridge', pp. 298–9.

64. Discussed above, Chapter 15, pp. 553–4.

65. John Maynard Keynes, introduction to D.H. Robertson, *Money*, Cambridge Economic Handbooks, Cambridge University Press, 1922, pp. v–vi. Marshall himself was very impressed with the Handbooks, as shown in his letters to H.D. Henderson (10 January 1922) and D.H. Robertson (14 January 1922).

66. John Vaizey, 'Keynes and the Cambridge Tradition, *Spectator*, 29 May 1976, p. 20.

67. Above, Chapter 17, p. 649 and n.115.

68. John Vaizey, 'Keynes and the Cambridge Tradition', p. 20.

69. John Maynard Keynes, *General Theory of Employment, Interest and Money, Collected Writings of John Maynard Keynes*, Volume 7, London: Macmillan 1973, p. xxix (my emphasis in the quotation).

70. T. Negishi, 'The Marshallian Foundation of Macro-economics', in *Economic Theories in a non-Walrasian Tradition*, New York: Cambridge University Press, 1985, pp. 169–81.

71. David Collard, 'Cambridge after Marshall', pp. 167–72; Robert Skidelsky, *John Maynard Keynes. Hopes Betrayed 1883–1920*, pp. 209–14.

72. H. Wright, obituary of Frank Lavington, *Economic Journal*, 1927, p. 504, reproduced in David Collard, 'Cambridge after Marshall', p. 180.

73. D.H. Robertson, *Lectures on Economic Principles*, paperback edition, London: Fontana, 1963, p. 12; and cf. his letter to H.M. Robertson, 3 November 1954 in H.M. Robertson, 'Alfred Marshall's Aims and Methods as Illustrated from his Theory of Distribution', *AMCA*, I, p. 364. J.R. Presley, *Robertsonian Economics*, London: Macmillan, 1978, p. 86 and n. 63, indicates that Marshall wrote to Dennis Robertson on at least two occasions to congratulate him on publishing two of his books: *A Study of Industrial Fluctuations* in 1915 and *Money* in 1922.

74. C.W. Guillebaud, 'Marshall's Principles of Economics in the light of contemporary thought', *Economica*, May 1952, in *AMCA*, II, pp. 186–7.

75. Peter Groenewegen, 'Alfred Marshall and the Establishment of the Cambridge Economics Tripos', p. 650. The seeds for that research program were explored in the context of Marshall's teaching in Chapters 9, 10 and 15, above, especially pp. 285–9, 317–20.

76. Marshall to Fay, 23 February 1915, in *Memorials*, p. 490.

77. Above, pp. 755 and n* and see, for example, Pigou, *Aspects of British Economic History 1918–1925*, London: Macmillan, 1946. For more recent assessments, see B. Glassburner, 'Alfred Marshall on Economic History and Political Development', *AMCA*, I, pp. 256–74 and R.C.O. Matthews and B. Supple, 'The Ordeal of Economic Freedom: Marshall on Economic History', *Quaderni di storia dell'economia politica* IX (2–3) 1991, pp. 189–214.

78. That is, T. Parsons, 'Wants and Activities in Marshall', and 'Economics and Sociology', in *AMCA*, I, pp. 179–231 and for a more recent appraisal, John Whitaker, 'Some Neglected Aspects of Alfred Marshall's Economic and Social Thought', in *ibid.*, pp. 453–86.

79. D.R. Stoddart, 'A Hundred Years of Geography at Cambridge', in *Early Geography at Oxford and Cambridge*, pp. 24–32, esp. pp. 24, 31.

80. See Peter Groenewegen, 'What is Political Economy?', *Methodus*, 4 (1), June 1992, pp. 16–18 and the references there cited, also above, Chapter 12, pp. 413–15.

81. *EOI*, p. 2: Marshall to Edwin Cannan, 22 September 1902, British Library of Political and Economic Science (Cannan Papers).
82. *P* VIII, p. 771; John Stuart Mill, *Auguste Comte and Positivism*, London: Trubner & Co., 1882, p. 83. It may be noted that both Marshall's page reference and quotation from Mill are inaccurate, a sign of how little he cared for scholarship in this sense.
83. Above, Chapter 16, pp. 574–5, Chapter 11, p. 389.
84. For a more detailed discussion, see A.W. Coats, 'Marshall on Ethics', in *Alfred Marshall in Retrospect*, pp. 153–77, and Stefan Collini, Donald Winch and John Burrow, *That Noble Science of Politics*, Cambridge University Press, 1983, Chapter 10, esp. pp. 332–6.
85. Adapted slightly from Marshall to James Bonar, 27 November 1898, in *Memorials*, p. 374.

21. A Man for all Seasons – and None: The Enigma of Marshall's Character

An often quoted remark from Joan Robinson argues that 'the more I learn about economics, the more I admire Marshall's intellect and the less I like his character'.[1] The biographer studying Marshall's life has a similar problem. Previous chapters have shown that there are different things to dislike about Marshall's character than the manner in which he constructed his economics, the specific cause for Joan Robinson's complaint. Examples are easy to find. His attitude to women; his ruthlessness in setting aside friendships and truth when he believed the occasion demanded it; his occasionally casual attitude to 'factual evidence' in argument, combined with an ability to manufacture such evidence if, and when, the need arose; his treatment of predecessors varying from the extremes of over-generosity to down-right niggardliness; his laborious, obfuscatory and sanitised prose when composing for publication as against the more casual flow of his personal correspondence, where spades were invariably called spades; his authoritarian streak in dealing with colleagues particularly when he himself was in a position of authority; his vanity, false modesty and egotistical self-centredness. It is easy to construct an unattractive picture of what was often a most unpleasant man. The behaviour giving grounds for such a construction has already been fully illustrated from Marshall's life in a variety of settings.

Fortunately for the biographer, there is more to the man. The preceding paragraph by no means presents the full picture of Marshall's complex personality and character. Important neglected characteristics are Marshall's frequent generosity, his humanity, his quality of inspiring others which made him such a good teacher, his hospitality, his willingness to assist in an extensive range of good causes, his lack of dogmatism on many questions and hence likewise his open mind, his strong attachment and loyalty to those for whom he cared and felt responsible, as well as for what he saw as the wider social interest. Portraits from the past have emphasised the teacher, the moralist, the do-gooder scientist, the hypochondriac, the crusading missionary, the compromiser, the synthesist, the romantic, the idealist, the misogynist, the misguided mathematician, the philosopher, the obfuscator, the family man, the devoted husband, the traveller, and above all, the great economist. No wonder Marshall's character has been described as an 'extraordinary enigma':[2] partly visible, partly hidden, revealing occasional glimpses of itself, often contradictory, often impossible to generalise, yet showing an interdependent whole of conflicting qualities to make his complex personality far from easy to comprehend. Was he a man for all seasons? Or for none?

The answers given so far to this question have been supplied implicitly in the framework of Marshall's activities. Virtually from necessity, these have focused on the mature Marshall. The young college Fellow and postgraduate reading philosophy, psychology, history and economics; the economic writer of occasional monographs and volumes; the economics teacher and university administrator; the participant in government inquiries, the person involved in his own way in the politics and institutions of his society, have all been encountered. In addition, there were glimpses and, where possible, longer looks at the husband, the traveller, the man with a social conscience, the correspondent, the friend, the uncle, the nephew and the son. Many of these pictures of Marshall's life are incomplete. In some cases, they are virtually non-existent. Very little is known about Marshall the son, even less about Marshall the brother; Marshall the schoolboy and the undergraduate are shadowy figures, only coming to a semblance of life from their background and from the flashes of their existence which history has preserved. The man is therefore difficult to construct from his youth; in fact, in Marshall's case the inverse seems more apt.

A general review of Marshall's person, partly constructed from activities already examined, partly from details of his life too small for chapters of their own, is therefore necessary. This further removes the disguise behind which Marshall so frequently hid his person. To eliminate features unsuitable for a great economist and to emphasise traits appropriate to the role assigned to him by history and by himself, Marshall sometimes adopted a convenient mask. The myth of Marshall to which he himself greatly contributed by selecting what he wished to leave for posterity, a process in which some of his favourite pupils ably aided and abetted him, needs deliberate exposure to the extent this still is possible. As Marshall himself always stressed, his activities shaped his nature and character; his environment and his age fashioned him to an extraordinary degree, making it all the more essential to uncover the hidden from the little that is known.

A SMALL, PHYSICAL PRESENCE WITH SHINING EYES

Without the possibility of meeting Marshall personally, his presence has to be constructed from his photographs and from the all too few physical descriptions of him which have survived. The last tend to focus on a small, physical appearance, with 'shining eyes' the most remarkable characteristic of the man. 'A small slight man with bushy moustache and long hair, nervous movements, sensitive and unhealthily pallid complexion, and preternaturally keen and apprehending eyes . . . [all] the youthfulness of physical delicacy' was how Beatrice Webb saw him in 1889 at a Cooperative Congress.[3] Holyoake likewise recalled Marshall's slender build and youthful appearance on that occasion, noting in addition his imposing presence on the podium but without remarking on his expressive eyes.[4] Eight years earlier, and about a year after Marshall's stones in the kidney had been first diagnosed, William Ramsay described Marshall as 'a thin ascetic man, all mind and no body', a physical description explicitly linked to the illness from which Marshall was then still very much recuperating.[5] Benians recalled Marshall's bearing on entering the lecture room: 'his head bent forward as if in thought, mounting his platform with a little fluster of manner, leaning on his desk, his hands clasped in front of him, his blue eyes lit up, . . . [lecturing] with rapt expression, his eyes in a far corner of the room'.[6] This was in 1900–1, when Marshall was aged 57, but the picture perfectly matches that recorded in less detail from the lecture room by others.

An acquaintance from Bristol, who saw Marshall in April 1924 before his final illness took its toll, drew a comparison between Marshall's physical appearance on these disparate occasions: 'He looked, it seemed to me, not so very greatly changed from the days when I knew him first. There was the same physical frailty – and courage, the same eager look on his face, the same unforgettable voice.' Previously, he had recalled, 'Professor Marshall looked, and I suppose he always was, a very delicate man, I used to watch him, in those early days at Bristol, walking up and down Apsley Road in the sun – in March I suppose it was, for I vividly remember that the crocuses were out on the sunny side of the road. I associated them somehow with him. It seemed to me, watching him then, as if an over-violent wind might blow him away.'[7]

In many respects the photographic record is equally meagre.[8*] The few photographs as a boy and young man which have been preserved, before the development of the 'bushy moustache' which had impressed itself on Beatrice Webb in the late 1880s, are particularly interesting. Marshall's school photo, at age 12 or 13, shows the familiar high brow, an abundant crop of hair, and his school nickname of 'tallow candles' notwithstanding, a considerable degree of that 'puppy fat' so often associated with adolescence. A fascinating feature of this photograph is the awkward positioning of the hands, imparting a sense of general anxiety to the sitter. What to do with his hands on such occasions was something which troubled Marshall for the rest of his life. Such concerns were confided to Rothenstein in 1908 during his preliminary stages of preparation when painting Marshall's official portrait, and is an awkwardness present in virtually all full-length photographs of Marshall which have been preserved. Marshall's hands are either artificially posed in action (simulating reading, writing, clasping bath chair or umbrella) or awkwardly placed across each other as in an 1877 photograph with Mary Paley Marshall taken after their wedding. This suggests the presence of a 'nervous angst' in Marshall, a sense of insecurity, explicable in terms of features of his disciplined upbringing and aggravated by his enforced mixing within the rather snobbish Cambridge milieu composed largely of people drawn from circles well above his own social class.

Two photos of Marshall in his twenties have also been preserved. One, full length and taken at Clifton College in 1865 when Marshall was 23, shows him for once in a casual, relaxed pose. It reveals his medium height comparable to that of the other Masters. Marshall is elegantly and fashionably dressed in light-coloured trousers with dark waistcoat and jacket, easily flowing graduate gown nonchalantly tossed on, a garb similar to that worn by Dakyns. Even Marshall's mortar board seems on at a rakish angle. This is Marshall the handsome second wrangler, by then secure in his intellectual achievement, comfortable in the midst of his peers, looking forward with confidence to that independence his virtually certain election to a college fellowship will bring later that year. The much more formal 1869 portrait taken for an unknown occasion shows Marshall the earnest new moral sciences lecturer. Marshall's hair is short and neatly brushed back, clean cut features draw

---

*   Marshall wrote to Ely in 1901 that he found 'photographing a nuisance' and that there were no large photographs or engravings of him. The letter responded to a request from Ely for a photograph, in which reference was made to a large photo he had seen of Marshall. Marshall explained this as an enlargement of a small photo for a special purpose and a 'very poor thing' (Marshall to Richard Ely, 23 November 1901, Ely Papers, Historical Society of Wisconsin). Eight years previously he had replied to Taussig about a similar request, 'My face is poor; my photo is ugly, but if you want it and will give golden armour for brazen, i.e. will return your photo, I shall have made a good bargain.' (Marshall to F.W. Taussig, 22 November 1893, Taussig Papers, Harvard University Archives).

attention to a high forehead and not very prominent chin. His countenance is still very youthful, despite his twenty-seven years. This last photo of a clean-shaven Marshall helps to explain why the moustache was subsequently adopted. It was a sure means of ageing the youthful impression the new lecturer imparted, hence adding to his authority. When precisely that Marshallian moustache was adopted, history does not record. Mary Paley's recollections of the early 1870s fail to mention it. Her account of their first meeting, for example, simply concentrates on his 'attractive face with its delicate outline and brilliant eyes'.[9] By the time of their wedding, the moustache is firmly in place, matching the thick long hair of its owner. This is also one of the last pre-illness photos of Marshall available.

Subsequent photos reveal what others had described. By 1885 both moustache and hair were greying and getting thinner, and show a disinclination on Marshall's part to frequent the hairdresser. Both this photo, and some taken in the 1890s reveal physical frailty and a still youthful face. A photo taken in his study, casually leaning on a mantelpiece, shows him at his middle-aged best. Health fully restored after the long decade of recovery from the effects of the kidney stones, this picture of a fairly robust constitution matches the bicycle riding and long walks which the Marshalls indulged in during the 1890s.[10] Photos from the twentieth century show a steadily ageing person, still fairly vigorous at its start but increasingly gaunt and weary as his years turn from seventies into eighties. The official photo for the National Portrait Gallery of 1917 in particular suggests the toll taken by old age, exacerbated in this instance by an illness of which he was complaining at the time in correspondence with Macmillan about his final volumes.[11] These photos fail to capture the bright, shining blue eyes as the striking feature of his face. They do, however, provide an inkling of that power for penetrating glances and never-ending quest of observation which was a striking hallmark of the man.

Other features of Marshall's presence are only recoverable from eyewitness accounts. Some suggest that conversation, clearly a major strong point in explaining the undoubted fascination his personality exerted over the young and the not-so-young, was often accompanied by much expressive movement of the arms and hands, as when explaining aspects of behaviour in primitive communist communities in the United States or imparting directions to guests and others during dinner in the cramped Balliol Croft dining-room. Whether from the assistance such movement provided or not, Marshall's power of conversation was greatly praised by Jowett, himself an arch conversationalist and connoisseur of the art from the famous dinner parties he arranged at Balliol College as its Master. A sample of the extraordinary range of Marshall's dinner conversation at Balliol Croft was preserved for posterity by one of his occasional 'working-man' dinner guests.[12]

Others were less impressed and more awed by Marshall's manner of conversation. Nephew Claude Guillebaud and former student Charles Fay recorded the fear and trepidation a Marshall invitation to lunch implied for young student guests. The young Guillebaud twins could never be certain on such occasions when Marshall's 'massive intellect' would crush them as makers of 'an inaccurate statement' or of an opinion 'of doubtful validity'; an experience Fay also highlighted. Fay's vivid memory of his first Balliol Croft lunch stressed that the little he contributed to the conversation was all certified to be highly ambiguous by Marshall as host who, avoiding the eating part of the proceedings, was disconcertingly sitting away from the table on a little foot-stool by the fireside.[13] Marshall as conversationalist was no bully exclusively of the young, however. In his later memoirs, Rothenstein recalled that conversation with Marshall called for a very high degree of circumspection, 'for everything one said he took literally, and . . . the most casual remarks [were] met with the full weight of his pedantry'.[14]

On this occasion, Rothenstein also recalled that 'not a gleam of humour lightened' Marshall's conversation. This personal characteristic was confirmed by Marshall's student and later colleague, Benians, in private conversation with Guillebaud. For one 'so patiently deficient in a sense of humour' as Marshall was, Benians 'had never known anyone who laughed so frequently during the delivery of his own lectures', a recollection, incidentally, he expressed much more gently in his official reminiscences on Marshall's death. 'Humour played an important part in his lectures' by the choice of illustrations and stories, which were never out of touch with life and the fun of which Marshall himself was the first to enjoy in the class by loud chuckling during their telling.[15] In Bristol, Mary Paley Marshall recalled his inclination to joke in evening classes, causing eruptions of laughter after an interval from Mr Grundy, a seemingly slower member of the class in catching the funny side of things.[16] Lynda Grier recalled his cleverness at coining epigrams in lectures, of which her previously quoted recollection give some samples.[17]

Few other instances of Marshall's reported humour have been preserved. His punch line in the character sketch of an American shop assistant in a hat store is one. Others occur in correspondence, such as the girdler pun to Maynard Keynes.[18] Marshall's final salutations for letters to intimates sometimes betray a schoolboy's humour by their inventiveness in devising forms appropriate to the contents of the epistle to be concluded. Examples are a 'yours foolishly' to Foxwell in 1887, 'your apologetic and grateful bore' to Keynes in 1888, 'yours most frankly. But with great admiration on all points but this' to Keynes in 1889, 'yours vernicularly trodden but turning' to Foxwell in 1890 and

<pre>
                    dreari)
                    sincere)
    Yours very   weari   ) ly
                    and yet)
                    hopeful)
</pre>

to Foxwell in a letter on the proposed Economics Tripos in 1902.*

During conversation, Marshall appears also to have been rather fond of making 'extreme statements', perhaps a consequence of that love of paradox he had acquired from his association with Clifford and Moulton during the second half of the 1860s.[19] Marshall was also capable of introducing an occasional piece of fiction to pass for fact to assist proving a point during an argument. Both John Neville Keynes and Beatrice Webb recorded instances of such habits when Marshall was still relatively young, while Mary Paley reported after his

---

*   This tendency appears to have started in the late 1880s but the small sample of Marshall letters preserved from an earlier period makes this uncertain. Another example was in a letter to J.N. Keynes congratulating him on his D.Sc. (above Chapter 18, p. 685 and n.*). A different genre of humour was noted in earlier Foxwell correspondence during the 1870s, which indicated the two were in the habit of exchanging jokes. The sample preserved from an evangelical tract then mentioned (Chapter 18, p. 671), did not seem particularly humorous to this contemporary reader.

death that 'I sometimes asked him where he got some odd story from and he pointed to his head'. No wonder 'imagination' was praised in the *Principles* with 'perception' and 'reason' among the three great qualities economists needed to have.[20]

Marshall could also monopolise conversation most effectively once he had embarked on a particular hobby horse, a characteristic which tended to increase with age. John Neville Keynes recalled an exasperating dinner conversation during the time of the Boer War in which Marshall did his best to provoke his guests by volubly airing his own decided views on the matter. Benians mentions an anecdote of Marshall haranguing the St John's senior fellowship on bimetallism in a 45-minute digression inspired by his praise of the qualities of silver as an appropriate college wedding gift for its Master. Wicksell remembered how his visit to Marshall at Balliol Croft in 1916, to discuss post-war international monetary reform was totally aborted because he could not get a word in edge-ways during Marshall's monologue on the subject.[21]

Marshall's speech had a tonal peculiarity which could occasionally startle his audience. At the climax of a prolonged pronouncement, 'his voice would rise to a very high pitch, almost squeak, followed usually by prolonged laughter'.[22] Likewise during lectures, Marshall often 'spoke with a laugh and choking exuberance of utterance ending in falsetto.'[23] Maynard Keynes, reporting on dinner parties he attended at Balliol Croft as an undergraduate, in remembering Marshall's 'great conversational power on all manner of matter', his unbroken 'cheerfulness and gaiety', his 'bright eyes and smiling talk and unaffected absurdity', also recalled the 'laughing, high-pitched voice and habitual jokes and phrases' evident on such occasions.[24]

THE PROFESSOR AT HOME AND AT LEISURE

There are only few glimpses of Marshall at home and at leisure. Leonard's description of the room in which his last visit to Marshall in 1924 took place, sets the stage for this aspect of Marshall's life. It portrayed the Balliol Croft sitting-room 'with its decoration – a Morris wallpaper, I think it must have been – its books, and some of the old pictures which vividly recalled his old home at Clifton'.[25] Other visitors to the Marshalls mentioned music from the auto-piano, art on the walls, books, as well as tea or more substantial meals, as part of the experience.

The simple, if not frugal, life style of the Marshalls had been noted by Jowett as a sign of their quiet practice of primitive Christian communism. It was likewise reflected in their, by contemporary standards, smallish, but comfortable, one-servant domestic establishment at Balliol Croft.[26] Marshall's abstemious eating habits during meals with guests were alluded to by Fay on the occasion of his first luncheon at the Marshalls. Marshall sat by the fireside while Fay (in the company of 'two Indians, one large-boned lady . . . a ferrety eyed undergraduate' and his hostess) enjoyed 'chicken and bacon, fancy pudding and ginger'.[27] He noted the informality of such repasts on other occasions, where the Marshalls adapted the hospitable notion that an additional plate and seat could always be found for one willing to share their humble supper. Not long after the First World War, tea at the Marshalls was accompanied with 'a round of buttered buns' for the guests, a cup of tea for Mrs. Marshall while Marshall himself partook of nothing.[28] Undoubtedly, such abstention on Marshall's part at this time was induced by the seemingly embarrassing consequences from increasing digestive problems. With lesser guests with whom conversation was not so urgent, these were kept at bay by the opportunity for Marshall to remain silent during, and after, the meal.

Marshall was probably never a very big eater. A 3d. potato pie at the Coffee Palace in Blackpool took care of the Marshalls' nutritional requirements during an evening while they were observing working-class amusements on holidays in the 1880s. More generally, there is little to suggest a Marshallian obsession with this form of bodily need. Apart from the odd remark contrasting French female culinary skills with the less imaginative and economical practice of the British housewife, there are few references to food and its preparation in the pages of the *Principles*, although on more than one occasion Marshall drew attention to the necessity of adequate food for a proper standard of life conducive to efficiency.[29] Marshall appears to have smoked until forbidden to do so by his doctor during initial treatment for his kidney stones. However, he would certainly have partaken of the occasional social glass of wine or port, an inevitable accompaniment to a college feast and University dinner party. While highly critical of over-indulgence, and especially of alcoholism, in parents and members of the working class, the evidence suggests he was never strict 'temperance'. Mary Paley had stronger feelings on this matter, and on her death, nephew Claude Guillebaud reported that a lot of wine which had probably been laid down by Marshall, had turned to vinegar.[30] In short, his self-denial at the table came more from health and habit than from strict principle.

Marshall's reading habits were likewise sober and restrained, though sometimes indicative of a tendency to romantic tastes. The last is evident from some of his literary preferences and visible in occasional utterances. A person who largely read for the facts books could give him, and, moreover, amply endowed with a vivid imagination himself, needed 'to care little for novels'. As a boy Marshall had read many Scott novels, perhaps a taste encouraged from his father's partial Scottish upbringing and 'he kept his love for them till the end of his life, in his last few years having [them] read to him over and over again'. At one stage, Dumas novels provided a source for Marshall's amusement, 'but in later years they rather disgusted him'. Mary Paley recalled 'he cared very much for George Eliot's novels', especially *Mill on the Floss*, to which he used to allude in his early lectures. He also liked Charlotte Bronte but 'never cared for Jane Austen', presumably because of the frivolous nature of her characters.[31] Guillebaud reported that his uncle had likewise enjoyed novels by Hardy, which were read to him by Mary Paley, as well as an occasional Dickens novel.[32] What Marshall made of the Tolstoi novels Jowett sent them for Christmas in 1891 has not been recorded, though some of Tolstoi's earnestness, as that of Eliot and Dickens, probably appealed to him.[33]

His taste in poets has also been recorded. Goethe, Shelley and Shakespeare were his favourites, the last used as a form of relaxation while studying for the Mathematical Tripos and as a source for pleasurable social readings with his coterie from St John's in the 1860s. Goethe was a companion on solitary mountain-climbing tours while he was learning German and, together with Shelley, would have catered for his more romantic inclinations so evident in his liking for Scott's novels, and more temporarily, those of Dumas. Marshall's own attempts at poetry did not survive, and his few sentiments on the subject are only preserved in a fragment of dialogue written as postgraduate and in his record of conversation with Emerson in defence of Swinburne. A taste for the last's avant-garde, and then decidedly *risqué*, poetry Marshall may possibly have acquired from Mary Paley and her Newnham friends.[34]

Music seems to have given Marshall greater pleasure than literature. Such tastes appear not to have originated with his upbringing at home, where with the exception of hymns, music seems not to have been encouraged, although his younger sister, Mabel, was apparently musical. Marshall's musical taste may well have been first stimulated from musical evenings at the Percivals while he was at Clifton in 1865. On Mary Paley's account, such tastes were nurtured by his attendance at concerts while learning German at Dresden in 1868. There are also references to musical entertainments at Bristol and Oxford.[35] Music production and consumption likewise feature relatively frequently in the pages of the *Principles*. An example is the cumulative impact of experience in stimulating musical pleasure and enjoyment as a way of illustrating the time dependence of utility functions.[36] The extent of Marshall's willingness to indulge his enjoyment of music as leisure activity and relaxation is measured by the purchase of the auto-piano, apparently a triumph over his reluctance to engage in material self-gratification. Beethoven piano sonatas and renditions of spiritual music (Bach? Handel?) became the comfort of old age. Music clearly played a quite important part in Marshall's long life.[37]

Marshall also appears to have had a considerable interest in painting, possibly inspired by Dakyns or Sidgwick.[38] His comments on the quality of the pictures he noticed in the houses of Carey and Emerson during his 1875 American trip was an early sign of such interest. In Dresden, Marshall visited its famous art gallery sufficiently often to venture comparisons between its Sistine Madonna by Raphael and a Holbein Madonna, in which the second gradually triumphed over the more facile, conventional appeal of the first. Art Gallery visits in Dresden were not a sudden fad for a culture-deprived postgraduate to make up for lost time. Mary Paley recorded that visits to art galleries were a regular part of their routine for visiting towns during summer vacations. Marshall himself wrote to Brentano that their enforced waits at Munich for train connections to the Tirol were frequently combined with art gallery visits in which modern art was observed as well as the great masters housed in its famous Alte Pinakothek. Although Mary Paley's artistic inclinations and talents would have undoubtedly reinforced Marshall's own interest in pictures, an enjoyment of art became a significant part of Marshall's life.[39]

Artistic illustrations were occasionally used in Marshall's writings. 'Raphael's pictures' were chosen to represent those non-reproducible commodities where demand, and in particular the means of those willing to buy, determined price.[40] Michelangelo and Leonardo da Vinci are mentioned in the *Principles* in different contexts.[*] More interestingly, when illustrating socially responsible and worthwhile spending by the rich, Marshall urged their investment in paintings and works of art, to be donated to the nation at their death or some other future occasion for the edification of the public at large.[41] Late in life, he commented on the important role of medieval art in spreading religious messages

---

[*] *P* VIII, p. 193 and n.780. As Pierre Bourdieu has argued, these examples fall all within the range of experience of those with the most elementary knowledge of art. See his *Distinction. A Social Critique of the Judgement of Taste*, London: Routledge & Kegan Paul, 1984, pp. 262–3; *The Love of Art*, Cambridge: Polity Press, 1991, p. 57.

before the development of printing; while two fragments on the importance and limitations of art were preserved among his unpublished papers.

The first of these, probably dating from the 1860s, reflects on the static nature of the plastic arts. These, Marshall argued, can 'only touch das Sein' and not 'das Werden', or reality as it exists rather than its future possibilities; more generally, a characteristic of all early artistic expression, including Shakespeare's literary art. Growth in the means of communication, however, had increased 'the self consciousness of the world and its artists have more involved and complicated mental phenomena to express'. Marshall doubted that those engaged in painting would generate the revolution required to accommodate such increased demands on expression. Notwithstanding this observation, he did not totally reject the ability of artists to develop more complex visions of the world. 'Yet the power of Rembrandt might be combined with the genius of Rafael in each of the many directions of which Rafael selected only one. In the direction of grouping, great progress may be made. Every day we get more completely whole scenes painted instead of a number of independent individuals standing together.'[42] These statements reveal general interest rather than a mastery in understanding developments in art.

Many years later Marshall wrote a further fragment on the usefulness of art and its association with social development. It linked art and economics and the difficulties in judging beauty in times of change, and was perhaps designed as a draft comment for later use on the artistic criticisms of political economy as voiced by Carlyle, Ruskin and Morris.[*]

> Life without art is not worth living, says Morris. I say no. Affection, and the conscious pursuit of noble aims have made a thousand lives happy for one that has been made happy by art, and their good has been unmixed with evil, whereas art has been a dangerous tonic, beautiful-making like strychnine and arsenic, but in its application more dangerous than they. These facts, so much overlooked by many, have for that reason all the more influenced the resolute and perhaps overstern men who have given a tone to economics and have carried them perhaps to see things a little out of proportion.
>
> An age in which plastic art is great is likely to be followed by an age in which art is fashionable. And hitherto when art has been fashionable, society has generally become vicious and a vicious age is always the beginning of a long period in which excitement is substituted for happiness and the alternative fever and despondency of ill-regulated passions take the place of the tranquil and peaceful.
>
> All this to lead up to that a man has no right to make things ugly or to be very [ugly]. That a railway may not be ugly; nor a factory, without need; that a healthy spirit of emulation is the best: but that when a parasitic race of money making men push down prices by destroying collective property in beautiful objects, there is a prima facie ground for interfering. This applies to access to beautiful scenery. Competition as spoiling beautiful scenery. Much nonsense [said] here. It is not certain that a railway is ugly. Every new scar is an evil. [But] the more picturesque things in nature are the results of terrible convulsions over which time has thrown a healing [hand].
>
> In judging of old things, we dwell on their scarcity, in judging new things only on their faults. . . . But we have lost through our hurry. It is the hurry of competition more than its definiteness and deliberateness of purpose that is injurious to art and to social life.[43]

---

[*] *P* VIII, pp. 22, 47, 780 n.1 dating respectively from *P* II, p. 76; *P* V, p. 47 and p. 780. Marshall knew Ruskin personally from his Oxford days. J.M. Keynes recounted, 'In December 1884, Jowett took Ruskin "to a lovely dinner *out* last night – with the Master at a quite nice couple's, Professor and Mrs. Marshall. Mrs. Marshall and I got into a discussion – very profound – about the difference between round and oval sections in girls' waists".' ('Obituary: Henry Higgs', *Economic Journal*, 50 (200), December 1940, p. 550). What Marshall and Ruskin conversed on has, unfortunately, not been recorded.

Conclusions are not easily reached about the extent of Marshall's appreciation of the fine arts. However, the few specific references to pictures and reproduction on the Marshalls' walls, both at Balliol Croft and at some of the Marshalls' earlier residences, suggest that exposure to art was a regular feature of Marshall's life. This is not to say that good taste in decoration was necessarily a strong point in Marshall's personal make-up. The slavish imitation of his furniture arrangements which Marshall communicated to Jowett in 1891, as well as Ramsay's caustic comments on the gloom of the furnished Marshalls' Clifton residence he had rented, suggest the biographer does not have easy generalisations to make on this score.

Marshall's 1906 fragments on art and beauty in relation to economics and competition also drew attention to the important role of nature and countryside for the complete life. This needs little further discussion in so far as the Marshalls themselves took account of this in their own practice. Communion with nature, particularly if in relatively unspoiled forms of lonely Alpine valleys in the then still unfashionable southern Tirol, or relatively uncrowded seaside retreats in Devon, Cornwall and Wales, played both an aesthetic and creative role in Marshall's existence. Summer excursions and shorter trips at other suitable times fully attest to this, and for once such activities can be explained both from Marshall's boyhood experiences and from the Marshalls' conventional adherence to the summer recreational pattern appropriate to their class in Victorian England.

As in the case of painting and other works of art, Marshall was anxious that all should have access to nature's gifts in fair measure. His strong concerns for clean air, parks, gardens, playing fields and his support of the Garden City movement indicate this. Such policy objectives were part of Marshall's 'tendency to socialism' and seem at least in part to have been inspired by his schoolboy experience in the far from clean air of the Merchant Taylors' schoolroom and its absence of playing fields of any description. Once again, Marshall saw the solution to these problems as a suitable opportunity for income redistribution and, despite his hostility to Henry George on the platform, recommended the appropriation for this purpose through appropriate taxation policy of at least part of the rent of land.[44]

Sports, games and creative hobbies also had their place in Marshall's leisure hours. Long, invigorating and bracing walks and later equally hardy bicycle excursions, were both parts of the Marshalls' recreation attuned to the spirit of the age. When his health allowed it, Marshall also indulged in sport. Cricket at school and rowing as an undergraduate were followed by tennis at Bristol, until ill health prevented this exercise on Marshall's part. In the context of industrial training, Marshall recalled this sequence of his short practice in the remark, that 'a good cricketer soon learns to play tennis well'.[45] A form of bowls, adapted from the Italian game, perhaps acquired during their Sicilian sojourn, became part of leisure during retirement at Balliol Croft, to be replaced in long winter evenings and at night by the relaxation of backgammon as a regular, hour-long communal game.

Marshall also had a workshop at the back of his garden, where he could indulge his wood-carving skills, carpentry and general handyman activities acquired in youth. From the nine pins and marking ink stand he had made for his younger brother and mother, Marshall graduated to the mechanical contraptions for long-distance operation of his auto-piano, getting tea up to his study on the first floor of Balliol Croft, as well as gadgets for more general domestic use. His obituaries recalled unsuccessful attempts to secure labour-saving devices in the home: electroplated knives which failed to cut; improvements for fastening galoshes which let the water in. Marshall apparently liked to give advice on all aspects of domestic work. He explained 'to ladies how to dust their rooms and what was the best thing for taking out a stain'.[46] A desire to be up to date with events in the world extended to technical inventions. While at Bristol, he was early in using gas fires for heating, thereby saving considerable cleaning time and the mess from traditional coal fires; in his administration he adopted an electric pen for more effective reproduction of written material by multiple copies; he had the first domestic telephone connection in Bristol to enable speedy contact between residence and university office. Space and labour saving was the key feature of his plans for Balliol Croft. Electric lighting was quickly installed there. In the last decade of his life he commented on the motor car, cinema and gramophone and their implications for social life and improvement. He was a photographer of sorts, as he informed Jowett. Old fashioned as he became in his morals, he tended to be up to date with, though not always fully accurate on, his technology.[47]

A PREPOSTEROUS, ODD AND IDIOSYNCRATIC INDIVIDUAL

Keynes described Marshall as a 'preposterous' human being, full of generosity and charm nevertheless; others noted him to be an odd and idiosyncratic individual.[48] These features of his personality can be reviewed by recapitulating some aspects of his relationships to predecessors, to college, to friends, and to his wife. Re-examining such major relationships in Marshall's life in this way also enables a review and summary which pulls together their essentials.

Predecessors. On this subject, Cannan mentioned as one of Marshall's 'besetting sins . . . [his] amiable but ruinous vice of excessive modesty', especially to the great masters Smith and Ricardo.[49] Twenty years later, Shove argued 'Marshall was not among the writers niggardly in their acknowledgements. He erred, if at all, in the direction of generosity.'[50] Marshall himself explained his practice of acknowledgement in correspondence with J.B. Clark. Without mentioning 'obligations either way', Marshall claimed to refer to all those 'whom I know to have said a thing before I have said it in print', a rule he established only after much soul-searching and invariably open, he also claimed, to much misinterpretation.[51]

When earlier a substantial part of this letter to Clark was quoted,[52] its substantial conflict was mentioned with the facts of Marshall's treatment in print of several contemporary economists. With respect to Jevons and, to a lesser extent, Walras and the Austrians, Marshall's recognition of his 'rivals' seems more to reflect strong pride in preserving his own priorities and reveals considerable meanness to those he thought were trying to steal such claims to fame from him.

Marshall's treatment of Jevons set standards in 'acknowledgement' abiding with the strict letter of those Marshall assigned himself. However, it seems contrary to the qualities on this score later ascribed to him by others. Marshall's review of Jevons was 'niggardly' in its praise and strong on criticism, explained *ex post* by Marshall's anger at Jevons's treatment of his 'masters', especially Ricardo. Marshall showed inordinate meanness of spirit in his failure to acknowledge Jevons's input into his own later treatment of marginal utility, its measurement and its associated notion of disutility. Marshall deliberately obscured these debts by claiming he had reached these results independently in lectures and by making obscure references – which interestingly only started during the year after Jevons's death – about the assistance provided on these subjects by Cournot and von Thünen. In reality, the significance of some of these acknowledgements, especially to von Thünen, is difficult to accept.

Marshall's personal association with Jevons during Jevons's lifetime was never close. Their temperaments clashed too much for any other outcome. Some of this is summed up in Keynes's comment that Jevons chiselled in stone while Marshall knitted in wool.[53] In addition, Marshall sensed a threat of rivalry he found hard to bear even after its major force was removed through Jevons's premature death. This fear is initially visible in Marshall's review with its carping critical tone, in the changes Jevons's book induced in Marshall's own publication strategy, and in Marshall's very selective praise for Jevons the applied economist while denying him any claim to 'startling' theoretical discovery in a memorial tribute.[54] The first edition of the *Principles* made many references to Jevons's *Theory* but only acknowledged one original contribution. 'The use of "indifference" seems to have been first applied to this use by Jevons', is the one concession Marshall made to this predecessor's theoretical originality, while the first reference to Jevons which then occurred in the *Principles* classed him mischievously among 'Mill's followers'.[55] Generosity is a quality conspicuously absent in Marshall's treatment of Jevons; the rule of only giving acknowledgement to those who said something first in print is rigorously applied to Jevons's disadvantage.[*]

Marshall's annoyance with the younger Austrians, especially Böhm-Bawerk, was also attributed by him to their mistreatment of early predecessors. Marshall's relationship with Menger had been formal, correct and minimal. However, a good case can be made out that Marshall's dislike of Böhm-Bawerk and von Wieser was inspired more by their criticism of himself, as he grudgingly admitted to Wicksell in the case of Böhm-Bawerk. 'The rough method of thumping' he had personally experienced from Böhm-Bawerk (to use the phrase he applied to such treatment in correspondence with J.B. Clark) explain his subsequent patronising references to Böhm-Bawerk and von Wieser. They were mere 'lads in school' when between 1870 and 1874 Marshall was completing his own economic system, although in actual fact they were only nine years younger than he was. Equally patronising is his comment to Wicksell that Böhm-Bawerk was guilty of mathematical blunders for which a twelve-year-old schoolboy would be severely punished. Umbrage at von Wieser probably came from Marshall's ingenious, but erroneous, attribution to von Thünen in the first edition of the *Principles* of first using the German word for 'marginal', an attribution grudgingly corrected in favour of von Wieser's claim by the time the second edition appeared. No wonder the well-documented encounter between Marshall and the Austrians caused such tremors in their respective households, despite the 'feast of reconciliation' which Marshall,

---

[*] Becattini has suggested in correspondence that Marshall's treatment of Jevons may have had an element of 'jealous spite' because of Jevons's sympathetic treatment of Mary Paley as a 'full blown' economist during her Tripos examination, as a result of which Mary became a much more ardent admirer of Jevons. Such personal aspects cannot be ignored.

as the 'soul of chivalry', arranged as recompense for earlier rudeness he had shown to Böhm-Bawerk. Relations between the leaders of Cambridge and Austrian economics ended in mutual but unspoken agreement to prevent recurrence of such encounters and was marked by increasing acidity in the tone in which Marshall referred to his Austrian colleagues.[56]

Associations with Walras are in a class of their own in so far as Marshall's uncollegiality and incivility are concerned. Despite Marshall's several later claims to have come into contact with Walras as early as 1873, contact by correspondence did not start until 1883, never led to personal meeting and fizzled out before the 1880s had ended. Perhaps a letter in 1882 from Foxwell to Walras praising Marshall, induced Walras to send Marshall a collection of his early theoretical papers. Marshall reciprocated by sending Walras the *Economics of Industry*, prompting a gift of Walras's *Elements of Pure Economics* not long thereafter. Marshall's response to this last gift showed his rudeness in the manner in which it raised matters of priority, demonstrating once again the high degree of sensitivity Marshall had on the subject. Subsequent lack of response to Walras's theoretical contributions is explicable from the fact that Marshall failed to read very far into the *Elements*. However, had he heard of it, Marshall would have been furious at Walras's approval of Rist's 1906 remark that both Pareto and Marshall had *continued* along lines which Jevons, Menger and Walras had *initiated*. Marshall always claimed his own niche of independent discovery in what was subsequently called the 'marginal revolution' of the 1870s. This was not unjust if the emphasis is on marginal rather than on the utility content of this 'revolution'. Walras was subsequently largely ignored by Marshall in his public utterances and, on some accounts, occasionally even actively censored.*

Relationships with these contemporaries show some interesting character traits not easily described as generosity or excessive modesty. Sensitivity to pressing claims on priority and to the pricks of criticism describe these relationships more aptly. This suggests a strong spirit of rivalry on Marshall's part with an overwhelming urge to be the eventual winner in the competition this generated, a desire for being first which other aspects of his life duplicated. Vanity, pride and ambition are attributes consistent with such behaviour. The reputation for generosity and modesty which Marshall later gained came more from the accolades he so freely bestowed on long dead rivals, a sign that Marshall really cared largely, and practically, about being first among the living in his more immediate

---

* Above, Chapter 13, p. 478 and for a discussion of Marshall's lack of collegiality with other economists in this context, John Whitaker and Kern O. Kymn, 'Did Walras Communicate with Marshall in 1873?', *Rivista internazionale di scienze economiche e commerciali*, 23 (4), 1976, pp. 386–91, esp. pp. 388–9. A comment to Foxwell on some other French economists may be mentioned here. The context is the book list for economics students. 'You will have noted that I have failed in the attempt to get good books in French. I expect Pareto is the ablest, but he is very unreal and cranky, I think. . . . Gide, is, I think, quite empty' (Marshall to Foxwell, 2 August 1903, Freeman Collection, 13/244).

Pascal Bridel has informed me that Walras's holdings of Marshall's work are also of interest. These included Marshall's inaugural lecture inscribed simply, 'From the author'. It is heavily underlined. Walras's copy of the later *Elements of the Economics of Industry* has some critical annotations on the measurement of utility by money while Walras appears to have owned only the French translation (1906–8) of the *Principles*. Pareto's holdings of Marshall writings included a copy of the second edition of the *Principles* without annotations, and two offprints inscribed by Marshall to Pareto, namely 'The Old Generation of Economists and the New', *Quarterly Journal of Economics*, 1897 and 'Distribution and Exchange', *Economic Journal*, 1898. Marshall owned a copy of the French edition of Pareto's *Manual*, unannotated.

environment. Hence Smith and Ricardo increasingly received his most generous praise, followed by von Thünen and, particularly later in life, by more qualified recognition given to the contributions of Cournot and John Stuart Mill.

Praise directed at the dead is most strikingly on show in Marshall's elaborate recitation in his inaugural lecture of the then recent demise of Britain's most eminent economists and hence, potential rivals, at the time of Marshall's own triumph in gaining acclaim through securing the Cambridge chair. The deaths in the decade prior to this triumph greatly facilitated the claims Foxwell made on his behalf in 1887 by proclaiming Marshall's pre-eminence in the British profession, even before his *Principles* had been published. Marshall retained that pre-eminence and leadership for the rest of his life. He greatly enjoyed the status it gave him, as well as the tributes it generated. A good example is his reaction to the letter sent him by the economists' community on the occasion of his eightieth birthday. Once at the top, magnanimity replaced competitive spirit. Hence, a posture of modesty and generosity were traits for which he became more easily venerated in the many of the tributes which followed his death.[57]

College. R.F. Scott wrote to Keynes after reading his Memoir of Marshall that 'Marshall was a bit of a mystery to us' at St John's, peculiar in both his habits of teaching as well as in his general college life.[58] Marshall appears never to have gained great popularity in his college. Apart from his appointment to position of Steward twelve years after his original election to a fellowship, he held no other college office. Given his post-1885 standing in the university, he was of course accorded the status of Professorial Fellow, and became member of the College Council. Lack of residential status, together with probable lack of interest meant that Marshall would have taken little advantage of such seniority. Foxwell's story about the transfer to the college of the Rothenstein portrait suggests little love for Marshall at St John's. There are in any case few other tangible monuments to Marshall's long association with his college. Its community was grateful for the honours Marshall secured for the college, from being a second wrangler to becoming a university professor. However, he cannot be seen as having ever being raised to anything like the position of favoured son.

At the same time, Marshall's undergraduate years at the college were never recalled by him as a highlight of his life. Mary Paley noted after his death that Marshall tended to speak of the 'glorious years 1864–67' and of his companions at this time, including presumably his narrow association with the Johnian circle for communal readings of Shakespeare in which, with his slightly younger contemporaries Clifford and Moulton, he took a position of leadership. Even if he was respected, Marshall cannot, however, be described as popular in these immediate postgraduate years. His exclusion from the Chit Chat Club is a good example of one type of ostracism, while Foxwell's comment on his cliquish association with Clifford (from Trinity) and Moulton suggests other peculiarities in his college social life. Although a member of the Johnian Boat Club, his undergraduate friendships were apparently confined to the sole, and not long-lasting association with Levett. As an undergraduate he probably had little time, and certainly no money, to spare for active socialising in college. His background, behaviour and class would also have made such socialising difficult, had he developed a taste for it. His tendency to come first in college examinations and the feelings this probably generated among his fellow students were also not designed to make him more popular. Such naked ambition and anxiety to do well would almost certainly have been frowned upon as the boorish behaviour of a swot by the social leaders at the college. By force of circumstance, these features made him a relative recluse as an undergraduate, a type of life for which he had already developed some aptitude while at school, a period rather devoid of friendships of much warmth and durability.

When the major Tripos prize had been won, albeit not to the extent which Marshall's ambition would have desired, more relaxation became feasible. However, even then there probably was little general unwinding. The picture of a recluse remains. The isolated thinker and reader of the 'wilderness' during the day, and the 'cloisters' by night, is one indication of such introversion. The select gathering of younger men among whom Marshall could feel relatively superior; and friendship developed with those working in the moral sciences is another. The latter constituted the circle to which his interests aided by ambition were gradually directing him as the 1860s were drawing to a close. Even these glorious years continued the inclination to shine apparent from his school-days and days as undergraduate. If an earlier hypothesis[59] is correct, and Marshall's choice of economics over psychology partly reflected the better chances for eminence economics provided, then the wish to succeed by the relatively unpopular boy and young man is easily seen as serving a strong psychological need for Marshall. Although in the context of the debate over degrees for women, Marshall pontificated about the unique value men students obtained from the collegiate life, his own student life exhibits little visible benefit from this privilege, apart from the path to greatness it provided via Tripos and subsequent academic career.

Friends. Marshall's friendships reinforce a picture of a proud, introverted, intellectually gifted, ambitious and often socially inept person. In addition, they reveal an occasional ruthlessness, an egotistical streak, a degree of insecurity from his choice of friendships combined with a fear of being rejected, and a social life thwarted and shaped by the vagaries imposed by the consequences of poor digestion. The lonely Alpine wanderer and mountaineer of 1867, pleased when the Mozley brothers, his earlier travel companions, departed to leave him alone in his mountain splendour, is in a way symbolic of the isolated man at his peak Alfred Marshall was to become. Likewise, when as ambitious professor with his eyes firmly fixed on posterity and on the more eminent role his subject had to play in the future of the nation, sacrifices had to be made for such lofty objectives, he did not allow friendship to stand in the way, even if such friendships were of nearly half-century standing. Marshall's loyalty was more to principle and propriety than to friends.

Such utilitarian features are visible in all four major friendships in which Marshall engaged. Sidgwick was useful as an early mentor and role model to learn from and admire, to be discarded when no longer needed or when he stood in the way of what Marshall conceived as his major task in university reform. Fear of Sidgwick's political economy as rival initially soured the good relationship they had enjoyed between 1867 and 1877, until this implied threat was dispelled first by Sidgwick's, and then by Marshall's own, elevation to a Cambridge chair in the Moral Sciences. There was a peculiar selfishness and brutality in Marshall's treatment of Sidgwick which was even noted by Fay,[60] though in fairness to Marshall, Sidgwick is not the blameless, long suffering 'saint' in which guise he was presented for posterity by his brother and widow.[61]

Foxwell, for long a genuine and loyal friend, invariably gave more than he received from the relationship, partly from the sense of duty friendship implies; partly, and perhaps increasingly, from the unqualified loyalty Foxwell believed the Professor in a subject was owed by his non-professorial staff. Marshall was very capable of abusing this goodwill on occasion: in the determination of teaching duties; in the re-arrangement of syllabus and booklists, in the appointment of staff and in his *ex-cathedra* campaigns against extending the rights of women in Cambridge University. The reciprocal camaraderie which exchanged rosewood desks and marriage gifts, advice and rare books, gradually gave way to bickering about bimetallism, the use of history, free trade and applied economics. Friendship was finally sacrificed in the choice of Marshall's successor where Marshall left no stone unturned, principled or unprincipled, to get Pigou elected for the sake of the Tripos and the reputation of Cambridge economics. Marshall could not risk the demise of the Tripos for which he had fought so hard by the appointment of the much older and less committed Foxwell. The breach then proved irreparable. Marshall's various attempts at reconciliation invariably came to nothing during these last sixteen years, revealing the inadequate grasp he had about Foxwell's sorely tried feelings.

John Neville Keynes, the third of Marshall's moral sciences friendships, was also perhaps the least intimate of the three. It likewise appears one-sided and ultimately only sustained by a sense of duty on Keynes's part rather than by the mutual like and respect on which friendships need to be founded. In sharp contrast to Keynes's rapidly developing rapport with Fawcett, and more especially, Sidgwick, Keynes warmed only slowly to Marshall's initial company, and then always in a critical and respectful manner. Marshall, on the other hand, used Keynes from the start. Keynes was immediately seen as a handy vessel for furthering the cause of economics through his sound and technically competent teaching, well trained as it had been by Marshall himself. On Marshall's departure for Bristol, Keynes was needed to maintain standards at Cambridge; on Marshall's resignation from Oxford, Keynes was immediately anointed as his reluctant, albeit temporary replacement. Later Keynes filled the role of major sounding board and adviser on administrative matters in moral sciences course reform politics. The most intimate part of their association came during their mutual exchange of proofs for the three years from the end of 1887; this coincided with the beginning of a relative trouble-free period at the Moral Sciences Board before new problems of course reform and the various manifestations of the women's issue generated cause for virulent ruptures. By the new century, Keynes was heartily sick of his colleague's ways and keen to avoid Marshall's company whenever possible. By 1905, if not earlier (recalling Maynard Keynes's presence at dinner parties during the 1904 Cambridge meeting of the British Economic Association), Marshall began increasingly to look to the son as a substitute for the father on which to build his hopes and ambitions as teacher and disseminator of economics, a transferred aspiration which father John Neville Keynes in the end was only able to thwart partially and temporarily. The former friendship had completely faded away by 1908. Marshall's retirement finally freed John Neville Keynes from any further professional obligations to his former colleague. Only sporadic contact was maintained in the subsequent years largely initiated by Marshall, and at his end, John Neville Keynes did not even attend Marshall's funeral, though, perhaps symbolically, the Keynes family was represented by son, Maynard.

The fact that Marshall ultimately and inevitably failed to sustain friendships because he pushed them too far and too selfishly to his own advantage is their major common element. However, the fact that these three friendships also had their common origin and ultimate *raison d'être* in the moral sciences is likewise significant, explaining the potential for their exploitation by Marshall, eventually so influential in their final termination.

Marshall's friendship with Jowett was quite different. It undoubtedly started with mutual respect and liking. Furthermore, it was nurtured on an official basis by the older man's role as Marshall's superior, first as member of the Bristol University College Council and later as Master of Balliol when Marshall joined it as teaching member. Marshall's election to the Cambridge chair removed any utilitarian qualities from the Jowett friendship, apart from Marshall taking obvious, but infrequent, advantage of the relationship by using Jowett's undoubted strong influence at Oxford in attempting to aid Keynes's academic career. This perhaps explains why the friendship survived, though the important role Mary Paley played in its perpetuation as loyal correspondent and exchanger of ideas cannot be ignored.

The two men were undoubtedly strongly aligned in mutually shared moral values and philosophical interests. This extended to political economy. They were also well attuned to their own mutually admired peculiar conversational talents. Mary Paley supplemented the friendship by being Jowett's companion on architectural excursions in Oxford, Cambridge and Ely. Jowett's sufficient seniority in age enabled him to play the father figure successfully, a role he perhaps consolidated by the cautious and unobtrusive advice and assistance he offered at crucial points during Marshall's Bristol career, and subsequently by introducing him to statesmen like Balfour and Asquith. Hence this was a relationship quite different from the others. It was unclouded by the problems which common membership of boards of studies and universities so often entailed. Moreover, Marshall did not need to feel the social inferiority from background with Jowett, which must have been ever present at Cambridge. Ultimately he came on a par with Jowett. He was after all a similar academic success story rising from relatively humble circumstances against substantial odds and on intellectual merit alone.

Marshall's few friendships help to illustrate his insecurity, self-centredness, introversion, ruthlessness and occasional generosity. Their course likewise suggests why in the end he only cared for some of his relatives and his more recent, former students.

Wife. 'Affectionate sentiment' and selfish exploitation; conflicting perspectives and mutual agreement in shared interests; liberal and enlightened tolerance and proscribing repression; such are the warring emotions in Marshall's relationship with his wife in a forty-seven year-marriage. He was highly dependent on her and could be fussily caring of her well-being, but not in the sphere of his work. No real intellectual partnership therefore ever existed. However, he relied on her judgement in every conceivable domain. She was said by him to have criticised his work and improved it continuously, yet in connection with the *Principles* she was assigned the most mundane research assistance in proofreading and preparing corrigenda for new editions. After marriage, he never attributed any major point in his economics to her, though they were co-authors on one book and she constructed a substantial part from his material for the final volume published under his name. She handled, and indeed contributed, much of the household's financial resources; ensured his material comforts at home and abroad, organised their extensive travel arrangements but yet, on the evidence of Maynard Keynes, was not permitted to participate in economic conversation at their dining-table and sitting-room. She greeted his students with tea, he greeted hers with condescension.[62] A wasted forty-seven years in which she was 'enslaved in self-denying servitude to Alfred' is one description of their married life.[63] This separated twenty-seven years of premarital life of a happy, but strict childhood, combined with the pioneering existence as woman student and resident lecturer at Cambridge, and a final twenty years of 'glorious rediscovery of the world', seeing old friends and making new ones, and presiding over 'her' library made up largely from his books. This particular post-Marshall Cambridge economist's account conflicts with others. Many acquaintances and friends described her devoted loyalty to his name and reputation, or her ability 'to relate what a jealous and selfish intellectual wretch Alfred had been' in the privacy of her sitting-room.[64] Claydon who, as librarian, worked closely with Mary Paley Marshall after her husband's death, told Becattini that she invariably described her married life as a period of 'uninterrupted bliss'; an exaggeration she was quite capable of contradicting on other occasions.[65]

About this relationship in particular, all too little can be resolved, yet there is much which points to the strange features in Marshall's life as husband and even as lover and person in love. There can be no doubt whatsoever that this marriage was mutually desired even if initial impetus in their courtship appears to have come from her. It is equally certain that from the start, their married partnership had unusual features beginning with their very selective and almost secretive wedding ceremony and its agreed deletion of the obedience clause from the order of service. Such unusual aspects continued with their interrupted honeymoon in Clifton and Cornwall; the childlessness of the union combined with her resumption with his agreement virtually within a year of paid employment as university teacher in the three universities in which he himself was employed. They had disagreements on many issues. They do not seem to have shared a mutual love for their own relations. Yet they spent all their subsequent summers and most of their other vacations together, he doing his writing, she engaged in her painting and both enjoying their sightseeing and observing factories and aspects of working-class life wherever they went. She was his eyes and ears at meetings of the Charity Organisation Society and the Cambridge Ethical Society; these experiences they re-lived together afterwards in shared discussion over late supper or breakfast. They also invariably corresponded when parted during infrequent brief absences, such as when he was in London to attend meetings of the Political Economy Club or Labour Commission hearings, or she was in Bournemouth to see her parents. A usual marital arrangement in many ways, a radical departure from the conventional in others; more than anything, Marshall's marriage captures the 'half ingenious, half absurd personal element in the man'.[66]

CHARACTER, METHOD AND FACTS

Marshall's ultimate aim in both writing and teaching economics was the hope that the economic knowledge his wider audience gained from his work would assist in the elevation of character by lifting society's standard of life. Mill's prospect of a science of ethology had attracted Marshall as a young graduate because it raised the possibility of a scientific approach to character formation. The need for an economic base to make general human improvement possible had been an important factor in directing Marshall's attention to the study of political economy. The perspective of the new liberalism from the 1860s to create the good life for everyone by making all men 'gentlemen' in the full sense of the word, all women to fulfil their designated role in the home and in society, required elucidation of the appropriate economic structure to make this vision of the future a reality.[67]

The demand this objective placed on Marshall's economic writing was twofold. It generated technical requirements for a sound theoretical structure capable of supplying the tools for solving problems of industry, markets, competition, regulation, production, accumulation and progress. In addition, his economics needed to be communicated not only to present and future academic specialists. It had to be read by the parties more actively involved in the process of social improvement and progress. Hence the *Principles* was consciously designed to be read by reforming clergymen and leaders of the working class and of charity organisation. For those incapable of grasping the prose of the *Principles*, an *Elements of the Economics of Industry* had to be prepared as an urgent necessity. The fact that Marshall sent free copies to scores of mechanics institutes and trade union leaders confirms its wider purpose and the need to add a chapter devoted to trade unions to this elementary version of the major work.[68]

The elimination of mathematics from the text is a well-known symbol of this strategy to increase his audience. It had been urged upon Marshall by friend Jowett, who was more concerned with the social purpose of the *magnum opus* than with its theoretical refinements of Ricardo. The deceptively easy style which hides the most intricate propositions is another device to achieve the end. Even organisation of contents was conscripted to this cause. Long, relatively easy introductory materials preceded the hard theoretical core of its Book V. In these matters of style the hand of the preacher, moralist and improver constrain the hand of the social and economic investigator.[69]

Aspects of Marshall's method of communicating the *Principles* in combination with his writing style tell as much about his own character as about the character-moulding intentions of his major book. It reflected a search for perfectibility which was part of the requirement for flawless solutions to difficult problems and partly a more egotistical ambition to provide a perfect elucidation of an intricate argument. The never-ending search for facts was part of that unachievable drive for faultless presentation of reality.[70] Continual revision to eliminate imperfections and demonstrated error from the text and to re-arrange and reconstruct existing content were part of that elusive search as well. How much arrogance, insecurity and scientific pride was mingled with a simple desire for the 'truth' in this ongoing process of modification and emendation is difficult to say. As Guillebaud once intimated, some of it certainly followed from a subconscious fear and association of punishment with mistakes going back to his father, who may have instilled Latin declensions in the young Marshall by the London equivalent of the Scots 'tawse'.[71]

Never-ending revision of the completed triumph was also a useful excuse for postponing the uncertain success of a second volume, particularly one about which there were such high expectations. Its early twentieth-century recasting into several 'companion volumes', following a decade's digression of devotion to a 'white elephant', has strong elements of procrastination disguised through the setting of unachievable targets for unflawed texts.[72] However, his personality allowed little to be written in 'white heat' as his wife recalled, all needed to be premeditated, weighed up and balanced, and the gradually evolving paragraphs and chapters submitted to the same careful analysis as to their relative merits in the manner that all decisions were scrutinised and evaluated in the Marshall household.[73]

The way of composing for publication as against writing for an individual audience in correspondence reveals the personality trait of a Marshall with his eye firmly on what the future will think. Letter writing was a spur-of-the-moment activity, enabling personal feelings to emerge, perhaps later to be regretted as incautious utterances. A grand treatise, even if scrap paper within a half century or even a generation, could not tolerate such treatment. It needed to be deliberate and produced in slow, careful batches.[74] Was it lack of strength or fear which caused this habit, learned at the end of his school-days by observing a Regent Street sign-writer.[75] Earnestness in desiring precision and humaneness mingled with caution and pride. The very slow composition of which Marshall told Hewins was the consequence of a great mixture of long ingrained personality traits.[76]

Aspects of method and characters can be strikingly illustrated from Marshall's attitudes to, and association with, facts. Marshall loved facts and was 'greedy' for facts. For much of his later life he only read for the sake of acquiring facts and his summer holidays were invariably intertwined with bursts of factual observation and casual empiricism. His books needed the realism that only acquaintance with the facts could give them; while this ambitious aim at the same time prevented their speedy construction or realistic design as to scope. Like friends, facts had their own capacity for generating conflicting relationship within Marshall's mind.

The use of facts made by Marshall in the *Principles* illustrate aspects of this paradoxical relationship. There is little telling use of facts to prove a point; they are largely chosen for their power of illustration, are often homely and give an impression of the anecdotal rather than being meticulously researched. Marshall's 'illustrations and generalisations about business facts not very much removed from common place, rather those of an outsider', was how Beatrice Webb reacted on her first reading of the book; more bluntly was her description of his approach to the facts some years later after she had visited the Marshalls in Cambridge. 'Professor Marshall is more footling than ever. . . . For really when one talks to him and he advances his little subtle qualifications to his own slipshod generalizations, one gets irritated, almost as irritated when, in order to controvert some "popular" notion, he makes an astonishing assertion which bears no relation to fact'.[77] On a different level, Marshall's time-consuming factory tours of the 1880s left few definite marks on the pages of the *Principles*[78] or, for that matter, of *Industry and Trade*, where the factual sources are largely confined to printed material. Marshall's thirst for facts seems almost a pathological urge to satisfy an insatiable curiosity, to know all, understand all, and hence to become truly expert.

A direct use for the information obtained seems rarely implied in the fact-gathering tours. It was a wish for comprehending knowledge that seems to have driven him to undertake them. Although he once explained to Flux that much of his factory research had been devoted to solving the Cournot problem of reconciling increasing returns with persistent competition, Marshall wrote to Foxwell he needed to clarify all his own 'difficulties' before he could satisfactorily complete his arduous writing goals,[79] an impossible quest in practice. This yearning is also visible in the objectives from his 'economic apprenticeship'. These included gaining the ability to 'reconstruct mentally the vital parts of the chief machines used in each . . . of the leading industries' and to guess, with a permissible margin of error of less than two shillings a week, the wages paid to labourers whose work he was observing.[80] Perhaps this is why some people compared Marshall to Casaubon[81], the husband of the heroine in George Eliot's *Middlemarch*, with his 'tenacity of occupation and an eagerness' to learn. Casaubon's quest for knowledge bordered on obsession but yet 'easily lost sight of any purpose which had prompted him to these labours'. His unfinished work and desire for authorship was plagued both by ill health and a misplaced desire for unachievable perfection, seen by others as the strange quest of a 'dried up pedant . . . and elaborator of small explanations'.[82]

Chapman correctly regarded this 'insinuation' as 'unjust', conceding only Marshall's growing belief 'that generalising from facts can yield fruitful results if the facts are exhaustive enough and representative enough' combined with Marshall's infinite dissatisfaction with ever having enough of them. Chapman further explained this realistic side was essential to Marshall to assuage a 'growing mistrust of the bare results of pure deduction' and perhaps also given his tendency' to underrate the value of abstract reasoning because it came so easy to him'.[83] Yet it was this critical side of the intricate business of life and life of business which was most difficult for the outsider to gain, particularly for one immured in the cloisters of the university in voluntary exile from the real world. Sidney Webb saw this as one of the major shortcomings of the *Principles*. 'Academic life . . . produces thoughtful work but its divorce from daily action, its inevitable "dilletantism", and its intellectual blindness is awful'[84] This weakness in Marshall's work was compensated for by its theoretical strength, a countervailing set of qualities in his work on which Foxwell commented more bluntly when writing to Walker on symmetalism:

> Marshall's reputation is deservedly high as a theorist, but increasingly low as a practical man. Within the last three days, two of his favourite and best pupils, Dr. Keynes and Henry Cunynghame, both observed to me quite independently that they found it useless and impossible to discuss matters with Marshall. Personally he is the kindest and most chivalrous man in the world, but he is sadly wanting in practical instinct. . . . Marshall and Edgeworth get more and more pedantic and doctrinaire. Neither mixes with practical men, nor is in sympathy with them. I perhaps except industrial matters where Marshall sees more of the human element but always, it seems to me, though distinctly academic spectacles.[85]

In sharp contrast to this virtual obsession with factual knowledge, Marshall occasionally displayed a most casual attitude to the facts. Beatrice Webb suggested he was quite capable of making up facts if the need arose to bolster a hasty generalisation; Mary Paley recalled that Marshall himself generously attributed some of his better and unusual stories to a vivid imagination. Mrs Sidgwick experienced to the full that for Marshall, as for Disraeli, the line between statistical inquiry and lies could be a very thin one in political argument. Edgeworth and many others among Marshall's correspondents sometimes felt the full weight of Marshall's factual pedantry when the Cambridge professor felt himself slighted.[86] Such weakness in debating ploys is a common ailment among economists, but all the same can never be excused.

Another feature of his relationship with the facts was Marshall's tendency to sometimes forget or suppress inconvenient facts. This was illustrated in the context of his perspectives on the women's issue and to a lesser extent in episodes such as his controversy with Pearson. A casual attitude to the truth when the occasion seemed to demand it was, however, not confined only to his more 'scientific' work. Foxwell experienced this less likeable quality of Marshall in abundance in the context of his unsuccessful attempt to get elected as Marshall's successor. He not only heard indirectly about the mischievous tricks Marshall was playing on his candidature to support his own campaign in favour of Pigou, he was himself confronted with the disingenuous lies Marshall was capable of telling in the letter he received after the event from his 'former' friend. Marshall's paradoxical association with the facts fits neatly with his complex character.

THE MAN IN HISTORY: EDUCATIONIST, SOCIAL SCIENTIST AND ECONOMIST – MORALIST, PREACHER AND SCIENTIST

The man in history has been widely documented in his various roles. Marshall the economist in particular has been extensively reviewed.[87] Homage was paid to his economics at the time of his death and subsequently at major commemorations of anniversaries of his birth and the publication of his *Principles*. There has been an enormous output of Marshall commentary. This has placed both the basics and the minutiae of his economic theory under the microscope for examination and assessment by both eminent and lesser-known successors. A few of these have been at book length, most take the more modest forms of articles and short notes. A process like this creates myths and misinterpretations as well as new insights and understanding. Some of these myths have been dispelled in earlier chapters.[88]

Most important has been the myth of Marshall as author of a single book, the *Principles of Economics*. Important though this book is for any historical assessment of the man, it embraces only part of his significant output. First of all, it needs to be joined by *Industry and Trade* as an additional, fascinating and quite different study in economics with its potential for continuing to supply economists with new insights especially about how to practice their craft. There are also a substantial number of articles and memoranda, more than have been reprinted in the *Memorials*; the two smaller texts, of which the earlier *Economics of Industry* provides subject matter not elsewhere discussed by Marshall at any length; and evidence supplied to Royal Commissions over more than two decades. A not really finished *Money, Credit and Commerce* which was published before his death, and the planned fourth volume visible only in sketchy outline, signal the presence of much unpublished manuscript material produced over the half century from 1867, the more important of which is now in print. Reviewing Marshall simply from the standpoint of the *Principles* does injustice to the magnitude of the scope of his intended work and thereby distorts its purposes. This life of Marshall displays the magnitude of Marshall's economic task as he gradually came to conceive it and the extent to which it was, and could have been, completed.

A second myth about Marshall the economist concerns his neo-classical credentials. These have been variously misunderstood. His manifold sources of economics, discussed in considerable detail,[89] show him as a neo-classical in the manner that word was coined by Veblen and originally used by others:[90] the reconstructor of the classical structure by both correcting and completing it as he himself liked to put it. In this process he altered the classical system and kept many of its features, not just from ancestor worship as some have argued but because they were useful and important to keep for the explanation of economic life and activity.[91] The work was never anti-classical in the sense that Jevons and, to a lesser degree, Menger and Walras opposed the older economics of Mill, Ricardo and Smith. As a supply and demand theorist Marshall is also often described as a neo-classical writer. This is a dangerous perspective if designed to infer that Marshall thought largely in terms of equilibrium positions reached by adjustments of supply and demand schedules envisaged exclusively as functions of price. As stressed previously,[92] supply and demand for Marshall were more than functional relationships. He saw them as two fundamental categories by which to analyse the dialectically related opposites of production and consumption, wants and activities. As a self-confessed marginalist, Marshall has also often been placed firmly within the modern neo-classical camp. Once again, this is a problematical classification. Marshall was no narrow praxiologist of resource allocation, no static re-arranger of scarce, substitutable resources to ends given from outside by an unseen hand. Marshall's more realistic and complex system of thought greatly surpasses this simplistic version of the so-called 'economic problem', warning in advance of its codification by Robbins that a person is not likely to be a good economist if the problem of value is simplified in this way.[93] More importantly, any Robbinsian focus to economics was far too narrow for the person whose evolutionary emphasis within his economics made him invariably conscious of change, of dynamics, of progress and time. For good and evil, *natura non facit saltum* captures the Marshallian evolutionary spirit which guides the contents of the *Principles* and his other work.[94]

Marshall can also not be depicted as a simple micro-economist, laying the foundations for the theory of value as it has been understood in contemporary economics after the Second World War. He would have staunchly opposed the obfuscation inherent in the distinction between micro- and macro-economics as both narrow and simplistic. First of all, Marshall would have described such a distinction as simplistic because it treats too many essential factors as exogenous from principle rather than from pragmatic analytical necessity. Marshall's motto 'The many in the one, and the one in the many' extols this methodological point as well as others. Secondly, Marshall would condemn it as narrow because its focus covers too small a range of interesting questions, and leaves too much of what is important to other disciplines. Although Marshall reserved questions of the state, money, international trade, combinations and trusts for his second volume,[95] he invariably reminded readers of his completed first volume that all the solutions presented were provisional in the absence of that discussion. His treatment of the rate of interest is a striking illustration, but it equally permeates his analysis of labour, of land use, and of price determination.[96] Marshall likewise rejected the positivism underlying so much of contemporary micro-economics, though not the quest for scientific detachment. He was continually aiming at maintaining the difficult balance between impartial observer and ardent, practical reformer. Marshall also placed his economics firmly within the social sciences, ever aware of its crucial associations with politics and history especially.

Reference to Marshall as social scientist gives an opportunity to dispel some myths about his work as educationist. Marshall's overriding educational reform ambition was to extend the opportunities for specialisation in economics at his beloved Cambridge. He combined this with strong concerns about widening the avenues for constructive economic debate. These last aims were evident in his support for the foundation of an economic association publishing a regular journal and in his paramount interest in first training, and then providing economic teachers for other educational institutions. However, Marshall's personal ambitions for widening Cambridge economics must be judged relative to the very limited position the subject had enjoyed previously. In the Cambridge of his youth, and extending to his initial period as Professor, economics' position in the syllabus had not been great. This reminder of the initial modest role of economics is necessary to emphasise that Marshall would have regarded excessive specialisation in economics as totally absurd and highly dangerous. Marshall fully subscribed to Mill's dictum that 'a person is not likely to be a good economist who is nothing else'.[97] His syllabus design, including that for the more specialised Economics and Politics Tripos, fully endorsed Mill's principle. It covered far more than just economics. In this, it followed his own practice in studying the subject during his economic apprenticeship. Marshall himself then read widely and voraciously in and around the subject. He subsequently encouraged his students to do likewise. His reading included history, philosophy, politics, town planning as well as economics, and he constantly tried to keep himself abreast of current affairs by reading newspapers and periodicals like the *Economist* and *Statist*, the *Times* and the *Guardian*. For him this was a matter of principle, taught to, and embraced by, all his better students.[98] This is illustrated by his fierce criticism of the concept of 'economic man'. He largely directed this at the false notion of artificially separating the economic from other motivation. Marshall saw such an approach to abstraction as totally illegitimate. Although he stressed the wide range of problems to the solution of which economic knowledge is useful, he never endorsed the epithet, 'man shall live and be guided by economics alone'.[99]

The educationist in Marshall is also very visible in the teaching methods he adopted. The lecture was for him a poor instrument of instruction except for assisting students in learning the art of thinking. As a device for inculcating a textbook message, Marshall regarded the lecture as positively harmful. Individual tuition and regular essays meticulously corrected were superior methods for getting students to come to grips with the subject. Many of his students recalled the benefits they derived from his teaching in this way.[100] Marshall likewise regarded good library access as crucial. This was needed to supply students not only with books but also with journal articles, newspapers, periodicals and blue books, from as many countries as possible to provide the necessary comparative breadth for understanding actual economic systems. Marshall devoted much of his own resources to repairing Cambridge deficiencies in this area. He was able to build initially on foundations for this left by Pryme, since Fawcett, Pryme's successor, was more a man of textbook and lecture and tended to neglect this student need.[101] A wide focus, a capacity to think, and emphasis on the need for fieldwork were the educational imperatives which allowed so many of Marshall's relatively few students to excel. For creating good economists these attributes retain their value, suggesting that the mass education of economists at schools and in large undergraduate lecture courses is a foolish and mistaken enterprise, which can only mislead by simplifying the complex.

The wide range of talents Marshall demanded for his chosen subject came from his own full appreciation that economics was both a social and a moral science. It was part of the science of man, more specifically directed at behaviour in the ordinary business of life.[102] This social science perspective which Marshall gave to economics arose both from his early Cambridge background and from his subsequent cumulative experience of the complexity of the subject. It combined the moralist and the scientist, the interventionist and the believer in competition, the man who could learn from blue books and 'socialist rhapsodies', the visitor of factories and the armchair theorist. It made economics by itself incapable of solution to any problem; it avoided the black and white approach which often passes for economic rationalism. Marshall's view of economics as part of a theory of progress, dangerous and misleading as some of its results sometimes were, always kept the limitations of the subject to the forefront. He likewise kept this constantly before the eyes of his readers. He was therefore less interested in gaining precise solutions to both practical and theoretical problems. All he wanted was to instruct on the manner in which others could reach such solutions, while now and then departing from this pedagogic principle to preach on what he called his own particular hobbies such as free trade and the desirability of garden cities.

The moralist, reformer, scientist and even politician were therefore always combined, constituting the one in the many, sometimes the many in the one. Marshall could preach on the role of women for the good of the race and on free trade. He could moralise on the drink question, the wickedness of gambling, and misplaced conspicuous consumption by the rich. He could advise on the political expediency of giving liberal outdoor relief to the unemployed and the aged and on inviting working-class leaders to Royal Commissions and other government advisory bodies. He could also discourse dispassionately on the difference between particular expenses curve and supply curve, on the irreversibility of increasing returns over time, and on the complexities of marginal cost in relation to value. *Qua* economist he could write letters to the newspapers on the role of the post office and on the morality of the German blockade during the First World War. In this way, he wished to serve his world, his nation, his students and his times. This wish to be of service manifested itself in writing for a general public, addressing all the special students of his subject whether theorist, businessman, or the philanthropic charity activist among the clergy in parish or bishop's palace. This gave his *Principles* the unusual distinction of being extensively reviewed in the newspapers and periodicals of the world. It enabled his astonished publisher to compare the sales performance of his *Industry and Trade* to that of a 'shilling shocker'.[103]

In noting this quality of Marshall's *Principles*, Schumpeter drew attention to another feature of Marshall's work. '[H]is views about social problems, his general outlook on the public as well as on the private sphere happened to coincide with the ideas, views, and outlook of his country and his time. . . . He accepted the institutions around him, the privately owned firm and the family home in particular, and entertained no doubt about their vitality or the vitality of the civilisation that had grown up around them.'[104] In so far as this makes Marshall a man of his time, this statement is unobjectionable. To the extent it emphasises Marshall's quality of leading from behind, to use Coats's felicitous phrase,[105] it is equally apt, as others, including the Webbs, have noted.* It errs, however, if it is taken to imply that Marshall accepted his environment uncritically and was invariably opposed to change. He was, it is true, cautious and gradualist about all proposals for change, and rarely impetuous or adventurous in his support for causes. This enabled him, as Schumpeter cogently put it,[106] to sympathise 'with the ideals of socialism and [to] patronisingly talk down to socialists', it likewise enabled him in his last major work to defend competition and the market as a bulwark against chaos followed by 'military despotism', while dreaming of a future with romantic hopes about what could be learned from other planets about the relation between individual and the state.[107] Yet he also vigorously and publicly criticised British imperialism in the Boer War and elsewhere, opposed the hate Germany campaigns during the First World War, was willing to sacrifice private property in land for the sake of clean air and the open space of gardens and playing fields for all, and supported substantial redistribution through capital and progressive income taxation in the interest of what he saw as the public good. His gradualist approach to reform cannot only be seen as an inherent conservative streak; it was also an acute awareness of the uncertainty in predicting the consequences of particular actions, especially if these had the potential to be very enduring.

This was the mixture which made Marshall. It produced a great economist and a cautious reformer. It created a scientist diligently seeking after truth but capable of hiding both his parental antecedents and his embarrassing place of birth. It created the moralist who unashamedly preached the worth, as aids to character building, of good consumption habits and general standards for living but who feared the social consequences of 'modern woman' being given the vote or a Cambridge degree. They showed in the educationist who battled valiantly and persistently for a greater place in the sun for his beloved economics 'men' but who, with equal vehemence and persistence, deplored the unresearched consequences of women teaching to mixed university classes and showed annoyance when two women topped his last Economics and Political Tripos. It formed the leader of a profession who laid down generous rules for the treatment of predecessors, but who, if need be, was willing to hurl himself into the controversy to protect both his own good name and his principles and who preserved an open door for the *Economic Journal* to combat notions of orthodox science as a contradiction of terms. Often humourless, pedantic, vain, selfish, ungenerous, even egotistical, he could at the same time be sensitive to the needs of others, courageous in his support of unpopular causes, generous of both time and money to advance teaching and students in the subject he professed and to which he made a lasting contribution in his writing. Much can still be learned in what to adopt and what to reject from the man and his life. In this sense, Marshall remains a soaring eagle.

---

* Sidney Webb to Beatrice Webb, 30 October 1890, in *The Letters of Sidney and Beatrice Webb*, p. 229 ('I do feel a sort of reverence for Marshall as "our leader" in Economics. . . . But I wish he would lead a little'); cf. my 'Marshall on Taxation', p. 103, which notes that Marshall followed the policy actually implemented in British fiscal policy pronouncement on progressivity and capital taxation.

NOTES

1.   Joan Robinson, *On Re-Reading Marx*, Cambridge: Student Bookshop Limited, 1953, p. 14.
2.   Sir Austin Robinson, 'Review of Mary Paley Marshall, *What I Remember*', pp. 123–4.
3.   Beatrice Webb, *My Apprenticeship*, p. 415.
4.   Cited above, Chapter 13, p. 456.
5.   William Ramsay to his mother, 16 March 1880, Ramsay Papers, UCL.
6.   E.A. Benians, 'Reminiscences', in *Memorials*, p. 78.
7.   G.H. Leonard, 'University College: A Charming Sketch of the Early Days', *Bristol Times and Mirror*, 6 June 1925; G.H. Leonard, letter to *Bristol Times and Mirror*, 8 October 1924.
8.   The photographs discussed in this and the subsequent two paragraphs are all reproduced in this volume; in order of discussion they are photos 11, 12, 13.
9.   Mary Paley Marshall, *What I Remember*, p. 11.
10. Cf. Chapter 17, above p. 653.
11. Above, Chapter 19, pp. 704–6, and illustration 49.
12. Above, Chapter 8, p. 246, Chapter 5, pp. 109–10.
13. C.W. Guillebaud, 'Some Personal Reminiscences of Alfred Marshall', p. 93; C.R. Fay, 'Reminiscences', in *Memorials*, p. 74.
14. Quoted above, Chapter 17, pp. 628–9.
15. Above, Chapter 10, p. 314.
16. Above, Chapter 9, pp. 284–5.
17. Above, Chapter 10, p. 321.
18. Above, Chapter 17, p. 638.
19. C.W. Guillebaud, 'Some Personal Reminiscences of Alfred Marshall', p. 92.
20. Quoted previously, p. 682–3, Chapter 16, p. 601; Mary Paley Marshall, 'MSS Notes' (NCA); *P* VIII, pp. 43, 46.
21. See Chapter 16 above, p. 604; Chapter 19, p. 721, and C.W. Guillebaud, 'Some Personal Reminiscences of Alfred Marshall', pp. 92–3.
22. *Ibid.*, p. 92.
23. E.A. Benians, 'Reminiscences', in *Memorials*, p. 80.
24. J.M. Keynes, 'Alfred Marshall', p. 214.
25. G.H. Leonard, Letter to *Bristol Times and Mirror*, 8 October 1924.
26. See above, Chapter 8, pp. 242–4.
27. C.R. Fay, 'Reminiscences', in *Memorials*, p. 74.
28. Above, Chapter 17, p. 638; C.R. Fay, 'Reminiscences of a Deputy Librarian', p. 88.
29. *P* VIII, pp. 119 n, 195–7, 689–90, and more generally on demand for food, 105–8.
30. As reported by Philomena Guillebaud to Rita McWilliams-Tullberg.
31. Mary Paley Marshall, 'MSS Notes' (NCA); Mary Paley Marshall, *What I Remember*, p. 19.
32. As reported by Guillebaud to Coase, and conveyed by letter to the author, 2 May 1991.
33. Above, Chapter 18, p. 690.
34. Discussed previously in Chapter 5, pp. 129–30; Chapter 7, p. 196; Chapter 8, p. 227.
35. Above, Chapter 5, p. 104; Chapter 7, p. 192, Chapter 8, pp. 290.
36. *P* VIII, pp. 94 and n.1, 108.
37. Above, Chapter 17, pp. 651–2.
38. Above, Chapter 5, p. 105.
39. W.G. Constable, 'Art and Economics in Cambridge', *The Eagle*, 59, 1963, pp. 23–6.
40. *EOI*, p. 93.
41. Alfred Marshall, 'Social Possibilities of Economic Chivalry', in *Memorials*, p. 344.
42. Fragment on 'Art', late 1860s?, Marshall Archive, Red Box 1.
43. Fragment on 'Art', dated 25 September 1906, Marshall Archive, Red Box 1. The references to strychnine and arsenic are obscure, though strychnine as a vermin killer, and arsenic as used in dyes may have been what Marshall was alluding to.
44. See above, Chapter 3, p. 64, Chapter 13, pp. 450–53, Chapter 16, p. 587, Chapter 17, pp. 633–4.
45. *P* I, 262, *P* VIII, p. 206.
46. *Times*, 14 July 1924; *Nation and Athenaeum*, 19 July 1924.
47. Above, Chapter 8, p. 243, Chapter 9, pp. 278, 288, Chapter 18, p. 691, Chapter 19, p. 727.
48. As cited in H.M.Robertson, 'Alfred Marshall', in *AMCA*, I, p. 443.
49. Cannan, 'Alfred Marshall 1842–1924', *AMCA*, I, p. 70.
50. G.F. Shove, 'The Place of Marshall's Principles in the Development of Economics', *AMCA*, II, p. 138.

51. Marshall to J.B. Clark, 24 March 1908, in *Memorials*, p. 416.
52. Above, Chapter 13, p. 479.
53. J.M. Keynes, 'W.S. Jevons', p. 131, cf. J.M. Keynes, 'Alfred Marshall, p. 185.
54. Above, Chapter 6, pp. 161–2.
55. *P* I, pp. 544 n.1 and 66.
56. Above, Chapter 13, pp. 476–7.
57. Above, Chapter 10, p. 309, Chapter 17, pp. 649–50, Chapter 20, pp. 739–42.
58. R.F. Scott to Maynard Keynes, 23 October 1924, (KMF).
59. Above, Chapter 4, pp. 127–8.
60. C.R. Fay to Maynard Keynes, 13 November 1924 (KMF).
61. That is, A.S. and E.M.S., *Henry Sidgwick: A Memoir*.
62. Above, pp. 258, 324.
63. Sir Austin Robinson, review of *What I Remember*, p. 123.
64. Above Chapter 8, p. 225.
65. Letter to the author.
66. A.C. Stenson to Maynard Keynes, 17 November 1924 (KMF).
67. Above, Chapter 6, pp. 141–3.
68. Discussed in Chapter 12, esp. pp. 426–8, 434.
69. Above, Chapter 12, esp. pp. 412–13, 434, 436–7.
70. Cf. Chapter 19 on *Industry and Trade*, pp. 714–15.
71. Above, Chapter 2, p. 23, Chapter 12, p. 426.
72. Above, Chapter 12, pp. 428–30, Chapter 19, p. 715.
73. In a letter to Maynard Keynes, cited above, Chapter 17, pp. 638–9.
74. Cf. Marshall's letter to Benjamin Kidd, quoted above, Chapter 1, pp. 14–15.
75. Above, Chapter 3, pp. 63–4.
76. Above, Chapter 12, p. 400.
77. Beatrice Webb to Sidney Webb, 9 August 1890, in *The Letters of Sidney and Beatrice Webb*, Vol. 1, p. 161; Diary, 23 February 1897, in *The Diary of Beatrice Webb*, Vol. 2, p. 109.
78. Above, Chapter 7, pp. 208–14, esp. pp. 211–13.
79. Marshall to Flux, 7 March 1898, in *Memorials*, pp. 406–7; Marshall to Foxwell, 14 April 1897 (Marshall Archive, 1:56).
80. Fragment, reproduced in *Memorials*, pp. 358–9.
81. Sir Sidney Chapman, *Autobiography*, p. 25
82. George Eliot, *Middlemarch*, quotations drawn from Chapters 20, 21, 42.
83. Sir Sidney Chapman, *Autobiography*, pp. 35–6.
84. Sidney Webb to Beatrice Webb, 17 October 1890 in *The Letters of Sidney and Beatrice Webb*, Vol. 1, pp. 221–2.
85. Foxwell to Francis A. Walker, 16 November 1896, Library of Congress no. AC.4539, cited in Rita McWilliams-Tullberg, 'Alfred Marshall and the Male Priesthood of Economics', p. 258.
86. Above, Chapter 17, pp. 634–6.
87. On this, see above, Chapter 12, pp. 434–7, Chapter 19, pp. 712–15, Chapter 20, pp. 760–2.
88. Above, Chapter 3, pp. 57–61, Chapter 20, p. 761.
89. Above, Chapter 6, pp. 145–54, 158–68.
90. A. Aspromourgos, 'Neoclassical', in *The New Palgrave*, Vol. 3, p. 625.
91. Above, Chapter 12, p. 411.
92. Above, Chapter 20, p. 761.
93. Lionel Robbins, *An Essay on the Nature and Significance of Economic Science*, London: Macmillan, 1934, p. 16, and passim; *P* VIII, p. 368.
94. Above, Chapter 12, pp. 411–12.
95. Above, Chapter 12, pp. 429–30.
96. *P* VIII, pp. 594–5, 722.
97. *P* VIII, p. 771.
98. Above, Chapter 6, pp. 154 n.*, 163–5, Chapter 10, pp. 317, 332, Chapter 15, Appendix, esp. pp. 568–9.
99. *P* VIII, pp. 20–7, esp. p. 27.
100. Above, Chapter 10, pp. 315–16.
101. Above, Chapter 10, pp. 331–2, Chapter 20, pp. 750–1.
102. *P* VIII, pp. 14–17, 38–48, 770–1.
103. Mary Paley Marshall, MSS Notes, (NCA).
104. J.A. Schumpeter, 'Alfred Marshall's Principles: A Semi-centennial Appraisal', *AMCA*, II, pp. 108–9.

105. A.W. Coats, 'Sociological Aspects of British Economic Thought', p. 711.
106. J.A. Schumpeter, 'Alfred Marshall's Principles: A Semi-centennial Appraisal, p. 109.
107. Above, Chapter 19, p. 712.

Acknowledgements

Apart from the people thanked in the Preface (above, pp. xii–xiv) and in the notes on sources below (pp. 796–800), I wish to thank the following persons and organisations for assistance in the preparation of this biography: Nahid Aslanbeigui, William J. Baumol, Melanie Beresford, Bob Black, Pascal Bridel, Robert Butler, James Claydon, Dr M.D. Cobcroft, William Coleman, Bernard Corry, John Creedy, Marco Dardi, Phyllis Deane, Eduardo de Fonseca, Giancarlo de Vivo, John Eatwell, H.G. Edwards, Jeremy Edwards, Tony Endres, John Foster, Dr Bryan Gandevia, Peter S. Gilbert, Flora Gill, the late Barry Gordon, Dr Reginald Green, Philomena Guillebaud, Arnold Heertje, James P. Henderson, the late Klaus M. Hennings, Geoffrey Hodgson, Miss Susan Horsfall, Thomas M. Humphrey, Alon Kadish, Jon King, Gerard M. Koot, David Laidler, Dr James H. Leavesley, Frederic S. Lee, A.D. McBriar, Bruce J. McFarlane, P.P. McGuinnes, Terence McMullin, John Maloney, Peter T. Marshall, Donald E. Moggridge, Ferdinando Meacci, Denis O'Brien, Rod M. O'Donnell, Paul Oslington, Mark Perlman, the late Sir Austin Robinson, Bob Rowthorn, Warren J. Samuels, Paul A. Samuelson, Bertram Schefold, Robert Skidelsky, D.J. Skipper, the late George J. Stigler, Paolo Sylos Labini, Peter Thal, Michael Tochtermann, Yanis Varoufakis, Philip Williams and Donald Winch.

I would also like to thank the Curator, Bank of England Museum and Historical Research Section; the Librarian, Cambridge County Council Records Office; the Archivist, Grays Inn Society; the Archivist, Guildhall Library; the Librarian, London County Council Records Office; the Archivist, Peterhouse, Cambridge; the Archivist, Public Records Office; Mrs M.C. Hislop, Secretary, Royal Statistical Society, and above all, the staff of Fisher Library, the University of Sydney.

I acknowledge permission from the Syndics of Cambridge University Press for being able to quote freely from Mary Paley Marshall, *What I Remember*; from Sheldon Rothblatt, *Revolution of the Dons* and from the Permissions Editor of Macmillan for permission to quote from the works of Alfred Marshall, published by them during his lifetime and subsequently, and from J.M. Keynes, 'Alfred Marshall', in *Essays in Biography*. I also acknowledge permission of the respective editors to use extracts from my articles which appeared in the following journals, *History of Political Economy*, *Scottish Journal of Political Economy*, *Journal of the History of Economic Ideas* and *European Journal of the History of Economic Thought*.

Notes on Sources, Especially from Archival Material

The heterogeneity of the subject matter in this biography makes it not appropriate or useful to include a list of books consulted or cited by way of bibliography. However, some such listings are provided. Marshall's published works and some other quite frequently consulted books are included in the list of abbreviations (above, p. xi); lists of articles dealing with Marshall's economics and associated subjects are obtainable from *AMCA*, and may be supplemented from the first issues of the *Marshall Studies Bulletin*, which review the Marshall collections published in commemoration of the centenary of the publication of his *Principles of Economics* in 1990. A listing of archival material used may, however, be helpful. It, moreover, enables an appropriate indication of the debt this book owes to the dedication of archivists and their staff in giving me access to the material in the collections they maintain, and in addition, allows convenient acknowledgement of permissions to quote from the material in their custody.

Marshall Archive

First and foremost, I have drawn heavily on the material contained in the Marshall Archive, Marshall Library, Faculty of Economics and Politics, University of Cambridge. A summary of its holdings was provided previously (above, pp. 749–50). In granting me generous permission to use and quote from this material, I express my gratitude to the members of the Faculty of Economics and Politics. For assisting me to find my way through it, to alert me to new material, to decipher some of Marshall's handwriting on occasion, I thank both the archivist, Dr Frances Willmoth, and a succession of Marshall librarians including the late A. H. Finkel, Donald Ross, Rowland Thomas and their invariably helpful staff of assistant librarians.

Cambridge University Library

I have drawn equally heavily on the vast resources of the Cambridge University Library, particularly on the material it contains relating to the history of the university, including manuscript material. Most extensively used and quoted were the Diaries of John Neville Keynes (Add MSS 7827–7867), the Minute Books of the Special Board for Moral Sciences and the Special Board for Economics and Politics, the Minute Book of the Cambridge Branch of the Ethical Society, the Chit Chat Club and Marshall correspondence with Lord Acton, Benjamin Kidd and a number of university librarians. I am grateful to the Syndics of the University Library of Cambridge for giving me permission to quote from the manuscript material in their possession and express my thanks for the invariably courteous assistance of the library staff in the main reading room, the special collections room and the photocopying department.

St John's College Library
I am indebted to the sub-Librarian, Mr Malcolm Pratt and the Librarian, Miss A. Saville, for assistance in drawing Marshall-related material in their collection to my attention. I was particularly pleased to be able to consult their collection of the college journal *The Eagle* from its inception, and to quote from college publications in their possession, more particularly the questionnaire to college lecturers and the responses thereto as circulated by the then Master, W.H. Bateson, in 1872. I am grateful to the Master, Fellows and Scholars of St John's College for permission to quote from this material in their possession.

St John's College Archives
I am indebted to Dr Marcolm Underwood, the College Archivist for providing me with facilities to examine relevant material relating to Marshall's period as student and Fellow of the College, correspondence including that relating to the building of his house, and general background on the college and its regulations. I am particularly grateful for his willingness to answer subsequent queries quickly in correspondence, and thank the Masters, Fellows and Scholars of St John's College for permission to quote from this material.

King's College Archive
I am indebted to Dr Michael Halls and his successor, Ms J. Cox, as Modern Archivists for the college, for giving me access to material relevant to Marshall in the possession of their archive, particularly that found among the Keynes Papers, the Oscar Browning correspondence and correspondence of, or relating to, other prominent former Fellows of the College such as A.W. Sheppard, A.C. Pigou and Sir John Clapham. For permission to quote from material contained in Keynes's Marshall File, especially the notes and correspondence from Mary Paley Marshall contained therein, from Keynes's Royal Economic Society File dealing with the publication of *Official Papers of Alfred Marshall*, the Oscar Browning correspondence, the Sheppard correspondence, Keynes's general correspondence with Marshall, and his essays as corrected by Marshall, I am grateful to the Provost and Scholars of King's College, Cambridge.

Newnham College Archive
I am indebted to the College Archivist, Dr Elizabeth M.C. van Houts for giving me access to parts of the collection relating to Marshall and to the Principal and Fellows of Newnham College for permission to quote from manuscript material in their possession, particularly from MSS notes prepared by Mary Paley Marshall for diverse purposes, including her published recollections, *What I Remember*, a talk to members of the Marshall Society and for use by the biographer of Jane Harrison, as well as from the Mirrlees typescript of Anabel Robinson's draft for a Jane Harrison biography.

Wren Library, Trinity College, Cambridge

I am indebted to Alan Kucia the archivist of Trinity College, Cambridge for giving me access to material relating to Marshall housed among the Sidgwick Papers and the Layton Papers. I am indebted to the Master and Fellows of Trinity College, Cambridge, for permission to quote from the following material: the correspondence of Marshall and Walter Layton (2^{31-8}), Layton's lecture notes, correspondence between Marshall and Erasmus Darwin on the Social Discussion Society housed with the Layton Papers; correspondence between Marshall and Mrs Sidgwick (c.103$^{80-1}$), Henry Sidgwick (c. 94.114–5), an autobiographical fragment (c.96 (20)) and the material relating to the Grote Club (Add MS 104.65).

British Library of Political and Economic Science (Archives)

I am indebted to Dr A. Raspin for giving me access to material relating to Marshall in her custody, with special reference to correspondence between Marshall and Beatrice Potter-Webb (in the Passfield Papers, 1(ii) 114, 116, 204, 205); Leslie Stephen (Coll. Misc. M1129); Edgeworth (M 469); Giffen (Collection I 84, II 25, 72); Courtney (Papers R(S)R 1003 VIII (15) (41) XIII 51, 104 XIX 49); Cannan (Cannan Collection 1020, 1021); and for the use of material in the Cannan Papers (909, 969) the Solley Papers (Coll. Misc. 154, 4a D11–12, 4b D45, D93, D162, D171 D 171, Folio B10 Item 2g), and from the unpublished biography of Sir Sidney Chapman (M1073, Coll. Misc. 664) and for permission to quote from the material in the Booth, Passfield, Cannan and Courtney collection for which they hold the copyright.

University College, London (Manuscripts and Rare Books)

I am indebted to the Librarian for giving me access to material relating to Marshall in the Sir William Ramsay papers as arranged by Morris Travers, pertaining to correspondence with his parents during the period while he and Marshall were at Bristol together, and for permission to quote from these letters.

University Library, London (Archives and Special Collections)

I am indebted to the Librarian, for giving me access to correspondence between Alfred Marshall and Charles Booth (Booth Papers MS 797: 1/1352, 1/1324, 1/1325, 1/1715, 1/2037, 1/1310, 1/1311, 1/1312, 1/5768, 1/5770–3) and to Mrs B. Norman Butler for permission to quote from these letters.

University of Warwick Library (Modern Records Centre)

I am indebted to the Archivist, for giving me access to the Clara Collet Papers, in particular her diaries (1876–1914, MSS 29/8/1/1–146, 2/1–146) and the Higgs–Foxwell correspondence (MSS 29/3/13/5/3) and to Dr Jane Miller for permission to quote from the diaries and this correspondence.

Bristol University Library (Special Collections)

I am grateful to Mr Michael Richardson, for assistance while giving me access to material held in this collection relating to the period of Marshall as Principal and his professorship at Bristol University College and to assist subsequently by answering a number of further queries by correspondence. Manuscript material consulted includes Marion F. Pease, 'Some Reminiscences of University College' (typescript, 23 February 1942), her 'Account of the Marshall Years at Bristol University College as told by Mary Paley Marshall, Notes from Memory' (MS Coll. DM 219), University College Bristol, Income and Expenditures, University College Bristol, Donations and Subscriptions, University College Bristol, Council Minutes 1878–83, University College Bristol, Local and Executive Committee Minutes (DM 506) and Testimonials for Alfred Marshall in support of his application for the position of Principal, and for permission to quote from this material.

Leeds University Library (Brotherton Library)

I am grateful to P.S. Morrish, sub-Librarian (MSS and Special Collections) for making available to me a photocopy of L.L. Price, *Memoirs and Notes on British Economists 1881–1947* (MS 107) and to the Librarian as well as the Trustees of the Price Estate for permission to quote from its first two chapters.

Foxwell Papers (Freeman Collection)

I am grateful to R.D. Freeman for giving me access to correspondence of Foxwell in his possession, and for permission to quote from these letters of Marshall to Foxwell.

Jowett Papers (Balliol College, Oxford)

I am grateful to the Master and Scholars of Balliol College in the University of Oxford, for permission to quote from the letters of Alfred Marshall and Mary Paley Marshall to Benjamin Jowett.

John Bates Clark Papers, Rare Book and Manuscripts Library, Columbia University, New York

I am grateful to the Librarian for permission to quote from correspondence between J.B. Clark and Marshall.

Newcomb Papers, Library of Congress, Washington

I am grateful to the Librarian for permission to quote from Marshall's letters to Newcomb.

Houghton Library, Harvard University

I am grateful to the Librarian for permission to quote from letters by Mary Paley Marshall and Alfred Marshall to William Rothenstein.

Taussig Papers, Harvard, University

I am grateful for permission to quote from correspondence between the Marshalls and Taussig.

Lund Universitets Bibliotek, Sweden
I am grateful for permission to quote from unpublished correspondence between Marshall and Wicksell.

Henry L. Moore Papers, Rare Book and Manuscript Library, University of Columbia, New York
I am grateful for permission to quote from correspondence between Marshall and H.L. Moore.

Kungl. Biblioteket, Stockholm
I am grateful for permission to quote from correspondence between Marshall and Gustav Cassel, and Marshall and E.F. Heckscher.

Seligman Papers (Columbia University, New York)
I am grateful for permission to quote from the Marshall–Seligman correspondence held with the Edwin R.A. Seligman Papers, Rare Book and Manuscript Library, Columbia University, New York.

Index